Little Elf
A Celebration of Harry Langdon

by **Chuck Harter**
& **Michael J. Hayde**

Little Elf: A Celebration of Harry Langdon
© 2012 Chuck Harter & Michael J. Hayde. All Rights Reserved.

No part of this book may be reproduced in any form or by any means, electronic, mechanical, digital, photocopying or recording, except for the inclusion in a review, without permission in writing from the publisher.

Published in the USA by:
BearManor Media
PO Box 1129
Duncan, Oklahoma 73534-1129
www.bearmanormedia.com

ISBN 978-1-59393-278-7

Printed in the United States of America.
Edited by Lon Davis.
Cover design by Chuck Harter. Front cover artwork by Chuck Harter and Veronica Hayde
Book design by Brian Pearce | Red Jacket Press.

Table of Contents

Foreword by Steve Massa 5
Acknowledgments 7
Personal Thank Yous and Dedications 9
Introduction by Edward Watz 11
Prologue 17
From Troublesome to Trouper 1884-1905 20
"The Langdons Is the Name" 1906-1911 32
"Goaheadativeness" 1912-1915 44
Big Time and Broadway 1916-1920 54
After the Ball and Hollywood's Call 1921-1923 74
From Lesser to Greater 1923-1924 86
"Legitimate Laughs" 1924-1925 110
"This Langdon is a Genius" 1925-1926 136
"The Saddest Stories Ever Told" 1926-1927 154
"Two of the Lousiest Pictures Ever Made" 1927-1928 176
"None of That High-Handed Stuff" 1928-1930 190
"The Tragedy of Marriage" 1931-1932 222
"Pictures Are Where I Belong" 1932-1934 236
"Ye Gods, Has it Come to This" 1934-1937 252
Laurel & Langdon & Hardy 1938-1940 270
"The 'O-Ouch-O' Comedies" 1940-1944 288
Epilogue 309
The Films of Harry Langdon 331
Theatrical Compilations 597
Television Programs 599
Appendix 603
Sources 681
Index 683
About the Authors 689

Foreword *by Steve Massa*

Harry Langdon is usually referred to as the comet that blazed across the silent comedy sky in the mid 1920s, only to crash and burn as sound came in. This is, of course, a generalization and only a small part of the entire story, as Harry had been a longtime vaudeville favorite before ever entering motion pictures and even after "his fall" he spent fifteen years starring in his own two-reelers, working as a writer and gag-man, performing on stage and appearing non-stop as a supporting character player in features.

With *Little Elf: A Celebration of Harry Langdon*, Chuck Harter and Michael J. Hayde have finally given Harry the biography he deserves, with all the aspects of his varied career thoroughly and lovingly detailed. Like "cinema bloodhounds" they've tracked down, devoured, and processed a wealth of sources and materials — newspaper archives, vaudeville sketches, trade magazines, genealogical information, pressbooks, interviews, studio financial records, scripts from unavailable films, personal letters, court proceedings, and his surviving comedies — in their quest to set the record straight on Langdon.

My own history with Harry began around 1960 when I discovered television programs such as *The Funny Manns*, where silent comedies were edited down and repackaged for kids. Harry turned up frequently, and although I didn't know his name I responded immediately to his mousey demeanor and blinking hesitations. Becoming hooked on silent comedies, it wasn't until I saw a couple of Robert Youngson's compilation features and stumbled onto Blackhawk Films that I started getting basic info on his career and films. There wasn't much more available until Frank Capra's 1971 autobiography *The Name Above the Title*, with its "Capra-centric" slant on Langdon. In the early 1980s, authors William Schelly and Joyce Rheuban started to put Harry's career in proper perspective with the information that was available to them at the time.

Now, Chuck and Michael have dug deep to present a three-dimensional portrait of Langdon the man, the comedy innovator, the father and husband, and the producer, all topped off with the most complete and exhaustive filmography to date. Their admiration and appreciation of Langdon's art informs every page of this biography, and in addition to my utmost respect for their skill and dedication, they have the sincere thanks of my inner five-year-old for the book I've been waiting 50 years to read.

Steve Massa is a research librarian in the Billy Rose Theatre Collection at the New York Public Library for the Performing Arts, and has organized comedy film programs for the Museum of Modern Art, Library of Congress, Smithsonian Institution, Pordenone Silent Film Festival, Museum of the Moving Image, and Eye Film Institute, Netherlands. In addition to being historian-in-residence of NYC's long-running Silent Clown Film Series, *he has written for* Griffithiana, The Chaplin Review *and* Slapstick!, *and has been a research consultant, writer and guest commentator for Facets' DVD set* Harry Langdon — Lost and Found, *plus others featuring Buster Keaton, Charley Chase, Roscoe Arbuckle and Max Davidson.*

Acknowledgments

The authors would like to acknowledge the support and contributions of many people, without whom this endeavor would have been impossible:

For generously sharing photographs, lobby cards, posters and other images from their personal collections, our sincere thanks to Buddy Barnett, Alan Boyd, Nico Cartenstadt, Bill Cassara, Harry Hoppe, Cole Johnson, Jim Kerkhoff, Steve Massa, John McElwee, Chris Seguin, Dr. Karl Thiede and Edward Watz. We'd also like to thank Richard Warner of The Historical Society of Pottawattamie County for providing images and information pertaining to Council Bluffs, Iowa, both old and new.

For helping us identify several of the uncredited players in Langdon's films, as well as placing names to a few unfamiliar faces in the stills, we are grateful to Steve Massa, Dr. Karl Thiede, Brent E. Walker and Edward Watz.

For providing invaluable secondary resources such as interviews, rare articles and copies of the films, we wish to thank Bill Cassara, Michael Copner, Rob Farr, David Kalat, John McElwee, Camille 'Brooksie' Scaysbrook, Chris Seguin and Edward Watz.

We extend our sincere appreciation to Rob Stone of the Library of Congress for arranging the screening of several otherwise-unavailable Langdon titles. We are likewise grateful to the research staff of the Katharine Hepburn Reading Room at the Margaret Herrick Library of the Academy of Motion Picture Arts and Sciences in Beverly Hills for providing assistance in navigating the special collections.

For reviewing portions of the manuscript and correcting errors, we especially would like to thank Steve Massa, Randy Skretvedt and Edward Watz. Also, words cannot express our gratitude and delight with Mr. Massa's Foreword and Mr. Watz's Introduction. Thank you both for going above and beyond the call of duty.

We thank Tim Greer, administrator of the *FeetOfMud.com* website, for permitting us space to publicize our work. Various contributors to *SilentComedyMafia.com, Nitrateville.com* and *SilentComedians.com* were also of enormous help (whether they knew it or not).

Our thanks to Dan Langdon, grandson of Harry's youngest brother, Claude Langdon, for sharing much of the family lore.

For writing the books that provided a springboard into a deeper appreciation of Langdon's genius, as well as their invaluable role in undoing so much negative revisionism surrounding his legacy, we salute William Schelly and Dr. Joyce Rheuban.

Our thanks to Ben Ohmart, Lon Davis and Brian Pearce for their part in making our vision a reality.

Most especially, we wish to extend our deepest gratitude to Floyd Bennett, who, from 1996-2000, created The Harry Langdon Society, authored nine quarterly newsletters and three annual journals, and helped spearhead a Harry Langdon celebration in Council Bluffs. His work yielded a great deal of information, particularly his interviews with Langdon's nephews, Donald and Harry, and ensured that the Little Elf's story would have a happy ending. Thank you for blazing the trail before us.

Personal Thank Yous and Dedications

Chuck: To Sue Quinn and Pud the Doggie for sanctuary; to my brother Erich Stollberger for his encouragement; to Elizabeth McCune for her artistic understanding and financial acumen; to Edna Martin for her friendship and spirituality; to Edward Watz for his expertise; and to my partner and closest friend, Michael J. Hayde, for his hard work, dedication and enthusiasm during this long project.

This book is dedicated to my mother, Luella Harter, for her belief and support.

Michael: To my father, John J. Hayde, for cleaning up several of the images; to my daughter, Elizabeth, for her assistance with the filmography; to my other daughter, Veronica, for coloring the front cover photo; to my partner, Chuck Harter, for shouldering all of the long, hard work with me; and to my wife, Myra, for her prayers for, patience with and devotion to her less-than-perfect husband.

This book is dedicated to my parents, John and Margaret Hayde, for giving me the gifts of life, love and laughter.

"WELL WELL WELL!
WHAT A PLEASURE TO
MEET TWO REAL PEOPLE.
HOPE WE MEET AGAIN
I DO – CONTINUED
HAPPINESS AND SUCCESS
YOURS FER EVER
Harry"

To
Mr and Mrs
Gadner –
With my compliments
and sincere best wishes always
Your friend
Harry Langdon

Introduction *by Edward Watz*

"If it wasn't for bad luck, I wouldn't have any luck at all."

So goes the old cliché, usually attributed to "anonymous." But this saying could also have been the mantra of Harry Langdon — although not in the way one might first imagine.

Over the course of his lifetime, most of it spent on stage and in film, Harry Langdon developed his unique comedy skills and created his lovable "Little Elf" characterization, earning his place as one of the 20th century's greatest and most iconic movie comedians. His career had its share of show business peaks and valleys, but overall Harry ended up having a very happy and fulfilled life. His story was the stuff of Hollywood legend: After a rapid rise to the top ranks of Hollywood stardom, Langdon's career suddenly and somewhat mysteriously plummeted. His greatest successes in film — and his greatest failures — occurred within a single five-year span, near the end of the silent film era. But Langdon was resilient. Gradually his film career recovered in the new "talkies" and he eventually re-established himself as a busy and prolific movie comic, securing a second-tier niche in two-reelers and the occasional role in features. Despite some financial setbacks in the 1930s (mostly due to back alimony demands from his two former wives), Harry Langdon persevered and prospered. He found a loving and devoted spouse when he married Mabel Sheldon, and became a proud and doting father with the birth of their only child, Harry Junior. When Langdon died in 1944, it seemed as though the only tragedy in his life was his early, untimely death.

Yet after his passing a new and mythic "tragedy" slowly evolved out of the Langdon mystique. It was the age-old fable of a once-famous clown who never understood what had made him so funny to his public, who didn't comprehend that his character could be wistful and funny at the same time, a performer who never recognized the natural pathos that was integral to his success as a great comedian.

Along the same lines, in his personal life, Harry Langdon wasn't being recalled as the happy-go-lucky and energetic dad who played toy musical instruments with pals like Vernon Dent, Stan Laurel and Red Skelton for his little boy's amusement (an event that wife Mabel captured in 8mm Kodachrome home movies), or who took his little boy for a private ride in a blimp over Los Angeles, or on a father-and-son outing to Columbia Pictures, just to say hello to his friend Buster Keaton.

Instead of a real-life picture of the man, Harry Langdon was being portrayed in a very different light: as an egotistical know-it-all who actually knew very little; a vain and self-important jerk that ruined his career while attempting to outdo the artistry of Charlie Chaplin. According to this scenario, Langdon was a figure to be pitied; he lost his audience because he never understood his own screen character — and, most damning of all, he didn't even create the character that made him a great star in the first place! A former employee of Langdon's own company said, "He didn't really know his character, though he could play it."

As ridiculous as this last notion might sound to anyone who has ever watched a Harry Langdon performance, it was blindly accepted by many as the gospel truth for years — primarily because the originator of these tall tales was Academy Award-winning director Frank Capra, "the most honored and well-liked director of his generation," as one cinema documentarian put it. Capra was one of Langdon's early collaborators in the movies, a top gagman who rode the wave of success as part of the Langdon team and who was later fired by Langdon over creative discord. Capra's own career rebounded after his split with Langdon and he went on to greater success as the director of Oscar-winning classics like *It Happened One Night* and *Mr. Deeds Goes to Town*. Gradually, though, Capra spent an increasing amount of time and effort extracting petty revenge on his one-time employer, and after Langdon's death, he began smearing the reputation Harry had achieved in film. Capra, whose personal credo had become "one man, one film," looked back to the early days of his career and attributed Langdon's greatest success primarily to one man — namely, Frank Capra.

Apart from some snippets of interviews and stories to be found in Capra's fictionalized autobiography *The Name Above the Title*, no first-hand accounts have surfaced about the breakup between the two men. Whatever their differences may have been, hindsight does reveal that Langdon was dead wrong to fire Capra. Besides making a spectacularly bad career move, Harry Langdon had acquired an enemy who would follow him to the grave — and beyond, if that were possible.

I learned something about Capra's deep-seated feelings while researching material for a proposed biography on Harry Langdon in the 1970s. One of the first people I interviewed was the actor Ben Lyon, remembered today by film buffs for appearing opposite Jean Harlow in Howard Hughes's *Hell's Angels* (1930). He appeared in two films with Harry Langdon and was directed in another film by Frank Capra. Mr. Lyon was an affable gentleman, extremely patient with the sometimes ridiculous questions from this neophyte teen scribe.

As I got to know Ben Lyon over several months he opened up and shared a peculiar story with me:

> Now, I just ask you not to repeat this story until after all the living participants are residing on the other side of the dirt, so to speak, because I believe Frank Capra is overall a good man. But I was making a silent picture in New York called *For the Love of Mike* (1927), and it was one of Capra's first pictures as a director. Claudette Colbert was also in it, but frankly, it wasn't a good film. Anyhow, one day I was riding alone with Capra in the backseat of a big Oldsmobile town car going to location filming, and we passed a theater where the latest Harry Langdon movie was playing. I knew that Frank had directed Harry Langdon, I had seen some of their earlier films, but I knew nothing of their working relationship. And I thought Harry Langdon was a great comedian, and he really was a very big star. So I said to Frank something like, "Gee, Mr. Capra, I really want to see that Harry Langdon picture you just made." And Frank kind of glowered back at me. And then he said, "I hope I never meet that so-and-so again, I'd probably break his neck!" I was given a quick lecture by Capra on what a terrible person Langdon was, told in colorful language that I wouldn't repeat back to a sailor.
>
> A couple years after this I made a movie with Harry Langdon [*A Soldier's Plaything*] and I went into the job dreading having to work with this man, based on the awful things Frank Capra told me. Lo and behold, we met and hit it off right away. Harry turned out to be a very nice fellow: funny, creative on the set, cooperative with our director Mike Curtiz and everyone else… very easy to work with. So I had to wonder whether Capra was off base about him.
>
> Some 40 years later, I ran into Frank at an event out in Beverly Hills; I think his book had just been published. He's one of our great directors, of course, so I kidded him and said jokingly, "I believe I'm the only man who can say with distinction that I starred in Frank Capra's one box office failure!" He sort of just stared at me — so I quickly added, "I'm Ben Lyon — we made *For the Love of Mike* together" — and then Frank nodded and said, "Yes, yes — we made that in New York, I had just been fired by that little so-and-so Harry Langdon…" And then for a minute Frank was reliving all of this intense dislike that he still harbored against Harry. It was as though he were back in that time all over again. I felt like telling him that maybe it was time to forgive and forget, you know? It was so strange that this enormously successful, almost revered director was still angry at an actor who died so many years ago.

During the 1970s Frank Capra's renewed celebrity as a successful author took him on the talk show and college lecture circuit, where he happily discussed his career in films to a public enthralled with his adventurous stories that, it was frequently noted, "sounded like a Frank Capra movie." Often during Q & A sessions he would be asked about his breakup with Langdon. Capra's public facade was always able to get his point across without appearing vindictive.

Comedy director and former soundman Edward Bernds worked with Capra and Langdon on separate projects at Columbia, and remarked how Capra would achieve a conciliatory tone:

> Whenever Capra spoke "on the record" about Harry Langdon in his later years, he was always quick to point out that Langdon was a great artist, a great pantomimist. But Capra wouldn't give Langdon any credit for coming up with that "little boy" character. Langdon's whole approach to comedy, the decision to slow things down and to react to them, gave Harry a unique slant that made him stand out from the rest. I watched Harry perform many times when I was a soundman. You really couldn't tell him how to act, he really did know better than anyone else. When Capra spoke with interviewers, he'd stress how he was wronged by Langdon, which was no doubt true. But then he would frequently go on to denigrate Harry on a personal level. Capra would finish up by saying, "Langdon was even greater than Chaplin, but because he was so simple, he never understood why he was greater." And who then is going to say that Capra must hate Langdon, after he makes a generous statement like that?

Frank Capra's public statements about Langdon had other, indirect ramifications as well. Shortly before Capra's autobiography appeared, film collector Raymond Rohauer had been negotiating with Warner Bros. to purchase the film rights and motion picture elements on Langdon's six silent features produced by The Harry Langdon Corporation. I went to work for Rohauer in 1977, assisting on a full-length Langdon biography. Rohauer told me that initially there had been plans to release all the Langdon features worldwide, in the same style revival that he orchestrated for Buster Keaton's films several years earlier. Said Rohauer: "But Capra kept on bad-mouthing Langdon everywhere he went, so that a lot of distributors turned me down flat. They figured the films must be terrible and wouldn't even look at 'em. I had to bribe theaters by offering the Keaton features if they would also accept a Langdon package. It didn't always work."

Rohauer, a shrewd businessman who often worked by intuition and hunches, was himself bamboozled into believing the entire Capra Myth. Over the four years I worked for him, I had to listen to Rohauer complain that Langdon's own ego had caused all the troubles in his life... never mind the fact that Rohauer created new title cards for all the Harry Langdon and Buster Keaton films he "owned," with his name prominently featured ahead of the star, and in giant-sized lettering!

Even Mabel Langdon, Harry's last wife who married him years after the Langdon-Capra feud, herself became an indirect victim of Capra's prejudices. Mabel only knew her husband as the warm-hearted *paterfamilias* and hard-working comedy star of two-reel shorts in the 1930s and '40s. But the more involved she became in promoting Harry's silent features, the more stories she heard from Rohauer about her late husband, as related by Capra.

After a while it became impossible to work with either Rohauer *or* Mabel on a Harry Langdon book. Rohauer was determined to include the Capra interpretation of events; and Mabel was equally determined that nothing of the kind would be included that might place Harry in a less than saintly light. Under those circumstances, there was nothing more I could do but disentangle myself from the project. The ever-paranoid Rohauer, fearful I would use my research materials to publish a Langdon book of my own, made *our* professional split as difficult as possible. It was all starting to seem very familiar.

During those 30 years since my own split with Rohauer, I never expected that anyone would be able to accomplish the impossible and so ably tell the definitive life story of Harry Langdon. I'm happy to report that Chuck Harter and Michael J. Hayde have not only proven me wrong, with a fair and balanced, wholly engrossing biography, but they have also taken this work further by including detailed synopses, critiques, and reviews on every one of Langdon's nearly one hundred films. It's actually like getting two complete books in one binding, and incidentally, they're both magnificent. Chuck and Michael have done justice to Harry Langdon's life and films. I feel that Harry himself, never one to rush things through onscreen, would agree that the wait for this book was well worth it.

Edward Watz is an American film historian whose field of expertise is the silent movie era, with a special interest in the lives and careers of the classic silent and early sound movie comedians. He saw his first Harry Langdon feature Tramp, Tramp, Tramp *in 1971 and has been a vociferous Langdon supporter ever since. Watz is the author of* Wheeler & Woolsey: The Vaudeville Comic Duo and Their Films, 1929-1937 *(McFarland, 2011), and co-author (with Ted Okuda) of* The Columbia Comedy Shorts *(McFarland, 1998). Watz's other work includes audio commentary tracks on DVD sets, including* The Buster Keaton Collection *(Sony Pictures), and* Harry Langdon — Lost and Found *(Facets). He has contributed articles to motion picture publications including* Filmfax *and* Classic Images *and contributed comedy lore to Turner Classic Movies.*

Little Elf

Prologue

This story begins at the end.

In November 2010, one of the authors wished to pay his respects at Harry Langdon's gravesite. He discovered that Grand View Memorial Park in Glendale, California, was in a state of extreme disrepair. It had been that way since 2006 and had recently been the target of a class action lawsuit for mismanagement and the mishandling of remains. The suit was settled in October 2009 and $500,000 had been earmarked for renovation and repairs. However, one year later, this work was just beginning and the cemetery was only open to the public for four hours on Sundays.

The author visited on November 7, and found the mausoleum containing Langdon's remains had clearly sustained extensive water damage. His nameplate was chipped and faded; the luster of its gold lettering only a memory.

To the author, this seemed like just one more undeserved indignity heaped upon Langdon, one of the few true legends of screen comedy — and easily the most misunderstood.

For approximately forty years, beginning with his 1944 death at age 60, Harry Langdon's legacy had been the province of two men: producer Mack Sennett, in whose studio Langdon became a comedy star, and director Frank Capra, who progressed from a Sennett gag man to the director of Langdon's second and third independently produced features. Both Sennett and Capra wrote autobiographies that were products of imaginative fancy rather than historical fact, and each dealt with Langdon in a way that reduced the comedian's own contribution toward his success to mere afterthought.

"Harry Langdon came from a small-town vaudeville act in which his specialty was helpless frustration with a balky automobile," wrote Sennett in his *King of Comedy* (Doubleday, 1954). "Langdon actually was as innocent as an infant. He had his routines, well learned in vaudeville, and he could do them on demand, but he seldom had the mistiest notion of what his screen stories were about....

"Langdon was as bland as milk, a forgiving small cuss, an obedient small puppy, always in the way, exasperating, but offering his baby mannerisms with hopeful apology. Frank Capra's enormous talents first showed themselves when he saw all this as something that would photograph."

In his book *The Name Above the Title*, (MacMillan, 1971), Capra took Sennett's cue and insisted that he'd actually invented Langdon's entire film persona: "Sennett had had Langdon's vaudeville act photographed. He insisted that directors and writers see it. It was my turn. I viewed it with [production manager] Dick Jones, [writer] Arthur Ripley and two other gag men....

"When the lights went on, Dick Jones said to us: 'Well, there he is, fellas. And we're stuck with him. I don't know what, but the Old Man [employees' pet name for Sennett] sees something in this Langdon. But so far, in films with other comics he's just another fresh little guy....' Ripley straightened up and coughed. 'What kind of magic could transmogrify that twirp (*sic*)? And since you're stuck with him, and my Aladdin's lamp isn't handy, I suggest prayer. Because at the moment I think only God can help us with Langdon.'

"I nearly jumped out of my skin. 'Wait — a — *minute*,' I said, getting up and pacing. 'Dick — that could be it! I think Arthur's got something...that only *God* can help an elf like Langdon. God's his ally, see? Harry conquers all with goodness....' 'But where's the comedy?' asked Dick, a little worried about being talked into something.

"'Where's the comedy in Chaplin?' I argued. 'It's in his character, the Little Tramp. Harry'll be the Little Elf. Look, Dick. Why don't you let Ripley and me kick it around? Give us Harry Edwards as the director....'

"Nearly everybody in the studio went to the preview of Harry Langdon's next two-reel comedy.... Next morning the lot buzzed with excitement. 'A new star is born!' was the word of mouth."

Subsequently, wrote Capra, success went to Langdon's head: buoyed by the attention received from important New York critics, he brazenly took credit for writing and directing his films, demanded "more pathos" in his scenarios and summarily fired Capra — who had by then become his director — when Capra wouldn't submit to Langdon's unreasonable and egotistical whims. Langdon took full control of his films, which failed miserably with audiences, and within a year he was washed up, toiling in cheap short comedies for the balance of his career. When Langdon died, Capra asserted, he was broke and forgotten, never understanding that, because he didn't create his screen character, he was incapable of guiding it.

In subsequent years, respected authors and film historians such as William K. Everson, Kevin Brownlow, Walter Kerr and Leonard Maltin, when chronicling Langdon's career, relied on the Sennett and Capra accounts as a foundation for their work. The facts, after all, were clear: Langdon's post-Capra silent features *did* fail at the box office. Langdon *did* work in low-budget two reel comedies almost literally to his dying day. His obituary notices, recounting various alimony hassles and declarations of bankruptcy over the years, *did* proclaim him broke and forgotten.

In 1983, Dr. Joyce Rheuban, a professor of cinema studies for City University of New York, penned a book-length scholarly analysis titled *Harry Langdon: The Comedian as Metteur-en-Scène*, in which, through extensive research, particularly of Langdon's vaudeville career, she argued that Sennett's and Capra's interpretations were false; that Langdon was unquestionably the creator of his own fully defined character; that the majority of his silent film work reflected his comedic vision, and his vision alone. Dr. Rheuban demonstrated conclusively that, far from "a small town vaudeville act," Langdon was a headliner on the major circuits, Keith and Orpheum, for several years. She argued that the key to understanding Langdon's character was not his "baby mannerisms"; rather, she saw him as "a victim of a pathological absentmindedness." She also compared him to Charlie Chaplin and Buster Keaton, demonstrating that Langdon was their equal in both uniqueness of characterization and comic inventiveness.

But Dr. Rheuban's thesis was itself built on a flawed foundation: namely an assumption that Langdon was a fully formed comedian as early as 1906. She maintained that from the start his stage character was fundamentally identical to his screen persona, and any changes made to his act in the ensuing years were cosmetic, designed to showcase the minimalism of his comedy. Consequently she saw no conflict in making a statement concerning the content of Langdon's act in 1906, then buttressing her point by quoting from a 1921 *Variety* review.

After Dr. Rheuban's book was published, a new generation of film scholars dug deeper into Langdon's body of work and found additional flaws with the Sennett and Capra accounts. Far from supporting Capra in the creation of Langdon's character, Arthur Ripley had been the lead writer of Langdon's films for several weeks before sharing that credit with Capra. Far from being assigned at Capra's suggestion, Harry Edwards had been directing Langdon's films for several weeks before Ripley began writing them. It was Capra who was very much the junior partner of the team.

Thus, for the past 20-odd years, the pendulum of posterity has swung away from Sennett and Capra toward Langdon himself. The time has come for a thorough reexamination of his genius.

This book is subtitled "A Celebration of Harry Langdon," and there is much to celebrate. Langdon's story is primarily one of perseverance. He entered vaudeville in the smallest of small-time venues armed with little more than a wife, a prop automobile, some song and dance and a few stunts. Within ten years, he was a regular on the big-time circuits and played the most prestigious theaters of them all: New York City's Palace and Chicago's Majestic. He wrote all his material, plus sketches for other vaudevillians. In 1920, his most popular turn, *Johnny's New Car*, was incorporated into a successful Broadway show. Three years after that, he entered films.

During the heyday of silent cinema's major clowns, Langdon was favorably compared with Chaplin and Harold Lloyd for creativity and audience popularity, and was considered ahead of Keaton in both realms. Of the four, only Chaplin had as swift a rise to the top as Langdon, who did it with fewer than half as many films. Of the four, Langdon graduated from shorts to independently produced features the fastest. Of the four, Langdon was the most prolific during the talkie era, during which he worked steadily in both shorts and features, co-wrote some of Laurel & Hardy's best-remembered films, and periodically returned to the stage, sometimes with his famous trick auto. To the end, his audiences remained loyal and he worked almost constantly.

As for Langdon's downfall: yes, it was swift but not debilitating. Upon the loss of his production company, he was immediately hired at big money for

stage appearances; in any case, he returned to films before his final silent feature had finished circulating. If a fiery ego played a role, it had been fueled and fanned by his second wife, Helen Walton Langdon, and by an entourage of yes-men and a coterie of pretentious film critics. More tangible contributors were the rise of talking pictures and the precarious financial position of his employers who were about to be acquired by a competitor. Ill-advised business decisions and artistic choices that didn't find popular favor also played a part… but in the end, Langdon not only survived but thrived, blessed with a happy third marriage and a child. Far from forgotten, he was in demand to the end of his life; far from "broke," he left his widow and son in comfort.

At the same time, we recognize that Frank Capra's self-serving account does contain elements of truth. Although even in his earliest films, Langdon displayed traces of his ultimate screen persona — traces he plainly originated in vaudeville — it is clear that the character did not emerge fully formed until the Edwards-Ripley-Capra triumvirate was complete. Having achieved success, it was no coincidence that Sennett kept them permanently assigned to Langdon, and that Langdon hired all three for his own company. But rather than having "created" Langdon's character, what these men provided were pieces of a puzzle. Assembled, what emerged was a framework to properly showcase Langdon's unique brand of comedy, brought with him from the stage, in *film*.

As funny as Langdon could be in the films made both before and after Capra — and at times he is supremely funny — those made with Capra's participation are clearly the ones that brought Harry Langdon to the heights of stardom, both critically and commercially. We believe Capra's label, "Little Elf," best captures the essence of Langdon's highly original character and have selected it as our title.

We also believe there was no cruel or arrogant motivation behind Capra's dismissal. Like any artist, Langdon had to pursue his own creative muse to the limit, and the results, while not considered successful at the time, have found a growing favor with modern audiences. As for Langdon's talking films, if they never consistently recaptured his magic, the majority showed him to be a multi-faceted performer and more than a few caught his particular lightning in a bottle. Of this we are sure: they're worthy of deeper examination.

We ask that you put aside all you may have heard or read about Harry Langdon, both pro and con. In the following pages, you'll learn his real story, much of it in his own words. You'll discover his childhood and early years as an actor. You'll know *exactly* what he did on stage throughout his vaudeville career, derived from his actual scripts. You'll follow his progression in movies from novice to major star, climbing from the bottom to the top. You'll understand all the factors that contributed to his fall, and how he got up, shook them off and resumed climbing. You'll discover the facts about *all* of Langdon's subsequent films, which have been sorely neglected even by historians, and find that many garnered critical and popular acclaim. To illustrate these points, you'll find over 500 images: photographs, advertisements, script pages; many unseen for nearly a century. You'll behold the most comprehensive Langdon filmography ever created.

Let the celebration begin!

CHAPTER ONE

From Troublesome to Trouper
1884–1905

Every celebrity life has its legends; in most cases, they're cheerfully provided by the celebrities themselves. In the case of the Little Elf, he shared his personal rags-to-riches story with various journalists over the years, and never the same way twice. Since his passing, employers and employees, biographers and historians have further stirred up already muddied waters.

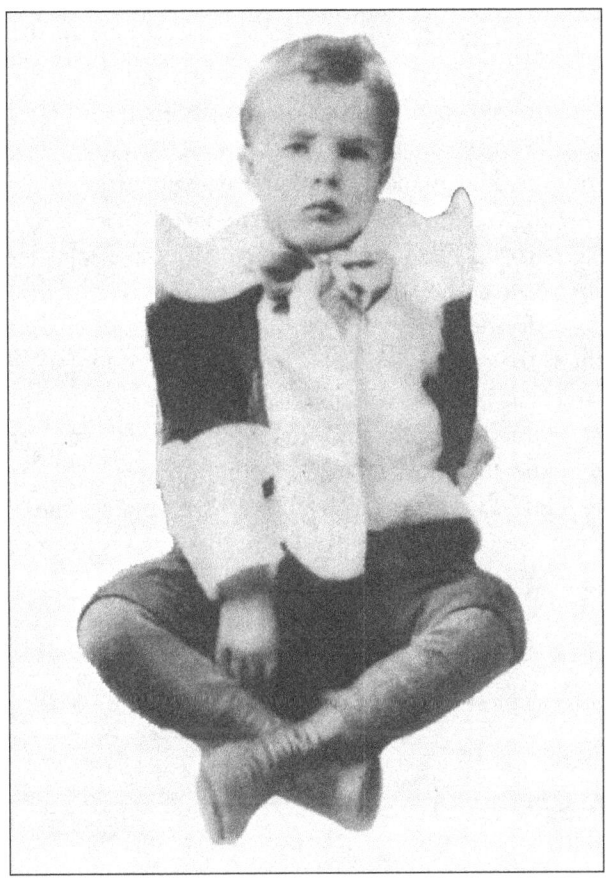

Harry Philmore Langdon, approximately three years old.

Most every reliable source states that Harry Philmore Langdon was born in Council Bluffs, Iowa, on June 15, 1884, the fourth of eight children. His father, Williamson Worley Langdon, hailed from Clinton, Missouri, according to family members. The Federal Census has the family in Boone one year before Williamson's April 1851 birth, and by the time he was nine, they could be found in Ozark. Harry's mother, Lavina Luchenbill (later anglicized to "Lookinbill"), was born in Illinois, where she met and married Williamson around 1874, at age 16.

Williamson was the fourth child of his parents' five. His father, Henry Langdon of Virginia, worked as a farmer, per the 1850 and 1860 Federal Census, as Williamson eventually would alongside three older brothers: Richard, John H. and James P., while younger sister Lydia assisted their mother, Polly, with the household chores. Lacking the necessary health and build in adulthood, "W.W.," as Williamson eventually labeled himself, abandoned farming and plied his trade as a sign painter.

W.W.'s older brother James chose the same career, and by 1880 had settled in Sioux City, Iowa, with his wife, Emily. W.W. and Lavina could be found there as well before moving to Council Bluffs in 1882, where Harry would join his brothers Charles Bartly (born in Illinois in April 1875), William Jr. (born in 1877) and John Henry (born June 5, 1879). The family would remain in Council Bluffs, through the births of James Tulley (December 22, 1890), Claude Haviland (February 4, 1894) and Gertrude Jane (January 21, 1897), and the death of William Jr. sometime prior to 1895. (A second daughter, Bertha, died in childhood.)

Omaha, Nebraska, was situated just across the Missouri River, and around the time his wife became pregnant with Harry, W.W. carried out a job that was impressive enough to earn mention in the Council Bluffs department of the *Omaha Daily Bee* on October 16, 1883: "The large, handsome sign, two feet high by forty-two feet long — one of the largest in the city — which now adorns the front of the store of Eiseman, Rodda & Co., was painted by W.W. Langdon, and is a credit to his skill." Gifted as W.W. could be with the brushes, like other artists he was overly fond of bottled spirits, and his next mention in the *Bee*, on September 26, 1891, would be far less flattering:

> The patrol wagon was called to the upper end of Harrison Street, in the vicinity of "Duck Hollow," last night to arrest W.W. Langdon, a painter. An information had been filed in Justice Hammer's court charging Langdon with committing an assault and battery on his wife. According to the woman's story, her husband [had] been out collecting during the afternoon and came home drunk. Something did not go to suit him, and he commenced to strike and kick her in a most brutal manner. She only

Opposite: Dohany's Opera House in Council Bluffs, where Harry Langdon worked as an usher and made his earliest stage appearance, circa 1898. PHOTO COURTESY OF THE HISTORICAL SOCIETY OF POTTAWATTAMIE COUNTY

escaped serious injuries by taking refuge at the house of a neighbor. Langdon could not give bail and spent the night in the city jail.

Clearly that day's wages went straight to the saloon. Family lore holds that Lavina became an officer in the Salvation Army as a means to enter bars and retrieve her errant husband, but once enlisted, she took the responsibility seriously. Eventually, W.W. joined her in the organization, possibly even by choice. The 1895 Iowa Census lists "Salvation Army" as their "Religious Belief," and by the end of that year, W.W. had risen within its ranks to captain. He leased a small building at 161 Broadway, next to the Ogden Hotel, and on January 22, 1896, opened the Langdon Mission, "free for people with or without religious convictions," according to that morning's edition of the *Bee*. "The charitable feature will consist in giving away to the worthy poor each Saturday evening 100 loaves of bread. W.W. Langdon of the Salvation Army will have charge of the work."

Despite their newfound piety — or perhaps because of it — W.W. and Lavina's boys were suitably rambunctious and troublesome, particularly their middle child. In May 1896, shortly before his twelfth birthday, Harry and another young man were apprehended for robbing Gallagher's grocery store. Both were represented by counsel and presumably received a light punishment. Two years later, Harry — by then a street vendor of the *Bee* — and two others were charged with assaulting Harry Snyder, a fellow newsboy. Such battles were common among "newsies" who were very protective of their turf; Harry's was the lucrative theatrical district, and young Snyder was allegedly selling his stock at a discount. Since the "assault" was merely knocking the papers from under Snyder's arm, the judge dismissed the case. After a few months, Harry and two other pals were arrested for creating a disturbance during the wee hours. "Judge Aylesworth," read a news report of the hearing, "let them off with a suspended fine of $10 and [court] costs during good behavior, but took occasion to read them the riot act. He told them that if found on the streets at night at an unreasonable hour they would be arrested and he would see to it that they served out this fine and another larger one on top of it."

Harry wasn't the only Langdon boy to cause trouble: in 1894, Charles and another youngster were

This photo of the Ogden Hotel shows the building that housed the Langdon Mission in 1896. It is the small structure to the left of the hotel. PHOTO COURTESY OF THE HISTORICAL SOCIETY OF POTTAWATTAMIE COUNTY

arrested for chicken stealing, but the case was dismissed when the victim failed to show in court. In 1898, John was cited and fined for swearing on the public streets. More seriously, in 1899, Charles was again arrested, this time for throwing a brick through a large plate glass window at the Creston House hotel, which he claimed was accidental: he was aiming at a stray dog and missed. Along with hiring an attorney, W.W. threatened to "commence proceedings to close the saloon in the hotel" if charges were pressed. Threats backed by the Salvation Army were not to be ignored.

Needless to say, Harry never mentioned these events in later interviews when the legend-creation began. Beginning with his earliest days at Mack Sennett's studio, he insisted that he began his acting career at age 12, but in true movie star fashion, he was trying to convince journalists and the public that he was younger than his actual age. In a 1920 interview he was more forthcoming: "I began to get my experience in stage life at the Boyd Theater [in Omaha], where my father was a scenic artist and [which] turned out many shows for the small Western towns. In those days, property boys didn't get very much money, and so to help along I sold papers on the corners during the daytime for the *Omaha Bee*.

"When I wasn't playing hooky from school, I used to draw pictures for my own amusement of the town notables. Then Admiral Dewey came along and I made a pen drawing of him. One of the boys took it to the city editor of the *Bee*, and he thought so well of it that he gave me an assignment, and I did several 'strips,' and became known as the newsboy cartoonist around the paper." Admiral Dewey's exploits occurred in 1898–99, when Langdon was 14, and this coincides with the Harry Snyder incident.

Langdon enjoyed drawing — he would do it all his life — but the theater fascinated him. In a 1926 article for *Cinema Arts*, writer Margaret G. Monks captured his perspective: "Watching people enter the doors of this house of magic every day, Harry noticed that they went in careworn, unhappy, frowning, and they came out carefree, happy, grinning. What sort of magic place was this which one entered sad and left glad? In a world of work and care the least bit of joy would have meant much to the little fellow, and the theater offered such a moment."

Having viewed some of the Boyd's productions, courtesy of his father's affiliation, as a youngster Harry and a friend created their own playhouse, calling it "The Grand Theatre of the World, and Omaha." He described this "establishment of no little importance" to a writer for the French weekly *Mon Ciné* in 1925:

> Half the yard behind my father's house was barely enough space for it…. We built it, my little friend and I, out of used planks, crates, and old curtains. I was the only actor, and my buddy was the entire public. Then he had the clever idea to bring in all the kids in the neighborhood, for free at first, then for money — when I say "money," beads and candy sticks were also accepted as payment — as soon as we were sure "The Grand Theatre of the World, and Omaha" would succeed. It was splendid. I had complete medieval knight's armor, assembled out of fruit boxes, and I played several roles I created myself, which, given the lack of actors other than me, were just long monologues ending only when I changed costume and character. Those were good times. I did anything I wanted to, before a public always ready to applaud me.

With such reward at the forefront, the lure of genuine show business inevitably followed. He'd already had a taste at Boyd's, but Dohany's Opera House was right in Council Bluffs. Having been caught one too many times trying to sneak in, Dohany's enterprising manager offered the eager teen a job as usher, which he cheerfully accepted. "The only remuneration I received was the privilege of watching the show when I wasn't seating customers," he related in a 1930 interview, "but I was satisfied. I also was permitted to go backstage, where I learned a great deal about actors and their work." Within a short time, he'd moved on to the slightly more prestigious responsibility of ticket-taker.

Despite the designation, local "opera houses" were not limited to music: theatrical and vaudeville troupes, minstrel companies and even medicine shows would set up shop in these establishments for a week of work. "Stock companies played our theater," wrote Langdon in 1932, "and I would watch them perform and dream of the time when I [would] be an actor and travel with the shows." It was at Dohany's, according to this account, that he first appeared before the footlights. A touring troupe player given to over-indulgence was too hungover to appear in the evening performance of *East Lynne*, the dramatization of Ellen Wood's 1861 novel that became a stock company perennial.

"Luckily it was a small part and they gave me a chance," Langdon recalled. "After the show the company manager congratulated me and asked me to join the company. You can imagine what a surprise that was to both the manager of the opera house and myself."

According to Monks, the company included "an old character actor who knew his lines so well from long repetition that he could ad lib at leisure. He often rattled other actors by his *sotto voce* lines and Harry was no exception." In a tale Langdon told more than once, he at one point was to tell the "old trouper" in an excited voice, "He jumped in the saddle and galloped off," but the actor decided to prompt him with the unscripted cue, "Come on, hurry up, you're terrible!" The nervous Harry blurted out, "He gumped in the jaddle and salloped off," much to the audience's delight.

The tour with the *East Lynne* company lasted only a week because "the show went broke," remembered Langdon; adding insult to injury, he never got paid. Yet despite these setbacks, the hopelessly stage-struck boy decided he'd found his calling, which led him to Micky Mullins' Music Hall, a sprawling Omaha honky-tonk that catered to the local farmers. There, as the story goes, he presented himself to the owner/manager as a dancer and singer, whereupon Mr. Mullins invited him to compete in the hall's amateur night. For the next several weeks Harry became a mainstay at this competition, where the occasional triumph over other contestants only whetted his appetite for more.

One evening, according to Langdon, Mr. Mullins greeted the youngster at the stage door:

"You can't work here no more."

"Why not?"

"'Cause you're a professional amateur now."

Harry took that as his cue to head for Des Moines, which had a dedicated vaudeville house. No contemporary record can be found of exactly when this was or what Harry did there, but we have a clue from a 1939 interview in which he spoke about this period, performing "a gag my dad once taught me. I bought an old oil painting and I'd whitewash it so that it looked like a blank canvas. This was mounted on an easel that was all daubed with colors.

"Then, with three brushes in each hand, I'd do a lightning 'painting' act. The paint pots actually held only water. I'd dip the brushes and swab off the

Dohany's Opera House, as it looked when Langdon worked there as usher and ticket-taker. PHOTO COURTESY OF THE HISTORICAL SOCIETY OF POTTAWATTAMIE COUNTY

whitewash so that the astonished customers would see a beautiful picture. The only trouble was that people started asking me to sell them originals."

It was while performing in Des Moines that he was invited to join the Kickapoo Indian Medicine Show, run by a Doctor Staley, or Gelcher, or Belcher; the name seemed to change each time Langdon was interviewed.

Medicine shows were a middle-America staple during the late 19th and early 20th centuries for one reason: the entertainment was free to all. The show would set up at a local theater or opera house — or, if necessary, simply pitch a tent — and stay for a week, with different acts each evening. The Kickapoo show also enticed crowds with prizes, such as a set of silverware to "the best looking lady in the audience." The following item from the *Des Moines Daily Capital* holds some idea of the mass appeal they enjoyed, while doubling as a splendid example of spin control:

> The first meeting of the Hickory Debating Society of this Village was held last Tuesday night at the town hall, and when we say that it was a glowing success we are putting it mildly indeed. True, the audience was exceedingly small and unresponsive, but when it is remembered that the Kickapoo Indian medicine show held forth here on the same evening, we should not be surprised at the meager attendance.

The Debating Society's topic was "resolved that Lord Byron was a greater poet than Ella Wheeler Wilcox," demonstrating that the masses have always favored vulgarity over refinement in their pop culture choices.

The Kickapoo show thrived, of course, on the sales of one-dollar bottles of Sagwa, "a remedy for all time and for all seasons. It restores the stomach, liver and kidneys to a state of perfect health; and if these organs are in good condition you need not fear disease. Rheumatism, Dyspepsia, Liver complaint, Disease of the Kidneys, Nervous troubles, Scrofula, Erysipelas, and all blood disorders are cured and prevented by the harmless and valuable compound of roots, barks and herbs." (A combination not unlike those found in the herbal teas of 21st century health food stores… minus the outrageous claims, of course.)

By all accounts, Langdon did his first professional comedy with the medicine show, in and out of various make-ups, including blackface, and speaking in Irish and German dialects. Additionally, he mixed and peddled Sagwa, and — perhaps inspired by his father — painted the signs touting the troupe. All told, he toured with the Kickapoo show for about six months before returning to Council Bluffs.

This puts us, depending on the source, somewhere between 1899 and 1901. The challenge in recount-

Young Harry Langdon, in blackface, demonstrates a skill he mastered while in the Kickapoo Medicine Show. Langdon designed this poster to promote himself between engagements.

ing Langdon's pre-vaudeville career is the lack of chronological detail found in most primary sources, as well as the inconvenient presence of other Harry Langdons in show business. One such Harry, a contemporary of Edwin Booth, was alleged to have left the stage in 1890 (according to his obituary notices), but actually performed right up to his 1902 admittance to the Actor's Fund Home in Staten Island, New York. His 1899 tour with the James-Kidder-Hanford company was credited to our Harry by at least one biographer. Another Harry toured with his wife, one Mae Cody Langdon, during our subject's formative years. Yet another was a member of S. J.

Poli's Stock Company in Bridgeport, Connecticut, a troupe that included Walter Huston.

In any case, secondary sources credit our Harry at this juncture with time in the Wallace Circus, where he mastered juggling and balancing tricks, and also dabbling in ventriloquism or traveling with the occasional minstrel show or touring company. When at home between jobs, he'd resume freelance cartooning

A poster for Ferris' Comedians. Langdon joined the troupe in July 1902.

for the *Bee*. The 1901–02 edition of the Council Bluffs City Directory lists him as a painter along with his father and brother Charles, with brother John listed as paperhanger; they all resided together in the Langdon home. But that state of affairs, if it ever existed beyond the printed page, wouldn't last long.

Not that Lavina wasn't earnestly trying to steer the lad away from the immoral theatrical world. She'd give him stern lectures, to which he barely paid attention, whereupon he'd receive a switch on the backside. One account holds that when a medicine show came through town she hid his clothes and made him dress as a girl until they left; whether true or not, he'd use the idea of enforced feminization in some of his films. When he followed the show anyway, she gave up and bought him a trunk.

In July 1902, he hooked up with one of the most famous of touring troupes: Dick Ferris' Comedians ("A Great Show for Little Money"). Ferris and his wife, actress Grace Hayward, formed their first company around 1894 and built a reputation for good showmanship almost from the start. "Ferris' Comedians do not offer a sugar coated pill filled with the wind of humbug, but they guarantee two and a

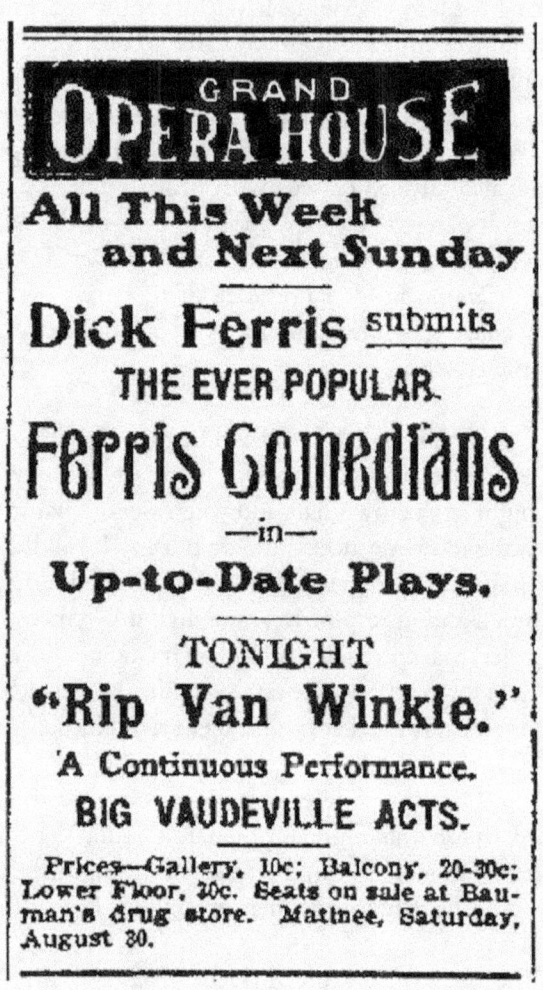

A newspaper ad for the Ferris troupe's performance of Rip Van Winkle *in Oshkosh, Wisconsin; August 27, 1902. Langdon played the title role.*

half hours of solid enjoyment, or refund your money before the last act," according to an 1895 press release. Eventually Ferris and Hayward would head up individual companies: two or more touring troupes that combed the Midwest, which would come together as a stock company in Minneapolis and St. Paul during the summer. All were marvelous training grounds for aspiring performers.

Harry auditioned and was accepted during one of these expansion periods, and it was with the Ferris troupe that he drew possibly his earliest favorable notice, courtesy of the *Daily Northwestern* of Oshkosh, Wisconsin, August 28, 1902:

> Ferris' Comedians drew another good audience to the Opera house last evening, and gave a fine presentation of that standard play "Rip Van Winkle." Harry Langdon as "Rip" was good while the supporting company was all that could be desired...At the matinee Saturday afternoon by request "Rip Van Winkle" will be repeated, and as a special attraction for the children the celebrated cake walking dogs will be introduced.

Like all troupes of the day, Ferris' Comedians would arrive in a town where they'd been booked by the local opera house or theater and stay for at least a week, putting on a different show each night. Both comedic and melodramatic plays were on the schedule, and between acts there would be specialty performers (such as "cake walking dogs"). Harry, when not cast in the evening's play, was called upon to do his juggling and balancing tricks, often in blackface.

The tour ended on January 3, 1903, after which the company went into stock at the New Metropolitan in Duluth, Minnesota, for several weeks. During these times, the troupe changed plays weekly instead of nightly, and performances were augmented with small-time vaudeville acts. At the conclusion of the regular season, Langdon was selected for Ferris' Lyceum Theater stock company, which alternated during the summer between the Lyceum in Minneapolis and the Metropolitan Opera House in St. Paul. During this stint, the company performed *My Friend From India*, *The Man From Mexico*, *Monte Cristo*, *All the Comforts of Home* and *Shamus O'Brien*.

The *St. Paul Globe* reviewed every play, sometimes more than once, and Langdon is mentioned in several:

> THE MAN FROM MEXICO (July 6, 1903): Dick Ferris, in the leading role, while hardly so pleasing as Willie Collier, made the most of the opportunities afforded him, and was liberally applauded by those who witnessed the performance.... Harry Langdon, as Sheriff

An ad from the St. Paul Globe *for the Ferris troupe's performance of* Monte Cristo, *July 19, 1903. Langdon held the role of Danglers.*

Cook, and Charles C. Burnham, as Von Bulow-Bismarck Schmidt, overdid their parts, their interpretations savoring very much of burlesque.

MONTE CRISTO (July 21): Another large audience witnessed the second performance of "Monte Cristo" by the Ferris company at the Metropolitan last night and received the stirring scenes with applause. Frederick Montague did even better work in the leading role than on the opening night, and the roles of Caderousse, Villefort and Danglers were well handled by Charles Burnham, Ernest Fisher and Harry Langdon.

SHAMUS O'BRIEN (August 10): The largest Sunday night audience which has been seen at the Metropolitan in years was there last night to witness the initial performance of that popular Irish melodrama, "Shamus O'Brien," with which the Ferris Stock company opened the week's engagement…The play, which was new to St. Paul theater-goers, was well received, and the audience expressed its sentiments by applauding the heros (sic) and hissing the villains and traitors. Frederick Montague appeared in the title role to the satisfaction of all. Harry Langdon, as Shadrick O'Finn, the traitor and informer, was seen at his best, and the hisses he received upon his every appearance indicated that he was performing his part well.

Having achieved such verifiable growth as an actor, Langdon continued with Ferris' Lyceum Company into the 1903–04 season. But not every performance was bouquet-worthy. In March 1904 the troupe, including Grace Hayward (who'd temporarily disbanded her own company), returned to St. Paul for two nights with *When We Were Twenty-One*. The *Globe*'s reviewer was decidedly unimpressed:

A painfully inadequate performance of Henry V. Esmond's delightful comedy, "When We Were Twenty-one," was given at the Metropolitan last night. Only one member of the company can be honestly commended, to wit, Joseph Totten, who contributed a spirited and spontaneous portrayal of the Imp that was

Dick Ferris, flanked by his wife, Grace Hayward (left) and Fannie Granger (right), in 1903, when Langdon was a member of Ferris' Metropolitan Stock Company.

altogether satisfying. As for the impersonation of Richard Carewe by Dick Ferris, it was quite perfunctory and monotonous, while the Phyllis of Grace Hayward savored of the rural drama, in accent and action. The three bachelor friends of Carewe were impersonated by actors who did not know their lines. The less said of the rest of the show the better.

not among them this time. Joining the troupe as the drunken "savage" Wah No Tee was a Canadian actor who would, within five years, transfer his allegiance to "the flickers" of New York's Biograph Studios: Dell Henderson. There he would befriend and collaborate with fellow Canadian Mack Sennett, the man who'd one day introduce Harry Langdon to movie stardom. But that day was still nearly two decades in the making.

Harry Langdon, in and out of costume, as a member of the Ferris stock company, circa 1903-04.

Considering the same company had successfully executed the play three weeks earlier at the Lyceum, this panning must have come as an unpleasant surprise. Harry was listed among the cast in a publicity blurb, but it's unknown if he portrayed one of the "three bachelor friends" or was among the "less said, the better" portion of the cast.

May 1904 found Langdon and the company back at the New Metropolitan in Duluth for a week's worth of *The Octaroon*, Dion Boucicault's melodrama of interracial romance in pre-Civil War Louisiana. No doubt some of the actors "blacked up" for their roles; Harry, as Mr. Sunnyside, a plantation owner, was

Shortly after *The Octoroon* concluded its run, actor Mort W. Sanford of the Lyceum troupe organized his own touring unit, the Girard Stock Company, with players having been chosen "from the best and most capable artists of Mr. Ferris' different road companies." Harry was among those selected, and the troupe opened at C. F. Brown's Opera House in Waterloo, Iowa, during the second week of June, staying for two weeks.

It was most likely during his stint with the Girard Company that Langdon met his future wife and show business partner, Rose Frances Musolff. Born on September 4, 1882, in Milwaukee, Wisconsin, Rose was the eldest of Paul and Rosalina Braun Musolff's eight children. Paul and Rosalina had emigrated from Poland only a few years earlier; as Catholics, they had been no less spared from harsh discrimination than their Jewish brethren.

Possessing a body that would best be described

> **WATERLOO DAILY REPORTER,**
> **SATURDAY, JUNE 11, 1904.**
>
> ## Brown's Opera House
> J. F. BROWN, Manager.
> BOTH PHONES
>
> ### ONE SOLID WEEK
> commencing
>
> ### Monday, June 13
> SANFORD and ARTHUR
> present the
>
> ## GIRARD STOCK CO.
>
> in repertoire of successful
> COMEDIES and DRAMAS
> Specialties Between Acts.
> A CARLOAD OF SCENERY
> Opening bill (MONDAY) Dick
> Ferris' great play
> "MY JIM."
> Prices 10 and 20 cents.
>
> LADIES FREE MONDAY NIGHT

The Waterloo Reporter announces the coming of the Girard Company, with which Langdon was then associated, on June 13, 1904.

as "statuesque" — tall and well endowed — and blessed with a pleasant singing voice, Rose left the crowded nest prior to both her 18th birthday and the arrival of Cecilia, the youngest Musolff, to test the show business waters. Details are sketchy at best, but at some point she appeared with the Gaskell Carnival Company and reportedly toiled in burlesque. Whatever she was doing when Harry appeared on the scene may be lost to history. The two were wed in Milwaukee on November 23, 1904, in what was presumably a Catholic ceremony witnessed by her family. More than likely, W.W. and Lavina did not discover their son's marital status for several months: in the 1905 Iowa Census, Harry is listed as a resident of the family's Council Bluffs home, with Rose's name conspicuously absent.

Also lost to time are Langdon's theatrical pursuits during 1904–05, although it's probable he and Rose either remained with the Gerard Company or returned to Minneapolis for what would be the Ferris troupe's final year at the Lyceum and Metropolitan. Whichever it was, the marriage led to an unexpected salary cut. In May 1924, Langdon recalled for columnist Jack Jungmeyer, "When I graduated from a [medicine] show to the stage, I drew $25 per week. Then I got married. With my wife a member of the company, we drew a total of only $30, whereas before our earnings had been at least $55."

Thus, for the 1905-06 season, Rose and Harry, calling themselves "The Langdons," fashioned their respective talents into a whole that might loosely be considered an act, then embarked on a dangerous, yet undoubtedly exciting, journey into the world of small-time vaudeville.

CHAPTER TWO

"The Langdons Is the Name"

1906–1911

In 1996, Floyd Bennett, president of The Harry Langdon Society and editor of its newsletter, sat in front of his library's microfilm machine with reels of *Variety* and *The Billboard* and painstakingly searched through issues printed ninety years earlier for documentation of Langdon's earliest vaudeville work. After adjusting his eyesight to the negative images common to library microfilm, Mr. Bennett struck gold: an itinerary for three Illinois cities during September 1906 and an advertisement in *The Billboard*'s September 8 issue:

THE LANGDON'S
IN VAUDEVILLE
With a Comedy Novelty Act, featuring their automobile. See Billboard as per route

Writing in the first official issue of *Wild About Harry*, the Society's newsletter, Mr. Bennett waxed enthusiastic:

> "Featuring their automobile." That could only mean the famous trick car. Gazing in awe into the microfilm reader, I saw it as if I were there: In September 1906, in Decatur, then in Springfield, and then in Quincy, Harry and Rose "drive" onto the theater stage in the wooden breakaway car he designed and built. The car stalls. Harry bobbles around helplessly, struggling to fix it and making things steadily worse, while shrewish Rose berates his every effort. Finally, the car "blows up." The audience howls for more. Future comedy superstar Harry Langdon is on his way.

The author's excitement is palpable and understandable, but in reality the Langdons' act, in 1906, bore no resemblance to this description of its contents. Nor in 1907, or for that matter, 1917, nor in any year Langdon was in vaudeville.

This description of helpless Harry and "shrewish" Rose is, perhaps, the last surviving myth brought to us courtesy of Frank Capra and his "autobiography." In his book, Capra, writing about a film of The Langdons' by-then famous car act, described action one might expect from Langdon the movie star: a flurry of frightened, hesitant gestures, with Rose delivering such captioned dialogue as, "Idiot! Is this what they sold you for a new car?" as the auto proceeds to fall apart at his touch. For lack of anything more definitive, subsequent authors have trusted this account, even while debunking the other, admittedly more damaging, parts of Capra's tale.

But this isn't Langdon the solo screen performer. This is Langdon the vaudevillian and his wife, who was, for a time, his equal in talent and audience appeal. And as it happens, and in fairness to Mr. Bennett, more information and resources have been made available in the years since his groundbreaking essay was written.

After the summer of 1905, Dick Ferris' Lyceum troupe was no more. Fifteen years later, Langdon told a reporter his memory of what happened next: "At the close of the season, I was told that there was a man in Chicago who had a vaudeville circuit and that I had better try and get into it, as it would tide me over the long winter lay-off. I framed a singing and dancing act, and that started me [in] vaudeville." The "man in Chicago" was Gus Sun, who was considered the smallest of small-time vaudeville "circuits" (a route of theaters controlled by a single booking agency), but Langdon himself is getting ahead of his tale. He and Rose didn't play in Sun's theaters until mid-1907.

The earliest booking for The Langdons that has surfaced is at the Electric Theater in Waterloo, Iowa during the week of February 5, 1906, and it includes a reasonably detailed description of their

TONIGHT--ELECTRIC THEATRE — BEST SHOW OF THE SEASON — PACKED HOUSES THE RULE
Everyone says, "A good show." See the following artists: Gilmore and Carroll, black face singers and dancers; Charles Bailey, acrobat and barrel jumper; The Langdons, novelty comedy sketch, singing, talking and dancing; Ben A. Tilson, singer of ballads; Motion Pictures, "The Miller's Daughter."
Special added attraction for this week
THE GREAT MILLIO BROTHERS, NOVELTY AERIAL GYMNASTS
The Greatest Gymnasts Ever Here.   Two Shows--8:00 and 9:30 o'clock.   Come any time; stay as long as you like.
Seats on sale at Brady Bros. Drug Store.   Prices: 10, 15 and 20 cents.

Opposite: The Langdons in 1906. Above: Newspapaer advertisement for the earliest known booking of The Langdons in vaudeville, February 5, 1906.

first vaudeville turn, courtesy of the *Waterloo Times-Tribune* of February 11:

> The comedy sketch… is unique and highly interesting. Taking the part of an Irishman, Mr. Langdon, ably assisted by Mrs. Langdon, created roars of laughter with their quips and funny expressions. A little song and dance was mixed with the comedy which was catching and pretty. Following the duo was (a) bottle balancing act, an unusual thing even in vaudeville. With the hind legs of a common kitchen chair balanced on the neck of two bottles, Langdon seated himself in the chair and assumed an attitude of repose, the seriousness of which was lost by the comical expression of Mr. Langdon and the extremely funny way he had of treating the performance….
>
> Perhaps the most interestingly unique part of the whole sketch is the automobile feature. This closes the Langdon sketch and is always the occasion for vigorous applause and enchores *(sic)*. Mrs. Langdon sings a song which has one of the most catchy choruses imaginable, as she reaches this portion of her song, the other member of the team comes onto the stage with a red automobile into which the lady steps and as the vehicle is driven across the stage the pair engage in one of the prettiest duets ever heard on this stage.

The reason for the detailed description is because Waterloo audiences didn't get to see it beyond opening night. On Tuesday evening, as Langdon assumed his "attitude of repose" while balancing, "one of the bottles broke, causing the fall of the performer, whose body struck the jagged edge of the broken bottle," reported the next morning's *Times-Tribune*. "The rear of the left leg was severed for three inches at a depth of over an inch. Doctor McMannus was called and sewed up the wound, and the suffered was removed from the theater" to the boarding house where he and Rose were staying.

Friday's *Waterloo Semi-Weekly Reporter* noted that Dr. McMannus "stated [Langdon] would be unfit for work for some time to come," but by the time of Sunday's *Times-Tribune* write-up, the prognosis had changed for the better: "Reports of the condition of Harry Langdon…are that he is recovering rapidly and will be able to resume his part of the sketch in a very short time."

As a result of the accident, wrote the *Times-Tribune* critic, "Mrs. Langdon has had to supply a little sketch of her own. She has more than made good in the single part she has taken since her husband's accident, and has greatly pleased her audiences. Her singing is good and her little dance is takingly

> SEMI-WEEKLY REPORTER.
> WATERLOO, IOWA.
> FRIDAY, FEBRUARY 9, 1906
>
> Accident at Electric.
>
> An accident occurred last night at the Electric theatre which will lay up one of the popular performers on the bill for some time to come. Harry Langdon, who does the very difficult and daring feat of balancing chairs on bottles, was doing his act last night when the neck of one of the bottles broke, letting Mr. Langdon fall, and he alighted upon the jagged edge of the bottle, making a very severe and painful wound. A surgeon was summoned to dress the wound, and stated he would be unfit for work for some time to come. He was removed to Mr. Johnson's home, 316 East Park avenue.

graceful." Nevertheless, opined the unnamed reviewer, the original act "has been greatly missed since Mr. Langdon has been out of commission, and patrons of the little playhouse here are hopeful that a return engagement can be made with them."

Nothing has turned up regarding such a return. The Langdons made their debut in *The Billboard*'s "Routing for Performers" pages in its February 24 issue. Alas, the pair had to postpone these listed appearances in Colorado and Missouri while Langdon's leg healed. He was able to return to work the week of March 5 at the Crystal Theater in St. Joseph, Missouri.

Unexpected bloodletting was only one of the potential hazards facing Harry and Rose. In these early days, they were dealing directly with the managers of the Midwest's smallest vaudeville houses, which meant writing letters describing the act, traveling and auditioning; building a reputation one theater at a time. It also meant the risk that if you failed to please either the audience or manager during your initial performance, you needn't return for the remainder… and there was no severance pay. On the up side, they'd arrived just as vaudeville was approaching parity with dramatic theater in salary and prestige; just as the era of continuous performances (minimum six shows a day) was drawing to a close. As their act became known, with press clippings and ads such as the one

John J. Murdock, head of the Western Vaudeville Managers Association, who booked The Langdons for his theaters in the autumn of 1906.

in *The Billboard*, the Langdons hoped they'd soon be deemed worthy of attention from the Vaudeville Managers' Association.

Which is what happened. Sometime that summer, John J. Murdock, a manager who not only owned several Illinois theaters, but was also head of the Western Vaudeville Manager's Association, saw or read about The Langdons. The W.V.M.A. was the western component of the Vaudeville Manager's Association, created in 1900 by the twin czars of vaudeville, Benjamin Franklin Keith and Edward Franklin Albee, and designed primarily to place theater booking under one manageable system (with the added benefit of keeping performers' salaries under control). Murdock booked Harry and Rose for those September appearances in Decatur, Quincy and Springfield mentioned earlier, among others, into the following year.

Murdock was a visionary as both a V.M.A. agent and theater owner. In the third edition of his book *The Stage in the Twentieth Century*, Robert Grau wrote of Murdock, "There is no question but that he was a power and influence among vaudeville men. He was never known to break his word, always fought for the right, and was loyal to his friends. He was undoubtedly one of the best friends the actors ever had… Many a performer owes his success to Mr. Murdock's interest in his behalf. He was the first to advocate the high salary.… Many performers who had trouble with managers appealed to Murdock, not in vain, to patch up their difficulties, and he placed them in a position to again receive booking." In short, J.J. Murdock was a powerful ally.

At the People's Theater in Cedar Rapids, Iowa, a reviewer from the *Daily Republican* was present: "The show started with the Langdons and their comic novelty in which they feature their automobile. The act contains some very clever balancing with tables and chairs, and ends with the team in their auto going back and forth across the stage, as they sing several of the latest automobile songs."

In the spring of 1907, they graduated to the Gus Sun Circuit for fifteen weeks. Sun, also affiliated with the W.V.M.A., had begun his managerial career by forming a minstrel troupe, with which Langdon reportedly spent some time during his formative years. In 1904, Sun opened his first vaudeville house in Springfield, Ohio. By 1907, he oversaw his own circuit in the heartland that, before the decade was out, would grow to 200 theaters. For his part, Sun remembered Langdon's audition and is reported to have remarked, "I figured that if he should turn out to be half as funny looking on the stage as he was the morning he wandered into my office, he would have them rolling in the aisles."

It was around this time that Langdon added electric lights to his auto, along with specific instructions for theater personnel for dimming the stage lights. A critic for Newark, Ohio's *Daily Advocate* caught them at the Orpheum Theater: "Other features of the bill are the Langdons in their new original auto novelty act. The finish is one of the prettiest scenes ever produced on the local stage, speeding away in their automobile singing their latest song hit." At least one

Gus Sun theater, along with the trade paper *Variety*, referred to them as "The Auto Langdons," so distinctive was the motoring portion of their act.

As yet, there wasn't much comedy other than the Irish dialogue opening. Posterity has credited Rose Langdon for helping to popularize "In My Merry Oldsmobile," composed in 1905 by Gus Edwards and Vincent Bryan, and presumably one of the "automobile songs" referred to by the *Daily Republican*. Langdon built the prop car and wrote the act, but hadn't created much in the way of a character for himself. Theater ads for this period tout the auto, along with singing, buck-and-wing dancing, balancing and juggling: it was a novelty act in every sense of the word. Nevertheless, theatrical manager John P. Goring was impressed enough with what he saw to invite "the Auto Langdons" to join his touring company of *The Show Girl* for the 1907–08 theatrical season.

B. C. Whitney's *The Show Girl* was a mostly plotless musical comedy revue, centered on a theatrical company stranded in Greece (of all places) and had debuted about five years earlier and played for over two hundred performances each in New York, Boston and Chicago before going on tour. For the new season, Goring, "at an expense of about $10,000, entirely rebuilt [the show] from the ground up [and] scoured the country looking for the best possible talent to make this *The Show Girl*'s best season," or so proclaimed his publicity. Another husband-wife team, Lillie Sutherland and Jack Curtis, were the biggest stars to sign on, having toured in vaudeville and musical comedies across the nation and in Europe for several years under the auspices of

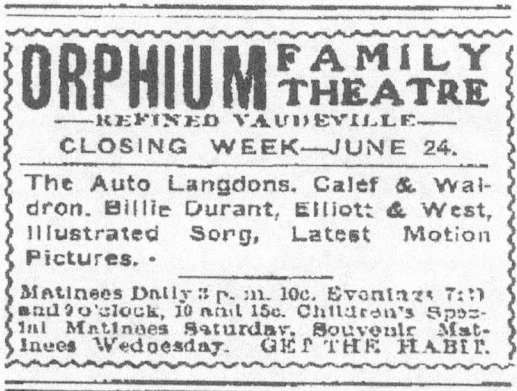

Above: A Billboard ad for the Gus Sun Circuit in 1907. Note the request that aspiring performers should "state lowest salary."

comedian-turned-impresario Lew Fields. "Seventeen Song Hits and Eight Specialties" were *The Show Girl*'s highlights, including the Langdons' automobile turn. Prominently mentioned in the ads was "Stately Rose Langdon," while Harry, "the cleverest of comedians," was consigned to publicity blurbs.

Rose may have received higher billing, but *The Show Girl* was far more important to Langdon's development: it was here that he became a character comedian, and not just a figure of amusement. The role he was handed, Johnny Jones the Property Man, gave him plenty of room for comic "bits," according to reviews. For the first time, he employed an eccentric costume and hat, along with exaggerated make-up, although photos show a lean figure looking more like future Sennett comedian Al St. John than the Harry Langdon cinema patrons would come to know.

Rehearsals began in mid-August in Detroit, Michigan. The tour was grueling: mostly one- or two-night-stands, with travel primarily by automobile (not, we presume, Harry and Rose's). Naturally the troupe began in Michigan, then traveled south into Indiana, turning west to Illinois, Iowa and Nebraska, making a sharp right toward South Dakota, trekking upward into North Dakota, pivoting westerly to Montana, veering south directly to Utah (somehow bypassing Idaho entirely), proceeding eastward with stops in South Dakota and Iowa again, then pirouetting into Minnesota, Colorado, Missouri and ultimately Kansas, where the whole shebang crashed and burned.

We'll get to that last part in a moment. At its start, the show held the promise of success. "The musical comedy *The Show Girl* opened a two nights' engagement at the Empire last evening and delighted a good sized audience," said the critic for Marshall, Indiana's *Daily Chronicle* on September 11. "The comedy equals many that are given long runs in the large cities…. Jack Curtis as 'Manager Fly' and Harry Langdon as 'Johnny Jones the property man,' were rivals for first place in the cast and yet there could be no hard feelings as their parts differ so much that the comedy could not dispense with either. Both are artists and both made good with the audience…. Those who failed to see *The Show Girl* missed one of the best attractions of the season, but another opportunity awaits them tonight."

The above represents The Langdons, in their trick automobile. They are booked solid for the season by the Western Vaudeville Managers' Association. The auto is proving a novelty in the continuous and the act is making a hit everywhere.

The Democrat of Washington, Indiana, was equally delighted one month later: "[*The Show Girl*] drew a bumper crowd at Coats & Momeny's opera house and every number on the program was encored. There were thirty-five members of the company. The equipment was good, the jokes new, the songs catchy and the dancing fine. Miss Lillie Sutherland, soubrette, caught the audience from the start. She is petite but oh

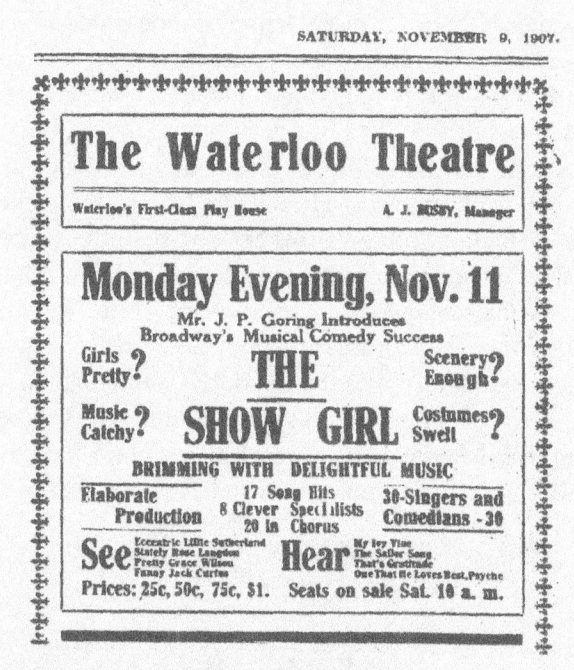

The Langdons in 1907, approximately when they joined The Show Girl.

my! she makes them all stand around and take notice of her…. Jack Curtis and Harry Langdon, comedians, caused many a hearty laugh and they knew how to do it without using 'slap sticks' or 'horse play.'"

But a catastrophe several hundred miles away soon turned this and other traveling companies toward disaster. October 17 initiated the infamous "Panic of 1907" when, in an ill-fated attempt to corner the copper market, Charles W. Morse — a Wall Street banker who'd once successfully cornered the ice market — lost a fortune, and saw a run on the six New York banks with which he was affiliated. This quickly spread to other banks and trust companies, leading to loss of confidence in, and bankruptcies of, financial institutions across the land. Had it not been for J.P. Morgan's propping up New York with his personal fortune, the Great Depression might have begun twenty-two years earlier. As it was, by the start of 1908 the stock market had lost nearly half its previous year's value and much of the nation had plunged into a deep recession.

Goring did what he could to spur attendance — "Comedy Is the Rage During Panicky Times" was the

new headline for one of his standard press releases in December — but nothing worked. Attendance was poor. Box-office receipts were sparse.

Other problems beset the company, including the perils of traveling through Montana when winter is nigh. According to the *Anaconda Standard* of December 10, Harry and Rose experienced a taste of their future act:

> "The Show Girl" did not please a Butte audience last night by a great deal. In the first place, the show began with an apology from one of the managers, who said that the company had attempted to reach Butte and had got stranded by the breaking down of an automobile. Then it was announced that another automobile had gone to the rescue and the players had arrived, breathless, but ready for the play. Judging from the expression of disgust on the part of the audience, the major portion of the people who had given up good money to see the show wished the second automobile had blown up. People left at the end of the first act. During the second act the actors were [audibly mocked] and more people left when the curtain dropped. The play did not please by any means, and it did not have a redeeming feature.

Fortunately, the company went from Butte to Salt Lake City for a three-day stay at the Grand Theater. The venue was filled, at least for opening night, and the players rose to the occasion. The Amusements critic for the *Salt Lake Herald* wrote, "The show apparently made a hit with the Grand patrons, the songs and music being of the whistling order and the jokes of the kind that you think of for awhile before forgetting. Taken as a whole, *The Show Girl* is a good show and worth the price…. One of the hits of the piece was the illuminated automobile specialty song by the Langdons."

But after Salt Like City, it was back to tank towns and uncertainty. Salaries were inconsistent and morale sunk. Sutherland and Curtis departed during the last week of January for a more reliably lucrative vaudeville tour, which didn't dissuade Goring from keeping their names in his newspaper ads, probably because he couldn't afford to revise them. In February, everything fell apart. The seventh marked the last time anyone in the company would be paid. In Iola, Kansas, on the fourteenth, the leading lady who'd replaced Sutherland refused to go on, feigning illness. One week later, in Lawrence, Goring was served with attachment papers for unpaid salaries. Upon being served, the manager swiftly departed with the music and suddenly life imitated art: the company that had portrayed a stranded company was stranded.

"From all accounts, the town did not lose much," wrote the *Iola Daily Register*. "*The Show Girl* has been getting roasted over the state and was preparing to go on the tallow candle circuit from here. After the company left there were some attachments run…This has been a hard year on the show business. All but the best have gone to pieces and the best ones have experienced rough sledding." The

Billboard, always impresario-friendly, simply noted in its March 28 issue, "Mr. J.P. Goring of the J.P. Goring Amusement Enterprises, Detroit, Mich., has closed all of his attractions owing to light business, but expects to reopen The Show Girl Company in the near future."

Harry and Rose, taking Sutherland and Curtis's cue, returned to vaudeville, which was not altogether a bad thing. Vaudeville shows were significantly cheaper than traveling theatrical companies, and so were not as hard-hit by the recession. Langdon took the opportunity to revamp the act, bringing the auto on stage at the start and building the comedy around it. And he gave the act a title: "Midnight on the Boulevard."

J. J. Murdock was more than happy to book them again, and so The Langdons' made the rounds of the Midwest. By June they were in Wisconsin. A review in the *Appleton Daily Post* was so enthusiastic that Langdon used it in a *Variety* ad:

> There is a team at the Bijou this week such as has never been there before, and while their act is a scenic production such as is seldom seen here, it is at the same time the most uproarious clean-cut comedy without any of the old jokes you have heard ever since you were a child, and makes an instantaneous hit with the audience. This act is entitled, "Midnight on the Boulevard," and an automobile is introduced into the action of the turn. It is perhaps the best new thing that has been at the little theatre in some time, and is put on by the Langdons.

Langdon promoted "Midnight on the Boulevard" in six consecutive *Variety* issues during July and August, most concluding with the line: "THE LANGDONS is the name." Meanwhile, J.P. Goring had summoned them for his revitalized *Show Girl*, for which he'd engaged one Helen Stuart, an actress-vocalist who'd recently appeared with a stock company in Goring's home state of Indiana. This tour would begin in Ohio and was designed to proceed eastward toward New York.

Whatever rosy future Goring described to entice Harry and Rose never materialized. This time the show disintegrated in less than a month. "Trouble has been rife in the ranks of the organization since a few days after the production took to the road," wrote Connellsville, Pennsylvania's *Daily Courier* of September 21. "The leading man was dismissed at Wheeling [West Virginia]. This started dissension in the ranks. Then at McKeesport [Pennsylvania, the previous week] the trunks of the company were attached and others left. The company was badly crippled when it arrived here, but by doubling up, two performances were given. But [the show] received its death blow here when Helen Stuart, leading woman, made a sudden departure…. Some of the members of the organization are here and the untimely end of the sprightly creature, *The Show Girl*, is regretted in several ways by them." One of which, no doubt, was in the pocketbook.

The Langdons wasted no time getting back on stage, scurrying to Ft. Wayne, Indiana's Temple Theater for the week of October 12. The W.V.M.A. routed them to such northeastern cities as New Rochelle, New York, and Hoboken, New Jersey, and even a brief stay in lower Manhattan, during the first week of June 1909 at the Fourteenth Street Theater, although only the *New York Dramatic Mirror* saw fit to write about them:

"The Langdons were successful in their presentation of *Midnight on the Boulevard*. They carry a scenic boulevard effect which was exceptional, and a prop auto full of good comedy and electric effects. There is no plot, it being a sort of conversational affair, replete with some clever comedy lines and original business. The male half of the team affect *(sic)* some unique comedy mannerisms, which helped his work, but was not so pleasing when he sang. Their musical numbers were 'Automobile Honeymoon' and a medley finale."

A *Variety* staffer named "Rush" caught the act in Hoboken a few weeks later, and duly filed his "New Acts" review for the July 24, 1909 issue. Terming *Midnight on the Boulevard* a "Novelty Singing Sketch" and clocking it at fourteen minutes, "Rush" failed to see anything uproarious:

> Certainly The Langdons have arranged a novelty. The curiosity lies partly in the fact that the team, man and woman, make their entrance in a "prop" automobile and partly in the fact that the woman does all the singing while her partner, introduced in the character of the chauffeur, does no singing but talks occasionally to no very good effect. Although appearing in eccentric clown make-up he does not work very hard for laughing points. The woman appears attractively attired in automobile costume. Upon the entrance there is a very short period of dialog when the woman goes into a song, leaving the man out of the proceedings altogether. Another interval of talk follows in which the man figures inconspicuously. Then comes a second song. At the finish an electric display is depended upon to arouse interest, a score or so of red electric lights attached to the automobile becoming illuminated. If the two people will evolve a straight specialty (meaning a specialty shorn of cheap spectacular effects such as the final illumination) they may work up into some notices. Light effects never yet made an act any more than a "claque." [Rather,] it is clever, skillful specialty material that gets across for solid success. It appears from the showing of the Langdons that the man has a comedy knack and the woman an agreeable voice. Why not work out a suitable vehicle in which the most is made of these gifts. If they desire, the mechanical incidentals may be worked in as a casual episode.

Upon reading the review, Langdon shot off a letter, which was published a couple of weeks later:

> Editor VARIETY:
> Rush reviewed our act this week and stated that the woman member of the team did all the singing while her partner did no singing at all but talked occasionally to no good effect. Rush made a mistake, which I wish to correct. There are two songs, and my wife and I sing them together and always did.
> As for the effect of my talking, two shows out of three the talking was a laughing hit, so it must have had some effect.

Despite this indignation, advice from *Variety* was generally not ignored by ambitious vaudevillians, and so, during the 1909–10 season, Langdon reworked his sketch. By April, he'd renamed it "A Night on the Boulevard, or Troubles with an Automobile." The Langdons' prop car was now officially uncooperative. He removed most of the lights from the auto and placed them on his boulevard backdrop depict-

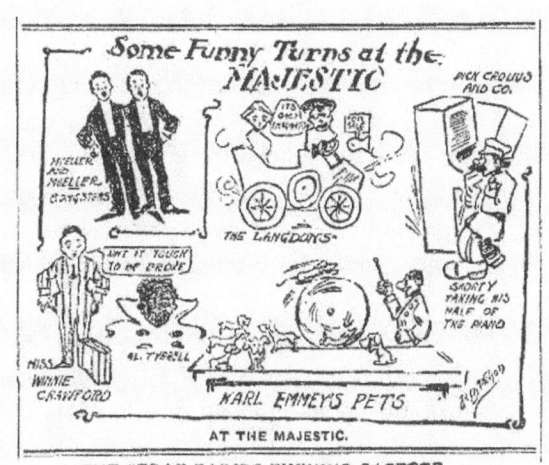

THE CEDAR RAPIDS EVENING GAZETTE, TUESDAY, SEPTEMBER 21, 1909.

ing an avenue receding in the distance; the painted street lamps would now be illuminated. The effect was remarkably convincing and impressive. A critic for the *Evening Journal* of Lewiston, Maine, who caught a split week engagement in the town's Music Hall, enthused, "The moment the curtain ascended upon this act, the audience liked it. When a stage setting receives the plaudits of an audience, then the eye sees something better than it is accustomed to [seeing]. The scene represented a boulevard, with its numerous lights and beautiful road-bed. The perspective was wonderful; the eye seemingly could traverse the painted curtain for miles." The opening applause became so commonplace, The Langdons would eventually advertise it: "Always a Reception at the Start."

The act played the Sullivan-Considine circuit in the West and Murdock's theaters in the Central. "For genuine 'funniness,' originality and staging, The Langdons in their novelty…is the best thing on the bill, and their songs and automobile troubles made the biggest kind of a hit," per the critic for the *Cedar Rapids Evening Gazette* on September 21, 1909. Given Langdon's hometown status, we would ordinarily allow for some partiality, but this was typical of the reception they were getting everywhere. The

Daily Journal of Buffalo, New York, raved, "The electrical effects are unusually clever. The comedians come onto the stage in their own automobile, which is quite different from anything ever seen in this part of the country. It is quite like all other automobiles in one respect, however, namely, it breaks down, and the accident happens on the stage. With the aid of mechanical effects, all the troubles of the chauffeur are depicted and the trials are, as in real life, very much enjoyed by the onlooker. The act is one of the most unique and comical ever seen here."

Langdon wasn't done tinkering, though, and in the autumn of 1910 added three additional parts: a waiter, a policeman and a second chauffeur. Since these tertiary characters never appeared on stage at the same time, he engaged his younger brother James to play all three. James elected for billing under his middle name, Tulley.

During a New Jersey appearance in early March 1911, a reviewer for the weekly *New York Clipper* was in attendance and wrote it all up for the March 18 edition:

The Langdons have a specialty in "A Night on the Boulevard" which gets away from the well-traveled route, and shows a new and ambitious turn of mind. The man is made up as a Simple Simon kind of character, a chauffeur, who is whirling the lady around town in the smell wagon. As the curtain rises on a darkened stage, with the electric street lamps of the pretty boulevard glowing in a long double line, the automobile, a practical dummy, comes into view, with the lady and her chauffeur seated in it.

They talk for awhile, the man gets a drink at the horse-head fountain, which works as well regulated fountains should, and he has some fun with a 'phone which persists in moving about. Another auto, a limousine, comes from the opposite direction and stops abreast of the first car. The spoony couple inside are seen in embraces through the curtain, and finally the limousine departs.

The occupants of the first auto have considerable fun with all these props, and in addition

A 1911 Variety *ad illustrated by Langdon.*

the talk is interesting and amusing, and a parody to the tune of "Give My Regards to Broadway" is introduced.

At the finish of the offering a medley is sung, the auto is cranked up and started, the stage is darkened, and a searchlight such as is used on touring cars is swung back and forth to send its rays into the audience while the auto slowly disappears into the wings. The act gave great delight to the Jerseyites last week. It ran about eleven minutes, on the full stage.

Behind the scenes, E. F. Albee's son, Reed Albee, joined forces with Frank Evans and Harry Weber to form a talent agency to represent top-tier acts. By the spring of 1911, Weber had inked The Langdons. As the agency was closely affiliated with the senior Albee's United Booking Office, it was only a matter of time for Harry, Rose and Tulley: United Time. There would be no need to settle for lesser circuits such as Gus Sun or Sullivan-Considine; the U.B.O. would route The Langdons for the entire season.

Even though "United Time" wasn't as prestigious as the Pantages, Keith or Orpheum circuits, the class and size of venues still went up a notch in the usual Midwest towns, not to mention the salary. As for the major Eastern cities, Albee had plenty of second- and third-rate theaters within his fiefdom, most of which were acquired by the crushing of competitors. These would do for now, but with Keith's prestige showcases in New York City within sight, Harry Langdon wasn't far away from Big-Time Vaudeville.

The twin czars of vaudeville, Benjamin Franklin Keith and Edward Franklin Albee.

CHAPTER THREE
"Goaheadativeness"
1912–1915

Presumably at the urging of Harry Weber, his agent, Langdon typed up *A Night on the Boulevard* and submitted it to the U.S. Copyright Office. He might have hand-delivered it; on the day it was received, May 8, 1912, The Langdons were appearing in Washington D.C. at the Academy Theater. The manuscript, preserved on microfilm in the Library of Congress, coupled with reviews and photographs,

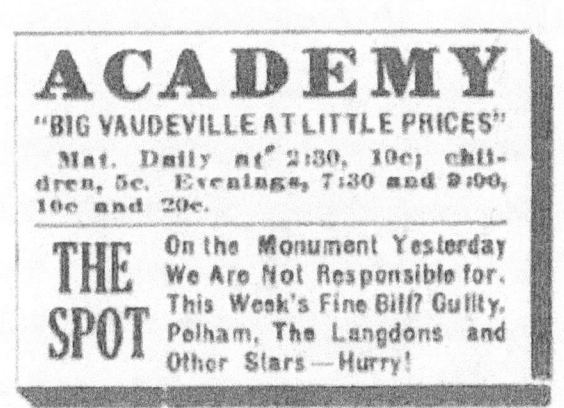

provide a fair idea of what The Langdons were doing while on the cusp of major vaudeville stardom. (Following is a basic description with selected lines of dialogue, and with grammatical errors corrected. The complete, original text may be found in Appendix I.)

The characters: Rose as "Katie Speedington," Harry as "Johnnie Flat-tire," and Tulley as Waiter, Chauffeur and Policeman. As the curtain slowly rises ("with lively music" from the pit orchestra), a clock is heard to strike twelve gongs. A blue light floods the stage; all others have been dimmed. "The scene is a drop in three (meaning the amount of stage space required is three-quarters deep), representing a boulevard with street lamps illuminated from back with electric lights." A café sits on stage left, and a drinking fountain, with water that emerges from a horse's head, is at stage right.

Enter, from the left, "a white touring car with [a] search light" on the front, four horns on the side (one of which is a French horn with a bulb), a toolbox on the running board, and illuminated headlights. A sign on the front of the car says "For Hire." Katie is in the back seat; Johnnie is her driver, outfitted in overcoat, cap and motoring goggles. The car comes to a stop aside the café, and the stage lights come up. A laughing Katie asks Johnnie if they were "scorching" (speeding).

JOHNNIE: No…

KATIE: Well, what are we stopping here for? Can't we go any farther?

JOHNNIE: No…

KATIE: Well, what's the matter?

JOHNNIE: The wheels are all <u>tired</u>.

Katie ignores the pun, looks around, and to her delight sees the café. She asks Johnnie to call for the waiter, which he does…very softly. Nevertheless, the waiter "jumps out quickly and surprises Johnnie."

KATIE: Waiter, you may bring me a crème de menthe.

WAITER: *(looking at Johnnie)* And what will you have?

JOHNNIE: Toothpick.

At the waiter's urging, Johnnie decides on "a nice high cold one," intending beer, but the waiter brings him a glass of water. Johnnie gripes, "Hey, I am thirsty, not dirty." Meanwhile, Katie sips her drink.

Having exited, Tulley blows a "Devil whistle" from off stage.

JOHNNIE: Listen to the wind.

KATIE: That wasn't wind, Johnnie, that was an automobile that just passed here just then. Look, here comes another one. My goodness, they must be running a race with each other! *(Tulley blows the whistle again.)* My goodness, that one came so close to us, he nearly took a wheel off our car!

Through all this, Johnnie is looking suspiciously at Katie.

JOHNNIE: Did you see automobiles going by here?

KATIE: Yes, going right by here.

JOHNNIE: Right by here???

KATIE: Yes, going right by here.

JOHNNIE: *(Looks over at Café)* Waiter, bring me a crème-de-menthe.

This is a cue for a song from Rose. Based on the *New York Clipper* review, it's probably the parody of "Give My Regards to Broadway"; more's the pity lyrics weren't included in the manuscript. Although not specified, it's possible that she and Harry dance a little, as the song concludes with the two of them "down stage standing together." This leads to a nice bit of visual comedy.

KATIE: You are now standing on the boulevard.

JOHNNIE: Yep.

KATIE: And the clock just struck twelve.

JOHNNIE: Yep.

KATIE: And you are all alone with me.

Johnnie looks at her out of the corner of his eye, then turns around and "blows out" all of the illuminated street lamps on the backdrop.

KATIE: Well, I just wanted to tell you that you will make a pretty good chauffeur for my father.

And with that, Johnnie turns around and whistles, and the street lamps come back on. Katie interviews Johnnie for a time, with such exchanges as:

KATIE: Suppose you were driving at the rate of 60 miles an hour, and a man was standing in the middle of the road. What would you do to let him know that you were coming?

JOHNNIE: Write him a letter.

KATIE: No, no, faster than that.

JOHNNIE: Send him a tele-scratch.

KATIE: No, no, what would you blow?

JOHNNIE: My nose.

KATIE: No, you would blow your horn.

THE LANGDONS.

In the merry travesty, "A NIGHT ON THE BOULEVARD," which has recently been increased to a three-people, three-automobile offering in vaudeville.

Johnnie walks over to the car and touches the French horn.

JOHNNIE: Here is a fine horn. *(Playing it)*

KATIE: Yes, Johnnie, it sounds just like a band, doesn't it?

JOHNNIE: Yep, that is a handy horn.

KATIE: It is?

JOHNNIE: Yes, every time I run over anybody, I give them music while they are dying.

While this is going on, Tulley has changed into a chauffeur's outfit and "drives" onstage in a prop taxi, stopping in left-center. He inquires for a preacher, as there is a couple in the cab that wants to get married right away. Johnnie informs him that his tires are punctured, at which point the chauffeur leaves. With the intention of getting a peek at the amorous couple, Johnnie tries hitting the hood of the taxi with an axe, but only succeeds in sending an adjacent street lamp six feet into the air and down again. Johnnie walks over to the fountain and fills a tin cup with water that emerges from the horse's mouth.

KATIE: Johnnie, what was that you were drinking?

JOHNNIE: Horse liniment.

Unseen by the audience, Tulley manipulates two cardboard cutouts of a man and woman's head, and these cast shadows on the cab's rear window. Johnnie therefore spies on the "couple," who, from the audience's viewpoint, appear to be kissing.

KATIE: Johnnie, what are you doing?

JOHNNIE: Sight seeing.

KATIE: You'd better try to fix up that man's machine.

JOHNNIE: *(Still looking at the shadows in the taxi's window)* It is already fixed.

KATIE: How are the connections?

JOHNNIE: (Observing that the shadows are "kissing" without moving) Solid.

KATIE: Do you think the connections will bust?

JOHNNIE: Not unless his face slips.

Tulley pulls down a shade in the taxi window, cutting off the view.

JOHNNIE: Show's over.

This leads into Johnnie trying to get his auto started, first with a crank, then by kicking the front tire. To indicate that this has started the engine, Rose surreptitiously rattles a tin can filled with buckshot; she also fires a .38 revolver through a hole in the bottom, to simulate an explosion. Johnnie opens his toolbox (the words "Get busy" are painted on the inside lid, which the audience sees), and tries cranking the auto again. Rose fires off a couple of .22 cap pistols to simulate backfire. At that sound, Tulley runs on as the policeman, yelling "STOP, STOP!" When another backfire is heard, the policeman, believing he's been shot, grabs his stomach and runs offstage.

Katie says she thinks there's a leak in the gas tank, which of course is Johnnie's cue to light a match to investigate, and the car "explodes" again. In what was probably the most spectacular visual gag, after Johnnie cranks the engine once more, he bends over to pick up a handkerchief. Rose manipulates a bellows with her foot that contains lycopodium powder (commonly used in fireworks) passed through a small flame of alcohol. The resulting burst of sparkling flame hits Johnnie in the rear end. Johnnie examines his pants.

JOHNNIE: Ain't it warm. That is a pretty bad leak in that tank.

KATIE: Yes, I have told you before that gasoline is very deceitful.

JOHNNIE: Yes, it talks behind your back, all right.

Katie tells Johnnie to phone the depot and see if her train is on time. She points to a prop telephone on a lamp post, which leads to more visual nonsense as the phone slides up and down the post (manipulated by the property man). Finally the mouthpiece comes flying off the phone and hits Johnnie in the mouth.

Katie cranks the auto, which starts up (in fact, the property man is shaking the tin can of shot). When Johnnie hears this, he gets into the car, as does Katie… and just as they get settled, the steering wheel flies out of its place and over the passengers' heads. Johnnie reaches for the "For Hire" sign and turns it over. It now reads "For Sale."

The orchestra strikes up a song, the stage lights go out (while the street lamps remain illuminated), and Harry and Rose sing a duet. As they sing, Harry flashes the search light through the audience, and the property man (using a rope attached to the bottom) pulls the car across the stage, where it exits on the right as the curtain descends.

Thunderous applause and encores follow.

The distribution of verbal and visual humor in *A Night on the Boulevard* is fairly even, but there's little in the dialogue or business that would suggest the "Little Elf" character to come. Johnnie vacillates between stupid (such as when Katie questions him) and streetwise (when addressing the waiter or commenting on the taxi shadowplay), and there's nothing written that suggests the shtick around which Langdon's screen persona would be forged. On paper, at least, his character comes across as an American Chico Marx; notwithstanding the fact that when The Langdons first performed this sketch, Chico hadn't yet joined his brothers' act. Given the reviews of the period, we can safely assume that Harry's automobile gags produced the loudest laughs and his musical interludes with Rose were suitably charming.

The Langdons spent just about all of the 1911–12 season on the Eastern seaboard, including, the week of November 6, 1911, a return to New York City at Keith-Proctor's Fifth Avenue Theater on West 28th Street. Being a more prestigious venue than the Fourteenth Street, this time *Variety* and a few newspapers sent critics to cover the bill, on which The Langdons were third. *Variety*'s "Dash" liked the act enough to award it a new adjective: "Everything they have in their laughable skit, *A Night on the Boulevard*, shows goaheadativeness. The pair [has] a prop auto that's a little dandy. They enter in it, and it is the best looking thing for a travesty buzz wagon yet shown. A pretty, attractive set is also carried. This, along with a second prop auto, and a company,

A 1911 Variety *ad illustrated by Langdon.*

makes the act look pretentious. The man and woman do very well with the comedy props and get a great deal from the material. The Langdons put it over 'No. 3.' For their newness and novelty, they should be welcome visitors around here."

Some of the city's daily papers also had kind things to say, which Harry dutifully quoted in a banner ad in the following week's *Variety*.

Keith & Proctor's 5th Ave. Theatre, where The Langdons were first seen by New York City newspaper critics.

Among the cities that season, the act played New Haven and Naugatuck, Connecticut; Lawrence and Springfield, Massachusetts; Philadelphia, Lancaster, Scranton, Altoona and Johnstown, Pennsylvania; Trenton, New Jersey (*Trenton Evening Times*: "As the curtain rises the audience sees a boulevard brilliantly lighted with a long row of street lamps, converging until they almost go together. An automobile brings the Langdons on and then the comedy begins. The lines are bright and the comedy is beyond the ordinary"); Washington D.C. (*Washington Herald*: "The Langdons, who rely on scenic effects and imitation automobiles for their comedy, got many a laugh over the footlights") and Atlanta, Georgia (*Atlanta Constitution*: "The Langdons…caused many hearty laughs, their act ending with a song that brought them several bows").

The start of the 1912–13 touring season found Harry, Rose and Tulley on their home turf, the Midwest. They opened in Racine, Wisconsin, for the Orpheum Circuit on August 26. "The Langdons in a spectacular travesty, *A Night on the Boulevard*, present a piece of acting, the automobile adding to the interest of the production," remarked the *Racine Journal-News*. "Rose and Harry are the principals; they possess sweet voices and are funny in the extreme."

The team hadn't been in Racine since July 1910, before Tulley joined, when they'd played the less prestigious Bijou. Which, of course, was the one great characteristic of vaudeville: an act could travel for two years or more without seeing the same city twice. But that was not to be the case this year, as U.B.O. routed them in the East once again, presumably by popular demand. And so, beginning in September, they trekked eastward into Cincinnati, then Philadelphia and Washington, D.C., Rochester, and other spots until, on Sunday, November 12, they played the Columbia Theater in Manhattan. And, except for a one-week return to Philadelphia in early December, they'd be exclusive to the city's five boroughs until January 4, 1913.

The Columbia was a burlesque house Monday through Saturday, but on Sundays it showcased refined vaudeville. The *New York Clipper* was there: "The Langdons, in their automobile act, showed a fine trick auto propelled and lighted by electricity, with many novel stunts, all of which were well liked and pronounced to be one of the best motoring acts. The lady sang well, and the he Langdon is a splendid comedian in make-up and action."

The next day saw the team in Brooklyn at Keith's Bushwick, followed by a split week at Keith's Colonial (Monday–Wednesday) and Union Square (Thursday–Saturday). Returning from Philly, they spent the week of December 9 at the Colonial, then north a few blocks to Keith's Alhambra, then further north to Keith's Bronx for Christmas week, followed by a return to the Union Square for New Year's week. They were well received everywhere, and their managers, Albee, Weber & Evans, made certain everyone knew it in another banner ad in *Variety*.

Show biz historians might be intrigued by the acts that were appearing near or with The Langdons during the season. In Brooklyn, as they played the Bushwick, the more prestigious Keith's Orpheum was hosting The Three Keatons: Joe, Myra and 17-year-old Buster, in "a mirth-provoking skit of the knockabout variety," according to the *Brooklyn Daily Eagle*. At the Union Square the final week, Harry and company shared the bill with a "singing comedienne" then known as "May West." It wasn't long before she spiced up the spelling of her first name to go along with her act.

Leaving New York, a brief tour of Canada followed, including two consecutive weeks in Montreal at the Orpheum. Then it was back into the States, pushing ever westward toward Chicago's Majestic Theater where, the week of June 21, the headliner was Marie Dressler, only a year away from her motion picture debut at Mack Sennett's Keystone Studios. The *New York Clipper* reported that The Langdons would spend the summer playing the Orpheum (outdoor) parks, followed by the Orpheum circuit proper beginning in late August.

October 20th found them on the West Coast at Oakland's Orpheum Theater, sharing the bill with Ed Wynn, among others. Working as an usher was a high school senior who would one day loom large in Langdon's screen career *and* personal life: Vernon Dent. Dent had already been bitten by the showbiz bug; the day before Langdon's opening, he had performed for his school's Thespians' club. Dent

biographer Bill Cassara speculates, "As an usher, Vernon had to catch that show for at least one of the performances. Knowing Vernon, he must have introduced himself to every act." A lifelong friendship may well have begun under these modest circumstances.

At the Pantages that same week, the Four Marx Brothers were also in Oakland headlining in *Mr. Green's Reception*, an expanded version of their earliest comedy sketch, *Fun in Hi Skool*. We'll never know what Harry thought about that, or if he realized that he'd been doing *A Night on the Boulevard* since the days when the Marxes were the Four Nightingales, yet there they were, headlining — albeit on a slightly lesser circuit — while he was still holding down the number three spot.

Being third on the bill was not an insult by any means, but it was the lowest of the "prestige" spots. The implications were that the latecomers had arrived, the shuffling of seats and chit-chat had ended, and now the *real* show would begin. The spot was always slotted with something that would snap the audience to attention; something flashy…and Langdon's car and special effects were just what the manager ordered.

For Harry, it had been a thrilling year, what with spending the winter holidays in and around New York City, and debuting in Canada and California,

but The Langdons were still considered on the fringes of "The Big Time." They'd made inroads on the Keith and Orpheum circuits but had yet to headline anywhere. Harry had been in vaudeville long enough to know that, however spectacular, an act lasting eleven-to-fourteen minutes was unlikely to achieve headliner status. At the same time, he was reluctant to make any drastic changes beyond sharpening the dialogue and

replacing worn-out jokes. Recognition of *A Night on the Boulevard* was growing, as was his reputation as a comedian of note.

Harry had another reputation, though, known primarily by his co-stars: he was superstitious. He wasn't the only vaudevillian with this trait, of course, but in him it ran deep. As a boy he'd found a safety pin and carried it for luck throughout his career. He also considered the overcoat and slap shoes he wore on stage as lucky; once, when a well-intentioned porter gave the shoes a shine, Harry was beside himself, certain their charmed effect had been polished away. Thus his innate wariness and penchant to keep to what was working often conflicted with a desire to take his career to the next level. As a motion picture comedian he would mine the conflicts and contradictions within his nature and emerge from those depths with a rich vein of comedy.

But it is unlikely Langdon was thinking of motion pictures just yet. Movies were still the lowly stepchild of show business in 1913, the only affordable entertainment for poor immigrants and a means to chase patrons out of theaters for everyone else. Mack Sennett, himself a non-U.S. native, was tap-

Portraits of Harry and Rose in character, 1914.

ping into these class distinctions for his Keystone Comedies, where cops, fops and dandies were forever being bested by the little guy (or gal) with few social graces but lots of gumption. Just as Langdon was gearing up for the new season, Sennett was reaching out to another vaudevillian — an English Music Hall comedian who was finishing up a tour on the Sullivan-Considine circuit — with an offer to join Keystone effective in December. The comedian, whose name was Charles Chaplin, accepted and started work in January 1914, and before Sennett knew what had happened, motion picture comedy evolved into art.

While Chaplin was making his earliest films, The Langdons trekked east again, but this season they'd be in New York City a single day, for another Sunday show at the Columbia Theater on February 22. *Variety*'s founder, Sime Silverman, caught them this time: "The Langdons were the hit of the afternoon in their *On the Boulevard* skit that employs a prop auto, with the man in a comedy make-up resembling John Burke's (John and Mae Burke). The Langdons should find booking on the big time very easy. If not, there is something wrong with the bookers, for there's nothing wrong with the act that also has a pretty woman for further recommendation."

After the Columbia, it was a week in New Brunswick, New Jersey, then westward again, to all the old familiar places: Racine, Wisconsin; Waterloo, Iowa; et cetera, finishing up at Chicago's Majestic Theater.

The following season brought more of the same: Keith's circuit theaters on the East Coast, again in the number three spot on the bill, including a four-week stint in New York City. Then on to D.C., then upstate New York (with two consecutive weeks at Keith's Grand in Syracuse) and neighboring Pennsylvania; then Ohio, Indiana, Georgia, Alabama, Virginia. There were two separate stints at Chicago's Majestic in April and June; in between, they inaugurated the summer season with a week at Coney Island's New Brighton Theater beginning May 17, 1915. Reviews also rang familiar, such as the *New York Clipper*'s for their June Majestic appearance: "The Langdons, including Rose, Harry and Tulley, got no end of laughs with [their] freak automobile. All old Ford jokes were revived with some new ones injected. Boulevard scenic arrangements unusually beautiful.

Advertisement for the Keith Grand Theatre, Syracuse, NY; January 2, 1915. By then, A Night on the Boulevard *was considered "a laughing success."*

Clean dialogue, full laughs." *Variety*, too, reviewed the performance: "The Langdons with their prop motor car was the most liked act of the early section. This act is always sure of enough laughs through the trick car and Harry Langdon's fun."

If it sounds like things had stagnated for The Langdons, Harry must have felt the same way. He returned to Council Bluffs — both he and Rose appear in the 1915 Iowa Census, living in W.W. and Lavina's home — and took some time during the summer to revamp the act, albeit in his cautious Harry way. The automobile remained the same, but it was now painted red (as it had been in 1906). The backdrop, sets and characters remained the same, but most of the situations and jokes were new. Most significantly, pantomime wouldn't be performed by cardboard cut-outs but by Harry himself. He also saw fit to remove most of the clown makeup from his face, and exchanged the chauffeur's cap and goggles for a simple fedora with an upturned brim.

After ensuring the new act was as acceptable as the old, by year's end Langdon changed its name. He tried *Troubles of a Jitney Bus* briefly, then settled on *Johnny's New Car*. At the same time, he made an even more significant alteration: The Langdons were now billed as Harry Langdon and Company.

PHOTO COURTESY OF ALAN BOYD

CHAPTER FOUR

Big Time and Broadway
1916–1920

Johnny's New Car runs twelve script pages to its predecessor's eight. Containing a great deal of suggested business, it ran a good 18–20 minutes in performance. The sketch was clearly intended to propel Harry Langdon and Company into a headliner spot.

Langdon submitted two scripts of *Johnny's New Car* for copyright registration: once in July 1916 and again in February 1921. Both are reprinted in full in Appendix II, and reviews give us a good idea as to when and which elements of the latter supplanted the former. Here we begin with a brief summary of the 1916 version:

The backdrop is identical to the one described in *A Night on the Boulevard*. Sets are almost the same; the drinking fountain is now "just outside of [the] café," which has moved to stage right, while stage left includes a milepost reading "One Mile to Garage." Rose is still "Katie Speedington," but Harry is now "Johnny Got-a-car." Tulley's chauffeur part has been dropped; he is still the Waiter and the Policeman. Johnny and Katie enter from the left and turn so that the front of the car is facing the audience.

KATIE: And you told me you knew every bump in this road.

JOHNNY: Didn't I find them?

KATIE: My goodness, but you're a fast and reckless driver. You make me nervous to ride with you. Don't get so excited when you are driving your car, take your time. And another thing: when you turn a corner, slow down to about thirty-eight miles an hour. I wish I had that wheel, I would show you how to run this car.

JOHNNY: Do you want to run this car? Well, there's the wheel. *(He removes the steering wheel and hands it to Katie.)*

KATIE: Get out and crank it.

JOHNNY: I won't crank the car. You're the only crank, and you'll have to crank it.

KATIE: Oh, how nice of you to stop right in front of the café!

JOHNNY: Well, I'll crank it up for you then.

Katie asks Johnny to call the waiter, and it's the same business as before, except that Katie's order has become more extravagant.

WAITER: What would you like to have, madam?

KATIE: You bring me a broiled lobster.

WAITER: *(speaking to Johnny)* And what do you wish?

JOHNNY: I wish you a Happy New Year, and I wish I hadn't stopped here.

Katie urges Johnny to order something for himself, so Johnny inquires about the cost of their chicken.

WAITER: We have chicken for one dollar, but of course the larger the chicken, the larger the price.

JOHNNY: I'll have an egg.

The waiter returns to Katie, who wants to order "some nice French roast, Welsh rarebit," but Johnny is blowing the horn on his car. The waiter turns to Johnny.

WAITER: I beg your pardon, sir, but I can't hear what the lady is saying.

JOHNNY: Couldn't you hear what she said?

WAITER: No.

JOHNNY: She wants a ham sandwich.

WAITER: *(to Katie)* Anything else you would like?

KATIE: Cancel that order and bring me a seltzer highball.

WAITER: All right, madam. *(To Johnny)* And I think I know what you want all right. *(Exits into café.)*

JOHNNY: If he brings me a nut sundae, I'll shoot him.

The waiter returns with a ginger ale highball, which he hands to Katie.

JOHNNY: Say, waiter, how do you like my little runabout?

WAITER: Fine. She has pretty eyes. *(Exits)*

JOHNNY: That's an insult to my runabout.

As the orchestra begins playing, Johnny gets out of the car and tries to get a drink from the fountain, but every time he approaches it, the water stops running. Finally he takes the cap off the radiator and removes water from a spring attached to the cap.

KATIE: Why Johnny, that water isn't fit to drink, is it?

JOHNNY: It ought to be, it comes from the springs.

At this point, Katie sings a song, walking back and forth across the stage. Johnny follows her, but eventually gets tired, and he blows a whistle, pretending to be a traffic cop. As the song finishes, Tulley appears in his policeman guise behind Johnny. And it's here that the first piece of bona fide Langdonesque pantomime has been documented:

Johnny stops blowing the whistle, looking frightened. Katie, standing to Johnny's right, is pointing to the policeman, but Johnny is afraid to look around. He starts whistling, looks around, and sees the policeman. The policeman turns to Katie and offers her Johnny's whistle, but she refuses it. Johnny takes it back and puts it in his coat. The policeman has moved to the right, so when Johnny turns to the left, he no longer sees the policeman and assumes he is gone. Johnny smiles, takes out the whistle and begins blowing it again, then turns around and sees the policeman on his right. Johnny smiles and tries to act unconcerned.

Katie signals to the policeman and he turns to look at her. At this moment, Johnny surreptitiously removes the policeman's badge and pins it to his vest, then begins blowing the whistle again. The policeman turns and grabs the whistle from Johnny, but Johnny pulls back his coat, showing the badge on his vest, whereupon the policeman gives the whistle back, salutes Johnny and departs.

KATIE: Why, I didn't know you were an officer.

JOHNNY: Don't you know who I am? I'm Sherlock Nobody Homes. I'm working on a case now. I'll have it all finished tonight.

KATIE: All finished tonight?

JOHNNY: Yes, I've only got three more bottles left.

The waiter returns with a bottle of champagne, which he opens "with a loud report." Startled, Johnny immediately examines his tires. Katie informs him that it is champagne.

JOHNNY: Who ordered that champagne?

KATIE: I did.

JOHNNY: Who's going to pay for it?

KATIE: Why, US!

JOHNNY: The "S" is off.

KATIE: Why, what's the matter?

JOHNNY: The "S" hasn't got any money, that's what's the matter.

KATIE: You haven't any money? Why, you owe this waiter two dollars and a half now. What are you going to do?

JOHNNY: Give him the automobile, and then I'll send him the rest.

Katie explains that this particular waiter is absent-minded. The previous evening, she and a friend stopped for refreshments; Katie's friend told the waiter some Ford jokes, and the waiter forgot to charge for the drinks. She encourages Johnny to do the same. Johnny whistles for the waiter.

JOHNNY: How much do I owe you?

WAITER: Two dollars and a half.

JOHNNY: That's very reasonable. Oh, say, waiter, did you hear the latest Ford joke?

WAITER: Why no, do you know some Ford jokes?

The waiter immediately starts laughing. Encouraged, Johnny orders another bottle of champagne. "I didn't know it was going to be so easy," he tells Katie. The waiter returns with the bottle.

WAITER: Now let's hear that Ford joke.

JOHNNY: Well, once upon a time there was some lightning bugs…

The waiter starts laughing. Johnny asks him if he has any twenty-five cent cigars.

WAITER: No, but we have some nice fifty-cent ones.

JOHNNY: Well, I'll have a nice fifty-cent one — what do I care how much they cost?

The waiter eyes Johnny suspiciously, and then departs. Johnny asks Katie if she's sure it's the same waiter. The waiter returns with the cigar, and demands to hear the rest of the Ford joke. (The joke is not specified in the script, as they were constantly being updated; automobile or "Ford" jokes were very much in vogue for several years.) When Johnny finishes, the waiter is no longer laughing. Johnny nervously looks at his cigar, then asks if he'd like to hear another.

WAITER: Now listen here — a fellow stopped here last night, got me interested in Ford jokes and I forgot to charge him for the drinks. Don't think you can put it over.

Johnny is "taken by surprise, gets weak in the knees, leans against the fountain, gets his hands all wet, collects himself." Anyone who has seen a Langdon film can readily imagine how this bit played. But then, Johnny addresses the waiter:

JOHNNY: You say a fellow stopped here last night, got you all excited and you forgot to charge him for the drinks?

WAITER: That's what I said.

JOHNNY: Well what's all of that got to do with my change?

WAITER: *(scratching his head)* Change? Why what did you give me?

JOHNNY: A twenty dollar bill.

WAITER: A twenty dollar bill? Well, I'm sorry anything like this happened. *(The waiter counts out Johnny's "change," handing him fifteen dollars.)* I thank you. Come in again.

JOHNNY: *(pocketing the money)* Sure, I'll come back tomorrow night.

Johnny heads to the car and begins cranking it, right-handed, then left-handed, then with his foot; forward and backward. At one point, the orchestra starts playing "imitating a hand organ, Johnny cranks to the time of music," then takes his hat off, acting as if he's making a collection.

KATIE: Why Johnny, you told me you had a self-starter.

JOHNNY: No, I have a combination starter.

There's a dial on the hood, which Johnny starts turning as if he's opening a safe; at one point he opens the hood to retrieve the "combination." When the car refuses to start, Johnny grabs and shakes it, whereupon it starts. Smiling at Katie, he gets into the car; the engine backfires and the auto guards start to shake. Johnny gets out again.

JOHNNY: I think my car has deliriums.

KATIE: Well, Johnny, maybe your engine's cold.

JOHNNY: It must be, look at it shiver.

Johnny cranks the car again, it starts; he gets in. The hood flies open, and the "engine jumps out on stage."

KATIE: And you told me there were six cylinders.

JOHNNY: They were sick, but I guess they're dead now.

KATIE: Well, what's the matter?

JOHNNY: Oh, I know what's the matter all right.

KATIE: Well, what is it?

JOHNNY: There's something wrong with it.

KATIE: Well, I think you have a leak in the gasoline tank.

This leads to the match business, and the flame-on-the-pants gag as Johnny is picking up the engine to put it back in the car. Johnny rushes over to the fountain, which of course stops working as soon as he approaches. In desperation, he fans himself with the car door. The joke about gasoline being "deceitful" is used. The waiter runs outside.

WAITER: The people upstairs are kicking about the noise you're making down here with this one-lung rattler of yours. *(During this, Johnny keeps shutting the hood, which keeps flying open.)* And I don't care much about it myself and if you don't stop it, I'll knock your block off.

JOHNNY: Are you looking for trouble?

WAITER: Sure, I'm looking for trouble!

JOHNNY: *(pointing to where the flame came out)* Well, look in there.

Johnny cranks the car once more, the engine starts; he gets in, the steering wheel flies away. Johnny gets out, picks up the steering wheel and the remnants of the engine and places them in front of the milepost. He places a mat of grass over them, and now it looks just like a grave. Johnny removes his hat and weeps.

KATIE: *(singing)* Something seems to tell me that I'll have to walk home. I'll have to walk home in the dark.

JOHNNY: *(singing)* I'll never let you walk home, Katie, it's too far. I'll take you home in my pleasure car.

KATIE: *(speaking)* Pleasure car?

JOHNNY: Sure, when you get out of it, it's a pleasure.

Katie continues singing about the car, and Johnny professes that she's "liable to have trouble with any automobile."

KATIE: Well, I'm sorry if I hurt your feelings, Johnny.

JOHNNY: Well, kiss me then.

KATIE: Kiss you? Why, what girl would kiss that face?

JOHNNY: All the girls kiss me. They kiss me or they walk home.

KATIE: Well, I would rather walk home.

JOHNNY: That's nothing, they all walk home.

Katie and Johnny sing a song, the stage lights go down, the headlights are illuminated and the searchlight is flashed into the audience. The auto backs off the stage and the curtain descends.

The most surprising aspect of *Johnny's New Car* is the plethora of wisecracks. After all that's been written by previous Langdon scholars about a hapless Harry berated and belittled by a domineering Rose, we find instead that, in the sketch, what little guff Katie does dish out, Johnny takes none of it. He labels her a "crank," asserts that a compliment paid to her is an insult to his car, and tells her "it's a pleasure" when she leaves. If, in *A Night on the Boulevard*, Harry's character was reminiscent of Chico Marx, here he seems to be channeling Groucho, with Rose serving as his Margaret Dumont, anticipating the genuine article by a decade. Yet the childlike glee he experiences while blowing the whistle, the growing apprehension when confronted by the policeman, the knee-buckling horror and queasiness after the waiter warns him about not paying, indicate that Langdon was zeroing in on his strengths. Such bits had developed gradually in *A Night on the Boulevard* (according to *The Billboard*, the whistle routine had been introduced by January 1915) and, going forward, would become ever more prevalent, eventually taking center stage.

It's likely that the concept of a motion picture career was emerging from the back of Langdon's mind. By the time of *Johnny's New Car*, movies were no longer a dirty word. Feature-length films running an hour or longer were introduced, and one in particular — *The Birth of a Nation* — stirred up such controversy and made so much money that everyone was convinced this was a powerful and profitable medium. Serious film criticism was published in *Variety* and elsewhere. Most significantly for Langdon, the little English small-time vaudevillian, Charlie Chaplin, had in one year progressed from Keystone to the Essanay Film Manufacturing Company for six times the weekly salary, and during 1915 became not just a star, but a national craze. Even if he'd never seen a Chaplin film, Langdon had to be aware of the Chaplin impersonators and Chaplin novelty songs invading vaudeville; he must have read news reports of the offers Chaplin was getting as the Essanay contract drew to a close.

By the time the calendar turned 1916, he and Rose and the prop car had been at it for ten years. They'd made steady creative progress during that time, with the result that their act was an audience favorite in the cities and the sticks. But they were both in their thirties and the incessant travel had to be getting old, especially since they were responsible for the automobile, stationary props and illuminating backdrop; all of which occupied the entire stage. Imagine having to get not only yourselves but all that gear to the station in time at least once a week, usually right after the final curtain and regardless of weather. In at least one instance, heavy snow prolonged their scenery's arrival to a New York theater, with the result that they went on later than billed.

In 1926, Harry told an interviewer, "Every time I came West I tried to get a hearing in pictures — but no one would listen to me. The less likely my chances became, the more enthused I grew over motion pictures." As noted, Langdon's first West Coast tour was in the autumn of 1913, with returns during 1917, 1918 and 1921. If he attempted to break into the movies during any of these stints, details have never surfaced.

In the meantime, troupers that they were, Harry, Rose and Tulley pressed on, comforted that *Johnny's New Car* was proving as successful as its predecessor:

> The Langdons' delightful satire on the joys of motoring is about the funniest act of the year. Langdon has a one-lung rattler that is troubled with insomnia, locomotor ataxia and a bad case of the heaves.
>
> *Waterloo (Iowa) Evening Courier & Reporter*, November 26, 1915.

> Rose, Harry and James Langdon made a big hit with *Johnny's New Car*, getting five curtain calls.
>
> *New York Clipper* review of Chicago's Palace Music Hall, December 13, 1915.

> The Langdons have changed their amusing turn in some sections, but the changes have all been to the good, though some will maintain that Harry Langdon should retain his silly makeup.
>
> *Variety* review of Chicago's Palace Music Hall, December 17, 1915.

> The Langdons dash right in and cheer up everybody. He's a droll bird, this Harry Langdon; Rose and James Langdon are splendid foils, and they surely kid and skid in *Johnny's New Car* to the delight of everyone.
>
> *Goodwins Weekly*, Salt Lake City, April 15, 1916.

> Rose, Harry and James Langdon prove to the audience that it is possible to extract comedy from an automobile that isn't called O'Henry. The name of the act is *Johnny's New Car*. It takes a girl, young man, waiter and blue coat to make the comedy stuff a go.
>
> *Des Moines News*, April 28, 1916.

> The Langdons in their amusing automobile act manage to produce many a hearty howl and to make for aching sides.
>
> *Boston Globe*, June 20, 1916.

> Harry Langdon and Co. closed the first part with *Johnny's New Car*, a comedy act that will stand out in any company. Langdon's dialog is bright and snappy and noticeably original. It runs along to semi-situations without any particular plot, but the collection is well pieced and makes a fine comedy vehicle.
>
> *Variety* review of Coney Island's New Brighton Theater, July 14, 1916.

The week of July 18 marked a milestone: the act was booked for a week at the Palace, the crown jewel of the Keith circuit. It was for the number four spot, a step up from their usual position, and success would convince everyone that Harry Langdon and Company belonged in the Big Time. The headline act — a benefit for the *New York Herald's* Permanently Crippled Soldier's Fund — was a comedy playlet entitled *The Flivver*, which fortunately didn't involve a prop automobile. Originally scheduled for second-after-intermission, after the Monday matinee it was decided that, however noble the cause, *The Flivver* was too lightweight to hold down such a prestige spot. Beginning with Monday evening's performance, *The Flivver* and *Johnny's New*

Car swapped places. A lucky break for Langdon, as it turned out, since most of the evening's audience arrived late, according to *Variety*.

Once again, Sime Silverman did the honors for his trade paper: "The Langdons have a new version of their former *Night on the Boulevard*, calling it *Johnny's New Car*. The Palace crowd liked the turn very much. There is some new business as well as dialog in the act, the backdrop of the boulevard being retained with some of the former business. Miss Langdon sings a solo and another song by the two principals close *(sic)* the turn." According to *The Billboard*, the cast took four curtain calls at the opening matinee.

Not two weeks after the thrill of the Palace, Harry and Company got an even bigger thrill: an invitation to join a major Broadway revue, *The Century Girl*. Langdon happily accepted; a lengthy run in a hit show was every bit as appealing as a motion picture career, and the odds for success were probably more realistic. Furthermore, this wasn't a shoestring operation like *The Show Girl*. Theatrical giants Charles B. Dillingham and Florenz Ziegfeld, Jr., were the producers, and *The Century Girl* would be the debut presentation in their newest showplace, the Century Theater.

As the New Theater, the Century had opened in 1909 and was intended to host academic performances; Shakespeare's *Antony and Cleopatra* was its first production. Although located at Broadway and 62nd Street, about twenty blocks' north of Manhattan's main theatrical district, Ziegfeld and Dillingham leased the theater intending to create "a thoroughly cosmopolitan place of amusement — a theatre providing the variety of entertainment and diversion which was to be found in every other great world capital except New York," according to the *New York Sun*. The two hired scenic artist Joseph Urban to supervise a renovation, and Viennese painter Raphael Kirchner to paint ten panels in the foyer. A separate ballroom was created, "where two bands will be stationed and where patrons can dance between the acts without extra charge." The roof was to become a glass-enclosed nightclub called the Cocoanut Grove for after-midnight drinks and dancing. Incredibly, separate sections within the theater were created

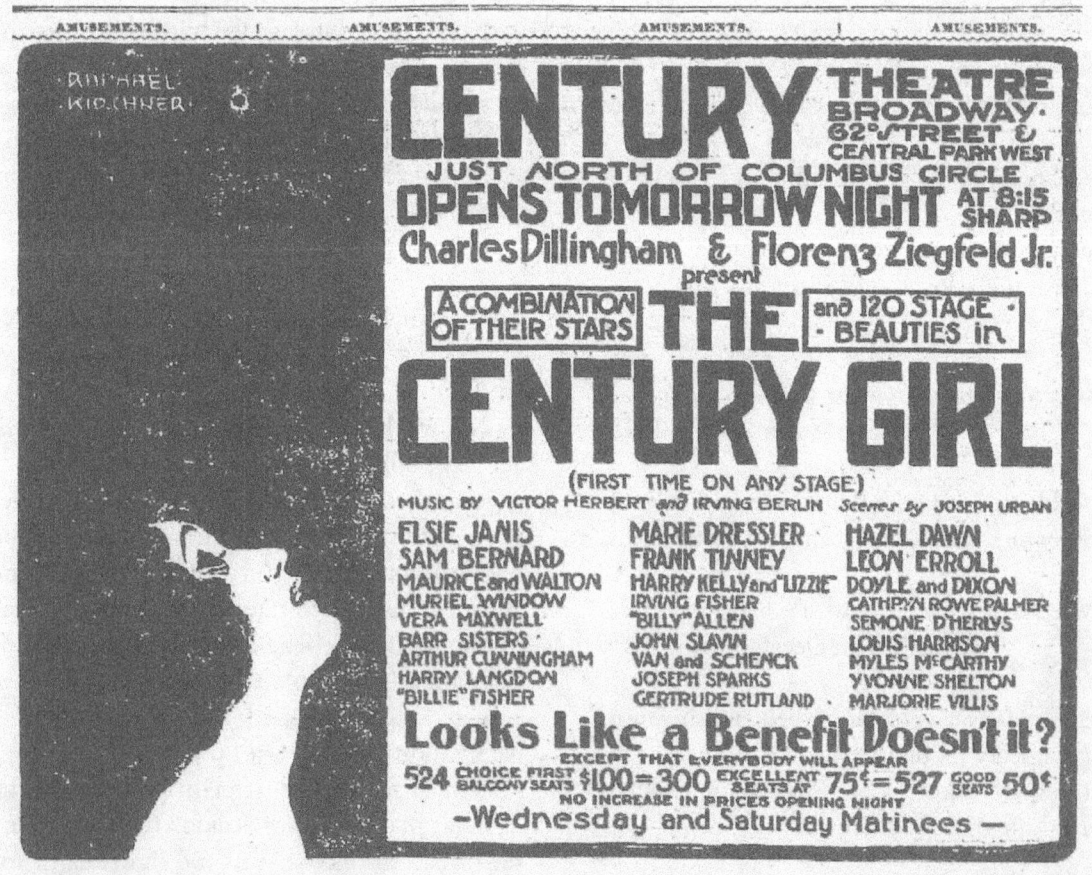

Langdon listed among the cast in this ad for The Century Girl; *he quit the show hours before the opening.*

for smokers, tea drinkers and those who like to talk during the show, "all being arranged so that the freedom and latitude allowed one variety of taste shall not be permitted to impinge upon that allowed to other and opposing tastes." In this, Dillingham and Ziegfeld were about eighty years ahead of their time.

For the show itself, the two impresarios pulled out all the stops: Marie Dressler, Eddie Foy, Leon Errol, Elsie Janis, Frank Tinney, Hazel Dawn, Sam Bernard, Van and Schenck, Irving Fisher, Harry Kelly, Doyle and Dixon, and a couple dozen other well-known vaudevillians were engaged along with the Langdons, and a chorus of 122 girls, chosen from a world-wide scouting operation, were the icing on the cake. They'd all be dancing, singing and cavorting to music provided especially for *The Century Girl* by Victor Herbert and Irving Berlin.

It was a monumental undertaking that quickly turned into a logistical nightmare. Eddie Foy realized the time limitations of such a talent-laden enterprise and dropped out fairly early on. Originally scheduled to open October 16, the premiere was postponed three weeks in order to whittle the show down to a manageable length yet keep the lineup intact. Harry, too, must have had reservations but he and his compatriots stuck with it all through rehearsals, right up until the Monday morning before the opening. The producers, still looking at a four-plus hour extravaganza, asked him to cut his turn down to *one minute* and to do it "in one," an impossible request that was doubtless calculated to yield an inevitable result. Langdon packed up his accessories, signaled for Rose and Tulley, and quit *The Century Girl*.

As it was, the premiere began at eight twenty-five Monday evening and the final curtain fell at two minutes-to-one Tuesday morning. Wrote Sime in *Variety*, "As there are only about 90 or 100 minutes to be taken out, it doesn't require much of a knife, just a hydraulic dredge." Elsie Janis, Leon Errol and a Victor Herbert march number staged by Ned Weyburn were the hits of the show, which enthralled the critics and ran for 200 performances, but without Miss Dressler, the Barr Twins and a few other acts cut over the next two days. *The Century Girl* was the only successful show staged at the Century Theater; it was both too large and expensive to maintain. Eventually the palace was sold to two other impresarios, Jacob and Lee Shubert, who razed it in favor of a new structure, the Century Apartments.

For Langdon, the lesson was obvious: keep away from shows with *Girl* in the title.

Fortunately there was consolation, courtesy of agent Harry Weber. He got *Johnny's New Car* back into the Palace as an "Extra Feature" for the week following *The Century Girl's* opening, then sent them out on the Western Pantages Time as the headline act, at a net sum of $475 per week, beginning Christmas week. Although the Orpheum was the West's A circuit, headlining the Pantages was nothing to be embarrassed about.

Especially since the act delivered the goods, as witness the *Tacoma Times* of March 20, 1917:

> From the ludicry of the mechanical genius of Johnny's new car, to the accidental stalling of the machine in front of a café, brings the biggest laugh that Tacomans have enjoyed for months, in the act on the new bill at Pantages' called "Johnny's New Car." His girl orders drinks, but even though Harry Langdon as Johnny is broke, he gets away with it.

Or the *Berkeley Daily Gazette*, April 14:

> Crowds are laughing this week at the troubles of an autoist, as portrayed at the Pantages by Harry Langdon. Everyone who has ever had an automobile has had Langdon's troubles, they are manifold, but he gets comedy out of them, whereas the man who breaks down on the road, especially if he breaks down in front of an expensive roadhouse, has a girl with him, and his pockets are empty, does not. But Langdon "gets by" and he really is the funniest autoist anyone ever saw in trouble. In fact, he's the talk of Oakland.

Or the *Ogden (Utah) Examiner*, May 18:

> Harry Langdon's face starts the smiles, but it takes his flivver to bring out the stuff that tickles the risibles. A sheet of flame, a cranky crank and a vociferous carburetor add to the fun. The appurtenant scenery was novel and original. This act is one no auto owner should miss, be he the holder of a much abused "roadlouse" or the proud possessor of a touring palace-car. Harry's fly-away down the pike is a wonderful bit of stage realism. The characters of the waiter and Katie Speedington were in capable hands.

The "fly-away down the pike" was an added special effect for the close. Langdon rigged a new set of lights for the backdrop, and new stage instructions: "Auto backs up on stage, as if turning around to leave, as curtain falls. [Then] curtain up, showing red tail light of Automobile in the dark going up the Boulevard [the center of the backdrop]. Red tail light diminishes to small light as it gets further away, when it is out of sight, curtain falls." Guaranteeing a giant round of applause from a suitably impressed audience.

Newspaper columnists quoted dialogue from the act, including an exchange not found in the scripts:

KATIE: What are you drinking?

JOHNNY: This is buck beer.

KATIE: How do you know it's buck?

JOHNNY: Because it gets my goat.

Further evidence that Langdon modified and refined his own performance while on stage, surprising even his co-stars, comes from the *Brooklyn Daily Eagle* of July 24, when playing the New Brighton in Coney Island:

> The most amusing thing on the long bill was the sketch entitled "Johnny's New Car," with Harry, Rose and James Langdon in the cast. Harry and Rose Langdon came on the stage in a marvelous auto, which cut up all sorts of side-splitting antics. Harry Langdon's air of stupidity would make a wooden Indian laugh, and it even convulsed the other players in the sketch.

While appearing in Denver, Colorado, on June 5, Tulley registered for the draft. America had officially entered the First World War on April 6, and the Conscription Act of 1917 had just passed, so all men aged 21–31 were legally obliged to register. Tulley was 27; he was also single and in good health. He remained with his brother and sister-in-law on the Pantages circuit into the following season until, in the spring of 1918, his number came up and he was shipped to France. (Back in Council Bluffs, 23-year-old Claude Langdon had also registered, but claimed exemption due to a "rupture" with no further specifics given.)

For 33-year-old Harry, draft registration was not required — yet. But a third member of his act *was* required, which brings us to the heretofore mysterious "Cecil Langdon," who joined for the 1918–19 season and remained until Harry entered the movies. Previous Langdon scholars, unable to trace the identity of Cecil, who was female, simply acknowledged her presence and let it go at that. She most definitely

PHOTO COURTESY OF ALAN BOYD

was not Harry's sister Gertrude, who had married Thomas Melroy in 1914 at age 17 and was raising a family in Council Bluffs. Genealogical searches fail to turn up any Cecil Langdons among his cousins. But a 1928 *Variety* article, along with nephew Harry N. Langdon, youngest son of Claude, affirm that "Cecil Langdon" had been recruited from the Musolff family, leading us to the only possible candidate: Rose's youngest sister, Cecilia, who was 18. All the other female Musolffs, like Gertrude Langdon Melroy, were wives and mothers.

Additional evidence: Langdon was in Milwaukee — still the Musolffs' hometown — just prior to the start of the season. While there, his (real) automobile, a Velie, was stolen; fortunately police recovered it swiftly.

"Langdon was called to headquarters to identify the machine," read a squib in *Variety*. "The auto rustlers had scratched his name off, and he didn't remember the motor numbers. Langdon finally thought of a baggage sticker which the Harry Weber agency gives its acts. He had pasted it underneath one of the muff-guards. That served as sufficient identification to obtain his 'boat.'"

WAITRESS: Why, the last time I saw her she was a brunette. *(Exits)*

JOHNNY: *(looking at Katie)* Yes, I had her all overhauled…

Keeping the policeman was easy, too, since "he" had no lines. But Cecil also had to be taught stage

"Johnny's Car" Is Comedy Hit

One of the funniest bits of comedy shown on a local vaudeville stage the past season is Harry Langdon's travesty, "Johnny's New Car," which heads the new Pantages program. It's an uproarious bunch of nonsense put together so cleverly that the entire audience keeps up a running fire of laughter during the entire act. Johnny and his girl go out for a ride in the new car. It is a trick auto and the funny capers that it cuts would arouse the humorous sympathy of any car owner.

The new bill is a credit to Mr. Pantages' fine theater. Rose Rosalind and her two beautiful white horses has a picturesque act. Dixie Harris and the Variety Four, singers, present their number with lots of pep. Frederica Harrison and Fred Jarvis are a stunningly dressed pair with a classy skit. The Cortez Trio of Neapolitan musicians have a pretty act, and George and Tony Florenz have a death-defying athletic stunt.

Headlining on the Pantages circuit, 1917-18.

Cecil's arrival meant making a few changes to *Johnny's New Car*. Converting the waiter to a waitress was easy; making the situations and lines appropriate was the work.

JOHNNY: *(to waitress)* How do you like my little runabout?

technique. It probably didn't help that one of her first engagements was at the Palace, the week of September 30, 1918, and that many eyes would be watching since the show was heavily advertised, with each performance including an appeal for the Third Liberty Loan. While the *New York Clipper*'s reviewer believed "Rose and Cecil, the other members of the comedy, did well in their respective parts," *Variety*'s Patsy Smith, who penned the "Among the

Women" column, wrote, "Sister Cecil will have to go into strenuous training for a stage career. Her voice is cold and hard and she is stiff and amateurish. Her maid's dress might be made a more graceful length (shorter or longer) and improve matters considerably."

Cecil learned her craft under the most nerve-wracking circumstances possible; after the Palace

BUY LIBERTY BONDS!
WE DID—DID YOU?
HARRY LANGDON
WITH ROSE AND CECIL IN "JOHNNY'S NEW CAR"
At B. F. KEITH'S PALACE THEATRE This Week (Sept. 30)
DIR. HARRY WEBER

engagement, the Langdons went on the prestigious Keith circuit in the headliner spot. The logical conclusion is that she succeeded, for her performance was never again negatively reviewed, and like any good trouper, she stuck with the act until its dissolution. All of which adds to our pleasure in finally providing Cecilia Musolff some long-overdue recognition for her modest place in Langdon's story.

Ratified on January 16, 1919, the Eighteenth Amendment to the U.S. Constitution officially prohibited the sale and distribution of alcoholic beverages. Prohibition, as the law was called, took effect exactly one year and one day later. Seemingly overnight, ordinary Americans became obsessed with breaking the law, and several criminal empires were built around the growing demand for "bootleg hooch."

In the act, Katie Speedington could no longer order highballs and champagne at the café, but that didn't mean alcohol wasn't available. Johnny created another unique feature for his "runabout," and now the policeman had something more serious to investigate than a rogue whistle-blower.

In the new version, Johnny "goes to his car and opens up the radiator, which discloses three Whiskey bottles, then he closes it up again quickly. [Katie] sees him do it, walks around car and opens up the radiator."

KATIE: Johnny, what is this?

JOHNNY: Tom, Dick and Harry.

KATIE: To me, it looks like WHISKEY.

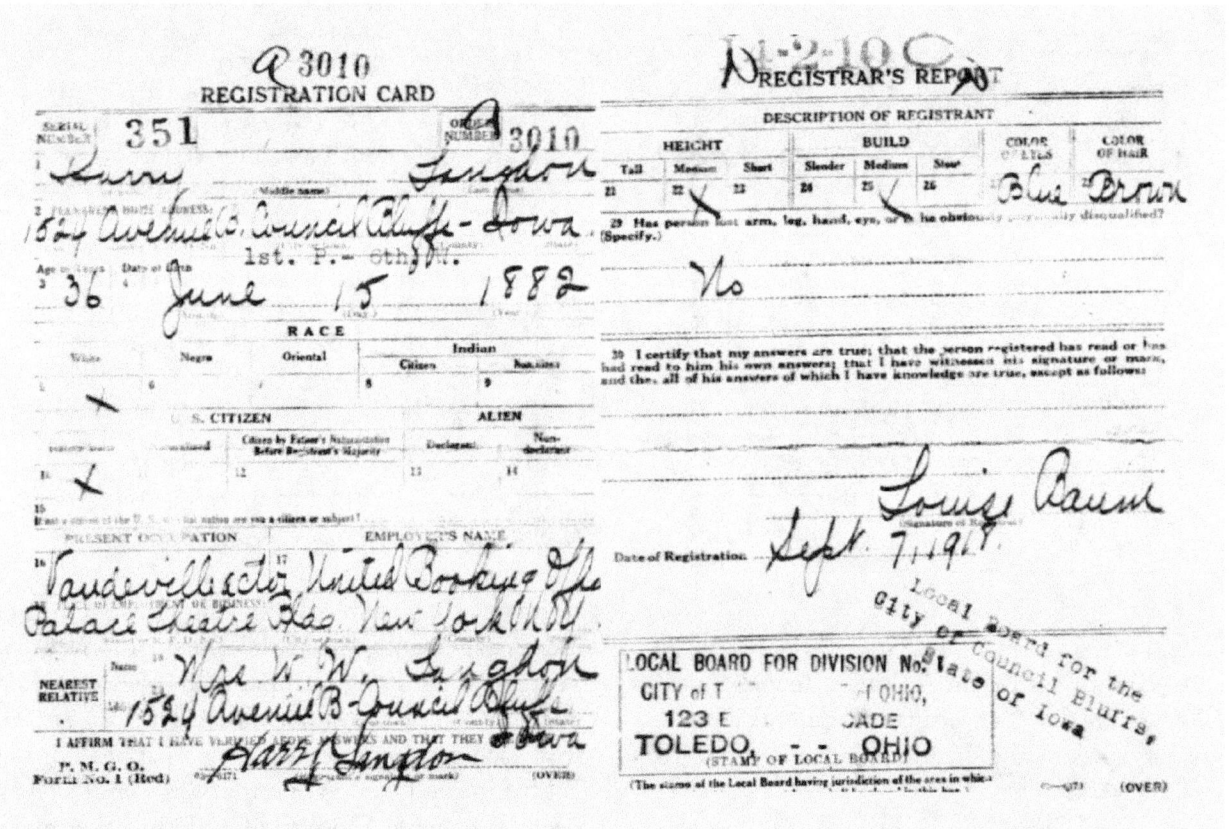

Langdon's draft registration card. By September 1918, the eligible age was raised to 35, so Langdon added two years to his birth date.

JOHNNY: Don't say that. *(Looks around to see if anyone is listening)* Don't you ever say what you said there.

KATIE: What, WHISKEY?

JOHNNY: Don't say that. Can't you say Schnapps? *(He removes a cup from the hub of the wheel.)* You'll find your cup on the other wheel.

Katie goes for her cup, while Johnny rests his foot on the bumper as if it's a bar rail. Katie returns.

KATIE: *(as Johnny pours)* Johnny, any kick?

JOHNNY: Oh, no one has said anything so far. Have you got enough?

KATIE: Oh, plenty.

JOHNNY: Well, after you drink that, just lay the money down any place but don't give it to me directly. *(Walks to the left side of the car, and lifts his cup toward her.)* Well, here's ago.

KATIE: Here's ago.

They both drink, but at this moment the policeman appears behind Johnny. Katie, of course, sees him and points, but Johnny "just looks at her as if he don't (*sic*) know what she means. He talks to her with his fingers, like a deaf and dumb person, then looks around and sees Policeman, tries to hide his cup then finds he cannot hide it. He dips his fingers into it and wipes his hands on his coat, then on his face, puts the cup in his pocket, acts innocent, turns to look at policeman."

The policeman walks around to Johnny's right while Johnny looks to the left. Johnny turns and sees him again, then impulsively tips his hat to Katie. The policeman turns toward Katie and this is where Johnny steals the badge and pins it to his vest, leading to his flashing the badge and ending the threat.

"Harry Langdon, assisted by Rose and Cecil, presented their 'Auto' satire," wrote a critic for the *New York Clipper* after a Palace performance in mid-March 1920. "Langdon is a funny fellow and has added several new bits that were well placed and registered strongly. Many laughs were gained…. The Langdons, in *Johnny's New Car*, are a sure-fire act."

Two weeks later they were uptown at Keith's 81st Street theater, home of six acts in support of a feature film. *Variety's* "Step" was there: "They must have been familiar with Harry Langdon and the funny automobile, for he got a reception in fourth spot even with the house dark and the drop illuminated by the avenue of lights…Langdon's…facial expression…can say something without a facial muscle twitching, and register mirth. The business of the automobile and the supplemented gags plus the annexation of the liquor stored in

PHOTO COURTESY OF ALAN BOYD

the radiator is evidence of priming and is in good taste."

There was no doubt that Harry Langdon and Company had reached vaudeville's top rung: always a welcome feature at New York's Palace and Chicago's Majestic, and the stars of the show everywhere else. But Langdon, growing ever more confident, continued to stretch himself. The contradiction between the smart aleck cracking wise and the timid little man whose visual bits were both sublime and hysterically funny had become apparent. If he was going to play the "boob" visually, his lines needed to reinforce that. Langdon penned new dialogue where innocence replaced cynicism. Once more the billing changed, this time simply to "Harry Langdon," with "assisted by Rose and Cecil" in much smaller type.

He also removed the songs. Rose was now just a foil, same as Cecil, and this may have driven the first wedge into their marriage. But Langdon was adamant his was to be a *comedy* act. And he succeeded: *Johnny's New Car* became, in *Variety*'s words, "the strongest little comedy offering in vaudeville."

The only scenery change is that the milepost sign now reads "Autos Park Here." Johnny and Katie have just driven to center stage:

KATIE: Johnny, your taillight is out.

JOHNNY: How did that get out?

KATIE: And your headlights are out, too.

JOHNNY: I'll bet they went out with the taillight.

KATIE: You had better get out and light up.

JOHNNY: I don't need any lights on this car.

KATIE: Why?

JOHNNY: *(pointing to car)* This is a Pathfinder.

Katie decides she wants to take a photograph of Johnny and his car.

JOHNNY: Shall I put the awning up?

KATIE: No, never mind the awning.

Johnny gets out of the car and immediately slips on the running board.

JOHNNY: Oh-oh. I will have to get that fixed.

KATIE: Now stand right down there. Put your hat back.

JOHNNY: Shall I put up the awning?

KATIE: Never mind the awning.

Johnny poses "with feet spread apart; one foot pointing one way, the other the other way."

KATIE: Well, make up your mind which way you are going.

The Big Time at last: Headlining on the Keith circuit, 1918-20.

JOHNNY: *(pointing to his feet)* Where they go, I go. Shall I put up the awning?

KATIE: Never mind the awning.

JOHNNY: Then be sure and get all the accessories in the picture.

KATIE: Why? The headlights are not in.

JOHNNY: How did they get out? *(Johnny shakes the auto and the headlights light up.)* Put the awning up?

KATIE: All right, put it up.

Johnny puts up the top, which is a garish striped thing.

KATIE: Is that a one-man top?

JOHNNY: No, that is my old shirt.

KATIE: Now, lean on the car as if you owned it.

JOHNNY: Oh, I can't lean on it.

KATIE: Why not?

JOHNNY: It is all damp.

KATIE: *(feels the car)* Say, it is damp, isn't it? What makes it so damp?

JOHNNY: There is so much due on it.

Katie takes the picture. Johnny gets back into the car and he falls through the bottom, "so that his feet are seen beneath [the] car."

JOHNNY: Now, what do you know about that?

KATIE: What's the matter, Johnny?

JOHNNY: Some one went and opened up my cut-out, and I fell right through it.

KATIE: And you brought me out with you, and you don't know a thing about running an automobile, and if I had that wheel, I would show you how to run this car.

JOHNNY: All right, here is the wheel.

Johnny detaches and hands her the steering wheel. Katie asks him to crank it.

JOHNNY: I refuse to crank it. You have the wheel now, you will have to crank it.

KATIE: Oh, Johnny, how nice of you to stop right in front of this café.

JOHNNY: *(Looks around at the café)* I'll crank it for you this time.

Katie insists on having dinner, and asks Johnny to call the waiter; the sole surviving verbal joke from *A Night on the Boulevard* follows, except a waitress emerges this time. She takes Katie's order, asks Johnny what he wishes, he wishes her a Happy New Year and asks her what she thinks of his runabout. When the waitress mentions the brunette, Katie is insulted.

KATIE: Are you going to sit here and let her insult me like that?

JOHNNY: No, I'll get out. *(He gets out of the car.)*

KATIE: The very idea of her talking to me like that.

JOHNNY: Yes, what do you know about that?

KATIE: Why, she insulted me.

JOHNNY: What do you know about that? I'll get even with her.

Johnny walks back and forth saying, "This place is unfair to organized labor." Then he asks Katie what the waitress said.

KATIE: She said the last time she saw me, I was a brunette.

JOHNNY: Yes? Well, just sit right here and I will settle this.

Johnny walks up to the café door and pounds on it. The waitress comes out.

WAITRESS: Well, what do you want?

JOHNNY: *(very meekly)* Can I have a drink of water?

The waitress returns with a glass of water, and Katie asks her if "there are any nice roads around here." The waitress responds enthusiastically, describing the various roads. As she speaks, she gesticulates with the glass of water, which Johnny is trying fruitlessly to retrieve. Finally he gives up and opens his radiator, revealing the three whiskey bottles and leading to the bit described earlier.

After the badge business, Katie tells him to "crank up and get away before the policeman gets back." Johnny cranks the car forwards and backwards, with no luck. He tries the "combination starter," no luck. He shakes the car. It works. Johnny climbs in. The engine stops. He gets out again, slips on the running board, and this time he pulls the door off as he falls. He puts the door back on.

JOHNNY: Leave the door open now, I want to get in quick. Say, when I crank the car, will you push that button there?

KATIE: *(pointing to button)* This button here?

JOHNNY: Yes, NO! Not that button.

KATIE: Well, what is this button for?

JOHNNY: That throws the hind wheel off.

Johnny takes a piece of the engine out and throws it away. He takes another piece out and throws it away. He takes out a third part and the engine stops, so he puts it back, and it starts again. He jumps into the car. As he does, the hood pops open and two tin cans come flying out. Frightened, Johnny jumps out and starts to run away.

JOHNNY: *(calling to Katie)* Come on, that's all. Every man for himself.

Katie gets out and looks under the hood.

KATIE: Why Johnny, there is nothing in there.

JOHNNY: *(pointing to the tin cans)* No it is all out here now.

KATIE: Why, where is the magneto?

JOHNNY: Where is the what?

KATIE: Where's the Maggy-neat-too?

JOHNNY: It went out with Dardenellie.

KATIE: I suppose you will have a blow out next.

JOHNNY: Well, I've got an extra tire.

Johnny removes the spare and it's a pitiful specimen, missing huge chunks of rubber from various blowouts.

KATIE: That's some tire.

JOHNNY: Yes, some of it. It's got a lot of rubber in it yet. See how it bounces. *(He attempts to bounce the tire, a piece of business that could have gone on for a while depending on audience reaction. Then he spots a hole.)* Oh-oh.

KATIE: Why, what's the matter?

JOHNNY: I've got a leak in it. *(He shows the hole to Katie)* Can you notice it?

KATIE: I can see it.

JOHNNY: *(puts his ear to the tire)* Yep, slow leak. Do you know what that hole reminds me of?

KATIE: No, what?

JOHNNY: That one. *(And he points to a different hole.)*

Johnny cranks the car again, and it starts. Then he goes to pick up the engine parts and gets hit with the flame in the pants. He runs around in a panic, finally fanning himself with the door. The waitress comes out.

WAITRESS: See here, young man, this noise will have to stop.

JOHNNY: It has stopped. I've been trying to start it.

WAITRESS: Well, don't start anything around here.

She hits the hood of his car with her pencil. Katie rebukes her; the two women argue, and Johnny tries to get a word in, to no avail. The waitress kicks a spoke out of the front wheel. Johnny yells out, but then starts coughing, using the auto horn to make a honking noise as he coughs. The waitress leaves.

KATIE: What was she kicking about?

JOHNNY: She was kicking my runabout, like this. *(He kicks out a spoke.)* Oh, anybody can do that.

He kicks out another spoke, and the car starts. As he sits down, the steering wheel flies out, knocking his hat off. Johnny gets out of the car, puts his hat on and starts to run away. Katie calls him back.

Johnny "picks up all the parts that are laying around and puts them at the bottom of [the] Parking sign… then he lays a grass mat over the parts, which resembles a grave, with the sign as the tombstone, then he places the old tire over the top of [the] sign for the wreath, takes his hat off in prayer."

JOHNNY: *(to Katie)* I'll bet you are disgusted.

KATIE: Yes, this thing has gone far enough.

JOHNNY: Yes, this is all the farther we will go.

KATIE: Do you think I will have to walk home?

JOHNNY: Noooo, don't be silly.

He picks up the spokes and carries them in his arms as if they were a cord of wood.

KATIE: Well, I want to go home in the worst way.

JOHNNY: We'll go in the car. Do you really want to go home?

KATIE: Certainly.

JOHNNY: Give us a kiss, kiddo, give us a kiss.

KATIE: Kiss you?

JOHNNY: Do you want to go home?

KATIE: Yes.

JOHNNY: Give us a kiss, kiddo, give us a kiss.

KATIE: Why what girl would kiss that face?

JOHNNY: All the girls kiss me when they go out in my Auto.

KATIE: They do?

JOHNNY: Yep. They kiss me or get out and walk home. I don't burn my gas for nothing.

KATIE: Well, I would rather walk home.

JOHNNY: That's funny, they all walk home. I think I will buy a Motorboat. *(He points to her forehead.)* What would you do if I would kiss you up there?

KATIE: Why, I would call you down.

Johnny kisses her. The stage lights go out, music comes up, the car backs up, the curtain goes down, then raises again for the "disappearing auto" light effect.

Langdon aficionados should recognize *this* Johnny. His speech patterns as written are identical to those Langdon used in talkies, especially his earliest ones: the simple response to problems ("Oh-oh"), the constant repetition ("What do you know about that?"), and the childlike wonder. By the end of the 1919–20 season, Langdon had emerged with not just a character but a comedic point-of-view, one that would stay with him 'til the end.

In the spring of 1920, Langdon was again invited to bring his act to Broadway, courtesy of impresario John Cort.

Cort had forged a sterling reputation for hit shows in San Francisco, and in 1912, brought his expertise to Broadway, building the Cort Theater at 48th Street. The Cort opened on December 29 with *Peg o' My Heart*, which ran for 607 performances, "a remarkable run…at a time when even 100 performances indicated a hit," wrote Ken Bloom in *Broadway: Its History, People and Places*.

In 1918, Cort produced a musical comedy, *Listen Lester*, which was a smash success, running for 272 performances, and continuing even after interruption by an Actor's Equity strike in August 1919. The show made a star out of its perky ingénue, Ada Mae Weeks, and its touring company provided a break to a young circus performer named Joe E. Brown. Both Weeks and Brown would be featured players in Cort's follow-up, *Jim Jam Jems*.

The book and lyrics were written by the same team responsible for *Listen Lester*: Harry L. Cort and George E. Stoddard, while an appropriate if raucous jazz score was provided by James F. Hanley. Billed as "a musical pastime," *Jim Jam Jems* focused on Miss Weeks as June Ward, a wealthy young lady

interested in a Broadway career. Her uncle (Stanley Forde) objects to her aspirations despite his own unhealthy nocturnal pursuits, and endeavors to hire a young man to squire her along the Great White Way and convince her of its unseemliness. However, he's unknowingly selected Johnny Case (Frank Fay), a reporter for the political scandal sheet *Jim Jam Jems*, whom June has engaged to find out just what her uncle does at those "board meetings" he claims to attend every night. Embarrassing predicaments abound for everybody and hilarity ensues, with more than a few musical interludes scattered throughout.

The show looked so promising, *The Billboard*'s May 22 issue announced that Langdon, "who has been one of vaudeville's best-known performers in his act *Johnny's New Car*, is about to forsake varieties for a new musical comedy production. His final appearance in vaudeville will be at the New Brighton Theater for the opening bill." The announcement was premature; when their Coney Island engagement ended, he, Rose and Cecil went on to appear in upper Manhattan's Fox Audubon and Chicago's Palace Music Hall before returning to New York for rehearsals.

Harry was originally envisioned as a tertiary character, "Auto Charlie, a speed fiend," but during the out-of-town rewriting phase he became the Wards' chauffeur, James, with Rose playing their maid, Annette. Along with Cecil, unnamed in the program, their specialty scene took place during Act I, Scene 3, set on 5th Avenue in front of the Plaza Hotel. This time, having been handed direction in advance, Langdon worked out the necessities to perform the act "in one." Brown portrayed Philip Quick, the Wards' butler, while the other major comedy role was a dour detective, played to perfection by Ned Sparks.

While Harry was rehearsing in the East, his parents were preparing to head west. Less than two years' earlier, Harry's older brother John Henry Langdon and his wife, the former Edna Grausbury, had settled in Los Angeles. Finding conditions to his liking, John encouraged his family to also make the move. W.W. and Lavina, their furniture ready for shipping, were to leave on Saturday, August 21, when W.W. "took suddenly ill Friday morning and passed away at 7 o'clock the same evening," according to the *Council Bluffs Nonpareil*. Cause of death was determined to be a cerebral hemorrhage. W.W. was 69 years old. Harry immediately left rehearsals and returned to Council Bluffs for the funeral. Although the obituary notice stated that his body would be "placed in a receiving vault and later will be sent to Los Angeles" for interment, W.W. was buried at Walnut Hill Cemetery in Council Bluffs, where he remains. Soon after, Lavina moved to Southern California, as did Charles, Tulley and Gertrude and her family.

Langdon returned to *Jim Jam Jems* in time for its out-of-town "preparatory" performances, which began in Baltimore, Maryland, on August 31. After two weeks at Baltimore's Ford Theater, it moved to Washington, D.C.'s National for a week, then to Syracuse for three days. *Variety* caught the show there: "Not so good as *Listen Lester*, perhaps, but nevertheless this new John Cort production is going to make them take notice in New York…a real laugh provoker, with good music, good dancing and good-looking girls for good measure. And the cast of principals, including Harry Langdon, Frank Fay, Ada Mae Weeks and Elizabeth Murray is all that can be asked."

The show was scheduled to reach Broadway immediately following Syracuse, on September 27, but required an additional week of fine-tuning. Cort brought in William MacGregor, renowned for musical comedy productions, to restage; another vaudeville specialty team known as Parish and Peru were cut at that time. *Jim Jam Jems* ultimately opened on October 4.

Reviews were mixed. Both the *New York Times* and *New York Post* took exception with Hanley's score. The latter's critic wrote, "*Jim Jam Jems*, a so-called musical comedy…takes all that has been done with that musical atrocity known as jazz in the past two years

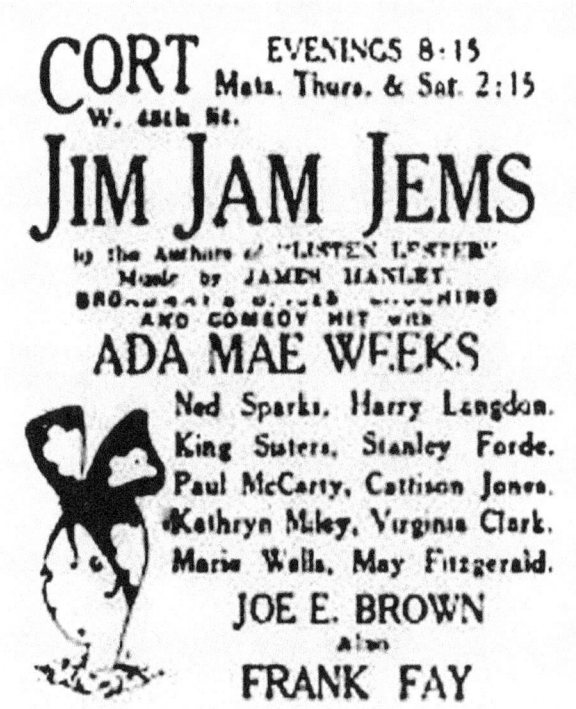

and goes it one better. This applies to music, dancing and singing. It is jazz gone insane." Added the *Times*, "Midgie Miller, the incarnation of Jazz, and her dancing partner, Roscoe Ails, with a violent jazz orchestra, injected a too liberal amount of musical barbarism into the score. Since, as we have been assured, jazz is a war reaction, the theatergoer might hope to be spared two years after the armistice." The same critic also opined, "The piece suffers primarily from a superabundance of comedians and a lack of wit."

On the flip side, the *New York Telegram* asserted, "*Jim Jam Gems (sic)*…does fairly well as a pastime in two acts and a half-dozen scenes…. As a reporter, Frank Fay is on the stage much of the time with his intoxicating smile and adds new laurels to his past performances. In the comedy roles of the butler and chauffeur, Joe E. Brown and Harry Langdon get away with a flock of clean-cut comedy, mostly through actions and not words. They are a scream, while Ned Sparks adds much to the humor of the show as the serious detective." The *New York Tribune* assured readers, "A gem of melody and wit flashed its rays 'cross Broadway last night. *Jim Jam Jems*…gives to New York its present season's prettiest musical comedy production…there is Joe E. Brown, the busy butler of the play, who is screamingly funny, Harry Langdon, with his trick automobile and his 'vacant stare,' brings a bit of vaudeville's very best into a new realm, and Ned Sparks, as a detective, in his monotone, is a splendid character." All critics agreed the charms of Ada Mae Weeks in the lead were considerable.

Attendance was reportedly sparse the first few days, until Cort made matinee tickets available through a cut-rate broker, one Joe LeBlang. Word of mouth took care of the rest, and by week's end, *Variety* was able to report a box-office take of nearly $14,000.

Variety's reviewer thought the show similar in nature to *Listen Lester*, but added "the production itself is much better than in any of the preceding Cort musical shows…. Mr. Cort, Sr., has dipped into vaudeville liberally in collating his cast. There are (*sic*) a trio of comedians all from that source in Frank Fay, [Joe E.] Brown and Harry Langdon…Langdon was a comic joy in the first act with his auto scene in 'one' with the aid of Rose and Cecil Langdon. It looked like a new version of the act as seen in vaudeville. For the rest of the evening, Langdon had to be content with bits, but he rarely came on without delivering a laugh." Gordon White, in a review for *The Billboard*, made a similar observation: "The Langdons do their well-known automobile skit to good results, and Harry Langdon roamed thru the piece, getting a laugh on every appearance."

A columnist known as "The Call Boy" for *Town Topics* magazine (a scandal sheet not unlike *Jim Jam Jems*) labeled the evening "vaudeville without dropping the curtain every time, and without the placards on the stage, [and] something runs through it which I suppose is intended to be a plot. A lot of people do a lot of things. Ada Mae Weeks…is something of the star, I fancy, but as most stars go nowadays somebody else is hauled in to steal the luster. Methinks that person is one Harry Langdon. At any rate, that is the way it seemed to me, for Mr. Langdon, albeit he does the oh, so familiar automobile stunt, does his with an originality that was about the only thing in the show — to me."

Midway through the second month, a problem arose. Publishers of the genuine *Jim Jam Jems* objected to the use of its name without permission or compensation, and threatened a lawsuit if the show was not retitled. Cort confessed he'd not made arrangements with the periodical for the use of its name, and agreed to make the change. He chose something safe and vaguely familiar, *Hello, Lester*. However, within two weeks the publishers agreed to let Cort use the original title, apparently having discovered that a Broadway show was jolly good publicity.

During the brief period that the show was called *Hello, Lester*, Langdon, killing time backstage, drew caricatures of the principal players, including himself and Rose. The *Brooklyn Daily Eagle* published them on November 28, along with a brief interview with Langdon, quoted earlier, in which he discussed his beginnings as a Council Bluffs newsboy and vaudevillian. "Mr. Cort saw my act last season and suggested that musical comedy might open up a new field for me, so he gave me an opportunity in *Jim Jam Jems*," concluded Langdon, deliberately omitting his prior, unhappy experiences with the genre.

Jim Jam Jems ran for 105 performances at the Cort; just enough to be labeled a hit but nowhere near the success of *Listen Lester*. It closed on New Years' Day, 1921. The next logical step was a road tour, but Cort was unwilling to finance one. Instead, he sold the show to Al Jones, a co-owner of the *Greenwich Village Follies*, who decided to recast. Ada Mae Weeks had already departed in a salary dispute with Cort, and Jones cut all but Joe E. Brown from the remaining original cast.

Once again, Harry, Rose and Cecil returned to vaudeville. Clearly Langdon's good fortune did not extend to Broadway. Perhaps movies were the answer after all. Charlie Chaplin had progressed to a million-dollar contract with First National Exhibitor's Circuit. A fellow named Harold Lloyd had become a big comedy star as well, and Buster Keaton — that kid from The Three Keatons who was ten when Langdon entered vaudeville — had recently been handed his own studio and production company.

If they could succeed in pictures, so could he. Maybe all he needed was to prove he could do more than the trick auto.

A Langdon-penned sketch of the cast of Jim Jam Jems, *a.k.a.* Hello, Lester.

CHAPTER FIVE

After the Ball and Hollywood's Call

1921–1923

With three months' stay in a single venue — and only two afternoons per week spent on stage — it's probable Langdon discovered golf during the run of *Jim Jam Jems*. The sport's popularity among ordinary citizens was certainly on the rise. Langdon himself commented on it in 1921:

> The game of golf has become what almost amounts to a national craze. I know of no other way to express it. Businessmen are on the links just as soon as the sun comes up. They are back again after business hours and remain until the sun goes down. In Chicago recently, I found it impossible during a week's stay to secure two hours in which to play on the principal golf courses. Every hour of the day had been reserved in advance.
>
> While golf may seem a childish game to many folk, it is rather a strenuous exercise. In fact, it is sometimes as full of possibilities as football or baseball. This is particularly so in the way of injuries. A crack from a golf ball, traveling at the rate of what seems like a mile a minute, has infinitely more potential damage than a kick from a cleat-shod shoe or the bad bounce of a baseball. Even a pitched ball cannot wreak the havoc of a golf ball poorly struck with a massy or a niblick. Yet fortunately the injuries suffered from the game are few and far between. As a rule, golf is conducive to good health. It gets people out in the open air. It keeps them active. It makes them walk, and sometimes swear, but whatever it does it builds up the tissues of the body. And that makes for health. So, if golf has one blessing to confer on the nation, it is this: red corpuscles.

So spoke the comedian who once peddled "Sagwa" for a living. With such a firm grasp on the dangerous side of the sport, it was only fitting that Langdon should capitalize on the craze with a sketch. Thus was born *After the Ball: A Satire on Golfing and Motoring, in Three Scenes*.

Each scene had a title: "In the Ruff," which took place on a golf course (with a house also utilized on the backdrop), was set "in one" and ran about six minutes; "Treated Ruff," set in front of the clubhouse on the full stage and running about eight minutes; and "Ruff Riding," which was basically an abbreviated version of *Johnny's New Car* with the action taking place in front of a hospital quiet zone "in two," occupying the remainder of the 30-minute running time.

In this sketch, Rose and Cecil portray "Rose" and "Cecil," but Harry is still "Johnny." Contrary to previously published accounts, Langdon does not portray a caddy; he's a full-fledged golfer along with his two

lady friends. A fourth actor, even more anonymous than Cecil since he was never identified in ads or reviews, portrays the golf course manager in Scene Two and a policeman in Scene Three.

The curtain rises as Rose and Cecil "enter with golf bag and sticks":

ROSE: Cecil, have you seen Johnny anywhere?

CECIL: No I haven't seen him. I suppose he is out in the ruff again.

ROSE: *(calling out)* Johnny! Oh, Johnny!

JOHNNY: *(from behind the drop)* I'm in here.

ROSE: In where?

JOHNNY: *(emerges from a door in the drop)* In here.

ROSE: What are you doing in there?

JOHNNY: I'm looking for my golf ball, it went in here.

ROSE: Did you find it?

JOHNNY: No, I haven't looked yet.

Rose and Cecil begin to swing their golf clubs back and forth in front of the door. Rose asks Johnny to come out and play, but he hesitates because of the clubs swinging in front of him.

JOHNNY: Let's play in here.

ROSE: No, come on out here and play with us.

Rose and Cecil continue swinging their clubs, and Johnny continues to hesitate. Finally he covers his eyes and walks through safely. He reaches for Rose's ball.

ROSE: Ah, ah! Didn't I tell you not to pick up other people's golf balls on this course?

JOHNNY: I don't pick them up 'til they've stopped rolling.

CECIL: Oh look, he's forgot his golf bag.

Johnny looks around for his bag, then goes to the door in the drop and retrieves it. It's "a large bag."

CECIL: Johnny, come here. Will you let me take your putter? *(Johnny looks confused.)* Your putter. You know, your putter. Putter, putter, putter!

JOHNNY: *(extending his hand to shake)* Putter there!

Cecil reaches into the bag and retrieves the club she wants.

JOHNNY: Be careful of that stick!

CECIL: Oh, I will Johnny. *(But with one swing, she breaks the club.)* I'm sorry, Johnny.

JOHNNY: *(dejected)* Oh, that's all right.

CECIL: I did not mean to do it.

JOHNNY: Oh, that's all right.

CECIL: I'm very, very sorry.

JOHNNY: Oh, that's all right.

CECIL: But I'll buy you a new one.

JOHNNY: Oh, that's...*(Brightens up)* all right.

Cecil exits. Meanwhile, Rose tries to hit her ball and keeps missing.

ROSE: What is the cause of me missing?

JOHNNY: What kind of gas do you use? You must keep your eye on the ball.

Rose continues to swing and miss "three or four times," with Johnny kibitzing ("Missed it again").

ROSE: What is the cause of me missing?

JOHNNY: Did you ever miss a train?

ROSE: Yes, I have missed a train.

JOHNNY: Well, how do you expect to hit that little ball?

Johnny removes a teapot from his golf bag. A string connects the pot to the bag. Johnny puts the ball on top of the teapot, cries "Fore!" then swings, but hits the bag. He moves the bag out of the way, but the teapot, being tied to the bag, moves with it. He "teas" up another ball, shouts "Fore!" then strikes the bag again. "Johnny repeats this bit, moving the teapot, then the bag." Meanwhile, Rose is searching for her ball, paying no attention to Johnny.

JOHNNY: Fore! Fore! Fore! *(to Rose)* Say, you women don't pay any attention to that figure, do you? Fore! *(to Rose)* Why don't you look around? Fore! Three-ninety-eight!

With that, Rose looks around.

ROSE: Where did my golf ball go to? You can't turn your head on this golf course or someone will take your golf ball.

JOHNNY: Was it the ball you were just playing with?

ROSE: Yes.

JOHNNY: Oh, you have been missing that all day. Johnny removes a stick from his bag, one with a nail attached to the end. Then he proceeds to pick up stray pieces of paper strewn along the course, like a trash collector. Rose, meanwhile, is griping that she loses her golf balls whenever she plays with Johnny.

JOHNNY: What seems to be the trouble with you?

ROSE: Every time I play golf with you I lose all my golf balls!

JOHNNY: Say, do you mean to insinuate that I take your golf balls?

ROSE: I am not only insinuating, but I am positive.

JOHNNY: Well, then you just be a little more careful what you say after this.

ROSE: Well, you just stand there 'til I search you. Rose searches him, but fails to find any golf balls on his person.

ROSE: Well, Johnny, I am sorry that I accused you of stealing my golf balls…Really, it was my mistake, won't you forgive me?

Rose puts out her hand to shake, and Johnny extends his, then notices that his glove is on backwards: "Instead of the black stripes being on the back of his hand, they are in the palm of his hand." He opts instead to tip his cap to her. "As he does, a bunch of golf balls roll out of his hat" onto the stage. Johnny grabs his bag and departs in haste. End of Scene One.

"Treated Ruff" begins outside of the country club. There is the clubhouse, a tee box and a spouting drinking fountain. Johnny enters with his golf bag. A ball whizzes by his head, just missing. A second ball whizzes by. Johnny takes out a club and assumes a batting stance. A ball comes from behind him, striking him on the rear end.

Cecil enters and "dumps a lot of rubbish in [Johnny's] bag." Johnny is about to hit a ball when Cecil picks it up. "Johnny just misses hitting her in the back." Cecil "gets on [the] tee box and addresses the ball in an eccentric manner, moving her body back and forth." This fascinates Johnny, so much so that Rose, who enters with her scorecard, fails to get his attention. He moves closer to Cecil, and she strikes the tee, knocking dirt in his face. Johnny "spits the dirt out of his mouth and dusts himself off."

CECIL: How do you like our golf course, Johnny?

JOHNNY: It is the best I ever tasted.

Cecil swings again and the sound of glass breaking is heard, implying that her ball broke a window. Cecil hands Johnny the club and dashes off. The clubhouse manager quickly enters, sees Johnny on the tee box with a club, and assumes he's responsible for the window. The manager asks if he intends to pay for the broken glass, to which Johnny replies he can't be expected to pay for something that is broken.

MANAGER: Well, you broke it!

JOHNNY: How do you know I broke it?

MANAGER: Because you have a club in your hand.

JOHNNY: Yes, you bet I've got a club in my hand.

MANAGER: *(growing angrier)* What are you going to do about it?

Johnny swings the club and we hear another window break. "Johnny lays his club down, motions for Cecil to come with him, both start to walk off stage (but) the Manager blocks Johnny's way." The manager grabs Johnny by the front of his coat and threatens to knock him around.

JOHNNY: I can tell by looking at you, you are sore about something. I can tell by the expression on your voice.

Johnny notices how high up his coat is and pulls it down, "like a girl would her skirt." The manager hoists it up again. Johnny pulls it down again.

JOHNNY: I don't know you very well. *(Pulls coat down again.)* Well, I've got to go now.

Johnny starts to go, and the manager "grabs him by the back of the collar and holds him."

JOHNNY: No…I don't like that hold as well as I do this one. *(Hands him the front of his coat as before.)*

The manager shakes Johnny. Harry makes a gurgling noise with his mouth, to put over that he's carrying a bottle of whiskey.

MANAGER: What have you got in there?

JOHNNY: Whist (*sic*) broom. *Johnny "shows the audience the [outline] of a bottle through his coat."* See the neck of the whist broom?

MANAGER: Take it out.

Johnny takes the bottle from his coat.

MANAGER: *(Interested)* What does this bottle contain?

JOHNNY: Contents…

MANAGER: Any kick?

JOHNNY: Nobody has said anything so far. After you drink that, just lay the money down anyplace, but don't give it to me directly.

With that, the manager exits, as Rose and Cecil enter with their capes on, ready to depart.

ROSE: Well, Johnny, we are going home in our car. Do you want to go along with us?

JOHNNY: Sure, but wait 'til I get a drink of water.

Johnny goes over to the fountain, which of course stops working as soon as he bends over to get a drink, and resumes once he walks away. He "sneaks up on the fountain and [it] stops running, but Johnny passes right by it as though he didn't see it. This is kept up to get the laughs. [He] stoops to drink water, stops — water shoots up in the air, striking Johnny in the face. He sits on the fountain." Just then, a golf ball whizzes by him and the sound of a window breaking sends him running off stage. End of Scene Two.

"Ruff Riding" opens as the automobile approaches a hospital, a "Quiet Zone" sign in full view. There is an oversized thermometer mounted on the hospital door. Rose and Cecil are in the front seat; Rose is driving, and Harry is in the back. The car stops in front of the hospital as the two ladies ad lib an argument as to which of them knows the most about running the car. Johnny notices the sign and tries to quiet them, but they don't pay any attention. He taps Rose on the shoulder.

JOHNNY: Would you mind pulling your car up a little further?

ROSE: Why?

JOHNNY: Because I can't stand that smell that comes out of that door.

CECIL: *(Angry, jumps up)* Well, if you don't like it, get out!

Johnny rises to get out, but Rose tells him to sit down. He sits down, Cecil orders him out again. This goes on until Johnny's feet fall through the bottom of the car.

JOHNNY: *(tapping Rose on the shoulder)* Say, you have left your cut-out open.

CECIL: *(to Rose)* Ah, c'mon, start it up.

This is the cue for surreptitious sound effects that mimic gears being stripped. "Johnny sits in the back seat as if he was frightened, tries to get out of seat, opens a little door in side of the car but it is only large enough to put his foot through. In trying to get out, he knocks the gas tank off the rear of [the] car." The engine stops and the girls are puzzled, while Johnny pretends he hasn't noticed. Rose and Cecil resume their argument over the car. Johnny gets out and tries to tell them about the gas tank, but they assume he's trying to tell them what to do and bawl him out. Finally he gives up and puts the tank back on the car, "and as he does a policeman enters and writes down the number of the car."

Johnny tries to get the girls' attention by winking at them. They think he's flirting and "tell him to mind his own business." The policeman walks up to the front of the car.

OFFICER: What do you girls mean by driving so fast?

ROSE: How fast were we driving?

OFFICER: You were driving fifty miles an hour. Rose turns to Johnny.

ROSE: Did you hear what he said?

JOHNNY: What did he say?

ROSE: He said we were driving fifty miles an hour.

JOHNNY: Are you going to let him get away with it? Go on and bawl him out. If he says anything, just mention my name.

OFFICER: I'll give you people just five minutes to move away from this hospital. Remember, just five minutes!

JOHNNY: Is that railroad time or central time?

ROSE: Johnny, crank the car for us.

Johnny gets out, cranks the car, the engine starts. Just as he starts to get back in, the hood pops open and "a lot of tin cans jump out." Johnny runs about as if excited.

JOHNNY: Come on, that's all!

Rose asks about the "Maggie-neato," as in *Johnny's New Car*, and gets the same joke in reply. She asks Johnny to crank it again. Johnny stoops to pick up part of the engine and gets the flame-in-the-pants, the one bit that has survived since *A Night on the Boulevard*. Johnny runs about fanning himself, then dashes inside the hospital, emerging with a thermometer in his mouth. He leans against the doorframe and the temperature rises on the large thermometer mounted on the door. When he walks away, the temperature drops.

CECIL: Do you smell something burning?

ROSE: Yes, I smell something burning. Johnny, do you smell something burning?

JOHNNY: I _feel_ something burning!

Rose takes out the owner's manual — which has the word "Packard" emblazoned on it — and begins to read. Johnny finds a gasoline can in the back seat and drinks from it. Then he starts coughing, with a horn sound effect. Eventually, Rose and Cecil turn to see what's the matter. Rose hits him on the back, Cecil hits him on the head; each time, Johnny coughs with the horn effect. Then Johnny blows his nose, and the horn sounds again.

Meanwhile, the policeman has returned and tells them he's issuing a ticket. Johnny steals the officer's badge, pins it to his vest. When the officer turns, Johnny flashes the badge; the officer salutes him and departs. The auto starts up and the Langdons drive off stage.

After the Ball is a curious mixture of old and new, where the old — at least on paper — doesn't seem as well integrated, nor as funny, as it did in *Johnny's New Car*. The balky fountain bit had a shred of context in the older sketch: not wishing to purchase something at the café/roadhouse, Johnny knew the fountain represented a free beverage. In *After the Ball*, it's just thrown in willy-nilly. Certainly Johnny's line about expecting payment for the illicit booze was funnier when directed at Katie Speedington than the golf course manager. Putting the automobile in front of a hospital was a novel twist, but little was made of the opportunity, or the policeman character. The conflict — indeed the whole sketch — simply stops with the old stolen badge gag. Lastly, without the boulevard backdrop there were no special effects for the finale.

The team broke in the act over the Western Vaudeville Circuit, starting with the Cedar Rapids Majestic the week of October 10, 1921. Four weeks later, they were in New York for appearances at Keith's Hamilton, Colonial, and the Palace.

Reviews were mixed. The *New York Dramatic Mirror* covered the act at the Hamilton, where apparently someone on the stage crew was expecting the usual Langdon ending: "Outside of Langdon's quaint humor, there is nothing to the act," wrote Gillespie, "even overlooking the miscues at the finish, which left the principals cold, owing to the negligence of whoever handled the curtain." Two weeks' later, the Mirror's Hal Elias reviewed the Colonial bill, and termed *After the Ball* "a skit of gossamer lightness.

The dialog is quite devoid of humor and we shudder to think of what this act would be without the whimsical Harry whose quaintness manifests itself throughout the act."

Covering the Palace opening in "New Acts," *Variety*'s "Fred" was guardedly impressed, positing that the material should — and eventually would — be sharper:

> Judging from the applause and laughs it is going to develop into a standard offering that will even eclipse "Johnny's New Car"… [although] it was noticeable that Langdon and his company were not at all sure of themselves as to the laughs.
>
> The first scene is on a golf course with Rose and Cecil clad in striking golf costumes, doing more gabbing than golfing…There are chances here that will be worked out. The second scene, in full stage…will build up to be as funny as the front of the road house in time. As it stands now it has a lot of laughs, but they are not of the "wow" quality.
>
> Finally, the auto bit is used for the closing scene. It is different than the old car stuff. This time it is a smart looking roadster with the girls in the front seat and Harry riding in the rear. Some of the copper stuff is used and still gets laughs. The prop tin cans in the hood and the blow torch backfire bit from the old act is still present and lands with the usual effect.
>
> The three scenes make pretty stage pictures and the two girls show to advantage in the smartly cut golf clothes with knicker[s] and hose. Harry is the same boob character as of yore and quite as funny in his inimitable way.

Conversely, a critic for the *New York Tribune* simply termed the sketch "one of the most vapid things ever perpetrated in vaudeville."

At Keith's Boston a few weeks later, *Variety*'s Len Libbey, after noting that a cold rain and a forthcoming local election prevented the theater from filling up, wrote that Langdon "was treading thin ice most of the time, and it wasn't his fault. His act depends so much on his quiet humor and facial expressions that a chilly house, such as he was bucking, is liable to miss. Langdon puttered along, however, with his comedy stuff, and with the automobile bit at the end got himself over."

By now, of course, Langdon was a pro at reading audiences, as quoted by *Photoplay*'s Jean North two years later: "In vaudeville…you can pretty well control the laughing of your crowd. If things were going well, I'd play along at a fairly slow tempo and keep my voice well down. If the laughs were too few and quiet, I'd increase my speed and raise my voice. It seemed infectious, for almost always it would make 'em laugh louder and longer."

Langdon continued on the Eastern Keith circuit for the duration of the season, with return visits to New York City in January and May 1922. Revisiting the Palace in May, *Variety* affirmed that there were still problems to iron out. "Harry Langdon got a halting start with the golf prolog *(sic)* to his auto burlesque," wrote "Lait." "In his new vehicle… he humors his slow personality a bit too much. It is a unique and laughable technique, but it does slow up business. He closed to very little, having tired the audience with repetition of gags and draggy delivery." Jed Fiske, who covered an appearance at Keith's 81st Street three weeks later for *The Billboard*, agreed: "Langdon is a delightful dumbbell, but his act drags and missed fire. It is about fifteen minutes and nothing much else."

In addition to concocting *After the Ball,* Langdon wrote a sketch for another act, not for the first time. Back in April 1920, the *New York Clipper* reported that he was writing for a new two-act, Tom McKenna and Sam Kline, who'd been touring with The Follies of Pleasure for two seasons. According to the article, McKenna and Kline were to open in May on United Time for six weeks with the untitled Langdon sketch, and then proceed to the Pantages circuit after the summer break. Unfortunately, neither the performers nor their act was mentioned in the *Clipper* or *Variety* beyond this point.

In 1921, Langdon wrote *A Brave Coward* for the team of Olive Briscoe and Al Rauh. This pair had been in vaudeville since 1916; Briscoe was a "singing comedienne" with a reputation for only using original material, while her "nut" partner mostly mugged in silence, but also joined Briscoe for duets. "*The Brave Coward* is a comedy and singing skit especially written by Harry Langdon," wrote the *Schenectady Gazette*. "Miss Briscoe and Mr. Rauh both possess pleasing voices and their offering is almost fifty-fifty song and fun." *Variety* caught its opening at the 23rd Street Theater in New York and briefly summarized the plot:

Before a silken drop Miss Briscoe appeared for a monologistic bit, the comment being anent beauty parlors, which included new stunts in male barber shops but ended by consideration of the dentist. The idea, she explained, was that the doctors often ordered the extraction of teeth for the alleviation of certain ailments and as she felt an attack of matrimony coming

Olive Briscoe and Al Rauh performed Langdon's The Brave Coward *for three seasons starting in 1921.*

on, she felt it might be cured by going to the tooth doctor.

Going into two found Rauh sitting on the dentist's door-step, trying to scrape up courage to go inside. The pair meet. She tells him she is going to have a wisdom tooth extracted and is so gay about it, he wants to know if she has already taken laughing gas. There was a duet, "Longing For You," after which Miss Briscoe exited into the dentist's office, suggesting Al gather his nerve and follow. He soliloquizes, finds himself in love with her, goes inside but comes flying out as a lusty scream is heard.

Miss Briscoe reappears, taunts Rauh over his cowardice. He promises to see the doc but whispers a request for a kiss. A slap in reply and out comes the aching molar. For a finish they sang, "In San Domingo," Miss Briscoe lightly yodeling.

Structurally, this sounds a lot like a recipe for Harry and Rose: pair a capable woman with a boob, put them in a situation rife with comedic possibilities, add a dash of flirtation, sprinkle in a couple of songs, and stir. Briscoe and Rauh toured with *A Brave Coward* for three seasons; unfortunately its exact contents are lost to the ages, as Langdon curiously didn't submit it for copyright registration.

What would turn out to be Harry, Rose and Cecil's final season began at Chicago's Majestic in September 1922, and ended on the Orpheum circuit, in most instances as the headliner. At the New Orleans Orpheum in October, a *Variety* reviewer noted simply, "Harry Langdon, who had a golf fol de rol, created merriment. He spotted perfectly." The critic for the *San Antonio Express* caught the act in November and enthused, "Harry Langdon's travesty on the ancient and honorable game of golf and the newer sport of automobiling is one of the funniest offerings the Majestic has staged in many weeks. *After the Ball* gives Mr. Langdon wide opportunity for his droll humor. His mannerisms, typical of a 'boob,' lead to just one thing after another even in the land of make believe and extricating himself from embarrassing situation, gives the onlookers much to laugh over. Assisting Mr. Langdon are Rose and Cecil Langdon. Their conspiracy to add to his troubles in general get admirable results." Langdon had done some tinkering with the sketch over the summer break; according to *The Billboard,* the hospital was replaced with a café, presumably the same one from *Johnny's New Car.*

The act swung up to Canada in January 1923, then back into the Western states, reaching California in mid-February. On March 5, Langdon began a week at the Los Angeles Orpheum. It wasn't his first appearance at the venue, but this one would at last open the door to Hollywood.

Langdon yielded the headliner spot to screen actor Bert Lytell, who'd been placed under contract by Principal Pictures Corporation, a firm headed by Sol Lesser. Lytell would be making a film, *The Meanest Man in the World*, for the company later in the year; meanwhile Lesser, who was also a vice president of the West Coast Theatres chain, arranged for Lytell's Orpheum appearance and, according to the *Los Angeles Examiner*, provided appropriate ballyhoo:

> Sol Lesser, the head of the West Coast Theaters and under whose auspices Bert Lytell is making his return to the stage at the Orpheum Monday, will entertain sixty guests at the theater Monday night to greet Mr. Lytell. Seats have been obtained in a body and a host of notable screen stars will be present. They will be entertained afterward at the home of Mr. Lesser with an after-theater supper and dance. Another large party is arranged, comprising some forty screen folk, and a host of other cinema luminaries have secured seats in smaller lots.

For this very special engagement, Langdon not only had his own act, but also concocted a clever afterpiece that utilized two of the other acts on the bill: The Seattle Harmony Kings, which consisted of a nine-piece orchestra plus a "colored" dancer and a girl sign-changer, and Johnson & Baker, a pair of hat jugglers who usually opened the show. Langdon labeled the four-page script *Dry Goods* and submitted it for copyright registration in February 1923.

The setting is a former bar that has been hastily converted into a dry goods store. All the trappings of the barroom remain, while the goods are advertised as follows:

Johnny Walker Whiskey Shoes
Manhattan Cocktail Shirts
Ginger Ale Highball Collars

Then there are the "hard" goods:

Old Crow-bars
Gordon Gin-erators
Kentucky Rye-ding Habits

A bartender, clearly outfitted as such, "serves" his customers with lines such as:

BARTENDER: Well, what are you wearing today, gentlemen?

CUSTOMER #1: I'll have a short neck tie.

The bartender hands him a necktie, then turns to another customer.

BARTENDER: And what are you going to have?

CUSTOMER #2: I'll have a soft collar; I am off the hard stuff.

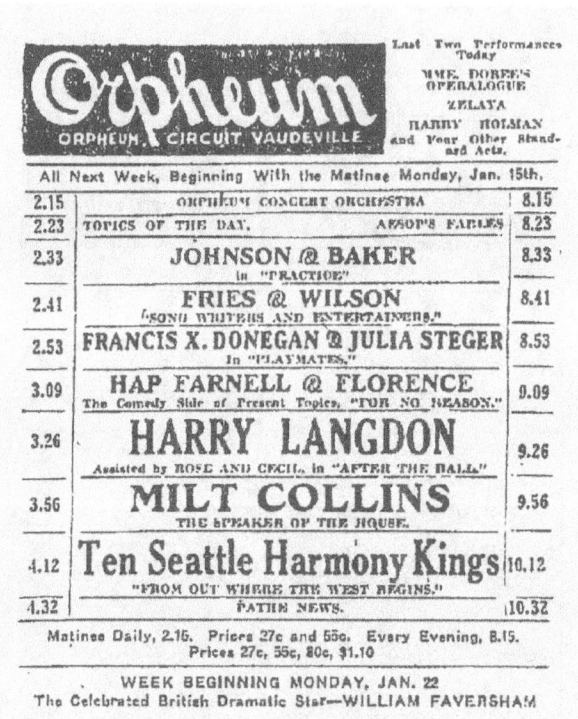

Occasionally, customers and/or the bartender burst into song, and there's a running visual gag of a "barroom bum" entering, going straight to the cellar, then leaving after a minute or two, only to return again. For the close, Langdon wrote, "Finish with [a] comedy quartette or a band. And as the band plays or the quartette sings, all the other vaudeville acts on the same program enter and go through their own individual acts, all simultaneously. Then at a given cue, all the acts on the program change places with the other acts on the program and do each other's act. FINISH." (The complete sketch can be found in Appendix IV.) The skit was such a success, it was utilized in subsequent engagements, with *The Billboard* calling it "the funniest and most clever afterpiece of the season, lasting for fifteen minutes and making a solid hit."

The L.A. newspaper critics enjoyed the show. The *Examiner* declared, "Harry Langdon, with his two assistants, Rose and Cecil, are the laughter hits of the bill. In three scenes this amusing number is a burlesque on golf 'in the ruff' as it were, and whether you ever chase the fugitive ball or not you must laugh at the experiences of those who do — on the stage." The *Herald*'s critic wrote, "There is some excellent by-play of Mr. Langdon's own devising. It is indeed a rare treat to watch and hear him. He's a cure for most of the ills, including those which are purely local to the cities he plays." And the *Times* asked its readers, "Do you remember Harry Langdon and his trick automobile? He is with us again, this time kidding in his own inimitable way through a comedy golf act, after which he trots out the old tin Lizzie. Langdon is awfully funny with his simp map and talk. He remains the life of the party in an amusing after piece."

One of the "cinema luminaries" in the audience on opening night was comedian Harold Lloyd. "I saw Langdon in vaudeville on the Orpheum circuit in a skit that he was doing," he recalled for an interviewer in June 1962. "I was with Hal Roach at the time, and I told Hal that here was a natural for the screen, and I suggested that we get him out there, and Hal talk to him and sign him up." Roach, who was also present, agreed. "And [Langdon] came out, and he was most willing, but they differed on [salary]. I think it amounted to a hundred dollars a week difference. And I said, 'Well, you're very foolish, Hal. He was easily worth that, and much more, to start with.'" Sol Lesser was equally impressed and tendered a contract with Principal Pictures.

In a press release some years later, Langdon recalled he had more than one offer on the table

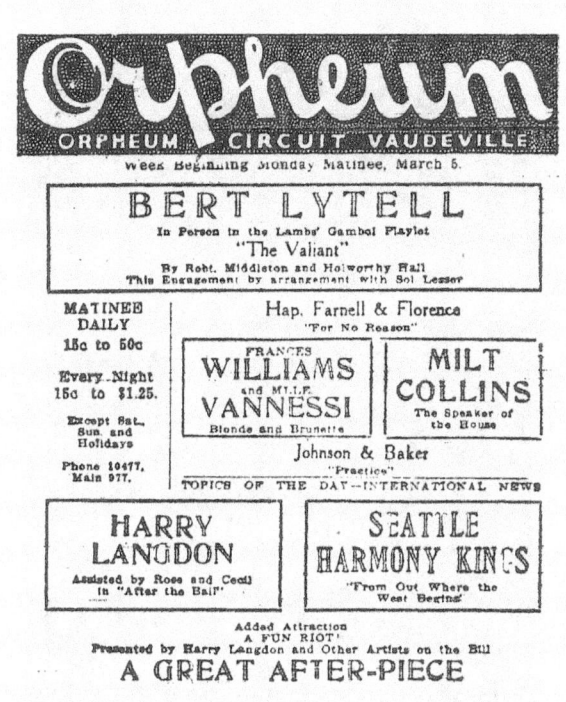

An ad for the Los Angeles Orpheum, and the appearance that won for Langdon a movie contract.

but didn't specify further, so it's unclear which producer approached him first. Roach was interviewed many times during the course of his 100 years, but never mentioned approaching Langdon in 1923, nor did he comment on Lloyd's recollection. In the end, Langdon chose to sign with Lesser.

It's probable, though, that more than money influenced his decision. At that time, Roach tended to start beginners in one-reelers, which generally ran about ten minutes. Langdon may not have known much about film acting, but he knew himself well enough to figure that a single reel would not be enough time to put over the comedy he did best. Lesser, on the other hand, offered him the title of Principal's Featured Comedian, meaning he would start in *two*-reelers, automatically ranking him in the elite class.

While Langdon finished up his Orpheum commitment, a vaudevillian named Jimmy Russell inquired about touring with *Johnny's New Car*. Now that it was certain he was leaving the stage, Langdon, through agent Harry Weber, made the appropriate arrangements. Russell appeared successfully with the act for over three seasons, proving its durability and delight with audiences. "Jimmy Russell and Company were seen in the Harry Langdon act… and obtained much laughter for comedy which is sure-fire," wrote the *New York Clipper* in April 1923, for a performance at Langdon's old stomping grounds, Chicago's Majestic Theater. "Russell is quite as good as his predecessor in the act."

It may have seemed to Langdon that a movie contract was years overdue, but in fact the timing was perfect. Chaplin and Lloyd had moved into features some months before, and Chaplin was pres-

Sol Lesser

A 1925 ad for Russell & Burke's version of Johnny's New Car, *"presented" by Langdon.*

ently engaged in directing his leading lady, Edna Purviance, in a drama. Keaton had just delivered his final two-reeler and was embarking on a feature. Until just recently, Mack Sennett was producing features with Mabel Normand and Ben Turpin. Roscoe "Fatty" Arbuckle had been banished from the screen after being tried and acquitted for manslaughter. The current king of short comedies, Larry Semon, was about to leave the Vitagraph Company (who'd been objecting to Semon's tendency to overspend) to sign with Truart Film Corporation for features. Second to Semon in popularity was Lloyd Hamilton, who was making two-reelers for Educational Pictures. Hal Roach's most successful shorts were his two-reel

Our Gang Comedies; he also starred Will Rogers in two-reelers, while lesser lights such as Snub Pollard, Paul Parrott and Stan Laurel (pre-Oliver Hardy, who was working for Semon) were grinding out single reels every month. After that came the generic series: Sunshine Comedies, Century Comedies, Mermaid Comedies, et cetera; symphonies of slapstick with more-or-less interchangeable plots and players.

There was ample opportunity for a new comedy star to arise, and Langdon was up for the task. The question was whether Principal Pictures, a relatively new concern, could pull it off.

CHAPTER SIX

From Lesser to Greater

1923–1924

By the time he signed Harry Langdon to a movie contract, Sol Lesser was on the verge of becoming one of the motion picture industry's titans, a mogul in the making. He might well have succeeded, if only he'd been more ruthless.

Born in Spokane, Washington, on February 17, 1890, Lesser was the middle son of German-Jewish immigrants. By the turn of the 20th century, the family was living in San Francisco. Papa Lesser worked as a shoe dealer, but four years later, he became the owner-operator of the Mission Theater. It was here, at age 14, that Sol started his first business: selling ice cream cones out front. At 20, he was running a film distribution company in San Francisco, and within four years had acquired his own theater chain, following the same career path from which emerged Adolph Zukor, Louis B. Mayer, William Fox and other cinema czars.

Lesser first made headlines in January 1916 when he brazenly walked into the office of William N. Selig, president of the Selig Polyscope Company, to inquire about distribution rights for *The Ne'er-Do-Well*, a 10-reel feature based on Rex Beach's novel. In an era when film distribution was handled on a "states-rights" basis, with individual firms supplying theaters for two-to-six states each, Lesser was particularly ambitious.

"Mr. Selig," asked the polite 25-year-old, "what is your price for all the United States rights for *The Ne'er-Do-Well*?" Preoccupied and in no mood to coddle a youngster, Selig snapped, "One-hundred and fifty-thousand dollars spot cash!" Lesser thanked Selig, walked out of the office, then returned within the hour with the full amount. Now local distributors had to go through Lesser if they wanted the film.

Based on the performance of his own theaters, the young entrepreneur had no trouble recouping his investment. "In the large cities, such as San Francisco, Los Angeles, Oakland and Sacramento, where the very biggest productions only play four days to one week, *The Ne'er-Do-Well* has played three weeks and in every instance is booked for a return," Lesser told a columnist that April. "In the smaller towns, where a feature plays for one day, [the film] is run from three days to one week."

Shortly thereafter, Lesser formed All-Star Feature Distributors Incorporated, which covered all of California, Nevada and Arizona, and placed his younger brother Irving in charge. In 1917, his theater chain became the West-Coast arm of the First National Exchange Circuit, for which Lesser became a vice president. The company, a nationwide band of exhibitors, made its first order of business the signing of the movies' two biggest stars: Mary Pickford and Charlie Chaplin. On behalf of All-Star Feature Distributors, Lesser acquired rights to several important films, including D.W. Griffith's *Hearts of the World* and Mack Sennett's third feature, *Yankee Doodle in Berlin*. On behalf of First National, he broke the stalemate between that company and Chaplin, finally securing the comedian's first independent feature, *The Kid*, which Chaplin had held back for better terms, with a hand-delivered half-million dollar advance.

At the same time, Irving Lesser signed Chaplin's co-star, five-year-old Jackie Coogan, to his brother's newest venture, Western Pictures Exploitation Company, designed to handle production as well as distribution. Irving produced Coogan's first post-*Kid* picture, *Peck's Bad Boy*, which was a smash. Sol wasted no time in gaining Coogan's services for five more films, all produced within 18 months: *My Boy*, *Trouble*, *Daddy*, *Oliver Twist* and *Circus Days*.

Fortunes were made from the Coogan films. Combined with his other business interests, by 1923 Sol Lesser was one of Hollywood's most powerful executives, holding the following positions: president of All-Star Feature Productions, president of All-Star Distributing Corporation, president of the First National Exchange of the State of New York, vice president of Associated First National Pictures (First National Exchange Circuit's new corporate name), vice president of West Coast Theaters and president of Golden Gate Film Exchange. That same year, Lesser, his brother and another associate, Michael Rosenberg of Seattle, took Western Pictures Exploitation Company and combined it with West Coast Theaters to create Principal Pictures Corporation. The company purchased (and spent $100,000 refurbishing) the Vidor studio at 7250 Santa Monica Boulevard, just west of the United Artists lot jointly owned by Douglas Fairbanks and Mary Pickford.

First order of business was to acquire some properties. Completed pictures were purchased from independent producers Irving Cummings (*East Side, West Side*) and Benjamin F. Zeidman (*The Spider and the Rose*). A deal was signed with George M. Cohan for *The Meanest Man in the World*. In March, Lesser announced plans to film Harriet Beecher Stowe's *Uncle Tom's Cabin*, but abandoned the project when Pat A. Powers informed him that F.B.O. was already producing the property. Next, Lesser acquired all of Harold Bell Wright's stories and announced that *The Winning of Barbara Worth*, starring Florence Vidor, would be first before the lenses. In May, citing "the great amount of research work and extensive plans and preparations necessary to adequately produce this popular novel," production was suspended until the fall, and the company instead chose Wright's more

straightforward western tale *When a Man's a Man*, with location filming in Arizona under the direction of Edward F. Cline.

Langdon signed his contract with Lesser on March 29. The deal called for ten two-reel comedies at a salary starting at $250 per week, with periodic raises up to $1,000, plus ten percent of the profits. Unsurprisingly, the profit participation was not publicized when Hollywood's trade papers announced the signing, and there was inconsistency when reporting the number of films. Since little tangible evidence of what Langdon did at Principal has survived, it's worthwhile to linger over the residual scraps.

Variety was among the first to break the news, with a San Francisco dateline of April 4: "A contract for a year to appear in Sol Lesser film productions has been entered into by Harry Langdon, the comedian in vaudeville." *Exhibitor's Herald* followed soon after with a Los Angeles dateline of April 10: "Harry Langdon, vaudeville comedian headliner, has been signed by Sol Lesser, president of Principal Pictures Corporation, to star in a series of comedies which Principal will distribute." *Film Daily* reported on April 12: "Production on the Harry Langdon comedy series for Principal will start in June. There will be 10 pictures all told in the group." In May, Lesser placed a banner ad in three consecutive issues of *Variety*, announcing that Langdon was about to begin movie work.

Upon concluding his tour of duty with the Orpheum circuit, Langdon arrived at Principal's studio on June 4. A press release was issued soon after:

Langdon, Mathilde Comont and a pair of helpers in The Skyscraper *(1923), Langdon's first short for Principal Pictures.*

VAUDEVILLE STAR ENTERS MOVIES

Harry Langdon, one of Vaudeville's most popular comedy headliners, has closed his footlight career and begun his picture work at Principal Pictures Corporation's studios in Hollywood.

His contract covers several years and calls for six feature comedies a year, two-reel length. Principal Pictures has gathered together the cream of the silent comedy field to support Langdon, and one of the best comedy directors in the business will be engaged.

Work on Langdon's initial story is being rushed while the comedian is studying the mysteries of movie make-up.

A similar story appeared in the June 23 issue of *Exhibitor's Herald*.

It's interesting that work on the first story was "being rushed," considering the company had two months to prepare for Langdon's arrival. On the other hand, a blurb in the *Exhibitor's Herald* issue of July 7 states, "Principal Pictures Corporation has contracted for a series of twelve two-reel feature comedies with Harry Langdon of vaudeville fame as their star. The first of these is now in production. It's an aeroplane story written by Langdon."

Shooting began during the week of Monday, June 25, according to the June 30 issue of *Camera*, another trade publication. The film's working title was listed as "The New Mail Man," and Langdon was credited as the assistant director. Acting, writing *and* assisting the director: such responsibility for a film novice was unprecedented.

The director in question was Alf Goulding, himself a vaude veteran who entered films in 1916, first (briefly) as an actor. At Hal Roach, Goulding helmed several Harold Lloyd one-reelers in the late teens, when Lloyd was migrating from the Chaplin-inspired character "Lonesome Luke" to the spectacle-wearing go-getter that made his fortune. The director also brought Stan Laurel to Roach's attention in 1918, initiating what would become Roach's most contentious, yet most profitable, relationship with any comedian; one that would directly impact Langdon's

Langdon poses in front of a major prop for The Skyscraper *in this gag photo.*

career several years later. Goulding left Roach in 1921, moving to Universal's Century Comedies unit for two years before arriving at Principal's doorstep.

Shooting wrapped in early July, after which the studio took a summer layoff, to resume in late August. But there was no vacation for Lesser or Principal's publicity people. In mid-July, Lesser signed a deal with scientist Louis H. Tolhurst, who'd perfected a means to shoot microscopic motion pictures, for a series of short subjects called *Secrets of Life*. Meanwhile, publicity blurbs about Principal, all mentioning Langdon, appeared in *Exhibitor's Herald* throughout July and August. On July 28, an article stated Langdon would make a "series of 12 feature comedies." On August 18, another Principal article mentioned "a series of eight Harry Langdon comedies."

Three days earlier, *Film Daily* reported that Principal had bought out West Coast Theaters' interest in their company for $750,000. The company's assets, of which the Lesser brothers and Mike Rosenberg were now sole owners, were estimated at $2 million dollars, consisting of "studio property, story rights, completed productions and the like." Nevertheless, the purchase took a huge chunk out of Principal's cash flow.

Langdon returned to work that month in a comedy western entitled *A Tough Tenderfoot*, scripted by John Grey, a former Sennett title-writer, and co-starring June Marlowe, who appeared in Principal's *When a Man's a Man* and is best remembered today as Our Gang's beloved schoolteacher, Miss Crabtree. According to *Camera*, Langdon was responsible for this story too.

The September 8 issue of *Exhibitor's Herald* mentioned that Langdon's first comedy, titled *The Skyscraper*, had been completed. The following week, *Camera*'s September 15 issue included this fascinating piece:

LANGDON BRINGS FAMOUS COAT TO SCREEN

Harold Lloyd and his horn-rimmed spectacles — Charlie Chaplin and his bamboo

June Marlowe and Harry eye each other with suspicion in a scene from A Perfect Nuisance, *later released as* The White Wing's Bride *(1925)*.

cane — Lloyd Hamilton and his checkered cap — and Harry Langdon and his triangle overcoat.

The short, flaring overcoat of Harry Langdon is as familiar to vaudeville fans as those other appurtenances are inseparable from the screen comedians. And Langdon has brought the overcoat with him to the screen. Or I should say, overcoats, for his wardrobe actually boasts eight.

It is an easy matter for a screen comedian to determine what is funny and what is not. He need only sit down in the projection room and examine his screen self at leisure — and the comedian himself generally knows better than anyone else what is funny. Whether or not a certain piece of wearing apparel, and the manner of wearing it will cause laughter, is decided before the picture leaves the projection room. Of course we don't always agree with the decision. But the stage comedian can't see himself. He's got to try out his ideas on an audience that has paid good money to be made to laugh. The measure of applause-or-otherwise that he receives from these first audiences decides whether or not his "stuff" is funny.

Harry Langdon had a slight advantage over his brother stage comedians. He was for many years a cartoonist, and knew pretty well what looked funny to people. A cartoon of his once made such a hit that Langdon set himself the task of discovering what it was about this particular figure that made it so funny. It wasn't the pose; it wasn't the face, or the hat — it was the lines of the overcoat! He forthwith adopted the style for himself for his vaudeville acts, with such success that the Langdon overcoat is as well known to vaudeville audiences as the acts themselves, "Johnny's New Car," and "After the Ball." A tailor in Chicago makes all the overcoats.

Langdon is busy now on his second two-reel comedy for Principal Pictures Corporation under the direction of Alf Goulding. June Marlowe plays opposite the star.

As it turned out, Langdon's overcoat wouldn't become as familiar to moviegoers as other aspects of his screen costume, but it can be seen in several of his films.

Immediately after completing *A Tough Tenderfoot*, Langdon went to work on his third film, also scripted by Grey and directed by Goulding, titled *A Perfect Nuisance*. In this, Langdon played a street-sweeper who inadvertently foils a jewel theft. By the last week of September, Principal had three Langdon comedies in the can… and no takers.

Not that Lesser wasn't trying. The constant mentions of Harry Langdon in *Exhibitor's Weekly*, including promotional photos in the June 15, September 8 and October 13 issues, were specifically designed to drum up interest. Lesser's West Coast theaters were a guaranteed outlet, but nationwide exposure was essential for the Langdon series to succeed, and there just weren't any offers. First National Pictures had agreed to take on Principal's features, and Educational Film Exchanges accepted the Secrets of Life shorts, but the Langdons went unsold.

Moreover, Lesser had a much bigger (and at the same time, smaller) fish to fry. On August 27, he signed Baby Peggy Montgomery, a four-year-old who'd made a splash in the Century Comedies, to a feature contract. The deal was speculated to be in the $1 million range, although Lesser later denounced the report as "entirely unfounded. No company could afford to pay such an amount to any one star if it wanted to stay in business."

"Mr. Lesser's able handling of Jackie Coogan gives us all confidence that Baby Peggy's acting abilities will be plumbed to their depths," spoke the starlet's father, James Montgomery. "Mrs. Montgomery and I are immensely pleased with this new affiliation." Lesser immediately bought Laura E. Richards's novel *Captain January* for Baby Peggy; the resulting film would make her a major star. The purchase was announced in *Moving Picture World*'s September 24 issue. On the same page was a brief blurb that the title of Langdon's first comedy had been changed from *The Skyscraper* to *The Greenhorn*.

Less than a week later, Lesser loaned Langdon to Mack Sennett. Originally this was announced as a temporary arrangement: after finishing two pictures with Sennett, Langdon was to return to Principal's studio "to begin work on a five-reel feature…based on the musical comedy success, *Listen Lester*," which we might recall had originally been written and produced by the creators of *Jim Jam Jems*. Instead, Sennett bought out Principal's interest in the comedian at the start of November.

In retrospect, Lesser's decision appears short-sighted, but in fact selling Langdon was a simple solution to a complex problem. For one thing, Lesser wanted to assign Alf Goulding to Baby Peggy, since he'd worked with her at Universal. For another, the films he'd made with Langdon weren't especially remarkable. Langdon's "aeroplane story"-slash-The New Mail Man-slash-The Skyscraper-slash-The Greenhorn was neither copyrighted nor released. The other two were sold to and issued by Pathé (under new titles) in the summer of 1925, after Langdon had achieved stardom with Sennett. Reviews for both were tepid; of the third one, a critic for *Moving Picture World* wrote, "It... is so full of gags familiar to audiences that Langdon hasn't a chance to be personally funny. All he is given an opportunity to do is to run around and grimace."

Extra weight must be given the criticism since the films cannot be reevaluated. Out of Langdon's three Principal two-reelers, or approximately 60 minutes of film, only about four minutes have survived, derived from a home movie condensation of *A Tough Tenderfoot* titled *The Capture of Cactus Cal*. It appears to consist of the final part of the film, when "Tenderfoot Teddy" (Langdon) captures the heavy by lassoing him and his gang and dragging them all to jail. Langdon's in about half the surviving footage, which is filled with the sort of mechanical gags that were by then commonplace in silent comedy: a hat popping into the air the moment its owner is frightened, a white canopy under which men are moving that looks like a multi-legged ghost, a car that loses its driver yet keeps going…and, naturally, a gang of toughs lassoed en masse and taken to jail by one man. This is Larry Semon material, and based on this excerpt plus the reviews, it's tempting to speculate that Lesser or his creative team envisioned Langdon as a Larry Semon-with-heart.

In its November 10 issue, *Exhibitor's Herald* ran a photo from Langdon's first film; since the caption gave its title as *The Skyscraper*, the trade magazine had presumably been sitting on it since September. By then it was too late for Principal Pictures, as Langdon was officially under contract to Mack Sennett Comedies.

As for the company, it simply lacked the muscle to compete with the big boys, all of whom had distribution sewn up tight. First National handled only two of Principal's features: *When a Man's a Man* and *The Meanest Man in the World*; neither did business enough to warrant continuation of the arrangement. *Captain January* was sold on a states right's basis, which failed to generate profits worthy of its critical and popular acclaim. Baby Peggy's parents would opt out of her contract after the first year. Future Principal releases, also states-righted, weren't nearly as successful. The owners finally threw in the towel in early 1926, when the rights for *The Winning of Barbara Worth* were sold to Samuel Goldwyn.

Sol Lesser would eventually thrive as an independent producer during the sound era, first by remaking his silent properties, such as *Peck's Bad Boy* and *When a Man's a Man;* then through a series of low-budget Tarzan movies after the jungle king had worn out his welcome at M.G.M. Before all that, however, he'd return for one brief yet significant moment in Langdon's story.

Mack Sennett called himself the "King of Comedy," but only because it was true.

Born Michael Sinnott in Richmond, Quebec, on January 17, 1880, Sennett went from boilermaker in an iron works factory to chorus boy, to Broadway actor, to movie actor, to film director, to director general of the Keystone Film Company in the space of fifteen years. Even then, he didn't stop climbing. In 1915, with Keystone only three years old, Sennett merged it into the Triangle Corporation, a joint venture with directors D.W. Griffith — who'd mentored Sennett when both were working at Biograph — and Thomas Ince. Two years after that, he left Triangle and joined the newly formed Paramount Pictures Corporation. In 1920, he progressed to feature film production for Associated First National.

Sennett's stock-in-trade was farce or burlesque mixed with slapstick, and no one did it better. Most subsequent comedy makers — even those who'd worked for Sennett — were never able to capture Keystone's perfect balance of social satire and crude knockabout, which left audiences limp from laughter. He also had an uncanny ability to spot raw talent and give it a chance to flourish. Chaplin, Mabel Normand, Roscoe "Fatty" Arbuckle, Gloria Swanson, Ben Turpin — these were the "discoveries" with which Sennett's name would be forever linked. It didn't matter if some of them came from other film factories; it was Sennett who served up their first taste of fame.

In December 1922, Sennett's feature deal with First National ended, and the following February, he contracted with Pathé Exchanges Incorporated to

Mack Sennett

presents

Harry Langdon

in Two Reel Comedies

Ask any vaudeville patron who Harry Langdon is.

They'll tell you!

Langdon not long ago was making 'em lie down and roll over, on the big time.

They'd start laughing as soon as his name went up.

"Picking Peaches" showed he brought from vaudeville into pictures two big assets: Personality and Popularity.

Beat 'em if you can!

P. S.—"Smile, Please," is the next laugh-gusher.

deliver 19 two-reelers. Six of these were to star Turpin, while the remaining baker's dozen were simply "Mack Sennett Comedies." Turpin's genuinely crossed eyes and comedic skill yielded popularity enough to carry his own series, but the rest of the stable consisted of second and third bananas such as Billy Bevan, Andy Clyde, Eddie Gribbon, Jack Cooper and Vernon Dent. The King of Comedy desperately needed another court jester.

How or where Sennett first became aware of Langdon may never be known. Although Sennett himself never confirmed it in interviews or his autobiography, a publicity release for his third Langdon release stated that he was among the Orpheum audience the previous March: "Mack Sennett, always on the alert for new types and faces, was immediately impressed with Harry Langdon's appearance while he was playing the Orpheum circuit in their Los Angeles theater. What most attracted the Comedy King was the positive comedy type possessed by Langdon. His easy manner in saying things with his eyes, or a mere shrug of the shoulders or tilting of his head. His walk is even something to laugh at."

In 1932, Langdon wrote a thoroughly unreliable account of how Sennett "discovered" him:

> I was making a train jump between two small towns in California to fill a vaudeville engagement. We had been speeding along at 60 miles an hour when the train suddenly stopped.
>
> It was about noon and all the passengers, yours truly included, filed out of the coaches to see what was up. About a hundred feet down the tracks was a big Pierce Arrow stalled on the tracks.
>
> Now here comes the surprise. Who do you think was near that car (he was smart enough to get out when he saw the train coming)? None other than Mack Sennett of the old silent comedies.
>
> At that time I did not know Mr. Sennett but had heard a great deal about him. We were introduced by a friend of his who happened to be on the train, and two weeks later he and I signed up for a year's contract to star in his comedies.

This entertaining yarn bears no resemblance to reality since, among other things, it completely omits Langdon's stint at Principal. If Sennett was one of the celebrities attending the Orpheum, perhaps he, like Hal Roach, made an offer that Langdon weighed and rejected. Or perhaps he subsequently viewed one or more of Lesser's pictures, saw whatever meager elements of characterization Langdon was able to get over and immediately realized, "I can do better for this guy." A *Motion Picture Magazine* article from 1926 quotes a more plausible Langdon recollection: "Sol Lesser gave me a chance and I made a few com-

Langdon greets "The Old Man," Mack Sennett, while shooting Picking Peaches *(1924) in November 1923.*

edies for him. Mr. Sennett saw these pictures — and you know the rest!"

It's a cinch Mr. Sennett had high hopes for Langdon. The same press report that announced the "temporary" loan arrangement began as follows: "Mack Sennett…claims he has found a second Charlie Chaplin. Harry Langdon, former vaudeville comedian, is Sennett's so-called "find." Langdon is under contract with Principal Pictures Corporation [and] was loaned to Sennett by Sol Lesser while the latter went to Europe. So impressed was Sennett with Langdon's screen personality and new brand of comedy antics, that he comes forth with the interesting announcement that Langdon can capably fill the gap left by the world's greatest comedian when Chaplin went in for drama."

For a subsequent piece in *Movie Weekly*, Sennett said, "I've been looking for years for a man as funny as Chaplin and I believe that I've found him in Langdon. He is really humorous, works quietly, but has a personality that bings the bulls-eye every time."

Sennett put his money where his mouth was. So anxious was he to bring Langdon into his fold that the two scripts he assigned had been intended for others. The first, "Look Pleasant," was originally written for Harry Gribbon, while the second, "Trifling," was for Jack Cooper. Then Sennett bought Langdon's contract before production on the first film of the loan arrangement had completed. On November 5, Langdon signed a year's deal beginning at $750 per week, with an increase to $1,000 after six months. The contract included an option for a second year, which was exercised on December 29; this paid Langdon $1,500 per week for months 13-18 and $2,000 per week for the remainder. Recognizing that his new star had been groomed as Principal's featured comedian, Sennett added clauses stating that Langdon's name would be showcased individually in large type on screen, and that no other leading comedian could be featured alongside him in any picture.

Next, Sennett got Pathé to put *their* money where his mouth was, selling them on a Langdon series, to consist of one two-reeler per month, in addition to the 19 films he was already contracted to deliver. Pathé would offer these to exhibitors in batches of three films each. The deal was announced to the trades in late November; *Motion Picture News* broke the story on December 1.

Concurrent with the signing of Langdon, Sennett announced the return of a concept he'd developed during the Keystone days: the Mack Sennett Bathing Beauties, to be reintroduced in Langdon's second production, according to another press release: "For the 'Trifling' cast, Sennett has selected fifteen attractive girls. Several of them have won prizes in various beauty contests. [However], in the present forthcoming Sennett comedies, the bathing girl will be called upon to do something other than stand around as atmosphere. A pretty face and an attractive figure without talent will be considered no longer. An applicant for a place in the new Mack Sennett beauty brigade…must act rather than pose. The girls so far chosen have all had previous experience. They must be able to swim, ride, drive a car, and to be otherwise athletic."

"Trifling" was briefly renamed "A Ribbon Clerk's Romance" before the final title, *Picking Peaches*, was selected. (Since Harry wound up portraying a shoe clerk, this was a wise decision.) During the course of production, another press release was issued, this one including the sum and substance of Mr. Langdon's philosophy, as of December 1923:

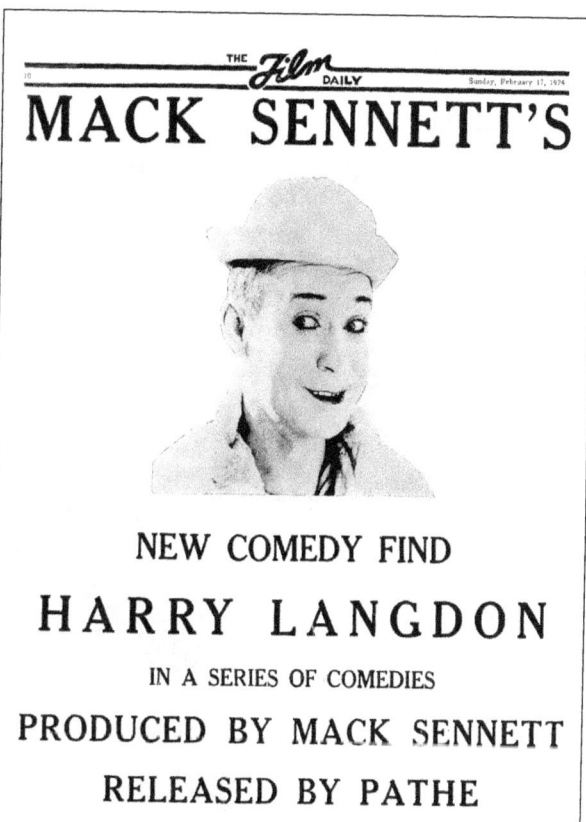

"Hard work never hurts anyone, especially a young kid. Hard luck and a few bumps are an aid to knowledge in later years. A silver spoon should never be forced between the lips of a child, nor should a parent interfere with the wishes of its offspring, even if it craves matches or dynamite as its toys.

"Them's my sentiments," says Harry Langdon, new star of the Mack Sennett comedy forces, who was recently signed to a long and much-to-be envied contract to appear in a special series of feature comedies.

Harry Langdon, well and favorably known across the continent as one of the cleverest comedians the stage has produced for many years closed his famous automobile act with which he was touring the Orpheum Circuit to create a new brand of laughs in Sennett comedies….He was known on the stage as the "King of Pantomime," and has a manner peculiarly his own of registering expression with the slightest facial movement.

In "A Ribbon Clerk's Romance," the comedy production now in the making, starring Langdon, the comedian is surprising everyone with the genuine mirth he is involving into his scenes.

No wonder Harry Langdon is scratching his head. The Mack Sennett comedian now occupies the same dressing room made famous by the names listed in the picture. He's only wondering if he'll rise to the same heights they did

This clipping from Photoplay *magazine's March 1924 issue illustrates the hype surrounding Langdon's arrival at Sennett's.*

While his first two were being previewed and adjusted accordingly at the editor's table, Langdon was working on his next one: "A Sailor's Honeymoon," which would also receive a title change, to *Shanghaied Lovers*. Roy Del Ruth, who directed "Look Pleasant" (itself to be retitled *Smile Please*), helmed the first Sennett film scripted specifically for Langdon. Meanwhile, preview audiences confirmed what Sennett had suspected in the screening room: *Picking Peaches* was a better crowd pleaser than *Smile Please*; consequently he announced the former as Langdon's first official release.

Although Pathé set the nationwide release date at February 3, *Picking Peaches* opened at Los Angeles's Mission Theater on December 17, in support of *The Virginian*. On January 9, *Variety* reported the film "is establishing a record for long runs for two-reelers. The comedy is now in its fourth week at the Mission…. The holding over of [*Picking Peaches*] along with the feature speaks well for Harry Langdon."

Hollywood columnist Jack Jungmeyer opined that Langdon had little to do with it, asserting the film had been stolen by the Bathing Beauties: "With so much stress on legs…it's rather difficult to keep Harry Langdon within the ken of critical appraisal. He was personable and seemed an earnest and deserving young man. But as to his ability, it would be rather unfair to judge by this his initial vehicle. The multiplicity of legs steal all the available laughs." Nevertheless, the film continued at the Mission for two additional weeks, setting the record predicted by *Variety*. For New York City's Central Theater, Sennett paired *Picking Peaches* with his final Mabel Normand feature, *The Extra Girl*.

Exhibitor reaction was overwhelmingly positive:

A real old-time Sennett. In Langdon he has made a real comedy find.

Antlers Theatre, Helena, MT.

I would say this fellow is there. More real laughs heard than in some time

Grand Theatre, Eldora, LA.

A comedy as good as the old Keystones, and the old-timers in this business know what that means.

Cozy Theatre, Winchester, IN.

Can't say enough for it. They all walk out smiling. People stopped me on the street to tell me how good it was.

Maxine Theatre, Croswell, MI.

(A sampling of exhibitor comments for the majority of Langdon releases can be found in the Filmography on page 331.)

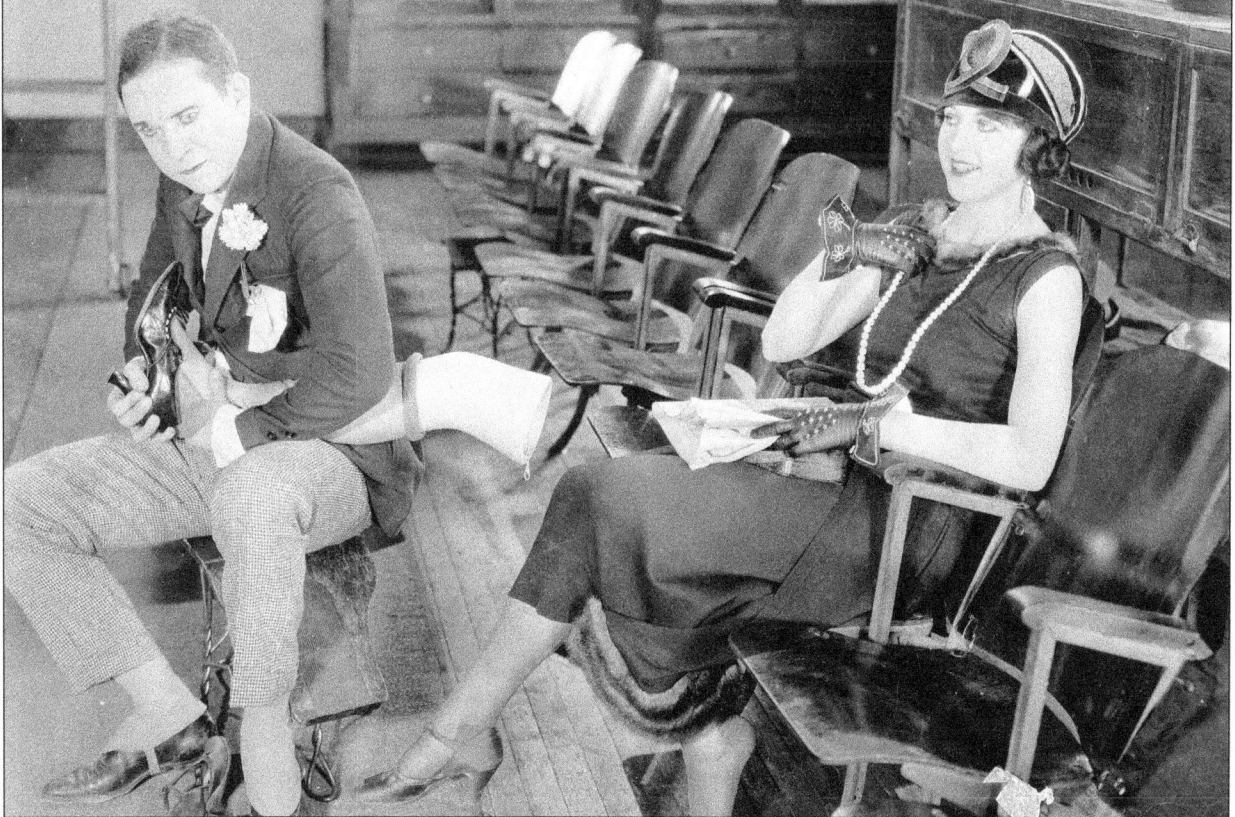

Top: Langdon and Alberta Vaughn in Smile Please *(1924). Bottom: Shoe clerk Harry has his troubles while Eugenia Gilbert watches with amusement in* Picking Peaches.

Smile Please and *Shanghaied Lovers* received similar praise, although a few pointed out that neither was as good as *Picking Peaches*. Still, the Langdon series, for which Pathé was charging a premium price, was shaping up to be a hit.

There are moments in all three of these films in which Langdon utilizes his gifts of comedic gestures and facial reactions. The very first we see of him in *Smile Please*, he spies Alberta Vaughn on a runaway horse and puts his hand up to his mouth in alarm before dashing to her rescue. It's a pose we will see again in due course. While marrying Vaughn later in the same film, he's inadvertently donned a suit jacket with the hanger still in it. He attempts to remove the hanger without calling attention to himself or annoying the minister, and is successful at neither. Between his movements and the growing dismay on his face, it is a richly amusing sequence, so much so that one of the female extras is clearly seen laughing.

Picking Peaches begins with Harry at breakfast, where he devours his wife's powder puff, thinking it's a pancake. As he laboriously continues chewing, his eyes make plain what he's thinking: "This doesn't much feel or taste like a pancake, but what else could it be?" A similar moment crops up in *Shanghaied Lovers*, when he serves up a soup that has been unexpectedly seasoned from a box of rubber bands.

But these are fleeting moments in films that race headlong into chaos and calamity. "It was difficult for us at first to know how to use Langdon, accustomed as we were to firing the gags and the falls at the audience as fast as possible," Sennett recalled in *King of Comedy*. Although Roy Del Ruth directed *Smile Please* and *Shanghaied Lovers*, and Erle C. Kenton helmed *Picking Peaches*, there was another guiding hand. Supervising director for all three films — indeed, for all of Sennett's releases — was F. Richard Jones.

Jones began his career at Keystone as a cutting assistant, then editor, followed by a promotion to director in 1915. He soon became Mabel Normand's pet director and oversaw all of her Sennett-produced

Ethel Teare is amused as she distracts Harry, while wife Alberta Vaughn is alarmed in Picking Peaches.

feature films. With the return to shorts for Pathé release, Jones became Sennett's supervising director. In his book *Mack Sennett's Fun Factory,* Brent E. Walker writes that Jones was "responsible for assigning writers, directors, actors, and for supervising the editing" of the studio's entire product.

Frank Capra, in his autobiography, recalled Jones saying of Langdon, "We're stuck with him. I don't know what, but the Old Man sees something in [him]." Yet according to the press book for *Shanghaied Lovers*, released several months before Capra ever set foot on Sennett's lot, Jones knew exactly what that "something" was: "In my opinion, Harry Langdon is one of the greatest exponents of pantomime the screen has introduced for a long time. He is naturalness itself, and a born comedian. He doesn't have to try to be funny in his actions nor does he resort to the usual 'mugging' tactics so noticeable in the work of other actors."

The challenge for Jones was not to figure out Langdon, but to assemble the combination of writing and directing that would showcase the comedian in the best possible light, while simultaneously appeasing the boss, whose life's work was dedicated to firing gags and falls as fast as possible. It wasn't going to be easy.

In fact, what excited Sennett most about Langdon's third film was his leading lady. Alice Day made her debut as a secondary player in *Picking Peaches*. Handed the co-starring role in *Shanghaied Lovers*, she rose to the occasion. Alice portrays Harry's new bride; when he's forcibly taken aboard a freighter, she sneaks on board and disguises herself as another "salt" by donning sailor's garb, cutting off a lock of hair and fashioning a mustache, then smearing "stubble" on her chin. After that, she stays as close to Harry as possible, gazing at him with moonstruck eyes, whispering in his ear, weeping on him, even kissing him…all to his uncomprehending horror.

A press release issued with the film describes what happened next: "Mack Sennett, producer of the comedies bearing his name, always on the alert for new talent, particularly noticed and was pleased with Miss Day's convincing portrayal of the difficult role allotted her in the picture, which, by the way, was her second part under his supervision. The policy on the Sennett lot has always been to reward conscientious effort with advancement, which in this case has made Alice Day one of the happiest little girls in Filmdom." Day continued as Langdon's romantic interest for four more films and was eventually given her own series; all resulting from a performance filmed barely a month past her seventeenth birthday.

Since *Picking Peaches* had received the best reaction of the first three, Jones assigned Kenton to Langdon's next one, "The Lady Barber," released as *Flickering Youth*. Unfortunately this and the follow-up, *The Cat's*

A Langdon sketch of himself in costume for Shanghaied Lovers.

Meow, are for the moment lost, but both received glowing reviews from the trade press. The latter title was filmed partially in Chinatown, which resulted in an appallingly racist publicity release:

MAH JONGG NOT CHINESE, CLAIM OF
COMEDY STAR

Since becoming a mah jongg fan, Harry Langdon, Sennett star comedian, has solved his problem of the tedious waits "between scenes" while the property boys dress the sets.

Top: Alice Day, Eli Stanton, Kalla Pasha and Harry in Shanghaied Lovers. *Bottom: Harry, Andy Clyde, Leo Sulky, Alice Day and unknown in* Flickering Youth *(1924).*

Recently when "The Cat's Meow" company went on location to Los Angeles' Chinatown, Langdon anticipated a thrill when he would have a game in the real Chinese atmosphere. Madeline Hurlock, the beautiful Sennett vampire, and Alice Day, Langdon's leading woman, looked forward to giving the yellow men a thrill, too, with their clever maneuvering of the bamboos, flowers, dragons and other characters.

But their disappointment was keen when a couple of loitering Chinamen watched the preparations for the game, and then sauntered lazily off in the opposite direction. Langdon then tried to attract the attention of another Chink in terms of pong, chow and mah jongg, but was informed with an apologetic shrug that the celestial "no speakee American."

The Sennett players thought this the last straw until they discovered a couple of Chinese children stealing off with several of their tiles, trying to eat them for candy.

Del Ruth's final Langdon short was *His New Mamma*, a minor milestone in the comedian's career. Interspersed within the usual Sennett madness, which in this case included a mad pursuit through the snow, another visit from the Bathing Beauties, and even a good old-fashioned Keystone Cop auto chase, was an unexpected vignette: Harry, in anticipation of Santa Claus, tiptoes downstairs to the fireplace, hangs his stocking and leaves a note. That's a basic description of the action; it's Langdon's eyes and face that bring the scene to life. This man-child expecting a visit from St. Nicholas is far more interesting and amusing than the aggressive cab driver he becomes in the next reel. For about a minute, the Little Elf wanders into a routine slapstick affair and quietly asserts his presence.

Perhaps this was the moment that inspired Dick Jones to change directors. "Harry Sweet has transferred his screen activities from featured comedian to director and will direct Harry Langdon in a comedy special for Pathé distribution," read

Production Manager F. Richard Jones and an unlikely waiter (Ben Turpin) in the Sennett commissary, 1924.

the report in the April 12 issue of *Motion Picture News*. "Richard Jones, supervising director for Mack Sennett, is responsible for this move. He feels that with the experience Sweet has had as a comedian he should get good results with the direction of another comedian."

Sweet, who'd just come to Sennett from Century Comedies, where he'd been directing himself, took the helm for *The First 100 Years*, a combination marital sitcom and haunted house farce. The film begins with Harry fighting a rival over Alice Day's affections. Fisticuffs aren't effective enough, so Harry throws him off a cliff. This alone represented a huge step backward from the previous comedy. The film then settles into domestic complications, such as the hiring of a new cook (Madeline Hurlock) who seems to be overly attracted to Harry, a houseguest (Frank J. Coleman) with designs on Alice, and threatening, shadowy figures lurking about their home. There are some choice facial expressions throughout the film, especially during the "haunting" sequences, but for the most part its humor is mechanical and plot-driven.

Assuming we can trust studio publicity, much of it was constructed on the set:

> The story that forms the basis for a Mack Sennett two-reel comedy is born in the studio scenario department. But it grows and matures and becomes mellow out on the set in the hands of the director and his "gag" men.

"Tiny" Ward joins Langdon in this gag photo from The Cat's Meow *(1924).*

A fearful Harry is comforted by His New Mamma *(Madeline Hurlock).*

> The story is often changed radically from the one originally written. In a new Harry Langdon comedy, called "The First Hundred (sic) Years," a clever plot theme was used: one that proved so rich with possibilities for comic situations that two changes were made in the story out on the set in order to take advantage of the "gags" that developed there.
>
> And to conform with the new trend of the story, the characterization of one of the players, Madeline Hurlock, was changed three times. Miss Hurlock began the picture as a "vampy" French maid, changing to a Russian princess and finally to a lady detective.

Moving Picture World had noted in April that the initial Langdon series "has proved very successful in all sections." Seven pictures in, the comedian was continuing to find favor with both critics and audiences. After seeing *The First 100 Years*, the *Los Angeles Times*'s Kenneth Taylor extolled, "Langdon can get over more comedy with one small motion of an eyebrow than some comedians can with a whole outfit of gags."

Small eyebrow motions, however, do not a character make, and without material to differentiate him from others comics he'd eventually wear thin with exhibitors, especially with the prices Pathé was charging.

Writer Tamar Lane clearly perceived what was happening — and what *could* happen — in an essay on comedians for *Motion Picture Magazine*:

> It is only at very rare intervals that a really fine comedian arrives on the screen. Of mediocre buffoons we have always had large numbers, but from the very inception of the silent drama there has been but a scant dozen of funmakers whose work has been marked by any appreciable degree of originality and superior talent....
>
> And now we come to Harry Langdon.
>
> This newcomer to the screen, in the few films in which he has appeared, gives every evidence of being the finest and most whimsical comedian that has flashed on the silver sheet since the arrival of Chaplin. He is droll, he is pathetic, and he has a most original and distinctive style of expression. But most important of all, the great percentage of his humor comes from within.
>
> I do not say that Langdon has shown any brilliance to date, but he does appear to have tremendous potentialities and, with proper handling, should quickly establish himself as one of the most popular comedians of the day.

Langdon himself thought he was capable of better, and sought out Harold Lloyd, his earliest champion, for advice. "Harry came to me," Lloyd recalled in 1962, "and said, 'What's wrong? I don't seem to be capturing what I was doing in vaudeville.'

"I said, 'Harry, they're working you too fast. They did the same to Chaplin. Slow down and let 'em work to *you*.'"

Dick Jones needed only the one film to decide Harry Sweet wasn't the answer, but his next choice was a curious one. Harry J. Edwards had entered

Langdon, possibly with cameraman Billy Williams during the shooting of His New Mamma *(1924).*

films in 1912 as a prop man for Universal, working his way up to director within two years. During the ensuing decade, he'd log time at such comedy shops as L-KO, Nestor, Kalem, Sunshine, CBC and Century, including a brief stint at Keystone during 1916. Unfortunately, Edwards had an intermittent alcohol problem; with drinking binges playing havoc with his reliability, employment at any one studio was never prolonged. Having arrived at Sennett's only a few weeks earlier, he'd completed one film — a typical slapstick romp titled *The Lion and the Souse* — when Jones assigned him to the Langdon unit.

Whether guided by knowledge or intuition, Jones's decision paid off. Langdon and Edwards formed an almost instantaneous bond. Their debut collaboration, *The Luck o' the Foolish*, is probably the most satisfying of Langdon's earliest films. The Elf hasn't yet emerged fully formed, but its nucleus is clearly there. It's apparent from the outset that Edwards has given Langdon room in which to create a screen presence. Twice the plot is suspended so Harry can indulge in routines designed to convey individuality.

The film opens with Harry and Marceline Day (Alice's younger sister) honeymooning on a sleeper train. Mix-ups among berth assignments, magnified by Harry's own clumsiness, culminate in one of Sennett's by-now trademarked melees: Harry opens a linking door, and a hurricane-force wind blows the interior of the sleeper car to smithereens, sending curtains and clothing flying and scuttling passengers around. Business as usual… but then we fade to the following morning, when Harry's off to the gentlemen's washroom for a shave.

The sequence is one of Langdon's best-remembered, owing to its use in Robert Youngson's classic compilation, *The Golden Age of Comedy* (1958). Harry is sharing a mirror with burly Yorke Sherwood, and armed with a very sharp straightedge razor. So we'll know just *how* sharp it is, a jolt causes another passenger to bump into Harry, who in turn pokes Sherwood with the blade. It stings. After a quick apology, Harry proceeds to shave. Swiping the razor across his face and under his nose with no more caution than if he were using a sponge, Harry makes short work of whatever whiskers he may have, while Sherwood looks on with a mixture of incredulity and horror. Finally, Harry digs out a bit of soap lodged in his ear by using the end of the blade… and Sherwood can't take any more.

The scene works for two reasons: First, Harry's innocence. It's not as though he's depicted as an idiot;

Harry shaves, Yorke Sherwood reacts in Luck o' the Foolish *(1924).*

rather, like a child he's blissfully ignorant of any possible danger. Second, Sherwood's reactions. *He's* the one to which the audience relates, not this otherworldly being wielding a very sharp toy. The bit is also brilliantly staged, the camera pointing directly at the mirror. From this vantage point, Harry stands to the left of and slightly behind Sherwood, so the latter actually appears closer to the camera. Thus we're drawn first to him and his reactions, but as he's focused on what Harry's doing, so are we.

Another remarkable sequence takes up a goodly portion of reel two. Having lost $500 in investment money through a theft aboard the train, Harry is forced to return to "his old job" of security officer for an upscale neighborhood. While parading up and down the sidewalk he strives for the attention of a fellow officer across the street, but is repeatedly ignored. He tries to match the other guard's steps, much like a child imitating an elder and seeking approval for doing so, but his gait is ludicrously stiff. At last, the older guard appears to acknowledge his counterpart with a wave and crosses the street with hand extended, but he's merely greeting two female residents standing directly behind Harry. The three walk off together, leaving Harry alone and unacknowledged.

Ah well, it's time for lunch. He sits down at curbside and takes out a sandwich. At that moment, a telegraph lineman above drops his chewing tobacco unnoticed into Harry's sandwich. What follows is another eating scene similar to those in *Picking Peaches* and *Shanghaied Lovers*, only slower and more effective. When he finally discovers what's wrong with his sandwich, Harry's thoroughly ill. Too dizzy

Marceline Day and Harry at the close of Luck o' the Foolish.

to walk, he opts to crawl across the street, and when two autos narrowly miss him, he simply lies down in the middle of the road and allows a third car to pass right over. At last, he makes it to a courtyard wall, struggles to his feet and, his face hidden from us by the wall, appears to be "losing his lunch." At one point, he stands upright and wipes his lips, but turns, bends and appears to relapse, his face again obscured by the wall. Then Edwards cuts to the other side, and we see Harry is merely using a water fountain.

The fruitless attempt to be noticed by his colleague (seen to be older and thus more experienced) has the deft touch of pathos that would eventually become Langdon's hallmark. This was relatively new ground for the comedian, who was content in vaudeville to portray a simple-minded "boob" with antics (and dialogue) designed to evoke laughter rather than sympathy. Even so, Langdon's "pathetic" expressions and gestures were evident to Sennett, at least, and he clearly encouraged his staff to exploit them. Around the time *The Luck o' the Foolish* was being previewed, a studio press release quoted "the Old Man's" thoughts about comedy:

Harry has his work cut out for him in The Sea Squawk *(1925).*

What isn't funny? It's the obvious attempt to be funny. Whenever a comedian shows he is trying to be funny, he is lost.

That's what makes both Chaplin and Harry Langdon funny. They have an air of being so much in earnest — little men trying so hard to do the best they can. Of all comedians, they best have achieved the art of being pitiful and funny at the same time. And there is something pitiful about all great comedy.

Once again Sennett was freely equating Langdon with Chaplin, and he was no longer alone. Langdon himself would become ever more intrigued with the concept of marrying comedy and sympathy as his career progressed. For the moment, his material wasn't consistently showcasing his natural ability, and Jones was still casting about for a solution to that problem.

Edwards's next two films, *The Hansom Cabman* and *The Sea Squawk*, were more heavily plot-driven than the first, with fewer opportunities for Langdon to stand out. In the former, Harry is a rich young man about to be married to Marceline. The film opens on the morning after Harry's bachelor party, and his butler seizes an opportunity for blackmail. He brings in Madeline Hurlock, ever the vamp, and tells Harry she's his wife, as of last night. The resulting complications find Harry locked up by a judge (Andy Clyde) who happens to be Marcie's father. Eventually he escapes and disguises himself as the titular cabman.

It's at this point Edwards is able to give Langdon some footage to play with. He's taxiing a pair of stereotypical opium-smoking Chinese, who request a ride to "the mah jongg club" (possibly intended as a dig at the Chinatown residents from the *Cat's*

Meow press release). Their smoke drifts upward from the cab right into Harry's face, and he becomes ever more sleepy and disoriented. While at a boulevard stop, he starts walking along the roofs of his cab and adjacent Model T's. Luckily, Marcie, who'd been present when Madeline and the butler confessed their plot to the judge, spies him and the two are happily reconciled.

Harry chats with pal Vernon Dent during a break in shooting The Sea Squawk. *After this film, the two would work together for the remainder of Langdon's Sennett contract.*

The Sea Squawk centers completely around a stolen jewel smuggled aboard a ship full of immigrants, including Harry, a kilt-garbed Scot. As it happens, he's bunking with the smuggler (Christian Frank), not at all a comforting prospect, especially since he's trying to impress a fellow immigrant (Eugenia Gilbert), described in a title as "a blue-eyed Bulgarian daisy." Made aware by his accomplice (Charlotte Mineau) that detectives are searching the ship, the smuggler forces Harry to swallow the jewel. Thoroughly nauseated now, Harry clobbers the crook with his shoe, and eventually disguises himself as a woman, seeking refuge in the captain's arms. The resulting mayhem includes a monkey making its way under Harry's dress as he and the captain are dancing. Eventually it comes out that Eugenia switched the jewel with a fake; she subsequently ID's the thieves for the detectives and wins Harry's devotion. Langdon's scenes in drag are interesting, but his character is hardly an innocent child-man. He's well aware of the dangers of the world and even carries a gun for protection, although it's dwarfed by the smuggler's weapon.

Behind the scenes, the "Old Man" had sold Pathé on another series, and added a fourth unit. This one would star Ralph Graves, who'd been Mabel Normand's leading man in *The Extra Girl* and whom Sennett was grooming as a young go-getter in the Harold Lloyd vein. To give the series some additional spark, Alice Day became Graves's leading lady. New writers were added to the fold, among them a couple of former Hal Roach employees: Tay Garnett and Frank Capra. After apprenticing on the Mack Sennett Comedies for about six weeks, each was reassigned. Dick Jones placed Garnett with Graves, then paired Capra with another recent arrival, Arthur Ripley, and put them in Turpin's unit. The two came up with a parody of *The Virginian* (the same film that had premiered with *Picking Peaches*) called *The Reel Virginian*.

Upon completing that script, Jones assigned them to Langdon. The assignment may have seemed more like an induction, since — according to Capra — it began with a training film.

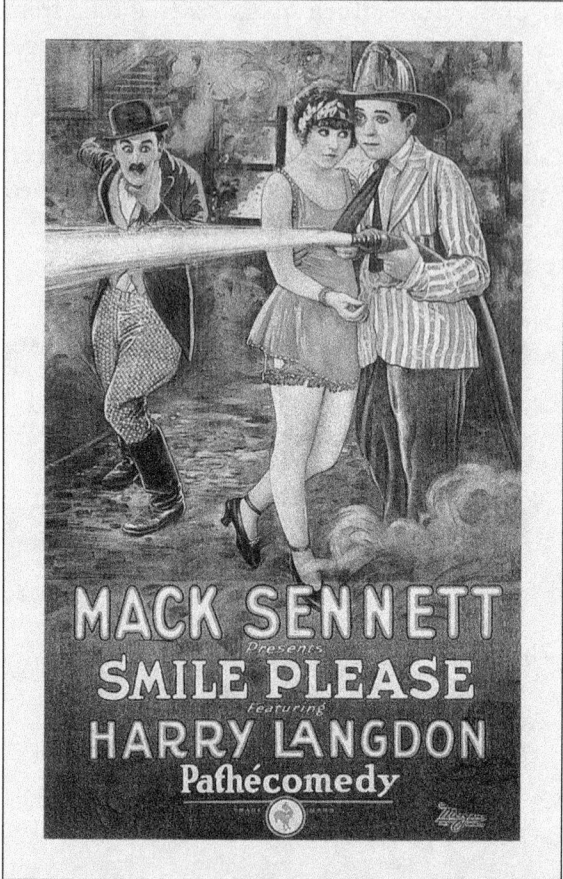

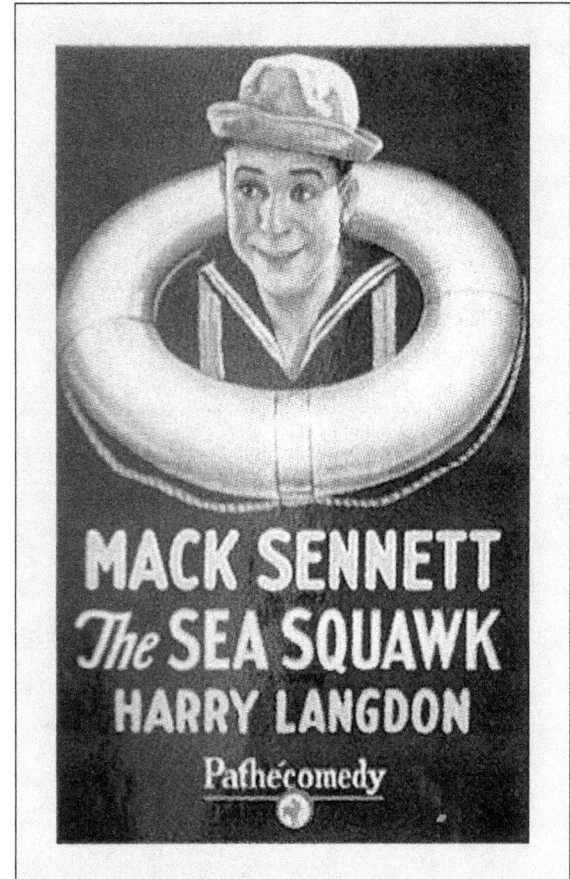

CHAPTER SEVEN

"Legitimate Laughs"

1924–1925

For creative souls, run-of-the-mill movie buffs, or those who simply enjoy well-written autobiographies, director Frank Capra's 1971 tome, *The Name Above the Title*, is wonderfully entertaining and at times inspiring. For cinema historians, however, it's damned near worthless, and a few have gone the extra mile to prove it.

Perhaps most infuriating to the film scholar is that Capra, from the outset, declared he would be playing fast and loose with facts and chronology. "This is not truly an autobiography," reads the third paragraph in the Preface. "Rather it is mostly random recalls of what went on in my head…. At times I will telescope conversations — which strung out over weeks and months — into one scene. I shall use real names; describe the kings, the queens and the rogues of Hollywood as I saw them from the inside of my own eyeballs. You may also sense a story: A cheap, egotistical punk grows into a man." That's indeed the "story" readers are handed, as Capra's growth is achieved at the expense of some prominent personalities, including Mack Sennett; Columbia studios' chief Harry Cohn and his M.G.M. counterpart Louis B. Mayer; screenwriter and collaborator Robert Riskin; stars such as Claudette Colbert, Frank Sinatra, Glenn Ford — and, most especially, Harry Langdon.

Historians, particularly those who have dug into Langdon's career and tried to ascertain exactly what, if anything, Capra brought to the party, have consistently emerged from *The Name Above the Title* with a different perspective. The story *they* sense: A cheap, egotistical punk grows into a highly successful, critically acclaimed, award-winning egotistical punk.

This isn't the place to deconstruct Capra's book, mainly because cinema studies professor Joseph McBride, in his 1992 volume *Frank Capra: The Catastrophe of Success*, did such a thorough job of it that Capra aficionados have never forgiven him. However, it's useful to recount the verifiable stops along the road to Hollywood taken by the man who, for a time, held a key position in Langdon's circle of trust, not by *creating* a screen character but by *affirming* it.

Born in Bisacquino, Sicily, on May 18, 1897, Francesco Rosario Capra "celebrated" his sixth birthday aboard the S.S. *Germania* on the eighth day of its 13-day journey to America. He was one of 1,401 immigrants crammed into the steerage hold, most of them combating seasickness and disease by clinging to a belief that they were headed to the Promised Land. But Southern California, where the Capras settled in 1903, was hardly paradise for the laboring illiterate poor, and young Frank — blessed with the ability to learn quickly and inspirational teachers who encouraged him to further his education — steeled himself to remain in school, even when mocked by neighbors, older siblings and his own mother. Somehow, despite overwhelming setbacks, including the tragic death of his father in a machine shop accident, the stubborn, scrappy Capra pulled it off, graduating from Throop College of Technology (later the California Institute of Technology, or Caltech) in September 1918. After a three-month stint in the Army, during which his major battle was with the flu epidemic then ravaging the nation, Capra set his sights on a film career.

In *The Name Above the Title*, Capra wrote that he stumbled into motion pictures in 1921 on a whim and a chance to bilk a novice producer out of a few dollars by feigning a prior Hollywood career. Despite a total absence of filmmaking know-how, he got caught up in his own enthusiasm and wound up directing the company's first production, a one-reel drama based on a Rudyard Kipling poem. Incredibly, the picture became a critical and popular success. As is the case with most of the book's tales, the true story was far less exciting. The Kipling-inspired *Ballad of Fisher's Boarding House* was indeed Capra's first solo directorial effort, but by the time it was made he was hardly the cinematic "greenhorn" he'd labeled himself.

Actually, Capra became interested in film while attending Manual Arts High School in the mid-teens. His Art teacher, Rob Wagner, wrote movie scenarios on the side and was the first person Capra sought out in 1918 when he was contemplating a career in the industry. A few early biographical accounts credit Capra with submitting "gags and situations" to Mack Sennett for extra money while at Throop. One of his first jobs post-Army was as an extra in at least one John Ford-directed Harry Carey western. Shortly after that, he worked as a janitor for a few months at Al Christie Studios, then the second-most prolific producer (after Sennett) of screen comedies.

Meanwhile, he'd been taking — then teaching — writing courses at the Plank Scenario School, one of many less-than-reputable organizations that promised to place movie scripts directly in the hands of Hollywood producers, for a fee. W.M. Plank's wealthiest "student," one Ida May Heitmann, had a yen to appear in pictures and in August 1919, she, Plank and Capra lit out for Reno to do just that. Together they formed the Tri-State Motion Picture Company, lined up investors and actually produced a five-reel feature, *The Pulse of Life*, directed by Plank and featuring Capra in a minor role (billed as "Frank Russell"), which went into limited release the following year. By then, Tri-State was bankrupt and its assets assumed by creditors.

Capra returned to Hollywood, and around April 1920 found a job with the C.B.C. Film Sales Company, which produced a series of two-reel comedies, *The Hall Room Boys*, and was branching out with a one-reel series touted as "a fan magazine on film," *Screen Snapshots*. The company was founded by two brothers, Jack and Harry Cohn, and a mutual friend, Joe Brandt; the initials of their surnames formed the company's moniker. In 1924, after years of hearing "C.B.C." disparaged as "Corned Beef and Cabbage," the company was rechristened Columbia Pictures.

As Jack Cohn and Joe Brandt operated in New York City, Capra was likely hired by Harry Cohn, a fact that played havoc with his fantasy that Cohn hired him on a blind hunch in 1927 after his unjust dismissal by Harry Langdon. Capra was put to work on *Screen Snapshots*, assisting co-producer Louis Lewyn, and likely did his earliest directing on the series, which was nothing more than publicity-minded footage of cinema stars at work and play. McBride speculates that Capra also did some assistant directing on *The Hall Room Boys*. All told, the C.B.C. job lasted about four months, for by August Capra was in San Francisco.

It was a curious choice. Though the Bay Area had its own film industry, it was dwarfed in every respect by Hollywood. Capra spent his first several months as a traveling drummer, hopping freight trains to small towns, selling photography sessions and books door-to-door, until he "graduated" to wildcat mining stocks. This period, which Capra wrote was from 1919 to 1921, actually lasted about ten months, but it was long enough to make him a pro at manipulating suckers. In the spring of '21, he met Walter Montague, a Shakespearian ham-turned-neophyte producer, as Capra saw him "from the inside of my own eyeballs."

In fact, Montague was another W.M. Plank, having once established a "school" that guaranteed each of its paying graduates an acting engagement; now he'd lined up investors in a movie company called Fireside Productions. Montague's idea was to film classic poems as one-reel dramas, with the actual stanzas serving as the title cards. The two men found each other when Capra was sniffing around the studio, located one block from Golden Gate Park, after reading a newspaper column about an unspecified film venture happening there. No doubt he inflated his résumé when selling himself to Montague, but it was Capra's genuine technical knowledge and sheer enthusiasm that convinced the would-be mogul to take him on.

In order to circumvent any possibility of being spotted as "a phony," Capra engaged retired stage

Trade ad for Frank Capra's first directorial effort, 1922.

actors and genuine waterfront tramps for the majority of the roles. His cameraman was an acquaintance from college days, and his leading lady was a chorus girl friend of the cameraman. All told, *The Ballad of Fisher's Boarding House* cost $1,700; Capra's salary was $75 per week. A representative from Pathé screened it, and shortly afterwards they purchased it for $3,500 and proffered a contract for 10 similar films at the same price. At least two more were made, but Pathé rejected both and Fireside Productions foundered. *Fisher's* would be released in April 1922 to positive reviews (Capra's favorite being *Film Daily*'s of April 2: "The scenes are all intensely dramatic.... The picture has dignity, beauty and strength."), and earned a Broadway booking with a Harold Lloyd comedy.

By then, Capra had long since set out to learn the nuts-and-bolts of filmmaking. *Fisher's* had been processed and edited in a small laboratory owned by

Waldon S. Ball, whose business mainly consisted of developing newsreel footage, local industrial films and home movies. Capra "demanded and pleaded" for an assistant's job, and the benevolent "Walt" Ball hired him to handle overflow work at night for $2 an hour.

In the autumn of 1921, Capra supplemented this with assistant directing for the Paul Gerson Pictures Corporation, whose work was processed in Ball's lab. Gerson was yet another actor-turned-teacher who'd formed his own school, followed by a film production company, but the difference was that he was able to consistently place his product with distributors (C.B.C. among them). His chief financial backer was William A. Howell, whose niece, Helen Howell, was an actress in the company. Apparently Helen viewed *Fisher's* and brought Capra to Gerson's attention. She and Capra would marry two years later.

In March 1922, Gerson initiated production of a two-reel series: The Plum Center Comedies, which were a blatant rip-off of the Toonerville Trolley shorts (based on Fontaine Fox's newspaper strip), an older series produced on the East Coast, starring Dan Mason as the Skipper and Wilna Hervey as the Powerful Katrinka. Mason and Hervey played identical types in the Plum Centers, and Helen Howell essayed the ingénue role. The films were written by A.H. Giebler, directed by Robert Eddy and distributed by Film Booking Offices (F.B.O.). Capra was the company prop man.

Because of his relationship with Helen, and by extension her uncle, Capra was perceived at first as a company *spy*, and the perception grew as he continually watched over production, appearing to monitor everyone's work. It was, in fact, his way of learning by observation, but his colleagues repeatedly shunned his attempts to be friendly and handed him the most menial tasks. Eddy simply ignored him. When after a few films Capra was promoted to editor, the cold shoulder grew even more frigid.

All of which changed the day he was asked to screen some rushes for a visitor from Hollywood, and happened to overhear the fellow tell Gerson, "If you make me director, I'll make the picture twice as good for half the cost." Later, Capra pulled Eddy aside and let him know about the potential usurper; Eddy was able to save his job and he and Capra became fast friends. Capra was promoted to gagman and co-writer with Giebler, and by the time the Plum Centers ceased production in May 1923, he'd become Eddy's personal assistant.

Eddy went to Hollywood, while Capra worked on a few features for Gerson and married Helen that November. In January 1924, Capra also went south. Eddy arranged for an interview at Hal Roach Studios, where Giebler was titling Will Rogers's films and Rob Wagner was directing them. Roach assigned Capra to write gags for the Our Gang Comedies, which were quickly becoming the most popular two-reelers on the market. But Capra, whose childhood on the streets of East Los Angeles consisted of equal parts fist-fighting and racist name-calling, was ill equipped to write for the clever, industrious middle-American youth that the Gang represented. Although Capra wrote that he voluntarily left Roach after six months, he was in fact released after eight weeks.

Between April and June 1924, Capra freelanced, including a few weeks spent as gag man for Eddy on a pair of college-themed shorts — a task for which he undoubtedly felt better qualified — called the Puppy Love films, released by F.B.O. By the end of June, he was working for Mack Sennett. Rob Wagner was writing there, and McBride credits him as the likely conduit for Capra's employment. But A.H. Giebler was also on staff as title-writer and probably better able to report on Capra's ability, having worked side-by-side with him on the Plum Centers. Such a reference would have been essential, considering the recent failure at Roach. Luckily Capra and Dick Jones were perfectly suited to each other, temperamentally and creatively, and Jones evidently decided that Capra, like Harry Edwards, might be another piece of the Langdon puzzle.

The biggest unsolved mystery in Harry Langdon's saga: did "the film" really exist?

"The film" would be *Johnny's New Car*, which Mack Sennett allegedly had photographed in order to plainly illustrate Langdon's individuality for the benefit of gagmen, scenario writers and directors. A training film intended for all creative personnel, yet Capra is the only one who ever mentioned it. Given the plethora of inaccuracies in *The Name Above the Title*, it's tempting to dismiss the film's existence as yet another of the book's fairy tales.

To be sure, as mentioned earlier, Capra misrepresented some key details about Langdon's famous act when describing the movie. In particular, Rose is described as "his wife, made up as a dominating, vulture-faced termagant…. Fixing Harry with a killing look, the disheveled, irate wife croaked the equivalent of (Title): 'Idiot! Is this what they sold you for a new car?'" The account bears no resemblance, physical or otherwise, to Rose's Katie Speedington.

At the same time, there's much that *is* accurate in Capra's recollection, starting with Harry's costume, "a small round hat with a turned-up brim, a coat tightly buttoned high but flaring out wide below," which is exactly the outfit Langdon wore during the act's heyday. Capra also described action that, barring a nuance or two, did occur on stage: "He turned the crank — nothing. He cranked harder — nothing. Impatient, he wagged a finger at the naughty car, like a child scolding a naughty doll. The Lizzie shook. Its motor sputtered into action. Harry jumped into the driver's seat, gave his wife a broad victory smile, and took the wheel. The motor stopped. Befuddled, he got out again. This time the car *door* came off in his hands."

Both McBride and Langdon biographer William Schelly assumed the film did exist in their accounts. Brent E. Walker, author of the encyclopedic *Mack Sennett's Fun Factory*, found nothing in the Sennett archives pertaining to the production of such a film. Rather than summarily dismiss its existence, Walker, like McBride, ascribed its creation to Sol Lesser in 1923.

In fairness, assuming either Lesser or Sennett made the film, it's possible Capra's memory was not playing him false. A movie version would have required staging, rehearsals — if only to set the lighting and figure the camera angles — and direction. The stage version, with its dependence on back-and-forth comedy dialogue, would not have been appropriate for film, and Rose's character might have been re-imagined by a director with this in mind. In the absence of movie and stills, we can't even be certain that Rose participated; based on Capra's description, one imagines an established screen "termagant" like Louise Carver or Phyllis Allen playing the part.

Whatever he watched, however it came about, one thing is certain: Capra, in Sennett's words, "wanted Langdon as soon as he set eyes on him." Jones assigned him to help gag up "Over Here," the working title of a World War I comedy written by Vernon Smith and Hal Conklin. One of his first contributions was a scene in which, having been passionately kissed by his sergeant's French girlfriend, Nanette (Natalie Kingston), Langdon's face slowly forms a serene smile and he tumbles backward through an open window into the street. Eventually getting to his feet, Harry stumbles around in a slow-motion stupor, still smiling, and tries to re-enter the house through the wall, eventually finding the door. Coming to, he confides to the appalled sergeant, "This is going to be *some* party!"

Vernon Dent portrayed the sergeant and the results were inspired; he brought a perfect combination of incredulity (when observing Nanette's growing romantic interest in Harry) and menace to the part.

Soldier boy Harry persuades his sergeant (Vernon Dent) to take him along on a dinner date in All Night Long *(1924).*

Born in San Jose on February 16, 1895, Dent, like Harry, was bitten by the show bug before entering his teens. He'd already been performing as a singer and comic in several amateur and professional venues when, as an usher, he likely met Langdon at Oakland's Orpheum Theatre during the week of October 20, 1913. Dent was multi-faceted: a musician-lyricist with a passion for acting and a talent for various dialects. Entering pictures in 1919 as a heavy for former Keystone Cop Hank Mann, Dent soon had his own starring series, playing a "Fatty" Arbuckle wannabe in the Folly comedies for the Pacific Film Company. After freelancing for a couple of years, he joined Sennett in early 1923, first as a bona-fide villain in *The*

Extra Girl, then alternating as comedian and heavy for the Pathé two-reelers.

Dent appeared briefly as Harry's boss in *Picking Peaches*, but that film moved too quickly from one slapstick vignette to the next to establish any noticeable bond. "Over Here," released as *All Night Long*, was a different story. The two play off each other as naturally as if they'd been teamed for years, which is as much a testament to Harry Edwards's smooth direction as to the chemistry between the two stars. It surely helped that both Langdon and Dent liked each other. Their off-screen friendship would last until Harry's death, and their film partnership would continue, off-and-on, for nearly as long. For now, Dent was assured of a part in every successive Sennett-produced Langdon comedy.

During the making of *All Night Long*, the studio prepared another press release in which Langdon commented on the difficulty in making people laugh. The *New York Evening Post*'s "News and Chat of the Photoplay" columnist utilized the piece in the August 23 edition:

Harry Langdon, newspaper cartoonist, vaudeville headliner and now screen comedian, should know how to make people laugh, but he is not certain of that. "The odd thing about the whole business of being funny," he says, "is that the public wants to laugh, but it is the hardest thing in the world to make them do it. They don't want to cry, yet they will cry at the slightest provocation."

But is he right about the crying? He might revise that statement a bit if he had ever watched the women at a play full of pathos which is well done. They fortify themselves with extra handkerchiefs before visiting a show in which they know they are going to cry, and they come out with tear-soaked linens and red eyes, avowing that they "have had a beautiful time." The public — one part of it — likes to cry.

But let Langdon tell the difference between the three ways of being funny. "Each is hard in its own way," he says. "Newspaper comics, because you have only four or five frames in

Wide-eyed Harry wonders if he's been blown in two, in All Night Long.

which to tell your comedy. You don't have the elbow room that you have in screen comedy. On the other hand you can get away with jokes that would be censored as too violent and brutal on the screen. Somehow the public does not think of it as brutal when they see a ton of coal fall on a fat old policeman in a comic strip, but they would send you to jail or have you burned alive or something if you tried it on the screen.

"Vaudeville is sometimes harder and sometimes easier than either of the other two ways of cracking jokes. If you have a good audience it is easier; if you get a cold audience it is harder than anything else in the world. The advantage of vaudeville is that you can change your act to suit each audience. When you have made a picture, there it is. It has to go just the same for Medicine Hat and Broadway. Coming for the first time into screen comedies, a funny man is surprised to find how difficult it is to get stories; you have to have more plot and a more logical and consistent plot than for a high-brow drama."

By then Langdon had grasped the pitfalls of motion picture storytelling, especially those that were indigenous to working at Sennett's. Having written his own comic strips and vaudeville sketches, no doubt he pressed for the opportunity to write his own films. Sennett recalled in 1928 that Langdon was "about the same case as Chaplin — same temperament…And in Langdon, the same restless energy and criticism of everything. Nothing was ever right because, like Chaplin, he had his own ideas, exactly, of how everything should be done. And he didn't want to be interfered with, although, of course, he was there under contract and had to take direction from others." Harry Edwards clearly offered some relief, handing Langdon the opportunity to create business whenever the story wasn't too restrictive. Perhaps *All Night Long* gave the comedian hope that the light at the end of the tunnel was drawing near.

In his book, Capra recalled that Arthur Ripley was present during the screening of *Johnny's New Car* and, equally excited by the potential of "the Little Elf," contributed to Langdon's ensuing films. No credits exist for verification, but it is unlikely that Ripley had a hand in *Feet of Mud*, Langdon's next scenario. The resulting film was another disjointed, gag-filled escapade in the manner of *Luck o' the Foolish*, with Edwards placing emphasis on Harry's facial expressions as he moved from football hero, to hapless street sweeper, to rescuing his girl (Natalie Kingston) from a Chinatown tong war. Ripley went to work on the next script, a lumberjack tale that would be titled *Boobs in the Wood*, and Capra would again serve as an anonymous gagman, with Ripley earning sole screen credit for the story.

Harry isn't much for football but Natalie Kingston doesn't mind in Feet of Mud *(1924).*

Arthur Ripley was born in Bronx, New York, on January 12, 1897, and entered films at age 12 as a negative cleaner for Kalem, progressing to film cutter at Vitagraph while still a teen. Curiously, during his years with Langdon, Ripley claimed to have apprenticed in writing for live theater, and even Capra believed he "came from the New York Stage — which gave him status as a theorizer of drama." In 1927, *Moving Picture World* reported, "In the theatrical world, Ripley was associated with Winchell Smith and Victor Mapes, from whom he learned the fine points of playwriting." However, according to Sennett historian Brent Walker, Ripley came to California as a cutter for director Rex Ingram in 1916, when he was just 19 years old.

In 1922, under the auspices of Universal's production head Irving Thalberg, Ripley edited Erich von Stroheim's *Foolish Wives*. Stroheim had intended the film to run a minimum of six hours over two evenings, while Thalberg and other Universal executives had no intention of indulging such a radical concept. Ripley came to Sennett in early 1924 as a story editor; his first credit a Sid Smith-Billy Bevan comedy, *Wandering Waistlines*, produced around the time Langdon was making *The Hansom Cabman*.

Director Sam White, who worked with Ripley in the early 1930s at R.K.O. and Columbia, recalled, "He was a very dramatic man, well-read. He was a college-educated man, [who] knew all the classics, the great plays in literature." Whether formally educated or self-taught, Ripley's knowledge and experience impressed all the right people throughout his career.

It was likely while working on *Boobs in the Wood* that Capra shared with Ripley his interpretation of Langdon as an elf "whose only ally is God." Armed with his axe, Langdon's character, Chester Winfield, happens upon a lumber camp just as Vernon Dent's men are bringing down one of the larger firs. They shout, "Timber falling — look out," but Chester stands transfixed as the tree collapses in his direction. Only after it hits the ground mere inches from his feet does it register that he might do well to get moving.

As in *All Night Long*, Langdon has unwittingly won the affection of Dent's sweetheart (Marie Astaire), who aggressively pursues him for a kiss, much to his alarm. At one point, he raises his axe to defend his honor from her intentions, but when she begins to sulk, he decides, after careful investigation, to pucker up. The result is another collapse into starry-eyed bliss. Naturally, Dent rebels, and a slapstick melee ensues. After an effects-laden ride on a log flume, the action shifts from the lumber camp to a nearby cantina, where Marie works as cashier and Chester as dishwasher/waiter/bouncer. Although episodic, *Boobs in the Wood* holds steady with a premise of Harry as an *inadvertent* hero. The film was shot partially on location at Big Bear in late September-early October.

Behind the scenes, there was upheaval. In September, Sennett had initiated his fifth unit, featuring Alice Day supported by Raymond McKee. Then, in mid-October, as production wrapped on *Boobs in the Wood*, F. Richard Jones resigned to take a similar

Some of the talent behind Langdon's films. Left to right: Frank Capra, unknown, F. Richard Jones, Arthur Ripley and Felix Adler.

supervisory position at Hal Roach Studios. Roach's pictures were also distributed by Pathé, and while his Our Gang Comedies were a critical and financial success, his other series weren't netting similar plaudits, and none were getting anywhere near the rental fees that Sennett was realizing for the Turpin and Langdon films. By hiring Jones, Roach was clearly seeking a little Sennett magic.

As Brent Walker noted in *Mack Sennett's Fun Factory*, Jones was so skilled at his job, "it took several men to replace him." John Waldron, Sennett's studio manager and personnel director, took over as supervisor of production. Under him was H. Lee Hugunin as production manager, assisted by Lonnie D'Orsa, who supervised editing. Arthur Ripley was promoted to scenario editor, with a staff "composed of Felix Adler, Rob Wagner, Jefferson Moffatt, Hal Conklin, Hal Yates, Tay Garnett, Frank Capra and Vernon Smith," per *Film Daily*. Adler would supervise titling.

Then Sennett suddenly lost *his* primary star. The health of Carrie Turpin, Ben's disabled wife, went into a sudden descent and he took a leave of absence to care for her, which would keep him off screen for over

A measure of Langdon's importance to the Pathé organization.

a year. "What's the use of all the money I got if it can't make my wife well," Turpin told one columnist. "She's all that counts. As long as she needs me, the movies can go hang." If he hadn't already become Sennett's most valuable property, Harry Langdon was now assured of that distinction.

Contractually, Langdon's salary would be rising to $1,500 per week the following month, and he decided it was time to hire a personal assistant. He also decided to keep it in the family, luring his youngest brother Claude out to the coast. Claude had been working at a grocery store in Council Bluffs, but on October 28, he headed west with his wife, Nellie, and son Donald. With mother Lavina and his other siblings having already settled in Los Angeles, there was presumably a happy reunion.

Film journalists continued to "discover" Langdon. In the December 9 issue of *Wid's Weekly*, editor Wid Gunning wrote an effusive piece under the title "Watch This Boy." "A good comedy star today is really a better business proposition than a star of the regular hero or 'shero' type. Mack Sennett has a boy coming along that is going to make all of the brothers sit up and take notice in the years to come. If you have seen any of Harry Langdon's pictures lately you have surely been impressed by the manner in which that boy puts his stuff over...

"I haven't been on the Sennett lot in a long time.... I don't know what sort of a contract Langdon has with [Sennett]. I have never met the boy. I do know that he has something which is of tremendous importance in putting across comedies. His stuff has earned laughs regularly, not only because of the gags, which have been good, but because of the manner in which he handles those gags.

"I have seen several of Langdon's short comedies in recent months, and they have all been very good. The other night I caught a thing [*All Night Long*] in which he and Vernon Dent checked back to their hectic days on the battlefield, and the Mack Sennett crowd certainly deserve credit for having filled that one full of a wonderful lot of surefire gags.

"I don't know how soon they are going to slip Harry Langdon into a real big comedy feature clean-up, but the boy is just about ready."

Only two weeks later, *The Film Mercury* ran an editorial titled "The Greatest Comedian on the Screen Today." The piece cited the accomplishments of Chaplin, Keaton, Lloyd and Semon, then summed up with the following:

> There is one on the screen today that comedy may well be proud of. He is a newcomer. If there was ever any actor or actress on the motion picture screen who could bring forth gales of delirious laughter by his or her mere appearance, this is the one. The writer has many a time sat through a draggy, sloppy feature to enjoy a few minutes of this comedian's antics afterward.

When Harry Met Helen: Helen Walton makes herself comfortable in a scene from The White Wing's Bride *(1925), filmed by Principal Pictures in September 1923.*

This maharajah of mirth, who has almost been overlooked in the mad scramble by highbrow critics to establish a great comedy king in one of the four others we have mentioned, in our belief — and we base our opinion upon his consistency in delivering the goods — the greatest comedian on the screen today is Harry Langdon.

Fan mail was on the rise and reporters from movie magazines were beginning to call. The "highbrow critics" weren't too far behind. It would be Claude's job to sort it all out.

Soon enough, though, Claude would discover his brother was leading a double life. Don Langdon was barely four years old, but in 1997 he recalled those days. "Rose was terribly jealous… and she'd call Mom at some weird hour, while Dad and Harry were up on location somewhere, and insist on the two of them driving up there to check on them." It wouldn't take very long for Rose's suspicions to be verified.

Her professional name was Helen Walton and she had met Langdon at Principal Pictures in 1923, when she played in his third film, *A Perfect Nuisance*. By the end of 1924, the two were romantically involved, despite his marital status — and hers.

Nellie Laura Walton was born in Toledo, Ohio, on January 20, 1891, although by the time she met Langdon, she was shaving nine years off that date. Her father, Arthur J. Walton, died prior to her eighth birthday, at age 32. By 1900, Nellie, her mother Laura, and younger brother Benjamin were living in Toledo with Laura's mother, Anna Harrison, plus a boarder.

In 1914, Nellie, who was now calling herself Helen, met Thomas J. O'Brien, an engraver by trade, and they married on November 26 of that year. A daughter, Virginia, was born to the couple the following September, but the union would always be stormy. The 1920 census sheds some light on the matter: the young family is living in an apartment in Highland Park, Michigan, with Helen's mother. Thomas is employed as the proprietor of a copper engraving business. Helen works as well, as a model

Langdon and Vernon Dent are directed by Harry Edwards in the days before rear screen projection; His Marriage Wow *(1925).*

for a dressmaking company, despite being the mother of a five-year-old daughter in an era when the concept of a working mom was nonexistent. Money and glamour were weaknesses for Mrs. O'Brien fairly early. As for Mr. O'Brien, *his* weakness was reportedly a short fuse. Their arguments were frequent, loud and occasionally physical, and there were several separations. "Our entire married life was a series of quarrels," she

Harry and Vernon Dent conspire in Plain Clothes *(1925).*

once said. "We quarreled ten minutes after the wedding ceremony and we quarreled ten minutes before we parted for good."

Not long after the 1920 census, O'Brien took a job in Southern California, and Helen made her way into the picture business, presumably by whatever means an ambitious and relatively young-looking woman with long blonde tresses would normally employ. On January 1, 1921, she appeared on a Tournament of Roses Parade float carrying "the six most beautiful girls in Southern California." "I thought it was like a beautiful dream," she once said. No one ever asked O'Brien what *he* thought about it, but in 1922, Helen moved out, taking Virginia with her. The following year, the up-and-coming actress met the up-and-coming screen comedian.

By January 1925, Helen's "friendship" with Harry had escalated considerably, much to O'Brien's annoyance. On the 9th, he followed Helen as she drove to a prearranged rendezvous with Langdon. After she'd parked and gotten into Langdon's car, O'Brien drove up and confronted his wife, saying, "You ought to be ashamed of yourself." That day's coupling was thus thwarted, but on the evening of January 28, O'Brien drove to his wife's home and saw Langdon's vehicle parked nearby. "I stopped and waited outside the windows of her bedroom from 11:45 until 1:30," he recalled in 1930, and when Langdon finally emerged, "I confronted him and… the lights flashed on inside the house. My voice had been heard. I told Langdon, 'I'll see you in the morning.'"

The next day, O'Brien drove to Langdon's home on Canon Drive, "and told him to get into my car, as I had something to say to him. I told him he was a first class scoundrel and said, 'You know what usually happens in cases of this kind, don't you?' Langdon said, 'Yes, gunplay.' I said, 'There won't be anything like that here.' Langdon asked me if I loved Helen. I told him I did and that if he was any kind of a man he would step out of the picture."

Langdon did step aside for a while in terms of physical presence, as the opportunity to take full control of his career occupied his time. Yet he continued to shower Helen with gifts, which only placed additional strain on both their marriages. For the sake of their daughter, the O'Briens officially reconciled in August, but the attentions of the newly rich and famous Harry Langdon would eventually prove too great for Helen to resist.

Ironically, while Langdon's off-screen relationship with Helen was approaching the point of passion, he was making a marital farce. Written by Ripley, *His Marriage Wow* focuses on bridegroom, then newlywed Harry Hope, who is gradually convinced by a lunatic (Vernon Dent) that his bride (Natalie Kingston) is interested only in his $50,000 life insurance policy. After drinking coffee inadvertently spiked with Bull Durham tobacco, Langdon is certain he's been poisoned and curls up on the parlor floor to die. Dent insists on taking him to a hospital and, in a marvelously filmed auto ride, Harry realizes to his horror that his driver is a nutcase. Unlike the previous comedy, *His Marriage Wow* tells a cohesive, if slightly gruesome, story that unfolds at a sure and steady pace. If not exactly the Elf, Langdon's character is a likeable simpleton, and the situation provides ample opportunity for his expressive eyes and mouth.

Beginning with the next production, *Plain Clothes*, Ripley and Capra would jointly script all but one of the remaining Sennett Langdon comedies. Their initial collaboration cast Harry as a private detective, one who is none-too-successful (his office furniture has been repossessed) but is promised a $10,000 payment for the recovery of a stolen necklace. He eventually learns the burglary gang, led by Vernon Dent, is residing at the same boarding house as his sweetheart (Claire Cushman). Although described in a title as "clueless about most everything," Harry is hardly a helpless man-child relying on providence for success; he does possess the cunning necessary to his chosen profession. He carries a gun, although, as in *The Sea Squawk*, it's not much more intimidating than a cap pistol. He also surreptitiously removes the necklace from its case before he's forced to hand it over, and turns on a gas lamp in order to subdue the gang, though he neglects to distance himself from his own trap and is overcome with dizziness. Luckily, providence *does* intervene, in the form of a timely arrival by the police.

Scenes in which Harry interacts with his girlfriend are similar to those in *All Night Long* and *Boobs in the Wood*. At Claire's insistence, he tentatively makes his way to the love seat from a chair on the other side of the room, with a stop at the piano bench in between; he's a willing, but extremely cautious, suitor. Some of the film's material would be recycled in Langdon's features. At one point, having spied a band of detectives, Dent slips the hot necklace into unknowing Harry's pocket, as Gertrude Astor would do with a roll of bills in *The Strong Man*. Later, caught in a gun battle between Dent and another detective, and unable to handle his own pistol with care, Harry resorts to hurling bricks, just as he would to divert a tornado in *Tramp, Tramp, Tramp*. But *Plain Clothes* demonstrates that, even at this late date, neither man had totally grasped the character that Capra claimed he and Ripley

Jean Hathaway (right) does not approve of Harry's relationship with Claire Cushman in Plain Clothes.

had "created" in the screening room in mid-1924. Something was still missing.

The final, *crucial* piece was Langdon himself. He'd already been seeking a measure of creative control, and would soon be getting it. In its February 14 issue, *Moving Picture World* noted, "Harry Langdon is fast becoming one of the most favored of comedians the screen has yet introduced. He has set a new standard

Vernon Dent seems to be telling Harry to pack his trunk and go, in Remember When? *(1925).*

for short length laugh films, in which a distinctive character has been introduced, and his subtlety of expression and action is being accorded surprising and enthusiastic reception wherever he appears, with the result that requests are received daily suggesting that he be presented in longer length stories. Rumor has it that his producer, Mack Sennett, will shortly announce feature length comedies for his comedy ace."

Later that month, Elmer Pearson — general manager of Pathé Exchanges, Inc. — met with Sennett to discuss signing Langdon to an extension. "The plan would provide for Langdon to appear in several additional series of two-reelers under the Sennett banner and then to star him in features," reported *Film Daily* in its March 2 issue. "In order to do this it is felt the contract must cover a period of years. Harold Lloyd's last comedy for Pathé will be released in the fall…. Therefore, there may be some significance in

the desire to build Langdon to the point where he can be starred in features."

Cannily, Langdon held off on signing any new deal, first pushing for more say in his current one. According to Capra's book, Harry Edwards asked Sennett's permission to have Ripley and Capra available on the set to "[think] up little goodies on the spot that Harry can stretch out into big laughs." Capra asked if he and Ripley could take Langdon to lunch once in awhile, "to dig into him, study him," with Ripley adding, "The theme, the key to Langdon, is innocence. That's a mighty frail reed, Mr. Sennett, not understood by many — not even by Langdon — not even by *us* really, yet."

Capra placed this sequence right after the premiere of *All Night Long*, but what transpired was more likely a gradual process, instigated by Langdon, that culminated in full-fledged collaboration beginning in the spring of 1925. Certainly once Capra began writing Langdon's comedies, the two got to know each other and discovered their similarities: two kids given to dreaming, in spite of stern mothers and older, less sensitive brothers; two scrappy newsboys toughing their way to more profitable street corners; two young adults bound and determined to succeed in the world of entertainment; two comedy creators that liked to think and de-stress while playing musical instruments; two now unhappily married men seeking fame and fortune as fuel for an escape.

Permitted to collaborate directly with the writers, Langdon spoke up. He wanted to do stories about his days with the circus and the Kickapoo medicine show, and had a brace of gag suggestions. At the same time, with Pathé's encouragement, Sennett wanted to make a Langdon feature. Ripley teamed with Clyde Bruckman, who was between assignments with Keaton, on the circus story, while Capra took first pass on the feature scenario.

In *Remember When?*, Harry is a tramp taken on as a helper for Mack's Circus, run by Vernon Dent. When the troupe sets up across from the orphanage where he spent his youth, he eventually discovers that the bearded lady (Natalie Kingston) is his childhood sweetheart. He discovers it about 30 seconds after she does, having given him a passionate hug and kiss that transfers the false beard from her face to his; whereupon he flicks it away in horror and stomps it to ensure its demise.

A sequence that clearly originated with Langdon appears during the first reel. Bumming his way

through a farming town, he steals a few chickens, a situation that would also make its way into *Tramp, Tramp, Tramp* (and was likely inspired by his brother Charles's chicken-stealing escapade). Having reached the woods with his bounty, he comes across a few fellow hoboes who have just been accosted by a sheriff seeking a chicken thief. The sheriff hasn't departed yet, but Harry doesn't see him as he shows off his catch, despite the other tramps' attempts to point out the threat. Eventually the law makes its presence known, and Harry slowly dissolves into flustered, futile and feathery protestations of innocence. The byplay harkens back to *Johnny's New Car* and the bits with the traffic whistle and bootleg whiskey.

During the making of *Remember When*, *Photoplay*'s Jean North came out to interview Langdon. The resulting piece appeared in the June 1925 issue, under the title "It's No Joke to Be Funny." Its subtitle might have been "It's Also No Piece of Cake to Interview Harry." North got so little out of Langdon that the piece began with a concocted tale of the comedian hurrying into a "well-known Hollywood portrait photographer" to order $1,950 worth of photos on a whim. "He's going to send a truck around to carry 'em to the Sennett studio when they're finished," says the unnamed photographer. North decides then and there to interview this "funny little chap with a full-moon face and large, serious, wistful brown eyes" that were actually blue. About 90 percent of Langdon's quotes in the article derive from the August 1924 press release discussed earlier.

The following month, *Motion Picture Classic* ran its own story, by Doris Curran, titled "The Sad-Faced Mr. Langdon." No attempt was made to interview or even quote Mr. Langdon. Instead, Curran culled press releases for raw data pertaining to his beginnings with the Kickapoo show, stock companies and the Gus Sun Minstrels, then freely embellished. (Both "It's No Joke to Be Funny" and "The Sad-Faced Mr. Langdon," along with several other vintage articles, appear in Appendix VI on page 657.)

By March, Capra, Ripley and various gagmen had whipped the feature scenario into Sennett-approved shape, and filming commenced that month, lasting into July. With so much time spent on a picture that had not yet been committed to a release schedule, it appeared there wouldn't be enough two-reel Langdon comedies for the year, until Principal Pictures, still fighting for a toehold in the industry, stepped up with its own backlog. Pathé purchased two titles: *A*

Tough Tenderfoot, rechristened *Horace Greely, Jr.*, and *A Perfect Nuisance*, which was going to be called "The Sea Gawk" until somebody realized that was too similar to *The Sea Squawk*. At the last minute, *The White Wing's Bride* became the new title.

Evidently, Sol Lesser sought to improve the old comedies through reediting and recaptioning. Having no comedy specialists on staff, he brought the films over to Educational Pictures' Jack White. Younger brother Jules was an editor, and he recalled in 1978, "Alf Goulding had directed them, and they were not good films. There was a fellow by the name of Robert Hopkins, who used to write funny titles for us; every one of them was a joke and a good laugh. I got him to title the pictures, and we recut them. [Lesser] was very happy with what we did. Hopefully he got his money back out of them." Released in June and July respectively, both films were considered several notches below the standard of Langdon's more recent output, were apparently never revived or resold, and are currently considered lost.

The feature, which would be released as *His First Flame*, is practically a treatise on misogyny. The single women in the film consist of gold-digger Ethel (Natalie Kingston), who loves Harry for his (apparently inherited) money, and her sister Mary (Ruth Hiatt), who loves Harry for himself but is not above playing the damsel in distress to win him. The married women, represented primarily by Dot Farley as Bud Jamison's near-homicidal spouse, are either battling shrews or hardened criminals. Vernon Dent is Harry's uncle, the

Rescuing Ruth Hiatt in His First Flame.

fire chief who is, after three failed marriages, a confirmed woman-hater. He breaks up his nephew's romance with Ethel by informing her that Harry is broke.

The plot (such as it is) concerns recent college grad Harry Howells's attempts to officially propose marriage to Ethel. Alas, he never comes close. First he meets up with his uncle, who enjoins him to avoid women at all cost; Harry timidly agrees, and presents his uncle with the candy and flowers intended for his intended. Straight away he buys another pair, but loses the flowers thanks to a taxi door — there's a marvelous moment where he inhales the stems dreamily, until he realizes there are no longer any blooms — and he throws the candy box out the cab's window, having mistaken it for the stems.

Next he encounters old pal Jamison, who slaps him on the back, causing him to drop his engagement ring. After a pointless but amusing search, the ring turns up in the cuff of Jamison's trousers. Harry's buddy excuses himself for a few moments, just as a couple pushing a baby carriage comes along; they are actually shoplifters and the carriage is to haul their booty. Harry follows them for a while ("I'll soon be pushing a carriage myself," he tells them), repeatedly trying to get a look at their "baby," but they manage to shake him. Finding himself in front of a store with a nursery display, Harry imagines having his own offspring. In a scene that has not survived in existing prints, what Harry visualizes is himself in a baby's nightshirt and bonnet, frolicking around an oversized carriage and high chair.

Jamison brings him home for supper, and Harry's attention is drawn to the battle royal of a couple in the apartment across the way. Staring out the window at the fracas, Harry fails to notice Jamison and his wife are equally combative. He's made aware when Mrs. Jamison threatens both men with a carving knife. Eventually Harry is forced to take sides, which he does based on the relative size of the vases each spouse is wielding; this gets him tossed into the street.

There he meets the shoplifting couple again, now being pursued by police. Harry runs along with them and gets knocked out by the woman. Utilizing one of his old balancing tricks, Harry sways from one side to another, eventually tipping over completely into an alley, where the woman switches clothes with him. Groggily, the gingham-clad Harry makes his way back to the firehouse. His disgusted uncle ("I thought college would make a man out of you!") hands him some trousers and sends him up to the bunk area, where the partially unclad firemen, seeing a figure in a dress, run and hide. Harry simply collapses in bed, exhausted from his ordeal.

From there, the scene shifts to an actual fire, at which the uncle ends up rescuing — and falling in love with — Ethel, thus demonstrating that no man can truly learn his lesson. Harry's reaction to this turn of events is Langdon's first all-stops-out attempt at pathos with no comedy to soften the blow. Returning to the firehouse, he actually cries over his loss, his tears shown striking the floor.

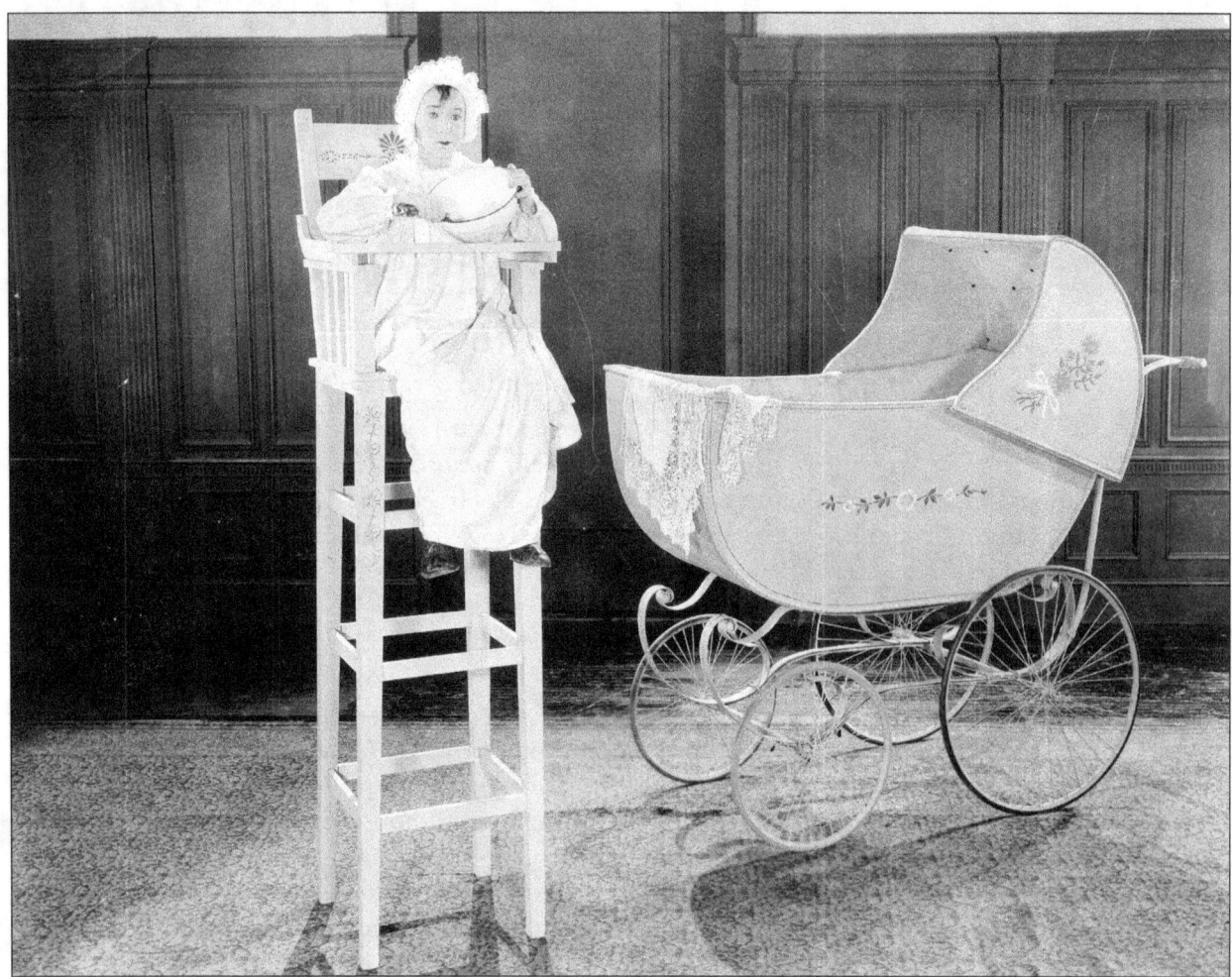

"Baby Face" Harry in His First Flame *(1927). Langdon's first feature was filmed in the spring of 1925.*

Having witnessed her true love's pain, Mary decides to stage her own fire, setting a match to a pair of nylons and placing them in a vase. Harry, who's alone at the station and not actually a fireman, is reluctant to leave, but is eventually persuaded to do so. He convinces the horses to be hitched to the fire engine simply by donning the appropriate hat. Stoking the boiler to a point where pedestrians are convinced the station itself is ablaze, Harry departs. When he's finally able to stop in front of the house, the engine's smokestack is doing more damage than Mary's "fire." The inside is so filled with smoke that Harry needs to light a match to see where he's going. Eventually he rescues Mary, who kisses him with heated passion, abetted by the fact that he's seated on the smokestack. At this moment, Harry's uncle arrives, and his wary nephew runs off with Mary in his arms, determined not to lose *this* girlfriend.

During production, LeRoy Green of *Movie Weekly* interviewed Langdon and at least found him agreeable if not exactly forthcoming. "Although I talked to him for some time there is little to quote," wrote Green in the resulting piece, "A Modest Clown." "I think he considers the whole process of interviewing aimless. It is only when the technical side of his work is mentioned that he responds with whole-hearted enthusiasm…. For a long time he couldn't get it into his head why he had to see the people from the papers and magazines. But he was getting a little better now. He would at least see them, even if he didn't talk much."

Green did manage to extract the following from Langdon, and it speaks volumes about his growth as both a comedian and collaborator:

> There are a lot of gags I don't like to use because they are a little raw. The other day somebody came to us with a wow of a gag — a sure laugh. I thought I'd use it and then I got to thinking it over. It was funny but a little shady. Still it wasn't any worse than a couple of hundred others you see in comedies every night. I don't think anyone would have found it offensive — but I wasn't sure. We decided not to use it. There are so many ways of getting legitimate laughs without getting raw about it.

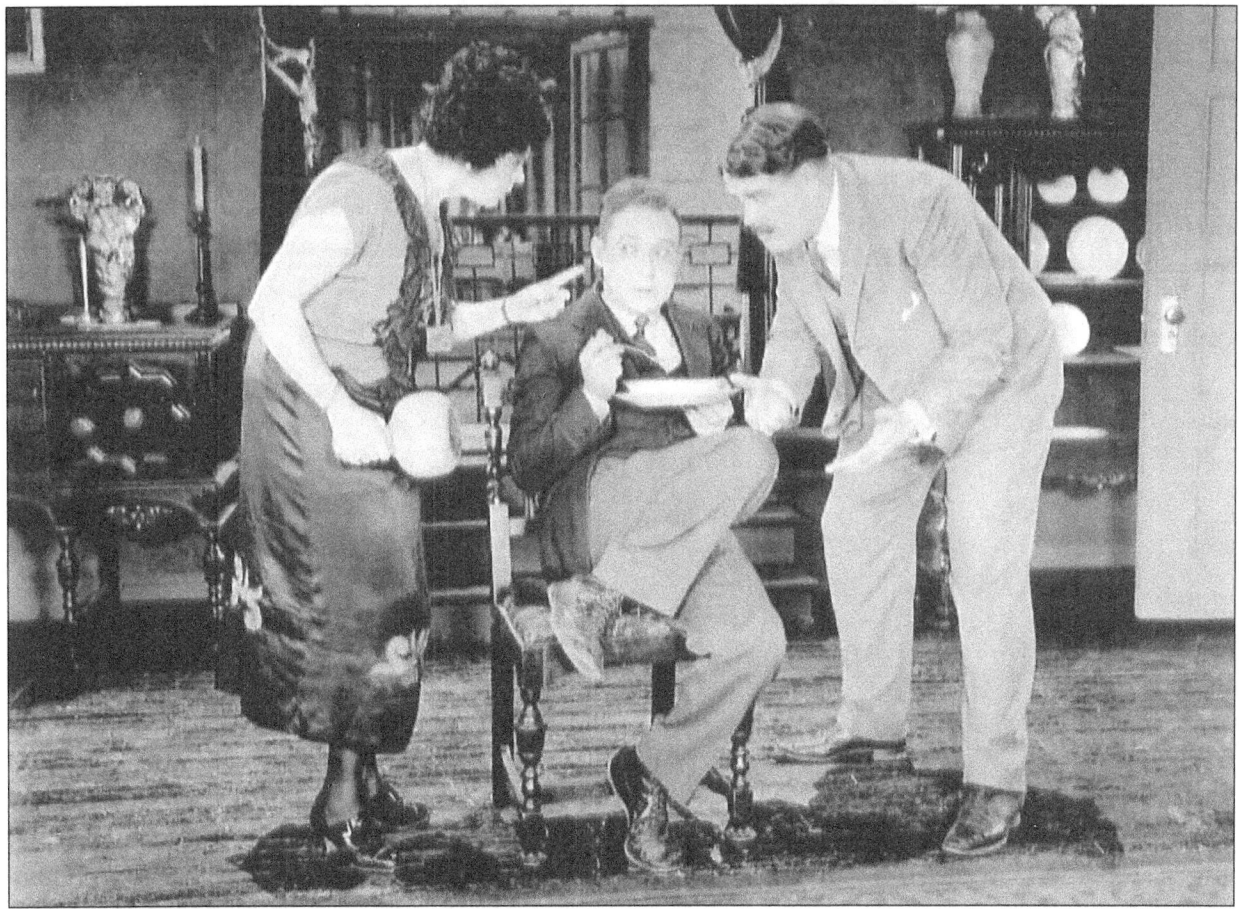

Harry contends with the marital strife of Dot Farley and Bud Jamison in His First Flame.

"Legitimate laughs" could also refer to the Langdon series in general. Impossible sight gags, such as powder emerging from Harry's ears, had pretty much vanished. Emphasis was placed on situations and Harry's one-of-a-kind reactions to them. His character was no more true-to-life than that of any other Sennett comic, yet he was able to reach through the screen and involve the audience through his expressions of bliss or terror, cowardice or bravery; his inability to comprehend danger until after it had passed; his inexplicable romantic effect on pretty girls.

By now, even newspaper writers were waxing enthusiastic. One of the first was Harry Carr of the *Los Angeles Times*: "If I were [Harold] Lloyd... I would ask Harry Langdon's cook, as a personal favor, to slip some arsenic into his soup.

"During the years I have been in Hollywood, Langdon is the funniest comedian, and one of the best actors, I have seen get started. He is funny for the same reason Chaplin is funny. All his comedy has an undercurrent of pity. Langdon realizes what Chaplin realizes: that comedy is not only akin to pity, but actually is pity. Only to the degree that it is pitiful is it also funny.

"Again, like Chaplin, Langdon's technique is slow, subtle and delicate. It has shades beyond shades.

"I say 'like Chaplin,' but the fact is he isn't in the least like Chaplin. He is like no one the screen has ever seen before — or is likely to see again. He is just Harry Langdon."

Responding to a *Film Daily* survey on short subjects, Arthur Sheekman — later to write for the Marx Brothers, but at the time a journalist on the *St. Paul Daily News* — declared, "Of the year's events concerning short film subjects, I think nothing was so important as the extraordinary advancement, altogether deserved, of Harry Langdon. He is unquestionably one of the most talented comedians that Hollywood has. In fact, I would place him second only to Chaplin. In the same survey, George C. MacKennon of the *Boston Advertiser* asserted, "With Langdon's new face, even the ancient gags take on new life."

Natalie Kingston seduces Harry in Lucky Stars *(1925).*

We presume Harry Howells and Mary will live happily ever after, but *His First Flame* makes absolutely no guarantees, stating its case right from the opening title: "Love is the only fire against which there is no insurance." McBride ascribes the film's misogynist viewpoint to Capra, but although Capra's marriage was in trouble — he worked longer and longer hours, and his wife had recently taken to drink to compensate for his absence — so was Langdon's. In fact, Harry's fascination with the gold-digging Ethel might well have been Capra's and Ripley's take on Langdon's involvement with Helen Walton.

With more than a century having passed since the event, with all who knew them as a couple also having left the scene, all that remains of Harry and Rose's marriage are photographs from and reviews of their stage work, a little word-of-mouth and some second-hand impressions. Miss Nellie Revell, a monologist from The Langdons' earliest vaudeville days (billed less-than-imaginatively as "The Woman Who Says Things"), recalled for *Variety*: "When Ed Hayman used to book Harry and Rose Langdon at Pete Weiss' Decatur or Danville for $60 for the team (and me for $30) they were the most congenial pair in the world." That would have been around 1908. But as Harry's focus shifted to building himself up as a comedian, then forsaking the stage for films, the two grew distant.

Anecdotally, among Harry's family members, Rose was nearer the cliché of a domineering wife in real life than she was on stage. She was the team's business manager, controlling their finances and doling out Tulley's, then Cecil's, salaries. Once they left the stage and Harry brought home paychecks befitting a Sennett star, he bought them a mansion on Hollywood Boulevard and engaged servants. "It's been said that at least one of the reasons Harry and Rose separated was because Rose was a party girl," according to Claude's youngest son, also named Harry Langdon, who was born after his uncle's marriage had ended. "Harry would often come home to a house filled with strangers, which didn't make this rather private person very happy."

Rose was also, as noted earlier, extremely jealous, and not without reason. Knowing her husband worked daily at the home of the Bathing Beauties, something that she assuredly had never been, must have played havoc with her self-esteem. What went on behind closed doors will forever remain unknown, but there's no question that as Harry sought more control over his screen work, so too did he seek the same in his personal life. Rose's sole comment on the situation came during the divorce hearing: "I tried to hold him, but he would only say, 'I have other interests in life. It is useless.'"

Once *His First Flame* wrapped, the team finished up a two-reeler, *Lucky Stars* — the "medicine show" story, production of which had been interrupted by the feature — then took a summer break for a few weeks. Harry used the opportunity to resume seeing Helen, thus demonstrating *again* that no man can truly learn his lesson. Rose sought an attorney, while Harry moved to the Hollywood Athletic Club. On the evening of July 18, he and Helen, after dining at the club, went auto riding together, possibly unaware they were being tailed by Rose, in *her* car. A friend had tipped her off; as a devout Catholic, she needed evidence of adultery to seek an annulment. Unfortunately, she was unable to negotiate a sharp turn as adeptly as her husband, and crashed into a telegraph pole. An ambulance was called, which took her to the receiving hospital. The end result was a broken nose, a wrecked auto and some unwanted publicity.

Almost immediately afterward, the Langdons reconciled, *Variety* reporting that "the couple are now seen together again at the Hollywood clubs and theatres. Mrs. Langdon has instructed her attorney not to begin a separate maintenance suit he had been authorized to file in the Superior Court." Regrettably, nothing had been resolved between them. The reconciliation was entirely pragmatic, as ever-increasing offers for Langdon's services were flying back and forth with ever-increasing frequency. It was not the time for a public backlash against a philandering husband.

Since May, columnists had speculated almost weekly about where Langdon would be going come November. "Warner Brothers, First National and M.G.M. are avowedly after him," wrote *Motion Picture Classic*'s gossip columnist for the July issue. Even Harold Lloyd reportedly made a tempting offer to become his rival's producer. It got to where Langdon had to release the following statement:

> It is very unfair to Mack Sennett personally, and to his company, also unfair to myself, to have such erroneous statements broadcasted. In deference to Mack Sennett, I want it known that he has been very fair. Through his genius and uncanny ability as a producer of comedy entertainment, he has aided me materially to attain my present position in the cinema world and although I have received flattering offers

from several producers to star me in feature comedy productions, there is a contract now in force, by the terms of which I will continue to enjoy Mr. Sennett's cooperation for many months to come. No definite plans as to my future activities have been decided upon, and until such announcement comes from my office, I trust no further rumors will be published.

Trouble finds Harry in There He Goes *(1925)*.

This diplomatic release notwithstanding, nobody doubted he'd be leaving Sennett and forming his own production company; all the major comedians had done something similar. None of the others, though, had reached that pinnacle so quickly.

Meanwhile, he exercised further control with his output, specifically requesting Peggy Montgomery for the ingénue part in his next picture, *There He Goes*, after seeing her at a preview. He even managed to obtain mood musicians for his set, a privilege Sennett had only ever granted to Mabel Normand.

Following *There He Goes*, which is the penultimate "lost" Langdon silent, work began on "King's Up," planned as a four-reel spoof of *The Prisoner of Zenda*. Harry is a doughboy in "Bomania," unaware that the Great War is over. While he's trying to capture a local farmer who's dynamiting some stumps on the "battlefield," the alcoholic Bomanian king, also played by Langdon, is kidnapped by an agitator interested in fueling a rebellion. Believing the true monarch to be dead, the king's aide (Vernon Dent) discovers Harry, forcibly brings him to the throne and has him sign a peace treaty. Meanwhile, the queen (Natalie Kingston), snubbed once too often by her drunken spouse, plots to kill him by stabbing him while they kiss. Each time Harry kisses her, though, she passes out in a swoon. Shortly after this, the film simply stops, with none of its plotlines resolved. Harry is merely a former doughboy, awakened by wife Natalie from a very vivid dream. Unfortunately, she's not so susceptible to his kiss in real life, even when he tries to help it along with a gentle shove. The finished picture was released in September 1928 as *Soldier Man*, in three reels. The end result was a disjointed tale with some nice moments that would reappear in future films.

After several weeks of cajoling his boss, Capra was granted the opportunity to direct "King's Up," but upon screening the first three days' rushes, an unimpressed Sennett replaced him with Harry Edwards. Neither Capra nor Sennett mentioned this incident in their respective books, and late in life Capra denied it had ever happened, despite the evidence in Sennett's files at the Motion Picture Academy library. Capra went back to the writer's quarters in Sennett's tower, where he and Ripley promptly turned out a masterpiece.

On August 27, while *Soldier Man* was still in production, the *Los Angeles Examiner* reported that Langdon had signed a two-year deal with Pathé worth $1,000,000. "The terms of the agreement are said to give Langdon complete supervision over his own productions," according to *Film Daily*. "He is to have his own unit, his own director and select his own stories. Three pictures a year are planned." Reached for comment later that day, Elmer Pearson said only, "I wish it were true." By then, "virtually every producing and distributing organization in the industry [is] seeking Langdon's services," according to the *Los Angeles Times*.

The bidding war genuinely ended on September 16, when Langdon signed with First National Pictures, Inc. Curiously, the deal was somewhat less attractive than the offer reportedly tendered by Pathé. Langdon was to make four feature-length pictures between 12-15 months, with First National holding an option for up to another four. He would receive a $6,000 weekly salary and percentage that, according to *Variety*, "will net him around $60,000 to $70,000 a picture." He was also guaranteed the same level of creative control as outlined in the Pathé deal. The latter was, in fact, the biggest sticking point.

"Though First National was reluctant to allow the contract to go through on the terms Langdon had made," continued *Variety*, "it is understood that the comedian's relations with John McCormick, general western manager for First National, are such that he will confer with the latter at all times on stories and cost problems. It was McCormick who engineered the deal for his organization, after Langdon had obtained propositions from others." The company's "reluctance" to pamper the artist was well known by at least one other great comedian. Had Langdon sought him out, Charlie Chaplin could have revealed the battle scars that led him to co-create United Artists. To the end of his days Chaplin insisted that, of all his employers, First National was the most "inconsiderate, unsympathetic and short-sighted."

On the other hand, Langdon probably expected McCormick to be agreeable to creative decisions, given he was also husband and producer of First National star Colleen Moore. Plus, signing the contract on behalf of the company, in his capacity as vice president, was the man who'd made Langdon's motion picture career possible in the first place: Sol Lesser. Clearly the comedian believed he was among allies.

Variety concluded, "First National will figure the cost of the Langdon pictures including the amount paid to him between $250,000 and $300,000 each. They propose to release three of these productions a year as super specials. Langdon will begin work on the first of the pictures about November 15 at the United Studios. Besides the one picture he is working on now, he has another to make before he can leave the Mack Sennett management."

The picture in progress was the three-reel *Saturday Afternoon*, arguably the most perfect short Langdon would ever make, at Sennett or anywhere else. The plot was pure situation comedy: Harry Higgins, assistant in a blacksmith's shop, is 100 percent henpecked by his wife (Alice Ward). However, pal Steve Smith (Vernon Dent) sets the two of them up with a couple of girls for an afternoon date. Complications ensue when Harry attempts to sneak a few coins past his wife, which actually works, and during the double date itself, when two other gentlemen discover their

Frank Capra, Langdon, Peggy Montgomery, Harry Edwards and a prop man mull over a gag for There He Goes.

dates are with Harry and Steve and engage them in fisticuffs. Harry's not so successful here, as he's repeatedly slugged into a state of semi-consciousness.

In *Saturday Afternoon*, the Little Elf is in full-flower. The character practically defies comprehension. He's a laborer who watches the clock closely when quitting time is nigh, and he's a small boy who calls home when he misses the trolley. He's a married man lengthy run on Broadway. Its situations fueled one of Langdon's features just two years later, and became something of a blueprint for several Laurel & Hardy comedies.

Langdon's final Sennett short, *Fiddlesticks*, was originally planned as a three-reeler. Ultimately released in two reels, what emerged amounts to little more than an anecdote, albeit a very amusing one.

The unlikely king of Soldier Man *(1928), filmed in 1925.*

Despite being married, Harry welcomes the attentions of Ruth Hiatt… sort of. Scene from Saturday Afternoon *(1926).*

transfixed by the sheer novelty of another couple's kiss, constitutionally incapable of any interaction with his own spouse beyond handing over his pay envelope. He's savvy enough to have *two* hiding places for his mad money, lest the wife discover one of them, yet so innocent that he can't identify a prostitute on sight; it's likely he has no idea what prostitution *is*. Faced with either running off with his pal to meet the girls or returning to the wife who is angrily summoning him, he's an indecisive child weighing the possible pleasure against the probable punishment…and, like most children, he chooses pleasure.

The film was a major success upon its release in January 1926, even returning late that year for a

Harry Hogan, the sole artistic lad in a family of rough laborers, spends his time learning the bass viol under the tutelage of Professor Von Tempo (Vernon Dent). Unfortunately he's hopeless and, under threat of eviction, Von Tempo gives him a diploma just to get him out of the building. At home, he proclaims himself "a naturalized musician," which gets him tossed out by his father and brothers. Seeing Von Tempo's band of street musicians, he joins them uninvited and turns what had been the throwing of coins into the hurling of blunt objects. This forces the professor to retrieve the diploma and return Harry's money. Undaunted, he makes the acquaintance of a junk peddler (also Vernon Dent, made up as a stereotypical hook-nosed

Jew) who literally witnesses the value of such a "musician." Before long, Harry returns home prosperous and triumphant, all from "just fiddling around."

Fiddlesticks does a fine job of keeping the Elf in perspective, although it's a bit of a letdown after the brilliant *Saturday Afternoon*. Langdon himself was anxious to complete it, so he could begin work on his debut First National feature and get it out ahead of *His First Flame*, which still hadn't been announced for release by Pathé. The company would also hold back *Fiddlesticks* (along with *Soldier Man*) for release during the 1927–28 season. Little did they know that by then Langdon's future as a screen comedian would be in serious jeopardy.

Aspiring musician Harry with Professor Von Tempo (left) and the Junkman (below), both played by Vernon Dent, in Fiddlesticks *(1927), Langdon's final Sennett short.*

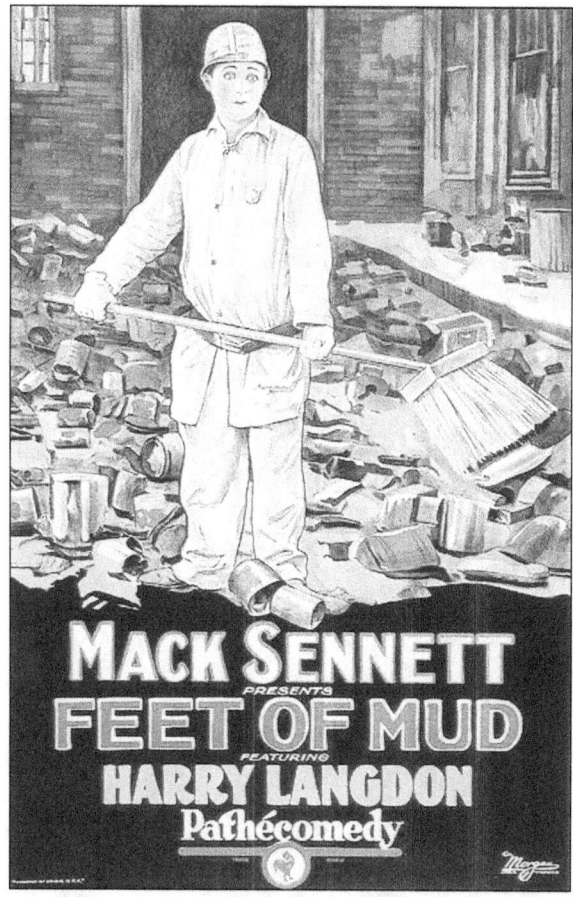

CHAPTER EIGHT

"This Langdon is a Genius"
1925–1926

Negotiations with First National were handled on Langdon's behalf by his business manager, William H. Jenner, and his Iowa-born attorney, Harold Lee "Jerry" Geisler of Woolwine and Geisler, the latter only four years from spearheading the retrial that overturned a statutory rape conviction for Alexander Pantages (creator of the Pantages Circuit). The publicity from that decision led to more high-profile cases, enabling

Motion Picture Magazine *cartoonist Chamberlain wryly comments on Langdon's contract and its effect on former employer Mack Sennett.*

Geisler's ultimate reputation as the "Attorney to the Stars." With $500,000 in working capital, Geisler, Jenner and Langdon chartered the Harry Langdon Corporation.

First National was leasing space at United Studio, 5341 Melrose Avenue in Hollywood, while simultaneously constructing its own plant in neighboring Burbank. Jenner immediately moved into United's administration building, using quarters recently vacated by Rudolph Valentino, but Langdon had no intention of sharing office or dressing room space with anyone but his own team. On September 29, he ordered the construction of a freestanding bungalow on the lot, for which he'd spend $5,000 of his own money. His team consisted of Jenner, his brother Claude, director Harry Edwards, and the writing staff.

According to *The Name Above the Title*, Edwards refused to take the director's job unless Frank Capra went with him. This might well have been true, but was probably unnecessary, as Langdon understood and trusted Capra's contribution to his comedies. Capra also wrote that he refused to leave Sennett without Arthur Ripley, which definitely was not true. Presumably due to Capra's altruistic claim, several historians and writers have assumed Ripley was an uncredited contributor to Langdon's initial production. Almost certainly invited to join the team, Ripley chose to remain at Sennett, where he continued as scenario editor and was even given the chance to co-direct (with Wesley Ruggles) a Ralph Graves comedy, *Hooked at the Altar*.

Another veteran of Langdon's Sennett comedies, Hal Conklin, accompanied Capra to United. Additional gagmen were Gerald C. Duffy, Murray Roth and J. Frank Holliday. Langdon secured Tim Whelan, co-writer of six straight Harold Lloyd features beginning with *Safety Last!*, to take the place of Ripley as story editor. From the perspective of box-office receipts, Lloyd was far and away the most successful of the major film comedians; bringing one of Lloyd's top writers on board was a stunning coup.

This staff, assembled by mid-October, had been shaping the storyline even before Langdon finished up *Fiddlesticks*, but by the comedian's own philosophy, developed during his last several months with Sennett and explained at a press interview in New York City, the real work would come during shooting:

> I write all of my own stories, but I have five gag men who work with me all through a picture. I have the main idea, and they embellish it as we go along. So far as possible the scenario is complete, but 60% of the laughs are built on the set. Comedy, first of all, must be spontaneous. The best laughs develop that way. That is one reason why I accept no original stories, returning all submitted with a form note which reads "Returned unopened and unread, with our cordial thanks." Another reason is that comedy ideas are more readily open to the charge of theft than dramatic ideas.

Casting began in late November. For leading lady, Langdon chose a Warner Bros. contractee, Alice Calhoun. "After two months' search through Hollywood," according to *Moving Picture World*, "Langdon found Miss Calhoun to be ideally suited to the role he had mapped out in his story. In addition to the fair Alice, Langdon secured the services of Edward Davis, Carlton Griffith, and Tom Murray for important parts." Left unmentioned was the not-so-coincidental fact that "the fair Alice" was a close friend to Helen Walton.

Langdon scored another triumph by hiring Elgin Lessley as head cameraman. Lessley began his career in 1911 with the Georges Méliès Star Film Company in Fort Lee, New Jersey. He worked at Triangle-Keystone during the mid-teens, and was hired by Roscoe "Fatty" Arbuckle when the latter went independent in 1917. Three years later, he joined Buster Keaton's company, becoming a key collaborator on all 19 of Keaton's solo two-reelers and first six independent features, especially the technically astonishing *Sherlock Jr.* Lessley joined the Langdon Corporation after wrapping up Keaton's *Go West*, and would prove indispensable, especially given the complex miniature and animated effects required for Langdon's initial production.

Shooting began near the end of the month under the working title of "Mr. Nobody," but by the end of December, for reasons lost to history, Alice Calhoun was replaced by another contract player: M.G.M.'s Joan Crawford. Contrary to legend, it was not Crawford's first big break; the former Lucille LeSueur had just completed an important supporting role in *Sally, Irene and Mary*, starring Karl Dane and Constance Bennett. Just prior to being cast in "Mr. Nobody," the Western Association of Motion Picture Advertisers included Crawford in their annual selection of WAMPAS "Baby Stars," along with Delores Costello, Mary Astor, Janet Gaynor, Fay Wray, Delores Del Rio and former Langdon leading lady Marceline Day.

With a contract in force, an independent company established and production humming along — even the film's release title, *Tramp, Tramp, Tramp*, had been selected — Langdon took care of one final loose end. On January 19, he and Rose officially separated. At least one snide Hollywood columnist spelled it out

Langdon and young Joan Crawford in Tramp, Tramp, Tramp *(1926).*

for the general public: "The Langdons have amicably agreed to disagree this week, and have divided their joint property. Under the peace terms, Mrs. Langdon acquires their Hollywood home and numerous skits and other odd bits they possessed when the Langdons were in vaudeville and thought celluloid was only used for collars. Harry, for his share, gets the air and the gate." He also agreed to a $70,000 property settlement in lieu of alimony, to be paid in installments, and promptly moved to the Hollywood Athletic Club. The fervently Catholic Rose still wanted conclusive proof that Harry had been unfaithful, which would be difficult given the morality clause in Langdon's contract that assured his utmost discretion.

The morality clause was a fairly recent occurrence, the byproduct of several Hollywood scandals involving sex, alcohol and drug addiction, and gunplay. Overall, the general public expected their movie favorites to be above reproach. Moreover, as had been true since the days of Chaplin's early contracts, many were appalled at the vast sums screen comedians were commanding.

Those who weren't appalled were envious. In its "Ask Them" column of January 31, *Film Daily* noted: "Sol Lesser has an interesting article in 'College Comics,' current issue. In part he tells of some of the mail which daily reaches producers. Among the letters received [is] the following:

> See you signed Harry Langdon's million-dollar contract. The kids in this town ask me to make faces for them every time I go down the street. I have been practicing this for years and am ready to go in the movies if you want someone just as good, but cheaper than Langdon.

Cal York of *Photoplay* came to call at the studio and was stunned by how much had changed in so short a time: "In the old days at Sennett's, the Langdon company was the only one which kept musicians on the set at all times — this was the only thing which distinguished him. Today he's surrounded by henchmen. An ex-pugilist sits at the door to the set and refuses any and all comers admission.... I sent in my own

Where's Buster? By May 1926, most critics had placed Langdon ahead of Keaton in the hierarchy of silent comedians.

card…and was told by the ex-pug that Mr. Langdon couldn't see me until after five in his bungalow….

"Harry really has a bungalow with a capital B…. [It] ought to help Harry make better pictures — perhaps better than Harold Lloyd — for Harold has no bungalow — just a nice little suite of dressing rooms in a building where mere mortals also dress. And I'll have to tell Harold about the ex-pugilist guarding the sacred portal…. Not even Doug Fairbanks, who seems quite over-run with scrappers and wrestlers, uses one at the door to his stage.

"When I got over to the bungalow…I found it almost filled with hangers-on. 'My gag men,' explained Harry, with a wave of the hand. 'All of 'em?' 'Sure — all six of 'em,' explained Harry, as we took a seat outside on the running board of a machine…. We had to. There wasn't room in the Bungalow — too many gag men.'

"Then I found Harry Langdon himself really hadn't changed — just his surroundings — and I was glad, for I like Harry and think he is a regular fellow."

Around this time, Langdon and other stars were queried by *Picture Play* magazine about the authors and books they enjoyed most. His response, printed in the February issue: "Perhaps it's strange for a comedian to pick humorists as favorite authors, but I can't claim to like philosophy and that deep stuff. I like the life that we see about us every day, chock-full of humor. I could chuckle over Nina Wilcox Putnam, Octavus Roy Cohen, Will Irwin, and Montague Glass by the hour.

"Sometimes I like my life dressed up a little with adventure. I devour detective stories. I've read Jules Verne's *Twenty Thousand Leagues Under the Sea* many times. As a kid, when I traveled with medicine shows, I always had my eyes glued to an exciting detective tale.

"Dickens, for his quaint characters and his charm of style, and O. Henry for his vitality and ingenuity, are the most highbrow authors I read."

Tramp, Tramp, Tramp opens on the Burton Shoes factory, in which the president and founder, John Burton (Edward Davis), boasts that their billboard advertising campaign, featuring his daughter, Betty (Joan Crawford), has boosted sales to the point where competitors are being crushed.

John Burton (Edward Davis) examines contestant Harry in Tramp, Tramp, Tramp.

One of those competitors is old-time cobbler Amos Logan (Alec B. Francis), who hasn't the money to pay the mortgage on his shop and is given a three-month deadline to do so. His son, Harry, promises to raise the money, although his attention can barely be turned from the Burton Shoes billboard: he's fallen in love with Betty's picture. No sooner has he left his father's shop, he encounters Nick Kargas (Tom

March 10, 1926: Boarding the train to New York for Tramp, Tramp, Tramp's *preview, Langdon takes time for a gag photo.*

Murray), who's not only his father's landlord, but also a world-champion walker, on his way to a cross-country walking contest, coincidentally sponsored by Burton Shoes, for a $25,000 cash prize. Harry becomes his "man Friday," but is so inept at it, Kargas fires him just as they reach town.

Betty, there to send off the contestants, witnesses Kargas's cruelty and encourages Harry to enter the race himself. Gradually he realizes he could win both the mortgage money and the heart of his true love, and enters the race.

That's the set-up, and the film follows Harry right to the finish line, gag by gag. Although there are periodic cutaways to Amos viewing his son's progress via the weekly newsreel, no emphasis is given to the irony that Burton's contest can provide the salvation for the old man's business. In fact, Burton is just a stick figure; he pretty much disappears as Betty takes center stage as Harry's ultimate goal. In the end, the two are married and living near his father, not hers. Some bits from previous films are reprised: the chicken-stealing routine from *Remember When?*, hurtling bricks at an enemy — in this case, a cyclone — from *Plain Clothes*, and Harry portraying his own baby from the still-unreleased *His First Flame*.

One choice moment reportedly required several takes. After Harry is dismissed by Kargas, he sits on a bench and stares dreamily at his billboard girl, not realizing that the flesh-and-blood version is approaching from behind to bring him shoes, sweatshirt and an entry form for the race. Once he spots her, his reactions range from surprise, to delight, to indecision, to fear, to recurring combinations of all four. After several attempts to take the scene with the two side by side, it was ultimately staged with Joan Crawford's back to the camera, because she couldn't keep from laughing at Langdon's antics. Capra related the tale in his book, while Langdon recalled it in a 1929 interview: "Joan is a wonderful girl, and she's never caused me any trouble. In fact, the only mischief she ever does is when I'm acting. Then she stands around and laughs so hard that the whole work is broken up and we have to take the scene over."

Production wrapped near the end of February, and on March 10, Langdon left Los Angeles by train to preview the picture in Rye, New York. Accompanying him were Jenner, Whelan and Capra, the latter for his editing experience, in case the preview determined that trimming was required. He and Whelan were also working with Langdon on the next feature, for the moment titled "The Yes Man," and at one point wired some set design sketches to the art director, Lloyd Brierly, in Hollywood.

Harry Edwards did not make the trip, and may have been released by this point.

There are two conflicting reasons why Edwards departed. In the absence of any statements by the man himself, both must be evaluated, as each contains elements of truth. According to a 1932 *Photoplay* article written by Katherine Albert, "Langdon's director had taken too much time on [*Tramp, Tramp, Tramp*] and run him into the red," and for that reason was dismissed. The negative cost had indeed gone over First

National's $250,000 budget by $50,037. Contrary to the article, though, that money didn't come directly out of Langdon's pocket. First National bore the extra cost and charged it to the film; Langdon wouldn't feel the pinch until it came time to collect profit percentages.

However, it's uncertain whether Edwards was to blame. Of necessity there had been reshooting after Alice Calhoun was replaced. Some of the sets were complicated, particularly a barbershop in which Harry takes refuge during the cyclone that is seen to sway from one extreme to another. The cyclone itself required special effects involving miniatures and animation that didn't come cheap. Lastly, Edwards completed the film within the 12 weeks allotted for shooting, making the claim that he'd "taken too much time" a dubious one.

The second reason, which originated with Capra, was that Edwards, "having guided Langdon from a frightened little actor to a star... couldn't take Langdon's present approval or disapproval of his every move," and actually resigned. In one sense, Capra's assessment was accurate: more than anyone, Edwards could lay claim to having made Harry Langdon a success in motion pictures. At Sennett's he'd been at the helm for all but the first seven, slowing down the studio's usual frenetic pace and, whenever possible, encouraging Langdon to bring his character into focus in his own way. On the other hand, how could Edwards not have expected to receive marching orders from Langdon? He was now more than just a star, he was Edwards's employer.

Capra also opined that Edwards "had qualms about accepting the more formidable feature film responsibilities," and based on Edwards's own actions upon completing *Tramp, Tramp, Tramp*, this might be the most likely explanation. On May 30, *Film Daily* announced that he'd signed with Universal to helm a new series of two-reelers entitled The Collegians. Edwards would primarily direct shorts for the remainder of his career, and in that capacity would again work with Langdon several years later.

The budget overage was a serious matter. On March 9, Richard A. Rowland, first vice president and general manager of First National who would be attending the preview, was instructed to "negotiate with the Harry Langdon Corporation and Harry Langdon to see whether, in view of the fact that the negative cost of the first Harry Langdon picture had greatly exceeded the maximum provided for in the contract, he could not persuade the producer to permit this corporation to take over the business supervision of the succeeding pictures so as to control expenditure." Mr. Rowland was unsuccessful in so persuading Mr. Langdon.

First National's next strategy was to persuade theatres to book the film and the public to see it. "Mac" Oracle of the *Exhibitor's Daily Review* attended the screening in Rye, apparently at Rowland's invitation,

and flipped: "For months picture fans throughout the country have been demanding a Harry Langdon feature picture. It's now here. This picture without question will establish him as one of the foremost comedians of the screen. *Tramp, Tramp, Tramp* is an achievement and it's going to "click" at the box office wherever it is played. Start working all the influence you've got with First National to get this picture on your screen as soon as possible, tell everybody in your town you've got it and it will be TRAMP, TRAMP, TRAMP of thousands of feet to your box office."

Other publications jumped on the same bandwagon. *Motion Picture News:* "Looks like an attraction surely destined to get the money at the box office." *Photoplay:* "Langdon has graduated and this picture is his diploma. *Tramp, Tramp, Tramp* will introduce him to a wider public, and the public which followed his two-reel career will be doubled or trebled." *Film Daily*: "Looks like sure-fire bet." *Variety*: "*Tramp, Tramp, Tramp* will be great for First National, ditto for the exhibitors." *Moving Picture World:* "It looks like good box-office stuff for any type of house, for it contains in generous measure the universal appeal of laughter." With such praise to guide them, First National confidently poured over $38,500 into advertising *Tramp, Tramp, Tramp*; the most they would spend on any of Langdon's features.

After the preview, Langdon spent several days in New York City meeting the press. From this, reporters subsequently printed blurbs about him and his forthcoming picture, while a First National publicist wrote up a press release for national consumption. The quotes within conclusively put the lie to *The Name Above the Title*, wherein Capra repeatedly asserted that Langdon never understood his character, "the Little Elf whose only ally is God." With Capra seated in the room one afternoon in mid-March 1926, Langdon was asked his thoughts on "the psychology of laughter." The various releases quoted him as follows:

> In the first place, the laugh is the reflection of one's own frailties — of everyone's weakness. We think we are laughing at the character on the screen, but in reality we are laughing at ourselves. All children at heart, we know subconsciously that when we laugh at the poor boob, who is the victim of circumstances, we might well be that same poor boob ourselves. Of course, we have grown up.
>
> Suppose you were to go into a bank and interview the bank president. You find him to be most austere and dignified. He apparently is a cold individual with little of heart and no sense of humor. Yet on Sunday you run over to Coney Island and find him throwing baseballs at the dolls, riding the roller coaster, eating hot dogs and generally having the time of his life. He's nothing but a big kid. And as a matter of fact we're all nothing but big kids. I've capitalized that side of my nature, though many of us would hate to admit that we have such a nature.
>
> To be successful at winning laughs one must first of all be sincere. I can't fool my audience and say, "I am funny and I'm going to make you laugh at me." When I do a part in a film I must really suffer. I must be wretched, and consequently ludicrous, but all the time I must play it real. Above all things, I must be a supreme though naïve optimist, suffering dumbly any harsh fate that may come my way. My optimism must be so all embracing, though pitiful, that nothing can ever rock it.
>
> In my pictures, I allow myself to be a victim of fate. But a sort of Divine providence always carries me through.

TRAMP, TRAMP, TRAMP—First National

THIS picture takes Harry Langdon's doleful face and pathetic figure out of the two-reel class and into the Chaplin and Lloyd screen dimensions. Not that he equals their standing yet, but he is a worthy addition to a group of comedy makers of which we have entirely too few. Langdon has graduated and this picture is his diploma. "Tramp, Tramp, Tramp" will introduce him to a wider public, and the public which followed his two-reel career will be doubled or trebled. The boy's good.

Harry plays a kid hobo, who enters himself in a transcontinental hiking contest. He's just got to win the race to win the gal, who is his inspiration, and Harry believes that all's fair in love and war, and he's in both. He isn't exactly on the level in the race, but you should worry about his sporting morals.

Review in Photoplay *magazine.*

First National released *Tramp, Tramp, Tramp* on March 21. In contrast to the trade reviewers, most newspaper critics were underwhelmed, although they blamed the story and gags, rather than Langdon's performance. The majority of New York reviewers pointed out that Harry's mishaps in the barbershop during the cyclone, and a scene where he's dangling from a fence over a precipice were strongly reminiscent of the windstorm in the cabin from Chaplin's *The Gold Rush*, released just a few months earlier. A scene where an electric fan sends the feathers in Harry's bed flying around his hotel room also reminded a few of *The Gold Rush* and Chaplin's willful destruction of a feather pillow. Mordaunt Hall of the *New York Times* summed it up for most of his peers: "Hitherto Mr.

Langdon's short comedies have had the spice of originality, but this effort will be really funnier to those few who may not have seen *The Gold Rush*."

If the reviews were tepid, exhibitor reaction was downright hostile. Most were unfamiliar with Langdon, since Pathé comedies rarely played in First National theaters, and had been swayed by the enthusiastic trade press. When the film failed to draw the expected crowds, they felt taken in. A sampling of comments submitted to *Moving Picture World* and *Exhibitor's Herald*: "Did not please here. Do not pay anything extra for this one." "[I] let the reviewers influence me against my judgment and shot this as a two-day special to a grand and glorious flop. He will run one day only in my theatres." "We've heard nothing but grief since showing this picture…. [It] is three degrees worse than terrible." "Did not make expenses on this one. They would not come and I don't blame them a bit." "My people were disappointed in this one. May not book second Langdon." "I bought this contrary to my better judgment, based on reports in the Herald. It is funny in spots, but…too slow and draggy…. Standing around and looking foolish isn't comedy."

Contrary to previous histories, the film's box-office performance was disappointing. All told, *Tramp, Tramp, Tramp* cost $407,235 and netted $339,482 combined domestic and foreign. In July 1927, with Langdon's consent, First National booked the $50,037 negative cost overage against the negative cost of what would be *Heart Trouble* (which didn't help, as Langdon would overspend on that film as well). A negative cost underage and profits from the second film were also applied, and by the end of March 1928, the ledger on *Tramp, Tramp, Tramp* was closed at the break-even point.

In April 1926, one month after *Tramp, Tramp, Tramp*'s release, word leaked out about First National's attempt to wrest financial control from Langdon, and rumors circulated that he was looking to break his contract. On April 21, *Film Daily* stated, "Harry Langdon denies any split with First National as reported and says his relations are most cordial."

The executive with whom Langdon was most cordial, John McCormick, asked him to make a cameo appearance in Colleen Moore's latest production, *Ella Cinders*. Langdon agreed, provided Frank Capra could direct his scene. Capra was champing at the bit to direct "The Yes Man," but before officially giving him

First National's campaign book publicizes Langdon's second film ahead of its change to The Strong Man *(1926).*

the nod, Langdon probably wanted to see his work, on both the set and the screen. It was a sort of dry run test for Capra, and Langdon wouldn't have to pay for it.

Capra got the nod but, realizing "The Yes Man" needed to be a big hit, Langdon sought out another key collaborator from the past, personally requesting that he join the team, go over the story and make whatever changes he deemed necessary. This time, Arthur Ripley said yes.

Ripley came on board around the time casting began. His precise contributions are shrouded in mystery, but he revised enough to earn the "Scenario by" credit. It was almost certainly Ripley's idea to make Langdon's love interest a blind girl, an idea that was objected to by several staffers, Capra apparently among them. Plus, during the course of filming, greater emphasis was placed on Harry's relationship with the muscular vaudevillian who employed him, prompting a change in title, from "The Yes Man" to *The Strong Man*.

Filming again took place at United Studios, even though it had just been sold to the Famous Players-Lasky Corporation, the company that released under the Paramount banner. First National, however, was still a few weeks away from opening its brand new plant in Burbank, so *The Strong Man* was the final independent production made at United before it became the nucleus of Paramount Pictures, which it remains to this day.

Priscilla Bonner was chosen as leading lady in late June. In an interview with author Edward Watz, she recalled, "I had appeared in a picture called *The Red Kimono* for Mrs. Wallace Reid. It was one of those films with a moral lesson for young people, informing them about the evils of narcotics. Someone at Harry Langdon's studio had seen me in it, and thought I might make a good leading lady for him.

"I went down to the studio and was shown into an office where I met Harry Langdon, Frank Capra and Arthur Ripley. They were all very cordial and complimented me on my performance in *The Red Kimono*. After a few minutes of small talk, Mr. Langdon said, 'Well, fellows, I think we've found our leading lady.' It wasn't much of an interview, but afterwards, Mr. Capra told me that Harry wanted me for the part because I didn't look like a hard-nosed flapper. I suppose he felt I could portray a fragile type of girl, which was what the role was supposed to be."

There were no distractions during shooting. Everyone was determined to make *The Strong Man* a great picture. Capra, by his own admission, was entirely focused on the job at hand: hashing and rehashing the storyline, prodding the writers for more and better gags. Along with Ripley, Whelan and Conklin, the writing staff now included former Sennett man Clarence Hennecke, Capra's mentor Bob Eddy and Harry's brother Tulley (billed as James Langdon).

The star, too, was immersed in his picture, keeping it always in the forefront and holding daily staff meetings to discuss its progress. Bonner recalled, "Mr. Langdon was always talking to his team about how he wanted to perform a scene. He would demonstrate so many different ways he could handle a funny bit of business, and he relied on Capra and Ripley to give their opinion on which worked best for the film. I got the impression that Langdon always knew instinctively what to do but didn't trust his own judgment completely. He trusted Capra and Ripley, and they guided him through these decisions."

Yet when cast or crew would socialize during lunch or between set-ups, he'd drift away. Co-star Gertrude Astor later commented, "He would wander a block away and sit alone on a bench until Frank Capra needed him for a scene. It was a contrast: Capra, so young and so serious, and Harry looking at you, blinking those pale blue eyes, and then glancing over his shoulder to make sure you weren't following him into his private world of silence." During one of these reveries, she approached him, asking, "Why do you sit over here alone?" Langdon replied, "Oh, I like it. I don't like people. I like to be alone and think."

An accident occurred during one of the film's final scenes. In an article published the following year by *Theatre* magazine, Langdon wrote:

> During the filming of "*The Strong Man,*" a trick cannon exploded as I pulled the lanyard to fire the final shot of the scene. In the noise, the smoke and confusion, I didn't even know there had been an accident. When the smoke cleared away, we found that one piece of the metal cannon had grazed the back of my head, struck a musician a glancing blow in the cheek and buried itself in the wall of the stage.

At the end of July, as shooting neared completion, Whelan resigned to take a staff position at Metro-Goldwyn-Mayer. Bill Jenner immediately signed Ripley to a long-term deal as head of Langdon's scenario department. Ripley was also to supervise editing, which must have taken Capra by surprise, since he fully expected to edit his film without oversight. In August, Jenner hired Reed Heustis, a Keystone veteran, to write the titles.

The final negative cost came in at $240,632, or $9,368 under budget. That had to please Langdon, even though First National eventually took the surplus and applied it to *Tramp, Tramp, Tramp*. He may also have griped that the company spent only $12,853 on advertising, roughly a third as much as for the first film, but all in all, business matters looked to be in solid shape.

On the personal life front, Rose had filed for separate maintenance at the end of June. About the time filming wrapped, Harry learned that Tom O'Brien had taken a job in San Francisco and resumed calling on Mrs. O'Brien, always bearing gifts. In return, Helen invited him to spend the night whenever he wished. For the sake of decorum, and because Helen's mother, Laura Walton, was also present, Langdon would occupy the master bedroom while Helen slept on the couch and her mother slept with Virginia.

Helen would later claim that she had separated from her husband once again at this time, but her own mother disputed that point. "Money went to Helen's head," Mrs. Walton testified in 1930. "Langdon gave her $1,000 at a time. She was carried away with the money and presents he gave her. [I told him] Tom O'Brien would not stand for that conduct when he returned." Harry's reaction was to lease a home on Hollymont Drive, at the foot of the Hollywood Hills, where Helen would be welcome to spend the night without her mother.

O'Brien did return in September, when the job ended up North, and confronted the couple on Vista Del Mar, the cross street nearest Langdon's home. "In view of this scandal," O'Brien reportedly told his rival, "I should think you'd use common sense." Helen evidently took exception to her husband's insinuation and the O'Briens once again parted with rancor.

In *The Strong Man*, Harry portrays Paul Bergot, a Belgian soldier during the Great War, who has been communicating with an American girl, Mary Brown

Immigrants Paul Bergot (Harry Langdon) and Zandow the Great (Arthur Thalasso) at Ellis Island in The Strong Man *(1926).*

(Priscilla Bonner), via letters transmitted by the Red Cross. Mary professes her love in the most recent letter, but while reading it, Paul is captured by a burly German soldier (Arthur Thalasso). After the armistice, the soldier becomes Zandow the Great, a performing "strong man" who lifts weights and shoots himself from a cannon onto a trapeze. Paul is his lackey. The two come to America, Zandow to enter vaudeville and Paul

Poor Harry Langdon! He has a nice, noisy gun and yards and yards of bullets, but the German soldiers in a nearby trench have just dropped off to sleep and he doesn't like to disturb them. Harry plays a dough-faced doughboy in his new comedy, "The Strong Man"

to find Mary, a task that causes him no end of trouble. As fate would have it, Zandow is booked in Cloverdale, a small town that has become a haven for crime and loose morals. Only the dedicated congregation of Pastor Josiah Brown — who is referred to derogatorily as "Holy Joe" — believe that God will smite the evil represented by the vulgar Palace Hall, as He did at the Wall of Jericho. Mary Brown is the pastor's blind daughter.

As with *Tramp, Tramp, Tramp*'s foot race, the search for Mary Brown in this film provides for a series of comedy routines that don't necessarily advance the plot. At one point, Paul is exhausted from peering hopefully into the faces of pedestrians on a New York City street corner, and rests for a brief spell. At that moment, Lil (Gertrude Astor), a gangster's moll, tucks a wad of bills into his coat pocket just before a detective searches her. Once the threat of the law is gone, she tries to retrieve the bills, but they've slipped through a hole in the pocket to rest within the seam of one of the coat's tails.

Desperate, Lil announces to Paul that she is his "Little Mary" and they go off together. But soon he doubts her claim, since she smokes cigarettes and brazenly invites him into her hotel. When he refuses and tries to leave, she pretends to faint…and now Paul must carry her inside to safety. Her room is at the top of a long flight of stairs; after two futile attempts, he decides the only way to get her there is to rest her on his lap and "climb" upstairs on his backside, one riser at a time. Unfortunately, there's a stepladder at the top, which he assumes is part of the staircase. Reaching the top of that, they both tumble over.

Once inside the room, things get steadily worse, as the revived "Mary" locks the door and attacks him bodily, seeking the money. Paul, naturally, believes her interest is much more carnal and he repels her as best he can, but finally submits himself when she pulls a knife. Lil embraces him, uses the blade to slice open his coat, and retrieves the wad. The deed done, she collapses on the bed, making sure to hand Paul the door key. "Don't let this leak out," he implores her. The scene was one of the comedic high spots of the film.

A second comic sequence, one noted by nearly all the critics, takes place on the bus to Cloverdale. Paul is suffering from a chest cold and is annoying all the passengers with his sneezing and coughing. One man in particular, seated right next to Paul, is particularly irritated, especially since Paul keeps sneezing in his direction. When it's time to take his cough medicine (apparently a nasty-tasting concoction), he struggles to bring it to his mouth only to sneeze at the last second, spraying the unpleasant gentleman. Helpfully trying to wipe the man off with his handkerchief, the fellow strenuously objects, as well he might. While on the receiving end of the man's tongue-lashing, Paul manages to down his medicine.

After a couple more hysterical vignettes, Paul rubs his chest with camphor, but soon he's inadvertently applying his boss's Limburger. This sets the other passengers even more on edge, and finally the grouch grabs him and throws him off the bus just as it's about to negotiate a hairpin curve. Through the courtesy of the "Divine providence" that surrounds the Elf, he rolls down the hill and crashes through the roof of the very same bus, much to everyone's surprise, landing directly into his seat. It's as if he'd never left.

At seven reels, *The Strong Man* is the longest of Langdon's features, but that's due mostly to the footage spent on the Cloverdale subplot. In *Tramp, Tramp, Tramp*, the comedy scenes were broken up only briefly with such moments as Harry's dad watching him in the newsreels (even some of these led directly into more comedy). With *The Strong Man*, the plight of

Cloverdale is depicted in full, with scenes of families broken over boozing and carousing members, and with Pastor Jones refusing to be bought off his campaign to reclaim the town by God's grace. In the end, it's Paul — fearful that the Palace patrons wish to corrupt his Mary — who, as a latter-day Joshua, "blows down the walls" of the den of sin by employing his boss's trick cannon.

There is, of course, a parallel in *The Strong Man* with the recurring theme in much of Capra's mature work: the triumph of the individual little man over the evil of bigger men and the indifference of the masses. For that reason, and because Paul Bergot is unquestionably the Elf as characterized in *The Name Above the Title*, it's easy to ascribe the film wholly to the director. Yet it's less likely the comedian placed himself completely in Capra's hands as it is that the two were simply operating on the same wavelength, along with Ripley, Whelan and the other writers.

"When we'd be actually filming a scene," said Bonner, "it was Capra in the director's chair who was in charge of everything in front of the camera. He'd confer with Langdon, Ripley and the other gagmen, but I don't recall Langdon ever contradicting him. It was all harmonious." Simply speaking, *The Strong Man* is Langdon and his creative team at their peak.

The film previewed in Los Angeles and to help ensure his box office wouldn't suffer at the hands of newspaper critics, Langdon invited a brace of them to one of the screenings. Tom Waller of *Moving Picture World* reported on the result:

> Clocked for laughs, Harry Langdon's new feature length comedy for First National, "The Strong Man," looks like one of the strongest winners that the saucer-eyed comic has ever had, according to Jed Buell, manager of the Deluxe Theatre, Los Angeles, where the final preview was held the other day, and William H. Jenner, head of the Harry Langdon outfit.
>
> Buell clocked 293 laughs emitted, expelled or otherwise projected by his amused patrons, while Jenner, at another performance, tabulated 225. The difference in the number of risibilities registered is explained by Mr. Jenner as due to

Paul will have to carry Lil (Gertrude Astor) up the stairs in The Strong Man.

his inability to determine exactly where one laugh left off and another began.

The average of 259 laughs for "The Strong Man" makes it a top-notcher, even bettering Harry's laugh-record in "Tramp, Tramp, Tramp." The preview audience at the Deluxe was not the sort generally given to indiscriminate chortling, consisting of hard-boiled newspaper critics. Buell states, nevertheless, that his "patrons laughed till they cried."

"The Strong Man" is now undergoing final revisions and will arrive in New York within a few days, with a trade showing to follow soon thereafter.

The trades responded with even more enthusiasm than before:

Watch out, Charlie and Harold! [*The Strong Man* is] a grand and glorious laugh from the start to the finish.

Photoplay

A whale of a comedy production that is bound to be a cleanup everywhere.

Variety

You won't have seats enough in your theater to accommodate the crowd so you'll have to show *The Strong Man* for at least several days.

Film Daily

Hail an artist! Hail the funniest long feature comedy ever made! Hail Harry Langdon! *The Strong Man* is worth at least a dozen *Tramp, Tramp, Tramp*s. It is worth a dozen miscellaneous Chaplin comedies, plus all the two-reelers Langdon ever made. It is the best long feature comedy ever manufactured.

Exhibitor's Herald

This time newspaper reviews from East to West were equally enthusiastic. There were some gripes that the story was at times inconsistent, but in almost every case, critics agreed that Langdon's performance more than compensated for any shortcomings. At year's end several critics would include *The Strong Man* in their Top Ten lists.

Dictionaries are incomplete. They won't be complete until Langdon leads the list of synonyms for laughter.... If there is any fault to be found with *The Strong Man*, somebody else will have to find it. While watching the picture I couldn't see its faults for laughing.

Roscoe McGowen, *New York Daily News*

Review in Photoplay *magazine.*

One carries away from *The Strong Man* a distinct notion that this comic person, Langdon, may succeed in topping them all before very long if events continue this auspiciously.

Wilella Waldorf, *New York Post*

As a pantomime artist Harry Langdon has no equal in screen ranks. Pathos is his meat, and pathetic he is throughout every reel of this loosely woven picture.

Grace Cutler, *Brooklyn Daily Eagle*

That curious minority that has so sturdily declined to recognize the distinguished comic gifts of Mr. Harry Langdon must certainly have been won over by *The Strong Man*. After his marvelous performance in this new screen comedy it is difficult to see how any one can fail to note that Langdon is one of the world's major clowns — standing at the moment but a few short steps behind the great Chaplin himself.

Richard Watts, Jr., *New York Herald Tribune*

If you want to spend a dismal weekend, keep away from Loew's State! For if you see Harry Langdon in *The Strong Man* you will certainly laugh for the next three days.... We confess to ignorance anent the past accomplishments of Frank Capra, who directed *The Strong Man*, but his handling of this picture marks him as a director of amazing scope.

Los Angeles Record

We visited the T. & D. yesterday to view *The Strong Man*, and found the first film of the year to send us into complete convulsions. In this film, Langdon justifies all the claims that were made for him and more.

Wood Soanes, *Oakland Tribune*

In *The Strong Man*, Langdon takes his place beside Lloyd or possibly a jot or three in front of him as a laugh producer. The big four among screen clowns are Chaplin, Langdon, Lloyd and Keaton, somewhat in that order. Lloyd has been funny more often than Langdon, but in the quality that robs laughter of its ruthlessness and brings it close to tears he has never quite equaled Langdon in *The Strong Man*.

William Morris Houghton, *Judge*

The review that most impressed First National publicists was that of Frances Comstock, who wrote, "Harry Langdon deserves the crown of clowns, be it a battered brown derby or his own inimitable felt hat. For the first time in the history of the movies, Chaplin has a real rival in creating comedy that is artistic as well as funny. This Langdon is a genius. Certainly Langdon has discovered that secret of great comedy, humor mixed with pathos."

With few exceptions the exhibitor reaction was a complete reversal from that of *Tramp, Tramp, Tramp*. A sampling of comments:

> One cannot help from laughing at this offering. A good comedy with plenty of gags to fill seven reels without padding.

To First National. Anthony lightly tossed away an empire and Cleopatra must have had plenty of "IT" to win the toss, hence we suggest Harry Langdon and Colleen Moore for the rôles, just to be different

First National's two biggest stars, as depicted in the November 1926 issue of Motion Picture Classic.

> Harry Langdon, you are great, you are an artist in pantomime, and your material is brand new and novel.... I did a nice business on your picture and they are still talking about it. It was a scream.

> If there were any more laughs in this one it would take a "strong man" to live through it. We had to shut the picture off three times so the audience could recover. Had to do it so they would not break down the seats.

If comedy is "it" this one has "it." The best comedy I have played in months.... Watched it run through four times and enjoyed it as much the last time as I did the first.

The film's success brought about an increase in fan mail, which in turn led to the creation of a national Harry Langdon Fan Club. The club's president was Doris Rondeau, a young woman in the Los Angeles area who impressed Langdon's publicity director, Don Eddy, with her enthusiasm. The Langdon Corporation officially recognized Rondeau's club and Eddy agreed to provide promotional material as membership grew. Autographed photos were distributed as prizes to those who actively recruited a certain number of new members. Usually included was a personal letter from Langdon, such as: "Miss Doris Rondeau has just notified me that you have qualified for a club membership prize and I hasten to send you a large autographed photograph…There is nothing that I can say except to thank you sincerely for your interest in the Club and in my efforts to entertain you." At its peak, the Club would boast about 200 members.

The Strong Man eventually turned a modest profit of $43,778, although it took nearly a year-and-a-half to do so. All of it would be allocated to less profitable films under the contract, negating any participation on Langdon's part for what would be his most successful independent production. For now, though, the trend was moving in the right direction and everyone expected his next picture to do even better.

France, among other European countries, took notice of Langdon's appeal.

Still, the comedian thought long and hard about the next picture. He already had the basic idea for a while, and believed the right team was in place to carry it out, but he wanted to ensure the story that emerged was cohesive. Isolated gag sequences, such as the chest cold scene, no longer interested him. Such sequences should help propel the story, he believed. He also felt there was room for his character to grow; to move beyond "the supreme optimist" of the Elf and become an individual with recognizable — and perhaps unreachable — hopes and dreams.

For inspiration, he turned to a recent best seller, a dramatic novel about a pathetic, misguided young man who commits a murder. The book so excited him it fueled the next film's scenario, which in turn created a conflagration that, in due course, left the Harry Langdon Corporation in cinders.

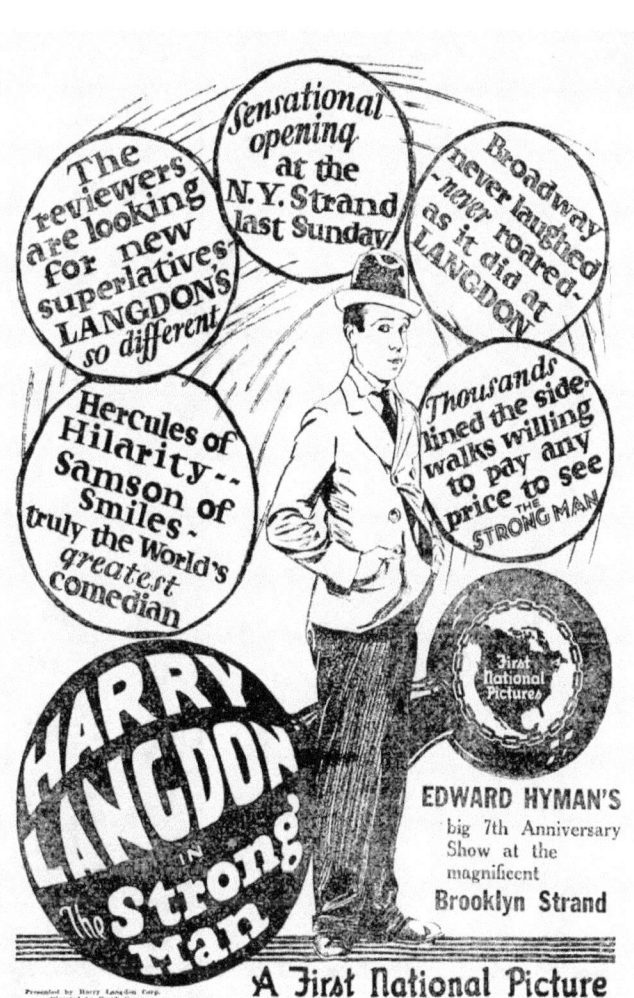

CHAPTER NINE

"The Saddest Stories Ever Told"

1926–1927

"Pathos! I want to do more pathos!"

This was the demand of comedian Harry Langdon, newly benighted by the cognoscenti as Chaplin's only rival, to his director, Frank Capra.

"Harry, the pathos is in your *comedy*," Capra countered. "If you deliberately *try* for pathos, it'd be silly, believe me."

"I believe the New York writers! Do you know more'n *they* do?"

So went the battle of *Long Pants*, Langdon's third independent feature, as described in *The Name Above the Title*. As it happens, we needn't rely on Capra's often-dubious memoir to ascertain Langdon's thoughts on this matter. He was quite straightforward in interviews made both during and after production:

> Humor finds its beginnings in pathos. This is the psychological fact upon which every real comedian builds his laughs. Underlying the necessity for pathos in laughter is the theory of the position of the audience — a theory I have dwelt on for years as a basis of creating chuckles.
>
> In serious plays, the hero is always the man in the audience. In comedy he is somebody else. That is why it doesn't hurt a moviegoer to laugh at the mishaps of a comedian, and that is why he weeps with the hero in misfortune. Comedies are becoming more tragic for that reason. Analyze Chaplin's "The Gold Rush" — brim full of misfortune and unhappiness for the leading character. Had John Gilbert or Ronald Colman essayed that role the picture might well have been another "American Tragedy."
>
> Another element of the present-day comedy which the future will see eradicated is the "gag." Comedies will not always rely on funny bits of business for laughs. Pantomime, story and situation will be the laugh-makers — not artificial bits of material constructed for the occasion. In five years I think the comedy which is just a string of irrelevant "gags" will be unknown. Comedies will be based on stories — good stories — and the greatest comedies of the future will be the saddest stories ever told.

This was a new Langdon: an articulate, informed creator of comedy with firm opinions and objectives, for which *Long Pants* would be the initial test.

Long Pants was conceived as "Johnny Newcomer" before *Tramp, Tramp, Tramp* had been completed. Langdon's original if somewhat vague idea was to portray "the joys and sorrows of naive adolescence," according to *Los Angeles Times* columnist Herbert Moulton. *Variety* reported the film "will be a story of mother love, eliminating the use of a leading woman, the first time this has been done in feature length comedies." Langdon was so certain of this approach that he loaned Priscilla Bonner to Famous Players-Lasky for *It*, which would be Clara Bow's breakthrough film.

Then Langdon read Theodore Dreiser's *An American Tragedy* and was immediately struck by its story of an ambitious yet misguided young man, drawn toward a wealthy woman of status, who murders the lowly female co-worker with whom he'd been intimate and who was pregnant with his child. He and Ripley conceived a similar situation for Harry's adolescent, who finally receives his first pair of long pants. Now dressed like the man he's imagined himself to be, he's attracted to an alluring city woman (who turns out to be a criminal), even though he's engaged to the small-town girl he's known all his life. Intent on pursuing his romantic ideal, he decides his only recourse is to shoot his bride-to-be on their wedding day. Leaving Ripley, Capra and his staff to work on the story's new direction, and with Bonner at work on the film version of Madame Elinor Glyn's novel *It*, Langdon took a few weeks off to play golf, enjoy Helen's company and rest up for production.

Capra and Ripley, though, were unable to see eye to eye. In Capra's opinion, "It was not in character for him that he wanted to kill in the first place. He might want to kill a fly, but not a human being." Since his boss was determined to play the scene, Capra imagined a lengthy prologue of Harry as a young boy, coddled and mothered and over-protected, designed to establish some semblance of audience sympathy that would carry him through the picture's darker aspects. Ripley thought it was all unnecessary fodder that delayed Langdon's entrance and slowed up the comedy.

When Langdon returned, Ripley and Capra brought their impasse before him. He tended to side with Ripley, but agreed to shoot the prologue and let preview audiences decide the matter. He also had another idea: a dream sequence in which Harry imagines himself a handsome, dashing prince who rescues the fair princess, to be portrayed by the same actress as the city woman. Once his dream is contrasted by the cold, hard reality of the woman, this, too, could create sympathy for Harry. He figured the sequence would last about a reel, and he wanted to shoot it in Technicolor.

Production began in October. Alma Bennett was cast as the beautiful city woman of Harry's dreams, and Betty Baker as another local girl who was to figure prominently in Harry's romantic pursuits; as the film now stands, she only appears briefly near the beginning.

When Priscilla Bonner returned, she could see that Langdon's relationship with Capra had changed since *The Strong Man*. From her perspective, the two were locked in a power struggle instigated by Ripley. "Capra and Ripley were no longer conferring together with Mr. Langdon," she told Edward Watz. "It was Langdon and Ripley going off on their own to discuss some bit of business. I got the impression that Ripley was cutting Harry off from [Capra]."

By that time, reviews for *The Strong Man* were out, and Capra had received his share of the plaudits ("this picture marks him as a director of amazing scope"). These only strengthened his desire to maintain control over *Long Pants*, not to mention his conviction that *he* was right and *they* were wrong. Said Bonner, "After a couple hours of working like this, Capra would hurry over to Langdon, and they'd speak quietly before going someplace away from the crew to discuss something. I was never privy to those discussions, but you didn't have to be a genius to figure out they were having disagreements. And Ripley seemed to materialize from nowhere [and] would quickly follow them off the set.

"Capra seemed unnerved by what was going on around him. He wasn't in control any longer and you could feel the tension." Yet he wouldn't openly challenge his employer-star. "There was never any flare up on the set," Bonner told Capra's biographer, Joseph McBride. "And it seemed to me that [Langdon and Ripley] gave him plenty of motivation." Capra kept his temper in check, but inside he was seething, developing an ulcer in the process.

Making matters worse, Helen began spending time on the set, and everyone got an unadorned view of the mistress that had been Langdon's obsession over the previous two years. Bonner had her pegged from the start, telling McBride: "She was a very grasping woman. She wanted his money. I sensed it, and I thought, 'Mr. Langdon is too good for this woman.' She was spending money like water and also she was feeding his ego. But he was completely overwhelmed with her charms." Cameraman Glenn Kershner summed it up for McBride: "We were a happy family on *The Strong Man*. We were going along fine until some woman spoiled the whole thing."

"She would come down on the set," Bonner told Watz, "and sit in Langdon's chair, or Capra's chair, and make herself at home there whenever we were beginning to shoot a scene. And she'd call out in this

Harry's just not interested in Priscilla Bonner in Long Pants *(1927).*

loud, sickly sweet voice, 'Oh, Harry! Harry, dear!' It would drive anyone up the wall!

"With *The Strong Man* being a big success, Harry had acquired this great confidence in himself and his own judgment, [and] I believe Arthur Ripley and Helen were behind this change in him. *Long Pants* was a very difficult picture to make and contained so many contentious memories that I didn't ever want to see it." (In fact, it would be 50 years before Bonner could bring herself to watch the film.)

While Capra felt that Ripley "was just a guy who wanted my job," the evidence suggests the director's chair was not his goal. *The Strong Man* had made big-time critics sit up and take notice of Harry's penchant for pathos, for which Ripley believed his story revisions, not Capra's direction, were responsible. His ultimate aim was to persuade Langdon to make the full transition to independence as writer and director. Langdon would become the movies' new comedy king, with Ripley installed as his sole trusted collaborator. Helen could see the advantages, too: fewer people on staff meant more money for Harry.

Between the lavishness of the production, and the constant distractions and discord, costs for *Long Pants* were mounting. Then, as if Langdon didn't have enough worries, Thomas O'Brien decided to turn up the pressure on his wife, reaching out to her with a new approach: abject humility and regret. Having obtained additional work in San Francisco, on October 23 he sent her the following letter:

Dear Helen,
  I am trying to accent things as they are — these thoughts come to bolster up courage for my final exit — you said that nothing is so dead as dead love.
  As a goodbye wish, I only hope you will attain the goal for which you are striving and that success may be yours in your chosen field.

Please forgive and forget the unjust things I have said and done.

On November 1, he wrote a follow-up:

My Dear Helen,
  I would give my life to undo the unhappiness and suffering I have caused you…You must believe me when I say that I did not realize until the past year just what I had done in killing the most wonderful love a man was ever blessed with. No one ever possessed a sweeter, purer and more innocent little girl. Is it any wonder that I suffer?
  Don't think that I don't realize how bitter you must feel in knowing that it was not your fault and that I am to blame.
  Way down in my heart I have always believed you to be the same pure, sweet, innocent little girl who gave herself to me thirteen years ago.

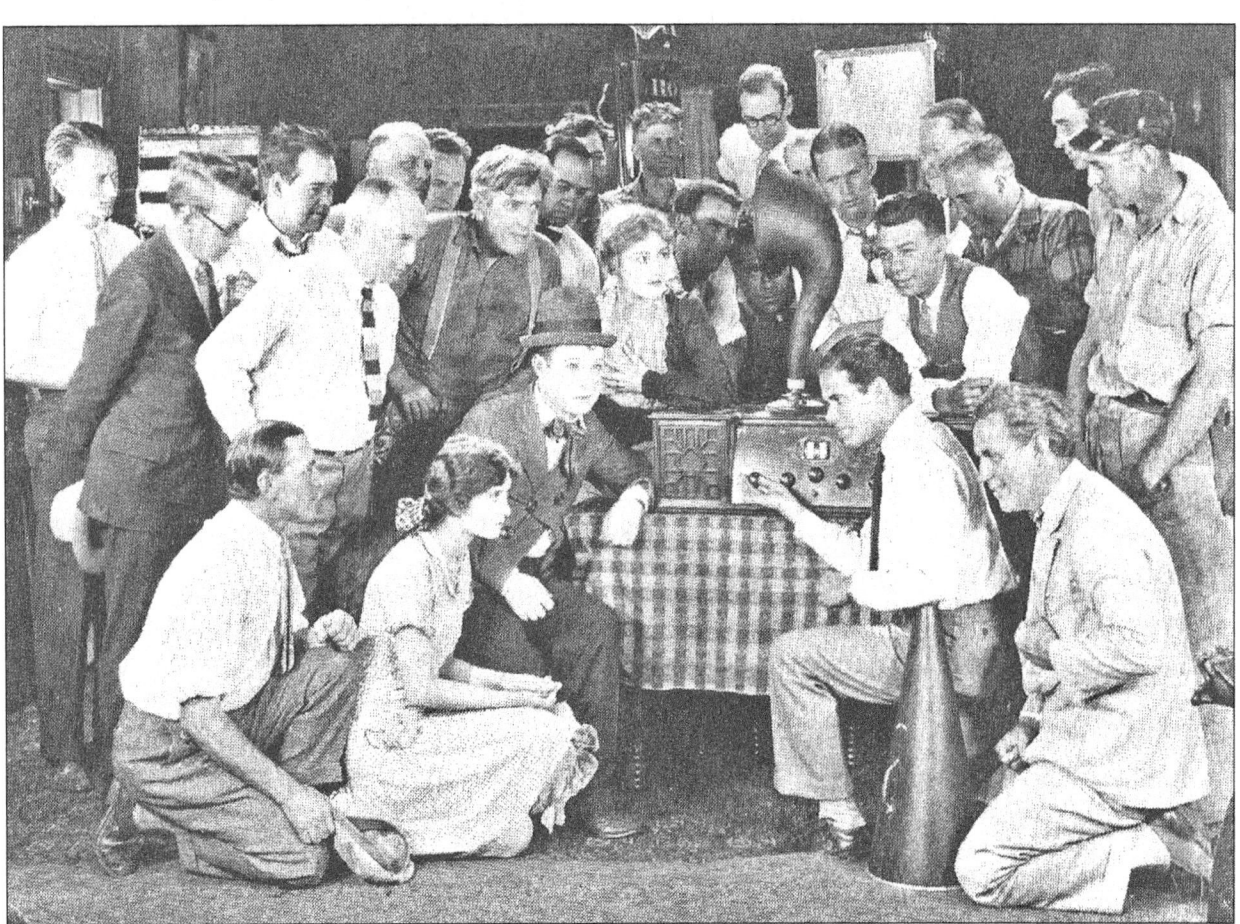

Frank Capra tunes in the Dempsey-Tunney fight of September 23, 1926 during the shooting of Long Pants. *Before long, he and Langdon would be in opposite corners.*

"Grasping woman" or no, the letters tore Helen apart. This was, after all, the father of her child. Moreover, her mother — a Catholic who never remarried after her young husband's death — continued to push Helen to reconcile with O'Brien.

Langdon panicked when he learned all this. That Christmas he outdid himself, giving Helen a diamond brooch, an $1,850 ermine coat, a $1,000 bill, a $150 gold case and a $500 Persian rug. For what it's worth, she returned the rug. She had no presents for Harry, but did purchase a new outfit of clothing for her husband.

During the week between Christmas and New Year, as O'Brien was traveling from San Francisco to San Diego, he stopped at a hotel in Glendale. Helen, accompanied by Virginia, went to visit on December 28. She and O'Brien remained together for five days and were intimate during that time. Wherever Langdon was when the calendar turned 1927, Helen wasn't there.

"One day when we were sitting alone waiting for the next scene to be lit," remembered Bonner, "and Helen wasn't there, Harry suddenly turned to me, looked me in the eye and out of the blue asked me, 'How could anybody love this funny face?' I was so taken aback that all I could say in reply was, 'Oh, Mr. Langdon!' But could you imagine — he already had this doubt about Helen." More likely it was a moment in which he permitted a deep-seated insecurity to surface. It's especially telling that his question was nearly identical to a line he'd written for Rose in *Johnny's New Car*: "Why, what girl would kiss that face?" With Helen gone, all he could do was continue to work on his picture, confer with Ripley on the next one and bicker with Capra about pathos.

Recently he'd taken to keeping a blackboard beside his bed so he could sit up and quickly jot down ideas that might come to him while sleeping. According to *Moving Picture World*, he conceived a gag sequence, went to the studio and, consulting neither writers nor director, stayed until 5:30 the next morning committing it to film.

Publicist Don Eddy brought some cheer: he'd arranged for the December 25 issue of *Hollywood Topics*, a local paper, to be a special "Harry Langdon Edition" with a look at *Long Pants* that included several photos and a biography by George Terwilliger. Even the ads had a Langdon twist to them; i.e., "Mother Dear — if I had LONG PANTS like Daddy…I'd go to the Bimini Furniture Company." Maurice Hart, a local member of the Harry Langdon Fan Club, personally ordered enough copies for all members, a gesture which impressed Eddy, as he was only able to secure 200 copies for the Corporation's use.

The issue included a lengthy "preview" of *Long Pants* by critic I.W. Irving, based on five-and-a-half reels (including the Technicolor sequence) viewed at the studio's projection room. "This writer, who

accounted himself 'hard boiled' in the matter of judging screen plays, has capitulated. With *Long Pants*, Langdon takes his place in the forefront of the screen's truly great artists.

"Langdon's name, of course, has become a box office standard. On the basis of *Tramp, Tramp, Tramp*, his first, and *The Strong Man*, his second big First National feature, he reached that point where only two other names could be mentioned in the same breath. After *Long Pants* is released, it is this writer's firm conviction that Langdon will stand alone."

Another Langdon booster was Tom Waller, West Coast representative for *Moving Picture World*. He, too, viewed the rushes, plus observed the shooting of scenes on the sidelines, and enthused, "If all that we have seen can be incorporated in the eight reels which will be the release length of *Long Pants*, then [it] will not only be unquestionably the most unusual picture in which Langdon has appeared, but also one of the few pictures which can be expressed [as] 'something stirringly different.'"

Waller observed filming of one of the closing scenes, where Harry discovers the truth about his city woman. "In the cold studio Langdon moves one way that makes even the hard-boiled gang on the lot, who know the tricks of the game backwards, double with laughter. An instant later they wonder how they could have laughed when what is before them is undoubtedly tragic. But before they can dope out this entanglement, there is another Langdon gyration which gets them going. Not gags, either. Just Langdon acting as though there were no camera recording his every movement.... While the camera is cranking, the musicians do not play the jazz accompaniment which one always hears around a set where a comedy is being made. The sobby strains of the *Camille* set orchestra would synchronize with that of the *Long Pants* musicians at this time. Langdon's right-hand man, Don Eddy, best sums up this condition with his description: 'A tragedy told in laughs.'"

Between takes, Waller asked Langdon if he liked the film "better than anything you have ever done" and why. Langdon replied, "Yes. It's the first thing of this kind I've ever done. It's sad and yet it is funny. There's a story all the way through it. And the story, while really dramatic, is funny. After all, the funniest things in real life spring from the saddest things. It's real. That's why I like it."

By the time of Waller's visit, *Long Pants* had been in production for eighteen weeks, with another four to go. Once Capra yelled, "That's a wrap!" in mid-February, the negative carried a $318,614 price tag. First National flatly refused to pay one cent over the contractual $250,000 advance, so Langdon covered the overage himself.

For Capra, the prospect of editing *Long Pants* was no less exasperating than directing it. Ripley, of course, was in charge and still pushing for the removal of the "Harry's boyhood" prologue (for which Frankie Darro had been cast), which only infuriated Capra. In the meantime, weary of defending his ambition against his director's narrow opinion of his strengths, Langdon solved his and Ripley's problem by dispatching Bill Jenner to fire Capra, apparently on February 21, the Monday after filming had completed.

In his memoir, Capra wrote that his firing took place shortly before Christmas, presumably to make his boss look especially cruel. As written, the director summons Langdon for an insert shot of his hand removing such books as *Don Juan* from the library shelf. "Directors don't use *stars* for stupid inserts," Langdon snaps. "They use *doubles!*" He then storms off with a parting crack about "making directors out of two-bit gag men." Concerned that Langdon's clouded ego is jeopardizing everyone's future, Capra decides to shock him back to reality. He confronts Langdon in his dressing room, labels him an ungrateful shitheel and "a little tin Jesus," and reminds him that he didn't create his screen character, didn't understand it, and "now that you believe your own interviews, you never will!" Summing up, Capra implores his boss to welcome and accept advice graciously and to "try thanking God for your success — and not yourself." Capra heads for home rather proud of himself...and that evening Jenner arrives with his closing check. Subsequently, when trying to land either a job or an agent, Capra discovers First National is telling everyone Langdon directed himself, while he was simply "a little gag man brought over from Sennett's for laughs."

As usual, the true story was not as colorful, nor as flattering to Capra. The Langdon Corporation made no official announcement about his dismissal. Instead, a dispatch dated February 22, which appeared in the next day's issue of *Variety*, stated simply that the director "has severed his connection with First National and will probably sign with United Artists." A somewhat longer blurb appeared in the February 23 *Los Angeles Times*. Future prospects weren't mentioned, but the piece did affirm "Capra's latest directorial effort, *Long Pants*, for Langdon, which will be released within the next six weeks, is expected to outshine his first directorial work in *The Strong Man* in box office value."

Not surprisingly, Capra wasn't the only one released. In its March 2 issue, *Variety* reported, "Harry Langdon has decided that he no longer needs a director to lead him through his paces.... The comedian feels no one can interpret his thoughts as well as himself, so he is going to hold the megaphone instead. Langdon is also said to feel that nobody can title his pictures like he can, so he is also going to title same. In the past, all ideas and gags used in the Langdon pictures were credited with having been conceived by the comedian, with the gagmen simply helping out in the construction."

On March 19, after two separate Los Angeles previews, *Moving Picture World* published another Tom Waller-penned piece about Langdon and *Long Pants*. In it, Langdon announced that "he is going to cut his corps of gag men or comedy constructionists, as they have been called of late, down to one man. Langdon's reasoning in this respect is that the trend of an excellent idea may be lost in its entirety after a half-dozen more of gaggists have made suggestions as to how it could be improved."

The article closed with the following paragraph:

Langdon directs himself in scenes in which he appears. He believes that he can do this best because he knows his story and he knows himself. He ventured the belief that a star, capable in these respects, directing himself would result in the motion picture industry probably turning out better pictures, or at least pictures more truly interpreting emotions as they really are.

Given that Langdon was the primary focus of his pictures, this was tantamount to labeling Capra (and Harry Edwards before him) a second-unit director, someone limited to working with the supporting cast and overseeing such things as establishing shots and "stupid inserts." In an article that appeared in the August 1931 issue of *Screen Play*, writer Bob Moak related, "Capra couldn't get an audience in another studio, for the word had spread…'Langdon says Capra never did pilot him.'" Moreover, unlike those for *The Strong Man*, trade and newspaper ads for *Long Pants* did not mention his name.

As nothing happened with United Artists, and no longer compelled to hold his temper, "the angry director wrote a letter to all the movie columnists," according to Katherine Albert's February 1932 *Photoplay* article. "He said that Harry was impossible to work with, that he wanted to have a finger in every pie, that he was conceited, egotistical and considered himself the biggest shot in pictures. That he gave himself airs and wore the high hat instead of the little battered felt of his films. It was a vitriolic letter from a disgruntled man." And it was far from the semi-inspirational, heartfelt speech, delivered to Langdon in private, described in *The Name Above the Title*.

Diligent research by McBride, other historians and the authors of this book have failed to turn up

Multi-faceted Harry. Langdon could play all those instruments, but by 1927 he was eager to expand his "do-it-all" skills into filmmaking.

Capra's letter, which he claimed was sent to one trade publication and was printed. Albert seemed to know all about it, but never specified her source. McBride presumed she'd interviewed Langdon, but the two quotes attributed to him in the piece came from news stories and columnist blurbs from around that time.

McBride concluded that Capra wrote his letter after reading the March 2 *Variety* article, but it's far more likely Waller's piece of March 19 is what set him off. Moreover, ten days before Waller's article was released, *Variety*'s "Inside Stuff — Pictures" columnist mentioned Hollywood's reaction to both Langdon's creative aspirations and a preview of *Long Pants*. Although the piece fails to mention Langdon by name, there's no mistaking the principal subject:

> Recently a picture comedian who has made three pictures for one of the larger releasing organizations decided that his producing unit would have to be a one-man organization, and that he would be the one man. He began by dispensing with the services of his director, some writers and a title writer. There was much talk around the West Coast studios that this comedian had let matters get to his head and that he was making a bad move. The last picture he appeared in was previewed around Los Angeles a few days ago.
>
> Though this man has been known on the screen as a great bet and his pictures in the past have been highly commended, the audience as well as picture wiseacres who saw [it] quickly realized that something was wrong.... [They] looked at 6,500 feet of film, which dragged along at a snail's pace and in which the comic saw to it that 95 percent of the celluloid used had him in the scenes as the principal figure.
>
> Those who saw the picture declare it was a gag affair lacking situations and romance. Though the comedian had a director on the job for this picture, he practically took away the megaphone and personally directed most of the scenes. In the past, the pictures of the comedian had been greeted with plenty of laughter and applause, but this got very little of either.

Even though it buttressed Langdon's claim that he directed himself in his scenes, the blurb made clear the state of his ego was being speculated upon within the industry. Burned by his firing and seeing his contribution diminished by the Waller piece, it was in Capra's best interest to confirm the gossip. "I had to counteract," he said in 1985, upon admitting to McBride that he did write and send such a letter. "Unless you defended yourself… nobody would know it. Langdon had achieved a tremendous reputation. Everybody was talking about him. I couldn't find a job. Nobody would believe me."

Indeed, Capra would not work again until late in April, when Robert T. Kane, another independent producer contracted to First National, hired him to direct the final film on the deal, *For the Love of Mike*. Even then, Kane assigned Joseph C. Boyle, director of his previous two pictures, to co-direct with Capra in case the rumor was true. Only when it transpired that Kane was running out of money, and Capra agreed to defer his salary (which in the end never materialized), was he permitted to go it alone.

The effect of Capra's letter on Langdon's career has been hotly debated since cinema historian Kevin Brownlow, in his 1968 tome *The Parade's Gone By...*, rediscovered Albert's article. At the time, though, any fallout was negligible. Langdon's "tremendous reputation," for a while, assured him of respectful press coverage. That would change once his first self-directed feature came out. Even then, critics mainly blamed him for trying to do too much at once to the detriment of his comic ability, a charge they also leveled at any screen clown not named Charlie Chaplin. It wasn't for another year that Langdon would be accused of rampant egomania.

It was right around the time of Capra's exit that Helen returned, tearfully. She was pregnant, she said. The baby was O'Brien's, a man she never wanted to see again, and she wanted an abortion right away. Barely two months after their New Years' tryst, they were battling once again. In the heat of an argument, O'Brien accused her of coupling with him to hide the fact that Langdon was actually the father. Helen vehemently denied it and stormed out, determined never to return.

What the press would term "an illegal operation" was secured and performed. Langdon, possibly uncertain himself about his responsibility, tried to talk her out of it, but she was adamant. He insisted she recuperate at his home, and later claimed that he proposed to her at this time.

Rose got wind of the resident at Harry's place and hired a private investigator, Mrs. Marie Firman, to report on her comings and goings. Mrs. Firman would testify that Helen did stay overnight in the nine-bedroom house several times. When going on outings, she and Harry were "nearly always" chaperoned by the maid, plus Helen's daughter Virginia and a second, adopted daughter, Edith; the two girls referred to Langdon as "Daddy Harry." (Edith, according to 1930 census data, was approximately one year *older* than Virginia. She does not appear with the

Helen Walton recuperates from "an illegal operation" at Langdon's home, March 1927.

O'Briens in the 1920 census, and evidence suggests that Thomas O'Brien didn't acknowledge her. Edith left Helen near the end of 1931, at age 17, and vanished from sight; her point of origin and subsequent life remain a mystery). Mrs. Firman's findings were enough to secure an annulment from the Church, but under California law, Rose would have to wait a year before filing for divorce (on grounds of desertion), and another year before it was finalized.

As for *Long Pants*, Langdon and Ripley supervised the editing, and the version that emerged ran for nine reels. Two previews were held in Los Angeles: one near the end of February at the West Lake Theater, the other at the Wilshire Theater approximately one week later. Tom Waller's article discussed both from Langdon's perspective:

Langdon comes forth again with his originality when he tells how a producer can gauge the success of a picture with a Hollywood preview audience: "It isn't so much how they applaud out there in Hollywood as it is if the picture has interested them enough to stand out in the street and look for the star."

[At] the first preview, *Long Pants*, edited for laughs rather than story, was shown in nine reels. The applause was there and probably a lot of people looked around for Langdon after the show but [he] was not to be seen…. Then *Long Pants* was taken back to the cutting room and this time edited for story essentials with a maximum length of six short reels. [At] the second preview… the applause thundered, and Langdon had a difficult time reaching his car.

Gone from the final edit was Capra's prologue, which wasn't surprising, but the publicity material and pressbook had already been released and they included billing for Frankie Darro, causing confusion when "Harry as a small boy" never appeared on screen. Additionally, the Technicolor daydream sequence, which had been planned for a reel (approximately 1,000 feet of film), then reduced to 326 feet in the first edit, emerged in the final version at a mere 52 feet. The sequence exists only in black-and-white in present-day copies, which mainly derive from a 16mm print (only reel two of the original domestic negative survived decomposition, making it doubly tragic that the foreign negative was junked in 1934). Lasting about 34 seconds, the scene contains no close-ups, so it's difficult if not impossible to recognize Alma Bennett as both Harry's fantasy princess and Bebe Blair, the notorious city woman.

Still, *Long Pants* represents a significant step forward from the previous two features in terms of storytelling. Nearly every frame centers on adolescent Harry Shelby's coming-of-age, starting with his attire (a boy's knickerbockers become a man's trousers) leading ultimately to his innocence (romantic fantasy turns into genuine disillusionment). There are three major gag sequences, all of which, as Langdon desired, propel the story forward. The first is Harry's initial encounter with Bebe Blair. She's clearly his ideal woman and he wants desperately to impress her, leading him to perform tricks on his bicycle, only some of which he handles with any degree of success. However, she's bored (her chauffeur is changing a flat) and thus eventually drawn toward Harry's show, and is just cruel enough to toy with this "boob," as she later describes him, by giving him a passionate kiss, which produces the usual Langdon effect of dreamy ecstasy.

The second is when he intends to shoot Priscilla on their wedding day so he can rescue the incarcerated Bebe. Every attempt goes miserably wrong, and each failure is ratcheted up a notch in ludicrousness

Harry's fantasy marriage to Babe London was cut from the release print of Long Pants.

and hilarity. Adding insult to repeated injury, once Harry resigns himself to failure, Priscilla discovers his gun and proves a crackerjack shot. The scene is marvelously double-edged: it's urgent that Harry escape this marriage in order to aid Bebe, and his impatience and frustration as he fails to rid himself of his innocent bride-to-be lead only to more self-inflicted punishment, which he absolutely deserves for even considering such a horrible idea.

The third comes after Bebe has escaped from jail. She's hidden in a large crate carried off by Harry, which is now positioned beside a theater's stage door. Having been warned to be on the lookout for cops, Harry's cautiously peering around street corners, and while his back is turned a prop man temporarily places a large dummy of a patrolman upon the crate. Harry spies the dummy and, from his distance, believes it

Langdon in costume for Long Pants's *Technicolor sequence, which was trimmed to a fare-thee-well in the final edit.*

to be real. He tries to convince it to follow him to an emergency, to thwart a holdup, and to come to his aid when he "passes out" on the sidewalk, but of course nothing works. Langdon's pantomime is particularly good, and although the bit may seem arbitrary, there is again an underlying purpose: he desperately wants to get Bebe out of that crate and into his life.

The Los Angeles and New York openings were quite successful. At the Strand in Manhattan, *Long Pants* pulled $36,230; not as good as *The Strong Man*'s $44,200, but still solid. In Los Angeles, Loew's State grossed $31,500 for one week, as compared to $28,000 for *Strong Man*. The theatre was, according to *Variety*, "the only downtown house that had a line each night." Based on this promising start,

First National committed $25,000 toward advertising the picture. They also exercised an option for two more features, for which the advance on each would increase to $260,000 and Langdon's weekly salary upped to $7,500.

Trade reviews were decidedly mixed. "As droll and hilarious a comedy as had been captured in a season or two is brought to light in *Long Pants*," the *Motion Picture News* assured readers. Unsurprisingly, given Tom Waller's previous write-ups, *Moving Picture World* agreed: "Once again Harry Langdon has come forward with mirth-provoking comedy that is sure to tickle the risibilities of the great movie going public." *Motion Picture Classic*'s Laurence Reid wrote, "*Long Pants* is studded with amusing gags, but with all of them clicking merrily, it is the very waggish star in whom you are most interested."

Among the naysayers were *Variety* ("A bit of a let down for Langdon. It hasn't the popular laughing quality of his other full-length productions, principally because the sympathetic element is overdeveloped at the expense of the gags and the stunts that made *The Strong Man* a riot"), *Harrison's Reports* ("The story, supposedly to be farce comedy, is unpleasant; it develops into vicious underworld melodrama that incites to crime. The action is slow. Outside of Langdon the principal players enact their roles seriously and what was intended for burlesque becomes ordinary bandit thrill material"), and *Film Daily* ("The situations aren't consistently mirth provoking and the repetition of some of comedy business slows

Harry intends to shoot bride-to-be Priscilla in the American Tragedy-*influenced scene from* Long Pants.

the tempo. Even Langdon shouldn't repeat his stuff if he wants it to hold to a brisk humorous pace").

Newspaper critics seemed to be baffled by Langdon's new direction, which is surprising given how their biggest problem with his previous two features was a lack of cohesion. "When Mr. Langdon is engaged in doing quaint things in his own quaint way…all is well. [But] not once during the proceedings does [he] take time out for an interlude comparable to the famous cold-in-the-head sequence in *The Strong Man*," stated the *New York Post*'s Wilella Waldorf. The *Brooklyn Eagle*'s Martin Dickstein wrote, "A two-reeler of hilarious possibilities, the film has been extended without sufficient reason to six, and thereby it manages too often to founder in chapters containing nothing to laugh about." On the other end of the country, Wood Soanes of the *Oakland Tribune* opined, "In this we have the estimable Master Langdon, so refreshingly comic in *The Strong Man*, endeavoring to make merriment out of tragedy in the way of a burlesque on Dreiser's [*An*] *American Tragedy*. Langdon attempts to make a humorous episode out of the murder of a bride-elect on her wedding day and it must be confessed that the incident emerges only gruesome."

"Rather a daring theme — that murder idea," wrote Marquis Busby in a profile for the *Los Angeles Times*'s April 17 edition, "but Langdon has made use of the daring before…. In discussing the proposed murder, which, of course, never came to pass, Langdon said that many people tried earnestly to dissuade him from introducing any such theme in a comedy. But the same people had voiced objections to a blind girl in *The Strong Man*, yet this character did much toward making the picture the human document that it was…. Consequently, Langdon feels that he will secure approbation for the almost-jazz murder in *Long Pants*."

It was not to be. In the end, *Long Pants* failed to turn a profit. Even after taking into account his footing the bill for the production overage, plus the application of profits from *The Strong Man*, the film still lost $79,620 by the time the books were closed in 1928. And the murder scene, however cleverly conceived and expertly performed, was most likely the root of the problem.

Audiences of 1920s middle-America, which had welcomed *The Strong Man* with open arms (and wallets), were appalled by *Long Pants*, at least according to exhibitors. "Many patrons said *Long Pants* was the worst picture we have ever shown," Guthrie Theatre, Kansas. "One big piece of cheese that patrons walked out on," City Theatre, South Dakota. "Might just as well hang a smallpox sign on the lobby. He just won't draw the crowds," Paramount Theatre, Illinois. "He had poor material to work with…[There were] many adverse criticisms," Capitol Theatre, Iowa.

Thirty years later, Buster Keaton, a man who'd never lost touch with his Midwestern roots, insisted the idea of turning Dreiser's novel into comedy was not just misguided but fatal. "Langdon and W.C. Fields were the two greatest film comedians, next to Chaplin," he told Columbia University's Robert Franklin. "I don't know whatever got [Langdon] off on the wrong foot. He started [making] feature

LONG PANTS— First National

IN the spring a young man's fancy turns to Long Pants—and when Harry Langdon gets his first pair of long pants he's sitting on top of the world. So much so that he casts aside the little country gal and falls madly in love with the vamp, who is incidentally a bandit. Harry soon realizes his mistake and returns home. Not much of a story for six long reels, but Langdon is always funny and so who cares a great deal about the story.

Review in Photoplay *magazine.*

Harry Langdon CORPORATION

FIRST NATIONAL STUDIOS   BURBANK CALIFORNIA

May 18, 1927.

Miss Lillian L. Doria
6312 Wentworth Ave.
Chicago, Ill.

My dear Miss Doria:

    Many thanks for your letter of May 3rd.

    I was indeed glad to hear that you enjoyed LONG PANTS, although I'm sorry you did not think it came up to THE STRONG MAN. However, I hope you will like the new one we are now making. We haven't got a title for it as yet, but if you will write me again in the near future, perhaps I'll be able to tell you what it is.

    I certainly enjoy your letters and your comments on our pictures, and hope you will favor me with your criticism and comments on future pictures.

    Let me hear from you again and rest assured of my sincere and continued friendship.

                                 Very truly yours,

                                   Harry Langdon

HL:KW

Langdon responds to a fan whose opinion of Long Pants *mirrored that of several critics.*

length pictures, and his first two were swell. They were good pictures. Then, for some silly reason, he picked out *An American Tragedy* to do a satire on; he thought he'd get a funny picture out of it and the situation....

"In the original, of course, the boy has been going with this little country girl for a long time, and her folks have taken it for granted they're going to marry. So the talk of the community is that it's just a matter

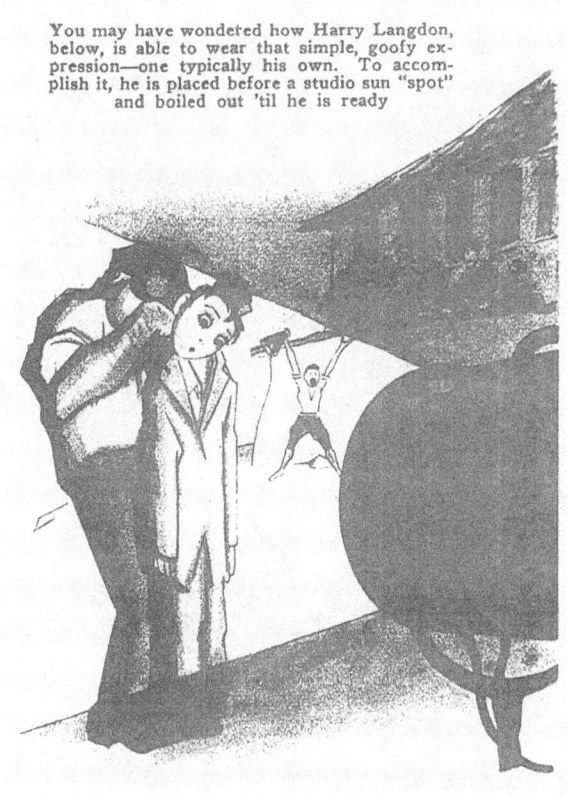

of time 'til they have the wedding. And he meets a city girl who's got money and who falls for him. To get rid of the country girl, he gets her out in a rowboat and drowns her....

"Langdon thought he was going to have an audience rooting for him, or laughing at him, taking a girl out to [kill] her! Now, the minute the comic had the idea of [murdering] somebody, he's killed himself and his picture. Even the thought, whether he goes through with it or not. Once he's thought of the idea, he's a dead character to a motion picture audience."

Behind the scenes, the balance of power was shifting at First National. In April, two theater chains assumed full control: the Stanley Company and West Coast Theatres. John McCormick remained in charge of production in Burbank and Richard Rowland remained first vice president and general manager, but Sol Lesser was gone; Stanley's president John J. McGuirk was appointed First National's president, and the board of directors mostly consisted of new faces. As with any business that changes ownership, financial performance and existing contracts would be heavily scrutinized.

Unfortunately for the Harry Langdon Corporation, Pathé finally brought out *His First Flame* a mere four

Another cartoonist-turned-screen comedian sketches Langdon, 1927.

weeks after *Long Pants* went into nationwide release, although it was not their intention to compete. The company had set its release date for the two-year-old Sennett picture back when *Long Pants* was expected to reach theater screens in February. The Strand in Manhattan, where Langdon's previous features had played to great success, cheerfully booked the film for a week, while the Keith-Orpheum theater circuit snapped it up for the rest of the country. *Photoplay* spoke for its brethren in a brief critique: "[*His First Flame*] was made about two years ago and the improvements in pictures in two years are remarkable. Langdon is, was and always will be funny but it is just a plain low trick to show this to audiences. The lighting is bad, the girl's clothes are a scream — in fact the picture looks like a number of two-reelers pasted together." Among newspaper reviews, perhaps the most telling comment came from the *New York Sun*: "*His First Flame* proves... that some years ago, Harry was doing the same round of tricks, doing them with more spontaneous gayety than he is now."

Perhaps in the interests of restoring some of that spontaneous gayety, First National purchased the play *The Butter and Egg Man* for Langdon. Instead he turned once again to an original story of his and Ripley's creation. As before, it began with a mere notion on Langdon's part, described in Busby's piece as "a waif of the wharves, unhappy in his drab surroundings and who dreams of happier days to come."

Harry admires Gladys McConnell in Three's a Crowd *(1927).*

On the personal front, these were Langdon's "happier days." In the battle for Helen Walton's affections, he was the victor, "funny face" and all. She'd officially renounced her husband, informing O'Brien she was filing for divorce and giving him $500 with the stipulation that he return to the East and stay there. Under California divorce law, both Helen and Harry would be free to wed by mid-1929. Langdon could now look forward to the promise of marital bliss with his beloved and her two delightful daughters.

But what if it hadn't worked out that way? When the year began, it certainly looked like this fairy-tale finish was doomed when O'Brien, apparently reformed and contrite, coaxed his estranged wife back into his arms. As it is, Langdon lost the opportunity to be a parent to a newborn, owing to Helen's determination to terminate her pregnancy, but at least he'd won her heart while she recuperated in his home. He could easily visualize his "waif of the wharves" pining for a family of his own and inheriting one by chance by taking in a destitute new mother and her infant son, only to lose them both to her true husband. Ripley is credited with the scenario

Above and Opposite: A pair of deleted scenes from Three's a Crowd.

for the finished film, *Three's a Crowd*, but the story was unmistakably influenced by Langdon's recent experience with Helen.

Under the working title "Gratitude," production began on April 22. Since Priscilla Bonner had moved on to presumably greener and assuredly less discordant pastures, Langdon engaged Gladys McConnell as leading lady. A relative newcomer, McConnell's motion picture debut had been in one of Hal Roach's feature westerns, *The Devil Horse*, filmed near the end of 1925. The following January she was placed under contract by the Fox Film Corporation, but she told

Edward Watz, "My career wasn't going anywhere. I was the leading lady in horse operas.

"Then I was selected to be a WAMPAS Baby Star [for 1927, among a class that included Helene Costello and Langdon's former Sennett co-star Natalie Kingston], and all of a sudden I was in demand for better pictures." McConnell opted not to renew her Fox contract and was freelancing when Langdon signed her. "I was chosen personally by Harry Langdon to appear in *Three's a Crowd*, and it meant a great deal to me, to be seen in what was going to be a major film, and with such an important star."

McConnell quickly discovered her employer/co-star's multi-faceted talents: "The set designers built this eerie-looking New York tenement with this very long staircase. I had seen sketches for this set drawn in a children's school notebook and Arthur Ripley noticed me looking them over. 'Harry Langdon drew that,' he told me. Harry carried the book with him and I noticed he had drawn many detailed sketches of how he thought different scenes should look. He had definite ideas on how he wanted this film to look on screen."

With Capra gone, the atmosphere around the studio was a complete reversal from that of *Long Pants*. "Harry and his collaborator, Arthur Ripley, had a great working relationship," McConnell observed. "Ripley was always behind the camera when Harry was performing. They watched the dailies together each day, and invited me once to watch the scenes with them. I just sat there quietly as they critiqued the footage. They seemed to be very much in accord with each other's ideas for the film, and their talk about comedy situations was always very serious."

Once again, *Moving Picture World*'s Tom Waller came out to the studio to observe production, and to wax enthusiastic in print. "On a garret 'set' several feet

in the air, built on a solid parallel, we found Harry pantomiming before the camera with his wonted tragic pathos," he wrote for the May 21 issue. "The current story shows him in a characterization similar to that of *The Strong Man* and from [the] little business we were fortunate enough to witness it is more than likely that he may even surpass his success in *The Strong Man*."

As with *Long Pants*, Waller attended two previews, and reported on the aftermath in a lengthy article for the August 13 issue: "Langdon, from now on, is letting his preview audiences make his pictures. What they want he puts in. What they do not want he clips out. He gauges their likes by the laughs and the dislikes by their silence…. Langdon is the only producer to place on record for the first time that instead of attempting to tailor a screen story for an audience he will provide them with the material and let them do their own tailoring.

"Several striking instances of how closely Langdon is adhering to this policy were afforded the writer… during the making of *Three's a Crowd*. The changes in this picture when it was first previewed and the state in which it will be shipped to exchanges are evident in the opening and closing scenes and in several sequences throughout the story as projected.

"In the picture, as it was previewed for the first time, Langdon gave way considerably to other characters on the screen. That this was obvious and at the same time disapproved by the first audience in a large local house with a cosmopolitan draw was evidenced by the applause toward the second or third reel every time that Langdon was flashed into full view."

The story as it finally emerged: Apprentice expressman Harry covets the companionship of a wife and child that his boss (Arthur Thalasso) enjoys, to the point of falling for a young woman (Gladys McConnell) he's only watched from a distance through his garret window. That winter, fate places an opportunity literally at his feet: the woman, apparently destitute, has collapsed in the freezing cold, exhausted and likely malnourished. We already know she's reluctantly left her husband (Cornelius Keefe) and his dissolute lifestyle. Harry brings her to his dilapidated "tenement with this very long staircase" (possibly the steepest continuous staircase in cinema history), and quickly discovers she's not only the girl he's spied from afar, but also pregnant. When the time comes, he summons every midwife and doctor in the neighborhood; between them the delivery is a success. Harry is ecstatic, throwing himself into the role of provider and parent, until the woman's penitent spouse turns up and reaffirms his devotion. In the end, Harry the waif is once again on his own.

The opening as first conceived shows the dreary neighborhood at dawn, with the street lamps going out as the sun comes up. It's five in the morning, and Harry rises as his alarm clock rings; he then dresses

for work. After the initial preview, Langdon lengthened the scenes of his awakening. In the film, he stretches and yawns and attempts to resume sleeping; a futile action, as the boss is yelling for him. He douses his own lamp and lights the stove, waters a plant, performs morning exercises and finally showers. By the time he's dressed and ready for work, it's after ten o'clock.

In a curious reversal of the *Long Pants* dispute, Langdon had deliberately included several scenes methodically tracing the history of McConnell's character and the romance with her young man. Clearly he'd taken to heart the criticism that he'd been the sole focus of his previous release. McConnell was firmly established as the daughter of a wealthy family that disapproves of her beau. The two young lovers meet clandestinely each evening, and during one of these, Harry, peering through a telescope from his window, spies her and immediately falls in love. These were all shot and included in the first edit but, due to preview audience reaction, exist today only in production stills.

"We filmed scenes at this beautiful estate, to establish where the girl came from," remembered McConnell. "Unfortunately, all of that footage was cut out. This left me with not much of a part, since I was supposed to be recuperating from childbirth. So there are lots of reaction shots of me smiling at Harry in gratitude, but it's not a real performance. I know that bothered Harry, and he said he'd make sure I had a better part in the next film we made together."

In the final edit, he spies the girl from his window after watering the plant (to the degree that the clay flowerpot is destroyed), and his reaction indicates that he's been admiring her for some time. He writes her a love letter and, since she lives in an adjacent building, secures a pigeon to deliver it. Unfortunately, this section decomposed over time and no longer exists in the negative, causing confusion among modern audiences when, later in the day, the pigeon appears out of nowhere and inadvertently delivers Harry's letter to his boss's wife. Because she is the only woman in the neighborhood who shows Harry any sympathy, the boss has repeatedly misinterpreted their relationship; the letter is the final straw. In eluding his livid employer, Harry accidentally falls through an open trap door in his home and, grasping his rug at the last second, winds up dangling several stories above ground in a thrill sequence similar to that in *Tramp, Tramp, Tramp*. Since the missing footage contains the set-up to the gag, what remains makes little sense. It's possible, in current prints, to interpret the letter as intended for its ultimate recipient, although we don't know when or why it was sent, or even if Harry wrote and sent it.

Finally, the original finish was more downbeat, with Harry standing outside in the cold after his "family" has departed, holding a small lamp. With the sun beginning to rise, he blows out the lamp at the exact moment the streetlights go out, which takes him by surprise. Audiences were expecting a bigger

Harry among the poor, buffeted by the elements, in Three's a Crowd.

laugh at the close, and Langdon obliged. First, he created a quick "plant" scene of Harry visiting a fortune teller, one Professor DeMotte, who assures him the wayward husband "will pass out of her life — and the girl will be yours." To wrap up the film, Harry is determined to toss a brick through this charlatan's window, but just can't bring himself to do it. Resigned, he tosses the brick aside, whereupon it dislodges a huge metal drum from the back of a truck that rolls into and demolishes DeMotte's entire storefront.

It's a wonderful gag, indicative of the Little Elf's "Divine providence," but Langdon places his first visit to DeMotte just *after* a scene in which we see the husband has indeed reformed and is earnestly seeking his wife by engaging a private detective. It's one of the novice director's few missteps. Because of this, we know from the outset that the prediction is wrong, and our frustration is with Harry for being taken in. Had the two scenes been reversed, the husband's reformation becomes more poignant, the audience can better relate to Harry's subsequent anger, and the demolition of DeMotte's store becomes more satisfying.

Three's a Crowd contains its fair share of comedy, especially a celebrated scene where Harry needs to change the baby. The newly washed diapers are hanging on a line, but as the flat is not heated on this winter's day, they're frozen stiff. No matter: Harry takes one down and proceeds to knead it, first with his hands, then a rolling pin, as one would a lump of dough. But he's so transfixed by the miracle of the child and the beauty of its mother, he loses himself in the task and proceeds to add flour, and some canned fruit, then crimps the mixture in a pie tin… and only when he's on his way to the oven does he realize what he's done.

Still, there's no question the Elf is meant to suffer in this film. The tragic framework of its story predominates, at times overwhelming the more gentle comedic moments. As his own director, Langdon saw to it that his desire "to do more pathos" wouldn't be denied, and by relying on preview audiences to do the final "tailoring," he was certain he'd produced a winner. "I have received such very fine reports on it [and] am convinced that we have a good picture," he wrote to fan club member Maurice Hart two weeks before it opened in New York City.

Langdon brought the film in under budget ($243,598), despite all the cutting and extra shooting, but First National never knew it because he'd kept the remaining $6,402, presumably to recoup some of his outlay for *Long Pants*. The company, meanwhile, crossed its fingers and allocated $22,000 for advertising, placing full-page pitches in such mainstream fare as *Vogue, Harper's Bazaar, Judge, Liberty, Vanity Fair, Good Housekeeping* and *American Boy*.

The trade press opted to tread lightly, basically dropping hints to Langdon that he was headed in a wrong direction. *Film Daily*: "There is some good incident and several clever gags that should draw a minimum of laughs but, on the whole, the picture is not the hilarious affair they look for from Langdon." *Variety*: "*Three's a Crowd*… shapes as fair program material with the comedian leaning toward the serious and stressing pathos more than is his habit. There are spots in the picture where Langdon is brilliant, but on the other hand slow passages also creep in. It's not a high geared vehicle and Langdon has held down the hoke, which may explain." *Moving Picture World*: "There is more pathos than comedy, more heart interest than laughter…. While retaining his familiar and amusing make-up and playing a character built along the same general lines, Langdon in this picture has wandered far from the straight gag comedy in which he made his reputation." *Exhibitor's Herald*: "The comedian with the droll personality and the mark of pathos on his countenance allows himself to become unduly tragic here. He's gone Chaplin — with the result that his own inimitable style is often buried. The pathos looks labored — and the comedy lacks spontaneity."

Poet and Abraham Lincoln biographer Carl Sandburg was writing film criticism for the *Chicago Daily News* in 1927. "Harry Langdon's new comedy, *Three's a Crowd*, is a slow-moving, rather sad affair which has little in it to stir a crowd to laughter," he wrote in his review. Sandburg sympathetically opined that Langdon could, like Chaplin, move audiences to tears as well as laughter, "but when the story has as little of humor and as much of tragedy as *Three's a Crowd*, the laugh stops in the throat."

Other newspaper critics saw no need to pull any punches. The *New York Post*'s Wilella Waldorf wrote: "*Three's a Crowd*, at the Strand just now, is poor from start to finish. Its gags are old and badly developed, its continuity is choppy and, worst of all, the film drags on interminably. *Three's a Crowd* is not funny, and Mr. Langdon, sad to relate, appears to be suffering from an acute attack of Chaplinitis." "Those who journey to the Strand this week anticipating again an

uproarious hour with the comedian of *The Strong Man* must, unfortunately, be doomed to disappointment," affirmed the *Brooklyn Eagle*'s Martin Dickstein. "The humorous moments in *Three's a Crowd* are weighed down by a false super-structure of tragedy, tragedy which resembles nothing so much as a clown who has smeared his make-up with a deluge of glycerin tears." The *Oakland Tribune*'s Wood Soanes griped, "If Harry Langdon is seeking the palm for mediocrity he has hit another bull's eye in *Three's a Crowd*.... In it we find him not only fumbling as a comedian, but wandering in a daze as an author and director. What comedy is in the picture is promptly strangled by Langdon in his attempt to drag it out to indefinite lengths."

Irene Thirer of the *New York Daily News* gave the picture her approval in the belief that Langdon couldn't possibly have expected anyone to take him so seriously: "This comedy-tragedy is indeed a decidedly impressive screen contribution. Its gags have been construed with much thought as to audience reaction. And most of them are novel and exceptionally funny. Its direction is subtle and quick-moving for the most part, with just a couple of lagging passages.... You actually feel for this lonely Harry, and yet you realize that he isn't really lonely and that this is all in fun and that you're supposed to laugh at it and you do." This was the antithesis of Langdon's intent, yet near enough to a rave review for First National to grab and reprint it in full in a subsequent trade ad.

For the most part, the "New York writers" in which Langdon placed his faith turned on him with a vengeance. Critic William Richmond, in his "On New York Screens" column, wrote: "No sooner does a screen comedian make his mark than he turns writer, director and what-not for his own productions. The minute he does that, it seems, his fame begins to dim. Lloyd, Keaton and numerous others are living examples of this rule. Chaplin, alone, has survived....

"Now comes Harry Langdon. During the last two years, this wistful tramp climbed to remarkable heights. As a matter of fact, he achieved genuine fame as a comedian. Then, having reached the top, he wheeled right around and committed the folly of greatness — he became his own author and director....

"Like Chaplin, Langdon aspires to the dramatic, the tragic, but unlike Chaplin, he does not possess that rare quality which would permit him to dally along the trail of fun-making and was serious for a flash or two. A capable director would have told him so — but Langdon, in *Three's a Crowd*, was his own director."

Playwright Arthur Kobler, in a piece for the *New York Sun* in which he welcomed and lavishly praised Chaplin's new release *The Circus*, couldn't resist adding: "Just when I was beginning to ignore the

absence of Chaplin from the screen by being amused by Harry Langdon, the helpless, frightened oaf, Mr. Langdon conceives a film in which he displays the pangs of fatherhood, goes inordinately hooey and sends me out into the night shouting frantically for my Chaplin."

Exhibitor comments fairly singed the paper upon which they were printed:

"So lousy and contaminated with nothingness that it has no rival."

"Some walked out on it, others demanded their money back and still others derived some satisfaction from insulting me. I had no comeback, knowing how justified they were."

"We like Harry, but he sure flopped in this one. Six reels with a few scattered laughs."

"Just three degrees worse than rotten. Harry Langdon is a favorite with me personally, too."

"Oh! What a lemon! No plot, silly from start to finish. Don't do it again, Harry, or you will ruin yourself for life."

One Fletcher Powers, manager of the Municipal Theatre of East Millinocket, Maine, was compelled to write the following to the local First National exchange in Boston, which was duly forwarded to the executives in Burbank:

Gentlemen,

I have just shown your picture, "Three is a Crowd" *(sic)* and will say that it was the worst beating I have ever received. Most of my audience left during the show and the remaining few spoke unfavorably of the picture. Under these conditions, I feel that I should receive the money I have paid for the picture.

I cannot understand that a company with your reputation would issue such a picture, and it would be appreciated if you would omit sending me any more pictures of this description.

Word-of-mouth finished off what the critics had started. After its first three months in release, gross receipts were down by more than 50 percent as compared to *Long Pants*. At the close of two years, *Three's a Crowd* wound up with $121,629 in red ink on its ledger.

It can be convincingly argued that the film — and Langdon himself — may have been victimized by over-exposure. When 1927 began, *The Strong Man* was still making the rounds, some of which were in return engagements, followed by *Long Pants* in April, then *His First Flame* in May. Complicating matters, Mack Sennett and Pathé released *Fiddlesticks* in November while *Three's a Crowd* was still in first run. Additionally, over the past year, other comedians had been utilizing Langdon-inspired make-up, gestures and routines. Lesser lights such as Billy Dooley, Lupino Lane, Stan Laurel (pre-Oliver Hardy) and even Larry Semon were slowing down, widening their eyes and reacting to the gags. Along with putting out the two older pictures, Sennett took a young comic named Eddie Quillan and turned him into a Langdonesque carbon copy.

Regardless of whether there had been too much Langdon on screen that year, or if all the harsh criticism sent moviegoers elsewhere, the comedian was stunned and stung by the blanket rejection of his artistic statement. Before starting work on his next production, he wrote a brief article for *Theatre* magazine, titled "The Serious Side of Comedy Making," which was published in the December 1927 issue. The piece began as follows:

> There are few more tragic businesses in the world than the making of funny pictures.
> There is the tragedy, for example, of working for weeks, sometimes months, on a sequence which the producer expects to be extremely funny, only to find that it fails to evolve even a ripple from the audience. In the producing of any big feature comedy this situation is certain to arise at least once. The producer and the star often find that their most cherished material is not funny when transmitted to the screen and the result is a tragedy not only for the audience, but for the makers of the picture.

That neatly summed up the reaction to both of Langdon's independent releases for the year. Unfortunately, there was much worse to come.

CHAPTER TEN

"Two of the Lousiest Pictures Ever Made"

1927–1928

"*Three's a Crowd* is not a Langdon picture. Langdon, the comedian, is gone. In his stead, another cavorts upon the screen — half mountebank, half maudlin dramatic 'ham'" (*On New York Screens*). "Now that Mr. Langdon has had his fling at art, perhaps he will snap out of it and give us another *Strong Man*" (*New York Post*). "He makes you wade through thick layers of oleomargarine pathos to get at the comedy.... May his next be louder and funnier" (*Photoplay*). "One of the poorest pictures we have run this season. If Langdon [doesn't] snap out of that marble face stuff, he is due for the discard very shortly" (*Exhibitor's Herald*).

Whether newspaper columnist or critic, fan magazine editor or exhibitor, the message was clear, at least to First National brass. West Coast production chief Richard Rowland was handed marching orders: ensure that Langdon's next picture "be louder and funnier."

To his credit, Langdon tacitly admitted that dismissing all those gagmen had been a mistake. Along with Bob Eddy and brother Tulley, he hired Harry McCoy, a veteran from Keystone days, and re-engaged Clarence Hennecke, who brought an idea to the table. According to *Variety*, the "story was developed through the first four reels, with the finish to be written during production." Shooting began at the start of October, and everyone worked for ten days at a cost of $20,000, when First National's bean counters got wind of what he was doing. "Langdon was persuaded ... to stop production until the story was fully worked out. This was to eliminate extra production costs while waiting for the writers to complete it.... Langdon's last two pictures, which he wrote, directed and starred in, were written as the shooting progressed. Innumerable delays and heavy expenses resulting were objected to by First National."

Of course, Langdon didn't actually direct *Long Pants*, but the industry had been convinced otherwise. He'd also brought in *Three's a Crowd* for less than his advance, but First National didn't know that. In any case, the company requested only a temporary respite until everything had been completed on paper; instead, to their horror, Langdon jettisoned Hennecke's story *and* the ten days' work, while he and Ripley concocted an entirely different scenario. Once *that* was completed, shooting resumed at the usual pace.

It was such blatant disregard for cost that gave his brother Claude, working behind the scenes on Harry's behalf, headaches. According to Claude's son, Don Langdon, "I remember Dad saying, when they had their film company, one of the bad things about Harry was that he was such a perfectionist. He wanted to have the scenes perfect. The trouble was, he'd have a whole bunch of camera people and extras standing around, on salary, running up the budget. Dad had to go in and talk with the people responsible for finance. And they were always jumping on him about overrunning [the] budget."

Feeling the pressure: a First National publicity picture from 1928.

William Jenner, production manager for the Langdon Corporation, endured a share of this abuse, but unlike Claude, he didn't feel obligated to stick around for more. Jenner resigned in September and Langdon appointed his publicity director, Don Eddy, to the post. Eddy, in turn, hired Weed Dickenson, formerly of United Artists, to assume his old job.

Meanwhile, Rowland assigned a studio manager to the company, ostensibly to watch over the budget, but Arthur Ripley soon discerned his true purpose. "Ripley informed me [the manager] was a spy for the front office," Gladys McConnell told Edward Watz. "I later learned he was to report back if Harry was trying to turn the comedy into a melodrama. There were complaints from exhibitors that *Three's a Crowd* wasn't funny enough, and so the studio expected

Harry Langdon to deliver a genuine comedy, with slapstick routines."

Under those conditions, it would have been nice if production could have proceeded without additional distraction. Unfortunately, like a bad penny, Tom O'Brien turned up again. Under the guise of a paternal visit, he spirited daughter Virginia away from her mother, while simultaneously declaring his intention to file a $250,000 alienation of affections suit against Langdon for "stealing Helen's love." The recent brouhaha over production, coupled with the anemic box office for *Three's a Crowd*, had already placed the comedian in a tenuous position with First National. He instantly realized that any publicity from O'Brien's threatened legal action would give them due cause to cancel his contract. Helen, of course, was bringing additional pressure to bear over her daughter's kidnapping.

Langdon immediately settled out of court, as O'Brien had no doubt expected. He handed over $15,000 cash; in return, O'Brien restored Virginia to Helen. Langdon also signed two promissory notes for an additional $11,500, his only stipulation being that they be made payable to O'Brien's lawyers rather than the man himself, so as to protect his reputation. At the time, it seemed a reasonable solution for all parties.

A few weeks after the O'Brien mess blew over, First National stunned the industry with an announcement that was essentially a vote of no confidence. *Variety* carried the scoop in its November 23 issue:

> First National will replace Harry Langdon's series of comedies with those produced by Douglas MacLean, if Langdon's current picture, "The Chaser," does not improve considerably over the previous features he has delivered ... First National feels Langdon is one of the best comedy bets in the business, but must be regulated to produce comedy features that meet market requirements and which would obtain wide distribution and grosses.
>
> If a satisfactory deal is made between First National and Langdon after his present contract expires, the releasing company will endeavor to make room for a series of two or three from MacLean, but if they do not get together with Langdon, MacLean will be moved in to take his place on the program.

Thus, even if *The Chaser* was a solid smash, Langdon would have a choice: remain with First National but surrender all creative and financial control, or take his act elsewhere. Not surprisingly, he began seeking a new distributor, with *Film Daily* reporting that United Artists was definitely interested.

Meanwhile, shooting progressed, and under First National's scrutiny, no gag was too old, odd or off-color to merit consideration. Old Roach and Sennett hand A. H. Giebler was engaged in November to

write the titles and contribute additional bits. "We had more gag men working on that picture than on *Three's a Crowd*," remembered McConnell, "and everyone was invited into the projection room to see the dailies. Everyone's ideas for some funny bit were carefully considered.

"My one contribution was when I suggested my mascara should run when I cry, after I believe Harry ran away from home. Harry thought that could be a human but also very funny bit, and everyone agreed. They filmed my face in this big close-up and the smeared makeup looked pretty grotesque! I was sorry then that I suggested the idea, but they left it in the picture."

The basic premise of the film was taken from the Sennett three-reeler *Saturday Afternoon*: Harry is a thoroughly henpecked husband, this time with a shrewish mother-in-law (Helen Hayward), who accuses him of "chasing" around with other women. In actuality, he's sneaking out to a roadhouse for some excitement, under the guise of attending a lodge meeting. Fed up with his behavior, wife (Gladys McConnell) and mother-in-law head for divorce court, presided over by Judge Limbsey (Charles Thurston, portraying what was intended as a jibe at Judge Ben Lindsey, a vocal proponent of "companionate marriage"; i.e., living together, as a means of reducing divorce and child custody problems). The judge decides that divorce "is not advisable in cases like this," and renders a "freak decision." Harry must dress and serve as "the wife" for thirty days.

His trials and tribulations while assuming this role fuel the comedy, some of which is in questionable taste. Ordered by Gladys to serve eggs for breakfast, Harry heads for the henhouse, grabs a chicken, holds it over a frying pan and waits. And waits. And waits. By the time he tries to force the egg out of his chosen hen, another chicken wanders under his dress (Harry is conveniently squatting) and lays an egg. Finally giving up, Harry stands, spots the egg beneath him and, like any badly written character, believes *he's* responsible.

Later in the film, a collections agent makes a visit regarding some unpaid merchandise. Harry retrieves the item, a baby carriage that has never been unwrapped, and gives it to the agent. He then recalls something else, and retrieves an unused training toilet seat, complete with chamber pot.

Still later, Harry, tired of being mistaken as the woman of the house and subsequently kissed (once on the mouth!) or propositioned by every male merchant in the picture, decides to end it all. He tries shooting himself, but the most impressive looking gun in the house is actually a water pistol. (And just whose is it? This couple has no children!) He opts for poison, but reaches instead for castor oil. Gulping it down, Harry lies on the kitchen floor awaiting death, but instead of eternal rest, his body feels an urgent need for a bathroom.

That's three "toilet" gags in a single film; all from the same comedian who, just three years earlier, was vetoing suggestions that seemed "a little shady," while proclaiming, "There are so many ways of getting legitimate laughs without getting raw about it."

Initial shooting completed during the first week of December, but after a preview at the Wilshire Theater in Los Angeles, some additional scenes were created. While filming these in the Verdugo Hills section near First National's Burbank studio, firemen were dispatched to a nearby forest fire. The Langdon company volunteered their assistance; unfortunately Langdon sustained minor burns in the process, and shooting was suspended for a few days.

At Langdon's invitation, Gladys McConnell attended the preview. "Harry had promised me that my role would not be trimmed, and I guess he

Harry stands safely behind Bud Jamison in The Chaser *(1928).*

figured if I came along I would see it for myself. I know the audience at the preview laughed quite a bit, but that's not always a guarantee you've got a successful picture."

Moving Picture World's Tom Waller attended a second preview at the Gateway Theater in Glendale, which resulted in a story about another Langdon innovation:

> Harry Langdon is reputed to have introduced a new one on filmdom — that of "clocking" laughs by the use of a dictograph.
>
> When Langdon previewed his latest comedy, "The Chaser," recently, he had three dictographs installed in the theatre for recording the

spectator's laughs so that they could be used as a reference chart in the final cutting of the picture.

The new Langdon comedy is based on a domestic theme and gives him plenty of opportunities for provoking laughs, giggles and chortles. Gladys McConnell has the leading feminine role, with Bud Jamison and Helen Hayward among those in the cast.

The dictograph "clocked" 267 laughs, which First National immediately used in its advertising as evidence that *The Chaser* was "funnier" than *The Strong Man*.

All retakes wrapped in the first week of January and Langdon, along with Don Eddy, took the final cut to New York on the 10th. Total negative cost came in at $261,040, Langdon once again personally footing the overage.

Later that week, First National, as required by state law, submitted *The Chaser* to the Motion Picture Commission of the State of New York for a seal of approval. The Commission maintained a censorship board that screened all films, and would either pass them without incident, or draw up a list of "eliminations" that were generally non-negotiable. Objectionable material fell within three categories: "Indecent," "Sacrilegious" and "[would tend to] Incite to Crime."

The Langdon films usually had little trouble passing the censors. Generally any complaints were minor: they didn't like the derogatory terms "Holy Joe" and "Psalm-singing idiot" as used in dialogue titles for *The Strong Man*, declaring them "sacrilegious"; they also objected to depicting the wet baby in *Three's a Crowd* as being "indecent."

However, after the board screened *The Chaser* on January 21, Langdon achieved a trifecta. Three days later, they sent the following eliminations list to First National:

REEL 1: *Change sub-titles: "In the beginning God created man in his own image" and "A little later he created woman."*

REEL 2: *In scene of Harry dressed as a woman holding hen over skillet — Eliminate rear view of Harry squatting on ground with skirt up where hen crawls under skirt.*

REEL 3: *Eliminate sub-title: "You don't seem to get along very well with your husband, do you?" (in connection with episode of bassinette and baby chair).*

Eliminate all views of baby chair after paper is removed from it.

Eliminate all views of chamber — including scene where Harry throws chamber at man and it lands on man's head.

In scene where Harry is contemplating suicide, eliminate all views of gun pointing directly at body and all views of Harry pouring contents of bottle marked poison into glass.

REEL 6: *Change sub-titles: "In the beginning God created man in his own image" and "A little later he created woman."*

The reasons for the above eliminations are that they are "sacrilegious," "indecent" and would tend to "incite to crime."

In a letter dated January 26, Samuel Lefkowitz, First National's office manager, cheerfully agreed to all cuts, adding:

We have made the following substitutions:

REEL 1: *Sub-title: "All men were created free and equal — but most of them get married."*

REEL 3: *Sub-title: "Your home is not a very happy one, is it?"*

We have also eliminated sub-titles in reel six, "In the beginning God created man in his own image" and "A little later he created woman."

Thus, the version of *The Chaser* as seen by New York residents — and presumably in other states with similar censorship boards — was approximately 150 feet and a few off-color gags shy of complete. The sensi-

bilities of the state's moviegoers were thus safeguarded, but one wonders if the reviews would have been different had the critics seen the entire film. As it is, First National's Manhattan picture palace, the Strand, opted to not book *The Chaser*; the film instead opened on Broadway at the Cameo, ordinarily a second-run house.

First National's advertising budget was the lowest yet — just a few hundred dollars shy of $10,000 — and all of it plugged *The Chaser* for its comedy:

"Latest Harry Langdon Comedy Based Exclusively on Laughs."

"The funniest film feast you've had in a month...."

"Will shake every laugh out of your funny bone!"
"Even funnier than the hits that made critics call him 'a genius.'"

"Will give you more laughs than any one picture this season!"

That turned out to be wishful thinking. Reviewers took one look at *The Chaser* and verbally sliced it to ribbons, starting with *Harrison's Reports*: "There are very few laughs in the would-be comical situations, and the interest is not aroused to any appreciable

degree ... Mr. Langdon seems to find pleasure in low comedy. In one scene he tries to make people laugh by putting a tin pan against the fat part of his back while he is a stooping position. In other scenes he introduces a baby chair, with pots and pans and the rest. These are the kinds of comedy attempts that were abandoned long ago."

From *Photoplay*: "*The Chaser* would seem to spell his doom as a leader in the screen comedy field. The picture is just a series of gags with little or no story. It concerns a henpecked husband with a nagging wife and a shrew of a mother-in-law. Several of the gags are rough.... If you miss this one you won't miss much."

From the *New York Herald-Tribune*: "It was not so long ago that a number of us were heralding Mr.

Langdon as one of the cinema elect; as virtually the legitimate successor of the mighty Mr. Chaplin. Today, unfortunately, we are forced to rush about in quest of alibis for our former ecstasy."

From the *New York Sun*: "The case of Harry Langdon is probably the saddest in the entire move clinic. With the attributes of the finest comedian of all at his command, he, somehow or other, has been guided along paths that are gagged to monotony ... [with] chases and the rest of the paraphernalia common to unimaginative slapstick."

From *Variety*: "No deluxe [downtown theater] will probably play the picture if they first see a couple of alleged comedy fun bits in it. For Langdon has some odd ideas about bathroom comedy ... Any screen comedian who thinks the castor oil and choking chicken bits are funny ... had better write idiotic after their names."

The editors of *The Film Mercury* summed it up for all the "New York writers" who had swooned over him nearly two years before: "It is heartbreaking to view the recent productions of Langdon, when we remember the superb performance of this comedian in *The Strong Man*. A few more films like this one and Langdon would have made the rest of the comedians worry about their popularity. Instead of living up to what he promised, we find reviews of his latest film, *The Chaser*, most unfavorable."

Welford Beaton, editor and publisher of *The Film Spectator*, agreed: "When I viewed *The Chaser* ... I found it such a pitiful thing that I refrained from reviewing it. Other screen writers were not so considerate. I know of no other picture that has been condemned so generally. I hope Harry reads all the criticisms and arrives at the conclusion that his last few pictures have forced the public to form: that he knows nothing whatsoever about film entertainment, and that to save what is left of his reputation, he should put himself in the hands of someone with such knowledge.... There was a time when he had the reputation for knowing something about acting. His lamentable failure as the master of his own destiny is creating the impression that he doesn't know much about anything."

Theater managers who ran the uncensored version lodged their complaints in the *Exhibitor's Herald*: "Absolutely the most vulgar, rotten, dirty, silly picture we have shown in the last 16 years. If producers are going to continue making pictures of this kind, here's hoping we get Federal censorship. Our patrons were disgusted with it and they told me so." "Positively vulgar. A very rotten comedy that had plenty of smut. Was funny at times but my patrons sure told me plenty when they went out." "Sequences which are intended to be humorous are based on plain muck. Patrons left in disgust."

The *Herald*'s critic asserted, "Only the past popularity of the star may draw the customers to the box-office window. The picture will get little word-of-mouth publicity. It has little to recommend it." In fact, word-of-mouth undoubtedly killed the picture. As of September 1929, *The Chaser* carried a loss of $187,541. It was the first Langdon feature where both domestic and foreign gross combined failed to exceed $350,000. Its total gross stood at less than $196,000, which didn't even equal the advance on production.

In December 1927, without knowing it, *Variety*'s "Along the Line" columnist 'Bland' hit upon the most plausible reason for *The Chaser*'s resounding failure: "Certain stars are the female's pets.... Harry Langdon plays to whole houses full of mothers. They feel 'Poor pale little thing!'" They also didn't want their intelligence insulted. If the attempted murder scene in *Long Pants* had damaged Langdon's relationship with this core following, *The Chaser* and its preponderance of unpleasant women and toilet humor utterly destroyed it.

Even so, Arthur Ripley's influence on Langdon held firm. Despite three consecutive box-office failures, the producer/director/star would not consider replacing his scenarist and story editor. No sooner had *The Chaser* been sent on its death march that the two were plotting out the next one. At least one trade paper announced that Ripley would direct the forthcoming film. If Langdon did offer him the job, Ripley either refused it or graciously surrendered screen credit to his boss and collaborator.

The story they concocted was set in 1917, and focused on Harry Van Hausen, a man of foreign descent, whose steady girlfriend expects him to enlist. Although he dreams of battlefield heroics, he's unfit for duty: too short, poor eyesight, flat feet and a weak heart. Another complication is that the U.S. is at war with his parents' homeland. Despite these and other setbacks, Harry becomes a hero when he stumbles into a plot surrounding a secret cache of weapons within his own hometown that are being smuggled to the enemy via submarines. He foils the plan and rescues an officer, both more by luck than design, and in the end is wed to his proud girl.

Langdon made a conscientious effort to control costs. Elgin Lessley was released; the crack cameraman returned to Buster Keaton, filming the comedian's first for M.G.M., *The Cameraman*. After that, Lessley left films to care for his ailing wife, Blanche, who was suffering from Wernicke's disease, a thiamine deficiency usually associated with alcoholism, to which she would succumb in 1931. Lessley apparently grieved for the rest of his life; he never returned to work. He died in 1944, at age 52, of heart failure compounded by his own alcohol abuse.

Langdon even sought cheaper studio space. Metropolitan Studios put in an attractive bid, but First National's Richard Rowland — probably not wanting Langdon's production unit to be more than a two-minute walk from his office — made price concessions to keep the comedian on the home lot.

In other matters, though, he was as financially reckless as ever. Gladys McConnell had requested her release in late January, which was granted, so a new leading lady was required. Langdon initially opted for a former colleague, Alma Bennett of *Long Pants*, to play against type as Harry's sincere girl friend. Although not yet ready to shoot, he kept Bennett on salary for five weeks. Then a relatively new contract player, red-haired Doris Dawson, caught Langdon's eye in a bit part, and he decided she was better suited to portray his love interest. Bennett was subsequently released without having stepped before the camera.

Dawson had been in pictures less than two years, beginning in 1926 as a Sennett girl, purely by luck and timing. "A girl I had known in New York was working at the Mack Sennett studio," she recalled in 1929. "I went to lunch with her one day and then went back to the studio to watch her work. They were shooting swimming scenes and needed some girls who could dive. My chum, knowing that I could, said that she would get me a job working in the picture. I declined at first, since I had never before given a thought to entering pictures. However, she urged me on and said we would have a lot of fun, so I went to work."

After six months with Sennett, Dawson signed as a leading lady for Al Christie, made a handful of shorts and then opted to freelance. At that point,

Doris Dawson is the cause of Harry's Heart Trouble *(1928)*.

work dried up. "I was just about to give up and go home [to New York]. I had already wired Daddy for money and bought my ticket when I got a call from First National. After waiting several days, I got a contract and wired Daddy that I was staying here." In a reversal of the norm, Dawson would be selected as a WAMPAS Baby Star the year *after* co-starring with Langdon.

Aside from the studio rental incident, there was no production interference from First National this time around. By the time filming was to start, the company had not so much surrendered control over Langdon as washed their hands of him. Once box-office figures for *The Chaser*'s first eight weeks were in, and made clear that it wouldn't do as well as *Three's a Crowd*, much less *The Strong Man*, the decision had been made for them. On April 3, the press was told that First National would not be renewing his contract.

At least Langdon's home life held no unpleasant surprises. Los Angeles Superior Court Judge Sproul granted Rose Langdon's divorce on April 28, on charges of cruelty and desertion. In her complaint, Rose asked the court to order her now ex-husband to remit the agreed-upon $70,000 property settlement, of which exactly $0 had been paid so far. Langdon began making payments, and as soon as another year,

as mandated by California's divorce laws, had passed, each of the one-time "Auto Langdons" would be free to wed new partners.

The only downside was an unfortunate accident in which Claude Langdon was injured by a faulty light. "At times he would go and help out on a set," son Don recalled in 1997. "Klieg lights were arranged above, and Dad was up there, looking them over. He heard a click and turned around to see what it was. One of the pins was loose, and he was practically looking right into the thing when it blew up in his face. He had surgery, but it got worse and they had to remove one eye, so after that he had a glass eye." By 1929, Claude had returned with his family to Council Bluffs and resumed working in the grocery store business.

On May 9, as production was winding down, an interesting item appeared from Dan Thomas, syndicated Hollywood columnist for the Newspaper Enterprise Association: "Harry Langdon was telling me the other day that his current film, as yet untitled, will be the best one he has ever made. Let's hope so as he hasn't made a good picture or a box-office success since *The Strong Man*. Unless his present production 'clicks,' the comedian in all probability will be through at First National — and a new release will be difficult to find. It's really a shame to see a comedian of Langdon's ability slip the way he's slipping. Harry's chief trouble is that he wants to be star, director, writer and gag man. And he won't listen to criticism from his staff, some of whom realize his predicament and could pull him out of it."

Evidently, Thomas was unaware that First National had already decided to drop Langdon the previous month. On May 31, he published a follow-up: "Just as we predicted in this column a short time ago, Harry Langdon is through at First National. It is understood that the comedian will go back to making two-reelers again. And he has only himself to blame. Langdon is truly funny. But he is so self-centered that he thinks he knows everything there is to know about making comedies. He won't listen to anybody. As a result, his feature-length productions have failed to draw the required number of laughs and box-office receipts."

Up to that point, Langdon's bad press had been mostly generic: he was just one of several comedians whose attempts to emulate Chaplin by producing and directing themselves didn't translate into critical or financial success. Only *Variety*'s column of March 9, 1927 inferred that Langdon's ego was being discussed in studio corridors, and in that piece the comedian's name was never mentioned. Thomas was the first journalist to call out Langdon publicly for conceit.

Other columnists filed similar pieces that same month, such as the *New York Sun*'s Eileen Creelman: "Two years ago, the baby-faced comedian made his first feature length comedy, which, unfortunately for Mr. Langdon, and for First National, was heralded by the critics as a rival to Chaplin films. Mr. Langdon was impressed. He decided to dispense with director and gagmen. His most recent pictures, written and directed by himself, have slid rapidly downward." Creelman got in another dig a few days later in an article about Langdon's former director: "Frank Capra, whose presence from the First National is mourned by all former admirers of Harry Langdon, is to desert comedy for a time. It was under Mr. Capra's direction that Langdon made his first feature comedies before deciding to take entire charge of his pictures. Capra has since joined Columbia for which he is about to make a melodrama, *The Way of the Strong*."

Capra's letter about Langdon's star trip had been written over a year earlier. It's possible Dan Thomas was a recipient, but he also knew Langdon personally during that time, as witness this item from September 1927: "Whenever Harry Langdon is in deep thought, he always makes pencil sketches of various objects.... While out at his house a few nights ago, I noticed sketches on the flyleaves and covers of many books and discovered a drawing on practically every page of the telephone directory. When the comedian wants to draw, he picks up the handiest object, regardless of what it is."

Was Thomas's assertion about Langdon's self-centeredness based on firsthand knowledge, a secondary source such as Capra, or both? There's no convenient answer. The upshot, though, was a reputation that hung over Langdon's head for a few years to come, and would forever taint his legacy.

The "as yet untitled" picture went through a couple of title changes. Production began as "Volunteers," then "Here Comes the Band" was chosen around the time shooting completed; exhibitor contracts were actually drawn up under the latter title. Because First National wished to play up the romance angle of the story in the advertising (presumably to woo back those "whole houses full of mothers"), at the last minute the film was christened *Heart Trouble*.

Langdon brought in the negative cost at $214,053, which ordinarily would have been cause for rejoicing given his contractual $260,000 advance. Unfortunately, owing to a deal he'd cut in July 1927, the $50,037 that was overspent on *Tramp, Tramp, Tramp*'s negative was to be deducted from the advance for this film, which meant he actually went *over* budget by $4,090.

Neither First National nor Langdon were interested in prolonging the inevitable. In June 1928, after handing over *Heart Trouble*'s negative, he quietly dissolved his company by selling all its assets to First National for a flat $5,000. At the time it was a bargain: fifteen months later, the books would be closed on the Harry Langdon Corporation at an overall loss of $511,497.

Langdon cashed out while First National was in upheaval, along with practically every other Hollywood film factory, over talkies. Sound had captured the public's fancy beginning in October 1927, almost from the moment Al Jolson spoke on screen in *The Jazz Singer*, which had been only a part-talkie. Warner Bros. had produced that film using Western Electric's Vitaphone sound-on-disc system. By the summer of 1928, Vitaphone was being challenged by RCA's Photophone; meanwhile, Western Electric's parent company, Electrical Research Products, had introduced a sound-on-film method called Movietone.

In early June, after William Fox attempted a hostile takeover, First National's board of directors reached out to Joseph P. Kennedy to serve as business advisor. Kennedy had been the head of the Film Box Office (F.B.O.) Corporation, and had recently arranged a merger with that company and the Keith-Orpheum theater circuit. He'd also signed a deal to utilize RCA's Photophone system, and the combination of all these interests would soon result in a new entity: Radio-Keith-Orpheum (later R.K.O. Radio) Pictures. The board members, who had pooled their stock holdings into an escrow account, offered Kennedy an option for up to 25 percent ownership over five years, which he accepted in late July.

Kennedy's first edict was for a 40 percent cut in production overhead. After outlining his blueprint for accomplishing this during a meeting of First National executives, immediate concerns were raised over the quality of the resulting pictures. An executive committee outlined its own cost-reduction plan, and also sought to reduce some of Kennedy's authority. Kennedy insisted on full corporate control; when the committee wouldn't budge, he resigned.

Meanwhile, Warner Bros. released their first all-talking Vitaphone production, *The Lights of New York*.

At the Strand in Manhattan (a First National-owned theater), the film grossed a whopping $50,000 during a week in which the weather alternated between stifling humidity or rain. The company was flush with success and cash, with net income for the first nine months of its fiscal year reaching $1,123,947. Warner stock acquired a blue chip rating. Both Paramount and Fox made offers to purchase Warner Bros. outright, with bids reaching up to $20 million at one point.

Not one week after Kennedy bowed out, rumors circulated that the Brothers Warner would be purchasing the Stanley Theater chain, and thus would end up controlling First National. Although denials were publicly issued on both sides, talks progressed behind the scenes, and the deal with Stanley was completed on September 12. Twelve days later, the Warners purchased 42,000 shares of First National stock for $3,800,000, giving them a controlling interest. Although each would maintain separate identities for a few more years, the two studios were now essentially one company.

Lost in the midst of all this turmoil was *Heart Trouble*. A mere $1,000 was allocated to advertising. Only $8,762 was spent on positives, which translated to about 90 prints, half as many as were struck for *Long Pants*. (The average for First National was about 140-150 positives.) It played in Manhattan for *one day*, as half of a double bill; for this reason, no New York-based critic other than *Variety*'s bothered to review it. In most cities, it had the misfortune of playing at the same time as *The Singing Fool*, Warner Bros.' second Al Jolson film (and Jolson's first all-talkie), which did even better business than *The Jazz Singer* and *The Lights of New York*.

Variety's review may have been the most charitable, its critic calling it "one of the best of the few he has made during the past two years. It can stand up without a supporting feature for a short run in any house. [Langdon] does less of the emoting he gave way to in his last two. He abandons to a great extent his ambition to be the complex of a tragedienne and a comedian.... That he is directing himself is less obvious."

Others were not as kind. "All the real laugh sequences could be boiled down into a two-reel comedy," wrote *Film Daily*. "That is what is wrong with it — strung out to make a feature when it did not have the material to make the feature comedy grade." *Photoplay* was especially harsh: "Just a lot of silly gags, no story and enough inane situations to spell the exit of Harry Langdon. It was his cue to give us a good picture. He didn't." *Exhibitor's Herald* also chimed in: "This can hardly be considered more than ordinary comedy and far away from the standard promised by the earliest of Langdon's feature releases. The laughs are scattered and the story is weak."

Most exhibitors passed on the film, which prompted a stern letter directed at the sales managers from Ned E. Depinet of First National's home

office on November 7, after the dust had settled from the acquisition:

TO ALL MANAGERS:

It has always been the policy of First National, in distributing pictures of outside producers, to use its best efforts in the utmost of good faith to obtain the largest gross rentals and the largest number of rental contracts that can be obtained by diligent, fair and efficient distribution of such pictures.

I want to call this to the attention of every manager with particular emphasis upon the following Langdon pictures:

*Aug. 28, 1927: Three's a Crowd
Feb. 12, 1928: The Chaser
July 29, 1928: Heart Trouble*

which are included in our Showman's Group. I want you to continue this policy with respect to the pictures of this producer till the very end of our contract. I want these pictures to receive the same undivided attention that we give all of our pictures. You should place each and every picture in every unsold spot, and, further, instruct your booker to insist upon playing time in proper order of availability and not to allow exhibitors to pass these pictures up for one reason or another.

Please issue the necessary instructions to your staff with respect to this matter.

That such a letter was even necessary spoke to the precipitous decline to which Langdon's popularity had succumbed. Further evidence came that same month when Pathé dumped its final unreleased Langdon short, *Soldier Man*, unheralded into the marketplace, where not a single trade publication bothered to review it.

When the books were closed at the end of September 1929, *Heart Trouble*'s total domestic gross was $134,989, and the foreign gross a miserable $17,435. The final figure reported was a loss of $199,708. Even so, Warner Bros. kept those 90 prints in circulation for as long as they could, until the film had run in every possible remote outpost that hadn't yet wired for sound. Its last known exhibition was on April 18, 1931 at the Goenelg Theater in Adelaide, Australia, almost three years after the demise of the Langdon Corporation. In 1953, the negative was deemed unsalvageable due to decomposition and was junked. Today, all that exists of *Heart Trouble* are still photos, the pressbook and the cutting continuity (see Appendix V, page 646, for an illustrated synopsis).

As for Langdon, he received no further overtures from United Artists, Pathé or any other studio. At the time, he blamed bad luck and poor business decisions for his fall from grace, but after a decade of reflection, hard work and few professional successes, the comedian became more philosophic. "I thought I was smart, but I was a fool. I went to the top… made a mess of things and faded out of the business," he would say in 1938. "No one could tell me I was on the wrong foot. I had to find it out myself."

As proof, he'd bring up *The Chaser* and *Heart Trouble*, labeling them "absolute stinkers" and "two of the lousiest pictures ever made." To Associated Press columnist Dan Deluce he confided, "They were so bad I never went to the [premieres]. I took one look at them in the projection room and was sick."

In the end, Langdon agreed with all the critics and exhibitors of ten years before: "They were terrible [pictures]. And they finished Harry Langdon as a movie star."

CHAPTER ELEVEN

"None of That High-Handed Stuff"

1928–1930

For the moment, motion pictures were closed to him. Studio heads were in a tizzy, converting stages and wiring theaters for sound, putting contract players through tests in front of microphones and scouring New York stages for potential replacements. Employing a master of delicate comic pantomime with four consecutive flops to his name was last on their to-do lists.

On the other hand, vaudeville was delighted to welcome Harry Langdon home.

Even before wrapping up *Heart Trouble*, Langdon, through the William Morris agency, made it known that he'd be happy to return to the stage for the right price; specifically $5,000 per week. The news reached Fanchon Simon and Marco Wolff, a brother-sister dance team who had graduated from vaudeville to establish their own production company in the mid-1920s. Fanchon & Marco specialized in creating live prologues of music and dance that were performed ahead of the feature film in various Los Angeles movie theaters. Their prologues were billed as "Ideas"; one of these, "The Feast of the Lanterns Idea," had preceded *Long Pants* during its run at Loew's State.

The pair also assembled their own touring companies, which were sent out to both movie and vaudeville houses along the coast.

On August 28 — barely two weeks after the release of *Heart Trouble* — the trade press announced that Fanchon & Marco had booked Langdon for a three-week tour, meeting his asking price and sweetening the deal with 50 percent of the gross above house average. He would not be incorporated into the F&M stage show (a musical fantasy entitled "A Trip to Mars"), but used as an additional headliner, expected to provide his own material. Unfortunately, as part of their property settlement, his balky automobile belonged to Rose, lock, stock and carburetor, along with all the gags and situations. He needed to write a new turn, and emerged with fifteen minutes of full-stage nonsense entitled *The Messenger*.

The tour began in Seattle, Washington, on September 24, then to Portland, Oregon, and lastly San Francisco. In Portland, Langdon was met at the station by the mayor, chief of police and several civic leaders, and received five invitations for breakfast while traveling to his hotel.

An unnamed critic for the *Motion Picture Herald*'s "Vaudeville Reviews" section caught Langdon's return to the stage in Seattle: "Making his first Seattle visit and serving as a forerunner of bigger attractions, under arrangements with Fanchon and Marco — Harry Langdon is this week admitted by capacity audiences to be funnier on the stage than on the screen. His act is highly diverting."

Variety's "Edwards" covered opening night at the Warfield Theater in San Francisco on October 8:

> Harry Langdon's return to the stage, this time as a special Fanchon & Marco feature for a limited tour of West Coast theatres. The screen comic is supported by Mia Marvin, charming, and an unprogrammed gal who plays a silent bit. It is preceded by announcement and trailer showing scenes of some of Langdon's screen comedy.
>
> Set is an elaborate interior. Langdon, as a goof, delivers a note to the sweetheart of one Jack. Business of forgetting object of call, for laughs. When gal gets note from her admirer, she essays to vamp Harry and there is a red-hot kiss scene.
>
> "Jack" phones he is on his way over. Business of Langdon trying to get away, but stopped by

the gal. She wraps her arms about him as knock sounds on door. The expected "Jack" turns out to be Langdon's "wife."

Hilarious hokum, with the screen actor at home in his talking role. A sure-fire skit. As arranged, act would fit picture or vaude house.

According to *Variety*, the box-office take was above average for all engagements, for which Langdon received full credit. Three more cities were quickly booked: Detroit, St. Louis and Chicago. None of this escaped the notice of a studio executive who'd courted him at least once before.

Times had changed for Hal Roach since tendering his first offer to Langdon, all for the good. After seeing that Pathé was openly favoring Mack Sennett's product over his, Roach signed a distribution deal with Metro-Goldwyn-Mayer, which commenced in 1927. It was a fortuitous move on both sides: Roach's films were assured of placement in the mighty Loew's theater chain, and M.G.M. were beneficiaries of the resounding success achieved by Roach's newly minted comedy team, Stan Laurel and Oliver Hardy, who were to loom large in Langdon's story a few years hence.

Still, Roach was never satisfied to be merely a producer of short subjects, regardless of their popularity. He'd had a taste of feature film success with both Harold Lloyd and a handful of westerns starring "Rex, the Wonder Horse," and was always chasing that horizon. With Langdon available, he saw another opportunity. In mid-October, he proffered a deal for a series of four-reel comedies that would be silent with synchronized scores, with filming to begin in January 1929, to which Langdon agreed.

Roach, however, failed to take two things into account. First was the unexpected success of — and demand for — talking pictures. He was still producing silent comedies, and his players were primarily visual comedians, extremely popular among exhibitors and the public. Only one month before reaching out to Langdon, Roach was quoted in *Motion Picture News*: "There isn't the slightest chance that dialogue ever will entirely displace pantomime on the screen. Dialogue can't possibly take the place of pantomime in causing laughs. There is no doubt, however, that sound synchronization of the score will be a great help to comedy subjects."

In other words, while Roach was willing to embrace the technology of sound, he wasn't convinced that "talkies" and screen comedy were meant to cohabitate. The marketplace persuaded him otherwise.

Second, M.G.M. was not as open to the idea of Roach-produced feature films as Pathé had been. Theirs was a self-contained film factory with their own ambitious feature program, and their contract with Roach was for two-reel shorts. (In fact, M.G.M. would twice borrow Laurel & Hardy during 1929 for

Langdon in October 1928 while on tour in the Northwest.

supporting parts in feature films.) Although Roach probably expected the four-reel length to be acceptable, M.G.M. was decidedly uninterested in any Harry Langdon "features."

Reports appeared in the trades and newspaper columns that Langdon arrived for work in January only to find Roach had closed his studio for three months in order to convert it for talking pictures, and that having turned down lucrative stage work, the understandably furious comedian tore up his contract. In fact, Langdon never signed this contract, which remained in his files for years after his passing. Roach did shut down his studio for soundstage construction in January, which only took about four weeks, while Langdon went back to the stage. Both sides expected to work together in some capacity before too long.

The William Morris agency submitted Langdon to the Keith-Orpheum circuit, but the latter balked at a $5,000 weekly salary. The two sides dickered through most of January, and an acceptable compromise was reached: $3,500 per week. Just in time, too, as Langdon was about to be sued by the federal government for $3,862 in unpaid taxes, based on profits his corporation was asserted to have realized in 1927. Apparently the fact that profits on *The Strong Man* were swallowed up by losses incurred on *Tramp, Tramp, Tramp* and *Long Pants* made no difference to Uncle Sam.

On February 3, Langdon began a tour of Keith-Albee theaters on the East Coast with *The Messenger* skit, opening at the 86th Street Theater accompanying a Universal talkie, *The Last Warning*. *Variety*'s "Rush" caught the Sunday evening show: "Straightaway vaude show made into a gala event by the comedy of Harry Langdon in a hoke sketch called *The Messenger* and new hereabouts. No question about the 'Lillian Gish of slapstick' being a draw. They were packed in to the last inch Sunday night by 7:30. Capacity is the rule here for that evening, but this was capacity plus...

"Langdon [presented] 16 minutes of unbroken laughter. This is his return to the stage after some half dozen years in flickers. He brings his amusing character of boob boy to the sketch, played with two unprogramed (*sic*) women and a roar. Sketch is a fast 11 minutes supplemented by five more minutes in one. Skit is the same as done last fall on the coast in one of the Fanchon & Marco Ideas. Has a riotous incident when the girl tries to vamp Harry who resists or yields with hilarious embarrassment. Some spicy bits here which heighten the frolic." (The "spicy bits" would have a considerably different impact outside of New York.)

In its February 27 issue, *Variety* reported that Langdon "is said to have received two offers for talkers. One is for full-length comedies, with three to be made within a year. The other is for talking shorts, not less than eight within the year. Langdon is reported undecided, not accepting either further vaude dates beyond a few weeks nor either of the talker proffers."

There was no question, though, that he wanted another chance in films. "Getting his voice in shape for the talkies," was the reason he returned to the stage, according to press reports. Speaking with a *Harvard Crimson* reporter, he observed, "Talking

Langdon's self-drawn Christmas card of 1928.

pictures are a howling success…[yet] the talkies are now just in their infancy. If one compares the automobile of 20 years ago to the present model, and then judges the talkies by the same rate of development, one can imagine what they will soon amount to."

Following the 86th Street, there were weeks in Newark, New Jersey (at Proctor's), and in Brooklyn (at the Albee). By then, he'd at least decided to accept one of his picture offers, although he wouldn't specify which one. *Brooklyn Eagle* columnist Rian James wrote, "See Harry (Flicker) Langdon, who has gone temporarily Vaude, at the Albee this week, chiefly because Mr. Langdon is every bit as oompah in the flesh as he is in the flickers. Harry Langdon, as it happens, is one of the few big 'names' whom we sincerely like. This chiefly because there's nothing of the 'ham' about him. He's quiet, restrained, gentlemanly — almost serious — and unlike most of his vocational brethren and sistern, his chief fear isn't that everybody won't recognize him, but that somebody will. Too, with the single exception of Charles Spencer Chaplin, Harry Langdon is our very favorite comic. Hence we were pleased as anything when he told us, over at the Paramount Grill the other night, that he goes to work on another flock of pictures again in May."

After a week in Boston, Langdon returned to Manhattan, and its famed Palace, on March 17, although it wasn't as triumphant as he would've liked. Frank Fay, who had starred in *Jim Jam Jems* all those years ago, was the headliner, ably assisted by his wife, Barbara Stanwyck; Langdon took second place on the bill. Also appearing was El Brendel with his then-partner Flo Bert. Brendel would soon bring his "dumb Swede" (*Variety*'s term) to Fox's Movietone productions, but it's a cinch neither he nor Langdon imagined that fate would one day partner them on a soundstage.

The *New York Times* didn't think much of *The Messenger*: "Langdon is a variety droll who, in recent years, has found favor in the films, to which his comedic gifts of pantomime and expression are especially suited. The sketch in which he displays himself at the Palace does not show these talents to best advantage, and certainly it could reasonably be expected to be a little funnier." Neither was *Variety*'s "Bige" impressed: "Harry Langdon opened the second [half] in his parlor skit, *The Messenger*, an act that, as an act, is 'way short of the talents of its principal player…Langdon would have done vastly better by returning to his old and well-remembered auto skit. Following the full stage action, which was laughless except for Harry's facial business, Langdon appeared before the drape for five minutes of intimate talk and topped off with a comedy dance. That dance, lasting about a minute, brought more response than all of the preceding 17 minutes."

Variety's "Among the Women" columnist was more favorable: "Harry Langdon's return to vaude, after his sojourn in pictures, should be of plenty interest to the local musical comedy producers. If ever a comic were a sure bet for productions, Langdon is the one. A corking natural comedian with a pantomimic sense and a very unique appeal." The comedian, however, wasn't entertaining offers from Broadway.

Two notable events occurred during the run. On Tuesday the 19th, Langdon made his radio debut from New York's NBC station, WEAF, as part of the network's "RKO Program." It's not clear what his contribution was, but the show included others from the Palace bill. At the end of the week, *Photoplay*'s Leonard Hall paid Langdon a visit "disguised as a Big Reel and Sprocket Man from Culver City." His superlative-laden article was published in the June issue under the title "Hey! Hey! Harry's Coming Back."

"Harry Langdon, if God is good, is coming back to pictures! It's a new Langdon we'll see, too — A Harry with a well-deflated skull, a head full of smart ideas and a soul that bulges with pepper, hope and the old confy!

"He had just wound up a red-hot week at the Palace Theater — which is to the vaudeville actor what Heaven is to the hell-bent…. Langdon's vaudeville act, as far as words went, was a weak sister. No, why quibble? It was terrible. But the star, using all the quaint, helpless mannerisms that made him famous in the flickers, was tremendous. In short, it was his superb film pantomime that put him over…

"We all remember the yarns that were whispered at the time of his box-office collapse — of how he had tried to write, supervise, direct and act — of how he suffered from night sweats, galloping ego, growing pains above the ears, and delusions of grandeur…. Don't ask me whether or not little doughface suffered from an inflated cranium. Harry himself says it was his tough luck. His producers, he declares, began clamping down on him as the doubloons started to slip away.…"

Among the "smart ideas" Langdon shared with Hall: "I believe that the day of the long gag comedy,

with the whole picture depending on the efforts of a starred comedian, is over. A kick in the pants isn't as funny in pictures as it was in 1910. The gag field has been worked bare. The story is the thing of today and tomorrow — the laugh picture with a tale to tell. Furthermore, no living comic can carry the whole burden of a seven-reel comedy and make it one long howl. No man can be that funny and live. He must have the help of a good story and two or three all-wool featured actors to help him play it."

After New York's Palace, it was on to Chicago's Palace, opening on April 1. Sime Silverman, *Variety*'s founder, who'd covered Langdon off-and-on since the *Night on the Boulevard* days, reviewed the opening: "Langdon is doing well enough for a draw name. He has nothing but himself in this little skit with two women. He finishes it off with an encore, also light. The house liked Langdon, probably on his picture comic rep. He is too capable a performer, stage and screen, not to be able to take care of himself under any condition."

Silverman made another observation: "To someone leaving town before this is printed, it remains a question if the Palace direction ordered out at least two of Ethel Waters' dirty songs after the Sunday matinee, or Harry Langdon's dirt gag, and, of course, his best laugh." As it happens, the house manager did order the gag — whatever it was — dropped from the act, but after appealing to Keith's New York booking office, Langdon restored it two days later.

After Chicago came a week at the Palace Orpheum in Milwaukee, which must have left Langdon uneasy, given that Rose's Catholic family was still living there (the divorce was just a few weeks from being finalized). This was followed by a week at Keith's Palace in Cleveland, where *The Messenger*'s "spicy bits" led to a brush with the law. It started on Monday, April 16, with William F. McDermott — another critic with a long memory — and his review for the *Cleveland Plain Dealer*:

Note on Vulgarity
Harry Langdon, better known as a film comic, and headline man on the current Keith Palace bill, knows his way about in vaudeville and could get along well enough on the

three-a-day stages without the momentum of his picture popularity.

He is also too experienced and adroit a comedian to have need of the vulgarities of which his present act is composed. It has all the delicate horsy flavor of an old-fashioned burlesque show when the police were not looking. Vulgarity is its first name, its middle name, and its last name, and it is nothing else.

Such stuff would not be permitted to permeate the night air at a respectable stag sociable, nor to smudge the screen in a picture honky-tonk. [Yet] it seems to be all right in a great family theater, among Mr. Albee's Corots, Israels and needlepoint tapestries.

The morning Mr. McDermott's column hit Cleveland's breakfast tables, the police department's Safety Director, Edwin D. Barry, received "about 50 telephone calls complaining about the act," as reported in the next day's *Plain Dealer*. It's unknown if these callers had actually attended the show or merely read McDermott's review. Barry sent a policewoman, Capt. Dorothy Doan Henry, to that day's afternoon matinee with instructions to report back. "As a result of her report," said *Variety*'s April 24 issue, "Frank Hines, manager of the Palace, got hauled up on the official carpet…. The meeting almost ended in a fight, with the big shot of the police force making it a personal issue against Hines and his theatre." According to the *Plain Dealer*, the exchange went like this:

BARRY: This is the first time we ever had any complaint about the Palace Theater. I'm telling you now to get that act of Harry Langdon's out of the show. It's vulgar and indecent.

HINES: You mean to take out his objectionable material?

BARRY: Yes, and that'll about take him out. If you don't, we'll take him out.

HINES: Would you mind telling me what lines are objectionable? We don't want to run an indecent show.

BARRY: We'll not tell you how to run your show.

HINES: But what might seem objectionable to me might not be regarded as objectionable by other people.

BARRY: That is the dirtiest, filthiest act ever put on in that theater. If John Royal *[previous manager of the theater, later a vice president of NBC]* was there, he wouldn't have permitted it.

HINES: John Royal saw the show Sunday afternoon.

Fuming, Barry ordered Hines to cut the dirt out of *The Messenger* or he'd shut down the entire bill for the rest of the week. Heading for the door, Hines replied, "I want you to know that I'll cooperate with you 100 percent. But I resent your attitude. You seem to be trying to make it a personal issue with me. The acts are sent here. I don't prepare them."

According to *Variety*, "At the next performance, several of Langdon's worst gags were cut, in spite of the fact that it was originally reported the act originally consisted of 75 percent dirt. Policewomen were assigned to cover the show for the rest of the week, but apparently they were satisfied."

With that, Langdon returned to Hollywood and Helen. On May 6, he was involved in an auto collision that resulted in serious injury for the other driver, Leon Sturgeon, and minor injuries for Sturgeon's passenger, Miss Christine Hirschman. "Police of the University Division, who reported the collision, said that the accident was unavoidable and did not hold Langdon," read a news account the next day. This wouldn't deter Sturgeon from filing a lawsuit some months later.

Lavina Langdon quietly passed away on May 29. She had never spoken to the press, not even during the heights of her son's fame, and remains an enigma to Langdon scholars. No doubt Harry loved her, even if he didn't always appreciate her religious scruples. She was laid to rest in Grandview Memorial Park in Glendale; within 24 years, four of her children would be joining her there.

Two days after Lavina's passing, Metro-Goldwyn-Mayer announced that Langdon had signed with Hal Roach. "Under the terms of his five-year contract," read the press release, "Langdon will appear in eight two-reel dialogue comedies each year, all of which pictures are on the Metro-Goldwyn-Mayer program. Langdon will join the Roach personnel which already includes, besides the Our Gang unit, Charley Chase, Stan Laurel and Oliver Hardy."

The announcement coincided with the publication of Leonard Hall's *Photoplay* article, while a much different piece appeared in the June issue of *Picture Play*, another magazine for movie fans. "Their Chaplin

Complex," by Nat Dyches, was a vicious, sarcastic tome that took every other screen comedian but one to task: "The other comedians know that Chaplin is his own director; know that every phase of a Chaplin comedy bears the stamp of his individual touch — they all know and aspire to the same impossible feat. And in the face of that impossibility, they rush to their doom like sheep plunging over a cliff in a blind rush after the bellwether. Their every move, it seems, must be made with one green eye on Chaplin."

Only Harold Lloyd got a pass from Dyches, because "Lloyd has brains. Any man who is big enough to listen to the advice of his subordinates has brains…. The lowliest underling at Lloyd's studio can gain his ear. Any suggestion for a gag or situation, be it even from an office boy, gets kindly consideration from the star. And if it is a good suggestion — miracle of miracles! — it is accepted."

Dyches proceeded to beat a dead horse, in turns castigating and taunting Buster Keaton, Raymond Griffith and even Clyde Cook, all of whom by then had given up — or lost — their own production units and were now mere studio contract players. As for Langdon, Dyches wrote, "Each star of comedy has one trait in which he approaches Chaplin. Harry Langdon has the pathos. There is something about this actor which makes one instinctively sorry for him. Unfortunately, Langdon insists on being sorry for himself. Where Chaplin is wistful, Langdon must be mournful. His mirth must be plunged into the murk of darkest tragedy — like Hamlet wise-cracking as he sticks a dagger into his hated uncle's gizzard. Tragedy is the Langdon obsession, hence one of the most talented graduates from two-reel ranks finds himself no longer on the screen.

"Langdon no doubt has been informed of his mistake. And there is this about Harry — he will listen. Oh, charmingly listen! Most gallantly, Prince Harry will give ear to his scenario men and advisers in the conference room — then go out forthwith and forget all that was said." Had he read this, Arthur Ripley would have begged to differ.

Dyches's snide essay is easily dismissible today, as time and tastes have since validated the artistic choices of most of its targets. But it's worth noting here for one reason. Langdon's Roach contract had been negotiated by the William Morris agency. When he was finally introduced to Hal Roach, his new boss reportedly greeted him with, "Now, see here, Langdon, none of that high-handed stuff you pulled at First National."

In 1932, *Photoplay*'s Katherine Albert cited this as an example of the fallout from Frank Capra's infamous letter about Langdon's ego trip. But assuming Roach made the remark, it's much more likely he was addressing the philosophical Langdon of yore; the comedian who, influenced by Ripley, pontificated to the press about the importance of pathos and released *Long Pants* and *Three's a Crowd*, in which the comedy

Langdon, Lew Foster and Hal Roach on the set of the Harry Langdon Announcement, *June 1929.*

was indeed "plunged into the murk of darkest tragedy."

M.G.M., too, wanted assurances that Roach's new employee would toe the mark; they were, after all, advancing the production money. This led to an unusual response. Langdon's *The Messenger* (presumably minus the spiciest "spicy bits") was to serve as the basis for his initial Roach two-reeler. The team created a variant of the opening scene, along with a short coda, and the result was a seven-minute "introduction" intended solely for M.G.M. brass.

Harry calls on "Mrs. Quimby" (Thelma Todd) to deliver a message; in the process, he asks her a series of embarrassing questions about her husband, Mr. Quimby (a nod to Fred Quimby, head of M.G.M.'s short subject sales department). Gradually, he gets to the point, asking Mrs. Quimby if she would "raise a rumpus" if her husband came home intoxicated. "I don't think so," she replies. "You sure you wouldn't slap him right in the face?" "Oh, no," says Mrs. Quimby. Satisfied, Harry drags in the disheveled, thoroughly drunk man he believes is Mr. Quimby (Eddie Dunn), who slurs, "Hello, honey!" Mrs. Quimby exclaims, "Why, Mr. Feist!" (Felix Feist, another M.G.M. sales executive) and the shocked Harry hastily drags him out of the house.

After a fade, the film returns to the set. Dunn reenters and addresses the viewers directly: "Gentlemen, if you'll just permit me to sort of step out of my character for a moment, I have an announcement to make. Mr. Roach has requested me to tell you folks out there that he has added another star to his already well-known firmament. A very great star, in fact: Mr. Harry Langdon. Mr. Roach has the greatest confidence in the world in Mr. Langdon, and I know that Harry is with Mr. Roach heart and soul."

Although the film ends on a gag — Harry and Thelma in a passionate embrace, causing Dunn some embarrassment — the intended message was clear and brutal: Langdon will follow orders.

Although not intended for public consumption, the film (restored by UCLA's Film and Television Archive and released to DVD in 2007) *is* Langdon's first "talkie" and the earliest example of how he must have sounded to vaudeville audiences at least since the start of the 1920s. Much of his dialogue has the same ring as that in the scripts for *Johnny's New Car* and *After the Ball*, including repeated exclamations like, "Oh-oh" and "Well, well, well." There's also a "spicy bit" that was apparently ad-libbed: after Thelma assures Harry she wouldn't "raise a rumpus" if her husband was drunk, Langdon adds, "You wouldn't raise one little rump?" causing Todd, who was off-camera, to hastily stifle a laugh. (Another line, "You got a bathroom in here?" could well have been the one that got him in trouble in Chicago and Cleveland.)

However, Langdon is clearly portraying his established screen character, the Elf. His outfit is the same as seen in his most recent films. He's as perplexing as ever: singularly focused on the simple task of knocking, he keeps it up even after Mrs. Quimby opens the door. He mixes childish questions and infantile motor impulses with such adult terms for drunkenness as "cockeyed" and "a snoot-full." Dialogue adds another dimension: in trying to reach for the correct words, he frequently stops mid-sentence and starts over.

Earlier in the year, Langdon explained the genesis of the character:

A few years ago, I got to watching children. I noticed how, when a baby came into a room and tumbled on the floor and looked surprised as if it was the floor that had suddenly come up and hit it, the way babies always do, everyone would laugh and say, 'How cute.'

Then I noticed how the guilelessness and simpleness (*sic*) of all children are among the things that make them appealing and at the same time makes us laugh when we see them making childish gestures to get out of difficulties. So I began to imagine a kid that would always amuse me and would be a great kid at the same time...At first I used to draw cartoons of him and sell him to the papers. Then the idea came to me: 'Why not act that kid?' From that time on I began acting that childish character [and] I got to love him.

A few days after the extra-short short was completed, the trades reported that Langdon was home in bed with influenza, although it might've been a bout of premarital jitters. At noon on Saturday, July 6, he and Helen emerged from the marriage license bureau to find a brace of reporters in their midst. Langdon was incredulous: "How did you find this out? It was a secret." Helen was much more accommodating, cheerfully spelling out exactly where and when their nuptials would take place. The next day, the couple hosted an engagement party for their friends. Photographers were present and M.G.M. would release several of the pictures for publicity purposes. Someone suggested they should have their wedding filmed, now that movies could talk. Langdon agreed and arranged to borrow the equipment from the Roach studios.

This news was also publicized, and at least one columnist, the *New York Journal*'s Rose Pelswick, had some fun with it: "When the future Mrs. Harry Langdon refuses to let her husband eat potato chips for lunch, all Harry will have to do, in order to get his own way, is to show her the movie of their wedding... Hal Roach, for whom Langdon is now doing two-reelers, has offered Harry the studio sound equipment, and the talkie record of the wedding will be on hand at the Langdon home for future reference. At the least squabble, no doubt, it will be run off instantly by either party when one of them needs to be reminded of certain promises."

During the three weeks leading up to the wedding, the first short on the contract, *Hotter Than Hot*, was filmed. This film and its follow-up, *Sky Boy*, are not distributed nowadays as their soundtrack discs are lost. Based on the dialogue and cutting continuity submitted to the Library of Congress, *Hotter Than Hot* takes *The Messenger* and adds a backstory of how Harry was sent to deliver a note to the girl (Thelma Todd). There's also a new conclusion: instead of Harry's wife showing up, Jack the boyfriend (Edgar Kennedy) arrives as Harry is trying to rescue the girl from a fire he's inadvertently started. Jack misconstrues the situation, and Harry winds up leaving via the window into a fire net. The picture was directed by Lewis R. Foster, who also helmed Laurel & Hardy's first talkie, *Unaccustomed As We Are*.

On July 27, at 8:30 p.m., Langdon's marriage to Helen Walton O'Brien was held in the home of Alice Calhoun, who apparently held no grudge over her dismissal from *Tramp, Tramp, Tramp*. The Reverend James Leishman officiated; local architect Carl Jules Weyl was best man, while Helen's daughter Virginia was maid of honor. One hundred guests were in attendance. With the camera strategically placed, someone gave the word to activate the lights and sound equipment. Instantly the house was plunged into darkness, its every fuse blown out. "People were frantically searching for matches and candles," said Priscilla Bonner, who wasn't present but was told about it later. "The story I heard was that in the darkness and confusion, Harry turned to his best man and whispered, 'Maybe it's an omen.'"

Amidst the soft glow of candlelight, the superstitious comedian went through with the ceremony anyway. A harpist, Hazel Schertzinger Brewster, provided the music; Helen's adopted daughter Edith sang

A mock-bashful Langdon announces his engagement to Helen Walton on July 7, 1929.

Harry doesn't trust Thelma Todd's intentions in Hotter Than Hot *(1929).*

"O, Promise Me." After a brief reception, the newlyweds left for a honeymoon in Canada.

After that, it was back to work. Charley Rogers, former English Music Hall trouper and a pal of Stan Laurel, directed the next two, *Sky Boy* and *Skirt Shy*. After seeing the former, *Variety*'s "Bige" had a few thoughts about Harry's character: "In his talk Langdon has adopted the same goof style he pantomimed with the silents. That may tend to change his type of story, for Langdon when talking in his goof way lends slight opportunity for love interest. A beaut going nuts over Langdon despite his talk would be pretty hard to take. Silent, he was cute." There was no romance in *Sky Boy*, although the plot dictated that Harry attempt to protect Thelma Todd from the overbearing Eddie Dunn, while the three are marooned on an iceberg.

Skirt Shy, which does exist in full, also has no love interest for Harry. He's a butler, and leading lady Nancy Dover is the maid, and she has the upper hand, ordering him around and slapping him when he messes up. Romance is reserved for their mistress, Maggie (May Wallace), who needs to marry wealthy Edgar (Tom Ricketts) in order to keep her

Above: Edgar Kennedy gets both Harry and Thelma in Hotter Than Hot.

heavily mortgaged home. Much of the film consists of knockabout violence, especially after a gun-toting rival from Texas shows up to court Maggie. The Texan was played by Langdon's former "strong man," Arthur Thalasso, which at least implies the comedian had some say in casting.

Roach himself decided to take the reigns for the next one, *The Head Guy*, with retakes helmed by Fred Guiol, who would be awarded sole directorial credit. In this, Harry plays the assistant to a railroad station manager (Edgar Kennedy) and is temporarily left in charge. Under Roach's guidance the Elf's childish repetitive dialogue is kept to a minimum, as is the slapstick.

There is, however, an astonishingly bizarre scene in which Harry, told by his girl (Nancy Dover) that she doesn't want to see him again, sobs and declares he no longer wants to live, which causes his eyes to noticeably widen, as though they were independent of his thoughts. At one point, he becomes indignant and decides a better solution is to find another girl, but he's quickly reminded of Nancy and resumes his sobbing death wish. Throughout his twisted monologue, he's cleaning his nails with a fountain pen and eating a sandwich — actions that connote anything other than suicidal tendencies. Eventually, after too large a bite, his words become unintelligible and he starts to choke. As when Harry tries to kill his girl in *Long Pants*, this scene is either remarkably funny or embarrassingly wrongheaded — or possibly both — depending on one's point of view. While not discussing the monologue directly, *Film Daily*'s reviewer noted, "Harry Langdon appears to be still experimenting to find out his forte in the talking line. In this comedy he is at his best when he confines himself to pantomime."

Guiol and Charley Rogers split the directing chores on Langdon's next, *The Fighting Parson*, filmed in mid-November. Set in the Wild West, it opens with a stagecoach journey, upon which Harry, a traveling entertainer, sings and plays banjo, and fruitlessly passes the hat. The song was Langdon's own

A "Movieland Puzzle" depicts an enhanced scene from Sky Boy *(1929).*

Harry with Nancy Dover in Skirt Shy *(1929).*

composition, according to *Film Daily*'s Ralph Wilk. There's a bit of borrowing from the past, as Harry eats a sandwich containing a plug of chewing tobacco and gradually feels its effects, as in *The Luck o' the Foolish*. Unconscious, he isn't aware that the stage is being held up and the Reverend Bob MacDonald, the titular parson, is shot. Arriving in town he's mistaken for MacDonald, who was supposed to "clean up" the town. The residents are quite surprised when, expecting to hear "Rock of Ages," Harry instead breaks into "Frankie and Johnny." In a setting that reminds of *The Strong Man*, he defends a young saloon girl (Nancy Dover), who is kept there against her will. Trade reviewers labeled the resulting boxing match "a scream" and "a panic."

Even more borrowing accompanied *The Big Kick*, directed by Warren Doane, who'd been piloting Charley Chase's talking comedies. Set at a rural filling station, Harry and Nancy find themselves dealing with bootleggers. Outside the station, Nancy yells for Harry; he rises and goes through a lengthy process of getting ready for work, mirroring his opening scene in *Three's a Crowd* right down to watering a single flower. The whole scene is played in mime, as

Director Charley Rogers, far left, discusses the action with Tom Ricketts, Langdon, Fred Guiol and George Stevens, on the set of Skirt Shy.

is the next one when a potential customer arrives in a very noisy vintage auto. Even face to face, he cannot hear what the man is saying over the engine noise, so Harry investigates under the hood. He tries putting a blanket over it, but it gets pulled inside. Using a routine straight out of *Johnny's New Car*, he starts removing parts of the engine and tossing them aside. When he gets to the fourth part, the motor comes to a dead stop; he quickly puts the piece back and it starts right up again.

Eventually the bootleggers arrive in a bus carrying mannequins that contain alcohol. Federal agents have staked out the station, which leads to a shootout. As in *Long Pants*, Harry believes the mannequins are real and signals for them to follow him to safety. Eventually he carries them into the garage, where he discovers the truth. He gets a hammer to smash off their fake heads. At that moment a uniformed patrolman arrives and investigates, and gets walloped by Harry. As depicted here, the routine is a pale shadow of the original, but includes the unique twist of Harry getting soused on the bootleggers' wares.

There's almost no dialogue in *The Big Kick*, for a simple reason: this was the first of Langdon's shorts to be made in a separate foreign language version, a practice that Roach, along with other producers, derived in order to serve foreign markets in the pre-dubbing era. Roach's other stars were doing the same. Laurel & Hardy were making two or three separate versions of their hugely popular films in German, Spanish and/or French, learning the lines phonetically, while Charley Chase and even Our Gang were doing one apiece. (In the case of the Gang, other children who spoke the languages were recruited to handle expository dialogue, leaving Hal Roach's Rascals to deliver "yes" and "no" responses.) A Spanish version of *The Big Kick* would be released under the title *Estaccion de Gasolina*.

Background music also debuts in this title, although the peppy original tunes composed by LeRoy Shield that would personify Hal Roach comedies were still in the future. In *The Big Kick*, as with concurrent Roach shorts, the music came from the Victor Talking Machine Company's record library, incorporating such popular tunes as "Wobaly Walk"

Harry serenades Nancy Dover in curious publicity still for The Head Guy *(1929), which actually takes place in a train station.*

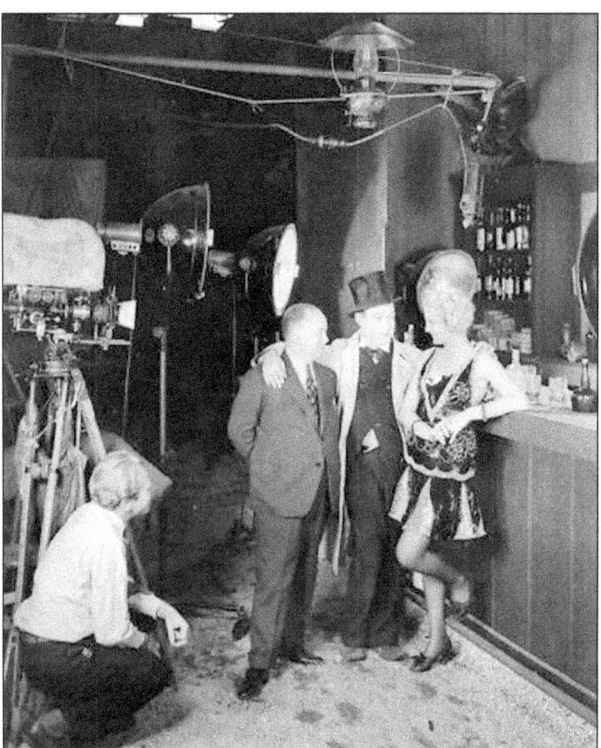

Langdon and Thelma Todd meet the Roach studio's new production manager, Fred Karno, on the set of The Fighting Parson.

and "What'll I Do?" Some of the themes heard in this short also turn up in Our Gang's *Bear Shooters*, in which the Rascals, on a hunting trip, have their own encounter with bootleggers.

As 1929 drew to a close, the country was embarking on the worst economic crisis of its history, although the full effect wouldn't be felt for about two more years. Like many other Americans with money to play with, Langdon had invested in the stock market, which crashed on October 29, wiping out most of his savings. Luckily he had a steady job and decent income, although his new bride's love of luxury doomed any possibility of establishing a new nest egg. Typical of Helen's extravagance was a New Year's Eve party that year, which Fred W. Fox wrote about for the *Los Angeles Mirror-News* in 1959:

> In the afternoon one Dec. 31, when I had dropped in to visit [Langdon] on the set, he insisted that I accompany him to his Beverly Hills house for the New Year's party that night. "Just an informal gathering," he said, but I was mortified when, upon arriving, we were confronted by a large gathering of formally dressed

Harry at the bar in The Fighting Parson *(1930).*

guests. Ready to flee in embarrassment, I was grabbed by the arm by a stunning blond who came out of the throng. "Come sit at our table," she said.

The "stunning blond" was Thelma Todd, who assumed a supporting part in the next film on the docket, *The Shrimp*. Charley Rogers returned to the director's chair, and a new arrival, Nancy Drexel, took the leading lady role, although the Spanish-language version, *¡Pobre Infeliz!* ("Poor unhappy one") replaced her with Linda Loredo. The story, which probably should have occurred to somebody much sooner, sets up Harry as a put-upon resident of a boarding house, the butt of everybody else's practical jokes… none more cruel than those of Jim (James Mason), the house bully. Nancy, the owners' daughter, encourages him to rebel, but it's no use. After enduring trips, kicks and having his face pushed into a bowl of berries, he's inexplicably brought to Dr. Schoenheimer (Max Davidson) as the test subject of an experiment, where the personality of a live bulldog is to be transplanted into a human being. Needless to say, it works and

A sozzled Harry carries off a liquor-carrying dummy in The Big Kick *(1930).*

James Mason gets the best of Harry, while Thelma Todd looks on…

a fired-up Harry is ready to exact revenge upon his fellow residents for all their abuse. Trade press critics were unanimously pleased and effusive with their praise.

On Monday, January 27, all of Roach's stars participated in a radio broadcast direct from the studio, *Voices From Filmland*, which aired over the CBS Network. This weekly series was sanctioned by M.G.M. and featured their players along with the Biltmore Trio (house band of the Biltmore Hotel) and other musicians. M.G.M. promoted the Roach segment in the trades, labeling it the launch of "Hal Roach Comedy Week" and enticing exhibitors to cash in by booking Roach shorts for their programs. Unfortunately, the broadcast itself isn't known to exist and seems not to have been reviewed, leaving historians puzzling over exactly what Langdon, Laurel, Hardy, Chase and the Our Gang kids brought to the airwaves.

One final film remained on the contract, which turned out to be *The King*, helmed by both Rogers and Horne. Harry portrays the title role, with Thelma Todd as the queen and young Dorothy Granger as the flirtatious wife of the king's new chancellor (James Parrott). The resulting short is possibly the worst of the eight, consisting of one slapstick contrivance after another as both Queen and Chancellor knock Harry around for his (mostly innocent) misdeeds. At one point, the queen labels him a "chaser," bringing to mind another hopelessly contrived Langdon film. Perhaps due to its vaguely European setting, a German-language version was produced, *Der Koenig*.

Long unavailable to most comedy fans and scholars, Langdon's Roach shorts — at least the six available for viewing — are a mixed bag, but the majority are quite funny, and for the most part successfully integrate the Little Elf into the sound medium. The fact that many incorporate routines and situations from earlier films proves conclusively that Langdon didn't merely follow orders but was an active participant in their conception.

Roach himself was evidently pleased, as he exercised his option to extend Langdon's contract, but the comedian still hoped to get back into features. "It's because of my golf more than anything else that I want to go back to making feature length films again," he told columnist Dan Thomas. "I would have much

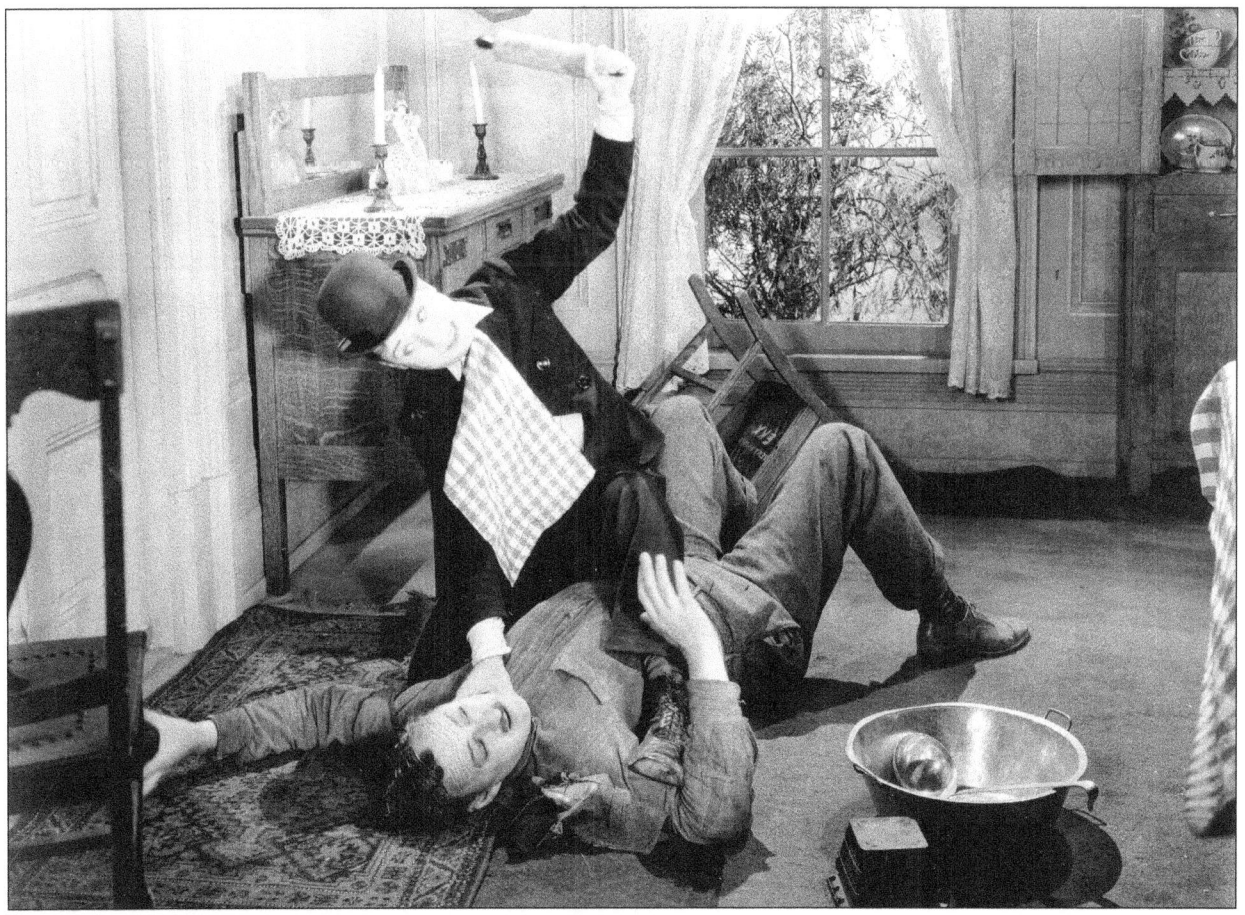

... but the worm eventually turns in The Shrimp *(1930).*

more time between pictures and therefore would have more time to knock that white pill around." According to Thomas, any day Langdon wasn't working, he'd be on the Lakeside course, rain or shine. "He shoots a good game, too, doing under 75 quite consistently," wrote Thomas for his "Seeing Stars" column.

The opportunity came sooner than expected. Within three weeks of Roach's extension, Warner Bros. offered Langdon a supporting role in "Come Easy," an original story by novelist Vina Delmar written for Austrian actress Lotti Loder, who, it was hoped, would be the studio's version of Dietrich and Garbo. That the offer came from the owners of the company that unceremoniously dumped him less than two years earlier was perceived as a good omen, plus there was Helen's unswerving faith that he was much too valuable a talent for two-reelers. Langdon immediately requested a release from the Roach deal, which was granted.

Handling the love interest was Ben Lyon, with Langdon as his comic pal. The story, such as it is, pits the two in the Army, stationed in Germany during the immediate postwar occupation. Langdon, as Tim, is a willing enlistee; while Lyon, as Georgie, hastily joins up to escape what he believes is a murder rap. As soldiers, the two engage in various comic mishaps that naturally involve their commanding officer (Noah Beery), who repeatedly assigns them to clean a stable of horses. Georgie falls hard for Loder's Gretchen, daughter of a local innkeeper, but when his hitch is ending, he doesn't want to take her to his homeland for fear of an eventual conviction. Only when he spies Hank (Fred Kohler), the fellow he thought he'd killed and who is among the replacement troops, does he realize he's free and clear to marry his German love.

The studio chose "Come Easy" as its entry in cinema's latest technological advance: wide film. By this point, sound-on-film was becoming the industry standard, but few filmmakers were happy that, as a result, picture width had noticeably shrunk. The solution seemed to be a graduation from 35mm to something larger; consequently — and not

King Harry contends with Dorothy Granger and James Parrott (pointing) in The King *(1930).*

surprisingly — various entrepreneurs came up with 56mm, 65mm and 70mm film widths. Unlike the Cinemascope revolution of 23 years later, few were interested in wide screen; the hoped-for result was a sharper, less grainy picture to completely fill existing screens, along with a wider, better-quality soundtrack. The Warners opted for 65mm film, labeling their process Vitascope.

The picture, directed by Michael Curtiz, was shot during April and May. Prior to completion, producer Darryl F. Zanuck changed its title to the titillating *A Soldier's Plaything*. The resulting film is a fast 56 minutes of episodic situations (all of which are heralded with text titles), mostly comic in nature. Langdon basically portrays the typical buffoon soldier, who turns left when the command "right face" is barked, and vice-versa. His best moment is a comedy song called, "*Oui, Oui*," during which he plays the piano. Langdon's singing talent was hinted at in *The Fighting Parson*; here it's on full display, with a few comic expressions and gestures added for good measure. His voice is pleasant and he puts over the tune quite nicely.

While the film was in production, lawyers for Helen's ex, Thomas O'Brien, filed suit to collect on the $11,500 in promissory notes that Langdon had written in October 1927. Langdon responded by filing a counter-suit against O'Brien for the $15,000 he'd already paid, claiming he'd been forced against his will to fork over the cash and the notes. The two suits jointly went to trial beginning Wednesday, June 11, in California Superior Court, before Judge Samuel R. Blake.

Right from the start, things got interesting. Langdon asserted, "I was forced into [the agreement]. I did it to protect the future of my wife and her little girl, and to avoid the notoriety and publicity of the threatened alienation of affections suit." Then Langdon's lawyers, Paul W. Schenck and J. M. Bowen, called Helen to the stand, whereupon O'Brien's lawyer, Bayard R. Rountree, objected on the grounds that the law prohibiting a wife from testifying against her husband extended to ex-wives as well. There being

This comic strip by Don Wootton accompanied Dan Thomas's SEEING STARS column of January 23, 1930.

no precedent to back up Rountree's assertion, Judge Blake called a halt and took the rest of the day to decide the matter.

The next morning, he ruled that Helen would be allowed to testify provided she limited her testimony to events that had been witnessed by others, and to acts of violence her ex had committed against her. She was forbidden to discuss their private conversations.

Harry flirts with Lotti Loder in A Soldier's Plaything *(1930).*

Members of the press, noting the significance of the ruling, subsequently settled in for the long haul.

They wouldn't be disappointed. Once on the stand, Helen swore that, far from being stolen by Langdon, her love for O'Brien began to die five minutes after they were married. "Mr. O'Brien and I began quarrelling in church, immediately after we were married. He was rude to me then because I was slow to in hastening out of church so that two other friends of Mr. O'Brien could be married.

"From that time on, until we were separated, my entire life with him was a succession of quarrels. When we got home from the church, he swore at me. Mr. O'Brien said to me, while I still had on my veil and wedding gown, 'I don't know why I married you, anyway.' On one occasion, he struck me in the face. After my baby was born, he called it 'a little devil' and often cursed it, and on one occasion, when it was about two years old, struck it in the mouth with his fist."

Helen's testimony continued the next day, in which she recounted a "humiliating and revolting" event: "My mother, my little girl Virginia, and myself were driving downtown with Mr. O'Brien. My mother wanted to go in one place and Mr. O'Brien wanted to go in another. He flew into a violent rage, and shouted and screamed curses at me. People passing by stopped to listen and a crowd gathered. I was never so ashamed nor so humiliated in my life...I made him drive straight home and then I left him and he didn't know where we were for three months."

Asked by Schenck of O'Brien's opinion of her, she replied, "He said I didn't have any brains at all. He said he was mentally my superior. He said he didn't think I ever would have any brains." Helen testified that she and O'Brien lived apart for three years, until the time in late 1926 when he wooed her back with letters she described as "pitiful." She affirmed she first met Langdon in September 1923, after a casting agency sent her to work at Principal Pictures, that they didn't become close until several years later, and that he didn't steal her love from her ex-husband.

With that, O'Brien's legal team, which included Rountree and also Otto Emme and Leo Rosecrans, the two attorneys to whom Langdon's notes were originally made payable, took over with what the *L.A. Examiner* termed "a merciless cross-examination." They began by recounting the story of Langdon's visit to her home in January 1925, where O'Brien saw him leaving at 1:30 in the morning. She vehemently denied it, choosing her words carefully. "It is not true he was caught in my bedroom.... He had come to my home at 6600 Sunset Boulevard to see me about a motion picture in which I was to act with him. He came through the back door because some guests were occupying the front room, and he didn't want to disturb them. It is not true I was in my night clothes."

The lawyers asked her about gifts Langdon had given her before their marriage; she admitted to receiving the $1,000 bill and a diamond ring, and pointed out she had refused the Persian rug. When they got to a question about her brief reunion with O'Brien at the end of 1926, she began sobbing. Judge Blake suspended the proceedings until the following Tuesday, June 17.

Helen remained on the stand all that day, too, as O'Brien's team continued to grill her. "My life until I married Harry Langdon was unbearable. I tried to forget all this unhappiness and would have, too, if Mr. O'Brien hadn't brought it all back… I wanted to forget all his cruelty. I hoped I was through weeping about the cruel things O'Brien has done to me, and I had succeeded in putting him out of my mind." She spoke about riding in the Tournament of Roses parade float, thinking it "a beautiful dream — just as I had thought my wedding day would be." This prompted Rountree to ask, "Was your wedding day a dream or a nightmare?" Helen's response was to burst into tears.

At that point, according to the *Examiner*, "Mrs. Langdon… suffered a slight heart attack. Langdon called Dr. E. C. Fishbaugh, who had medicine sent to the courtroom immediately. She was finally able to resume her testimony after a half-hour of rest."

It didn't get easier. O'Brien's lawyers asked her about an encounter with Rose: "Isn't it a fact that the first Mrs. Langdon called you a blonde hussy and accused you of stealing her husband?" "No, it is not!" she snapped. "I heard she talked like that, but never in my presence. I would have called the police!" The interrogation continued:

ROUNTREE: Mrs. Langdon, isn't it true you were very flattered when, during your engagement in a motion picture with Mr. Langdon, you received certain attentions from him?

HELEN: No, I am not subject to flattery.

ROUNTREE: Didn't you consider it a feather in your cap to have him for a friend and to have him call on you?

HELEN: No, I have had many film stars call on me besides Mr. Langdon.

ROUNTREE: When did you first realize you loved Harry Langdon?

HELEN: I don't know the exact date, but I know it was when Mr. O'Brien had taken my baby away from me and Mr. Langdon stood by me and helped me get her back.

ROUNTREE: Didn't you know Mr. Langdon was married?

HELEN: Yes, I knew he had been married at least, but I knew he was not living with his wife at that time.

ROUNTREE: Just when did Mr. Langdon propose to you?

HELEN: I think it was in March 1927.

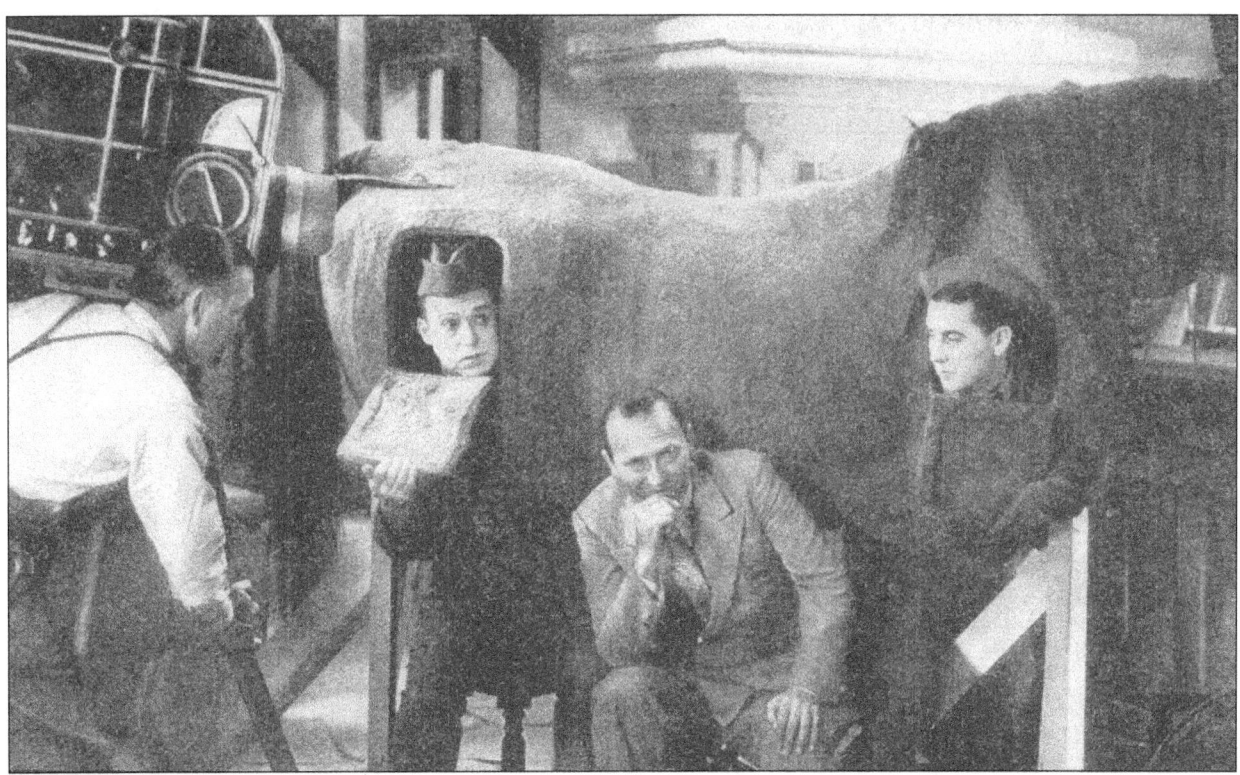

Langdon and costar Ben Lyon wait for director Michael Curtiz to get out of the shot on the set of A Soldier's Playthjng.

That was, of course, the exact time she was recuperating in his home following her abortion, an event that would become the next line of questioning. Rountree began by bringing up the $1,000 bill Langdon had given her. "Wasn't that money given to pay for an illegal operation, a condition for which Langdon, and not O'Brien, was responsible?" Shocked, Helen cried out, "You know O'Brien was responsible and he knows it, too!"

Rountree persisted, demanding that she confess to meeting with O'Brien in Glendale for the express purpose of intimacy, to "cover up" her misconduct with Langdon. "It's a lie! A deliberate lie!" she screamed. Sobbing hysterically, she added, "Tom O'Brien knows it's a lie! How that man can sit there and build up lies against the mother of his child is more than I can understand!" Rountree addressed Judge Blake: "Your honor, I move these comments be stricken from the record," to which Helen cried out, "You cannot strike out an answer that protects my honor and that of my little girl!"

During this, Langdon stood up and headed toward the stand, but was restrained by both his lawyers. At

Langdon sketches the principal figures in his "love balm" trial, June 1930.

that point, court was adjourned until the next day when, once again, Helen took the stand for cross-examination. This time, as reported in the *Examiner*, she became "militant," barking her answers at the lawyer:

ROUNTREE: Did not Mr. Langdon accompany you to your home on the night of June 15, 1927, enter with you and remain in the house the rest of the night?

HELEN: No, he may have visited me at my home but he never stayed all night.

ROUNTREE: Well, didn't he go into your home at a late hour several nights during that summer and on one occasion didn't you turn out the lights? And wasn't Mr. Langdon there as late as two a.m.?

HELEN: I don't remember the dates, but I repeat that Mr. Langdon never stayed at my home all night. I'll tell you, Mr. Rountree, you have accused me of wasting Judge Blake's time, but it seems to me that you are wasting it more than I have when you keep insisting on these questions. My answers will always be the same.

ROUNTREE: Well, didn't Mr. Langdon accompany you home several nights during the summer of 1927?

HELEN: I daresay he did. A gentleman usually accompanies a lady home after he takes her out.

ROUNTREE: And you insist Mr. Langdon never spent the night in your home?

HELEN: Certainly I insist that. Mr. Langdon did everything to protect me against gossip. He wouldn't do anything to hurt me. I tell you, Mr. Langdon is a man of honor. He would not do the things you insinuate.

With that, attention was turned toward Mr. Langdon, who testified under his own lawyer's questioning that O'Brien "had no grounds for a love theft suit." When attorney Schenck asked why he agreed to the settlement, he replied: "I was forced to do that. I had a motion picture contract at the time, and feared notoriety resulting from a trial of such a case would jeopardize my future as an actor."

Rountree got his chance at Langdon when trial resumed the next morning, and immediately made it personal:

ROUNTREE: What did you give your present wife for Christmas, when she was still Mrs. O'Brien, in 1926?

LANGDON: A diamond ring and a $1,000 bill to get herself a fur coat.

ROUNTREE: And what was your relation at that time?

LANGDON: We were just friends — I admired her very much.

ROUNTREE: Weren't you in love with her then?

LANGDON: No — well, I thought an awful lot of her.

ROUNTREE: Didn't the then Mrs. O'Brien, in the spring of 1927, stay in your home for a time?

LANGDON: Yes, on two occasions — when she was ill. Altogether she stayed probably four or five days.

ROUNTREE: In fact, you took her there, didn't you?

LANGDON: Yes, I did.

Under further questioning, Langdon stated, "The first time I knew I loved her was when her little girl had been kidnapped. I did not propose to Mrs. Langdon until long after she was separated from her husband. But in 1927, when her little girl had been kidnapped and when an alienation suit was threatened and all this trouble came up — well, it brought us together and I knew I loved her." Rountree pressed the issue:

ROUNTREE: Mr. Langdon, when was the first time you ever kissed your present wife?

LANGDON: Well, it was around that time.

ROUNTREE: And when was the first time you ever put your arm around her?

LANGDON: The same time I kissed her.

ROUNTREE: And you didn't do any of these things before that time?

LANGDON: No, I don't remember doing it.

ROUNTREE: Wasn't the present Mrs. Langdon married to Mr. O'Brien at that time?

LANGDON: Yes, but she was separated from him.

ROUNTREE: And were you married at that time?

LANGDON: Well, yes, but I also was separated from my wife.

Langdon's cross-examination continued on the 20th, and according to the *Los Angeles Times*, he got a few laughs from courtroom attendees. The first came when he was asked about his divorce from Rose, and "admitted paying $70,000 to [her] as a settlement in 1928. 'Sev-enty thou-sand dollars,' sighed the pensive comic, sadly. The courtroom audience greeted this with laughter." Had she been present, Rose might have objected since to date she'd only received a fraction of that amount. Another laugh came when the nervous comedian stated he'd married Helen "July 27, 1908 — ah! Ah! Pardon, 1928!" Schenck had to remind him their marriage was in 1929, meaning they hadn't yet celebrated their first anniversary.

When trial resumed on Monday the 23rd, Benjamin Walton, Helen's younger brother, recounted his own observations of his sister's marriage to O'Brien, including the events on their wedding day. He also stated, "O'Brien told me in 1927 that he could spread stories in the newspapers to ruin Langdon's career. He said a Los Angeles friend, not a newspaperman, had assured him that all he had to do was to say the word and they'd 'get' Langdon."

Tuesday brought Langdon's final witnesses, beginning with actress Helen Barnes, who knew Helen during the time of her August 1925 reconciliation with O'Brien. According to an Associated Press report, "She said she observed that O'Brien was not affectionate and Mrs. O'Brien was cool. 'I asked her why she did not divorce him,' Mrs. Barnes said. 'She replied that she tolerated O'Brien only for their daughter's sake.'" Three more associates, casting director Nan Collins, and actresses Julia Griffith and Marie Estabrook, testified they'd been told by Helen in 1926 that "she always had been unhappy with her first husband [and] quoted her as saying she had permanently separated from him."

Then O'Brien took the stand. Up to now he'd been stoic, emotionless, even in the midst of his ex-wife's hysteria. He stated his belief that "Harry Langdon broke up our home and stole my wife." The next day, Schenck put him under cross-examination. To start

A smiling (and surprisingly matronly-looking) Helen poses with Harry at the trial. Her ordeal on the stand would not be so pleasant.

things off, Schenck read from the two letters O'Brien had sent Helen in October and November 1926, in which he assured her "it was not your fault... I am to blame," as proof that he alone was responsible for "killing" his wife's love. O'Brien, in turn, responded with vivid detail the circumstances of their reconciliation in Glendale during the last week of December. "Matters of most intimate nature were told," is how the next day's papers described his testimony.

Mrs. Marie Firman, the private detective hired by Rose to shadow her husband and Helen during March of 1927, took the stand in the afternoon and described that Helen and her two daughters were living in Langdon's home at that time, that they'd go on automobile drives and that Langdon "put his arm around" Helen during a visit to Ocean Park. She also noted that both girls called him "Daddy Harry." She was cross-examined by Schenck the following morning, as he attempted to prove that she couldn't have witnessed such activity from her vantage point.

A blackboard was brought into court so Mrs. Firman could illustrate exactly where she was stationed and its proximity to Langdon's house.

O'Brien returned to the stand to detail his various encounters with Langdon, beginning in January 1925, which pretty much took up the rest of the week. When the case resumed on Monday the 30th, a letter from Helen to her ex, written on August 29, 1925, was

The Hearst press has some fun at Langdon's expense.

read into evidence. "In it, she asks O'Brien to reaffirm his faith in her innocence of any wrongdoing… and never question her relations with Harry Langdon," according to the *Examiner*, "a request which O'Brien declared prompted his letters in which he expressed his confidence in her. O'Brien testified…that he did not have the faith in her that he said he did in his letters."

The final bombshell came that afternoon in the form of a deposition from Helen's mother, Laura Walton, which Rountree read into evidence. "I never had any difficulties with Mr. O'Brien," her statement began, along with an assertion that he was "a loving, kind and dutiful husband." O'Brien and her daughter got along fine, she'd continued, "with only ordinary squabbles," until Langdon came into the picture. She had spelled out the occasions when he'd spent the night, and affirmed she'd seen Helen "emerging from his bedroom" during one of these. She detailed the gifts he gave Helen at Christmas 1926, noting that "money went to Helen's head and her mother was not good enough for her. It was not a question of affection. I never saw [her] show any affection for anyone except herself."

Mrs. Walton said she didn't want to believe there was anything improper between Helen and Langdon, but "seeing is believing." She related her own conversations with Langdon; specifically that O'Brien "would not stand for that conduct," upon learning Helen was living in his home. While denying any bitterness toward her, Mrs. Walton couldn't resist adding, "I sacrificed thirty-six years for my daughter and never got even a 'Thank you.' I am 63 years old and still earn my own living." She also threw in one final slap: "She says she is 30. She will be 40 her next birthday."

Thus, in one fell swoop, Laura Walton had potentially sent her daughter's entire testimony — not to mention her trustworthiness — down the drain. Had she appeared in person, the damage might have been more severe, but she was determined to avoid Helen. Theirs must have been a contentious estrangement, and the deposition was undoubtedly the final straw. On July 1, both sides rested, and at that point it was anybody's guess as to which way Judge Blake would rule; indeed, he took the rest of the week to decide the matter.

On Monday, July 7, Judge Blake rendered his decision. "The most important issue in the case has been whether or not Langdon stole the affections of O'Brien's wife. I find that long prior to Langdon's entry into the then Mrs. O'Brien's life, O'Brien had lost the affections of his wife. The court is forced to the conclusion that the loss of affection was not due to acts of Langdon. The drama presented in this court was not a result of Langdon's acts but due to O'Brien's own acts. The blame lies with O'Brien and not the acts of a third party.

"I find further that O'Brien knew he had lost the love of his wife through his own fault and that, therefore, he knew at the time he first made his claim upon Langdon for payment of money that he was not acting in good faith.

"I find further that, although there were meetings between Langdon and his wife while she was still Mrs. O'Brien, there were no improper relations between them. Those are stern words charged by O'Brien. Such a charge strikes at the very heart of society and must be considered carefully, especially when the welfare of minor children is involved. At best it is mere suspicion, rebutted by denials of both principals…. After weighing all of the evidence, I am not prepared to find that there was anything wrong between Mr. and Mrs. Langdon before their marriage."

As for the $15,000 that Langdon had paid, Judge Blake stated, "Although I believe that this money was not demanded by O'Brien in good faith, the statute of limitations prevents me from restoring this money to Langdon. If Langdon had come to court to ask for this sooner he might have recovered it."

As Judge Blake delivered his ruling, and it became clear her husband had won, Helen burst into tears, later telling reporters, "I'm crying because I am so happy, and because my honor has been vindicated." Harry's sole comment was, "I'm happy for my wife's sake. Now I won't have to walk down alleys." As for O'Brien, he'd try appealing the decision, but was officially rebuffed a few months later. Thomas J. O'Brien was finally gone from Langdon's life.

More good news followed the next day, when Universal Pictures signed Langdon to co-star with their resident comedian, Slim Summerville, in a picture titled *See America Thirst*. The story was conceived as a satire on gangster pictures that had recently come into vogue. Summerville (as "Slim") and Langdon (as "Wally") are two hoboes mistaken by a crime syndicate to be hired hit men: "Shivering" Smith and "Gunkist" Casey. For the most part, Summerville plays straight for Langdon, who is saddled with perhaps the most insipid dialogue of his career.

Still, it was work. Shooting took place during August and September, and production went smoothly, although leading lady Jeannette Loff was replaced early on by Bessie Love. At the time filming began, the Langdons moved from their Los Angeles residence of 7720 Sunset Boulevard to a bona fide Beverly Hills home: 510 N. Alta Drive.

Producer Carl Laemmle, Jr. liked *See America*

Langdon and Slim Summerville in *See America Thirst (1930)*.

Thirst enough to commission a second Summerville-Langdon script from the same writer, Edward Luddy. It was not until the film was about to be released that trouble arose, courtesy of the Motion Picture Commission of the State of New York. Once their board of censors screened the picture, they sent a two-page list of "eliminations" to Universal that made their demands for *The Chaser* seem like mere nitpicking:

> REEL 2: *Eliminate spoken subtitles in dialogue:*
> "Well, I want his throat cut."
> "Yes sir."
> "Well?"
> "I'm sorry, Mr. O'Toole, they made a mistake — they shot him."
> ----------
> " — When I ask to have a guy's throat cut — you shoot him! When I want a man put on the spot — you take him for a ride!"

> *Eliminate underlined words in spoken subtitle in dialogue:* "Gunkist Casey and Shivering Smith arrive within the next few days — they look us up — but they'll do the job themselves — we give them all the help we can."

> REEL 4: *Eliminate spoken subtitle in dialogue:* "Here's your first payment — one hundred grand — you get the rest after you get McGann. S'matter — ain't it enough? Here — here's a hundred and fifty more — you get the rest if you do a good job."

> REEL 5: *Eliminate scene of beds being riddled by bullets.*
> *Eliminate spoken sub-titles in dialogue:*
> "Say — what kind of a funeral will we give Shivering Smith and Gunkist Casey?"
> "When the boss gets through with them, there won't be enough left for a funeral."

> REEL 6: *Eliminate spoken sub-title in dialogue:* "And I filled those two babies so full of lead that they'll have to bury 'em in a ten ton truck."

> *Eliminate underlined words in spoken subtitle in dialogue:* "This is the idea — see — Spumoni gives us half a million bucks to bump you guys off — now what's it worth to you for us to get him?"

> *Eliminate spoken subtitles in dialogue:*
> "To get Spumoni? I'll give you three quarters of a million."
> "Tell you what I'll do — I'll give you a million for Spumoni, dead or alive — Now that's a lot of dough — for that guy ain't worth a nickel to me."
> "Here's your million."

> *Eliminate scene of actual exchange of money between gangster and men.*

> *Eliminate underlined words in spoken subtitle in dialogue:* "There was no train this afternoon because my gang derailed that Special."

> REEL 7: *In scenes of rival gangs shooting at each other across road, eliminate all views of machine guns in action.*

Eliminate spoken subtitle in dialogue: "Don't get discouraged, boys — you're bound to hit 'em if you keep on shootin' — come on — keep it up."

Eliminate underlined words spoken in subtitle in dialogue: "I think you're right at that — it's time for the attack — come on."

REASONS: "WILL TEND TO CORRUPT MORALS" and "INCITE TO CRIME."

The changes were addressed to Charles E. Fallis of Universal's Big U Film Exchange of New York City. Upon receipt, the executives at Big U were aghast, and concluded that whoever wrote up the list had no idea what they were watching. One R.H. Cochrane saw fit to address the situation directly with James Wingate, head of the State's Motion Picture Division, in a letter dated November 11:

Dear Mr. Wingate:

I hope you will view our picture SEE AMERICA THIRST in an entirely different light than that in which it was seen by some of your reviewers. They have evidently taken it seriously as they might take some straight underworld picture, when as a matter of fact it is the broadest kind of burlesque, purposely done with such broad strokes that no one can take offense. It is as utterly harmless in its present form that it should not be judged on a serious basis. Two of the best known screen comedians are the leading characters, which, in itself, is enough to stamp it as nothing more nor less than slapstick comedy.

It is in no sense offensive to either drys or wets and it contains no vulgarities.

Heaven knows the people need all the laughs they can get in these depressing times, and I sincerely hope you will see eye to eye with me on this.

On November 13, the Motion Picture Commission responded to this plea by re-screening the film, and sending a two-page letter of eliminations that was identical to the first. Apparently Big U objected again because on the 19th, Mr. Wingate himself screened *See America Thirst*. The next day, he composed a list of eliminations that was only slightly less demanding. All of the material in reel five could remain, as well as the lines in reel six about "filling those two babies

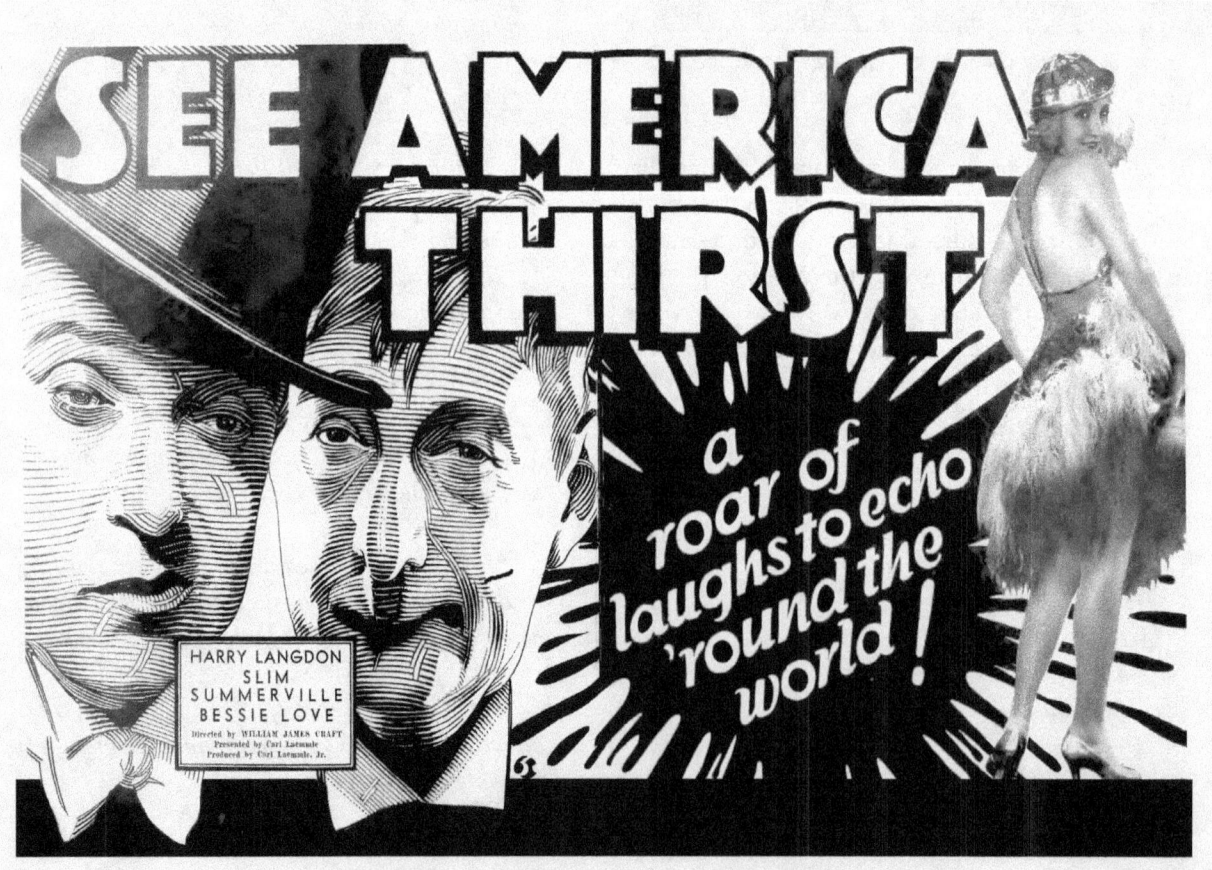

full of lead" and of derailing "that Special," and also the dialogue in reel seven. Everything else would still need to be cut.

Big U's Charles Fallis wrote to Mr. Wingate on December 4, hoping that with a little schmoozing he might broker a compromise:

Dear Mr. Wingate:

In resubmitting our picture, SEE AMERICA THIRST, for your approval, I wish to explain just what we have done with the picture, in an effort to meet with your requirements and at the same time, to avoid breaking up of the sense of the story.

In reel two, we have eliminated all of the dialogue which you required.

In reel four, we have eliminated all of the spoken dialogue which you required, with the exception of the first four words, "Here's your first payment."

In reel six, in the underlined spoken words in dialogue, "This is the idea — see — Spumoni gives us half a million bucks to bump you guys off — now what's it worth to you for us to get him?" we have eliminated the spoken words "to bump you guys off."

And in the next spoken dialogue, "To get Spumoni? I'll give you three quarters of a million," we have eliminated the spoken words, "To get Spumoni?"

The rest of the spoken dialogue and the scene of actual exchange of money, have been eliminated in this reel.

In reel seven, the objectionable scenes and dialogue have been eliminated.

Having eliminated almost six hundred feet in this picture, in an effort to meet with your approval, I feel sure that you will pass upon it favorably in its present form.

Thanking you for your many favors, and with my best personal regards.

Mr. Wingate was unmoved, responding on December 5:

Gentlemen:

I have this morning rescreened Reels 4, 6 & 7 of your picture entitled SEE AMERICA THIRST — Synchronized and Dialogue Version. Reel 7 has been satisfactorily cut. I am unable to modify our directions relative to the eliminations in Reels 4 and 6, as suggested in your letter. The dialogue which you desire to retain and which we directed to be eliminated is the key which carries the objectionable parts.

With that, Big U gave up the fight.

Harry and Slim enjoy the pause that refreshes on the set of See America Thirst.

While this was going on, Warner Bros. released *A Soldier's Plaything* in regular 35mm. Although the studio claimed to have manufactured "a special projector head, which can be used for either 35 or 65mm…and have already turned out enough to equip all of the company's theaters," according to *Film Daily*, the Society of Motion Picture Engineers were undecided as to whether 65 or 70mm should be the uniform standard, and exhibitors refused to invest a penny until that question was settled. Vitascope made its theatrical debut in October with *Kismet*, a First National feature, and *Motion Picture News* reported

Two months prior to its release, Universal heavily plugged See America Thirst *to exhibitors.*

that, out of thirteen New York newspaper reviewers, only two commented favorably on the process. Seven ignored it altogether, and the remaining four didn't care for it. These percentages basically mirrored audience interest as well. "Wide film" was put on the shelf for a couple of decades, while other technical matters, such as improved color and sound reproduction, were pursued.

As for *A Soldier's Plaything*, it flopped badly. Most critics were decidedly underwhelmed; *Film Daily* labeling it "a miscue production that offers very little in the way of entertainment," and the *New York Times* calling it "an insignificant item." Domestic rentals amounted to $185,000 and foreign bookings were a paltry $22,000. With a negative cost of $344,000, the overall loss equaled $289,000.

Along with anticipating a second picture at Universal, Langdon also signed with a new concern, Liberty Productions, for a comedy entitled *The Ape*, written by Earl Snell. Owing to a lack of financing, Liberty Productions sank without a trace. Unfortunately, something similar was about to happen to Langdon's film career. He didn't realize it, but once shooting wrapped on *See America Thirst*, he would not stand before a motion picture camera for 16 months.

A SOLDIER'S PLAYTHING
—Warners

IF you like romance seasoned with plenty of laughs, some slapstick and hot thrills, catch this. It's great, though heaven knows what to call it. A war story that isn't a war story; not a musical, but has some grand music; not slapstick, yet happy with it—well, call it just a darned good talkie! That will cover it. Ben Lyon, Harry Langdon and Lotti Loder have head honors of a fine cast.

Review in Photoplay *magazine.*

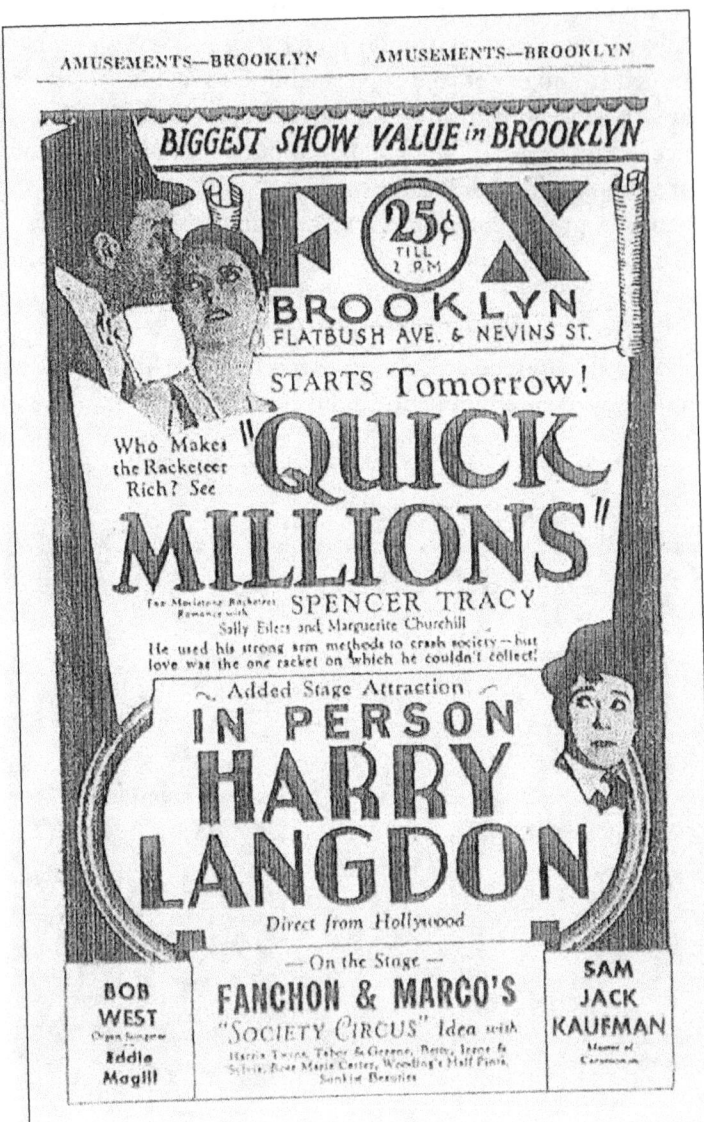

CHAPTER TWELVE

"The Tragedy of Marriage"

1931–1932

If 1930 had been a year of promise, 1931 would be a year of defeat. Month after month, like wildfire, the bad news just kept coming.

In early January, a handful of columnists reported that Langdon had received an invitation from Florenz Ziegfeld to co-star in the next edition of the *Ziegfeld Follies*. A response was sent that Langdon would come to New York to discuss terms. Looking for details, the *New York Telegraph* went straight to the showman, who denied he'd ever sent such an invite. "When the wire was read to [Ziegfeld], he responded: 'I have never seen Langdon. I don't know anything about his work; in fact, I never heard of him until this minute.'" A rather surprising quote, given Langdon's long-time stage fame, not to mention his near-participation in Ziegfeld's and Dillingham's *Century Girl*.

As it turned out, "the Great Glorifier" was just trying to downplay any publicity that might drive up Langdon's price. Negotiations were conducted long distance and, according to *Variety*, "It's all a matter of dough. Langdon wants $2,500 [per week]; Ziggy says it's too much. No counter-propositioning." This was unfortunate, since he needed the money. Before January was over, he and Helen would be served notice to vacate their Beverly Hills home of five months.

On February 7, James F. Dickason, former owner of the Alta Drive house, filed an eviction suit in Municipal Court, declaring no mortgage payments had been received since the initial $1,000 down payment the previous August. Langdon directed his attorney, John M. Bowen, to file a demurrer the next day, which stated Dickason's suit "is ambiguous and uncertain and does not state how or in what manner the complainant is entitled to possession of the property." The lawyer also told Dickason's attorney, Ernest E. Noon, that the Langdons would vacate the house in any event.

Having been so informed, on February 9, Dickason drove by the home at 10:30 p.m. in time to witness furniture and other belongings being loaded into vans for warehouse storage. Among the items removed were an awning and lighting fixtures that the landlord believed to be his property. The next morning, he swore out a complaint against the Langdons for petty theft, whereupon the Beverly Hills police came by that afternoon and arrested a frantic and frightened Helen, and threatened the housekeeper and chauffeur with the same when they tried to interfere.

Attorney Bowen assured Justice of the Peace Billings that both Langdons would be in court later in the day for arraignment, whereupon Billings released Helen of her own recognizance. According to a local newspaper account, "Mrs. Langdon said their troubles with Dickason are due to his asserted failure to place certain improvements in the house as specified in their contract of purchase." Adding to the spin, Helen also said, "Her husband is to leave in a few days for New York to enter negotiations with Florenz Ziegfeld about his appearance in the new *Ziegfeld Follies*."

While the couple moved into the El Royale Apartments in Hollywood, the J.W. Robinson Company, having read about Langdon's furniture being placed in storage, checked their records and found that they, too, had not been paid since August 1930 for $2,085 worth of merchandise. The store filed suit to attach the furniture, for which the Langdons had remitted only a $600 down payment at the time; Harry and Helen were served on the 11th, while in court for *l'affaire* Dickason.

The couple produced receipts proving they'd purchased the awning and fixtures that had been removed. Noon tried to argue that "the articles had become permanent fixtures and therefore no longer belonged to the Langdons," but Justice Billings would have none of it, and delivered a verdict of acquittal. Later in the year, Langdon would file a $500,000 suit against Dickason charging "false arrest and malicious prosecution."

The court decision was one of Langdon's few victories that year, tempered by the fact that, around that time, Universal was getting a look at how *See America Thirst* was under-performing at the box office and shelved the follow-up, "Two Weaks." However, there were overtures from Beatrice Lillie's *The Third Little Show*, a revue that was being assembled by Dwight Deere Wiman and Tom Weatherly, with sketches by Moss Hart, S. J. Perelman and other notables. The producers were targeting an early June Broadway opening and sought Langdon for lead comedian.

With no compelling reason to remain in Hollywood, Langdon and his pal, fellow vaudevillian Eddie Shubert, headed to New York and the friendly confines of the R.K.O. Circuit during the week of March 1. "I think they made the trip by themselves, as Mrs. Langdon refused to go with them," wrote gossip columnist John P. Medbury. "However, she might have left at the last minute. A wife's negative is never positive." R.K.O. agreed to the $2,500 figure that Ziegfeld scorned, but it was noticeably less than the $3,500 weekly he'd received during pre-crash 1929.

Since *The Messenger* had been cannibalized for *Hotter Than Hot*, Langdon opted to revive *After the Ball*. It's open to conjecture whether he or his agent cleared this with Rose. Given he was in arrears on her settlement, Langdon likely bypassed her entirely,

Edith, Helen and Virginia Langdon send Harry off to New York in style on February 12, 1931.

unless she waived a rights fee in the interests of getting him a salary, in the hope of a resumption of payments. Shubert played the clubhouse manager (Scene 2) and cop (Scene 3), while two musical comedy veterans, Lillian White and Berta Donn, essayed the roles originated by Rose and Cecil.

Langdon's troupe opened in Boston the week of March 7, then in Providence, Rhode Island, the following week. Both gigs did well from a box-office perspective, with *Variety*'s stringer in Providence noting that "most of the credit [went] to the comedian." On March 21, they returned to New York for four days at the 86th Street Theater, where an unnamed critic, unaware that the sketch was nearly ten years old, reviewed it for *Variety*:

Harry Langdon returns to vaude with a sure-fire offering. His new act gives the comedian ample scope for his pantomime.

Carrying quite an expensive act, from the scenery angle. Four scenes, first in "one" representing a golf course, second in "full," club house, third a street scene in front of a hospital and closing before the regulation "one."

Two girls and a man, latter Eddie Shubert, support. Opening scene has Langdon spearing golf balls and hiding them, with the three assists wondering what became of them. Second scene has one of the girl's *(sic)* breaking the windows of the clubhouse while attempting to tee off, with the blame thrown on Langdon. He monkies around a stalled prop auto in the third scene.

Through it all Langdon weaves in his familiar dumb gestures and expressions. He does more talking in this act than he's done in some of his talkers. His patter with the support is of the nut variety. For finish Langdon does a short comedy dance.

Langdon closed to a whale of a hand. Every movement was familiar and relished.

The day after the engagement closed, *Film Daily* reported that Langdon had been signed by Vitaphone for a series of 12 short comedies. By now, the Vitaphone moniker was owned by Warner Bros., and the name used for its Brooklyn-based shorts studio. For reasons unknown, but most likely financial, the deal collapsed. The studio opted instead for the presumably less expensive Joe Penner, a younger vaudevillian who would achieve a burst of nationwide attention a few years later on radio with a catch-phrase: "Wanna buy a duck?" One of Penner's Vitaphone comedies was a remake of Langdon's *Fiddlesticks* titled *Sax Appeal*. "Penner is a sure pinch hitter for Harry Langdon," said *Motion Picture Daily*'s review.

After a few weeks, *The Third Little Show* also fell through. "Harry Langdon was set for the revue," wrote *Variety* when the show opened out-of-town in April. "Material did not fit him, and it was called off"; Ernest Truex, who specialized in meek characters, took the comedian's spot. Langdon spent a week at the Brooklyn Fox, opening on April 24. "[He] will entertain with an act called *After the Ball* [and] will immediately thereafter leave Brooklyn for

Hollywood, where he'll go flicker again," said the *Brooklyn Eagle*. It was wishful thinking on somebody's part.

There were no offers from Hollywood, and precious few from vaudeville. Therefore, he had time to wax philosophic when writer J. R. Milne came calling, for a piece that was published in the Sunday magazine section of the *Omaha World and Herald*. The article, titled

Harry Langdon, the movie comedian, as he seems on the stage at the Fox Theater this week.

"Whoopee Isn't Fun," consisted of Langdon's definition of what it means to have a good time ("I can have a pretty good time taking a nap in the afternoon"). In the process, the older-but-wiser comedian shared some revealing remarks about, in his words, "the overrated matter of success," especially in Hollywood:

> Half the people I meet are yearning for the day when their ship will come in and dock without wrecking the wharf. That's when they're going to have their good time — when they have plenty of money, and can travel, and burn up the town, and ride in limousines and say "Keep the change."

> That is applesauce. It's hooey. It's bunk.

> Take it from one who has scraped his foot on every rung of the ladder, the best time of all is when you're working your head off to get somewhere. It isn't when you get there. When you get up to the top you're scared to death of falling off. Life is full of grief. The same critics — I'm speaking as an actor — who lifted you up will be just hanging around waiting for the day when they're destined to pull you down. You know it. You don't blame them. It's their job.

> When you're on the way up you can keep your eyes up, enjoy working your head off, and think only of the success you are going to make and what a fine job you're doing. When you reach the top — well, then you have a chance to look down. And the danger of a dive makes you dizzy.

> There's nothing but grief in the movies — even for those who win. In fact, they have the most grief.

Langdon went on to say that he was having a good time in vaudeville, in part because he was able to easily overcome any nervousness, and because "you have a chance to live like a human being." But deep down he knew that motion pictures were still the most desirable occupation from a financial standpoint; if he ever forgot it, Helen was there to remind him.

On May 15, Langdon's lawyers filed the "false prosecution" lawsuit against ex-landlord James Dickason, asking $500,000 for damages ("humiliation and loss of sleep and weight" among them), and an additional $2,500 in legal fees. Dickason retaliated by filing his own suit to recover $11,129 pledged by the Langdons in two promissory notes.

Broadway came courting again, in the form of a new musical comedy production to be written by Moss Hart, Morrie Ryskind and Irving Berlin, and produced by Sam H. Harris. Langdon was actually placed under contract, along with Andrew Tombes, Lulu McConnell, Joseph Macaulay and Jack Whiting. Rehearsals were to follow at an unspecified future date.

The next immediate booking was for vaudeville: a tour of Middle America's less-populated cities, beginning on May 25. Places like Louisville, Kentucky; Logansport, Indiana; Youngstown, Ohio; and other towns he'd not seen since before "going flicker." Now

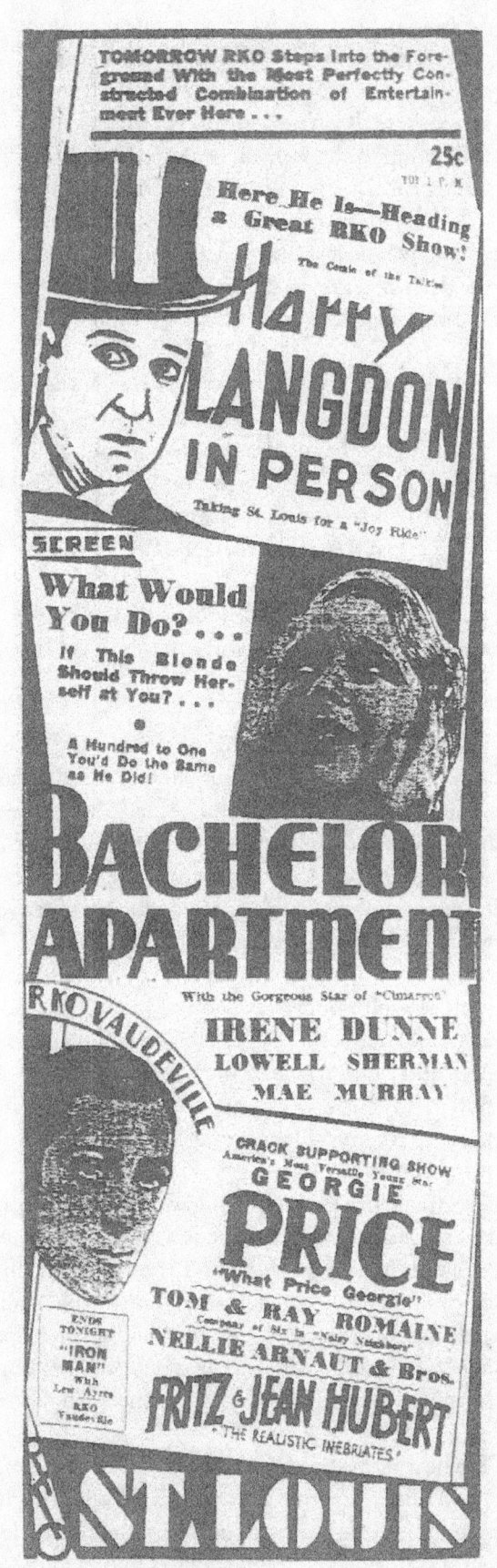

that the months were warmer, Helen had moved east and came along as his dresser. "[She] stands in the wings and hands me my little coat and helps me change and we listen to the laughs together," he told one reporter.

All was not so idyllic behind the scenes, however. A primary reason he asked her along was in the hope of curbing her tendency to spend his salary as soon as (and sometimes before) he'd earned it. Three years after the glory days had come to a resounding halt, Helen had not lost the taste for glamour and finery that "Harry, dear" had so recklessly cultivated before their marriage. Later would come reports that she'd persistently make wisecracks about his work, and insist that he find more lucrative employment. Being arrested, losing both a house and furniture, and schlepping wardrobe backstage in the heartland were *not* what she'd signed up for.

In Ohio the third week of June, in between stints at Youngstown and Cincinnati, the Langdons took a 10-day vacation, some of which was spent in Helen's old hometown, Toledo. *News-Bee* reporter Donald Pond was there with a photographer to cover the couple's visit with one of Helen's old school chums, Mrs. V. R. Alberstett. "Harry's conversation," wrote Pond, "liberally sprinkled with laugh-getting lines that were spontaneous and occasionally cutting, dealt with the show business, Hollywood, New York, his vaudeville tour and the musical comedy that will claim his services in the near future. It did not turn personal at all except to remind his interviewers that he met Mrs. Langdon when she was playing with him" in pictures.

"I played in musical comedies in New York before I went into the pictures, of course. Worked for Dillingham, you know," Langdon told the reporter, stretching truth to the breaking point. "Why shouldn't I love the stage, anyway? Made my first appearance when I was 12. I'm glad to be back playing in front of people. It's nice, you know, getting your pay in applause and laughs as you do your stuff." Presumably the actual paychecks were unworthy of the comparison by that point.

The photo that ran with the piece shows a smiling Helen in a wicker lawn chair, wearing a smart summer dress and a hat to shade her eyes, looking every inch the hometown girl who'd wed a Hollywood star. Harry, half-resting beside her on the arm of her chair, looks decidedly less comfortable in a full three-piece suit and tie, squinting as the sun beats down.

HARRY LANGDON, WIFE VISIT FRIENDS HERE

Film Actor Stops in City on Way to Fill Stage Engagement

By DONALD POND.

HARRY LANGDON, famous as the pathetic, eager little dummy who has stumbled across countless cinema screens in almost every land, Saturday stopped in Toledo for breakfast and proved to be a substantial, middle-aged gentleman who looks like a successful auto salesman.

With him was his wife, the former Miss Helen Walton, of Toledo. They were breakfast guests of Mr. and Mrs. V. R. Alberstett, 1246 Craigwood road, and later visited Mrs. Alberstett's parents, Mr. and Mrs. W. W. Southerland, 52 Birckhead place. Mrs. Alberstett, whose husband is head of the commercial department of Woodward High school, is a girlhood friend of Mrs. Langdon.

Harry's conversation, liberally sprinkled with laugh-getting lines that were spontaneous and occasionally cutting, dealt with the show business, Hollywood, New York, his vaudeville tour and the musical comedy that will claim his services in the near future.

It did not turn personal at all except to remind his interviewers that he met Mrs. Langdon when she was playing with him for Metro-Goldwyn-Mayer.

The musical show, written by the authors of one of the last year's hits, has not been titled as yet and Harry has not seen the book. All he could tell about it was that he was enthusiastic. He hopes it's going to be a smash hit and he waits with just a little impatience for the rehearsal call.

"I'm glad to be back playing in front of people," said Langdon. "It's nice, you know, getting your pay in applause and laughs as you do your stuff. Helen stands in the wings and hands me my little coat and helps me change and we listen to the laughs together. It's better than the studios, in a way."

He made it plain that he wasn't too tired of pictures to plan the making of a series of shorts and a feature or so at the New York studios of Paramount before they close Oct. 1. It was just, he intimated, that it was pretty nice

Mr. and Mrs. Harry Langdon say "Hello!" to Toledo.

t oget back on the stage.

"I played in musical comedies in New York before I went into the pictures, of course," he explained. "Worked for Dillingham, you know. Why shouldn't I love the stage, anyway? Made my first appearance when I was 12."

Toledo News Bee, *June 13, 1931.*

For such a normally reticent man to speak so insistently — and with "cutting lines" — about himself and his profession signifies that he was starved for attention — or at least meaningful conversation — during this break.

July began with an injury. Opening on the 4th at the Cincinnati Albee, he punctured a blood vessel in his left eye when struck by the license plate on his prop auto. He continued with the act through the finish, and then sought treatment. The doctor advised him to take several days off to heal. Langdon refused; he couldn't afford it.

The rest of the month brought the insult that inevitably follows injury. Back in February, just prior to leaving for New York, Langdon had borrowed $1,532 from a friend, William Koberle, to buy some new furniture for his Hollywood apartment, where Helen had chosen to remain. For security, Koberle secured a chattel mortgage on the furniture in exchange for the loan. On July 9, having received no repayment, and unable to track down Langdon, he seized the furniture and auctioned it. On July 30, James Dickason won his suit, and Langdon was ordered to pay the $11,129 plus legal fees.

This particular tour ended on August 21, at Shea's Theater in Toronto. Then it was back to New York City to see if the Moss-Ryskind-Berlin musical comedy was any closer to opening rehearsals, which was not the case. Based on the lack of trade and newspaper coverage, nothing was happening for Langdon, except behind closed doors, where his patience would finally run out.

Another vaudeville gig was lined up for October, a week at the Cleveland Palace beginning on the 10th. Before leaving the 57th Street hotel-apartment where he and Helen were residing, he placed a notice in the major New York dailies, announcing he would no longer be held responsible for his wife's debts. On October 4, he packed his bags and lit out for Ohio. By the time the notice was published, he'd arrived in Cleveland and had registered under an alias.

New York's tabloid press, sniffing a scoop, descended upon Helen and asked point blank if she and Harry were washed up. The former actress — unwilling to disembark from the Langdon gravy train, despite its derailing — gave a bravura performance: "Heavens, no! We're happy as two turtledoves. Somebody has been using my charge accounts at the stores and both Harry and I are very angry about it. Harry inserted the advertisements to forestall any other purchases in my name. But no, no, no, it does NOT mean that we have come to the parting of the ways. Far from it!"

Helen's exclamation appeared in the papers on October 9. When Langdon saw she wasn't going to take the hint, he immediately wired Nathan Lieberman, his New York lawyer, to file a suit for separate maintenance. For emphasis, he labeled his

wife "a persistent nag [who] makes herself generally obnoxious," and accused her of extravagance. "Her bill for cosmetics alone would sometimes be over $350 a month." Lieberman's filing stated Langdon would agree to "reasonable" alimony, without naming a figure.

On stage, he was his usual self. Reviewer Glenn C. Pullen, who had critiqued his films going back to the First National era, caught opening night and wrote it up for the *Cleveland Plain Dealer*: "Harry Langdon, at the Palace this week, is one of the few film comics who doesn't lose his screen personality when appearing behind the footlights. With his dinky hat and baggy suit, his 'frozen-face' and plaintive gestures, he looks as if he had just stepped out of one of his old movie comedies.

"Langdon, who belongs more in vaudeville than to Hollywood, is particularly comical when he tells a whimsical joke in a stuttering and gesticulatory style. His horseplay in a 'prop' auto and at a trick organ is amusing, too. A few of his gags are rather blue. His clowning with a voluptuous singer is laughable but more fit for a burlesque house." (Luckily, there were no threats to shut down the show this time.)

For her part, Helen raced to Cleveland in an attempt to charm her way back into his life, but Langdon steadfastly refused to see her, preferring to let his lawyer do the talking. Only when he was certain she was headed back to New York did he open his mouth:

> I don't feel like making an audience laugh after I have had a quarrel with a woman. I have been married twice, and I have learned women just must quarrel. Women are like that.
>
> My wife is a wonderful woman with high ideals, but she was not intended for me. Nor was any other woman. Women like to quarrel and I am not much of a fighter. In order to be a good comedian, I must escape the tragedy of marriage.
>
> After listening to a woman's quarrelling for about three hours, I feel like going to Europe or the mountains or to Mexico, and not onto the stage.

Langdon continued to lay low after his Cleveland appearance ended, and except for issuing denials to the press about her alleged extravagance, Helen wasn't pressing the issue, evidently still angling for a reconciliation. On November 6, another professional blow had landed: for unpublicized reasons, Sam Harris called off the proposed musical comedy and dismissed the cast, releasing them from their contracts. Langdon returned to the vaudeville stage on November 22, at the Brooklyn Albee. On Wednesday the 25th, putting matters into terms he was certain Helen would finally grasp, he filed a voluntary petition of bankruptcy in federal court. Despite his current engagement, plus an upcoming week at Proctor's in Newark, he listed his occupation as "Actor, Unemployed," and attributed his situation to a lack of success in talking pictures.

"Langdon listed his liabilities as $62,637, of which $30,400 is owed to the United States Government in income taxes," read the papers the next morning, "and his assets as $700, consisting of an automobile valued at $200, props, scenery and trunks at $300 and $200 owed to him by his lawyer. His clothing, which is exempt in the bankruptcy action, is valued at $400." Those to whom he owed money included James Dickason for $12,113 "and more than 100 small debts to trades people and individuals in Hollywood and Los Angeles." Langdon actually understated his liabilities, as he still legally owed Rose nearly $60,000 in unpaid property settlement, along with interest that had been accruing since payments ceased in August 1930.

With that, Helen finally woke up. On December 18, she filed her own suit of separation in Westchester County court, charging abandonment and hiring a former judge, William D. Cunningham, to represent her. "She will ask $1,000 a week alimony," read the account in the *New York American*, "to support herself and a daughter by a previous marriage." The action took Langdon and lawyer Lieberman by surprise, as they'd been expecting an out-of-court settlement, but hell hath no fury like a "grasping woman" scorned.

Helen's complaint stated that Langdon frequently drank alcohol to excess, his pet name for liquor being "Woof-Woof." She also detailed an odd habit: whenever traveling, he would carry ten $1,000 bills, and attach each one underneath chairs and tables with thumbtacks. In his response, Langdon agreed not to contest her suit, but objected to the alimony figure. He restated her extravagance, declared she drank every bit as much as he did, and explained that he carried the cash with him because, were he to deposit it into a bank, Rose would attach it. He pointed out Helen had already cost him $15,000 paid to her ex-husband, and added "[she] crabs my acts and cramps my style by wisecracking." Lieberman added that her alimony request was "impudent," noting his client had filed for bankruptcy.

Helen's team requested a week to answer Langdon's "scurrilous and scandalous" accusations, and the lawyers took over once the case went in front of Justice Joseph Morschauser on December 30. Both sides made it clear that alimony was the issue.

Pointing out the $1,000 bills habit, Cunningham told the court Langdon had filed "a dishonest bankruptcy" and accused him of recently "drinking heavily of 'woof-woof' [with the result that his earnings] have probably fallen off." The alimony figure, he asserted, was based on his $2,500 weekly vaudeville salary, an offer of $10,000 per week from Paramount Pictures Corporation that he'd not yet accepted (Paramount, in a statement for the trades, denied such an offer existed), and "a large salary for drawing cartoons for a syndicate, also unaccepted." Letters written by Langdon to Helen were produced, dated as recently as the previous summer, containing "many endearing phrases." Cunningham accused Eddie Shubert of turning Langdon against his wife, based on a friendship with Rose.

Lieberman, in turn, pointed out, "When [Helen] married Langdon, she came to him with two pieces of broken furniture and a daughter. He had to repair the furniture and the 16-year-old daughter has been a constant expense." In a recent column for the *New York Evening Graphic*, Julia Shawell reported, "His foster child ran up a bill of $350 just for food at a Manhattan hotel." Presumably this referred to Virginia, since Edith, then 17, had recently departed for pastures unknown. He spelled out his client's $62,000 bankruptcy, exclusive of the $60,000 owed to Rose, and that his only salary is $2,500 per week in vaudeville, but "he isn't always working."

Since neither side was contesting the separation, Justice Morschauser ordered the trial set for February 23, and ordered temporary alimony of $100 per week, which would be superceded by whatever figure was agreed upon at trial. Both counsels agreed to the ruling.

Langdon went back to work, but as 1931 gave way to '32, his bad luck didn't change. On January 6, he along with eight other acts walked out of an engagement at the independent Palace Theater in Baltimore, Maryland. They'd performed nine shows over the previous three days, and two more that Wednesday, but it became apparent that salaries would not be forthcoming. "The [walkout] came just before curtain time, forcing refunds to reserved seat customers already present," reported *Variety* on January 12. "The bill would have cost $7,300 if paid. Under the scale and the exceptionally heavy stage nut for a town like

Putting on a brave face for the industry.

this, the venture had a tough battle from scratch. The no-payoff was just another worry for Harry Langdon, who had plenty others while here." It was the first time he'd been stranded since the bad old days of *The Show Girl* nearly a quarter-century before.

It was around this time that *Photoplay*'s February issue went on sale, containing Katherine Albert's "What Happened to Harry Langdon." Billed as "The amazing story of how a two-page letter ruined the career of a grand funny man," Albert's piece began by recounting the recent headlines pertaining to the separation and bankruptcy, "but the most amazing story of little Harry Langdon's rise and fall has never been printed. It is as fantastic as Hollywood itself."

The article (which can be found in Appendix VI) tells how Langdon, "an itinerant vaudevillian," found stardom at Sennett's, went on to independent feature production, released his first director for going over budget, to replace him with "a poorly paid gag constructor…whose name cannot be mentioned here." The anonymous director "turned out a jim dandy of a piece in *The Strong Man*. It was made in record time, under cost and…put Langdon right on the top of the heap." Subsequently, he and his (also unnamed) writer quarreled on the next film, which "was completed in all the maddening discord of a school girl squabble," followed by "the angry director" writing his "vitriolic letter," as discussed earlier.

"Langdon is a highly sensitized fellow," she continued. "The thing completely got him…. Fearful, lest he prove true to the statements made in the letter, he took anyone's advice…would listen to any prop boy's suggestion for a gag and try to use it. He also heeded the advice of one of the other producers who told him he should shoot his stuff fast, turn out pictures and cash in quick…. The critics panned these quickly turned out films….

"Well, it got him down — that's all. He couldn't be funny when he knew that they were all whispering about him, that they all believed the stories of his conceit…. His life is a mess. In real life, he's playing that beaten, knocked about little fellow he made popular on the screen…. He knows he's still a good comedian, but every time anybody looks at him sideways he remembers the letter and its tragic results."

It's unclear how the West Coast-based Albert got her information. Langdon was in the East, and the article contains only two direct quotes, both of which had appeared in columnist blurbs from that time. She surely didn't talk to Capra, who in any case wouldn't have known what went on behind the scenes after his departure. The most logical source is Ripley, at that time back at his old post as Mack Sennett's scenario editor. If so, he put an interesting spin on First National's front office furor surrounding *The Chaser* and their utter disregard of *Heart Trouble*. Aside from possibly having his own score to settle with Capra (whom Albert described as "successful and prosperous and powerful in Hollywood"), Ripley remained a loyal friend to Langdon, and in two years would initiate the comedian's longest-lasting affiliation with any Hollywood studio.

As for the "knocked about little fellow," somebody must have taken Albert's article to heart. After playing a split week in Massachusetts and New Jersey between January 16 and 22, Langdon inexplicably received backing for a return to the screen. The proposal was for a series of two-reel comedies to be independently produced in the East, using staff from Paramount's recently shuttered Astoria studios: production manager Joseph Boyle, cameraman George Weber, soundman Percy Glenn and assistant director David Thursby. For the pilot, Langdon would direct his own script, which he wrote over the course of two weeks and titled "The Show Goat." Facilities would be rented inexpensively at the newly renovated Royal Studios in Grantwood, New Jersey, originally built during the movies' formative years.

Langdon wrote a foreword for his script:

> The story deals with the dramatic incident in the community of a small mid-western town. The wife of the proprietor of the Sheva-Lade Auto Company, the town's leading automobile agency, promotes the idea of selling to the community a motor fire truck to replace the old horse driven vehicle. To do this — she, being the town's social leader — conceived the idea of raising the money by means of the presentation of a play which she writes and directs herself, getting the local townspeople to act in it. Among them is Harry. Harry has a sweetheart, Sue, to whom he is very devoted. Sue's father, Seth, is the only paid fireman in the town — being the driver of the old horse drawn fire engine. If the play is a success Seth will lose his position because of the fact he has never driven a motor vehicle of any kind — much less a fire truck. This, Sue explains to Harry, and while he is in sympathy

with Sue and her father, he is also filled with the ambition of being an actor. This puts him in a spot of being torn between love and ambition. Then, through great ingenuity, he succeeds in showing the town officials that Seth, Sue's father, much against his own will, and entirely by Harry's effort, seemingly can and does drive the new fire truck. In this way Seth becomes the hero of the moment, but it is Harry alone that is the real hero, and all ends happily.

I have tried to give the story a note of real sincerity. The part of Harry is a real boy — simple — sincere and human — one that really lives and not an exaggerated cartoon. This also goes for all the other characters: Mr. Glom, the town undertaker; Mrs. Winters, the social leader; Mr. Guthers, the butcher; Mr. Talburt, the town barber; and Mrs. Talburt, his jealous wife; Miss Lottie Barnes — the public stenographer who was to Chicago once; Sue Carroll, Harry's sweetheart; Mrs. Lathrup — the giggly dressmaker; etc. down the line.

These are true to life types that could and do live in a small community. I would like to have you picture them as I have.

The script opens on the poster that announces Mrs. Winters's play, *Her First Wrong Step*. Looking it over, Seth Carroll and his pal Hank discuss the fact that if the town acquires the fire truck, he'll be out of a job. Sue tries to comfort her father, then heads over to Mrs. Winters's home, where the actors — all of whom are townsfolk, not professionals — are gathering to rehearse. Sue speaks to Harry just as he's being summoned by Mrs. Winters:

MRS. WINTERS: Harry — come, come, come. You know we need our little property boy!

HARRY: Goodbye, Honey — I got to go in and act.

SUE: Yes — you are going in to act in something that is going to take away my father's job — our bread and butter!

Harry, script in hand, is torn between comforting his girl and getting to the rehearsal.

HARRY: Everything will turn out all right, Susie — your dad can drive the new engine.

SUE: No he can't — he don't know how to drive an automobile — he can only drive horses.

HARRY: Well — maybe — or something — you can't tell — well, well, well, I'll have to go in and act now.

SUE: All right — go in and ACT!! If you can't act any better than you did with me last night on the front porch — you're rotten!

During rehearsal, Miss Barnes, the leading lady who is displaying some ill-advised temperament, is unhappy with the quality of the doorbell sound Harry is making. The leading man, Mr. Talburt, has his own problems as his wife is exceedingly jealous and is causing a disturbance. Before long the rehearsal devolves, especially when Harry inadvertently reveals a hidden bar behind a curtain, which distracts all the actors. Eventually Mrs. Winters gives up and allows everyone to have a drink. Mrs. Talburt throws her drink into Miss Barnes's face, Mrs. Winters gamely tries to close the bar and resume the rehearsal, and before long, Harry is thoroughly drunk.

The night of the show is no better. All of the "actors" are suffering from stage fright, except Miss Barnes, who is simply too temperamental to go on stage first. Mr. Guthers, playing Miss Barnes's father, refuses to enter until Harry beans him a couple of times with a club, then revives him with smelling salts. Mrs. Lathrop, playing his wife, also refuses to go on, until she sees Harry is about to give her the same treatment. Meanwhile, Mr. Talburt misses his cue because his wife has knocked him out with a brick. Harry revives him and literally drags him on stage. Mrs. Winters orders Harry to keep Mrs. Talburt away.

Eventually, Mr. Glom, portraying the villain, makes his entrance and starts the "fire" that concludes the play. As Mr. Glom delivers his concluding line ("My proud beauty, you will never leave this house alive! Ha! Ha! Ha!"), Mrs. Winters asks Harry if the fire truck is outside. Harry checks and tells her there's only a bicycle. She sends him to retrieve the fire truck, and attempts to drag out the conclusion by having Mr. Glom repeat his lines again and again. By the time Mr. Glom makes his seventh reappearance, the audience says the line for him.

While this is going on, Harry runs to the firehouse and, in a moment of inspiration, puts Seth in the drivers' seat of the new engine. Seth protests that he can't

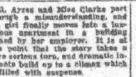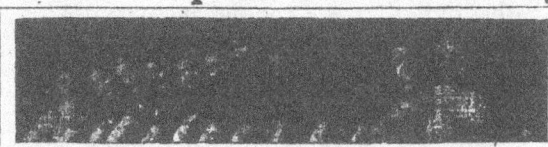

When Harry Langdon comes to Madison Wisconsin for 3 days in May 1932, merchandisers jump on the bandwagon.

drive, but Harry starts it up and puts Seth's foot on the gas pedal. Two townsfolk, Ryan and Leonard, see Seth driving and follow on foot. When the engine literally crashes onto the stage, the audience stands and cheers. Ryan arrives and tells Seth, "You're the man we want to drive that fire truck! There ain't no one in this town or any other that could drive it as you did!" As for Harry, Sue runs up and smothers him with kisses.

Production began on February 8 and continued for two weeks. A few changes were made to the action during filming; not uncommon where comedies were concerned. Instead of Harry accidentally revealing the hidden bar, the film has Mrs. Winters's husband (portrayed by Langdon's crony Eddie Shubert) showing it to him, and plying him with various alcoholic drinks, while Harry tries to protest; all he's interested in is beer. The character of Mrs. Winters is less haughty than scripted, and a scene in which Harry inadvertently tears the back of her dress was changed so that it happens to the snippy Miss Barnes. Assuming everything else was shot nearly as written, Langdon evidently wound up with a solid three-reeler.

While Langdon was tied up with filming, his lawyer, Lieberman, was reaching out to Helen's team, hoping for an out-of-court settlement, but although her demand was halved to $500 per week (still too much in Lieberman's opinion), Helen was pushing for a trial. "I must refuse to settle as long as Harry's charges against my character have been unanswered," she told the *New York Mirror*. "How can I let the matter drop without demanding exoneration? Harry recklessly made those accusations against me, and now I intend to force him into court to back them up."

At a press conference in her Yonkers hotel, she elaborated: "He said I was extravagant — said I spent $350 a month on cosmetics alone. The truth is I never was inside a beauty parlor once in my life." Evidently the reporters present were too gallant to point out the difference between a cosmetics counter and a beauty parlor. As for the alimony, Helen declared, "I despise women who bleed men for alimony. My lawyer made me ask for $500 but I know Harry is not making so much as he used to, and I'd be more than satisfied with $250. That would be enough to keep me and my daughter Virginia."

How noble of you, Langdon must have thought disdainfully, while visions of diamond brooches and ermine coats and gold trinkets and money spent like water danced in his head.

Helen testified on the morning of March 1, before Justice Morschauser, but he withheld granting the separation until Langdon appeared later in the afternoon and testified as to his earning capacity. "Questioned by Mrs. Langdon's attorney, he said his gross earnings in 1931 were $48,000 and his net earnings $25,000," read one news account. After that, Morschauser set alimony at $150 per week for the first six months, to be increased to $250 weekly thereafter. Langdon was also ordered to pay $2,500 in legal fees. Langdon stated he was "fully informed" of the terms and signed the papers. It was over…for the moment.

On March 6, *Film Daily* reported, "The comedy which Harry Langdon recently completed at the Royal Studios is now in the process of being cut for early release. Those who have seen the 'rushes' claim that Langdon stages a real comeback in the picture which has a side show background." The same paper reported on March 20:

Harry Langdon's new picture, which was being produced at the Royal Studios as a short subject comedy, has been changed to a feature. Those who have seen the picture claim that Langdon staged such a marvelous comeback… that it was decided to make it into a feature.

A few days later, another blurb stated that work would begin on additional scenes starting March 24.

Before that could get started, however, Langdon was summoned to substitute for his *Soldier's Plaything* co-star, Ben Lyon, at the RKO in Flushing, New York, beginning March 23. Shortly after that Martin Beck, RKO's head of booking, sent him and Lillian White on a tour into the Midwest with *After the Ball* that would last until mid-May. With two wives to pay off, he had to follow the money. In fact, "The Show Goat" would never progress beyond its short subject origins, and wouldn't be released until September 1933.

Whether due to the strong word of mouth on "The Show Goat" or the loss of Helen — or both — he was becoming a hot property in Hollywood again. In April, Paramount approached him for a role in their upcoming satire of the Olympic Games, *Million Dollar Legs*. United Artists, planning an offbeat feature musical for Al Jolson, sought him as a co-star. Trade papers and columnists also reported feelers from Fox Film Corporation and Warner Bros.

On May 13, with his tour wrapping up in Kansas City, Langdon signed for the Jolson film, which was then titled "Living High." As "Egghead," a radically communistic street-sweeper at odds with Jolson's hobo, he'd have more visibility than in the comedian-studded *Million Dollar Legs*; also UA's contract put him on salary immediately. He flew back to Hollywood — his first airplane trip — on the 16th. "It seems more like twelve years than twelve months," he told the local press; it was actually fifteen months, but the comparison was apt. "I hope that I won't have to leave again."

Asked about his recent matrimonial misadventure, he replied, "I am glad a divorce was not granted, for marriage has not been successful for me, and I don't want to try it again." No doubt he was sincere, but — as was made clear in *His First Flame* — "Love is the only fire against which there is no insurance."

CHAPTER THIRTEEN

"Pictures Are Where I Belong"
1932–1934

On May 14, the day after Langdon signed his contract, background footage for "Living High" was filmed in New York's Central Park, where much of the story would take place. Joseph M. Schenck, United Artists' head of production, hired Lewis Milestone to produce the picture and Harry d'Arrast to direct. It was to be a comeback picture for Al Jolson, who'd fallen from popularity since his unprecedented success in Warner Bros.' earliest talkies, and had been off screen for about two years. Richard Rodgers and Lorenz Hart were composing the music for Ben Hecht's original story.

Hecht and Schenck wanted to evoke the fantasy feeling inherent in the films of French director Rene Clair; hence the engagement of d'Arrast. Rodgers and Hart worked with S. N. Behrman to create a script brimming with "rhythmic dialogue," a phrase that would be heavily promoted, in which principal characters would speak in rhyme while moving in concert with the music, to be orchestrated by a very young Alfred Newman. There were still problems to iron out, so casting was temporarily put on hold with only three principals — Jolson, Langdon and leading lady Madge Evans — engaged and drawing salary to date.

The day Langdon arrived in Hollywood, the press reported that Bert Wheeler and Robert Woolsey had broken up their five-year association over a contract dispute. "Wheeler and I never really formed a team at any time," explained Woolsey. "He had his manager and attorney and I had mine. Wheeler's manager advised him to cancel [a pending contract with Columbia Pictures]. He did and started east, ending what professional relationships we may have had." Consequently, Woolsey had his manager reach out to Langdon's, hoping to replace Wheeler for the Columbia contract. Langdon, though, was committed to "Living High," the starting date for which had still not been set. In mid-July, shortly after the team made the exhibitors' annual list of the Top Ten box-office attractions, Wheeler and Woolsey reconciled.

On May 23, Langdon signed a contract for four two-reel comedies, with an option for two more, to be released through Educational Pictures. The contract was not with Educational, however, but with Arvid E. Gillstrom, who began his career in 1911, worked at Keystone and had been directing for Charles and Al Christie since the 1920s. With the Christie Brothers preparing to file bankruptcy, Gillstrom opted to branch out with his own production unit. Gillstrom also signed Vernon Dent as supporting actor/second banana; he and Langdon had not worked together in nearly seven years. Harry Edwards was expected to split directing chores with Gillstrom for the six shorts. Langdon would receive $2,000 per picture to start, and was free to accept feature film and stage work.

In need of a permanent address, Langdon rented a home from Rose, who'd entered the real estate business upon their divorce. A columnist for *New Movie* magazine elaborated:

> Wonder how it would feel to rent your house from your former wife? Harry Langdon is finding that out! He is renting his former wife's home on a Hollywood hill, and up she comes each month for the rent.
>
> Harry says he talks real fiercely to her every time she comes — and has the time of his life. He says he never could talk that way and get by with it while they were living together and now is his chance. "If she talks back, I'll move," grins the irrepressible Harry.

"Living High" finally got under way on Monday, June 13 under a new title: "The New Yorker." Reportedly, it was d'Arrast's first and last day. Latter-day accounts have it that he didn't care for Jolson's style and requested permission of Milestone to recast the part. The request was refused and d'Arrast quit. Whether the account is fact or legend, it wasn't very long into production before d'Arrast was replaced with Chester Erskine.

Mabel Sheldon around the time she met Langdon in the summer of 1932.

Production took up most of the next two months, with location shooting in the Pacific Palisades (doubling as Central Park) during the height of summer. One evening, Langdon's agent, William Gill, invited him to a dinner party at the home of his girl friend, Janice Snoden. She, in turn, invited a friend of hers, Mabel Sheldon, to keep him company. Mabel recalled in 1997:

> My high-school chum — we would be the ones who would ditch classes — became a beautician. I was working in an insurance office. We used to go out on double-dates, and one night she called up and said, "Mae, I'm having a dinner party, and I was wondering if you'd like to come and be a companion to one of the customers that's coming." I said,
> "Sure, but I've just come back from the beach, and I'm sunburned and peeling and I look horrible." She said, "Oh, well, you'll probably never see him again anyway, so come on over." So I went to the party and was introduced to Harry Langdon. My friend says, "He's the comedian!" I said, "So what?" I didn't know who he was.

Sheet music for Harry Langdon's "Lulu" (1932).

Apparently that impressed Langdon. With no knowledge of his career, she had no preconceived notions of his net worth. Moreover, with an obvious sunburn, she had to be uncomfortable yet wasn't complaining about it. The two hit it off and he decided this was someone he wanted to see again. "After the dinner party, we went on another date," Mabel told Edward Watz. "He asked me to accompany him with another couple. After that evening, we became steady."

Mabel Georgena Sheldon was born in Portsmouth, England, on February 3, 1906, exactly two days prior to Harry and Rose's vaudeville debut. Reportedly her grandfather and father, both natives of India, were in the military, and despite living in Southern California as a young adult she had no inclination to pursue a show business career.

Sparked by the budding romance, or possibly his "rhythmic dialogue" in "The New Yorker," Langdon tried his hand at songwriting. He came up with two tunes: "Calling All Cars" and "Lulu." The latter was published, and by December Phil Harris and his Orchestra had added it to their repertoire during their engagement at Hollywood's Cocoanut Grove.

Langdon was finally able to begin work for

Gillstrom during the last week of August. In the interim, Educational had signed Harry Edwards to direct Andy Clyde, whom they'd hired away from Mack Sennett. The director's reunion with his former star was postponed while Gillstrom took the helm himself. Nevertheless, there was a burst of nostalgia awaiting Langdon: Educational's studio had been the home of Principal Pictures, where he'd made his first ill-fated comedies only nine years before.

Their initial effort was *The Big Flash*, written by long-time Sennett comic Bobby Vernon, in which Vernon Dent uses amateur photographer Harry in his quest to become a big shot in the newspaper business, as well as impress Betty (Ruth Hiatt), the editor's receptionist. Harry has his own crush on Betty and finally wins her when he inadvertently overpowers the notorious gangster Brick Dugan (Matthew Betz). Langdon pretty much picked up where he left off at Hal Roach, highlights being a scene where he's "vamped" by Lita Chevret (as Dugan's moll) and a reprise of the *Long Pants* routine of attempting to get an indifferent cop's attention, with the variation that it's a genuine patrolman and not a dummy. The street scenes were shot on the Chaplin studio backlot, using storefronts built for *City Lights*.

Trade critics were delighted to see Langdon back in action. Lou Jacobs of the *Hollywood Filmograph* attended a local preview in September. "Harry Langdon is at his best ably assisted by Vernon Dent. His frozen pan blundering in the character of an assistant newspaper photographer snapping the robbery of a jewelry store, kept the audience at the Uptown screaming. Who ever said Harry Langdon is to make a comeback in pictures is absolutely wrong. As far as the public is concerned he never went away." *Film Daily* enthused, "Plenty of gags and nice comedy

Harry and Lita Chevret in The Big Flash *(1932).*

work on the part of Langdon make this look like a strong laugh number," and *Motion Picture Herald* proclaimed, "The picture moves along in a zippy style. Careful restriction of the amount of dialogue coupled with abundant use of many of the oldtime gags that featured [in] the silent short subjects gives the picture plenty to amuse your patrons."

Educational had been one of the top comedy studios of the 1920s and the only one with its own sales exchanges to handle distribution. The increased production cost that accompanied sound, coupled with stronger competition from M.G.M.-Roach, Vitaphone and Paramount, including the loss of Mack Sennett to the latter company, plus a misguided foray into feature film production (under the name World Wide Pictures) took its toll on the resulting releases and significantly diminished Educational's standing among exhibitors and patrons. Shortly after Langdon joined their release roster, the company had been forced to divest itself of its exchanges, while creditors took ownership of its two West Coast studios. Fox Film Corporation assumed the distribution of the shorts.

The Langdon comedies, along with the studio's own Andy Clyde series, would be the most successful Educational product of the season. Part of this was due to Gillstrom's comedy know-how and ability to stretch a dollar. He was unafraid of location shooting, as witness the second of the series, *Tired Feet*, most of which was shot at Lake Arrowhead during late September into October. Although more of a slapstick affair than *The Big Flash*, the film does include a scene where Harry encounters a water faucet that mysteriously turns off every time he approaches it, a gag Langdon first used in *Johnny's New Car*. Bobby Vernon again provided the story.

In late September, Reliance Pictures, an independent company helmed by producers Edward Small and Harry Goetz, proposed a series of features starring Langdon, to be distributed by United Artists. *Film Daily* broke the story on the 28th, and a follow-up in early January stated Langdon would play the title role in a feature based on the Joe Palooka comic strip. The story died after this, which suggests Reliance couldn't get financing. There were similar false alarms to come.

While *Tired Feet* was in production, "The New Yorker" got its title changed again, to "Happy Go Lucky," and was undergoing previews. Apparently Joe Schenck was not pleased with the results and instructed Lewis Milestone to re-shoot. Langdon was notified on October 17 that he'd need to return to UA for additional scenes; enough were filmed for Milestone to take the director's credit. Around this time, he made a cameo in Paramount's sixth *Hollywood on Parade* entry, another series of stars-at-play shorts produced by Louis Lewyn, founder of the original, *Screen Snapshots*. In a bit taken from Scene One of *After the Ball*, Jimmie Thompson, Viola Dana's golf pro husband, accuses Harry of pocketing his ball. When searched, he's clean, but after Thompson apologizes, Harry makes the mistake of tipping his hat, sending balls cascading to the ground.

On November 12, he and Vernon Dent appeared on the *California Melodies Hour* over the CBS Network. It its review, *Variety* erroneously labeled it "the film comic's air debut"; it was Langdon's third radio appearance at least. Their reviewer, "Abel," continued: "It was a laugh productive interlude, simply

Vernon Dent orders Harry to get downstairs for breakfast in Tired Feet *(1933).*

contrived, including the ole slapstick-bladder to punctuate the gags, with Langdon on the receiving end. Script had to do with a rehearsal of their vaude act. Dent was an able foil and was on a par with Langdon in the total effect."

One week later, Langdon did a screen test at M.G.M., "with parts for two pictures in mind for him," according to *Variety*. One of them, *Whistling*

in the Dark, wound up with Ernest Truex in the lead; the same comedian who'd replaced him in *The Third Little Show* the previous year. The studio also had an idea of pairing Langdon with Jimmy Durante and Cliff "Ukulele Ike" Edwards for a series of musical comedies, but that fell through.

Just days after that, Nat Levine, head of Mascot Pictures, signed Langdon for a serial, *The Whispering Shadow*, to star Bela Lugosi. The deal was engineered by William Gill, but Arvid Gillstrom cried, "Foul." As noted in the *Hollywood Reporter*, "Gillstrom declares that his agreement with Langdon stipulates that the player may not work in short subjects for any other producer although he is granted the right to appear in features. A serial, the producer claims, is classified as a group of short subjects, since it is used in two-reel sections." Gill claimed he wasn't told the deal was for a serial. Levine asked if an exception could be granted in this case; Gillstrom replied the decision rested with Educational's head, Earle W. Hammons, "and he sees small possibility of securing the consent." Langdon was released from the deal and replaced with Karl Dane.

The third Gillstrom short, *The Hitch Hiker*, went into production near the end of the month. Its chief distinction is a reprise of the "chest cold" scene from *The Strong Man*, this time taking place on an airplane and with Dent as the disagreeable passenger. It's a matter of debate whether the soundtrack enhances the comedy or induces nausea, but one thing is clear: as he'd done with the Roach shorts, Langdon was contributing to these films, and his Elf character remained consistent, demonstrating again that he never lost sight of who he was.

Film Daily's "Along the Rialto" columnist, whose pen name was "Phil M. Daly," picked up on what Gillstrom was doing for Langdon, and vice-versa: "In analyzing the recent comedies of Harry Langdon, it becomes quite apparent that it is team work that counts with a screen comic… team work with his director. There is only one Charlie Chaplin, capable of directing and acting simultaneously. Harry has recently learned that fact, after trying to put on the entire show by himself, and his last three pictures with Arvid Gillstrom directing have helped tremendously in putting him back where he rightfully belongs: as one of the screen's ace comics.

"He is one of the few real pantomimists in the realm of comedy; he talks less than any comedian on the modern screen. He is thoroughly sold on the idea that unless he can get a gag over in ACTION alone, then it just ain't a gag. His style of working is entirely his own; he starts with a running gag, and builds up the incidental business while the cameras are clicking. Director Gillstrom gives him full rein. In this way, they get a degree of spontaneous comedy that hours of rehearsals could not achieve. It is simply a case of director and actor being in full accord…and working harmoniously."

Langdon was quite happy to be "working harmoniously," free from the responsibilities of everything except creating and doing the gags, as he told *Motion Picture*'s Sonia Lee right around that time:

> Pictures are where I belong. I don't especially care if I'm never a star again. I am much happier now — I'm down to earth, to the essential values of living. I enjoy having carpenters shake me by the hand. I get a thrill when the

prop boys greet me with the old familiar, "Hello, Harry." I didn't have that friendliness when I was a star — I haven't had it since those happy and peaceful Sennett days. Somehow, stardom isolated me, removed me from human contacts.

In reality, I don't care how small my roles are, as long as they give me a chance… I am not afraid of people anymore — or even injustice. I've regained my old assurance, my faith in myself. If it's in the cards that some day my name will again be important — that's fine! If not — I'll be content.

Part of that contentment was due to his budding romance with Mabel Sheldon. "We went together for about two years before we were married," she told Edward Watz. "We'd be together every evening. After work, I'd go to his home, and we'd go out to dinner. Next day, he'd come over to my home. He made me laugh. He was good company and we found a lot to talk about."

Bobby Vernon moved on to greener pastures, so Gillstrom engaged William Watson, an old Christie hand, to write the next picture alongside newcomer Dean Ward, who'd assisted Vernon with the last one. The result was released as *Knight Duty*, and according to *Film Daily*, "Harry Langdon achieves a record… speaking less than 100 words" through the whole two reels. After production wrapped, Gillstrom flew east with the negative to confer with Hammons about additional films. The option for two more was exercised, and Langdon received a modest increase: an extra $250 per film.

Meanwhile, "Happy Go Lucky" received its final title change, to *Hallelujah! I'm a Bum* and was released on February 3. The resulting film handed little in the way of visual humor to Langdon, who admitted years later that, despite the similarity of hat and clothes, the character of Egghead was not the Elf: "The guy was a radical — a fast talker," he told columnist Reed Johnson in 1941.

Reviews were mixed. Among the trades, *Hollywood Filmograph* and *Variety* caught a preview screening in Glendale that was only three-fourths complete. The former was entranced: "Lewis Milestone's genius, shining brightly again is responsible for a picture that will rank in 1933's list of 'best.' The cast of *Hallelujah[!] I'm a Bum* is an excellent one, down to minor roles. Al Jolson has the most prominent part, and gives his best motion picture performance. His singing is far above his past performances. Harry Langdon gives his best performance since the memorable *Tramp, Tramp, Tramp*." *Variety* was guardedly impressed: "Here is a light, ethereal musical fantasy, entertaining and airy. But it hasn't the socko and that lack keeps even the nicest ideas from paying negative costs. Jolson does a first-rate job as [a] hobo and bursts into song frequently, but it's a new type of vocal delivery for him. He has but

Harry and Nell O'Day at the climax of Knight Duty *(1933).*

one regular type of a number, 'Hallelujah, I'm a Bum Again.' Rest is all singing dialog and short snatches. Same applies for every other member of the cast…. Secondary honors are split between Frank Morgan, as the mayor, Harry Langdon, as a Red street cleaner, and a tiny ebony pal of Jolson's, played by Blueboy Conners…. Direction, photography and musical recording showed cleverness and unusual touches."

Other critics weren't as excited. *Film Daily*'s termed it "a curious combination of foreign musical technique and a thin American story. It is over-brimming with songs, most of which are handled by Jolson in the same Jolson style which characterized his early talker successes. Particularly clever are the lyrics. The supporting players, particularly Frank Morgan and Harry Langdon, are good but are unable to overcome the tremendous handicap imposed by the story, sluggish with songs."

Among newspaper critics, the *New York Post's* Thornton Delahanty wrote, "The picture which we have under consideration is Al Jolson's latest starring vehicle, which came last night to the Rivoli. Ben Hecht is credited with the story.... With what appears to have been his left hand, he has provided a rambling and incoherent travesty on municipal government, contrasting a beloved vagabond who dominates the transient inhabitants of Central Park to a splendiferous pre-depression ruler of City Hall." Martin Dickstein of the *Brooklyn Daily Eagle* passed judgment on the novelty aspect: "Prior to its Broadway premiere... this production was hailed as a new departure in talking-and-singing pictures, possessing a brand new element of entertainment known as 'rhythmic dialogue.' *Hallelujah! I'm a Bum* really isn't much of a departure at all, and that extravagantly heralded 'rhythmic dialogue' turns out to be nothing more than a few badly written lyrics which at intervals are recited by the actors instead of being sung to music."

Between the prolonged scripting phase, the shuffling of directors and the need for extensive retakes, the final product bore a whopping $1.2 million negative cost. Even a blockbuster hit had no chance of

Left: This cartoon from a 1933 trade ad depicts Langdon with fellow Educational comedy stars Andy Clyde, Tom Howard and Moran & Mack. Below: Review in Photoplay *magazine.*

HALLE-
LUJAH,
I'M A BUM—
United Artists

NO great shakes as a story, but if you go for Al Jolson, you should get a kick from the swell music and lyrics present. Al, as "King of Central Park," or in other words, head of the bums, delivers the ditties as incidents of his effort to straighten but a tangled heart-affair between the mayor of New York (Frank Morgan) and his girl (Madge Evans).

recouping that kind of outlay in 1933, possibly the worst year of the Great Depression. The stock market finally reached rock bottom as unemployment scaled new heights. With Franklin Delano Roosevelt primed to close America's banks once he assumed office the following month, citizens were now counting every penny and selecting their movie nights judiciously.

Hollywood Filmograph's Harold Weight had closed his review with, "Mark *Hallelujah[!] I'm a Bum* down as one of those pictures which must be seen," but hardly anyone agreed with him. The final take was $339,000 domestic and $128,000 foreign. The best that can be said is that Langdon shouldered no blame for its failure. He and Frank Morgan are probably the most enjoyable performers in the film, although the latter's line "There's no place like home" unintentionally resonates with modern audiences, given that Morgan went on to play the title role in 1939's *The Wizard of Oz*.

By March 1933, Arvid Gillstrom discovered the same thing as had Mack Sennett the previous year: Educational Pictures was neither timely nor proficient at paying its producers. Sennett sought relief by switching his distribution to Paramount, but soon realized he was at a distinct disadvantage. Out of its previous five production years, his company had sustained net income losses for four; while by the start of 1933, Paramount was facing receivership, hastily reorganizing and filing for bankruptcy in order to protect its assets from creditors. Having built a costly new studio from the ground up in 1928, then forced by the marketplace to invest in sound equipment, Sennett could no longer afford to put off paying the debts that resulted. He ceased production, relying on rental income to stay afloat. It wasn't enough, and by the end of the year the one-time King of Comedy also filed for bankruptcy.

However, Paramount still needed shorts for its theaters, and on March 31, signed a deal with Gillstrom for a series of 12 two-reelers: six starring Langdon, and six with Bing Crosby, whom Paramount had signed once his contract with Sennett had been completed. As it turned out, Crosby would only make two comedies before moving permanently into Paramount's firmament of feature stars; Gillstrom would engage vaudevillian Leon Errol for

Nell O'Day helps Harry board their honeymoon train the hard way in Tied for Life *(1933).*

the balance. As for Langdon, the deal meant another raise, to $2,500 per picture.

There were still two pictures to go on the Educational contract. The first had begun production on March 27 under the title "All Aboard"; it would be released as *Tied for Life*. A dubious item in *Film Daily* claimed, "Gillstrom was shooting scenes at the Santa Fe station [and] Harry was doing stunts on the observation platform of the train, with the cameras clicking. The train started, with Pasadena as its first stop. Gillstrom and his crew had to hold up production for an hour until Harry's return by motor." If true, some unit manager didn't do his job.

The final Educational comedy, "Down and Out" (released as *Hooks and Jabs*) began shooting immediately upon completion of *Tied for Life*. In it, leading lady Nell O'Day portrays a Salvation Army-type and was appropriately costumed. "I played a Salvation Army girl trying to stop these gruff characters from going into the saloon to drink," she recalled for Edward Watz. "I just came out on the set from my dressing room, wearing my costume, looking very prim in navy blue, with the bonnet tied under my chin and the cape around my shoulders. I believe it's the same type of uniform that the Salvation Army women have always worn; they still wear it today.

"I was walking towards the crew when Harry saw me and said 'Wait there a moment, Nell. Please, stop where you are.' I stood there framed by the doorway as Harry looked at me in my costume, from perhaps ten feet away. He didn't say a word and his expression was

Life is becoming more agreeable for Langdon in this candid photo from 1933.

very serious. Then he finally said in a quiet voice, 'You look exactly the way my mother did, in her Salvation Army uniform.' I recall that everyone on the set — Vernon, Mr. Gillstrom, and all the crew — stopped what they were doing and also looked over towards me. That occasion seemed to be a very emotional moment for Harry." Shortly afterwards, Langdon began sculpting a bust of his mother, which depicted her in her bonnet; when it was completed, he had it bronzed. The bust remains in the Langdon family to this day.

Both *Tied for Life* and *Hooks and Jabs* were scripted by Dean Ward and Vernon Dent. Gillstrom, happy with their work, signed them to write not only the six Langdons under the Paramount contract, but the Bing Crosby shorts as well. Dent was also given a contract to appear in all twelve films.

Educational would have liked to keep Langdon; to prove it, they purchased "The Show Goat," releasing it in September under the title *The Stage Hand*. In cutting it down to precisely two reels, all subplots but one — the jealous wife of the play's leading man — were trimmed to the bone. Introductory scenes that established Harry's girlfriend and her fireman dad who can only drive horses were jettisoned. When the girlfriend suddenly shows up during the second reel, we have no idea who she is or where she's come from.

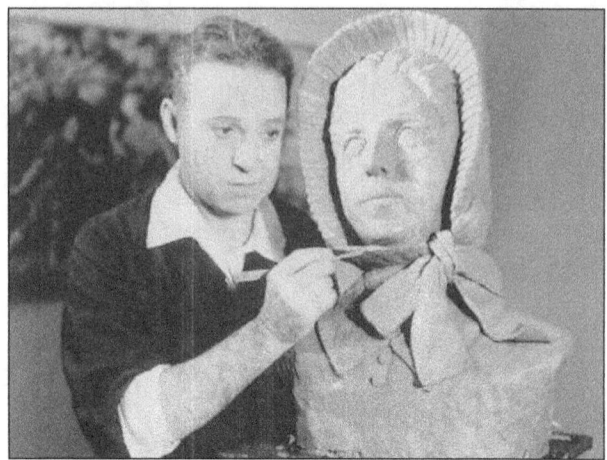

Harry admires Salvation Army crusader Nell O'Day in Hooks and Jabs *(1933).*

Her father makes his first appearance when Harry forces him to drive the new fire engine to the theater, and we have no idea who he is, either, nor of the significance of Harry's action. Finally, the closing scene was shot by Educational with doubles, although the soundtrack seems to be from the original production. The resulting film was, to put it mildly, a confusing mess that did no favors for Langdon's reputation as a director.

Around the time *Hooks and Jabs* was wrapping up, Langdon signed with another independent company, Screen Art Productions, for a feature "of a new and novel type," according to *The Hollywood Reporter*. The firm was headed by Dr. Eugene Frenke and director Slavko Vorkapich. "Dr. Frenke has written the story and will direct. The picture will specialize in beautiful outdoor locations and in high class music." There were to be only two players: Langdon, "and the leading woman will be Bebe Farnum, an unknown." A second blurb in the *Reporter* stated, "The picture [will be] entirely in pantomime." The

A 1933 photo session shows Langdon sculpting his mother, dealing with a jigsaw puzzle, and playing one of his favorite tunes.

premise sounds intriguing at least, but once again an actual film failed to materialize; likewise Miss Farnum's career.

Langdon did secure a feature assignment with an almost equally intriguing role. Fox Film Corporation cast him as Dan Cupid for their entry in the big-budget musical sweepstakes that was proving so profitable for Warner Bros. and M.G.M.: *My Weakness*. It was

Harry as Cupid in My Weakness *(1933).*

a logical choice: who better to play such a whimsical character than Hollywood's most whimsical comedian?

Like *A Soldier's Plaything*, *My Weakness* was conceived to introduce a foreign actress (Germany's Lilian Harvey) to American audiences. Unlike *A Soldier's Plaything*, *My Weakness* actually has a sturdy plot, albeit one lifted wholesale from George Bernard Shaw's *Pygmalion*. The film opens with Cupid addressing the audience in song (or rather, in "rhythmic dialogue," although no one dared call it that) about his toughest assignment: Ronnie Gregory (Lew Ayres). This womanizing wastrel finds his allowance cut off by his uncle (Henry Travers), but manages to charm the old fellow into relenting by promising to turn a cleaning woman, Looloo Blake (Harvey), into an appetizing dish for the purpose of marriage to the uncle's eccentric son, Gerald (Charles Butterworth). Ronnie calls upon his bevy of gorgeous girlfriends to assist him with this task, but of course as she transforms, an awkward romance blossoms between Looloo and her personal Henry Higgins.

Vernon Dent's not happy with the attention Harry is getting from Mrs. Dent (Ethel Sykes) in Marriage Humor *(1933).*

The film, which received a rapturous reception from critics, audiences and exhibitors, was the most popular and profitable feature in which Langdon had appeared since *The Strong Man*, but it didn't turn into any immediate assignments. He would not appear in another feature for two years. For the short term, though, it didn't matter: upon concluding as Cupid, Langdon went to work on the first Paramount short, *Marriage Humor*, which reunited him with director Harry Edwards for the first time since *Tramp, Tramp, Tramp*.

Unfortunately, the Paramount two-reelers are not available for reappraisal. Negatives reverted to Gillstrom, which meant they weren't included when Paramount sold its pre-1948 library of short subjects and non-Popeye cartoons to U. M. & M. TV Corporation in December 1955. At present, all that has survived from Gillstrom's Paramount tenure is one of the Crosby shorts.

One cannot fairly assess a film from a continuity transcript of its action and dialogue, but one can get an idea of the type of material used, as well as its influences. A reading of the continuities for the Paramount shorts suggests that Langdon and Dent were moving toward situations that would have suited Laurel & Hardy; not surprisingly, since the latter's two-reelers were unquestionably the most popular comedies on the market.

In *Marriage Humor*, Vernon has argued with his wife and prods his manservant, Harry, to do the same with his wife; the two go stepping out after that. *On Ice* has Vernon as the owner of an ice delivery business and Harry as his employee doing all the heavy lifting. Vernon sets up a double date with a pair of lady café owners; Harry objects because he's already married, but manages — in the best Stanley tradition — to slip out of the house. In *A Circus Hoodoo*, both are working under the big top — Vernon is the front end of a fake horse and Harry brings up the rear — until the manager fires them because Harry is "a hoodoo" and causes bad luck to his performers. The two revert to a prior scheme: Vernon sells umbrellas to a gathering crowd as Harry provides "rain" with a handy hose. Of course it backfires when a customer gets wise and a cop is summoned.

There's some borrowing from the past as well. In *On Ice,* Harry meekly hands over his pay envelope, then retrieves some coins from a hiding place and is caught by the missus, just as in *Saturday Afternoon.* In this film, however, he doesn't outsmart her; he merely swallows the coins. When she hears him start to "jingle," she pounds on his back, forcing him to cough them up. *A Roaming Romeo* repeats the golf ball business from *After the Ball* and the *Hollywood on Parade* short, as well as Harry stealing fruit from a farmer as in *Tramp, Tramp, Tramp. Petting Preferred* borrows the business of Harry trying to retrieve something from the front of a fainted woman's blouse, only to be spied by her husband, from *Hotter Than Hot,* which was itself inspired by Langdon's *The Messenger. A Circus Hoodoo,* which introduces a gangster subplot in

Harry's wife (Ethel Sykes) and her sister aren't pleased with Harry and his boss's (Vernon Dent) nocturnal pursuits in On Ice *(1933).*

the second reel, reworks the mistaken identity gambit of See America Thirst.

Curiously, the final gag of *Petting Preferred* has Harry throwing a brick at a dog, in hopes of chasing it away, and breaking a nearby window instead. Older brother Charles Langdon, we may recall, actually did this (and was arrested for it) back in Council Bluffs, when Harry was 15.

The films also contain brief snatches of dialogue that would have been at home in *A Night on the Boulevard* or *Johnny's New Car*. Drinking at a swank café in *On Ice*, Harry sips some "Egyptian tea" (actually liquor) and tumbles backward to the floor. Vernon is incredulous:

VERNON: Say, what's the matter with you? Can't you stand a little tea?

HARRY: Was that tea?

VERNON: Certainly. Egyptian tea!

HARRY: Egyptian?

VERNON: Yes.

HARRY: They must've left a mummy in it!

Although stills show Harry in his typical costume, the transcripts suggest little of the Elf. At times, his character is aggressive and not entirely stupid, much like his "Johnny" in vaudeville. Both he and Dent split the slapstick indignities fairly evenly. "I know that Harry had discussed with me in the 1930s that it would be great if Vernon and he were more like a team," Mabel Langdon told Edward Watz. "But with Laurel & Hardy being so prominent, it wouldn't have worked out at that particular time." Based on the existing evidence, the Gillstrom-Paramount shorts were the closest the two came to realizing that goal, although they would continue working together, off and on, into the next decade.

On December 1, a story broke that Helen Langdon, according to her friends, was about to file for divorce from Harry. The friends were mistaken; she was merely petitioning the court for a judgment against him for overdue alimony and legal fees. Since their separation was granted on March 1, 1932, Langdon had paid only $671.43 in alimony, plus $250 toward the $2,500 her lawyers had charged. Nevertheless, as 1933 drew to a close, Langdon decided to give himself a Christmas present, and initiated a quickie Mexican divorce from Helen, which would free him to marry Mabel.

On February 1, 1934, Justice Frederick P. Close awarded Helen a judgment amounting $21,078.57, the full amount due. One week later, Rose filed suit

Given Madam Guessora's costume, it doesn't take a psychic to read Harry's mind in A Circus Hoodoo *(1933).*

for $64,717.47 that Langdon owed her. She would be granted a judgment for $66,424, which presumably included her own court costs. Langdon responded to both actions by doing nothing.

The Mexican divorce was finalized around the time *Petting Preferred*, the fifth short of the series, had wrapped, and on February 12, he and Mabel, accompanied by William Gill and Janice Snoden, drove across the border to pick up the papers. Mabel recalled, "The four of us drove 'way down into the hinterlands of Mexico, to some little small town. And he picked up his divorce papers.

"Now this was over by the Arizona border. So he said, 'Well, why don't we go over to Arizona? Let's get married, Mabel! Let's get married in Arizona!' This took me off my guard! So I said, 'Sure!'"

At Trinity Presbyterian Church in Tucson that evening, Reverend Karl P. Buswell looked over the divorce papers, declared them valid, and married

Harry and Mabel; Gill and Snoden serving as witnesses. Once word got around, the press descended upon them as they dined in a local restaurant. Feeling puckish, Langdon told reporters he found Mabel "out here on the prairie behind one of these cacti."

A few days earlier, Gillstrom had conferred with Paramount execs to request a budget increase for the sixth Langdon short, which he wanted to turn into a mini-musical. "Arvid Gillstrom's comedies for Paramount during the past year have hit so well that in one case, Leon Errol, an original one-picture deal has been extended to three pictures," said *The Hollywood Reporter*'s Feburary 12 edition. Noting that the budget increase had been approved, the trade paper summed up, "It has all combined to put Gillstrom in a choice spot as a shorts producer."

The newlyweds returned to Hollywood on the 16th, to be greeted by the local columnists. He referred to his bride as "the girl of my dreams," and affirmed, "Contentment means much more to me now than money. I've seen all the Hollywood parties and nightlife that I want to see. What I want now is a fireplace, a wife and my police dog."

Then, in an unexpected move, Paramount decided to produce its own shorts, severing both Gillstrom and their second comedy contractor, Phil Ryan. Lou Diamond, head of the studio's shorts department, had opted to focus on musical product, which would be cheaper and where production could be divided between both coasts. The studio, still on shaky financial ground, was counting every possible penny. The mini-musical short was canceled. There was no chance that Gillstrom would find another "choice spot"; everyone else had their shorts programs sewed up.

Suddenly Langdon was unemployed and would remain that way for the next several months. Complicating matters, Mabel became pregnant about five weeks after their wedding. Gill, his agent and best man, was unable to scare up work and Langdon had to let him go. Along with the usual bills, basic living needs and regular doctor visits for Mabel, he had two ex-wives with the law on their side demanding a combined total of $87,500.

It was looking like a frighteningly barren summer when, in late June, an old colleague came to the rescue, initiating a working relationship that would literally continue until the end of Langdon's life.

Langdon and Mabel Sheldon wed in February 1934. The third time is the charm, even though the press thinks it's the fourth.

This 1932 photograph of Harry in character was one of Mabel Langdon's favorites.

CHAPTER FOURTEEN

"Ye Gods, Has it Come to This"

1934–1937

"In 1933, I was put in charge of all of Columbia Pictures' short subject production, and it was one Herculean job — to set up a company, pick comedians, directors, writers, and supervise thirty-odd pictures," Jules White recalled in 1978. White had started out as editor for his older brother, Jack White, about ten years earlier at Educational Studios, then progressed to director around the time sound had arrived. He moved to Metro-Goldwyn-Mayer in 1930, co-creating and directing the Dogville comedies, one-reelers in which a cast of live canines performed spoofs of various movie genres. White signed with Columbia in July 1932, but because of his M.G.M. contract, he couldn't start until the following year. Once he arrived, the first thing he did was hire as many comedy veterans as were available, whether or not he'd worked with them before.

"Arthur Ripley came to work for me as a writer in 1934. He hadn't worked for a while. I knew him by reputation rather than personally. He'd been in charge of Mack Sennett's editorial department; he supervised the writers and watched over production, direction and everything. We were kicking around ideas [and] he said, 'What would you think of Harry Langdon?' I said, 'None better. Where is he, what's he doing?' He said, 'Harry is flat broke. He's absolutely *destitute*. He needs work and he needs it badly.'

"I had heard about what transpired with him and Frank Capra. He was a great, great comedian…but like many actors, he wasn't satisfied with just acting. Many actors think they know better what kind of material they should have, what scripts should be written and who should write and direct them. They want to be the whole show. This was my fear, [but] Ripley said, 'He'll be a good boy. Would you like to meet him?'

"I said, 'I sure would. There's no question about the man's talent, and talent doesn't die. Will you bring him in?' He said, 'No. I want to make him think you're coming for him, because he's very demoralized. All it would take is just one little boost to make him feel great, you know what I mean?' I said, 'I sure do.'"

Ripley set up the meeting at Langdon's preferred golf course, the Lakeside Country Club. White remembered, "I saw this little guy sitting out there at this table, and I knew he was going to put on a front for me and I had to put on one for him. I [thought], 'Well, it can't do any harm, it can only do us both some good.' Ripley introduced us, and I said, 'I'm sure glad to meet you. I've always been one of your great fans.' Well, his face brightened [but] I had to lead him to talk. He wouldn't say much. So finally I said, 'How would you like to make some pictures for me?' He said, very softly — almost surprised — 'I'd like it.' I said, 'Well, great, how about coming to the office tomorrow, and we'll sit down and talk turkey?' He said, 'Fine!'

"So he came in. He had no agent; I made the deal directly with him, and we drew up a contract for two pictures with options, at one thousand dollars per picture."

Although White's offer was double the amount paid to most other Columbia comedians, it was still a huge comedown from the last contract with Arvid Gillstrom. Langdon, though, was in no position to quibble. He knew that when Mabel's pregnancy entered its advanced stages, she would have to leave her own job.

The trades announced the deal near the end of June, but production wouldn't begin until the first week of September, so there were still two months of hardship. Part of it was due to Gillstrom, who filed a motion on June 30 to stop Columbia from using Langdon, claiming the comedian was still contractually obligated to him. There was indeed one more short owed on that deal, but Gillstrom had failed to secure distribution after Paramount cut him loose. Somehow Columbia took care of that dilemma, but the details and timetable were never reported. Gillstrom eventually went to England to direct for several months, returning to Hollywood in April 1935 for what was intended as a brief visit. Instead, he was stricken with pneumonia, to which he succumbed on May 21, 1935 at age 45.

Two days after Gillstrom's legal action, Jed Buell, formerly Mack Sennett's publicity director (and before that, manager of the Deluxe Theater where *The Strong Man* had its 293-laugh preview), announced the formation of Rainbow Pictures for the production of feature-length comedies at Sennett's studio. The second one was to be a jungle farce, "They Go Wild," that would co-star Langdon with his fellow Sennett alumnus, and current Columbia stable mate, Andy Clyde. Once again, the realities of the Depression crushed an entrepreneur's hopes; Buell's producing career wouldn't be launched for another two years.

On August 24, Rose Langdon filed a court order demanding Langdon pay up the balance of their property settlement, which by then amounted to $66,424, thanks to accumulating interest. A 30-day continuance was requested and approved.

Langdon's first Columbia short started shooting on September 6. Dan Thomas stopped by during production in search of a few quotes; between takes the columnist who once publicly called out Langdon for egomania got a handle on the comedian's new perspective:

> All this business of being a "big shot" — I've found it really doesn't mean much after all. It wasn't many years ago that my name was in lights [and] emblazoned on billboards in huge letters. Certainly it was pretty swell and all that. I can't deny that I enjoyed it.
>
> But Fate, or whatever it is, played tricks with me. I sat around relaxing and writing and sculpting for quite awhile. That became tiresome. So I decided to go back into pictures. They're not feature length anymore, but that's nothing. And they've taken away the sloppy clothes that were so much a part of my character and are dressing me up like a fashion plate. That's not so bad. I rather like it.
>
> And last but not least, if I didn't have anything else to be ridiculously happy about it wouldn't matter at all, for I'm going to be a father pretty soon! That's enough to take care of any amount of unhappiness that might come along!

Co-written and directed by Ripley, the resulting film, *Counsel on De Fence*, was both something different and more of the same since their last collaboration. As Langdon told Thomas, the traditional screen costume was gone, replaced by a tailored business suit. Gone as well was the clown-white face with exaggerated eyeliner and lip makeup. A dapper mustache added a finishing touch to the destruction of the screen's Little Elf. Part of this was calculated to evoke actor Warren William, as the short was a burlesque of William's 1932 feature *The Mouthpiece*.

The film also brought back the tastelessness in gags and situations that marred *The Chaser*, thanks to Ripley's love of unpleasant bodily functions. The film's big comedy payoff is when hapless lawyer "Darrow Langdon" swallows a bottle of poison that he thinks has been switched with a harmless tea. When he learns otherwise, he hails a taxicab and commands

the driver to get him to a hospital. The cab ride is a wild one, complete with several 360-degree spins on a wet road. As Darrow emerges, he dabs at his lips with a handkerchief and claims to be fine and hungry, the implication being that he's regurgitated the poison. Unfortunately for him, the acquitted woman has summoned an ambulance, which pulls up; he's dragged inside and his stomach is pumped. Once that's over, he's grabbed by two of his legal associates and made to endure another pumping. In both cases, he tries to object as the tube is inserted down his throat, leading him to make disturbing gargling sounds. It's all rather nauseating, and subsequent shorts, while restoring a clean-shaven Langdon, were nearly as gross, with gags based on smallpox, torture, bloodstains and other unpleasant situations.

On September 28, Langdon went to court, accompanied by Mabel, to face the music with Rose and her lawyers. After Judge Dudley S. Valentine called Langdon to the stand, he addressed the court.

JUDGE: Is Mrs. Langdon in court?

MABEL: Yes, your honor.

JUDGE: Do you want Mr. Langdon sent to jail for contempt of court?

MABEL: Oh, no, I certainly do not! That's what his first wife wants. I'm Mabel Langdon.

Counsel on De Fence *(1934)*.

Above and opposite: Welcome to Columbia — Langdon clowns with Monty Collins and the Three Stooges, 1935.

It was quickly determined that Rose had failed to appear, "a misunderstanding," according to her lawyer. Judge Valentine ordered the case be continued another month, but nothing further happened, as Rose's quest for justice vanished from subsequent press coverage. Future news stories about the first Mrs. Langdon would focus solely on her work as an extra in such films as *Many Happy Returns* with George Burns and Gracie Allen, *Poppy* with W.C. Fields and *Destry Rides Again* with Marlene Dietrich and Jimmy Stewart.

No official reason for Rose having thrown in the towel has survived, but it's tempting to speculate that she'd read Dan Thomas's column, saw the news about his impending fatherhood, and decided to drop the matter. A member of the Musolff family, Rose's niece, has claimed that Harry and Rose lost a child of their own in the mid-teens; if so, this may have played into the decision. In any case, Rose had remarried in 1929 to Jack J. Clark, a fellow ex-vaudevillian. Her real estate ventures were successful and she was again dabbling in show business. Possibly, in keeping with her Catholicism, Rose decided the time had come for mercy and forgiveness.

Unfortunately, Mrs. Langdon #2 was not similarly inclined. On November 8, two days before Langdon started work on his second Columbia short, Helen Langdon's lawyer, Harry A. Goldman, announced he was filing a divorce complaint on her behalf. In Helen's view, her ex's Mexican divorce was illegal and she was prepared to seek a division of property from 1929 through the present day. The "grasping woman" was poised to bare her claws.

The second Langdon-Ripley comedy, *Shivers*, finished up during the week of November 12. In it, Langdon is Ichabod Krum, the author of several mystery novels and his wife, Minerva (Florence Lake), has rented the house for him as inspiration. The loquacious Minerva is delighted as the leasing agent tells of a murder that was committed and points out the bloodstains, while Ichabod recoils in fear. However, rather than being haunted, Chinese smugglers use the house as a transfer point, and several Chinese laborers are held captive within. One of them insists Ichabod is a blood brother, and as they argue, Ichabod begins speaking in Chinese. Suddenly his loving wife is appalled that she has married "a Chinaman," and refuses to sleep with him. "Well, can I help it if my father was a sailor?" he replies. Although Langdon's Chinese gibberish is funny, the whole concept has a distasteful air about it and mars what would otherwise have been a reasonably amusing short.

While waiting for Columbia to pick up his option, which they would do on December 6, he signed with Audio Productions, a short-lived subsidiary of Educational, for an industrial short on behalf of tire and rubber manufacturer B.F. Goodrich. The comedy, titled *Love, Honor and Obey (the Law)*, would co-star fellow Columbia comic Monty Collins as bridegroom Harry's two-faced pal, a former rival who's serving as

Harry insists he's not a Chinaman, but he is... much to Florence Lake's dismay, in Shivers *(1934).*

best man while surreptitiously trying to doom the marriage by having Harry ticketed or arrested for violating traffic laws. Production took place in December.

The following spring, Goodrich sponsored road show screenings across the country, in conjunction with their authorized dealers. *Love, Honor and Obey (the Law)* accompanied a specially produced newsreel about the everyday use of rubber and a feature-length

Helen Walton Langdon at her divorce hearing, December 1934.

docudrama titled *Highway Patrol*. No admission was charged and tickets were obtainable at various retail outlets. The Langdon two-reeler was part of a contest in which viewers, having been handed a special "package" upon entering the screening, were encouraged to note all of the traffic violations Harry commits during the film. They would submit their answers, along with a 200-word essay about the importance of safe driving habits, in hopes of winning one of four "valuable prizes."

As the free show made its rounds, local exhibitors filed protests with the Motion Picture Theatre Owners of America (MPTOA), especially when news (or rumor) leaked that other concerns, such as Chevrolet, Ford and General Electric, were considering similar promotions. According to *Daily Variety*'s May 24, 1935 issue:

Exhibs here are viewing with alarm reported widespread production of dramatic feature length pictures, utilizing well known screen players, by national advertisers to promote sale of their products…Goodrich company of Akron, O., is reported to have on the road a feature advertising picture, "Highway Patrol," that is being shown in halls, auditoriums, unused theatres and largely in school auditoriums as part of a two hour show. Program includes a Harry Langdon comedy, newsreel and prize contest, with no admission charged. Portable projection apparatus is used. Protests have been made to the Goodrich company by MPTOA, with exhibitors taking a stand that such shows, if given on a large scale, would rapidly fold up picture houses.

The practice dried up and the furor died down.

Six days after his Columbia option was lifted, Langdon was officially divorced (again) from Helen. At their separation hearing three years earlier, she'd testified about his penchant for consuming "woof-woof" (alcohol), a practice that was then illegal. She turned the melodrama up a notch for the divorce hearing: "Once he beat me with his fists for fifteen minutes without cessation," she told Judge Lewis Howell Smith, "but I'm sure he wouldn't have done so had he been sober." Under guidance by her lawyer, Goldman, she testified that all she knew about the Mexican divorce was what she'd heard over the radio, and that she understood Langdon had remarried and was living with his third wife.

Helen's testimony of the alleged beating made three-column headlines in the local newspapers. With all the knowledgeable parties dead and gone, it's impossible to say whether or not she was lying. On one hand, she had long been skilled at never letting the truth stand in the way of her well-being. On the other hand, we know that drinking to excess turned Langdon's father into a violent brute at least once, and that such reactions can be hereditary.

Upon granting the divorce, which would take a year to finalize, Judge Smith decided, "Until such time as it can be determined what Mr. Langdon can earn in pictures," he ordered the payment of $25 weekly to Helen for maintenance. Presumably Langdon sent a legal representative, although he himself was not in court, owing to Mabel's advanced condition.

On Sunday morning, December 17, Harry Philmore Langdon, Jr., was born at Good Samaritan Hospital. The child weighed a strapping ten pounds and was completely healthy. Two weeks later, on December 31, mother and baby were permitted to go home, and the press was there to see Langdon hold his son. "It's the happiest New Year I have ever known," he crowed. "I've looked forward to this event for many years. Now I'm the happiest man in the world.

"I'm telling the world a man has never known happiness until he has become a father. Pardon me for bubbling over with parental joy."

"Every moment he was at home he had that baby," Mabel recalled for Edward Watz. "He used to tie a diaper around his neck like a hammock, and he'd carry little Harry around in the diaper, even when playing the piano. Once we had a nurse and she didn't want Harry to handle the baby so much. Harry said, 'Well, you can just leave.' He fired her. That child just meant so much to him."

Langdon went back to work on January 23 for his third Columbia comedy, *His Bridal Sweet*. This one didn't involve Ripley; it was written by John Grey and directed by none other than Alf Goulding, who'd last worked with Langdon at Principal Pictures. It was no improvement, with situations involving a smallpox quarantine and a dangerous lunatic. Ripley and Langdon collaborated once more on the next picture, *The Leather Necker*, a half-hearted remake of *All Night Long* that included some tasteless references to murder and torture.

Shortly after this, Ripley left Columbia to direct the Edgar Kennedy shorts at R.K.O. Radio, and would go on to alternate between writing and/or directing, and teaching film courses, becoming the first professor of cinema arts at the University of California, Los Angeles in 1954. One of his proudest accomplishments was the founding of UCLA's Film Center. He and Langdon would never work together again, although they remained lifelong friends. Summing up his years with Langdon for an

Billy Gilbert and a pie-eyed Harry in His Bridal Sweet *(1935)*.

interviewer, Ripley simply commented, "To him, I owe everything."

It's not as simple to discern what Langdon owed Ripley. As part of the Sennett team that crystallized Langdon's screen persona, his main contribution seems to have been an impeccable talent for story construction. Certainly the Ripley-driven scenarios, both at Sennett and First National, were the most

Sgt. Wade Boteler and Pvt. Harry Langdon in The Leather Necker *(1935), a loose remake of 1924's* All Night Long.

linear Langdon had made for those companies, but he had little interest in the whimsical, trusting side of the Elf, which had been Capra's forte. Ripley, by all accounts a dour man in real life, liked his humor black, and as Langdon's interest in comedy's tragic side grew, the comedian found himself more in synch with Ripley's sensibilities than Capra's.

Ripley was always welcome at the Langdon home, although Mabel never really warmed up to him. "Arthur Ripley and I didn't get along very well," she told *Cult Movies'* Michael Copner. "He worked pretty well with Harry, but his thoughts were always so morbid. We'd have him over to our house if we were having a party, but Arthur liked to spend a lot of time in the kitchen — and he wasn't cooking!" She would never forget, however, that Ripley brought Harry a lifeline, in the form of Jules White, when they most needed one.

On March 4 — about three weeks before *The Leather Necker* went into production — Langdon went to court to defend himself against a charge of contempt, brought about by Helen, who'd received nothing of the weekly $25 he'd been ordered to pay. "My present wife and three-month-old baby must be fed and clothed," he told Commissioner E. D. Doyle, adding that the expense of maintaining

Langdon during a courtroom break, March 4, 1935.

his home amounted to $400 per month. "I owe my first wife $59,000, $40,000 to the Government and $5,000 to attorneys," he said, explaining further that as soon as he finished a picture, he exhausted the money paying debts. Of his last movie salary, only $22 remained.

Then it was Helen's turn. With the authority of California's divorce laws beside her, she declared, "I am still Harry's legal wife. He is a bigamist and he knows it! It is only because I loved him that I wouldn't sign a bigamy complaint against him last year."

Furthermore "I am starving," she cried. "All I have had to eat for ten days is a soft-boiled egg. I've gone without food, and the landlord told me if I didn't pay my rent tonight, I would have to move." Sobbing, she added, "I lost everything by my marriage to Harry and now I am destitute."

Commissioner Doyle found Langdon in contempt; ordered a one-month continuance before passing sentence and commanded him to pony up the $25 weekly sum. Langdon promised to "try to borrow money" in order to meet the court's demand.

The Leather Necker had wrapped up Langdon's second two-picture commitment; White was happy to option two more, but production on those would have to wait until work began on the next release season in July. On May 28, Langdon swallowed his pride and penned a letter to fellow vaudevillian-turned-movie comedian — and golfing buddy — W.C. Fields:

> Dear Billy,
> I am not really as nervie as this letter may sound to you. But desperate circumstances forces *(sic)* me to ask for help. The X wives and the income tax authorities accomplished their purpose, and left me temporarily flat, financially.
>
> Two hundred dollars will pull me through until I start my new Columbia contract, which starts in July.
>
> This amount will save my furniture, automobile, and supply kid Jr. with milk, etc. My credit is good for other necessities, until I start to work.
>
> Can you?...and confidentially?
>
> Ye Gods, has it come to this.
>
> Very gratefully yours,
> Harry Langdon

Fields dispatched the full amount on June 3. Right around then, Langdon scored a two-week gig in Columbia's B-unit: a fast-paced romantic drama called *Atlantic Adventure,* which starred Nancy Carroll, an early talkie star on the downside of her career, and newcomer Lloyd Nolan. Langdon played "Snapper" MacGillicuddy, the photographer pal of

Harry shmoozes with perennial movie cop Fred Kelsey in Atlantic Adventure *(1935).*

Nolan's Dan Miller, a rather self-absorbed reporter. Unfortunately, Langdon brought nothing distinctive to the film, but then neither did anyone else in the cast.

Old pal Vernon Dent, now with Columbia, is credited with the story for Langdon's late-August return to Jules White's slapstick factory. The resulting film, though, is something of a cross between two

Langdon bums a smoke from a costumed player for The Girl Friend *(1935), during the making of* Atlantic Adventure.

of Langdon's better Sennett comedies. Harry Pierce intends to wed Nellie (Dorothy Granger), but his Uncle Elmer, played by Dent, objects. As in *His First Flame,* Uncle tries to interfere, first by warning Harry that he's engaged to an axe-murderess. His nephew tries to escape the church but inadvertently winds up in front of the preacher just as the ceremony begins. After the marriage, Elmer tells Nellie that Harry is insane. At one point, Harry sees Elmer with his arm around her shoulder, and sadly assumes his uncle has stolen his wife, reminiscent of a similar moment in *His First Flame.* As it happens, Bertha Sharp the axe-murderess, also played by Granger, shows up and, like the mad Professor McGlumm in *His Marriage Wow,* takes Harry on a wild ride, only slightly marred by some obvious process screen work. Overall the film, titled *His Marriage Mix-Up,* nicely showcases Langdon's comedy-of-innocence and is the most enjoyable of his early Columbia shorts.

His Marriage Mix-Up was directed by Jack White under his pseudonym Preston Black, as was Langdon's next, *I Don't Remember.* White used the moniker on most of his Columbia work; when asked why, brother Jules would jokingly say, "He didn't want to sully the wonderful reputation of Jack White on these [films]!" In *I Don't Remember,* which White also wrote, Harry is hopelessly absent-minded and it costs him both his furniture (since he has used the installment payment to buy an Irish Sweepstakes ticket), then his marriage to Geneva Mitchell. Vernon Dent is the goodtime pal who encourages Harry to split the cost of the ticket; after Mitchell leaves him, Harry decides to commit suicide, until Dent shows up and he opts instead to commit homicide.

A mad scramble through city streets takes place, as Harry fires shots at Vernon with a rifle and a policeman's pistol, until the two discover they are the Sweepstakes winners. They head to the Sweepstakes office, but as Harry produces his half of the ticket, it blows out the window, leading to another mad scramble. A street sweeper ultimately washes the ticket down a sewer drain; Harry dives in after it and is washed out to sea!

While these were in production, the William Morris agency was negotiating to place Langdon in a touring company of *Anything Goes,* the Cole Porter-Guy Bolton musical that had opened on Broadway the previous year. The show was a huge hit for its star, Ethel Merman, and several of its songs — the title tune, "You're The Top," "I Get a Kick Out of You" — would become standards. Langdon was cast in the role of "Moonface" Martin, a fugitive posing as a clergyman, essayed by timid Victor Moore on Broadway.

This particular tour would cross Australia, under the auspices of manager J.C. Williamson. Among show people of both American coasts, the "land down under" was considered a haven for has-beens and wannabes, but Langdon didn't care. For one, even in a supporting role, he was the biggest "name" in the show. For another, it was a chance to flex his creative muscles as part of something with merit, something more challenging than the mostly contrived tripe of the past year. Just days after wrapping up *I Don't Remember,* Langdon, Mabel and their baby boarded the S.S. *Mariposa* in Los Angeles and set sail. Harry, Jr. celebrated his first birthday at sea while passing Honolulu. The ship docked at Sydney on December 30.

"He is pleased with the prospect of appearing in a theatre again," reported the next day's *Sydney Morning Herald*. "'It is fine,' he said yesterday, 'to get an immediate response from an audience as you do in the theatre. If anybody laughs while you are making a talking film they are likely to be shot or hanged. That is a swell way to make a comedy; when it's a crime to laugh at it. It was not so bad in the days of silent films, because then there were people around the set snickering and laughing, and that was fine for the comedian.'"

To publicize the upcoming tour, members of the cast made a few personal appearances. One was at a nursery, another at the Deaf, Dumb and Blind Institute in Darlington. Langdon was in his element at both places, mugging and clowning with the children.

After about five weeks of rehearsals, *Anything Goes* opened on February 8, 1936 at the Theater Royal, but apparently the performance was not as sprightly as expected. A review in the next day's *Morning Herald* noted, "The present incarnation of *Anything Goes* will probably have its admirers. But, somehow or other, a subtle something seems to have evaporated from the production during its transpacific voyage.

"Brought out in New York, this sort of play travels at a rattling pace [and] the audience is swept up into a crescendo of unthinking joviality. That was really what was missing on Saturday night. Approached in too cautious a spirit, the fun simply went off the boil.

"Yet one's visit to the theatre was not entirely time wasted. A catalog of the play's virtues must now be brought forward. This list embodies the clever fooling of Mr. Harry Langdon.

"Mr. Langdon looks exactly as one remembers him in his diverting series of silent films. To pantomime, in which he still luxuriates, he now adds a thin, mournful little voice, which exactly matches the visual aspects of his personality. It is a voice entirely without accent, and the queer, helpless gestures were what drew most of the laughs on Saturday night."

Harry didn't intend to marry Dorothy Granger in His Marriage Mix-Up *(1935)*.

Langdon working on the Columbia Ranch for a scene in I Don't Remember *(1935).*

According to the *Morning Herald*, Mabel served as Harry's "dresser and prompter" backstage; presumably she did so more agreeably than did Helen five years earlier. When the paper ran a piece about husbands and wives that quarrel in its Sunday supplement on February 6, it was followed up on the 20th with a "conversation" between Harry and Mabel that, whether genuine or not, makes for interesting reading in light of Langdon's previous union:

MR. LANGDON: Have you read this piece about husbands and wives and the way they nag each other?

MRS. LANGDON: Yes, I did, and I guess I'm thinking the same as you are. Why do they waste their time quarreling when they could be so happy in each other's company?

MR. L: I don't know. It's always been a mystery to me. I guess the reason is because they're not suitably mated, or something like that.

MRS. L: But, why don't they find that out before they get married?

MR. L: Because all the time they are courting they are acting a part. They deceive each other — conceal their real selves. Instinctively they know that if they are natural the whole thing would be a flop. This goes on until the "I will" part of the business and then, piece by piece, they throw off their masks and cloaks of virtuousness and both discover that they are married to a couple of devils!

MRS. L: That sounds all right in theory, but how are they going to get the "low-down" on each other's temperaments, faults, and all that?

MR. L: Easy. Watch 'em at sports games. Take 'em driving a car in a congested area. If they're selfish or intolerant they will want the whole thoroughfare to themselves. They might be roadhogs — have no regard for pedestrians — curse the driver of the car ahead for not clearing the road for them. If this sort

An ineffectual solution to repossessed furniture in I Don't Remember *(1935).*

of conduct happens on the streets it will happen in the home.

MRS. L: This article says men grumble about their food. Now you never complain about the food I serve you — eggs, for instance. I give you eggs every morning. Why don't you squeal about it?

MR. L: I guess I like eggs. Besides, you always serve them different styles, and I know by the way you dish them up that you are endeavoring to please me, and I feel I appreciate your efforts.

MRS. L: Of course, mothers-in-law usually are supposed to cause a lot of trouble.

MR. L: That's where we are lucky. I like your mother around because she takes such darn good care of Harry, junior. Anyhow, if a mother and daughter get along well, a man shouldn't worry. You can't say we haven't had single row yet, though.

MRS. L: Oh, Harry!

MR. L: Oh yes we have. You remember that time you wanted to buy six pairs of silk stockings all at once, and I insisted on you having a dozen? That was a real row — and I won it — easily.

Two days after the above was published, the *Australian Women's Weekly* ran a column penned by Langdon, which was a reflection on his years in Hollywood and the rise to fame of many with whom he'd worked. Among the stars, Joan Crawford, of course, topped the list, but there were some surprising names as well, such as Clark Gable ("He worked for me as an 'extra' and bit-player. Then he started to climb"), Claudette Colbert ("I worked on a picture once in which Claudette was featured. Temperamental? Why sure, most of 'em are, but a peach of a girl for all that"), William Powell and even Greta Garbo ("She still remembers enough about the tough sledding of the early years of the colony to say, 'Hello, Harry,' if we happen to meet some place").

Langdon began the article, though, by recalling his days with a prominent director:

The SS Mariposa arrives in Sydney, Australia for Anything Goes, *and Harry (with Harry Jr.) is quite relieved; December 30, 1935.*

Langdon and the cast of Anything Goes *appeared at a nursery and the Deaf, Dumb and Blind Institute of Darlington, January 1936*

Although I'm in Australia now… I still read my "Esquire," a real he-man American paper. And going through it last night, I noticed an article by a very old friend and co-worker of mine, Frank Capra, one of the finest directors in the film business.

Capra's article, titled "A Sick Dog Tells Where it Hurts," forcefully castigated the concept of Hollywood as a production factory and its output as a commodity rather than an art form. "We have a magic carpet, but we don't fly with it….What we need are more individuals with artistic honesty; writers with a sincere desire to say something of merit rather than writing to order; directors honest enough and big enough to make their own pictures; actors who give more thought to their parts than they do to the temperatures of their swimming pools…in other words, more MEN and not prostitutes. [The] business of making pictures is in the hands of people who lack the intestinal fortitude to assert their artistic independence."

Langdon's piece continues:

Quite apart from its contents, that story of Frank's made me think.
"Why, say!" I said to myself, first thing. "Here's Frank busting into print. Why, it's only the other day…"
Well, I pulled myself up in time. That other day was quite a few years ago. Things move so fast in Hollywood that time seems to jump by you…it is only yesterday, to me, that I was working on the old Mack Sennett lot, turning out comedies that the public of those days went into fits about…
But it was Capra's name that started me off on this. Good old Frank — a fine guy if ever there was one. Wonder if he has time these days to remember the way the two of us worked together when he was starting off in the business as a gag-man, and I was everything from director to cutter and emergency scenario writer for the small producing company that paid both of us our dough. Maybe he's too busy, although I hardly think so. Last time we met up — middle of last year it was — we spent a few hours and some canned beer going over those days.

As cheerfully friendly as this appears on the surface, there's some obvious bitterness between the lines. Capra was, of course, more than "a gag-man" during his days with the Harry Langdon Corporation, the "small producing company" to which Langdon refers, but that is, of course, how he was allegedly portrayed after his firing in 1927. Then, after having labeled him a "gag-man," Langdon takes credit for every other function Capra had performed in reality. As for the "canned beer" reunion, one suspects Langdon employed the same imaginative license that produced his dubious 1932 article in which he described meeting Mack Sennett when the latter's car stalled on train tracks. The reality is that, after nine contentious years apart, neither man had any great desire to "meet up."

The troupe appeared in Sydney until March 20, and then proceeded by rail to Brisbane, the next stop on the tour. The *Brisbane Courier Mail* caught him in an introspective mood: "'Eighteen years of the quick-fire life of Hollywood, and now this quiet contrast — it will do for me, your Brisbane,' said Mr. Harry Langdon, the American comedian leading the cast of 'Anything Goes'…. 'My wife and I are not the right kind for the popular conception of Hollywood life…'

"The whirl of Hollywood was awful, Mr. Langdon declared — not because of social gaiety but of the intense, high-speed work, the competition, and the struggle to excel the highest standards of previous achievement. He would like to stay in Australia for a few years and relax."

The show opened at His Majesty's Theatre on March 24. By now, everyone had ironed out any performance problems, and both the play and Langdon in particular, received excellent notices. The *Courier Mail* noted, "[There] is the sheen and sparkle of sumptuous settings as a brilliant backing for the synthesis of comedy, dancing, music, costume and lighting… adroit management of high-speed dialogue dulls any double edges.

"Mr. Harry Langdon holds the stage almost throughout… he seems to get as much fun out of his role as the audience, and in the suggestion of spontaneity is not a little of his success. His part is the figment of a playful conception, cunningly conveyed with a droll drawl… There is fine team work among the cast, and while he is the central figure in the fun, Mr. Langdon refrains from overshadowing those whose function also it is to amuse."

The *Daily Telegraph* agreed: "'Anything Goes' is a mixed musical comedy in that there is a lot of everything and plenty to go in it. The comedy runs on smoothly, constant ripples of merriment being interspersed with positive gales of mirth...

"Harry Langdon... is a thoroughly good comedian, with plenty of new tricks in his bag. He works quietly, has a funny face, uses it well, and last night scientifically courted and won an audience that seemed determined to make him win on his merits. Before the end of the first act they had wholeheartedly capitulated."

After Brisbane came Melbourne, the tour's final stop. Again, the press notices were glowing: "For the first time a musical comedy has been written and composed for adult audiences," asserted the *Melbourne Argus*. "Not for [Langdon] the boisterous horse play of the knock-about comedian, nor the hand springs of a red-nosed clown. 'Tread the step lightly, my pretty Louise' is a good enough motto for him. His impersonation of the gangster masquerading in clerical garb is a comic masterpiece of understatement."

Off-stage, Langdon submitted cartoons to a Melbourne-based magazine, *Table Talk*, the offices of which he visited while in town. He would continue to do so off-and-on for the next several years; finally, in 1943, the magazine officially appointed him as a staff cartoonist.

The theatrical season wrapped on May 25, after which cast and crew dispersed. Langdon and his family departed June 4 from Australia's Western Coast, aboard the R.M.S. *Narkunda*, ultimately bound for London. The next day's *Adelaide Advertiser* noted his departure: "After 18 years' continuous work at Hollywood, during which he has taken prominent roles in a number of silent and sound films, and five months in Australia playing the lead in *Anything Goes* with the J. C. Williamson Company, Mr. Harry Langdon, an American film actor, accompanied by his wife and son, is going to England [on] the *Narkunda*, which left the Outer Harbor yesterday afternoon. From England, Mr. Langdon and his family will return to Hollywood, where Mr. Langdon will probably give up acting to become a director."

During its 37-day journey, the *Narkunda* docked for a while at Bombay, India, and the Langdons took time to visit some relatives of Mabel's father. While there, she discovered her husband had more knowledge than she of certain Indian customs, telling Edward Watz, "We had lunch in a hotel that was recommended to Harry by one of the officers from our boat. And I had to use the ladies' room at the hotel restaurant. When I went to the restroom, I saw that there were no doors on the compartments. But there was this large man sitting in the corner of the ladies' room with a tip basket in his lap! I figured the guy was some kind of a weirdo or pervert and rushed outside to tell Harry.

"I made him come over to me and was barely whispering, I guess because I was so nervous, and all he kept saying to me was, 'What? What're you saying, Mabel? I can't hear a word you're saying...' Finally I blurted to him, 'There's a big guy sitting in there, he was gonna watch me!' Harry said, 'Wait a minute...' and he looked around to make sure the coast was clear, and he peeked in. Then Harry looked at me, smiled, and said, 'It's okay sweetie, he's just a harmless eunuch doing his job. Have you got a coin in your purse you can give him?' I got so embarrassed! You would guess that I'd know about eunuchs because of my Indian heritage, but Momma raised me as a proper English girl in Southern California. Eunuchs were like mythical characters out of an Arabian Nights fable to me!"

On June 29, while the Langdons were at sea, brother James Tulley Langdon passed away at age 45. Obituaries called him a "veteran vaudeville player" of the Keith and Orpheum circuits, while failing to note his contributions to his brother's films. As the family's lone veteran, he was buried at Los Angeles National Cemetery in Westwood on July 3. Oldest brother Charles also died that year, on October 31 at age 61; he was laid to rest beside his mother at Grandview.

As it happened, the Langdons ended up staying in England for ten months, enabling Mabel and Harry, Jr. to spend time with family, and Langdon to accept motion picture work. His first assignment was directorial, which somewhat validated the *Advertiser*'s claim that he hoped to forsake acting permanently. *Wise Guys* was a vehicle for Charlie Naughton and Jimmy Gold, two members of The Crazy Gang, a sort of Depression-era Monty Python that regularly appeared at the London Palladium and Victoria Palace. The film casts Naughton and Gold as the downtrodden nephews of one Phineas MacNaughton, who wishes to retire and turn over his business to family members. The two attempt to raise the cash necessary to accomplish this, but are outsmarted by a pair of American swindlers, Flo and Eddy. Although produced by Fox British, the film never received a U.S. release and does not circulate, although it apparently does exist. In 1984, David Quinlan, author of *British Sound Films: The Studio Years 1928–1959*, summed up *Wise Guys* in two words: "Nothing special."

Langdon's next assignment put him in front of the camera as a supporting player. *Mad About Money* stars three other Hollywood names: Ben Lyon, Wallace Ford and Lupe Velez. The film, directed by Melville Brown, is set in the Melbrow Film Studios where Lyon and Ford are attempting to raise money for a new musical picture. Langdon plays Otto Schultz, a potential backer that inherited a brewery when its owner, his uncle, failed to make out a will. Velez portrays a showgirl who crashes the studio gates by posing as a cattle heiress, which causes all sorts of complications.

Mad About Money's chief distinction is that it was filmed in color, although not very competently, according to *Variety*: "Film can't make up its mind whether to stick with a bad pale yellow-pink tint or one equally bad in greenish blue. Coloring is brutal to the faces and thins the photography until players can hardly be recognized except in close-ups." Grand National Studios acquired stateside distribution, releasing it in May 1938 under the title *He Loved an Actress*, while British Lion didn't release it on the home continent until November.

No other work presented itself. Having exhausted all they'd earned overseas, and then some, the Langdons booked passage on the R.M.S. *Berengaria*, and set sail for New York on May 15, 1937, arriving four days later. "We stayed in New York for a few weeks, then returned to Hollywood," remembered Mabel. Back home, Langdon scrambled for work. He sold a script for Al Jolson's weekly radio series, made an appearance on a local air program, *Pick of the Pictures*, and returned to Columbia for a one-shot two-reeler. Three months into 1938, he was once again "absolutely *destitute*," and once again, an old comrade came to the rescue.

Harry reacts to Olive Sloane in this reissue lobby card for Mad About Money *(1938), original U.S. title:* He Loved an Actress.

CHAPTER FIFTEEN

Laurel & Langdon & Hardy

1938–1940

On March 24, 1938, Langdon returned to Commissioner Doyle's court at the behest of ex-wife Helen and her quest for overdue alimony, plus the judgment of $21,078 she'd been awarded in 1934. Of her ex-husband, who was described in the *Los Angeles Herald* as "unshaven and rather unkempt in appearance," Helen declared, "He hasn't paid anything since November 1935."

"I'm flat broke," Langdon told Doyle, explaining that his earnings since returning to the U.S. ten months earlier totaled only $1,090, most of this being his net pay for a single Columbia short, *A Doggone Mixup*, filmed the previous October, plus $200 from Columbia in February for an original scenario titled "The Ambulance Chaser." Confessed Langdon, "Before that, I lost money on a personal appearance in Europe. I've been borrowing money from my friends. The amount runs into hundreds of dollars." Mabel, who accompanied him, added, "We have nothing except fifteen dollars." Doyle ordered the case be continued in July. The story made its way, via the next morning's papers, to the eyes of fellow vaudevillian-turned-screen comic Stan Laurel, who may well have been one of the friends from whom Langdon was borrowing money.

Laurel, having been teamed with Oliver Hardy for over a decade, had of late been producing their pictures for Hal Roach. He immediately hired Langdon as a gagman for his and Hardy's latest feature, "Meet the Missus." Laurel could sympathize with Langdon's predicament, having more than one vindictive ex-wife of his own (one of whom would be taking *him* to court just three weeks later). Yet that likely had little to do with the decision. Laurel had every reason to believe Langdon could write effectively for his character, because it owed so much to Langdon's own.

Born Arthur Stanley Jefferson in Ulverston, England, on June 16, 1890, Laurel was the son of a theater owner, and from childhood dreamed of a career before the footlights. After a few years of working in music halls and his father's theater chain, occasionally appearing in sketches written by the senior Mr. Jefferson, 19-year-old Stanley hooked up with Fred Karno's London Comedians, playing supporting roles and understudying Charlie Chaplin. Stan joined Chaplin on the company's American tours in the early 1910s and, like Chaplin, decided to stay.

Chaplin, of course, went to Sennett's Keystone and on to cinema greatness; Laurel opted for vaudeville, initially as a Chaplin imitator in an act first called The Keystone Trio, then The Stan Jefferson Trio. In 1917, he took on a partner, Mae Dahlberg of Australia, who later became his common-law wife and gave him his new surname when he realized, in a moment of Langdonian superstition, that "Stan Jefferson" contained 13 letters. With his Karno training, Laurel was also sought for movies, but lacked Chaplin's intimate appeal. Sporadically during 1917, 1918 and 1921, he'd

'Flat Broke'

With the exception of $15, Harry Langdon is "flat broke." The once famous comedian of the screen told the court yesterday that was the reason he was unable to pay Helen Walton Langdon $25 a week, as ordered when they were divorced in 1935. She says he is in arrears $2920. Langdon's present wife (pictured with him above) told the court "we have nothing but $15.00." — *Los Angeles Examiner* photo.

make films for one company or another, including Roach, but little or nothing would happen with them and he'd return to the stage.

For a week in June 1920, when Harry, Rose and Cecil were headlining at the Fox Audubon in upper Manhattan's Washington Heights, Stan and Mae could be seen on the lower east side at the small-time City Theatre. Winning over what *Variety* termed "a hard-boiled crowd of regulars" on an especially balmy day, reviewer "Con" was decidedly impressed and right on the money in deducing Laurel's training ground:

Stan and May *(sic)* Laurel... achieved the seemingly impossible with an assortment of English low comedy songs, dances and pantomime bits. The male enters as a burglar and is mistaken for a doctor by the girl, who has just phoned for a dentist. After this the act devolves into a succession of comedy business by the man which was good for screams. He is a comic who reminds of the Karno school and has a fine knowledge of travesty values and an unusual amount of pantomimic talent. He will make any gathering laugh.

In 1922, Laurel made a series of comedies for Metro release under the supervision of G.M. "Broncho Billy" Anderson, once the "Ay" of the defunct Essanay Film Manufacturing Company. In these, Laurel took his "fine knowledge of travesty values" and made burlesques of popular costume dramas. *Mud and Sand*, a parody of Rudolph Valentino's bullfighting epic *Blood and Sand* (Stan portrays "Rhubarb Vaseline"), brought him his first positive notices; he followed this up with more: *When Knights Were Cold* (*When Knights Were Bold*) and *The Soilers* (*The Spoilers*), but such things would only carry him so far. As a character comedian, Laurel was found wanting. A second stint with Roach in 1923, then one with producer Joe Rock the following year, failed to yield anything resembling stardom. Finally, in 1925 he gave up performing and returned to Roach as a writer-director. Oliver "Babe" Hardy was among the supporting players, having arrived at Roach after Larry Semon's profligate spending ended their association along with Semon's employment.

Future director George Stevens, who later photographed the earliest Laurel & Hardy comedies, saw Laurel's problem: "Some time before beginning at Roach, I had seen Stan work and thought he was one of the unfunniest comedians around...He laughed and smiled too much as a comedian. He needed and wanted laughs so much that he made a habit of laughing at himself as a player, which is extremely poor comic technique. How he changed!" Indeed he did, and upon close examination it's apparent that Langdon's success was a primary motivator.

As early as his work with Joe Rock, Laurel toned down the brashness and became what writer Chris Seguin called "a prissy, petulant, easily agitated fop." This approach, too, lacked the wide appeal that builds a following. Director Leo McCarey, who is generally credited with seeing and shaping the potential of Laurel and Hardy as a team, recalled that in 1926, "the [Roach studio's] head of production, a very clever man named F. Richard Jones... taught Stan many things about moviemaking. Jones saw Stan's great potential as a performer." This is, of course, the same F. Richard Jones who oversaw Langdon's transformation from "fresh little guy" to Little Elf at Sennett's.

Having just settled into a comfortable niche behind the camera, Laurel initially refused when Jones asked him to portray Harry Myers's butler in an All-Star comedy, *Get 'em Young*. Jones persisted: the role had been intended for Babe Hardy, who'd been injured (scalded while cooking over the weekend). A suitably comic replacement was urgently required to keep production on schedule. Hal Roach dangled a $100 bonus and Laurel acquiesced. Cast in supporting roles were Eugenia Gilbert as leading lady and Charlotte Mineau as a fortune-hunting bride-to-be, both Sennett alumni who'd worked with Langdon.

Late in life, Laurel recalled this picture as the one in which he evolved his "crying" bit, and it appears rather frequently. This butler is such a timid, easily distressed character that it's nigh impossible to picture Hardy playing it. Clearly some hasty re-writing was performed before the camera rolled. Apart from the cry, though, there's a much more telling moment for Laurel. Clad in wig and white gown, contemplating the unpleasant prospect of posing as a bride so his boss can inherit $1 million, Laurel downs a bottle of liquor. Slowly his morose expression vanishes; he takes a long blink and gradually realizes that the liquor is making him feel better. The moment lasts only a few seconds, but it's got "Harry Langdon" stamped all over it: the luminous blue eyes, the vacant stare, the three-second blink, the measured transformation of facial expression.

"In the all-too-short span of Harry's superstardom," wrote Seguin for *Blotto* magazine, "his influence was everywhere. So it was inevitable that it would reach Stan Laurel. Stan had been struggling for years to define his comic persona.... Ultimately, Stan did learn from Harry. Here's what he learned: to take it slow. Slooooooow. This seemed to be the trigger Laurel required to re-evaluate his comic style — and it would change everything."

Persuaded by Jones to remain in front of the camera, Laurel decided to make a two-reeler out of a music hall sketch written by his father, "Home From the Honeymoon." Two tramps, in evading the police, wind up in a mansion owned by a millionaire who has gone on an extended vacation, and are mistaken for the actual householders by a pair of would-be renters. Eventually the real owner returns home unexpectedly and disposes of the impostors. Laurel portrayed one of the tramps, and Hardy was cast as his cohort. The results were glorious. It must have been evident in the screening room that the two men fit together seamlessly, but it would take several months — during which the film, titled *Duck Soup*, made its way around the world's theaters — before the decision was made to build Laurel & Hardy as a team.

The pair appeared on the scene not long after Langdon had deserted shorts for features, and it's probably more than coincidence that their rise to fame occurred at the same time as Langdon's descent. Laurel may have transitioned into a slow-moving, dim-witted, Langdonesque innocent, but he had something Langdon did not: a rotund, fussy, self-important, yet equally dimwitted companion. In essence, Laurel & Hardy took Langdon's comedy of reaction, added slapstick, and effectively doubled the laughs.

Over the course of the next decade-plus, Stan and Babe two-stepped easily into talkies, conquered the short subject field, won an Academy Award for their three-reeler *The Music Box*, and had successfully transitioned to feature films. In between, they used and reused the basic premise of Langdon's classic *Saturday Afternoon* for a silent short (*We Faw Down*) and a talkie feature (*Sons of the Desert*). Laurel & Hardy became the gold standard among comic duos; so much so that, as we have seen, many of the talkie shorts Langdon made with Vernon Dent were undisguised attempts to mirror the pair that they, themselves, had mildly influenced.

And so, Langdon returned to the Hal Roach lot for the first time since leaving his own starring two-reel series eight years before. The initial script for "Meet the Missus" amounted to about four reels' worth of action, but Roach was contracted to deliver a full-length feature as the last under his Metro-Goldwyn-Mayer contract. The producer had recently signed a new deal to produce for United Artists and was anxious to wrap up old obligations.

Three minds without a single thought: Laurel, Hardy and Langdon between takes on Block-Heads *(1938).*

Langdon immediately suggested a prologue taken right from his own *Soldier Man*. Stan would be a doughboy unaware that the war had ended twenty years before. He'd be returned to the U.S. and placed in a veterans' home, where Ollie would retrieve him. This would lead into the body of "Meet the Missus," which was actually an extended remake of the team's first talking two-reeler, *Unaccustomed As We Are*. Ollie

June 19, 1938: Hardy, Langdon, Hal Roach Jr. and Minna Gombell help Stan Laurel celebrate his 46th birthday on the set of Block-Heads.

brings Stan home for a home-cooked meal, but Mrs. Hardy strenuously objects and walks out on her husband. Attempting the task himself, Ollie makes a mess of things until the neighbor's wife volunteers to help. Alas, she has a jealous husband, and when he returns home, followed soon after by a contrite Mrs. Hardy, things unravel for the boys. 'Twas ever thus.

Filming took place during all of June, and Langdon remained on the set most days, ready to chime in with a suggestion. One such bit involved the gurgling of a water cooler, which Stan mistakes as the churning of his stomach. Making the cooler gurgle on cue was the problem, and with the help of the prop department, the problem was solved by a large tube, masked by the cooler, and a hidden assistant blowing into it whenever a red light was switched on. Langdon would use the gag himself in a 1940 Columbia short, *Cold Turkey*.

There were a few former co-workers on the Roach lot. Fellow gagmen included Charley Rogers, who'd directed the majority of Langdon's Roach shorts, and Felix Adler, a title-writer during his stint at Sennett's. Another colleague was Nancy Carroll, with whom he had appeared in *Atlantic Adventure*. Ms. Carroll was playing a small role in Roach's first United Artists production, *There Goes My Heart*, the story of an unlikely romance between a newspaperman (Fredric March) and the wealthy daughter of a successful department store owner (Virginia Bruce). Although based on an original story by then-columnist and future variety show host Ed Sullivan, the film's plot bore more than a passing resemblance to Frank Capra's classic *It Happened One Night*. Carroll suggested Langdon for the role of the minister who wraps up the story

The celebration continues at the Laurel household when work is over.

by subtly offering to marry the two leads. Milton H. Bren, vice president in charge of production, agreed.

Roach's UA deal included up to four Laurel & Hardy pictures annually, so the future was looking bright enough that he was able to make partial payments on the money due Helen; just enough to stay out of trouble. On June 20, he and Mabel secured a marriage license in Ventura County, where they wed a second time, a purely sentimental gesture. Having attended her sister's marriage in Ventura, Mabel had promised the family to also be wed there one day. The press, of course, found out; Harry's answer to their query was, "Weddings are such fun that we want to be married again and spend another honeymoon." It's tempting to assume such statements were calculated to annoy Helen as much as to entertain readers.

Four days after the ceremony, he took a short break from Stan and Babe's set, and returned to Columbia to make a two-reel quickie of his original story "The Ambulance Chaser." The resulting film, which would be released in September as *Sue My Lawyer*, would be his first directed by Jules White. White was not a particularly inspired director, favoring fast-paced, violent sight gags, which were never Langdon's forte. Co-starring was Ann Doran, and according to her, the production played host to a brief, and unlikely, professional reunion.

Frank Capra was now firmly established as Columbia's — and Hollywood's — most successful director, and Doran had worked on two of his Oscar-winners: *Mr. Deeds Goes to Town* and *You Can't Take it With You*. Capra was in post-production for the latter and Doran had seen him around the lot. She knew his history as both a Sennett gagman and a member of Langdon's old team. "I told Mr. Capra that I was working with Harry Langdon across the street and to come over if he found the time," she told Steve Randisi for *Filmfax* magazine. Doran elaborated:

> He came over and I saw him way off in the background. We were coming up to a point where we needed a gag, and we tried to find something funny but it was just not working. So I saw Mr. Capra and he waved to me. I called him and he walked over, still out of the lights of the set. I went over to him and said, "Mr. Capra, will you please gag it for us?" He asked, "Do you suppose Harry will take it?" And I told him, "At this point he'll take anything because we are in a spot." Then I went over to Harry and asked, "Do you mind if I bring over a friend of mine to gag it for us?" And he said, "God, no. Anything to make it funny!" Capra came on and there was electricity all over the set, but we needed that gag. Capra said to Harry, "Let's do the old going-up-the-stairs thing..." Harry said, "That's wonderful, wonderful!"

Langdon and Ann Doran in a gag photo from Sue My Lawyer *(1938).*

Lending credence to Doran's account is that the sequence is nearly identical to the version in *The Strong Man*. Although Langdon authored *Sue My Lawyer*'s original story, it's unlikely Ewart Adamson's screenplay would have so closely mirrored the original gag's construction, whereas between Capra and Langdon it could have easily come into focus. Doran wants to get Harry into her apartment and pulls a mock fainting spell. Harry lifts and tries to carry her up the stairs in standard fashion. Owing to the type of slapstick contrivance that tickled White's fancy, there's a corkscrew protruding from a hole in Harry's pants, which jabs Doran's backside with every alternate step. Annoyed, she surreptitiously pulls the pin from her lapel flower and gives him a taste of the same. He stops with a jolt and, as in the original film, places the woman on the banister, whereupon she slides back down to the bottom. Harry picks her up again, tries charging up the stairs, but hasn't the stamina to make it. He sits on the steps, positions her across his lap, and takes her up the stairs backward, proceeding onto a stepladder, then over for what appears to have been a very painful tumble for some stuntman.

In *The Name Above the Title*, Capra related the barest portion of the backstory, claiming that he only watched the filming from afar, never making his presence known. "My heart sank," he wrote. "I left — and I could have cried," because White was yelling, "Faster, Harry, Faster!" to "that great, great artist — whose art was the very essence of slow, slow pantomime." Adding to the melodrama, he misrepresented the film as a one-reeler, White as a nameless "irreverent slapstick director" and the svelte Doran as "an enormous fat lady," and never mentioned that what he termed "a grotesque replica of the famous scene we did" had been filmed at his suggestion. The only apparently true statement was that it was the last time he and Langdon would ever see each other.

"I don't know that they became buddy-buddy friends again," concluded Doran, "but at least for the moment they tolerated each other because the gag was more important than the personal problem.... To good comedians, directors and gagmen, the laugh is more important than personal relationships."

Meanwhile, Stan Laurel's personal relationship with Hal Roach had deteriorated to the point where

Bud Jamison can't believe Harry has the evidence in Sue My Lawyer.

laughs couldn't save it. Theirs had long been a contentious alliance. The producer was first and foremost a businessman, and even after Laurel and Hardy had been established as a team, he'd kept them under individual contracts that did not run concurrently, negating the pair's bargaining power. Second, although admiring his gagging ability, Roach had no confidence in Laurel as a story constructionist, which led to recurring battles over creative control.

Twice before, when Laurel's contract was up, he'd tried holding out for a better deal. In 1935, Roach countered with a proposal to create a two-reel series called The Hardy Family, teaming Babe with Patsy Kelly and Our Gang's popular Spanky McFarland. When Laurel tried again in 1937, Roach announced he'd pair Hardy with Langdon, even though the latter wasn't under contract, or in the United States for that matter.

In August 1938, things came to a head. To begin with, on January 1, Laurel had married a third time, to Illiana Shuvalova, a self-styled Russian "countess" he'd met while auditioning singer-dancers for his previous film, *Swiss Miss*. Turning Laurel's head with charm, flattery and a well-endowed physique, Illiana turned out to be something akin to Helen Walton on steroids. Making matters worse, Laurel's most recent ex, Virginia Ruth Laurel, immediately went to court claiming their divorce had not yet been finalized. Over the following months, Illiana suffered two nervous collapses (allegedly brought on by Virginia's action), announced she and Stan would separate, then married him two more times (presumably to make it doubly legal), and while under the influence of alcohol, smashed a rental car into two parked autos and a tree (for which she attempted to blame the rental company for letting her, an unlicensed driver, have the car in the first place). The non-stop publicity from these antics failed to engender sympathy from Laurel's boss.

Then he and Roach bickered over the ending for *Block-Heads*, the release title for "Meet the Missus." The plot wrapped up with Billy Gilbert as a jealous husband chasing Stan and Ollie with his hunting rifle, and Laurel conceived a closing shot: his and Hardy's heads mounted like trophies on Gilbert's wall, with Hardy glaring at Laurel in full "Here's another nice mess you've gotten me into" mode and Laurel poised to weep. Roach hated it and demanded Laurel return for retakes. When the comedian refused, Roach suspended him and filed suit for breach of contract.

This time Langdon *was* under contract, and preview audiences for *There Goes My Heart* had actually cheered his brief appearance. After smoothing some ruffled feathers in UA's front office, on August 17 Roach made it official: Laurel was out and Langdon was in as Hardy's partner.

Much like his screen character, Langdon displayed several emotions at once: excitement, concern, confi-

Harry the preacher in There Goes My Heart *(1938).*

dence, wariness, joy. Mostly, though, he was grateful to be signing a contract that would pay him $1,000 per week. "Looks like all my troubles are over," he reportedly remarked as he picked up the pen. "All I can say is that it's swell."

Reporters and columnists from all the wire services swarmed the studio to interview Langdon, and all of them had the same question: "What went wrong all those years ago?" Bemused by the attention, he seemed to derive pleasure out of giving a different answer each time:

To United Press's Frederick C. Othman: "By 1927, I was producing my own pictures and I was palling around with a stockbroker. He lived in swell style. I envied him. He said I ought to quit spending so much money on my pictures and play in the stocks. So I took his advice. I cut down on my budgets [and] played the stock market… It wasn't long before I lost all my money. My wife left me and there I was, broke, after earning a literal fortune."

To Associated Press's Dan Deluce: "I made a mistake when I signed a contract which cut the production budget of my pictures from $250,000 to $125,000. I said 'yes.' I should have said 'no.' I can't even remember the names of the last two pictures I made on that contract."

To NEA's Paul Harrison: "I really started on the skids back in 1928. Some people had been comparing my work with Charlie Chaplin's, but I knew even then that I was headed out. The last two features I made were absolute stinkers, and scarcely anybody saw them. Then [I went] into short features. And in 1934 I made a series of very bad shorts for Columbia. Then I was through."

To columnist Robbin Coons: "I had to turn out a feature in 10 weeks, where Chaplin and Harold Lloyd were spending up to two years on each of theirs. It couldn't be done — the public quickly tired of the character, and there I was, in '29 — out. I'm not the type who could make good as his own producer. The responsibility got me down [and] I finally said, 'Oh, nuts.'"

The dissolution of Laurel & Hardy was such a huge story that, inevitably, a handful of correspondents missed the key details and assumed there'd been a feud between the two stars. To his credit, Langdon kept the facts straight: "Stan got me my writing job here at Roach's. I never dreamed that his partnership with Oliver Hardy would be broken, but the studio claimed Stan failed to appear for retakes for his last picture, and canceled his contract. I honestly hope they'll patch things up, even if it means Hardy and I won't play in a picture together.

"[Stan] understands this thing now. He knows that if I hadn't taken it, someone else would have — and he's glad I got the break. Great fellow, Stan." At the same time, he couldn't resist comparing Laurel's current predicament to his own of a decade before: "He's just the way now I used to be. I hope Stan isn't following in my footsteps. I really mean that, but the irony of the situation is one that keeps me awake nights, wondering."

As to his present and future, he was invariably consistent: "I never want another build-up," he

August 27, 1938: Harry and Mabel Langdon at the wedding of Vernon and Eunice Dent.

assured Coons, "I'm tired of the top. I'm happy. My wife and I get along fine, we have a fine four-year-old boy, and — well, everything's right." He told Deluce, "It may sound like Pollyanna talk, but I think I've learned a lesson from all the hard knocks. I have a fine wife and a healthy young son, whom I didn't have when I was in the big money." To Othman, he elaborated, "I got married to a girl who loved me for myself, and not for my money. I knew she did, because I didn't have any money. We have a little boy and we're happy. I used to wish I could live my life over again. Now it looks like I'm going to do that very thing."

The United Press report included the following: "[Langdon's] income is around $1,000 a week and not one cent of it is going for champagne. 'I'm buying nothing but federal bonds and insurance annuities,' he said. 'There isn't much fun in that, maybe, but neither is there any trouble.'" True, until Helen summoned him into court on October 7. Telling the judge he was "back in the money," he agreed to remit 25 percent of his earnings to Helen going forward. "I guess I won't be coming back here anymore," said the woman who, years before, witnessed Langdon's failure to pay off his first ex-wife, proving she hadn't lost her capacity for self-delusion.

There was only one shadow cast across this sunny future: the first Langdon & Hardy picture was shaping up to be a disaster. Based on an H. C. Bunner short novel titled *Zenobia's Infidelity*, it was a period piece, set in the immediate post-Civil War South, in which Hardy plays Henry Tibbett, a courtly country

Langdon and Hardy seem optimistic about the script for their first film together.

A publicity still that doesn't quite depict the Langdon-Hardy relationship as seen in Zenobia *(1939).*

doctor with a heart of gold, and Langdon is Professor McCrackle, a medicine show huckster with a performing elephant, Zenobia. When the elephant suddenly takes ill, Tibbett reluctantly treats her, then discovers to his horror that he's won her undying loyalty. She follows him everywhere, destroying his social life and jeopardizing the romance his daughter, Mary (Jean Parker) shares with Jeff Carter (James Ellison), who hails from a wealthy society family. Making matters worse, McCrackle takes Tibbett to court for alienation of Zenobia's affections, a fascinating turnabout for the comedian who, in real life, had been sued for the same thing.

As the story had originally been purchased for Roland Young, star of Roach's 1937 success *Topper*, some rewriting was essential, and Langdon chimed in as much as possible. However, by December, with the film in production, he had decided it was "merely an experimental step up from the bit part in *There Goes My Heart*," according to columnist Thornton Delehanty. "There is to be no Laurel and Hardy slapstick in this Hardy and Langdon combination. Hardy, in fact, has about 90 percent of the picture, while Langdon estimates his contribution will be about 30. That is why he speaks of it reservedly and why his eye lights when the next picture after that is mentioned. As yet untitled, it will be a genuine starring proposition for the team…. Bert Kalmar and Harry Ruby are working on it."

Settling on a title for "Zenobia's Infidelity" was itself a headache. The first one announced was, surprisingly, "Zenobia," quickly followed by "This Time It's Love," then "It's Spring Again," which lasted through most of production into previews. "We, the People" was considered for a time, until finally and definitively the studio opted for *Zenobia*, having come full circle. (In other English-speaking countries, *Zenobia* was titled *Elephants Never Forget*.)

Production began in November and continued into 1939, with Gordon Douglas directing. It was Douglas's first feature assignment after two years of helming the Our Gang shorts. Throughout, the publicity kept on coming. "Take six fine actors and actresses, inject a little rivalry and it should spell 'swell entertainment.' That's what Associate Producer A. Edward Sutherland expects from his cast of 'It's Spring Again,'" according to one early blurb. "First there's Oliver Hardy and Harry Langdon, both consummate actors and long versed in the art of creating laughs. For Langdon the picture is an opportunity to 'come back' to the stellar rating and multi-figured salary he once enjoyed. He's working as he never worked before.

"For Hardy, the picture means a new type of characterization of even wider appeal, and while he and Langdon are pals off-screen, he's not going to let the funny-faced little fellow be one whit better than he is before the camera.

"Sutherland says it's the most potential cast he ever had in a picture. Each player is prodding himself or herself without any coaxing from the sidelines.

Examining Zenobia.

Sutherland says it's the kind of a situation a producer always dreams about but usually wakes up before he gets it."

Even Queenie — the real name of the elephant playing Zenobia — was grist for the publicist's mill:

> Queenie is an elephant. Her size has nothing to do with the way in which she fills the lens, because a camera can back away to where even an elephant looks no bigger than a marble. But somewhere during her career with circuses, carnivals and in the studios, Queenie picked up every trick known to man or beast that'll succeed in stealing scenes.
>
> [Should] Oliver Hardy try to emote in a scene with her, she simply attracts all the attention by wriggling her nose. There is something fascinating about a wiggling nose that is seven feet long and Queenie knows it.
>
> [Should] Harry Langdon try to do a medicine selling routine with her, she simply keeps backing away an inch at a time, until Langdon's completely turned around and all that's left for the camera is Queenie's face...
>
> The elephant's trainer, George Emerson, says Queenie, who will be known in the picture as "Zenobia," really isn't a lens-louse at heart. He says she's just shy and timid, and basically a rather retiring soul, but there's nobody on the set who subscribes to such ideas....
>
> Since Langdon started to work with her, and discovered her trick of backing away and making him turn around, he doesn't bother to put on make-up anymore. He just daubs a little grease paint every morning on the back of his ears and the nape of his neck and lets it go at that.

Supposedly Roach liked what he saw of the rushes enough to offer Langdon a long term deal as Hardy's partner. "Pact replaces one which still had several months to go, and provides for [a] considerable pay hoist," *Daily Variety* reported on December 7. This was the day after Stan Laurel filed his own breach of contract suit against Roach, and the possibility exists that this particular contract, if tendered at all, was calculated to send Laurel a message.

Intentionally or not, Louella Parsons aided Roach in this goal, telling readers in her column of January 2, 1939: "Hal Roach and Milton Bren ran the first rough cut of 'It's Spring Again' in the projection room with the result that Harry Langdon is set as a full-fledged star again. What a swell break, for Harry has had so much bad luck in the last five years, professional and personal. Hal couldn't have given him a better New Year gift than the long term contract calling for three feature pictures a year, co-starred with Oliver Hardy. He'll take Stan Laurel's place, and any doubts anyone

Behind the scenes on Zenobia.

may have that Harry couldn't fill his comedy shoes were dispelled when the studio gang took a look at the first Hardy-Langdon opus."

The film's real test, though, was not in a screening room but with audiences, and the previews weren't promising. "The continuance of Oliver Hardy and Harry Langdon as a team will depend on the reception of their first picture together, 'It's Spring Again,'" read a February 3, 1939 account. "The film was sneak-previewed the other night, and since then eleven-hundred feet have been eliminated. It will have another sneak showing [and] the fate of the Hardy-Langdon combination will then rest with the Hal Roach salesmen."

Judging by the results, the salesmen, whether from Roach or United Artists, were at a complete loss. Unlike M.G.M., UA had no theaters of their own upon which to rely; the company was wholly dependent on the desirability of the product. Their ultimate strategy was to turn their problem into a contest, offering "$500 in cash prizes" to be split between the exhibitors with the best campaign. Acting as judges would be Hal Roach, three UA executives, and a brace of trade magazine columnists and critics.

Meanwhile, the marketing materials turned this lightweight romantic comedy into a mystery. "Who is Zenobia?" asked the posters and ads. "What's she got that every girl could use?" The pressbook, daring to call this a "fresh, sparkling, patron-pulling ad approach," added, "Ask your whole town 'Who is Zenobia?' and your whole town will flock to find out!"

Evidently not, according to the few theaters that could be persuaded to book the film. "We couldn't get them in to see this one," said Ontario, Canada's Harland Rankin, no doubt speaking for his managerial brethren. "'Zenobia' is the elephant; we were the goats." With a negative tab of $637,000, *Zenobia* returned a dismal $220,000 in domestic rentals and $131,000 in foreign. It was far and away the biggest loser of the Roach-UA partnership. As far as most exhibitors were concerned, there was room on their program for only one period piece set in the Civil War-era South, and that would be *Gone With the Wind*.

Late in life, Gordon Douglas accurately summed up *Zenobia*: "Harry Langdon was a great comic, but there's no way to break up a combination like Laurel and Hardy. It wasn't Laurel and Hardy by a long shot; there were more dramatics, [with Hardy playing it] straighter than he'd ever been. It wasn't set up as much for comedy, and I'm sure the audience wasn't as happy as they would have been with Laurel and Hardy."

That's an understatement. When it comes to marketing a product, there is a saying: "There's no such thing as bad publicity." *Zenobia* is an exception to the rule. All the hype Roach employed to promote Langdon as Oliver Hardy's new partner backfired when their first effort failed to deliver on those lofty expectations. They have only two fairly lengthy scenes together, both of which involved examining

the elephant; otherwise, they occupy separate frames for most of the picture. Critics were caught off-guard, exhibitors felt betrayed and audiences kept away. However, the hype was also designed to put Stan Laurel in his place. From that perspective, *Zenobia* was a howling success.

Just what was Laurel doing during the *Zenobia* fiasco? The answer is, "Not much." In September, he briefly hooked up with Mack Sennett, of all people. The King of Comedy Emeritus announced a new company, Senate Pictures Corporation. Laurel was to star in its first production, "Problem Child," in which he would play the son of two married midgets. Sennett's associate producer would be former employee Jed Buell, who'd just produced an all-midget western, *The Terror of Tiny Town*, considered a classic by aficionados of very bad movies. Alas, Sennett was unable to secure a distribution deal and the venture faded away.

On December 6, the day after a drunken-driving arrest, Laurel filed his breach of contract suit to the tune of $700,000. A few weeks after that, wife Illiana filed a separation action, accusing her husband of cruelty, drinking too much and allowing his two ex-wives to harass her. She called it off in January, after serving seven hours in jail for the rental car incident while Stan patiently waited outside.

Laurel had nothing but his dysfunctional home life to keep him occupied until April, when Roach realized that Hardy and Langdon had no future together, at least as far as United Artists was concerned, and opted to mend fences with his troublesome star. Their respective suits were called off and, on April 8, Laurel signed a new one-year deal for up to four "short features" as Hardy's co-star, each film to be four reels. The next day, Illiana filed yet another separation suit, complete with a $1,000 weekly alimony request; this time Laurel countered by filing for divorce, ending once and for all the stormy union with his personal "grasping woman."

At around the same time, Laurel worked out a deal with an independent producer, Boris Morros, for an outside Laurel & Hardy picture that would be released through R.K.O. In the interests of keeping Laurel happy, as well as in making some easy cash, Roach agreed to

J. Farrell MacDonald and Olin Howard try to quell a sales pitch in Zenobia.

Gag men Charley Rogers and Langdon join Laurel & Hardy and director Alf Goulding in a little off-track betting on the set of A Chump at Oxford *(1940).*

loan not only Hardy, but cameraman Art Lloyd and Laurel's corps of gag-writers, including Langdon, to Morros once the first four-reeler was completed.

Thus the team of Langdon & Hardy (or Hardy & Langdon) was consigned to history. The Kalmar and Ruby screenplay, whatever it was, vanished into thin air, as the two veteran songwriters and scribes went down the street to M.G.M. to pen a script for the Marx Brothers that also wouldn't be used. Another potential Hardy-Langdon opus, *Road Show*, would be re-written for Adolph Menjou and Charles Butterworth and filmed the following year.

The "considerable pay hoist" contract was canceled, and Langdon returned to gag man status; Laurel, who truly bore him no ill will, wanted him kept on the writing team. He, Rogers and Adler concocted *A Chump at Oxford*, in which street sweepers Stan and Ollie, by inadvertently thwarting a bank robbery, are awarded an education at Oxford University. Fellow students (a young Peter Cushing among them) haze the hapless pair and just when all seems lost, Stanley is struck a blow on the head that changes him into Lord Paddington, Oxford's long-lost champion athlete and scholar. The haughty Paddington makes long-suffering Ollie (whom he persists in addressing as "Fatty") into his manservant, until the worm inevitably turns.

This was the crux of a 42-minute feature, a length that was deemed acceptable for U.S. audiences, but United Artists had requested a six-reel version for the European market, and there just wasn't enough material left over to fashion an additional 20 minutes. By the time Roach realized a whole new sequence was needed, Stan and Babe were shooting the Morros picture, "Deuces Wild," in Hollywood.

Originally planned as an adaptation of a French comedy entitled *Les aviateurs*, Laurel, with the help of Langdon and Rogers, had spent July turning it into an extended reworking of a four-reeler made in 1931, *Beau Hunks* (which M.G.M. had reissued only two years' previously). Stan and Ollie are in France, and Ollie is pining over Georgette (Jean Parker), a woman who cannot have him, as she's married to a certain François (Reginald Gardiner). He decides to end it all by drowning. He also decides that Stan should accompany him. The two are talked out of suicide by none other than François, who encourages them to join the Foreign Legion, which they do. The complications that ensue, especially when they fail to escape from camp, and when Georgette arrives and is once more accosted by Ollie, lead to a rousing finale in which they avoid execution by piloting an airplane with their usual flair. Filming concluded in August.

R.K.O. released "Deuces Wild" under the title *The Flying Deuces* in October. Since *A Chump at Oxford* wasn't ready, Morros was able to publicize his picture as the return of Laurel & Hardy after a fourteen-month absence. Although posterity deems it far from Stan and Babe's best work, both the public and most exhibitors received *The Flying Deuces* joyously.

When they returned to Roach in September, the team filmed an unrelated prologue that was actually a remake of one of their silent shorts, *From Soup to Nuts*. In this, the two are hired as butler and maid for a newly wealthy couple, but turn their dinner party into a slapstick melee. Fired from that, they become white wings, which leads into the original four-reeler. The new sequence was so well done that Roach and UA, after resolving financial and contractual logistics, opted to sell the 63-minute European edit domestically. (U.S. audiences wouldn't see the original 42-minute version until a 1943 reissue.) This decision, which delayed the film's release until January 1940, enabled UA to sidestep competing with *The Flying Deuces* for box-office dollars.

With *A Chump at Oxford* finally in the can, Laurel, Langdon, Rogers and company went to work on the next Roach film, *Saps at Sea*, toiling on the script before shooting commenced in mid-October. This time there was story enough for six reels, and Roach bypassed the whole idea of issuing a shorter version in the U.S. In this one, Stan and Ollie are working in a horn factory when the latter has a severe nervous breakdown caused by the constant honking. The doctor (James Finlayson) prescribes a sea voyage, but the boys are not too thrilled with the idea of being tossed about the ocean. They lease a yacht intending to keep it tied to the dock, but a hardened criminal (Rychard Cramer), to escape from the police, sneaks aboard and sets sail. This puts our two heroes in the uncomfortable position of having been shanghaied aboard their own boat, and their attempts to solve this dilemma reflect their usual track record of success. At one point they concoct a meal designed to make Cramer horribly ill. Unfortunately, he's wise to the plan and, at gunpoint, forces *them* to eat it. The results call to mind the many scenes of Harry eating such things as rubber band soup and chewing tobacco sandwiches.

While the film was in pre-production, Langdon received an offer from Lou Brock, R.K.O. Radio's short subjects producer, to star in a two-reel comedy with an eye toward a possible series. As Langdon's recent deals with Columbia were single-picture contracts, he was free to accept, signing at the start of October. Brock permitted Langdon to write the screenplay from a treatment conceived by former Keystone Cop George Jeske and Arthur V. Jones. Filming started on October 25.

NEA's syndicated columnist Paul Harrison ventured over to R.K.O., where he found "somewhere in the middle of the excitement (on Stage 5) a bewildered-looking little man named Harry Langdon.... For the first time in 11 years he was back in the character that made him famous." Choosing not to recall the two-reelers made for Roach and Gillstrom, Langdon told Harrison, "After talkies came in, I never got a chance to do my character. Slapstick was out, but it's back in now. I worried some about making the character speak, but my normal voice seems to fit pretty well, and anyway I stick mostly to pantomime... Back in the days when I was in the big dough, we'd take maybe a month to do stuff like this, and now they've cut it down to three days. I was glad to see that the stories still come easy. The character practically flows along by himself; all we have to do is think up some new motivation to get him started. I hope it goes all right. Anyway, it's fun."

The comedy, titled *Goodness! A Ghost*, indeed brought back the simple-minded innocent of Langdon's earlier work, as opposed to the aggravating moron he'd been portraying at Columbia. Here he's Harry O'Toole, an aspiring actor working as a sound effects man for an amateur stage production, a situation nearly identical to that of *The Stage Hand*. He's also the owner of the vintage policeman's uniform used in the play, and when the actor playing the cop abruptly quits, Harry's cast in the role. The uniform once belonged to his grandfather, a genuine policeman, whose ghost (also played by Langdon) has taken issue with its use. Thus, Harry is led into confronting an actual criminal gang, and his attempts to get out of danger peacefully conflict with the ghost's aim to make him a hero. It's slapstick fun, minus the tastelessness and contrivances that had been marring his

Rogers and Langdon confer with Laurel & Hardy for the final scene of The Flying Deuces *(1939).*

Columbia comedies. Although clearly getting older, Langdon's makeup still manages to evoke the Elf, and he's more energetic than in *Sue My Lawyer*, made over a year earlier.

Brock put the film into the "Radio Flash" series of one-shots, but R.K.O.'s sales force didn't put much effort into placing it. Issued in July 1940, *Goodness! A Ghost* went completely unnoticed by the trade press and no exhibitor that ran it saw fit to send in a comment. In the end, the studio opted not to expand on its current comedy roster of Edgar Kennedy and Leon Errol. When the short came out, Langdon was back at Roach, handling rewrite duties on *Road Show*, which at one time was planned as his and Babe Hardy's picture.

Meanwhile, upon completion of *Saps at Sea*, Laurel's one-year deal with Roach expired, and Hardy's contract had reached its natural end. The two were finally in a position to sell themselves as a team, and promptly formed Laurel & Hardy Feature Productions, Inc., with former Roach Studio attorney Benjamin Shipman as treasurer. Stan, unwilling to forget the many power struggles with Roach over the years, honestly believed he and Babe would do better creatively on their own. Subsequent events would prove him wrong. Although probably neither realized it at the time, Laurel — no longer free to handpick his writing staff — would never work with Langdon again. Fortunately for Langdon, it wouldn't be detrimental in the long run.

There had been one silver lining to the dark cloud of *Zenobia*: it put Hollywood on notice that Harry Langdon was still around. The old reputation of pretentious prima donna had been forgotten, as most things are in Hollywood, by virtue of recent events. He was now perceived as a capable and conscientious comedian, and as the film industry moved into a new era of prosperity, prolonged spells of unemployment became a thing of the past. In some cases, as with *Goodness! A Ghost*, he'd be permitted to resurrect a near-approximation of the Little Elf. If the material wasn't as strong as it had once been, he could still be counted upon to put his all into whatever he'd been given.

Throughout, Harry remained friends with Stan and Babe, their families socializing on many occasions. In his twilight years, Laurel was asked his opinion of Langdon, and his response spoke not of his gagman and friend, but of his long-ago inspiration: "A great comedian, who had it in him to be a great actor, like Chaplin."

CHAPTER SIXTEEN

"The 'O-Ouch-O' Comedies"

1940-1944

For the most part, these were Harry Langdon's tranquil years. Work was reasonably steady, and he was grateful to have it. More importantly, his home life was idyllic. A loving wife and a strapping son: no man could ask for more.

"No one realizes how much Harry wanted to have a child," Mabel Langdon told *Cult Movies*' Michael Copner. "He deeply loved our son. He'd do 'soft shoe' routines and pantomime little bits to entertain the boy, and was a real gentle father." Home movies, which show a delighted father and son chasing each other about and rolling around on the lawn, attest to this devotion.

In 1997, Harry, Jr. told Edward Watz, "I remember how much fun my dad was. He was always clowning around, as fathers will with their kids. The best picture I have of him was doing a soft shoe in the living room while clowning around with a banjo, and playing the piano. He and my mother would have these barbecues on Sunday afternoons, with Stan Laurel, Oliver Hardy, Red Skelton, Jules White… there would be all these other friends of my dad from the whole motion picture world, and they'd have a tremendous amount of fun."

He also thought nothing about bringing Harry, Jr. to work with him, which led to a cute item in *Daily Variety* one morning, when Langdon was working on the *Road Show* script:

> Harry Langdon had his career straightened out for him by his five-year-old son while breakfasting together at Roach studios. Youngster queried, "Are you writing or acting here now, daddy?" "Writing," Langdon replied. Junior munched his toast thoughtfully for a moment, then paused for a succinct, "Good!"

In addition to writing for Roach, 1940 included another Columbia short, an industrial film and the lead in a feature. The Columbia film, *Cold Turkey*, was Langdon's debut in Hugh McCollum's unit. McCollum was a former First National man who had accompanied Langdon to New York in 1926 for the preview of *Tramp, Tramp, Tramp*. When Warner Bros. acquired First National in 1928, he went to Columbia, first as Harry Cohn's secretary, then as business manager for the shorts department, handling cartoons and the *Screen Snapshots* series. In 1937, McCollum was given his own production unit for two-reel comedies.

Discussing McCollum in his book *The Great Movie Shorts*, Leonard Maltin wrote, "His style was distinctly different from [Jules] White's — gentler, and more tasteful." To be sure, *Cold Turkey* has a fair share of gratuitous slapstick within its tale of Harry winning a live turkey in an office holiday raffle, but it also takes time for a minute or two of Langdonesque pantomime. Especially memorable is the moment when Harry needs to convince his boss that the cup of champagne on his desk is water. Dreading the idea,

Writing gags at the Roach studios. The open script on Langdon's desk is for Topper Takes a Trip *(1938).*

he forces himself to gulp it down, and his face gradually transforms from apprehension to drunkenness, with a few stops in between.

The industrial short (produced right around the same time as *Cold Turkey*) was *Sitting Pretty*, produced by the Jam Handy Organization, a Detroit-based firm that primarily made industrial films screened at sales conventions and such. One of Handy's biggest clients was the automobile manufacturer Chevrolet; in *Sitting Pretty*, the spirit of an unconscious Harry seeks a place to rest and finds it in the comfortable new Chevy model. The premise sounds intriguing, and as the film was likely silent with music and narration, it may have given Langdon a better chance to shine than in his recent theatrical work. Unfortunately, *Sitting Pretty* seems to be lost, as no prints reside in the Jam Handy archives or any other repository. To confuse matters, Handy produced at least two other films with the same title, also for Chevrolet.

The feature was *Misbehaving Husbands*, produced by Jed Buell for the relatively new concern, Producer's

Releasing Corporation (P.R.C.), a B-movie factory. If the film's pressbook is to be believed, Langdon's involvement came about this way:

> Jed Buell... is the man to be thanked for Harry's return. Buell spent six weeks pleading with Harry to read the script and, although he knew that producers in Hollywood and London had tried without success to persuade the comedian to emerge from his semi-retirement, he stuck to his guns until finally, more in hopes of getting rid of Buell than for any other reason, Langdon agreed to scan the screenplay.
>
> "From then on it was a cinch," grinned Buell when he told film reporters about it, later. "Harry hadn't read three or four pages when he began pacing the floor, suggesting bits of action and at one point was acting five characters at once."

Any reluctance on Langdon's part was more likely fueled by his prior failed association with Buell in 1934, along with Stan Laurel's in 1938.

P.R.C. was ensconced at the old Principal Pictures studio on Santa Monica Boulevard, the former home as well of Educational, which had gone under in 1937. Once again, Langdon returned to the lot where it all began, and was guided by William Beaudine, who'd been helming comedians since the mid-teens. *Misbehaving Husbands* was the first of four Langdon would do with the veteran director.

Langdon's character, Henry Butler, is an absent-minded husband, although not to an absurd degree; basically he's singularly focused on his department store to the exclusion of everything else, including his own 20th wedding anniversary. Effie, his wife (Betty Blythe), is understanding of Henry's lack of focus, and it's only through a combination of unfortunate circumstances that she comes to believe he's having an affair, and — led by an unscrupulous lawyer (Gayne Whitman) — decides to file for divorce. The pathos is gentle and thoroughly rooted in character. Langdon is both funny and believable and a few critics commented that the role might open up a new career.

Henry Butler (Langdon) gets tough with "Gooch" Mullgan (Frank Hagney) in Misbehaving Husbands *(1940).*

With the money made from these ventures, Langdon decided in early 1941 to pack up his family and spend some time in New York City. Harry, Jr. told Watz, "My mother and father [would] drive across country to New York, and I'd sit in the back seat. So we'd see the country, and it was a lot of fun. I remember it being winter in New York. To keep me occupied, they'd send me out with the chauffeurs; they'd take me to Central Park and keep me occupied with sleds in the snow."

In mid-February, Hollywood columnist Harrison Carroll reported, "Harry Langdon postcards from New York that he has a yen to go back on the stage and is looking for a play." An opportunity cropped up with *Hellzapoppin'*, the madcap Broadway vehicle for the team of John "Ole" Olsen and Harold "Chic" Johnson that opened in 1938 and was still going strong. Universal Pictures had signed Olsen & Johnson for the movie version; prior to leaving for Hollywood, the two were auditioning their replacements.

In between auditions and negotiations, Langdon was able to secure at least one stage appearance: three shows per day at Paterson, New Jersey's Majestic Theater from March 28–31. On April 5, the *New York Times* reported: "Two comedians are competing for the role Harold Ogden (Chic) Johnson will vacate when he and his partner, John Siguard (Ole) Olsen, retire from *Hellzapoppin'* about April 26. Each of the contestants — Harry Langdon and Happy Felton — will give their interpretation of the part at separate performances next week. The victor will be selected by Lee Shubert and the Messers O. & J. The Olsen role already has been assigned to Jay C. Flippen." Felton won the role, so Langdon returned to Hollywood, arriving no later than the first week of May.

Shortly after returning, Langdon was in an auto accident, injuring his back and shoulder when struck by a truck. Luckily, Mabel and Harry, Jr. escaped harm, but Harry Sr. was laid up for a few weeks. After that, Hal Roach studios called with an offer to work as a gag man on a script for producer-director LeRoy Prinz. Jimmy Fidler later elaborated in his column:

Hellzapoppin's Chic Johnson, left, and Ole Olsen, right, meet with Langdon in New York City, April 1941.

SHORT TRUE STORY: Harry Langdon, once an ace comedy star but now fighting for a comeback as both writer and actor, was offered a job concocting gags for an independent picture, at $100 a day. Estimating the job would last no more than three days, Harry was about to turn it down but was swayed by the frantic protests of his brother, an amateur astrologer. After studying the heavens, the brother assured Langdon that it was the wrong time of the moon to turn down anything. Reluctantly, Langdon took the job. Once started, he noticed an excellent possibility of writing in a role for himself. He did, sold the producer the idea — and collected an additional $1,000 a week while doing it!

The film was *All-American Co-Ed*, one of Hal Roach's "Streamliners," a series of short features (usually running about 45 minutes) deliberately intended for the lower half of a double bill. Although the dollar figure quoted by Fidler was for publicity purposes only, Langdon does get a couple of brief comic vignettes in this swing time collegiate take on *Charley's Aunt*. As "Hap" Holden, Langdon plays a press agent trying to publicize a struggling all-girls' horticultural university. If nothing else, the role showcases his versatility; not every character has to be meek or bewildering to be funny.

In September, Monogram — another B-picture factory — signed Langdon for a series of films that would costar his former director and writing partner at Roach, Charley Rogers. The first would be titled *Double Trouble*, which introduces the pair as Albert and Alfred Prattle, refugees from war-torn England, who are adopted by a wealthy American couple under the mistaken impression that they are children. When we first see the two men, Harry (as Albert) is wearing his traditional costume, complete with the "popover" fedora, as he greets his benefactors with the old hand wave. The Elf has returned.

"It's like coming home to be in [these clothes] again," he told columnist Reed Johnston during shooting. The film was directed by William West, who, as Billy West, was the silent screen's pre-eminent

Harry is seated between Marjorie Woodward and Marie Windsor in All-American Co-Ed *(1941).*

Chaplin impersonator and thus no stranger to visual comedy. Throughout *Double Trouble*, Langdon and Rogers display a natural rapport. Although some of the gags are old-hat, the two are clearly having fun, particularly in a lengthy scene where both are dressed as women to avoid the police.

West and producer Dixon Harwin kept things so informal that seven-year-old Harry, Jr., was able to watch the filming, and even suggested a gag for the closing scene:

> They were trying to think of an ending. My dad and Charley Rogers were hitchhiking somewhere, right at the end of the film, and a car comes by and picks them up. They were trying to think of a little hook for the ending. They both had umbrellas like canes, and I said, "Why don't you have the umbrellas stay behind and continue hitchhiking, waving back and forth like a hitchhiker would do?" So that was the ending of the film.

During the making of *Double Trouble*, producer Sam Coslow tapped Langdon for a brief musical short. *Beautiful Clothes (Make Beautiful Girls)* was produced for Soundies Distributing Corporation, intended for use in a video jukebox known as the Panoram, usually found in upscale cafés or similar establishments. In it, Langdon lip-synchs to Cliff Nazzaro's recording of the title song while preparing a department store fashion show.

On November 6, Langdon found himself once again before Commissioner Doyle to face contempt charges due to being $1,079 in arrears on the $25 weekly alimony he owed Helen. Langdon testified his earnings for 1941 would not exceed $2,007. Doyle, possibly weary of seeing the clearly aging comedian in his courtroom, dismissed the charges, stating, "He is just a man who is having a hard time." As for Helen, from this point forward she would vanish from the purview of columnists and gossipmongers. She never remarried and died in Los Angeles on June 17, 1963, at the age of 72.

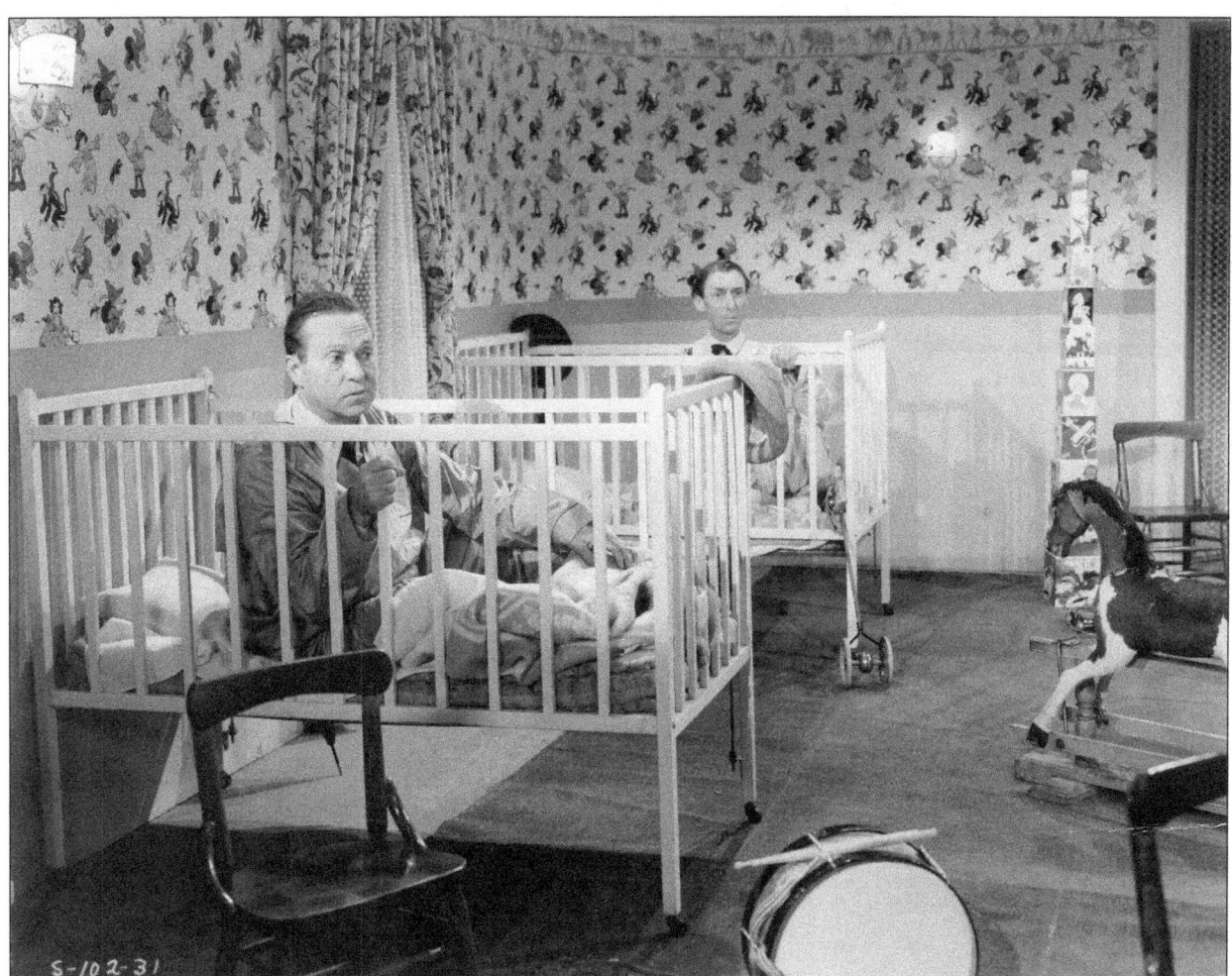

Langdon and Rogers are tired of being "babied" in Double Trouble *(1941).*

Langdon appears in a Mother Hubbard...

Coyly primps and flirts until...

LANGDON BRITCHES FALLING DOWN—

Back in the days when movies were the strong, silent type, and Mack Sennett was the two-reel king, Harry Langdon began his cinema career. Now after many years, Monogram Pictures has lured him out of retirement, and starred the little man in their new farce, *Double Trouble*.

Halp! This guy ain't kiddin'!

For reasons unknown, the second Langdon-Rogers film was produced at P.R.C. at the end of 1941 and into the following year. *House of Errors* was based on an original story by Langdon, and scripted by Ewart Adamson, who'd turned another Langdon scenario into *Sue My Lawyer* at Columbia, and Eddie M. Davis, a P.R.C. scribe. The tale concerned Bert and Alf attempting to get a newspaper story about a new machine gun by playing houseboy and butler, respectively, for the gun's inventor (Richard Kipling). They are beset on one hand by a fellow reporter (Ray Walker), who's in love with the inventor's daughter (Marian Marsh), and on the other hand by a pair of swindlers (John Holland and Guy Kingsford) trying to steal the gun. Given the nation's recent entry into World War II, the subject was topical if nothing else. Langdon has a couple of funny vignettes both with and without Rogers, but the film is smothered by a good deal of lesser talent in the supporting roles, coupled with the uninspired direction of Bernard B. Ray, who was more at home piloting the studio's many horse operas.

Evidently, *House of Errors* was not a success; it barely received any mention in the trades. There being no further interest in vehicles with Charley Rogers, Langdon went back to Columbia in February 1942, where he would spend the next 12 months turning out six — for want of a better word — "comedies." At first, he found himself teamed with Elsie Ames, a raucous comedienne who'd previously partnered with Buster Keaton in five two-reelers for the studio. The experience pretty much convinced Keaton to not renew *his* contract, and Langdon filled the breach. The two shorts they made together run the gamut from merely unfunny (*Carry Harry*) to positively dreadful (*What Makes Lizzy Dizzy?*). Of the other four, there are some isolated moments of interest, but only one — *Piano Mooner*, with a story by Langdon and direction by Harry Edwards — came close to providing him a vehicle worthy of his gifts.

By 1942, the Three Stooges comedies were the most successful of Columbia's roster, and the studio's other two-reel series were emulating them. From this point on, Langdon's Columbia output became, more often than not, slapstick affairs complete with Stoogeian sound patterns to accompany blows to the head, biting, fist fighting, sitting on springs or stepping on pincushions. Langdon did fare somewhat

Ray Walker unknowingly keeps Langdon and Rogers at bay in House of Errors *(1942).*

better in Hugh McCollum's unit because his most frequent director was Edwards, who tried to give him some space for pantomime.

Edwards, though, was on the downside of his career, as alcoholism played havoc with his skills. "Harry Edwards was a drinker," recalled director Edward Bernds in 1980. "He was past his prime; probably a very fine director in his day, but he made mistakes… and [McCollum] was dissatisfied with him. He ran over budget, and that was one thing the front office would whip the producers for doing.

"I wish that I would've had the chance to direct Harry Langdon. I don't know if I would've had the 'sensitivity' that early in my career, but I'd seen his films. I like to think that I would've been able to use what he had. Harry Edwards was quite jealous, and I think he deliberately kept Langdon from me. Edwards was insecure, and with good reason, because eventually I did replace him."

Admittedly, it is easy to disparage the Columbia two-reelers nowadays, especially when compared to the best of Langdon's other work, but audiences were not so picky during the war years. Columnist Jimmy Fidler probably spoke for many ticket buyers when he penned the following in February 1943:

> Columbia, presumably convinced that the dual bill system is on the way out, is going in for two-reel comedies — not the sophisticated, snicker-inducing type that most studios have offered in recent years, but the full-bodied, slap-happy variety that used to give America a surplus of belly-laughs in Hollywood's lustier days. And, in order to put a blue-seal on their laugh-potions, they've rounded up an all-star aggregation of veteran comics.
>
> Heading the eight comedy units now working here are the Three Stooges, Hugh Herbert, Harry Langdon, Slim Summerville, Billy Gilbert, Andy Clyde, Una Merkel and El Brendel — most of them names to conjure with in the comedy world long before the screen found a voice.
>
> I'm looking forward to their output with a whetted appetite. I'm tired of a pink tea diet of polite titters; I'm bored with the smart-alecky

Elsie Ames, Monty Collins, Dorothy Appleby and Langdon in the abysmal What Makes Lizzy Dizzy? *(1942)*.

Above: Harry's had his palm read, while Dave O'Brien is unimpressed, in Carry Harry *(1942).*

Below: Harry and his fellow Americans overpower Vernon Dent's nest of Fifth Columnists in A Blitz on the Fritz *(1943).*

puns and cynical wisecracks of parlor-type humorists — I want to let my hair down and roll in the aisles while watching the slapstick antics of real, honest-to-gosh clowns.

Movie comedy, for the past ten years, has been subservient to radio comedy. It's been conversational, rather than visual. Laughs have been created mechanically by radio-trained gag men. The "lines" have been considered first, and the manner of delivering them second.

Think back — those of you who are old enough to remember — to the uproarious comedies of the '20s when Arbuckle, Keaton, Langdon and the Sennett Gang were in their heyday. I believe you'll agree that Columbia is on the right track.

For the most part, exhibitor comments bear out Fidler's observation. "Our patrons love these comedies and actually ask for more in preference to some of the so-called features which we are forced to show to them," wrote one theater manager about *A Blitz on the Fritz*. Of *Carry Harry*, another exhibitor asserted, "This comedy sure got the laughs out of my patrons."

As for Langdon, he had no illusions about the lack of artistic merit in the shorts. By the time the last of the season, *Here Comes Mr. Zerk*, had wrapped, he was gleefully engaged in a new challenge. Producer George Banyai brought Francis Swann's Broadway comedy *Out of the Frying Pan* to Hollywood's Music Box Theater, and cast Langdon in what had originally been a woman's part. The play, loosely based on the real-life experiences of Swann's sister Lyn, focused on three actors and three actresses rooming together in a boardinghouse and attempting to land work by staging "performances" there. The show opened on Broadway in March 1941; among its original cast was an 18-year-old newcomer, Barbara Bel Geddes, later of *Dallas* fame. The Hollywood version starred former child actress Edith Fellows.

The original play had featured a persistent, if slightly daffy, landlady; Langdon convinced Banyai to let him rewrite the part as a male. It opened on February 4 to mostly positive reviews:

> That hilarious comedy *Out of the Frying Pan* opened at the Hollywood Music Box and promises to keep mirth and merriment at a high pitch in its neighborhood for the coming fortnight. George Banyai has made an excellent production of this Francis Swann opus and has provided a cast which fits the roles to a T. Starring Harry Langdon, as a dumb apartment house landlord, and pretty Edith Fellows, as the flighty Muriel, the entire company of young actors does full credit to the amusing lines and situations.
>
> Producer Banyai won unanimous approval from his audience for his current offering and is now planning to maintain a company, in the order of a permanent group with guest stars, and change the bill every two weeks. The Hollywood Music Box was well filled last night to greet the laughable offering, and capacity houses are indicated for the week-end performances.
>
> F. B. L., *Los Angeles Examiner*

HARRY LANGDON
He fits his whimsical routines into farcical doings in "Out of the Frying Pan" at the Music Box.

Another wacky apartment farce of the *My Sister Eileen* type came to the Hollywood Music Box last night. After a groping first act it came to life and laid out on the line fast and amusingly, the matters referred to in its title, which is *Out of the Frying Pan*.... Langdon is very amusing as the landlord, working in the whimsical buffoonery for which he is known. It is wild stuff, depending on timing and pace. When the show gets them, there is a chance that it may be very good fun.

Los Angeles Evening Herald & Express

Out of the Frying Pan is a comedy of the screwball genus. Its greatest fault lies in the fact that it doesn't get screwball soon enough. Producer George Banyai could well have thrown away Act 1 and a goodly portion of Act 2. Act 3, now, is a fine piece of stage business. The production, first of a series which Mr. Banyai says he will produce at the Music Box, is made notable — yes, and nostalgic — by the presence of Harry Langdon, Edith Fellows, and George Beban, son of the late dialect master, in the cast.... Langdon, wandering lost through the maze of incomprehensible goings on, provides moments of great mirth.

Hollywood Citizen-News

Only the *Los Angeles Times*'s Philip K. Scheuer perceived more minuses than pluses: "It is a little early in the game to be making predictions — but Mr. Banyai will have to do better than this, even in a free-spending, easygoing show time, if he hopes to stick around for long. The producer is played by a pompous-sounding gent named Robert H. Harris, who also directed. He appeared to be more of a professional than others in the cast. Among these are Harry Langdon, the pantomimist, who seemed more like a would-be actor trying to imitate Harry Langdon than himself, and two erstwhile children of the cinema: Edith Fellows and Ann Gillis."

Unlike the *Anything Goes* cast, *Out of the Frying Pan*'s troupe would not have the luxury of time to work out the kinks. There was no tour to follow; the show was scheduled to close on February 21. Nevertheless, Langdon enjoyed himself thoroughly. In a burst of sentimental nostalgia, he installed eight-year-old Harry, Jr. as an usher during the matinees. The boy's salary: one 25-cent war stamp per day. Between shows, Langdon would head over to the Hollywood Canteen to entertain visiting troops, per

Harry and his brassy girlfriend, Iris Adrian, in Spotlight Scandals *(1943).*

Louella Parsons: "Between the matinee and evening performance he goes through all his dance routines for the boys." Harry, Jr. recalled for Michael Copner that Langdon also did caricatures of the men: "I'd see twenty or thirty soldiers lined up to get their picture drawn by my dad."

According to the *Los Angeles Times* of February 18, "Since [Langdon] opened at the Music Box in *Out of the Frying Pan* he has had many stage and screen offers, even from New York, but he won't leave his family here, saying he's a 'sissy' about them." He also spoke freely about his screen character, touching on his real feelings about the Columbia two-reelers in the process:

> A comedian should establish a character with human appeal. For instance, in developing my character I use little childish gestures — and children are always appealing. Such a comedian isn't a machine. I know the limits of my character — a little too aggressive, for instance, and he's gone. I've tried to inject this character into parts offered me, but if the director interfered the character would be lost.
>
> Without character the comedian is lost. When I play in what I call the O-Ouch-O comedies, where the comedian runs about, is hit on the head, etc., I am just an animated suit of clothes.

Langdon also demonstrated that he had learned a few things over the years, or at least since Arthur Ripley had moved on: "Women have a keener sense of humor than men, are more observing and responsive. Women care more for comedy than men do, too. You have to get dirty to get men to laugh."

"Going Hollywood" columnist May Mann caught one of the final performances, and noted, "Amazing the audience reaction when movie favorites appear in the flesh on the stage. 'Why he's just like he is on screen,' we heard all about us when Harry pulled his inimitable tricks in pantomime."

A few days after *Out of the Frying Pan* closed, Langdon signed another two-pictures-with-options contract with Columbia. After nine years, the company proffered a raise, to $1,250 per picture. However, they had nothing ready for him at the moment. Monogram signed him for a supporting role in a quickie musical comedy, *Spotlight Scandals*, directed by William Beaudine and intended as the first in a series that would pair Frank Fay (he of the lead in *Jim Jam Jems*) and former Hal Roach supporting player Billy Gilbert. Evidently the film didn't do any better financially than the Langdon-Rogers features, as the team's debut was also its finale.

As the war escalated during 1943, live entertainment became more and more valuable, and the offers Langdon received from the East became more lucrative. He reunited with Edith Fellows and proposed a tour of the eastern theaters that were playing live shows ahead of the feature film. The Loew's chain snapped it up. Langdon's idea: an updated *Johnny's New Car*, with Fellows taking the singing spot that had once been Rose Langdon's. Harry, Jr. recalled his father "building a wooden automobile" in the garage; after which "he would rent out or borrow the 10th floor of the Bekins Storage building downtown in Los Angeles, and he and his participants in the play would rehearse in the quiet of the storage vault."

Unfortunately, a script was not accessible, but according to press reports and reviews, the new version consisted of a formally gowned Edith trying to persuade Harry to give her a ride in his red car (also described as a "Jeep"), despite his fear of doing so. "You can look at my tattoo instead," he tells her, although at one point he also confesses, "I go to day school so I can chase around nights and get a practical education." Edith turns on her charm by singing "Kiss Me Again," from the Victor Herbert operetta *Mlle. Modiste*. Naturally, Harry's auto fails spectacularly before she gets the ride; according to *Variety*, it "disgorges various and sundry articles, including a fried egg."

Apparently it wasn't spectacular enough. *Variety*'s "Arke" caught the opening performance on August 12 at Loew's Capitol Theater in Washington, D.C., and had this to say: "Harry Langdon, wide-eyed comic of the silents, has a 20-minute act which seems to have been hastily thrown together. Makes his entrance in a prop jeep, around which much of the laughs are evolved....Act needs solid laughs. Business which might have been rib-tickling in pantomime fails to register in this mammoth house, where Langdon's expressions are lost."

A critic for *The Billboard* was also present: "Harry Langdon, vet film comic, moved into the Capitol this week, accompanied by Edith Fellows, and although opening audience gave him a big hand the management is going to be fully appreciative of the supporting bill before the week is out....Audience sat on its hands thru most of the act, although there was a mild hand when Miss Fellows warbled 'Kiss Me Again.' Comic works in familiar deadpan style, but lacks good material and situations. There wasn't a first-rate gag in the act."

One week later, Langdon and Fellows opened at Loew's State in Manhattan, where they were third on the bill and their act trimmed by about

four minutes. "Rose" of *Variety* was especially harsh: "Harry Langdon and Edith Fellows, latter the film starlet, are singularly ineffective in a skit that's too reminiscent of small-time vaude to get by today, particularly in this ace Broadway house.... When caught, the laughs came few and far between, with almost embarrassing lulls spacing. Miss Fellows is a cute number with lusty pipes that register well in the upper cadenzas… but as a foil for Langdon there's little opportunity of determining her comedic talents.…He's likewise handicapped by [an] inability to use his facial expressions and pantomime to full advantage on the stage. It's his chief stock in trade and fails to get across as it did via the screen close-ups."

The Billboard was there as well: "Vet screen comic, Harry Langdon, with gag act using prop car and diminutive Edith Fellows. Comedy relies on both getting a pushing around. Langdon bears down on old movie technique of worried, ineffectual gestures, but laughs stem from knockabout nonsense…The little Fellows is easy to look at and vocals one number, 'Kiss Me Again,' to good reception. Hits high notes right on the nose and with amazing power for pint-sized chanteuse."

So it seemed things had come full circle. When Langdon began in vaudeville nearly 38 years earlier, it was the singing that was the hit of the act. Now, if

Una Merkel gets drilled in this gag photo from To Heir Is Human *(1944).*

the reviews were any indication, Edith Fellows was carrying *him*. What had once been "the strongest little comedy offering in vaudeville" was considered too "small-time" for modern audiences.

Two days after the New York opening, Langdon received a telegram from Hugh McCollum: "Advise when you expect return to Hollywood." Langdon wired a reply on the 22nd: "At present can postpone future eastern engagements if you can start picture within two weeks stop can leave here twenty sixth august otherwise difficult to arrange definite future date at this time." McCollum replied that, due to productions already underway, stage space wouldn't be available until September 21 at the earliest.

Langdon finished up at Loew's State on August 25, and sat tight for a couple of weeks, but the underwhelming reception in D.C. and New York City versus the salary he was getting cooled the Loew's chain on future engagements. He packed up his props and returned once more to Hollywood, where the McCollum picture *To Heir is Human* began production on October 6. In this one, Langdon co-starred with Una Merkel, who'd provided comedy support throughout the 1930s, but was now reduced to toiling in Columbia's slapstick factory. Merkel handles the indignities well, but the film is paced so briskly, one knockabout turn after another, it's impossible to judge if she and Langdon have any chemistry at all. For his part, Langdon looks and sounds old; in the nine months between *Here Comes Mr. Zerk* and this short, he appears to have aged at least five years.

It was Jules White's contention that all the years of struggling, all the money problems and alimony hassles "had taken a toll on him. His baby face [now] had wrinkles. The only time babies have wrinkles is when they're first born." Coupled with that, White realized "the short subject business was going to hell. Theaters were running double features everywhere, and if they ran a short at all, it would be a cartoon. It got so we couldn't make any money on them. We were lucky if we broke even." In a few years, the front office would tell White they only wanted the Three Stooges pictures: "We can still sell those."

At the moment, the studio was interested in developing a team that might compete with Universal's Abbott & Costello and 20th Century-Fox's Laurel & Hardy features for box-office dollars. White had the brainstorm of teaming Langdon with another ex-vaudevillian, El Brendel, whose specialty was a Swedish dialect. Brendel had been with Columbia for about five years and, like Langdon, his gentle innocent character had morphed into a brainless nincompoop. In January 1944, the pair went before the cameras in *Defective Detectives*, written and directed by Harry Edwards. "There is talk of features to follow, if the short turns out to be a success," wrote columnist Edwin Schallert. The resulting tale of two dimwitted maintenance men-turned-detectives who shadow the

Harry and El Brendel trip up Snub Pollard in Defective Detectives *(1944).*

wrong couple was only successful enough to warrant additional two-reelers.

Whenever work dried up at Columbia, Langdon found it at Monogram, a studio dedicated to filling the double-feature demand. At the end of 1943, he was cast in *Hot Rhythm*, a low-budget musical in which the numbers take place on two sets: a recording studio and a nightclub. Dona Drake portrays Mary Adams, a jingle singer who wants to break into big-time show biz. Love struck tunesmith Jimmy O'Brien (Robert Lowrey) tries to help Mary get into a band led by Tommy Taylor (Jerry Cooper), despite the latter's having no interest in adding a girl singer. Irene Ryan, known to later generations as the beloved Granny of *The Beverly Hillbillies*, furnishes most of the comedy as a ditzy secretary mistaken for the chanteuse by two competing executives (Tim Ryan and Robert Kent). Langdon does some fine work as her foil.

After the first short with El Brendel, he returned to Monogram for *Block Busters* with Leo Gorcey, Huntz Hall and the rest of the East Side Kids. His role here is brief and not especially memorable; the same goes for the film. At the time, these pictures were about 50 percent melodrama and 50 percent malapropisms from the Kids, particularly Gorcey. It wasn't until later that directors such as Del Lord and Ed Bernds arrived to steer the series, renamed The Bowery Boys, toward farce and slapstick in the Columbia tradition.

On the evening of February 21, 1944, Harry's youngest brother, Claude Langdon, suffered both a heart attack and stroke, and was taken to Mercy Hospital in Council Bluffs. He lingered for 18 days, dying on March 10 at age 50. His eldest son, Don, was in the Army Air Corps, but stationed at Lincoln, Nebraska, so he was able to join his mother and brother, 16-year-old Harry, for the funeral. Presumably Harry and Mabel, older brother John and sister Gertrude attended as well.

Possibly it was Claude's death that prompted Langdon to seek less strenuous work than the "O-Ouch-O comedies." He signed with R.K.O. as a gag man (now termed "comedy constructionist") for a romantic comedy titled "That Hunter Girl" (eventually released as *Bride by Mistake*), and scripted an audition for a radio series, *Mr. Fixit*, in which he would star. Caryl Coleman, producer for the Blue Network (soon to be renamed the American Broadcasting Company), co-wrote with Langdon and supervised the recording of a transcription during the week of April 17. *The Billboard*'s radio columnist claimed, "It is reported that quite a bit of agency interest has already been shown" in the program, but *Mr. Fixit* was not picked up and the pilot aired only on the West Coast, as part of a summer anthology sponsored by Bullock's Department Stores.

So it was back to Columbia for *Mopey Dope* and another short with El Brendel, *Snooper Service*. The work may have been unfulfilling, but the $1,250 per film was essential. Meanwhile, Republic Pictures bought the rights to the *Mr. Fixit* pilot from

Irene Ryan drives Harry to distraction in Hot Rhythm *(1944).*

Above: Christine McIntyre finds Harry's watch where his egg should be in Mopey Dope *(1944).*
Below: El and Harry find themselves in a tough spot in Snooper Service *(1945).*

Coleman, for reasons that will remain hidden until either the show or a script emerge from the shadows. Not hidden is the fact that Republic also hired Langdon for a role in one of its low-budget musicals, *Swingin' on a Rainbow*. The part — and for that matter, the plot — is similar to that of *Hot Rhythm*, with a female singer-composer (Jane Frazee) getting her big break with an unwitting male bandleader (Richard Davies) while romancing a songwriter (Brad Taylor), except that the activity is centered around a radio station, not a recording studio. Adding to the similarity is that William Beaudine directed both films. As Chester Willoby, an artists' representative for the radio program central to the plot, Langdon's job is to be suitably befuddled by the goings-on.

On November 27, he went to work on *Pistol Packin' Nitwits*, another short with El Brendel. This one was based on an original story he co-wrote with Edward Bernds, though the latter told Edward Watz, "Harry Edwards completely rewrote my script. I noticed that Edwards claimed full screenplay credit. I wrote a screenplay though it wasn't used." As it emerged, the film is a devastating parody of western clichés and gives Langdon a chance to display a little of his musical ability, as he strums a banjo near the opening. Later he does a bit of soft-shoe with Brendel, but he looks older than ever and his steps don't have as much energy as his partner's.

Shooting evidently took a full two weeks, mostly due to Edwards's rapidly deteriorating skills. A scene that was mainly improvised involved Harry and El serving an unpalatable dinner to Vernon Dent, cast as a sheriff. According to Watz, who co-authored *The Columbia Comedy Shorts* with Ted Okuda, "The sequence played disgustingly. Edwards had Dent spitting out the food and slobbering over himself in a protracted routine that was deleted after the film was previewed. Hugh McCollum was fed up with Edwards after this."

Mabel Langdon never forgot the fateful final day, telling Raymond Rohauer, "Harry came home from work the evening of December 8, 1944, while he was working on *Pistol Packin' Nitwits* at Columbia. He complained of doing a very strenuous soft-shoe tap routine for this film, and that he was not feeling well.

Harry listens to Jane Frazee's compositions in Swingin' on a Rainbow *(1945).*

He had pains in his head." She told Michael Copner, "I took him to our doctor and he ordered Harry to bed. We kept him at home while he was conscious. On the thirteenth, our son went in to his bedside and said, 'Daddy, my birthday's coming up.' And Harry couldn't speak, but he held up four fingers. It was four days before our son's birthday and he was aware of that. But after that, he lost consciousness."

On December 21, Mabel took him to St. Vincent's Hospital on the orders of Dr. Francis E. Browne. "Harry had made me promise that I'd never put him in the hospital if anything happened to him, but the doctor said, 'Mrs. Langdon, the man is unconscious. You've got to put him in the hospital.' And they made me put him there. Harry Edwards went to the hospital with me. And he died there on December 22."

As happened to his father 24 years earlier, Langdon succumbed to a cerebral hemorrhage; he'd also suffered a heart attack the day he went to the hospital. He was 60 years old. "The sad thing," said Mabel, "is that Harry was dead for six hours before the hospital called to let me know."

Almost as sad was how a wire service completely botched his obituary: "Langdon never became bitter when his money was gone and he was earning $22 a week — 'some weeks,' as he testified in one alimony suit," read the Associated Press account, which mistook what he had left over after paying debts for his total earnings. The notice, which appeared in countless newspapers, continued: "Four wives divorced him. His fifth divorced him, too, but they were remarried, after a few months, in 1938." This must have come as a shock to Mabel, who was, of course, his third and final wife, and who remarried him for sentimental, not legal, reasons. Capping off the AP's misinformation, the obit concludes, "This wife and their daughter, Virginia, survive, together with his son Harry, Jr., now nine, the child of his third wife, Helen."

How many errors can one notice hold?

Harry, El and a Wild West version of the Rockettes in Langdon's final film, Pistol Packin' Nitwits *(1945).*

Funeral services were held at Pierce Brothers Mortuary the day after Christmas, and were conducted by the Reverend Neal Dodd of St. Mary of the Angels Church, who also portrayed clergymen in several Hollywood films (including three directed by Frank Capra). Capra was then in the Army, but Harry Edwards and Arthur Ripley attended the funeral, as did other colleagues: Andy Clyde, Chester Conklin, Jerry Geisler, Priscilla Bonner, Charley Rogers, Stan Laurel, Jules White, Hugh McCollum and El Brendel. Vernon Dent made the funeral arrangements; Charlie Chaplin sent an arrangement of white carnations. Langdon was cremated and interred in Grand View Cemetery, where his mother and brother Charles were also laid to rest.

For ten-year-old Harry, Jr., life would never be the same. "I thought that all kids had famous motion picture people over to the house on Sunday afternoons, or got to go backstage in the theater, or had fathers who built life-sized automobiles out of wood in the garage," he told Edward Watz. "So when my dad died, it was a tremendous shock. All of a sudden it was, 'This is the real world.' I had to go to public school, and my mother had to go to work, and we moved out of the big house in the Hollywood Hills. It was tough, but it drove me to be an achiever. Who knows what would have happened if he'd lived? I might have been a recluse somewhere, just living off of my dad's fame. I had to make my own career."

That he did, becoming a commercial photographer in the 1950s, and building a reputation for his glamorous, stunning portraits of movie, television and recording stars. Among the celebrities of the last 40 years, Harry Langdon Jr. has taken many of their most iconic photographs, and these have appeared on magazine and album covers as well as in publicity releases. As of this writing, he continues in this work.

His mother found employment with the Motion Picture Television and Relief Fund soon after Harry's passing. Mabel became head of the Studio Deductions Department, handling the contributions that funded the Motion Picture and Television Country House and Hospital in Woodland Hills, where so many professionals who spanned her husband's Hollywood career, from Mack Sennett to Edith Fellows, spent their final days. Retiring in 1971, Mabel used her spare time to assist Harry, Jr. with the financial aspects of his photography business.

Four years before her passing on March 17, 2001, *Cult Movies*' Michael Copner asked Mabel if she'd ever remarried. "Friends have asked me about that," she replied. "I don't want to. I'm still in love with Harry."

JOIN IN TRIBUTE—Left to right, El Brendel, Andy Clyde, Rev. Neal Dodd, Jimmy Finlayson and Chester Conklin, pictured at funeral of Harry Langdon, veteran comedian of stage and screen who died at 60 years.

Harry Langdon

THE GALLERY OF MODERN ART
Including the HUNTINGTON HARTFORD Collection
Two Columbus Circle, New York, New York 10019
RAYMOND ROHAUER (Film Curator and Program Director)

Epilogue

At the time of his passing, Langdon still had films awaiting release. The final Columbia shorts, *Snooper Service* and *Pistol Packin' Nitwits*, along with Republic's *Swingin' on a Rainbow*, would reach theaters during 1945. Columbia also released a *Screen Snapshots* reel, "Doctors in Greasepaint," that featured early footage of 69 famous comedians, Langdon among them, early that year.

Interestingly, Warner Bros. was releasing two-reel shorts consisting of silent footage from their library, which dated back to the days when Larry Semon was churning out comedies for Vitagraph in the late teens. Some would be assembled by Robert Youngson, then directing documentary shorts for the studio. At one point, in 1947, an inquiry was made to Warners' legal department to ascertain if footage from Langdon's First National features could be utilized in the shorts. One R. C. McMahon replied in the negative: "I find, unfortunately, that [Langdon's] contracts include an express prohibition against the use of any portions… as a part of any other motion picture.…Consequently, since I understand that Langdon is dead, claims might be asserted both on behalf of Langdon's estate and also by the successors in interest of the Harry Langdon Corporation, whoever they might be." McMahon's research failed to determine that for a $5,000 fee his employers became the "successors in interest." Studio lawyers will always err on the side of caution.

Sadly, the specter of premature death had not finished with the Langdon family. On February 5, 1948, Harry's sister Gertrude Langdon Melroy died; she had just turned 51 about two weeks earlier. She was survived by her husband, five children, seven grandchildren and one brother. Only John Henry Langdon lived beyond his sixties, passing away at age 73 on March 7, 1953. Gertrude and John, like Harry, Charles and Lavina, are laid to rest at Grandview Cemetery in Glendale.

One of the tragedies of Harry Langdon's passing was that he missed the rise of television and its hunger for talent. Even so, he was no stranger to the home screen. In 1948, a distributor called Atlas Television acquired 350 of Educational's talking comedies, including the seven featuring Langdon. That same year, Hal Roach licensed a chunk of his film library to Regal TV, in packages that not only included six of Langdon's eight two-reelers, but also *Zenobia*. Soon after, another distributor, Motion Pictures for Television, picked up more recent titles such as *Double Trouble*, *House of Errors* and *Hot Rhythm*. Much of Langdon's silent work could be seen periodically on *Howdy Doody*, NBC's hit children's program, which utilized the Mack Sennett Pathé library, among others. All of this made him a recognizable figure to the first television generation.

But Langdon's death put the matter of his legacy into others' hands, and the first of these was critic James Agee. His essay, "Comedy's Greatest Era," appeared in the September 5, 1949 issue of *Life* magazine, in which Langdon was named one of silent comedy's four greatest clowns, along with Chaplin, Lloyd and Keaton. The article was instrumental in creating a market for their films for both television and home use.

Labeling Langdon "The Baby," Agee wrote, "It seemed as if Chaplin could do literally anything, on any instrument in the orchestra. Langdon had one queerly toned, unique little reed. But out of it he could get incredible melodies…. His walk was that

Opposite: A photo from The Strong Man *graces the program for The Gallery of Modern Art's 1967 Langdon retrospective.*

of a child which has just gotten sure on its feet, and his body and hands fitted that age. His face was kept pale to show off, with the simplicity of a nursery school drawing, the bright, ignorant, gentle eyes and the little twirling mouth....Twitchings of his face were signals of tiny discomforts too slowly registered by a tinier brain... a virtuoso of hesitations and of delicately indecisive motions."

Agee was loaned, through the courtesy of Warner Bros., 16mm screening prints of the first four of Langdon's First National features for his analysis, which led him to seek out the most prominent name on the credit roll for an interview: Frank Capra. Consequently, the author's Langdon profile was reflected through Capra's prism, which included the following quote: "If there was a rule for writing Langdon material, it was this: his only ally was God. Langdon might be saved by the brick falling on the cop, but it was *verboten* that he in any way motivate the brick's fall." That certainly summed up Capra's interpretation of Langdon's character, but it failed to account for every other contribution to the complexities that formed the Little Elf, particularly those of Langdon himself.

"Langdon came to Sennett from a vaudeville act in which he had fought a losing battle with a recalcitrant automobile. The minute Frank Capra saw him he begged Sennett to let him work with him," wrote Agee. "Langdon was almost as childlike as the character he played. He had only a vague idea of his story or even of each scene as he played it." Five years later, Mack Sennett (or his collaborator, Cameron Shipp) relied heavily on this paragraph when introducing Langdon in the pages of *King of Comedy*.

In 1928, Sennett told Theodore Dreiser that he considered Langdon "the greatest of them all... greater than Chaplin. Langdon suggests a kind of baby weakness that causes everybody to feel sorry for him and want to help him out. He's terribly funny to me. On the other hand, Langdon knows less about stories and motion picture technique than perhaps any other screen star. If he isn't a big success, [it is] because he doesn't understand the many sides to picture production. He wants to do a monologue all the time; he wants to be the leading lady, cameraman, heavy and director all in one. So far in my experience that attitude has never proved successful."

Dreiser interviewed Sennett around the time Langdon was released by First National; writing a quarter-century later, Sennett's opinion hadn't much changed: "I thought for a while Langdon was as good as Chaplin. In some of his pathetic scenes he was certainly as good....The two were the same in their universal appeal. They were the little guys coping with a mean universe....

"Langdon became important and unfortunately realized it.... He decided he was also a businessman. His cunning as a businessman was about that of a backward kindergarten student and he complicated this by marital adventures, in which he was about as inept as he was on screen. He was soon behind in alimony payments.... Poor Langdon failed wretchedly as a producer." Sennett was speaking, of course, from a business perspective, not an artistic one.

In summing up his ex-employee, Sennett wrote: "His sly charm and his gentle humor have yet to be matched on the screen. I wish he had stayed with me. He was a quaint artist who had no business in business," this last an opinion Langdon himself expressed more than once. It is tempting, however, to speculate on what might have been had Sennett's wish come true. With no Tim Whelan on staff, and Sennett not trusting Capra to direct, posterity would likely have been denied the pleasures of *Tramp, Tramp, Tramp, The Strong Man* and *Long Pants*, while *Three's a Crowd* would not have been so personal a statement. On the other hand, without the pressures of business matters and a squabbling creative team, Langdon might have risen to even greater heights, prolonging his star stature and perhaps Sennett's company as well.

As the 1950s progressed, more of Langdon's films made their way to TV when the major studios began leasing their libraries to various distributors. These were mainly the talking films, but his pantomime skills were still in evidence in most of them. In a January 1956 Sheila Graham column, the comedy team of Dean Martin and Jerry Lewis named their ten favorite comedians of all time. Langdon was Lewis's choice for number eight: "Whimsical, a touch of pathos, and a flair for the ridiculous, he was truly beautiful to watch."

With Langdon having passed on, former vaudevillian Gene Sheldon brought a pantomime character to the home screen on several of its variety shows. Garbed in a tight coat, slightly oversized trousers and a round-brimmed fedora; silent but for an ever-present banjo, Sheldon's humor was also "whimsical, a touch of pathos and a flair for the ridiculous." For viewers with a modicum of silent comedy knowledge, there was no mistaking its influence.

After apprenticing in his father's magic act, Sheldon began his own stage career as a Langdon impersonator, and by 1928 was billed as "The Harry Langdon of Stage Land," which was ironic, since Langdon himself had been that a mere five years earlier. Even after the original had returned to vaudeville, Sheldon kept his Langdonesque persona intact. For a February 1933 stage performance, *Variety* pegged him as someone who "saw Harry Langdon once and never forgot him." According to Mabel, Harry was

The Langdonesque Gene Sheldon, circa 1957.

irked at Sheldon's derivative character, but when she suggested filing an injunction, he simply replied, "No, dear, I've been in court often enough."

While costume and gestures were nearly identical, Sheldon didn't overtly steal any of Langdon's material or routines. He worked "in one," a stool and his banjo his only props, ideal for vaudeville and in musical revues as a spot act while stage scenery was being changed behind the curtain. By the time television came along, its many variety shows, which were always live, had similar staging requirements and he found a warm welcome there.

Reviewers with long memories always pointed out the influences. "Gene Sheldon of the *NBC Summer Comedy Hour*," wrote critic Jack O'Brian in 1954, "is getting a warm weather popularity among folks who do not remember Harry Langdon, Harpo Marx and many Chaplinesque trademarks." It didn't matter: audiences thoroughly enjoyed the wistful little man who always seemed to struggle with, yet really could play that tenor banjo. Sheldon kept busy in nightclubs, movies and on TV well into the 1960s, and passed away in 1982.

By 1957, Robert Youngson had left Warner Bros. and gone independent. Partnering with Hal Roach, Jr., he produced a feature-length compilation, *The Golden Age of Comedy*, which primarily relied on silent Laurel & Hardy material owned by Hal Roach Studios, but was augmented with scenes from various Roach and Sennett comedies. Lloyd and Keaton footage was unavailable, and public opinion surrounding

Chaplin's controversial exile from America by the Department of Immigration precluded the use of his public domain material. That left Harry Langdon as the only one of *Life* magazine's four comedy greats to be represented, in scenes from reel one of *Luck of the Foolish*, and *Life* saw fit to devote a picture spread to the film when it was released in February 1958.

Youngson's labor of love was a tremendous success with both critics and audiences, and he would follow it up with three more popular compilations, all of which featured Langdon: *When Comedy Was King* (1960) (an abbreviated version of *The First 100 Years*), *The Days of Thrills and Laughter* (1961) (battlefield scenes from *All Night Long*) and *30 Years of Fun* (1963) (clips from *Feet of Mud* and *Smile Please*). *When Comedy Was King* includes, in its narration, an eloquent, sympathetic explanation of Langdon's decline in popularity: "At the height of his career, he turned, in films directed by himself, to a new, strange, offbeat kind of comedy, full of pathos and even despair. It was like a trumpeter reaching for a celestial high note somewhere beyond human range. Audiences stopped laughing."

"Youngson's *The Golden Age of Comedy* introduced a whole new generation to the art of silent film comedy," writes Brent Walker in *Mack Sennett's Fun Factory*, especially once the film reached television in 1964. Spurred on by the compilations, writers began looking more closely at Langdon's work. The first was 1959's *Classics of the Silent Screen*, a book by Joe Franklin, host of ABC-TV's *Memory Lane* program, with considerable assistance by film historian William K. Everson. In the section on Langdon, Franklin declares, "Langdon was one of the greatest. Unfortunately, his genius was of a very specialized kind. It needed careful, delicate handling.…Directors like Harry Edwards and Frank Capra knew what he was trying to do, perhaps better than he did — and they knew how to handle him, how to express it best. When Langdon took over, he became bogged down in his character for its own sake."

This marked the first appearance in print of an assertion that Langdon's directors knew his character and comedy better than he did, one that would be repeated in subsequent accounts for years to come.

Franklin's book also called *The Strong Man* "not only Harry's best picture, but also probably the best film its director (Frank Capra) ever made," in a separate entry for that film. The previous year, Capra had revived the "going-up-the-stairs-backwards" gag once again, giving it to Frank Sinatra in *A Hole in the Head*.

Heading into the 1960s, universities, colleges and film societies were including Langdon shorts in their silent comedy programs. Footage from the Sennett films also found its way into two kid-oriented film packages: *Comedy Capers*, produced by National Telpix, and *The Funny Manns*, produced by NBC's California National Productions. Langdon also cropped up in a network series, *Silents Please*, created by Paul Killiam and airing on ABC.

The First National features, though, were missing from revivals and on television, until Raymond Rohauer entered the scene in 1964. Rohauer was a film enthusiast who, in 1950, took over the Coronet Theater in Los Angeles and began screening classic movies. In 1954, he met Buster Keaton, who brought him several reels that had recently been discovered in a vault at Keaton's former home by its new owner, actor James Mason. Rohauer and Keaton formed a partnership that led to their securing all rights to

A scene from The First 100 Years *(1924) used in 1960's* When Comedy Was King.

and ownership of Keaton's silent shorts and independent features, and sent Rohauer to such disparate places as Algiers and the Soviet Union in search of prints. Once that was done, he spearheaded Keaton programs at various institutions and art houses that put the comedian's finest work before the eyes of the world's most prestigious film critics. The results benefited both men: Rohauer basked in the acclaim for demonstrating Keaton's importance to film history, and Keaton remained in constant demand until the end of his life.

Then Rohauer turned his attention to Harry Langdon. In 1956, Warner Bros. had sold rights to its pre-1948 product, silent and sound, to Associated Artists Productions, a television film distributor. Two years later, United Artists bought A.A.P. and all its properties. The Langdon films were of little importance to UA; their interest was solely in the classic Warner talkies and cartoons. In April 1964, Rohauer acquired UA's copyrights to the six First National features, "to the extent that we have any rights in the pictures," according to the legalese.

UA had never received prints of the Langdons from A.A.P., and as discussed above, Warners' own legal department was unable to determine if any rights ownership resided with the defunct Harry Langdon Corporation, which probably exempted the films from the A.A.P. deal in the first place. Rohauer sought out Mabel Langdon, who transferred to him all but one share of the Corporation's otherwise worthless stock. That made Rohauer majority owner, and on April 20, 1965, his lawyer, who happened to be

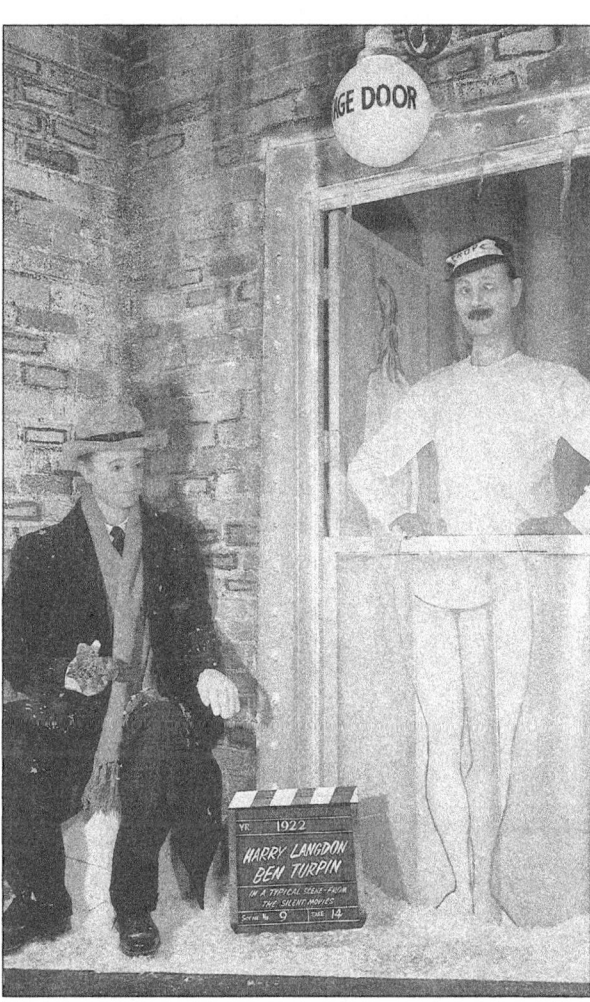

Harry shares exhibit space with Ben Turpin at the Movieland Wax Museum, 1963.

W.C. Fields, Jr., sent a letter to Warner Bros. detailing all of this and to "respectfully request your assigning to Mr. Rohauer any and all copyrights you may hold to these pictures."

It was at this point that Warners evidently discovered First National had bought out the corporation and its assets long before, and they responded by charging $60,000 — $10,000 per picture — for said copyrights, along with delivering any surviving prints and preprint materials. Rohauer paid in $5,000 installments, the last one made on October 1, 1970.

In 1967, Rohauer launched two Langdon retrospectives: one at the Huntington Hartford Gallery of Modern Art in New York City (where he was then its film curator and programmer), and the other at the 17th Annual Berlin Film Festival. Mabel participated in both events.

That same year, writer Vernon L. Schonert penned a Langdon profile for *Films In Review* magazine. Schonert relied heavily on Agee's article and Sennett's *King of Comedy* as a foundation for his piece, coupled with his own choices for films that constituted Langdon's best work. He termed *Saturday Afternoon* and *Soldier Man* "two of the funniest three-reelers ever filmed," and considered *The Strong Man* "Landgon's most successful film." Describing *Three's a Crowd*, Schonert wrote, "Instead of being tender, the pathos of this sentimentality cloys. Comedy is feeble and infrequent." His opinion of *The Chaser* was even harsher: "His magic — or, more accurately, Capra — was gone. [The story] is warmed-over Sennett, good for two or three reels but much too thin for six." The author might well have relied solely upon the reviews of the day for his assessment.

However, Schonert was the first journalist to call attention to Langdon's talkies. "The tone of his voice exactly suited his screen image.... In general, the eight two-reelers Langdon made for M.G.M. successfully combined his pantomime with dialogue." He also pointed out that the Educational films "differed very little from the ones he had made for Sennett. Even Vernon Dent and Ruth Hiatt were often in their casts. Harry talked, it is true, but the emphasis was on action, not dialogue." Schonert was more impressed, though, with Langdon's work in *Hallelujah! I'm A Bum* ("He had the important role of Egghead [for which] critics thought him 'delightful' and 'effective'") and *My Weakness* ("Langdon played an impish cupid, with entirely satisfactory results") than with his two-reelers of the same period.

Schonert has little to say about the later films, mainly because he hadn't seen them. Among the more glaring errors in his article is an assumption that co-star Charley Rogers is Charles "Buddy" Rogers, former matinee idol and husband of Mary Pickford. Aside from terming him "occasionally quite funny" in *Zenobia*, there is nothing of substance about Langdon's

Raymond Rohauer interviews Harry Jr., and Mabel Langdon for The Gallery of Modern Art, 1967.

Columbia shorts or post-1933 features. Still in all, it is the most comprehensive career assessment the comedian had received in print to date and would remain so for years afterward. The article concluded with an equally comprehensive filmography; its chief flaws being the inclusion of four Educational shorts in which Langdon did not appear, and the crediting of Harry Edwards as director of *The Stage Hand*.

The following year saw a book by Donald W. McCaffrey, *Four Great Comedians: Chaplin, Lloyd, Keaton, Langdon*. Even though the author limited his scope to Langdon's silent work, only a handful of the Sennett films are singled out for attention. McCaffrey went directly from *Picking Peaches* to the Ripley-Capra *Lucky Stars*, noting that "considerable growth in story line and character development was displayed," while failing to account for the progression of that growth in the many films made in between. Discussion of *Remember When?* and *Soldier Man* (the latter at length) followed before he moved on to the First National features.

McCaffrey cited the episodic nature of the first two features as a fundamental weakness, although he believed several of the sequences, including the attempted "rape" by Lil and the chest cold scene in *The Strong Man*, to be Langdon's finest work. However, he felt *Long Pants* "can be rated as Langdon's best picture if the film is viewed as a total work. Capra's control of the story, the camera, and his actors makes it one of the best silent screen comedies." This is an impressive observation, given the sterling reputation *The Strong Man* was enjoying as "Langdon's best" even then. Of course, McCaffrey had no idea of the struggle Capra endured to maintain *any* control over *Long Pants*.

"Unfortunately," wrote McCaffrey, "the comedian was not satisfied with Capra as a director and dismissed him from his company. It was a fateful decision that spelled the rapid fall of Langdon's career.... Evidently he was not the judge of his comic skills that Capra had been." Once more the assertion is made that Capra knew better, and still years before the director's own account appeared on the scene. McCaffrey ended his analysis with *Three's a Crowd*, claiming that Langdon "never recovered from this failure." True, but then First National refused to give him a genuine opportunity to do so.

In April 1971, Rohauer programmed another Langdon retrospective in New York City, this time at the Elgin Theater. All five of the surviving First National features were included, along with nine Sennett shorts, and even two talkies: *Hallelujah! I'm a Bum* and the Educational short *Hooks and Jabs*. The week it opened, Penelope Gilliatt wrote a Langdon profile for *The New Yorker*. Although Agee was again trotted out as a resource ("Capra apparently understood Langdon's comic personality perfectly, and begged to be allowed to work with him"), the balance of Gilliatt's piece was her own perspective:

> Harry Langdon looks like a small girl with high hopes of one day being eight. The exquisite Bessie Love face is hung with panniers of puppy fat. The makeup, which weirdly manages to not seem androgynous, gives him the likeness of a child who has been mooning for hours in front of a looking glass with its mother's lipstick and mascara....As a 1914–18 private in "The Strong Man," he takes abstracted aim at a tin can and then at a German [with] biscuits slung from a catapult. Only a girl would find such a rotten form of bullet, and only a girl would be so thrilled and surprised to get a hit.... Langdon automatically goes his own way, without troubling himself to get in touch with the rest of the world.

Rohauer brought the festival to Los Angeles's Los Feliz Theater that July, by which point Capra's *The Name Above the Title* had been published. Having thoroughly dissected the book's myths elsewhere in these pages, there's no need for a rehash here. Its impact, though, was evidently immediate. When Charles Champlin, entertainment editor for the *Los Angeles Times*, offered up his perspective of the

comedian as the festival was winding down, he noted, "In his recent autobiography... Capra characterizes Langdon as a thorny and difficult off-camera personality, peremptory and jealous. In all events, Capra and Langdon split, and Langdon undertook to do his own films, like *The Chaser* (which was then the only picture remaining to be screened).

The Chaser certainly will convince no one that Langdon was under-rated. It is a slow, thin, posturing tale.…There is no evidence in *The Chaser* that Langdon had anything more going for him than his unique look — the white make-up, the wide, dumb eyes, the pork pie hat, the gestures of a nail-biting little boy and a quite Chaplinesque waddle.…

It's not possible to judge a comic on one film, but one bad film can certainly suggest how much any comic (and, I suspect, Langdon more than most) was at the mercy of his gag-writers.… The Langdon figure was applied, like the white makeup, by other hands, and he himself seems to have had no idea what people were laughing at.

Champlin can be forgiven his ignorance of the pitiful circumstances under which *The Chaser* was created, but his devastating view of Langdon's off-screen personality and comic instincts would soon become the norm.

Fortunately, Langdon had his champions even then, one of which was British composer Harold Truscott. Less than a year after *The Name Above the Title* was released, Truscott's lengthy profile, titled simply "Harry Langdon," appeared in *The Silent Picture*'s winter-spring 1972 issue. Truscott goes into very specific detail about Langdon's comedy, citing examples from several films, both silent and sound, but mostly from personal memory, abetted by reviews and other contemporary resources. One of the more surprising revelations is that he viewed *Heart Trouble* more than a dozen times in his youth, because it "was booked for a week and stayed for three.… This extended run happened at two different cinemas in Ilford at different times, each time for *Heart Trouble*, a three-week run each time." If Truscott's recollection is valid, the city must have accounted for a substantial chunk of that film's miserable foreign gross.

Capra's book was evidently not available to Truscott, but this didn't stop him from attacking the perception surrounding the director's actual contribution as well as the negative consequences of Langdon's self-directed films. Using Sennett's *King of Comedy* as his launching pad, Truscott mistakenly assumed that if, as Sennett claimed, Capra directed Langdon "as soon as he set eyes on him," it must have been for Langdon's earliest films, which bear no director credits on screen. "If Capra did direct Harry Langdon for Sennett it was within those first five films… the only bad films in which I have ever seen Langdon."

With added emphasis, Truscott continued, "If Capra did *not* direct any of these first five films, his *first* connection with Langdon as *a director* was with *The Strong*

Man; admittedly magnificent, but *not* made for Sennett. But Harry's mature screen character was already formed and in operation by this time, and not by any direction of Capra. Either way, what becomes of the legend that Capra first perceived how best to handle Langdon? The director who knew more of Langdon, from a film point of view, was Harry Edwards. I have often wondered why there has never been a word quoted from him on this subject." This is easily answered: Edwards had died in May 1952, long before this particular controversy progressed from spark to flame.

Moving on to Langdon's own direction, Truscott notes, "He has also been adversely criticised as a director. I have no idea why.... I saw all these films as well as the bulk of his sound films, and *Three's a Crowd*, *The Chaser* and *Heart Trouble* were as tautly made, with as much evidence of fine direction, as the first three of these six.... What one finds in Langdon's best work, as in Keaton's, is a taut although often simple story, in which the laughter grows naturally out of that story and out of the main character or characters who motivate the story and make it move. Films such as *The General* and *Long Pants*, *Steamboat Bill, Jr.* and *Three's a Crowd*, *Seven Chances* and *Heart Trouble* are of this order, and are among the most perfectly constructed and organic films ever made....Now, this tautness is as much present in the last three of the First National films, the three Langdon directed, as it is in the earlier ones, and it could not be if Langdon had been the failure as a director that he has been described."

Maurice H. Zouray, a Brooklyn-based entrepreneur that acquired 335 Educational talkies in the early 1970s, including the seven Langdon titles, tried in various ways to capitalize on the library...none particularly successful.

In the U.S., then-film student Richard Leary offered up a quick treatise on "Capra & Langdon" for the journal *Film Comment*'s November 1972 issue. "That Langdon is not now completely forgotten is due in no small part to the intimidating reputation of James Agee," wrote Leary. "Many writers who invoke the departed Golden Age of Chaplin, Keaton, Langdon and Lloyd clearly include Langdon in this ritual roll call on the basis of Agee's say-so rather than out of any personal enthusiasm for — or even acquaintance with — the comic's work. Unfortunately, even as he rescued Langdon's reputation, Agee solidified some misconceptions, notably the image of Langdon as Galatea to Frank Capra's Pygmalion."

After citing his own perception of Langdon's comedy, buttressed with his favorite gags and scenes from specific films, Leary posits, "The Langdon character was both too complex to be developed in shorts and too passive to keep a feature length plot moving... the pace of his movies had to be fast enough to prevent the fragile whimsy from becoming irritating, yet not so fast as to kill the delicate humor by rushing it....

"So despite Langdon's genius as a clown, his films depended on careful craftsmanship and firm, knowledgeable control in writing and direction. Langdon was lucky to receive the necessary support and guidance from the Edwards-Capra-Ripley team, although the problem of building a steady crescendo while staying within the confines of an undisciplined, unassertive character was never satisfactorily resolved." He notes that even Capra violated his own "principle of the brick" in *The Strong Man*, in which the director "creates a slam-bang climax at the cost of character consistency."

Toward Langdon's own films, Leary was sympathetic but failed to see Truscott's parity with those of Keaton. "Langdon's downfall came not from firing Capra, but from taking the directorial reigns himself, instead of entrusting them to a professional. Langdon's direction wasn't bad for a novice, but his amateurishness was most conspicuous when contrasted with the dazzling finesse of the films of Keaton, Chaplin, and others in the late silent era.... Still, his later films are not the disasters of legend; if nothing else, they are irrevocably personal works, especially in their melancholic misogyny and their acceptance of a malevolent universe."

Gerald Mast's book-length study on film comedy, 1973's *The Comic Mind*, included a chapter on Langdon. By then, Capra's account had become prevalent, and Mast recounts it, simultaneously trying to give Langdon the benefit of the doubt: "Though audiences did not like the [post-Capra] films, the pictures were certainly as entertaining and interesting as the weaker [Harold] Lloyd comedies. And the weirdness of Langdon's comic situations unmistakably link the films he directed himself with the films directed by Capra. Perhaps Langdon would have developed a unique cinema style if he had had more time, if the audience's tastes had been more harmonious with Harry's, and if sound had not come along to stifle further possibilities." He also understood the motivation behind Capra's dismissal, when discussing *Three's a Crowd*: "Langdon is trying to do something different and personal, reaching much further than Capra tried to take him," but Mast concludes that he fails, owing to an absence of "stylistic mastery [and] intellectual control."

An unlikely re-release in the 1970s.

Perhaps appropriately, Langdon's most vocal supporter was a teenager. Edward Watz was approaching his 13th year in April 1971 when he saw *Tramp, Tramp, Tramp* at the Elgin Theater. Highly impressed, he returned for *The Strong Man* and *Long Pants*, and sought out more of Langdon's films wherever possible, which eventually led him to collect them on 16mm from dealers such as Blackhawk Films. Starting in 1974, he penned a series of 12 articles for *Classic Film Collector*, a quarterly magazine that later morphed into the still-vital *Classic Images*. Among his other accomplishments, Watz was possibly the first U.S. aficionado to argue the merits of *Three's a Crowd* and *The Chaser*.

Over the next three years, Watz's thoughtful essays, covering Langdon's work in both the silent and sound arenas, were well received, and so impressed Raymond Rohauer that the latter invited him to collaborate on a planned Langdon biography that, sadly, never reached fruition (and ultimately ended with Rohauer's death in 1987).

These works were all a sign of the times: silent film comedy had reached a new pinnacle of interest, spurred not only by the many recent retrospectives, but also the return of Charles Chaplin to the United States in April 1972 to receive a special Academy Award. The previous year, Chaplin had arranged to release his silent classics in the U.S. for the first time since the early 1950s. The films played in mainstream cinemas to mainstream audiences, and were quite successful. The 82-year-old "Little Tramp" received a hero's welcome upon his arrival, and was fêted on both coasts. One noted critic took stock of these events and decided it was time for a thorough examination of the genre's greatest names.

It took 26 years, but the influence of Agee's famous *Life* article was finally eclipsed by the appearance of Walter Kerr's affectionate-yet-scholarly 374-page book, *The Silent Clowns*. The longtime dramatic reviewer for New York's *Herald-Tribune* and *Times* newspapers effortlessly meshed his critic's eye with an unabashed love for the form with which he had grown up. The result was a comprehensive tribute to the genre that not only influenced but also practically birthed at least two generations of silent comedy historians, scholars and writers, including the authors of this book.

Although Kerr focused mainly on Keaton, Chaplin and Lloyd (in that order of importance), he also discussed other once-prominent comedians, as well as the comedic philosophies of the Sennett and Roach studios. Two chapters were devoted to Laurel & Hardy's impact on silent comedy during its waning days. The six chapters that opened the book dwelt on a discussion on the form of silence in general, and why the coming of sound was a boon to screen drama and a disaster for visual comedy.

The Silent Clowns was important enough that, in advance of publication, one of its chapters was printed in *American Film*, the magazine of the American Film Institute. The chapter selected for the November 1975 issue was the first of three devoted to Langdon. One of the book's more charming aspects was Kerr's habit of sprinkling anecdotes into his narrative; the chapter "Who Was Harry Langdon?" begins with one of these:

> When I was about twelve, a friend and I began showing films on Friday nights in the auditorium of the school we attended. I suppose we really wanted to see the films again for ourselves — naturally, we weren't allowed to book current features, but had to wait six or eight months until they had exhausted their commercial runs....
>
> At the end of a year and a half we had earned some six hundred dollars for the school, or just enough to equip the auditorium with splendid new seats. And, as it happened, the project took its impetus from the work of a single man: the comedian Harry Langdon.... We made our debut as showmen with Langdon's initial feature, "Tramp, Tramp, Tramp," in 1926, and included his subsequent films on our programs as rapidly as we could get our hands on them.

Kerr then touched on his enjoyment of the booking process; of visiting the various film exchange offices in Chicago and "talking film 'shop'" with the employees. He related how, in visiting First National's exchange to book *Long Pants*, he "asked — out of personal interest — when [Langdon's] next might be appearing in the theaters. 'Oh, I don't know,' the booker said casually, 'we'll be dumping the little son-of-a-bitch soon.'"

Kerr the youngster was astonished that Langdon, seemingly at the height of his popularity, "was being dismissed out of hand — and by the very men who had been tucking away profits for two exhilarating years." Kerr the author used this anecdote in part to confirm Capra's assertions about Langdon's ego trip. His long-ago conversation with First National's booker, however, was based on an entirely different reality.

As we now know, of Langdon's first three films, only *The Strong Man* turned a profit, and a rather modest one at that. Contrasting Kerr's timetable with release data, he would have begun his exhibition project around December 1926, after *Tramp, Tramp, Tramp* had been supplanted in theaters by *The Strong Man*. Assuming the average of six–eight months' lead time between initial release and availability, Kerr would likely have booked *Strong Man* around April–May 1927 and *Long Pants* around November–December. According to the quarterly statements submitted to the Langdon Corporation, all three had yet to show a profit; *The Strong Man* didn't go into the black until the following March.

By the end of 1927, of course, "Langdon's next" would have been *The Chaser*, which was in production, *Three's a Crowd* having been released in August. First National had just publicly declared that Langdon's future with their firm would depend on how well *The Chaser* did at the box office. If there's any revelation to be gleaned from the booker's "dumping" comment, it is probably that he and his peers had gotten an earful from exhibitors about how poor *Three's a Crowd* had been and they weren't holding out much hope for the next one.

In *The Silent Clowns*, Kerr's summation of Langdon's appeal rests on his observation that the Elf possesses an "ambiguity" in age. To him, Harry is ideally a "five-year-old and not a five-year-old. A twelve-year-old and not a twelve-year-old. A full-grown functioning male and not a full-grown functioning male. Langdon was and was not all three at once, with nary a seam showing."

This ambiguity was indeed part of the complexity of Langdon's screen character, but it was only a part, just as Capra's "principle of the brick" was also a part, as was Langdon's assertion that he "must be a supreme though naïve optimist." Kerr's thesis fails to distinguish these other aspects, to the point where Langdon's "successful" films are discussed in a chapter subtitled "Creating an Ambiguity" and the "failures" in another chapter, "The Ambiguity Dissolves."

Most tragically, Kerr does not even consider that, unlike his peers, Langdon was able from time to time to wholly resurrect his comic persona in talkies. He simply concludes, "Langdon's career as a star of features had so disintegrated by 1928 that no one was going to bother to discover whether or not he could speak, and he did what he could to keep alive by making catch-as-catch-can two reelers and

Left to Right: Raymond Rohauer, organist Lee Irwin, Mabel Langdon, Ed Watz and Kristian Chester (Rohauer's business partner) at the SILENT CLOWNS retrospective in 1979.

occasionally appearing as minor support in other men's full-length films." It's an almost equally apt description of Buster Keaton's career after 1933. While there are paragraphs discussing Lloyd's and Keaton's sound work near the end of *The Silent Clowns*, there's not even a sentence or two about Langdon's Roach and Educational shorts, not to mention later *starring* features for P.R.C. and Monogram.

video formats, took its toll on film collecting as that decade progressed.

The year 1982 saw the publication of the first Langdon biography in America, simply titled *Harry Langdon*. Written by William Schelly and published by Scarecrow Press (as part of its *Filmmakers* series for academic use), the book basically summarized Langdon's life story as culled from available resources,

The 1970s saw the peak of classic film collecting. Various merchants offered Langdon titles, including Blackhawk Films (left) and Niles Films (above).

Raymond Rohauer capitalized on Kerr's book twice: first in 1976 with a comedy festival titled "Mirth of a Nation" and again in 1979, when a paperback edition was published, with "The Silent Clowns." *The Strong Man* was screened at both events, while the latter also included *Tramp, Tramp, Tramp* and *Three's a Crowd*.

The publication of *The Silent Clowns* coincided neatly with the peak of film collecting. Blackhawk Films, which was founded in 1949 as a clearinghouse for used 16mm prints of all genres, had begun specializing in vintage silent material in 1952. Some 20 years later, the firm offered films from all the great comedians, including Langdon. Having expanded into the 8mm gauge, for three decades, Blackhawk was the premier source from which enthusiasts could actually own many of the classic titles seen at retrospectives, or read about in various publications. In fact, film collecting spawned its own periodicals, such as *The Big Reel* and the aforementioned *Classic Images*, both of which featured additional Langdon overviews by various authors into the 1980s. But a sharp increase in the price of silver, coupled with the rise of home

which were hardly numerous. Langdon's stage career is summarized in a few paragraphs mostly derived from articles and press releases issued during the film years, along with Capra's description of *Johnny's New Car*. The bulk of *Harry Langdon* is spent discussing the films themselves and it is the book's greatest strength, representing the first in-depth analysis of the majority of Langdon's output.

Curiously, Shelley begins his biography with an unsourced assertion that, in early 1923, Langdon was considering giving up show business, changing his mind only when offered his first film contract. There's no contemporary evidence to suggest such a thing; indeed, Langdon spent what would be his last vaudeville season tinkering with *After the Ball* and writing *Dry Goods*, the afterpiece performed at the Los Angeles Orpheum. Shelley also recounts the Capra-Ripley-Jones conversation in the screening room, in which Capra "creates" the Little Elf, and decides it "rings true."

The following year brought Dr. Joyce Rheuban's book-length treatise on Langdon's comedy, *Harry*

Langdon: The Comedian as Metteur-en-Scène. The tome did much to reestablish the most basic truths about Langdon's status as a vaudevillian, which had been obscured by Sennett and Capra, but as discussed earlier, her basic thesis of Langdon as a fully formed comedian right from the start was based upon some ill-advised conclusions about his vaudeville act. Regardless, it was an important work and opened the eyes of many who failed to understand Langdon's lofty reputation during the 1920s.

Still, the "Capra myth" continued to dominate, not helped by Thames Television's otherwise-excellent *Hollywood* program. Produced by Kevin Brownlow and David Gill, and narrated by James Mason, this 13-episode British mini-series respectfully celebrated the American silent film, with generous helpings of clips from all the genre's greatest stars. Langdon was featured in the episode "Comedy: A Serious Business," which first aired on February 26, 1980. All four of Agee's Kings of Comedy were represented, but while Chaplin, Keaton and Lloyd were basically presented on their own merits, Langdon was "explained" by Capra, by then the only survivor of the comedian's creative team. The series reached U.S. shores later in the decade via PBS.

By the mid-1980s, home video had grown into a thriving business. As the popularity of VHS tapes ascended, HBO Video released *The Strong Man* in 1985, which was the first time one of Langdon's First National features, still controlled by Rohauer, became legally available for purchase in any format. Nostalgia Merchant, which held the video rights to the Hal Roach library, released *The Head Guy* on a compilation tape entitled *Hal Roach Comedy Classics*. Independent concerns such as Video Yesteryear and Videobrary offered many of the Sennett shorts, *His First Flame* and even an Educational talkie or two; all public domain material derived, for the most part, from 16mm prints originally sold by Blackhawk and other companies.

Langdon scholarship continued into the 1990s, as his work became more accessible. In 1992, *Films In Review* revisited Langdon from the perspective of his nephew, Harry N. Langdon. Named for his famous uncle, Claude's youngest son became the drama instructor for Abraham Lincoln High School in Council Bluffs, and directed the school's plays. In his article, he rejects most of the Capra viewpoint, although he innocently repeats the myth that *Johnny's New Car* "was about a little guy plagued with a nagging wife and a car needing repairs."

In describing the later First National features, his nephew wrote, "Perhaps Langdon's separation from Capra was not the sole reason for the lack of public enthusiasm….The material he selected was too surrealistic and expressionistic for the mass audience that

Harry Langdon on VHS in the 1980s.

films had attracted by the late 1920s. Cinema buffs may even prefer certain sequences in *Three's a Crowd* and *The Chaser* to the more obvious humor of *Tramp, Tramp, Tramp, Long Pants* and *The Strong Man*." It was not an unfounded observation. Changing tastes triggered a reevaluation of these films; the result was a gradual distancing from the staid views of Champlin and Kerr.

The newly formed Harry Langdon Society looks for members in 1996. Ad from Classic Images.

A relatively new publication, *Cult Movies*, occasionally ran Langdon-related pieces in its pages, mainly because its publisher, Michael Copner, was a fan. Copner even sought out Mabel Langdon and Harry, Jr. for interviews (which appeared in 1997 and 2001, respectively), and penned articles about *Heart Trouble* and one of the homes in which Langdon lived (evidently the Hollywood Hills structure he had bought with Rose during his early years in films, then rented from her in 1932), which was alleged to have hosted some supernatural phenomena.

The two most significant events of the 1990s surrounding Langdon's legacy took place within months of each other. In late 1996, after communicating with other fans located through *Classic Images*, Floyd Bennett, a resident of Downer's Grove, Illinois, founded The Harry Langdon Society. It was the first Langdon fan club since the original had dissolved in the late 1920s. Bennett had been a fan for several years, and even hosted a Langdon "birthday bash" every June 15 at his home, where his friends and family could watch and evaluate the films. That fall, he decided to take his appreciation to the next level, placing ads in relevant publications.

Membership in the society included a filmography and membership list, both revised annually, and a quarterly newsletter, *Wild About Harry*. In stating the society's mission, Bennett set some impressive goals: "I want us to have fun with Harry, and I look forward to sharing with others the delight he's given me. But I want more, too. Here's *my* idea of success:

> Name recognition. By rights, Langdon's name should be on a par with Chaplin's....
>
> Availability of his films... on the shelves of everyday video stores. Chaplin's there, let's put Langdon there, too! This is vital: People won't embrace Harry if they can't even watch him.
>
> Setting the record straight. The conventional mythology...may never be completely overcome [but] correction of inaccurate stories from the past (and present) should be a priority.
>
> Some long overdue honors. Examples come readily to mind: a suitable memorial in his hometown, some highly visible events commemorating his art, perhaps a postage stamp in his honor.

It's a tribute to Bennett that, although the society only lasted about four years, some of its goals were accomplished. In collaboration with the Bluffs Art Council and the Iowa Humanities Board, Harry Langdon Day was celebrated in Council Bluffs on September 20, 1997. Bennett attended, brought materials to share, and interviewed nephews Don and Harry Langdon.

Harry Langdon Day floated the idea that a Council Bluffs street be named for the comedian, and Bennett naturally editorialized for it in *Wild About Harry*. The first vote, taken in September 1998, failed due to objections from local merchants and citizens. The town's newspaper, *The Nonpariel*, came out in favor of the renaming "to mark the career of a man who has a star on Hollywood's Walk of Fame but whose career is not recognized in his hometown." Don Langdon wrote a lengthy letter about his uncle's career and ties to Council Bluffs. Although erroneously stating that Langdon had married Rose there, the letter was a positive step.

It was soon learned that a renovated section of Highway 375 was going to be renamed regardless, and on October 12, 1998, the Council Bluffs City Council voted to call it Harry Langdon Boulevard. The dedication ceremony was held on May 15, 1999. Langdon's grandson, Harry Langdon III and his family were present, along with Don Langdon. In lieu of a ribbon, a strip of motion picture film was cut to open the newly named street. Vintage automobiles took part in a special parade, and there was even a Harry Langdon look-alike contest, which was won by five-year-old Adam Beck.

Bennett ran the Harry Langdon Society for four years, retiring in 2000.

Only four months after the society had prepared its first newsletter, Langdon was back in the news, courtesy of Kino On Video. The company, a subsidiary of Kino International, originally specialized in its own library of art films, but found great success in the restoration and release of classic early-American cinema. In March 1997, they issued digitally mastered versions of *Tramp, Tramp, Tramp*, *The Strong Man* and *Long Pants* on VHS and Laser Disc formats under the umbrella title *Harry Langdon: The Forgotten Clown*. Along with the feature, each volume contained one of Langdon's Sennett shorts: *All Night Long*, *His Marriage Wow* and *Saturday Afternoon*, respectively. The films were tinted and accompanied with new scores.

Mainstream newspapers and magazines reviewed the collection, and although many of the writers drew upon the Capra account (probably unavoidable since he was credited on all three features), the gist of the articles focused on the comedian.

"Though capable of slapstick, [Langdon] was primarily an inspired mime with a way of becoming flummoxed all his own," wrote David Everitt for the *New York Times*. "His comedies center on his reactions, which are often hilariously slow. Sometimes his funniest moments come when he is completely still, staring wide-eyed as he tries to make sense of the world around him, usually without success.…Only Jack Benny could get as many laughs out of doing nothing.…

"The videos include Langdon's three best feature films.…All three were released to theaters in 1926 and 1927, coinciding with Langdon's brief fling at

Council Bluffs dedicated Harry Langdon Boulevard in 1999. PHOTO COURTESY OF THE HISTORICAL SOCIETY OF POTTAWATTAMIE COUNTY

superstardom. That any historical reputation sprang from such a short starring career is a tribute to Langdon's talent. His films on tape show how remarkable that talent was." Susan King of the *Los Angeles Times* agreed: "Now comedy fans can see for themselves why Langdon endeared himself to both critics and audiences 70 years ago."

In 2003, Kino re-released the films (without the accompanying shorts) on DVD. Two years later, a Langdon overview appeared in *Film Quarterly*, a journal of University of California Press. Written by Joanna E. Rapf, professor of Film & Video Studies at the University of Oklahoma, "Doing Nothing: Harry Langdon and the Performance of Absence" was another scholarly examination of Langdon's comedic style, in the same vein as Joyce Rheuban's book. In making a point about Langdon's minimalism, Professor Rapf dares to compare him with Jerry Seinfeld's TV situation comedy: "[Quoting] Jacques Derrida: 'To risk nothing is to start to play.' And play is behind so much of the comic impulse, including the way *Seinfeld* and Langdon turn our expectations upside-down by, paradoxically, allowing nothing to happen."

In December 2007, Facets released *Lost And Found: The Harry Langdon Collection*, a four-DVD box set produced by David Kalat that was clearly a labor of love. The first three discs gathered 17 surviving Sennett shorts plus *His First Flame*, all with newly composed scores. Disc four included three talkie shorts: *Knight Duty*, *Hooks and Jabs*, and *Love, Honor and Obey (the Law)*, plus a 75-minute Langdon documentary. A 20-page booklet included essays from various silent comedy experts and scholars, among them Brent Walker, Edward Watz and Steve Massa. The same people provided commentary tracks for every one of the titles on the set, and Watz supplied archival audio of Nell O'Day, Mrs. Vernon Dent and Jules White.

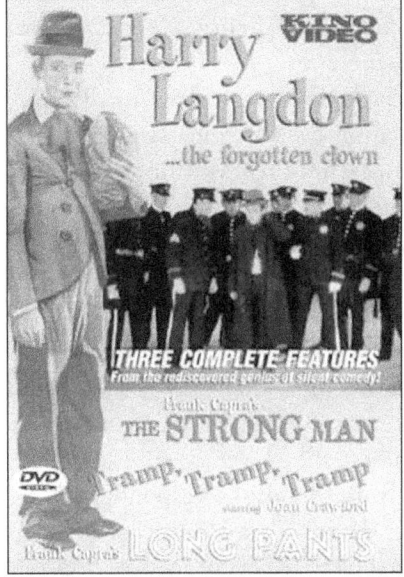

By 2008, nearly all of Langdon's silent films (and a sampling of his talkie shorts) were available on DVD.

Bonus material included the excerpt from *Horace Greely, Jr.*; the *Harry Langdon Announcement* that Hal Roach produced for M.G.M. executives, the *Voice of Hollywood* and *Hollywood on Parade* shorts in which Langdon appeared, the *Beautiful Clothes* Soundie, episodes of *The Funny Manns* and *Comedy Capers*, and even some of Langdon's home movies. Playing under the on-screen menu was Langdon's cameo in *Ella Cinders*.

This release, too, received attention from the mainstream press. "*Lost and Found: The Harry Langdon Collection* is a generous four-disc set with the avowed aim of establishing Langdon alongside the Holy Trinity of silent comedy: Chaplin, Keaton and Lloyd," wrote the *New York Times*'s Dave Kehr. "The jury may still be out on that, but the case that Mr. Kalat presents is strong." In *The New Yorker*, Richard Brody proclaimed, "Harry Langdon, the fourth and most elusive of the great silent comics...is also, in some ways, the most modern — which explains why he remains on the margins of movie history. The films featured in [this set] suggest both the grandeur and the limits of his art."

Perhaps inspired by the reaction to *Lost and Found*, Kino released the Langdon-directed features *Three's a Crowd* and *The Chaser* on DVD the following year, as part of their *Slapstick Symposium* series. *The Chaser* looked fine (albeit a brief section had to be mastered from a 16mm reduction print), but *Three's a Crowd* was marred by severe decomposition in one of its sequences and the loss of a key scene, both discussed earlier in the text. Nevertheless, the two most contentious Langdon films could finally be evaluated — and enjoyed — on their own terms.

All of these releases, which remain in print as of this writing, have brought the Little Elf into the 21st century, where, ironically, he may find himself more at home than he did in his own time.

Harry Langdon's legacy has suffered from a lot of myth: some of it malicious, some of it well intentioned, but myth nonetheless. Perhaps it would have been different if he had not died so soon. Had he lived another decade or two, Langdon might have brought his own perspective to James Agee's article and Mack Sennett's book; he might have provided some creative input to *The Golden Age of Comedy* and its successors; he might even have brought *Johnny's New Car* to television and put to rest all speculation about the act and its contents.

Or perhaps he might simply have kept plugging away at various film roles, his focus on providing for the wife and child he loved so much; content, like Keaton, just to be in demand. Unfortunately, genetics exacerbated by a lifelong cigarette habit robbed him — and us — of any of these happy endings.

One puzzle, though, remains: Langdon had 16 years to definitively address the public speculation about his alleged "swelled head," and did not. At times he hinted it was never true ("Don't ask me whether or not little doughface suffered from an inflated cranium. Harry himself says it was his tough luck"; Leonard Hall in *Photoplay*, June 1930); at others, he hinted that it was ("I thought I was smart, but I was a fool....I went to the top years ago, made a mess of things and faded out of the business"; as quoted by columnist Frederick C. Othman, 1938). He opted instead to deal with his reputation by example, presenting himself as a cooperative worker and willing collaborator.

Indeed, among co-workers not named Capra, Langdon was generally described as a kind, easygoing, down-to-earth, likeable fellow not too far removed from his screen character. "Mr. Langdon was absolutely charming," recalled Nell O'Day. "He had very much the same kind of personality off screen that he had as his character in films — a sort of sweet helplessness." Another co-star, Ann Doran, asserted, "Harry was an absolute doll... a sweet, gentle man who never hurt anybody. I really enjoyed working with him." Jules White was delighted that "he was not the man of the reputation that I had heard. He was a very subdued, quiet, nice guy... and he worked like a Trojan. When we called him anytime we wanted him, he was Johnny-on-the-spot."

Yet consider: Mack Sennett was personally comparing him to Chaplin even before Langdon's first comedy had finished shooting. Within 16 months, trade and newspaper critics were in enthusiastic agreement, and with Chaplin taking two or more years between pictures, they along with moviegoers and exhibitors urged that Langdon be moved into features.

Closer to home, Priscilla Bonner perceived Helen Walton as guilty of "feeding [Harry's] ego." He also had a retinue of crewmembers who were unlikely to disagree with him, lest they be released. Plus, there were regular visits from friendly correspondents such as *Moving Picture World*'s Tom Waller, who wrote lengthy articles portraying his every creative decision as a masterstroke of genius that would revolutionize the industry. It might have been impossible for him to avoid, in Capra's words, "the barnacles of conceit."

And if Langdon *was* so afflicted, so what? He wouldn't have been the first such artist, nor would he be the last. Certainly Chaplin wore his self-assuredness and arrogance as a badge of honor to his dying day. As the head of a company that bore his name, Langdon, like Chaplin, had every right to follow his muse wherever it led him. Chaplin, though, had the luxury of time — all that he wanted — to fine-tune his work with precision and infinite care. Langdon had to churn out features every four-to-six months, all but one of which failed to turn a profit. In the end, the paying public determines the validity of a filmmaker's artistic choices and the guidance he chooses to accept or disregard.

Moreover, Chaplin relished the power of being in charge of his own company; Langdon dreaded it. He tried in earnest to meet the demands of his contract — even though his instincts told him they were unreasonable — and just get the pictures out. He didn't have the stomach to push back or the financial resources to take as much time as he believed necessary, as Chaplin did on both counts. As far as he was concerned, *that* was the catalyst for everything that subsequently went wrong, from the dissension with Capra to the failure of his corporation.

In late 1932, he told *Motion Picture Magazine*'s Sonia Lee:

> The trouble with me was that I was pushed through pictures too fast…I was turning them out without preparation — without giving situations a chance to mature, or to be worked out with the infinite care comedy requires.
>
> When superlative praise was given to "Long Pants," I knew the curtain was slowly coming down for me. The extravagant terms critics used were in reality a death knell for me. I knew, if no one else realized at the moment, the fundamental weakness of the picture — and the difficulties under which it was made.
>
> I had been talked into producing my own pictures — and they were financially fatal. I trusted directors and writers, and business managers. When I needed every bit of energy for a scene before the camera, I was harassed by business squabbles and by internal strife — as unnecessary as it was selfish. The worries of management destroyed my peace of mind — I couldn't concentrate.
>
> There's no doubt that fear of criticism licked me. If I had gone ahead, depended on my own judgment, insisted on a schedule of picture-making that would permit me to do good work — I would have continued to be Harry Langdon, the star.

This is as close as Langdon ever came to describing the heartbreak of the First National years; even then, he omitted the many personal distractions engendered by his separation from Rose and courtship of Helen. It is significant that this interview took place near the outset of his romance with Mabel Sheldon. Once they married and their son was born, he pretty much closed the book on the past. His greatest screen triumphs went hand-in-hand with the most painful years of his life, so there was little desire on his part to revisit the past beyond reworking a few of the better gags in new films.

Among film historians, critics and fans, a perception exists that Chaplin and Lloyd were the most successful of Agee's "Big Four," while Langdon and Keaton were mostly wasted in inferior vehicles once the silent era ended. The perception is true only if "success" is defined by the amount of money each man earned and saved. In truth, during the sound era Chaplin and Lloyd turned out a handful of films that were less adventuresome and free-spirited as their older work, and spent the majority of those years in the comfort of their respective mansions. Lloyd indulged a passion for hobbies such as 3D photography; Chaplin, when not traveling and greeting dignitaries, toiled over scripts and produced films that found little favor among critics or the public. Meanwhile, Langdon and Keaton kept busy in unpretentious features and shorts, providing moviegoers with a welcome presence and nearly always adding a spark or two of genuine humor to some occasionally banal proceedings. By *that* measure, Langdon and Keaton share the crown.

Happily, nearly all of Langdon's films survive. A close examination demonstrates conclusively that once he, Edwards, Ripley and Capra got a handle on how to adapt the comic instincts of a successful vaudevillian into those of a screen star, his future was assured. Like any stage performer coming to films, he needed to learn cinema technique; at Sennett's he had the best teachers possible.

Langdon never forgot those lessons. Sometimes his character was overshadowed by poor writing, indifferent direction, or some other form of interference. Sometimes, despite a similarity in costume and gestures, it was completely submerged by a different character altogether. Sometimes Langdon was asked to put "Harry" completely aside and portray a Professor McCrackle, a Henry Butler or a Chester Willoby, and he always acquiesced.

But given an opportunity to bring the Little Elf to life, Langdon nearly always rose to the occasion, and demonstrated once more the greatness promised by his earliest films and realized in the silent classics. Those who insisted he never understood his character merely resented his lack of emphasis upon one aspect or another to which they felt proprietary. The heart and soul of the character was always his alone.

Whatever pain he endured during his meteoric rise and descent, however damaging the tales that have been told and retold, time is on Harry Langdon's side. If in doubt, merely attend a screening of one of his films. His brand of humor clearly resonates with modern audiences, and the availability of his greatest work on home video ensures that future generations will embrace him, long after the myth has faded from memory.

Harry Langdon received a star on the Hollywood Walk of Fame in 1960. Photo taken in 2012.

The Films of Harry Langdon

This filmography purports to list every original film in which Harry Langdon appeared in his lifetime, as well as films that he directed and/or co-wrote. The list is chronological by release date, not production; thus two of the three films Langdon made in 1923 for Principal Pictures appear at the point of their 1925 release. The third Principal title, *The Skyscraper* (a.k.a. *The Greenhorn*), appears to have never received a release and is not listed here. A handful of films are, at this writing, considered lost or were otherwise unavailable for screening. In those instances, we have obtained production and plot details from written sources, such as copyright submissions, pressbooks and cutting continuities. Otherwise, the authors have personally viewed every title.

In addition to a detailed synopsis, we have provided analysis for the films that we viewed. These entries are, of course, subjective, but both authors have expressed disappointment in books that do not include the writers' opinions on the work of their subjects. Even when there is disagreement, such analysis can spur a healthy debate or at least make us want to view the work. That's our goal here.

We have also included, wherever possible, each film's "Harry Moment." The authors define this as a scene or gag in each film that is most Langdonesque; something that no other comedian could have pulled off as successfully. This is also subjective. Some of the least amusing titles in Langdon's canon contain such a moment, and some otherwise very funny films do not.

Finally, we have gathered reviews from the trade and mainstream press, and also exhibitor comments, for each film in which they could be located. The authors plowed through various Internet databases and microfilmed periodicals to retrieve this material, and we believe it provides an excellent snapshot of how Langdon's comedy was perceived by both critics and moviegoers, without the bias of latter-day revisionist criticism.

The list concludes with the most significant theatrical films and television programs in which Langdon appeared via archival footage.

Picking Peaches

A Mack Sennett Comedy Released in Two Reels. **DIRECTED BY** Erle C. Kenton. **SUPERVISED BY** F. Richard Jones. **TITLES BY** John A. Waldron. **PHOTOGRAPHED BY** George Spear. **CAST**: Harry Langdon, Alberta Vaughn, Ethel Teare, Andy Clyde, Jack Cooper, Alice Day, Vernon Dent, Cecile Evans, Dot Farley, Eugenia Gilbert, Thelma Hill, Si Jenks, Irene Lentz, Horace "Kewpie" Morgan, Leo Sulky, Roscoe "Tiny" Ward, Joe Young, Mack Sennett's Bathing Beauties (Mary Akin, Marceline Day, Dorothy Dore, Evelyn Francisco, Elsie Tarron, Gladys Tennyson, Hazel Williams). **WORKING TITLES**: "Trifling," "A Ribbon Clerk's Romance." Copyright January 9, 1924, Registration Number L19812. Released by Pathé Exchange, Inc., February 3, 1924.

SYNOPSIS: Harry is a married shoe salesman for a department store. A frugal man, he refuses to allow his wife to purchase a second-hand hat. After an unfortunate breakfast, during which he'd mistaken his wife's new powder puff for a pancake, he heads to work. He unintentionally offends some of the female customers, and his boss threatens to fire him.

Later in the day, one of his "regulars" — a middle-aged woman — lures him away for some fun and games at the beach. Meanwhile, Harry's wife is also there with a friend. She spots her flirtatious husband playing games with some bathing beauties. Later, Harry and his customer friend take in a beauty and diving contest. Harry's wife enters masked, and with a spectacular (animated) dive, she wins the grand prize: a $3,500 wardrobe from the department store.

Back at work, Harry sees his wife obtain the wardrobe and is puzzled. He examines the bill of sale, approved by his boss, and assumes the worst. He follows his boss home, mistaking the boss's wife for his own, and confronts him with violence. Once he realizes his mistake, he tries to escape only to wind up in the bed of a married man, who mistakes him for the wife. When that ruse is discovered, more violence follows.

Emerging from the hospital with his wife, a bandaged Harry briefly imagines how a pretty nurse would look in a bathing suit, and then decides he'd best stick with the woman beside him.

Although the second to be produced, this was Harry Langdon's first motion picture release for Mack Sennett, as well as Sennett's 13th release for distributor Pathé Exchange, Inc. Langdon's role was originally intended for Jack Cooper, who appears as the Fashion Show's master of ceremonies.

ANALYSIS: A very disjointed comedy filled with typical Mack Sennett gags and very little characterization. Langdon wears little facial makeup, which exposes his true age, and he essays the role of a middle-aged flirtatious husband in the standard Sennett manner. Action moves from Harry's home life, to his work life, to the beach, to the beauty contest, back to work, to his jealous pursuit of his boss, to a married man's bed, to a hospital; all of it appearing arbitrary, as if the whole film had been built from scratch during shooting.

The slapstick is also arbitrary and mostly mechanical, with such standard Sennett devices as bursts of powder emerging from Harry's mouth and ears, the animated high-dive, the jealous husband shooting literal daggers from his eyes (also animated), and Harry being knocked out of a window and hanging from

a ladder. That said, these gags seldom fail to draw laughter from audiences.

Overall the film is a cut-and-dried slapstick opus that does not show Harry to any great advantage.

HARRY MOMENT: Far and away the highlight is when Harry mistakes his wife's powder-puff for a pancake. Unlike other comics, he doesn't react immediately and perform a spit-take or exaggerated grimace after one bite. However unpleasant, he's determined to get that pancake down, and his expressions are priceless. It's fitting that, in a film that almost never stops moving, Langdon puts his very first stamp on a scene in which he is sitting still and his eyes do all of the work. The laughs are genuine and they build steadily throughout. Only when his wife cries out does Harry realize what he's eaten, and when he exhales a burst of white powder, it's a perfect topper. Unfortunately, it's carried too far when powder also emerges from his ears.

WHAT THE CRITICS SAID:
The Manitowoc (WI) Herald-News, *January 11, 1924; Reviewed by Jack Jungmeyer*

Just as the affliction of chilblains was becoming almost unbearable throughout our fair land, Mack Sennett thaws out some of the frost by parading his 1924 Bathing Girls on the screen.

Sennett used the same picture, Picking Peaches, *to launch his new star, Harry Langdon, hailed as his "latest and greatest comedy find," and also as another potential Charlie Chaplin. Be that as it may,* Picking Peaches *gives Langdon the role of a shoe clerk with a handsome lady clientele, notably Dot Farley and Eugenie Gilbert, and a brand of comedy which will not go over the head of the simplest viewer.*

It is as funny as an eye-straying married man looking at a strange woman's walking appendages (these censors are certainly making us brush up a vocabulary) and eating his wife's powder puff instead of a hotcake in his embarrassment. As funny as the shoe clerk trying to detach another woman's nether limb in the, to him, reasonable belief that it is a shoplifted wooden leg. As funny as the cat scratching a fair customer's upper ankle, eliciting her sharp query of the clerk over a newspaper, "Is that necessary?" and her further enraged outburst, "You fresh thing!" as the hidden cat encores its performance.

As funny as — well, you get the drift of Mack Sennett's latest and greatest comedy. It's as funny as a phallic sign — and no funnier.

With so much stress on legs (let's call 'em that just this once, Mr. Censor) it's rather difficult to keep Harry Langdon within the ken of critical appraisal. He was personable and seemed an earnest and deserving young man. But as to his ability, it would be rather unfair to judge by this his initial vehicle. The multiplicity of legs steal all the available laughs. Indeed, even the bathing beauties introduced later in the picture, suffer by the preliminary pedal

"Tiny" Ward, Langdon, Vernon Dent and Irene Lentz in Picking Peaches.

pulchritude, for the surprise element has been sunk in surefeit. Those tired business men and the sidewalk sheiks for whom animated hose always contains the element of film-temple comedy, have completely exhausted their hearty outbursts before the bathing bevy promenades its pranks. So it was, at least, at the Picking Peaches *premiere here.*

Motion Picture News, *February 2, 1924; Reviewed by Chester J. Smith*

This first of a new series of Sennett Comedies reveals a new comedian in Harry Langdon and a new batch of bathing beauties, but apparently there is nothing else in the Sennett repertoire. Langdon, in the role of the disgruntled husband eventually discovers that beauty, like charity, begins at home. At the seaside with a fair companion he is a witness to a beauty contest, in which his wife, as a masked bather, is the winner. Not knowing her identity he becomes enamored of her and the truth is ultimately revealed to him.

The story is somewhat lacking in humor, though Langdon makes the most of the various situations. However, in this picture at least, he is hardly up to the standard of some past Sennett comedians.

Sennett still retains his eye for beauty of face and figure and introduces some bathing girls who are good to look at either in ballroom gown, or as they pose in bathing costumes in the beauty contest.

Moving Picture World, *February 2, 1924; Reviewed by M.K.*

Mack Sennett introduces a new screen comedian in this — Harry Langdon — who proves an expert in humorous expression. He has the art of getting a wealth of laughter out of small incidents. The scene, for instance, where he attempts to masticate a powder puff, thinking it a pancake and is trying to convince himself that it must be a pancake is a fine piece of captivating nonsense. His adventures and thrills as a shoe clerk are thoroughly amusing. The title refers to the diving contest, an angle that will be appealing to a great many, as many attractive girls, bathing beauties, are seen. There is something new about Harry Langdon's personality and technique that holds out a flattering promise for the series of comedies in which he is to be starred.

WHAT THE EXHIBITORS SAID:
Exhibitors Herald, *March 15, 1924*
A peach of a comedy. Langdon, if handled right, should come along.
W. H. Mart, Strand Theatre, Grinnell, IA.
College town patronage.

Exhibitors Herald, *April 5, 1924*
A1. In a class by itself. A scream. Very high class. 100 percent entertainment.
A. F. Jenkins, Community Theatre, David City, NE.

Moving Picture World, *April 13, 1924*
A good bathing girl slapstick comedy. Moral tone fair. Not suitable for Sunday here. Had fair attendance. Draw farmers in town of 2,500.
E. J. Longaker, Howard Theatre (350 seats).
Alexandria, MN.

Moving Picture World, *May 17, 1924*
This new Mack Sennett comedy is certainly a peach. It's a laugh from start to finish. A real old-time Sennett. In Langdon he has made a real comedy find. The 1924 bathing suit girls make quite a splash in *Picking Peaches*. Book it. Draw mixed class in city of 12,000.
C. B. Hartwig, Antlers Theatre (500 seats),
Helena, MT.

Exhibitors Herald, *June 28, 1924*
Very good. A comedy that is worthy of the designation. Plenty of Sennett bathing girls present to add luster and spice. I would say this fellow is there. More real laughs heard than in some time.
L. F. Woolcott, Grand Theatre, Eldora, IA.
Small town patronage.

Exhibitors Herald, *July 26, 1924*
This fellow is funny, but [I] fail to see another Chaplin in any possible way. Pathé advertises him as a "find," but he just makes a good comedian as far as I can see.
Henry Reeve, Star Theatre, Menard, TX.
Small town patronage.

Exhibitors Herald, *August 2, 1924*
Right here you have a comedy as good as the old Keystones, and the old-timers in this business know what that means. A real knockout that makes 'em laugh right out loud and they are not ashamed to do it. Yes, Mack Sennett is hitting on high and I, for one, appreciate his efforts.
W. H. Brenner, Cozy Theatre, Winchester, IN.

Exhibitors Herald, *August 9, 1924*
One of the best Mack Sennett has ever made. Has plenty of bathing girls, and everything.
W. E. Elkin, Temple Theatre, Aberdeen, MS.
Neighborhood patronage.

Exhibitors Herald, *September 6, 1924*
This one is a riot. Can't say enough for it. They all walk out smiling. Give us more like this one. People stopped me on the street to tell me how good it was.
Mrs. W. J. Carter, Maxine Theatre, Croswell, MI.
Small town patronage.

Exhibitors Herald, *September 20, 1924*
A peach of a comedy. My first from Pathé in a long time, but if this is a fair example it won't be the last by a long shot. People said best comedy in months.
Mrs. Linnie M. Carter, Court Theatre, Huntingdon, TN.
Small town patronage.

Exhibitors Herald, *November 29, 1924*
They laughed at this one and that is what we want comedies for.
F. L. Johnson, Johnsonian Theatre, Ripley, NY.
Small town patronage.

Exhibitors Herald, *February 7, 1925*
   Like all other exhibitors have said, it is good, but it is better for adults. The kids didn't like it.
J. J. Eagen, American Theatre, Wautoma, WI.
Small town patronage.

Exhibitors Herald, *April 24, 1926*
   Langdon is good and I've had many favorable comments, Some good laughs in this one and would call it a first rate comedy.
Ross & Miller, Community Theatre, Surprise, NE.
Country patronage.

Smile Please

A Mack Sennett Comedy Released in Two Reels. DIRECTED BY Roy Del Ruth. SUPERVISED BY F. Richard Jones. TITLES BY John A. Waldron. PHOTOGRAPHED BY George Spear. CAST: Harry Langdon, Alberta Vaughn, Jack Cooper, Madeline Hurlock, Roscoe "Tiny" Ward, Jackie Lucas, Billy Armstrong, Louise Carver, Andy Clyde, Cecile Evans, Cameo the Dog. WORKING TITLE: "Look Pleasant." Copyright January 9, 1924, Registration Number L19811. Released by Pathé Exchange, Inc., March 2, 1924.

SYNOPSIS: Harry, a portrait photographer, doubles as the sheriff in a small town. When a young woman out riding is unable to stop her runaway horse, Harry "rides" to the rescue in his auto. He also thwarts a rival's rescue attempt and wins the girl's affection. The rival attempts revenge, first by setting Harry's studio aflame, but this backfires when Harry rescues the girl from the fire, which ensures her devotion. At the wedding, the rival tries to convince the girl that her husband-to-be is unfaithful. This almost works when Harry is called away to stop a burglar at a married woman's home, but it turns out the invader is the woman's husband. After the wedding, Harry photographs some of his wife's relations, and must contend with a mischievous lad who not only gets underfoot, but also brings a hornet's nest and a skunk onto the premises.

Louise Carver, Billy Armstrong, Cameo the Dog, Alberta Vaughn and Jackie Lucas are being photographed by Harry in Smile Please.

Smile Please was the first Harry Langdon comedy produced by Mack Sennett, filmed during October 1923. Langdon's role was originally intended for Harry Gribbon.

ANALYSIS: Less disjointed than *Picking Peaches*, *Smile Please* is also less amusing. Its gags are almost entirely of the mechanical and wire-work variety that could be competently delivered by any comedian. A particularly cartoonish gag: kicked by the girl's horse, Harry winds up with the imprint of a horseshoe on his face that has disappeared by the next shot. Many of the jokes were considered old in 1924. Called to Harry's studio, the fire department sees fit to engage in some calisthenics before attempting to douse the fire, a gag that Chaplin used to better advantage in *The Fireman* from 1916. Certainly the hornets' nest and skunk were old wheezes by this time. Langdon has pitifully few moments of comedic facial expression, but makes the most of what he's been given.

HARRY MOMENT: All dressed up for his wedding, Harry is alerted by the Best Man that he left the coat hanger in his jacket, the handle of which is visible at the back of his neck. He tries to remove it without causing a disruption, but the minister becomes angry at his gyrations. Once again, in a film filled with frenetic movement, Langdon delivers solid laughs mainly through facial expression and in trying to remain as still as possible while removing the hanger.

WHAT THE CRITICS SAID:
Moving Picture World, *March 1, 1924; Reviewed by C.S.S.*

In the second comedy in which he has been starred by Mack Sennett, Harry Langdon does good work and there are a goodly number of laughs, however it does not measure up to the high standard as a fun producer attained by his first comedy, Picking Peaches. *Langdon appears as a sheriff who is a photographer on the side and much of the fun takes place in a studio. There are scenes involving the losing of his trousers, recovering them with a hornet's nest therein and also a chase where he is clad partially in lady's underwear which many will probably consider a bit off-color even though these scenes are quite amusing.*

Harry keeps an eye on Jack Cooper, who is eyeing Alberta Vaughn, in Smile Please.

Motion Picture News, *March 17, 1924; Reviewed by Tom Hamlin*

Rough tactics by a rough comedian will amuse the lovers of the familiar old style slapstick comedy and all the old business is dragged back in.

This is the second of the Mack Sennett comedies featuring Harry Langdon and the action is placed in a photographic gallery with the comedian as the photographer.

Jackie Lucas is in the family about to be photographed and his antics help provide the comedian with most of the opportunities. The cast is good and the action fast throughout.

WHAT THE EXHIBITORS SAID:

Exhibitors Herald, *June 21, 1924*

Ran this with Harold Lloyd in "Grandma's Boy" and it made a dandy program. If all the Langdon comedies hold up to this I am not sorry that I bought them, if I did have to pay above the average.
A. L. Veatch, Princess Theatre, Morganfield, KY.
Small town patronage.

Exhibitors Herald, *July 26, 1924*

Good, but not quite as good as "Picking Peaches," his first one.
I. F. Woolcott, Grand Theatre, Eldora, IA.
Small town patronage.

Moving Picture World, *July 26, 1924*

A knockout comedy by a new star for us. One, however, who will take his place with Lloyd, Keaton and Semon with a few more like this. Tone, okay. Sunday, yes. Small town class. Town of 2,900.
C. L. Smith, Victoria Theatre, Winnfield, LA.

Exhibitors Herald, *September 6, 1924*

Not as good as *Picking Peaches*, but you couldn't hear the music in a couple of places. You can't go wrong on these. Print good.
W.T. Waugh, Empress Theatre, Grundy Center, IA.
Small town patronage.

Exhibitors Herald, *September 20, 1924*

A very good slapstick comedy that got oodles of laughs. At times my "customers" just roared at the situations.
Frank L. Browne, Liberty Theatre, Long Beach, CA.
General audience.

Exhibitors Herald, *September 20, 1924*

This was my first Langdon and it was good. It seems that the price is a little high, but if bought right they should satisfy any exhibitor.
Pugh Moore, Strand Theatre, McKenzie, TN.
Small town patronage.

Exhibitors Herald, *November 8, 1924*

A good comedy. Our first Langdon and he pleased. Print good.
W. T. Waugh, Strand Theatre, Conrad, IA.
Small town patronage.

Exhibitors Herald, *November 15, 1924*

My first Langdon and it is far ahead of the ordinary comedies. Very, very good.
H. J. Eagan, American Theatre, Easley, SC.

Exhibitors Herald, *December 13, 1924*

Not exactly a comedy for a Sunday school, but it caused more laughter than the usual comedy.
Dinsmore & Son, Majestic Theatre, Weinder, AR.
General patronage.

Exhibitors Herald, *March 7, 1925*

A very good comedy. All of this star's work has been good.
C. E. Holt, Legion Theatre, Elmwood, WI.
Small town patronage.

Exhibitors Herald, *March 28, 1925*

This is an extra good one. A little risque in spots but he keeps 'em laughing so much that they kinda overlook it.
Wm. E. Tragsdorf, Trags Theatre, Neillsville, WI.
Small town patronage.

Exhibitors Herald, *May 26, 1927*

A very good comedy. Harry knows how to make a successful job of his situations.
Stoddard brooks, Rex Theatre, Madisonville, TX.
General patronage.

Scarem Much

A Mack Sennett Comedy Released in Two Reels. DIRECTED BY Del Lord. SUPERVISED BY F. Richard Jones. TITLES BY John A. Waldron. PHOTOGRAPHED BY William "Billy" Williams and George Unholz. EDITED BY William Hornbeck. CAST:

George Cooper, Madeline Hurlock, Kalla Pasha, Andy Clyde, Jack Cooper, Sunshine Hart, Gordon Lewis, Grover Ligon, Roscoe "Tiny" Ward, Joe Young, Mack Sennett's Bathing Beauties (Margaret Cloud, Dorothy Dore, Cecile Evans, Evelyn Francisco, Thelma Hill, Elsie Tarron, Gladys Tennyson, Hazel Williams). Ringside audience members (visible in stills): Harry Langdon, Charlie Murray, Fanny Kelly, Marvin Loback, Leo Sulky. Copyright March 20, 1924, Registration Number L20011. Released by Pathé Exchange, Inc., March 23, 1924.

SYNOPSIS: This film was unavailable for viewing. Following is the synopsis submitted to the U.S. Copyright Office:

> Violet Ray, a beautiful girl, has many suitors — among them being Edison Watts. Needless to say she has a very rough father who dislikes every suitor she ever had and quickly gives them notice to leave. But Edison is more persistent than the others and determines to elope with Violet. They do elope and get aboard a ship where many things happen not scheduled on a regular honeymoon, but eventually persistence wins out and they meet with the reward that true love should always get.

In stills taken of a boxing match during the first reel, Langdon can clearly be seen among the spectators, but it's unknown if he appears in the finished film.

Shanghaied Lovers

A Mack Sennett Comedy Released in Two Reels. DIRECTED BY Roy Del Ruth. SUPERVISED BY F. Richard Jones. TITLES BY John A. Waldron. PHOTOGRAPHED BY George Spear. CAST: Harry Langdon, Alice Day, Kalla Pasha, Roscoe "Tiny" Ward, Billy Armstrong, Andy Clyde, George Cooper, José Sanchez Garcia, Gordon Lewis, Eli Stanton, Joe

George Cooper has defeated Roscoe "Tiny" Ward while Madeline Hurlock and referee Andy Clyde look on, in this scene from Scarem Much. *The crowd consists of several Sennett stars, including Langdon in the front row (visible under Cooper's arm).*

Young. WORKING TITLE: "A Sailor's Honeymoon." Copyright April 18, 1924, Registration Number L20100. Released by Pathé Exchange, Inc., March 30, 1924.

SYNOPSIS: Newly married, Harry and Alice miss the ship that was to take them to their honeymoon destination. While at the dock, Harry is knocked out

and shanghaied aboard a freighter. As new man on the crew, he is ordered by the burly captain to assist the cook, which he does with mixed results.

Unbeknownst to Harry, Alice has stowed aboard and disguised herself as another sailor. She tries to cling to her husband, who doesn't realize "the new gob" is his wife and objects strenuously, especially when they're forced to bunk together. Eventually Alice is found out, and when the captain and other crewmembers attempt to have their way with her, Harry manages an inept, but effective, rescue. In the ensuing chaos, the freighter veers into the rocks and is split apart. Luckily, Harry and Alice have salvaged a buoyant section, and enjoy a honeymoon cruise into the sunset.

Incomplete for many years, the film survives thanks to television. The first reel turned up in a kinescope of NBC-TV's *Howdy Doody* program that had been released to home video, while most of the second reel was used in an episode of *The Funny Manns*. Since Langdon appeared several times during the "old movie" section of *Howdy Doody*, it's possible that his other "lost" or incomplete Pathé films will eventually surface in this manner.

ANALYSIS: The first film written specifically for Langdon, *Shanghaied Lovers* is a mixed bag, with several fleeting moments that suggest the Harry to come, combined with some tried-and-true Sennett slapstick.

It's tempting to ascribe the opening sequence to Langdon himself, since it plays on his superstitious nature. Newlyweds Harry and Alice exit the church, whereupon a horseshoe falls from the door frame and strikes Harry on the head. He tosses it away, breaking a mirror in the process. Worried about what this means, Harry is gently scolded by his bride about the folly of superstition. When the couple misses the honeymoon ship, Harry lets Alice know with a glance that he believes the broken mirror to be the cause.

After this, Harry is knocked cold and brought aboard the freighter, and the situations and several

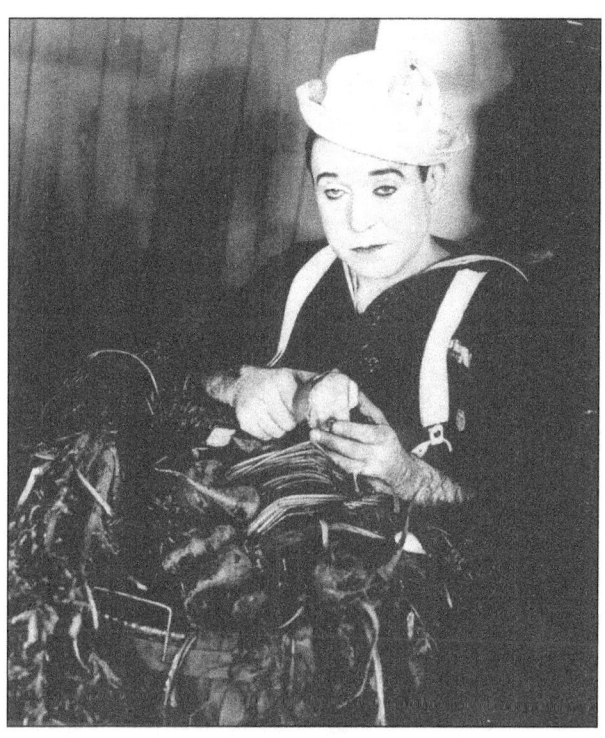

gags are lifted right out of Chaplin's 1915 two-reeler *Shanghaied*. (Interestingly, Billy Armstrong plays a crewman in both films, leading to speculation about his contribution to the plot.) Langdon, like Chaplin, assists the cook, inadvertently spoils the soup, is made queasy by the ship's rocking and becomes doubly seasick when the captain "seasons" his food with kerosene. Of course, Langdon brings his own persona and facial expressions to these scenes.

A novel twist comes when Alice stows aboard, although how she managed it is never explained; she's just there. Her scenes with the apprehensive Harry, who is seriously disturbed by the new "man" staring at him with lovesick puppy eyes, are marvelous. It's easy to see why Sennett eventually gave Alice Day her own starring series; she very nearly walks off with this film.

Until the coming of Harry Edwards, Roy Del Ruth was Langdon's most frequent director at Sennett, but as with *Smile Please* his guidance here is uninspired, with repeated emphasis on slapstick over characterization. To cite one example: near the close, Alice and Harry have settled down to domestic bliss on their little honeymoon craft, with Harry fishing for their dinner. Some character comedy, perhaps Harry struggling with his catch, would have been a nice touch, but Del Ruth is more intrigued with a fish that expectorates tobacco juice.

As Alice Day clings to him, Harry looks unusually heroic in Shanghaied Lovers.

HARRY MOMENT: Harry brings soup to the captain, not realizing a box of rubber bands has emptied into it. Having struggled with its chewy contents, the captain orders Harry to partake, which he does with extreme difficulty. As with the "pancake" in *Picking Peaches*, Harry's facial expressions enhance the scene (although in the existing print, the rocking of the ship causes him to periodically disappear from the frame).

Worthy of honorable mention is the moment when Harry takes pity on the new sailor, actually his wife, reluctantly inviting "him" to share his bunk. As she watches Harry sleep, she can't resist giving him a lengthy kiss. Of course, Harry awakens and his horrified reaction calls to mind the effect that aggressive women will have on him in later films.

WHAT THE CRITICS SAID:
Motion Picture News, *March 29, 1924; Reviewed by Tom Hamlin*

Mack Sennett cast Harry Langdon as the groom and Alice Day as the bride and this comedy is well mounted. Most of the slapstick is resorted to continuously.

Some people may be able to see comedy in a row of apparently seasick men leaning over a rail but such a scene is revolting to many and should not be too prolonged, as in this picture…

This will get by where they like their comedy rough but will never make a hit with the too fastidious audiences.

Moving Picture World, *March 29, 1924; Reviewed by C.S.S.*

Harry Langdon, the vaudeville comedian who has successfully starred in a couple of Mack Sennett Comedies, is the star of Shanghaied Lovers*… There is good opportunity for comedy action, much of it of a familiar type but a lot of it quite different. Langdon is excellent, his personality being finely suited to comedy work, and Alice Day as the bride is fine. She is a very attractive girl and will make a hit with the audience when she appears in rough togs with a heavy moustache, so disguised that she even fools her own husband. Some of the comedy involving seasickness and the supposed cooking of a cat in place of a rabbit will probably rub the wrong way with some patrons, but on the whole it is an enjoyable comedy, not quite up to Langdon's previous offerings, but well up to the average Sennett standard.*

WHAT THE EXHIBITORS SAID:
Exhibitors Herald, *June 7, 1924*

Pretty good comedy. Some new gags in this one.
Miller and Wilcox, Lake View Theatre, Lake View, IA.

Exhibitors Herald, *August 2, 1924*

A good comedy. Plenty of action and laughs.
A. F. Jenkins, Community Theatre, David City, NE.

Exhibitors Herald, *September 27, 1924*

A good comedy, but not as good as his previous ones. — Print good.
W. T. Waugh, Empress Theatre, Grundy Center, IA.
Small town patronage.

Exhibitors Herald, *October 4, 1924*

Good comedy. The few of Langdon's that I have played have given almost universal satisfaction.
Pugh Moore, Strand Theatre, McKenzie Theatre.
Small town patronage.

Exhibitors Herald, *June 20, 1925*

Another good Langdon comedy. This boy is certainly a winner. My patrons like him better than Lloyd. Some good trick stuff in this one.
E. F. Ingram, Ingram's theatre, Ashland, AL.
Small town patronage.

Exhibitors Herald, *November 14, 1925*

About two laughs in two reels.
E. H. Brechler, Opera House, Fennimore, WI.
General patronage.

Flickering Youth

A Mack Sennett Comedy Released in Two Reels. DIRECTED BY Erle C. Kenton. SUPERVISED BY F. Richard Jones. TITLES BY John A. Waldron. PHOTOGRAPHED BY George Spear and Bob Ladd. EDITED BY William Hornbeck. CAST: Harry Langdon, Alice Day, Charlie Murray, Ray Grey, Charlotte Mineau, Louise Carver, Andy Clyde, Dorothy Dore, Cecile Evans, Eugenia Gilbert, Roscoe "Tiny" Ward, Kalla Pasha, Marvin Loback, Budd Ross, Eli Stanton, Leo Sulky, Harry Sweet, Joe Young. WORKING TITLE: "The Lather Pushers." Copyright May 6, 1924, Registration Number L20168. Released by Pathé Exchange, Inc., April 27, 1924.

SYNOPSIS: This film was unavailable for viewing. Following is the synopsis submitted to the U.S. Copyright Office:

Harry Langdon is about to wed a nice Society girl when a hated rival steps in on the scene and by a series of circumstances brought on by his cunning devices, succeeds in breaking up the match and has Harry almost married to another woman who has nothing but an inclination for wealth and a good time and at all times. Despite all these circumstances, the sweet young girl still has faith in Harry who overcomes the plots of his rival and eventually marries the girl.

No prints of this film are known to exist.

Charlie Murray looks after Harry in Flickering Youth.

WHAT THE CRITICS SAID:

Exhibitors Herald, *April 26, 1924; Reviewed by Tom Hamlin*

Harry Langdon appears as a wealthy young idler aspiring to the hand of a beautiful girl in his own set.

His trouble commences when he is boldly taken in hand by a robust woman barber, who later sues him after a free for all fight in his home that affords enough excitement for all, including the audience.

The court scene is especially funny and this is one of the best comedies made with Harry Langdon to date.

Our hero finally wins back the charming heroine after an automobile chase that is full of surprises, thrills and laughs.

Moving Picture World, *April 26, 1924; Reviewed by Tom Waller*

This Mack Sennett attraction presents Harry Langdon in a role admirably suited for his type of acting — appearing as a society slob, with lots of money and no brains, he is easily made the butt of practical jokes by a clever lawyer who is in love with his girl. But with all his shortcomings, the girl loves him and he goes through a series of jaw-breaking complications to a wholly unexpected success. A strong arm lady barber misconstrues his intentions when he shows her the engagement ring he is about to give his girl. Laughs don't describe what is provoked by his antics with the "barbaress." He is almost married to her when her friends, who have invited themselves to his home, decide to indulge in a free-for-all. Several of Sennett's bathing beauties are shown to advantage in this battle. A burlesque on the breach of promise courts will also prove a big laugh getter.

Cleveland Plain Dealer, *April 28, 1924*

There is a fine Mack Sennett comedy in this new State bill, called Flickering Youth. Done in the new Mack Sennett style with a promising young comedian named Harry Langdon, it stretches the laughs consistently. The bathing beauties are absent, but there are some touches of genuine, sparkling burlesque and satire.

Alice Day isn't pleased with the attention Harry's getting from lady barber Charlotte Mineau in this lobby card.

WHAT THE EXHIBITORS SAID:

Moving Picture World, *November 8, 1924*

Good comedy and that's all you want. Print good. Sunday, yes. All classes in big city. Admission ten cents.
Stephen G. Brenner, Eagle Theatre (298 seats), Baltimore, MD.

Moving Picture World, *January 2, 1925*

This brought the laughs pretty well. A few elaborate, Mack Sennett slapstick stunts are employed, but Langdon's mug and posture are chiefly relied upon. Tone, okay. Sunday, okay. Audience appeal, okay. Rural and small town class town of 400.
E. L. Partridge, Pyam Theatre (250 seats), Kinsman, OH.

Exhibitors Herald, *August 15, 1925*

A pretty fair comedy. Print not very good.
Andrew Rapp, Theatorium Theatre, Emlenton, PA. General patronage.

Exhibitors Herald, *August 22, 1925*

Very good comedy.
Nyman Kessler, Atlantic Theatre, Atlantic, MA. General patronage.

Exhibitors Herald, *October 10, 1925*

Very poor comedy. Nothing in it for kids and too silly for grown-ups. Had to cut several places.
F. A. Millhouse, Star Theatre, Sumner, NE. Small town patronage.

Exhibitors Herald, *November 28, 1925*

If this bird is a find I wish he would strut his groceries. Haven't run any of his comedies yet that could be rated more than fair. One or two attempts to be vulgar and lack of comedy makes this very ordinary.
A. F. Botsford, Palace Theatre, Long Pine, NE. Small town patronage.

Exhibitors Herald, *December 12, 1925*

A very poor comedy, as are all of Langdon's I have run.
E. H. Brechler, Opera House, Fennimore, WS. General patronage.

Exhibitors Herald, *May 1, 1926*

This is a good one.
Julius Schmidt, Grand Theatre, Breese, IL. General patronage.

Exhibitors Herald, *May 8, 1926*

Fairly good comedy. Pleased the kids very much.
William Wiske, Community Theatre, Red Granite, WI. Small town patronage.

The Cat's Meow

A Mack Sennett Comedy Released in Two Reels. DIRECTED BY Roy Del Ruth. SUPERVISED BY F. Richard Jones. TITLES BY John A. Waldron. PHOTOGRAPHED BY Billy Williams and Leland Davis. EDITED BY William Hornbeck. CAST: Harry Langdon, Alice Day, Kalla Pasha, Lucille Thorndike, Roscoe "Tiny" Ward, Madeline Hurlock, Louise Carver, Budd Ross, Cecile Evans, Marvin Loback, Andy Clyde, Gordon Lewis, Eli Stanton. WORKING TITLE: "A Southern Exposure." Copyright May 6, 1924, Registration Number L20167. Released by Pathé Exchange, Inc., May 25, 1924.

SYNOPSIS: This film was unavailable for viewing. Following is the synopsis found in the film's file, from the Mack Sennett archive at the AMPAS Margaret Herrick Library:

As the story opens, Harry Langdon is courting Alice Day. He pays the girl a visit to meet her parents, Buddy Ross playing the father and Mrs. Thorndike, character woman, the mother.

Alice lives in a big, palatial home, and when Harry arrives he is met at the door by a liveried butler, Tiny Ward. He makes an undignified entry, falling on the polished floor and sliding into the living room, then gets his fingers mixed up with some dried chewing gum, stuck on a chair. This he transposes to the father's fingers, when he shakes hands with him. He is showing his photographs to the family when an automobile horn summons the mother to a window.

In answer to the horn, Mother says she will be right down, and with Father and a visiting friend they get their hats on, to take a trip to the slums, as they all belong to an Uplift Club. The elders go in one car to do some investigating, while Harry and the girl go to see sights for themselves in another car.

As the second car reaches the Tenderloin section of the city, Alice's gaze hits upon a notorious café sign reading, "The Cat's Meow," and wants to go in. Harry is somewhat afraid and tells her she is apt to get hurt with all the roughnecks present and suggests that they go to the drugstore for an ice-cream soda

instead. The girl wins out though, and they approach the entrance where they hesitate until the check-boy grabs Harry's hat and coat, and a waiter insists they follow him to a table in the very center of the smoke filled room. Harry realizes they are very much out of their element, but is scared to death for fear someone else may see his fear, and he tries hard to look at ease under the conditions.

To those familiar at all with the queer little cafés in New York's Greenwich Village section, the café scene in *The Cat's Meow* will be interesting, as they are quite true and not too far fetched. Langdon and Alice are the center of attraction as they sit at a table dressed in evening clothes, and their presence is almost resented by some of the tougher element, all of which goes to make some of the most humorous material ever screened. As is usual in such places, the evening breaks up in a grand free-for-all-fight, and Harry's endeavor to protect Alice is greatly mussed up in the melee. So much so that when the cops come to clear the place, Harry is carried out on a streetcar, announcing, "Well we'll go to the drugstore anyhow, won't we, dear?"

As a result of this experience of her daughter's, also their own observations of conditions in the Latin Quarter of their fair city, Alice's mother and the other members of the Purity League, decide to appoint a special policeman who, with their aid, will help clean up the city. The honorary position goes to Harry and he assumes the unpleasant duty of whipping the toughs of the neighborhood into submission. As a policeman, he was a great duty dodger.

The antics of Langdon in an ill-fitting, odd looking uniform of semi-English cut, with high pointed helmet, goes out to meet his Waterloo. Almost immediately, he comes across a crap game, but on second thought he decides it best to let it progress and not interfere. Instead he approaches two young children fighting and warns them they will be punished one day for their actions and gets a punch in the eye from a little boy for his trouble. Following this he is approached by an Italian woman, in the person of Madeline Hurlock, who asks his protection from her husband whom she claims has given her a terrible beating. She asks for his arrest and points the brute out to Langdon. One look at his seven feet in height and the new cop gets cold feet. However, having sworn he will do his duty even at the risk of his own life, the new cop crosses the street to where the wife-beating husband is standing on the corner with a dazed and stupid expression on his face. As Langdon gets closer to him, he does not move, although the cop does not know he has been hit on the head just a minute previous and, though standing, he is not conscious. When Langdon learns this he bravely takes him by the arm and leads him towards a police call box, to ask for the patrol to be sent, after his victim. When the other toughs see this cop leading their champion to the lock-up, they stand back in admiration for his nerve, and with just a look, they all scamper away from him.

As he leads his man down the street, his sweetheart, her mother, father and other members of the Purity League drive in range, see him with the giant and admire him too, also compliment him on taking the biggest man first. Langdon's actions while leading the dazed giant down the street, provides some of the most humorous comedy to be imagined. Arriving at the call box, the new cop handcuffs himself and his prisoner together so he can use both hands more easily. While he is calling, a laborer in a building empties a pail of water out of the window and it falls on the giant's head reviving him. When he sees he is fastened to the little shrimp of a policeman, he picks him up and throws him over his head, and a chase begins, which finishes with Langdon leading all the roughnecks into the patrol wagon, locking the door behind them, then giving orders for the driver to start toward the police station with the load of human terrors.

No prints of this film are known to exist.

WHAT THE CRITICS SAID:
Film Daily, *May 18, 1924*

Harry Langdon does exceedingly good work in this. He's funnier than ever before. He is seen as the very timid sweetheart of a sweet young thing whose imposing mother is the head of a purity league the purpose of which is to clean up the slums. "The Cat's Meow" is a cabaret and dance hall of most doubtful nature. Langdon and his girl on a slumming party go in to look it over. The comedy ensuing is really funny. Langdon's facial expressions put it over in great shape. The second reel shows Langdon appointed policeman by the purity league to clean up the slums and incidentally, "The Cat's Meow." The chase stuff is different and funny. Don't miss this one. Get it sure.

Motion Picture News, *May 24, 1924; Reviewed by Tom Hamlin*

Comedy business reminiscent of former releases of both Chaplin and Lloyd appear in this Mack Sennett comedy but the comedian Harry Langdon also has an original style of his own and provides plenty of merriment throughout.

This one is very well produced and has a large and all-sufficient cast...

In spite of some crudeness, occasionally encountered, this is a comedy that will register the hearty laughter in great volume with the average audience.

WHAT THE EXHIBITORS SAID:
Exhibitors Herald, *November 29, 1924*

A good comedy, although not as good as *Smile Please* and *Picking Peaches*. Print good.
W. T. Waugh, Empress Theatre, Grundy Center, IA.
Small town patronage.

Exhibitors Herald, *December 6, 1924*

This fellow is genuinely funny. In a day when many of the comedies are just a collection of gags (notably Educationals) he builds up his business cleverly and is making a name for himself.
Henry Reeve, Star Theatre, Menard, TX.
Small town patronage.

Exhibitors Herald, *December 20, 1924*

Fairly funny.
Wm. E. Tragsdorf, Trag's Theatre, Neillsville, WI.
Small town patronage.

Moving Picture World, *February 14, 1925*

This is a wow. Star and stunts original. This bird Langdon introduced in this comedy as an open faced youth lives up to the name and sure gets the laughter. Tone, good. Sunday, yes. Audience appeal, one hundred per cent. Small town class town of 2,500.
A. L. Middleton, Grand Theatre, (500 seats), DeQueen, AR.

Exhibitors Herald, *May 23, 1925*

This Langdon comedy has too much cheat stuff in it to take in a small town. A few clever stunts, but mostly rough joint brawls.
W. L. Douglas, Strand Theatre, Newman Grove, NE.
Small town patronage.

A wild, wild slapstick which pleased the majority.
I. R. Gavin, Hammond Theatre, Hammond, WI.
Small town patronage.

Exhibitors Herald, *July 18, 1925*

Not as good as some of his pictures, but my patrons get a kick out of Langdon's looks alone. He would not have to act.
Phillip B. Peitz, Rialto Theatre, New England, ND.
Small town patronage.

Exhibitors Herald, *August 22, 1925*

Good comedy, though not as funny as some his others. He makes a good "cop" just the same.
Nyman Kessler, Atlantic Theatre, Atlantic, MA.
General patronage.

Exhibitors Herald, *October 17, 1925*
   This is a very good two reel comedy with several good laughs.
W. J. Shoup, De Luxe Theatre, Spearville, KS.
Small town patronage.

Exhibitors Herald, *November 21, 1925*
   I billed this independently. We advertised Langdon as the latest comedy find who was climbing up the electric ladder to stardom. Also advertised the comedy as "wild, wild slapstick" (quoted from the "Box Office Record"). Result: All the long distance laugh heavers in the country were present and the uproar was terrific. Guards had to be summoned from the State Funny House to take away one young dame who couldn't stop shrieking and two others are being held under close observation for volcanic eruptions. Oh, Harry, be careful!
Phillip Rand, Rex Theatre, Salmon, ID.

Exhibitors Herald, *June 5, 1926*
   This is O. K.
J. W. Schmidt, Breese Theatre, Breese, IL.
General patronage.

His New Mamma

A Mack Sennett Comedy Released in Two Reels. **DIRECTED BY** Roy Del Ruth. **SUPERVISED BY** F. Richard Jones. **TITLES BY** John A. Waldron. **PHOTOGRAPHED BY** Billy Williams. **EDITED BY** William Hornbeck. **CAST:** Harry Langdon, Madeline Hurlock, Alice Day, Andy Clyde, Jack Cooper, Roscoe "Tiny" Ward, Mack Sennett's Bathing Beauties (Mary Akin, Margaret Cloud, Dorothy Dore, Ceclie Evans, Evelyn Francisco, Eugenia Gilbert, Thelma Hill, Natalie Kingston, Elsie Tarron, Gladys Tennyson). **WORKING TITLE:** "The Taxi Scab." Copyright May 28, 1924, Registration Number L20250. Released by Pathé Exchange, Inc., June 22, 1924.

SYNOPSIS: At a drafty cabin on a snowy Christmas Eve, Harry's papa introduces him to "his new mamma," who is unfortunately a gold-digger interested in the old man's fortune. When interaction between "mamma" and her new son seems a little too flirtatious to his liking, Papa forces Harry to sleep beside him. Harry's excited about Santa's imminent arrival, though, and heads downstairs to the fireplace. But a couple of balloons come loose from the tree and frighten him, so he races upstairs and takes refuge in a closet, in the room where mamma sleeps. Papa catches him there and, after a wild chase through the snow, throws him out.

A title card reads: "A new job, a new life." Now a taxi driver, Harry is at the train depot waiting for a fare. By grabbing a disembarking passenger's valise, he forces its owner to accept a ride. The man is the wealthy guardian of Alice, who takes a shine to Harry. The Sennett Bathing Beauties enter the cab and ask to be taken to the beach, where they frolic before the camera. Harry doffs his own bathing suit and joins them, then happens to spy his "mamma" with a new wealthy escort. He calls his papa, who informs him, "She and that big chauffeur took everything but the snow shovel!" Meanwhile, "mamma" directs the bulky chauffeur to keep Harry and Alice at bay until she's married her new "bankroll." A wild auto chase, involving a fire truck and a police contingent not unlike the Keystone Cops, ensues. Nevertheless, Harry arrives at the church and successfully warns his "new mamma's" next conquest.

The opening few minutes of the film, where Harry is introduced to and interacts with his father's new fiancée, are missing from current prints.

ANALYSIS: Although Roy Del Ruth has not lost his affection for mechanical gags (such as sentient balloons) or animated effects (such as a diving beauty flying over Harry and into the ocean), more character comedy emerges here than in his earlier Langdon films. Until *Flickering Youth* and *The Cat's Meow* can be reexamined, *His New Mamma* stands as the earliest example of what Walter Kerr termed Langdon's "ambiguity." He's adult enough to threaten Papa's relationship with the new woman and to hold a job, yet child enough to expect Santa Claus to fill his stocking. The makeup isn't quite right, yet — Harry's lined brow is plainly visible when in bed, his sleep persistently disrupted by his father's beard — but we're getting closer to the Elf, at least during the first half.

The second reel features a more aggressive Harry, who basically forces Alice's guardian into his cab by stealing the man's bag. The rest is dominated by auto gags: first Harry's taxi, which causes his passenger to somersault whenever it hits a bump in the road, then a typical Sennett climactic chase, with a fire hose that sends cars skidding in circles and cops flying into curbs. In between these extremes is the interval with the beach-bound Bathing Beauties, who get up a softball game for the camera and engage in some fancy diving (for which they steal the inner tubes from Harry's cab), with shots almost identical to those in *Picking Peaches*. But Harry gets the last laugh: inadvertently knocked cold by a wooden plank, he slowly collapses onto Alice's shoulder, welcoming oblivion with a serene smile.

HARRY MOMENT: "Too excited to sleep," as the title card reads, Harry creeps downstairs, looking around for Santa. Convinced that the parlor is empty, he goes over to the fireplace, removes the stocking hung on the mantle, tosses it away disdainfully and replaces it with a much longer one. Pleased with himself, he then carefully removes a note for Santa tucked into his dressing gown and pins it to the stocking.

WHAT THE CRITICS SAID:
Film Daily, *June 15, 1924*

Harry Langdon succeeds in being really funny especially in the first reel of this. His facial expressions are sure-fire laugh getters. Madeline Hurlock looks very well in this too, and there is a good cast including in addition to the Sennett bathing girls, Alice Day, Andy Clyde and Jack Cooper. The early sequences, in which Langdon comes down the stairs in a nightshirt with a lighted candle in his hand, to look for Santa Claus are very funny, as is the sequence in which the old man chased him out into the snow. Altogether, it is an entertaining comedy.

Motion Picture News, *June 21, 1924; Reviewed by Thomas C. Kennedy*

Harry Langdon's rather individualistic work shows off to good advantage in the Mack Sennett two-reeler…

The picture starts off to a good opening scene in which the featured comedian hangs his stocking over the mantle piece in the front parlor in anticipation of a visit from Santa Claus. It's a little farm house and outside the wind howls and the snow drifts up into enormous drifts. From this Way Down East-Old Homestead setting the picture swings into ultra modern stuff, with bathing girls and all that sort of thing. His New Mamma *is a highly*

Andy Clyde, Madeline Hurlock and Langdon.

diverting picture and it should make a hit in all types of Theatres. Alice Day, Andy Clyde, Tiny Ward and Jack Cooper are also in the cast.

Moving Picture World, *June 21, 1924; Reviewed by Sumner Smith*

In this Mack Sennett subject Harry Langdon is assisted by Madeline Hurlock, Alice Day, Andy Clyde,

Andy Clyde's not happy with son Harry in His New Mamma.

Tiny Ward, Jack Cooper and other comedians who seldom fail to score. In the role of farmer boy whose dad brings home a Broadway chicken for a wife, Langdon is immensely funny. The gags are well thought out and put over perfectly — so well, in fact, that reviewers who like to make a pretense of being hard-boiled forgot themselves and laughed right out loud. Langdon has an ideal comedy face and knows how to use it.

He shops that plain in this comedy, from the very start, where he lies in wait for Santa Claus, until the closing scenes on the bathing beach. One of the best gags is where he is in bed with his father and a wind blows the elder man's whiskers so that they tickle Langdon's face. In the second reel Sennett introduces several of his very chic and pleasant-to-the-eye bathing girls. The number is a pippin.

WHAT THE EXHIBITORS SAID:
Exhibitors Herald, *October 25, 1924*
A very good comedy that certainly made them laugh. Would say pleased young and old alike.
R. C. Getting, Lyric Theatre, Chappell, NE.
Small town patronage.

Exhibitors Herald, *November 22, 1924*
One of the very best. Book it and boost it. When I say "boost it," I mean boost way up there.
Pugh Moore, Strand Theatre, McKenzie, TN.
Small town patronage.

Exhibitors Herald, *January 3, 1925*
There are a lot of laughs in this one. Mack's bathing girls also do their stuff.
Wm. T. Tragsdorf, Trags Theatre, Neillsville, WS.
Small town patronage.

Exhibitors Herald, *January 10, 1925*
A real comedy. All of his are good and they get the laughs. Print good.
W. T. Waugh, Empress Theatre, Grundy Center, IA.
Small town patronage.

Exhibitors Herald, *February 14, 1925*
This one is okay.
T. A. Shea, Palace Theatre, McGehee, AR.
Neighborhood patronage.

Exhibitors Herald, *March 21, 1925;*
Moving Picture World, *March 21, 1925*
Barring none, here is one of the best two reel comedies I have ever seen. Plenty of action, pretty girls and everything pep from start to finish.
W. E. Elkin, Temple Theatre, Aberdeen, MS.
Neighborhood patronage.

Exhibitors Herald, *July 11, 1925*
What I call a good comedy. Langdon very popular here. And this one pleased. Has some new stuff and lots of good tricks.
E. F. Ingram, Ingram's Theatre, Ashland, AL.
Small town patronage.

Exhibitors Herald, *September 19, 1925*
Good comedy of the slapstick variety and with the bathing girls on hand. Poor print with cut-outs between reels.
P. G. Eatee, S. T. Theatre, Parker, SD.
Small town patronage.

Exhibitors Herald, *June 12, 1926*
Extremely good.
A. N. Miles, Eminence Theatre, Eminence, KY.
General patronage.

The First 100 Years

A Mack Sennett Comedy Released in Two Reels. DIRECTED BY Harry Sweet. SUPERVISED BY F. Richard Jones. TITLES BY John A. Waldron. PHOTOGRAPHED BY George Crocker and Billy Williams. EDITED BY William Hornbeck. CAST: Harry Langdon, Alice Day, Frank J. Coleman, Louise Carver, Madeline Hurlock, Fanny Kelly, Leo Sulky, Roscoe "Tiny" Ward. Copyright May 28, 1924, Registration Number L20251. Released by Pathé Exchange, Inc., August 17, 1924.

SYNOPSIS: Black Mike, a villain, is forcing his attentions on Alice. Harry arrives and knocks the villain off a cliff.

He and Alice are soon enjoying marital bliss when the new cook arrives. She is a tall, unattractive woman who immediately takes command of the household. Roland Stone, an old pal, arrives for a visit and starts to flirt with Harry's wife.

At Roland's urging, Harry attempts to confront the aggressive cook, with disastrous results. He brings in a dog to frighten the cook but she, in turn, scares the dog, who runs away with Harry. Later, when Harry objects to a party the cook is throwing in the house, she is offended and quits.

Soon, Harry arrives with the attractive Miss Gainsbourg, the new cook. She immediately caters to Harry's every need, much to the annoyance of his wife.

That evening, the new cook reads Harry's fortune. A storm causes the lights to flicker. Several mysterious strangers enter the house and one frightens the new cook in her room, causing her to faint. Harry spots one of the men and runs away from him. Roland gives Harry a pistol and urges him to confront the men.

Harry finds the cook out cold on the floor and revives her. As she is expressing her thanks, Roland and his wife see them and believe him to be romantically involved with her. When they leave the room, a dagger, with a note attached, suddenly lands beside Harry. He tries to read it, but his eyes are obscured by the beard of a tall, dark man standing behind him. Harry flees in terror.

Roland encourages Alice to move out. Harry finds another note stating that his wife is going to leave

with a dangerous criminal. Harry heaves a brick at the departing Roland and knocks him out. All of the mysterious strangers appear and pounce on the criminal; they are actually the police. The cook shows Harry a "Wanted" poster that identifies Roland as Willie Cheatham, a criminal with a $5,000 reward. She reveals that she is a detective.

No copies of the complete short are known to exist; all that remains are the excerpts used in Robert Youngson's *When Comedy Was King* (1960) plus about a minute of additional footage, augmented with recreated title cards obtained from the files on this film housed at the AMPAS Margaret Herrick Library, Mack Sennett Collection.

ANALYSIS: Overall, *The First 100 Years* is an enjoyable romp mostly in the tradition of "haunted house" comedies that everybody from Buster Keaton to Bob Hope has done. With the exception of the opening scene, where an overly aggressive Harry hurls "Black Mike" off a cliff, Langdon portrays a timid, easily confused man caught up in events he can barely comprehend, much less control. Fortunately, the "Black Mike" sequence is over so quickly that it doesn't detract too much from the balance of the picture, and Langdon is able to put his stamp on most of the subsequent scenes. Alice Day, in her last appearance with Harry, turns in her usual fine work, while Madeline Hurlock as Miss Gainsbourg succeeds in a rare sympathetic role, a break from her usual scheming vamp characterizations.

HARRY MOMENTS: As Harry confronts the first cook, he loses his nerve and backs away against a wall. The cook inadvertently flings a meat cleaver that lodges in the wall just above Harry's head and causes a bottle to drip ketchup on his head. His hesitation, then shock at believing he has been cut is conveyed through his expressive eyes.

As Harry reads the first note, the bearded stranger comes up from behind and lowers his beard over Harry's face. Harry slowly lowers his hands until the stranger takes the note from him. While the stranger reads the note, Harry slowly pushes the beard aside, his face now registering pure fear. It's one of the earliest examples of Langdon's unique ability to get laughs by doing almost nothing.

WHAT THE CRITICS SAID:
Film Daily, *August 10, 1924*

The fine hand of Mack Sennett and Harry Langdon's penchant for making two laughs grow where only one grew before put this two-reeler on a plane with the finest of comedy films. The plot revolves around the oft-worked subject of hiring a new cook, but the director and the principals manage to produce enough newness in gags and in the method of presentation to give the thing the air of something entirely new. Several scenes, in which the collection of weird noises shatters the stillness of the night, strange figures scurry across the darkened rooms of the love nest and a surprised close, furnish incidents which are full of interest and rollicking moments.

Motion Picture News, *August 16, 1924; Reviewed by Tom Hamlin*

Here is another combination of Harry Langdon with Mack Sennett. It will make them laugh practically anywhere and is ambitiously mounted. It's the ghost and mystery thing with final denouement that satisfactorily accounts for many of the seemingly far-fetched things that happen during the course of the comedy.

Louise Carver is the fighting cook, and she looks and acts the part to perfection. Alice Day, Madeline Hurlock and Frank Coleman are in the cast and the fun is lively throughout.

Moving Picture World, *August 16, 1924; Reviewed by Tom Waller*

Mack Sennett's The First Hundred Years *(sic) presents Harry Langdon and a cast including Alice Day, Frank Coleman, Louise Carver and Madeline Hurlock in a two-reel sketch into which seems to have been conglomerated all the various phases of human encounter as interpreted in stageland. It starts off as one of those types of comedies which have no particular point of view. Then it seems to develop a plot and finally does in time to secure a highly dramatic ending. The ending eliminates the bewildering middle portion… The whole thing is rather a hodge-podge of about everything. From this standpoint it is certainly an innovation.*

Photoplay, *November 1924*

The most amusing Mack Sennett comedy that Harry Langdon has appeared in thus far.

WHAT THE EXHIBITORS SAID:
Moving Picture World, *November 1, 1924*

A good comedy. Langdon is funny. Not foolish. Watch for his leading lady in this. Miss may to be starred in features sure. Family and student class town of 4,000.
R. J. Self, Star Theatre (600 seats), Decorah, IA.

Exhibitors Herald, — *December 6, 1924*
　Very good indeed. Lots of laughs. Excitement stunts. They want good comedies. Got so they call up and ask what the comedy is.
A. F. Jenkins, Community Theatre, David City, NE. General patronage.

Exhibitors Herald, *March 21, 1925*
　The poorest Langdon we ever ran. All the others were good. This wasn't much.
Dinsmore & Son, Majestic Theatre, Weinder, AR. Small town patronage.

Moving Picture World, *April 4, 1925*
　Good comedy and will please all. Langdon always good. Tone, okay. Sunday, yes. Audience appeal, ninety per cent. Town and country class town of 1,200.
C. R. Self, New Radio Theatre, Correctville, IA.

Exhibitors Herald, *July 11, 1925*
　This bird can sure make them laugh. One of his best. Print fair.
W. T. Waugh, Empress Theatre, Grundy Center, IA. General patronage.

Exhibitors Herald, *September 5, 1925*
　Not so much excitement, but good humor and got lots of laughter.
Geo. J. Kress, Hudson Theatre, Rochester, NY. Neighborhood patronage.

Exhibitors Herald, *April 3, 1926*
　Very good one of that sort. Some fellow said that this was raw in spots, or words to that effect. He must have got a different print than I, because there was nothing smutty in mine.
H. G. Stettmund, Jr., Odeon Theatre, Chandler, OK. Small town patronage.

Exhibitors Herald, *May 26, 1927*
　Fair: Nothing to rave over.
Schaghticoke Amusement Assn., Odd Fellows Hall, Schaghticoke, NY. General patronage.

Newlyweds Harry and Alice Day with their imposing cook, Louise Carver, in The First 100 Years.

The Luck o' the Foolish

A Mack Sennett Comedy Released in Two Reels. DIRECTED BY Harry Edwards. SUPERVISED BY F. Richard Jones. TITLES BY John A. Waldron. PHOTOGRAPHED BY Billy Williams. EDITED BY William Hornbeck. CAST: Harry Langdon, Marceline Day, Madeline Hurlock, Frank J. Coleman, Eli Stanton, Yorke Sherwood, Leo Sulky, Roscoe "Tiny" Ward, Louise Carver, Barney Hellum. WORKING TITLE: "Watch Out." Copyright August 2, 1924, Registration Number L20458. Released by Pathé Exchange, Inc., September 14, 1924.

SYNOPSIS: Harry is trying to get to sleep on a train while Marcie curls her hair. Harry's pants fall out of the sleeping compartment and passengers track the contents down the aisle. He retrieves his possessions, which disturbs his fellow travelers. In the morning, while shaving, Harry bothers a man who is also shaving. The man finds a newspaper clipping describing Harry Hedda, a barber who goes crazy when he sees his wife cut in a can of sardines with his favorite knife. Harry continues to irritate the man.

Marcie examines a note from her Uncle Bill asking for $500 and promising a job for Harry. She checks Harry's wallet and sees that the money is safely inside. Marcie's friend Frank, who is a loudmouth, spots her counting the money. Harry fumbles his way through the passenger car. A sheriff arrives with his prisoner, the infamous McGraw. Harry is frightened of the criminal and is informed by the sheriff that the prisoner's comrade has escaped in a handcart. The comrade pulls up alongside the train and beckons to Harry through a window. The sheriff spots him and handcuffs his prisoner to Harry while he leaves to capture the comrade. The prisoner reveals two pistols strapped to his legs and gives one to Harry, proclaiming them partners. The prisoner begins a shooting match with a train official and Harry is caught in the gunfire. In the confusion Frank lifts Harry's wallet. A shot breaks the handcuffs and the prisoner leaps from the train. As the passengers disembark from the train, Harry discovers his wallet missing.

As a result Harry returns to his old job of uniformed security officer for an upscale neighborhood. He walks a beat before pausing to eat his lunch. As

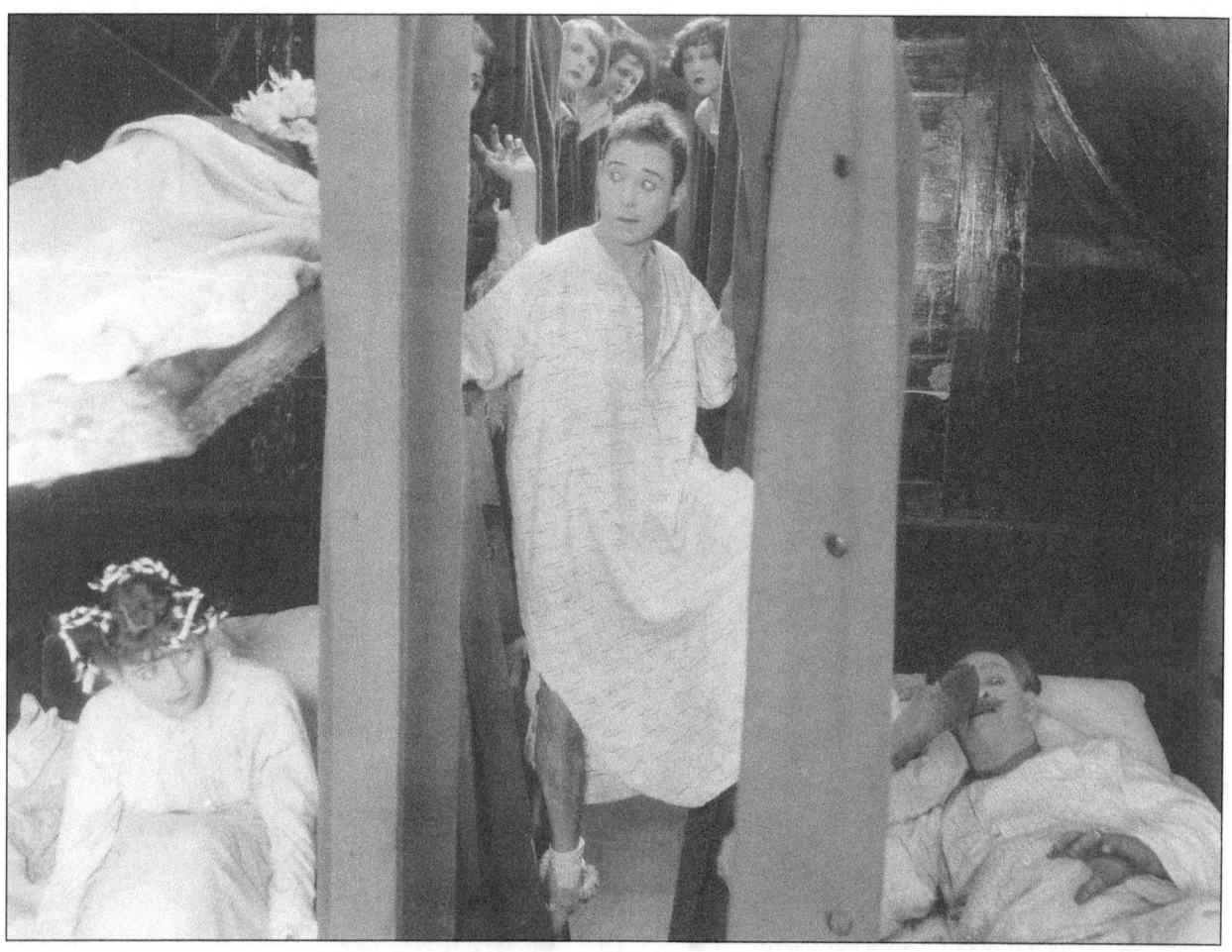

Harry sits and prepares to eat, a telephone operator drops a plug of chewing tobacco, which falls onto Harry's sandwich. Harry doesn't see this and begins to eat. He soon notices that something is wrong and discovers the tobacco after he has eaten much of the sandwich. His vision becomes blurry and he is soon crawling through the street, where he narrowly escapes being run over by a car. As he struggles to his feet, he appears to be regurgitating the offending tobacco but is actually drinking from a water fountain.

Meanwhile, Marcie is working as a seamstress and in the evening delivers some clothing to Madeline's mansion, coincidentally in the same neighborhood that Harry is patrolling. Harry has his first case while on the night shift. He sees an owl and thinks it to be a bad omen. Madeline asks Harry to stop a dog from howling. He enters the backyard and is discovered by the criminal from the train who is casing the joint. Madeline asks Marcie to stay at a party being held in the house. Frank, who is attending the party, drops Harry's wallet. Marcie sees this and agrees to attend the party. Frank retrieves the wallet and shortly thereafter is embracing Marcie. Harry sees this through a window and thinks Marcie is romancing Frank for money. As Marcie is embracing Frank, she retrieves Harry's wallet. Meanwhile, Harry has crawled onto the roof for a better look and falls into the swimming pool. Frank demands the wallet back and begins to chase Marcie. The criminal arrives and throws a bomb at Frank, which lands in the pool. The explosion catapults Harry up onto the ledge outside the room and he grabs a round top of a pillar for a weapon. During the subsequent melee, Harry ends up with another bomb in place of the pillar top. The criminal and Frank react to this and fall into the pool. Marcie shows Harry the wallet and money. In his excitement he drops the bomb; after the explosion they are flung onto the top of a telephone pole. Harry salutes a fellow officer.

The exterior of Madeline's mansion was Mack Sennett's actual home at 141 Westmoreland Place, since demolished.

Footage from the first reel was used in Robert Youngson's *The Golden Age of Comedy*.

Marceline Day, Frank J. Coleman, Eli Stanton and Langdon in Luck o' the Foolish.

ANALYSIS: In his first assignment with Langdon, director Harry Edwards amply demonstrates why he would helm all of the comedian's subsequent films for Sennett. For the most part, he skillfully guides Langdon away from the Sennett formula of snappy pacing and outlandish sight gags into a slower, gentler world. Only the scenes of wind blowing through the train's sleeper car and the explosion that provides a rousing slapstick finale have the typical Sennett touch. Although the costume and makeup aren't there yet — he looks too dapper in his suit and straw hat, and his brow still shows the telltale lines of his true age — Langdon's ultimate screen personality of a too-trusting, eager-to-please, grown-up child emerges with remarkable consistency throughout the film, most especially in his scenes as the neighborhood guard.

HARRY MOMENT: Harry's eating scene with the tobacco is pantomime at its finest. His face runs the gamut from satisfaction to unease to worry to nausea and dizziness. He shows these emotions mostly through his remarkably communicative eyes. At one point they are lidded and he does appear to resemble the "baby dope fiend" perceived by critic James Agee. The scene is shot in one continuous take, during which Harry remains quite still.

WHAT THE CRITICS SAID:
Moving Picture World, *September 13, 1924;*
Reviewed by Tom Waller

Harry Langdon, supported by Madeline Hurlock, Marceline Day and Frank Coleman, under the supervision of F. Richard Jones, appears in one of the best funmakers of his career in The Luck of the Foolish. *This Mack Sennett comedy burlesques a melodrama to such an extent that there is a laugh with every third breath.*

Motion Picture News, *September 20, 1924;*
Reviewed by Thomas C. Kennedy

Harry Langdon provides some pleasant amusement in this Mack Sennett two-reeler. This comedian has an individualistic style and is bringing into comedies something which is a bit out of the beaten track. His eloquent facial expression never fails to amuse and in this play there is a piece of pantomime which registers excellently. The episode referred to is that in which he eats his humble meal of a sandwich, into which a plug of chewing tobacco has found its way…

The Luck of the Foolish should be well received by all picture fans.

WHAT THE EXHIBITORS SAID:
Exhibitors Herald, *April 18, 1925*

The first reel of this is a dandy, as it shows Harry's troubles on a Pullman. The second reel shows him as a night watchman and does not move fast enough. The only reason I have ever discovered for 2-reelers is that they can nick you 3 or 4 times more for them than they do for 1 reelers.
Wm. E. Tragsdorf, Trags Theatre, Neillsville, WI.
Small town patronage.

Exhibitors Herald, *June 20, 1925*
Very good. Got lots of laughter.
W. L. Douglas, Strand Theatre, Newman Grove, NE.
Small town patronage.

Moving Picture World, *November 14, 1925*
This is a good two reel Sennett comedy which furnishes a number of good laughs. Draw town and country class, town 900.
Chas. L. Nott, Opera House (450 seats), Sutherland, IA.

Exhibitors Herald, *November 21, 1925*
A real good two-reel comedy. Nothing to rave about but just one that is a little better than most of them.
W. J. Shoup, De Luxe Theatre, Spearville, KS.
Small town patronage.

Exhibitors Herald, *December 19, 1925*
Harry always gets the laughs for me.
H. M. Retz, Strand Theatre, Lamont, IA.
Small town patronage.

The Hansom Cabman
A Mack Sennett Comedy Released in Two Reels. DIRECTED BY Harry Edwards. SUPERVISED BY F. Richard Jones. TITLES BY John A. Waldron. PHOTOGRAPHED BY Vernon Walker and Leland Davis. EDITED BY William Hornbeck. CAST: Harry Langdon, Marceline Day, Madeline Hurlock, Leo Sulky, Charlotte Mineau, Andy Clyde, Roscoe "Tiny" Ward, James Donnelly, Charles Force, Yorke Sherwood, Bill Blaisdell, Thelma Hill, Elsie Tarron. Copyright August 2, 1924, Registration Number L20466. Released by Pathé Exchange, Inc., October 12, 1924.

SYNOPSIS: Harry, soon to be wed, awakens with a hangover in a hotel. His future bride, Betty Brief, calls him but her voice is too loud and Harry goes back to bed.

A butler arrives in Harry's room and begins preparing breakfast. Harry says he doesn't want any and is informed that his bride, who he married at last night's party, wants to eat there. A vampish woman

Harry hands Mother a pistol and tells her to shoot him. Betty and her mother leave and Harry removes a metal plate which was intended to stop a bullet. She comes back and somehow shoots Harry in the rear. They both leave. The woman, now angry, throws a vase at Harry and says she'll knock those bigamist ideas out of his head. She throws a knife at Harry, followed by a dresser drawer that sails out the window, striking

Marceline Day will help Harry escape in this gag photo from The Hansom Cabman.

a cop on the street below. Confusion results and when the cop arrives the woman asks to arrest Harry as a wife beater. The cop hauls him away.

Meanwhile, Betty and her mother are telling their troubles to Betty's father, Judge Brief. Harry is brought before the judge, who orders him to be taken away and that he'll hear the case later that day. Harry is thrown in a cell with some toughs, who mock him as a sissy. A crazy inmate imagines some bugs that he "kills." After spotting another, Harry "kills" it, to the delight of the inmate. Harry is then hauled to do work in the kitchen. He vigorously swabs the floor before being informed that he using the evening's soup. He then stumbles upon some inmates playing a dice game and advises one of the players, who subsequently loses

enters and announces that she is Harry's bride. When Harry says he's never seen her before, she falls tearfully into his arms.

Shortly thereafter, Betty and her mother arrive and see Harry in the arms of the woman. Mother demands to know who she is. Harry looks puzzled and says the butler and the woman say she's his wife.

everything. The con chases Harry, who falls down an elevator shaft and finds himself free in an alley.

The butler and woman are brought before the judge. She tells the judge that the butler was scheming to get Harry's money. The judge calls the prison to order Harry's release and is informed that he has escaped. The judge vows to put every man on Harry's trail. Harry has disguised himself as a cabman and spots a "Wanted" poster. He notices that a man looking at it is indeed the face on the poster and runs to get a cop. The man rips down the poster and leaves. Another cop puts up a "Wanted" poster of Harry as he brings up a cop to inspect the poster. The cop recognizes him and the chase is on. Harry ends up on his cab and picks up two Chinese men who are smoking opium. Harry gets a buzz and ends up on top of a car. He manages to end up on several cars before winding up on top of a police wagon containing Betty and her mother. They spot him and tell him of the woman's confession. They all decided to head for the minister, but Harry's horse sits down and refuses to move. Harry gets it to move with some sugar cubes and the horse and cab skid down a long hill.

ANALYSIS: This film harkens back to the Keystone days, when suspected infidelity and mistreatment of the upper classes were favored subjects. Harry pretty much serves the timeworn plot with very little to differentiate him from any other Sennett comedian, except perhaps during his interaction with the prisoner who is hallucinating invisible insects, and the scene in which he is exposed to the effects of opium.

HARRY MOMENT: Harry's pantomime in killing and disposing of the invisible bug while in jail is excellent. He really seems to make the viewer "see" the bug and uses his whole body to excellent effect.

WHAT THE CRITICS SAID:
Film Daily, *October 5, 1924*

This is one of the most amusing comedies made so far by Harry Langdon and that's saying a lot. Don't miss it. Langdon has a way with him that's all his own and is sure to be liked and laughed at by your folks.

Cleveland Plain Dealer, *January 7, 1925; Reviewed by W. Ward Marsh*

The newcomer on the comedy horizon is Harry Langdon, who is a member of the Sennett ranks. If you haven't seen him yet — and can weather the sex sirocco in Wife of the Centaur *— go to the Allen this week and "discover" for yourself the newest comedy talent in the fold.*

Langdon makes The Hansom Cabman *much funnier than the material in it has any right to be. You can't praise a comedian any more than that.*

He has the best low comedy face in the world, an asset ascribed to the well known Merton Gill of Merton of the Movies *fame.*

Langdon's face is not so sensitive as Chaplin's, nor does his style have the flexibility and pathos of Chaplin's, but as a comedian Langdon is infinitely better than Harold Lloyd. In the race which this column sees, the newcomer and Keaton are neck-and-neck at this minute — and Langdon hasn't made a feature comedy yet!

The finish is as blah as some of Sennett's best comedies. In fact there is no real end to this kind of plot. It finishes with the cabby's horse sliding down hill. Had it ended with the lovin' couple reaching the minister's house, one would feel that the story at least had ended. This plan of chopping off a story in the middle of a laugh is not a good one. But Langdon is worth a visit.

WHAT THE EXHIBITORS SAID:
Exhibitors Herald, *September 19, 1925*

This bird may be a knockout on the stage or in some places, but he hardly ever gets a titter around here. His stuff moves too slow. He tries to put his stuff over by making faces at the camera. 'Zabunk.
Wm. E. Tragsdorf, Trags Theatre, Neillsville, WI. Small town patronage.

Exhibitors Herald, *October 17, 1925*

Pretty good comedy. Would like to see Langdon in about a five reel comedy.
R. L. Nowell, Idlehour Theatre, Monroe, GA. General patronage.

Moving Picture World, *August 7, 1926*

One of Langdon's best; lots of laughs. Draws all classes.
D. W. Strayer, Mt. Joy Theatre, Mt. Joy, PA.

All Night Long

A Mack Sennett Comedy Released in Two Reels. **DIRECTED BY** Harry Edwards. **SUPERVISED BY** F. Richard Jones. **STORY BY** Vernon Smith and Hal Conklin. **TITLES BY** John A. Waldron. **PHOTOGRAPHED BY** Billy Williams and Leland Davis. **EDITED BY** William Hornbeck. **CAST:** Harry

Langdon, Natalie Kingston, Fanny Kelly, Vernon Dent, Billy Gilbert, Vance Veith, Leo Sulky, Andy Clyde. WORKING TITLES: "Over Here," "War is Swell." Copyright October 29, 1924, Registration Number L20713. Released by Pathé Exchange, Inc., November 9, 1924.

SYNOPSIS: Harry finds himself asleep in an empty theatre. Upon awakening he finds a note from his wife, informing him that she left with a wide-awake man. Meanwhile, three burglars are in the theatre office attempting a robbery. When Harry bumps into them he is recognized by their leader as an old Army buddy from the days in France.

In a flashback, soldier Harry is peeling potatoes beside a huge pile. Sergeant Gale Wyndham, the lead burglar seen earlier, receives a note from his girl, Nanette, inviting him and a friend for supper. Harry receives a letter from his girlfriend, Gwendolyn, who tells him that she is proud of him for being promoted to KP. Harry ends up being invited to go along with the sergeant for supper. Upon arriving, Harry is introduced to the beautiful Nanette and her parents. She gives Harry a kiss and he falls out of a window into the street. In a state of bliss he has trouble returning to the house. At the dinner table Nanette makes eyes at Harry and he is smitten. He looks at the photo of Gwendolyn, compares it with Nanette and tears it up. Suddenly explosions fill the air with the sound of an air raid. As the sergeant is leaving he sees Harry kissing Nanette. He throws Harry to the ground with a warning that Nanette is *his* girl.

In the theatre office, Harry asks the thief if he remembers how he got even. Back in the war, Harry and Sergeant Wyndham are in the trenches. They advance onto the field of battle when Harry gets caught on some barbed wire. A live grenade falls under Harry, who uses it in an attempt to free himself. He tosses it away and it explodes. Harry finds himself buried up to his neck in a mound of dirt with his legs sticking straight up. Harry is pulled loose and discovers the legs are not his. Harry pulls on the legs and frees the sergeant, who points out a building called Suicide Post. He tells Harry that this is his post and to stay in the open so he doesn't miss anything. Harry is caught in a searchlight's beam. He climbs atop a long pole and dodges a shell, which tears off a piece of the pole. Another shell removes an additional chunk. Harry starts to climb down when another

shell knocks it down. Harry mistakenly picks up a long stick instead of his rifle. Harry patrols Suicide Post, carrying the stick. A sudden barrage of artillery fire blows Harry into the air. He finds himself attached to another soldier and they retreat to safety. Harry discovers that the other soldier is the colonel.

In the theatre office Wyndham reminds Harry that the colonel made him a lieutenant. Back in the Army, Harry, in his new uniform, pays a call on Nanette. As he describes his exploits, he notices that the sergeant is present. Harry tells him to salute a superior officer. The sergeant chases Harry out onto the street and accidentally knocks out an officer.

In the theatre office, Wyndham reminds Harry that he got the girl and the sergeant got the guardhouse. Suddenly, two policemen arrive. Wyndham puts on a guard's cap and hides Harry behind a door with a stranglehold. He tells the policemen to arrest the two burglars. They leave with the crooks as Wyndham tosses a cigarette, which falls on the fuse of some dynamite intended for the robbery. Harry and Wyndham fight as the dynamite explodes.

Some days later, Nanette, alongside some children, is seen pushing a large carriage, which contains the bandaged Harry and Wyndham. He tells Wyndham that they named one of the kids after him. They spot a parade of marching soldiers and both men stand and salute.

Some of the flashback scenes were used in Robert Youngson's *Days of Thrills and Laughter*.

ANALYSIS: *All Night Long* marks a turning point for Langdon. The flashback sequences during the Great War showcase Harry's innocent, put-upon character to the hilt. Moreover, Vernon Dent makes a superb foil. Their teamwork is so natural that it's easy for the uninitiated to assume a Laurel & Hardy influence, except that this picture predates Stan and Ollie's teaming by three years.

The framing device of the attempted movie theater burglary is not as effective; it's almost as if the material was thrown together in order to beef up the footage. Throughout, Harry is fully aware of the danger his former sergeant poses, and basically engages him in reminiscing in order to avoid being injured or worse. The explosion of the dynamite, followed by the injured Harry and Gale being "walked" by Nanette (along with Harry's children), seems almost arbitrary. It is gratuitous slapstick that pales in comparison to the more linear tale set during the war.

HARRY MOMENT: At the dinner table Nanette flirts with Harry. In a single continuous shot of Harry over her shoulder, he expresses joy and infatuation followed by ripping up his girlfriend's photo. Harry is very appealing in this sequence and really registers with his facial pantomime.

WHAT THE CRITICS SAID:
Film Daily, *November 2, 1924*

This boy, Harry Langdon, is fast becoming one of the funniest comedians, if not the funniest, in short length comedies. His work in this is fine. As the hungry doughboy in Flanders who is taken by his superior officer to dinner at the latter's sweetheart's home, he is a riot… Don't miss this. The humor is immense.

Moving Picture World, *November 8, 1924;*
Reviewed by Sumner Smith

Give the average comedian a good vehicle and he'll usually turn out a good comedy; give Harry Langdon only the thread of an idea to work on and he makes it into two reels of side-splitting fun. This Mack Sennett comedian certainly is coming along fast. That's more and more apparent with each new product of his, and All Night Long *is the latest evidence of it. Here is a subject built of conventional comedy stuff but rendered superbly hilarious by Langdon's proverbial crutch — and then some… Book this comedy and hear your audience laugh its head off.*

Motion Picture News, *November 14, 1924;*
Reviewed by Thomas C. Kennedy

The laughs lurk in every scene of All Night Long, *a two reel Mack Sennett offering in which Harry Langdon achieves one of the cleverest comedy performances developed in the short length pictures. Those who for some time have felt that Langdon is destined for a place among the screen's truly great comedians may go see* All Night Long *and have their convictions confirmed. If Langdon's swoon after the French girl kisses him, his irrepressible desire to point out his favorite cut of the chicken served up at the table of his hostess, his bewilderment and fear on the field of battle, and the other bits he scores with her, if these do not reach the peak of the screen comedian's art, we are very much deluded for we consider them flashes of real genius.*

It is a well done comedy and there should be praise for Harry Edwards, the director, and Vernon Dent, Natalie Kingston and Fannie Kelly, the other players. In moments All Night Long *is as funny as Chaplin's* Shoulder Arms, *though totally different except for the war atmosphere and there is no similarity between the two comedians — save an ability common to both to be uproariously funny.* All Night Long *can be booked, and boosted, with confidence that the audience, irrespective of the type of Theatre in which it is gathered, will respond to the hilarity and fun which abound in this picture.*

WHAT THE EXHIBITORS SAID:
Exhibitors Herald, *January 31, 1925*

It's a pleasure to report on this fellow's comedies, for I have yet to play a poor one, and have shown several. Chock full of laughs.
H. E. Patrick, Palace Theatre, North Rose, NY.
Small town patronage.

Moving Picture World, *January 31, 1925*
This is positively a knockout. Langdon great drawing card here. A few more like this and we shall see Langdon up where Lloyd is now. Tone, good. Sunday, yes. Audience appeal, 100 per cent. Suburban class town of 2,000.
H. Warren Rible, Mayfield Theatre (210) seats; Mayfield, CA.

Exhibitors Herald, *March 7, 1925*
A good two part comedy. All comedies I have used so far in which Langdon was featured have been good. I consider him one of the best comedians in the business.
Adolph Kohn, Pastime Theatre, Granville, NY. Small town patronage.

Moving Picture World, *June 6, 1925*
Where do they get this stuff that Langdon is stepping after Chaplin, Lloyd and Keaton's honors? There are a dozen better. He has a silly manner that is all his own, but it is anything but funny. Some good story work and stunts by the gag men have gotten laughs. General class, city of 15,000.
Ben L. Morris, Temple Theatre, Bellaire, OH.

Exhibitors Herald, *October 17, 1925*
Good comedy. Most of Langdon's are good.
Henrietta Eckhardt, New Palace Theatre, Wisconsin Rapids, WI. General patronage.

Exhibitors Herald, *December 12, 1925*
An extra good comedy. The comedian has a style all his own. Something unusual now-a-days.
Bert Silver, Silver Family Theatre, Greenville, MI. General patronage.

Exhibitors Herald, *March 20, 1926*
Langdon may have made some good comedies, but *All Night Long* isn't one of them.
Palace Theatre Co., Inc., Lyric Theatre, Frostburg, MD. General patronage.

Exhibitors Herald, *June 5, 1926*
Boys, this is a dandy. The best I ever saw this fellow put out, and it's clean.
J. W. Schmidt, Grand Theatre, Breese, IL. General patronage.

Exhibitors Herald, *July 3, 1926*
Rattling good comedy.
Phillip Rand, Rex Theatre, Salmon, ID. General patronage.

Exhibitors Herald, *November 20, 1926*
Our favorite comedian, so please pull for us for a photo.
R. B. Maxwell, Illinois Theatre, Sullivan, IL. General patronage.

Exhibitors Herald, *June 11, 1927*
Laughs came few and far between.
Robert Wygant, Heights Theatre, Houston, TX. General patronage.

Feet of Mud

A Mack Sennett Comedy Released in Two Reels. **DIRECTED BY** Harry Edwards. **SUPERVISED BY** F. Richard Jones. **TITLES BY** John A. Waldron. **PHOTOGRAPHED BY** Billy Williams and Leland Davis. **EDITED BY** William Hornbeck. **CAST:** Harry Langdon, Florence D. Lea, Natalie Kingston, Yorke Sherwood, Vernon Dent, Malcom Waite, Leo Sulky, Silas D. Wilcox, Andre Bailey, Betty Bird, Claire Cushman, Eugenia Gilbert, Elsie Tarron. Copyright December 3, 1924, Registration Number L20823. Released by Pathé Exchange, Inc., December 7, 1924.

SYNOPSIS: Harry is a football player, seated bench side as a substitute, at a game. He is in love with campus sweetheart Nina, who is watching from the stands.

His mother is also watching, just as she used to watch his father. Harry "receives" the ball in the back of his pants and runs for the winning touchdown.

He is congratulated by Nina and his mother. Later, Harry pays a call on Nina in her family's expensive home. Her father, made rich in the stock market, wants a son-in-law who can do likewise. He informs Harry that he can't marry Nina and then gives him a card that will provide a job with the city engineer. If Harry sticks with it the father will reconsider the marriage.

Harry's engineering job turns out to be that of a street sweeper. He sweeps some bricks into an open manhole and crowns a worker. He accidentally stabs a cop with his paper retriever and is subsequently arrested. Harry spots his mother on the street and runs away from the cop into a subway entrance. After being jostled by the crowd on a car, Harry exits in Chinatown. There is a tong war going on between the Wa-Hoos and the Pa-Jonggs. Harry is handed a card with some Chinese writing on it and shows it to several Chinamen, who run in terror. He then shows it to an older Chinaman, who asks where he got it. Harry shows him the location and the man runs away. As

Harry begins to sweep the streets he knocks the head of his brush against a metal trashcan. Inside a room, a group of Chinese thugs believe it to be the enemy's gong. Their leader bangs his own gong and suddenly a hail of debris is flung into the street from buildings. Within moments the street is filled with garbage.

Suddenly, a touring car appears on the street with a guide describing the neighborhood with its drug addicts. Among the tourists are Nina, her father and Harry's mother. They enter a Chinese hop house to observe the locals on drugs. Harry is discovered in one of the compartments of the house. As he hugs his mother an angry Chinaman, armed with a meat cleaver, rushes into a room and orders everyone to get out. They quickly leave; once outside, they notice that Nina is not among them. Harry falls through a trick door and finds himself in a large ornate room. He accidentally spears a dummy and fights it. Spotting

the Chinaman with the cleaver, Harry hides under a long table and pokes his head through a hole. He is in line with several fake heads. A Mandarin puts burning incense in front of each head and Harry reacts to the smoke. He gets woozier and the Chinaman kneels before the table and asks if Buddha is with him. Harry smites him and is chased. The Chinaman flings a cleaver at Harry, which smashes a large vase,

Here's the original caption for this photo taken by George F. Cannons on the set of Feet of Mud: *"Harry Langdon is the favorite star of John, Herman and William White, triplets, working in Mack Sennett Comedies. Harry has devised a game whereby Herman, John and William earn extra quarters. Harry makes a two bit bet with everyone who comes on the lot that they can't tell the triplets apart after looking at them thirty seconds. William, John and Herman always win."*

exposing Nina inside. Harry grabs a sword and begins to fight the Chinaman. He and Nina fall through a trapdoor and land in the street outside, knocking down her father. Harry says he couldn't find the door, and covering the father's face with a hat, kisses Nina.

ANALYSIS: One year into his tenure as a Mack Sennett comedian, Langdon has mastered the ability to rise above his material. The story is without structure or logic, the situations are nothing new, and countless comedians have endured football mishaps and even tong wars in Chinatown. Any resemblance to characterization is purely coincidental. Nevertheless, Harry puts his stamp on nearly all his scenes, keeping his highly expressive face in the forefront.

HARRY MOMENT: Harry's reaction to the incense, although brief, is yet another example of his skill at facial pantomime. He convincingly and hilariously conveys the numbing effect of the smoke. No doubt it was scenes like this that earned him the "baby dope fiend" label from James Agee.

WHAT THE CRITICS SAID:
Film Daily, *November 30, 1924*

Harry Langdon is extremely funny in the opening sequences of this. He is seen as a football substitute player who has to play but hopes he doesn't. The baggy uniform, the pathetic eyes and manner will undoubtedly get this off to a fine start. The rest of the comedy is funny, too.

Harry is given a political job (street cleaning) by his girl's father. He gets mixed up in a tong-war, and rescues the girl. That doesn't sound very "different" but it's the style that Langdon gets his stuff across with that makes it enjoyable, and after all that's what every good comedian has to have. Langdon knows the art of facial expression, too. Harry Edwards directed.

Motion Picture News, *December 6, 1924; Reviewed by Thomas C. Kennedy*

Harry Langdon scores again in a snappy comedy from the Sennett studios. Feet of Mud is not one of Langdon's best, but it is better than the majority of two reel comedies, and can be highly recommended…

The play presents the absurdities common to comedies of the type and the star of the picture scores with them as only an actor of his talent can score. Natalie Kingston, York Sherwood, Vernon Dent, Malcolm Waite and Florence D. Lee make up a fine supporting cast. The picture was directed by Harry Edwards. It is a sure-fire laugh getter.

Moving Picture World, *December 6, 1924; Reviewed by Tom Waller*

There are a number of laughs in the picture and Langdon, as usual, does highly amusing work.

WHAT THE EXHIBITORS SAID:
Exhibitors Herald, *December 20, 1924*

These Harry Langdon Mack Sennett Pathé comedies are all pleasing. Extra good. Have run four or five, but they do not as yet mean any extra money at the box office. Making a star overnight is a thing of the past.
Frank G. Buckley, Princess Theatre, Superior, WI. Downtown patronage.

Moving Picture World, *August 8, 1925*

This very much overrated comedian has a dandy comedy in this. His stunt and gag workers were doing overtime on a polo game that gets lots of laughs. I believe a half dozen other comedians could have done the same stunts and gotten more laughs. Draw general class, city 15,000.
Ben L. Morris, Temple Theatre, Bellaire, OH.

Exhibitors Herald, *August 22, 1925*
Good comedy.
L. V. Feldman, Orpheum Theatre, Pipestone, MN. Small town patronage.

Exhibitors Herald, *October 17, 1925*
Excellent.
E. Korenowski, A-Mus-A Theatre, Pittsburg, OK. Small town patronage.

Exhibitors Herald, *December 12, 1925*
Kept the crowd in good humor.
A. G. Weiner, Grand Theatre, Rainer, OR. General patronage.

Exhibitors Herald, *April 17, 1926*
Langdon draws well but they better keep him in two reel comedies.
R. M. Smith, Mission Theatre, Mission, TX. Mixed patronage.

Exhibitors Herald, *May 1, 1926*
We feel sorry for the exhibitors that have to buy Langdon from First National as a star. This comedy was terrible; One man comedy.
F. K. Shaffer, Lyric Theatre, Frostburg, MD. General patronage.

Exhibitors Herald, *May 22, 1926*

This is a funny comedy, better than average. Langdon's a comedian.
Bert Silver, Silver Family Theatre, Greenville, MI. General patronage.

The Sea Squawk

A Mack Sennett Comedy Released in Two Reels. **DIRECTED BY** Harry Edwards. **SUPERVISED BY** F. Richard Jones. **TITLES BY** John A. Waldron. **PHOTOGRAPHED BY** Vernon Walker and George Unholz. **EDITED BY** William Hornbeck. **CAST:** Harry Langdon, Eugenia Gilbert, Christian J. Frank, Charlotte Mineau, Budd Ross, Eddie Baker, Leo Sulky, Louise Carver, Fanny Kelly, Andre Bailey, Alice Day, Dorothy Dore, Louise Gallagher, Thelma Hill, Elsie Tarron, Hazel Williams, Pat Kelly, Grace Gordon, Edwin Hubbell, Roscoe "Tiny" Ward. Copyright October 2, 1924, Registration Number L20629. Released by Pathé Exchange, Inc., January 4, 1925.

SYNOPSIS: Captain Hennessey commands the three-star liner, the S.S. *Cognac*. A detective is conferring with him. Also aboard is Blackie Dawson, a jewel thief in possession of a large stolen ruby. Flora Danube, a Bulgarian beauty, strums a mandolin. Harry, clad as a Scot complete with kilt, gazes fondly at her. He wanders over and accidentally knocks her off a hammock. Embarrassed, he leaves and enters the cabin he shares with Blackie. The thief asks him if "I will shoot" or "I shall shoot" is correct. Harry doesn't reply and begins changing his clothes. He watches Blackie load a large pistol. Harry pulls out his own tiny pistol and attempts to twirl it. Blackie spots the gun and tells Harry they speak the same language. The thief crawls into his bunk and attempts to sleep. As Harry gets in his own bunk he accidentally pops a balloon, which startles Blackie. They both reach for their pistols, with Harry trembling in fear. Blackie takes his pistol and tells him to go to sleep.

Meanwhile, on deck, the detective is conducting a thorough search for the missing ruby. Flora, covered in a shawl, enters Harry's darkened cabin and quickly leaves.

A hand tosses a paper airplane through a porthole into the cabin. Blackie opens the plane and reads that detectives are searching the ship. He is advised to swallow the ruby. Upon hearing a knock on the cabin door, Blackie quickly forces the ruby down Harry's throat. Blackie tells him to keep quiet. The detective and an officer search Blackie and Harry. After they leave, Blackie tells Harry he swallowed a million-dollar ruby and to keep his mouth shut. Harry is shocked and imagines himself strapped to an operating table while Blackie sharpens a knife. Harry attempts several times to leave the cabin and is restrained by Blackie. Harry knocks him cold with a shoe, and leaves. Harry heads for the railing in an attempt to regurgitate the ruby and is stopped by Blackie, who tells him to keep a stiff upper lip. Harry runs away from the thief and winds up in the cabin of Pearl Blackstone, Blackie's accomplice. He spots a dress and changes into it. After donning a blonde wig Harry reappears on deck as a woman. He bumps into Blackie, who initially takes a shine to "her." As Blackie continues to flirt, he begins to get suspicious. Harry falls down and knocks his wig loose. Blackie and Pearl realize who he is. Harry puts his wig back on and enters a ballroom where a dance is in progress. The captain begins to dance with Harry. As Blackie and Pearl dance nearby, the thief presses a pistol into Harry's back. After the dance, Harry begins to pull a string from the back of a tall woman's dress. He ends up popping her corset, which knocks a man down. The woman attempts to strike Harry, but he seeks protection from the captain and begins to dance with him again.

A small monkey runs into the ballroom and ends up under Harry's dress. The monkey's tail pokes out of the back of Harry's dress as he dances. Harry keeps reacting to the unknown monkey. He runs around the dance floor in shock, with the captain and Blackie in close pursuit. As he dances near the band, the monkey's tail flicks at a drummer. He raps the tail with a drumstick, causing the monkey to pop out of Harry's dress. Harry winds up in a ladies' changing room. A woman puts a lit cigarette on Harry's rear, causing it to catch fire. He runs around the room until a pitcher of water puts out the fire. Harry flees and winds up on deck with the captain and Blackie.

Blackie drags Harry down the deck and punches him. Pearl warns Blackie away and gives Harry some reviving liquor. Several other women also give Harry liquor. After Harry staggers to his feet, Blackie chases him. Harry falls down some stairs and winds up on the ballroom floor. Flora tells the captain and the detective that Blackie is the crook. Blackie begins firing at them, using Harry as a shield. He breaks free and climbs up the mast, with Blackie and the others in pursuit. They all fall into a cabin.

Flora reveals the real ruby and says that Harry only swallowed paste. Blackie is taken away in handcuffs. Harry embraces Flora and warily eyes the real ruby.

ANALYSIS: Filmed before the previous two comedies, *The Sea Squawk* is mainly notable for Harry's female impersonation. Although he would appear in drag in future films, it's a rarity when he is consciously trying to imitate a woman. Unfortunately, the heavy-handed plot of the jewel robbery overshadows everything, including most of Langdon's performance. Had this been produced after *Feet of Mud*, it's likely the comedian and his director would have found additional ways to emphasize Langdon's gifts. He briefly deals with nausea brought on by both the rough seas and the "jewel" he's swallowed, but it's a pale shadow compared to the "tobacco sandwich" scene in *Luck o' the Foolish*. Only in the ballroom, where Harry must contend with a monkey as he dances with the ship's captain, affords him any opportunity to use his face and body in ways that set him apart from other screen comics.

HARRY MOMENT: Harry's facial reactions to the monkey's movements under his dress are wonderful. His pantomime skills are so good that the viewer can almost feel the monkey's presence.

WHAT THE CRITICS SAID:
The Pre View, *August 20, 1924; Reviewed by H. M.*

To anyone who has an incipient, ingrown or chronic grouch, I cheerfully recommend Mack Sennett's latest comedy starring Harry Langdon. It may not, in the case of the chronic ailment, effect (sic) a complete cure, but it should at least result in a step toward normalcy.

The Sea Squawk *boasts of more plot than most two-reelers usually have. Langdon portrays a Scotch immigrant who becomes the victim of a particularly large, dark, burly villain. Victimizing in this instance means that the hapless Scot is forced to serve as a depository for a stolen jewel the size of an egg. In other words, it is forced down his throat. Ordinarily, the gem would be safe in its human safe deposit vault, but even a Scotchman can be forced to relinquish certain things if the sea becomes rough enough. But Langdon, despite his seasickness, has to fight nature. "Remember," admonishes the villain darkly,*

Eugenia Gilbert and Harry serenade each other.

pressing a revolver against helpless Harry's heart, "Mum's the word, regardless of what comes up!"

Of course, after that there isn't much to do but sink down in the chair, loosen one's belt, and go on a rampage of laughs. And in all justice to Mr. Langdon, it is he who provides most of them. He has in many respects abandoned the ways of slapstick comedians (although others in the cast dispense broad humor with good effect) and earns most of his laughs by little whimsicalities of manner and expression.

Eugenia Gilbert has a small part, and appears to good advantage in most of her scenes with the star. The role of the villain (the jewel thief) is enacted by Christian Frank. His villainy is laid on with a heavy hand, a practice which would be open to criticism in the majority of cases, but one which here serves as forceful contrast to the personality of the meek and easy-going hero. Charlotte Mineau and Leo Sulky are acceptable in their respective character bits.

Harry Edwards, the director, and F. Richard Jones, under whose supervision the comedy was filmed, are both to be commended for their efforts in making one of the best and smoothest-running short comedies of recent months. J. A. Waldron's subtitles, too, are deserving of praise, not only because of their cleverness, but also in view of their consistency and mirth-provoking proclivities.

Langdon appears to be one of the best bets among the rising generation of film comedians. His screen personality is greatly in his favor; much of his humor is put across by facial expression, and he is droll and whimsical — and seldom inane.

Frankly, Langdon is one of the few short-subject comedians who can really act. Many of his Sennett releases have been crude and unworthy of him, but in The Sea Squawk *he appears to strike a stride which should carry him far on the cinema highway.*

Film Daily, *December 28, 1924*

Harry Langdon is starred in this. To those who have seen any of his recent comedies this will be enough to bring them in. If you aren't playing them you are missing one of the best series — really funny stuff — on the market. Langdon is funny no matter what the material he works with, and that's saying a lot.

Motion Picture News, *January 5, 1925; Reviewed by Thomas C. Kennedy*

As the title indicates this is a burlesque. However, it does not particularly make travesty of the famous Sea Hawk. *Burlesque of a broad — occasionally too broad for general exhibition purposes — is the substance of the action in which Harry Langdon is starred as a Scotchman riding as a steerage passenger on a ship bound for the States...*

There are several bits of comedy built of more elegant and more effective material than nausea, and they are diverting.

WHAT THE EXHIBITORS SAID:
Exhibitors Herald, *July 4, 1925*

The most over-rated in the movies. Gags must be getting scarce on the Sennett lot when they have to resort to vulgarity to get a laugh. If you have a critical bunch, look it over first. If you do you will probably use the scissors before you dish it up for your patrons. Yes, he is being groomed for feature length comedies, but I think he needs a lot more grooming, for I don't think he's the big "it" just because the exchange men say he is. Personally, I give him nothing and *The Sea Squawk* very much less.
Stephen D. Brown, Mission Theatre, Santa Paula, CA. Neighborhood Theatre.

Exhibitors Herald, *November 14, 1925*

Very silly comedy that seemed to produce a fair share of laughs, so why worry? Not up to Langdon's standard, in my humble opinion.
Henry Reeves, Star Theatre, Menard, TX. Small town patronage.

Exhibitors Herald, *June 5, 1926*

This man will run Harold Lloyd ragged in feature comedies.
C. H. Studebaker, Elk Theatre, Worland, WY. General patronage.

Exhibitors Herald, *August 28, 1926*

One of the best yet. Langdon is a natural comedian. You'll laugh when you look at him.
H. M. Face & Sons, Star Theatre, Nashville, MI. Small town patronage.

Boobs in the Wood

A Mack Sennett Comedy Released in Two Reels. **DIRECTED BY** Harry Edwards. **STORY BY** Arthur Ripley. **TITLES BY** John A. Waldron. **PHOTOGRAPHED BY** Billy Williams and Leland Davis. **EDITED BY** William Hornbeck. **CAST:** Harry Langdon, Marie Astaire, Vernon Dent, Leo Willis,

William McCall, Barny Hellum, Leo Sulky, Mary Hunt. Copyright December 11, 1924, Registration Number L20882. Released by Pathé Exchange, Inc., February 1, 1925.

SYNOPSIS: Harry is Chester Winfield, an aspiring lumberjack wandering in the North Woods. Big Bill Reardon, boss of the camp, warns some passersby on horseback to move back as a cut tree is about to fall. A huge tree falls and just misses Harry, who runs in fear. He decides to cut down his own tree, which turns out to be a slender sapling. He attempts to chop at a big tree, with no result except to break a water bucket and douse Big Bill. Meanwhile, Hazel Wood, the camp waitress, runs into Bill, who warns her that if she has another sweetie, she can start feeling sorry for him. She considers this threat and goes after Harry. She offers Harry a cracker and asks for a kiss. He is unsure and hesitates. She acts hurt by his indifference and gives him a kiss, after which he sinks to the ground. Bill observes all of this and tells Harry that a fast worker like him is entitled to a long rest. He tells Harry to sit on a big log then releases it down a long chute. As the log pulls away, a chain catches Bill's foot and he is dragged along. When the log stops, Harry is hurled through the air and comes to rest, sitting atop a small pole. An angry Bill gives him a thrashing and tells him to beat it while he's still able.

Later, a disheveled Harry wanders into camp. He overhears Hazel urging Bill to give him another chance. After a scuffle with Bill, Harry and Hazel depart. Hazel is working as a cashier in a saloon and is told by the owner that Harry can work as a dishwasher. She calls Harry, who soon arrives at the saloon. The owner sizes him up and offers him a drink for luck before starting work. Harry takes the drink and falls to the floor. In the kitchen Harry encounters a burly cook who also offers him a drink for luck. Thinking quickly, Harry sits on the ground before taking the drink. Harry picks up a huge stack of dishes and struggles with them. A small worker in the kitchen breaks a plate and is beaten by the cook. Harry puts down the dishes and prepares to leave. Out in the saloon a tough customer is inquiring about his soup order. Harry causes a lamp to leak oil into a soup pot and then to fall in. Harry is told to serve

Leo Willis expects Harry to be careful in Boobs in the Wood.

the customer his soup. The cook straps a holster and gun on Harry to strengthen him. Meanwhile, Hazel tells the owner and the customer that Harry's got six guns full of notches. The owner urges the customer to eat whatever Harry brings. After some complications, the customer flees the saloon. Hazel tells everyone inside that Harry is called the Crying Killer. Back in the kitchen the cook discovers the lamp in the soup pot. Somehow, he is kicked by a mule and believes Harry to be the one doing the damage. He flees in terror, calling Harry a brute. Everyone recoils in fear when Harry comes out of the kitchen.

Later that evening, Mike, a tough customer, enters and is told that the new bouncer has his eye on him. Harry has rigged a series of strings to various points in the saloon. Mike pulls a pistol and shoots a bottle on a table. Harry shoots his gun, pulls a string, and a bottle falls. He does this again, and when the he fires a third time the short worker pulls all the strings and havoc ensues. Harry accidentally fires the gun again, causing Mike to flee the saloon. He then places a chalk notch on a chair.

Big Bill enters the saloon and warns Hazel not to trifle with his heart. Harry tries to get Bill to leave and is rebuffed. He then strikes Bill and another patron. Suddenly, someone turns out the lights and a brawl begins. When the lights come back on he is the only one standing. He puts many notches on the chair as Hazel congratulates him.

ANALYSIS: *Boobs in the Wood* is similar to Langdon's earlier Sennett comedies in that it consists of two distinct situations that comprise about a reel apiece. The first deals with Lumberjack Harry, the second with Dishwasher/Waiter Harry. Only the presence of Vernon Dent's Big Bill ties the two threads together.

However, the resemblance ends there. This first known collaboration between Arthur Ripley and Frank Capra (although Capra is uncredited) features Langdon in a consistent characterization of the innocent, with a minimum of gratuitous slapstick. A scene that best illustrates this new direction comes during the second reel. Once again, a soup has been "flavored" with kerosene oil, but in this film Harry notices it. Ordered to serve it to a demanding patron, Harry is extremely cautious and polite, repeatedly offering a sip of beer after every spoonful and helpfully wiping the man's lips. The laughs come not from an explosive reaction, but in Harry's determination to lessen the customer's ultimate discomfort.

HARRY MOMENT: In the scene in which Hazel flirts with Harry while offering him a cracker, Langdon's hesitancy and odd body rhythms are very reminiscent of a small child. He definitely has an interest but is very unsure and nervous. This is an early example of what Walter Kerr termed the Little Elf's "ambiguity."

WHAT THE CRITICS SAID:
Film Daily, *January 25, 1925*

In his latest, Harry Langdon makes a strong bid for being the perfect screen boob. Throughout this comedy his face registers a perfect blank with the exception of his expressive mouth. His lip pantomime is a perfect barometer of his varied emotions. We can recall no other comedian who does so little to express so much. And all with his mouth. He seems to work without effort in the midst of the wildest scrambles of this fast moving riot of laughs. He escapes from a logging camp with the sweetheart of the boss. They get jobs in a restaurant — she as cashier and he as waiter. And the boob waiter crowds fast moving fun into every foot. It is a new brand of hilarity Harry Langdon uncovers. All the old stuff is discarded. This bland-faced comedian springs a lot of original gags that are bound to get a lot of laughs. Arthur Ripley, author and Harry Edwards, director deserve to be placed near the head of the class with this one.

Moving Picture World, *January 31, 1925; Reviewed by C.S.S.*

The title of this two reel Mack Sennett comedy distributed by Pathé, with Harry Langdon in the stellar role, indicates the nature of the picture, which is a travesty on the type of vigorous north woods and logging camp melodramas…Harry Langdon is extremely amusing in this characterization, even his appearance being good for laughs and he has been given a number of which are out of the ordinary. Marie Astaire is entirely satisfactory as the girl. Altogether it is a comedy that should please a large majority of patrons in any type of house.

Motion Picture News, *February 7, 1925; Reviewed by Thomas C. Kennedy*

Harry Langdon is the star of this amusing two-reeler from the Mack Sennett studios. He appears as a shy, timid "bouncer" at a very rough saloon on the edge of the great timber country where he tried but failed to make good. The story is rather cleverly gagged, presenting a number of situations which contrive to make the quaking hero appear as one of the most courageous and fearsome fighters in his neck of the woods.

The starred comedian makes splendid use of his opportunities. He has the able support of Vernon Dent as the rival for the girl's hand, and Marie Astaire as the heroine. It was directed by Harry Edwards. Boobs in the Woods *(sic) is not up to the best we have had from Langdon, but it succeeds admirably as brief entertainment.*

Cleveland Plain Dealer, *April 9, 1925; Reviewed by W. Ward Marsh*

Boobs in the Woods *(sic) is the title of the Harry Langdon comedy in the Allen this week. Harry (these first names!) is always funny. He has, as I have already said, Chaplin's trick of bordering his comic antics on genuine pathos. Boob is not Harry's best, but it is pretty funny. Some of the situations strain even the amusing Harry to get them over.*

It's ailing in the ending, which doesn't keep up the fun that is found in the earlier part.

WHAT THE EXHIBITORS SAID:
Exhibitors Herald, *May 23, 1925*
Very good. One of the best of the Langdon comedies.
*W. L. Douglas, Strand Theatre, Newman Grove, NE.
Small town patronage.*

Exhibitors Herald, *July 18, 1925*
His comedies are not what they're cracked up to be. Hardly a laugh in the entire two reels.
*R. Pfeiffer, Princess Theatre, Chilton, WI.
Small town patronage.*

Exhibitors Herald, *April 3, 1926*
An average comedy with several laughs.
*J. G. Kennedy, Empress Theatre, Akron, IA.
Small town patronage.*

Exhibitors Herald, *April 17, 1926*
Langdon good in this one. Has a style of comedy all his own. Lloyd and Chaplin had better watch this fellow.
*R. M. Smith, Mission Theatre, Mission, TX.
Mixed patronage.*

Exhibitors Herald, *April 24, 1926*
This comedy very good. It has some new gags that sure get the laughs.
*Wilcox and Miller, Lake View Theatre, Lake View, IA.
General patronage.*

Exhibitors Herald, *July 19, 1926*
Harry Langdon — This guy is funny in all of his comedies.
*Bert Silver, Silver Family Theatre, Greenville, MI.
General patronage.*

His Marriage Wow

A Mack Sennett Comedy Released in Two Reels. **DIRECTED BY** Harry Edwards. **STORY BY** Arthur Ripley. **TITLES BY** Felix Adler and A.H. Giebler. **PHOTOGRAPHED BY** Billy Williams and Leland Davis. **EDITED BY** William Hornbeck. **CAST:** Harry Langdon, Natalie Kingston, Vernon Dent, William McCall, Ronald Tilley, Thelma Hill, Art Rowlands, Silas D. Wilcox, Jack Murphy, Thelma Parr, Georgia Hale. Copyright December 26, 1924, Registration Number L20951. Released by Pathé Exchange, Inc., March 1, 1925.

SYNOPSIS: At the Highland Park Church, a wedding is about to take place. Agnes Fisher is to be the bride. Her father is concerned as there has been no sign of the groom. In another deserted church, Harold Hope is waiting in a pew. Back at the first church, Professor McGlumm, a student of melancholia and pessimism, warily eyes everyone. He suggests that the groom may have met with an accident. In the other church, Harold is found by the reverend and soon finds out he is at the wrong church. He leaves and gets directions to the correct church from a traffic cop. Back at the first church, McGlumm suggests that the bride is now a widow. Harry pauses on his way to the church by a car and drops his wedding ring, which becomes embedded in a rear tire. After some difficulty chasing the car, Harold manages to slash the tire and recover his ring. Arriving at the church Harold attempts to explain and is greeted with a kiss by Agnes, which results in a dreamy smile. The professor asks Harold why a beautiful girl would marry him and could he leave her well fixed if anything should happen? Harold shows him a $50,000 life insurance policy and is told that Agnes's sister is enjoying her *late* husband's policy. Harold looks shocked and frightened by this news. The ceremony begins, and when the reverend asks if anyone objects to the marriage, Harold looks expectantly at the wedding party. As he reaches for the ring, he spots the professor looking at him and winds up tossing the ring into a glass of water. The bride feels faint and is revived with the

Langdon and Natalie Kingston in His Marriage Wow.

water glass. She discovers the wedding ring in her mouth. Soon after this, they are pronounced man and wife. After some mix-ups with the wedding car, the couple is on their way.

After the honeymoon, the family — consisting of the professor, Agnes's widowed sister and her father — moves right in. At the dinner table, Agnes notices that her wine glass is full and switches it with Harold's, which is not as full. The professor warns him not to drink it. Harold switches his glass with the father's. When Father drinks it with no ill effects, Harold downs his own glass, while smirking at the professor in triumph. In the kitchen, the cook has discovered that Harold's pouch of tobacco has fallen into a coffee pot. A maid, unaware of this, fills some cups and serves the coffee. The professor drinks first and spits out the offending brew. He warns Harold not to drink the coffee. Harold ignores him and drinks, noting that there is nothing like coffee for the finish. As he drinks he begins to feel nauseauted and his eyes become heavy lidded. He tells the professor, "They've got me." He staggers out of the room and lies down on the floor of the hallway. The professor places a call to an attendant and says to have the operating room ready. The guard, who is at an insane asylum, says that he's located Looney McGlumm. The professor helps Harold on with his coat and drives him away in a car.

Just then, some attendants from the asylum arrive and are told that McGlumm drove away with Harold. Passenger Harold notices that the professor is driving recklessly. McGlumm stops the car, gets out and begins yelling at a pole for being in the way. They get back in the car and drive away. Meanwhile, a wagon from the asylum is in pursuit. McGlumm stops the car again. They get out and grab some bricks and head for a marriage license shop. The professor throws a brick at the window, breaking the glass. They both run to the car and speed away. As they drive along, McGlumm begins laughing hysterically. Harold asks him what is so funny and McGlumm explains that he is Barney Google. He continues to drive erratically as Harold climbs in the back seat. The professor joins him as Harold panics and climbs in the front seat and takes the wheel. Shortly thereafter, McGlumm pulls the steering wheel off and throws it away, causing the car to crash. The asylum wagon pulls up and McGlumm points to Harold, who is sitting awkwardly in front of the wreck. Agnes kisses Harold; he smiles with relief.

ANALYSIS: *His Marriage Wow* is, in every respect, the quintessential Arthur Ripley screenplay: an oddball, slightly sinister plot containing many elements that will reappear throughout Ripley's work with Langdon. Here, Harry is not the hesitant, sexually immature creature of Capra's gags — he's in love, he wants to get married, and he knows what will follow — but he's still too trusting and childlike for his own good.

In Ripley's universe, innocents like Harry are ripe for manipulation by the Professor McGlumms of the world, particularly when it comes to their attitudes toward women and marriage. Similar characters would turn up in *His First Flame* (Harry's uncle) and *The Chaser* (pal Bud Jamison). During the course of the film, Harry believes himself to be poisoned; this also occurs in *The Chaser*, as well as a later Ripley-Langdon collaboration, *Counsel on De Fence*.

HARRY MOMENT: At the dinner table, when Harry discovers that the wine is not poisoned and he smirks at McGlumm, he perfectly portrays a small boy's attitude. It's a charming shift from an adult to a little boy and showcases the strange ambiguity of age that is a large part of Langdon's appeal.

WHAT THE CRITICS SAID:
Film Daily, *February 22, 1925*

Harry Langdon has made another really laughable comedy in His Marriage Wow. *The gags are funny in themselves, but it is Langdon's comedy sense and excellent work that really put it over…[The] real kick comes when Langdon is forced to ride in a machine with the doctor, whom he gradually discovers is a lunatic. This ride is one of the funniest things done in comedies in a long while. Get this one, sure.*

Moving Picture World, *February 28, 1925; Reviewed by Sumner Smith*

It seems safe to say that Harry Langdon, Mack Sennett's comedy find, is rising in the public's favor faster than any other comedian on the screen. This latest vehicle should increase his prestige, for it is a pippin for humor. Some of the gags are new, but the principal idea behind the picture is well known. Nevertheless, Langdon's exquisite sense of comedy values and his wonderful facial expressions make one forget that they have ever seen the plot before…Book this. You can't go wrong on it. That applies to any class of patronage.

Motion Picture News, *March 7, 1925; Reviewed by Thomas C. Kennedy*

Now that Harry Langdon seems to be pretty generally "discovered" it is quite permissible to grow enthusiastic over his acting in these two-reelers from the Sennett studios. This one is amusing, entertaining, and it is rich with that skillful and eloquent pantomime which stamps Langdon as the most promising comedian outside the ranks of the real top-notchers…

Several neatly contrived gags are distributed through the film and ample opportunity is afforded the star to interpolate his individualistic and highly amusing comics…. Harry Edwards directed the picture, and he as well as the players deserves applause for the excellent results.

Cleveland Plain Dealer, *July 8, 1925; Reviewed by W. Ward Marsh*

A new Harry Langdon comedy, His Marriage Vow *(sic), is on exhibition in the Stillman this week, and if Langdon had not proved himself before, this Sennett marriage vow would do it.*

The material in it frequently creaks under the strain of age, but a lot of it is genuinely amusing…

Langdon makes His Marriage Vow *funny. Anyone may see that the gag men were taking half-holidays when they wrote it.*

WHAT THE EXHIBITORS SAID:
Exhibitors Herald, *March 28, 1925*

Hate to pour cold water on Pathé's efforts to make a Lloyd out of Langdon, but honestly, we can't see where Langdon sets the world afire in the comedy line. The "Gang" series do *(sic)* twice the comedy business.
O. R. Oatee, Bridge Theatre, Petersburg, WV.
Small town patronage.

Exhibitors Herald, *April 3, 1926*

A funny comedy.
Bert Silver, Silver Family Theatre, Greenville, MI.
General patronage.

Exhibitors Herald, *May 8, 1926*

Patrons did not think very much of this one.
M. J. Babin, Fairytale Theatre, White Castle, LA.
General patronage.

Exhibitors Herald, *June 5, 1926*

Pretty fair comedy, I always enjoy Harry myself and he is a distinct personality to be played up strong here. Cannot say that this particular effort is anything to rave about.
Henry Reeve, Star Theatre, Menard, TX.
Small town patronage.

Exhibitors Herald, *June 5, 1926*

Real good comedy. Our patrons like Harry in most all his comedies.
Leeman Marshall, Iris Theatre, Terrell, TX.
General patronage.

Plain Clothes

A Mack Sennett Comedy Released in Two Reels. DIRECTED BY Harry Edwards. SUPERVISED BY John A. Waldron. STORY BY Arthur Ripley and Frank Capra. TITLES BY Felix Adler and A.H. Giebler. PHOTOGRAPHED BY Billy Williams and Earl L. Stafford. EDITED BY William Hornbeck. CAST: Harry Langdon, Claire Cushman, Jean Hathaway, Vernon Dent, William McCall, Leo Sulky, Evelyn Sherman. Copyright February 13, 1925, Registration Number L21143. Released by Pathé Exchange, Inc., March 29, 1925.

SYNOPSIS: Police are still baffled by the robbery of a $100,000 diamond necklace owned by Cecile Rhodes.

Members of the Ferrett Gang are eating a meal in their boarding house. One of them holds a jewelry case and says that it's hot stuff and should be disposed of quickly. The landlady's daughter, who is clueless to the boarder's real identity, cleans off a table. She answers a knock at the door and is handed a rose. She returns a kiss to Harvey (Harry Langdon), who enters the room. He is described as her boyfriend, who is clueless about most everything. She invites him to join her on the settee. Soon she is sitting on his lap and they begin to snuggle. They are discovered by the landlady, who looks on with disapproval. Harvey attempts to leave but is restrained by the girl. The mother dismisses her daughter and sits next to Harvey to have a talk. She asks him what kind of thing he is. He proudly shows her his detective badge. Harvey accidentally pulls down some curtains and leaves. At the bustling offices of Mr. Harvey Carter Private Eye, Harvey finds his office furniture being removed for non-payment. Cecile Rhodes places a call to the Carter Agency. She tells Harvey that she'll send a promissory note right away. When the note arrives, Harvey reads it and finds an offer of $10,000 for the recovery of the necklace. He later sees the landlady's daughter in a shop and shows her the promissory note.

Meanwhile, one of the crooks is seeking a good fence to get rid of the hot ice. He's rejected by a pawnshop owner who phones the Detective Bureau after he leaves.

Harvey begins to follow a suspicious-looking man, not realizing he is a fellow detective. At the Detective Bureau office, Harvey attempts to persuade the man to follow him. In the struggle he notices the man's badge. Suddenly, several detectives converge on the Bureau office, armed with shotguns, and leave with Harvey in tow.

Many of them pile into an open car with Harvey in their midst. As the car pulls away, one of them loads a shotgun, prompting Harvey to load his tiny pistol. As the car speeds along, Harvey spots the landlady's daughter and tells her that he's on a raid. The car comes to a stop and the detectives plan their actions. Harvey tells the crooks' leader that they're on a raid. The crook slips the jewel case into Harvey's pocket. The pawnshop owner points out the crook who quickly punches a detective, knocking him into Harvey. They chase the crook into an alley and gunplay ensues. Harvey eventually begins hurtling bricks and accidentally knocks out the detective in the process.

The crook chases him, recovers the necklace and tells Harvey that he's a good egg. They leave together and return to the boarding house. Upon surprising the others, who quickly draw their guns, the leader tells them that Harvey is okay. They tell him that with his honest face, *he's* the one to hock the jewelry. They give him the necklace and as he's leaving he encounters the landlady's daughter, who exposes his identity by mistake. After she leaves, the crooks discuss how to get rid of him. Harvey removes the necklace from the case and hides it behind a couch. The leader retrieves the empty jewel case and knocks Harvey around, breaking a gas lampshade in the scuffle. Harvey thinks for a moment and decides to turn the gas jet to full. As he is getting woozy from the gas, he tells the gang that crime never pays. Harvey staggers around and falls behind the couch; just then, the crooks smell the gas. After they turn it off, the police burst into the room and arrest the crooks. Harvey is sitting on the couch and is accused by the landlady of being a home wrecker. Her daughter intervenes and ends up on the couch with Harvey. She finds the necklace and, while kissing, they both fall behind the couch.

ANALYSIS: With *Plain Clothes*, Capra was promoted to full-fledged scenarist alongside Ripley, and the results are uneven. Harry's character resumes his sexual wariness as seen in *Boobs in the Wood*, and when he proudly displays a detective's badge to his girlfriend's mother, he seems much like a child showing off a new toy. At the same time, he also displays more aggression and cleverness than usual. Such moments as painting furniture on the walls to impress a potential client, slipping the necklace out of its case and hiding it, and turning on gas to subdue the crooks are not the kinds of behavior that are expected from Harry, who usually has to depend on luck or circumstance for his successes.

HARRY MOMENT: Harry's facial pantomime as the gas fumes overpower him is delightful.

WHAT THE CRITICS SAID:
Variety, *March 18, 1925*

Another Harry Langdon comedy, this time Plain Clothes, *was exposed to continuous laughter. It is getting bromidic to say that Langdon is one of the screen's great comedians, but it is definitely shown by audience after audience that the multitude of slapstick comics and the nance-like funny men aren't four, five, six with Langdon as a favorite. This one is a Pathé-Mack Sennett, as are the others, and with the "Our Gang" group, that firm is sitting pretty insofar as comedies are concerned. Langdon's film ran 22 minutes — not long enough!*

Film Daily, *March 22, 1925*

Harry Langdon is funnier in this than almost any of his previous releases. As always, it isn't so much what he does, but the way he does it. Some of the gags are screams. In one scene, the furniture in his office is taken away because the installments are unpaid. Harry is a correspondence school detective. While he is dejectedly looking at his empty office, the telephone rings and a client — the first and only one — makes an appointment to call. Half an hour later the office looks as if it had furniture, but that which isn't made of wrapping paper is drawn in pencil on the walls. The sequence in which Langdon interviews his client and endeavors to keep her from sitting on any of the furniture is extremely funny. So is the comedy as a whole. Don't let this one get away from you. Get it.

The secret's out: Harry's a detective. Vernon Dent's gang, Claire Cushman and Jean Hathaway look on in Plain Clothes.

Motion Picture News, *March 28, 1925; Reviewed by Thomas C. Kennedy*

This latest Harry Langdon vehicle is everything that a comedy should be — which to say that it is funny. Indeed one could not reasonably ask for more laughs, or a greater quantity of genuine humor in the space of two reels than this picture affords. To outline the story, or describe any of the several gags, presents a difficulty which the reviewer cannot easily surmount. Langdon's acting is so decidedly individual — one thinks of Chaplin alone in making comparisons — that the mere telling of the incident is inadequate to convey the richness of the pantomime, the extraordinarily clever timing of the action, and the subtle play of humor and pathos suggested by the comedian....

Langdon plays the blank-faced and simple-minded detective with a sense for its full comic values which gives more testimony in his rare talents. He is more than a "silent actor" employing gesture and grimace as a substitute for words. He not only registers emotion, but projects it with an ease and grace which remove from the business of acting all obviousness and effort.... Plain Clothes *is the kind of two-reeler the screen has need for, and there is no hesitancy in recommending the picture of a "spot" on any program.*

Moving Picture World, *March 28, 1925; Reviewed by Tom Waller*

As a detective, more insipid than bashful, Harry Langdon in Plain Clothes, *a Mack Sennett two-reeler, is a howl. The whole comedy is filled with laughs and should add greatly to Harry's staff of fans.*

WHAT THE EXHIBITORS SAID:
Exhibitors Herald, *December 5, 1925*

Langdon will never make 'em any better. This one was a scream.
Jack Cairns, Brooklyn Theatre, Detroit, MI.
Neighborhood patronage.

Exhibitors Herald, *April 3, 1926*

Harry takes well here and all enjoy his work fine.
Jack Greene, New Genesco Theatre, Genesseo, IL.
Small town patronage.

Remember When?

A Mack Sennett Comedy Released in Two Reels. **DIRECTED BY** Harry Edwards. **SUPERVISED BY** John A. Waldron. **STORY BY** Arthur Ripley and Clyde Bruckman. **TITLES BY** Felix Adler and A.H. Giebler. **PHOTOGRAPHED BY** Billy Williams and Leland Davis. **EDITED BY** William Hornbeck. **CAST:** Harry Langdon, Natalie Kingston, Vernon Dent, Sam Lufkin, Irving Bacon, William McCall, Anna May the Elephant. Copyright February 13, 1925, Registration Number L21142. Released by Pathé Exchange, Inc., April 26, 1925.

SYNOPSIS: As a small boy, Harry is given a locket to remember his friend Rosemary. Young Harry escapes from the Hillcrest Orphanage. Some 15 years later, he has the world at his feet and is a wandering tramp. He encounters several tramps running from an officer on horseback. He sends them all across the state line into California as they specialize in tourists. Meanwhile, Mack's Circus is traveling to the next town. Included in the troupe is Rosemary, who plays the bearded lady and walks a wire in the show. Harry stumbles across a deserted picnic table laden with food. He begins reaching for the food but has so many choices that he doesn't actually eat anything.

Abruptly, a group of people arrives and sends Harry on his way. He soon arrives at a farm and attempts to purloin some chickens. He manages to entice some chickens to leap into his coat, after which he makes his escape. An official arrives at a hobo camp and announces that he's laying for a chicken thief. After he leaves, Harry wanders into the camp. He shows the tramps a chicken in his coat and fails to notice the official's return. Soon the official jumps on Harry and retrieves the chickens. After leaving the camp, Harry accidentally picks up a hornet's nest. He soon discovers it and hurls the nest toward the picnic table he saw previously. The diners run away in terror.

As Harry continues on his way he encounters the circus; meanwhile, a hornet is working its way into his pants. Harry immediately begins doing backflips and more to dislodge the pest. This is noticed by the manager of the circus, who promptly hires Harry as an acrobat. Soon the tents are going up in a new town. Harry pulls a big wagon with the help of an elephant and delivers several large trunks to the bearded lady's tent. He doesn't notice her but does notice the orphanage. Harry tells some fellow workers that this was where he got his start in life. Meanwhile, the bearded lady writes a letter to the orphanage asking what became of Harry Hudson. Harry sees the bearded lady for the first time and is shocked. He offers her a cigar and is refused. She asks him to take the letter to the orphanage and he inquires if she was acquainted there. She tells him of her youth when she played on a swing with young Harry. He feels her beard and is puzzled, but takes the letter to the orphanage.

Meanwhile, the bearded lady is doing her show. As Harry leaves the orphanage, a boy asks if he can be let into the circus. Harry acquiesces, and soon a dozen more boys appear around him. Harry lifts up a section of the main tent and lets them in. He's almost

Harry and Natalie Kingston. Gag photo from Remember When?

caught by the manager, who gives him a warning. Inside, the boys knock the manager down in their haste to get to their seats. The manager asks who let them in and they reply that the boss did, and they point to Harry. He admits to letting them in and asks the manager to let them stay and he'll wash the monkeys. The manager fires him and tells him to leave. As he's leaving, Harry gives the orphanage's reply to the bearded lady. The note reads that he is Harry Hudson. Rosemary, delighted at the news, kisses Harry, causing her beard to come off. Harry recognizes her and they embrace.

ANALYSIS: With this film, Ripley was joined by Clyde Bruckman, one of Buster Keaton's favorite collaborators. Ripley's penchant for a neat storyline with an oddball twist — in this case, Harry's childhood sweetheart becoming the circus's bearded lady — is nicely enhanced with some Keatonesque physical gags, such as the hornet in Harry's pants. Langdon, too, has grown considerably as an artist since appearing in the uneven, herky-jerky comedies of only a year earlier. Given a situation loosely drawn from his own performing career, his range here is marvelous. He convincingly shifts from broad yet believable gags, like those in the chicken-stealing scene, to the wistful longing for the girl he left behind. Topped off with Harry Edwards's sharpest direction to date, *Remember When?* is one of the most satisfying of Langdon's short comedies.

HARRY MOMENT: When tramp Harry discovers the deserted picnic table, he sits down to eat. He becomes a young child and is so wide-eyed with wonder at the possibilities that he doesn't eat anything. His pantomime and sudden shift to infantile behavior is fascinating and very believable.

WHAT THE CRITICS SAID:
Film Daily, *April 19, 1925*

Harry Langdon's comedies have been so well received generally that all you'll have to do to get them in is say that this is his latest. Remember When? *creates plenty of opportunity, besides, for Langdon to be as pathetic as possible. This particular type of comedy is Langdon's forte. He is as funny as he is pathetic and as pathetic as he is funny. He at times reminds one of Chaplin. One of the best bits seen in a two-reel comedy in many a day is the sequence in this in which Langdon is accused of being a chicken thief. This he denies, but the several dozen live chickens under his overcoat, protest, and he is caught with the goods. You've got to see this to appreciate it. Harry Edwards directed.*

Motion Picture News, *April 25, 1925; Reviewed by Thomas C. Kennedy*

The sobby, sentimental tale of the boy and girl who were childhood sweethearts in an orphanage and then were separated, only to meet again as members of a circus troop (sic), is burlesqued in this Harry Langdon vehicle from the Sennett studios. We hold no brief for the scenario, but Langdon has a few moments to himself, and that is enough for the fruition of splendid comic effects. He blends cupidity and stupidity in one of the most expertly acted comedy scenes we have witnessed. This is where a sheriff, hunting for a chicken thief, meets the hero while his coat is stuffed with pilfered fowls. There are other entertaining bits — enough of them to make this a first rate two-reeler.

Harry Edwards directed, while Natalie Kingston and Vernon Dent play the leading parts in support of this always amusing star.

Moving Picture World, *April 25, 1925; Reviewed by E.W.S.*

Though this film carries less story than some of the other Harry Langdons, it offers a wealth of good gags and the comedy situations pile up nicely... The story is rather bald, but the gags are fast moving and well connected. It's a laugh maker.

WHAT THE EXHIBITORS SAID:
Exhibitors Herald, *December 5, 1925*

Chaplin gets the crowd with his funny shoes. Langdon does the same with his funny face. A high class comedy. A valuable addition to any program.
Jack Cairns, Brooklyn Theatre, Detroit, MI.
General patronage.

Horace Greely, Jr.

A Principal Pictures Production Released in Two Reels. **DIRECTED BY** Alf Goulding. **TITLES BY** Robert Hopkins. **CAST:** Harry Langdon, June Marlowe, William Blaisdell; all others unknown. Originally filmed in 1923. **ORIGINAL TITLE:** "A Tough Tenderfoot." Copyright May 4, 1925, Registration Number L21476. Released by Pathé Exchange, Inc., June 7, 1925.

SYNOPSIS: Except for a fragment, this film was unavailable for viewing. Following is the synopsis submitted to the U.S. Copyright Office:

The story of a bashful young chap who goes out west to look for gold. He has many wild experiences in the toughest saloon in Coyote Junction. Eventually, more by good luck than anything else, he beats up the bums and wins the heart of the pride of Coyote Junction.

No complete prints of this film are known to exist. A four-minute fragment, which appears to be the finale, survives in a 9.5mm Pathex home movie condensation titled *The Capture of Cactus Cal.*

WHAT THE CRITICS SAID:
Motion Picture News, *June 6, 1925; Reviewed by Thomas C. Kennedy*

Harry Langdon is the star of this two-reel comedy produced by Principal Pictures under the direction of Alf Goulding. It provides an effective setting for the actor, who is seen in the wild, wild West, where he meets rough men and becomes a hero in spite of his tremendous respect for their superior fighting abilities.

The picture presents some effective situations and not a few sure-fire gags, but at the same time it is felt that Langdon has traveled far along the road since this offering was made. Langdon is now in the position where his pictures just have to be something more than merely "good" to satisfy his fans. But while Horace Greely, Jr. *is only good, still it stars an increasingly popular comedian and since there is some diversion in the film we expect it will succeed wherever shown.*

Moving Picture World, *June 6, 1925; Reviewed by Tom Waller*

Horace Greely, Jr. *is a burlesque on a western, featuring Harry Langdon. It is a comedy without any beginning or end with a goulash of things that make many people laugh. Langdon as a reader of dime novels flivvers into a town of hard men and painted women. Dumb luck makes it possible for him to knock out the toughest guy in a saloon and thereafter he is looked up to as a real hero. He later rescues a girl from a motley horde which he lassoes into the local jail.... Langdon is given plenty of latitude and those who like this comedian's work will be well satisfied with* Horace Greely, Jr.

WHAT THE EXHIBITORS SAID:
Exhibitors Herald, *April 24, 1926*

This is an extra good comedy.
Bert Silver, Silver Family Theatre, Greenville, MI.
General patronage.

Exhibitors Herald, *June 5, 1926*

Darn good comedy to run on a Saturday in a small town. Langdon is sure fine, though, anytime.
Henry Reeve, Star Theatre, Menard, TX.
Small town patronage.

The White Wing's Bride

A Principal Pictures Production Released in Two Reels. DIRECTED BY Alf Goulding. TITLES BY Robert Hopkins. CAST: Harry Langdon, June Marlowe, Helen Walton; all others unknown. Originally filmed in 1923. ORIGINAL TITLE: "A Perfect Nuisance." ALTERNATE TITLE: "The Sea Gawk." Copyright May 18, 1925, Registration Number L21476. Released by Pathé Exchange, Inc., July 12, 1925.

SYNOPSIS: This film was unavailable for viewing. Following is the synopsis submitted to the U.S. Copyright Office:

Harry, a sailor on a boat, gets hold of a famous jewel that is the object of a couple of robbers. He gives it back to the owner. Later he gets a job as a street cleaner. He goes to a fancy ball and gets the jewel again. After the robbers chase him all over the place, he finally manages to get them arrested and wins the hand of his sweetheart.

No prints of this film are known to exist.

WHAT THE CRITICS SAID:
Motion Picture News, *July 11, 1925; Reviewed by Thomas C. Kennedy*

Harry Langdon's rise to fame throws a new light on an old picture — "old" in the sense that it was made before Langdon joined the Sennett organization and started to display the extraordinary abilities which have made him one of the most talked of comedians acting before the camera today. The "new light" is something corresponding to an interest and absorption in the work of the featured player which lends attention value to a picture which on its own account is little better than a mere routine affair in two reels. It was produced by Prinicpal Pictures Corporation under the direction of Alf Goulding. Mr. Goulding also has traveled a long way since The White Wing's Bride *was made.*

Langdon's acting in this picture differs from his later performances mostly in the finish which he has acquired in achieving comedy effects and characterization. The distinctive mannerisms which are his now were part of his equipment when he essayed the inconsequential role of the white wing who suddenly is projected into a plot concerning the theft of a valuable jewel. His make-up, too, is much the same, the main features being over-sized coats and under-sized hats.

The White Wing's Bride *will not bring the laughter which is now expected of Harry Langdon comedies. It is conventional slapstick, introducing a plot merely for the purpose of supplying here and there an excuse for action, action and more action. There is the ever-present "chase" and it does not seem different from many others which have been done time out of mind in the two reelers. Langdon is set upon by a pair of fearsome-looking*

Harry admires June Marlowe in The White Wing's Bride.

Orientals, who are in pursuit of the jewel which has been stolen from the idol....

The players who support the star provide all the assistance that is possible under the circumstances.... The picture is lacking more in gag material than in quality of performance and production. It has some amusing moments and may ride along to fair success on the reputation and appeal of the star.

Moving Picture World, *July 11, 1925; Reviewed by Sumner Smith*

This is the second Harry Langdon comedy of a series of two made by Principal Pictures Corporation under the direction of Alf Goulding. It varies from the usual Langdon comedy in that it is so full of gags familiar to audiences that Langdon hasn't a chance to be personally funny. In a few scenes he appears as a street cleaner, but most of the time is dressed up. All he is given an opportunity to do is to run around and grimace. His best humor is of the more subtle and leisurely sort, and this is very broad and the subtitles are forced attempts to be funny. Audiences that like burlesque undoubtedly will find much to enjoy in The White Wing's Bride, but Langdon's ever increasing throng of followers won't consider it typical of his work.

Cleveland Plain Dealer, *January 6, 1926; Reviewed by W. Ward Marsh*

Harry Langdon, former Sennett comic who recently joined First National, appears to have weakened considerably in the final ones made for Sennett. His first for First National, which has the title of Tramp, Tramp, Tramp, *has not been completed.*

The Allen is showing his latest Sennett release (sic), however. It is called The White Wing's Bride. *One doesn't expect much plot in a two reel comedy, but no rhyme and little reason got into the make-up of this two-reeler.*

The audience which saw it Monday afternoon was an unusually quiet one. It saw nothing funny in Langdon's antics on ship board (sic), or later in his work in the streets as a white wing.

Langdon has splendid comic ability. One or two good ones will easily lift him in the ranks with Chaplin, Lloyd and Keaton. A few more bad ones will finish him off. Perhaps First National will save him.

Lucky Stars

A Mack Sennett Comedy Released in Two Reels. DIRECTED BY Harry Edwards. SUPERVISED BY John A. Waldron. STORY BY Arthur Ripley and Frank Capra. TITLES BY A.H. Giebler. PHOTOGRAPHED BY George Crocker. EDITED BY William Hornbeck. CAST: Harry Langdon, Natalie Kingston, Vernon Dent, Andy Clyde, Ruth Taylor, Roscoe "Tiny" Ward. WORKING TITLE: "The Medicine Man." Copyright July 20, 1925, Registration Number L21665. Released by Pathé Exchange, Inc., August 16, 1925.

SYNOPSIS: Harry Lamb, a trusting and naive man, is sitting on the sidewalk next to a man with a telescope. The man tells him to follow his lucky star and he'll find fame and fortune. He's handed a card with some prophecies. One is that he should be a doctor and another is that he will take a long journey and fall in love with a dark woman.

The man tells Harry that his lucky star rules his destiny. The next day, Harry arrives at a train station. He asks a porter to drop his trunk from atop a big pile on a wagon. After he does so, Harry loads several pies into his trunk. Unfortunately, the porter drops another trunk, which crushes Harry's into pieces. He is dismayed by this and leaves with his banjo. Harry runs toward a moving train and jumps aboard. Once inside, he seats himself in a car. A conductor asks him for his ticket and Harry unfolds a handkerchief, revealing a large wad of money along with the ticket. He is informed that he is on the wrong train. Harry darts about in confusion and leaps from the train. The train stops and the conductor brings a bedraggled Harry back on board. A doctor is summoned and Hiram Healey, a quack, tends to Harry's distress. He tells the doctor that he jumped from the train to follow his lucky star. The quack notices his large roll of bills and is told that Harry intends to spend it all to be a great doctor like him. After he pockets Harry's roll, the doctor tells Harry that heaven must have sent him and that he can teach him all he knows in a very short time. The doctor's destination is San Tabasco, a town of hot hate, hot love and hot tomatoes.

In the town a sign advertises Dr. Healy's Health Herbs, with a free show that evening. After arriving in town with the doctor, Harry goes into a bar and emerges with a glass of beer. The doctor tells him to leave it in the street. Harry hesitates back and forth toward the glass until they both enter the bar for a beer. As they leave, Harry still wants to retrieve the glass and is advised not to do so. They climb onto a stage atop a wagon and the doctor hands Harry a banjo. He tells the crowd that Harry will play the genuine Honolulu Banjo. As Harry begins to play, the doctor tells the crowd about his miracle medicine. It cures measles, mumps, pip, corns, and that tired feeling — all in one day.

Señorita Mazda, the druggist's daughter, arrives on the scene. She tells her father that she'll fix those quacks for spoiling his business. She holds a knife and contemplates her next move. Meanwhile, the doctor and Harry are examining a man and inform the crowd that he has a case of Hyphenated Milligatowney. The man buys a bottle of the "medicine" and soon others are buying as well. Harry tries to sell a bottle to a large man, who refuses. Harry examines the man and offers to pay for the bottle himself. The man gives the bottle back and takes Harry's money. Later, as Harry continues to play the banjo, he sees the señorita, who flirts with him. Harry consults his prophecy card and notes the line about his finding love with a dark woman. He soon joins her as she pretends to faint. Harry listens for vital signs as she caresses his neck.

He rests his head on her shoulder as she reaches for her knife. He is saved by a call from the doctor, urging him to return to the stage. Harry is told to mix up another tub of medicine. The señorita tells a friend to put something in the medicine to make people sick. The man puts some noxious liquid into the tub and departs. Harry returns and adds several ingredients to the tub. He fills several bottles and approaches a

man with an injured foot. Harry pours some of the medicine onto the foot, which burns the man. He tosses aside the bottle and it explodes on impact. He tells the doctor that something has happened to the medicine. A couple of men react violently to the medicine, and the crowd is in an uproar. People begin hurtling bottles at the doctor, who flees for his life. The wagon supporting the stage rolls away, revealing Harry mixing up another batch of the medicine. He is blissfully unaware of the confusion.

Harry eventually ends up, alone, and on the street. He sees the doctor, in tatters, still running for his life. Suddenly, the crowd appears and chases both of them. The doctor is put before a firing squad and is told, "So long" by Harry, who runs away. The doctor then escapes by jumping aboard a moving wagon. Harry continues to run away as the bottles he is carrying slip and fall onto a street, causing explosions.

ANALYSIS: Another instance of Langdon drawing from his professional life for a story, *Lucky Stars* is the first tangible example of one of his most curious notions: the absence of romance with a leading lady. In this film, Natalie Kingston is actually the "heavy," attempting to rid the town of the two medicine show quacks in order to save her father's practice. All featured comedians, even the stoic Buster Keaton and cartoonish Larry Semon, actively wooed leading ladies in their comedies, and the device was considered indispensable among those who moved into feature films. Whether due to Arthur Ripley's influence or Langdon's own judgment, the comedian would repeatedly attempt to create comedies without venturing into romantic situations, especially during the First National period.

Harry's scenes with Vernon Dent, who portrays his less-than-honest mentor, strongly prefigure Stan Laurel teamed with Oliver Hardy. The burly Dent maintains a false dignity and continually orders the subservient Harry around, much as officious Hardy would do with meek Laurel.

HARRY MOMENT: Harry's hesitation in attempting to get the glass of beer off of the street is shown in a long shot. He wants the beer, but he also wants to obey Dent, who is insistently summoning him. Harry's herky-jerky movements, both strange and wonderful, really are unique among the silent clowns.

WHAT THE CRITICS SAID:
Film Daily, *August 9, 1925*

Here's Harry Langdon again. That should be enough for you. It will undoubtedly be more than enough for your audience regardless of the type [of] house you operate. Langdon's popularity is growing by leaps and bounds. It isn't what he does. It's the wonderfully funny way he does it. He makes all his little ineffectual movements register to the n'th degree. Vernon Dent does good work as a quack medicine man who uses Harry to help him sell the cure-all. Harry makes a mistake in mixing the medicine, and the crowd runs the doctor out of town. That's all there is to the plot, but Langdon goes through it in his own inimitable fashion and wrings all the laughs possible out of every tiny situation. Harry Edwards directed.

Motion Picture News, *August 15, 1925; Reviewed by Paul A. Yawitz*

A curb astronomer advises the naïve Harry Langdon to go in search of his fortune under the guidance of a star that the telescope has picked out for him. Harry gathers his few earthly belongings and sets forth on his way in life only to meander into the pernicious hands of an itinerant snake-oil salesman. With this much for a beginning much might have been expected of the story but it develops into insignificant and meaningless hokum held together by nothing other than the two reels of raw stock.

There is something deliciously artistic in the movement of this comedian; he has the understanding which most comics lack; and to this reviewer, it seems more than shameful that so meager a story and so inept direction should be given him.

The bulk of the humor rests upon the time-worn slapstick that results when the quack doctor gives a crowd of burly Mexicans several bottles of medicine in which has been mixed a dangerous chemical. When the bottle drops it explodes and with it the possibility of holding audience interest.

Langdon is supported by Natalie Kingston, a more than beautiful Miss of Spanish type, but the cutter (or perhaps it was the director) decided they would have as little of her as necessary. And so you have less of her than is necessary to give the comedy a touch of pulchritudinal pleasance....

With a little effort the producers might have made of this an excellent comedy feature. The gags carry little punch and the action is constantly slowed up for no palpable reason. Harry Langdon's work is amusing when he is given free rein of a situation, and may get the laughs in the neighborhood theatres.

Moving Picture World, *August 15, 1925; Reviewed by Sumner Smith*

This is a more or less routine slapstick subject, with few chances for Langdon to display his unique type of comedy. He is funny but hardly any more so than any other comedian would be in the same role. Natalie Kingston is as charming as ever as the vampish señorita and Vernon Dent has a good part as the chief quack.

Film Daily, *November 8, 1925*

Harry Langdon in Lucky Stars *is another good laugh getter with amusing situations and a good share of new comedy gags.*

WHAT THE EXHIBITORS SAID:
Exhibitors Herald, *December 12, 1925*
I did not think much of this one and believe it is one of Langdon's poorest.
L. V. Feldman, Orpheum Theatre, Pipestone, MN. General patronage.

Exhibitors Herald, *March 20, 1926*
Absolutely nothing to this. I would like to know where Pathé gets a special at special high price out of this one. Lay off, boys.
A.O. Lambert, Monticello Opera House, Montincello, IA. General patronage.

There He Goes

A Mack Sennett Comedy Released in Three Reels. **DIRECTED BY** Harry Edwards. **STORY BY** Frank Capra and Arthur Ripley. **CAST:** Harry Langdon, Peggy Montgomery, Frank Whitson, Vernon Dent, Andy Clyde, Leo Sulky, Irving Bacon, Silas D. Wilcox, Charles Force. **WORKING TITLE:** "Big Bug Story." Copyright August 28, 1925, Registration Number L21780. Released by Pathé Exchange, Inc., November 29, 1925.

SYNOPSIS: This film was unavailable for viewing. Following is the synopsis submitted to the U.S. Copyright Office:

Harry is in love with the daughter of an executor of an estate who has been threatened by some crooks. Harry comes to the house and accidentally opens the safe and a bag of money falls out. Cops on the trail of the crooks chase him all over town. The crooks come to Harry's place and start to divide the money. Harry finally subdues as the cops arrive and he gets his sweetheart.

No complete prints of this film are known to exist.

WHAT THE EXHIBITORS SAID:
Exhibitors Herald, *August 20, 1927*
If you buy comedies for laughs, this one is not worth carrier charges. Disappointing.
F. G. Roberts, American Theatre, Ada, OK. General patronage.

Exhibitors Herald, *December 24, 1927*
Good.
R. Pfeiffer, Princess Theatre, Chilton, WI. Small town patronage.

Two scenes from There He Goes *(1925)*.

Saturday Afternoon

A Mack Sennett Comedy Released in Three Reels. DIRECTED BY Harry Edwards. SUPERVISED BY John A. Waldron. STORY BY Arthur Ripley and Frank Capra. TITLES BY A.H. Giebler. PHOTOGRAPHED BY Billy Williams. EDITED BY William Hornbeck. CAST: Harry Langdon, Alice Ward, Vernon Dent, Ruth Hiatt, Peggy Montgomery, Leo Willis, Anna Hernandez, Joe Young, Roscoe "Tiny" Ward. Copyright January 23, 1926, Registration Number L22306. Released by Pathé Exchange, Inc., January 31, 1926.

SYNOPSIS: Mrs. Harry Higgins is a staunch believer is wearing the pants in her marriage. While ironing her husband's pants, she finds a packet. She tells her mother that she gave him a nickel for popcorn and he bought tobacco. The mother tells her that she is too hard on him. The wife argues that the first step in losing any man is to let him get his own way.

We first see Harry Higgins on the job, at a metal shop. The noon whistle announces that it's lunchtime. He telephones his wife and tells her that he'll be two minutes late as he missed his trolley car. She gives him an earful of abuse and he runs for home. Meanwhile, his friend Steve Smith is chatting up Pearl and Ruby, two beauties. Harry runs into them and Steve tells him that the one with the swell lamps is dying to meet him. He's told to get that worried look off his face and they'll never know he's married. The two couples stroll down the street. Harry's girl gives him a kiss and runs into her house. Steve says goodbye to his girl and tells Harry to be ready for a date at two o'clock. He removes a coin from his pay packet and tells Steve that *he'll* buy the hot dogs. Steve's girl returns and Harry stands between them as they bill and coo. He is fascinated by their romantic behavior and whistles for his girl to return. Her dog comes running instead, and chases Harry down the street. The girl retrieves her dog and blows Harry a kiss, which he wipes off before entering his house. He timidly approaches his angry wife and gives her his pay packet. He hides his coin under a corner of the living room rug; under which there are other coins he's previously stashed.

As he is counting his money, the wife enters and sees him. Harry gives her the coins and says he was saving for a rainy day. After his wife storms out of the room he begins telling her off. She returns through

another door and catches him in the act. He lets it slip that he has a date with a pair of beautiful lamps. His wife, not believing him, gives Harry a dime so he can get his date a soda. After she leaves, Harry goes to another area of the rug and retrieves more coins. His wife tells her mother that she called Harry's bluff about going on a date.

At two p.m. Steve shows up and he and Harry go off to meet the girls. Harry informs Steve that he told his wife, who wears the pants. After some confusion on Harry's part they drive to the agreed-upon meeting place. The girls are not there and Steve blames Harry for making them late, so Harry looks for two other dates. He returns with two floozies. Steve tells Harry that they won't do. Harry informs the floozies and one slaps Steve and the other slaps him. Harry heaves a brick at them, but it shatters a shop window.

The boys hurry from the scene and run into Pearl and Ruby. Steve and the girls get into his car and Harry ends up in the rumble seat. They drive alongside Harry's wife, who is driving her own car. Harry hides under the rumble seat. Steve eventually spots Harry's wife and drives away down a bumpy road. When they finally arrive on level ground, Steve sends the girls back down the road to search for Harry. He opens the rumble seat and finds the bedraggled passenger within. He is quite dazed from his ordeal. On the road, the girls encounter two tough guys driving by. They stop and grill the girls about their escorts. The girls point to Steve and Harry, enraging the guys; they promptly start a fight with Steve. Harry tries to help but is knocked to the running board of Steve's car. He hands Steve a hammer to fight the duo and is knocked back to the running board when the hammerhead flies off.

One of the girls grabs a cup of gasoline by mistake and gives it to Harry to drink. He becomes energized and joins the fight, but is punched to the ground. He crawls back to the two cars and positions himself on each car's running board. A cop frightens the brawlers and they speed away, with Harry caught between the two cars. He ends up wrapped around a post and is helped by two passing men. His wife pulls up in her car and she and Harry drive off. She tells Harry that it is all her fault for giving him that dime. He puts his head on her shoulder as they drive along.

ANALYSIS: *Saturday Afternoon* captures the Langdon-Edwards-Ripley-Capra collaboration in full bloom: Ripley's insistence on linear storytelling, Capra's sense of whimsy, and Langdon's solid grasp of characterization, driven by Edwards's cinematic know-how. Topped off with Vernon Dent's role encompassing both instigator and foil, the result is perhaps the most perfect comedy Langdon would ever make.

The story moves along at such a good clip, with every sequence progressing logically from one to the next, the three-reel length is hardly noticeable. The Little Elf is so intriguing a character that the laughs come not just from the strength of the gags, but directly out of Harry's implausible existence. He's a

married man, yet gazes at Steve kissing his girl with such acute concentration that you suspect he's never done such a thing before. He can watch the clock with the rest of the laborers, and secret away some cash for himself like any henpecked husband, but can't comprehend what to do with the free time or the money without his pal's guidance. Even his domineering wife understands how utterly blameless her husband is, no matter the degree of trouble he's in.

HARRY MOMENT: Harry's scene in which he tells off his wife only to be caught by her reveals his pantomime skills at their peak. He seamlessly portrays a wide spectrum of emotions, from anger, to confidence, to embarrassment, to abject fear.

WHAT THE CRITICS SAID:
Film Daily, *January 24, 1926*

Here's another Langdon knockout. It's a three reel comedy with a laugh every minute. They'll chuckle when they're not laughing and laugh when they're not chuckling. Langdon with all his typical, ineffectual mannerisms is seen as a dutiful day-laborer who is in the habit of letting his wife scare him into faithfulness... Get this one.

Moving Picture World, *January 30, 1926; Reviewed by Sumner Smith*

Here's another Harry Langdon-Mack Sennett scream, with Harry as the dutiful husband of a domineering wife until a friend takes him on a joy ride with some chickens. From beginning to end it's a series of laughs. It isn't choked with gags, but moves at a pace leisurely enough to allow Harry footage for real comedy acting. And he can act! Another great thing about the comedy is the titling. A. H. Giebler has provided some pippins, including, "Just a crumb from the sponge cake of life," in introducing our hero... The cast includes Vernon Dent who is very effective, Ruth Hiatt and Peggy Montgomery. Harry Edwards directed Langdon in most intelligent style. The subject ought to tickle highbrows and medium brows alike.

Variety, *September 22, 1926; Reviewed by Fred*

The selection of the three-reel Harry Langdon comedy as part of the Rialto program with Thomas Meighan in Tin Gods *was a fortunate one.* Tin Gods *failed to click with the audience, and* Saturday Afternoon *saved the bill. Langdon is a funny guy, and this three-reeler, coming along when he has just scored in* The Strong Man, *should mop up.*

Langdon has the role of a browbeaten blacksmith's assistant. It's Saturday afternoon, and on the way home a pal meets a couple of "pips" and dates them up. He rings Langdon in on the date. Langdon does a holdout of two bits from the pay envelope, but the wife catches him counting his hidden hoard, and cops it all. But he fools her, as he has another cache.

The keeping of the date, the fights that follow and the automobile ride with the half-unconscious Langdon sitting on the running board of one car with his feet resting on another, is all business that will bring howls.

Of the supporting cast Vernon Dent as the pal gets over, while the brow-beating wife of Ruth Hiatt registers. The Girls are typical Mack Sennett beauties.

Film Daily, *September 24, 1926; Reviewed by Kann*

That Langdon man is irresistible. Before leaving Mack Sennett, he made several short subjects which had yet to reach the market. One of them, Saturday Afternoon, *is at the Rialto. It's a riot. Langdon is a real comic, if ever there was one.*

WHAT THE EXHIBITORS SAID:
Exhibitors Herald, *March 12, 1927*

A very good comedy. If you have a weak show this is just what you want, it's a little feature.
Wilcox and Miller, Lake View Theatre, Lake View, IA. General patronage.

Exhibitors Herald, *November 24, 1928*

A very funny comedy.
Bert Silver, Silver Family Theatre, Greenville, MI. General patronage.

Tramp, Tramp, Tramp

A Harry Langdon Corporation Production Released in Six Reels. **DIRECTED BY** Harry Edwards. **STORY BY** Arthur Ripley and Frank Capra. **ADAPTATION:** Tim Whelan, Hal Conklin, J. Frank Holliday, Gerald Duffy, Murray Roth. **PHOTOGRAPHY BY** Elgin Lessley and George Spear. **CAST:** Harry Langdon, Joan Crawford, Alec B. Francis, Brooks Benedict, Tom Murray, Edwards Davis, Carlton Griffith. **WORKING TITLE:** "Mr. Nobody." Copyright March 7, 1926, Registration Number L22515; Renewed March 4, 1954, Number R126537. Released by First National Pictures, Inc., March 21, 1926.

SYNOPSIS: John Burton, head of Burton Shoes, boasts to the company's board members that his advertising "is gradually wiping out competition." This includes small businesses, such as that of Amos Logan, who is facing eviction from his cobbler's shop. The landlord, Nick Kargas, gives Amos three months to raise the mortgage money. Amos, in turn, sends his son Harry out to make good. Harry will try, provided he's not too distracted by the Burton Shoes billboard girl, as he's fallen in love with her image.

Harry becomes an assistant to Kargas, who is also a champion long-distance walker, on his way to compete in Burton's latest publicity scheme: a cross-country walkathon, from Massachusetts to California, with each competitor outfitted in Burton shoes and a sweatshirt that advertises the company. The winner will receive a $25,000 cash prize, to be presented by Betty Burton, who is not only John Burton's daughter, but also the girl in the billboard.

By the time they arrive the evening before the contest, Kargas has been irritated by both Harry's ineptitude and inability to tear himself away from the billboards, and fires him in front of everyone, including Betty. She sympathizes with the little man, and decides he is entitled to compete. While Harry admires her picture on the billboard, she approaches him with the needed accessories, taking him completely by surprise. Once he gets past the shock and fear of being so close to her, she presents him with an entry form, tells him she hopes he wins the $25,000 prize, and assures him she'll meet him in California. Harry realizes this is his chance to obtain both the money for his father and the girl of his dreams.

Harry is asked by the hotel manager to share his room with a fellow contestant, who turns out to be Kargas. When Kargas enters, Harry is covering the walls with Betty's image, which he's taken from several billboards. Kargas tears down most of the pictures and orders Harry to "forget that woman and let me sleep." One of the photos is over Kargas's bed, and when it falls over, Harry climbs upon the bed to hammer it back into place, causing the bed to collapse. Kargas hurls a pillow at Harry, who ducks; the pillow knocks an electric fan onto Harry's bed.

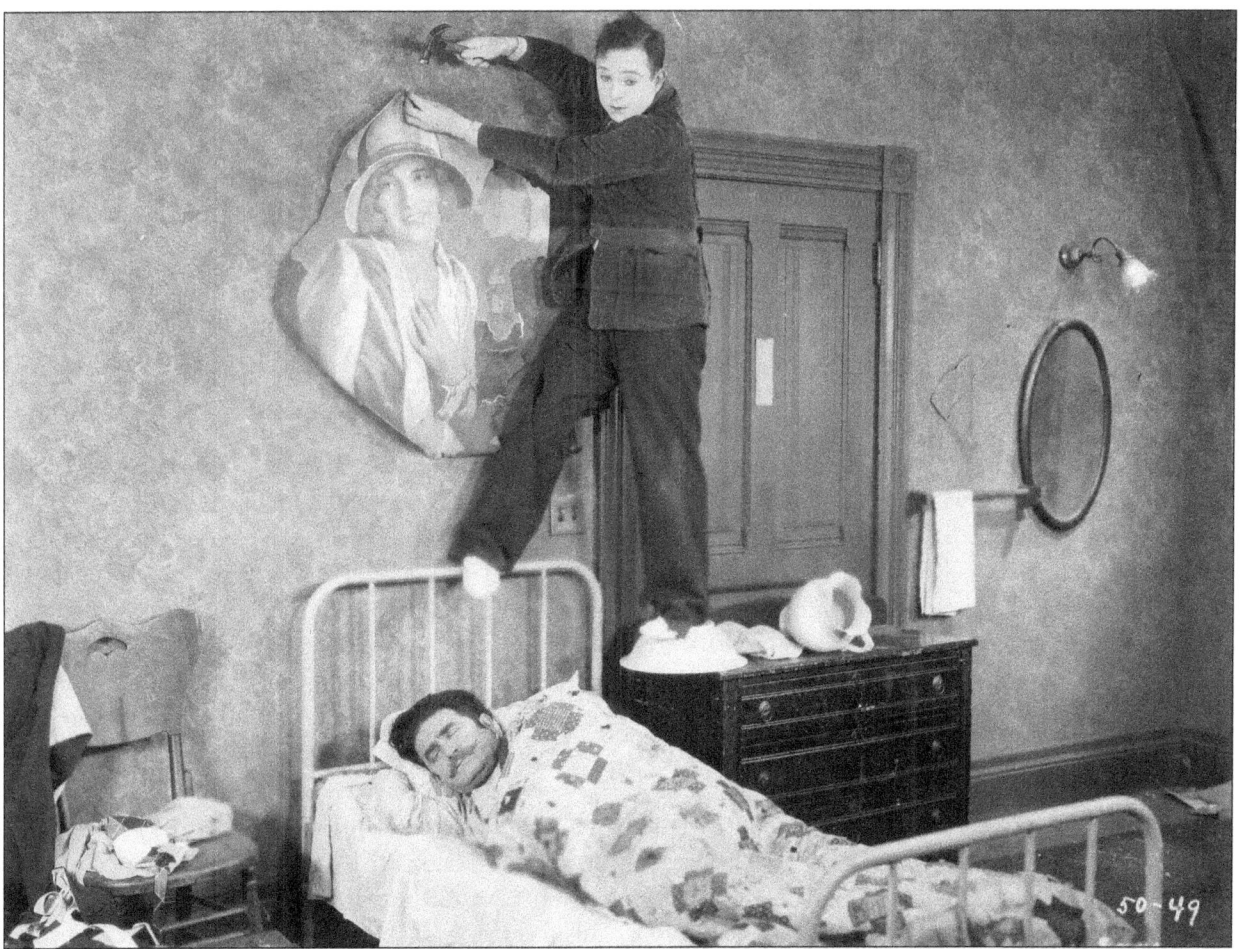

Disaster is about to befall Tom Murray in Tramp, Tramp, Tramp.

Believing he's turning out the light, Kargas throws a wall switch, and it activates the fan, sending feathers flying around the room.

Harry insists he can't sleep. Kargas pulls out a bottle of sleeping tablets, for which the recommended dosage is one, and gives Harry a handful. Harry takes them and gradually fades out, falling asleep on the floor. The next morning, the race is ready to begin. The announcer calls Harry's name, but he's still unconscious in his hotel room. The hotel manager awakens him and helps him dress for the race, but Harry's still extremely groggy. He arrives in a taxi and can't seem to comprehend that he needs to pay a fare. Harry tries to find money but the sleeves on his "Burton Shoes" sweatshirt are so long, he can't get his hand into his pocket. In frustration, the cab driver threatens to fight him, removing his coat and rolling up his sleeves. Harry, in turn, rolls up his sleeves, then reaches into his pants pocket, retrieves a coin and pays the driver.

Betty is there to see him off. Harry hands her a note and tells her, "Don't forget, we got a date in California." The note reads:

Dear Sweetheart –

I love you, I love you, I love you, I love you, I love you, I love you, I love you.

And hope you are the same.
Harry

Harry rushes to catch up to the other competitors, then dashes past them. He fails to see that they've all veered off the road he's on. Harry stops to remove something from his shoe, and notices that the walkers are now ahead of him on a different road. He tries to take a shortcut and winds up in a sheep pasture. To escape the sheep, he decides to climb over a fence, but doesn't see there's a sheer drop of at least a mile on the other side. As he climbs over, a nail catches his sweatshirt and belt. He removes the sweatshirt, and as he starts to undo the belt, he happens to look down. With a start, he realizes he's in serious danger. His solution is to refasten the belt and replace the sweatshirt around the nail, and then to hammer more nails into the shirt. He gets the nails by prying them from other parts of the fence, but this causes the section to which he's attached to come loose. Eventually, Harry removes one nail too many and winds up sliding down the cliff-face, with the fence serving as a toboggan. Amazingly, the fence comes to a stop along the proper road, just in time to block the other walkers, while Harry is free to proceed.

Amos Logan follows his son's progress by watching newsreels at the local movie house. In the first of these, the race leaders are in Cleveland, Ohio, where John Burton greets them at one of his stores. Betty is there, too, and Harry can't resist giving her a kiss.

The walkers are headed through farm country, and a farmer is complaining to the law that his fruit has been disappearing. When they notice fruit dropped along the road, they proceed to follow the trail with guns drawn. Eventually they catch up to Harry, with a mouth smeared with berries and a watermelon tucked in his sweatshirt. He tries to hide the melon, but it causes his pants to fall. At the same time, a live chicken pokes its head out of the shirt. Harry is taken into custody and placed on a chain gang.

Ordered to grab a hammer and start breaking rocks along a roadside, Harry chooses the smallest hammer in the lot, but one of the guards insists he take a bigger one. When Harry does so, the head falls off the handle. As both Harry and the guard reach for another hammer, Harry winds up with the guard's rifle. When the guard raises his hands in alarm, a frightened Harry tosses the rifle to the ground, which goes off. He picks up his ball and chain and starts to run, but another guard holds him at gunpoint. With that, Harry raises his hands, dropping the ball on the second guard's foot. Both guards insist Harry take a hammer, whereupon he chooses the small one again.

While Harry breaks up the tiniest rocks around, another group of prisoners have dug up a hidden chest containing loaded weapons. These are passed out to all the prisoners, including Harry, who mistakes his pistol for the hammer, and proceeds to use the butt to break a rock — which discharges a shot. This alerts the guards and a melee breaks out. The guards are overpowered, and the convicts, including Harry, escape. The majority of the convicts climb into a moving boxcar, shutting its door before Harry can board. He tosses his ball into another car, and in trying to climb inside, he disengages the boxcar containing the convicts. The train picks up speed and Harry has to run to avoid being dragged.

"Forty miles later," a title tells us, the train comes to a stop. Harry removes his ball, sits down and examines his feet. Both shoes and socks are a wreck, the soles completely gone. He dips his feet into a puddle of water for a few minutes. As he prepares to move on, the train pulls out, severing Harry's chain, which had been draped across the rail. However, Harry fails to notice this, and picks up the ball when he spies one of the walkers. It is Kargas. When Harry tries to hide the ball in his coat, Kargas takes it from him. While Harry tries to explain, the broken chain hooks onto Kargas's pants; when Kargas hurls the ball away in disgust, he is pulled off the road into a ditch. Harry turns and realizes that the man he's speaking to is no longer there, but neither is the ball. He smiles and moves on.

Amos catches another edition of the newsreel: Harry and Kargas are the two "surviving contestants" of the Burton Race, and are in Silver City, Utah, preparing to cross the desert. John Burton and his daughter are at Sand City, at the western edge of the desert, waiting to greet the pair when they emerge. Burton predicts that the first walker to arrive "will undoubtedly win the race." It's Kargas, and as he drinks from a pitcher of water, Betty asks about Harry. Kargas laughs and tells her, "Haven't seen him for weeks. Guess the wolves got him in the desert."

The next day, a refreshed Kargas is ready to leave Sand City and complete the race's final leg. The wind is starting to pick up, and Burton points out that ominous clouds are forming, but Kargas is unafraid. However, before Kargas can leave town, a telegraph operator runs out and warns the onlookers that a cyclone is nearing. Everyone, including Kargas, rushes to shelter.

As the winds pick up strength, Harry appears from around a corner, running. He's stunned to see the town is apparently empty, but is delighted that "a breeze" is cooling him. As the winds grow stronger, Harry dashes into a barbershop. "Am I next?" he calls out, but no one else is there. He prepares to take a bath, but as the cyclone draws nearer, the shop starts to vibrate back and forth. Suddenly, Harry is blown out the front door. He grabs the door and hangs on for dear life, while Kargas is blown into the shop through the rear entrance. Kargas manages to close the back door, which enables Harry to re-enter the shop. As the two spy each other, Harry cheerfully greets his rival; Kargas explains about the cyclone and

Edwards Davis, Langdon, Joan Crawford in Tramp, Tramp, Tramp.

begs Harry to save him. As the twister comes into town, buildings start to topple and the shop is violently buffeted by the winds. Harry tries to telephone for help just as the shop collapses. He's blown into the street and watches the damage being wrought. He tries to keep a building from collapsing and hears a cry for help from within. It's Betty Burton. Harry rushes inside and rescues her.

The storm is getting worse, and in order to protect Betty, Harry decides to take action. As the cyclone approaches, Harry hurls bricks at it. Suddenly the twister veers down a side street and away from the town. Harry returns satisfied that his brick throwing has saved the day.

Another newsreel depicts the finale of the Burton Race. Harry and Kargas are running neck-and-neck, but Harry dashes forward at the last second to be declared the winner. The moviegoers congratulate Amos. With the prize money, Harry has paid off his father's debts and married Betty. As Harry and Amos are walking together, Betty greets them and tells Harry, "The baby is calling." The couple watches their young son, who is the spitting image of his father, playing in his bassinette.

ANALYSIS: Overlooked due to the widespread acclaim for *The Strong Man*, erroneously credited in part to Arthur Ripley, and misrepresented as a Frank Capra film that happened to be directed by Harry Edwards, *Tramp, Tramp, Tramp* is, in many respects, Langdon's most uncharacteristic film. Its latter-day reputation is due mainly to Capra having assigned himself and Ripley most of the credit for its story, as well as labeling himself its co-director alongside Edwards. The film, though, belies all the revisionism. Credit for the story and structure of *Tramp, Tramp, Tramp* belongs, first and foremost, to its head writer and scenario editor: Tim Whelan, formerly of Harold Lloyd's writing staff.

The plot of *Tramp, Tramp, Tramp* exactly mirrors Lloyd's almost patented formula of the young man who must succeed at a formidable task to not only save the day but also win the girl. Capra and the other gagsters may have molded the individual gags to suit Langdon's character, but the situations are tailor-made for Lloyd. The thrill scene at the cliff's edge — for many, the most memorable moment of the film — is unmistakably Lloyd-influenced, but everything else applies as well. One can easily imagine Lloyd (perhaps as "Harold Logan") encountering and overcoming every single obstacle placed before Harry in this film. This is not the case with any subsequent Langdon feature, or even with *His First Flame*, made several months earlier.

That said, Langdon brings his individuality to each scene. No other comedian could have pulled off the moment where Harry encounters his dream girl face-to-face for the first time, as he veers between elation and horror, with every stop in between, all in a matter of seconds. When confronted with the theft of the farmer's fruit and chicken, he's not bright enough to realize that his berry-stained face gives him away, or that shifting a watermelon into his pants will cause them to fall. And only Harry could be convinced that a cyclone can be chased out of town by hurtling bricks at it. It's through sheer force of personality that a Harold Lloyd story becomes a Harry Langdon film.

Audiences, though, were conditioned by Lloyd to expect decisive action when presented with such a premise, and a few critics commented on the lack of it in *Tramp, Tramp, Tramp*. Yet Langdon's entire persona was built around reacting to life's crises, not resolving them. What he needed were stories that were constructed around his strengths, rather than have them shoehorned into ready-made situations. That problem would be rectified once Ripley rejoined the team.

HARRY MOMENT: The scene at the fence is undoubtedly the film's best-remembered highlight. Harry fails to notice the drop, as he's concerned only with escaping the sheep. His double-take, upon looking down, is a marvelously funny moment, but then he again becomes focused on only one thing: avoiding a fall. Consequently he doesn't notice how his "solution" is jeopardizing his safety.

WHAT THE CRITICS SAID:
Exhibitor's Daily Review, *March 16, 1926.*
Reviewed by "Mac" Oracle

Irwin Wheeler, of the Playhouse Theatre, Rye, N.Y., was host to the entire sales force of First National Pictures Corporation and their friends Friday night at the eastern preview of Harry Langdon's first comedy super-feature, Tramp, Tramp, Tramp.

For months picture fans throughout the country have been demanding a Harry Langdon feature picture. It's now here. This picture without question will establish him as one of the foremost comedians of the screen. It is the story of a foot race from Massachusetts to California and it's a riot, nothing less. A "Race Riot." It's one long, solid laugh with a breathing spell here and there to catch your breath and wipe the tears out of your eyes.

The audience displayed every brand of laughter known, giggles, grins, chuckles, mirth, topped with loud, uncontrolled, exploding side-splitting laughter. Everyone laughed at the drolleries of Langdon, then at the way others in the audience laughed and then at themselves.

Hats off to Richard Rowland and his entire production organization. Tramp, Tramp, Tramp *is an achievement and it's going to "click" at the box office wherever it is played.*

There isn't a gag in the picture that doesn't register. There are many the audience will carry home to tell their friends. The person that made the remark that there is nothing new under the sun should see the new gags in this picture.

This picture is a "Nineteen Twenty-Seven" Model with a 250 HP "Non Stop Mirth" Motor and no breaks. It's a triumph for Langdon, whose pantomime never misses. Titles are few but fit like a glove. And the windup is a "WOW" with the usual happy ending with a baby and the happily married couple. Langdon's acting as the baby in the crib starts everybody off again in convulsive laughter just when they thought they could pull up and rest their aching sides.

Start working all the influence you've got with First National to get this picture on your screen as soon as possible, tell everybody in your town you've got it and it will be TRAMP, TRAMP, TRAMP of thousands of feet to your box office to get in on the good time.

Motion Picture News, *April 10, 1926; Reviewed by George H. Pardy*

Looks like an attraction surely destined to get the money at the box office. It is clean, wholesome comedy, mixing up mirthful situations with snappy thrill shots, smoothly directed and racing along with electric speed. You couldn't pick out a more likely picture for the family trade, and in fact it's pretty sure to please all classes of fans, for even its most comic absurdities are excellent specimens of fooling. They keep Harry Langdon busy all the way through and there's no denying his originality or power or personal appeal in the character of the lovable young hobo hero. Also the superfluity of subtitles that has marred many a jestful feature, don't handicap this film. There are just enough, and no more, to help out the continuity and the action is much benefited thereby. Joan Crawford a vivaciously pretty Betty; support good, photography excellent.

Summary: Has universal audience appeal. Comedy with real human interest, puts over lively gags, snappy farce punches, thrills by the score. Harry Langdon at his best, a sure laugh-creator, with a little romance to balance the fun.

Cleveland Plain Dealer, *April 19, 1926; Reviewed by W. Ward Marsh*

There have been times when I considered Langdon one of our funniest slapstick comedians. At least one of his two-reelers I rate almost on a par with Chaplin's best.

But Tramp, Tramp, Tramp *does little more than permit Langdon's fans to witness the metamorphosis of a comedian; that is, the change from an expert two-reel comic to a fair-to-bad feature length comedian.*

Tramp, Tramp, Tramp *is only occasionally funny. Langdon possesses certain facial expressions which exercised invariably send me into mild convulsions; these appear in this film. But the photoplays demand action and the deadpans both of Langdon and Keaton haven't enough action to keep things completely lively for six or seven reels. Keaton, however, is much more successful in obtaining funny stories.* Tramp, Tramp, Tramp is Langdon's first, and his story is merely a two-reeler stretched out. He may improve; there certainly is room for it, and he has my prayers, for a good story next time.

The picture is about a cross-country foot race and the fun is largely obtained from the roadside — where the film's many authors apparently have rested in an effort to "think up" laughs.

Photoplay, *May 1926*

This picture takes Harry Langdon's doleful face and pathetic figure out of the two-reel class and into the Chaplin and Lloyd screen dimensions. Not that he equals their standing yet, but he is a worthy addition to a group of comedy makers of which we have entirely too few. Langdon has graduated and this picture is his diploma. Tramp, Tramp, Tramp *will introduce him to a wider public, and the public which followed his two-reel career will be doubled or trebled. The boy's good.*

The Reel Journal, *May 22, 1926*

Consider this one of the cleverest comedy productions ever offered the American public. Langdon steps to the head of the class in this triumph. Congratulations on this big success to First National. Exhibitors should win with Langdon.

New York Times, *May 24, 1926; Reviewed by Mordaunt Hall*

While viewing Harry Langdon in his first feature-length production, Tramp, Tramp, Tramp, *one is impelled to feel a greater respect for Charlie Chaplin's genius than ever, for although Mr. Langdon undoubtedly has a keen sense of the ridiculous there are in this new film several episodes that are strongly reminiscent of* The Gold Rush *and which suffer by comparison with the Chaplin comedy. You are able to enjoy Mr. Langdon's control over his features in portraying a very simple young man, but at the same time you can't help thinking how much more finished were the situations in Chaplin's picture. This, of course, is hardly Mr. Langdon's fault, but rather that of the half dozen authors who contributed to the gags in his story.*

One of the passages mindful of Mr. Chaplin's effort is that in which Harry Logan (Mr. Langdon) climbs over a fence, only to discover that on the other side is a precipice. He is stopped from falling, from what appears to be a dizzy height, through his sweater catching on a single nail. Mr. Chaplin depicted much the same idea in the cabin sequence in The Gold Rush *when he swung through the door while the frail frame structure was balanced on the edge of an Alaskan ravine. Then, in this current picture, there is a series of scenes in which Mr. Langdon battles against a high wind, as Chaplin did in the cabin, and also a glimpse of flying feathers from a pillow, similar to that in* The Gold Rush *where Chaplin was ecstatic over the promise of the girl to dine with him on New Year's Eve. In each instance the actual fun in the Langdon film is pictured more mechanically than that in* The Gold Rush. *The scenes in this new photoplay are invariably abrupt in their termination.*

This is quite a jolly entertainment and it was obviously enjoyed by the majority of the Mark Strand audience yesterday afternoon.

New York Evening Post, *May 24, 1926*

Harry Langdon is the latest comedian to step from the two-reelers into the realm of full-length comedy, his first ambitious effort being Tramp, Tramp, Tramp, *at the Strand this week. There have been many comedies better than this one beyond a doubt, but there are few comedians at work today who top Mr. Langdon when it comes to quaintly idiotic pantomime. He has, it seems, a technique all his own, and the near-hysteria at the Strand yesterday indicated beyond a doubt that Chaplin, Lloyd, Keaton, Griffith, MacLean, Hines and Company have a new junior member of the firm, and not so junior at that.*

Mr. Langdon is engaged in this, his first lengthy opus, in a strenuous effort to win a cross-country walking contest arranged for advertising purposes by the Burton Shoe concern. The prize is $25,000 and our hero has every reason to believe that victory may bring him the Burton daughter as well, for he has fallen violently in love with that lady from her picture on a billboard and she has — Heaven be praised! — smiled upon him as the race starts. The question, however, appears to be "Will She Smile in California as She Did in Massachusetts?" and then came the cyclone. Many of the Langdon cyclonic antics are funnier than similar house-teetering episodes in Chaplin's The Gold Rush, *and nothing more need be said concerning this engaging gentleman except that he should by all means be seen by anybody who likes to laugh.*

Brooklyn Daily Eagle, *May 25, 1926; Reviewed by Martin Dickstein*

Reports from out of town where Harry Langdon's latest comedy, Tramp, Tramp, Tramp, *was presented preparatory to its New York showing, indicated that here, indeed, was the farce of the century. From San Francisco, from New Orleans, from Charleston and other way places there had wafted to this desk the hosannas of the film writers. And so, with great expectations, your correspondent went yesterday to the Strand Theater in Manhattan to laugh himself into a state bordering upon coma.*

But Tramp, Tramp, Tramp, *at least as it may be seen now in Manhattan, fails to bear out the superlative adjectives which have gone into those advance reports. It is not such a thing as to cause couples to pair off and dance where 47th Street crosses Broadway.*

There are one or two situations in the Langdon piece which were suggested, it seems, by Chaplin in The Gold Rush. *There is the episode in a hotel room where an electric fan, tossed into a bed, stirs up a storm of feathers.*

"I can't sleep," subtitles Langdon with that infantile stare as he picks the feathers from his mouth.

And then there is that business of climbing over a fence only to discover that there is a drop of several hundred feet on the other side. This was treated of in The Gold Rush *in the cabin sequence in which the shack, swept away by a windstorm, hangs dangerously over the edge of a precipice.*

Tramp, Tramp, Tramp *is a slow moving and often dull comedy. It is not to be compared with Harold Lloyd's* For Heaven's Sake *nor even with* Wet Paint, *which occupied the same screen a week ago.*

Variety, *May 26, 1926; Reviewed by Sisk*

First big picture by a man who played in vaudeville several years ago, and who wasn't even a headliner, although a well-rated standard act. Into the movies he went, taking his vaudeville tricks, and within six months his two-reel comedies were much sought.

In Tramp, Tramp, Tramp *he has done it. The film has a finish that will cause as much talk as Peggy [Hopkins] Joyce's romances. That scene is where the hero and the girl are married a year or so later and look in through a window to call to their baby. And in the cradle is Langdon, dressed in baby clothes and goo-gooing away for dear life. The effect, of course, was gained by use of a large scale cradle and everything else is scale, so that his body might be properly dwarfed...*

Langdon does some remarkable work in Tramp, Tramp, Tramp. *Aside from the expert handling of the gags assigned him, he does several very long scenes in which facial expression is the only acting. Joan Crawford is borrowed from Metro to be a nice leading lady with little to do, while Tom Murray as a mighty hard-boiled walking champion is the only other member whose assignment amounts to more than a bit.*

Tramp, Tramp, Tramp *will be great for First National, ditto for the exhibitors. If Langdon can follow it with something as good or better, he is automatically installed as a pretty high muckety-muck among the Chief Screen Comedians.*

The New York Times, *May 30, 1926; Follow-up by Mordaunt Hall*

Baby-faced Harry Langdon was seen last week at the Mark Strand in his first long production. It is called Tramp, Tramp, Tramp, *and is the sort of comedy which is funny, but which at the same time in several chapters is quite like Chaplin's comedy in* The Gold Rush. *Of course, Chaplin no more than Lloyd has any corner on the fun to be obtained through placing a character at a seemingly dizzy height. It is also true that Charlie Chaplin has not copyright on a scene in which feathers fly all over a room nor in producing one in which a pathetic character battles against a wind. However, Mr. Langdon, thanks to his half a dozen authors, has such scenes in* Tramp, Tramp, Tramp, *and they are not nearly so well pictured as those in the Chaplin comedy.*

One can, however, enjoy some incidents in the Langdon film. There is, for instance, one where he is working with a ball and chain gang in breaking stones, and Mr. Langdon's efforts rather remind one of a man cracking nuts. The high-spot in this particular chapter is where Langdon, although his heavy chain has been severed, still believes it to be intact and, therefore, carries the iron ball around with him.

The idea of the story is an entertaining one, as Langdon is supposed to be walking from "Burton," Mass., to California to win a prize. There are various incidents through which the rival pedestrians are defeated, some of the ideas being quite hilarious. Even the episode in which Langdon climbs over the fence, only to discover that once on the other side he faces a drop of several hundred yards, is mirth-provoking, although it is not nearly as cleverly pictured as Chaplin's experience in the cabin when that frail structure is balanced on the edge of an Alaskan ravine. In trudging along the road Langdon's walk often reminds one of Chaplin's well-known waddle. Hitherto Mr. Langdon's short comedies have had the spice of originality, but this effort will be really funnier to those few who may not have seen The Gold Rush.

Brooklyn Daily Eagle, *May 31, 1926; Reviewed by Martin Dickstein*

Harry Langdon, the moon-faced comedian with the baby stare is revealed at the Brooklyn Strand Theater this week in his first feature length comedy, Tramp, Tramp, Tramp. *Langdon is a cum laude graduate of the variety* stage and two-reelers for Mack Sennett. His face, in truth, is his fortune. I cannot recall an eyelid flutter or a lip tighten to better comedic advantage than those of this fellow Langdon at the Strand.

Toward the story itself, however, I am not as generously inclined. In the first place, Tramp, Tramp Tramp is one of those pictures in seven reels which could very nicely have been scissored to four. To report that it is consistently amusing would be to exaggerate its smile-provoking quality. It is one of those things which evoke a grin here, a chuckle there and sighs of tolerance in the places that go between.

Considering duly Langdon's excellent close-camera pantomime and one of two other droll situations, Tramp, Tramp, Tramp manages to be fairly entertaining.

Photoplay, *June 1926*

The first feature length comedy featuring Harry Langdon — and the boy's good. Worthwhile.

Film Daily, *June 1, 1926; Reviewed by Lilian W. Brennan*

The past two weeks have not brought forth any great array of fine pictures, but there have been several notably excellent performances by players not usually found holding sway in the headlines.... One of the best of the week was Harry Langdon's comedy Tramp, Tramp, Tramp. The picture, his initial feature to be released, was replete with a lot of new gags and fine comedy business. Langdon's work, especially long sequences when he held the screen alone and through sheer clever pantomime kept the laughs coming, is high class comedy.

Harrison's Reports, *June 5, 1926*

A good comedy! Some patrons may even consider it excellent entertainment. There are laughs all the way through, and some thrills of the Safety Last[!] sort. Such thrills are caused when the hero attempts to lower himself on the other side of a fence, ignorant of the fact that the

Langdon and Joan Crawford in Tramp, Tramp, Tramp.

ground is several hundred feet below. The scenes showing him hanging in mid-air, his blouse having been caught on a nail, gives one chills. Suspense is mingled with laughs when the broad fence breaks and he, riding down on the broken part of it, slides down a hill. Toward the end the cyclone scenes thrill one as well as make one laugh. There are other comical situations all the way through. Mr. Langdon possesses a comical style all his own; his facial expression is that of a pantomimist. With good stories, he ought to work up a following as big as that of Chaplin or Harold Lloyd. Joan Crawford takes the part of the heroine well in the love affair. Harry Edwards's directorial work is good. Good for week-run theatres.

Film Daily, *June 6, 1926*

Langdon's First Feature Comedy To Be Released Comes Through With Fine Lot of Laughs and an Array of New and Amusing Gags.

Star: Another of the sober faced comedians who gets most of his laughs over without breaking a smile himself. Has a few stunts in this that are real gems.

Cast: Not important. Joan Crawford is the girl and Tom Murray is Harry's chief competitor in the cross continent walk.

Type of Story: Comedy. Harry Langdon's success in two reel comedies lead the way to his initial feature comedy release, Tramp, Tramp, Tramp, *a picture replete with laughs and a quantity of amusing slapstick that assures good comedy entertainment. Judging from the reception given it by the Strand audiences the picture is a complete success. Not all of Langdon's gags, in spite of the fact that six people claim authorship, are new. The comedy thrill bit is reminiscent of Lloyd, and the cyclone episode has been used for comic effect before. Nevertheless, there are plenty of new stunts and the idea of the cross country hike for a basic theme is a corker…*

The picture has few slow spots but on the whole it maintains a fine average and to all appearances was sending them out of the Strand chuckling over the comedy.

Box Office Angle: Looks like sure-fire bet. Langdon promises to set new pace for himself, if they give him the material.

Direction: Harry Edwards; good.
Photography: Fair.

Moving Picture World, *June 12, 1926*

Possessed of the attributes which immediately placed him well up in the front as a comedian in two-reelers, it was inevitable that Harry Langdon would eventually find his way into comedies of feature length. The plunge has been made in Tramp, Tramp, Tramp, *released through First National, and Harry emerges triumphantly…*

With the space of the whole continent to deal with and a multitude of different situations at his disposal, Director Harry Edwards had an ample field from which to choose his material, and that he had done his work well is shown by the fact that Tramp, Tramp, Tramp *develops a succession of smiles, chuckles, laughs, roars and some thrills, too, that have all been handled with the comedy angle in view.*

Harry's big card is his thoroughly amusing personality in make-up. In several of the scenes, such as his entry in the race and his coming into the western town during a cyclone, his appearance is good for a spontaneous laugh before he does a thing. This is backed up by a genius at handling his hands, feet and face for comedy effect, nothing boisterous, but always subdued, which scores with a bang.

Of course, no matter how good a comedian is he must have the material. Harry has a lot of new gags and even those which are along familiar lines are given a new twist through his handling… Tramp, Tramp, Tramp *is good, clean wholesome fun, suitable for the entire family and of the type that will amuse every member. It looks like good box-office stuff for any type of house, for it contains in generous measure the universal appeal of laughter.*

Rochester (NY) Democrat and Chronicle, *June 21, 1926*

Now that Comedy is King in the world of the cinema and that theater managers are striving to bring in the crowds that turn instinctively to the great highways of nature in the summer season, there should be at least some alleviation of the latters' energies. Many a motorist will bethink himself when a good comedian is heralded for a local screen and decide in favor of the theater. If there be any such who are hesitating right now concerning the advisability of seeing Harry Langdon in his first feature-length comedy at the Eastman Theater, let them decide once and for all that here is a comedian worth their attention. As fair a beginning as this screen play, titled appropriately Tramp, Tramp, Tramp, *is promise of achievement extraordinary for Mr. Langdon. A distinctively original type for comedy roles, a screen personality that combines admirably a suggestiveness of pathos and a peculiar style of sheer foolishness, he brings to the spectators of his foolhardy goings-on in this ridiculously comic tale a two-fold reaction of laughter and tears. This, as the discerning know, is well-nigh the perfect tribute.*

Not that Tramp, Tramp, Tramp *is a perfect picture. Far from it. Comedy sequences that have been used before* mar the novelty most fans desire in their screen fare, and there is the seemingly inevitable fault of slowing down in the comedy action in spots, resulting in more or less spasmodic continuity. However, so excellent are the other qualities of the photoplay and so arresting is the comic personality of the star, the picture maintains, despite its faults, a high standard of entertaining value.

The story itself, entirely original in its fundamental idea, tells the comic experiences of Langdon who enters a cross-country walking contest to pay off the old mortgage. The jaunt becomes excruciatingly funny for beholders and curiously pathetic and comic, by turns, for the contestant. Merry for the most part, audiences beholding it for the first time with the writer yesterday felt no doubt about their enjoyment of the mishaps that befell the comedian, Langdon, to whom everything from prison to a cyclone became an experience fraught with comedy possibilities. Specific details of these comedy sequences are intentionally omitted in order to make them more enjoyable for prospective patrons.

Motion Picture Classic, *August 1926; Reviewed by Laurence Reid*

Harry Langdon has finally won his spurs or laurels or colors or what you care to call the honors of stardom. Having been bound to the two-reel comedy, he has come along so fast that he is entitled to a seat among the comedians who have graduated into the feature class. Which means that he deserves to ranked with Lloyd, Keaton, et al.

Surely no one is equipped with a sounder knowledge of what makes and sustains the Big laugh than this same Langdon. He has a firm acquaintance with pantomime and expresses comedy and its allied ingredients, pathos, with fine appreciation of their values. But he waited to make his feature debut until he found something good. And it arrived in Tramp, Tramp, Tramp.

No comedian could be more adaptable to the part of the contestant in a hiking tour than Langdon. I found him very amusing. He doesn't trespass on the lines marked out by other ranking fun-makers. He has an individuality all his own. His best asset is his wistful expression. On most of his journey he sees to it that he suffers like Chaplin, tho he is no imitator.

He experiences several difficulties which have been well timed to provoke laughter. Still there are moments when the piece pauses occasionally — as if it was out of breath and wanted to catch up with itself. So that is why it loses some of its spontaneity.

I shall dismiss these few errors and pin upon it the blue badge of excellence. For indeed, Langdon releases oodles of fun in his cross-country tramp. There is a worthy thrill in the scene wherein the comedian scales a fence to avoid a flock of sheep. While perched on top, he lets himself down slowly, trying to find a landing place for his feet. But he looks around and discovers himself on the edge of a cliff which has a sheer drop of a few hundred yards. His coat catches on a nail of the fence and soon the structure gives way — with Langdon descending as fast as Mother Earth and gravity can attract him.

This is but one of many ludicrous and original episodes in the picture. The piece is more quiet than The Gold Rush, and not as effervescent as The Freshman. But, nevertheless, it has comicalities. There is a final moment which contains a rollicking bit. It shows by trick photography the gag of Langdon placing himself in a crib — and made to represent his own offspring. The comedian's cherubic expression comes in handy for this hilarious finish.

Picture Play, *September 1926*

Harry Langdon's familiar role of a sap, which was all very well in the short comedies of Mack Sennett, is not strong enough or interesting enough to sustain Tramp, Tramp, Tramp, his first picture of feature length. In consequence it is pretty thin in spots although six good men and true are credited with the story and the gags that embellish it. All, including Langdon, have worked hard to make a showing but it seems to me that Langdon has short changed the bunch for while they have gagged for dear life he has given us his accustomed characterization of a simpleton and let it go at that…

Tramp, Tramp, Tramp isn't exactly dull but it is only mildly amusing when it should have been much more to warrant Langdon's debut in features. He shines in the shorts but grows monotonous for an hour at a stretch.

Rushville (IN) Daily Republican, *March 17, 1927*

Harry Langdon exceeds expectations. We thought he would be good. Now we know that he is great. He is as great a comedian as Charlie Chaplin and Harold Lloyd.

Tramp, Tramp, Tramp, which had a premiere showing at the Princess Theatre last night, definitely establishes Langdon as a top-notcher among film comedians. He is beyond the shadow of a doubt as funny an actor as has ever been seen in the films.

Langdon's humor is enigmatical. He is the picture of innocence involved in all sorts of complications. Very, very funny indeed.

WHAT THE EXHIBITORS SAID:

Exhibitors Herald, *July 3, 1926*

Nothing extra. Not the comedy First National would make you believe it is. Will stand a boost in admission. Advertised heavy; only ordinary business.
Ray McGuire, Peery Theatre, Darlington, MO.
General patronage.

The Reel Journal, *July 24, 1926*

It is not nearly what people expected. In fact, it was a poor picture.
D.R. Martin, Oregon, MO.

Exhibitors Herald, *August 14, 1926*

Not a good comedy. Did not please here. Do not pay anything extra for this one.
Rae Peacock, Mystic Theatre, Stafford, KS.
Small town patronage.

Exhibitors Herald, *August 14, 1926*

Not a box office knockout but to an intelligent theatregoing audience it is a wow. I liked it better than *For Heaven's Sake*, because of its originality and cleverness. Small towns who depend on farm trade don't pay too much. Most of your patrons won't get it.

R. E. Palmer, Postville Theatre, Postville, IA.
General patronage.

Exhibitors Herald, *August 21, 1926*

Harry, go back to two reelers and stay there. Let the reviewers influence me against my judgment and shot this as a two-day special to a grand and glorious flop. He will run one day only in my theatres.
S.B. Johnson, Regent Theatre, Cleveland and Shaw, MS.
General patronage.

Exhibitors Herald, *August 28, 1926*

You've sowed your wild oats, Harry. Get back where you belong. We've heard nothing but grief since showing this picture. When you go above two reels you're out of your class. This picture is three degrees worse than terrible.
Russell Armentrout, K. P. Theatre, Pittsfield, IL.
General patronage.

LANGDON REALLY TRAMPED IN THIS CHARLOTTE LOBBY
James Cartledge put a caricature body on the cutout head and geared the legs to a motor that never tired. The star and title cards are used to hide the mechanism. It made a hit with the patrons.

Exhibitors Herald, *August 28, 1926*
Did not make expenses on this one. They would not come and I don't blame them a bit. Harry better go back to two reelers.
Rae Peacock, Mystic Theatre, Stafford, KS.
Small town patronage.

Exhibitors Herald, *September 4, 1926*
Not so good. My people were disappointed in this one. May not book second Langdon.
C. M. Vail, Blende Theatre, Benton, WI.
General patronage.

The Reel Journal, *September 18, 1926*
Very good comedy, bought right. Langdon is a comedian. Good service from First National. Print and advertising good.
H.P. McFadden, Reel Theatre, Natoma, KS.

Exhibitors Herald, *September 25, 1926*
Advertised big and drew a large crowd. Everybody seemed 100 percent pleased with Harry and his first picture comedy.
C. A. Gallo, Auditorium, Red Cloud, NE.
Small town patronage.

Exhibitors Herald, *October 9, 1926*
Picture drew fair but failed to please. Not much of a story.
J. W. Bascom, Shastona Theatre, Mt. Shasta, CA.
General patronage.

Exhibitors Herald, *November 6, 1926*
We ran this picture following *For Heaven's Sake* and it sure pleased much better. Several people told me if I had to charge 40 cents admission for either picture they would rather pay for *Tramp, Tramp, Tramp*. Neither picture is entitled to a raise in admission, but the Langdon picture is a good comedy and will please.
L. D. Metcalf, Grand Theatre, Ash Grove, MO.
Small town patronage.

Exhibitors Herald, *November 27, 1926*
I bought this contrary to my better judgment, based on reports in the HERALD, but the curly-tailed film hound bunked me into buying it and wrapped it around my neck while I was looking out the window. It is funny in spots, but the spots are too few and far between. The comedy in it is very good but it is too slow and draggy. They had better give this guy a shot of something before he starts any more pictures so there will be more action in them. Standing around and looking foolish isn't comedy.
Wm. E. Tragsdorf, Trags Theatre, Neillsville, WI.
Small town patronage.

Exhibitors Herald, *December 8, 1926*
Good, but not big. Kept audience in good humor throughout and several good laughs. No comment and did not hold up second day. Played October 28–29.
C. M. Staples, Y. M. C. A. Morenci, AZ.
Small town patronage.

Exhibitors Herald, *December 8, 1926*
Very funny in parts but draggy and stretched out too much. Suitable for ordinary program. Played November 1–2.
Casio Theatre, Edmundston, N. B. Canada.
General patronage.

Exhibitors Herald, *January 8, 1927*
30%. Personally thought it was one of the cleverest and funniest productions I have ever witnessed. Bad weather prevented any box office gain. Pleased the few who braved the blizzard. Played December 12–13.
J. C. Kennedy, Empress Theatre, Akron, IA.
General patronage.

Exhibitors Herald, *January 8, 1927*
Pretty thin, but at that our people liked it better than *For Heaven's Sake*.
F. Haygood, Grand Theatre, Waynesboro, GA.
General patronage.

Exhibitors Herald, *February 5, 1927*
50%. One jump and Harry lands at the top rank. Now stay there old fellow, for we all are for you, and don't let your managers gouge the exhibitors as Lloyd and Chaplin have done. One-half of this play is very funny, whenever Harry could get in facial expressions it went big; when he was sidetracked for the story, everyone went to sleep. Sliding down the mountain on a fence, the cyclone scene, and the trick ending where Harry sees himself in his new born baby; these are as good as any of Chaplin's or Lloyd's gags. Trouble with this is that a walking race is too tame. Try an auto race next time, Harry. However, whatever we think of the play, we think you are a real comedian.
Phillip Rand, Rex Theatre, Salmon, ID.
General patronage.

Exhibitors Herald, *February 5, 1927*

These are the kind of pictures that are welcome. Business increased a few dollars more the second night. It is the kind of pictures the exhibitor is looking for, especially in a small town.
F. I. Thompson, Strand Theatre, Curwensville, PA. General patronage.

Exhibitors Herald, *February 26, 1927*

80%. Excellent comedy. Langdon and Syd Chaplin, in our estimation and according to our box office, the two best comedians going. Picture pleased and had many favorable comments. Played December 25.
W. S. & W. W. Woodworth, Border Theatre,
Rock Island, P.Q., Canada. General patronage.

Exhibitors Herald, *April 23, 1927*

20%. Only a few came out. Weather fine, roads good, had enough to pay film rent and express. Some said great, some said fair, some said no good. Personally thought it was a very passable comedy. It takes a good crowd to enjoy a picture like this.
Dr. F. M. Childs, Cozy Theatre, Villisca, IA.
General patronage.

Exhibitors Herald, *April 23, 1927*

78%. March 29–30. This may be his first but he is already as good as Harold Lloyd, and the film rental is only 10 per cent. Didn't kid my patrons in order to give them a good laugh. Harry, old boy, I have given you a good send off at my Theatre, so "*Tramp, Tramp, Tramp*" on to success. I advertised an old pair of shoes would admit anyone free and I admitted about 300 with shoes and that's a lot of people for a small town like this. After giving away all these passes I still had a big increase at the box office.
Perry G. Walker, Amusu Theatre, Statesboro, GA. General patronage.

Exhibitors Herald, *June 11, 1927*

67%. May 13–14. This was my first of Harry Langdon and I believe that he pleased, for the laughs were numerous and the comments after the show were favorable.
L. N. Crim, Crim's Theatre, Kilgore, TX.
Small town patronage.

Exhibitors Herald, *June 18, 1927*

A good clean comedy. Not half as bad as some of the reports would lead one to believe. I was all ready to hide when my patrons came out, but when I heard the noise inside I changed my mind. Just foolish enough to be good. Cyclone scene fine. Good comments.
A. F. Jenkins, Community Theatre, David City, NE. General patronage.

Moving Picture World, *July 2, 1927*

As for all the panning that this picture has received, I don't think that it deserves it. Nothing to crack your head about, of course, but a lot of fun, well enjoyed by audiences. Good comments. Tone, generally good. Sunday, yes. Special, no. Draw general class, town 2,300.
A. F. Jenkins, Community Theatre, David City, NE.

Exhibitors Herald, *August 27, 1927*

Here is a flop for the grownups. Rather tame and wishy-washy, silly story in parts. But for the children it went over great. They laughed and screamed. Harry Langdon is fine but he should have something better than this silly and impossible vehicle. He deserves better unless someone is trying to run him in a blind-siding. The boy has talent and deserves better treatment.
Giacoma Brothers, Crystal Theatre, Tombstone, AZ. General patronage.

Exhibitors Herald, *September 17, 1927*

A comedy drama with lots of laughs. Everybody pleased.
L. C. Boldue, Bijou Theatre, Conway, NH.
General patronage.

Exhibitors Herald, *September 24, 1927*

78%. August 18–19. Good business on this one but dissatisfied patrons. Too silly. However, I don't see how the boy could act otherwise and because they are not used to him.
Anthony Swearingam, Crescent Theatre, Woodville, TX. Small town patronage.

Exhibitors Herald, *October 1, 1927*

30%. This one put out as a special, but we bought it very reasonable and played two nights to small houses and come out just a little ahead. Think it pleased most of the patrons.
W. C. Synder, Cozy Theatre, Lamont, OK.
General patronage.

Ella Cinders

A John McCormick Production Released in Seven Reels. DIRECTED BY Alfred E. Green. PRODUCED BY John McCormick. STORY BY Mervyn LeRoy and Frank Griffin. TITLES BY George Marion, Jr. PHOTOGRAPHY BY Arthur Martinelli. EDITED BY Robert Kern. ART DIRECTOR: E.J. Shulter. CAST: Colleen Moore, Lloyd Hughes, Vera Lewis, Doris Baker, Emily Gerdes, Mike Donlin, Jed Prouty, Jack Duffy, Harry Allen, Alfred E. Green, D'Arcy Corrigan, Harry Langdon (unbilled). Copyright May 27, 1926, Registration Number L22779. Released by First National Pictures, Inc., June 6, 1926.

SYNOPSIS: Ella Cinders (Colleen Moore), mistreated by her stepmother and stepsisters, enters and wins a spurious beauty contest for which first prize is a Hollywood movie contract. When she arrives, she finds no welcome from the studio. Determined to realize her dream, she slips into the studio and after some comic evasion from the authorities, is eventually spotted by a director and cast in a film. Ella becomes a star, ironically by portraying a servant girl, but is eventually "rescued" by her hometown boyfriend.

Langdon has a cameo lasting about two-and-a-half minutes. As Ella is pursued by the studio guard, she stumbles onto Harry's set, and he assists her in evading capture by throwing a tablecloth over her and pretending to eat lunch. When she rises, a bowl of hot soup spills onto his lap.

This scene was presumably filmed near the end of production of *Tramp, Tramp, Tramp*, as Harry is wearing his "Burton Shoes" sweatshirt underneath his comedy overcoat from vaudeville. In an interview, Colleen Moore recalled that Frank Capra directed them in the scene.

WHAT THE CRITICS SAID:
Variety, *June 9, 1926; Reviewed by Fred*
There is a brief minute of Harry Langdon in the picture, he playing one scene with the star for laughs, although not billed.

The Strong Man

A Harry Langdon Corporation Production Released in Seven Reels. DIRECTED BY Frank Capra. ASSISTANT DIRECTOR: J. Frank Holliday. STORY BY Arthur D. Ripley. ADAPTATION BY Tim Whelan, Frank Capra, Tay Garnett, James Langdon, Hal Conklin, Murray Roth. PHOTOGRAPHY BY Elgin Lessley and Glen Kerschner. EDITED BY Harold Young. CAST: Harry Langdon, Priscilla Bonner, Gertrude Astor, Arthur Thalasso, Brooks Benedict, Robert McKim, William V. Mong, Robert Kortman. WORKING TITLE: "The Yes Man." Copyright August 31, 1926, Registration Number L23063; Renewed July 29, 1954, Number R134077. Released by First National Pictures, Inc., September 19, 1926.

SYNOPSIS: It is the time of the Great War, where Paul Bergot (Harry Langdon) is a Belgian soldier in No Man's Land. He practices firing his machine gun at an empty can, but cannot seem to hit his target. He finally uses a slingshot, and is successful. Pleased with himself, he is nevertheless bothered by "cooties." As he stands watch, a German in a trench is firing shots at him. At first he mistakes the grazing bullet as a cootie bite, but a subsequent shot draws his attention to the sniper. Paul aims his machine gun, but a shot from the German disarms the weapon. Paul employs the slingshot, striking the enemy's helmet and face with hard tack. He then "shoots" a crushed onion, which strikes the German right between the eyes. The German tries to don his gas mask, but Paul shoots that from his hands. The enemy soldier retreats his position, as Paul repeatedly fires his slingshot.

A friendly soldier approaches Paul and hands him a letter. It is from Mary Brown in America, who has been corresponding with him through the Red Cross. Paul opens the letter and reads:

I hope you are better. Your letters have been a great joy to me, and my heart is warmer for knowing I have as a dear, dear friend, a brave soldier from another nation...

Because an ocean rolls between us, and we are never to meet, I find the courage to put my whole heart on paper and to tell you,

I love you, I love you, I love you.
Mary Brown

While Paul dwells on the letter and a tiny enclosed photo of Mary, the German soldier quietly approaches from behind. Confronting the small Belgian, the muscular German grabs him, places him under his arm and dashes off.

After the Armistice, the German soldier immigrates to America to perform as "The Great Zandow, Strongest Man in the World." Paul is now his assistant and has crossed the ocean in the hold with the luggage. They arrive at Ellis Island. Zandow is concerned about his trunk, which contains a silk top hat given to him by "the Crown Prince." A baggage handler sends a heavy crate down a ramp where it crushes Zandow's trunk and the hat. As Zandow sobs, loyal Paul picks up a paddle and summons the baggage handler, intending to beat him for his carelessness. The handler, however, is a big man, so Paul smiles and winks at him, in hopes he'll "play along" with the scolding. Paul strikes a doorframe while shouting, "Take that! And that!" When another baggage handler emerges, he is struck with the paddle, causing Paul to grab Zandow and run off. In so doing, he knocks over a bench, which in turn knocks over another bench in front. As benches collapse like dominoes, Paul is incapable of stopping them.

In New York City, Zandow visits the offices of booking agent "Harry Veber" (a mildly ethnic take on Harry Weber, Langdon's real-life vaudeville agent). "I lift the heaviest weights in the world," Zandow brags, "and when I shoot myself from a cannon to a trapeze, it's a sensation!" Meanwhile, Paul is on a street corner, stopping various women in hopes of finding Mary Brown; one of them objects strenuously. Deciding on a different approach, Paul shows Mary's tiny photo to a hotel doorman and asks if he knows her. The doorman, trying to suppress his laughter, points and says, "Sure — she passes that corner every day!" Paul heads to the corner, sits, and waits.

Lily, a gangster's moll fresh from jail, approaches the corner, where her guy passes her a roll of bills and asks her to hide it, as he's being trailed by a detective. Lily takes the roll and places it in her purse, but the detective sees her. Quickly, she drops the bills into Paul's jacket pocket. The detective takes her purse, but finds it empty. She taunts the detective, who wanders away. She then reaches for Paul's pocket, but when a new group of pedestrians arrive, he starts wandering around, looking for Mary. When they've all passed, he sits down again. Lily discovers that the bills have gone from Paul's pocket through a hole in the seam and settled into the tail of the jacket. Desperate now, she introduces herself as "little Mary." Elated, Paul walks off with her, past the hotel doorman, who is incredulous when Paul introduces him to Lily and thanks him.

Paul buys a bag of popcorn for them to share, but "Mary," nervous about getting the roll back, isn't interested and repeatedly knocks popcorn from Paul's hand. They enter a cab and Lily tells the driver to go to the Russell Apartments. When Lily lights a cigarette, Paul becomes suspicious of her. They arrive at the apartment building, and when Paul refuses to enter with her, Lily stages a faint. Paul tries to leave anyway, but the cab driver tells him he must take her inside. The cabbie picks up Lily and places her in Paul's arms.

Once inside the building, "Mary" murmurs, "Room Three, upstairs." He gets about halfway upstairs and needs to rest, so he places her on the banister. While he gathers himself, she slides back down to the bottom. He retrieves her and tries to head up the stairs a little faster, but he lacks the requisite stamina. He sits on the stair, places "Mary" in his lap and proceeds up the stairs on his backside. He reaches the top, but there is a stepladder present. Unknowing, Paul continues up the stepladder and over, causing he and Lily to tumble to the floor. Stunned, he picks up a rolled carpet and carries it into Lily's room. Depositing it on the bed, he notices that it isn't "Mary."

He retrieves the now genuinely groggy Lily, brings her into the room and pours some champagne from an open bottle into her mouth. Seeing she has revived, he starts to straighten up her bed; from behind, she strikes him with the bottle and he collapses. Lily locks the door, tucks the key into her bosom, and gets down to business. She tries to reach into Paul's coat, but this revives him and he's petrified of her intentions. She grabs a knife and chases him around the room. Trapped, Paul submits to her; as they kiss, she uses the knife to remove the bills from his jacket, and then collapses from exhaustion. She retrieves the key and hands it to Paul, who warns her, "Don't let this leak out!" In the hallway, he overhears a woman ask for "the studio of Madame Browne." He watches the woman enter the art studio, where inside, Madame Browne is doing a sculpture of a nude model. Paul enters the studio and, upon spying the nude, frantically runs out of the studio, falls over a railing and tumbles down the stairs.

Zandow has been booked in Cloverdale, which had once been "a peaceful little border town," until bootleggers transformed it into a rowdy haven for drink, gambling and lust. The Town Hall has been converted into a saloon called "The Palace." Families have been broken apart, and only the loyal congregation of Parson Joseph Brown — whose blind daughter, Mary, is Paul's long-ago correspondent — hold fast to the simple values of old. Parson Brown encourages his flock to join him in marching and praying for the miracle of Joshua, in the belief that the saloon will fall like the walls of Jericho. Employees of "Mike" McDevitt, owner of The Palace, dismiss the Parson as harmless "Holy Joe," but McDevitt intends to stop "these demonstrations against me," and threatens to "have his daughter in here as the main attraction."

At the moment, Mary is entertaining the children of the town with stories about "the Belgian soldier who won the war." As her father listens from the window, she talks about a "plain little girl who dared to love a brave soldier…but when he wrote that he was coming to America, she stopped writing and hid — for she had never told him she was blind." Meanwhile, on the bus to Cloverdale, Zandow sits up front with the driver in comfort. Paul is seated in the main cabin, nursing a very bad cold, which is disturbing the other passengers, particularly a surly gentleman seated on his left. Paul attempts to take some liquid medicine, carefully pouring it into a spoon, but it's a nasty-tasting remedy. He hesitantly brings it to his mouth and suddenly sneezes, spraying it all over the annoyed passenger, who loudly objects when Paul tries to wipe him off with his well-used handkerchief. While Paul finally manages to down his medicine, the man gives him a stern lecture. The fellow has finished, but Paul gives him a glare of contempt, forms a fist and gives him a tap on the chin; he, in turn, socks Paul in the jaw and knocks him down. Paul takes his seat again, resumes his glare, forms a fist again and threatens to throw a punch, but decides not to retaliate when the man slaps his fist. As he resumes coughing, Paul opens his shirt and tries to remove the "heat patch" on his chest a little at a time, but decides against it. The man spies it and tears it off, much to Paul's alarm. He decides to apply camphor rub to his chest; at the same time, Zandow has partaken of Limburger cheese from a similarly shaped jar, which tumbles through a vent to land beside Paul. Deciding that the camphor is working, Paul reaches for some more and winds up applying the Limburger. This causes much distress among the passengers. When Paul applies some to each nostril, he announces with joy, "My head's clear! I'm beginning to smell!" The surly man agrees, and hurls Paul toward the rear of the bus, where the remaining passengers toss him out. Paul rolls down a hill as the bus is negotiating a curve. He lands through the roof of the bus and back into his seat, much to the shock of the other passengers.

The bus arrives in Cloverdale, and Zandow is welcomed with news that "the whole town's crazy to see your Cannon Act." While Zandow is over-indulging in beer and women in "The Palace," Paul is backstage trying to sew a pair of tights. He asks a stagehand where he can fill a bucket with water. "Behind the church," the stagehand responds. "Ask Mary Brown."

Paul heads for the door, then stops with a jolt. "WHO?" he asks.

"MARY BROWN."

Paul immediately looks out the door toward the church, where he sees Mary at the water pump. He runs back and forth in excitement, straightens his shirt and tie, hurriedly retrieves his coat, and then picks up the bucket and calmly heads outside. He stands behind Mary and watches her water the garden. He drops the bucket and she turns. Paul asks if she is the girl who wrote to the Belgian soldier. When she says yes, he leaps with joy, and parades back and forth in front of her. He then tells her that the soldier is in town. When she asks where, he replies, "I'm him." Mary is stunned, and when Paul asks her, "Aren't you happy to see me?" she is too overwrought to speak and momentarily forgets where she's standing. She extends her arms around until she feels a nearby tree, sits down on the bench that surrounds it and sobs, while Paul watches attentively.

Before long, Mary is laughing as Paul tells of his attempts to locate her, vividly describing his encounter with Lily. He "shows" her he has kept the photo

she sent him by placing her hand on it. Paul sits beside her and takes her hand, examines it carefully, traces her love line with his finger, positions his hat so no one will see them holding hands, then removes the hat to give her hand a quick kiss. Inside the dressing room, Zandow is thoroughly intoxicated, unable to perform. McDevitt and the stagehand grab Paul, drag him into the dressing room, and put him into Zandow's costume. The crowd is yelling, "Bring on the Strong Man!" McDevitt orders Paul to do the act. Paul gives McDevitt "the glare" and taps him with his fist; McDevitt socks him in the jaw, knocking him to the floor. Paul gets up and heads onstage.

Unsure of what to do, he strikes a few poses, and then tries to lift a 400 lb. weight. Unsuccessful at this, he proceeds to dance and strike a few more poses. He positions a trick bucket over a hole in the stage floor, and rolls two heavy balls into the bucket, which pass through. With great effort, he lifts the empty bucket over his head and the crowd cheers. When he tries to duplicate the feat by placing a barbell into the bucket, the secret is given away as the barbell weight gets caught and forces the bucket through the hole in the floor. Paul tries dancing again, then spies a poster of an acrobat performing a split. He tries to duplicate the pose, but his legs will only go so far. A stagehand manipulates a barbell onto his shoulders; he grabs it and is lifted above the stage, where a few pigeons are nesting. He loses his grip and lands on a counterbalance, which sends a weight into the air, when it lands, Paul is sent flying, does an aerial somersault and lands perfectly, as the crowd cheers. Discovering that a few of the pigeons have lodged in his trunks, he rolls up his sleeves and proceeds to do "magic," releasing the pigeons one-by-one. The crowd whoops and hollers its approval.

Paul leans against the stage, which causes the backdrop to rise, revealing Zandow's trick cannon. The crowd calls for the cannon trick. Panicked, Paul runs backstage to try and wake Zandow, but is unsuccessful. He dons his hat and coat and tries to escape. Meanwhile, Parson Brown is again leading his hymn-singing congregation past The Palace. Paul sees them from the window and removes his hat, assuming it is a funeral procession. When the crowd shouts for the cannon act, Paul returns to the stage and hushes the crowd. "There's a funeral," he explains, but they mock him. Then a beer-sodden mug cries out, "The kid's right! Let's bow our heads and pray for poor old 'Holy Joe!'" The crowd laughs and grows unruly, much to Paul's confusion. When the mug cries out, "And may we soon have the honor of entertaining Mary Brown in our midst," Paul becomes indignant. He approaches the mug and strikes him in the face — and gets a sock in the jaw and is knocked down. He tries again, with the same result. Groggily, Paul swings and misses, and the mug picks him up and throws him onto the trapeze.

As he swings from above, Paul grabs a bottle; returning, he breaks it over the mug's head, knocking him out. This stuns the crowd, but when someone tries to steal the till, a full-fledged brawl breaks out, as Paul continues swinging overhead. McDevitt orders two goons to "lock the doors and protect the money." Paul reaches a balcony, but when several men start to rush him, he climbs back onto the trapeze. Tables and chairs are hurled and miss him, knocking out patrons. Paul lands on a supply of bottles and kegs; he knocks out a plug and sprays beer into the crowd. He grabs a case of bottles and resumes swinging on the trapeze, knocking out the toughest members of the crowd. Heading toward the stage, he grabs hold of the curtain and pulls it over the length of the saloon, covering the brawlers.

Running across the curtain, Paul reaches the stage and loads the trick cannon with gunpowder. The resulting blast knocks the crowd back. When they try rushing him again, Paul discharges the cannon. McDevitt takes a shot at Paul, who promptly places a small weight into the cannon and returns fire. Hit by the weight, McDevitt is knocked through a window and lands in a trashcan. As Parson Brown's congregation gathers outside, Paul loads several weights into the cannon, which proceed to blow down the Palace walls. The crowd flees in terror, chased from town by the inspired congregation.

Cloverdale is restored to a law-abiding community, with Paul as a duly sworn policeman. He leaves on his rounds; Mary asks to go with him, but he insists she should return home. However, he relents when she starts to cry. They go off together, and when Paul trips and falls off the curb, Mary helps him to his feet.

ANALYSIS: Having ascended to director, Frank Capra rose to the occasion and produced not only Harry Langdon's most successful feature, but also the first of a long series of movies in which a little man, with right on his side, can defeat evil despite overwhelming odds. Anyone who doesn't believe *The Strong Man* is a Frank Capra film has never seen a Frank Capra film.

Arthur Ripley deserves a healthy share of credit as well. Although he reportedly came aboard at the time filming began, his contribution was substantial enough to earn sole story credit, despite Whelan, Capra and Langdon having prepared the initial scenario in tandem. The original, with its title "The Yes Man," may have been another Harold Lloyd situation, with an emphasis on Harry's relationship with his muscular benefactor, Zandow, mirroring films where Lloyd is befriended by one-time adversaries, such as *A Sailor-Made Man* or *Why Worry?* Evidently, Ripley switched the emphasis to Paul's search for Mary and added to the poignancy by making her blind, and just as timid as her suitor.

Topping everything, though, is Langdon's performance. It is simply brilliant. The opening war scenes are marvelously funny. Maybe Paul can't handle a gun, but his slingshot prowess is formidable. With the love of his American sweetheart, he can conquer any army, at least until Zandow carries him off. The scenes at

Ellis Island, and especially with Lily, where he is victimized by circumstances beyond control, are keyed to the Elf's one-of-a-kind reactions to everything that transpires, and they all register.

HARRY MOMENT: Beyond a doubt, Paul's chest cold on the bus is *The Strong Man*'s outstanding laugh-getter. The surly passenger is entitled to object when Paul sneezes and sprays medicine on him, or when being wiped by a well-used handkerchief, but he continues to administer a stern scolding even after Paul has downed his nasty syrup. The glare Paul shoots his tormentor is priceless, mirroring the look any child would give an unpleasant adult behind his back. He takes it further by giving the grouch a tiny punch in the mouth, and is repaid with a full-fledged sock in the jaw. (This actually becomes a running gag, as twice more Paul deals with unpleasant people with his tiny punch, only to get knocked silly in return.) The conclusion, as Paul is thrown out of the bus only to fall right back into it, is the Elf's "Divine providence" at its most effective.

WHAT THE CRITICS SAID:
Hollywood Filmograph, *August 21, 1926 (Preview at the Belmont Theatre)*

For the first two thirds it was a fast moving comedy, going from one clever situation into another, then the action slowed down and from there on out it was mostly drama. Even the finish was slow. It makes one think of a fighter who is fighting ten rounds, the first six or seven rounds being the whale of a fight, but the fighter fought himself out and just hung on the rest of the way because he was determined to go ten rounds.

Harry Langdon gave the best and most natural performance we have ever seen him give, but watch your make-up, Harry; it looked bad in places. His business with Gertrude Astor was the outstanding sequence of the entire picture. Astor looked great.

Priscilla Bonner looked sweet, but had little to do. Wm. V. Mong's part was good while it lasted. Robert McKim did some good work. Arthur Thalasso, the Strong Man, fed Langdon some good gags and did good work himself. Brooks Benedict played the traveling salesman.

Direction good, titles very funny, and photography O.K.

New York Herald-Tribune, *September 6, 1926; Reviewed by Richard Watts, Jr.*

Harry Langdon, that sad-faced cinema clown, who goes in more completely for wistfulness than does even the eminent Mr. Chaplin, is appearing at the Strand this week in an amusing slapstick farce called The Strong Man, *wherein he reveals once more his amazing skill at gently farcical pantomime.*

Langdon, as you must certainly know, is that round-faced comic, whose propensity for running around in futile little circles remind critics of everything from Lillian Gish to a personification of the Nietschean slave class…

The picture is completely Langdon's. He appears in practically every scene and in the few minutes that he is absent the film slumps into boredom. During long periods of time he appears alone upon the screen and these scenes give the picture its chief distinction.

The star is particularly fine in an episode where he is trying desperately to fight off a cold. Here he indulges in such skillful comic pantomime that even a somewhat

unpleasant bit, wherein he rubs Limburger on his chest by mistake, assumes a minimum of offensiveness. It is difficult to pay any actor a higher tribute than that.

The chief fault of Langdon's comedies is their lack of smoothness, and The Strong Man is no exception in that respect. In fact, it is greatly to be doubted whether the star has yet learned how to make long comedies.

Brooklyn Daily Eagle, *September 7, 1926; Reviewed by Grace Cutler Cutler*

That round-faced comic of diminutive proportions, Harry Langdon, entertains this week with a one-man show at the Manhattan Strand. In The Strong Man, Harry is cast as assistant to Zandow the Great. It is not surprising to find that he has to take the place of this husky brute before a mad audience in a lawless saloon. It is Harry's show.

As a pantomime artist Harry Langdon has no equal in screen ranks. Pathos is his meat, and pathetic he is throughout every reel of this loosely woven picture. His efforts rise to the greatest height when he is shown in the act of trying to ward off a cold. He is funny, even when he is rubbing his chest with Limburger.

The Strong Man moves in jerks. It looks like parts of several farces, not like a finished picture. This is a minor fault, because the sad-eyed one is amusing throughout the film.

His stiff arm gestures convey every emotion from happiness to terror. His walk is as funny as Chaplin's. His expressions give the effect of comic masks adjusted with incalculable speed.

The picture is Langdon's, but Gertrude Astor, as an Amazonian crook, manages to help the entertainment along considerably. Priscilla Bonner is a capable and pretty heroine.

This is one comedian who doesn't need to swim the Channel or keep pet alligators to attract the multitudes. He doesn't even need a good scenario.

New York Daily News, *September 7, 1926; Reviewed by Roscoe McGowen*

Dictionaries are incomplete. They won't be complete until Langdon leads the list of synonyms for laughter. My enthusiasm for the little moon-faced comedian is unbounded. If there is any fault to be found with The Strong Man, somebody else will have to find it. While watching the picture I couldn't see its faults for laughing.

And the picture will be a hit, no doubt of that. As I left the Mark Strand yesterday afternoon it was difficult to get through the crowds waiting to get in.

Langdon is almost the whole picture. Yet a great amount of credit must be given those who support him, notably Gertrude Astor. The scenes between Langdon and Miss Astor are the most side-splitting in the film and the girl plays no small part in making them so.

The sequence wherein Langdon holds the girl in his arms and goes upstairs backward by the simple expedient of getting partly up and sitting down one step higher is

In "The Strong Man" at the Strand Theatre

the highlight of comedy. When he continues on up a stepladder at the top of the stairs a number of ribs must have been cracked in the audience.

Then when Harry fights the girl desperately to protect himself against what he imagines to be her amorous advances the action supplied on of the funniest, and at the same time most satirical, bits ever screened.

His business with a slingshot in a Belgian trench; his work on the swinging trapeze over the heads of the Palace saloon crowd; his act as the substitute strong man; his putting to rout the crowd with the trick cannon — everything is superbly funny.

Nor must mention of his pantomime while suffering from a bad cold be overlooked. It must be really difficult for some of the players who work with Langdon to keep the straight faces demanded. In fact, I think I noted some evidence of that difficulty.

New York Evening Post, *September 7, 1926;*
Reviewed by Wilella Waldorf

Harry Langdon, the quaint little man who stepped competently from short comedies to long ones a few weeks ago, thereby reaching in one bound the pinnacle occupied by Chaplin, Keaton, Griffith and the rest, appears to have established himself comfortably in his perch, with furtive glances over and anon at the difficult places higher up.

The Strong Man, his latest comedy at the Mark Strand this week, registers in individual scenes a distinct improvement over that first venture into the realm of feature films, Tramp, Tramp, Tramp. *As a whole the new picture suffers from a bumpy continuity, all ups and downs, the ups very high, the downs very low indeed. That smooth pleasant flow so necessary to sustain interest in any moving picture is not in* The Strong Man, *yet in only one or two painful spots does interest actually wander away from the screen. Langdon himself shoulders the whole responsibility in that shy, half-witted fashion of his, carrying the thing through to a hilarious finish. Those few scenes wherein attention wanes represent the comedian's few absences from the screen.*

One of the most amusing pantomimic sequences this department has ever witnessed takes place in the course of The Strong Man. *Mr. Langdon, riding cross-country in a bus, has caught a very bad cold in the head. He is forever sniffing and coughing and choking and rubbing salves on his chest and swallowing cough medicine, much to the discomfiture of the other passengers, who resent the germs and the fumes in no uncertain terms. One passenger in particular, in the next seat, exhibits extreme annoyance, and the series of indignant looks which pass between these two irritable ones manages to keep whole audiences in a state of hysteria for a considerable time. This scene and several others almost as funny are the impressions one carries away from* The Strong Man, *along with a distinct notion that this comic person, Langdon, may succeed in topping them all before very long if events continue thus auspiciously.*

New York Times, *September 7, 1926; Reviewed by Mordaunt Hall*

Harry Langdon's latest comedy, The Strong Man, *leaps from gag to gag, always giving the protagonist ample opportunity to show his talent as a screen farceur. These interludes of fun, which are like short sketches, have precious little bearing on a coherent narrative. Nevertheless they serve their purpose in stirring up gales of laughter, the audiences being immensely tickled by Paul Bergot's complete and faithful illustration of the discomforts of a cold and also by his pathetic search for one Mary Brown…*

If Mr. Langdon would study psychology in constructing his narratives, his films would be more than mere laugh-makers. He and his director, Frank Capra, do wonderfully well with the ideas or gags, but as soon as they have finished with one of these chapters they dismiss it rather abruptly for another sequence, and sometimes a character or two falls by the wayside. It is questionable whether in such a vehicle it is necessary to enlist the Scriptures, and it is perhaps in bad taste to have a sightless heroine in a broad farce, even though the girl's optimism is pointed out.

In this comedy the Mark Strand organist is kept continually on the alert watching his screen cues, for it would never do to play "Onward, Christian Soldiers," during a cabaret scene, and it would be equally disastrous if "How Dry I Am" were rendered as the church people of Cloverdale march through the streets. Yet these two selections follow one another in the unfurling of this comedy.

Mr. Langdon's work in this production displays true ability, and it is to his credit that he is more effective in the more sober scenes than in the turbulent streaks. Priscilla Bonner is sympathetic as the little blind heroine, and Arthur Thalasso is by no means unimpressive as Zandow the Great.

Variety, *September 8, 1926; Reviewed by Rush*

A whale of a comedy production that is bound to be a cleanup everywhere. It has a wealth of slapstick, a rough-and-tumble finish and in the earlier passages bits of pantomimic comedy that for a legitimate and effective hour are notable in the whole range of screen comedy.

Langdon, until not long ago a maker of short subjects of the familiar gag school, has a comic method distinct from all the other film fun makers. The quality of pathos enters into it more fully than the style of any other comedian with the possible exception of Chaplin. His gift of legitimate comedy here has a splendid vehicle.

There is one scene where the awkward hero is engaged in fighting off a bad cold while traveling in a crowded stage coach. He earns the enmity of his fellow passengers and his pantomimic display of helpless suffering mingled with indignation is an epic of laughable absurdity. In the same scene the business with a porous plaster was greeted with howls.

One of the remarkable things about the picture is the fact that its action and its comedy values are sustained for more than an hour. Besides this the finale rises to a climactic punch, although the finish as might be expected goes into roughhouse of the most violent kind. Something of the sort was imperative to provide mounting interest, and this the closing does.

At another point there is a rich episode of an adventure with a woman crook. The girl has "planted" a roll of money in Langdon's pocket to get rid of it when she is threatened with arrest. To recover the money she lures the boy to her apartment. He imagines she is making cave woman love to him, while she really is trying to salvage the loot and his coy retreat from her attack is the last word in comic misunderstanding. Gertrude Astor handles the crook role admirably here.

The story has a sentimental side that helps to give it light and shade.... A rich comedy that should take Langdon a step toward the class of stars whose pictures figure for more than a week's engagement.

Harrison's Reports, *September 11, 1926*

Very comical, the comedy being caused by the situations as well as Mr. Langdon's acting. There is one situation that is altogether different from what has been seen in pictures of the past. The hero returns home from the war and seeks a girl by the name of Mary Brown: she had written him love letters while he was fighting in France. A detective follows a crook who had stolen a roll of bills from someone; the crook hands the bill roll to a woman confederate. The confederate, seeing the detective coming toward her, slips the roll into the hero's pocket. After the detective had gone, the woman tries to entice the hero into her apartment for the purpose of finding an opportunity to get the bill roll back; it had slipped into the back pocket of the hero's coat and she could not reach it without letting the hero know that there was money in his coat. She pretends to be Mary Brown. The hero becomes suspicious and refuses to follow her. But she in some way succeeds in dragging him into her apartment, in the last resort pretending that she had fainted. Once in the room, the crook woman tries to unbutton the hero's coat for the purpose of taking the bill roll out of it. The hero misinterprets her motive and tries to get out of the room unsuccessfully. The whole thing is comical in the extreme. Though it sounds risqué, it will not offend any spectator, even the most particular; it has been done cleverly.

Good for any theatre, vaudeville houses included. In the small towns it should make an excellent Saturday bill; it should not, however make a bad Sunday bill. Children should enjoy it immensely.

Film Daily,, *September 12, 1926*

Knockout comedy that delivers laugh upon laugh and makes a picture audience sound like a crowd of professional laugh starters. Certainly lands its comedy.

Star: One of the really clever pantomime artists of the day. Variation adds much to the success of his playing. Must be accumulating a great following.

Cast: Gertrude Astor fine in one sequence. Priscilla

Bonner pretty as Harry's blind sweetheart. Arthur Thalasso first rate as the strong man, and others, [including] Wm. V. Mong and Robert McKim.

Type of Story: Comedy. If Harry Langdon hasn't already "arrived," he certainly slides right to the home plate in The Strong Man. You wouldn't have to take anyone's word for it. The howls, and even screams, of the Strand audience are sufficient proof that Langdon delivers the laughs. His methods are distinctive and he doesn't rely solely upon gags to keep a crowd amused. There are long stretches where the comedian holds the screen alone and through sheer pantomime keeps the folks out front in a continuous uproar. The taxi episode, where Harry doubts the maneuvers of the dizzy blonde who slipped a roll of bills into his pocket to avoid a "dick," is a wow and the piece showing Harry trying to carry her into her apartment after she has fainted is two wows. Harry's trick method of getting her burden up stairs by holding her on his lap and lifting himself from step to step, backwards, is a scream and when he continues on up a ladder, thinking he is still on the stairs — well, the audience yelled so loud you couldn't keep your mind on Langdon. There is a story for a framework but Langdon is the whole show... Like Chaplin, Langdon employs a certain amount of mild pathos which shades off effectively into more laughs.

Box Office Angle: You won't have seats enough in your theater to accommodate the crowd so you'll have to show The Strong Man *for at least several days.*

Exploitation: Hardly requires any go-getter advertising but it's up to you to convice them that this is the laugh hit of the current season.

New York Herald-Tribune, *September 12, 1926; Follow-up by Richard Watts, Jr.*

That curious minority that has so sturdily declined to recognize the distinguished comic gifts of Mr. Harry Langdon must certainly have been won over by The Strong Man. *After his marvelous performance in this new screen comedy it is difficult to see how any one can fail to note that Langdon is one of the world's major clowns — standing at the moment but a few short steps behind the great Chaplin himself.*

It should be remembered, too, that while Langdon's work grows in maturity with each picture, Chaplin gives indication of remaining where he stands. In The Strong Man, *you are permitted to see the most complete portrait yet revealed of the comic character Langdon is creating, just as* The Gold Rush *showed the most carefully considered picture extant of the American Pierrot Chaplin has been developing throughout his career. But while the Chaplin portrayal showed no advance over the earlier and briefer performances,* The Strong Man *marks a noticeable increase in stature for its star. I don't say Langdon will ever surpass or even equal Chaplin, but such a thought, I insist, is not as absurd as might first appear....*

The outstanding characteristic of the Langdon screen figure is his disarming friendliness for all the world. He has a profound confidence that the rest of mankind is as open-hearted as he is, and from that misplaced trust in the world around him arise his humor and his pathos. He is the little brother of all the universe, and the universe repays him by socks in the jaw.

Yet, apostle of non-resistance, trusting youth and the brotherhood of man that he is, the Langdon character grows less the pacifist by the moment. In The Strong Man, *Langdon, fighting off for 200 feet or more of the most delightful comic pantomime of ages a furious cold that is assailing him, is tormented by a neighbor. He ceases for the moment to apply lotions and innumerable home remedies to himself and just glares at his oppressor. It is the most devastating glare at present on the records, and into it he puts all of the hopeless contempt of generations of the meek against their oppressors. That one glance is, I suspect, one of the great things in film history....*

So gentle and wistful and immature is the Langdon mask that his appeal to the feminine must be mainly maternal. In The Strong Man, *though, the comedian reveals an unexpected and amazing gift for — of all things! — sex appeal. It is in complete keeping with his characterization that his romance should be with a blind girl. And how beautifully he plays his love scenes.... This skill at serio-comic love making, this gesture of revolt against his oppressors, both are, so far as I remember, new sides of the comedian. Once he has learned to make his long pictures smooth entities rather than a number of amusing but loosely linked short comedies, he is likely to be unbeatable. He is very close to that now.*

Moving Picture World, *September 18, 1926*

After scoring exceptional success in two-reelers, Harry Langdon, following the example of Chaplin, Lloyd and Keaton, entered the feature comedy field as the star of Tramp, Tramp, Tramp, *and, for his second venture he is now appearing in* The Strong Man. *While not quite so hilarious, it has more heart interest and pathos, which is quickly turned into smiles and fully measures up to it as a laugh-getter.*

A reading of the bare details of the plot easily accounts for the abundance of pathos, for it leans toward emotional melodrama, but in the hands of the gag man and Director Frank Capra and backed up by Langdon's inimitable and amusing personality and genius at pantomime, situations that read like drama are invested with humor made even more amusing for the element of pathos that is retained. For example, the situation where he gets into all sorts of trouble by stopping girls on the street trying to locate the one who wrote him letters during the war...

While there was (sic) not many loud guffaws, the audience at the New York Strand was kept in smiles and chuckles, and, the quiet humor of Harry's pantomime in a sequence where he is in a stagecoach and has a terrible cold, is one of the best bits of comedy acting we have ever seen.

Audiences generally should find The Strong Man *amusing.*

Los Angeles Times, *September 19, 1926; Reviewed by Barbara Miller*

"Have you seen Harry Langdon's latest?"

This is certain to be the prevalent query within the next few months, when The Strong Man *is presented to the movie-going world.*

For the comedian has followed his cross-country laugh epic, Tramp, Tramp, Tramp, *with a film that is a true triumph for Harry Langdon. This, despite obvious crudities of plot and consistent lack of humorous talent on the part of other members of the cast.*

The Strong Man *is amusing because Harry Langdon is amusing.*

For all credit is due one sad-faced comedian since from the instant when first he is glimpsed by the audience blandly carrying on a little private war out in the wastes of No Man's Land, until the successful denouement of his diffident love-making, he is funny — and strangely appealing.

You are sorry for Harry, when everyone treats him so badly, even though you laugh at his predicaments.

The Strong Man *boasts plot as well as multitudes of gags, which should be of material help in making the picture a consistent hit…*

While the other members of the cast are not funny, they are interesting from the viewpoint of characterization.

As the blind girl, Priscilla Bonner is appealingly helpless. Gertrude Astor, as the flamboyant Lily of Broadway, gives an authentic characterization, done with broad strokes.

Of the men, William V. Mong is his usual capable self as the crusading parson, and Robert McKim is effective as the evil personage of the village.

Cleveland Plain Dealer, *September 27, 1926; Reviewed by Glenn C. Pullen*

In The Strong Man, *Harry Langdon has one of the funniest slapstick comedies that I have seen on the screen for some time. If Chaplin's* The Gold Rush *tickled your funny bone, if Richard Dix in* Let's Get Married *made your ribs ache with laughter, if you went into hysterics over Harold Lloyd's* For Heaven's Sake *— then you are due for a hilarious party at the State this week.*

As if to make up for the uneventful Tramp, Tramp, Tramp, *Langdon has made his second feature picture a thing of ACTION. It is a farce that depends wholly upon gags. And although they aren't tied together very snugly, no one will mind such flaws, as the gags are refreshingly original in humor and expertly worked out.*

Langdon has always been considered an unusually good comic. In The Strong Man *he demonstrates conclusively that he is one of the best buffoons in the movies; in fact, I would say he ranks only a few steps below the great Chaplin himself. His vivid pantomime and ability to inject pathos in the most amusing episodes are gifts that not many of our film humorists possess…*

It is difficult to refrain from philosophizing on the comic Mr. Langdon. Certainly it is not his "dead-pan" and eloquent gestures alone that make him funny. The secret, I believe, lies in his realistic air of Peter Panish bewilderment and naïve friendliness. He tries in his characterization to be a little brother to the world, and the world repays him with socks in the jaw. And to the audience, that is intensely amusing. For with all our civilization, we are still barbarians enough to find a cruel enjoyment in scenes of another's misfortunes.

But such Nietzschean reasoning is not necessary to enjoy The Strong Man. *It is not a perfect comedy but it is great fun. I highly recommend it to you.*

Cinema Art, *October 1926*

Since humor is by its very nature a flashing, short-lived affair, the feature-length comedy must invariably contend with certain difficulties. In this instance they are overcome by padding, but where there are so many excellent scenes such fillers can easily be forgotten.

The best incident, to our mind, is that in which Harry misunderstands the intentions of a young woman, who is trying to steal a roll of bills from his pocket. He first believes she is his sweetheart, "Mary Brown," whom he has never seen, but who had written him frequently when he was in the trenches. Langdon achieves a shy, terrified embarrassment which is somehow never vulgar and never painful. First he sees the girl of his dreams smoking a cigarette — and nearly collapses. Then as things go on, he becomes sure she is not a nice girl, and his embarrassment becomes almost hysterical. Even when she locks him into her room and tries to tear from him the coat containing the money, he maintains his equilibrium and keeps the thing funny.

There is something almost monstrously pathetic in his eager search for "Mary Brown" whom he expects to find at any street corner, or behind any door. And when he finally does reach her, he discovers that she is blind!

Another unusually successful episode is that in which he takes care of his cold. While he is traveling in a crowded bus he decides to take his medicine and rub his chest. Well, you can just imagine what happens.

Gertrude Astor is effective as the terrifying city girl, and Miss Bonner is pretty and sweet in a small part.

Photoplay, *October 1926*

Marching into stardom with Tramp, Tramp, Tramp, *Harry Langdon's second laugh-provoker firmly establishes the wistful comedian in the front ranks of the screen's mirth-makers. Watch out, Charlie and Harold!*

It's a grand and glorious laugh from the start to the finish. It begins with one laugh overlapping the other. Chuckles are swept into howls. Howls creep into tears —

and by that time you're ready to be carried out. And we don't mean maybe!

The story runs along at a merry gait with Langdon keeping pace with his clever pantomime. Wait and see his interpretation of a cold. Gertrude Astor is outstanding as a big-blonde-mama vamp.

Don't be selfish — treat the whole family.

Los Angeles Evening Herald, *October 2, 1926*

Harry Langdon as The Strong Man *at Loew's State shows himself to be a stronger comedian as the film progresses.*

As for the story, its weaker moments are many and manifest. However, the thread of the plot is strong enough to hold, and it has Langdon. That any admirer of funny films will like it a great deal is a foregone conclusion.

Los Angeles Record, *October 2, 1926*

If you want to spend a dismal weekend, keep away from Loew's State! For if you see Harry Langdon in The Strong Man *you will certainly laugh for the next three days.*

The Strong Man, *which opened at Loew's yesterday, is that rare thing, a really funny comedy with a plot. There are gags aplenty, of course, but the picture is based on an idea. And the idea is a knockout.*

Harry Langdon is seen as a Belgian ex-soldier, who, during the war, received letters from an American girl. After the war he comes to the United States to search for her and, incidentally, to assist a professional strong man in his vaudeville tours.

His efforts to locate the girl, whose picture he has, gives rise to some of the funniest episodes since Shoulder Arms. *There is a sequence in which the noble hero is lured into a lady crook's apartment so that the wicked vampire may recover a roll of bills he had dropped into his pockets, which for sheer and unadulterated humor is unparalleled.*

But the big climax comes when Harry, the proverbial underdog, "cleans up" the border town in which his war-sweetheart lives. Cleans it up quite definitely, conclusively, and — unintentionally.

There is a vein of idyllic charm running through the side-splitting slapstick of it all. A thread of tenderness and pathos which reaches its climax in one scene of almost exquisite charm.

We confess to ignorance anent the past accomplishments of Frank Capra, who directed The Strong Man, *but his handling of this picture marks him as a director of amazing scope.*

Living up to the film's title, Harry Langdon carries the vehicle on his shoulders practically unaided. His pathetic appeal and delicious humor were never shown to better advantage than in The Strong Man.

Oakland Tribune, *October 11, 1926; Reviewed by Wood Soanes*

There must be something in that old saw about the third time being the lucky one.

At any rate we have suffered twice through Harry Langdon feature pictures convinced that, while the stage lost a good comedian when he started housekeeping in Hollywood, the screen hadn't gained anything but an owl-eyed, solemn youth who was anything but funny.

Then, to complete the cycle, we visited the T. & D. yesterday to view his third feature release, The Strong Man, *and found the first film of the year to send us into complete convulsions. In this film, Langdon justifies all the claims that were made for him and more.*

And the beauty of it is that he rises triumphant over an ordinary manuscript and the efforts of the cutting room to ruin the film. When a comic manages to remain funny under conditions such as Langdon is furnished with in The Strong Man, *he is indeed worthy of the name.*

The Strong Man *contains some of the most hilarious scenes that have ever been depicted on the screen. There is the matter of the cold, for instance. A gentleman suffering from the grippe is, in life, a melancholy figure, but it remained for Langdon to develop him into the richest and most laughable of fellows.*

Then, too, Langdon did not depend solely upon buffoonery for his heavy laughs. He has a gesture in The Strong Man *designed for the votaries of satire, in which he, as the modest and virtuous young man, goes through all the agonies suffered by heroines in countless melodramas as he endeavors to escape the attentions of what he believed to be a designing woman.*

The picture is replete with new comedy situations and at no time are they presented without having a solid foundation laid by the comedian. It is obvious that these scenes are his contributions to The Strong Man *and that the newest office boy wrote the rest of the story, while the janitor wielded the scissors in the cutting room.*

But, while The Strong Man *may annoy you with its outrageous melodrama and its incredible story, and while the presence of a blind heroine in a comedy may be a trifle abhorrent, there is laughter in abundance for the most exacting and entertainment for the most lachrymose when Langdon is working.*

Exhibitors Herald, *October 23, 1926*

Thursday evening, October 14, Oriental Theatre, Chicago. Audience reaction — cataclysmic.

Hail an artist!

Hail the funniest long feature comedy ever made!

Hail Harry Langdon!

Maybe you will not "hail" all these things with exclamation points, but if you don't you will be suspected of obstinacy by this reporter and the 3,000 people who sat and laughed and cried and yelled with him on the occasion denoted above.

What this reporter thought of Mr. Langdon's short feature comedies may be remembered. It may be recalled that violent objection was raised against the comedian's invasion of the long feature field, the same being regarded as rank desertion and an unnecessary risk of possible disaster. Anyhow, it looked from this chair to be a bad idea.

Tramp, Tramp, Tramp seemed to prove that the switch was a good thing, but when reports began coming in from exhibitors who had played it there was room for doubt. "You've had your fling, Harry; now go back to work," is the language in which one exhibitor summed up the somewhat prevalent sentiment.

But that's history.

The Strong Man *is worth at least a dozen* Tramp, Tramp, Tramps. *It is worth a dozen miscellaneous Chaplin comedies, plus all the two-reelers Langdon ever made. It is the best long feature comedy ever manufactured. That's strong, but not so strong as* The Strong Man.

They've taken the oldest recorded burlesque bit — the one about the gal who vamps the goof to pinch his poke — and built it up to what must be the dimensions of a standard two-reeler and is funnier in itself than 99 out of every 100 comedies of any length. They've set Langdon on the end seat of a closed bus and let him doctor a bad cold for about ten minutes — and if there's a dry eye in the house after the first ten seconds of it the ventilating system needs adjustment. The final caption in this section, which has almost no captions, is funnier than all the writings of Mark Twain, Charles Hoyt and Joe Miller rolled into one.

But is this the peak? It is not. The peak is reached in the final sequence which gives the picture its name. Langdon's performance of a strong act before an audience composed of bootleg outlaws who shoot — as they drink — from the hip. Anyone betraying the contents of this scene via printed or spoken word is guilty of the thing Shakespeare charged in that crack that began, "Who steals my purse steals trash…"

Langdon took chances in making this one. It has a religious slant that has no business in comedy and would wreck a less triumphant one that this. It has a blind girl angle that proved disastrous two or three years ago in short features by Al St. John and an unremembered one of the Century comedians. It has the re-built burlesque bit, not entirely shorn of its burlesque aspects, which wouldn't get by if done with one whit less genius than is Langdon's. Yet the man is so good, so supremely funny of face, gesture and thought — even the thoughts show through in this picture — that these items serve merely to build up the comedy.

People associated with Langdon in the picture just fit. Priscilla Bonner is beautiful in a sheer, modest sort of way that is what the doctor ordered. Gertrude Astor may never get out of comedy roles again, as reward for her splendid handling of the difficult burlesque section. Arthur Thalasso is to Langdon in this what Mack Swain used to be to Chaplin, and how! Robert McKim is just such a slicker as he's been in dozens of mellerdrammers, and William V. Mong does a straight clergyman under circumstances wherein the blink of an eye might have wrecked the picture.

Frank Capra is down on my record as director of this comedy, and why is his name unfamiliar to me? If he has made comedies previously, it has been kept a secret from this reporter. I believe it will be just as impossible to keep secret any future product manufactured under his direction as it will be to keep me from seeing it.

Boston Herald, *November 2, 1926*

Harry Langdon's latest laugh, The Strong Man, *now playing at the Washington Street Olympia Theatre, is the best comedy he has made.*

You will be interested in this lonesome boy who strolls across the screen in the personality of Harry Langdon. Peculiar, this comedy is. If it had been an actor who considered himself an emotional dramatist playing the role of the ex-Belgian soldier searching for his American guardian angel, The Strong Man *would have been hailed as one of the most poignant films of the year. As it is, with Harry Langdon in the title role, we have a curious yet remarkably attractive mixture of laughter and sobbing. Chaplin has a rival at last for pathos-humor.*

Motion Picture, *December 1926*

Perhaps we have no funny-bone. We can't have, for while the audience at the Mark Strand Theater were convulsed, ransacked, doubled over with mirth at Harry Langdon in The Strong Man, *we felt more like weeping over the mishaps of the futile little fellow. Actually, we neither laughed nor cried, and yet on that borderland between the two we found ourself (sic) watching with an absorbed interest…It's good entertainment, it's comedy based on truth. Whether you laugh at Harry or weep over him, don't miss seeing him.*

Picture Play, *December 1926*

Harry Langdon in The Strong Man *offers another expensively produced comedy. I am sure you will agree it is the funniest of them all because, in spite of the utter nonsense of it, Langdon has contrived to create a human character. His Paul is essentially like all the other wide-eyed, shambling little men he has brought to life, but the little fellow called Paul is, in my opinion at least, the first one with a heart.*

He is first seen in a battlefield sequence, fondling a picture of Mary Brown with whom he has been corresponding. His return to America, as an assistant to a professional strong man, begins his search for Mary, a quest that develops many farcical difficulties, as you may imagine. These include his capture by and escape from Gold Tooth, a siren played by Gertrude Astor with such amazing gusto that one wonders why she hasn't done this sort of thing before.

Paul's eventual meeting with Mary, who is blind, is genuinely moving — a moment when Langdon's art of clowning reaches its highest estate. For while he remains a clown he becomes also a yearning, timid, pathetic figure of dreams frustrated and denied. For a moment he makes us see ourselves at some moment in our lives.

But these tears would never do to end a farce with, so Langdon gives us the hilarious amusement of watching his efforts to substitute for the strong man at a show from which the Hercules has defaulted. Some things cannot, however, be described. This is one of them.

WHAT THE EXHIBITORS SAID:

The Reel Journal, *October 30, 1926*

We did a fair business on this picture. Print and accessories good.

J.W. Weigard, Marshall Theatre, Manhattan, KS.

Exhibitors Herald, *December 25, 1926*

One cannot help from laughing at this offering. A good comedy with plenty of gags to fill seven reels without padding. It is a farce comedy. A family picture. Langdon has not yet reached the box office figure of Harold Lloyd and Sid (*sic*) Chaplin. Played November 18–19.

Chas. H. Ryan, Irving Theatre, Chicago, IL.
Neighborhood patronage.

Exhibitors Herald, *January 15, 1927*

A dandy good comedy. Played this one for the Legion and almost tickled the boys to death. Hook up with them on this one. Paper won't get them in.

T. M. Morris, Iris Theatre, American Falls, ID.
General patronage.

Exhibitors Herald, *January 22, 1927*

We exploited this strong. Had poor crowd first night and second night dropped off over 50 percent. We lost money on the engagement. Our patrons do not care for this star. It is fair comedy, not as funny as *Tramp, Tramp, Tramp*, but should get over with those that like Langdon.

Cragin & Pike, Majestic Theatre and Airdome, Las Vegas, NV. General patronage.

Exhibitors Herald, *January 22, 1927*

While there are many funny situations in this, I am here to tell you the time has arrived to cut feature length comedies in the class with this. I think that Harry Langdon is good and his pantomime is

fully as good as Chaplin, much better than Keaton, and for the good of the industry, which does not require feature comedies, Harry should go back to two reelers.
W. H. Brenner, Cozy Theatre, Winchester, IN.
General patronage.

Exhibitors Herald, *January 29, 1927*
80%. About the poorest picture that we have ever shown. Had I seen it beforehand would never have ruined a Saturday night with it. Drew fairly well but was a 100% flop and disappointment. Hope next one is better.
Marion F. Bodwell, Paramount Theatre, Wyoming, IL.
General patronage.

Exhibitors Herald, *February 19, 1927*
Harry Langdon — Now here is where I come to bat. I don't like to argue with anyone, but when any exhibitor pans this picture he is either too dumb to appreciate it or else he failed to do big business on it. Ruben and Finkelstein in the Northwest, A. H. Bland and Balaban and Katz played it in their first run houses. The *Photoplay Magazine* also picked it as one of its six best in November. When you pan a picture like this you are insulting the intelligence of the big showmen in this part of the country.

Harry Langdon, you are great, you are an artist in pantomime, and your material is brand new and novel. Here's success to you. I did a nice business on your picture and they are still talking about it. It was a scream. Stay in feature length comedies.
L. E. Palmer, Postville Theatre, Postville, IA.
General patronage.

Exhibitors Herald, *March 5, 1927*
Excellent comedy. Little drawn out but as a whole it pleased.
R. V. Fletcher, Lyric Theatre, Hartington, NE.
General patronage.

Exhibitors Herald, *April 23, 1927*
85%. March 8. Very good. Harry sure kept 'em giggling. Played with Dempsey-Tunney fight picture and used a tieup ad which drew a big crowd. This means another star made good for me.
L. F. Heitzig, Star Theatre, Madelion, MN.
General patronage.

Exhibitors Herald, *April 30, 1927*
If there were any more laughs in this one it would take a "strong man" to live through it. We had to shut the picture off three times so the audience could recover. Had to do it so they would not break down the seats. My cashier laughed so much she gave a fellow five dollars back in change for a one dollar bill.
P. T. Moon, Star Theatre, Neiligh, NE.
General patronage.

Exhibitors Herald, *April 30, 1927*
Better than *Tramp, Tramp, Tramp*, but Langdon would do better by staying in the short reel subjects.
T. J. Potter, Star Theatre, La Grande, OR.
General patronage.

Exhibitors Herald, *April 30, 1927*
All reports favorable. We consider this as good if not better than *Tramp, Tramp, Tramp*. Lots of laughs and drew a good crowd. People liked this one.
T. J. Beam, Beam's Auditorium, Red Cloud, NE.
General patronage.

Exhibitors Herald, *April 30, 1927*
Very comical. The comedy being caused by some funny situations as well as Mr. Langdon's acting. Paid a special price for this one but screened it at regular admission. I would consider it a good Saturday night bill in any small town.
M. D. Williams, Community Theatre, Red Granite, WI.
General patronage.

Exhibitors Herald, *June 4, 1927*
If comedy is "it" this one has "it." The best comedy I have played in months. Laughed so hard a couple of times that I couldn't see the picture. Watched it run through four times and enjoyed it as much the last time as I did the first. A sure test of comedy situations.
Homer P. Morely, Princess Theatre, Buchanan, MI.
Small town patronage.

Exhibitors Herald, *July 9, 1927*
35%. Excellent. The story is rather weak but the antics of Harry save the picture. Should please 100 per cent in communities where good clean comedies are liked.
O. B. Junkins, Manzanita Theatre, Carmel, CA.
General patronage.

Exhibitors Herald, *September 24, 1927*
August 21–22. A pretty good comedy drama but too long drawn out. Would have been better if it was in five reels. It drew a fair crowd and I broke even. Print good.
P. G. Held, Strand Theatre, Griswold, IA.
Small town patronage.

September 5. A good comedy but failed to draw. Title poor and paper worse. If you can get them in they will enjoy it, but we lost money.
Guy B. Amis, Princess Theatre, Lexington, TX.
Small town patronage.

Exhibitors Herald, *October 1, 1927*
49%. September 3. Langdon's pantomime is clever, although play is not much, but gets by with most of the people.
O.A. Halstead, Cozy Theatre, Ducheane, UT.
General patronage.

25%. April 7–8. Our first Langdon picture and went over fairly well with the few that came out. Played two nights to very small houses and lost money.
W. C. Synder, Cozy Theatre, Lamont, OK.
General patronage.

Exhibitors Herald, *October 29, 1927*
From the ridiculous to the sublime. This is so ridiculously funny that we nearly fell out of our seats ourselves and the fans laughed until they cried. Some pronounced it the silliest thing they ever saw, but they laughed just the same. Where Harry fell down the stairs after glimpsing the artists model was a riot.
Dinsmore & Son, Majestic Theatre, Weiner, AR.
General patronage.

60%. Just fair. Only a program picture.
W. Fahrenkrog, Lincoln Theatre, Bunker Hill, IL.
General patronage.

Exhibitors Herald, *November 5, 1927*
50%. A very poor thing to call a special or anything else.
Orio M. Rolo, High School Theatre, Sun City, KS.
Rural patronage.

Exhibitors Herald, *December 24, 1927*
Not much to this one. Would not advise showing it.
Nathan E. Frank, Regent Theatre, Wayland, MI.
Small town patronage.

Exhibitors Herald, *January 14, 1928*
November 22. Not much of a drawing card here.
A. J. Wallace, Pacific Community Association Theatre, Columbia, SC. General patronage.

Exhibitors Herald, *February 4, 1928*
Special cast — 25%. *The Strong Man* developed a glass arm and it was over before it started. Harry, as a drawing card you are a false alarm. The only thing special about this was the price asked. Oh, Yes, quite a few liked it, but we are in business for profit. We have one more of yours Harry and then it's over well forever.
Phillip Rand, Rex Theatre, Salmon, ID.
General patronage.

Exhibitors Herald, *April 21, 1928*
March 17. Good comedy that seemed to please. I myself didn't like the way the church was brought in. The church and the minister were made to appear ridiculous. No minister is foolish enough to expect such miracles these days and that part of the picture is all wrong. Print and photography good.
Robert Yancey, Bonny Theatre, Mansfield, MO.
General patronage.

Long Pants

A Harry Langdon Corporation Production Released in Six Reels. DIRECTED BY Frank Capra. STORY BY Arthur Ripley. ADAPTATION BY Robert Eddy. PHOTOGRAPHY BY Elgin Lessley. EDITED BY Alfred DeGaetano. CAST: Harry Langdon, Priscilla Bonner, Alma Bennett, Gladys Brockwell, Alan Roscoe, Betty Francisco, Bill Wolfe. Cut from final release print: Frankie Darrow, Babe London. Working title: "Johnny Newcomer." Copyright March 22, 1927, Registration Number L23766; Renewed February 8, 1955, Number R144082. Released by First National Pictures, Inc., April 10, 1927.

SYNOPSIS: From the Oak Grove Public Library, Harry Shelby retrieves all the lurid romance novels such as *Don Juan*, and reads them in the solitude of his parents' attic. He imagines himself as a suave, dashing prince, winning the heart of a beautiful dark-haired princess by climbing the ivy strewn on a castle wall to her balcony. He emerges from his reverie upon hearing two young ladies outside his window. He calls out to one flirtatiously, but is told, "Little boys should be seen and not heard." For Harry is still wearing knickerbockers at his mother's insistence: "Short pants are keeping him off the streets and out of trouble."

Today, though, is Harry's birthday and his father has bought him a pair of long pants. Mother doesn't want Harry to have them, but Father is determined, assuring her that "those pants will never go to his head." When Harry puts them on, mother begins to cry. Harry immediately imagines that he's ready for real romance.

As it happens, Bebe Blair, a dope smuggler and thief, is passing through Oak Grove when one of her car's tires is punctured. As the chauffeur is changing the tire, Bebe re-reads a note given her by a lover:

Don't be downhearted. I haven't deserted my Baby Face.

Believe me, as soon as I get back we'll be married.

Walking around a corner, Harry spies Bebe in the car and realizes she's as beautiful as the princess of his imagination. Now that he's dressed like a man, he decides to impress her with his prowess on a bicycle, performing riding stunts — a few not very successfully. However, Bebe is bored and watches Harry's tricks. When he's through, she summons him into her car and gives him a passionate kiss, and he blissfully tumbles into the street. Upon coming to, Harry's mother calls for him, and he's forced to leave. The tire repaired, Bebe demands that they go "before that boob comes back," causing her love note to be blown out of the car. When Harry returns, he finds the note and believes Bebe has written it for him.

Harry's parents have arranged a match-up between their son and Priscilla, a local girl who loves him. When Harry returns after finding Bebe's note and tells his parents, "Don't be surprised if I get married soon," they assume he's referring to Priscilla and begin planning the wedding. On the big day, though, Harry reads that Bebe has been caught, tried and convicted. "'All plot and frameup!' Cries Bebe As Jurors Return Verdict of Guilt," reads a headline over her picture. Harry is more determined than ever not to marry Priscilla. He tries to explain this to his father, who will have none of it. Harry imagines the only way to avoid his marriage is to shoot his bride-to-be.

After sending a telegram to Bebe ("Thought you had forgotten your promise.... Must take desperate steps before I can join you. Be brave little girl."), Harry goes to Priscilla's home, where she is dressed for their wedding. From outside her window, he invites her for a walk in the woods.

As they walk, he reaches for a pistol but it has fallen through a hole in his pants and drops to the ground. He suggests a game of hide-and-seek. At first, as he sneaks off, she follows behind him, mim-

icking his skulking gait. He insists she return to her spot and count. She does, and Harry tries to draw a bead, but can't remove the gun from his pocket until just as she finishes. When she turns to face him, he drops the gun to the ground and orders her to count to 500. After this, nothing goes right. He mistakes a similarly shaped stick for the gun; in tossing a horseshoe for luck, it rebounds and smacks him on the head; he steps in a bear trap; he gets his head jammed into his top hat so that he can't see. Giving up, he sits upon a log in frustration. Priscilla joins him, removes the stuck hat and dusts him off, but he's too morose to notice. She finds his pistol, tacks a newspaper to a tree and fires several shots, which snaps Harry to attention. Each shot is a bulls-eye, with one going right into Bebe Blair's picture on the front page.

Later, Priscilla is on the Shelbys' front porch, telling Harry's mother that "he said he was sorry, but he couldn't marry me — and that his father would explain everything," but "all we can get out of father is — 'DON'T WORRY! HE'LL BE BACK!'"

Harry has gone to San Francisco to rescue Bebe, who has just managed to escape. Pacing outside the jail, he spots her and helps elude her pursuers by hiding her in a nearby crate. He nails it shut and carries her off. Once they're on the streets, Bebe warns him to look out for cops. He places the crate down beside a theater's stage door and looks around, while a stagehand places a dummy policeman on top of the crate. From a distance, Harry is convinced the cop is genuine, and tries several different ways to summon him from the crate. Before long the stagehand returns and removes the dummy, much to Harry's chagrin. While Harry's face is turned, a real cop arrives and takes a seat. Believing this to be a dummy as well, Harry tosses a brick at him, and is chased away.

Upon returning, Harry mistakes a crate containing a live alligator to be the one with Bebe, and drags it off. Just as he's opening the crate, a cop arrives to phone the station. Harry sits upon the crate and the alligator takes a few bites. Once the cop departs, Harry opens the crate, sees the alligator and runs away. In doing so, he trips over Bebe's crate, and helps her out. "Stick with me and you'll be on Easy Street," she tells him and he kisses her. Unbeknownst to Harry, she's armed with a pistol and robs a nearby steamship company office. Having stolen a fancy suit for him, she dresses Harry and they set out together. Bebe surreptitiously sticks her gun into a pedestrian's side, whereupon the gentleman hands Harry all his valuables, which the puzzled boy gratefully accepts.

Out for revenge, Bebe goes to a club where the girl who squealed on her works as a dancer. The girl gets a tip-off that she should leave town after her last performance, but while she's on the dance floor, Bebe and Harry arrive and hide in her dressing room. The girl returns, and though Harry believes it to be a social call, Bebe's intentions are much more sinister. The two women land into each other while an astonished Harry can only watch.

Bebe wins the fight, throws the disheveled dancer into the street, and revives herself by finishing off a nearby bottle. She sits beside the stunned Harry and puts her arm around him, but he's seen enough.

"Why — I'm surPRISED!" he tells her. "I'm sorry but we must part. I'm through." Just then, the tipster enters the room and spots Bebe, who shoots him. As he falls, he reaches for his gun; more shots are fired, and Bebe is hit. So is Harry, in his right arm. The nightclub crowd bursts in; police arrive and there is chaos.

Most of the crowd, including Harry, is taken to jail, but he is swiftly released. Still stunned, he heads

Langdon with Priscilla Bonner in a publicity still for Long Pants.

for home, and enters the house just as his parents, and Priscilla, are saying grace. Silently he takes a seat and bows his head. The prayer finished, they all look up to see him. As he offers a wan smile, they rise as one to embrace him, knocking the table and all the food onto him.

ANALYSIS: *Long Pants* is arguably the cleverest and best constructed of all Langdon's silent features. Its emphasis on black humor is ahead of its time, making it the Langdon film most likely to please modern audiences. Unfortunately, the circulating version derives from such an inferior source (primarily a 16mm dupe print), that it's also the poorest-looking film in the comedian's First National canon; this plus Frank Capra's harsh opinion has hurt its reputation. Should a 35mm nitrate emerge one day (perhaps with its Technicolor sequence intact), a critical reevaluation will doubtless follow. More prints were struck of *Long Pants* than any other Langdon feature, so such a find is not beyond possibility, although time is running out.

In retrospect, it's easy to understand why Capra was dismayed. His costume notwithstanding, the Harry of *Long Pants* is not the Little Elf. There's nothing comically perplexing about him or his actions or reactions. He is solely an adolescent, perhaps in his upper teens, whose father believes it is past time for him to stop wearing knickers and whose mother fears what will happen if he does. He is fixated on romance and adventure, having long been denied both. In *The Silent Clowns*, Walter Kerr writes that Harry's Elfish "ambiguity is restored" once it's revealed that he's old enough to marry Priscilla, but in farm country, where Harry is clearly being raised, it was not uncommon to be wed at 16 or 17. Members of Langdon's own family, including his parents and at least one sibling, married at that age.

As discussed in the text, the scene in which Harry intends to shoot Priscilla engendered a great deal of controversy at the time and has its detractors to this day. Robert Farr, silent comedy historian and founder of the annual Slapsticon festival in the Washington, D.C., area, has written, "There is nothing else like it in any comedian's body of work. Not even the crudest, most vulgar slapstick practitioners would willingly throw away audience empathy to that extent." Curiously, 20 years later, Chaplin would create an entire film around his portrayal of a man who marries wealthy women only to murder them. The film, *Monsieur Verdoux*, includes a comic scene in which he attempts and fails to drown one of his wives, drawing nearer to the actual situation in *An American Tragedy* than even Langdon dared, though the slapstick indignities he endures are remarkably similar. However, Chaplin's would-be victim is not an innocent childhood sweetheart like Priscilla, but an obnoxiously abrasive broad, memorably essayed by Martha Raye. Regardless, even in the postwar 1940s, movie audiences found such humor tasteless and unpleasant.

If there is anything ambiguous about *Long Pants*, it is the ending. Harry, clearly disillusioned by his "romantic adventure," makes his way home. He sits at table while his parents and Priscilla are at prayer, and bows his head. At the close of grace, all look up and are stunned to see him. Their reaction swiftly turns to joy, and they rise as one to offer an effusive welcome, even as they knock over the table, spilling it and the dinner all over him. As he rises, he looks every bit as stunned as he did when Bebe was shooting it out to her fatal finish. The film ends here, with no sense

of resolution. Has this boy learned anything? Is he happy to be home? Will he marry Priscilla, or even learn to love her? There are no answers; like a book with its final pages missing, *Long Pants* just stops and leaves us guessing.

HARRY MOMENT: The scene where Harry attempts to rouse the dummy policeman is a tour-de-force of remarkable pantomime. As he acts out several different emergency scenarios, each more urgent than the last, his utter befuddlement at the "cop's" disinterest is the punctuation that demonstrates Langdon's mastery of comic timing.

WHAT THE CRITICS SAID:

Brooklyn Eagle, *March 28, 1927; Reviewed by Grace Cutler Cutler*

Harry Langdon's newest comedy, Long Pants, *at the Manhattan Strand, might be judged on the merits of the gentle art of pantomime. It shows Langdon to be one of the very best in this type of screen flattery — a subtle pantomimist who has found the advantage of eloquent acting as against the grimness of subtitled wisecracks.*

In Long Pants, *Langdon follows the blazing trail of Chaplin. He remembers the Oceana Roll of* The Gold Rush *and decides that with caution he may do the same. Accordingly, the picture has two sequences of ineffable drollery — the one in the woods where Langdon takes his rustic bride-to-be and attempts to shoot her so that he may be free for the seductive city vamp — and the other in which he rescues the vamp from prison and encounters the law in the person of a stage dummy policeman. With the exception of Chaplin, these two bits of acting show him to be probably the most enterprising and courageous of the comedians. Which is something for Gilbert Seldes to crow about…*

Long Pants is probably Langdon's funniest picture. It contains sustained and genuine humor throughout, with just that touch of pathos which transforms the stock comedy wheeze into something short of a work of art. Its gags are few and better, and if they are occasionally predominant mark it down as a last obeisance to the demigods of Hollywood.

New York Evening Post, *March 28, 1927; Reviewed by Wilella Waldorf*

Possibly a little flustered at the rousing reception accorded his last comedy, The Strong Man, *Harry Langdon has tried hard to do something even better in* Long Pants, *at the Strand this week, and succeeded in stringing together an extraordinary combination of novel ideas and stock comedy situations.* Long Pants, *as a whole, is not so much the funny Mr. Langdon as it is a picture of the comic things which happen to the funny Mr. Langdon. Unfortunately, several of these things have happened before to other funny men and are, therefore, lacking, not unnaturally, in freshness and spontaneity.*

Long Pants has not run on very long before it shows signs of having been "gagged" almost to death. When Mr. Langdon is engaged in doing quaint things in his own quaint way — such as riding his bicycle circus fashion round and round a broken-down Rolls-Royce, occupied by a lady whom he would impress — all is well. Later on, however, when the small-town boy goes to the city and becomes involved with a gang of crooks, a series of slapstick doings sets in reminiscent of all the slapstick comedies extant and a good many dead and gone. Not once during the proceedings does Mr. Langdon take time out for an interlude comparable to the famous cold-in-the-head sequence in The Strong Man.

The very fact that this is a Langdon comedy, however, insures a number of perfectly legitimate laughs and there are times when he is very funny indeed. Almost invariably these moments occur during the less elaborately planned sequences. Alma Bennett and Priscilla Bonner also appear from time-to-time, Miss Bennett in a particularly strenuous role demanding jail breaking and hair pulling.

New York Times, *March 29, 1927; Reviewed by Mordaunt Hall*

Some hilarious passages enliven Harry Langdon's latest film oddity, Long Pants, *which is on view at the Mark Strand. Although these incidents are acted with consummate skill, except for an occasional repetition, it is obvious to any male who has made the decisive change from short to long trousers that the idea offers possibilities far greater and more genuine than those that greet the eye. The answer is that Mr. Langdon has once again capitulated to his omnipotent band of gag-men. It may be all very well for Harold Lloyd to rely on mechanical twists, but Langdon possesses a cherubic countenance which offers him a chance in other directions.*

Mr. Langdon does begin in a modulated fashion, but afterward he officiates wonderingly in a series of whirlpool effects. First he appears as the boy in knee-length breeches, who is absorbed in the great lovers of history, including none other than "Don One."

That he should become awestruck by the attractive presence of a young woman whose fingerprints are known to many police authorities is not unnatural. But the idea of her permitting him to embrace her is quite another matter. It is very comical to look at the Boy taking one stance after another as he looks down at his full-length trousers. The idea of having the Boy ride around the Vamp's car, doing tricks on his bicycle, is side-splitting, even if he indulges in a couple of falls before this piece of business….

The Vamp is apprehended as a "snow" smuggler, and while this Boy endeavors to officiate as the gallant rescuer he espies a dummy policeman whom he believes to be a minion of the law in the flesh. Langdon's efforts to tempt this bluecoat to follow him would probably cause a real policeman to look upon him as a candidate for a psychopathic ward of a hospital. However, this does not mean that this stretch is without its degree of humor.

Mr. Langdon is still Charles Spencer Chaplin's sincerest flatterer. His short coat reminds one of Chaplin, and now and again his footwork is like that of the great screen comedian.

Variety, *March 30, 1927; Reviewed by Rush*

A bit of a letdown for Langdon. It hasn't the popular laughing quality of his other full-length productions, principally because the sympathetic element is over-developed at the expense of the gags and the stunts that made The Strong Man *a riot.*

By anybody else the picture would be hailed as a great production. Langdon's name and work will make it a substantial box office property. The pull of the name was evidenced at the Strand Saturday and Sunday, when queues were continuous. The point is that the picture is amusing and satisfying, but it is not up to this up and coming comedian's best.

The opening is exceedingly quiet. It is here that the picture seeks to build up a sympathetic background for the Boy, giving a semi-serious twist calculated to heighten its subsequent clowning.

Langdon does the boyhood scenes in his inimitable style, but the humor is a bit fine for the generality of fans.

Later on, when they get into rougher material, there are several highly effective comic passages. One of the best was the incident where Langdon, who has unwittingly helped a woman criminal to escape jail in a packing case, sees what he thinks is a policeman sitting on the box. He takes up a position across the street and tries by half a dozen absurd ruses to draw away the cop.

The picture builds up in speed of action when the lady crook the hero innocently rescued from jail gets into a fist fight with a woman cabaret dancer whom she blames for her arrest. Harry all this time registers merely his typical nervous futile protest, and for the moment the story gets out of his hands.

A swift finish is used. The whole situation elaborately built up, is unceremoniously dropped, and Harry is seen returning from the nest of crooks he has stumbled into to his quiet home and his simple sweetheart. This brusque transition is rather confusing. Besides the incident with the cop there is an elaborate comedy situation about half way. Langdon has become enamored of a woman criminal without, of course, knowing her character. While he wants to go to her in the city, his parents force him into a marriage with a village girl. In his absurdly naïve way he decides the only way he can escape is to take the village bride out into lover's lane and shoot her.

Much laughable material is used here in Harry's painstaking but futile preparations for his scheme, and his decisions not to carry it through when he loses his pistol, gets caught in a bear trap and jams his hat down over his eyes as he takes aim. Some pretty obvious devices are employed here, such as his slipping trousers and efforts to control his suspenders.

The opening shows Johnny, a kid in knickerbockers, reveling in super-heated romances from the public library. When he gets his first long pants he starts out to do a Don Juan, with such complications as can be imagined.

Harrison's Reports, *April 2, 1927*

The entertainment values of Long Pants *are not very high. Harry Langdon's slapstick comedy gets the laughs here and there but it is not of such strength as to off-set the picture's shortcomings. The story supposedly to be farce comedy, is unpleasant; it develops into vicious underworld melodrama that incites to crime. The action is slow. Outside of Langdon the principal players enact their roles seriously and what was intended for burlesque becomes ordinary bandit thrill material. A holdup of an express office by the girl crook is followed by a scene where she sticks up a man in the street, aided by the hero. A situation, sure to prove offensive in many localities, particularly in small communities, is that in which the hero, takes the girl, which his father and mother are trying to make him marry into the woods and make several unavailing attempts to shoot her. Making a joke about attempted murder in this way leaves an ugly taste in the spectator's mouth. It is just like making fun of a funeral. Harry Langdon's antics and pantomime are always amusing, but in this case his talents are wasted on a thin plot that outlines a bad moral. There is little suspense.*

Film Daily, *April 3, 1927*

Langdon [is] thoroughly capable of keeping the audience in laughs although the gags are not consistently good all the way through.

Cast: Again scores in his long solo scenes where by sheer comedy pantomime he keeps the crowd in stitches. Alma Bennett the vamp and Priscilla Bonner the country sweetheart. Al Roscoe and Gladys Brockwell are Harry's ma and pa.

Story and production: With little effort on his part Harry Langdon can eke more laughs out of an audience than the best gagsters could secure with a series of top notch stunts. Again in Long Pants *it is purely Langdon's way of doing things that keep the crowd laughing. The situations aren't consistently mirth provoking and the repetition of some of comedy business slows the tempo. Even Langdon shouldn't repeat his stuff if he wants it to hold to a brisk humorous pace. His encounter with a vamp who turns out to be a crook provides the nucleus of the comedy with Harry a victim of the well known "it." He returns home, disillusioned to marry the country girl.*

Direction: Frank Capra; fair.

Photography: Elgin Lessley-Glenn Kershner; good.

Film Daily, *April 3, 1927; Reviewed by Lilian W. Brennan*

Harry Langdon reached Broadway in his latest, Long Pants, *and sent Strand audiences out in a happy frame of mind. Langdon is a master pantomimist.*

Motion Picture News,, *April 8, 1927; Reviewed by Laurence Reid*

As droll and hilarious a comedy as had been captured in a season or two is brought to light in Long Pants. *Here is a typical Langdon title adorning a typical Langdon film — which means that it's full-grown, charged with bright and effervescent gags and humor and continuously funny. It may be a little lengthy and repetitious, but there's no denying its appeal as a rib tickler. The comedian dons his baggy costume to bat around on a bicycle — and certainly plays his trumps. Which is another way of saying that he doesn't forget to apply his pathos to temper the comedy. His is an individual art — and he has certainly capitalized it to a fare-you-well.*

He jogs along on his "bike" and is captured by the beauty of a girl seated in the tonneau of a dashing car (yes, the Rolls-Royce is all of that). As he spies her he forgets all about the village belle. He even goes so far as to forget his impending marriage to rescue the vamp from jail, for, to be truthful, the girl is something of a bandit. When he discovers what a jam he is in he returns to his sweetheart — and is forgiven.

In telling this one cannot account for all the play of comic incident. Let it be said that it packs one hilarious episode after another — and the entire series of gags are well timed.

Theme: Comedy of rustic youth who falls hard for a vamp and forgets his village sweetheart. He returns to her when he learns a thing or two.

Production Highlights: The bicycle gags. The episode with the dummy policeman. The gag showing effort to shoot the belle. The titles.

Exploitation Angles: Bill as Langdon's best. Feature the gags. Play up the pathos which always marks star's comedies.

Drawing Power: Should break records. For any type of house.

Moving Picture World, *April 9, 1927*

Once again Harry Langdon has come forward with mirth-provoking comedy that is sure to tickle the risibilities of the great movie going public. Long Pants, *his third and newest starring vehicle for First National is plentifully supplied with smiles, chuckles and hearty laughs and should put any audience in good humor.*

This is a typical Langdon vehicle made to his measure by competent gag men and expertly directed by Frank Capra…

Possibly the story reads like straight drama and this gives Harry opportunities to play upon pathos and human interest as well as comedy, but of course it is the comedy that is predominant. The story in truth is slight and wavers, at times, being halted for long periods while innumerable gags are worked out. In fact, it is a typical example of a gag comedy, episodic in nature, with the laughs clustered around four scenes, his meeting with the vamp, his attempt to get up courage to shoot his sweetheart to get rid of her, his aiding the vamp to escape by putting her in a box and carrying through the streets and his part as a surprised witness to her outburst against husband and double-crossing rival. Each of these sequences has been held for considerable periods and between them the continuity is at times jumpy, being bridged by subtitles. There is also a noticeable tendency to repetition in some of the gags which weakens them and the result is that while Long Pants is screamingly funny it is not as fast or snappy as The Strong Man.

Langdon appears in his familiar type of make-up and has a congenial role, he is the Langdon that the fans have learned to laugh at, although there is the novelty of seeing him as a kid in short pants and, what is more striking, as a romantic lover in uniform in a bright Technicolor sequence when he dreams of his amorous conquests which are to come.

Alma Bennett is dashing and satisfying as the vamping female bandit and all-round crook, and Pricilla Bonner is well cast as the demure country girl. Gladys Brockwell and Alan Roscoe are satisfactory in the minor roles of the boys' mother and father.

There are a lot of original gags in this picture, such as his stunts on a bicycle while trying to attract attention. Although held rather too long, the sequence where he carries the vamp through the streets is a scream, especially when he mistakes a dummy cop for a real one and vice versa, hitting the real policeman with a brick and starting a chase.

Cleveland Plain Dealer, *April 11, 1927; Reviewed by W. Ward Marsh*

Harry survives a rather weak and sometimes too aimless story. He is always funny to me.

His combination of childlike trustfulness, even when the world wallops him most severely, and his eagerness to please, to be considered as a man, is a fine and an accurate plumbing of pathos. As with all comedians, this pathetic quality colors and gives a new and vital interest to his comic antics.

Two splendid pantomimic scenes stand out in this picture which is so repetitious that in another's hands it would have been completely ruined. The initial one is when Harry, encased in long pants, feels love's first awakening. He longs for adventure and wilder women than his village sweetheart can offer.

And adventure and romance arrive in a high-powered motor car, at his door. He circles this automobile on his bicycle while Alma Bennett boredly reclines in its luxurious rear seat. He does tricks. He is the male of the species trying to engage the eye and the attention by queer and hilarious tricks from the insect world.

But the scene is smashed into a too definite reality when Harry climbs in and is so thoroughly kissed that he remains kissed even on the eve of his wedding to Miss Bonner.

Influenced by An American Tragedy, *without doubt,* Harry plots to kill her, and then in a far too long sequence, he fails to carry out his threat.

The second splendid scene comes after he has aided the other woman in her escape from jail. He believes

the dummy policeman, sitting on the box in which the temptress is concealed, is a real one and he pulls some most amusing gags to draw the policeman from his post.

This one will make you laugh, but it is not up to Langdon's standard. He shows the effects of too many gag-men, with whom he was at odds, as well as with the director, during the filming of the production. Langdon is always, however, well worth recommending in spite of the fact that the painted "drops" look as real as the urban settings in the "fotygraph" album.

Brooklyn Eagle, *April 18, 1927; Reviewed by Martin Dickstein*

There have been few funnier incidents on the screen than the one in Long Pants, *current at the Brooklyn Strand Theater, where Harry Langdon, the baby-faced comic attempts to draw the attention of a dummy policeman sitting on a packing box in which his sweetheart lies hidden from the eyes of the law. Even fewer funnier film passages have come this way than the one in which this comedian is discovered pedaling his bicycle round and round a motorcar to win a smile or recognition from the lady who sits placidly in the tonneau. And yet, while these episodes are uproarious in high degree, the remaining moments in* Long Pants *must be reported as disappointingly dull and uneventful. A two-reeler of hilarious possibilities, the film has been extended without sufficient reason to six, and thereby it manages too often to founder in chapters containing nothing to laugh about.*

In Long Pants, *you have the story of the boy who grew older, who acquired simultaneously his first long trousers and a longing for worldly romance. You are told of his infatuation for a beautiful stranger who subsequently turns out to be a notorious trader of narcotics. Inadvertently, this bumpkin hero helps his beloved to escape from prison and thus he is discovered in the amusing pantomime with the dummy policeman mentioned early in this account.*

Did you enjoy (sic) The Strong Man *or even* Tramp, Tramp, Tramp, *you may find less cause for amusement in* Long Pants, *for, generally, it does not reveal Mr. Langdon at his best.*

Davenport (IA) Democrat and Leader, *May 1, 1927*

If as they say, love is the strongest of all emotions, then Harry Langdon's mad actions in Long Pants, *his latest picture, are accounted for. The capers he cuts are for Harry little short of cyclone.*

Over that well-nigh immobile but almost transparent face rage conflicts of desire that for Harry mount into the spectacular.

Into Harry's actions, engendered by the force that makes the world go round, come speed and freedom that must have astounded even the actor himself as he previewed his latest creation.

But for all the change Harry retains the ability to make the fan titter and laugh in short spasmodic jerks. No audience is ever convulsed by his antics. Attention is required to appreciate his pantomime…

High spots in the show are hard to pick out but watch for the place where Harry goes round and round on his bicycle while his head does the same. Catch his pantomime with the police, and right at the first of the story before he has attained to long pants — notice that, too.

There was some evident cutting of the film which gave the appearance of effect without cause. That seems to be its chief fault.

Motion Picture Classic, *June 1927; Reviewed by Laurence Reid*

In his ridiculous baggy costume, Harry Langdon comes forward with what many will consider his drollest comedy. Long Pants *is studded with amusing gags, but with all of them clicking merrily, it is the very waggish star in whom you are most interested.*

A smart fellow, this Langdon. He knows that to succeed in comedies one must project a personality. So in exploiting his innocent manner and his goofy expression he has emerged as an artist, a showman and a judge of good tricks.

Long Pants, *like its forerunners, builds from preposterous situations — and Langdon, painstakingly, sees to it that they present him in pathetic loneliness. Thus he always balances his scenes by alternating comedy with pathos.*

In Long Pants, *Langdon takes to the bicycle and as he pedals over the road he becomes interested in a girl seated in the tonneau of a Rolls-Royce (that's a good car, too). Well, the upshot of it is he forgets the bucolic belle of the village and falls for the vamp.*

On the day set for the wedding he takes his sweetheart to the woods for the purpose of shooting her. But the gun is rusty and refuses to work, so, leaving her in the lurch, he goes to the city to rescue his fair vamp from jail. When he learns that she has a fondness for collecting jewels — other people's — he returns home and carries on his rustic romance.

Simple enough, you say? You don't know the half of it. The fun is evolved as the incidents develop — and they literally tumble over each other as Langdon strives to be heroic. Some of the gags are repetitious, but all of them are well timed. And so it becomes a neat strip of celluloid — one worth anybody's time and money.

Photoplay, *June 1927*

Not much of a story for six long reels, but Langdon is always funny and so who cares a great deal about the story.

Picture Play, *July 1927*

Harry Langdon will break your heart in Long Pants, *to the tune of laughter and chuckles; but he will break it just the same — if you're past the age of discretion…*

This slight tale, employing only three sequences, is embellished with all manner of byplay and gags, which brings it to the length required of a feature. Whether it is as funny as The Strong Man, *I cannot say, but it seems not to matter, so long as, underlying the laughs, is the pathos of loneliness and through it run the fever and futility of adolescence.*

Alma Bennett is highly effective as THE VAMP, and so is Priscilla Bonner as the deserted bride, while Albert Roscoe and Gladys Brockwell are THE BOY'S parents.

Oakland Tribune, *October 11, 1927; Reviewed by Wood Soanes*

When a low comedian — and a good one — elects to be subtle and satiric, extraordinary things are likely to happen and they do in Harry Langdon's Long Pants, *current at the Grand-Lake.*

In this we have the estimable Master Langdon, so refreshingly comic in The Strong Man, *endeavoring to make merriment out of tragedy in the way of a burlesque on Dreiser's [An]* American Tragedy. *Langdon attempts to make a humorous episode out of the murder of a bride-elect on her wedding day and it must be confessed that the incident emerges only gruesome.*

Of course there have been leading women whose acting deserved a parade to the guillotine and others who merited a visit to the electric chair, but up to the time Langdon makes up his mind to slay Priscilla Bonner she is displaying all the attributes of an attractive young actress who deserved if not a bronze plaque, at least a friendly pat on the shoulder.

Long Pants *otherwise has merit if not great hilarity. Langdon uses some interesting photography in his opening scenes of the boy achieving manhood and introduces some side-splitting low comedy into the sequences with the dummy policeman. Otherwise it falls considerably short of perfection. Langdon is naturally funny and an adroit pantomimist, he deserves a much better and faster script.*

Important in his histrionic aid are Alma Bennett, excellent as the vampire who lures the youth from his rural habitat; Gladys Brockwell and Al Roscoe as his doting parents, and Miss Bonner. Frankie Darrow is given on the program as "Langdon as a small boy," but that section must have been eliminated from the version we saw yesterday, else these old eyes are growing rheumy and strabismic.

WHAT THE EXHIBITORS SAID:
Exhibitors Herald, *May 5, 1927*
70%. April 21. Best Langdon comedy so far. Chock full of good comedy spice and good homey story, just what the masses want. Back it up with pep.
Jack Hoefler, Washington Theatre, Quincy, IL.
General patronage.

Exhibitors Herald, *May 7, 1927*
Outside of Harry Langdon's expressions and good acting, absolutely nothing to this picture. He had poor material to work with and believe he should be assisted by an able cast. Many adverse criticisms. Some liked it. Don't pay much for it. It's only medium program.
C. H. Sartorious, Capitol Theatre, Hartley, IA.
General patronage.

Exhibitors Herald, *May 28, 1927*
You can go back to two reelers any time you want to, Harry. You mean less than nothing here in features.
Leslie Hables, Reel Joy Theatre, King City, CA.
Small town patronage.

Exhibitors Herald, *July 23, 1927*
70%. July 2. A good comedy, but it lacks a lot having the laughs that were in *The Strong Man*.
Homer P. Morley, Princess Theatre, Buchanan, MI.
Small town patronage.

Exhibitors Herald, *July 30, 1927*
24%. One big piece of cheese that patrons walked out on. Will be glad when he strikes.
Art E. Trotzig, City Theatre, Vermillion, SD.
General patronage.

Fair comedy drama that failed to do much business. They don't seem to care much for Langdon.
Ernest Vetter, Majestic Theatre, Homer, MI.
Small town patronage.

This star puts crepe on the box office. Might just as well hang a smallpox sign on the lobby. He just won't draw the crowds and will not please what few stragglers that do venture in. This is just about as poor an attraction as you can get outside of *The Strong Man*.
Marion F. Bodwell, Paramount Theatre, Wyoming, IL.
General patronage.

Exhibitors Herald, *August 6, 1927*
25%. If Harry makes another one like this we won't wish him any bad luck, but hope he breaks a leg in the first reel. No sense, no story, no nothing.
Elva Miller, Liberty Theatre, Tremonton, UT.
General patronage.

Not a laugh in it. Absolutely rotten. Langdon is a failure with me in his long comedies. Used to be fair in two reelers.
A. Mitchell, Dixie Theatre, Russellville, KY.
Small town patronage.

Exhibitors Herald, *October 22, 1927*

Many patrons said *Long Pants* was the worst picture we have ever shown. Personally consider it a very poor feature. Would be good as a short comedy. Business poor.
P. K. Grant, Pollard Theatre, Guthrie, KS.
Small town patronage.

Exhibitors Herald, *November 19, 1927*

Only mildly amusing, and I might say poor. There is very little real comedy or action. I only heard one or two giggles during the screening. We expect more than this from you, Harry.
O. B. Junkins, Manzanita Theatre, Carmel, CA.
General patronage.

Moving Picture World, *December 24, 1927*

A knock-out comedy drama that pleased, but failed to draw for me. Langdon pleased them all but will not draw at my box-office. Not a special.
L. O. Davis, Virginia Theatre, Hazard, KY.

Exhibitors Herald, *April 21, 1928*

64%. March 16. Just fair as a picture, but think it's the best one he's made to date. It holds the Friday night's record here. Why, I don't know, but the audience seemed to like it.
E. N. McFarland, Pine Grove Theatre, Port Huron, MI.
General patronage.

His First Flame

A Mack Sennett Production Released in Five Reels.
DIRECTED BY Harry Edwards. **SUPERVISED BY** John A. Waldron. **STORY BY** Arthur Ripley and Frank Capra. **TITLES BY** Tay Garnett. **PHOTOGRAPHED BY** Billy Williams. **EDITED BY** William Hornbeck. **CAST:** Harry Langdon, Ruth Hiatt, Natalie Kingston, Vernon Dent, Bud Jamison, Dot Farley, Irving Bacon, Thelma Parr, Margaret Cloud, Evelyn Francisco, Thelma Hill, Elsie Tarron. Originally filmed during March–July 1925 in between two-reeler production. Copyright February 6, 1926, Registration Number L22377. Released by Pathé Exchange, Inc., May 8, 1927.

SYNOPSIS: Ethel Morgan, who is very stuck up, receives a telegram from Harry. She is invited to come to his college and hear his graduation speech. She tosses the telegram aside and it is then picked up by her sister Mary, who is sweet and romantic. Ethel says that she'll hear enough of his speeches after they're married. It seems that Ethel is just after Harry's money. Mary says she'd love Harry if he didn't have a cent.

It is graduation day at Bliss College. The students are told that Harry Howells will address them on "Women and — Why." He looks out on the students

and realizes that they are all women. Harry tells them that this country needs more matrimony and less alimony. He further says that women need no eulogy because they speak for themselves. His speech goes over very well with the women.

In a local firehouse stands Harry's uncle, Amos McCarthy, a confirmed woman hater. He tells his fellow firemen that if he ever hears of his nephew getting married he'll…

Harry, carrying flowers and candy, arrives at the station. His uncle asks him about his plans after getting an education. Harry tells him that the first thing he's going to do is get married. Amos tells Harry that any girl who wants to marry him is just after his money. Harry tells him that he'll think it over. He tells his uncle that he brought the flowers and candy for *him*. After Harry leaves, Amos sees Ethel's name on the flowers and tosses them into a spittoon. He then looks up her phone number and calls her.

When Ethel answers she is told that Harry doesn't have a cent. She stomps on her bridal veil and tosses Harry's photo into a fireplace.

Harry, engagement ring in hand, is on his way to see Ethel. He runs into old pal Hector Benedict. Harry drops the ring and believes that he has lost it. After some confusion the ring is found in Hector's pants cuff.

Meanwhile, two shoplifters posing as a married couple with a baby carriage full of stolen goods pass by. Harry walks with them and is restrained from cuddling the "baby." He goes to Hector's house and sees him fighting with his wife. He tries tp patch things up, to no avail. The couple continue to fight and argue, with Harry stuck in the middle. After a while he realizes that he's overstayed his welcome and leaves.

The two shoplifters are on the run from the cops. The "wife" begins to chase Harry. Ethel sees this and hopes the pursuing woman gets Harry. Shortly thereafter, the woman knocks Harry on the head and steals his clothes. He ends up wearing *her* clothes and is dazed from the blow. Harry arrives at the firehouse, where his awaiting uncle is aghast at his attire. Amos brings him a fireman's uniform, and Harry is soon asleep in a bed on the top floor of the firehouse.

A fire breaks out and a bell summons the firemen to the scene. After the fire trucks leave, Harry and Amos are left behind. They run toward the burning building. Harry watches his uncle climb a ladder to enter the building. A woman leaps from the top floor and lands in a safety net held by the firemen. Harry then spots Ethel in a window of the building. Harry enters the building, unaware that Amos has carried Ethel to safety. He emerges with a female mannequin and descends down the ladder. He soon realizes his mistake and sees Ethel and Amos getting into a car. Harry observes them kissing on the back of the car, which leaves the scene. Mary sees all of this and is saddened.

Later, Mary decides to start a small fire so Harry can rescue her. She burns some stockings in an ashtray and calls the firehouse. Harry, who has been crying, answers the phone and is told that Mary's house is on fire. He informs her that he'll tell the firemen when they return. Harry also tells her that there's nobody at the firehouse except him and two horses. He turns the horses loose and attempts to stuff a mattress into the fire wagon. Billows of smoke result and people

begin running toward the firehouse. Convinced by Mary to come to her aid, Harry manages to get the horses hooked up to the wagon and takes off toward the fire. Mary sees the wagon heading toward her house and readies herself to be rescued. Smoke from the fire wagon's smokestack billows into the house and Mary begins to panic. He enters the smoke-filled house and lights a match to find his way around the fire. He rescues Mary, and while carrying her, runs into Amos, who has arrived on the scene. Harry eyes Amos warily and runs away, carrying Mary.

ANALYSIS: In retrospect, it's a pity that this, Harry Langdon's first feature, was the fourth released, for it was deserving of more respect and attention than it received at the time. It is the only feature produced by the entire team that created the best silent shorts: Edwards-Ripley-Capra, plus Langdon himself.

Surprisingly, given the four had not yet progressed beyond the two-reel length, *His First Flame* does not feel padded or overlong.

Admittedly, there isn't much in the way of a plot. Harry Howells wants to propose to Ethel Morgan, unaware that she loves only his money, but circumstances keep interfering. The incidents that hinder his progress, however, are quite amusing and enjoyable. Too, because we're rooting for Mary, Ethel's less materialistic sister, to win Harry's heart, we can enjoy the various distractions on a second level. Rather than rely on nature, Mary takes matters into her own hands and eventually accomplishes her goal, which makes perfect sense in the universe of Harry.

HARRY MOMENT: After seeing Ethel leave with Amos, Harry is depicted in the station from behind. Two teardrops fall on the floor. The sudden realization

Vernon Dent initially doesn't recognize his nephew Harry in His First Flame.

that he's crying reveals a layer of vulnerability to the Little Elf character. Though fleeting, it is a characteristic example of Harry's sweet nature.

WHAT THE CRITICS SAID:

Film Daily, *April 3, 1927; Reviewed by Lilian W. Brennan*

Pathé is offering a Harry Langdon feature with comedian doing very good work and containing a comedy climax that will send them out laughing. The gags would have served as a first rate two reeler but they are far too few for a feature.

New York Times, *May 2, 1927; Reviewed by Mordaunt Hall*

Judging by the comedy in Harry Langdon's film, His First Flame, *now on view at the Mark Strand Theatre, Mack Sennett, the producer, had better beware or he will find himself wallowing in a more sophisticated strata of humor than that to which he has accustomed himself. Mr. Sennett and Mr. Langdon do their parts in this nice mile of fun. Mr. Sennett, who failed as a blacksmith and amassed millions as a maker of film humor, deserves no little credit for the hilarious situations in this picture. And Mr. Langdon is to be congratulated on a generous supply of sad smiles and wide-eyed effects.*

Sometimes the wit in this mirthful piece is as appealing as the sound of a well-hit anvil; on other occasions it is as if the hammer had missed its mark or struck a log of wood.

The story of this comedy is credited to Arthur Ripley and Frank Capra. It is a series of gags that are wonderfully suitable to Mr. Langdon's genius as a screen clown. Possibly the best effect of all in this current venture, which was produced several years ago, is where the wistful Harry gazes into a shop window and visualizes his own offspring, impersonated by himself. The child Langdon is beheld seated in a baby carriage, while its would-be father is looking dreamily through the window. The eyes are, of course, those of the father, and so is the queer little mouth. The actions of the infant have evidently been inherited from the father.

Another splendid episode is where Harry Howells, impersonated, of course, by Mr. Langdon, decides to answer a fire call. After informing the owner of the charming voice over the telephone that he will tell the boys about the fire when they return from the blaze they are at that moment fighting, Harry goes below and pats his knee to make the fire horses come out. The animals ignore him, but when he dons a fireman's helmet they immediately respond. Thereafter, as one might imagine, the incidents are uproarious, for Harry knows as much about running a fire engine as he does about training the guns of a battleship.

Mr. Langdon is at his best in this humorous piece of work.

Brooklyn Daily Eagle, *May 4 1927; Reviewed by Martin Dickstein*

Time was, before The Strong Man, Tramp, Tramp Tramp *and* Long Pants, *when Harry Langdon was a Mack Sennett comedian whose amusing cinema antics were distributed to eager exhibitors through Pathé Freres. Then the moneyed Associated First National Company came along and wooed the baby-faced Harry away from the Sennettian lot, leaving the ordinarily good natured Mack and the fraternal Pathés holding the bag which contained a last lone relic of Langdon in a slapstick comedy called* His First Flame. *Cannily enough, the frustrated Sennett and the garcons Pathés retarded the release of this film until a day, following the exposure of* The Strong Man *and* Long Pants, *when Langdon should have become an undisputed darling of the box offices of the land. Thus you have at the Manhattan Strand this week the naively ridiculous Langdon in a picture which dates something like three years. If you observe it carefully enough you will discover that it retains many of the near-custard pie mannerisms of that faded era.*

It is not unlikely that in the beginning His First Flame *was intended to be a two-reel potion of slapstick. But two-reel comedies, unfortunately, have lost caste in these days of de luxe programs in the million dollar movie emporia. Therefore you may watch* His First Flame *in five or six reels, not because its humor justifies a wider breadth but for the ample reason that a six-reel picture, by all existing etiquette of the motion picture tradesman, elicits more lucrative largess than a two-reel picture.*

His First Flame, *lest you allow the subtlety of its title to escape you, finds Langdon as an inadvertent fire laddie, who single-handedly rescues his sweetheart from the clutch of blazing death and otherwise conducts himself along the way of all Sennett flesh. Silly and stupid in the majority of its sequences, the film is hardly up to the standard of Langdon's more recently manufactured drollities.*

New York Evening Sun, *May 4, 1927*

His First Flame *proves…that some years ago, Harry was doing the same round of tricks, doing them with more spontaneous gayety than he is now.*

Moving Picture World, *May 7, 1927*

Several Amusing Gags in Harry Langdon Comedy produced by Sennett and Distributed by Pathé.

Before Harry Langdon began starring in feature length comedies he achieved big success in a series of two reelers produced by Mack Sennett and distributed through Pathé. This combination is now offering him in a five-reel comedy His First Flame *directed by Harry Edwards from a script by Frank Capra and Arthur Ripley.*

Characteristic of the Langdon vehicles, this is an out and out gag comedy and although there is a story it is exceedingly attenuated, serving only as a basis on which to build the comedy business…

The gags are all good, and even though some of them are familiar, they are all handled in Langdon's inimitable and highly amusing style and should get the laughs. In building the picture up to its feature length, however, many of the comedy situations are held too long and lose some of their force through repetition and the story interest is too slight to hold the interest at high pitch between the highlights. There is some corking good material but hardly enough for the footage allotted.

His First Flame, however, has enough laughs to make it a fairly popular attraction.

Variety, *May 11, 1927; Reviewed by Sime Silverman*

A gag picture, running through a story of no consequence, but with laughs enough from the Harry Langdon gags to make this picture stand up as that kind of comedy. It's the last full length Langdon made for Mack Sennett, and its release (Pathé) at the Strand, New York, shortly follows Langdon's latest First National (Long Pants).

It's about a blundering boy home from college with a bachelor uncle, foreman of a fire company and deadly on all women, trying to thwart his nephew's ambition to marry.

As a rule — and it seems inviolable in pictures — all dead pan comics must follow the gag line. That means padding to lead up to the laugh punch. It's so here, but Langdon, when he laugh-punches, does so with a kick, and you laugh, no matter who you are or what you think.

Still there's quite a lot of padding as in the fire rescue scene. Here the comedy punch is the weakest.

For immobility Langdon holds to about the most stern mug of all time. He barely broke into a slight smile once during the running. A funny guy who seems to be steadily forging forward, one of those slow but sure sort that eventually lands in the Chaplin-Lloyd class.

Quite a nice production even to exteriors, with support correspondingly. A couple of misses with reminiscent vaudeville names, Natalie Kingston and Ruth Hiatt, prettily show before the camera as sisters. They care nicely for their comparative little, and the same goes for the others. It's a Langdon picture.

Wherever Langdon has made himself this can follow right in, either before or after Long Pants.

Harrison's Reports, *May 14, 1927*

Not up to the standard of Harry Langdon's best pictures. It is a farce comedy, consisting mostly of the sort of slapstick fun one looks for in Mack Sennett two-reelers. The first part of the film is slow but it speeds up in the second half. Harry Langdon puts over a lot of gags that are really funny, if not very original, and that will amuse those who are not too critical. There is nothing to the plot, it simply serves the purpose of showing how the hero gets constantly into trouble and makes fresh blunders. Harry Langdon's pantomime is good.

It is not a week-run attraction but will probably amuse audiences in the smaller houses.

Exhibitors Herald, *May 20, 1927; Reviewed by Laurence Reid*

This picture, marking Harry Langdon's first and last five-reeler for Mack Sennett, comes as a belated release.

Since the comedian has blossomed out into Higher Celluloid his pictures are carrying a spontaneity which this earlier effort lacks. The piece has an uneven continuity — there being none of the rhythm and sparkle which accompanied The Strong Man and Long Pants.

The chief weakness is its length. It would click far better if condensed into two reels. Still it has its moments — moments in which the round-eyed Langdon indulges in plenty of highfalutin action. He is inimitable, as always, in his role of a youth who is frustrated in his effort to win the girl. She prefers his fire-chief uncle. A good deal of the comedy centers around Harry answering a fake fire alarm — and running away with the girl in his arms. He also provokes merriment when dolled up in antiquated feminine clothes and gewgaws.

His First Flame *is gagged all the way*. Langdon does his baby act which was used in Tramp, Tramp, Tramp, and casts his innocent stare into the camera time and again. Yes, the man knows his stuff. The picture is good here and there.

Theme: Comedy of boobish youth whose sweetheart is stolen away from him by his fire chief uncle. But he wins her back.

Production Highlights: The titles, The gags. The scene of Langdon running around in feminine attire. The fire alarm sequence, etc.

Exploitation Angles: Be sure to run stills of Langdon in his various disguises. Play up his air of innocence which has made him a star. Bill as sure-fire comedy stuff.

Drawing Power: Will please Langdon fans. O. K. for any type of house.

Photoplay, *July, 1927*

This is Harry Langdon's first feature length comedy and for reasons best known to Harry's former employers, it has just been released. It was made about two years ago and the improvements in pictures in two years are remarkable. Langdon is, was and always will be funny but it is just a plain low trick to show this to audiences. The lighting is bad, the girl's clothes are a scream — in fact the picture looks like a number of two-reelers pasted together — but Harry is always worth the price of admission.

Cleveland Plain Dealer, *September 12, 1927; Reviewed by W. Ward Marsh*

A season or so ago, before Harry Langdon left the famous ranks of Sennett for the fatter contract offered him by First National, this rare comic made several pictures which have been dribbled out to the public from time to time.

His First Flame *is, I believe, the last of that lot. Its age is as apparent as an old Chaplin comic. It is particularly noticeable in the style of feminine garb. The ladies were just beginning to discover they had legs which would be cooler if not so completely hidden, and since everyone has them, the sin of exposing at least a modest part of them passed out along with many other ancient taboos.*

His First Flame *is funny — in places. Those are the places where Langdon is given the freedom of the celluloid. His graduation speech, opening the picture, is a tremendously funny bit of pantomime — to me, at least. There is a pretty consistent letdown after that…*

Langdon is always funny. His story isn't so much this time.

WHAT THE EXHIBITORS SAID:
Exhibitors Herald, *October 27, 1927*

Terrible! I would think Mack Sennett would hide his head in shame after turning out such a piece of junk. Not worth showing.
Walter Hohfield, Elite Theatre, Greenleaf, KS.
General patronage.

Three's A Crowd

A Harry Langdon Corporation Production Released in Six Reels. **DIRECTED BY** Harry Langdon. **STORY BY** Arthur Ripley. **ADAPTATION BY** James Langdon and Robert Eddy. **PRODUCTION MANAGER:** William Jenner. **PHOTOGRAPHY BY** Elgin Lessley and Frank Evans. **EDITED BY** Alfred DeGaetano. **ASSISTANT DIRECTOR:** J. Frank Holliday. **TECHNICAL DIRECTOR:** Lloyd Brierly. **ELECTRICAL SUPERVISOR:** Wayne Harmon. **CAST:** Harry Langdon, Gladys McConnell, Helen Hayward, Cornelius Keefe, Brooks Benedict, Arthur Thalasso, Henry Barrows, Frances Raymond, Agnes Steele. **WORKING TITLE:** "Gratitude." Copyright August 17, 1927, Registration Number L24303; Renewed August 5, 1955, Number R154107. Released by First National Pictures, Inc., August 28, 1927.

SYNOPSIS: It is five o'clock in the morning, and as the milk wagon makes its rounds and the streetlights go out, Harry reluctantly rises at the sound of his alarm clock. He lives at the top of a long staircase in a dilapidated shack, in the poorest tenement district of the city. He's the assistant of a transport driver, and much as he'd like to go back to sleep, his boss is yelling for him from the street. "How do you expect the boy to get up at five when he works for you till after midnight?" asks the boss's wife.

Urged on by his boss, Harry begins his day, which includes preparing the coffee, watering a plant, some stretching exercises, and so forth. Included in this is the writing of a love note to a girl he's been admiring from a distance. He secures a pigeon to deliver the note, which reads:

Dear Sweetheart,

Perhaps you don't know that there is someone in this world that loves you more than everything — that's me.

I know I have no right to tell you and you can never be anything to me. That is why it will be best not to tell you how much I love you.

Good Bye Honey.

*Love and kisses,
a Lonesome Boy*

After sending the pigeon on its way, Harry resumes his routine. As he gets into a makeshift shower, his impatient boss hurls a stone toward his window, but it strikes the stovepipe, which collapses into Harry's shower stall, covering him with soot.

By the time Harry's cleaned, dressed and ready to work, it is ten o'clock. He retrieves an old rag doll from a trashcan, and while his boss playfully tosses his son in the air, Harry does the same with the doll. The boss laughs at how much the doll resembles Harry before tossing it away. The boss's wife notices this and assures Harry that one day he'll have a wife and child of his own. When the boss sees Harry talking to his wife, he misconstrues and puts Harry to work. However, the lunch whistle blows and Harry sits down to eat. The boss returns and threatens Harry with a gun, accusing him of trying to break up his home. He orders Harry back to work. When the wife offers to sew a tear in Harry's pants, he retreats, afraid that he'll be shot.

The boss apologizes for over-reacting, just as the pigeon lands and delivers Harry's letter — to the boss's wife. When his son brings the letter to his father, Harry runs for dear life. The furious boss chases him clear up to his shack. Harry falls through a trap door that he'd left open earlier. He grabs a carpet, but continues to fall. The trap door snaps shut on the carpet, leaving Harry to dangle several stories from the ground. He repeatedly climbs up the carpet to the door, but when he opens the door, the carpet is no longer held in place, causing Harry to drop until the door snaps shut again. Meanwhile, having given up the chase, the boss backs up his truck for loading. When the final piece of carpet is released, Harry

falls into the back of the truck. The boss sees Harry emerge, then looks over at the rag doll on the ground, and laughs.

The abandoned doll is tossed in the trash, thrown into the street, dumped into a horse trough, dragged off by a stray dog, covered in snow and eventually tossed by winds into the telegraph wires above. In the midst of a blizzard, a disheveled man awakens with a hangover; he finds a note on a chair beside his bed, which concludes, "You have lost everything you hold dear through your dissipation and I am leaving you only because I cannot put up with this life any longer. I am sure if you will listen to your father, he will give you another chance — and so will I, because I love you." Through the blizzard, a woman carrying a bundle wearily makes her way through the neighborhood.

As Harry shovels snow from the roof of his shack, he notices that someone has collapsed in the street below, and he rushes down to investigate. Finding no one else around, he picks her up and carries her to his home, and places her in the bed. On closer examination, he realizes she is the woman he's been admiring. He tries to warm her, covering her with a meager blanket and giving her hot liquids. As he is about to give her medicine ("For Measles," reads the bottle) he notices the bundle she'd been carrying contains baby clothes. In a panic, he rushes down the stairs and calls for "Help! Storks!" The women of the tenements answer his frantic call while Harry locates every doctor in town. As the doctors gather at the foot of the stairs, each tries to pass off the job to one of the others. Finally, Harry takes all their bags upstairs so that they must follow. The doctors are admitted, but Harry is told to remain outside.

Eventually, Harry hears the sound of a baby from within, and decides to tell his boss that he's now a proud papa. The doctors and midwives leave, and the women congratulate Harry on his "son." Harry has bought some toys for the baby. The final midwife tells him he must be quiet and let the mother and child rest. Harry stands in awe, not moving a muscle, for several minutes.

Elsewhere, the woman's husband, who has evidently reformed, hires a detective to locate his wife. "When she finds that Father has taken me back and I'm making good, she'll surely forgive me." At the same time, Harry's boss is having dinner with his family, explaining to the wife about Harry's new "family." The wife agrees that "it sounds just like some fairy tale," but the boss is certain that "some day the husband is coming back and you can tie a tin can to your fairy tale." As for Harry, he's visiting Professor DeMotte, a neighborhood fortune teller, who assures him, "Your worries are ended. The husband will pass out of her life — and the girl will be yours."

Harry returns home to see to the girl's comfort, and notices the photo of her husband beside her. He takes it and walks away from her so he can scold the photo, then reluctantly returns it. The baby cries, and after carrying it awhile, Harry realizes it needs changing. He brings in the diapers that were drying outside, but they are frozen stiff. Harry decides he can warm and soften them by kneading them on a table. At first he uses the flat end of an axe, then moves on to a rolling pin. While engaged in the task, he watches as the new mother interacts with her child, and is so lost in admiration that he adds flour, places the diaper in a pie tin, adds canned fruit, and trims the edges. Holding the pie in his hand, he looks down at the remainder of the diaper and realizes what he's done. Not wishing to appear totally useless, he places the pie in his oven.

Taking the baby again, he places some curved handles on the table, turns it upside-down on the floor, and it becomes a cradle. He steps inside, sits the baby on his lap and proceeds to rock back and forth. The baby continues crying, so Harry entertains him with funny faces, one of which involves crossing his eyes. When one eye doesn't uncross, Harry panics, but eventually it returns to normal. He rocks the baby until they both fall asleep.

Harry dreams that the husband, depicted as a laughing, maniacal figure, is lurking outside the shack. His wife sees him and screams, awakening Harry. She takes the baby from Harry and urges him, "Don't let my husband stand in the way of our love!" The husband enters as Harry is donning boxing gloves. The husband dons gloves of his own, and Harry's boss appears as a referee. Suddenly the room becomes a boxing ring, with the wife at ringside, encouraging Harry. His glove swells to three times its normal size, giving him confidence. The wife offers him a brick to put in his glove, but he refuses it. The bell rings, and Harry dances around the motionless husband. He urges the wife to cover her eyes, which she does. When she looks again, Harry is down for the count. As the boss/referee counts, he repeatedly strikes Harry on the head with a hammer. The wife calls to him, he crawls over to her and as he passes out, she kisses him.

At that moment, the dream ends and the husband arrives for real. He enters the shack and sees his wife dressing their child. As he marvels at them both, she turns, sees him, and starts to cry. He drops to his knees and pledges his devotion, just as Harry awakens. Seeing that the husband has reformed and that wife and child will be leaving, Harry is stunned. The departing couple conveys their gratitude for all he's done, telling him, "We'll always be glad to see you, Harry — and some day we hope to show our appreciation." After the chauffeur takes the child, the husband carries his wife down the stairs. The car pulls away, and Harry stands with his lamp, as we see the torn rag doll tangled in the telegraph wires. It is early morning now, and as Harry blows out his lamp, the streetlights go out as well.

Making his way over to Professor De Motte's shop, Harry is determined to toss a brick through a window. He repeatedly raises the brick, but just can't bring himself to do it. Resigned, he tosses the brick away. When he does, it knocks the gate off the back of a truck, which causes a huge metal drum to roll across the road and destroy De Motte's storefront. Swiftly, a frightened Harry runs to the safety of his shack.

Current prints do not contain the scene where Harry writes the love letter and sends it off with the pigeon.

ANALYSIS: *Three's a Crowd* is, in many respects, Langdon's masterwork. It is the film that defines the Little Elf as Langdon ultimately perceived him.

From a technical standpoint, apart from a couple of minor problematic matching shots, and the placement of the initial fortune teller scene discussed previously, there's nothing wrong with *Three's a Crowd*. Over the years, many movie critics and historians have taken Langdon to task for his direction, accusing him of meager skills in this area, but having called the shots for 17 years in vaudeville, coupled with four years of film experience plus a competent production staff at his disposal, he possessed all the proper tools. Most of the film's scenes are beautifully composed, the editing is taut, the story progresses at an agreeable tempo, and there's certainly no more emphasis on Harry here than in any of the previous films. The problem with *Three's a Crowd* is that Langdon is so determined to evoke sympathy he repeatedly initiates what should be moments of gentle melancholy and bludgeons the audience with them.

The discarded rag doll is the obvious example. Harry finds the doll, which looks exactly like him for no discernable reason except for what's to follow, and he uses it to practice throwing a child in the air and catching it, as the boss is doing with his son. This is strongly reminiscent of other moments in which the Elf has imitated his superiors. Then it's carried too far: Harry's boss notices him, sarcastically points out the doll's resemblance to Harry and laughs, confident in the knowledge that this is as close to fatherhood as his pathetic employee will ever get. The boss tosses the doll away and, in a lengthy sequence (marred by severe decomposition in current prints), it's subsequently knocked around, chewed by a dog, windblown in a storm, and finally left disfigured and tangled in telegraph wires. Symbolism is served up like a punch in the mouth. We get it: Harry is doomed to disappointment.

Indeed, the film's devastating flaw is that the outcome is a foregone conclusion, even without the rag doll. The expectant mother leaves her spouse reluctantly, assuring him in a letter that once he straightens up, she'll return because she still loves him. The entire time she's recuperating in Harry's bed, the husband's photo rests nearby. There's no evidence, outside of Harry's own imagination, that she's falling in love with her benefactor. Moreover, we've seen that the husband has indeed mended his ways and is eager to reunite with her and the child he knows is due. Langdon the storyteller gives us a tale that, by design, should compel us to root for his success, but Langdon the filmmaker insists that to do so is a waste of time.

The promise of eventual heartache permeates the picture and eclipses the comedy.

Contrast all this to Chaplin's *The Kid*, a film to which some critics, in reviewing *Three's a Crowd*, drew comparisons. In *The Kid*, we know from the start that the unwed mother regrets the loss of her child, and when she and her son meet by happenstance, each unaware of the other's identity, we suspect an emotional reunion will be forthcoming. However, these are but fleeting moments in a film that rest primarily on the Tramp's growing attachment to his orphaned "son," in scenes that are comical first, sentimental second, and which take place over five years, not a few days. Moreover, Chaplin is canny enough to have pompous, unfeeling authorities, not the mother herself, attempt to remove the child from him, giving him a logical reason to fight back; the boy is finally taken away while Charlie sleeps, by a seedy flophouse attendant desiring only to cash in on a reward. Lastly, once "the kid" is restored to his mother (their official reunion taking place offscreen), she has no intention of shutting Charlie out of her son's life, but rather welcomes him into their home. There's no chance of this happening in *Three's a Crowd*, because, as the opening cast list tells us, the wife and new mother is One, her penitent husband is Two, and Harry is Three.

HARRY MOMENTS: Harry tosses the rag doll in the air in imitation of his boss, who's playing with his son. The boss takes the doll away and invites Harry to practice with his son, but Harry isn't strong enough to lift him.

When Harry reluctantly decides he can't throw a brick through Professor DeMotte's window, he tosses it away. The brick dislodges a huge drum from the back of a truck, which rolls into DeMotte's storefront and demolishes it. It's another example of Divine providence looking out for the Elf.

WHAT THE CRITICS SAID:
Film Daily, *August 28, 1927*

Not the laugh riot they expect of Langdon. Some first-rate gags but picture doesn't hit an even comedy tempo.

Cast: Langdon is fine and has little trouble landing his laughs when the situations permit. But this is not often enough.

Story and Production: The Chaplin comedies have always contained a degree of pathos developed along with the humor in the plot. Now Langdon has taken to the same sort of theme, building a comic situation along with a sympathetic strain. In Three's a Crowd he is the unhappy outcast who, just when he has attained his heart's desire, loses it and is back right where he started. There is some good incident and several clever gags that should draw a minimum of laughs but, on the whole, the picture is not the hilarious affair they look for from Langdon. He rescues a young girl from a snowstorm and works to provide for her and the baby born in his rooftop shack. Just when he is supremely happy her husband turns up and she goes off with him.

Direction: Harry Langdon; fair.
Photography: Elgin Lessley-Frank Evans; good.

Harrison's Reports, *September 10, 1927*

This is not a comedy — it is a drama; and if it were directed as a drama it would perhaps have caused many heart throbs. There are a few situations where laughs are caused, but they are few and far between. The picture on the whole is tiresome, and the theme unpleasant. The hero is shown loving babies but he is not married, the girl he loved having married another man, leaving him heartbroken. Later the girl abandons her husband because of cruel treatment. The hero finds her in a snowstorm and takes her into his home three flights up in a dilapidated building. There she gives birth to a child.

It is the details of the birth that is the most unpleasant part of the picture. Dealing with birth of babies is unpleasant even in drama, however delicately handled; in comedy it is offensive, particularly when they are handled somewhat crudely. During these scenes Mr. Langdon is seen going back and forth, showing indecision as to what he intends to do. This is irritating to the spectator, who, as always, wants action.

Whatever comedy there is, it is caused by the fear the hero has of his employer, a bully.

Being a truckman, the employer forces the hero to move things. The scenes where the hero slips and falls through a trap door in the floor of his home three stories high, hanging from the carpet he has taken hold of while falling produces considerable comedy, and holds the spectator in suspense. Every time the hero, still hanging from the edge of the carpet, pushes the trap door up, the carpet, with its human load, slips more until only the edge of it is "bitten" between the trap door and the floor, saving him from a

A HOME MADE POSTER USEFUL FOR NICE LOBBY WORK
Another example of how the Everett Theatre, Everett, Wash., makes up its lobby smash. The center is either home drawn or utilizes a cutout from some lithograph, while there is room at the sides for a still display.

hard fall. But the fall eventually happens. The last time the hero pushes the trap door open, the carpet is disengaged entirely, and he falls on top of his employer's van, driven by the employer.

Cleveland Plain Dealer, *September 12, 1927; Reviewed by Glenn C. Pullen*

This picture presents a rather thin and uneventful tale, yet that always funny feller, Harry Langdon, contrives to make it a beguiling comedy, although it is not one of his best.

Langdon has been hailed as a "male Lillian Gish" and Chaplin's successor by his admirers; unfeeling critics have been less complimentary.

At any rate, there is a genuine artistry about his eloquent pantomime, a note of sincere pathos in his naïve Peter Pan-like characterization that stamps him as an unusually talented pantaloon. This pathetic quality of his is emphasized strongly and interestingly in Three's a Crowd.

The story shows Harry as a timid tenement roustabout for a moving company. Living in a shack that threatens to fall apart in a wind, he admires a girl in an adjoining house. His desire for a wife comes when the girl, a young mother, needs help and he befriends her.

The final scene has a stirring "La Bohème" touch. In the midst of his happiness, the girl's dissolute husband returns, now reformed, and takes her away. It is an odd ending but true to life.

In striving for pathos, Langdon has made humor take second place. The gags are good but few, and the sentiment is a trifle cloying at times. While this does not compare with Harry's [The] Strong Man, it is commendable, with a fine "human interest" angle.

Chicago Daily News, *September 22, 1927; Reviewed by Carl Sandburg*

Harry Langdon's new comedy, Three's a Crowd, is a slow-moving, rather sad affair which has little in it to stir a crowd to laughter. The story has too much of heartbreak for the poor, lonely fellow to make one wish to laugh at him.

Something of Chaplin's genius lies in his thoughtful moments and the artistic way he handles situations and undoubtedly he can move his audiences to tears and to laughter also, given half a chance, but when the story has as little of humor and as much of tragedy as Three's a Crowd, *the laugh stops in the throat.*

Photoplay, *October 1927*

Harry Langdon reaches for the moon in this and grasps — a feeble glow-worm. He has tried to stuff the plots of Chaplin's The Kid *and Charlie Ray's* The Girl I Loved *into one picture. The result is an absurd, unbelievable story. To top the blunder, he makes you wade through thick layers of oleomargarine pathos to get at the comedy. We like Harry Langdon and hate to hear the sound of his flops. May his next be louder and funnier.*

New York Daily News, *October 2, 1927; Reviewed by Irene Thirer*

Harry Langdon's Three's a Crowd *grasps that sober-faced comedian out of the rut into which he has been lowering himself, and shoves him right back to a place among the stellar lights of picturedom.*

This comedy-tragedy is indeed a decidedly impressive screen contribution. Its gags have been construed with much thought as to audience reaction. And most of them are novel and exceptionally funny. Its direction is subtle and quick-moving for the most part, with just a couple of lagging passages.

And Harry is grand. He has found himself again.

There isn't any too much of plot, but what matter? You'll probably, as this reviewer did, get a great kick out of what there is.

Hardly anybody in the movie game could have called this comedy and made his audience walk out of the theatre feeling that it really and truly is comedy — but comedy with a sadness. Not the frozen Buster Keaton kind. Pathetic, heart-rending comedy. You actually feel for this lonely Harry, and yet you realize that he isn't really lonely and that this is all in fun and that you're supposed to laugh at it and you do. Because in spots it is so laugh-provoking that you'll be kept in stitches.

Harry, you see, is a tenement boy — and you ought to see the tenement sets. Not much like New York. He's a lonely guy; works for a moving van owner and longs for a wife and children.

One day, as a furious storm rages, he comes upon a pretty girl, lying exhausted in the snow. He takes her up a steep flight of steps into his shack, and almost immediately calls out to all his neighbors:

"Help, storks!"

After her baby is born, the girl lingers with Harry. She has left her husband, it seems, and won't return to him although she still loves him. For a while, our Harry is happy. Then friend hubby comes along. Wifey admits she's ready to go back and it's proven thereby that "Three's a Crowd."

Now, you can't find much comedy in what has been reported in the aforementioned paragraphs. Can you? Yet you can take our word for it — there are giggles galore.

New York Evening Post, *October 3, 1927; Reviewed by Wilella Waldorf*

Harry Langdon should take himself in hand quickly before his past efforts are forgotten. The Strong Man will long remain in the minds of many people as a remarkably fine comedy, but if Mr. Langdon insists upon following it up with pictures like Long Pants *and* Three's a Crowd, *the memory will fade sooner than it might otherwise.* Long Pants *did contain some good scenes, but* Three's

a Crowd, *at the Strand just now, is poor from start to finish. Its gags are old and badly developed, its continuity is choppy and, worst of all, the film drags on interminably.* Three's a Crowd *is not funny, and Mr. Langdon, sad to relate, appears to be suffering from an acute attack of Chaplinitis. As someone remarked at the Strand on Saturday, his next picture will probably be a screen version of* Hamlet.

Encouraged by the plaudits that greeted his first few efforts as a "feature film comedian," Mr. Langdon has discarded a number of assistants and directed this so-called comedy himself. It looks very much as though he also wrote the story as he went along, and it is very obvious that his prime intention was pathos interspersed with humor. Unfortunately, the only pathetic thing about Three's a Crowd *is the fact that a good comedian has gone so rapidly down hill. Now that Mr. Langdon has had his fling at art, perhaps he will snap out of it and give us another* Strong Man.

New York Times, *October 3, 1927; Reviewed by Mordaunt Hall*

As Harry Langdon toddles through his new film, Three's a Crowd, *one is impelled to observe that this screen clown has a mouth like the Mona Lisa and eyes like a Raphael angel or a Lorelei Lee. His current shadow adventure is a mixture of gentle pathos and Big Bertha exploits. In some respects it gives one a foggy notion of Chaplin's picture* The Kid, *but it happens only too often in this present production that the bright bits are followed by a barrage of buffoonery that has about as much right in the narrative as a chimney sweep would have in a flour mill; the consequence is that these boisterous attempts to wring laughter from audiences have all the humor of Babe Ruth playing Peter Pan or Betty Bronson trying to make a home run in a World Series game.*

Mr. Langdon in some sequences again reveals himself to be a gifted player, and the pity is that he has been inveigled into using gags that detract from the continuity of the subject. The story of Three's a Crowd *begins a little late, for the initial chapters are concerned with showing, sometimes in no deft fashion, that Harry (the character) is an ingenious young man who longs to be a husband and a father.*

Brooklyn Daily Eagle, *October 5, 1927; Reviewed by Martin Dickstein*

In Three's a Crowd, *which may be seen at the Strand Theater in Manhattan this week, Harry Langdon tries desperately to flavor his comedy with the table salt of pathos with the not surprising result that pathos, over-flavored, has turned to bathos. Langdon is, of course, essentially a comedian who, having tasted of the fruit of comedic success, has arrived at that inevitable conclusion of clowns that tragedy is a longer art than farce. In a way, Chaplin has ventured into much the same frame of mind with, as he demonstrated in* The Gold Rush, *something less than fatal effect. Harry Langdon is, however, not a Charlie Chaplin and where Charlot might have made a tragicomedy of no little importance out of the thin skein of sentiment at the Strand, the less accomplished Langdon has had to be content with only moderate success.*

Three's a Crowd introduces the baby-faced comic as a lonely heart amid domestic happiness, a pitiful and ludicrous fellow who envies other men their wives and kiddies. Into this boobish Pagliacci's life one winter's morning comes a ray of sunshine in the form of a young woman, who, it is brought out, has run away from her bounder of a husband and who accepts the slender hospitality of the lonely one's shack until her baby is born. When the husband has turned over a new leaf he comes to take his wife and child away with him, leaving the sad young man to bewilder at the barrenness of life that fate has yielded him.

Most of this seemingly was not meant to be funny. Accordingly, those who journey to the Strand this week anticipating again an uproarious hour with the comedian of The Strong Man *must, unfortunately, be doomed to disappointment. The humorous moments in* Three's a Crowd *are weighed down by a false super-structure of tragedy, tragedy which resembles nothing so much as a clown who has smeared his make-up with a deluge of glycerin tears.*

Variety, *October 5, 1927; Reviewed by Sid*

Harry Langdon had previously threatened to direct his own pictures and in this one he's done it. Three's a Crowd *is no sensation but neither is it a cluck. So it shapes as fair program material with the comedian leaning toward the serious and stressing pathos more than is his habit.*

At the Strand juvenile patronage seemed particularly delighted Sunday while the more elderly secured their share of laughs.

Those who don't like Langdon aren't going to be won over by this release. It's too quiet and lacks the necessary explosive mirth to overcome that handicap. Those who do favor the comic, however, will be satisfied. There are spots in the picture where Langdon is brilliant, but on the other hand slow passages also creep in. It's not a high geared vehicle and Langdon has held down the hoke, which may explain.

A moderate production forms the setting as the action takes place in a tenement district. Photography is average. In this respect the director-comedian reveals a penchant for lingering over fadeouts at the end of scenes, pausing almost a full minute over some of these with himself as the central figure.

Three's a Crowd *is not of the spontaneous type but it's clean and jogs along at a fair gait with enough laugh incidents to hold interest. Supporting cast members handle little more than bits.*

Moving Picture World, *October 8, 1927*

There is more pathos than comedy, more heart interest than laughter in Three's a Crowd, *Harry Langdon's newest starring vehicle for First National, which is of a different type from his previous offerings.*

While retaining his familiar and amusing make-up and playing a character built along the same general lines, Langdon in this picture has wandered far from

the straight gag comedy in which he made his reputation. Either from a desire to get away from dependence on gags and to depend more on situations and "acting" or from belief in the idea of "Pagliacci" that the world will laugh at the misfortune of a clown, the greater the laughter, this comedian has introduced more drama and more dependence on situations in Three's a Crowd.

Whatever the reason, he appears to have overshot the mark in this picture, there are only a few gags and some of these are old ones. While his personality and make-up amuses as heretofore and he has some funny situations, obvious opportunities for slapstick and gags are overlooked, the heart interest plot built-up with pathos stressed even to an unhappy ending to his romance, although an added gag provides a laugh for a finish.

The plot is really a melodrama treated too seriously to be burlesque so that it will scarcely register either as comedy or melodrama, and it would certainly seem that his fans who expect hilarious comedy from Langdon will be disappointed by the lack of it in Three's a Crowd.

Utica (NY) Observer-Dispatch, *October 9, 1927; Reviewed by William Richmond*

Of all our screen comedians, Charlie Chaplin seems to be the only one capable of standing fame without crumbling. No sooner does a screen comedian make his mark than he turns writer, director and what-not for his own productions. The minute he does that, it seems, his fame begins to dim. Lloyd, Keaton and numerous others are living examples of this rule. Chaplin alone has survived as comedian, author, director and, mayhap, property man.

Now comes Harry Langdon. During the last two years, this wistful tramp climbed to remarkable heights. As a matter of fact, he achieved genuine fame as a comedian. Then, having reached the top, he wheeled right around and committed the folly of greatness — he became his own author and director. This week we watched the first picture of his since assuming these many roles — Three's a Crowd. *A large audience at the Mark Strand must have felt, as did this chronicler, that Langdon, too, had joined the others who have failed because they succeeded.*

Three's a Crowd *is not a Langdon picture. Langdon, the comedian, is gone. In his stead, another cavorts upon the screen — half mountebank, half maudlin dramatic "ham" — directed, all too apparently, by an inefficient director who is one of the finest comedians on the screen, but one of the worst directors in Hollywood.*

Like Chaplin, Langdon aspires to the dramatic, the tragic, but unlike Chaplin, he does not possess that rare quality which would permit him to dally along the trail of fun-making and wax serious for a flash or two. A capable director would have told him so — but Langdon, in Three's a Crowd, *was his own director.*

Exhibitors Herald, *October 14, 1927; Reviewed by Laurence Reid*

Harry Langdon has been working too steadily producing his pictures instead of taking his time and concentrating upon fresher ideas and gags. If he made his screen appearances six or eight months apart the intervening period could be devoted to better workmanship. The new comedy is not so hot and lags far behind The Strong Man. *There's scarcely an up-to-date gag in it and the story runs along in a slip-shod way without any semblance of continuity. Langdon is too finished a comedian to be projected in a work of this calibre. Perhaps he's taken on too big a burden in trying to be the chief cook and bottle-washer of his productions. Directing this effort himself, it appears as if he concocted it as he went along.*

There are a few funny spots in it, but they are overwhelmed by the sad ones. The comedian with the droll personality and the mark of pathos on his countenance allows himself to become unduly tragic here. He's gone Chaplin — with the result that his own inimitable style is often buried. The pathos looks labored — and the comedy lacks spontaneity.

The star plays a lonesome chap of the tenements whose only companion is a rag doll. Eventually he meets the Girl. After many strong bids for pathos everything ends tip-top for Harry. There will be those who will see it because of the Langdon fame, but they can't truthfully admit it's a wow.

Theme: Comedy of lonesome chap who after pining for romance meets the Girl.

Production Highlights: Langdon's pantomime. Sets and atmosphere.

Exploitation Angles: Tease title. Play up Langdon as one of the few top notch comedians.

Drawing Power: Langdon's popularity will draw them. For any house.

Photoplay, *November 1927*

Harry Langdon attempts too much in this one. The boy's good, but he's not Chaplin yet. Better luck next time.

Picture Play, *January 1928*

Harry Langdon is the same plaintive little fellow and adept comedian in Three's a Crowd *as he always has been, but the sum total of his efforts is not altogether satisfactory. The picture is monotonous in spite of some clever gags, because no one else is allowed to do anything, and there is little variety in the sets. The story is no story at all, but an incident merely. A boy rescues a runaway wife in a snowstorm and takes her to his squalid lodgings, where her baby is born. He adores her with dumb and futile devotion, living in a dream until her unworthy husband finds her. At first sight of him, she deserts the boy forever. All this is put across in Langdon's characteristic manner. Unique as that is, it hasn't succeeded in saving* Three's a Crowd *from slowness.*

Oakland Tribune, *May 7, 1928; Reviewed by Wood Soanes*

If Harry Langdon is seeking the palm for mediocrity he has hit another bull's eye in Three's a Crowd, *which will be on display at the Hippodrome for the last times today.*

In it we find him not only fumbling as a comedian, but wandering in a daze as an author and director. Possibly it was his view of himself in triplicate that prompted him to select the title. There was no other possible reason for it that this reviewer could adduce.

The story of Three's a Crowd is too utterly banal to warrant the space that would be needed to give it a résumé. What comedy is in the picture is promptly strangled by Langdon in his attempt to drag it out to indefinite lengths. Match these up, then, with a second-rate supporting cast and you have an idea of the entertainment value of this opus.

WHAT THE EXHIBITORS SAID:
Exhibitors Herald, *October 22, 1927*

Just three degrees worse than rotten. Harry Langdon is a favorite with me personally, too.
Russell Armentrout, K. P. Theatre, Pittsfield, IL.
General patronage.

Moving Picture World, *October 29, 1927*

Good comedy. This star is a comer. Tone, good. Sunday, yes. Special, no. Appeal good. Draw mixed type. Town 1,800.
Fred S. Widmore, Opera House (492) seats, Belvedere, NJ.

Exhibitors Herald, *November 12, 1927*

Langdon does some good acting, but the picture is not a "knockout" comedy. Should give satisfaction at regular admission.
L. L. Bascom, Liberty Theatre, Dayton WA.
Small town patronage.

The fellow who said it was three degrees worse than rotten was too modest. Hope First National will condense the rest of his pictures into two reels and at that have somebody to direct it. My folks waited through six reels for something to happen and then went home. Too draggy and silly.
W. H. Hardman, Royal Theatre, Frankfort, KS.
Small town patronage.

Hear ye! Exhibitors, hear ye! So lousy and contaminated with nothingness that it has no rival. There is no room in this industry for such talent. Because he is dumb looking, some think he should command a premium. Whether Langdon lives 100 years or dies tomorrow this picture bids him farewell. It's too bad the lot falls on First National, but the truth shouldn't hurt.
R. C. Metager, Cozy Theatre, Wagner, SD.
General patronage.

Exhibitors Herald, *November 26, 1927*

I herewith and hereby award Three's a Crowd first, second and third prizes for the poorest picture of the last five years. Some walked out on it, others demanded their money back and still others derived some satisfaction from insulting me. I had no comeback, knowing how justified they were. If you have bought, shelve it and thank your lucky stars that you are able to do so.
W.J. Powell, Loney Theatre, Wellington, OH.
Small town patronage.

Exhibitors Herald, *December 10, 1927*

November 27–28. Too bad! We like Harry, but he sure flopped in this one. Six reels with a few scattered laughs, and occasionally some mild pathos. Can't give it a percentage rating, as I played it with another attraction.
Roy A. Adams, Pastime Theatre, Mason, MI.
General patronage.

Exhibitors Herald, *May 12, 1928*

50%. Harry slipping here. I'll have to buy him for less money or let him alone.
M. W. Hughes, Colonial Theatre, Astoria, IL.
General patronage.

Exhibitors Herald, *May 19, 1928*

One of the poorest pictures we have run this season. If Langdon don't snap out of that marble face stuff he is due for the discard very shortly.
H. E. Gilman, Club Theatre, Weed, CA.
General patronage.

Exhibitors Herald, *June 30, 1928*

No good. He may be all right in two reelers but in six he is a bore.
J. L. Seiter, Selma Theatre, Selma, CA.
General patronage.

Exhibitors Herald, *July 28, 1928*

Oh! What a lemon! No plot, silly from start to finish. Don't do it again, Harry, or you will ruin yourself for life.
Charles A. Hagan, Crossett Theatre, Crossett, AR.
Small town patronage.

Fiddlesticks

A Mack Sennett Comedy Released in Two Reels. DIRECTED BY Harry Edwards. SUPERVISED BY John A. Waldron. STORY BY Arthur Ripley and Frank Capra. TITLES BY Tay Garnett. PHOTOGRAPHED BY Billy Williams. EDITED BY William Hornbeck. CAST: Harry Langdon, Ruth Hiatt, Vernon Dent, Anna Hernandez, Leo Sulky, Roscoe "Tiny" Ward, Billy Gilbert, Jack Murphy. WORKING TITLE: "The Junkman." Originally filmed in November 1925. Copyright March 29, 1926, Registration Number L22545. Released by Pathé Exchange, Inc., November 27, 1927.

SYNOPSIS: The men of the Hogan family are seated at table. One of the sons asks his father if they have to wait on dinner for the son who never brings home a dime. The father then tells the mother that they're through supporting a loafer and he'll have to make his own way. She tells him not to be hasty; that their son might be a great musician some day.

In the studio of Professor Von Tempo, a music teacher, Harry is practicing on his bass fiddle. He attempts to play "My Wild Irish Rose," with disastrous results. A note is placed under the door. Harry retrieves it and gives it to the professor. The note is from the neighbors, who want him to get rid of the guy making that noise. The teacher tells his student that if he can guess what he's playing he'll get a diploma. Harry is soon awarded the diploma from the relieved professor.

When Harry gets home he tells the family about his new diploma. They ignore him until the father tells him to get out. Harry kisses his mother goodbye, and leaves.

The next morning Harry awakens in a flophouse room. He has slept in a chair to avoid the bed bugs. Outside the hotel, a band led by Professor Von Tempo, is playing.

Residents of neighboring buildings throw down coins for the musicians. Harry stumbles upon the band and runs back to the hotel to get his bass. As he is leaving, he runs into the landlord, who tells him to pay for the room — or leave the bass. He lowers the instrument from his window, which catches on a hook outside of a pawnshop. Harry attempts to get the bass down and is told by the pawnshop owner that

the bass isn't his. He tells that owner that it *is* his bass, but the owner disagrees. Harry gives it back, and the owner replaces it on the hook, and then goes inside the shop. Harry sits down in a state of frustration. A man picks up a violin and gives Harry the money. He gives the owner the sum and gets his bass. Soon, he reaches the band and begins playing with them. People begin throwing junk instead of coins. Harry tells the professor that he was told he was a musician, and shows him the diploma. The teacher immediately gives Harry his money back, tears up the diploma and tells Harry he *isn't* a musician.

Meanwhile, a junk dealer, atop his wagon, is on the lookout for new items. He offers Harry $10 for the bass, but is refused. The dealer asks him to play something to see how the instrument sounds. As Harry plays "My Wild Irish Rose," a metal stove is thrown onto the street. The surprised dealer picks it up and urges Harry to join him. He offers Harry $5 to play the tune again. Junk rains down on the street and the dealer rubs his hands in happiness. He tells Harry that they are partners and that he must get a bigger wagon. Soon, Harry, encased in a wire cage, is playing as junk falls on him. Sometime later, Harry brings a small piano that he has found to the dealer. He says there is a lot of stuff around the corner. The owner of the piano arrives and is offered $50 for it by the dealer; he accepts. Soon after, Harry arrives, driving a steamroller. He runs over the piano and flattens it. The dealer cries over his loss. A man arrives and chides a driver for letting the steamroller get loose. He gives Harry $300 to cover the loss. Harry gives it to the dealer and tells him that there's lots of money in music.

Harry arrives home, outfitted in an expensive suit. The father tells him that he looks prosperous, and inquires how he did it. Harry replies, "By fiddling around." His mother asks him to play for the family. Harry cautiously closes a window and begins to play.

ANALYSIS: This, the final film Langdon made as a Mack Sennett employee, is another comedy in which the idea of romance is completely jettisoned. There is no leading lady, since Harry Hogan's only love is his music, horrible as it may be. The plot, such as it is, is quite charming but contains little of substance; it's more a diversion than a story. Langdon is the seasoned pro he became during his final year at Sennett, eliciting solid laughs out of miniscule situations. It's also a superb example of the "supreme optimism" that he considered a major facet of his character. Even when Von Tempo takes back his diploma and refunds his money, Harry is incapable of comprehending that he might not have any musical talent.

One of the most interesting aspects of *Fiddlesticks* is Vernon Dent's dual role. Through make-up and his own unique talent, he creates two distinct and convincing portrayals, as Von Tempo and the junkman. Anyone unaware of Dent's remarkable ability could easily need convincing that one actor is playing both parts.

HARRY MOMENT: When Harry's bass viol winds up at the pawnshop, he gets it back through no effort of his own. It is the providence of the man who mistakenly thinks he was the shop owner, leading him to give Harry some money, which causes the return of the bass. This is an example of Frank Capra's concept of Harry's good fortune that must not occur by his own actions but by external forces.

WHAT THE CRITICS SAID:
Moving Picture World, *November 19, 1927*
Clap hands, here comes Harry Langdon in what should be a rarity at this time of his film career — a two-reeler. From a sheer showmanship angle the ticket would be to sign up quick, but it has other virtues besides that of a box-office name. Langdon's baby stare endows it with the wistful quality that sticks up over and above the comedy nonsense, and the latter element, too, is packed tight with gags and business that get the laughs.

Film Daily, *November 20, 1927*
Any picture that features Harry Langdon stands an excellent chance of being entertaining to [the] nth degree. Fiddlesticks *is all of that, far better than some of his productions since he graduated into the feature class.*

Exploitation Herald, *November 25, 1927; Reviewed by Chester J. Smith*
Harry Langdon is seen again in one of the two-reelers which launched him on the road to fame and fortune. It is not so humorous as some of the other Langdon comedies have been, but it has its moments.

WHAT THE EXHIBITORS SAID:
Exhibitors Herald, *October 13, 1928*
Just fair. Would consider this about the weakest of the Langdon series.
Stephen G. Brenner, New Eagle Theatre, Baltimore, MD. General patronage.

The Chaser

A Harry Langdon Corporation Production Released in Six Reels. DIRECTED BY Harry Langdon. STORY BY Arthur Ripley. ADAPTATION BY Clarence Hennecke, Robert Eddy, Harry McCoy. PRODUCTION MANAGER: Don Eddy. ASSISTANT DIRECTOR: Ben Critchley. TECHNICAL SUPERVISOR: Lloyd Brierly. ELECTRICAL SUPERVISOR: Wayne L. Harmon. TITLES BY A. H. Giebler. PHOTOGRAPHY BY Elgin Lessley and Frank Evans. EDITED BY Alfred DeGaetano. CAST: Harry Langdon, Gladys McConnell, Helen Hayward, William "Bud" Jamison, Charles Thurston. WORKING TITLE: "The 19th Hole." Copyright January 23, 1928, Registration Number L24904; Renewed January 19, 1956, Number R165260. Released by First National Pictures, Inc., February 12, 1928.

SYNOPSIS: Gladys Larkin, a very angry wife, is yelling into the telephone, when her mother comes to call. The mother has a few words of her own to add — and soon both irate ladies are speaking into the receiver simultaneously. On the other end is husband and son-in-law Harry, patronizing a nearby roadhouse. He listens for a while, but eventually has to keep the receiver away from his ear, lest he lose his hearing. However, he's incapable of placing the receiver anywhere else without repercussions. Eventually his wife and mother-in-law hang up, and a relieved Harry returns to the crowd in the roadhouse. Before long, though, a brawl breaks out, and Harry dashes out to safety. He stops along the road and retrieves a lodge uniform, as he's told Gladys he's attending a lodge meeting. Donning the uniform, he returns home.

Gladys is not very pleased to see him, which makes Harry nervous. Her mother is convinced that Harry is "a chaser," one who runs around with loose women. She follows him through the house telling him off, until he leaves through the kitchen door. When she follows him outside, he crawls back in, shuts the door and barricades it with a table, chair and lamp. Just in case, he rigs a booby trap: a ceramic pitcher on a shelf that will land on her head with the pull of a string. It's no use; mother has simply returned via the front entrance and when Harry turns around, there she is. Humiliated, she produces a pistol, intending to shoot Harry, but Gladys intervenes, and the two women wrestle for the gun. Harry tries to protect himself by crawling under the sink and covering his rear end with a metal bowl. As the wrestling continues, Harry checks the chamber and sees that the gun isn't loaded. Gallantly, he offers to let his mother-in-law shoot him. He pulls his coat open and points directly at his heart, then spreads his arms wide, one of which jostles the string and releases his booby trap. The pitcher breaks over his head, knocking him into a stupor, as his mother-in-law threatens to see him behind bars.

Soon, she's testifying against Harry in divorce

court. However, Judge Limbsey believes a different sort of punishment is in order. He sentences Harry to serve 30 days at home in his wife's place, garbed in women's attire and deprived "of all the privileges of manhood," while Gladys becomes the breadwinner. The newspaper terms it a "freak decision" that has spurred nationwide interest, but Gladys is delighted and her mother believes it will "make him a perfect husband."

Dressed in a suit and tie, Gladys demands eggs for breakfast. Harry, in his usual coat and hat but wearing a long skirt over his pants, is in the henhouse. There are no eggs ready, so he chooses a hen and holds it over a frying pan. When the hen fails to produce, he tries squeezing it out. Meanwhile, another hen wanders underneath the squatting Harry's dress and lays an egg. Giving up, Harry rises and notices the egg beneath him. He looks around, but sees nothing. Afraid that he might be responsible, he kicks the egg away with his foot and buries it. He checks the vegetable garden, retrieves a few onions and potatoes, and

inadvertently drags a hen's nest along. Luckily there's an egg in the nest. Excited, he runs into the house with the egg, but slips and falls. The egg lands on the tie in the back of his skirt, and he cannot see it. After serving his wife, he sits down and becomes acutely aware of the egg. To hide this mistake, he grabs an apron and attaches it so it's covering his backside.

After Gladys leaves for her office, Harry resumes housework. A collections agent arrives to inquire about unused merchandise. Harry goes upstairs and retrieves an unwrapped item. He removes the wrapping, revealing an unused baby bassinette. The man is surprised that it is not wanted. Harry decides to double-check, and calls Gladys at work. She rebukes him, and he indicates that the bassinette must go. In fact, there's a second item and Harry retrieves that as well: a toilet training apparatus. The agent is astonished, and says, "You don't seem to get along very well with your husband, do you?" Harry simply sighs, and the agent offers a flirtatious smile. Livid, Harry flings various objects at him, then grabs a broom and chases him out of the house. Hopping mad, he jumps up and down in indignation and creates a hole on the porch, which he drops through, scaring several cats that had taken up residence there.

The iceman arrives at the back door, and after admitting him, Harry grabs a brick in order to defend himself against unwanted advances. The iceman proceeds right to work, and Harry relents, puts down the brick, sits in a chair and proceeds to tie his shoe. However, on the way out, the iceman stops, lifts Harry's head and kisses him full on the lips. Harry rises, looks at himself in the mirror and declares he is a sissy. He writes a suicide note to Gladys:

Dear ~~husband~~ wife,

Goodbye for <u>ever</u> and <u>ever</u>. I don't want to wear dresses.

No woman knows what it is to go without pants.

Harry

P.S. don't trust the iceman.

He pulls out the gun used by Gladys's mother and points it at various parts of his anatomy, but it isn't loaded. He then opts for another weapon, aims it at his head and pulls the trigger. It's a water pistol, with a spray that knocks him to the floor. Deciding on poison instead, he gathers several bottles, but the first thing he pours into a glass is castor oil. He puts that aside, and pours several poisonous liquids into a second glass. He's not looking forward to drinking it, so he covers his eyes and reaches for the glass, choosing the one with castor oil by mistake. He lies down on the kitchen floor, covers himself with his apron, places the note on his chest and waits to die. After several seconds pass, he rises, in urgent need of the upstairs bathroom.

That evening, Gladys returns home with several women, anxious to show them "how I drive my husband." She enters, sees the disarray from Harry's battle with the collections agent, and is furious. As she looks for him upstairs, one of the women comments, "From the way things look, her husband should have been driven slow for the first thousand miles!" When she returns downstairs, another woman tells her, "Something terrible has happened in the kitchen!" The women investigate; Gladys finds the gun, the bottles of poison, and Harry's note. Stunned, she sits down as the other women excuse themselves. As they leave, Gladys sobs, causing mascara to run down her face.

The next morning, the newsboys are hawking an Extra: "Skirts drive man to suicide." The headline blames Justice Limbsey for his "freak decision," and the judge fears for his career. At home, a remorseful Gladys hugs Harry's pants, while her mother tells her, "I have a feeling we'll find him very much alive." The two set out in the auto to search. As it turns out, Harry's been sleeping in the henhouse, and arises for another day's labor. He checks his garden and returns to the house as the milkman makes a delivery. Resigned, Harry offers his cheek for the milkman to kiss, which he does.

As Harry sweeps the front porch, his pal Bud drives up, ready for some golf. "Take off those skirts," he demands. "Be a man before your voice changes." Harry decides to tag along, but just in case, he takes both his skirt and lodge uniform with him. Out on the links, the overbearing Bud gets frustrated with his inability to drive the ball, and breaks several of his clubs. Seated, Harry spots what appears to be a tombstone and warns Bud that they're in a graveyard. Meanwhile, a dog is burrowing into a rabbit's lair and starts to emerge on the other side of the tombstone, which is actually an advertisement for "Grave's Golf Togs." As the ground in front of the stone gives way, Harry and Bud are spooked, until they see what happened. Suddenly, Bud gets stuck in the ground, and demands that Harry help him. Harry laughs and, seeing that Bud is now smaller than he is, decides to punch him around a bit. Eventually, Bud manages to free himself and chases after Harry.

They stumble over a campsite where a number of young, attractive girls are tossing a ball around. Bud decides to join in, telling Harry, "You're married — you don't know anything about women." The girls welcome Bud's participation, so Harry runs off to don his lodge uniform. One of the girls sees the now-uniformed Harry, approaches, caresses and embraces him, then offers herself for a kiss. Once he kisses her, she passes out. He summons Bud, who runs over with a couple of the girls. When the fainted girl revives,

Harry is taken aback by Bud Jamison's drive in The Chaser.

she spots Harry and passes out again. Bud carries her back to the campsite. An older woman approaches, and Harry decides to test his prowess again. He strokes her head, embraces and kisses her, and she also passes out. Meanwhile, the girls' guardian arrives and declares, "Somebody will pay for this — with his life!" Bud and Harry exit in haste.

They get into Bud's car and depart, Harry swiftly donning his skirt. They drive behind a truck that loses its canvas top; it lands on the car, covering them. Unable to see, Bud veers off the road and across some bumpy terrain, which throws him from his car. The auto continues, with Harry in the back, until it stops halfway past the edge of a cliff. Teetering back and forth for a moment, the car goes over the edge and proceeds down the hill, much to Harry's astonishment. He makes his way to the front seat and tries to steer, but the wheel comes off. He gets on the running board, but the car is proceeding too fast for him to make a safe jump. He decides to sit in the back seat and patiently waits to see what will happen.

The car crashes through several billboards and a fence, and is stopped by Harry's back porch, throwing him from the car through his kitchen door and into a table, which dislodges a bucket of flour that empties all over him. He rises just as an inconsolable Gladys returns with her mother. The ghostly white Harry emerges from the kitchen, frightening both women. As her mother runs out the front door in terror, Gladys approaches and sees that Harry is real and alive. Smiling, she embraces him, puts her head on his shoulder and closes her eyes in gratitude. The film ends as Harry tries to comprehend what this means.

ANALYSIS: If *Three's a Crowd* was Langdon's brave advance to newer, dramatic ground, then *The Chaser* marks a hasty retreat to the tried and true of gag comedy. Alas, most of the gags had worn out their welcome long before, after 15 years of two-reelers made by every screen comic under the sun. Practically anything that ever got a laugh is here: from the opening scene, where a telephone receiver scorches Harry's lap and sends waste paper flying through the air; to the middle, where he attempts suicide with a water pistol; to the conclusion, where he's thrust into a barrel of flour, thus appearing as a "ghost" that sends the meddlesome mother-in-law fleeing. Even the hoary bit of a car that has lost its driver yet continues merrily along, which appeared in Langdon's second-ever film, is recycled.

Also reused is material from *Saturday Afternoon* (henpecked Harry meekly greeting his wife), *His Marriage Wow* (Harry believing himself to be poisoned), *Soldier Man* (Harry's kiss causing women to faint) and *Tramp, Tramp, Tramp* (Harry dangling from a cliff's edge then plunging down the incline in a vehicle he cannot control). Throughout, it's impossible to escape the feeling that this material is here solely because it worked before and should therefore work again…only it doesn't.

Consequently, if there were a single word that would best sum up *The Chaser*, it would be "contrived." Its premise is contrived: the judge offers no justification for his bizarre sentence except to say that divorce "is not advisable in this case." Its gags are contrived, and awfully convenient: a chicken happens to lay an egg underneath Harry while he's squatting; a dog happens to be digging his way out of an underground tunnel, next to an advertising sign that happens to look like a tombstone; the runaway car, after plunging down a random cliff side, happens to wind up at Harry's back door so he can be sent flying into the flour and emerge looking like a ghost.

This is not to dismiss the film as entirely worthless. There are a few inspired moments of brilliance that fairly shimmer. One of the best is a marvelous tracking shot of Harry walking across his house, from parlor to dining room to kitchen, with his wife and mother-in-law haranguing him every inch of the way. Langdon continues out the back door into the night, swiftly followed by the rebuking mother-in-law, at which point we see Langdon crawl back inside and close the door. The payoff may be old-hat, but the progression through the house that precedes it is beautifully timed, intelligently staged and extremely funny. Another gem that never fails to draw laughs from modern audiences is Harry's ultimate resignation to being kissed by deliverymen.

On the other hand, when Harry trips, the egg he'd been carrying magically lands on the knot of his skirt and remains in place until he sits on it. After having been accosted by the collections agent, Harry repeatedly leaps up and down on the front porch in fury, until he creates (and vanishes through) a hole in its floor. Gags of this sort are reminiscent of the best — or worst — Mack Sennett or Larry Semon two-reelers.

As noted in the text, *The Chaser* was heavily criticized, and in some places censored, for its bathroom humor. The egg-laying scene and the suicide by castor oil were particularly scorned. When the collections agent turns up regarding unpaid merchandise, and we see that it's an unused baby carriage, at first it's taken as a (perhaps too easy) ploy for sympathy. But in fact it's merely the set-up for another off-color gag, when Harry retrieves the next piece of unused merchandise: a seat and chamber pot designed for toilet training. After taking the castor oil and having not died, Harry sits up with a jolt, and urgently runs upstairs. Once he disappears, the shot holds for a full 12 seconds before fading out, for no other reason than to force viewers to imagine the unpleasant prospect of Harry contending with diarrhea.

Harry's personality is based solely upon the whim of each gag. When Gladys is leaving for work, he sits on a stair and pats the empty space next to him, encouraging her to sit beside him. He sports a coy smile, appearing every bit the devoted wife, and when Gladys looks away, uninterested in such nonsense, his feelings are hurt. A few minutes later, though, when the collections man flirts with him, he flies into a rage, furious that he could possibly be mistaken for a woman. As for Gladys, she absolutely relishes the role of the "man," delighted to be putting her useless husband through a virtual castration. When it appears he's dead, though, all of that is conveniently forgotten, and she unexpectedly (and unbelievably) transforms into a remorseful, loving wife once he's restored to her. Even Harry's reaction says it can't possibly be genuine.

There's nothing in *The Chaser* that tells us anything about Harry. Instead, the situation is set up and then things happen, sometimes — as in the sudden appearance of Bud Jamison — at random. The sacrificing of characterization for the sake of a cheap laugh is perhaps the film's saddest aspect, especially after the major strides toward personality humor found in *Long Pants* and *Three's a Crowd*. If, as Gladys McConnell inferred, *The Chaser* is a byproduct of First National's demands, it would not be the last time that front office interference played havoc with an artist's vision.

Since it contains neither gags nor situations uniquely tailored to Langdon, the authors are unable to identify a singular "Harry Moment" from this film.

WHAT THE CRITICS SAID:
Harrison's Reports, *March 3, 1928*

Mediocre. It seems as if Mr. Langdon's style of acting is not adapted to comedies of the feature length. That is what one may deduce from the fact that, although Mr. Langdon has made many a good two-reel comedy, he has made only one good comedy of the feature length — Tramp, Tramp, Tramp. There are very few laughs in the would-be comical situations, and the interest is not aroused to any appreciable degree. In places, the action is monotonous and, as a result, tiresome...

Mr. Langdon seems to find pleasure in low comedy. In one scene he tries to make people laugh by putting a tin pan against the fat part of his back while he is a stooping position. In other scenes he introduces a baby chair, with pots and pans and the rest. These are the kinds of comedy attempts that were abandoned long ago.

Photoplay, *March 1928*

Possibly Harry Langdon was chasing after a new contract when he was making this picture. If that was his idea he failed miserably. The Chaser would seem to spell his doom as a leader in the screen comedy field. The picture is just a series of gags with little or no story. It concerns a henpecked husband with a nagging wife and a shrew of a mother-in-law. Several of the gags are rough, especially the castor oil gag and the "when I kiss 'em they stay kissed" episode. Gladys McConnell as the wife doesn't get much of a chance. If you miss this one you won't miss much.

New York Herald-Tribune, *April 9, 1928; Reviewed by Richard Watts, Jr.*

Another example of Why Comedians Go Wrong is on display at the Cameo where Harry Langdon's The Chaser *is on view. It was not so long ago that a number of us were heralding Mr. Langdon as one of the cinema elect; as virtually the legitimate successor of the mighty Mr. Chaplin. Today, unfortunately, we are forced to rush about in quest of alibis for our former ecstasy.*

On our behalf, however, it should be stated that, though the Langdon vehicles grow wan and unimaginative, the work of the comedian remains admirable. The trouble is that he has grown self-conscious, not as an actor, but as a director. Scorning imaginative comic business, he spends time and footage on lengthy close-ups that glorify little but his passion for being an exhibitionist and he delights in a slow paced movement that is probably intended as emphasizing his tragic side. Even though the star wants to be a tragic figure, he could never have imagined how really tragic he is in The Chaser.

New York Sun, *April 9, 1928; Reviewed by John S. Cohen, Jr.*

The runner-up to Charles Chaplin in the matter of comedy genius, the sprite known as Harry Langdon, may be seen in The Chaser, *his latest and weakest photoplay, now at the Cameo. He is the same Langdon, the Langdon whose appearance is almost sufficient in itself to cause an audience to burst into warm and sympathetic laughter, but his film is so dull that he is wasted.*

The case of Harry Langdon is probably the saddest in the entire movie clinic. With the attributes of the finest comedian of all at his command, he, somehow or other, has been guided along paths that are gagged to monotony.

Once or twice in The Strong Man *and in* Tramp, Tramp, Tramp *his producers managed to sustain interest from the first reel to the last, so that his various pantomimic solos, his intermittent sparks of genius, could be seen in adequate settings, but gradually his pictures became worse.*

And The Chaser, *despite a few bright ideas and a few killing whimsies on the part of the star, is the worst of all.*

Here the diminutive Harry is forced by the judge before whom his wife has laid the complaint that he chases too many girls, to don petticoats and retire to his kitchen for six months. There he is to cook and scrub and pay homely attentions to his mate in the way of cooking her breakfasts, etc., and this leads to the first and funniest episode in the film.

In this, Harry, retiring to the garden to find a lone egg, seizes an unsuspecting hen and tries, the innocent elf, to shake one out of her. Meanwhile another hen sneaks into the folds of his petticoat and lays an egg under him, and Harry, after giving up the first fowl in disgust, turns around and finds it. I have never seen a child, a gypsy, nor even a Palmer Cox Brownie, express such laughable wonderment as does Harry over the sudden appearance of this egg.

The rest of the film, however, dissolves into chases and the rest of the paraphernalia common to unimaginative slapstick. And Harry Langdon's disarming presence, his childlike gestures and sense of fascinating nonsense go a-begging once again for a decent setting.

New York Evening Post, *April 10, 1928; Reviewed by John Hutchens*

Probably nothing is quite as unhappy as a production labeled "simply screaming" by the always retiring press agents during its process of manufacture, but at whose completion no one can find even a tendency to titter. And that sad state is dismally near the truth about Harry Langdon's latest, The Chaser, *now — but not for long — at the Cameo Theatre. It's like a funeral that has its lighter points.*

This reviewer, cordial to Mr. Langdon for his past performances, received one laugh (count it) from The Chaser. *It was when the comedian was dressed absurdly in his lodge meeting hat and cape and equipped with a dragging sword. He didn't act. He merely stood in front of the camera and looked magnificently foolish and simple-minded, as aforetime, for a few seconds. But it took the better part of an hour to reach that point, and even it wasn't worth those other sequences that dragged on at a dirge-like pace. Elsewhere were only dim hints of the days when Mr. Langdon didn't direct his own pictures; the days when no one had infected him with the idea that someone other than Mr. Chaplin might cash in on Mr. Chaplin's technique. Hardly any further argument is necessary.*

New York Morning-World, *April 10, 1928; Reviewed by A.J.*

Allegedly, according to the playbill, The Chaser, *at the Cameo, is a film "based on laughs." Its formula is as laugh-worn and senile as could have possibly been culled from Hollywood's old film archives now buried beneath years of film dust. The central figure in this comedy is Harry Langdon, a rather favored comedian who, in this latest production of his, proves to be as fair an imitation of Charlie Chaplin as has ever been pushed before the eyes of the film public.*

There is little in The Chaser. *And this bodes no good for Mr. Langdon, who it is said, ambitiously wrote and directed it. The audience which attended this showing, from which this report is prepared, did not receive it kindly. One very fair spectator was heard to liken Mr. Langdon's facial expression to the blank and unintelligent look of a two-year-old, while others near an exit were for stepping out into the cool air.*

New York Times, *April 10, 1928; Reviewed by Mordaunt Hall*

In Harry Langdon's comedy, The Chaser, *now on exhibition at the Cameo Theatre, the comedian impersonates a husband who has an extraordinarily good-looking wife. This is not an auspicious beginning, for while queer comedians with strange sartorial notions may fascinate charming girls, it is an unwritten law that they shall not marry while the story is being told. They may leave you engaged and very happy, or, better still, they may appear as the victims, with aching hearts, who give way to big broad-shouldered men with glossy hair.*

But this is not the only mistake in The Chaser. *It was, unfortunately, directed by Mr. Langdon, who is a far better actor than he is a director. He also probably had a great deal to say about the story which is seldom plausible and not often funny. Mr. Langdon's expressions occasionally elicited laughter yesterday because of the absurdity of character, but the idea of a few flying bricks, a husband meditating on doing away with himself, a hole in the porch of the little gray home, a missed golf ball, fainting women or fleeing cats need more raison d'etre than they have in this production.*

Stupidity on the part of a character does not necessarily make him a comic genius. Spectators get tired of laughing at a character who obviously is not quite right in his mind, just as they give a hollow laugh when the conventional automobile chase is brought on.

This story gives Mr. Langdon a chance to wear skirts. He is sentenced by some freak-minded Judge to do the housework for a month in his own home or go to the workhouse for six months. His wife and her mother proceed to worry the little fellow to the extent that he starts to cajole a hen into laying an egg. He is surprised at what happens, and so perhaps were a few spectators yesterday afternoon. At any rate the little husband's nice wife gets her egg for breakfast.

Mr. Langdon's pathetic face with his Gish-like lips is used capably during the course of this slip-shod and rather tedious affair. He is wistful, appealing, awestruck and not infrequently surprised. Consider the stretch where he is meditating on hearth and home when suddenly the grass a few yards away from his feet begins to move. He shuts his eyes a few times to make sure that he is not a victim of a wild imagination. The earth continues to shake and a humped line is formed. Eventually, the reason for all this is cleared up for him when he sees a dog come to the surface after underground mole-hunting.

Mr. Langdon is clever throughout, but it is quite evident that he needs a really good story and a new director. Gladys McConnell does very well as the wife, and Helen Hayward plays the garrulous mother-in-law effectively.

Variety, *April 11, 1928*

Poor judgment is in evidence in comedy, [The] Chaser (First National) at the Cameo, on its Broadway first run. Since the Strand has the F.N. franchise for New York that's a tip off as to the merit of the picture all by itself. No de luxe downtowner will probably play the picture if they first see a couple of alleged comedy fun bits in it.

Mr. Langdon is starred and slide-announces he directed the picture, so the fault is all his own, although as he likely is responsible for the gags, his blame can go double. For Langdon has some odd ideas about bathroom

comedy and both of them are in the first 30 minutes of the picture. Whatever is worthwhile is in the latter section.

While one might suspect that Langdon's greatest needs are a director and author, still it might be a personal mental balance that would permit him to select newer and better subjects, the latter taking in ideas and gags. Or else be content as a dead pan comic who apparently can get more out of his face than he can out of his head.

Any screen comedian who thinks the castor oil and choking chicken bits are funny to even 15 percenters in the deaf and dumb racket had better write idiotic after their names. Yet for children the castor oil bit may be a laugh and in the neighborhoods perhaps the whole thing will be thought funny enough, but Mr. Langdon must figure someone else beside the kids and the women after wash Mondays.

For the first 30 minutes of The Chaser, *it's drear. But the last half is better with the best laugh of the film gotten by William Jaimison (sic). Langdon probably had to let the Jaimison laughs go to get the picture anywhere. The most Langdon could show was a runaway auto going over bumpy ground and then down hill, most of it done before…*

Now and then a laugh in the titles, but only now and then. Gladys McConnell does fairly as the girl and Helen Hayward the usual type mother-in-law, with Jaimison grabbing the picture for any worth grabbing there.

New York Evening Post, *April 14, 1928; Follow-up by John Hutchens*

The last half of a dozen new pictures to open during the week, Street Angel *was doubly refreshing because it followed at least three comedies which were varyingly dreary:* Ladies' Night in a Turkish Bath, Why Sailors Go Wrong *and* The Chaser.

The first two may be dismissed with the petulant comment that, if they are comedies, a new and more searching term should be brought into use to describe something that is funny.

But in the case of The Chaser, *it is otherwise, and the present position of Mr. Harry Langdon borders more nearly upon tragedy.*

A year ago, Mr. Langdon was considered in the same realm with Mr. Charles Chaplin, and not without reason. His capacity for bewildered foolishness was seen as a close approach to the inimitable comic spirit of the one genius of the cinema.

But apparently Mr. Langdon didn't think that Mr. Chaplin really was inimitable, and probably he suspected that the capacious picture world had room for at least one

more genius. Didn't his fan mail say so? And so, proceeding under this delusion, he took to writing and directing his comedies himself and adopting other Chaplinesque measures.

It didn't work. Long Pants *was a pale imitation lightened only by those rare sequences when Mr. Langdon was Mr. Langdon.* Three's a Crowd *was even weaker. And here now is* The Chaser, *in which, if you listen closely, you may discern the sounding of "taps" for what might have been a long and notable comedy career.*

This is an unpleasant forecast, and Hollywood can boast a ringing record of "comebacks." But we hazard the prediction that one or two more pictures like The Chaser *will seal the case of Mr. Langdon.*

Film Daily, *April 15, 1928*

Not at all hot. Pretty good comedy idea, outlandishly handled, makes picture implausible. Langdon gets over few laughs — very few.

Cast: Langdon funny at times. Weakens his efforts by planting himself too much before camera in every sequence. Others, unimportant including Gladys McConnell, Helen Hayward, William Jamison and Charles Thurston.

Story and Production: Langdon and his screen wife don't hit it off too well. Divorce proceedings enter the picture, but the judge, instead of granting the papers, determines to teach Langdon a lesson by reverting the situation at home. Langdon is to take the wife's place for one month. So Harry dresses like a femme, gets kissed by the iceman and the milkman, etc. The idea was not all bad, but the development — let's gloss that over. It's kinder that way. Sufficient to say a lot of utterly impossible things happen. The story was far too thin for the footage. Therefore, you get episodes that are strung to the main idea in very loose fashion. Has a few laughs. Spotty and minutes apart.

Director: Harry Langdon; so-so.

Author: Harry Langdon.

Scenarist: Harry Langdon.

Photography: Elgin Lessley and Frank Evans; satisfactory.

Film Daily, *April 15, 1928; Reviewed by Kann*

Imitating Caesar: The famous Julius is reputed to be the only fellow who could do two or more things at one time and get away with a good job. This noted personage of antiquity thereby started an argument which has been mighty keen ever since his day. And in the picture business it is in Hollywood that the pros and cons wage more fiercely than anywhere else. For instance: The case of Harry Langdon and The Chaser. *Langdon, a splendid* comic, wrote the story, prepared the scenario, directed and appeared in the picture.

Which, perhaps, explains as well as anything else why The Chaser *is the picture that it is. Langdon bit off far more of a task than he could handle. He naturally wrote a fat part for himself. The director had to follow the script and since Langdon was completely the works, you get such long — and often unfunny — sequences of the comedian that it appears most obvious how tough it was for him to keep outside of the camera lines. For the sake of Langdon and good comedies, Harry should know better.*

Cleveland Plain Dealer, *April 16, 1928; Reviewed by Glenn C. Pullen*

Seemingly discouraged by his unsuccessful efforts to capture pathos and high-browish art in his pictures, Harry Langdon goes back to out-and-out slapstick comedy in The Chaser. *The net result, one is sorry to report, is only an average, mildly entertaining film.*

Langdon's new opus is just a series of gags that revolve around — and frequently fly off tangent — an interesting but slight plot. Denounced by his shrewish mother-in-law and nagged by his wife who is divorcing him, Harry is sentenced by the judge to don women's clothes and do her housework for 30 days. Just why he deserves a divorce or such a sentence is not quite clear; but that's the way with so many other things.

The gags, some of which are rather unpalatable and drawn out to the breaking point, are not the kind over which you will crack a lip laughing. There are, however, several bright and hilarious moments of sport, such as Harry's attempts to cook a meal, his rebellion and "ghost" reconciliation with his wife. But these moments, being in the minority, do not make the comedy click as it should.

Gladys McConnell, who is made an unattractive and unsympathetic character, does not have a chance to show what talents she may possess. Langdon continues to capitalize his "dead pan" face and pantomimic clowning, both of which are very funny if you like them, and not so funny if you don't.

While The Chaser *may amuse you, it will be disappointing to Langdon's fans, who once considered him one of the "white hopes" of the films. Here's hoping his next one will be better and funnier.*

Exhibitors Herald, *April 21, 1928; Reviewed by Chester J. Smith*

Harry Langdon, through this latest opus, will lose a lot of the popularity he gained when he quit the two-reel ranks to star in feature-length comedies. In The Chaser *he is right back to the two-reelers, a two-reeler that is padded and poorly gagged out to feature length.*

There is hardly the thread of a story in this picture; there is no continuity, and the direction, by Langdon himself, is poor. The gags are only fair and what there are of them are poorly executed. They are allowed to drag out to such length that they lose what little humor there is to them.

Langdon, unfortunately, is the whole works. There is not another role in the story worthy of mention, and aside from his usual comical makeup, he falls absolutely flat. He slowed down what might have been a fair two-reeler to the lackadaisical and languid pace of the personal character he always assumes. There is (sic) not as many gags nor as much action in this full feature film as usually characterize the two-reeler. Langdon needs better material than this and far better direction if he is to again assume the popularity he once enjoyed.

Drawing Power: Only the past popularity of the star may draw the customers to the box-office window. The picture will get little word-of-mouth publicity. It has little to recommend it.

Exploitation Angles: There is little in the angles of the story or the gags that can be exploited. The star and the title seem to be the only bets open.

Photoplay, *April 1928*

Harry Langdon and a lot of gags — some of them too rough to be in good taste. Don't cry if you miss it.

The Educational Screen, *June 1928*

Pitiful failure as a Langdon comedy. He has done such good ones.

WHAT THE EXHIBITORS SAID:
Exhibitors Herald, *April 7, 1928*

50%. March 15–16. This is the best Langdon picture since *The Strong Man*. There are a good number of laughs in it. There are a couple of sequences that didn't hardly need (*sic*) to be put into the picture such as the castor oil gag and kissing scenes. Nevertheless they are about the biggest laugh getters so I guess they deserve a place somewhere.
Homer P. Morely, Princess Theatre, Buchanan, MI. Small town patronage.

50%. Would have made a good three reel subject but had no excuse for being so long about nothing.
W. G. Wright, Colonial Theatre, Troy, MO. General patronage.

Exhibitors Herald, *April 21, 1928*

March 14. Positively vulgar. A very rotten comedy that had plenty of smut. Was funny at times but my patrons sure told me plenty when they went out. Business is bad enough without having to overcome such features as these.
Leslie Hables, Reel Joy Theatre, King City, CA. General patronage.

Exhibitors Herald, *April 28, 1928*

75%. February 4–5. Absolutely the most vulgar, rotten, dirty, silly picture we have shown in the last 16 years. If producers are going to continue making pictures of this kind, here's hoping we get Federal censorship. Our patrons were disgusted with it and they told me so.
O. H. Lee, Star Theatre, South Range, MI. General patronage.

March 27. The most unsatisfactory picture we have had this season. Not a real laugh in it. Sequences which are intended to be humorous are based on plain muck. Patrons left in disgust. Too bad pictures are not shelved.
Cragin & Pike, Inc., Majestic Theatre, Las Vegas, NV. General patronage.

A little better than *Three's a Crowd* but both are rotten. Can't see why First National don't (*sic*) pay him off and kiss him goodbye. More results of block booking.
Hollis H. Chase, Diamond Theatre, Lake Odessa, MI. General patronage.

Exhibitors Herald, *July 7, 1928*

29%. Not up to Harry Langdon's usual standard. Would have been better if shorter and snappier.
C. E. Mallory, Liberty Theatre, Brewster Theatre, Brewster, KS. General patronage.

Heart Trouble

A Harry Langdon Corporation Production Released in Six Reels. DIRECTED BY Harry Langdon. STORY BY Arthur Ripley. ADAPTATION BY Earl Rodney and Clarence Hennecke. TITLES BY Gardner Bradford. PHOTOGRAPHY BY Dev Jennings and Frank Evans. EDITED BY Alfred DeGaetano. CAST: Harry Langdon, Doris Dawson, Lionel Belmore, Madge Hunt, Bud Jamison, Mark Hamilton, Nelson McDowell, Blanche Payson.
WORKING TITLES: "Volunteer," "Here Comes the Band," "Cock-A-Doodle-Doo." Copyright August 17, 1928, Registration Number L25537; Renewed August 7, 1956, Number R175134. Released by First National Pictures, Inc., August 12, 1928.

SYNOPSIS: This film was unavailable for viewing. Following is the synopsis submitted to the U.S. Copyright Office:

The Van Housen family, father, mother and son found America the most wonderful country in the world in which to live and prosper until the war clouds gathered in 1918, and then came the conflict of love for their native country and the U.S.A.

Harry, their boy, found his love for Doris to be the most wonderful thing in the world, until war clouds blocked out their sunshine of happiness.

So, Harry makes the decision. He'll enlist. He'll show those relatives of his on the other side that the Van Housens can be loyal.

And so it comes to pass that Harry, instead of meeting his sweetheart at a rendezvous from which they were going to elope, meets her with tears in his eyes.

From that day on, Harry's efforts to become a soldier are fruitless. He is refused by the recruiting officers everywhere he applies for an examination — he has every ailment known to man or beast.

Underweight; four inches too short; fallen arches; halitosis; dandruff; myopi; you-tell-'em and what-have-you are among his ailments.

Nevertheless, his many disappointments are not without their reward, for one night he accidentally stumbles across some information which results in one of the most startling exposés and most gigantic explosions the World War ever knew, and he becomes a hero overnight — but all unknowingly.

To his home town, his parents are holding a celebration, brass band, mayor, medal for valor, gigantic newspaper headlines — all proclaiming their home town boy the pride of the world — and Harry is nowhere to be found.

And we then learn that, after all, it is love that makes the world go 'round.

No prints of this film are known to exist. Reportedly the original preprint materials were unsalvageable due to deterioration and discarded by Warner Bros. (successors to the First National catalog) in 1953.

WHAT THE CRITICS SAID:

Photoplay, *September 1928*

If this is shown in an open-all-night theater near some midnight mission where you pay fifteen cents for the privilege of slumber — buy a ticket. It won't keep you awake a moment. But if you wish to enjoy a "movie," stay away. Just a lot of silly gags, no story and enough inane situations to spell the exit of Harry Langdon. It was his cue to give us a good picture. He didn't.

Film Daily, *October 7, 1928*

Just a fair comedy. Langdon works hard on a ragged script that is not too well gagged to get any laughs.

Cast: Harry Langdon does his usual innocent boob trying to enlist at the outbreak of the war. When he gets a good gag, he manages to keep the laughs coming.

Story and Production: Comedy. A little bit of everything was thrown into this one in order to make the footage, but all the real laugh sequences could be boiled

Exhibitor's Daily Review, *September 24, 1928*

This can hardly be considered more than ordinary comedy and far away from the standard promised by the earliest of Langdon's feature releases. The laughs are scattered and the story is weak. If Langdon's name still means anything, the fans who come in will be disappointed.

Perhaps the answer to this story can be found in the fact that Langdon, as has been the case in the past two or three flops, insisted on handling the direction. In addition he has gotten away from the characterization that brought him screen fame almost overnight. There may be those who can direct their own comedies, but it is clearly evident that Langdon would do better if he is interested in his screen future, to remain a comedian, in which field he is almost without a peer.

down into a two-reel comedy. That is what is wrong with it — strung out to make a feature when it did not have the material to make the feature comedy grade. Harry is trying his darnedest to enlist at the outbreak of the war in order to show his gal that he is a hero. But they turn him down as being physically unfit. Then Harry gets mixed up by accident in a plot to smuggle arms and ammunition out of the country to the enemy. In the secret arsenal the climax takes place, with a lot of meller mixed with the comedy.

Direction: Harry Langdon; ordinary.

Photography: Dev Jennings and Frank Evans; fair.

Variety, *October 10, 1928*

Probably because it is his last for First National, Harry Langdon's Heart Trouble comes into Manhattan unsung. Yet it is one of the best of the few he has made during the past two years. It can stand up without a supporting feature for a short run in any house.

The comic does less of the emoting he gave way to in his last two. He abandons to a great extent his ambition to be the complex of a tragedienne (sic) and a comedian. Heart Trouble is more compact and the story is more actionful.

That he is directing himself is less obvious.

A novel angle on conscription during the war, with a small-town locale and with Langdon in one of his regular moron roles, is used. Failing to get into the army after pestering a recruiting colonel, Harry, through a coincidence, saves that officer's life and blows up an enemy ammunition depot.

Doris Dawson shapes up physically as a comely leading lady, more sex appeal than a lot of the peaches Harry has picked in the past. The gags are not so numerous, but the ones used are good.

The Educational Screen, *October 1928*
Nonsense war-film, rather funny but marred by vulgarities.

Photoplay, *October 1928*
Harry Langdon writes his own finish in pictures.

WHAT THE EXHIBITORS SAID:
Motion Picture Times, *September 15, 1928*

They came on the second night to see him; had been a poor drawing card for me previously. Proved to be a good comedy and pleased all.
W.T. Briggs, Adair Theatre, Adair, IA.

Movie Age, *January 12, 1929*

While I didn't make much money on this picture, people here liked it.
J.C. Scott, Lyric Theatre, Tekamah, NE

Soldier Man

A Mack Sennett Comedy Released in Three Reels. **DIRECTED BY** Harry Edwards. **SUPERVISED BY** John A. Waldron. **STORY BY** Arthur Ripley and Frank Capra. **TITLES BY** A.H. Giebler. **PHOTOGRAPHED BY** Billy Williams. **EDITED BY** William Hornbeck. **CAST:** Harry Langdon, Frank Whitson, Natalie Kingston, Vernon Dent, Yorke Sherwood, Silas D. Wilcox, Andre Bailey, Connie Dawn, Muriel Montrose; Andy Clyde (part removed from final release print). Originally Planned for Four Reels. **WORKING TITLES:** "King's Up," "The King," "Soldier Boy." Copyright April 28, 1926, Registration Number LU22654. Released by Pathé Exchange, Inc., September 30, 1928.

SYNOPSIS: It is November 11, 1918, Armistice Day: the Great War has ended. American soldiers return home in triumph after their victory. It seems that every soldier that went overseas has returned except one. Harry is the soldier who didn't know the war was over. He is seen wandering the countryside in search of the Army. He was taken prisoner on his first day overseas and today escaped from his captors while they were celebrating something or other. A farmer intends to blow up some stumps with dynamite. Harry hears the explosions and jumps into a foxhole, believing he's being fired upon. He shoots at a scarecrow, knocking its head off. The farmer then jumps into the foxhole to avoid a blast. Harry sees him and leaves the hole to take refuge by the stump which is about to explode. The farmer tries to warn him but Harry doesn't understand the language. As Harry crawls to the foxhole, the butt of his rifle catches on the dynamite and it is carried along. Harry chases the farmer, who runs in terror.

In the capital of Bomania, a large group of the people are agitated outside the palace. Inside is King Strudel the 13th, who likes to drink and is an exact double of Harry. As he sits on the throne, one of his aides requests that he stop the rebellion as they haven't paid for the last one. This is observed by General Von Snootzer, who wants the rebellion to go on. The queen approaches and watches as the king passes out on his throne. She brings the king around and reminds him that it is their wedding anniversary. She is rebuffed and is told that he is thinking.

Meanwhile, Soldier Harry is still chasing the farmer, who gives him the slip. Harry kneels underneath a cow for cover. As he gets into a firing position he notices the cow's udder and touches it in a hesitant manner. After the cow gives him a look he leaves to get some water to put out the fuse; just then, the farmer appears and hurls the dynamite away. A passing man with a basket containing chops and sausages sees the dynamite. He drops the basket and runs away. Harry returns to the cow, discovers the dynamite missing, and guesses that the cow ate it. He tells the cow to spit it out, and turns away in anticipation of the blast. When the explosion occurs, the cow runs away and Harry sees the meat falling to earth, followed by the basket, which is on fire. He smiles as he begins to cook some ribs.

In the palace, the king is drunk. One of his aides asks him to sign a treaty. He refuses and staggers off for his royal nap. General Von Snootzer kidnaps the king and sends him away on horseback. The king is put into a cabin and the general informs his men to get rid of him when he has seized the throne. The king's men conduct a search but conclude that he must have been done away with. As they return to the palace, Soldier Harry is spotted and the aide surmises that he can take the king's place. They grab Harry and return him to the palace. Later, the aide announces that the "king" is coming to sign a peace treaty. Harry is dressed as the king and is puzzled by the bowing

Natalie Kingston and Langdon in Soldier Man.

of the servants. The queen appears and vows to make the king pay for his drunken insults. Harry is seated on the throne and is told that he's to be the king no matter what happens. He signs the peace treaty, which pleases his aide as the standing Army can sit down. The palace celebrates, while General Von Snootzer suspects that something is rotten in Denmark. The general announces that Harry is an impostor. The aide advises Harry to punish the general for his insults. The king orders his men to have the general beheaded, and he is led away. Harry rocks with glee upon the throne at his command. He then realizes what he's done and goes to investigate as a mannequin's head rolls out from behind a curtain. The general laughs and rolls out a headless dummy on wheels. Harry runs away with the dummy caught on his robe and following him.

In her chamber, the queen secrets a long knife in her robe. Harry is told that the queen would like to see him in her boudoir. Harry goes to her side as she reminds him of the time they picked daffodils together. The queen asks for a kiss as she positions her knife. Harry's kiss makes the queen swoon. She soon recovers and asks him to kiss her again, which causes the same result. Harry, feeling tired, goes to sleep on her bed as she recovers and begins to shake him.

Soldier Harry is asleep in his own bed and is being shaken by his wife, who tells him to wake up so he won't be late for the parade. Harry asks her to slip him a kiss. She tells him to be himself as she has dishes to wash. He kisses her, expecting a swoon, and she doesn't fall. Harry looks puzzled as she helps him with his uniform.

ANALYSIS: *Soldier Man* was produced before *Saturday Afternoon* and *Fiddlesticks,* and despite its three-reel length, gives the impression of being incomplete. Its closing sequence, where Harry awakens from a very vivid dream, appears to have been tacked on at the last moment so as to wind up a story for which inspiration had flagged. None of the plot threads are resolved: the real king is still missing; the revolutionaries have not been thwarted; the king's wife doesn't know the man who's kissed her into submission isn't her husband.

That said, there are some wonderfully funny moments in *Soldier Man,* and Harry maintains his Elf personality throughout. His attention repeatedly drawn toward a cow's udder and away from his own safety, his obliviousness to the dynamite in the "battlefield," his delight with himself for ordering a decapitation, his preoccupation with food over the advances of a beautiful woman in her boudoir are all among the greatest highlights of Langdon's screen career, even if the film as a whole is less than the sum of its parts.

HARRY MOMENT: Harry's childlike fascination with the cow's udder beautifully expresses the innocent nature of his character. There is nothing distasteful about the sequence, and it's doubtful whether any other comedian could have played it so well.

WHAT THE EXHIBITORS SAID:
Exhibitors Herald, *December 8, 1928*
    This is certainly a real comedy. Very funny. None of them have a thing on Langdon in two-reel comedies, where he should stay.
Bert Silver, Silver Family Theatre, Greenville, MI. General patronage.

Harry Langdon Announcement

No production credits available. CAST: Harry Langdon, Thelma Todd, Eddie Dunn.

SYNOPSIS: An extremely short (about seven minutes) "trailer," made by Hal Roach to screen for M.G.M. executives, which introduces Harry Langdon as a member of the Roach Company. Inspired by Langdon's recent vaudeville sketch, *The Messenger*, Harry appears at Mrs. Quimby's door and asks her a series of progressively embarrassing questions about Mr. Quimby, leading up to his friendship with Mr. Howard Dietz and their drinking habits. Once Harry is satisfied that Mrs. Quimby will not be angry if her husband arrived home "cock-eyed," he produces a drunken gentleman he believes to be Mr. Quimby, but he's in fact another man, a Mr. Feist. The names used in the short are all M.G.M. employees: "Mr. (Fred) Quimby" was head of sales for short subjects; "Mr. (Felix) Feist," a sales manager; Howard Dietz, the director of advertising. At the close, Dunn breaks character and assures the audience that "Mr. Roach has the greatest confidence in the world in Mr. Langdon, and I know that Harry is with Mr. Roach heart and soul." Screened for M.G.M. around July 1929.

ANALYSIS: That such a film was even produced spoke to M.G.M.'s concerns about Langdon's temperament. As documented in the text, Langdon's colossal failure as his own producer and director (at least from a box-office perspective), coupled with the negative publicity surrounding some of his business decisions, gave him a perhaps unjust reputation as an uncooperative egoist. Eddie Dunn's closing comments were designed to reassure M.G.M., whose funding paid for Roach's productions, that Langdon would not disregard his new boss.

In light of this, though, it's ironic that Langdon's first two-reeler for the company, *Hotter Than Hot*, would be taken directly from his most recent vaudeville turn.

HARRY MOMENT: Harry is so absorbed with the idea of knocking that he continues to do so after Thelma opens the door.

Hotter Than Hot

A Hal Roach Production Released in Two Reels. A Victor Recording, Western Electric System. DIRECTED BY Lewis R. Foster. PHOTOGRAPHY: George Stevens. FILM EDITOR: Richard Currier. RECORDING ENGINEER: Elmer Raguse. STORY EDITOR: H.M. Walker. CAST: Harry Langdon, Thelma Todd, Edgar Kennedy, Frank Austin, Edith Kramer, Eddie Dunn, Lyle Tayo. WORKING TITLES: "Hot Stuff," "Red Hot." Based on "The Messenger," a vaudeville sketch written by Langdon. Copyright August 26, 1929, Registration Number LM805; Renewed September 13, 1956, Number R176920. Released by Metro-Goldwyn-Mayer, Inc., August 17, 1929.

SYNOPSIS: This film was unavailable for viewing. Following is a description based upon the cutting continuity submitted to the U.S. Copyright Office:

In an upscale apartment, Thelma dismisses her butler and maid for the evening. When she hears a knock on the door, she reclines on the davenport, expecting it to be her boyfriend, Jack. Instead, Harry enters, impressed and a little wary. When Thelma asks him who he is and why he's there, he starts to explain as the film flashes back to a scene in the street. Engines and wagons are racing toward a fire, as is Harry on foot. He is stopped by Jack, who is standing in front of a cigar shop. Jack asks Harry to deliver a note to his girlfriend; Harry protests because he wants to see the fire. Jack gives him a lighter, and Harry takes the note. He absentmindedly puts a firecracker into his mouth and lights it. The explosion is mild, and he tosses the firecracker away, after which there is a much bigger explosion. Harry runs away, and a cop, his pants blown to shreds, emerges from where Harry tossed the firecracker.

Back at Thelma's, Harry is talking into a glass of ice water. He takes a piece of ice out of his mouth and it drops into his pants. Thelma continues to query about his visit, and Harry jumps up each time he feels the ice. In between jumps, he explains that he was told to give her something, and shows her the lighter. He lights it and puts it into his pants to melt the ice. Then he jumps up, removes the lighter (which is still lit) and tosses it out into the hall, where it lands on the fringe of a rug, setting it on fire. Harry eventually produces the note, which causes Thelma to scream. Harry falls off his chair. The butler enters and moves threateningly to Harry, but Thelma tells him to leave. She decides to get even with Jack by romancing Harry. She gets up, locks the door, and drops the key down her bosom. Frightened, Harry protests, but he winds up on Thelma's lap.

Thelma picks up the telephone receiver and calls Jack, but he's not there. As she's doing this, Harry plays with a doll. The doll loses its undergarments, and they fall by Thelma's feet, causing Harry to think they're Thelma's. Meanwhile, a neighbor couple sees the carpet on fire by Thelma's door. The man knocks; Thelma thinks it's Jack and laughs maniacally. Calling through the locked door, the man tells Harry, "Your house is on fire. Get out as quick as you can!" Thelma screams, faints and passes out on the davenport. Frantically, Harry ties her up with a drape cord, then uses the vacuum cleaner to retrieve the key. During this, Jack enters the burning hallway and bursts into the apartment to see Harry "embracing" the collapsing Thelma. As Jack lunges toward Harry, a tapestry falls on them. Harry pokes his head through and tries to run, but Jack is pulling on it. Thelma enters and calls for Jack, who responds "Honey!" and they embrace.

Harry falls backwards out a window. He slides down the drainpipe, reaches into an open window for an umbrella, opens it and jumps. The umbrella turns inside-out, but firemen appear with an open net. Harry falls into the net, bounces into the air, and lands on his backside in the fire engine's smokestack.

At present, no soundtrack discs for this film are known to exist.

WHAT THE EXHIBITORS SAID:
Motion Picture Herald, *February 22, 1930*

The best Langdon I've ever seen. If the rest are as good as this one Langdon will soon be popular here. *Harold Smith, Dreamland Theatre, Carson, IA. General patronage.*

Motion Picture Herald, *April 12, 1930*

Another good Langdon comedy. Hal Roach is certainly turning out some extra funny stuff this season. *R. D. Carter, Fairfax Theatre, Kilmarnock, VA. General patronage.*

Frank Austin, Thelma Todd, Edith Kramer and Langdon in Hotter Than Hot.

Very good comedy which kept our patrons laughing most of the time. Disc recording good.
Parkside Theatre, Clinton, IA.
General patronage.

Motion Picture Herald, *June 21, 1930*
Glad to see Harry back with us. He goes over nicely here.
Jack Greene, New Geneseo Theatre, Geneseo, IL.
Small town patronage.

Sky Boy

A Hal Roach Production Released in Two Reels. A Victor Recording, Western Electric System. **DIRECTED BY** Charley Rogers. **PHOTOGRAPHY:** George Stevens. **FILM EDITOR:** Richard Currier. **RECORDING ENGINEER:** Elmer Raguse. **STORY EDITOR:** H.M. Walker. **CAST:** Harry Langdon, Thelma Todd, Eddie Dunn. Copyright September 23, 1929, Registration Number LM806; Renewed December 19, 1956, Number R182600. Released by Metro-Goldwyn-Mayer, Inc., October 5, 1929.

SYNOPSIS: The soundtrack for this film was unavailable. Following is based in part upon the cutting continuity submitted to the U.S. Copyright Office:

An airplane crash-lands nose first on a deserted frozen tundra, and Eddie and Thelma emerge from the craft. Eddie complains that it's Thelma's fault that they didn't have enough gasoline to make it. When he realizes they are stranded and alone, he tries to kiss her, but she runs back to the plane and screams. "There's no one here to help you," says Eddie, but Harry, a stowaway, calls out and waves his hand. He is in a sort of "rumble seat" in the tail section, and asks when they will be taking off again. Eddie resumes chasing Thelma, and as she calls for help, Harry reaches into the food he's packed and grabs a pie. It slips out of his hand and slides along the top of the plane, dropping into the snow. Then Harry trips and he also slides, until he is seated upon the pie. Outside of the plane, Harry notices that there are bear tracks, and calls out, "Oh-oh! Monkeys!" Eddie demands their attention: "We're stranded alone on an iceberg and there's got to be some discipline." Eddie proclaims that he's in charge, as Harry stands beside him and snow falls on both of them.

Fade in on a tent from which Thelma emerges. She calls out that she sees a ship, but Eddie tells her it's "the tail of a whale." Disgusted, Eddie walks off, and Harry is unsure whether to laugh or cry. Thelma tells him not to get discouraged: "You can't make anything better by worrying about it. So just laugh and be happy and smile." Harry starts to laugh and to sing, but Eddie tells him to shut up. A makeshift fishing pole begins to bob up and down. Harry grabs it and tries to catch the fish, but winds up with his hand in its throat. He throws things at the fish and his foot slips into the water. When he pulls it out, his shoe is gone.

Meanwhile, Eddie is heating up some water, and calls for Harry, who has a piece of burlap over his foot. He asks Harry to give him a shave. Harry has a little trouble with the hot towel, putting it and the scarf around his neck on Eddie's face. When he turns to get the scissors, the scarf pulls the towel onto the floor. Harry discovers the towel is gone and searches for it. When he finds it, he puts it back on Eddie's face. As Harry sharpens the razor, Eddie asks if he thinks Thelma will like him better if he's clean-shaven. "Maybe," says Harry, so Eddie tells him to ask her. When he does, Thelma makes a motion with her finger indicating that Harry should cut Eddie's throat.

As Harry shaves Eddie, he's got a fish line tied to his wrist, which begins to jerk his hand, causing him to cut off pieces of the towel. Harry puts the razor down, but it gets caught on the fish line, and the razor slices Harry's hat, and then his belt, which causes his pants to drop, revealing that he has wrapped his legs with newspaper. Harry pulls up his pants, not noticing that an oil can has fallen into them. It's snowing now, and there's a hole in the tent above Eddie, causing snow to gather on his face. Harry tries to catch the snow, but it's falling too fast. He climbs up on a shelf and tries to plug the hole, as oil leaks from the seat of his pants. Meanwhile, a bear enters and proceeds to lick the lather off Eddie's face. As the fish line continues its tugging, Harry gets pulled off the shelf, causing the tent to collapse. Harry runs as the bear follows.

Outside, Thelma hears a motor. A zeppelin is above them, and its officers see Thelma and drop a rope ladder from the side. Harry is trying to elude the bear, and the fish line causes him to be pulled into the water. Thelma tries to climb the rope ladder, but Eddie pulls her back, telling her she can't leave until she promises to marry him. They struggle. Harry emerges from the water with a fish, which he spanks ("You little dickens, you!"), then notices the struggle. He throws the fish at Eddie, which knocks him back onto the tent, which collapses. Thelma and Harry climb the rope ladder, pursued by Eddie. Using the razor, Harry cuts the rope ladder from above him, causing them both to fall into the water. The rope ladder descends again, and Harry grabs hold of it, rising out of the water, clad only in his underwear.

As of this writing, the soundtrack disc for reel one has been located, but has not yet been restored to the film.

Thelma Todd, Langdon and friend in Sky Boy.

WHAT THE CRITICS SAID:
Variety, *December 25, 1929; Reviewed by Bige*

Laughs are scattered and the waits between them sometimes long, taking away chances for this to be a wallop two-reeler. Laugh total is fairly high if not consistent, however, that and Harry Langdon insuring Sky Boy *against floppage.*

In his talk Langdon has adopted the same goof style he pantomimed with the silents. That may tend to change his type of story, for Langdon when talking in his goof way lends slight opportunity for love interest. A beaut going nuts over Langdon despite his talk would be pretty hard to take. Silent, he was cute. Yet it may be to Langdon's credit that he adheres so closely to his old style in his new talk. They'll just have to pick his stories from a different angle.

Langdon is the star of the playing trio in Hal Roach's Sky Boy. *Eddie Dunn, comedy heavy, and the blond Thelma Todd support him. Story about forced airplane landing in snow wastes. Langdon is a stowaway. Reverts frequently to the old-time slapstick for gags, such as the fish and bear stuff. A comedy shaving scene gets the howl and is stretched for all its worth.*

Some cutting would quicken Sky Boy's *pace.*

Rochester Democrat and Chronicle, *March 10, 1930; Reviewed by C.L.M.*

Harry Langdon's talking comedy called Sky Boy *is full of laughs. Sound has taken no cubits from Langdon's stature as a comedian.*

WHAT THE EXHIBITORS SAID:
Motion Picture Herald, *February 8, 1930*

A good comedy. Langdon very good in shorts again. He has knockout voice.
*J. C. Kennedy, Empress Theatre, Akron, IA.
Small town patronage.*

Motion Picture Herald, *March 29, 1930*

Pleased the kids, but our grownups can't see anything funny about Langdon. He flopped hard in silent comedies and his talking doesn't help much.
*A. F. Botsford, Royal Theatre, Ainsworth, NE.
Small town patronage.*

Skirt Shy

A Hal Roach Metrotone Production Released in Two Reels. **DIRECTED BY** Charles Rogers. **PHOTOGRAPHY:** George Stevens. **FILM EDITOR:** Richard Currier. **RECORDING ENGINEER:** Elmer Raguse. **STORY EDITOR:** H.M. Walker. **CAST:** Harry Langdon, May Wallace, Tom Ricketts, Nancy Dover, Arthur Thalasso, Charlie Hall. Copyright December 9, 1929, Registration Number LM890; Renewed, December 19, 1956, Number R182604. Released by Metro-Goldwyn-Mayer, Inc., November 30, 1929.

SYNOPSIS: Edgar, an elderly and wealthy gentleman, is sitting on a couch with dowager Maggie. She is expecting him to propose, but he leaves before doing so.

She informs Harry, the butler, and Nancy, the maid, that the house is heavily mortgaged and that she was counting on marriage to save it. She tells them she is going to the bank for one last attempt to save the situation and that they should begin packing. Edgar returns, bearing flowers, and Nancy decides that she and Harry must keep him around until Maggie returns.

She dresses Harry in drag as "Maggie" and manages to lift Edgar's glasses so that he can't see very well. "Maggie" plays hard-to-get while Edgar is persistent with his intentions.

Meanwhile a loud, gun-bearing cowboy shows up and declares that he is Maggie's old flame; he goes on to say that he hasn't seen her in 20 years, and that he intends to marry her.

Edgar and the cowboy fight over "Maggie" and at one point Harry loses the boxing gloves that provided "her" bosom, when they're caught on a tree branch. In an attempt to get them back, Harry ends up boxing with the gloves. No matter how or where he ducks, the gloves manage to strike him in the head.

Later, Harry ends up under a tree as a piece of fruit drops into his hand. He takes a bite, and then spits it out as sour, whereupon another piece of fruit plops into his hand. The cowboy then discovers Harry's false identity and more mayhem occurs. Maggie returns as the cowboy drops a beehive in the greenhouse, where they are cowering. Harry sends the hive toward the cowboy, who kicks Maggie, believing her to be Harry in disguise. She hits the cowboy over the head with a shovel, and the greenhouse falls on Harry.

ANALYSIS: The emphasis is on visual comedy in *Skirt Shy*, but most of it is pretty clumsy and not just because this is an early talkie. When the cowboy greets "Maggie" by repeatedly lifting "her" up in the air (causing Harry's head to strike the roof of the porch), it's patently obvious that Langdon is on a wire. As Harry and Edgar crawl along the ground to avoid the cowboy's gunplay, Harry is dragging a machete that cuts down a row of small trees in a very improbable fashion. There's also an unusually large amount of knockabout: Nancy slapping Harry in the face and later hitting him on the head so she can dress him in Maggie's clothes;

May Wallace, Langdon and Tom Ricketts in Skirt Shy.

Harry's suspenders being pulled back and released, smacking him on the backside, which knocks him over the back of the couch; the encounter with the boxing gloves; and the finale, when the real Maggie clobbers the cowboy. This kind of humor was more prevalent with Mack Sennett than with Roach.

Langdon's pantomime is fine, while his dialogue is mostly insipid. He's incapable of comprehending that he's supposed to be impersonating Maggie, which

gets a little frustrating. Fortunately, the film moves at a good clip, never remaining too long in one place. The longest sequence is Harry's encounter with the boxing gloves, and it's fine. The glare on his face as he strikes (and is struck by) the gloves is reminiscent of *The Strong Man* and the scene on the bus with the surly passenger.

HARRY MOMENT: Harry's childlike expression of bewilderment as the pieces of fruit continue to drop into his hand is a fine example of the innocent Elf character.

WHAT THE CRITICS SAID:
Variety, *December 18, 1929; Reviewed by Sid*
   Rates showing on the major screen without threatening to be riotous. Harry Langdon's name may catch interest and the dumb pan clown should make good on the promise through the hoke involved.

   Two-reeler is somewhat overboard on footage and could be advantageously sliced. Tells of an elderly woman on the verge of being dispossessed unless her aged suitor rises to the occasion with a proposal.

   Langdon, as the butler, and a maid go to the front, the girl dressing Langdon as the matron to fool the aged Lothario, who loses his glasses to make it easier. Mix-up arrives with former flame of the woman, a two-gun totin' six-footer from the West. Chase and shots in the garden, including brick throwing, which sends a bee-hive into action.

   Gaiety $2 audience accepted it mildly, perhaps because of becoming somewhat impatient to see the feature, Sky Hawk *(Fox), as a dual newsreel, a cartoon one-reeler and a screen piano solo of "Annie Laurie" had preceded.*

   Some funny stuff at various spots in this two-reeler with Langdon, vaude and screen vet, knowing how to cash when opportunity arises. He's also capable of giving slow spots some pace.

   Langdon is a pleasant prospect for shorts, it being a question with him, as with others, of material.

WHAT THE EXHIBITORS SAID:
Motion Picture Herald, *April 12, 1930*
   A very, very good comedy. Few, indeed, can make a better comedy than Langdon.
R. D. Carter, Fairfax Theatre, Kilmarnock, VA.
General patronage.

   Fairly good. Langdon okay. Recording fairly good.
G. B. Orne, Richmond Theatre, Richmond, VT.
Small town patronage.

The Head Guy
   A Hal Roach Production Released in Two Reels.
DIRECTED BY Hal Roach (uncredited) and Fred L. Guiol. **PHOTOGRAPHY:** George Stevens. **FILM EDITOR:** Richard Currier. **RECORDING ENGINEER:** Elmer Raguse. **STORY EDITOR:** H.M. Walker. **CAST:** Harry Langdon, Thelma Todd, Nancy Dover, Eddie Dunn, Edgar Kennedy, Gus Leonard. Copyright December 26, 1929, Registration Number LM938; Renewed September 10, 1956, Number R198850. Released by Metro-Goldwyn-Mayer, Inc., January 11, 1930.

SYNOPSIS: During a rainstorm at the Elmira Train Station, Nancy informs Manager Kennedy that he is the father of twins. He tells her he's alone and can't leave, but Nancy suggests he put Harry in charge, which he does, reluctantly.

Nancy, his girl, tells Harry that she's proud of him, and leaves. He fumbles with the telegraph receiver, and goes outside to greet an arriving train, whereupon he's knocked down by a mailbag.

A troupe of chorus girls enters the station. Their egotistical director calls for a rehearsal while they wait. Some ducks get loose and Harry pursues them, disrupting the rehearsal. He meets Thelma, who asks him to walk her dog, which he does. He then ends up dancing with the chorus girls as they rehearse.

Nancy returns, gets mad at him for dancing with the girls, and tells him that they are through. Harry sits and alternately cries and gets angry with her, then haphazardly eats a sandwich.

Meanwhile, Nancy has caught the director's eye and he suggests that she dance with the other girls. He then offers her a job and suggests she leave that evening with the troupe. Harry protests and socks the director, who sends him reeling. He fumbles with his pistol as a train arrives.

After the troupe has left the station to board the train, Harry kicks the director into a mud puddle. As the train departs, he sadly waves goodbye then sees that Nancy has remained behind.

As he hugs her, Harry observes that the rain has stopped; he tells her, "It ain't gonna rain on us no more!" He then pulls a cord by mistake, which opens the water tower. They are both drenched.

ANALYSIS: The rough-and-tumble slapstick of the previous short is set aside in favor of some (admittedly slight) romantic comedy, resulting in a much better film. In Langdon's case, both dialogue and delivery are vastly improved. Thelma Todd returns, but only for a minute, as the haughty owner of a fancy dog that Harry "takes outside" so it can relieve itself. Surprisingly, although we don't see what the dog is doing, there's no attempt to fool the audience with a sight gag showing something other than the obvious. When Harry returns the dog to Thelma, she gives him a questioning look, to which he responds with a nod as if to say, "Yes, he did go."

During his brief moments with the dancing girls, Langdon performs an agreeable soft-shoe, followed by a more hyper version. Nancy clearly loves and believes in Harry, so it's more than a little bizarre that, immediately after walking out on him for fraternizing

with "that kind of women," she joins their rehearsal, freely discarding her skirt in front of director Eddie Dunn. When Harry objects, she simply pouts and ignores him, proving to be as childish as he.

The film's most memorable scene, of course, comes after Nancy has told Harry she doesn't want to see him again. It's both fascinating and cringe-worthy. Left alone, he cries and says he doesn't want to live, and cries again. He cleans his fingernails with a fountain pen and cries some more and declares that he will die. He seems to calm down, cleans his nails some more and, in defiance, decides he'll find another girl, "a bigger girl…. Maybe one who smokes!" Then he remembers Nancy doesn't smoke, and cries some more. He reaches into his lunch box for a sandwich while declaring he will die "like I've never died before!" He bites into the sandwich and cries some more. He talks while eating, so the words are unintelligible. He chokes a bit on the sandwich. He takes an apple from the lunchbox, looks at it and decides, "I don't want no apple now, I don't want no apple now. I'll eat my apple after now," and puts it in his pocket.

To label the scene "surreal" is barely adequate; it takes the Elf into new realms of perplexity. Harry's cry, although not on the same level of ludicrousness as Stan Laurel's, is quite funny and provides just the right punctuation to his off-the-wall monologue. Meanwhile, his actions are in complete contrast to the words and enhance the other-worldliness of the character. No other comedian could have portrayed the scene with such positive and negative aspects to his performance.

HARRY MOMENTS: His dancing with the chorus line is both eccentric and funny. Several of the extras portraying the girls genuinely smile at his wild steps.

Despairing over Nancy, in one stationary shot he alternates between a blubbering child and a bitter boy while professing an adult longing for his girl. This really reveals the ambiguity of age in the Elf character.

WHAT THE CRITICS SAID:
Motion Picture Times, *February 4, 1930; Reviewed by A.F.S.*

Harry Langdon puts over a neat little comedy in The Head Guy. *The dialogue is fairly humorous, but Langdon's familiar antics and clowning supply the main fun.*

Film Daily, *March 22, 1930*

Harry Langdon appears to be still experimenting to find out his forté in the talking line. In this comedy he is at his best when he confines himself to pantomime, and there is enough of this to make the short acceptable most anywhere. The story concerns a simpleton, played by Langdon, who is left in charge of a hick-town railroad depot while the station master is away. A theatrical troupe arrives for a stopover between trains and starts using the waiting room for a rehearsal hall. Langdon starts cutting up with the girls of the show and gets into hot water with his own

Thelma Todd asks Harry to walk her dog in The Head Guy.

local sweetie. Both of them are given a tryout by the manager of the troupe and their antics are good for quite a few laughs. Rather long considering its strength, but should answer satisfactorily for the not too fastidious audiences.

WHAT THE EXHIBITORS SAID:
Motion Picture Herald, *March 29, 1930*

A good enough comedy. Disc recording good.
J. C. Kennedy, Empress Theatre, Akron, IA. General patronage.

Motion Picture Herald, *July 26, 1930*

Good but not quite as good as *Skirt Shy* and some of the other Langdons that had more action in them. Above average present day comedies.
R. D. Carter Fairfax Theatre, Kilmarnock, VA. General patronage.

The Fighting Parson

A Hal Roach Production Released in Two Reels. **DIRECTED BY** Charles Rogers and Fred L. Guiol. **PHOTOGRAPHY:** George Stevens. **FILM EDITOR:** Richard Currier. **RECORDING ENGINEER:** Elmer Raguse. **STORY EDITOR:** H.M. Walker. **CAST:** Harry Langdon, Nancy Dover, Thelma Todd, Eddie Dunn, Leo Willis, Charlie Hall, Gus Leonard. Copyright January 6, 1930, Registration Number LM973. Released by Metro-Goldwyn-Mayer, Inc., February 22, 1930.

SYNOPSIS: In a western saloon, a cowboy tells his rowdy pals that Bob McDonald, the Fighting Parson, is on his way to clean up the town. Inside a stagecoach, Harry is singing a song while playing the banjo. After the coach hits a bump, the driver's plug of tobacco falls into a piece of bread held by Harry. As he eats, Harry begins to feel ill and falls over. The coach is held up by bandits, who make everyone get out. They overlook Harry, who is still inside as the startled horses run away with the coach. Before long, Harry takes the reins and regains control.

Meanwhile, Nancy, an unwilling saloon girl, is lamenting her situation. The stagecoach pulls into town as the cowboys exit the saloon. Harry goes into the saloon and drinks a beer as the cowboys watch him. He then sits on the stage and sings "Frankie and Johnnie" while playing the banjo. Harry yodels as he continues to play. The cowboys sway and tap their feet in appreciation. They throw coins on the stage as Harry does an eccentric dance to piano accompaniment.

A big cowboy attempts to grab Nancy and is punched by Harry. The cowboy suggests they fight it out on the stage. Harry dons boxing gloves and watches as the cowboy knocks down a sparring partner. Nancy grabs a pair of gloves that contain long poles and has Harry put them on. The bell rings and the fight is on. Harry, with long arms due to the poles, keeps punching the cowboy. After a while, the cowboy is punched through the floor. Nancy tears off one of Harry's long "arms" and declares him the winner. They embrace.

ANALYSIS: As director Charley Rogers returns, so does the slapstick. The boxing scene is fairly well choreographed (and certainly more imaginatively thought out than the one in Our Gang's *Boxing Gloves* earlier that season), and the use of gloves-on-long-poles

The locals don't know what to make of Harry, who is mistaken for The Fighting Parson *(1930).*

provides some very funny visuals. Thelma Todd has even less to do here than in the previous film; she's basically a background player with no lines. Nancy Dover again serves as a minor romantic interest, playing the unwilling captive of the town tough guy. Langdon gets some nice moments; we finally get to hear him sing and play a banjo, and he performs an eccentric dance that probably mirrored the one with which he closed his vaudeville turn during the previous year.

HARRY MOMENTS: After the runaway horses finally come to a dead stop in the center of town, Harry quietly says, "Whoa." This is similar to other times when his character reacts to danger after it has passed.

Harry's singing and playing "Frankie and Johnnie," his yodeling and eccentric dancing are all delightful and endearing. They are charming examples of what parts of his live performances must have been like, especially in the minstrel and medicine show days.

WHAT THE CRITICS SAID:
Motion Picture News, *December 11, 1929*

Harry Langdon is the star of this burlesque western comedy. It is brimful of laughs after it once gets under way, but the stagecoach sequence at the opening is too long and rather tiring. On the whole, however, the picture will get a lot of laughs from the average picture house audiences… A lot of good hoke here. Directed by Fred Guiol.

Film Daily, *December 29, 1929*

Though the action is a little slow at times, there is enough fun in this one to put it across. One sequence especially, a comedy boxing scene in which Harry uses a pair of false long arms to reach for his opponent, is a scream.

Motion Picture Times, *January 28, 1930*

Hal Roach comedy with Harry Langdon. Slow in spots but enough laughter to put it across. Story built around Langdon, a trouping banjoist, mistaken for a fighting parson. A comedy sequence in which Langdon uses lengthy false arms to reach his opponent is a panic.

Photoplay, *October 1930*

Another Harry Langdon that needs story and good dialogue, though this has its amusing moments. Harry plays his usual sappish character, with a little guitar plunking, singing and dancing. In the supporting cast are such superlative girls as Thelma Todd and Nancy Dover.

Voice Of Hollywood #A-7

A Tec-Art Studios Production Released in One Reel. **PRODUCED BY** Louis Lewyn. **CAST:** Taylor Holmes, Montague Love, Beth Mehaffy Hawaiians, Harry Jolson, Lola Lane, Gus Edwards and Armida, Lew Cody, Harry Langdon. Copyright, March 7, 1930, Registration Number LM1231. Released by Tiffany Productions, Inc., March 7, 1930.

SYNOPSIS: From the studio of Station S.T.A.R., Taylor Holmes introduces various performers. After Holmes introduces Lew Cody and Harry Langdon, the two alternately introduce each other. Harry tries to tell a story, but is distracted by the piano (which he calls a "ukulele" at first).

ANALYSIS: As a rule, the *Voice of Hollywood* shorts have not stood the test of time, and this one is no exception. The series had a reputation for wasting the talents of its participants. With the possible exception of Gus Edwards (co-author of Rose Langdon's best-remembered song, "In My Merry Oldsmobile") and his youthful protégée, Aramida, no one in this slipshod reel is shown to any great advantage, including Harry.

WHAT THE CRITICS SAID:
Film Daily, *February 16, 1930*

Another of the series of Hollywood's leading stars doing special bits before the camera and mike. Taylor Holmes officiating as master of ceremonies offers Lew Cody and Harry Langdon, Armida (sic) and Gus Edwards, Beth Mehaffy Hawaiians, et. al. Audience liked it.

Variety, *February 19, 1930; Reviewed by Char*

A new one in the Voice of Hollywood *series in which various Hollywood stars and personalities do their little bits in an impromptu manner. Different and intimate, short invites booking all over, even if some of the material fails to click. The novelty should hold it up.*

…Harry Langdon and Lew Cody kid around without doing anything in particular.

The Big Kick

A Hal Roach Production Released in Two Reels. **DIRECTED BY** Warren Doane. **PHOTOGRAPHY:** George Stevens. **FILM EDITOR:** Richard Currier. **RECORDING ENGINEER:** Elmer Raguse. **STORY EDITOR:** H.M. Walker. **CAST:** Harry Langdon, Edgar Kennedy, Nancy Dover, Bob Kortman, Sam

Lufkin, Robert O'Connor. WORKING TITLE: "Bootleg Gas." Copyright February 17, 1930, Registration Number LM1075; Renewed January 13, 1958, Number R206642. Released by Metro-Goldwyn-Mayer, Inc., March 29, 1930. SPANISH VERSION TITLE: *Estaccion de Gasolina.*

SYNOPSIS: Two agents are pursuing bootleggers. They stop at a gas station and ask Nancy if she's seen the criminal's car. She says yes and points them in the right direction. She then tells lazy Harry that it's time to get up. He gets dressed and cleans himself with water and an air hose.

A car belching smoke and making loud noises pulls into the station. There is so much noise that Harry can't hear what the driver is saying. He then pulls out parts of the engine and throws them away. Additional parts fly out and smash windows in the garage. After Harry finally stops the engine, the driver asks for directions to Petaluma. Shortly thereafter, a car pulls into the station with two girls who also ask for directions to Petaluma.

Later, two more agents appear and ask Harry to hold the bootleggers if they should arrive. He's also warned that they are killers. While waiting, Harry inadvertently inflates a balloon with a face painted on it that he normally uses as a punching bag. The balloon grows larger under Harry's coat and he begins to rise into the air. The balloon explodes.

A bus filled with mannequins and liquor arrives, and the bootlegger driver demands a fill-up. Agents begin shooting at the bootleggers, who return fire. Harry believes the mannequins are passengers and signals them to follow him into the station. The shooting creates holes in the side of the bus. Liquor begins flowing out of the holes and Harry gets drenched. He drinks some by mistake — and then deliberately — and gets very happy.

Becoming increasingly loaded, Harry begins carrying mannequins into the garage. Once inside, he notices that a female figure has lost her head, and a male's head is detachable. Meanwhile, the agents capture the bootleggers. Inside, Harry attempts to keep all of the mannequins standing. One of the agents tells Nancy that she and her boyfriend will be rewarded.

A policeman enters the garage and begins examining a row of fallen mannequins. Harry grabs a hammer and begins knocking the heads off the figures. He hits the policeman by mistake and takes off running down the street.

Nancy Dover and Langdon in The Big Kick.

ANALYSIS: Chock-full of routines that originated in other films, plus one from *Johnny's New Car, The Big Kick* is an enjoyable romp. With dialogue kept to a bare minimum, Langdon performs one pantomime bit after another; all are enjoyable and demonstrate that Harry's character and sound weren't incompatible under the right circumstances. Some of the situations, such as the balloon lifting Harry off the ground, and the alcohol spraying from the bullet holes, strain credibility, but not to an outlandish degree. Mainly *The Big Kick* reflects the Roach studio philosophy of comic exaggeration without overdoing it, making the short a sure crowd pleaser.

HARRY MOMENT: From outside the station, Nancy tells Harry it's time to wake up. He rises and goes through a lengthy silent routine of watering a plant, washing up and doing some calisthenics. It's a variation on the opening scene of *Three's a Crowd*.

WHAT THE CRITICS SAID:
Motion Picture News, *January 25, 1930*
  Harry Langdon and Hal Roach — 'snuff said! They feature several gags in this which are bound to tear [the] house down with laughter. The funny antics of Harry, as the owner of a gas station on a lonely road frequented by desperate rum runners, offer comedy that is ace-high.

Variety, *January 29, 1930*
  Okay anywhere. Hoke comedy, and though not riotous, this short is well spattered with laughs. Comedian's dumb panto cheers generally. Ed Kennedy and Nancy Dover assist.
  Langdon does a gasoline station lad with a girl assistant. Two are unwittingly showed into the centre of a battle between rum runners and agents. In the clear the girl emerges as heroine when she prevents the bootleggers from making a getaway by planting their auto over an hydraulic pump. Fadeout, however, is Langdon running off from a lone policeman with whom he jammed in error.
  Photography and recording good.

WHAT THE EXHIBITORS SAID:
Motion Picture Herald, *April 12, 1930*
  The best Langdon yet. But my objection is that he's too silly.
  Lee Brewerton, Capitol Theatre, Raymond, Alta., Canada. General patronage.

Motion Picture Herald, *June 7, 1930*
  This was a good comedy and well liked.
  Frank Shepard, Majestic Theatre, Biggar, Sask., Canada. General patronage.

Motion Picture Herald, *June 14, 1930*
  A very good comedy.
  J. C. Kennedy, Empress Theatre, Akron, IA. Small town patronage.

The Shrimp

A Hal Roach Production Released in Two Reels. DIRECTED BY Charley Rogers. STORY EDITOR: H.M. Walker. PHOTOGRAPHY BY Art Lloyd. SOUND ENGINEER: Elmer Raguse. FILM EDITOR: Richard Currier. CAST: Harry Langdon, Nancy Drexel, James Mason, Thelma Todd, Max Davidson, Frank Alexander, Helen Gilmore. Copyright March 3, 1930, Registration

Thelma Todd and Langdon in The Shrimp.

Number LM1116; Renewed January 13, 1958, Number R206643. Released by Metro-Goldwyn-Mayer, Inc., May 3, 1930. SPANISH VERSION TITLE: *¡Pobre Infeliz!,* with Linda Loredo replacing Drexel.

SYNOPSIS: In a boarding house, the various tenants gather in the dining room. Nancy, the owner's daughter, cautions Harry not to let them push him around. Harry arrives for dinner and is bullied relentlessly. The tenants laugh at his misfortunes and refer to him as the Shrimp. At the dinner table, Harry falls asleep after Grace has been said. Jim, a big bully, and Thelma sit on either side of Harry. They elbow him, reach in front and generally keep him from being able to eat. Jim asks Harry if he likes berries. Harry says no, and has his face shoved into a big bowl of them.

Meanwhile, a newspaper headline announces that Professor Schoenheimer's theory has amazed the world. He has apparently been able make timid men acquire the ferocity of bulldogs. Later, the professor is going to give a demonstration to a group of students. Harry, a timid man, is brought to the professor for his demonstration. Harry is injected with the glands of a ferocious dog. When he comes to, he announces that he can lick any man in the place. Recalling what Jim the boss. Harry then shoves Jim's face into a large bowl of berries.

The professor and his colleagues arrive and declare the experiment a success. Just then, Harry eyes a cat and takes off in hot pursuit. He pauses momentarily to eye a telephone pole, and then resumes the chase.

ANALYSIS: *The Shrimp* is the best of the available Roach shorts. Its opening scenes, with Harry abused

Langdon's two leading ladies: Nancy Drexel in The Shrimp *(left), and Linda Loredo in the Spanish language version,* ¡Pobre Infeliz! *(right).*

has done to him, he suddenly leaves the room, and is pursued by the professor and his associates.

Harry returns to the boarding house, intent on vengeance. He administers retribution to Thelma and is only stopped from striking her by Nancy's plea. Harry tells Mother that she shouldn't have to work anymore and to stop scrubbing the floor. He tells the lazy Father to clean the floor instead. Jim returns, and after being filled in by Thelma about Harry's "change," announces that he's going to wring the Shrimp's neck. Instead, Harry knocks him down with a turkey leg. He and Jim get in a fight, and Harry prevails. Jim admits defeat and agrees that Harry is and belittled by the other residents, manage to evoke the gentle pathos that marked his best work with Mack Sennett. The cruelty is believable and one genuinely feels for Harry, making the second half, after the personality transplant, all the more satisfying as the worm finally turns on Thelma, Jim and the rest.

The science-fiction aspect of the plot isn't overplayed, with Max Davidson bringing just the right touch of eccentricity to his character. No attempt is made to depict the medical procedure, which keeps things moving. Once Harry is infused with the bulldog's personality, he's eager to exact revenge on Jim, and we're eager to see it.

HARRY MOMENT: Harry's falling asleep at the dinner table during grace is a good, though brief, example of the sleepy aspect of his innocent character.

WHAT THE CRITICS SAID:
Motion Picture News, *February 15, 1930*

Harry Langdon is right up to snuff, with a bushelful of laughs in a two-reeler centering around a timid boarder, much abused by his room-mates, who is the subject of an experimental operation performed by a big scissor-and-knife man. He claims to have discovered the secret of transplanting the fighting spirit of a bulldog into man. And he succeeds. Langdon runs right back to the boarding house and does his stuff. Good comedy; moves at a fast clip. Directed by Charles Rogers. Running time, 20 minutes.

Film Daily, *February 23, 1930*

Harry Langdon with a minimum of effort manages to make this one a real laugh-getter. The film is built around a novel idea. Langdon appears as a timid young boarder who is made the butt of the other boarders' jokes. He falls into the hands of a scientist who has discovered the secret of transforming meekness into combativeness. A slight operation turns him into a wildcat, with the result that he wins domination over those who have been bullying him. Decidedly a fine comedy.

Motion Picture Times, *March 4, 1930; Reviewed by A.F.S.*

Harry Langdon makes this one a winner; novel story of a scientist who applies secret of changing the meek and mild into the hardboiled and wild to faint-hearted Harry, who has been the object of bullying at his boarding house. Title tells the story. Tough on the folks who have been romping on Harry, but decisively a comedy with a wallop in laughs. You can bill it that way.

Variety, *May 7, 1930; reviewed by Bige*

Harry Langdon, staging a return in talker shorts of the old silent two-reel slapstick comedy type, hits again in The Shrimp. The laughs are secured by Langdon's

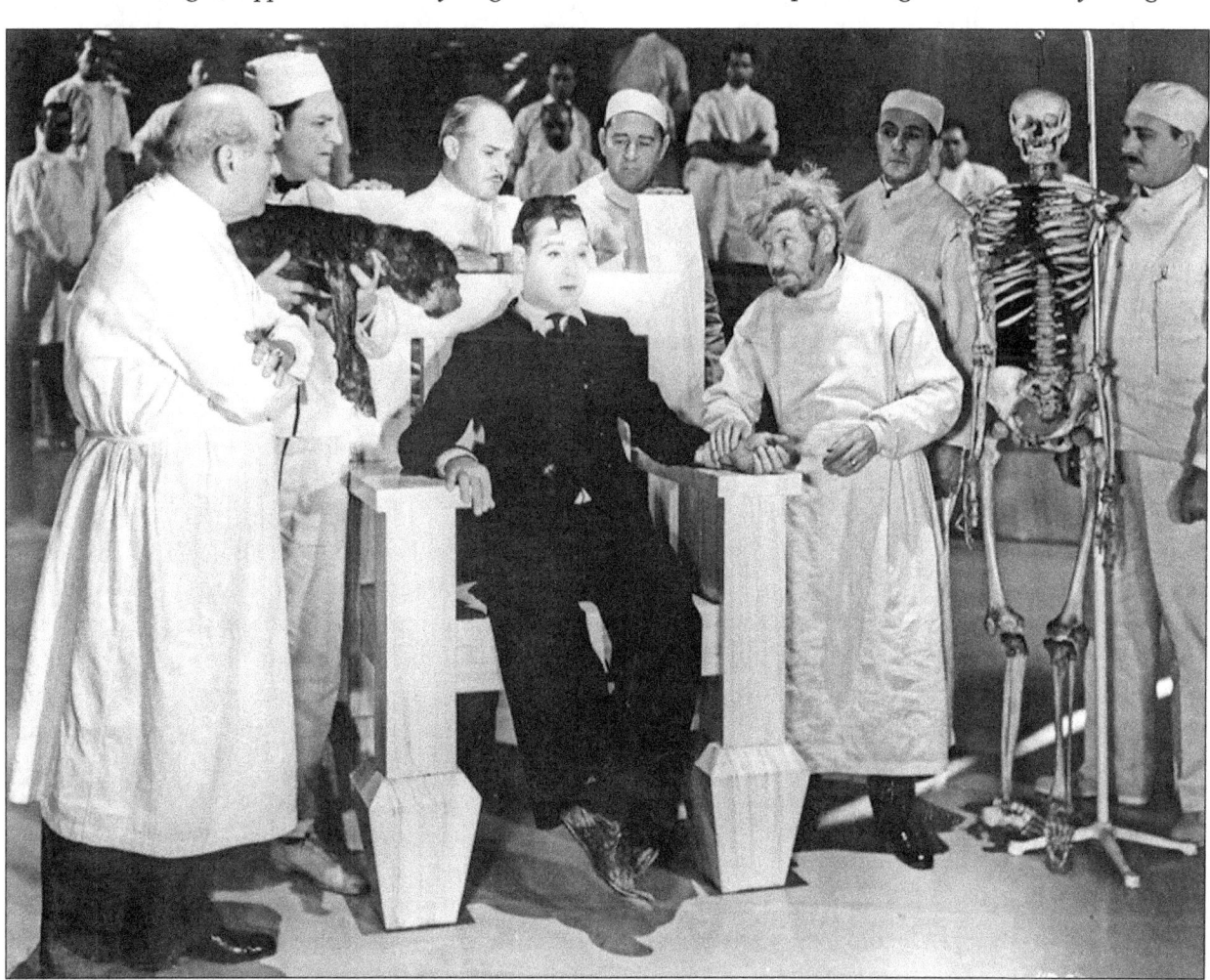

Max Davidson (right) wants to give Harry a bulldog's personality in The Shrimp.

goofing — he's "cute" — and some plate throwing around a good situation.

Langdon, as the worm, turns. He's the punching bag of a boarding house. A Dutch dialect doc uses him for an experiment — injection of bulldog serum in a timid man. After the shot, he cleans up his tormentors. At the finish the dog stuff tells and he dives out the window after a cat. He stops for a moment at a lamp post but changes his mind and keeps on going after the cat. Post biz subtle as done and not too rough.

WHAT THE EXHIBITORS SAID:
Motion Picture Herald, *May 10, 1930*

M.G.M. COMEDIES — All good but Langdon's, and he will pass out in these as in silents. Do not look for him on Metro's next year's comedy list.
H. R. Cromwell, Bedford Theatre, Bedford, PA. Small town patronage.

Motion Picture Herald, *June 21, 1930*

One of Langdon's best, which is not saying much. Why does he act so silly?
Lee Brewerton, Capitol Theatre. Raymond, Alta., Canada. General patronage.

The King

A Hal Roach Production Released in Two Reels. **DIRECTED BY** James W. Horne and Charles Rogers. **PHOTOGRAPHED BY** Len Powers. **RECORDING ENGINEER:** Elmer Raguse. **EDITED BY** Richard Currier. **DIALOGUE BY** H.M. Walker. **CAST:** Harry Langdon, Thelma Todd, Dorothy Granger, James Parrott. Copyright April 21, 1930, Registration Number LM1233; Renewed January 13, 1958, Number R206646. Released by Metro-Goldwyn-Mayer, Inc., June 14, 1930. **GERMAN VERSION TITLE:** *Der Koenig.*

SYNOPSIS: In a palace, the queen sits on her throne and asks where the king is. It seems that King Harry is hunting in the woods. He fires his rifle, hitting several things by mistake when his new advisor tells him that the queen requires his presence.

The queen arrives and catches the king kissing another girl. She spanks him for his indiscretion. He then eludes her and meets another girl from a different kingdom. They kiss, and the king swoons and falls to the ground. Shortly thereafter, the advisor pummels a man because he kissed his wife. It turns out that the girl that the king kissed is the advisor's wife. She faints, and the king is drenched by water in an attempt to revive her. When she begins to come around, she tells the king to kiss her again. King Harry tells the angry advisor that she's talking in her sleep. The king walks away, laughing, and after a safe distance tells the advisor, "So what if I kissed your wife." The queen hears this and throws things at the fleeing king. He runs into a large room, followed by

the queen, who tells him he's a little chaser, just like his father.

She attaches a bracelet with a chain to his wrist and puts the other end on her own wrist. They retire to twin beds, separated by a curtain. As she gets undressed she repeatedly pulls on the chain, much to the king's distress. He says that he's going to peek at her, and gets a slap in the face.

When the queen sees King Harry asleep, she undoes her end of the chain to be able to take a bath. He escapes and runs into the advisor's wife. Thinking it's a gift, she puts on the other bracelet, causing she and the king to be joined together. They hear her husband, the advisor, approaching and run into another room. In the confusion, her dress is ripped off and she hides under the covers of a large bed. The king stands next to the bed as the advisor asks him questions.

A mouse crawls under the covers, causing the advisor's wife to thrash about. King Harry sits on the bed to stop the movement, and the mouse runs into his pajamas. He begins to twitch as the advisor looks on. The king puts a mousetrap into his pajamas, then falls, revealing the advisor's wife. The chain breaks, and the advisor chases the King; he then throws him out a window, into a pond.

As the queen arrives, two footmen bring in the soaked king. She tells them to put him to bed. She then asks the king if he's going out. When he says no, she knocks him cold, stating that he *is* going out.

ANALYSIS: A rather poor finish to the series, *The King* leaps from one implausible situation to another. None of the characters, including Harry, are particularly likable. At one point, he threatens to end it all by jumping out a window, into the water, but the queen coldly replies that he hasn't the nerve to do it. Later, when he's returned to the queen, who is told he was pulled from the water, she seems to become sympathetic, and then inexplicably knocks him unconscious with a sneer. Combined with some overly gratuitous slapstick, the whole thing misses the mark.

HARRY MOMENT: When the advisor's wife kisses him, Harry collapses.

WHAT THE CRITICS SAID:
Photoplay, September 1930

Harry Langdon again, this time in another royal travesty. Wistful Harry playing a philandering King who gets mixed up with the pretty blonde wife of his chancellor. The dialogue is deadly dull and the fear grows upon us that Harry's enormous gift of pantomime is lost in talkies.

WHAT THE EXHIBITORS SAID:
Motion Picture Herald, *June 14, 1930*
A very good comedy.
B. J. Vanderby. Strand Theatre, Springfield, S.D. General patronage.

A Soldier's Plaything

A Warner Bros. Production. 56 minutes. **DIRECTED BY** Michael Curtiz. **ORIGINAL STORY BY** Vina Delmar. **SCREENPLAY BY** Perry Vekroff. **DIALOGUE BY** Arthur Caesar. **PHOTOGRAPHY BY** Barney McGill. **EDITED BY** Jack Killifer. **GENERAL MUSICAL DIRECTOR:** Erno Rapee. **ORCHESTRA CONDUCTED BY** Louis Silvers. **CAST:** Ben Lyon, Harry Langdon, Lotti Loder, Jean Hersholt, Noah Beery, Fred Kohler, Otto Matieson, Lee Moran, Marie Astaire, Frank Campeau. Copyright October 11, 1930,

Registration Number LM1630; Renewed February 14, 1958, Number R208827. Released by Warner Bros. Pictures, Inc., November 1, 1930.

SYNOPSIS: It's 1917, and while Georgie's in a hot-and-heavy poker game, his pal Tim is barker for a shooting gallery. Outside, an Army recruiter gives an inspirational speech. Georgie's disgusted and closes the window, but Tim decides to enlist. He comes up to say goodbye. Although Georgie's upset with Tim for enlisting, he freely offers some money and the two remain buddies. The game is down to two players, Georgie and Hank. When Georgie has won $1,220, he decides to take his winnings and go. Enraged, Hank orders him not to go to Lola's apartment, but Georgie tells him, "It's Todd Green I go to see, not Lola!" Hank warns him to see Todd someplace else, "or you'll be pushing up a lot of daisies." Georgie laughs it off and leaves. At the window near Georgie's seat, Hank finds the Ace of clubs, realizes he's been cheated, and wrongly suspects Georgie.

Todd's sister Lola is lounging at the apartment when Georgie arrives. She comes on to him but he gently refuses her advances. He gives her the money he owes his brother, as Hank enters. Hank accuses him of cheating, which Georgie vehemently denies: "I don't have to cheat playing with you and your dumb gang!" Hank slugs Georgie and the two take the brawl into the hallway. Georgie knocks Hank into a banister; he loses his balance and falls several stories to the bottom floor. Believing Hank to be dead, Lola panics and directs Georgie to the fire escape.

Three members of Hank's gang spot Georgie trying to escape and follow him, pistols in their pockets. At that moment, a parade of newly enlisted soldiers, including Tim, are in the streets. Georgie meets up with Tim, who helps protect him from the gang. Georgie winds up enlisting and is still in the Army, stationed in Belgium, at the time of the Armistice.

A title card reads: "Fifi, who tended bar at the little café across the road from the barracks, was no Cleopatra — but she would do till one came along." Fifi is being romanced by a soldier when Georgie arrives, diverting her attention. Georgie playfully razzes the soldier, then retires with Fifi to a back room for some mouth-to-mouth. It turns out the soldier

is the company's new captain, and he deals with Georgie by placing him and Tim (wrongly accused of giving a "raspberry") in the horse stalls where they must clean up manure, much to the amusement of the other soldiers.

The company puts on a show, as Georgie and Tim scrub the stage floor. Tim loses the soap and gets slapped around by a dummy. Three "Musketeers" are rehearsing swordplay, and Georgie shows them how to do it, but pokes Tim in rear end. After getting knocked around, Tim takes the sword away and throws it; it cuts the rope for a sandbag, which falls on captain, who puts Tim and Georgie back on manure duty.

The division is told they're going to Coblenz in Germany. A title card explains: "The Army of Occupation looked it over and decided they liked it," although the gruff captain issues orders restricting the company to barracks and forbidding them to associate with civilians. Georgie rustles another soldier to sneak out with him, but the guy wants to sleep. Tim asks to go along, and Georgie reluctantly agrees. Tim makes noise while trying to leave the barracks.

There's only one nightclub in Coblenz. When Georgie and Tim arrive, they find several of their buddies there. Georgie tries coming on to Gretchen, the owner's daughter, but she rejects him. Tim is talked into trying his luck with her. After some very inept small talk, he tries for a kiss, and gets slapped. Georgie sits down at the piano and sings a love song, and Gretchen slowly melts.

A soldier calls out, "And now we'll hear from the little shrimp," which is the company's nickname for Tim. He sits at the piano and sings a flirtatious song, "If you will 'Oui, Oui' me, I'll 'Oui, Oui' you" to one of the patrons, a French girl. When he tries romancing her, he's told she is deaf. Tim sighs, "When they're not deaf, they're dumb!"

Some M.P.'s arrive to arrest the soldiers that have disobeyed orders. Tim and Georgie try to escape by wearing a horse costume that is used by two performers in the nightclub, as the captain settles in with a beer. Tim lures the two performers away with some racy picture-postcards, and then he and Georgie suit up. They let the owner know it is they in the costume, but the captain sees this and gives chase. Before long, they're back on manure duty. Their bad luck continues when Georgie is posted as a sentry, and he shows off for Gretchen by barking orders. The company overhears him and proceeds to march in various directions, causing chaos. Tim, who's directionally challenged, winds up marching in a major's office. He and Georgie return to the manure pile.

Georgie falls in love with Gretchen. Under a tree, he promises to take her to Coney Island, and describes "Lady Liberty" and the skyscrapers of Manhattan. They kiss and tumble off a bridge into the water. Elsewhere, Tim does sleight-of-hand tricks for

the deaf French girl. He mimes that he'd like to walk with her, but she shakes her head no. Discouraged, he pulls out his picture-postcards, looks at them, and shows them to the girl. She surprises him by speaking: "How dare you, you little shrimp!" and slaps his face.

Sitting beside a stream, Georgie promises to marry Gretchen right away and take her to America "on the first boat!" As they embrace, he recalls Hank sprawled out on the floor after falling. He tells her it would be better if they didn't marry right away. "I'd be doing you the dirtiest trick in the world if I married you right now." She doesn't understand, and runs away.

Georgie is morose, even when Tim tells him they'll be headed back to "good old Brooklyn" soon. Gretchen is miserable too, especially when Papa happily declares the division is going home and new soldiers will be arriving. As the men prepare to leave, a depressed Georgie crosses the road and is almost hit by a truck — driven by Hank! Georgie's elated, even when Hank threatens to knock his head off for causing a nasty scar on his face. Georgie kisses Hank and runs off to find Gretchen, while Tim explains everything.

Back in the city, Georgie marches through the streets with the returning troops, arm-in-arm with Gretchen. Afterwards, at Coney Island, Tim is accompanying a girl who wants to ride the carousel. Tim takes one look at the backside of one of the horses and, remembering all the manure duty, refuses and quickly walks away from the ride.

ANALYSIS: *A Soldier's Plaything* is an enjoyable little film, but certainly no classic. Considering the project began as a vehicle to introduce Lotti Loder to U.S. audiences, it's curious that she doesn't appear until the film is half over, and is barely in it afterwards. The lion's share of the footage goes to Ben Lyon and Langdon as the soldiers who keep getting into trouble and are repeatedly forced to clean up after the horses.

Langdon's not the Elf here, although many of the familiar hand gestures and exclamations ("Oh-oh!") are present, and it's interesting that other characters call him "the little shrimp," which calls to mind his best Roach short. There's nothing unusual or perplexing about his character. Tim is more of a typical comedy relief buffoon; paired with Georgie, the two make a sort of poor man's Abbott and Costello. Lyon is nowhere near the bully that Bud Abbott portrayed, but the Army setting and Langdon's voice — surprisingly similar to Lou Costello's — give rise to the resemblance. Of course, this film was made 11 years before *Buck Privates*, but there's a touch of foreshadowing in such scenes as Tim's inability to march in the correct direction.

The film itself is a curious hybrid of silent and sound. Its scenes are "all-talking," but transitions and plot exposition are handled via text titles, which are numerous. Lyons's Georgie, established as something of a ladies' man, falls in love with Gretchen rather suddenly, because the budding romance is explained in writing rather than shown. Their few romantic scenes are brief, and are all followed by scenes of Langdon engaging in some sort of shtick.

HARRY MOMENT: The flirtatious song Tim sings in the café is cute and rather amusing. It's a good showcase for Langdon's vocal ability, and it's easy to see why music was a part of his vaudeville act for many years.

WHAT THE CRITICS SAID:
Photoplay, October 1930

If you like romance, seasoned with plenty of laughs, some slapstick and hot thrills, catch this. It's great, but heaven knows what to call it. A war story that isn't a war story; not a musical, but has some grand music; not slapstick, yet happy with it — well, call it just a darn good talkie! That will cover it. Ben Lyon, Harry Langdon and Lotti Loder have head honors of a fine cast.

Harrison's Reports, *January 3, 1931*

Fair entertainment of its kind. For those who like their comedy rowdy, and sometimes bordering on vulgarity, A Soldier's Plaything *offers many laughs. Generally, it is a collection of situations that have proved laughable in similar comedies. While some of the rough humor might not be called in good taste, the picture is no worse in that respect than other comedies. The nature of the story places little demand upon the principals or the director but Harry Langdon and Ben Lyon do good work; they are the best in the cast. Children will be entertained in the usual run of slapstick gags...*

There are many comic interludes which have nothing to do with the story but which lengthen the running time. There are two songs in the production. Sound is just average or less.

New York Times, *May 2, 1931; Reviewed by A.D.S.*

The Beacon, a mile or more removed from the feverish Broadway scene, is enjoying a film opening of its own this week in the form of A Soldier's Plaything, *an insignificant item which should never have ventured even that near the Rialto.*

The story is by Vina Delmar and the imposing cast includes Harry Langdon, Ben Lyon, Lotti Loder, Jean Hersholt, Noah Beery and Fred Kohler. That should mean a great deal, but it does not.

A Soldier's Plaything *presents Mr. Langdon and Mr. Lyon as the cut-ups of the army of occupation after the armistice. They seem to have loads of fun, one of their richest escapades reaching its height when they drop a large weight on their captain's head. The title is a mystery —* A Soldier's Plaything *could have been called "The Locomotive Driver's Revenge" and meant just as much.*

Film Daily, *May 3, 1931*

This is the type of material that they use in the two-reel shorts, with the story of the doughboy overseas and the mixups with the girls. There wasn't enough plot in it to stretch to feature length, and the whole thing shows it all too plainly. Ben Lyon is the hero, with Harry Langdon as his buddy. They eventually land in Coblenz on the Rhine, with the Army of Occupation. Langdon is continually pulling his dumb plays, and manages to score some laughs. He is the only bright spot in the entire affair. The sentimental angle is very weak, the dialogue is trifling and banal, and altogether it is a miscue production that offers very little in the way of entertainment. The title is misleading for there is nothing in it of a real sexy slant, and any way you figure it, it is just a filler, and a very weak one at that.

Direction: Poor. Photography: Okay.

See America Thirst

A Universal Pictures Release. 75 minutes. PRODUCED BY Carl Laemmle, Jr. DIRECTED BY William James Craft. SCREENPLAY BY Jerry Horwin, Edward Ludwig, Vin Moore. PHOTOGRAPHED BY Arthur C. Miller. EDITED BY Harry W. Lieb. CAST: Slim Summerville, Harry Langdon, Bessie Love, Matthew Betz, Stanley Fields, Lloyd

Whitlock, Richard Alexander, Tom Kennedy, Lew Hearn, LeRoy Mason, Mitchell Lewis, Walter Brennan. Copyright November 20, 1930, Registration Number LM1745; Renewed August 29, 1958, Number R220715. Released by Universal Pictures Corporation, November 24, 1930.

NOTE: The authors were unable to view this film, and gratefully turn over the entry to their colleague Edward Watz, who provides the Synopsis, Analysis and Harry Moments:

SYNOPSIS: A freight train speeds across the countryside. Railroad workers discover two hoboes "riding the rails" and roughly toss them off the fast-moving train. Rolling down the embankment, the transient buddies Wally (Harry Langdon) and Slim (Slim Summerville) land at the bottom of a ditch. Wally suddenly reacts in typically nonplussed fashion as he extracts a huge jagged rock from beneath his posterior.

Assessing their new surroundings, Wally and Slim try to guess their location. Examining the dirt on the ground, Slim figures that they've landed somewhere in Tennessee. Wally disagrees, saying, "No, we're in Boston."

"Tennessee!" shouts Slim.

"Boston!" counters Wally.

This debate continues back and forth until Wally notices what he believes to be a pile of baked beans. He holds them up to Slim for a close look. "See," he beams, "we're in Boston, all right!" A cutaway shot reveals farm goats grazing in close proximity to our heroes. Slim disgustedly slaps the "beans" out of Wally's hand. Hungry for food, the boys have a run-in with a local policeman who's looking for thieves near a farmhouse. The cop fails to see a white duck stick its head out from beneath Wally's coat. Wally shoves the duck inside his clothing as the policeman increasingly grows suspicious. Cries of "Quack!" emanating from beneath Wally's coat are passed off as animal calls made by the boys to amuse themselves. Finally, the cop spots the stolen duck and gives chase.

Wally and Slim hop aboard the back of a delivery truck loaded with crates of bootleg liquor. The truck speeds away, followed by another vehicle in hot pursuit. Rival gangsters try to hijack the truck, firing bullets that whiz past Wally and Slim, who fail to realize that they're in great danger. Slim wonders what all the commotion is about. "Fourth of July!" Wally replies matter-of-factly. Dynamite sticks are next flung into the vehicle. Finally coming to their senses, Wally and Slim dive out as the truck crosses a bridge and explodes. Landing in the river below, Wally begins to panic.

"Slim," he cries, "I never swam a stroke before in my life!"

"Well," Slim replies, "now's a good time to start learning!"

Slim Summerville and Langdon in See America Thirst.

As Wally continues to wail that he can't swim, he propels himself like a marathon swimmer and gets to dry land far before Slim does. Among the wreckage from the dynamited truck, the boys discover a satchel. Slim opens up the bag, revealing it to be filled with banknotes. "Money-money-money-money-money-money-money!" Wally exclaims in disbelief as he points at their discovery.

Wally and Slim immediately begin enjoying their newfound windfall by indulging themselves outrageously. Resplendent in top hat, tuxedo and white-tie outfits, the boys rent a sightseeing bus to escort them through the nightlife of the Chicago underworld. Visiting a nightclub run by gangsters, Wally and Slim are smitten by Ellen, a cute little showgirl who sings a specialty number, "Is You Is or Is You Ain't," finishing the song amid giggles while playfully sitting on Wally's lap. At that moment, Ellen's mobster boyfriend arrives, Insect McGann, with murder in his eyes for Wally. As the other patrons back away, Wally is so overcome with fear that he stands in place and begins to shake furiously. Wally's frightened gyrations are mistaken for the style of Shivering Smith, an out-of-town hitman sent for by the rival Spumoni Gang to "bump off" Insect McGann. For no particular reason the gangsters assume that Slim is another vicious killer from back East, Gunkist Casey.

Because of their newfound notoriety, Wally and Slim are treated with respect by the mobs of both the Spumoni and McGann factions. To ensure his own safety, Insect McGann pays the boys a fortune for protection insurance against his enemies. Ellen reveals to Wally and Slim that she isn't a gangster's girl at all; she's really employed by the district attorney's office. The boys plot with Ellen to instigate a gang war and force the two families to liquidate each other. Wally and Slim look forward to spending the gangs' money, and vying for Ellen's affections. Meanwhile, the Syndicate Kingpin "Tarface" Spumoni is enjoying a Miami vacation when he encounters the real Shivering Smith. Spumoni realizes that somebody is double-crossing him back in Chicago, and Smith is furious that he is being impersonated. Vowing revenge, Spumoni and Smith take to the skies in Smith's airplane, *The Spirit of Homicide*, bound for the Windy City.

All the city streets are abandoned on the day of the gang war. Wally, Slim, and Ellen take refuge in an armored bunker, safely overlooking the battlefield site. But when Spumoni and Shivering Smith arrive, explaining to the mobs that Wally and Slim are impostors, all the gangsters unite with one common goal: to murder Wally and Slim! Fortunately, a friendly inventor has come up with a formula for a knockout gas to anesthetize the combatants. Wally and Slim stealthily patrol the neighborhood with giant-sized spray guns, neutralizing their enemies. The unconscious gangsters are rounded up and Wally and Slim are heroes of the day. But to their shock they discover that Ellen isn't in love with either of them; her fiancé is the district attorney. They console themselves with the thought of their money, only to discover that someone has substituted hand grenades for the loot in their satchel.

Slim and Wally are seated on a curbside. Slim regrets that their money is gone, but at least they're alive. Wally, however, admonishes Slim because he lost something even greater than money: his love for Ellen was unrequited. Wally complains about the woman he loved: "She broke my heart — she broke

it into pieces — and then she stepped on the pieces!" Wally lectures Slim about his heartache, wagging a finger reproachfully as he vows to remain "an unmarried bachelor." Suddenly Slim notices, as his buddy gestures, that wads of money are being shaken farther and farther out of Wally's sleeve. Wally has stashed the gangster's loot inside his tuxedo! With a knowing look on his face, Slim gets up and walks towards an alley, sweetly beckoning Wally to follow so he can show him something. Wally only reluctantly follows Slim, who pulls Wally in, away from the sidewalk. From inside the alley we hear a terrific clatter as Slim attacks Wally for "holding out" on him. For the fadeout, Wally, off-camera, speaks the film's final lines (and his verbal running gag in the film): "Oh Slim! I apologize! I apologize!"

ANALYSIS: *See America Thirst* has the dubious distinction of containing what is likely the worst performance given by Harry Langdon in a feature film. When one considers how well Langdon adapted the Elf to sound film technique, and his exceptional performances in several of the Roach talkies and *A Soldier's Plaything*, then *See America Thirst* becomes all the more frustrating to watch. It's as if Langdon has forgotten everything he learned during his first year in talkies. His dialogue comes across as though it was unscripted at best, and his instinctive sense of timing has completely left him. He interrupts himself nearly every time he speaks, stopping in mid-sentence, and then repeating his dialogue, sometimes twice in a row, effectively killing any amusing punchlines. When a routine recalls a sequence from silent days (e.g., the duck hidden under Wally's coat harkens back to *Remember When?* and *Tramp, Tramp, Tramp*), the comedy is dragged out by an overabundance of unnecessary talk.

Universal Pictures in 1930 was just at the threshold of its Horror Film cycle, but *See America Thirst* emerged as a horror of another kind. Among all the major studios that year, Universal was least capable of producing good feature-length comedies. Director William James Craft did not know how to pace a comedy, and many of the scenes suffer from an apparent lack of rehearsal. When Slim Summerville tells Matthew Betz (portraying Insect McGann), "You may be a big bug to your friends — but you're not even a ladybug to me," you can see Betz starting to "crack up" and stifle a laugh.

As team partners, there is no chemistry between Langdon and the Keystone Comedy veteran Summerville. Their styles don't clash like Buster Keaton and Jimmy Durante in their talkies together; it's just that Summerville comes across as a loner who's supposed to be both Langdon's pal and straight man. As the nominal star comedian, Langdon's pantomime skills are mostly overlooked save for a few choice "Harry Moments," otherwise it's all dull talk and very little action. Bessie Love, as the film's nominal ingénue, is given a totally thankless role and has to perform an equally thankless musical number, the inane "Is You Is or Is You Ain't."

The scene that holds the most promise involves Wally and Slim perched on cannons high atop the gangster penthouses, in an obvious attempt at a Harold Lloyd "thrill comedy" sequence. However it quickly becomes apparent that most of this Langdon footage was filmed silent with a stuntman taking his place. Langdon's own voice is crudely dubbed over the action. Apart from the exaggerated moans and groans coming from Wally, the sequence is seen mainly in long shots with no attempt to personalize the comedy, or to make an ordinary gag episode something that becomes uniquely Langdon's. It might just as well be El Brendel or Benny Rubin or Gus Shy out there — the qualities that made Langdon special are altogether missing from *See America Thirst*.

HARRY MOMENTS: Wally finds himself cornered on the street by several gangsters who are prepared to "rub him out." He begins spraying the thugs with his knockout gas, only to discover that his canister has run dry. Stalling for time, he tries to talk his way out of a bad situation. Gesturing with his hands, Wally points at one of the gangsters, who suddenly becomes drowsy and collapses to the pavement. He then points his forefinger at another gangster, and the same result occurs. We learn that Slim is hiding above the men in an awning and spraying knockout gas on each gangster. Wally, however, believes it's his finger that contains this magic power and regards with wonderment this heretofore "hidden talent."

Near the end of the film, Wally rushes in to propose to Ellen, only to find her in the arms of her boyfriend. Without a change of expression on his face, he watches them silently in utter disbelief, while the flower he is holding in his hand slowly wilts and dies. It's a totally unexpected throwback to the poignancy of *Three's a Crowd*, and perhaps because Langdon plays it so eloquently (he doesn't say a word), the moment works beautifully.

WHAT THE CRITICS SAID:
Motion Picture News, *October 18, 1930; Reviewed by Dick Crenshaw*

Harry Langdon and Slim Summerville are seen at their best as the innocents in this farce of underworld life. This picture will hold appeal to admirers of the Langdon type of humor, although some of it will not go over with those who care for a rational story.

Plenty of box-office value in this with the Langdon and Summerville names. Will stand up in the week-run houses and subsequent bookings.

Underworld life is portrayed as being quite comical and collegiate, with its theme songs and gang yells. Trick forts built on the tops of skyscrapers furnish the novel setting for a large part of the picture and plenty of action is seen.

A good supporting cast of Hollywood's ugliest and toughest hombres adds to the atmosphere. Summerville shares the acting glory in this film, making a perfect partner for Langdon. Bessie Love furnishes the love interest, although her part is rather unconvincing…

The picture has plenty of comedy appeal and should click with any audience.

Film Daily, *November 23, 1930*

There's enough nutty comedy and action in this satirical burlesque on the underworld to put it over with audiences everywhere. In addition, the names Harry Langdon, Slim Summerville and Bessie Love will count at the box-office…Miss Love's role is small. She furnishes an incidental love interest, leading the two tramps on and finally giving them the air for her district attorney boy friend.

Direction: Good. Photography: Okay.

New York Evening Post, *December 12, 1930; Reviewed by Thornton Delehanty*

That one-time popular screen comedian who was temporarily abashed by the talkies, causing him to relapse for awhile into making two-reel comedies, now comes forward in a full-length picture called See America Thirst, *which had a formal premiere yesterday at the Globe. Not to keep you in suspense any longer, the comedian's name is Harry Langdon, one of the best of the slapstick pantomimics.*

In his present vehicle he does not get much opportunity to indulge those wry facial contortions and half-witted gestures which marked his particular brand of comedy. For one thing the dialogue slows him down, just as it has stultified others of the old school of screen actors; and since the dialogue of See America Thirst *is only moderately funny it automatically imposes that much of a handicap on Mr. Langdon.*

Aside from the slight disappointments of its acting and dialogue, See America Thirst *is a wholesome and breezy satire on the much-belabored gangster film. It has at least the courage of an idea, and since both courage and ideas are all too conspicuously absent from the general run of Hollywood products, this combination of the two in* See America Thirst *furnishes an hour of refreshing entertainment.*

There is very little in the exciting panorama of underworld life that does not receive a degree of sly comment and spoofing. The beer barons and high-powered racketeers are shown dining sumptuously if dangerously in a dazzlingly modernistic nightclub, holding conferences in a paneled office where an oil painting of their beloved leader

Langdon, Bessie Love and Summerville in See America Thirst.

scowls at them (Tar Face Spumoni is his name, and he's sojourning in Florida for his health) or lounging elegantly in penthouse apartments.

It is Harry Langdon and Slim Summerville who are unwittingly injected into this atmosphere and are accepted by the gangsters under the impression that they are two of the most lethal gunmen at large. Terrified at their predicament, but not knowing how to escape, they involve themselves in a series of escapades which include perilous danglings from the skyscraper roots à la Harold Lloyd and triumphant if accidental annihilation of their enemies à la Harold Lloyd.

If the satiric note is evident throughout the picture in the modernistic settings it is no less so in such directorial touches which show rival gangs lined up in trenches on either side of a street and shooting it out in a heavy machine-gun barrage while the police apparently are keeping discreetly out of the way, or in the incident where a gunman, who has been hijacked on the road, is handed a pistol by his superior as the only honorable way out of his disgrace. He salutes and goes into the next room; there is a muffled shot, and instantly he pokes his head back through the door and says, "I missed."

Slim Summerville and Harry Langdon are diverting if not always hilarious. Bessie Love is agreeable in an unimportant part, and the others of the cast are realistically ferocious. It is a healthy sign when the film producers begin satirizing themselves, and for this reason See America Thirst is worthy of imitation.

New York Times, *December 12, 1930; Reviewed by Mordaunt Hall*

Timid Harry Langdon and brusque Slim Summerville are partners in crime in See America Thirst, a talking film now at the Globe. This effusuion may be intended as a satire on gangsters, but it is really a burlesque on the bad men of America with a strong suggestion of a nightmare. There are sequences that recall Harold Lloyd's mid-air exploits and others that bring to mind those old silent comedies.

In the settings for some of the scenes no little ingenuity is displayed, but it is a pity that a similar cunning was not devoted to the dialogue, for there is seldom anything said that is laughable. Virtually all the amusement is aroused through the actions of the players. The sight of Messrs. Langdon and Summerville having a hectic time on a racketeer's penthouse cannon poked out over Broadway is apt not only to make persons laugh, but also to make them a bit anxious for the poor, benighted Wally and Slim. These two are mistaken by gangsters for desperate chieftans who revel in the names of "Shivering" Smith and "Gun-kissed" Casey.

Wally (Mr. Langdon) is about as dense as any slapstick comedian was ever supposed to be and Slim (Mr. Summerville) is scarcely rational any of the time. During this hardy adventure, buttons that are pressed may bring forth almost anything, including an armored covering for a gangster's bed and monster pieces of artillery, that jut out from the top of a skyscraper. Doors close mysteriously and, the racketeer may find that the covered platter before him is meant for his end and not for nourishment — a pistol pops up where food was expected.

A mysterious gas concocted by a crazy inventor helps Wally and Slim to get out of their difficulty when the real "Shivering" Smith and "Gun-kissed" Casey, accompanied by the snobbish Spumoni, come North to put them on the spot.

The audience yesterday afternoon appeared to be thoroughly amused at many of the incidents. Mr. Langdon's voice at first sounded very far away, but finally he, or the sound apparatus, gained confidence and the words were clearer. It is, however, hardly a vehicle suited to Mr. Langdon's particular style of comedy. Mr. Summerville enters into the spirit of the events with gusto and he gets more out of the banal lines than does his colleague.

For the sake of romance, Bessie Love is called upon to officiate as a gangster's favorite, but soon the spectator is taken into the producer's confidence and one learns that Ellen (Miss Love), is really a brave girl working for the district attorney.

Variety, *December 17, 1930; reviewed by Shan*

In the metropolitan centers this film will get its own laughs and support. Not an undue attracter, but a fair programmer. Picture looks as if it had been aimed at satire, but it pops travesty. Hitched together for farce, it pulls slapstick. That makes it curved for exploitation, with the romance angle not helping. Title should help.

Part of the story is great, at other times it is dull. More pantomime and less dialogue for the Langdonian characteristics of misty eyes and pasty face would have created some subtlety that is wholly lacking. Instead, this system was used on Summerville. Langdon's voice is known through his shorts. This is his first feature to be released, and without too much talk he'd whiz by anytime. He's from vaude[ville] anyway.

Here he is a goofy hobo pal of Summerville, both being snapped up mistakenly for gangster killers and adopted by one gang to wipe out another. Funny things follow for complications, but the windup is blah. On the roof, where rival gang chieftains are imagined with French 75's, the film reverts to the old-fashioned hoke made acutely prominent by Harold Lloyd. Shows both Langdon and

Summerville hanging in mid-air from the cannon mouths. Here it's too long and half as much is more than enough.

Bessie Love plays the heart and has little to do. Summerville is the most serious histrionically. He actually has the biggest part, and on performance is okay.

Direction shows silent technique throughout, and is unmindful of the talker advent. Rub is that this system got reversed in the important sequences.

Maybe the fact that only one woman and her being used so slightly will hurt. Some café stuff with unintelligible music also shown, but there seems only enough legit laughs to really punch for two and a half reels.

Harrison's Reports, *December 20, 1930*

A fairly amusing burlesque on gunmen; but it becomes boresome after the first two reels because of the slow action. The dialogue is not funny, but the situations Harry Langdon and Slim Summerville find themselves in when they are mistaken for two notorious gangsters are amusing and at times suspensive. One such scene is where they both find themselves in the penthouse of the leader of one of the gangs. In trying to make their escape, they go out on the terrace. Langdon sits down on what he thinks is a seat but it turns out to be a battleship gun and Summerville, playing around with the machinery, unknowingly pushes a lever and the barrel slides out, leaving Langdon suspended in the air. In the next scene, Summerville finds himself in a similar predicament. These situations are somewhat similar to those in Lloyd's Safety Last[!].

The talk is clear.

The Big Flash

A Mermaid Comedy Released in Two Reels. PRODUCED AND DIRECTED BY Arvid E. Gillstrom. STORY BY Robert Vernon and Frank Griffin. CAST: Harry Langdon, Vernon Dent, Lita Chevret, Ruth Hiatt, Matthew Betz, King Baggot, Jack Grey, Bobby Dunn. WORKING TITLE: "The Photographer." Copyright November 6, 1932, Registration Number LM3590. Released by Educational Film Exchanges, Inc., November 6, 1932.

SYNOPSIS: Mr. Hinkle, editor of the *Daily News*, is asking his reporters to get a photo of Rick Dugan's girl. They tell him that Dugan, a gangster, will bump them off if they try.

Harry is a janitor in the newspaper building. He flirts with Betty, the secretary, until Krause (Vernon Dent), the electrician, tells him that she's *his* girl and that they're going to married. She says that she won't marry either of them.

Krause soon discovers that Harry took a photo of the editor and his girlfriend. He shows the photo to the editor and takes the credit. Hinkle then gives him an assignment to get a photo of Dugan's girl. He quickly makes Harry his assistant. Dugan's girl gets a tip that two men are coming to her apartment to get a photo. When Krause and his assistant arrive,

Harry pauses to get some uncooked popcorn; he tells Krause that he likes it that way. After they enter the apartment Dugan's girl changes into a slinky dress and flirts with Harry. While Krause is making time with her maid, Harry assembles a large camera from the newspaper and poses Dugan's girl on a couch. She responds by kissing him, which causes him to sway, then drop in a swoon. Dugan and some gangsters arrive and Krause and Harry depart in haste.

Later, in the editor's office, Hinkle gets a tip from Dugan's girl that he's going to rob a jewelry store. The editor tells Krause to cover the story, and gives him a machine gun. Outside the office, Krause tells Harry that he's going to photograph a gunman at work. Harry says he's scared of gunmen. He ends up firing the machine gun and causing havoc.

Krause and Harry set up a trashcan and a tent in front of the bank. Dugan eventually shows up, but Harry tips him off about the filming and breaks the jewelry store window with a brick. Dugan grabs some jewels and Harry is caught in a gun battle between a cop and the thief. Harry ends up chasing Dugan and causes him to be knocked out by bricks. The arresting cop informs him that he'll get a reward of $1,000. Betty shows up and embraces Harry, and they kiss. Betty's kiss is so hot that the popcorn in Harry's pants begins to pop. Krause then sets fire to some film attached to some flash powder in Harry's pants, which soon explodes. Harry asks Betty if she feels a draft; she says, no, she doesn't. He says it must be imagination on his part. As they walk off together, it is revealed that the seat of Harry's pants has been torn away.

ANALYSIS: Off the screen for two years, the Little Elf returns full-force in *The Big Flash*. It's similar to the later Roach shorts in some respects, especially in the reappearance of gags and routines from the silent days. However, the addition of Vernon Dent adds a new element. Dent's character, Krause, freely uses an unwitting Harry to further his own career, enabling the audience to root for Harry's success. Krause isn't an overt bully like Jim in *The Shrimp*; he's an opportunist who is not much higher in status than Harry. Ultimately, it isn't Harry's ability that wins the day; neither his nor Krause's schemes prove successful. Rather, it's the Elf's Divine providence that enables him to finally get the photo he needs, overpower Dugan and win Betty.

HARRY MOMENT: When Dugan's girl kisses Harry, his arms fall to the side and he teeters back and forth before swooning. This is a great example of his innocent character and his naïveté regarding women. The teetering act is one he performed in his earliest stage appearances.

WHAT THE CRITICS SAID:
Hollywood Filmograph, *September 10, 1932; Reviewed by Lou Jacobs*

Here we have an Educational short that is truly spice for any man's program. For a laugh-getter, The Big Flash *is unexcelled. It is pure hokum of the slappiest order, yet has a plot burlesquing the newspaper angle of the crime wave that hangs together despite the absurdities. The gagging is novel, particularly the pocketful of raw popcorn that pops under the heat of a fervid love scene.*

Harry Langdon is at his best and is ably assisted by Vernon Dent. His frozen pan blundering in the character of an assistant newspaper photographer snapping the robbery of a jewelry store kept the audience at the Uptown screaming. Who ever said Harry Langdon is to make a comeback in pictures is absolutely wrong. As far as the public is concerned he never went away. He is more welcome than ever.

Ruth Hiatt provides the love interest and Lita Chevret the vamp devilment. The latter gave evidence of possessing fine balance and understanding of values and is very pleasing to look at.

Great credit should be given Bobby Vernon for the story. Frank Griffin, too, for the adaptation and dialogue, shares honors. The photography of Gus Peterson was exceptional, especially the novelty fadeouts. Arvid Gillstrom did a sweet job of directing, losing no opportunity for milking every situation of its fun possibilities. This short subject should rate high in the yearly score.

Film Daily, *October 15, 1932*

Harry Langdon does a comeback with Vernon Dent as his comedy partner in this Mermaid Comedy. They are porters in a newspaper office, and get promoted to news photographers. Harry has a dinky little camera that he experiments with. They are sent out to cover a robbery of a jewelry store on a tipoff. Langdon gets between the yegg and the cop shooting it out, and automatically takes pictures of the gunman, then captures him through a fluke and wins the reward. Plenty of gags and nice comedy work on the part of Langdon make this look like a strong laugh number.

Motion Picture Herald, *October 15, 1932*

Besides marking the return of Harry Langdon, this comedy is an excursion into the technique of the silent days. Langdon as a combination janitor-assistant news photographer, is assigned to get a picture of a robbery for his newspaper. The way he considers and goes about his assignment creates a load of laughs and provides farcical entertainment for the kids as well as grownups. Everything is done as it shouldn't be done and in the most foolish way. The picture moves along in a zippy style. Careful restriction of the amount of dialogue coupled with abundant use of many of the oldtime gags that [were] featured [in] the silent short subjects gives the picture plenty to amuse your patrons.

Variety, *October 25, 1932; Reviewed by Shan*

Interest in this two-reeler comes first from the fact that it brings Harry Langdon back to the screen. As a panto artist Langdon has few superiors. Herein, as in the past comedies by Langdon, his biggest moments come when he is pantomiming.

In that short sequence where Langdon finger talks to Vernon Dent and perepares to give the cop a distracting boot in the pants Langdon pulls a hearty laugh. But in the slight chatter moments, where the dialog he uses comprises more than a single exclamatory expression, the reaction is not so hot.

However, the makers of the short have done something here that bears study. That's the injection of serious dramatic moments by fairly able players in a scene with a newspaper editor.

The short, while from a photographic and technical angle being well made, fails to sustain the fullest comedy intent and falls short of fulfilling big-time laugh expectations. Okay outside the bigger combos and deluxers.

Motion Picture, *January 1933; Reviewed by James Edwin Reid*

The Big Flash *is the signal for a long, sustained clapping of hands — for it brings back Harry Langdon, the wistful-innocent comic, to two-reel comedies, where he once reigned as king. And this trial effort is so successful that he has just been handed a contract for a series. He is a downtrodden assistant janitor in a newspaper office, who has a flair for taking snapshots, and gets orders, first, to photograph a gangster's sweetheart and then a big robbery. With a minimum of dialogue and some skillful pantomime, he carries out his assignments with sly humor. And he has two helpful companions in Vernon Dent and Lita Chevret.*

WHAT THE EXHIBITORS SAID:
Motion Picture Herald, *January 21, 1933*
Another dandy two-reel comedy from Educational.
Charles Wiles, Wiles Theatre, Anamose, IA.
Small town patronage.

Motion Picture Herald, *January 28, 1933*
If all of Langdon's new comedies are as good as this one, we certainly want them. This is one of the best two-reel comedies ever on our screen. Running time, 20 minutes.
A. N. Miles, Eminence Theatre, Eminence, KY.
Small town patronage.

Motion Picture Herald, *February 4, 1933*
A good comedy. This little guy is funny.
Bert Silver, Silver Family Theatre, Greenville, MI.

Tired Feet

A Mermaid Comedy Released in Two Reels. PRODUCED AND DIRECTED BY Arvid E. Gillstrom. STORY BY Robert Vernon and Frank Griffin. CAST: Harry Langdon, Vernon Dent, Shirley Blake, Maidena Armstrong, Eddie Baker, William Irving, Leslie Goodwin. Copyright January 1, 1933, Registration Number LM3854. Released by Educational Film Exchanges, Inc., January 1, 1933.

SYNOPSIS: Mr. Krause, sitting at the breakfast table, tells Aunt Hattie that he's bought another garage and is going to take a trip to the mountains. Upon hearing an alarm, he remarks that the dumbbell mailman must be sleeping in again. Krause goes upstairs and finds Harry in bed with an alarm clock. After being nudged, Harry struggles to wake up. Eventually, he arrives for breakfast, but is too late. Katie brings a cup of coffee and reminds him that it is his day off. As they agree to go to the beach, Aunt Hattie announces that she and Katie are going to the mountains. Harry states that they are going to the beach. Later, in the mountains, Aunt Hattie, with Katie as a passenger, drives Harry's car. It is laden with supplies, upon which Harry sits. He is soon knocked off by an overhanging pipe, which goes unnoticed by the girls.

The car develops engine trouble and grinds to a halt; Krause pulls up alongside and suggests the girls accompany him. As they prepare to continue, Harry shows up and is told to tie his broken car to the rear of Krause's auto. Shortly after they move away, the front wheels of Harry's car are pulled off and he is left behind. What's left of his car begins to roll backward down the mountain road and Harry struggles to regain control. As Krause and party pull into a camp they notice that Harry is missing. His car soon rolls down by them and crashes, leaving Harry hanging from a tree branch. He manages to get down and is ordered to carry all the supplies up to the camp.

He barely manages to do so, and winds up with sore feet in the process. Harry gets a bucket of water and manages to drench Aunt Hattie. He spots a girl using a punching bag and begins to hit a bee's nest, enraging the insects. Krause brings a chicken, and Harry is told to fix lunch. Instead, he lets the chicken escape and Krause pursues it, only to fall in a lake. Sometime later, Harry clangs a bell and announces that the food is ready.

This announcement attracts three tramps that sit down at the table expecting to be fed. They chase away Harry, who joins Krause in trying to evict them.

They repel Krause, who tells Harry to put on women's clothes and evict them. Harry flirts with two of the tramps and leads them to a tent, where Krause knocks them out. The second tramp accidentally knocks out Krause inside the tent. As Harry flirts with the third tramp his dress is accidentally removed and he gets in a scuffle. The last tramp is knocked out inside the tent. Harry grabs the beehive and tosses it into the tent.

Krause and the three tramps lift up the tent and run away. He tells Katie that his feet are killing him and as they sit on a rock by the lake Harry dunks his feet in the water. A cloud of steam arises as he breathes a sigh of relief.

ANALYSIS: *Tired Feet* goes heavy on slapstick, with the result that it's a bit of a letdown after *The Big Flash*. Also, unlike the prior film, there's no background music, possibly due to the extensive location shooting and its impact on the budget. An appropriate score could have livened up the proceedings.

Harry is beleaguered by both his girlfriend's mother (who's also his landlady) and Vernon Dent: he's forced to go camping in the mountains, he has problems with his car, and he is forced to dress in drag to deal with the hoboes. Surprisingly, although the balky waterspout gag is resurrected from *Johnny's New Car*, the scenes in which Harry tends to his decrepit automobile bear no resemblance to the action described in his most famous vaudeville act. The situations have cast him not so much as the perplexing Elf as a poor soul.

There's also a bit of risqué humor in the sequence when Vernon dresses Harry in drag. The two argue while pushing Harry's fake bosom from side to side.

HARRY MOMENT: Water stops flowing every time Harry approaches the spout. Although not a uniquely "Harry" gag, it was one of the oldest in his repertoire, as he used it in *Johnny's New Car*.

WHAT THE CRITICS SAID:
Hollywood Filmograph, *November 5, 1932; Reviewed by Hal Wiener*

Harry Langdon's latest laughie, Tired Feet, *will be a credit to any exhibitor's program. This Educational release has what it takes to make audiences laugh. Slapstick? Sure, but the type that just can't help but bring gales of chuckles. It was written by Bobby Vernon and Frank Griffin…*

Typical Harry Langdon gags are constructed throughout the picture to the best of advantage by Director Arvid Gillstrom. And he knows how to anticipate [what an] audience wants. At the Fairfax Theater preview, showgoers were delighted at the various antics performed by Harry Langdon.

Vernon Dent, Gladys Blake, Maidena Armstrong, Eddie Baker, Bill Irving and Les Goodwin supported the comedian in his rampage of comedy.

We noticed, also, that the minimum of dialogue was used, thereby assuring the greatest amount of laughs through the natural form of funmaking — pantomime.

Hollywood On Parade #A-6

A Paramount Picture Released in One Reel. PRODUCED BY Louis Lewyn. CAST: Alvin "Shipwreck" Kelly, El Brendel, Viola Dana, Jimmie Thompson, Bing Crosby, Harry Langdon. Seen in silent footage: Joe E. Brown, Charlie Chaplin, Paulette Goddard, Harold Lloyd, Charles Farrell, Robert Montgomery, Edmund Lowe, Johnny Weissmuller, Lupe Velez, Mary Pickford. Copyright January 12, 1933, Registration Number LM3746. Released by Paramount Publix Corp., January 13, 1933.

SYNOPSIS: "Shipwreck" Kelly, world's champion flagpole sitter, shows a bevy of starlets how to do the stunt. While perched at the top of the pole, each uses a periscope to view various Hollywood stars at play: El Brendel receives a workout by a masseuse; Joe E. Brown does calisthenics on his lawn; several stars are viewed at the racetrack; and golf pro Jimmie Thompson shows his wife, Viola Dana, how to swing a club; Bing Crosby also demonstrates his technique, but his ball winds up in the lake.

When his own ball disappears, Thompson asks Harry Langdon if he's found any golf balls. Harry replies that it's a dirty lie. Jimmy asks him if he's positive that he hasn't found any balls. Jimmy then shakes Harry's hand and prepares to leave. Harry raises his hat and golf balls fall to the course. He then walks away.

ANALYSIS: One year after the demise of Tiffany's Voice of Hollywood, Louis Lewyn moved over to Paramount to inaugurate the Hollywood on Parade series. Backed by a major studio, the resulting shorts were much more interesting, if equally as contrived.

Langdon's bit was filmed at a nearby golf course. He is nattily dressed in golfing togs, he wears glasses and his hat is not the usual round-brimmed felt. He does his bit perfunctorily; one suspects that he resented having his game interrupted to perform without compensation. Nevertheless, the gag idea clearly originated with him, and he would repeat it in another Paramount short, *A Roaming Romeo*.

HARRY MOMENT: After being cleared of stealing Jimmie Thompson's golf ball, Harry tips his hat and several balls come cascading out of it. This bit closed Scene One of *After the Ball*, Langdon's vaudeville turn during 1921–23 and 1931–32.

Hallelujah! I'm a Bum

Joseph M. Schenck presents a Lewis Milestone Production. 89 minutes. DIRECTED BY Lewis Milestone. ORIGINAL STORY BY Ben Hecht. ADAPTATION BY S.N. Behrman. MUSIC AND LYRICS BY Richard Rodgers and Lorenz Hart. PHOTOGRAPHED BY Lucien Andriot. ART DIRECTOR: Richard Day. RECORDING ENGINEER: Oscar Legerstrom. CAST: Al Jolson, Madge Evans, Frank Morgan, Harry Langdon, Edgar "Blueboy" Connor, Chester Conklin, Tyler Brooke, Dorothea Wolbert, Tammany Young, Louise Carver. Working title: "The New Yorker." Reissue title: "The Heart of New York." Copyright February 6, 1933, Registration Number LM3665; Renewed February 29, 1960, Number R252953. Released by United Artists Corporation, February 3, 1933.

SYNOPSIS: Bumper (Al Jolson) is considered the "Mayor of Central Park" by all its other homeless hobo denizens. Although street sweeper Egghead (Harry Langdon), who is a devout believer that the workers will soon unite in a revolution against capitalism, often harasses him for flouting his nomad status, Bumper and his "manservant," Acorn, revel in their lives as "bums." Yet Bumper is also a man of principle and strives to do right by everyone; consequently, he's beloved by everyone. Even Sunday, the sleepy driver of a horse-drawn cab, laughs with delight when he finds that the passengers he's transported to a local restaurant are Bumper and Acorn.

Bumper also shares a friendship with the New York City's actual mayor, whose life he once saved. As it happens, the mayor has a steady relationship with a showgirl, June Marcher, but he repeatedly (and

unjustly) doubts her fidelity. When she loses her purse, which contains a $1,000 bill given her by the mayor, he accuses her of having given the money to a lover. Through neglect, the purse winds up in Egghead's trashcan, and then into the hands of Bumper. He tries to return it, but Miss Marcher has decided to leave town. The mayor comes to her apartment and finds Bumper there. When Bumper gives him the purse, and he sees the money is still there, he's elated and gives the bill to Bumper, who distributes the cash amongst his hobo pals and Egghead. The mayor alerts the police to search for June.

That evening, June attempts to commit suicide by jumping off a bridge into Central Park Lake, but Bumper witnesses this and rescues her. The shock of the attempt has given June amnesia. As Bumper takes care of the girl he calls "Angel," they fall in love. He finds her an apartment and, through the mayor's intervention, gets a job for himself and Acorn in a bank. This alienates him from his hobo pals, and they place him on trial in the park, via a makeshift "Kangaroo Court." Egghead defends him, and after stating his case, Bumper is found not guilty by reason of insanity.

Meanwhile, the mayor has not been successful in locating June, and has taken to drink. One evening he turns up very drunk, and Bumper escorts him home. The mayor bemoans the loss of his love, and shows Bumper her photograph. Bumper realizes that June is his "Angel," and takes the mayor to her apartment. Once she sees him, she faints; when she comes to, her memory has returned and she no longer recognizes Bumper. The mayor pledges his love to June, and Bumper willingly returns to his former life.

ANALYSIS: As far as musicals go, *Hallelujah! I'm A Bum* is charming and agreeably free from overacting, so that its contrivances don't seem too overt or convenient. Al Jolson, as ebullient a performer as ever trod the boards, practically underplays the role of Bumper, and the rest of the cast is equally restrained. The "rhythmic dialogue," for the most part, is clever and catchy and foreshadows a time when musicals would use production numbers not simply for entertainment value but to advance the plot. Alas, its staggering production costs, coupled with the state of the economy, doomed this modest, diverting film of any hope of box-office success.

As Egghead, Langdon portrays a political radical, and the role is a radical departure for him. He makes the most of what he's given, but doesn't really get a chance to shine, and one wonders just how much all the reshooting impacted the size of his part. His outfit is that of his usual screen character, and makeup continued to mask his true age (he was then 48); basically he looks just as he did in the silent days. His past experience with music on stage serves him well, as he handles the "rhythmic dialogue" sequences with ease. Yet considering his reputation for pantomime, Langdon is given next-to-nothing by way of visual

comedy. One or two "silent" comedy sequences might have tempered those critics who thought the film was too verbose.

HARRY MOMENT: After Bumper distributes $1,000 among his friends of the park, Egghead uses his share to get very drunk. As Bumper walks by, Egghead gives him the typical "Harry hand wave," then passes out.

WHAT THE CRITICS SAID:
Variety, *December 23, 1932*

As different from any previous Jolson picture as Edna St. Vincent Millay is from Al Smith. And Ben Hecht has become an active competitor of Hans Christian Anderson or Mother Goose. Here is a light, ethereal musical fantasy, entertaining and airy. But it hasn't the socko and that lack keeps even the nicest ideas from paying negative costs. Unless, however, the Jolson air plugging of the pictures has built up enough interest to send them boxofficewards....

Jolson does a first-rate job as [a] hobo and bursts into song frequently, but it's a new type of vocal delivery for him. He has but one regular type of a number, "Hallelujah[!] I'm a Bum Again." Rest is all singing dialog and short snatches. Same applies for every other member of the cast. Therefore, despite the great scoring and lyrical job performed by Rodgers and Hart, there's nothing to carry out of the theater to associate with Jolson, which was a great factor in his past successes. What is in the picture is entertainment for the moment it is seen and heard.

Secondary honors are split between Frank Morgan, as the mayor, Harry Langdon, as a Red street cleaner, and a tiny ebony pal of Jolson's, played by Blueboy Conners (sic). This picture should make Conners, who has a pert, bright personality and a perfect set of molars for smiling. Madge Evans makes an appealing feminine lead. Chester Conklin and Tyler Brooke handle their smaller roles with neatness and dispatch. Tammany Young, as the most prominent of the park bums, was the shrewdest casting of the picture.

Opening sequence was a bit dim in sight and sound. Outstanding musical scenes were "Going to New York," "Laying the School Cornerstone," "Bumper Found a Grand," and "Kangaroo Court." Finale drags a little in tempo. Aside from that, direction, photography and musical recording showed cleverness and unusual touches. (Reviewed at preview screening, Alexander Theater, Glendale, CA, December 18, 1932.)

Hollywood Filmograph, *December 24, 1932.*
Reviewed by Harold Weight

We who have been wailing for a Rene Clair touch in American musical pictures need wail no more. Three-fourths of Al Jolson's first United Artists' picture, Hallelujah[!] I'm a Bum, *previewed in Glendale Sunday night, is as good as the justly celebrated Frenchman's best. Lewis Milestone's genius, shining brightly again, is responsible for a picture that will rank in 1933's list of "best." Two others to whom a major slice of credit is due are Richard Rodgers and Lorenz Hart, the men responsible for the music of this charming film.*

The cast of Hallelujah[!] I'm a Bum *is an excellent one, down to minor roles. Al Jolson has the most prominent*

"Blueboy" Connor, Dorothea Wolbert, Al Jolson, Langdon, Tammany Young and John George in Hallelujah! I'm A Bum.

part, and gives his best motion picture performance. His singing is far above his past performances. I would [praise] Harry Langdon as the communistic park cleaner, and Edgar Connor as Acorn, Jolson's colored pal. Harry Langdon gives his best performance since the memorable Tramp, Tramp, Tramp.

Frank Morgan played the Mayor of New York with a sure, polished hand. Particularly was he good when impersonating a drunk. Chester Conklin was another to attract attention. Madge Evans was charming in the leading feminine role. Tyler Brooke and Louise Carver were excellent.

Ted Billings did a very find job of "The Fiddler." His work stood out very far above the many bits in the picture, and is worthy of special attention and commendation.

This is not an actor's picture, however. It is, as should be the case, a film rising above its elements. Upon the shoulders of director, musician, and camera man lies the burden and the credit. Lucien Andriot photographed the picture in outstanding fashion. The adaptation was by S. N. Behrman from an original story by Ben Hecht.

To me, the outstanding hit of this film is the singing of "America" by the school children, while the camera cuts from face to face with each note. The effect is grand, resembling, but from a comedy angle, the effect of the closing moments of Eisenstein's Romance Sentimentale. Another great bit is Jolson's singing of the hit number of the piece, "Hallelujah[!] I'm a Bum Again." During this, the camera occupies itself with pictures of everything but Jolson's face, and the effect is a swinging tune in pictures.

Mark Hallelujah[!] I'm a Bum down as one of those pictures which must be seen. Hallelujah, what a show!

Film Daily, *January 27, 1933*

This one presents a curious combination of foreign musical technique and a thin American story. It is overbrimming with songs, most of which are handled by Jolson in the same Jolson style which characterized his early talker successes. Particularly clever are the lyrics. The supporting players, particularly Frank Morgan and Harry Langdon, are good but are unable to overcome the tremendous handicap imposed by the story, sluggish with songs. The picture includes a number of very expert bits of business.

Direction: Fair, Photography: Fine.

New York Evening Post, *February 9, 1933; Reviewed by Thornton Delehanty*

The unfortunate thing about Rene Clair is the baleful influence he exerts on the producers who try to imitate him. Being an original and elusive personality, his tricks have a way of defying reproduction, and nowhere can you find a more lamentable form of flattery than in the devices whereby the authors of Hallelujah! I'm a Bum have sought to capture the peculiar irresponsibility which is the distinctive characteristic of his work.

The picture which we have under consideration is Al Jolson's latest starring vehicle, which came last night to the Rivoli. Mr. Jolson has been in more or less of retirement since his fabulously successful The Jazz Singer, and his emergence as a hobo hero in Hallelujah has all the earmarks of bewilderment. You can't exactly blame him if he flounders through the story, because it is the kind of story which practically imposes floundering on any one who plays in it.

Ben Hecht is credited with the story and Mr. Hecht must have gone berserk after attending a preview of A Nous la Liberte. With what appears to have been his left hand, he has provided a rambling and incoherent travesty on municipal government, contrasting a beloved vagabond who dominates the transient inhabitants of Central Park to a splendiferous pre-depression ruler of City Hall.

The bond which unites these divergent individuals is encased in the person of June Marcher, an errant beauty who bounces from the jealous arms of the mayor into the Salvation Army embrace of the beloved vagabond. Miss Marcher serves throughout the story as a kind of lady-in-waiting to the two heroes, and she provides the means by which Mr. Jolson is able to make a noble renunciation in favor of the silk-hatted mayor.

If there is any more story to Hallelujah than this, please forgive us for refusing to tell it. We have had our spell of German and French films, minus subtitles, and we would much rather recount their plot than attempt to elucidate the intricacies of the Rivoli offering. Evidently Mr. Hecht and those others who worked on the shaping of the story were loathe to expose their formula. Rather than tramp out in the open with an honest-to-goodness tale, they preferred to cloak their intentions under a series of drawing-room experiments by the talented team of Rodgers and Hart, who in turn slyly hid their light under a bushel of what the publicity department is pleased to call a blanket of "rhythmic dialogue." As near as we can make out, "rhythmic dialogue" is a lot of words which, when run together and spoken by Al Jolson, sound like Ben Jonson with a stomach ache.

Though the story radiates a vague confusion, it is pulled together at sundry moments by the richly humorous performance of Frank Morgan as the (guess who?) mayor. Mr. Morgan is a splendid comedian, and last night we were grateful to him for a notable drunk scene.

Harrison's Reports, *February 18, 1933*

Boresome! The story is thin, and half of the dialogue is spoken rhythmically. A good deal of the dialogue among the tramps is given over to preachments about the social system, and although this is done in a comedy strain it becomes rather tiresome…

Suitable for children and Sunday showing, if they can stand for it.

Brooklyn Daily Eagle, *April 1, 1933; Reviewed by Martin Dickstein*

Al Jolson, who you may remember was the talkies' first star (in The Jazz Singer*), is again presented in a film with music — this time in* Hallelujah! I'm a Bum, *at Loew's Metropolitan. Prior to its Broadway premiere a few months ago, this production was hailed as a new departure in talking-and-singing pictures, possessing a brand new element of entertainment known as "rhythmic dialogue."*

Hallelujah! I'm a Bum *really isn't much of a departure at all, and that extravagantly heralded "rhythmic dialogue" turns out to be nothing more than a few badly written lyrics which at intervals are recited by the actors instead of being sung to music. In fact, if the truth must be told,* Hallelujah! I'm a Bum *is a much less satisfactory vehicle for Mr. Jolson than* The Jazz Singer. *And* The Jazz Singer *was produced "way back in the talkies" Stone Age, or nearly six years ago.*

Mr. Jolson enacts (and sings) the role of a genial tramp, who is a sort of headman of all the tramps in Central Park. What is more, he is a friend — in fact, a bosom pal — of the Mayor of New York. And when His Honor's sweetheart becomes the victim of an attack of amnesia, Bumper (Mr. Jolson) save her from drowning in the park lake and takes care of her like a good tramp until she recovers her memory and goes back to her beloved Mayor.

That's about all you need to know about Hallelujah! I'm a Bum, *aside from the fact that Director Milestone has attempted (but not always very successfully) to imitate the musical-film technique of Rene Clair. Mr. Jolson now and then bursts into song, singing such pieces as "Hallelujah! I'm a Bum Again" and "What Do You Want With Money?" but nary a single mammy sing (sic).*

Madge Evans plays the part of June, the Mayor's darling, and other important supporting roles are filled by Frank Morgan, Harry Langdon, Chester Conklin and Tammany Young.

Connor, Langdon, Jolson and Madge Evans in Hallelujah! I'm a Bum.

WHAT THE EXHIBITORS SAID:
Motion Picture Herald, *April 29, 1933*

A well-written play. Revised and polished to the last rub. Dialogue clever and painstakingly poetic with much of it in rhyme. Music so directed that the play is a mere appendix to the music, with the acting synchronized to the music. The delivery in rhyme quite suggestive of school days in sixth grade. Story thin, not to hurt anybody's head. Fantastic motions synchronized to music takes the place of acting. Jolson good but not quite up to his standard. There is no hokum in this play; therefore, there was absent the usual noisy applause of common people in waving the flag and singing the national anthem (the flag was not waved) which is usual at a community gathering or corner stone laying. Instead, the idiotic expressions and idiotic faces, often seen in a mixed gathering, were brought out. Nobody missed the hokum but they did miss the patriotism and didn't like the substitute. I again express my admiration for the work and finish of this play. But as to results: a good house the first night, with a number of walkouts. Second night: not enough people to keep from feeling lonely. Manager Jones just weepingly remarked "there will be nobody tonight." As to expressions heard in the lobby: "Nothing to it." "Another night gone to waste." "I waited and waited and nothing happened."
A.J. Gibbons, Illinois Theatre, Metropolis, IL.
General patronage.

Motion Picture Herald, *May 13, 1933*

Very ordinary entertainment, sez I. If Al would open his mouth, and pronounce his words so all could understand him, perhaps it might be a fairly good picture. His colored running mate is almost understandable. There are times when one can catch a word or two of what he is talking about. "A Bum" picture would be a fitting title for it. No business, and I don't wonder. Played April 25–27.
Jack Greene, Geneseo Theatre, Geneseo, IL.
Small town patronage.

The Hitch Hiker

A Mermaid Comedy Released in Two Reels. PRODUCED AND DIRECTED BY Arvid E. Gillstrom. STORY BY Robert Vernon and Frank Griffin. CAST: Harry Langdon, Vernon Dent, Ruth Clifford, William Irving, Chris Marie Meeker. WORKING TITLE: "The Pest." Copyright February 12, 1933, Registration Number LM3840. Released by Educational Films Corporation of America, February 12, 1933.

SYNOPSIS: Harry, a wandering hobo, has been sleeping by a movie location, and is told to leave by the irate director. Two actors, playing a scene, cause a baby carriage to fall in a lake. Harry hears their cries of distress, dives into the lake to save the "baby" and ruins the scene. Later, Harry, now with a cold, is hitchhik-

ing on a road. He is continually passed by and goes to an airport to hitch a ride on a plane. He has no luck and bumps into Vernon, causing a suitcase to be emptied of its contents. Vernon and his wife wait in line to catch their plane. Harry causes the wife to leave and a preoccupied Vernon hands him his wife's ticket by mistake. He boards with Vernon and soon the angry wife arrives, having purchased another ticket. The plane takes off as Harry sits between Vernon and his wife.

He begins coughing and sniffling, which annoys the married couple. Soon the other passengers register disapproval as Harry sneezes, causing a man's toupee to flip forward. Vernon becomes increasingly annoyed and begins to sneeze. Harry sprays his throat and spritzes Vernon by mistake. He manages to send his cough medicine into Vernon's face and is warned that if he sniffles once more he'll be tossed out the window. Harry waits, and then throws a tiny punch at Vernon, only to be slapped down in return. Harry timidly attempts to remove a mustard plaster, which is yanked off by Vernon, who laughs. As the sick one attempts to apply VapoRub to his chest, a jar of Limburger cheese falls near him. Harry rubs the offensive smelling cheese on his chest, to the distress of the other passengers. After applying dabs of cheese to his nostrils, Harry announces that he's getting better and beginning to smell. Vernon grabs the jar of cheese and throws it out a window. Harry throws a second puny punch at Vernon and is knocked down again. The angry husband puts a parachute on Harry and drops him from the plane.

The chute opens and, as Harry floats down, he begins to cut the cords with a knife. He then notices that he is falling to earth, and becomes afraid. Meanwhile, another take of the scene that Harry ruined is being attempted. The director calls for the baby carriage to be sent in as Harry falls in the lake, causing the whole crew to fall in the water.

ANALYSIS: *The Hitch Hiker* is a laugh-out-loud romp. The best-remembered moment from *The Strong Man* is given a modern setting, that of a passenger airplane, and loses nothing in the updating. All of the sight gags surrounding Harry's chest cold make a welcome reappearance. While the sound of coughing and sneezing can be a little disconcerting, and the pacing is just a tad sluggish, most of the gags are enhanced by the presence of Vernon Dent in the role of the surly passenger. Dent is given a few opportunities to react with Oliver Hardyish exasperation at Harry's predicament, and when Harry periodically responds with his own look of scorn, the result is actually funnier than in the original film.

The set-up for the situation, with Harry disrupting the filming of a melodrama, is wholly believable as is the moment when Dent, believing his wife is behind him, hands Harry her ticket without looking back. Although it's not explained how Harry gets to the airport, or how he expects to "thumb" a ride while standing aside a runway, the multitude of laughs significantly diminishes these problems. Even the obvious use of miniatures and process shots for

Sleepy Harry imposes on Vernon Dent in The Hitch Hiker.

Harry's parachute descent don't detract from the film, especially since the closing gag of his disrupting the same movie production a second time is quite clever.

HARRY MOMENT: The whole scene aboard the plane in which Harry struggles with his medicine shows his childlike concentration. He still looks quite youthful.

WHAT THE CRITICS SAID:
Hollywood Filmograph, *December 3, 1932; Reviewed by Harry Burns*

The Harry Langdon comedy The Hitch Hiker *has many hearty laughs in it. In fact, if you fail to laugh at this funmaker's antics in this one, you better hunt up a doctor very pronto. It has everything that a comedy should have. Langdon is one of those easy going happy-go-lucky kind of individuals who catches the eye of the audience the minute he appears on the screen. This comedy moves so fast that they will have to keep their optics glued on him not to lose a single mannerism or point of the funmaking. He is so ably assisted by Vernon Dent, who in a way, is another one of those Babe Hardy menaces. He acts as a foil for Harry Langdon, and helps to carry the burden of the story. Ruth Clifford, who plays Vernon Dent's wife, adds much to the picture; in fact it is the seriousness with which she plays her part that makes the comedy situation develop with such keen interest. Chris Marie Meeker, a new personality, imitated Greta Garbo in a very clever manner. William Irving, as the director, deserves special mention. Dorothy Vernon, Jack Gustin, Ralph Brooks, Les Goodwin, Hugh Saxon, Helen Curtis, Bruce Guiver and others helped the story along to a good comedy tempo. The direction of Arvid Gillstrom commands attention, for he brought the best out of Harry Langdon that we have seen and heard since he started making the two-reel Educational series.* The Hitch Hiker *was written by Robert Vernon and Dean Ward. They surely know their* LANGDON *and what he can do best. Excellent photography by Gus Peterson, and a good job of editing by Jack English. It tells the take of what* EXHIBITORS ARE TO EXPECT IN HARRY LANGDON'S LATEST FUN-FILM *— which Educational is to release in the world's best theaters.*

Film Daily, *January 12, 1933*

One of the best products in which this comedian has ever starred. The gag sequences are closely knit together, and the film moves along with a steadily ascending crescendo of laughs. Langdon is immense all the way… Harry pulls some great laughs with the help of the leading lady who does a Greta Garbo that is a scream. Arvid Gillstrom directed. Vernon Dent and Ruth Clifford are in the cast.

Variety, *January 12, 1933; Reviewed by Char*

Harry Langdon develops a cold and for intended purposes of comedy tries to make funny a cough and some sneezing. At first it's a little annoying, but finally his condition elicits a laugh or two. For the smaller houses.

On pantomime Langdon doesn't seem to be there in this one. He upsets a filming scene by diving into a lake to pull out a drowning baby dummy, thus contracting the cold. From there on his efforts to hitch-hike end in a plane, where he annoys everyone with his incessant coughing. It's done in that weak manner, along with sneezing, and eventually has Langdon looking as though he went through a wringer. Somehow or other it isn't as funny as it may sound. But when he goes into a wrong jar, getting Limburger cheese instead of Vapo-Rub to smear on his chest, the situation takes on some promise. For a finish an over-annoyed gent sitting close to Langdon knocks him cold, pins on a parachute and tosses the poor mugg (sic) out. He lands in the same lake where a director is trying to film another water scene, spoiling it again.

WHAT THE EXHIBITORS SAID:
Motion Picture Herald, *June 24, 1933*

Not as funny as the star's previous comedies, but got by to a few hearty laughs.
A. N. Miles Eminence Theatre, Eminence, KY. Small town patronage.

Knight Duty

A Mermaid Comedy Released in Two Reels. **PRODUCED AND DIRECTED BY** Arvid E. Gillstrom. **STORY BY** Dean Ward and William Watson. **CAST:** Harry Langdon, Vernon Dent, Matthew Betz, Lita Chevret, Nell O'Day, Eddie Baker, Billy Engle. **WORKING TITLE:** "Wise Dummies." Copyright May 7, 1933, Registration Number LM4001. Released by Educational Films Corporation of America, May 7, 1933.

SYNOPSIS: While in the park, a lady painter has her purse stolen. Harry, who is sleeping in a hammock, falls on the fleeing robber and knocks him out. He returns the purse and is praised by the painter for overcoming the brute. A cop arrives and scares Harry away; the artist explains his heroism and points out the crook, who manages to get away. Harry drops his hat near a water hose and is sprayed while trying to retrieve it. He makes several attempts and succeeds in getting completely soaked before he finally gets the hat. He boards a truck that soon leaves the park. The truck contains several wax figures.

Upon arriving at a museum, a waxen cop falls over and knocks Harry cold. All of the figures, including a stiff Harry, are carried into the museum. Harry regains consciousness by a bar and attempts to eat the free lunch. To his amazement, the food and beer are fake. He then eyes two wax gunmen aiming their weapons at him. He holds his hands up while construction workers outside use a drill that sounds like gunfire. Harry runs into the main part of the museum and asks a wax cop for help. When he gets no reply, he punches the cop and pulls its head off. Harry then reads a sign and realizes that he's in a wax museum.

The painter and the cop from the park arrive as Harry eludes a museum guard. The painter shows the cop an expensive ruby on display and worries about the possibility of theft. The cop reassures her and is promptly knocked down by a large vase.

Two crooks, a man and a woman, arrive and plan to disguise themselves as wax figures and steal the ruby. They are soon dressed as a cop and a scarlet lady. They steal the ruby and slip it in Harry's pocket to avoid detection. Harry disguises himself as a wax sultan and is soon discovered by the lady crook, who attempts to wrestle the jewel away from him. The park cop suggests to the museum guard that the crooks may be disguised as wax figures. The guard suggests sticking pins in the figures to find the criminals. The crooked cop forces the museum owner and the painter under a large basket.

The crooks chase Harry while he continues to elude the guard and the park cop. The crooks eventually grab the ruby from Harry, who soon frees the museum owner and painter from the basket. Harry ends up falling on the crooks and returns the ruby

Vernon Dent, Nell O'Day and Langdon in Knight Duty. *(Photo inscribed by Nell O'Day to author Edward Watz.)*

to the museum owner. He then gets in a car and is joined by the painter, who tells him he's wonderful. They drive away through the museum as a flap falls from the back of the car reading "So Long."

ANALYSIS: *Knight Duty* is perhaps the best and most consistent of all Langdon's sound shorts. It contains a lot of genuine laughs and some terrific pantomime.

This, plus *The Hitch Hiker* and the earlier comedy *The Shrimp*, prove beyond doubt that Langdon's character could, with the proper material, thrive in the talkie era.

The *Long Pants* gag in which Harry attempts to gain the attention of a dummy policeman is revived, as is the business from *The Strong Man* of a lady crook slipping something valuable — in this case a $200,000 ruby — into Harry's coat pocket and then having to forcibly retrieve it. Setting most of the action inside a wax museum was a novel concept, and the most was made of the opportunity. A running gag was created whereby a cop and the museum watchman attempt to identify the thieves by stabbing them with pins. Naturally it's Harry who bears the brunt of this punishment.

Vernon Dent, although second billed, is largely wasted as an incompetent cop who repeatedly gets clubbed over the head, forcing his helmet over his eyes. There's no variation to the business, which gets tiresome after awhile. Nell O'Day seems a little stiff and self-conscious at the start but becomes more comfortable as the film progresses. Fortunately, Langdon is in top form and carries off all the laughs.

HARRY MOMENT: Langdon displays exquisite full body pantomime skill when he attempts to control the water hose. His timing, gestures and gagging completely portray the playfulness of the Elf character.

WHAT THE CRITICS SAID:
Film Daily, *March 15, 1933*
  A Mermaid Comedy featuring Harry Langdon in a fast moving bit of fun that carries the laughs liberally through the entire footage… Some very ingenious gags are worked out, and the entire film is done practically in pantomime. It moves fast, and is one of Langdon's best.

Variety, *April 18, 1933; Reviewed by Rush*
  Shrinking Harry Langdon in a slapstick idea serves very well for a while, but wears thin toward the end of a two-reeler.
  Harry's a sleeping tramp who falls out of his roost in time to knock out an escaping purse snatcher, only, of course, to be mistaken for the thief. Chase leads to a wax museum, where there is the familiar mixup, Langdon posing as a figure while a jewel thief chase goes around him.
  Trick finish has the comic climb into an antique Ford exhibit, which miraculously starts up to carry him to an exit with the heroine.
  Fair stuff for a filler. But why doesn't somebody use this amusing clown in a real comedy? He's passé only because he has appeared for a long time in cluck material. Standard variety stage comedians don't die, but they can be starved to death.

Motion Picture Herald, *May 13, 1933; Reviewed by McCarthy, Hollywood*
  A lot of clowning in a wax museum. Langdon, fleeing from a fat park cop, finds refuge among the dummies. A man and woman, crooks, seek to steal a fabulously priced jewel. Laugh-exciting scenes as police and owner scout through the museum jabbing pins and wielding nightsticks trying to ascertain which are wax and which has feelings. Langdon finally gums things up so that the crooks are caught and as a reward he wins the owner's daughter. Absence of much dialogue and plenty of "sock 'em" action combine to make this short plenty comic.

WHAT THE EXHIBITORS SAID:
Motion Picture Herald, *July 1, 1933*

This is not an uproarious comedy, but it is decidedly good. Laid in a wax museum, the setting is different and interesting.
A. N. Miles, Eminence Theatre, Eminence, KY.
Small town patronage.

Motion Picture Herald, *January 20, 1934*

This is a fairly good two-reel comedy with Harry Langdon and should produce many laughs. It is of the slapstick variety and very funny. Our entire audience seemed well pleased and many laughed through the entire two reels.
J. J. Medford, Orpheum Theatre, Oxford, N. C.
General patronage.

Tied for Life

A Mermaid Comedy Released in Two Reels. PRODUCED AND DIRECTED BY Arvid E. Gillstrom. STORY BY Dean Ward and Vernon Dent. CAST: Harry Langdon, Vernon Dent, Nell O'Day, Mabel Forrest, Elaine Whipple, Eddie Baker. WORKING TITLE: "All Aboard." Copyright July 2, 1933, Registration Number LM4024. Released by Educational Films Corporation of America, July 2, 1933.

SYNOPSIS: Harry awakens to the sound of a quartet singing about his upcoming marriage. He brings them some beers, only to be doused with buckets of water. Meanwhile, his bride, Nell, is being dressed as her mother complains that Harry hasn't arrived for the wedding. In his room, Harry is dressed and checks to see if he has the ring. He looks into a mirror, which shatters, and as he leaves the house a black cat crosses his path.

He trips on a hose and drops the ring onto the street. A car, driven by Vernon, pulls up and a tire stops on top of the ring. As the car leaves, the ring becomes stuck to the tire. Harry jumps on the running board and slashes the tire with a knife as the car drives on. The tire becomes shredded; after the car stops, Harry retrieves the ring. He hands a jack to Vernon, and leaves. Harry arrives just in time for the wedding to begin. Shortly after, Vernon, a rival for Nell's affection, arrives; he sees that the ceremony is in progress and departs. As Harry kisses the bride, her flowers wilt.

Later, on the honeymoon train, Harry sits with Nell and suggests turning in. Her mother glares at him as his wife says that she isn't sleepy. Harry reminds her that they'll both be in berth nine. Harry gets his pajamas as his wife retires to their berth. Vernon, disguised as a porter, turns the numbers on berths nine and six to read the opposite. Harry goes to berth "nine" and makes cooing sounds before entering. He kisses who he thinks is his wife as her husband returns. Harry suggests the angry husband thinks

Vernon Dent, Nell O'Day and Langdon use a novel means of transportation to get to the Tied For Life *set.*

that something is wrong and the spouse punches out another passenger by mistake. Harry pulls a cord and the train stops, causing the passengers to fall out of their berths. He climbs over the pile of bodies and is reunited with his wife in the real berth nine, much to the frustration of both Vernon and Nell's mother.

Much later, Vernon, his wife and their baby are strolling through the park. They meet Harry, who says he's been traveling and asks if they only have the one baby. They say yes. Nell arrives with Harry's baby carriage, which contains quadruplets. With that, Vernon's wife glares at her husband.

ANALYSIS: This film marked the first collaboration between Vernon Dent and Dean Ward as scriptwriters on the Langdon shorts. Unfortunately, the result is basically some routine slapstick while Harry attempts to join his bride aboard a Pullman car, material that was much more imaginative in *The Luck o' the Foolish*. Also revived is a choice gag from *His Marriage Wow*, in which Harry must retrieve his future bride's ring from the tire of a moving automobile, which he does by slashing it to ribbons.

Near the close, when Harry inadvertently pulls the emergency cord to escape the furious husband, some crude animation is used to depict the train coming to a stop. Although operating as an independent producer, Arvid Gillstrom was hamstrung by Educational's miniscule budgets.

HARRY MOMENT: When he approaches what he thinks is his wife's berth, Harry makes cooing noises, as if speaking to an infant. Although he's anticipating intimacy, his view of romance is very childlike and innocent.

WHAT THE CRITICS SAID:
Film Daily, *August 15, 1933*
Slimness of material keeps this comedy in the tepid class. Harry Langdon is the suitor who wins out in competition with Vernon Dent, so the latter pulls a few little tricks to annoy Harry on his wedding day. Comedy is built up around Harry getting ready for the wedding, while the bride and her mother waits, then the church ceremony, followed by a lot of roughhouse in a Pullman car as the newlyweds go on their honeymoon, mother-in-law tagging along.

WHAT THE EXHIBITORS SAID:
Motion Picture Herald, *February 24, 1934*
This one was very well received.
Marion F. Bodwell, Paramount Theatre, Wyoming, IL. Small town patronage.

Marriage Humor

An Arvid E. Gillstrom Production Released in Two Reels. **DIRECTED BY** Harry Edwards. **STORY BY** Dean Ward and Vernon Dent. **PHOTOGRAPHED BY** Gus Peterson. **FILM EDITOR:** Jack English. **RECORDED BY** William Fox. **CAST:** Harry Langdon, Vernon Dent, Nancy Dover, Ethel Sykes, Eddie Shubert. Copyright August 17, 1933, Registration Number LP4066. Released by Paramount Productions, Inc., August 18, 1933.

Nancy Dover, Langdon and Ethel Sykes in Marriage Humor.

SYNOPSIS: This film was unavailable for viewing. Following is a description based upon the cutting continuity submitted to the U.S. Copyright Office:

Scenes of war battle and a victory parade appear over the opening titles, which dissolve to a crowd listening to a voice from a public address speaker: "Our symbol will be the dove. On land, sea and in the homes there shall be naught but peace. And let us hope there will be no more battles abroad or at home." Vernon and Ethel are in their upscale dwelling, and she is pounding on the bathroom door in anger. Vernon is singing in the bath, but his wife is furious over her husband's playing of a bridge game the previous night. When he emerges from his bath, the argument becomes full-blown.

Harry and Nancy are married and serve as butler and maid for the Dents. Observing the argument, Nancy closes her eyes and puckers up for a kiss from Harry; he rests his hand on a grapefruit, causing Nancy to be hit in the face with juice. She accuses him of doing it on purpose and storms off. Meanwhile, Vernon and Ethel are hurling things at each other, and Harry is hit with a vase, then gets a pincushion stuck to his rear end. Ethel declares she is leaving.

Vernon, fed up with all women, orders Harry to fire the maid. Harry objects, but Nancy willingly leaves with Ethel. The wives gone, Vernon reveals a hidden cache of liquor, which he and Harry take for a night on the town. They make the rounds of various nightclubs and get very drunk. Eventually the wives spot them; Nancy is remorseful and worried that the men will be arrested, but Ethel insists, "We may have been a little hasty, but they need a lesson."

Eventually Vernon and Harry wake up in bed in the apartment, which also contains various wild animals. Vernon, extremely hungover, eyes a kangaroo and believes he's seeing "pink elephants," but Harry tells him it's not real. Outside, a trainer approaches the gardener, and explains that he's come to retrieve his animals. Apparently, Harry and Vernon purchased them during their wild night out, but the check was no good. Inside, Harry sees an ostrich, which he mistakes for a coat rack, and a zebra that he believes is a picket fence.

Harry returns to bed. A gorilla enters the room and climbs into bed between Vernon and Harry, and pushes Harry out of the bed. When the gorilla growls at him, he realizes it's real, and so are the other animals. Vernon, still badly hungover, is unconvinced and tries to resume sleeping, but the gorilla, playing with a seltzer bottle, squirts Vernon and himself. Harry winds up riding the zebra into the living room and is thrown to the floor; he runs away.

The trainer enters the house via a French window and summons his animals by name. The zebra, kangaroo and gorilla leave, followed by a bear, a monkey, and the ostrich. Meanwhile, Harry discovers the wives asleep in the servants' quarters, and he kisses

They may be hung over but Vernon Dent and Harry aren't imagining that kangaroo in Marriage Humor.

his wife. Thrilled, he skips out of the room and tells Vernon that the women are here. Vernon is furious: "Didn't I tell you we're through with women? I'll get rid of them! Let me at 'em, I'll kill 'em!"

The wives, hearing this, get out of bed and place dummies there. Harry tries to stop Vernon by tripping him, but he's determined. "I'll keep women out of this house! I'll annihilate them!"

Harry objects, "No, no, don't annihilate them! We'll both go to the caliboose!" He grabs Vernon by the vest, which then comes off in a tear, sending Harry into a backwards somersault. He crashes against the radio, which knocks a vase onto his head.

Vernon is choking one of the dummies as Harry rushes in to stop him. Its head comes off, and Vernon tosses it to Harry, who's mortified. "Nancy, Nancy, forgive me, Nancy!" he says in earnest. "I'm sorry we quarreled! Oh, Nancy, it wasn't me!" Vernon throws the dummy out the window. As Harry looks out the window, Vernon cries out, "What have I done?"

The distraught Harry replies, "You've not only killed your wife, but you've killed mine!" At that point, the wives, who were hiding in a cupboard, emerge.

"Spooks!" screams Harry, and he and Vernon dive out the window.

Filmed after, but released ahead of *Hooks and Jabs*, *The Stage Hand* and *My Weakness*. No prints of this film are known to exist.

WHAT THE CRITICS SAID:
Variety, *August 8, 1933; Reviewed by Waly*
It doesn't take much of a story to make the average short, but Harry Langdon and a novel gag provide Marriage Humor with plenty of laughs.

Running the slapstick gamut, usual dish and crockery heaving, Langdon and Vernon Dent wake up with a hangover and imagine they see kangaroos, ostriches, etc. For a time the audience also thinks it is imagination, despite the appearance of the animals, until a tamer makes his appearance.

Rows with their wives started the throwing and spree.

Motion Picture Herald, *August 12, 1933*
Harry Langdon, possessing that good touch of proper pantomime, is effectively comic and provides the bulk of the rather plentiful laugh material in this comedy. Harry is the servant, and when his master and mistress go at each other with murder in their eyes, Harry and his wife, the other servant, contribute their share to the excitement. When the wives leave, the husbands go on a real spree, wake with big heads and see terrible animals about them. The wives return, place dummies in their beds, and the husbands throw them out the window, following them when they see their wives, whom they take to be ghosts. It moves rapidly, is amusing and has numerous laughs.

WHAT THE EXHIBITORS SAID:
Motion Picture Herald, *December 23, 1933*
Good comedy.
Roy W. Adams, Mason Theatre, Mason, MI.
Small town patronage.

Motion Picture Herald, *January 6, 1934*
Good comedy, lots of laughs.
D. E. Fitton, Lyric Theatre, Harrison, AR.

Motion Picture Herald, *January 20, 1934*
A very amusing comedy with plenty of action. Give us more of 'em.
W. F. Roth, New Palace Theatre, Gallatin, TN.
Small town patronage.

Motion Picture Herald, *February 10, 1934*
Good slapstick and well received.
Hobart H. Gates, Garlock Theatre, Custer, SD.
Small town patronage.

Hooks and Jabs

A Mermaid Comedy Released in Two Reels. **PRODUCED AND DIRECTED BY** Arvid E. Gillstrom. **STORY BY** Dean Ward and Vernon Dent. **CAST:** Harry Langdon, Vernon Dent, Nell O'Day, William Irving, Frank Moran, Johnny Dundee. **WORKING TITLE:** "Down and Out." Copyright August 25, 1933, Registration Number LP4272. Released by Educational Films Corporation of America, August 25, 1933.

SYNOPSIS: Harry gives away pies from the back of a truck to several kids. He's caught by the driver while eating a pie and is taken away. Later, he leaves the city jail and meets a Salvation Army lady, who tells him to be a good boy. She gives Harry a dollar for food.

Meanwhile, Vernon is singing "When You and I Were Young, Maggie" to a group of men in a bar. Harry wanders in, asks the bartender a question, and is pointed to the bathroom. Upon returning, he asks for a glass of milk and loses his dollar to a barfly. The barfly promptly orders ten beers, refusing to return Harry's dollar. Vernon wins all ten in a strange game of checkers, and as the barfly skulks away, Vernon orders Harry to pay up. Harry then helps himself to the free lunch at the bar, but is told to sweep up the gym to pay for the beers. He watches a punch-drunk fighter working out and ends up being a referee to an imaginary opponent. After the fighter "wins" the bout, he knocks Harry cold. Other fighters enter the gym and begin sparring with a tough pug, who is coached by Vernon. Harry gets worked up watching the sparring and is sent into the ring by Vernon. As Harry and the pug spar, another fighter knocks the opponent out with a club. Vernon is knocked down as well. The men in the bar react with fear when Harry enters.

Outside the bar, a Salvation Army band led by the lady who loaned Harry the dollar is preaching against drink. He leaves the bar and encounters the band as the girl complains that the bar's patrons are making too much noise. Harry goes inside and tells them to be quiet. They ignore him and then force him backwards until he accidentally switches off the lights. A brawl ensues and a policeman enters to find everyone knocked out and Harry sitting on the bar. He tells that the cop that "beer is back." Vernon, Harry and the cop exit the bar.

After the policeman departs, Vernon tells the Salvation Army band to scram. Harry punches him and tells them to sing all they want. Vernon tries to punch Harry and puts his hand through a phone pole. Harry ties a stick to his hand and traps Vernon. As Harry leaves with the band, the lady tells him that a man may be down but he's never out. Harry then falls down an open manhole.

ANALYSIS: *Hooks and Jabs* is a step up from *Tied For Life*, with some lively sight gags. Although the short is rather episodic, Langdon has a number of marvelous pantomime sequences, especially in the tavern's "back room," where Vernon Dent manages a pug with a mean "left hook." Most of this material is original to Langdon, although some of it appears to have been borrowed from Chaplin's 1915 comedy, *The Champion*. The scene in which Harry "counts" out the pug's imaginary opponent is a reworking of the "invisible insects" scene in *The Hansom Cabman*.

HARRY MOMENT: Harry's pantomime sequence as the referee is light, comedic and very believable. For a few fleeting moments, he's in complete control of his skills.

WHAT THE CRITICS SAID:
Film Daily, *June 10, 1933*
   A Mermaid comedy that is cleverly gagged, with Harry Langdon busting in on a gymnasium where a pug that Vernon Dent is managing is in training. After the bruiser has knocked out about six sparring partners, Langdon is sent in against him, with an iron weight accidentally dropping in his glove as he puts it on. He knocks the pug cold, and then all the rough mugs around the place greet him as the coming champ. The comedy comes in the fact that Langdon really thinks he has got a terrific left, but when he tries it out on some of the gang without the gloves he is soon disillusioned. Harry Langdon sends this one in strong.

Motion Picture Daily, *June 17, 1933*
   Frozen faced Harry Langdon makes for good comedy. His antics are genuinely amusing, and he has the ability to make the most of pantomime, which still remains one of the most effective methods of comedy portrayal...It is good comedy, well done.

Film Daily, *July 26, 1933*
   Harry Langdon plays the part of a goof who wanders into a tough beer joint and gets himself in wrong with Vernon Dent, the proprietor. The latter is managing a prize fighter on the side, and Dent sends Langdon in for a bout. The comedian knocks the pug cold as a fluke, and immediately becomes a great guy with all hands among the assembled plug-uglies. But soon they discover that Langdon is only a phoney, and the film winds up in a free-for-all fight. Moves fast, with some highly original gags. It should please generally.

WHAT THE EXHIBITORS SAID:
Motion Picture Herald, *March 31, 1934*
   Not so good. Very few laughs from my audience.
A.N. Miles, Eminence Theatre, Eminence, KY.
Farming patronage.

"HOOKS AND JABS"
A MERMAID Comedy
with
HARRY LANGDON
and VERNON DENT

The Stage Hand

A Mermaid Comedy Released in Two Reels. **DIRECTED BY** Harry Langdon. **STORY BY** Harry Langdon & Edward Davis. **PHOTOGRAPHY BY** George Weber & Frank Zucker. Sound Technicians: Percy Glenn & Andy Weber. **ART DIRECTOR:** Walter Keller. **FILM EDITOR:** Frank Melford. **PRODUCTION MANAGER:** Joseph Boyle. **CAST:** Harry Langdon, Marel Foster, Eddie Shubert, Ira Hayward, Rollin Grimes, Maryen Lynn, Harry Hamill. **WORKING TITLE:** "The Show Goat." Copyright September 1, 1933 by Producer's Share, Inc., Registration Number LP4340. Released by Educational Films Corporation of America, September 8, 1933.

SYNOPSIS: The residents of a small town are staging a play, hoping that the proceeds will enable the fire department to acquire a new fire engine. Actors are rehearsing a scene when Harry is reminded that it's time for his cue. He utters very unimaginative doorbell sounds, which displeases the lead actress. Soon after, the jealous wife of the leading man quarrels with the actress. The director's husband tells Harry that he's built a speakeasy and hands over a drink. Harry drinks and falls down. He sits on the floor before taking a second drink. After some more drinks, Harry becomes tipsy. The actors soon find the speakeasy and discover Harry covered in beer foam.

Later, in the theatre, a large audience applauds the beginning of the play. Backstage, Harry prepares to ring a bell. A fellow actor asks him if he has a union card. Harry replies that he doesn't. As they argue he's pushed onto the stage, and his appearance is met with applause. He greets the crowd and does a little dance. He then goes backstage and joins the other actors. Harry is told that an actor is afraid to go on the stage. He pushes the actor out front, and the play continues.

The leads are rehearsing their love scene backstage when the jealous wife hits her husband with a brick. Harry brings him around with smelling salts, and then causes the back of the actress's dress to be ripped off. He covers her rear with a small curtain as she enters the stage. She turns around, which causes the curtain to raise, exposing her rear end, to the delight of the audience. Backstage, the jealous wife punches her husband, who falls unconscious. Harry brings the actor around and drags him onto the stage.

Meanwhile, the company is preparing for the fire scene when they discover that the fire engine has not arrived behind the theatre. Harry is sent to get the fire engine, while on stage the villain has tied up the heroine. Upon arriving at the fire station, Harry convinces an elderly fireman to drive the engine to the theatre. The old man protests that he doesn't know how to drive it, but he manages to careen through the streets toward the playhouse. The engine crashes into the theatre and the audience surrounds it and laughs.

Later, Harry is walking down a country road and is embraced by a woman who tells him that he saved her father's job and that she loves him. He utters a silent reply and they embrace once more.

This short was made in February 1932 as an independent production, and was filmed at Royal Studios in Grantwood, New Jersey.

ANALYSIS: Anyone unfamiliar with the backstory of this film can only deduce that Langdon was hopelessly inept as a director. The short has the same clumsy feel as the earliest talking pictures, with such things as stock shots of an applauding audience over a barren soundtrack (and visually sped up, to boot).

Characters, such as Harry's girlfriend and her father, the fireman, appear out of nowhere. Although the supporting players are supposed to be amateurish while in Mrs. Winters's stage show, many of them carry this over into the rest of their performances. Only Eddie Shubert as Mr. Winters shows any sort of comedic skill as he plies Harry with liquor in his secret "shpeakeasy." Finally, the closing shot, as his girl runs up and thanks Harry for saving her father's job, makes absolutely no sense. Not only are doubles used for both Langdon and Maryen Lynn, the two are seen out of doors, yet the soundtrack was clearly done indoors; the girl can be heard running on a hard floor!

Unfortunately, *The Stage Hand* is a poor stepchild compared to the original shooting script, "The Show Goat." As related in the text, Langdon probably wound up with about three reels' worth of material. Having since decamped to Paramount, he and/or his original backers left it to Educational to shorten the film to the conventional two reels. Presumably, everyone made back their investments, but the finished product is just muddled, and certainly compares unfavorably to the comedies Langdon was turning out under Gillstrom's supervision.

HARRY MOMENT: When Harry is pushed onto the stage, he smiles and joyfully acknowledges the audience's laughter and approval. He exhibits genuine warmth and, as he does his little dance, shows the charisma that delighted audiences during his long stage career.

My Weakness

A B.G. DeSylva Production. 72 minutes. DIRECTED BY David Butler. WRITTEN BY B.G. DeSylva. ADAPTATION BY David Butler. ADDITIONAL DIALOGUE BY Bert Hanlon, Ben Ryan. PHOTOGRAPHY BY Arthur Miller. RECORDING ENGINEER: Kenneth Strickfaden. MUSIC AND LYRICS BY B.G. DeSylva, Richard Whiting, Leo Robbins. Copyright September 18, 1933, Registration Number LP4143; Renewed October 20, 1960, Number R264441. Released by Fox Film Corporation, September 22, 1933.

SYNOPSIS: From his home in the clouds, Cupid (Harry Langdon) tells us in rhyming couplets about "the toughest job I ever had," involving playboy Ronnie Gregory. Ronnie has been dropped from the payroll of his late father's brassiere company by his uncle Ellery, co-owner of the business. Ellery was encouraged to do this by his young girlfriend, Jane, a gold-digger. As Ronnie tries to persuade his uncle to reinstate his income, and that Jane is only interested in marrying for money, Looloo, a dowdy maid, arrives to tidy up the room. Ronnie insists, "Every woman is a bag of tricks," and claims he could take any woman and "marry her off to a man in the social register." Looloo overhears and begs Ronnie to do it for her: "I don't want to be a maid all my life." She also dreads the idea of marrying her boyfriend Maxie, a cab driver. Amused, Ellery tells Ronnie to "fulfill this young girl's dream...and I'll re-establish your income." Disgusted, Ronnie leaves, but Looloo follows. She tries to convince him that she is attractive to men, but fails miserably in her attempt.

Cupid introduces Ronnie's overly studious cousin Gerald ("I gave up on him years ago"). Ronnie tells Gerald, "Get your father to release my money." He refuses because all Ronnie thinks about is women. Ronnie insists it isn't true as a number of his girlfriends arrive. Some of them flirt with Gerald, but he's uninterested and departs. Meanwhile, Looloo appears, hoping to convince Ronnie to take on his uncle's challenge. With no alternative, he agrees and his girlfriends set to work improving her appearance. Ronnie decides Gerald will be the perfect beau for Looloo, and each of the girls will teach her the art of capturing a man. As they fix her up, Cupid flies into the room and conducts a choir of dolls and figurines, who sing "You Can Be Had."

Two months pass and Cupid points out the bills for Looloo's makeover are driving Ronnie to distraction, until the girls tell him they're finished. In her apartment, she practices talking and walking and converses with an imaginary Ronnie, with whom she's fallen in love. Ronnie arrives and tells her how to win Gerald's heart, explaining his interest in stamp collecting and diet of raw carrots. He says, "I want to see how you are at something a girl can't teach you." They practice kissing. Maxie enters and objects, but Ronnie assures him he's not interested.

At the fashion show where she is to meet Gerald, Ronnie takes Looloo aside and gives her some last-minute instructions: "If he asks you something you don't understand, just say 'What do you think?'" Ronnie introduces her to Gerald, and they sit together. After one of the models sings, Looloo says she's bored and wishes she were home with her stamp collection. At this, Gerald perks up: "Are you really an ardent philatelist?" "What do you think?" she replies.

As they talk further, Gerald becomes more interested, while Looloo realizes he's a bore. She asks him to dance, but he graciously declines, so she begins singing the song the model performed earlier. She scoffs at the idea of lovemaking, while holding his hand, putting her arm around him and kissing him. When the clock strikes twelve, she declares it's time for supper and tells him raw carrots are "my weakness." Won over, Gerald proclaims his love.

Ronnie congratulates Looloo for pulling it off, adding, "Don't let him escape now. Can you imagine Uncle Ellery when he wakes up and finds his son married to a maid!" Back in her apartment, she again addresses an imaginary Ronnie: "You think it's very funny that Gerald should fall for me, don't you? Well, maybe I can find *your* weakness, too!" A telegraph boy delivers a letter; as he leaves, Ronnie's butler arrives and tells her that although his boss wishes to see no one, he'll let her in whenever she wants. She thanks him and opens the letter, a marriage proposal from Gerald. Leaving, Looloo runs into Maxie, who tells her he's going to be "indifferent" about her until she comes crawling back.

Looloo meets with Ronnie's girlfriends. When they ask if Gerald has proposed yet, she lies and says no. Each gives her more tips: compliment his teeth, use baby talk, and if all else fails, stage a faint. She visits Ronnie, who is depressed about not having an income. She tries the girls' suggestions, but he is unresponsive until she stages a faint. He orders his butler to bring water to the "poor darling," and she immediately perks up: "Did you mean that?" He calls her a fraud and tells her to get out.

Cupid comments: "Can you imagine a fellow throwing a girl out of his apartment? It's usually the other way around." He takes us to Gerald, who's being tailed by Ellery and Jane. Ellery tells her Gerald "went completely haywire" and lost several big accounts for the company. Ellery finds him at Looloo's apartment, confronts him and sends him away. Then Ellery asks Looloo to break up with Gerald. When he admits Ronnie tried to break up his relationship with Jane, Looloo comes on to Ellery and pours him a highball. She sings as he gets intoxicated, and he falls for her.

At Ronnie's apartment, Looloo tells the butler her plan: when Ronnie hears that she's going to marry his uncle, he'll object and profess his love. Jane shows up, furious that Ellery has broken up with her, and tells the butler she intends to marry Ronnie for spite. Immediately, Looloo fights with Jane until Ronnie intervenes. When Jane storms out, Looloo tells Ronnie she's going to wed Ellery. Ronnie is delighted: "Now I'll be even with the lot of them: Jane, Gerald and Ellery!" "All you ever think of is yourself," Looloo replies. "I hate you! I hate all men!"

Leaving, she encounters Maxie in the hallway and shoos him away; the same with Gerald, who commiserates with Maxie.

Ronnie has second thoughts about Looloo marrying Ellery. His butler believes he loves her, but Ronnie is reluctant to admit it; instead, he professes concern about gossip his uncle will endure. Ellery arrives, announcing that he and Jane are through and that he intends to marry Looloo. Ronnie confesses that she's the maid from their original bet, but Ellery doesn't care, admitting Jane was the cause of their troubles. When Ellery tells him his income has been restored, Ronnie instead asks for a job. Ellery is delighted.

Looloo returns and tells Ellery she's too young to marry him. She also tells Ronnie, "I once thought I could marry for money and ease, but I've learned enough about men in the last three months to know that I'll never marry anybody. So thanks for the education." She walks out.

His eyes finally opened, Ronnie goes to her apartment and professes his love, asking, "Won't you forgive me for taking so long to find it out?" She replies, "What do you think?" and they kiss. Cupid winks and addresses the audience: "Well, I put it over…and look out I don't do it to you, and you, and you…."

ANALYSIS: *My Weakness* is a cute, slightly risqué, pre-code musical comedy; no classic but very good for its type. Lilian Harvey is quite charming and tries hard, but lacks the extra quality a Carole Lombard would have brought to the role. Consequently, she failed to 'click' in America. Lew Ayres is competent as Ronnie and the supporting players are all good. Sharp-eyed viewers will note, among Ronnie's girlfriends, Susan Fleming, who would marry Hollywood's other pixyish comedian, Harpo Marx.

As Cupid, Langdon is slightly reminiscent of Harpo; adorned with wig and eccentric costume, he's very youthful looking. His voice is perfect, just cute enough to endear without being saccharine. For most of his scenes, he addresses the audience directly, in close-up, and it's very effective. He participates in the film's highlight: the "You Can Be Had" sequence. As the girls give Looloo a makeover, a miniature Cupid leads a choir of dolls and figurines. At one point, photos of Fox's four major stars are shown: Will Rogers, Clara Bow, Warner Baxter and Janet Gaynor; each sings a verse in voice-over.

HARRY MOMENT: Every time he's on screen. The whole of his performance is one extended Harry Moment.

WHAT THE CRITICS SAID:
Film Daily, *September 22, 1933*

Light in texture but quite charming withal, this B.G. DeSylva production makes very pleasant entertainment for any class. Though in the musical comedy class, and quite tuneful in that respect, its footage is mostly devoted to romance and comedy. Lilian Harvey, a maid and apparently ugly, is taken in hand by Lew Ayres on a bet with his uncle that he can in a few weeks transform her and teach her the feminine wiles necessary to ensnare a rich husband. If he wins the bet, Lew is to have his income restored, the uncle having been seduced to cut him off by a golddigger who transferred her designs to the older man when the younger one turned him down. Although it is obvious that Lew is to fall for the re-made Lilian, he does not do so for quite some time, and meanwhile the plot unwinds a lot of amusing incidents, song numbers, feminine pulchritude, comedy and novelties, all-in-all making it an agreeable satisfying picture.

Direction: Fine, Photography: Fine.

New York Times, *September 22, 1933; Reviewed by Mordaunt Hall*

The vivacious and charming Lilian Harvey, an English actress who has spent several years in Germany, is now to be seen at the Radio City Music Hall in the first of her two Hollywood productions to be released. It happens to be known as My Weakness, *and was produced by B. G. DeSylva. It is a fluffy piece of work with no more of a story than most musical comedies. It is, however, handsomely staged and virtually all the members of the cast contribute highly satisfactory performances, but as the scenes come to the screen it is disappointing to hear so many silly and antiquated jokes and painful puns.*

But Miss Harvey's presence atones for most of the shortcomings. She sings and she prances about the various settings in a blithe and happy fashion. And the audience at the first exhibition of this film laughed heartily even over several none too original ideas, such as Looloo Blake (Miss Harvey) falling down several steps and the sudden shrinking of a taxi driver's trousers…

A familiar countenance pops up here and there as a mature Cupid. After thinking it over, one decides that this person who is shooting darts now and again is none other than Harry Langdon.

My Weakness *is perhaps more of a musical fantasy than a musical comedy, for not only is Mr. Langdon supposed to be up in the skies overseeing affairs of the heart but now and again the ornaments, including dogs, cats, monkeys and a statuette of Rodin's "Thinker," lift their supposed voices to the melodies, which are quite amusing and tuneful, particularly one called "Gather Lip Rouge While You May."*

The elderly Cupid takes it into his head occasionally to relate parts of the story and then the tale goes on with the characters. Occasionally the persons involved choose to converse in rhyme, notably in the episode when Looloo, or, as they call her on one occasion, the Lady known as Looloo, is being prepared to appear as the girl who is to win the wager for the redoubtable Ronnie.

Reverting to Mr. Butterworth, it is rather comic to hear him ask the pretty Looloo if she is "really an ardent philatelist," and it is bound to tickle the risibles of many when Henry Travers falls a victim to Looloo's undeniable beauty and permits her to make his hair look absurd.

But, notwithstanding the good points of this production, it is a pity that Miss Harvey was not presented in something less rowdy — a whimsical piece, for she knows how to capture the favor of her audience. Her last Continental film was Congress Dances, which was infinitely better suited to her talent.

Mr. Ayres is quite good as Ronnie. Henry Travers does extraordinarily well by the part of the numbskull uncle. Mr. Langdon, Barbara Weeks and Irene Bentley are among others who do creditable work.

Variety, September 26, 1933; Reviewed by Abel

Lilian Harvey's American screen debut in a Hollywood made production — a musical — is highly favorable. On personality she impresses herself to the degree it should stand her in good stead when outfitted with a more substantial story. Buddy DeSylva has turned out a good if light musical comedy for the screen, deficient in story sturdiness as is the usual shortcomings of the average musical comedy libretto.

Lightness of the theme is offset by a naïve manner of presentation and self-kidding through the medium of a hokum Dan Cupid played by Harry Langdon. He's an amorous talking reporter who recognizes the obviousness of Lew Ayres's romantic possibilities but almost gives up Charles Butterworth as a possibility. When Butterworth finally falls, it makes for much of the comedy in the picture...

Miss Harvey and Ayres are costarred, with Butterworth, Harry Langdon, Sid Silvers and Irene Bentley sub-featured and distinguishing themselves. Silvers was in DeSylva (and Laurence Schwab's) musical comedy hit Take a Chance on Broadway last season, and in exchange for bolstering the book with some supplementary dialog and other material, DeSylva promised him a break in pictures. He takes every advantage of his opportunities.

The fashion show idea permits for some sartorial flash and is the setting for the big laff sequences. Three songs, "Gather Life (sic) While You May," "You Can Be Had" and "How Do I Look?" the latter distinguished by its manner of delivery by Dixie Frances, a saucer-eyed, personality hot songstress.

Reunion of David Butler, the director, and DeSylva seems a happy one. Butler and the former team of DeSylva, Brown and Henderson did quite well on the Fox lot in the first screen musical vogue in 1929 with Sunny Side Up.

Production ideas are novel and fresh. There are toy animals, part of the apartment adornments, which are utilized for some dubbed reprise of a song chorus, their mouths moving in ventriloquial fashion. A fan magazine also exposes four Fox stars, Will Rogers, Clara Bow, Warner Baxter and Janet Gaynor, who similarly are heard in their own styles of vocalizing a chorus.

In toto, Miss Harvey's initial fan introduction, while not auspicious, is highly favorable. She can become as big for the American market as during her Ufa days, but she seems worthy of sturdier stuff than a light musical comedy, although she is equally adept on the song end.

Harrison's Reports, September 30, 1933

Fairly pleasant entertainment, suitable mostly for the better class audiences. The story is thin, but the production end is excellent, and the interest is held because of the charming performance by Lilian Harvey, the new Fox star. There are some good comedy situations brought about by the heroine's attempts to marry a wealthy man...

The plot was adapted from a story by B.G. DeSylva and Leo Robbin. It was directed by David Butler. In the cast are Sid Silvers, Harry Langdon, Susan Fleming, Barbara Weeks, Dixie Francis, Henry Travers and others.

There are some suggestive remarks; this may make it unsuitable for children, adolescents and for Sundays.

Rochester Democrat and Chronicle, October 13, 1933; Reviewed by George L. David

Lilian Harvey, the delightful wisp of charm and talent who, as a European favorite, won American favor in Congress Dances, has become more thoroughly Americanized in her first Hollywood film, My Weakness, than Maurice Chevalier did in his. She plays American farce in this new film, which came to the Century yesterday, and plays it so fetchingly that she will please you considerably, we imagine.

My Weakness is a very fresh and fluffy thing of musical comedy libretto tenuousness, and of no more seriousness. It is a comedy cocktail effervesced by Miss Harvey, a Cinderella whimsy done quite sophisticatedly. David Butler, the director, deserves the long yell for handling the thing with such an excellent sense of sprightly, airy farce. The piece has numerous clever lines, absurd lines even, and it has players who make the most of them in Miss Harvey, Charles Butterworth and Sid Silvers. By the way, Silvers, a former "stooge," does a capital comedy sketch as Maxie, a taxi driver. And Butterworth, his old dumb rather bewildered self has some very funny moments.

My Weakness is so fresh and bright that it doesn't need the exhibition in a girls' locker room of a swimming pool, but as Buddy De Sylva, the producer, was formerly not only a composer but a Broadway musical comedy producer, the feminine display is accounted for. De Sylva contributes a new song, sung by Miss Harvey, that appeals, and the background music is right.

Miss Harvey plays with elfin lightness, humor and wistfulness. She completely captivates. Ayres is good, except for bits of diction. Harry Langdon is clever as a neatly used Cupid.

WHAT THE EXHIBITORS SAID:

Motion Picture Herald, *October 28, 1933*

At last Fox has come through with an audience picture. This is clever and different. Some good music, three good songs and Lilian Harvey. This gal has everything. She is versatile and has a flair for comedy, cute as a button and she is going to make some of these other stars step, if she gets the break. Did the audience go for her? I'll say they did. The girl is clever and she had to be to carry this story. It would be well when advertising this picture to stress that she is a new star and her first picture and they will not be disappointed.
A.E. Hancock, Columbia City, IN.
General patronage.

Motion Picture Herald, *November 11, 1933*

Now here is a picture that's different and pleased all 100%. Many favorable comments. Lilian Harvey very clever. Picture has a little bit of everything, good comedy, beautiful clothes to please the women, good story. Sends the customers away happy.
W.A. Collins, Regal Theatre, Elvins, MO.
Small town patronage.

Nice picture but did less than average business. Music with this was very nice. Played October 22.
Edward M. Starkey, Rex Theatre, Berlin, WI.
Rural and city patronage.

Motion Picture Herald, *November 25, 1933*

Another good picture from Fox. The first one from this star, and fine comments. She seemed to go over in nice shape. Business picked up the second night, which is a good sign. The picture was well liked. Good for your best nights. Played Nov. 2–3.
R.W. Hickman, Lyric Theatre, Greenville, IL.
General patronage.

Motion Picture Herald, *December 2, 1933*

It is a light comedy story, but oh, boy, it has class. Big draw second and third nights, and they did come the fourth night and called for it.
Walter Odom & Sons, Dixie Theatre, Durant Theatre, Durant, MS. General patronage.

Pleasing picture, made with good cast. Two or three tuneful songs with a lot of comedy. Drew just ordinary business and didn't hurt or help the cause.
Mayme P. Musselman, Princess Theatre, Lincoln, KS.
Small town patronage.

Motion Picture Herald, *December 16, 1933*

Musical comedy that pleased. Charles Butterworth the hit of the show. The song "Gather Lip Rouge While You May" is very good. Played November 13–14.
J.E. Ross, Jr., Strand Theatre, St. George, S.C.
Small town patronage.

Now here is a motion picture. Man, man, you will want to attend every show yourself when you run it. My folks thought it the best entertainment of the year. And I have recently played the two big musicals. But this has them both beat a mile as far as pleasing the public.
M.W. Larmour, National Theatre, Graham, TX.
General Small town patronage.

Failed to draw. No title, but it is a very pleasing picture. If you can get them it will please. Played Nov. 20–21.
G. Carey, Strand Theatre, Paris, AR. Family patronage.

Motion Picture Herald, *December 23, 1933*

Drew well and pleased 90 percent of my audience. Plenty of good laughs and an abundance of beautifully dressed girls. Charles Butterworth ran away with the show. Fox's new star, Lilian Harvey, is easy to look at and has a pleasing voice. She will improve with experience. Played Dec. 1–2.
W.J. Powell, Lonet Theatre, Wellington, OH.
Small town and rural patronage.

Book this before *My Lips Betray* and it will help the latter, as Lilian Harvey is a new type and they'll like her in this musical comedy romance. No dancing, but good songs, a fashion show and plenty of laughs.
M.P. Foster, Granada Theatre, Monte Vista, CO.
General patronage.

Motion Picture Herald, *December 30, 1933*

My patrons enjoyed this breezy comedy very much. Lilian Harvey is charming. Her English accent is not so pronounced as some of our own American stars, who have acquired theirs. Average business. Played Dec. 15–16.
M.R. Williams, Texon Theatre, TX. Rural patronage.

America's Weakness! A glamorous new star. The cutest thing in pictures in a rapturous, spicy romance set to lively music, fascinating! Played Dec. 10–11.
Horn & Morgan, Star Theatre, Hay Springs, NE. Small town patronage.

On Ice

An Arvid E. Gillstrom Production Released in Two Reels. DIRECTED BY Arvid E. Gillstrom. STORY BY Dean Ward and Vernon Dent. PHOTOGRAPHED BY Gus Peterson. FILM EDITOR: Jack English. RECORDED BY William Fox. CAST: Harry Langdon, Vernon Dent, Eleanor Hunt, Ethel Sykes, Kewpie Morgan, Glen Cavender, Ruth Clifford, Diana Seaby, William Irving. Copyright October 5, 1933, Registration Number LP4149. Released by Paramount Productions, Inc., October 6, 1933.

SYNOPSIS: This film was unavailable for viewing. Following is a description based upon the cutting continuity submitted to the U.S. Copyright Office:

Vernon and Harry are icemen; Vernon, the boss, drives the truck and Harry does the hauling. Vernon parks in front of a café owned by Min and Marge. He finds Harry sitting on a cake of ice and warming himself by a small fire. "Say, what are you trying to do — melt away my business?" says Vernon, and he knocks the fire out of the truck. "Bring in fifty pounds of ice to Min and Marge." When Harry stands up, the back of his coat is torn off.

In the café, while Vernon chats with Min, Harry struggles with the ice. He pushes it through a revolving door; it slides across the café floor, and Harry has to chase it. Vernon tells Min he has tickets for four at the El Toro nightclub; Min agrees provided he gets a date for Marge. Meanwhile, Harry has gotten to the icebox. He opens its door and heaves in the cake on the top shelf, at which point another cake slides out from the lower shelf. He kicks that cake aside and exits. Vernon explains that he's taking Harry to a party, for which Marge is his date. Harry protests that he's married, but Vernon tells him not to worry about it.

As they leave the café, Harry's tongs get caught on a man's jacket. Vernon tugs at it and tears the coat, making its owner angry. Vernon rushes out of the café as the man approaches; Harry leaves as well, although he goes completely around in the revolving door first. Vernon puts the truck in reverse and backs into the man's car, demolishing it. Harry gets into the truck as it pulls away. The customer sees his ruined car, retrieves a whiskey bottle from the front seat and puts it in his pants pocket. Just then, the car door swings open and causes the bottle to break, sending the liquor streaming down his pant leg.

Harry returns home to his wife. He pays her several compliments, but she simply holds out her hand, expecting his pay envelope, which he hands over. She tells him to get ready for dinner, and leaves the room. He heads to a bookshelf and pulls out a "map" that shows where he has some money stashed. He removes the book *(Hidden Treasure)* from the shelf and opens it; it's hollow inside, with a sardine tin that contains some coins. His wife calls for him and he frantically puts the coins in his mouth. When she enters the room and says, "Why don't you answer me?" he tries to speak and swallows the coins. She hears them and slaps him on the back; he spits them into a glass bowl.

As his wife calls him for dinner, he emerges in a nightgown, moaning. The wife tells him to go to bed, but her sister warns her that she "wouldn't trust any man." They enter the bedroom and Harry's in bed, still groaning. His wife says, "I think you'd better have some castor oil."

Harry perks up: "No. I feel better already."

Treating him like a child, the sister says, "Will you take some if I take some?"

"Maybe," he replies.

The two women pour out one glass of castor oil and one of water, but via a mirror Harry sees which is which. When the sisters leave the room, Harry switches the glasses, so that the sister drinks the castor oil. She leaves the bedroom quickly, followed by Harry's wife. Harry rises, grabs his silk hat and jumps out the bedroom window. He hops on a bicycle and rides off.

Outside the El Toro, Vernon assures Min and Marge that Harry will be there soon. Meanwhile, Harry's wife and her sister discover that Harry has left the house. "I'll find him if I have to search every place in this city," says the wife, and the two women leave together. Harry rides up to the El Toro, still in his nightgown, which Vernon rips off; luckily, he's wearing his frock coat underneath. Marge orders some "Egyptian tea" and, as Vernon and Min head for the dance floor, she sidles up to Harry, who backs away from her. "You're not afraid of me, are you?" asks Marge.

"No, but I'm cautious!" says Harry. In backing away, he falls on the dance floor and a couple tumbles over him.

At the table, drinks are poured. Harry takes a sip of his "tea" and tumbles off his chair. The girls help him up. The man whose auto was wrecked is one of the waiters; he spots Vernon and Harry and goes over to their table. He takes their bill for the drinks and adds $75 for auto repairs, telling Vernon, "I want that paid before you leave here, or else." Trying to keep this a secret from the girls, Vernon signals to Harry that he'll pass the money to him under the table. Harry slips under the table, but Marge feels him and winds up taking the money. She smiles, winks at Vernon, and slips the cash into the front of her dress. Harry returns from under the seat, puzzled.

While Harry has another sip of "tea," Vernon writes a note on his hand: MARGE HAS THE MONEY. He holds up his hand. Harry points to Marge. Vernon nods and points toward Marge's bosom. Harry points to Marge again, and Vernon nods. Suddenly, Harry grabs Marge and kisses her. They fall to the floor, while Min and Vernon watch. Harry gets up and takes his seat; followed by Marge, who slaps Harry in the face and storms off. Harry shows Vernon the money.

Vernon sees Harry's wife and sister enter. They, in turn, spot him. Harry quickly ducks under the table, while Vernon and Min head for the dance floor. The sister sees a compact belonging to one of the girls and the two women sit down. Under the table, the sister is nervously kicking her leg back and forth, unknowingly striking Harry on the chin. The wife sniffs the "teapot," discovers that it's liquor, and empties it under the table, into Harry's face.

The waiter approaches the women and is told by Harry's wife, "This is my husband's table."

The waiter tells her, "You'll take care of his check, I suppose," and when she refuses, he takes her purse. The wife slugs the waiter, who staggers backwards and hits a wall, falling to the ground. Harry stands up, knocking the table over. Vernon, who has seen this, yells, "Help! Police! Raid!" and turns the lights out. Patrons scream and run outside, joined by Vernon, Min and Marge. Harry, tangled up in a tablecloth, runs outside and jumps on his bicycle, but it's propped up on a parking stand, so when he pedals it goes nowhere. The police arrive; one squad car drives up to the curb, knocking Harry away.

At one o'clock in the morning, there's a knock at Harry's door. Garbed in pajamas, Harry answers to find his sister-in-law and apologetic wife. Harry scolds his wife for causing him so much worry, when suddenly Vernon's voice is heard, crying, "Woof! Woof! I'm a big bad wolf!" Harry explains it's the radio. Then a drunken happy Vernon emerges from inside, clad in a bearskin, and he leaves the house. "That's television," explains Harry, and he also starts to leave when Min and Marge suddenly emerge and chase after Vernon, yelling, "We're not afraid of the big, bad wolf!" Harry runs outside and holds the door shut so his wife and sister-in-law can't open it. It begins to rain, and Harry pulls a cord to activate an awning, but it unfolds and dumps water all over him.

No prints of this film are known to exist.

WHAT THE EXHIBITORS SAID:
Motion Picture Herald, *November 11, 1933*
   Good two-reel comedy.
D. E. Fitton, Lyric Theatre, Harrison, Ark.
Small town patronage.

A Roaming Romeo

An Arvid E. Gillstrom Production Released in Two Reels. DIRECTED BY Arvid E. Gillstrom. STORY BY Dean Ward and Vernon Dent. PHOTOGRAPHED BY Gus Peterson. FILM EDITOR: Jack English. RECORDED BY William Fox. CAST: Harry Langdon, Vernon Dent, Nell O'Day, Richard Cramer, Jack Henderson, Leslie Goodwins. Copyright December 28, 1933, Registration Number LP4369. Released by Paramount Productions, Inc., December 29, 1933.

SYNOPSIS: This film was unavailable for viewing. Following is a description based upon the cutting continuity submitted to the U.S. Copyright Office:

Nell and Vernon are at a local swimming pool. Vernon complains that the water is too cold for swimming, so Nell playfully pushes him into the pool. He grabs her leg and pulls her in. He asks her, "When are you going to wear my engagement ring?"

Nell replies that she "can't make a choice until Harry arrives."

They both watch a boy make an impressive dive, and Vernon boasts that he can do as well. As he heads for the diving board, Nell puts on her bathing cap. Vernon jumps in, which splashes the people at a table alongside the pool. When we look into the now-drained pool, he, Nell and four others are sitting at the bottom.

Meanwhile, a farmer is showing a local sheriff how his trees are barren of peaches. The two spy Harry in the orchard; his mouth has peach residue around it, and his coat is protruding with stolen fruit. The farmer calls out to him and he starts to run. The sheriff gives the farmer permission to shoot. When the farmer fires his rifle, about 20 other poachers emerge from behind trees and bushes and run off. The farmer and sheriff chase after these men. Harry finds himself behind the sheriff and farmer; he hears more shots and runs off.

Harry runs into a mobile cottage elsewhere on the farm. As he climbs up the porch steps, he sees a pigpen, and dumps the contents of his coat for the pigs to eat. Once inside, he goes to the kitchen, puts some peas on the table and checks himself in the mirror. Not liking what he sees, he tries turning the mirror sideways. He goes to the sink, then washes and dries his face. He turns on the gas stove, lights a match and tosses it in, holding his hands over his ears. The stove "explodes," filling the room with smoke and causing the furnishings to jump. He picks up a coffee pot, fills it, then notices the can of milk is empty. He sees a cow grazing outside from his window. He smiles, picks up some empty bottles and heads out.

Harry climbs through a hole in a wire fence and places one of the bottles under the cow, then stands and waits. Nothing happens. He tries shaking and pushing the cow, without success. He looks off and notices a calf nursing from another cow. When he turns back to "his" cow, she has raised her tail, causing him to jump back. Then he "pumps" the tail up and down, and the cow starts filling the bottle with milk. With one bottle filled, Harry sets down another and resumes pumping when the farmer and sheriff spot him.

The farmer yells and Harry ducks through the fence. The farmer shoots, causing Harry to drop all but one of his bottles. He runs into the rear door of his house. Chasing after Harry, the farmer clears the fence, but the sheriff gets his trousers caught on it and ends up losing them. They both reach the rear door and demand entrance. Harry ducks out the front door, jumps in his car and pulls the cottage away, leaving the porch behind. The sheriff jumps toward the house as it departs, but misses and he lands on the ground. The farmer shoots as the house recedes in the distance.

Harry arrives in a residential neighborhood. He has a letter in his hand, and as he stops beside a house, he checks the address. At that moment, the garage door opens and a car pulls out, with Vernon and Nell in the front seat. Vernon sees the cottage and says, "He must be a tourist." Nell recognizes Harry and gets out of the car. She embraces him, and Vernon is surprised. Nell comments on the "cute little cottage," and Harry explains that he built it. She asks if she can go inside. He escorts her into his house, while Vernon fumes.

Nell notices a button beside the mirror and presses it. A folding bed comes down from the wall. She pushes it again and the bed folds up. She pushes another button and a filled washbowl swings out from a panel. "That's for when we get dirty," explains Harry. She asks about a third button. "That's the emergency," he tells her. She pushes it and a large crockery jar falls out at Harry's feet. He puts it back.

Meanwhile, Vernon gets tired of waiting and heads for the cottage. He climbs the steps of the front porch, and his weight causes the house to tilt. Harry and Nell lose their balance; they weave from side-to-side a little, then Harry falls into a chair, and Nell lands on his lap. Vernon enters the house and slams the door, causing all the pictures to fall off the walls with a loud crash. Harry notices that a vase of flowers didn't fall and pushes it over.

Inside, Vernon is laughing derisively at Harry's home. Harry greets him affably, then suddenly socks Vernon on the nose. "There's a doorbell out there for visitors!" He walks off, but jumps as if expecting Vernon to kick him.

Vernon follows him. "Who is this?" he demands of Nell.

"Why, this is Harry, that I've been telling you about."

"That she's been telling you about," agrees Harry. "This is my house, and that's my girl, and this is the marriage license." He pulls the license out of his pocket. Vernon produces his own license, and claims it has a later date. Harry tries to trade his for Vernon's.

"You can't use that! My name is on it," says Vernon, so Harry takes his back and returns Vernon's. Vernon produces his engagement ring, as does Harry, and Nell exclaims she doesn't know what to do. As the three pace back and forth, Nell suddenly changes direction, causing Harry and Vernon to embrace each other.

Vernon asks Harry if he plays golf. Harry shakes his head "no," but when Nell gives him a sweet smile, he changes to "yes." Vernon declares that they'll play a match, and Nell agrees to be engaged to the winner. Harry agrees, then reaches for Nell's hand to give her the ring. Vernon sees this and pushes Harry away. Trying to regain his balance, Harry's hand rests on one of the buttons, causing the bed to emerge from the wall and knock Vernon to the floor.

On the golf course, a small crowd follows Harry, Vernon and Nell as the two men play. Vernon tees up his ball, and Harry tells him to play to the right because his house is parked to the left. Harry crouches down to watch, and Vernon tells him to get back. Harry takes two walnuts from his pocket and tries to crack them in his hand but is having difficulty.

Vernon cries, "Fore!"

Harry responds, "No, two," and shows him the two walnuts.

Vernon tells him to keep quiet, then swings. A reaction shot of the crowd shows them following the ball, making a complete circle before it lands on the ground. Harry offers to shake Vernon's hand, but Vernon slaps Harry's hand away.

Harry tees up his ball, swings at it and misses, and his body goes into a complete circle before he connects with the ball. The observers rush in front of him to follow the ball, and he has to crawl between various legs. The crowd laughs and a man comments, "Those two dubs think they are playing croquet." They disperse. Harry selects a club, swings, misses, and then hits the ball on the backstroke. It lands in a deep gully. Vernon laughs and tells him he'll have to play it from where it lies.

Harry removes an umbrella from his bag. He stands on the bank of the gully, then jumps, using the umbrella as a parachute. The umbrella falls into the gully, then Harry rolls down behind it, stopping beside his ball, which he picks up and kisses. Harry continually swings at and misses the ball, even after changing clubs. Finally, he notices that it's resting on the edge of a stick, so he jumps on the other edge, sending it into the air; it lands on the green, beside the hole.

Later, Vernon's ball has landed beside a sprinkler. Harry tells him to "play it from where it sets." Vernon asks him to show a little sportsmanship, and with Nell's encouragement, Harry agrees. He picks up the hose and folds it, shutting off the water. Vernon hits the ball. Harry, holding the hose, watches the ball fly. "Oh, boy! What a shot!" he enthuses. He absentmindedly drops the hose, soaking Vernon and Nell.

A ball lands beside him and he looks around; he then produces a sharp-ended stick from his bag, which he uses to pick up the ball. He places it in his bag, as a woman golfer walks up, asking him if he's seen a golf ball. He tells her he hasn't. The woman searches him, but finds nothing. She apologizes and starts to walk away, as Harry tips his hat, releasing a bunch of golf balls. As she reaches for a club with which to hit him, he runs away.

Harry runs up to the soaked Nell and Vernon, and apologizes. Vernon accuses him of doing it on purpose; Harry raises his fists, as Nell declares that she'll cancel the agreement if the two can't be good sportsmen. She leaves to change clothes; Harry tries to follow, but Vernon pulls him away. At the 17th hole, Harry tries to hit his ball while up in a tree. ("Tough shot," he tells Vernon.) At the 18th, Vernon's ball lands just short of the hole, while Harry's ball has gone inside a hose. Vernon says he'll have to play it there.

"What'll I use?" asks Harry.

"Your brain," Vernon replies, reminding him that if he misses this shot, "I win the match."

After figuring out where the ball is nestled, Harry swings and misses but hits the lever that turns on the water, which forces the ball from the hose. It rolls past the 18th hole, to a sign that reads "Pitching Balls To This Green Not Allowed." The ball bounces off the sign and heads back to the hole, where it rolls in. Harry begins cheering that he won the match; a disgusted Vernon walks off.

At the clubhouse, Nell hears that the match has ended, and spies Harry on the front porch of his cottage. Nell tells him that he won, and he replies, "I'm tickled, too!" They both go inside. Vernon asks if anyone has seen Nell, and they point toward Harry's house. He sees a window shade being pulled down and gets angry. He notices a truck parked nearby. He climbs into the truck and releases the brake, then jumps off…but his foot gets caught on a rope and he is dragged off. The truck crashes into the cottage, demolishing it. Vernon is freed and staggers off.

Two windows lie on the ground, shutters closed. One set of shutters opens and Nell emerges. She calls for Harry, who emerges from the other window.

"What happened?" she asks him.

"Somebody must have knocked on the door!" replies Harry.

They hear a pig squealing, and look around. Harry finds it trapped inside a jar. He frees the pig, and turns to Nell. They exchange loving looks and embrace.

No prints of this film are known to exist.

WHAT THE EXHIBITORS SAID:
Motion Picture Herald, *December 23, 1933*
   Harry Langdon — one of his best.
D. E. Fitton, Lyric Theatre, Harrison, AR.
Small town patronage.

Motion Picture Herald, *February 10, 1934*
   Pretty fair.
H. H. Gates, Garlock Theatre, Custer, SD.
Small town patronage.

A Circus Hoodoo

An Arvid E. Gillstrom Production Released in Two Reels. **DIRECTED BY** Arvid E. Gillstrom. **STORY BY** Dean Ward and Vernon Dent. **PHOTOGRAPHED BY** Gus Peterson. **FILM EDITOR:** Jack English. **RECORDED BY** William Fox. **CAST:** Harry Langdon, Vernon Dent, Eleanor Hunt, Matthew Betz, Diana Seaby, James C. Morton, Tom Kennedy, Joe Bordeaux, William Irving. Copyright February 15, 1934, Registration Number LP4490. Released by Paramount Productions, Inc., February 16, 1934.

SYNOPSIS: This film was unavailable for viewing. Following is a description based upon the cutting continuity submitted to the U.S. Copyright Office:

Watching his trapeze act, the manager of a circus sees one of his men falling, and declares, "There's someone in this circus who's a jinx and a hoodoo." Vernon and Harry are working inside a dummy horse. Vernon is the front end; Harry the back end. Vernon tells Harry to cut out a certain gag, but Harry insists, "Every horse does it." The manager complains about the jinx on the circus: he's lost two animals, and his best bareback rider broke her leg. At that point, Harry sneezes, causing his eyes to cross. The manager reacts and declares that Harry is the "hoodoo." Vernon uncrosses Harry's eyes by striking him on the back of the neck, and says it's just a coincidence. Harry sneezes again. His eyes cross, and when he looks into a mirror, it cracks. The manager fires both of them. Vernon takes his trunk and summons Harry.

Vernon sets up an umbrella stand on the midway, while Harry wanders off. He sees a hot dog vendor and orders one. The hot dog is too small for Harry, so he leaves it and walks off. The vendor blows up a balloon and places it in a bun, then calls Harry. The vendor smothers it with mustard. Harry takes a bite; the balloon bursts, which sends mustard into the vendor's face. As Harry walks off, he bumps into a girl leaving a tent and wearing a slinky costume. He smiles at her, and she slaps his face, knocking him to the ground. From the ground, he notices the name on the tent: "Madame Guessora, Mind Reader." He gets up and leaves, tripping over the tent rope.

On the midway, Vernon is drawing a crowd to his umbrella display. He assures his audience that the umbrellas will protect them from both sun and rain. "You never can tell when it may rain…remember the Johnstown Flood!" At that moment, water starts to fall, and some folks purchase umbrellas. We see that Harry is operating a hose. He sneezes and goes cross-eyed, and misdirects the hose, hitting a balloon vendor. He corrects the hose, just as Vernon sells the last umbrella to a man. The buyer walks off as the umbrella comes apart. He notices that water is only falling on one side of him. Realizing he's been conned, the customer summons an officer.

Harry sees the cop approaching and tries to hide the hose behind his back. The cop orders him to stick out his hands. Harry does so, one at a time. When the cop demands he show both hands at once, Harry — still holding the hose — squirts the cop in the face. The cop tells him, "Give me that hose!" Harry does so, and then runs away. The cop hands the hose to the disgruntled customer and runs after Harry.

Harry tells Vernon, "Cops!" and the two hide in the wild animals tent. The cop, joined by his chief and the crowd who bought umbrellas, head into the tent, which collapses. Harry and Vernon both escape. Harry runs past the mind reader, admires her again and slaps his own face before running off. Meanwhile, the cop and chief have emerged from the collapsed tent and continue their search.

Elsewhere on the midway, a barker is calling attention to two hula dancers. They are soon joined by Vernon, dressed in a hula outfit with a veil over his face. When the barker notices the new "girl," he proclaims, "Two hundred and fifty pounds of female and not a wasted ounce!" The cops approach while Vernon dances, and the veil slowly slips from his face. From inside the tent, Harry sees this and distracts the cop by "wrestling" with a dummy female. The cop enters the tent to investigate. Harry hides behind the dummy; the cop asks, "Which way did he go, Miss?"

Harry gestures with the dummy's hand and replies, "Down that way!"

Vernon, now dressed in his own clothes, sees Harry hiding behind the dummy and grabs his arm. The two run off the circus grounds, the cop in pursuit. Now in the city, they hide at a shoeshine stand. Harry gets a shine, his face hidden by a newspaper. He sneezes and his eyes cross. Vernon strikes his neck and mimes that the cop is nearby. They try sneaking away, but the cop sees them and follows. As they become aware, Harry and Vernon dash off; the cop starts to run, but trips over a cart. The two realize they've lost the cop, and duck inside a pawnshop.

Elsewhere, gangsters are reading a newspaper story about how the mayor and city treasurer are starting a "vigorous campaign" to rid the city of crime. Chick, the gangster boss, points out the story to his two molls and orders them to intercept both men in front of the Grove City Bank. One of the gangsters, "Cocaine" Joe, objects: "These two dames couldn't pull a job like that." Chick shoves Joe to the floor, and leaves with the two molls and the rest of his gang. Joe picks up the telephone receiver and calls police headquarters to warn the chief.

Outside the pawnshop, Vernon and Harry emerge in fancy suits. Harry now appears to be at least a foot taller than Vernon, and declares he's the boss from now on. When Vernon responds with mocking laughter, Harry pops him in the nose. Vernon kicks Harry in the shin, causing him to topple off the stilts under his pants. From a short distance, the cop sees them. As Harry rises, Vernon demands to know

Umbrella peddlers Harry and Vernon Dent are in trouble with Officer James C. Morton in A Circus Hoodoo.

who's the boss now. Harry picks up one of his stilts and declares, "I'm the boss now!" He brings it back to strike Vernon, and knocks out the cop, who was approaching from behind. The two run off, as the cop groggily comes to and resumes his pursuit.

At the bank building, the cop enters, looking for Harry and Vernon, whose heads pop up to observe. From inside, the mayor and city treasurer are heading for the bank's revolving doors, and we see that their suits are almost identical to those of Vernon and Harry. The cop, believing them to be his quarry, strike the mayor and treasurer each time they go around the revolving door. He grabs them both as the driver tells him who they are. The cop doesn't believe it and hauls both men away, with the driver continuing to protest. Vernon and Harry leave the bank and are spied by the two molls.

As the molls approach, Harry's eyes cross again and Vernon fixes them. One of the molls faints in Harry's arms. Vernon offers to call an ambulance, but the other moll tells him, "She has these often. Please take her up to the apartment." Harry has to carry her.

In the apartment, Harry sets the moll down on the chaise lounge, and sneezes again. Vernon fixes it and asks what Harry did with the girl. They both look around until Vernon accidentally sits on her, causing her to scream. Vernon orders Harry to get a hot water bottle. Meanwhile, the other moll telephones Chick and tells him the two officials are at her apartment.

Harry brings various pans and utensils from the kitchen, and Vernon rejects each one as inadequate. Vernon takes the girl's pulse, while Harry uses a small tube as a stethoscope. He puts one end into her mouth, and gets a squirt when he looks into the other end. Harry pulls out a big thermometer as Vernon goes to the next room for the other moll. "I think your friend needs you," he tells her, but she acts unconcerned and begins to flirt with him.

In the first room, the "fainted" moll is sitting up and she suddenly embraces Harry, calling him "Darling." Harry calls for Vernon, who finally comes outside with "his" moll, and she encourages Harry to humor her friend. Chick and two other gangsters, carrying camera and flash equipment, creep into the

Vernon about to fix Harry's "hoodoo" in A Circus Hoodoo.

apartment. As the two molls continue flirting with Harry and Vernon, one of the gangsters takes their picture. With the flash, Chick realizes that they are not the mayor and treasurer, but "a couple of bozos!"

A fight breaks out, overheard by three federal agents outside the door. They enter and take the gangsters into custody. One of the agents hands Harry one thousand dollars in bills as a reward "for the capture of these two crooks." Harry tosses the bills onto a nearby table. They land in an ashtray containing a burning cigarette. Vernon tells Harry they can buy a half-interest in the circus. Harry sneezes and Vernon fixes his eyes again. They look down and see that the thousand dollars has gone up in flames, and begin to weep loudly.

No prints of this film are known to exist.

WHAT THE EXHIBITORS SAID:
Motion Picture Herald, *March 24, 1934*
   Fair.
E.E. Holmquist, Broadway Theatre, Centerville, SD. General patronage.

Petting Preferred

An Arvid E. Gillstrom Production Released Released in Two Reels. DIRECTED BY Arvid E. Gillstrom. STORY BY Jack Townley. ADAPTATION BY Dean Ward and Vernon Dent. PHOTOGRAPHED BY Gus Peterson. FILM EDITOR: Jack English. RECORDED BY William Fox. CAST: Harry Langdon, Vernon Dent, Dorothy Granger, Eddie Baker, Alyce Ardell, William Irving, Billy Engle. WORKING TITLE: "Get Along, Little Dogie." Copyright April 26, 1934, Registration Number LP4644. Released by Paramount Productions, Inc., April 27, 1934.

SYNOPSIS: This film was unavailable for viewing. Following is a description based upon the cutting continuity submitted to the U.S. Copyright Office:

In the maternity ward of a hospital, a man is seen pacing back and forth. A doctor assures him that everything will be fine in a few minutes. The man continues pacing until Harry, an intern, enters carrying a basket covered with a blanket. He pulls back the blanket, and shows the man a litter of pups. When the man cries, "Oh, boy!" Harry responds, "Yeah, two-thirds!"

At the Vernon Dent household, Dorothy is pampering her dog, Snookums, much to her husband's displeasure. She's been brushing her dog's hair with his brush, and he angrily tells her, "You get rid of that mutt or I'll get a divorce!"

"Suits me," she haughtily replies, and he leaves the room in a huff.

The dog follows him into his bedroom. As he undresses, the dog grabs onto Vernon's pants and the two have a tug-of-war, until one trouser leg is completely torn off. Vernon picks up the dog and proceeds to the window, but Dorothy enters and stops him. She takes the dog from Vernon, pampers it, and then summons Colette, the maid. She orders Colette to take Snookums for a walk.

In the park, Colette is spooning with her policeman boyfriend and ignoring Snookums, who is resting beside a much bigger dog. Vernon sees this and surreptitiously removes the dog, attaches its leash to the bigger one, and sneaks away. When Colette finally stands up and sees the wrong dog, she screams and faints into the policeman's arms.

At a nearby pet store, Harry is sweeping up with a monkey on his shoulder. He sweeps everything into a corner where he thinks it won't be noticed. Vernon enters and asks if the shop stuffs dogs. Harry answers yes, and Vernon hands him Snookums. "Stuff this! He's driving me made and he's breaking up my home!" Harry argues that the dog "is too good to stuff." Vernon tells Harry to do it anyway and to keep the dog there until he calls for him, and leaves the shop. Harry puts Snookums on the counter and starts teaching tricks, which the dog obeys. Harry looks toward the door and defiantly states, "Not going to stuff this dog!" He puts Snookums in a cage at the back of the store.

Back at the Dent home, Colette and the policeman are with Dorothy. Colette tells Dorothy, "Somebody stole Snookums!" Dorothy panics, and orders the cop to "call a policeman!" She tells Colette, "If you don't find little Snookums at once, I'll discharge you!" Colette leaves, while the cop tries to calm Dorothy.

Colette goes to Harry's pet store, shows him a picture of Dorothy holding Snookums and asks to see a dog "just like that."

"We're all out of dogs just like that," Harry tells her. "We'll have a shipment in tomorrow." As Harry is showing her other animals, she sees Snookums in its cage. She takes Snookums out, as Harry objects. "You can't take that dog out of there!"

"Pretty please?" asks Colette.

"No 'pretty please!'" says Harry.

Just then the proprietor of the store tells Harry, "Murphy's dog is having kittens! Help me! Do something!" The proprietor runs off, and Harry is torn between Snookums and his job. He chooses to follow his boss, and Colette leaves with Snookums.

At the Dent household, Vernon enters with a cage covered in a blanket. Dorothy is delighted, until the blanket is removed, revealing a duck. Dorothy scolds him for getting her hopes up. As Vernon lowers the cage, a cat is seen climbing up his coat front. Dorothy gets angrier. "I don't like cats! I want my Snookums!" Vernon claims not to know where the dog is, which only makes Dorothy grow hysterical. She orders him to find her dog and lets out a loud, shrill scream. Vernon tells her to shut up, and she begins to sob uncontrollably. Feeling remorseful, Vernon agrees to look for the dog.

Vernon returns to the pet shop and upon seeing him, Harry becomes very nervous. Vernon reminds him, "I left a dog here to be boarded," and asks for it. Flustered, Harry claims to remember Vernon and the dog, and tells him that the dog asked to go for a walk outside, so he let it go.

"What are you trying to do, kid me?" asks Vernon.

Harry gets even more nervous as Vernon threatens to make trouble. The proprietor enters, and as he and Vernon talk, Harry notices the photo that Colette brought in. He turns over the photo and sees it is stamped with an address. The proprietor takes Vernon to the back room to show him the boarded dogs, as Harry grabs his coat and quickly exits.

Meanwhile, Colette returns home with Snookums. Dorothy is overjoyed and cuddles the dog, talking sweetly to it. The doorbell rings and Colette answers. Harry tells her he's come for the dog, and she slams the door in his face. He enters and follows her, and demands the dog. She tries a kiss to quiet him. "No, certainly not!" he shouts, and she puts her hand over his mouth. He bites it and she screams. Dorothy asks what's wrong.

"Mice, ma'am," says Colette.

Harry continues to demand the dog as Dorothy enters the room, and Colette kisses him, which makes him grow docile. "I want that dog," says Harry, and she kisses him again. He grows even weaker and sweetly asks, "Got a little puppy around?" She kisses him again.

Dorothy asks Colette, "What is the meaning of this?" Colette introduces Harry as "Dr. Puppy," her fiancé. Impressed, Dorothy leaves the two of them alone. Harry tries to object again, but Colette resumes kissing him.

Snookums appears at the doorway, and Harry dives for him. He and Colette wrestle with the dog on the ground, until Dorothy enters. She assumes they're getting physical, and tells Harry, "Doctor, please! After all, there's a time and a place for everything!" A buzzer is heard and Colette excuses herself: "I think the ice man wants to see me." Dorothy escorts Harry to the door.

Back at the pet store, the proprietor and Vernon are looking at various dogs, when Vernon spies the photo of his wife and Snookums. "How did that photo get here?" he asks, and the proprietor tells him that she's Harry's sweetheart. "That's my wife!" cries Vernon, and he quickly leaves the store.

Harry is outside the house and is trying to figure out how to get back in. Stopping to think, he leans on the door, which opens, causing him to fall into the hallway. Snookums climbs on his back. The dog licks his face and falls to the floor as Harry gets up. The dog crawls on its stomach into the living room and Harry does likewise. The dog proceeds to the kitchen, where Colette is entertaining her boyfriend the cop. The cop stands up and trips over Harry. Colette introduces him as "the doctor," and escorts him out the back door.

Harry looks in an open window and sees Dorothy with Snookums beside her. She shifts the dog to another position as Harry's hand reaches in. He grabs Dorothy's hair and she screams. At that moment, Colette is on the cop's lap; he gets up to investigate and she falls to the floor. Harry hears this and lets go of Dorothy's hair; she faints. The cop and Colette rush into her room. Colette tries to revive her, while the cop rushes outside. He finds Harry and tells him, "Doctor, Mrs. Dent has passed out. You'll have to come in and take care of her."

Entering the room, Colette offers to get water and exits. The cop tells Harry to "loosen her dress so she can breathe."

"Oh, no," says Harry. "You do it."

"You do it, Doctor. It's your duty," says the cop.

Harry starts to undo Dorothy's dress with one hand, covering his eyes with the other. As the cop leaves, Harry instead tries feeling her pulse, checking it against his watch. He realizes something is wrong. He opens the watch and sand comes out. Checking Dorothy's pulse again, he puts the watch down on her chest, and it slips down the front of her dress. Harry tries to figure out how to get the watch. He places his head on her chest to hear the watch ticking.

At that moment, Vernon walks by the window, looks inside and sees Harry's head on his wife's chest. He heads to the front door and quietly enters. He finds a gun and draws a bead on Harry as the cop comes up from behind and clubs Vernon with his nightstick. Vernon collapses onto a couch.

Colette quickly enters as the cop tells her, "I got that burglar!"

"Oh, no," says Colette, "that's the master!"

The cop offers to get the doctor. He brings Harry into the room to revive Vernon. Harry gets some water from a pitcher and sprinkles it over Vernon's face. Reviving, Vernon sees Harry and grabs him. "You little runt! I'll teach you to fool around with my wife!"

At that moment, Dorothy revives, sees the fracas, and runs to her husband. "Darling, don't do that," she tells him. "That's the doctor! He's engaged to marry Colette!" Hearing that, the cop grows angry. The cop lunges for Harry but strikes his chin on the mantelpiece and collapses. Harry runs off, pursued by Vernon. He ducks into another room and closes the door in Vernon's face. Harry holds the door to keep Vernon from opening it, but Vernon sneaks around to another entrance.

Harry continues to pull on the door, then gets a long cord and ties it around the doorknob. Meanwhile, Vernon is behind Harry, watching. Harry turns to his observer and points out his clever tying job, until it dawns on him that it's Vernon. Harry dashes off, accidentally knocking over a table, which Vernon trips over. Harry notices the cop coming toward him, and turns back toward Vernon. The cop and Vernon run into each other, as Harry ducks away. Vernon and the cop wrestle, each thinking the other is Harry.

Outside the house, Harry comes out and is pursued by Snookums. "Go away! Go on back," Harry tells the dog. "I don't want anything to do with you." He continues running but the dog still follows him. He picks up a brick and throws it, thinking Snookums will chase it. The brick goes through the pet store window, and all the dogs that had been on display run into the street Harry runs down the street, chased by all the dogs.

No prints of this film are known to exist.

WHAT THE CRITICS SAID:
Variety, *March 20, 1934; Reviewed by Chic.*

Harry Langdon and Vernon Dent in a comedy with few good moments. Opens with the stale gag of the anxious father in the hospital and a litter of pups. Flat finish. Business is familiar and too much horseplay to be funny to other than lowbrow audiences. Style of stuff that went out some time ago. Sound is very bad.

Counsel on De Fence

A Columbia Short Subject Released in Two Reels. DIRECTED BY Arthur Ripley. STORY AND SCREENPLAY BY Harry McCoy. PHOTOGRAPHY BY Benjamin Kline. EDITED BY Al Clark. CAST: Harry Langdon, Renee Whitney, Earle Foxe, Marjorie "Babe" Kane, Jack Norton, William Irving, Charles Dorety, Lew Davis, Robert "Bobby" Burns. WORKING TITLE: "The Barrister." Copyright October 29, 1934, Registration Number LP5070; Renewed July 2, 1962, Number R297689. Released by Columbia Pictures Corporation, October 25, 1934.

SYNOPSIS: Newspaper headlines describe the recent Drake poison case. In an office, lawyer Travis is in conference on the Drake case and feels that Toni Drake is innocent. Lawyer Darrow Langdon soon arrives and manages to disrupt the conference. One of the lawyers present describes Travis's theory that Drake committed suicide to put his wife on the spot for refusing to reconcile. Darrow acts out the lawyer's theory then announces that he can prove that Toni poisoned her husband. Travis reminds him that they're trying to prove the wife's innocence.

A phone call, which Darrow answers, announces that Toni has escaped custody. She arrives at Travis's office and they embrace. Travis soon removes Darrow's clothes and tosses them to Toni, who is hiding behind a screen. He then gives Darrow $50 and tells him to buy a new suit. The stripped lawyer puts on a long coat and leaves. Toni, now dressed in Darrow's clothes, follows him and reveals her true identity. Darrow agrees to help her and hides her in a hamper on wheels. While Darrow is distracted, a worker pushes the hamper away and someone puts a dummy dressed as a cop on top of it. Darrow then tries to get the "cop's" attention, with no success. He then sees the fake cop carried away but fails to notice that a real cop now sits on the hamper. Harry flings a brick, knocks down the cop, and the chase is on.

Darrow runs into Travis, who is on a stretcher and is being loaded into an ambulance. The police capture Toni; Travis ends up in a hospital, where he receives a telegram stating that Darrow will defend Toni in court. At the trial, Darrow tells an assistant to switch a prop bottle for the bottle of poison, which is being used as evidence. Before he can do this, Darrow drinks the whole bottle of poison, which shocks the courtroom. The jury finds Toni not guilty and Darrow is told he drank real poison. He hails a taxi and tells the driver to go to a hospital. The taxi spins in the street causing Darrow to regurgitate the poison. An ambulance pulls up and attendants grab Darrow and pump his stomach. Soon after this his stomach is pumped yet again and he finally ends up in Travis's office. While he is being congratulated, the prosecuting attorney arrives and announces that he's going to have Darrow's stomach pumped. He quickly faints.

ANALYSIS: Harry McCoy and Arthur Ripley, who worked on *The Chaser*, reunite to hand Langdon another series of labored gags in poor taste. *Counsel on De Fence* is based in part on a 1932 Warner Bros. feature called *The Mouthpiece*, in which Warren William plays a sleazy attorney who willingly swallows a bottle of slow-acting poison to achieve an acquittal for his guilty client; he then calmly submits to a stomach pump once the verdict is in. The dapper mustache Langdon sports in this film was probably intended to evoke William's character, but it no longer resonates with audiences and undercuts the effectiveness of his facial pantomime.

When his assistant fails to switch bottles, Darrow Langdon is forced to endure two stomach-pumpings, neither of which is necessary because, it is implied, he's already vomited up the poison. It's astonishing that Ripley, McCoy or Jules White — or Langdon, for that matter — could possibly have thought audiences of the day would laugh as Darrow emerges from the taxi wiping his lips and thanking the driver for relieving him of the need for a hospital.

The "dummy policeman" gag from *Long Pants* is revived yet again; clearly it was one of Langdon's favorite bits, given the number of variations he used previously in the Roach and Educational shorts. In this case, the situation is identical to that of its inspiration: Darrow has concealed Toni Drake and, as he checks the street, the receptacle winds up beside a theater and a stage hand places the fake cop on top of it. As would become typical of Langdon's Columbia comedies, the bit is badly staged and marred by gratuitous slapstick, when Darrow's girlfriend secretary tears his overcoat in anger.

HARRY MOMENT: Harry's brief pantomime of the lawyer's theory is delightful and convincing.

WHAT THE CRITICS SAID:
Film Daily, *October 27, 1934*

Harry Langdon does a role that is away from his usual characterization. Here he has a dressed up part as a young law partner with a firm of criminal attorneys. When the head of the firm meets with an accident, Harry undertakes to defend the girl accused of poisoning her husband. The comedian swallows the poison to prove that it wasn't poison to the jury, and the results are quite hilarious as different groups insist on rushing him to hospitals to have his stomach pumped out.

Film Daily, *December 1, 1934*

Some mild tomfoolery in which Harry Langdon, as the witless member of a law firm, goes to the defense of a woman accused of murdering her husband and, after a burlesqued court trial, wins her freedom. To put over his arguments to the jury, Harry drinks from the bottle supposed to contain some of the poison given by the woman to her husband. Harry's assistant doesn't get a chance to switch bottles as they had arranged to do, but there is no fatal effect nevertheless, and for the windup the comedian has his stomach pumped a few times.

WHAT THE EXHIBITORS SAID:
Motion Picture Herald, *March 16, 1935*
   Good comedy.
   Sammie Jackson, Jackson Theatre, Flomation, AL. Small town and rural patronage.

Shivers

A Columbia Short Subject Released in Two Reels. **DIRECTED BY** Arthur Ripley. **STORY BY** Arthur Ripley. **PHOTOGRAPHY BY** George Meehan. **EDITED BY** William A. Lyon. **CAST:** Harry Langdon, Florence Lake, Richard Elliot, Chester Gan, Louis Vincenor. Copyright December 21, 1934, Registration Number LP5192; Renewed November 2, 1962, Number R303629. Released by Columbia Pictures Corporation, December 24, 1934.

SYNOPSIS: Minerva Krum, wife of mystery novelist Ichabod Somersault Krum (Harry Langdon), is renting a house in which a gruesome double murder was committed, in order to inspire her husband's next book. A rental agent shows them around, pointing out bloodstains and other aspects of the crime. After the agent departs, they head upstairs to the bedroom. Minerva offers to prepare Ichabod's typewriter while he dresses for bed. She's delighted the house is so spooky, believing it will put Ichabod in the proper mood to compose a mystery. However, she doesn't care for the strange ring he wears, and thinks he's hiding something from her even after he explains that the ring came from his mother.

As Ichabod begins typing, a window slams and other noises are heard. A Chinese man crawls through a secret opening in the wall. He tells Ichabod that the house is used by smugglers and that he and his brothers are being held against their will. He begins talking to Ichabod in Chinese, telling him that they are blood brothers, and shows him that not only do they wear the same ring but also have identical marks on their knees. Ichabod objects, but soon both are arguing in Chinese.

Minerva is horrified to learn that she's married to a Chinaman. ("I see it all now. That's why you always wanted to do the family laundry.") She refuses to come to bed with him, and instead crawls up to the "top bunk," which is actually a canopy, through which she falls onto the mattress, and the force sends Ichabod up onto a ceiling lamp. The lights go out and a knocking sound is heard. Minerva orders Ichabod to see who it is.

Florence Lake and Langdon in Shivers.

As Ichabod comes down off the lamp, he falls through a trap door, and runs back to the bedroom. His wife accuses him of being afraid. As he goes downstairs, one of his suspenders gets caught on the railing. When released, he ends up on the couch and sits on an accordion that attaches to his backside. Each time he moves, music is heard. He finds nothing downstairs and returns to the bedroom, and Minerva removes the accordion. A voice calls out, "Get out of this house!" Ichabod wants to leave, but Minerva refuses — until she sees a disembodied head in a trunk ordering them to get out, after which she falls through the trap door. Together they try to get out, going through one door, only to find another door that is locked. As they push, we see that the door leads directly to the outside, with a sheer drop from the second floor. The door opens and they fall out.

The scene shifts to a train. Inside, Ichabod is furiously typing and Minerva is egging him on. Everything that happened previously was the story he has been writing. They discuss different aspects of the tale, and Minerva says he still needs "a good smashing finish." At that moment, another train approaches from the opposite direction. Both trains crash into each other, and as they emerge from the wreckage, Minerva asks Ichabod if he's got the finish.

"What finish?" is his dazed reply.

ANALYSIS: *Shivers* purports to be a typical haunted house romp, except that Ripley, who both wrote and directed, can't leave well enough alone. From the rental agent pointing out bloodstains on a carpet, to Minerva's glee that rats roam the halls and birds occupy the fireplace, to her ultimate distaste that her husband is actually part Chinese, the film's atmosphere is one of discomfort rather than thrills. This is a pity, because many of the gags are quite enjoyable: Ichabod stepping into another room (the one with the rats) to change into his night clothes, emerging dressed for bed in a split second; he and the Chinese man arguing in gibberish; the bit with the accordion. The short also utilizes background music to enhance the mood, a rarity for Columbia. *Shivers* is primarily situation-driven, and Langdon is given scant opportunity to put his individual touch on its scenes, unlike his previous "scare" comedy, *The First 100 Years*.

HARRY MOMENT: While the accordion is attached to his rear, Ichabod alternates between large and small steps and turns, varying the sounds the instrument makes, while not comprehending that he's the one making the music.

WHAT THE EXHIBITORS SAID:
Motion Picture Herald, *February 2, 1935*

A good comedy. Plenty of laughs. Our Saturday fans sure like Langdon.
J. O. Smith, Paramount, Ashland and Dixie Theatres, Ashland and Linesville, AL. Small town patronage.

Motion Picture Herald, *June 8, 1935*

A pretty good comedy. Both kids and grown-ups liked it.
Chas. Nelson, Fay Theatre, Jasper, FL. Small town and rural audience.

Motion Picture Herald, *July 27, 1935*

Kept the audience in an uproar from start to finish. Langdon is one who never lost his comedy through talking pictures.
W. M. Allison, Mission Theatre, Clayton, NM. General patronage.

His Bridal Sweet

A Columbia Short Subject Released in Two Reels. DIRECTED BY Alf Goulding. STORY AND SCREENPLAY BY John Grey. PHOTOGRAPHY BY Benjamin Kline. EDITED BY William A. Lyon. CAST: Harry Langdon, Geneva Mitchell, Billy Gilbert, Bud Jamison, Lew Kelly, Robert "Bobby" Burns, Alice Belcher, Eddie Baker. Copyright March 12, 1935, Registration Number LP5409; Renewed December 5, 1962, Number R306051. Released by Columbia Pictures Corporation, March 15, 1935.

SYNOPSIS: Harry and his new bride are riding in their car as he tries to kiss her, with no success. She spots their honeymoon cottage and insists on stopping to see it before they catch their train. Inside, people are hearing the virtues of the all-electric house. Harry is soon pummeled by various electric appliances. He stumbles into a room and meets a drunk named Lush, who pushes a button, causing Harry to vanish behind a wall as a bar appears.

His new wife asks him to the buy the house, and he agrees. A strange man approaches Harry and sits next to him on a couch. He begins to twitch, and Harry calls for a doctor. A doctor arrives and declares that the man has smallpox. Everyone in the house is quarantined, and the doctor departs. The people inside the house are told that the husbands will have to stay in one room and the wives in another.

Harry ends up in another room with the drunk, who locks him in. The souse tells Harry that he can be violent and once killed a man with a razor. He also says that he might get hazy and forget he knows Harry. He then tells him to quack so he'll remember him. Harry quacks to remain safe and the drunk now "sees" a lion in the room. Harry "shoots" the lion, and the drunk is relieved. The drunk then gets banged up in a mechanical bed and calls for a doctor. Harry dresses as a doctor, but the drunk hallucinates that his pal has become a giant liquor bottle. He opens the "bottle," pours out the sauce, then disposes of the bottle by throwing Harry out a window. The other people break down the door to Harry's room, and his wife soon joins him outside. They hail a car and tell the driver to hurry them to the depot, but Harry's coat gets caught and he winds up being dragged along the road.

ANALYSIS: *His Bridal Sweet* has some clever ideas marred by poor pacing and execution; the result is a pretty weak comedy. Even without Ripley, the bad taste parade continues with references to smallpox and Billy Gilbert's claim to have murdered someone with a razor. Harry, of course, tries to humor the lunatic by "seeing" what he sees, with bits that recall the jail scene in *The Hansom Cabman*. Such material worked well in silent films because of the unreality of the characters and swiftness of pacing. With sound, everything is leaden. Langdon musters up a few chuckles as he reacts to the house's various quirks and Gilbert's eccentricities, but nothing flows naturally from his personality. A few less mechanical gags and a bit more emphasis on Harry might have resulted in something far greater than this middlingly amusing short.

WHAT THE CRITICS SAID:
The Philadelphia Exhibitor, *April 1, 1935*
   Wild time in a sample, modern house where electricity operates everything. WEAK.

Motion Picture Herald, *April 13, 1935*
   There are numerous laughs in this more or less slapstick comedy, featuring the "dead-panned" Harry Langdon. Harry, just married, stops with his bride on their way to the train to see the demonstration house of the type they plan to buy. Everything in it is of the electrical gadget type, and Harry's troubles begin before he gets inside. When the house is quarantined for the night, things get worse and worse, as Harry is locked in the bedroom with a burly inebriate. He and his wife escape finally, but it is by way of a window.

Film Daily, *April 22, 1935*
   At a house party one of the guests develops smallpox, so all the gang are quarantined. Harry Langdon, about to depart on his honeymoon, is separated from his bride, and finds himself forced to occupy a room with a very violent nut. The comedy consists in Langdon's frantic efforts to

Billy Gilbert and Langdon in His Bridal Sweet.

humor the goof, and to keep him from doing him bodily injury. The trouble with the "comedy" in this picture is that many in the audience may not find much humor in the antics of a demented person, and Langdon doesn't lighten it up very much.

Box Office, *May 18, 1935*

Amusing in spots, although the humor is dragged out somewhat. Harry Langdon and his bride join a party of prospects inspecting the latest in electric houses. Some laughs are caused by the modern appliances working in an unexpected manner but the comedy ideas gave out when the entire party is compelled to spend the night due to a smallpox scare. Here Harry is forced to sleep with a lunatic and his efforts to keep him quiet may fail to impress audiences as being particularly humorous. Geneva Mitchell makes an attractive leading woman. Below average short.

WHAT THE EXHIBITORS SAID:
Motion Picture Herald, *August 10, 1935*

A very good comedy that brought plenty of laughs. Chas. T. Nelson, Fay Theatre, Jasper, FL. Small town and rural patronage.

Love, Honor and Obey (the Law)

A Goodrich (B.F.) Company Release in Two Reels. **PRODUCED BY** Audio Productions, Inc. **DIRECTED BY** Leigh Jason. **WRITTEN BY** Stanley E. Rauh. **CAST:** Harry Langdon, Monty Collins, Diana Lewis, Fred Toones, Robert Graves, Robert "Bobby" Burns, Dick Curtis, William McCall. Copyright May 23, 1935, Registration Number LP5561. Released by Goodrich (B.F.) Company, April 29, 1935.

SYNOPSIS: In the Freckled Arms apartments, some workers are discussing Harry's forthcoming wedding to the police chief's daughter. A car pulls up with Harry and his equally inebriated friend Bob. Bob was a rival for the daughter's affections but lost out to Harry. They stumble out of the car into the apartment building, where Harry gets a stack of messages from his intended bride. He calls his girl and is told that her father was burned up about Harry getting a ticket and that if he breaks another traffic law the wedding is off. Harry tells her that he got her a canary as a pet and vows to get to the next day's wedding without getting a ticket.

The next morning, Bob turns back Harry's alarm clock so that he will be late for the wedding. When it goes off, Harry leaps to his feet and asks for a carpet sweeper for his tongue. Bob spies a cop near Harry's car and tells him to get going to his wedding. Once they get in the car, Harry notices the cop's watch and realizes that they're going to be late. The car speeds off toward the wedding as Bob encourages Harry to drive faster.

After a while, Bob reminds Harry to get the canary he promised to his bride. They pull up next to a "No Parking" sign and Harry runs into a pet store to get the bird. Bob tries to get a cop's attention but fails to do so; they move on. Bob then tells Harry that he forgot the ring and that he must get a new one from a store. Two motorcycle cops pull them over and prepare to give Harry a ticket. Suddenly, some crooks shoot their way out of a bank robbery and the cops leave in hot pursuit, failing to issue Harry's ticket.

Harry goes into a jewelry store to get a ring. Bob calls the police and reports that a crazy driver is causing havoc and gives them Harry's license number. At the wedding, the police chief wonders where the groom is. He tells his daughter that if Harry gets another ticket then the wedding is off. Harry soon arrives and brings in the canary for his bride. As the ceremony begins, the bird manages to get drunk and loudly annoys Harry. A cat eyes the bird and ends up eating it. The ceremony is a success and they are married. The police chief gives the newlyweds a car as a wedding present. Harry then gives his old car to Bob and the couple leaves for their honeymoon. A group of policemen appear and arrest Bob, whom they believe to be the crazy driver.

Filmed before *His Bridal Sweet*, but released after.

ANALYSIS: One of the more unusual shorts in Harry's canon, *Love, Honor and Obey (the Law)*, as mentioned in the text, was paid for by tire manufacturer B. F. Goodrich as a promotional gimmick. Since the emphasis is as much on driving infractions as it is on Harry's upcoming wedding, the short isn't executed as smoothly as an average theatrical comedy. There's also an unfortunate lapse into 1930s racial humor, with two stereotypical black laborers providing the exposition at the film's opening (Fred "Snowflake" Toones, who sounds a like a cross between Eddie "Rochester" Anderson and Stepin Fetchit, is a receptionist who'd rather read a recipe book for fried chicken than answer the telephone). Characterizations such as these had been nonexistent in Langdon's earlier films, an aspect that makes them timeless.

Beyond the stereotypes, the comedy is rather good, with Monty Collins striking the right note as the suitor who seems to be a pal but is actually trying to sabotage Harry's wedding. There are some good sight gags, such as Harry absent-mindedly picking up a small trashcan outside the church, instead of the birdcage; also the canary drinking altar wine and doing some wild swinging on its perch until a cat eats it. There's also a choice bit as Harry tries to discern which top hat is his. Overall, the film is on par with Langdon's Educational shorts; this is appropriate, since it was produced by one of Educational's units, despite the "Audio Productions" screen credit.

Presented in traveling road show engagements with no admission charged, the short was never reviewed by trade or mainstream publications.

HARRY MOMENT: After the wedding, Harry is looking over a table containing four top hats, trying to identify his own. His is collapsible, so he pushes on one hat, then another, but they are simply crushed under the weight. Upon ruining the second hat, he's unsure if he should continue. After a brief hesitation, he crushes the third hat, and realizes (with a pleased smile) that the remaining one is his.

The Leather Necker

A Columbia Short Subject Released in Two Reels. Written and **DIRECTED BY** Arthur Ripley. **SCREENPLAY BY** John Grey. **PHOTOGRAPHY BY** John Stumar. **EDITED BY** James Sweeney. **CAST:** Harry Langdon, Mona Rico, Wade Boteler, Bud Jamison. Copyright May 18, 1935, Registration Number LP5539; Renewed December 12, 1962, Number R306574. Released by Columbia Pictures Corporation, May 9, 1935.

SYNOPSIS: Harry is being chased by two men in their auto. The passenger says that the reason they are chasing Harry occurred when he was in the Marines in South America. The man's name is Donegan and he was a sergeant who was chasing Polero, the bandit. In a flashback in South America, Sergeant Donegan has a letter from his girl, Lolita. She invites him to

Harry can't wait until grace is over in The Leather Necker.

dinner and wants him to bring a friend. Donegan reluctantly invites fellow soldier Harry to dinner, where they meet Lolita and her family. She begins to flirt with Harry and kisses him. He swoons and falls out the window. When he gets back inside the house they sit down to dinner.

Lolita dances with Harry as Donegan simmers with anger. Gunfire signals the arrival of bandits, who capture Harry, Donegan and other soldiers. Later, in the bandit's camp, Donegan suggests that the bandits might torture Harry, who would reveal the whereabouts of other soldiers and the location of ammunition. He then says Harry should be killed to avoid talking. Another soldier, Casey, tells Donegan to give Harry a chance. The sergeant asks Harry if he would talk if tortured and the answer is yes. Casey tells Harry that since he might talk, Sergeant Donegan is going to choke him to death. Harry then says that he wouldn't talk, but Donegan doesn't care.

Donegan and Casey get in a fistfight, during which Harry is knocked cold by a rock. Other soldiers arrive and, in the confusion, Donegan is knocked out. He comes to and chases Harry, who climbs atop a long pole. As the sergeant attempts to shoot him, Harry fires back with a slingshot. Artillery shells knock off pieces of the pole, which then breaks, dropping Harry on top of Donegan.

Back in the present day, the car chasing Harry pulls to a sudden stop and flings Donegan into the street. He tells his driver that Harry married his girl while he spent a year in the hospital with a broken neck. Harry pulls up beside them and asks for directions. Realizing who it is, he drives away and the chase continues.

ANALYSIS: One of Langdon's greatest silents, *All Night Long*, is thoroughly plundered and what emerges is more sad than amusing. Whether or not Ripley was involved in the original scenario is open to conjecture, but his plodding direction kills the comedy in *The Leather Necker*. Scenes such as Harry amidst the mountain of potatoes, his eagerness to accompany the sergeant on a dinner date, and his swooning reaction to being kissed, all highlights of the original film, fall sadly flat in this one.

Not helping matters is Wade Boteler, who is no Vernon Dent. His Sergeant Donegan is all sadistic bluster without a trace of comic shading. He talks of torture and of murdering Harry, ostensibly to protect the other men but in reality because of Lolita. Even Harry's pop-eyed reactions to these threats are overpowered by the sheer bad taste of it all. The framing sequence, with Harry in his car obsessively pursued by Donegan, is woefully unfunny; it's also diminished by some sloppy process work and, worst of all, is never resolved.

WHAT THE CRITICS SAID:
Film Daily, *May 31, 1935*

A lot of typical Langdon humor and slapstick gags worked into a U.S. Marines background. Harry, a K. P. private is invited to dinner by Sergeant Wade Boteler where Boteler's girl makes a play for the comic. They are captured by bandits and most of the humor comes in while Boteler is trying to kill Harry to get rid of him. A bit slow except for some automobile chase scenes which open and close the film.

Motion Picture Herald, *June 1, 1935*

Harry Langdon, in the lead of this comedy, is the chief reason for the amusement that is in it. The story offers little, but the comedian is really amusing.

The Philadelphia Exhibitor, *June 1, 1935*

Not as good as some of the Langdons, with a tropical country background, the usual army background, with Langdon and the officer fighting for the girl. There is a chase, as well. Langdon is up to standard. SO-SO.

Box Office, *June 8, 1935*

The Harry Langdon fans might enjoy this bit of nonsense, but the former silent star won't win any new admirers through his latest effort. It's of the slapstick variety and contains little that is fresh…Fair.

Atlantic Adventure

A Columbia Pictures Release. 68 minutes. **DIRECTED BY** Albert Rogell. **STORY BY** Diana Bourbon. **SCREENPLAY:** John T. Neville and Nat Dorfman. **PHOTOGRAPHY BY** John Stumar. **CAST:** Nancy Carroll, Lloyd Nolan, Harry Langdon, Arthur Hohl, Robert Middlemass, John Wray, E.E. Clive, Dwight Frye, Nana Bryant. Copyright August 5, 1935, Registration Number LP5701; Renewed January 22, 1963, Number R310927. Released by Columbia Pictures Corporation, September 10, 1935.

SYNOPSIS: Dan Miller, the Daily Chronicle's self-proclaimed "ace" reporter, is forever postponing dates with his sweetheart, Helen, because he's been ordered to cover a story. After one too many of these, she snubs him for someone else. He tries to win her back by choosing her over an interview with the city's district attorney, but loses her after punching out his rival. Making matters worse, he turns in a fake interview, only to discover that the D.A. was murdered; the editor fires him for not covering the story.

Having lost both girlfriend and job, Dan determines to get both back by covering the murderer's arrest, on a tip from a friendly detective. He asks his photographer pal "Snapper" MacGillicuddy (Harry Langdon) to get Helen on board the ship where the arrest is to take place. However, the murderer has slipped aboard in disguise, and Helen is unwittingly mistaken for an accomplice in a major jewel theft. Once at sea, the murderer and jewel thieves discover each other and combine forces. When that happens, Dan, Helen and "Snapper" find themselves in grave danger, from which only Dan's moxie can extract them.

ANALYSIS: In keeping with his other work at Columbia, Langdon's role in *Atlantic Adventure* is not an approximation of the Little Elf, but merely a comedy relief character that could have been essayed by any competent supporting player. "Snapper" MacGillicuddy is a little slow on the uptake and certainly likes to eat, forever reaching for some kind of snack and eager to sit down to dinner. Since Lloyd Nolan's Dan Miller is something of a con artist, and none too good at it, the two could have formed a comedy duo with more "Abbott & Costello" potential than Langdon shared with Ben Lyon in *A Soldier's Plaything*. Alas, team comedy is not the object of this script, which quickly bogs down in tired gangster melodrama and romantic complications between Nolan and Nancy Carroll, who's actually top-billed, yet barely registers any emotions beyond fear and anger. The best thing about *Atlantic Adventure* is that it moves like lightning, but its situations are trite, its dialogue is tepid, and its comedy is uninspired.

WHAT THE CRITICS SAID:
Brooklyn Daily Eagle, *August 30, 1935; Reviewed by C.G.*

When a Hollywood-type reporter, his girl-friend, jewel thieves, hijackers, and a murderer are thrown together on

Langdon sketches costar Nancy Carroll between takes on Atlantic Adventure.

an ocean liner, a film of familiar screen pattern, such as *Atlantic Adventure*, results...

Much of the humor in the presentation is of the unintentional brand, due to implausible situations, and the fact that a nimble brain is needed to follow with the constant jackrabbit movements of the characters. Harry Langdon, the veteran comedian, supplies the intentional farcical aspects entertainingly.

Nancy Carroll returns to the screen as the somewhat bewildered sweetheart and has little to do but look pretty. The bulk of action centers around Lloyd Nolan, the Dan Miller of the film, whose breezy portrayal of the gentleman of the press is effective for purposes of plot.

Box Office, *August 31, 1935*

A picture of the loves and duties of a newspaper man who goes to extremes to get his job back after losing it through carelessness and because of a woman. Film is not very entertaining and too fantastic for any lifting out of the ordinary programmer class. The ace reporter of a big newspaper has a date with his girl. He has broken date after date and in desperation to keep this one decides to fake an interview with the district attorney. On this particular occasion the D.A. is murdered and the reporter is fired for his negligence. On a tip he hops a boat and encounters jewel thieves and the murderer. After a series of complications comes the usual happy fadeout.

Variety, *September 4, 1935*

Only lack of cast names keeps this in the dual pix classification. It has a familiar but well-worked out story which has received a fine adaptation. Added to this, Al Rogell has done a bang-up job of megging and the well-chosen cast comes through. This one is good enough to rate more than ordinary exploitation mention by intermediate houses....

[Plot] has been done on previous occasions, but it's largely good cast performances and clean-cut direction that makes it jell. Actually, the seemingly involved action on the high seas is developed to such fashion that one climax after another is stacked up until the story eventually bursts in flaming action with the newspaper scribe and ship officers corralling the four crooks.

Romantic passages subordinated for the sake of action and plot build-up. Scenes in city news room are astonishingly restrained for a feature production. Selection of Lloyd Nolan, who did similar role in *Front Page* road production, a neat bit of casting. Harry Langdon, as news cameraman, provides droll laughs and is splendid foil. After suffering from English accent at outset, Nancy Carroll comes through. She looks particularly well here. John Wray also very good as murder suspect.

Camera job by John Stumar measures up and production value high for story of type. A strong pix for double programs and can solo in some spots.

Film Daily, *September 10, 1935*

Though it hasn't a great deal of strength for marquee purposes, and the story develops no special punch, this is a generally absorbing yarn that should do all right in the popular-price houses.

Direction: Good, Photography: Good.

Schenectady Gazette, *September 14, 1935*

Atlantic Adventure made us grind our teeth in that well known impotent rage we are always getting into. It was another story of a reporter, this time played by Lloyd Nolan. And it had the same kind of city room we are always seeing in the movies — the kind that makes us grumbly and dissatisfied for weeks.

And the reporter led the sort of life we always imagined before we were disillusioned. Great fires where one climbs with the firemen up ladders. And murderings (sic) of attorney generals with the reporter on the spot. And diamond robberies with the reporter trailing them out on the high seas. And everything.

We were so jealous that we even hate to admit that we thought the movie very funny and well played in a somewhat mad manner by Nancy Carroll, Nolan and Harry Langdon. We were almost glad when Nolan got the story and the girl. One more picture like that and we're through. Our city editor doesn't have nine phones on his desk. He doesn't even look stern. He has never pointed at the door and shouted to us, "Get that story."

Harrison's Reports, *September 30, 1933*

A pretty good melodrama. The action is fast and one is held in suspense throughout because of the danger to Nancy Carroll and Lloyd Nolan, who had unwittingly become involved with crooks. The closing scenes, in which the crooks hold Nancy and Nolan captives, are the most exciting. Comedy is provoked by Harry Langdon, a newspaper photographer, who is more interesting in eating than in doing his work. The romantic interest is pleasant...

Not for children, adolescents, or Sundays. Harmless for adults. Class B.

His Marriage Mix-Up

A Columbia Short Subject Released in Two Reels. DIRECTED BY Preston Black. STORY BY Vernon Dent. PHOTOGRAPHY BY Benjamin Kline. EDITED BY Charles Hochberg. CAST: Harry Langdon, Dorothy Granger, Vernon Dent, Robert "Bobby" Burns. Copyright October 26, 1935, Registration Number LP5903; Renewed January 22, 1963, Number R310950. Released by Columbia Pictures Corporation, October 31, 1935.

SYNOPSIS: Harry Pierce (Harry Langdon) sends his uncle Elmer a wedding invitation that includes a photo of the bride-to-be. Uncle Elmer is aghast that the photo matches one on his newspaper's front page of Bertha Sharp, an escaped criminal who has murdered three husbands with an axe. As he leaves, Elmer tells his wife, "I've got to stop him before she chops his brainless head off!"

It's the wedding day and Nellie, the bride-to-be, and her family wonder where the groom is. Harry is in a taxi on his way to the church, when he checks his pockets for the ring. He removes several gumballs and other trinkets, placing them on the seat. When it appears the ring has fallen through a tear in the cab's seat, he uses his pocketknife in an attempt to retrieve it. Only after he has thoroughly destroyed the seat cushion does he remember that the ring is attached to a chain around his neck.

At the church, Elmer signals Harry and shows him the newspaper. Harry doesn't believe it, until he overhears Nellie claim she could fix something "better with an axe." Elmer encourages his nephew to sneak away, but Harry inadvertently enters the main church just as the ceremony begins. He marries Nellie, cries out for his uncle, and immediately faints.

At home in bed, Harry is still passed out. After Nellie leaves the room to get some water, Harry sits upright. Elmer tells him, "Pretend that you're crazy and I'll get you out of here." Harry's not sure how to do that, until a grasshopper lands in his shirt. He leaps out of bed and wildly gyrates. Elmer tells Nellie that Harry is "mentally unbalanced" and has been all his life. As Elmer and Nellie leave the room, Harry manages to kill the grasshopper. He peeks through

Husband killer Dorothy Granger has Harry and Vernon Dent trapped in this lobby card.

a door, sees Elmer talking to Nellie with his arm around her, and misconstrues their conversation.

Meanwhile, Bertha Sharp is eluding the police, and enters Harry's home via an open window. In the bedroom, Harry is both saddened and angry that his uncle is planning to make off with his wife. He turns and sees Bertha, and believes it is Nellie. He offers to get her a drink of water. As he does, Uncle Elmer tells him he can escape, but Harry orders Elmer to leave. He brings back the water and hears a knock on the door. He assumes it's his uncle, until Nellie calls out, but he refuses to let her in. Nellie gets Elmer to break open the door, and when Harry spies her, he thinks she's Bertha. He grabs the real Bertha and they leave through a window. Elmer tells Nellie that Harry's left with the axe murderess and tells her to call the police.

In the car, Harry turns on the radio, and hears a bulletin reporting that Bertha is traveling with a man fitting his description. He realizes whom he's with, and she declares that she's going to kill him. She drives wildly. Harry gets her axe and throws it out of the car, but she simply stops at a hardware store with a display of axes in the front window; she breaks the window and steals the axes. Elmer attempts to stop her, but she drives more crazily. He throws a lasso and gets both Harry and Bertha. Eventually, the auto crashes, and the police nab Bertha. Harry is thoroughly tied up and Nellie gets one of the axes to cut the rope. Harry sees her lift the axe and runs away.

ANALYSIS: *His Marriage Mix-Up* is the most entertaining of Langdon's early Columbia shorts, built on the foundation of two of his best Sennett films: *His First Flame* and *His Marriage Wow*. Uncle calls him "brainless" and Harry's aunt terms him a "nincompoop," yet Harry is neither; he is merely the wide-eyed innocent. Although not dressed like the Elf (understandable, since he's about to be married), his demeanor is that wonderful, perplexing manchild; one who carries gumballs to his wedding.

Although the axe murderess theme could have been distasteful, this is avoided by the wonderfully over-the-top performance of Dorothy Granger as Bertha Sharp. About the only "gross" moment is with the grasshopper that jumps into Harry's shirt, and then falls into his pants. In most instances of this type of gag, once the insect is no longer useful, it simply escapes. Here, the gyrating Harry slaps his backside, then calmly shakes the carcass out of his pant leg, stepping on it to ensure its demise. It's funny, until one thinks about how it would actually feel to do it.

Credited onscreen as "Preston Black," Jack White's direction is taut and the film moves at a brisk pace, with an occasional lapse into some unfortunate ethnic humor. The auto chase at the close is mostly genuine and quite funny. Overall, Vernon Dent's screenplay remains true to the Elf character, and even though they'd collaborated on stories during the Arvid Gillstrom years, and would continue to work together on screen, Dent would never pen another Langdon script. It was our loss.

HARRY MOMENT: As Harry searches for the wedding ring, he removes several gumballs and toys from his pockets, showing his childlike aspect, even though he's about to be married. It's another example of his charming ambiguity.

WHAT THE CRITICS SAID:
Film Daily, *November 4, 1935*

Harry Langdon has been given a very good laugh vehicle that moves fast and with plenty of original gags. His brother-in-law (sic), *Vernon Dent, informs him that the girl he is about to marry (Dorothy Granger) is the maniac hatchet killer that the cops are searching for. He tries to help Harry avoid the marriage ceremony. But into the house comes the escaped lunatic hatchet woman with her axe. The fun consists of Harry mistaking her for his fiancée, for they are doubles. The nut takes Harry for a wild ride in his car that furnishes a very hilarious chase sequence for the windup. Produced by Jules White.*

The Exhibitor, *November 15, 1935*

Not very funny, except when Harry Langdon looks extremely dumb. Langdon is about to marry. His uncle, thinking bride is actually notorious "axe-murderess" at large, attempts to save him. Not preventing the marriage, he tells bride that Harry is insane. Along comes real axe-murderess to further confuse things. She kidnaps Harry and the uncle, is finally captured in usual auto chase finale. FAIR.

I Don't Remember

A Columbia Short Subject Released in Two Reels.
PRODUCED BY Jules White. **DIRECTED BY** Preston Black. **STORY AND SCREENPLAY BY** Preston Black. **PHOTOGRAPHY BY** Benjamin Kline. **EDITED BY**

Charles Hochberg. CAST: Harry Langdon, Geneva Mitchell, Mary Carr, Vernon Dent, Robert "Bobby" Burns, Lynton Brent, Harry Semels, Al Thompson, Charles "Heine" Conklin, Bobby Barber, Gertrude Astor, Jack "Tiny" Lipson, Harry Tenbrook. Copyright December 27, 1935, Registration Number LP6039; Renewed January 25, 1963, Number R309312. Released by Columbia Pictures Corporation, December 26, 1935.

SYNOPSIS: Harry's wife welcomes his mother for a visit and complains about his being absent-minded. He doesn't recognize his mother and ends up looking for his shoes, which are, in fact, on his feet. Oscar and his wife arrive and she complains that Harry has caused her husband to think about gambling. Later, Harry works on one of his strange paintings. His wife tells him that unless a payment is made, the finance company will take their furniture away. She gives Harry the money to make the payment but he has trouble remembering the address. His mother says that when he was a boy they made him remember by hitting him on the head. She hits Harry with a tray and he remembers the address and departs.

Harry then runs into Oscar, who convinces him to hand over the money to buy a ticket for the Irish Sweepstakes. They go to a gambling den and, after getting the ticket, Oscar tears it by half and gives Harry his half as the police arrive. The room is quickly transformed into a massage therapy clinic, with Harry as the subject. As the cops look on, Harry has his legs and neck twisted by the "massage therapist." The cops leave, but return suddenly, causing Harry to jump out a window and land on a trashcan.

Back at the house, the furniture is being removed. Harry arrives and tells his mother that he didn't make the payment. He's told that his wife will be furious and will probably leave him. Harry paints furniture on the walls. His wife returns, discovers the ruse and the ticket purchase, and leaves. Harry decides to commit suicide with a rifle. Before he can do so, Oscar shows up and Harry rigs the gun to fire when his friend opens the door. The shot knocks down the door and Harry chases Oscar out of the building. He grabs a cop's pistol and continues to chase Oscar down the street.

His friend hides behind a stack of newspapers. The headlines reveal that they have won $75,000 in

This still was taken after Harry decides to commit murder instead of suicide in I Don't Remember.

the sweepstakes. They go to collect the money and Oscar presents his half of the ticket. Harry finally finds his half, then sneezes and blows it out the window. They chase after it as it blows in and out of various windows, into the street and down a sewer drain. In the end Harry finds the missing half — in the ocean!

ANALYSIS: Leonard Maltin famously dissected this film in his landmark book *The Great Movie Shorts*. In it, he wrote that *I Don't Remember* "sounds funny... but it doesn't play funny," and labeled it an example of "how the ingredients for a good comedy can be present but, if not treated carefully, can fall flat."

Indeed, there are some clever ideas in *I Don't Remember*, notably the gags involving the painted furniture, as well as Harry's absent-mindedness and the concept of his memory being restored with a blow to his head. All of this, unfortunately, is lost within a film that is smothered by mechanical contrivances. From his painting of a lion that "roars" because a child is taunting him with a noisy toy for no reason, to Harry's "examination" in the bookie joint that is spoiled by the use of rubber legs, to the sweepstakes ticket clearly manipulated by a wire, the fakery is both obvious and overwhelming.

What's more, director Jack White had no clue as to Langdon's strengths. A scene in which Harry inadvertently puts his breakfast egg into his coffee, then proceeds to eat the shells, is rushed through with no emphasis on comic facial reaction. Even the otherwise lightning-fast *Picking Peaches* took the necessary time to make the most of Harry's pantomime when he's served the powder-puff pancake. It's one of several missed opportunities that characterize this comedy...and, sadly, most of Langdon's Columbia output.

WHAT THE CRITICS SAID:
The Philadelphia Exhibitor, *February 1, 1936*

Harry Langdon is in this generally dull comedy. There may be a few laughs for those who find Langdon amusing, but plot is too generally burlesqued to afford real humor. Langdon is shown as fellow about to lose wife and furniture because of inability to remember where he puts money. By lucky stroke, he wins sweepstake prize, but loses half ticket through window. From then on, he chases it. Last shot shows him going into sewer for ticket, ending out in the ocean. Which gives an idea. So-so.

Personality Parade

A Metro-Goldwyn-Mayer Short Subject Released in Two Reels. Producer: Ralph Staub. CAST: Jimmie Fidler. Released by Metro-Goldwyn-Mayer, Inc., January 8, 1938.

SYNOPSIS: Hollywood columnist Jimmie Fidler introduces and narrates this compilation of archival footage showing stars of the silent screen. Langdon is seen on a golf course: he hits the ball, and mimes that it has traveled in a complete circle and is about to strike him, whereupon he runs off. The footage was reportedly filmed for a Screen Snapshots short of the 1920s.

ANALYSIS: Tantalizingly brief, Langdon's mime is spot-on, and the gag was reused during the sound era in *A Roaming Romeo*. Fidler's narration calls Langdon "one of the funniest clowns of them all. His decline from stardom is still a Hollywood mystery." It's worth noting that he'd been off the screen for two years when this short appeared.

A Doggone Mixup

A Columbia Short Subject Released in Two Reels. ASSOCIATE PRODUCER: Jules White. DIRECTED BY Charles Lamont. STORY AND SCREENPLAY BY Elwood Ullman, Al Giebler and Charles Nelson. PHOTOGRAPHY BY Benjamin Kline. EDITED BY Charles Nelson. CAST: Harry Langdon, Ann Doran, Vernon Dent, Bud Jamison, James C. Morton, Eddie Fetherstone, Bess Flowers, Sarah Edwards, Blanche Payson. Copyright January 10, 1938, Registration Number LP7721; Renewed December 17, 1965, Number R376156. Released by Columbia Pictures Corporation, February 4, 1938.

SYNOPSIS: In a busy office, Harry shows a fellow worker two ties that he bought. Another worker sells him a large dog collar for it seems that Harry can't resist a bargain. He ends up buying a doghouse and a bag of dog food even though he doesn't have a dog. When he gets home, Harry's wife is angry that he bought the doghouse. He explains that he just can't resist a bargain.

"Herbert," a large dog, enters their apartment and Harry explains that he bought him to match the collar. Herbert eats their dinner and is put outside. The pooch then knocks over trashcans and wrecks a neighbor's laundry, keeping Harry busy all night. Meanwhile, Harry's wife has prepared another dinner, and Herbert eats that as well. Furious, she makes Harry take the dog away. Herbert leaves but sneaks back into the house and meets up with Harry. In the morning, Harry's wife discovers that the dog has returned. Herbert then chases a cat and wrecks the apartment. They are evicted, and Harry, with his wife, is driving their car with a trailer and a doghouse on wheels behind it. They arrive at a lot that Harry has purchased, and proceed to set up camp.

At breakfast, Harry tosses a piece of bacon to Herbert, which ends up on the rope that ties the trailer to their car. The dog causes the trailer to get loose and it rolls to the edge of a cliff. The rope catches and the trailer now dangles over the cliff's edge. Herbert pulls the trailer to safety. Harry then causes the trailer to roll down a hill, where it crashes. Harry's wife emerges and warns him not to ever buy anything again. An insurance agent arrives and attempts to sell Harry an insurance policy. Harry's wife clobbers the agent, and then chases Harry down the road.

ANALYSIS: Although it has a reputation as one of Langdon's better Columbias, *A Doggone Mixup* is generally weak tea that might serve for students as an example of Uninspired Slapstick 101. Between Harry and the dog, belongings are constantly knocked over, shattered, or thoroughly destroyed, and as the film progresses, these objects get bigger, as if to make the short "funnier." Langdon's character is a milquetoast, albeit a likable one, but his wife has no respect and precious little love for him, and emerges as basically unpleasant. As in *Counsel on De Fence*, Langdon sports a mustache, to no good effect. There are a couple of sweet vignettes between him and Herbert, and thankfully no distasteful gags or situations, but these things do little to salvage a less-than-mediocre comedy.

HARRY MOMENT: After Harry has sent Herbert away, he prepares for bed. He drops to his knees to pray, and asks God to "take good care of Herbert and please send him back to me sometime." He turns and sees Herbert (who entered from an open window)

A mustached Harry is distracted by the lovely faces and shapely legs in A Doggone Mixup.

beside him, then looks up and says, "Thanks." It's a sweet moment, one that is reminiscent of the Elf's trusting innocence.

WHAT THE CRITICS SAID:
Film Daily, *February 9, 1938*

Harry Langdon is the comic who gets involved in all sorts of headaches at his office and home as he allows his mania for buying things that lead him into the purchase of an oversize dog collar. He buys a kennel for the dog he hasn't got, and finally purchases a big St. Bernard to wear the collar. Arrived home, the fun begins. The big dog creates such havoc that he has all the neighbors up in arms, and ruins all the furniture. The finale has Langdon and his wife living in a trailer, which he buys at a bargain. The trailer is wrecked as the St. Bernard goes on a rampage.

Box Office, *February 12, 1938*

The years haven't dealt kindly with Harry Langdon and neither have the scripters with this ludicrous attempt at comedy. Langdon, a mere shadow of his former self, is the "goat" for every high pressure salesman. Having been fast-talked into a dog's collar, biscuits and a house big enough for a toy bulldog, he waltzes home with a St. Bernard. The apartment likewise being too small for the animals' activities, amidst a welter of damage, Langdon and his wife are forced to take up life in a trailer. From this point on all credulity is tossed to the winds, with the net effect a mere ripple.

He Loved an Actress (*a.k.a.* Mad About Money)

A Henry Barnes Production for British Lion. 76 minutes. **PRODUCED BY** William Rowland. **DIRECTED BY** Melville W. Brown. **ORIGINAL STORY BY** John E. Harding. **SCREENPLAY BY** John Meehan, Jr. Dances by Larry Cebellos. **PHOTOGRAPHY BY** John Stumar. **SPECIAL EFFECTS BY** Len Lye. **EDITED BY** Julian Caunter. **MUSICAL SCORE:** James Dyrenforth and Kenneth Leslie-Smith; **ARRANGED AND CONDUCTED BY** Peter Yorke. **CAST:** Lupe Velez, Wallace Ford, Ben Lyon, Jean Colin, Harry Langdon, Cyril Raymond, Mary Cole, Ronald Ware, Olive Sloan, Arthur Flinn, Philip Pearman, Andrea Melandrinos, Olive Sloane, Peggy Novak, John Stobart, Albert Whelan, Ronald Hill, Alan Shires. Reissue Title: "Hollywood Racketeers." Produced in the United Kingdom in 1937. Released in the United States by Grand National Pictures, Inc., March 25, 1938.

SYNOPSIS: Roy Harley and Peter Jackson, two hotshot producers who have recently struck out on their own, are about to shoot a movie with a new technique for color film when their star and primary backer is offended and storms out of the studio. Upon reading that cattle heiress Carla de Huleva is arriving in London, Jackson goes to her and attempts to woo her into financing the studio. Carla isn't an heiress at all, but she pretends to agree with Jackson so that her best friend, Diana West, can get an audition for the starring role. Diana agrees to go along with the charade, so long as nobody gets hurt. Harley and Jackson make their movie, despite the scheming of their former employer, who wants the color film process; Diana's former employer Eric Williams, who wants a love affair with Diana; and columnist Jerry Sears, who wants a juicy story to publish, apparently at anyone's expense. During production, Carla and Jackson fall in love, as do Diana and Harley. The night before the film's premiere, Carla is revealed as a fraud, and the two girls discover that without Carla's non-existent fortune, the studio goes under. Diana goes to Eric to bargain for the money needed to pay for the film. He agrees to give it to her if she'll accompany him to Berlin, but Sears eavesdrops on this exchange and reveals that he knows some dirty little secrets of Williams's and keeps him distracted with blackmail threats until the film's premiere. Diana returns to Harley, and Jackson and Carla reconcile.

Produced before *A Doggone Mixup*, but released after.

ANALYSIS: *Mad About Money* takes the old standby plot of a producer who needs funding for a show and transplants it into a motion picture studio, providing an opportunity for some visual effects during the production numbers that are rather engaging, if not state of the art. The balance of the film is the usual 1930s musical mélange of romance mixed with false identities and former suitors, only less compelling than most due to some shoddy editing. The only color film in which Langdon appeared (other than the dream sequence of less than a minute in *Long Pants*), unfortunately neither the British original nor the U.S. release, *He Loved an Actress,* currently circulate except in black and white prints.

Langdon's role as Otto Schultz, another backer of Harley and Jackson's production, is minor and appears to have been reduced in editing. He has some nice moments at the start as he attempts to see the two producers, only to be thwarted by their ever-diligent receptionist, and is later chased about by a gold-digging actress. He also gets to sing a verse of the film's show-stopping number, "Dusting the Stars," when a drunken Otto dreams that he and the leads board a Flash Gordonesque rocket for Saturn. Once they arrive, the singing and dancing take place among the stars, hence the tune's title. No attempt is made to integrate his character into the main storyline, which is unfortunate; his brief scenes ironically provide a better showcase for his unique comedic ability than his recent U.S. productions.

HARRY MOMENT: Otto attempts to enter Mr. Harley's office, but is stopped by the receptionist. He repeatedly tries to sneak past her and she continually scolds him, sending him away like a disobedient child.

WHAT THE CRITICS SAID:
The Exhibitor, *April 1, 1938*

This importation emerges as nothing more than fodder for the duallers. English-made, it has the benefit of four American names, little more, although some musical numbers, tunes should please. It tells the tale of two movie makers who need cash, think that a cattle queen, Lupe Velez, may help. But she, in turn, is a phony, uses them to promote a chorus girl friend. Windup finds all the complications taken care of, with some sloppy cutting not helping. In short, this is just another picture; its names are the sole salable assets.

Estimate: Dualler; bottom half.

Variety, *May 25, 1938; Reviewed by Barn*

Biggest drawback on this English cut musical is the color faulting. Film can't make up its mind whether to stick with a bad pale yellow-pink tint or one equally bad in greenish blue. Coloring is brutal to the faces and thins the photography until players can hardly be recognized except in close-ups.

For American audiences, its marquee power is light, even though Lupe Velez, Wallace Ford and Ben Lyon are well known in the minors, and Harry Langdon, once a two-reel fav, is making his first appearances in a long time. Jean Colin, new on this side, is a fancy tow-head, who has a pretty fair set of pipes in spite of bad recording, which dulls all the voices.

Story is one of chiseling and chiseler, Lyon and Ford trying to make an indie film and promising Lupe Velez, a showgirl masking as a cattle heiress from down under, for the shekels. Langdon, having inherited a thriving beer biz because his uncle died without leaving a will, finally comes to the rescue. There's some other pure English slow motion, which garbles the running, but that's about all there is to it, except a couple of misunderstandings and four tunes.

Latter, penned by James Dyrenforth and Kenneth Leslie-Smith, include "Oh So Beautiful," "Perpetual Motion," "Little Lost Tune" and "Dustin' the Stars." One number tends to swing the Strauss ditty "Blue Danube" adding to the general dimness of the picture by having ghosts appear by double exposure. "Oh So Beautiful" gets the most frequent call, and is the best.

Film is doomed to the sluff spots, too slow for a satisfactory musical as this country sees them.

Monthly Film Bulletin of the British Film Institute, *December 1938*

Mad musical comedy. A confused plot tells how two hard-up film producers manage to find the money to buy the option on a new colour process in the nick of time. Mixed up with all this are plenty of blackmailers, spurious South American "cattle queens," music and romance. In addition, for no apparent reason, there are some surprising "effects" introduced by Len Lye, including a rocket trip to Saturn with a ballet of the stars, and the trial of a modern composer by the ghosts of past musicians. These interludes of pure fantasy help to redeem a film which otherwise suffers from lack of continuity and bad cutting. Jean Colin makes a charming heroine, Lupe Velez a sufficiently exotic "cattle queen," and Ben Lyon is amiable and handsome enough as the young producer.

Sue My Lawyer

A Columbia Short Subject Released in Two Reels. **ASSOCIATE PRODUCER:** Jules White. **DIRECTED BY** Jules White. **SCREENPLAY BY** Ewart Adamson. **STORY BY** Harry Langdon. **PHOTOGRAPHY BY** George Meehan. **EDITED BY** Charles Nelson. **CAST:** Harry Langdon, Ann Doran, Monty Collins, Bud Jamison, Vernon Dent, Don Brody, Cy Schindell, Charles Doherty, Jack "Tiny" Lipson, Robert "Bobby" Burns. Copyright August 15, 1938, Registration Number LP8201; Renewed July 12, 1966, Number R389210. Released by Columbia Pictures Corporation, September 16, 1938.

SYNOPSIS: Attorney Harry arrives at the districty attorney's office. He wants to see the D.A. but is told that the official wants nothing to do with him. It seems that the Pruitt murder case is driving the

D.A. crazy because suspect Red Burton won't confess. Inside of the office, the D. A. is grilling Burton. Harry tells the official that he knows enough to send Burton to the chair. This is overheard by Burton's sister and her boyfriend. The D. A. throws Harry out of the office.

Later, at the Krumola Apartments' lobby, Burton's sister and boyfriend are searching for Harry's name in a phone book. Harry is sitting in the lobby as well and manages to get his foot stuck in a pail of water. Burton's sister tells her boyfriend to ignore him. Harry announces that he's a lawyer and gives them his card. The sister flirts with Harry and suggests that they go up to her room. He refuses, and she pretends to faint. Harry carries her partly up some stairs but manages to drop her down to the floor. He carries her up again by sitting on the steps and moving backwards up the stairs. He continues to back up onto a ladder at the top of the stairs and they fall to the floor.

Inside her apartment, Burton's sister revives and slips away from Harry to get her boyfriend. The D. A. and an associate arrive and begin to search the apartment for evidence. Harry hides and observes them. The sister and boyfriend return and are told by the D. A. that he's going to find the evidence. Harry causes the D. A. and associate to argue and lifts and gun and evidence. Upon discovering Harry, the D. A. throws him out of the apartment.

Later, in the courtroom, the D. A. argues that Burton is guilty. Harry produces the gun and evidence and a melee breaks out in the courtroom. Harry flees and ends up on a pole outside the building. The D. A. calls him a genius and promises to make Harry his assistant. Harry's joy at the news causes him to slip on the pole.

ANALYSIS: Another three-day Columbia calamity, *Sue My Lawyer* is not only unfunny, but painfully so. The "staircase" gag, one of the best-remembered moments in *The Strong Man*, is poorly staged and ploddingly paced. It's not surprising that Langdon hadn't revived the gag in his talking films to date; in the real world of sound, it's more painful than amusing. The tumble off the stepladder taken by Langdon's stunt double looks especially dire; the poor fellow appears to have landed on his neck. For all the lies in Frank Capra's book, his assessment of how far Langdon the artist had fallen was sadly accurate.

WHAT THE CRITICS SAID:
Box Office, *October 1, 1938*

Not one of Harry Langdon's best, but he works hard and takes a lot of punishment before convincing the district attorney he has what it takes to make an able assistant. The comic is a lawyer turned down by the D.A. when applying for a job. The D.A. is trying to convict a notorious murderer, but lacks the evidence. Langdon promises to get it, but how the comedian comes through is more than he can understand. Langdon's antics will probably garner a good quota of laughs. He has already graduated from the short subject division and is now a partner of Oliver Hardy.

Film Daily, *October 3, 1938*

The attempts of Harry Langdon, a young lawyer, to be made as assistant district attorney. Harry learns that the D.A. is trying to get the evidence against a murderer, Red Burton, so he starts out to get it. His misadventures, when he meets the killer's moll, are funny and good for the laughs.

WHAT THE EXHIBITORS SAID:
Motion Picture Herald, *November 23, 1940*

Whoever gave this guy an idea he was funny? I have never seen one of his comedies yet that produced even a smile.
Ray Peacock, Onalaska Theater, Onalaska, WA. Loggers and mill workers patronage.

There Goes My Heart

A Hal Roach Production. 81 minutes. PRODUCED BY Milton H. Bren. DIRECTED BY Norman Z. McLeod. SCREENPLAY BY Eddie Moran and Jack Jevne. ORIGINAL STORY BY Ed Sullivan. PHOTOGRAPHY BY Norbert Brodine. EDITOR: William Terhune. ART DIRECTOR: Charles D. Hall. MUSICAL DIRECTOR: Marvin Hatley. CAST: Fredric March, Virginia Bruce, Patsy Kelly, Alan Mowbray, Nancy Carroll, Eugene Pallette, Claude Gillingwater, Arthur Lake, Etienne Girardot, Robert Armstrong, Irving Bacon, Irving Pichel, Sid Saylor, J. Farrell MacDonald, Tommy Mack (unbilled), Marjorie Main (unbilled), Harry Langdon (unbilled). Copyright October 6, 1938, Registration Number LP8333; Renewed December 2, 1965, Number R374809. Released by United Artists, Inc. October 15, 1938.

SYNOPSIS: Joan Butterfield, heiress to the Butterfield department store chain, is kept a virtual prisoner by her over-protective grandfather. She rebels and runs away to New York, where, posing as "Joan Baker," she becomes a sales clerk at Butterfield's. Reporter Bill Spencer, a down-to-earth guy, is assigned against his will to get the dirt on Miss Butterfield's "disappearance." Spencer discovers where she is and plays along with her charade for a story. He discovers that, behind the wealth, there's an ordinary girl looking for fulfillment and romance, and they fall in love. Spencer tears

up his story, but his editor pieces it back together and prints it, which causes a rift between the two lovebirds. However, Joan's friend and fellow sales clerk Peggy and her boyfriend scheme to get them back together.

ANALYSIS: Hal Roach producer Milton Bren saw to it that *There Goes My Heart,* Roach's entrée into A-picture production for United Artists, would be loaded with entertainment. Although the basic plot is lifted from *It Happened One Night,* the screenplay by Eddie Moran and Jack Jevne contains a number of original touches and is remarkably free from contrivance. Along with the sparkling performances of Fredric March and Virginia Bruce in the leads, and the delightful Patsy Kelly in support, this sweet romantic comedy includes a plethora of fine character actors. There are also a few unscheduled bonuses: radio's Tommy Mack as a café manager, complete with his catch-phrase, "Excited! Who's excited?!? I'm not excited!!!" (Mack would return for a similar cameo in Langdon's next film for Roach); Marjorie ("Ma Kettle") Main as a stoic, lower-class homemaker seeking "a fireless cooker"; and, of course, Langdon as the minister who wraps up the tale. Bren and director Norman McLeod gave them all the opportunity to make the most of what could have been, in other hands, merely bit parts.

HARRY MOMENT: Although his screen time is less than two minutes, Langdon brings himself completely into the role of the minister, infusing him with the Elf's wide-eyed innocence and trusting smile. There's also a marvelous double-take when, after a crash of thunder and lightning, he peers into the window, and then shows us in pantomime that the two lovers are ready to be wed.

WHAT THE CRITICS SAID:
Daily Variety, *September 23, 1938*

Call it romantic comedy, if you will, but "riotous fun" better describes There Goes My Heart, *first of Hal Roach's more pretentious efforts under his United Artists releasing deal. Made up of a chain of stand-out performances, elaborately and efficiently mounted, the picture is sure-fire from the box-office angle, and should pile up receipts that will equal or surpass the cream of Roach's previous money-makers.*

While Fredric March and Virginia Bruce occupy the co-starring niches, and turn in portrayals as fine as any they have yet had camera-recorded, they by no means carry the histrionic burden. Turning in equally brilliant portrayals are Patsy Kelly, Alan Mowbray, Eugene Pallette and Claude Gillingwater. Shining in roles of lesser importance, yet taking advantage of every opportunity offered them, are Nancy Carroll and Harry Langdon, both too long absent from the silver sheet.... [Norman] McLeod's piloting gleams brighter than his accomplishments of the past.

Box Office, *October 1, 1938*

Bright, romantic comedy with moments of entertainment for any and all tastes, it is Producer Hal Roach's first for release under the UA banner and, incidentally, his first million-dollar picture, reflecting in production values this open-handed expenditure. Fredric March is impressive in the male lead, while Patsy Kelly romps home with the comedy honors in a characteristic rowdyish role into which has been written the film's choicest laugh-garnering bits.

Brooklyn Daily Eagle, *October 16, 1938; Reviewed by Herbert Cohn*

Hal Roach deposited his first United Artist (sic) feature at the Music Hall. Its title is There Goes My Heart *and it marked the initial — though brief — appearance of Harry Langdon as a talking-film comedian, and the return of Patsy Kelly, streamlined, to the front ranks of screen comediennes.*

There Goes My Heart *is a bright, frolicsome comedy with shrewd showmanship by Director Norman Z. McLeod and top playing by an admirable cast (headed by Fredric March and Virginia Bruce) cloaking the fact that its Ed Sullivan newspaper story is ragged from hard wear. The story is the least of its virtues, retelling the miraculous experience of a newspaperman who scooped the town with a yarn about a disguised heiress and had the consummate luck, besides, to scoop up the heiress in his haul.*

Patsy Kelly makes the largest contribution to the collection of fun, not so much with what she does but how she does it. Eddie Moran and Jack Jevne, who adapted the story, supplied it with a wealth of witty cracks which not only made Mr. Sullivan's work seem to be more original but also afforded Mr. Roach a jolly comedy to break the ice with United.

Harrison's Reports, *October 22, 1938*

A fairly good comedy. Lacking a substantial plot, the picture depends mostly on gags and wisecracks for its entertainment value; for the most part, these are good. Patsy Kelly provokes most of the laughter; two situations in which she appears, one, as a customer in a cafeteria and, another, as a demonstrator for a vibrator, are extremely comical and should provoke hearty laughter. As a matter of fact, each time she appears there is something to laugh about. The action lags a bit in a few spots; this is so particularly towards the end. Fredric March and Virginia Bruce make a pleasant romantic team, despite the routine way in which the romance is developed.

Suitability: Class A.

WHAT THE EXHIBITORS SAID:
Box Office, *March 25, 1939*

Audience reaction varied from very good to terrible. Light comedy with lots of laughs. Business just fair.
H. Workman, Shakopee Theatre, Shakopee, MN.
Population: 2,000, Theater Capacity: 570.
Small town patronage.

Box Office, *April 1, 1939*

Very good, many favorable comments. A couple scenes outstanding. Get behind this one.
E.L. Danielson, Castle Theatre, Mabel, MN.
Population: 700, Theater Capacity: 200.
Rural Patronage.

Motion Picture Herald, *March 16, 1940*

Played this somewhat later than necessary even though we are a third and fourth run situation. Without the Warner hit *The Oklahoma Kid* to bring them in, the attendance would have been just fair. The title a handicap for our spot. However, this is really a swell comedy and it kept the house in stitches part of the time and certainly entertained them very much.
E.P. Grindley, Community Theater, Missoula, MT.
General patronage.

Zenobia

A Hal Roach Production. 71 minutes. **PRODUCED BY** A. Edward Sutherland. **DIRECTED BY** Gordon Douglas. **SCREENPLAY BY** Corey Ford. **STORY BY** Walter DeLeon and Arnold Belgard. Based on "Zenobia's Infidelity" by H.C. Brunner. **PHOTOGRAPHY BY** Karl Struss, ASC. **SPECIAL PHOTOGRAPHIC EFFECTS:** Roy Seawright. **EDITOR:** Bert Jordan. **ART DIRECTOR:** Charles D. Hall. **SOUND:** William Randall and W.B. Delaplain. **MUSICAL SCORE:** Marvin Hatley. **CHORAL ARRANGEMENTS:** Hall Johnson. **CAST:** Oliver Hardy, Harry Langdon, Billie Burke, Alice Brady, Jean Parker, James Ellison, June Lang, Stepin Fetchit, Hattie McDaniel, Philip Hurlic, Olin Howard, The Hall Johnson Choir, Tommy Mack, J. Farrell MacDonald, Robert Dudley, Chester Conklin (uncredited), Arthur Thalasso (uncredited). **WORKING TITLES:** "It's Spring Again," "We The People." Copyright April 11, 1939, Registration Number LP8778; Renewed January 17, 1967, Number R402832. Released by United Artists, Inc., March 14, 1939.

SYNOPSIS: It's 1870 in the village of Carterville Mississippi. Mary Tibbett and Jeff Carter are in love and want to marry, but there's a problem. Mary's father is Dr. Henry Tibbett (Oliver Hardy), once a prominent physician to Carterville's wealthiest citizens, until he decided to turn his attention to the poorer folks, who are often unable to pay. Jeff's mother,

Mrs. Emily Carter, widow of the town's founder and one of Dr. Tibbett's ex-patients, is very focused on her family's social status, and Mary fears she won't approve of the marriage.

Dr. Tibbett's wife, Bessie, sends their servant Zero to fetch him so Jeff can ask his permission for Mary's hand. The flighty Bessie has thoroughly confused Zero and by the time he reaches Dr. Tibbett — who has just helped deliver a baby boy for the poor parents of five girls — the details of the message are forgotten, and the doctor thinks there's an emergency. Once at the house, he tries to determine the problem, but nobody gives him a straight answer, as they're all preparing for company. Finally, Zeke — the young son of Zero and the Tibbetts's cook, Delia — tells the doctor that Mary is getting married.

As Dr. Tibbett tries to ask Mary about the marriage, Jeff approaches him and after a couple of failed attempts, asks the doctor for his daughter's hand. He beams and approves. But when Mary expresses her doubts about how Mrs. Carter will react, and suggests that Jeff not tell her right away, her father is hurt and leaves the room. Mary follows and asks him why he had to sacrifice his high standing in the community, as well as their financial status. He points to a framed copy of the U.S. Declaration of Independence that hangs over his desk, and tells her it says, "All men are created equal" and entitled to "life, liberty and the pursuit of happiness." He explains he was unhappy catering to the wealthy — especially the hypochondriac Mrs. Carter — when there are less affluent people in town that really need his services and are deserving of those rights.

Elsewhere in town, Zeke is at a carnival where Professor McCrackle (Harry Langdon), a patent-medicine huckster, is peddling his wondrous elixir. The professor has a performing elephant, Zenobia, but when he calls on her, she lays down. He tries giving her some of the "medicine," and she sprays it all over him. Worried now, he asks if there's a doctor in the crowd. Zeke says he knows a doctor and runs off to the Tibbetts's house.

Dr. Tibbett arrives and, after some confusing conversation with McCrackle, discovers his patient is an elephant. Zeke implores him to help her, so he takes her temperature, checks her pulse, and advises the professor to keep her warm. At the Tibbett household, everyone's nerves are on edge as they prepare dinner for Jeff and his mother. When the Carters arrive, Virginia Reynolds, the young woman Mrs. Carter hopes Jeff will marry, is with them. In between whiffs of smelling salts, Mrs. Carter boasts of her many ailments, and objects to various types of food, which causes Bessie to repeatedly revise the dinner menu. At one point, Bessie asks her daughter to sing something, but Mary objects, saying that she doesn't sing very well. Dr. Tibbett returns home and tells Mrs. Carter she's looking healthier than ever, causing her to become more frigid. Jeff announces that he's planning to wed Mary, whereupon his mother strenuously objects, immediately becomes faint and forces him to leave with her.

Forced to throw a reception in honor of the upcoming nuptials, Mrs. Carter tries to figure out how to convince Jeff that Mary is "too ordinary" for him. Virginia reminds her that Mary cannot sing; Mrs. Carter smiles and adds "with music" to the invitation. The Tibbetts notice this, so Dr. Tibbett and Bessie rehearse an old song they used to sing. While doing this, Professor McCrackle arrives, worried about Zenobia, and the doctor hastily leaves with him. Dr. Tibbett decides to examine Zenobia in sections, and has McCrackle draw them on her skin with chalk. He crawls underneath her to listen to her heart, just as a mouse appears in the barn. The frightened elephant lowers to the ground, almost crushing the doctor.

Soon after, the doctor notices that Zenobia's tail is in a knot. He unties it, and she recovers so quickly that, in gratitude, she lifts him up with her trunk. Although McCrackle assures him it means she likes him, the frightened Dr. Tibbett hastily departs. That evening, as the professor sleeps beside her, Zenobia breaks her chains and leaves the barn. McCrackle awakens and chases after her.

As the Tibbetts dress for the reception, Zeke helps the doctor with his boots and complains that he's unable to go to parties with other little boys because they're white and he's black. Dr. Tibbett reminds Zeke that he can't go to colored folks' parties, and reminds him of the Declaration of Independence on his office wall. He tells Zeke to memorize the document a little bit every day and, if he is successful, he will be given a quarter.

When the Tibbetts arrive at the reception, Mrs. Carter coolly informs them that she's sent Jeff to pick up Virginia. As they make their way across the room, Bessie greets several women and is given a cold shoulder in return. The musicians strike up a waltz, and guests begin dancing. Dr. Tibbett dances with his daughter, as Jeff and Virginia enter the room; she urges him to dance with her. When the doctor sees them, he cleverly cuts in, freeing Jeff to dance with Mary. Meanwhile, Professor McCrackle continues to pursue Zenobia.

Mrs. Carter announces that Mary will sing. Mortified, Mary whispers to her father that she can't. "Even if you can't, Pumpkins…do it anyway," he tells her. She musters her courage and sings beautifully, impressing all the guests. They congratulate the Tibbetts on their talented daughter, but just then Zenobia enters the house and frightens everybody. Dr. Tibbett tries to calmly depart with Bessie, but Zenobia follows him and lifts him with her trunk. When McCrackle enters, the guests learn the truth: that the elephant had been a patient. Upset that this has disrupted their daughter's reception, Bessie locks her husband out of the house, forcing him to sleep outside beside the elephant.

The next morning, after having been seen by all the neighbors, Dr. Tibbett tries to shake Zenobia, but it's futile. Meanwhile, Mrs. Carter sees this as an opportunity to disgrace the Tibbett family, and hires a lawyer so McCrackle can sue the doctor for alienation of Zenobia's affections. At trial, Dr. Tibbett, who is representing himself, cannot enter the courtroom because the elephant will follow him in, and so must question witnesses and testify from a window. On the stand, Jeff is forced to admit that the elephant displayed much affection for Dr. Tibbett and caused his mother anguish for ruining the party. Dr. Tibbett asks the judge what the penalty is for stealing the affections of an elephant. The judge calls for a recess to research the matter.

Mary is upset with Jeff for his testimony. Outside, Dr. Tibbett pitches horseshoes with his friends, and Jeff confesses that he's confused as to what he should do. The doctor calls for Zeke and asks the boy if he's ready to earn that quarter. Zeke recites the introductory passage of the Declaration, and everyone stops what they're doing to listen, including Mrs. Carter and Virginia. When Zeke is through, Dr. Tibbett

The principal cast of Zenobia. *Front row: Jean Parker, June Lang. Second row: Billie Burke, Alice Brady. Third row: Oliver Hardy, James Ellison, Langdon.*

gives him the quarter and Jeff tells his mother that, whether she approves or not, he refuses to jeopardize his own happiness and intends to wed Mary.

Inside the courtroom, a chastened Mrs. Carter refuses to take the witness stand, and says she'll reimburse Professor McCrackle for any damages. She explains that her selfishness almost cost her son's happiness, and tearfully apologizes. Bessie and Mary offer her comfort as the case is dismissed.

As it turns out, Zenobia did indeed urgently require the doctor's services: she was pregnant. After assisting with the delivery, Dr. Tibbett quickly returns home for his daughter's wedding, while Professor McCrackle and his two elephants depart for another town.

ANALYSIS: To call *Zenobia* "unusual" is a little like saying the Johnstown Flood was "wet." A better description for the film might be "schizophrenic." It veers from light romantic comedy, to broad farce, to ethnic (and, when Stepin Fetchit is involved, demeaning) humor, to slapstick, back-and-forth in much the same confused manner as the Little Elf once veered from one emotion to another in mere seconds.

Alas, there's no trace of the Elf in this film; in fact, Langdon can hardly be said to have any character at all. Professor McCrackle is little more than an excuse for Zenobia's existence. There's a cute bit at the opening where, while delivering his sales pitch, he feigns hoarseness so he can be "cured" by a swig of his elixir, but this is too quickly followed by Zenobia's illness. Langdon's interaction with Hardy is minimal and the material is too thin to offset the pair's lack of chemistry. In the courtroom, Langdon tries hard for laughs as he repeatedly launches into his prepared "testimony" that, at one point, turns into another tonic sales pitch. Unfortunately, Olin Howland, as prosecuting attorney Culpepper, is a woefully inadequate foil.

As for Hardy, for whom *Zenobia* is actually a starring vehicle, he brings his natural Southern charm to his part, and for the most part succeeds admirably in making Dr. Tibbett real. However there are several moments in which "Ollie" surfaces: double takes, "tie-twiddling" (in this case, stethoscope-twiddling), exasperated looks into the camera, the disgusted sotto voce repeating of a perceived inane comment on Langdon's part. When these occur, our attention is immediately drawn to the absence of Stan Laurel and the sad fact that Langdon is incapable of bridging the gap.

WHAT THE CRITICS SAID:
Film Daily, *March 14, 1939*

Because an elephant never forgets, an enjoyable comedy was created. A new Oliver Hardy is introduced. His work is a cross between the slapstick for which he is noted, and a straighter sort of role. It should appeal to grown-ups as well as to children. Teamed with him is Harry Langdon who, too, supplies a lot of laughs, and Billie Burke whose type

A Swedish poster for Zenobia.

of scatterbrained humor is always entertaining. The affair depends on gags for its hilarity, and since they are present in most of the footage, the piece should be well liked. Jimmy Ellison does right well with the love interest, the object of his affections being Jean Parker. Others who do well are Alice Brady, June Lang, Olin Howland and J. Farrell MacDonald. Stepin Fetchit supplies his quota of laughter, as does Hattie McDaniels (sic). A little Negro boy, Phillip Hurlic, recites the Declaration of Independence in a manner that everyone will understand. To a great number of people, this will be their first association with the contents of the notable document which they know only by name and spirit. A hand to Hal Roach for presenting it in a most significant

fashion. Gordon Douglas did a splendid job on the direction, making the gags count for their full worth and delivering them in good taste. He maintains an ever-moving tempo throughout and gains some excellent performances. Corey Ford contributed the screenplay from an original by Walter DeLeon and Arnold Belgard. Marvin Hatley's musical score is noteworthy. A. Edward Sutherland produced this amusing comedy which Hal Roach presents.
    Direction: Splendid. Photography: Swell.

Variety, *March 16, 1939*

After these many years, Hal Roach introduces Oliver Hardy in straight comedy. Teamed with Harry Langdon — drafted to replace Stan Laurel — Hardy gives out with a minimum of slapstick antics and knockabout stunts. A few of Hardy's double-takes remain, but the rest is a straight portrayal. Zenobia *is mild entertainment and will provide support in the key duals. In the subsequents it will aim for kid patronage and followers of Hardy.*

Slender story provided does not warrant the amount of footage. Script is a series of incidents tied together in not too compact form. There are several spontaneous moments, but on the whole, comedy is strained. Things just seem to drift away without achieving much audience interest....

Hardy demonstrates he can easily handle straight comedy without [resorting] to familiar slapstick, but is handicapped by material provided. Langdon has but a few moments to work with Hardy, so an estimate on their work as a team must wait for future pictures.

Box Office, *March 18, 1939*

A far cry is this from the hysterical comedies with which the name of Hal Roach was connected of yore. It is slow-paced and overlong for the niggardly quantity of humor and straight story elements that have been written into it, a failing that not even the most tasteful and expensive production, and the work of an exceptionally fine cast, are able to overcome. The story is a queer hodge-podge with the South of 1870's as its background, and Oliver Hardy playing a near-straight role as a village doctor. Into this scene drifts Harry Langdon — teamed with the corpulent Hardy for the first time — with a sick elephant, Zenobia, on his hands. Hardy cures Zenobia's ailment and the elephant conceives an undying affection for her benefactor which almost ruins his and his family's reputations.

Box Office, *March 18, 1939. Reviewed by Ivan Spear*
    Hal Roach's Zenobia, *for United Artists release... misses its mark by a wide margin, despite the galaxy of comedy stars heading the cast, principally because the script is sadly lacking either in logical story construction or the side-splitting antics which the Roach name usually guarantees. Director Gordon Douglas showed to best advantage in slapstick sequences.*

Motion Picture Herald, *March 18, 1939; Reviewed by William R. Weaver*

The first picture in which Harry Langdon appears with Oliver Hardy in place of Stan Laurel is, in view of the wide news mention made of the Hardy-Laurel separation, something of a "must-see" on any theatergoer's list. Clearly the first thing to tell the customers about Zenobia *is that it's that picture. There is plenty more to tell them, including the news that Billie Burke, Alice Brady, June Lang, Jean Parker, J. Farrell MacDonald and Step'n (sic) Fetchit are among the substantial personalities also present in the cast, and Hal Roach, wise in his veterancy, has taken steps to see that showmen presenting the picture boldly as the first Hardy vehicle without Laurel will be in no danger of an audience kick-back from such billing.*

A less experienced showman than Mr. Roach might have been expected, as no doubt he was, to simply substitute Mr. Langdon for Mr. Laurel, as a baseball manager substitutes a pitcher in the ninth inning, and leave him on his own. Mr. Roach proceeded differently. He made of Zenobia *a quite different kind of comedy, pairing Messrs. Hardy and Langdon only intermittently in the action, and he furnished all those first flight supporting players with plenty of material for individual and collective entertainment. He has thus made it impossible for* Zenobia *to be directly compared with any Hardy-Laurel comedy, favorably or otherwise, and has started the Hardy-Langdon series off on a new note....*

To Gordon Douglas, former Our Gang comedy director moved up here to direct this unique production as his first feature picture, congratulations are definitely due. The film is likewise an achievement for A. Edward Sutherland, the former director, here bowing to the industry as a producer. The period is 1870, the setting is a small town in the Old South and the humor is of the kind the whole family can appreciate.

Previewed at the Alexander Theatre, Glendale, Calif., where a general audience responded with genial laughter to the whole and with a burst of applause to the Declaration of Independence sequence.

Harrison's Reports, *April 22, 1939*

That a producer of Mr. Hal Roach's experience should have produced a piece of junk such as this is indeed discouraging. Oliver Hardy, an excellent short-subject comedian, is bad enough when he is put in a feature, but when he is coupled with an elephant, that is unbearable. If Mr. Abram F. Myers (Allied Association) had this picture in Washington to show it to the Subcommittee of the Senate Committee on Interstate Commerce, holding the hearings on the Neely Bill, he would have need no other arguments to persuade its members to report the bill favorably. It is supposed to be a comedy, but I doubt whether any one else but Mr. Roach will find it such....

Morally, there is nothing wrong with it — it may be put in the "A" class, but it is doubtful if it will amuse even children.

Brooklyn Daily Eagle, *May 15, 1939; Reviewed by Herbert Cohn*

The happiest thought about Zenobia, Hal Roach's comedy at the Globe Theater, is that it probably won't happen again. According to latest reports from the studios, Stan Laurel will rejoin Oliver Hardy so that our corpulent friend will be spared the embarrassment of another try at straight comedy.

It isn't that Oliver is alone at the Globe. He pairs off alternately with Harry Langdon of yore, and with the clever Billie Burke; Stepin Fetchit is on hand with his peculiar brand of incoherencies; Alice Brady sports the accent of a Southern matron, and Zenobia, who is — without further ado — an elephant, performs helpfully. But all of the 75 minutes consumed by this lineup of popular comics is less than fair exchange for a single scene involving the long-jawed Laurel. Without his runty partner, Hardy falls as flat as Floogie's foot.

The story, which finds Hardy as a Mississippi doctor in a swallowtail coat back in 1870, doesn't make matters better either. Neither does Gordon Douglas's direction, which lavishes a heavy-handed slapstick style on the tattered problem of a middle class girl (Dr. Hardy's daughter), in love with the son of a proud and wealthy Southern dame who gave up the Mississippi doctor long ago because he insisted she was healthy. Zenobia's fondness for the doctor develops after he has straightened out her knotted tail, and with it comes a batch of complications that only the preamble to the Declaration of Independence, precisely delivered by little Phillip Hurlie, can untangle. Unfortunately, the pursuit of happiness today does not lead to Zenobia.

New York Post, *May 15, 1939; Reviewed by Archer Winsten*

The 1939 vote of this reviewer for the queerest picture of the year goes to Zenobia, now at the Globe Theatre. If I told you all about it, you would not believe me. At times it has the appearance of a very old picture, one that Hal Roach might have made fifteen years ago. Supporting that theory are a few slapstick antics of Mack Sennett vintage and the presence of Harry Langdon in a supporting role. The story itself reinforces that notion with its legend of a graceful elephant, Miss Zenobia, who embarrasses her benefactor, a small-town doctor, played by Oliver Hardy, by following him after he has cured her of a tail tied in a knot.

On the other hand, more recent notes are sounded by Billie Burke in her absent-minded, twittery condition and Alice Brady trying to act silly, too. This period is further represented by Stepin Fetchit in his lazybones characterization.

Coming down to the next period, we have James Ellison, Jean Parker and June Lang acting themselves as much as the script will allow. They date from, let us say, 1937–8.

And finally, the crowning datemark, there is March 1939 represented in little colored Philip Hurlie who sounds the popular Americanism-and-freedom-for-all-people note by reciting the entire Declaration of Independence for a quarter. Oliver Hardy had previously stressed the "life, liberty and pursuit of happiness" part.

The Hall Johnson Choir lends yet another flavor to this incredible mixture by singing a snatch of one of the standard Southern songs.

I cannot be so bold as to predict whether or not you would like the picture. At rare intervals there are soundly conceived slapstick laughs. But the general level of entertainment is juvenile, and you are apt to be puzzled as to which response the film calls for more strongly, boredom or embarrassment.

WHAT THE EXHIBITORS SAID:
Box Office, *September 2, 1939*

This one didn't get much from trade papers, but it seemed to please those who came looking for a laugh. It didn't break any house record.
G. B. Woodbury, Bethel Theatre, Bethel, VT.
Population: 1,500, Theater Capacity: 250. Rural small-town business.

Box Office, *September 16, 1939*

Only one comment on such a picture and that is that. It set me a new low. Better skip this one if you can.
J. M. Plasterer, Strand Theatre, Steelton, PA.
Population: 13,000, Theater Capacity: 500. Town Patronage.

Motion Picture Herald, *March 16, 1940*

Can't say much for this picture. They have taken comedy material, it seems to me, and attempted to stretch it out feature length. Sequences were very unrelated. Might be all right for some houses but not here.
Simon Galitzki, Coed Theater, Topeka, KS. General patronage.

Motion Picture Herald, *June 29, 1940*

We couldn't get them in to see this one. Just a very mediocre picture. "Zenobia" is the elephant; we were the goats.
Harland Rankin, Plaza Theater, Tilbury, Ontario, Canada. General patronage.

Sitting Pretty

A Jam Handy Picture Service Production, #M-824. CAST: Harry Langdon. Copyright April 26, 1940, Registration Number LU9601. Released by Jam Handy Picture Service Inc., 1940.

SYNOPSIS: This film was unavailable for viewing. Following is the synopsis submitted to the U.S. Copyright Office:

Harry Langdon, assistant to Freddie, world's champion flagpole sitter, is all tired out after a long night's vigil. In the morning, while trying to wake Freddie up, a water bucket falls from atop the pole and knocks Harry unconscious. From the state of suspended motion, Harry's phantom body rises out of his real body and goes in quest of a nice comfortable place to sit down.

Inside a museum he tries to find comfort on a throne chair, a bed of nails, and in Napoleon's coach, but to no avail. Then he discovers a modern motorcar which has all the comfort features he's been looking for.

After a series of humorous incidents in the car, Harry hears an announcement over the radio telling about his accident. This brings Harry's phantom back to where the real Harry's body is still laid out on the sidewalk — unconscious. The real Harry wakes up and once more commences his weary grind of playing nursemaid to the flagpole sitter.

An industrial short made for Chevrolet; not screened for general audiences.

Goodness! A Ghost

A Radio Flash Comedy Released in Two Reels. PRODUCED BY Lou Brock. DIRECTED BY Harry D'Arcy. ASSOCIATE PRODUCER: Clem Beauchamp. STORY BY George Jeske and Arthur V. Jones. SCREENPLAY BY Harry Langdon. Director of PHOTOGRAPHY: Harry Wild, A.S.C. FILM EDITOR: John Lockert. Recordist: Earl Mounce. CAST: Harry Langdon, Tiny Sanford, J.C. Morton. Copyright July 2, 1940, Registration Number LP9745. Released by R.K.O. Radio Pictures, Inc., July 5, 1940.

SYNOPSIS: The Community Dramatic players are presenting *Love Conquers All* at a theatre. Actors are rehearsing a melodrama as Harry, backstage, provides sound effects. An actor, playing the small part of a policeman, quits the show. Harry is assigned the role after telling the director that the cop's uniform belonged to his grandfather. Later, Harry, clad in the uniform, rehearses his line, "Did anybody call an officer?"

His grandfather's ghost appears and straightens out Harry's hat. He runs out of the theatre into an alley. The ghost reappears and advises Harry on posture and sense of duty. A woman appears and drags Harry into a nearby building. She tells him that a gang of killers is in a room and he should be careful when he enters. Inside the room are three crooks who are playing cards when Harry enters. He's told to pick which of the three should annihilate him. The crooks then decide to play a hand of poker to see who plugs Harry. If he wins the game, they'll let him go. Harry is dealt three queens and the ghost advises him to discard them. They are all dealt another hand, and Harry wins with a straight. The thugs refuse to let him go, and prompted by the ghost, are sprayed with seltzer water.

The ghost, now in miniature form, climbs into a model biplane and flies it around the room, pummeling the villains. Harry finds a slingshot and shoots blasting caps at the plane. The thugs think it is gunfire and get trapped behind a foldaway bed. The real police arrive and arrest the three thugs. Harry returns to the theatre and discovers that he missed the play. His grandfather's ghost rips off the uniform and Harry is left standing in his long johns.

ANALYSIS: A marked improvement over the Columbia comedies, *Goodness! A Ghost* resurrects, if not the bewildered and bewildering Little Elf, then at least Harry, the trusting innocent. Langdon looks somewhat younger than in recent shorts, with the slapstick indignities saved for the members of the gang who deserve the punishment. The concept of the ghost of Harry's grandfather pushing his descendent, much against his will, toward heroism is cleverly handled, with convincing effects. On the down side, the film is a little rushed. At one point, Harry is torn between releasing his would-be killers, who are trapped behind a Murphy bed, and admitting the genuine policemen, who are pounding on the door. In earlier days, this indecisiveness would have been milked for laughs (and possibly given the film a Harry Moment); here it's thrown away as the police abruptly knock the door down. Still, in terms of laughs, *Goodness! A Ghost* is Langdon's most enjoyable two-reeler since *Knight Duty*.

Cold Turkey

A Columbia Short Subject Released in Two Reels. PRODUCED BY Del Lord and Hugh McCollum. DIRECTED BY Del Lord. STORY AND SCREENPLAY BY Harry Edwards and Elwood Ullman. PHOTOGRAPHY BY Lucien Ballard. EDITED BY Arthur Seid. CAST: Harry Langdon, Ann Doran, Monty Collins, Bud Jamison, Vernon Dent, Eddie Laughton. Copyright October 17, 1940, Registration Number LP9982; Renewed September 6, 1968, Number R442795. Released by Columbia Pictures Corporation, October 18, 1940.

SYNOPSIS: In the office of the Caldwell Coughdrop Company, the boss reminds his workers that Christmas vacation doesn't start at 4:59. After he leaves, they start celebrating with drinks and party hats. Harry is offered a drink but refuses. He eventually has a glass of champagne and becomes tipsy. He wins a live turkey in the office raffle.

Harry walks home, pulling the turkey on a string. The bird gets loose and Harry finds it on top of a store awning. When he gets home, he brings the bird inside and tells it to be quiet. He puts a balloon on the bird's beak to silence it. The turkey inflates the balloon, which pops and wakes Harry's wife. Not realizing that it's a live bird, the wife tells Harry to put it in the icebox. The turkey gets loose, goes into the living room, and wrecks the apartment. The superintendent arrives outside their front door and overhears Harry's wife telling him to kill "him." The superintendent, not realizing they are referring to the turkey, thinks they mean to do him in. He runs in fear into his apartment and barricades the door. Harry finds an axe with which to kill the turkey, and the superintendent is scared that *he's* going to be killed. Harry, hearing the superintendent's cries, believes that a maniac is on the loose. He runs around, yelling, and upsets the other tenants. When the superintendent does see Harry, he screams, "Maniac!" and everyone runs away from the man with the axe. In the rush, Harry gets knocked to the floor, thinks for a moment until he remembers what he was doing, then gets up and runs off, yelling, "Maniac!"

ANALYSIS: In *Cold Turkey*, some clever ideas are interspersed with routine slapstick; the result is a mixed bag. As in *A Doggone Mixup*, Harry brings home an unwieldy animal, much to Ann Doran's displeasure. Harry's much more likable here, because he wins the turkey, as opposed to being bamboozled into purchasing it, plus there's no mustache to obscure the character's childlike innocence.

This was Langdon's first short in Hugh McCollum's unit. McCollum's films were generally less violent than those of Jules White, but in this instance, Del Lord directed and co-produced, bringing a penchant for slapstick in which he'd been schooled under Mack Sennett. Thus we're given gratuitous moments such as superintendent Monty Collins dripping paint on Doran's face, a telephone that jerks around the fellow on the other end when you give its cord a healthy tug, a turkey that can blow up a balloon, and similar gags. The film's biggest laughs aren't among the knockabout shtick, but rather when the superintendent overhears Harry and Ann discuss killing the turkey and believes they mean to do him in. In trying to avoid Harry, Collins continually encounters him and effectively puts over comic fear without overdoing it. Harry, meanwhile, can't comprehend that his superintendent considers him a threat. These scenes help lift *Cold Turkey* a notch or two above the usual lackluster Columbia product.

HARRY MOMENT: Harry has one drink of champagne, and his facial pantomime veers from fear of how he'll feel, to bliss, to giddy intoxication in a delightfully skillful transition.

WHAT THE CRITICS SAID:
The Exhibitor, *October 30, 1940*
　Harry Langdon wins a turkey in a raffle and is made to wish he hadn't. There are several amusing moments, but at times the script strains so hard for laughs that it produces the opposite reaction. FAIR.

Misbehaving Husbands

A Producers' Releasing Corporation Production. 65 minutes. PRODUCED BY Jed Buell. DIRECTED BY William Beaudine. SCREENPLAY BY Vernon Smith and Claire Parrish. ORIGINAL STORY BY Cea Sabin. PHOTOGRAPHY BY Art Reed. EDITOR: Robert Crandall. ART DIRECTOR: George Van Marter. ASSISTANT DIRECTOR: Eddie Munfort. PRODUCTION MANAGER: Peter Jones. CAST: Harry Langdon, Betty Blythe, Ralph Byrd, Esther Muir, Gayne Whitman, Florence Wright, Luana Walters, Frank Jacquet, Charlotte Treadway, Byron Barr, Frank Hagney, Fred Kelsey, Hennie Brown, Billy Mitchell, Mary MacLaren, Gertrude Astor. Copyright December 13, 1940, Registration Number LP10164. Released by Producers' Releasing Corporation, December 20, 1940.

SYNOPSIS: Henry Butler (Harry Langdon) is the owner of a booming department store, to which he dedicates more energy and attention than he does to his wife, Effie. It's the morning before the store's big annual sale, and Henry is neglecting everything else, from eating breakfast to the fact that it's his 20th wedding anniversary. Effie is disappointed but pragmatic, as by this point she's used to Henry being preoccupied with his business. She is planning to throw him a surprise party that evening.

A friend of theirs, Grace Norman, is newly divorced, and has pretty much written off all men as lying, cheating jerks. When Effie pays her a visit and tells her that Henry forgot their anniversary, Grace starts hinting that Henry might have the same sort of wanderlust as her ex-husband. Grace's attorney, Gilbert Wayne, drops by to deliver Grace's settlement, as well as his bill. Grace introduces Gilbert to Effie, and asks if she might bring him as her guest to the party, to which Effie agrees. That evening, while setting up for the party, Effie walks under a ladder, and the superstitious servants, Memphis and Opal, lament the imminent bad luck.

Henry once again works late, losing track of time until 7:00 p.m. He tries to rush home, but more work falls in front of him: Mr. Sibley needs his approval for three outfits to be displayed at tomorrow's sale. The outfits are on three beautiful models, and between Henry and Mr. Sibley, they disapprove of two of the outfits and send the models out to change. Sibley brings him to a window display for his approval, and Henry nitpicks over "Hedy" and "Carol," two ceramic

Waiter,----(Enters with Large beer glass filled with water)
              walks up to Katie gives her the Cream-De-Minth,)
              hands Johnie the glass of water)- and heres your
              drink,""
Johnie,----(bus"looking at beer,)- whats this water,?
Waiter,----(bus" talking to Katie,looks at Johnie)-yep good
              water,"
Johnie,----hey, I am thirsty, not dirty,"
Waiter,-----Exits,
Katie,------Well Johnie you had better order somthing to eat,"
Johnie,-----Somthing to eat," all right, Waiter,Waiter,
Waiter,--- (Jumps out,)
Johnie,------How is your chicken,??
Waiter,------Fine I saw her last night, (Exits)
Johnie and Katie,(looks at each other dont no what to make
              out of it,)
Waiter,-----(blows devil/ Devil whistle on out side,)
Johnie,-----Listen to the wind,"
Katie ,------That wasnt wind Johnie, that was an Automobile
              that just past here just then, look here comes
              another one, my goodness they must be runing a
              race with each other(another whistle blows,)
              my goodness that one come so close to us he nearly
              took a wheel off our car,"
Johnie,- ---(looks at her suspiciously,)- did you see
              Automobiles going by here,?
Katie,------Yes going right by here,"(bus looking after Antols
Johnie,------Right by here,???
Katie,--- --Yes going right by here,"
Johnie,-----(Looks over at Cafe,) Waiter,Bring me a Cream-De-
              Minth,""
              (Cream-de-menth is cue for song,)After song Johnie
              and Katie are down stage standing to gether.)
Katie,------You are now standing on the Boulevard,"
Johnie,---- Yep,"
Katie,-----and the clock just struck twelve,""
Johnie,-----Yep,"
Katie $----- ~~so do not make any noise~~ and you are all alone
              with me,"
Johnie ------(looks at her out of corner of his eye,)
              then turns around and blows out all the street
              lamps on scenery,)
Katie,--- Well, I just wanted to tell you that you will make
              a pretty good chauffeur for my father,""
Johnie,-----(turns around and whistles,for lights. come
              up,)
Katie,-----my Father wants a man that can drive a Machine 60
              miles an hour, how fast can you drive,??

(4)

Johnie,----- 60 miles a week, down hill,
Katie,----- Before I go any further I want to ask you a few questions,"
Johnie,----- Shoot,"
Katie,----- What is your name,?
Johnie,----- Johnie,"
Katie,----- No I mean your full name,
Johnie,----- It is Johnie wheather I am full or not,
Katie,----- are you married,?
Johnie,----- Yes,
Katie,----- how many children have you,?
Johnie,----- We got one children,
Katie,----- Boy or girl,?
Johnie,----- I think she is a boy.
Katie,----- By the way Johnie I heard you were arested for speeding, is that right,??
Johnie,----- Yes, I told the judge I was driveing 60 miles per hour,
Katie,----- Wha did the Judge say?
Johnie,----- Fine,"
Katie,----- (grabing Johnie by the hand and speaking,) suppose you were driveing at the rate of 60 miles an hour, and a man was stanhing in the middle of the road, what would you do to let him know that you was coming,?
Johnie,----- write him a letter,
Katie,----- No no faster than that,
Johnie,----- Sendhim a telema scrach,
Katie,----- No No, what would you blow,?
Johnie,----- My nose.
Katie,----- No you would blow your horn.
Johnie,----- (walkin back to Auto, and touching french horn) Here is a fine horn, (playing it,)
Katie,----- Yes Johnie it sounds just like a band, does'nt it,?
Johnie,----- Yep, that is a handy horn,
Katie,----- it is,?
Johnie,----- Yes every time I run over any body I give them music while they are dieing.
Katie,----- By the way Johnie, What be came of that little run-a-bout you use to have,?
Johnie,----- Oh it run a bout a week then,---Blowed up.
Katie,----- Thats a fine Machine you have there what make is ----SHE,?
Johnie,----- That is not a she,
Katie,----- No, well what is it,??
Johnie,----- That is a touring car, not a Run-a-bout,"

Katie,----I suppose you are a good machinist,?
Johnie,----Oh yes I am a good machinist,
Katie,----you are,? do you know what a machinist is,?
Johnie,----Yes, a machinist is a man that can take an Automobile
           apart then put it all back to gether again,
Katie,----And you are one of those fellows,?
Johnie,----Oh yes, the other day I took a machine apart then
           I put it all back to gether again,
Katie,---- oh fine,"
Johnie,----then I had three pieces left over,"

(Waiter changes to chauffeur, enters in prop taxie cab at cue
Three pieces left over, enters very fast honking horn, stops
left center.)

Johnie,----Who left that door open,?
Chauffeur,--Hay boy, do you serve lobsters there,?
Johnie,----(Standing near Cafe) - yes what will you have,?
Chauffeur,--Well what have you got,?
Johnie,----(scraching his side,)- the hives,"
Chauffeur,-- Say can you tell me where I can find a preacher,?
Johnie,----Look what wants a preacher,"
Katie,--- What do you want with a preacher this time of the
          night,?
Chauffeur,---Why, I got a couple in my cab that wants to get
             married," say bub have you ---
Johnie,---- Stop, your tires are punctured,"
Chauffer,--Tires are punctured,""well just keep your eyes on
           this car till I get back,(exits like he is leaveing
           stage, but stops behind taxie to work cues,)
Johnie,----(walks behind his car and gets a large prop axe
           then walks over to taxie cab,)
Katie,----He is having some trouble is'nt he Johnie,?
Johnie,----Yes I am going to fix it up,
Katie,----What are you going to do with it,?
Johnie,----I am going to see how hard I can hit it,(swings Axe
           over head then strikes at front of Auto an misses
           it,)
Chauffeur,--(hits slap stick on floor behind taxie,)
Johnie,----(Grabs his pants)- there goes my other button,"
           I bet I will hit it this time,(hits the top of
           hood with axe.)Property man shoots lamp post on
           set wall up in the air 6 feet and down again,)
           (chauffer rings a bell back of taxie) Johnie looks
           up at post, walks over to horses head on set wall
           pulls his ear down, property man pores water in
           funnel back of horses head there is a small hose
           attached to funnel, water flows down hose to mouth

of horse.,Johnie catches water in tin cup and drinks it,)
Katie,---- Johnie, What was that you were drinking,?
Johnie,----Horse liniment.
Chauffer,(Puts to shadows made out of card board to represent a man and a women. holds them close to window of taxie, an electric light hanging back of taxie throws the shadows on window, window is made of tracing paper.) Johnie sees the shadows kissing in window. sits down on floor looks up at window and sings)--Every bodies doing it, doing it,"
Katie,---- Johnie," what are you doing,?
Johnie,----Sight seeing,"
Katie,----You better try and fix up that mans machine,"
Johnie,---(still looking at shadows in taxie window) it is all ready fixed,
Katie,----How is the sparking plug,?
Johnie,----(looks up at shadows, man has plug hat,) He has got his plug hat on to night,"
Katie,----Well how are the conections,?
Johnie,----(shadows are now close together kissing with out moveing,) -- Solid,"
Katie,--- Do you think the conections will bust,?
Johnie,----Not unless his face slips,"
Chauffeur,-(Pulls curtain down in taxie cab window, cuting off view of shadows,)
Johnie,----Shows over,""(gets up starts to walk around taxie chauffeur enters gets into taxie and backs off stage. Johnie cranks his Auto, with a ratchet for a crank, when machine wont start he kicks the front wheel and jars the car, from the force of the kick, the engine starts going, the effect is made by Katie seated in back seat of Auto, shaking a tin can filled with shot. When machine starts, Johnie steps in Auto, Katie shoots a 38 revolver through a hole in bottom of Auto, which gives the effect of an explosion. Johnie mugs and crawls out of car, katie pulls a string that lifts lid off of tool box on the runing board facing audience, the words " get busy " are painted beneath lid so when opened the audience can read it. Johnie cranks Auto again, Katie shoots a cap pistol in the car, Johnie walks around to see what the matter is, Policeman runs up to front of car yells,)- STOP, STOP,"
(another 22 revolver is conceald in the front end of Auto, Katie shoots it by means of pulling a wire attached to trigger of revolver, policeman turns about and runs off stage holding his stomach.

Johnie,--(~~watches~~ watches policeman runing,)- He must of been
     trying to steal a ride,"
Katie,----This reminds me of the battle of bulls-run,"
Johnie,--(looks off stage in direction of policeman,)
     Yes he is runing yet,
Katie,---Johnie, do you know what I think,
Johnie,-- No what do you think,?
Katie ,--I think you have a leak in your gasoline tank,"
Johnie,---(lights a match holds it up so audience can see it)
     "yes I am going to find it,(then sticks match ~~in front~~ in side of car as though looking for leak,)
     Katie pulls a string attached to a cap pistol on prop dog back of Auto, it explodes, Katie wags dogs
     tail by means of a fine thread attached to tail.
     Johnie takes an oil can with a very large spout
     and oils the dogs tail while wagging. after oiling
     he takes salt celler and sprinkles salt on tail.
     then walks to front of car, cranks it engines starts
     as before, johnie turns around to pick up handkerchief
     Katie pushes a small bellows with foot, bellows is
     filled with lycopodium, which blows through a small
     blaze of alcohol, flame hits Johnie in seat of pants
     while stooping for handkerchief. Johnie jumps up and
     holds his pants, looks behind to see if he is burnt,
     then speaks,)- Aint it warm," that is a pretty bad
     leak in that tank,?
Katie,-- yes I have told you before that gasoline is very
     ~~desiptull~~ deceitful,"
Johnie,--- yes it talks behind your back all right.
Katie ,---You had better telephone to the Depot and find out
     if my train is on time,(Pointing to prop telephone
     on lamp post near Cafe.) Johnie walks over to
     telephone puts receiver to his ear and speaks)
     Hello," (telephone slides down post through a
     tin grove, worked by property man, Johnie looks
     down at Phone,)- Hello," (Phone slides up post,)
     Johnie speaks again,)- Hello," (Phone slides down
     as before,) Johnie gets made and yells,) What the
     hell-O (Phone goes back up and stays there ,
     Johnie Speaks,) Hey central give me the Depot,"
     (turns around to Katie who is standing on left stage
     Johnie still speaking,) She wont give it to me,
Katie,--- Why what is the matter,
Johnie,-- It is nailed down.
Katie,-- Ask central for ONE.

Johnie,--- Give me one,"
 (Props Shoves mouth piece out of Telephone and hits Johnie in the mouth,) Johnie holds his mouth then speaks,) It is a good thing I did'nt ask central for Ten. (then he picks up the receiver and walks over to Katie,)

Katie,--- How are you going to talk now,?

Johnie,--- Long distant, (bus) walking up to put receiver back on Phone,) Katie Cranks Auto Props shakes can off stage for engine effect. Johnie hears the engine going an runs with Katie in the Automobile, they dont no more than get seated when the steering wheel flys out of its place over Johnie and Katies head,(Steering wheel is worked with a spring attach -ed in tube. the wheel flys off stage back of Auto. there is a signe on front of car that reads For Hire. When wheel flys out Johnie Turns the signe around which reads For Sale.
For Sale, is the music cue for song, while Johnie and Katie sing song the stage lights are out with street lamps on scenery still illuminated. Johnie flashes serch light through the audience while singing, at the close of song , props pulls Auto off to the right of stage, with a rope attached to the bottom of the Car.

<u>FINISH</u>

APPENDIX II
Johnny's New Car 1916 & 1921

The two versions of *Johnny's New Car* document how thoroughly a vaudeville act could be honed and reworked over several seasons. The first script was submitted about six months after Langdon abandoned *A Night on the Bouelvard*; the second about six months before he wrote *After the Ball*. As Langdon discovered his pantomimic strengths, verbal comedy eventually took a back seat to visual routines and reactions. Note how the business with the prop auto has been expanded upon, with the garish striped awning, the radiator that contains liquor (a nod to Prohibition), the door that comes off in Johnny's hands, and the engine parts that fly onto the stage.

```
                               Jul 22, 1916
                                4 4537


                    Vaudeville Act
                       entitled
                   "JOHNNY'S NEW CAR."
                Written and Produced by-Harry Langdon.

    Scene:-  On a Boulevard.
    Cast:-
         Katie Speedington..............Miss Rose Langdon.
         Johnnie Gotacar................Harry Langdon.
         Policeman & Waiter.............James Langdon.
```

(Curtain rises on boulevard scene with illuminated lamp post. Cafe at Right of Stage. Drinking fountain just outside of cafe. On left side of stage Mile Post reading "One Mile To Garage." Katie and Johnnie enter in runabout, coming from left entrance. Turning and running down center stage, facing audience.)

KATIE.

And you told me you knew every bump in this road.

JOHNNIE.

Didn't I find them?

KATIE

My goodness, but you're a fast and reckless driver. You make me nervous to ride with you. Don't get so excited, when you are driving your car take your time. And another thing when you turn a corner slow down to about thirty eight miles an hour. I wish I had that wheel I would show you how to run this car.

JOHNNIE.

Do you want to run this car? Well, there's a wheel. (Bus. handing Katie steering wheel)

KATIE.

(Takes wheel and at the same time looking around, noticing cafe at the Right, speaking) Get out and crank it.

JOHNNIE.

I won't crank the car, you're the only crank and you'll have to crank it.

KATIE.

Oh how nice of you to stop right in front of the cafe.

JOHNNIE.

Well I'll crank it up for you then.

KATIE.

Now don't try to get out of it Johnnie, I knew you were going to buy me supper to-night; won't you call a waiter?

JOHNNIE.

Sure. (speaking in a weak voice) Waiter, waiter. (Waiter jumps out of cafe)

WAITER

Good evening.

JOHNNIE.

You're not hard of hearing this evening, are you waiter?

WAITER.

Why certainly not; won't you step out and come in?

JOHNNIE.

No I'm afraid someone will steal my car if I step out and come in.

WAITER

Oh very well, I have a little table; I'll bring it out here and put it on the car. (places small table on the Right side of car)

KATIE.

Oh Johnnie isn't this nice service?

JOHNNIE.

Yes, but I don't like service a la carte.

WAITER

What would you like to have madam?

KATIE.

You bring me a broiled lobster.

WAITER.

(speaking to Johnnie) And what do you wish?

JOHNNIE.

I wish you A Happy New Year, and I wish I hadn't stopped here.

WAITER.

Why you shouldn't wish this- come on and have something.

JOHNNIE.

How much is your chicken?

WAITER

We have chicken for One Dollar, but of course the larger the chicken the larger the price.

JOHNNIE.

I'll have an egg.

WAITER.

Anything else you'd like, madam?

KATIE.

Yes, I'd like to have some nice French roast, Welch Rarebit (Johnnie blowing horn on automobile, trying to interrupt Katie.)

WAITER.

I beg your pardon, sir, but I can't hear what the lady is saying.

JOHNNIE.

Couldn't you hear what she said?

WAITER.

No.

JOHNNIE.

She wants a ham sandwich.

WAITER.

Anything else you would like? (speaking to Katie)

KATIE.

Cancel that order and bring me a seltzer highball.

WAITER.

All right, madam (speaking to Johnnie) And I think I know what you want all right. (waiter exits into cafe)

JOHNNY.

If he brings me a nut sundae I'll shoot him.

WAITER

(enters with ginger ale high ball, speaking) Here's your highball madam, and I am sorry I haven't got what you want.

JOHNNIE.

You haven't got any water? And my radiator is dry.

WAITER.

Well I'm sorry (picking up table from car, starts to exit)

JOHNNIE.

Say waiter how do you like my little runabout?

WAITER

Fine, she has pretty eyes.

JOHNNIE.

(looking at Katie's eyes) Gets out of car, speaking. That's an insult to my runabout. (MUSIC CUE.) (Johnny walks over to fountain, starts to drink water, water stops running, tries same thing again and unable to get water, walks over to automobile, takes the cap off the radiator and gets water from springs of the automobile.)

KATIE.

Why Johnnie that water isn't fit to drink, is it?

JOHNNIE.

It ought to be, it comes from the springs. Won't you have a drink?

KATIE.

No I don't care for water. (SONG) (During song, Katie walks back and forth across stage, Johnnie following. Johnnie gets tired following, blows whistle, imitating traffic cop, at finish of song, policeman enters behind Johnnie, blows whistle. Johnnie stops blowing, looks frightend

(Katie- bus. continued--)(Katie standing Right side of Johnnie keeps pointing to policeman- Johnnie is afraid to look around- talks deaf and dumb to Katie. Johnnie starts whistling, looks around, sees policeman- policeman turns to Katie, offers her the whistle- Katie refuses it- Johnnie puts it in his coat- looks around where policeman was standing. As Johnnie looks around, steps on the other side of him. Johnnie thinks he has left and starts blowing whistle- turns around, sees policeman standing there- smiles and tries to act unconcerned. Katie attracts policeman's attention- policeman turns to look at her Johnnie takes policeman's badge off his coat, puts it on his own vest- then starts blowing whistle again. Policeman turns grabs the whistle from Johnnie- Johnnie pulls back his coat showing badge. Policeman gives whistle back to Johnnie, salutes and exits.)

KATIE.

Why I didn't know you were an officer.

JOHNNIE.

Don't you know who I am? I'm Sherlock Nobody Homes. I'm working on a case now. I'll have it all finished to-night.

KATIE.

All finished to-night?

JOHNNIE.

Yes, I've only got three more bottles left. (Waiter enters with bottle of champagne. Opens bottle with a loud report. Johnnie turns quick examining all of his auto tires.

KATIE.

No tire, Johnny, a bottle of champagne.

JOHNNY.

Who ordered that champagne?

-6-

KATIE.

I did.

JOHNNIE.

Who's going to pay for it?

KATIE.

Why US.

JOHNNY.

The S is off.

KATIE.

Why what's the matter?

JOHNNY.

The S hasn't got any money, that's what's the matter.

KATIE.

You haven't any money? Why you owe this waiter Two Dollars and a half now- what are you going to do?

JOHNNIE.

Give him the automobile, and then I'll send him the rest.
(pushing guards to one side.)
    auto

KATIE.

Well if you haven't got any money to pay the waiter, I have a good way out of it. I stopped here last night with a friend of mine and we had some refreshments. This friend of mine got the waiter interested in some Ford jokes and the waiter forgot to charge my friend for the drinks.

JOHNNIE.

You think I can do that?

KATIE.

Sure tell him some Ford jokes.

JOHNNIE.

(whistles for waiter) waiter enters) I thought I would call you out because we are going to go away. How much do I owe you?

WAITER.

Two Dollars and a half.

JOHNNIE.

That's very reasonable. Oh say waiter, did you hear the latest Ford joke.

WAITER.

Why no, do you know some Ford jokes? (starts laughing)

JOHNNIE.

(surprised at waiter laughing orders another bottle of champagne) (Waiter exits after champagne.) (speaking to Katie) I didn't know it was going to be so easy. (waiter enters with another bottle of champagne speaking)

WAITER.

Now let's hear that Ford joke.

JOHNNIE.

Well once upon a time there was some lightning bugs (waiter interrupts by laughing) Say waiter, have you got some nice twenty five cents cigars?

WAITER.

No but we have some nice fifty cent ones.

JOHNNY.

Well I'll have a nice fifty cent one- what do I care how much they cost. (waiter looks at Johnnie suspiciously) (waiter exits) (to Katie) Are you sure that's the same waiter?

WAITER.

(enters with cigar.) Now let's hear the rest of that Ford joke. (JOHNNY TELLS JOKE.) (WAITER REFUSES TO LAUGH-LOOKING DISGUSTED AT JOHNNIE.) (Johnnie laughs at his own joke- turns and sees waiter looking solemn- then looking at his cigar speaking)

JOHNNY.

Yes, here comes papa. You want to hear another funny Ford joke?

WAITER.

Now listen here- a fellow stopped here last night, got me interested in Ford jokes and I forgot to charge him for the drinks. Don't think you can put it over.

JOHNNIE.

(taken by surprise, gets weak in the knees, leans against fountain, gets his hands all wet, collects himself, speaking.) You say a fellow stopped here last night, got you all excited and you forgot to charge him for the drinks?

WAITER

That's what I said.

JOHNNIE.

Well what's all of that got to do with my change?

WAITER.

(scratching his head) Change? Why what did you give me?

JOHNNIE.

A Twenty Dollar bill.

WAITER.

A Twenty Dollar bill? Well I'm sorry anything like this happened. (takes money out of his pocket, speaking) The wine if five, well here is five, ten, fifteen dollars change. I thank you. Come in again. (waiter exits)

JOHNNIE.

(puts money in his pocket) Sure I'll come back to-morrow night,(gets into automobile, shows Katie the money- waiter steps out of cafe with telephone in his hand speaking)

WAITER.

Hello Central, connect me with the police station. (Johnnie hears him talking, gets out of auto and lays the money down on the table near the waiter) (Waiter continues talking)

Hello, police station? Send a policeman up here at once and shoot my dog he's gone mad. (Johnnie picks up the money and puts it in his pocket, walks around in front of car, cranks with his right hand as if in a hurry to get away. Gets tired of cranking with his right hand, used his left with right hand on hip, cranks engine backwards, then starts to crank with his foot. (Orchestra starts music playing imitating hand organ, Johnnie cranks to the time of music, takes his hat off as if asking for a collection.)

KATIE.

Why Johnny you told me you had a self starter.

JOHNNIE.

No, I have a combination starter. (with dial on front of hood, starts turning as if trying to find combination. Loses combination, studies for a minute then raises automobile guard up where combination is hidden and chalk marks- goes back to combination but refuses to work so Johnnie shakes car, jar of the car starts engine. Johnnie gets into car, smiling to Katie gets prepared to start, engine back fires, auto guards commence to shake. Johnnie gets out unable to understand what it is.) (speaking to Katie) I think my car has deliriums.

KATIE.

Well Johnny may be your engine's cold.

JOHNNY.

It must be, look at it shiver.

KATIE.

Oh, it's a six cyclinder, isn't it?

JOHNNIE.

Yup, six cyclinder,(cranks car, engine starts, Johnnie gets

into cab, top of hood flies open, engine jumps out on stage)

KATIE.

And you told me there were six cylinders.

JOHNNIE.

They were sick but I guess they're dead now.

KATIE.

Why does it always act like this?

JOHNNIE.

No, only when I try to start it up.

KATIE.

Well, what's the matter?

JOHNNIE.

Oh, I know what's the matter all right.

KATIE.

Well what is it?

JOHNNIE.

There's something wrong with it.

KATIE.

Well I think you have a leak in the gasolene tank.

JOHNNIE.

(Looks into hood with lit match) No there's no leak in the gas tank. (Johnny cranks car again, then runs off to one side, holding his ears expecting another explosion but the engine runs all right. Johnnie starts to get in car, Katie speaking)

KATIE.

Pick up the engine, Johnnie. (Johnnie stoops over to pick up engine as he does, a large flame of fire shoots off from side of car, hitting Johnnie in seat of pants. Johnnie runs around car to water fountain, starts to get a drink, water stops running, Johnnie runs to car again and fans himself on the

the back with car door, speaking) Isn't it warm?

KATIE.

I told you gasolene was very deceitful.

JOHNNIE.

Yes, it talks behind your back all right.

WAITER.

(runs out of cafe, speaking) The people upstairs are kicking about the noise you're making down here with your one lung rattler of yours. (Johnnie keeps shutting lid on hood and lid keeps flying open again) And I don't care much about it myself and if you don't stop it I'll knock your block off.

JOHNNIE.

Are you looking for trouble?

WAITER.

Sure I'm looking for trouble?

JOHNNIE.

Well look in there. (pointing to where fire came out. (waiter exits) (Johnnie cranks car, engine starts, Johnnie gets in car, steering wheel flies out of car, going up into the air, dropping on stage, Johnnie gets out, picks up remains of steering wheel and the engine placing them both in front of mile post, then places grass mat over them, representing a grave, takes off his hat and weeps.)

KATIE.

(Singing) Something seems to tell me that I'll have to walk home. I'll have to walk home in the dark.

JOHNNIE.

I'll never let you walk home Katie, it's too far, I'll take you home in my pleasure car.

KATIE.

(speaking) Pleasure car?

JOHNNIE.

Sure, when you get out of it, it's a pleasure.

KATIE.

(Singing) If I had this car I would only ride at night. I wouldn't let my friends see me in broad daylight.

JOHNNIE.

Well I'm surprised to hear you talk that way about my car. You're liable to have trouble with any automobile.

KATIE.

Well I'm sorry if I hurt your feelings, Johnnie.

JOHNNIE.

Well kiss me then.

KATIE.

Kiss you? Why what girl would kiss that face?

JOHNNIE.

All the girls kiss me. They kiss me or they walk home.

KATIE.

Well I would rather walk home.

JOHNNIE.

That's nothing, they all walk home, but I'm going to fool them. I'm going to buy a motor boat.

KATIE.

Don't buy a motorboat Johnnie.

JOHNNIE.

Why?

KATIE.

Because I love to go. (SONG) (Bus. moving headlights that are illuminated, throwing a search into audience. (Exit backing off stage in automobile. FINALE.

mannequins. He goes about making little adjustments to Sibley's display, infuriating the man. Henry wants to pose "Carol" on the bed, but Sibley won't hear of it. When the models return to get approval for their new outfits, Henry beckons them over one at a time.

Outside, Clara Drake, one of Effie's party guests, has pulled over for a quick stop, and she sees the silhouette of Henry adjusting the girl's outfit. She peeks into the store and sees Henry posing the girl on the bed (still trying to convince Sibley to put "Carol" there), and assumes the worst. Her husband, Wilbur, also sees, and orders Clara not to say anything to Effie. After Sibley and the models leave, Henry tries to pose "Carol" on the bed, but gets his feet tangled up in a cord, trips, and breaks her. He fetches a toolbox and tries to glue her back together.

Effie is entertaining the party guests while waiting for Henry to come home. The Drakes arrive, and Clara almost spills the beans to Effie. Guests begin to grumble that Henry is late. As Grace and Wayne arrive, Clara starts whispering to one of the other guests about what she saw. The news spreads from ear to ear. Worried about Henry, Effie tries to call the department store, but there is no answer. As Effie is returning to the party, she overhears, "I'm so sorry for poor Effie. If she ever finds out it will break her heart." The speaker goes on to describe Henry sitting on a bed with a beautiful blonde. She goes to Memphis and asks him to drive down to the store to check on him. Memphis remarks that he wishes Effie hadn't walked under that ladder.

The glue having failed, Henry tries to find a repairman who can fix the mannequin by morning. He does, but has to drive it to the repair shop right away. Memphis pulls up to the store just in time to see Henry carrying "Carol" to his car, and believes it to be a real woman. As Henry pulls away, Memphis and a couple of pedestrians see the mannequin slumped over in the back seat, with the crack on her face looking like an open wound. The pedestrians make note of the car's license plate number and rush off.

A police call goes out for Henry's car, with "a body of dead woman" reported in the back seat. The call goes on to say that the man is dangerous and may be armed. Henry drops "Carol" off at Max's Wax Works, where Max assures him that it will be ready for the window display by morning. By now it's 9:30 p.m, and Effie is finally giving in and serving dinner to her guests, while Henry gets arrested and is questioned by the police. Nervous, Henry's answers give the cops the wrong idea. When Henry tells them he didn't have a *girl* in his car, the police show him a corsage and a high-heeled shoe as evidence. Memphis is brought in as well, having apparently driven his car into the city hall fountain from the shock. The police accuse him of being in on the "murder" and lock them both up; they then proceed to Max's Wax Works to investigate.

The party breaks up, and Grace and Clara give their "condolences" to Effie. Late that night, the police finally get things straightened out, and release Henry and Memphis. They try to sneak into the house, and Henry finds the remains of the anniversary dinner. When Memphis tries to sneak into his room, Opal yells at him, waking Effie, who hides and watches as Henry sneaks into their room. As he's about to enter, he realizes he still has the corsage and the high-heeled shoe, as well as a strand of blond hair on his jacket. Effie watches as he tries to hide them under a chair cushion. She takes the items and confronts him about his sneaking. The next day she takes the items to Grace, who convinces her to take Gilbert Wayne as her divorce attorney.

The next day, Henry is listless and depressed, sleeping on his office couch. But he wakes right up again when Wayne comes into his office to inform him that his wife is suing for divorce. Henry tries to call his wife, but Effie refuses to speak to him. Henry then calls for his lawyer, Mr. Kimble.

Kimble and Wayne argue furiously on behalf of their respective clients, while said clients sit fuming silently. The pressure finally gets too much for Henry when he is informed that he will either have to move out of his house or install a witness to testify that he and his wife are living apart. When Wayne tells him to be quiet one too many times, he has a loud, angry outburst that shocks and frightens Effie.

Effie's niece, Jane Forbes, is to be her witness. Jane is stunned at the news of the divorce and laughs at the idea of her uncle having an affair, until Effie shows her the corsage and shoe. Jane brings some of Henry's clothes to the guest room, where she meets Henry's witness, a law student named Bob Grant. Bob and Jane hit it off instantly, and agree that this divorce seems all wrong.

Wayne sends a private detective/body guard named "Gooch" Mulligan to the Butler house to protect Effie, in case her husband gets violent again. Gooch is cruel to Memphis and harasses Henry the second he comes in the door, going so far as to frisk him as he's reaching for his pipe. Elswhere, Wayne is talking to his fiancée, Nan, who's concerned that he is running around on her since he's always representing women. Wayne points out that the lawyer who represents the woman always gets more money. He asks Nan to tag along on his next visit to the Butlers' just in case Effie is having misgivings.

Indeed, Bob and Jane have talked the Butlers out of the divorce, as Wayne finds the four playing bridge together, all very friendly with one another. Nan comes in during the bridge game and asks to see Henry, calling herself "Evelyn." She greets him with an enthusiastic kiss, and asks why he "left so early the other night, when the party was just getting hot." She also asks him why he ran away with "her" shoe. She does this loudly enough for everyone in the parlor to hear, and this starts the divorce proceedings once again. Effie signs the papers and runs off to her room. Henry tries to follow, but Gooch won't let him in. Jane and Bob realize that "something is rotten in Denmark."

The next day, Effie and Henry rant to Jane and Bob, respectively. Henry insists that he's never seen "Evelyn" before in his life, becoming more and more upset. Grace Norman invites Effie to a party, and Effie decides to celebrate her divorce and "get tight." Effie dresses up and storms out, declaring that she won't be home until morning. Hurt, Henry decides to go out as well. Jane and Bob discuss the shoe that Nan claimed to be hers. Jane says she took note of Nan's feet and that she's "no Cinderella," and also noticed a wise look she'd passed with Gooch. She's sure that Gooch knows her, and might know where she lives.

Effie arrives at Grace's party, and Grace immediately plies her with alcohol. Elsewhere, Henry stumbles out of a café after a single bourbon highball. He drunkenly complains about his situation to a guy on the corner, who just watches him with bemusement until Henry declares he's "Got it!" and stumbles away.

Jane calls Gooch to the telephone, pretending that a girl has called for him. When Gooch answers and hears no one, Jane says she "must have hung up." Gooch remarks that only one girl knows he's at the Butlers' home. Jane and Bob go upstairs to eavesdrop

Fred Kelsey wants Harry and Billy Mitchell locked up in Misbehaving Husbands.

on the extension while Gooch calls Nan. Gooch gives the operator Nan's address and asks to be put through. Jane takes note of the address, and she and Bob go to investigate. At the apartment, Nan is excitedly waiting for Wayne to take her dancing. But when he arrives, he tells her that a business date has just come up. Bob and Jane arrive at the apartment and eavesdrop on Nan and Wayne arguing. Wayne storms out and goes to Grace's party. Bob enters Nan's apartment and tricks her into revealing the plot.

Henry, still drunk, has decided the solution is to bring "Carol" home to his wife. He puts her on roller skates, walks her home, and stumbles with her on the stairway. At the same time, Bob, Jane and Nan have gone to the police station, where it's revealed that Wayne is a con artist who's been pulling similar divorce scams all over the country. When Wayne arrives at the Butler home with Effie, the police are there to arrest him. Although Nan confesses the whole scam to Effie, she's still suspicious about the original shoe. Just then, Henry, still struggling to get "Carol" up the stairs, tumbles down. Effie rushes in, sees Henry with the mannequin, and finally understands where the shoe came from. Although he persists in explaining everything, she repeatedly kisses him, while Bob and Jane quietly slip away for some quality time of their own.

ANALYSIS: A charming, fast-moving comedy, *Misbehaving Husbands* hits the bulls-eye, and emerges as one of Langdon's best sound features. The plot moves along swiftly, and the characters are all well defined. Both Henry and Effie Butler are sympathetic as they find themselves caught up in a wholly believable sequence of misunderstandings. As the husband and wife plunging toward a divorce neither wants, Langdon and Betty Blythe rise above the material and emerge with just the right touch of pathos. The "witnesses," Bob and Jane, represent the audience in knowing that the divorce action is wrongheaded.

Although Langdon portrays a timid, absent-minded husband similar to those in *A Doggone Mixup* and *Cold Turkey*, here he's given every opportunity to bring his unique brand of comedy into the proceedings, and comes across as more energetic than in the shorts. Nearly every scene includes some little gesture that evokes the Elf, even though Henry Butler is not the otherworldly character of old. He wears glasses throughout, and like the mustache in earlier films, it tends to reduce the effectiveness of Langdon's facial expressions. However, glasses do fit the character, and along with the absence of extreme makeup, keep him grounded in reality. Blythe's character is also gentler and more understanding than the hot-tempered harpies with whom Langdon contends at Columbia.

The film includes a touch of ethnic humor in "Memphis" and Opal, the Butlers' black servants, but it's not too overbearing or tasteless. Perennial screen cop Fred Kelsey makes a welcome appearance as a desk sergeant who is befuddled by Henry's explanation of the "body" in his car, but on the whole, the film belongs to Langdon. Producer Jed Buell, who managed the Los Angeles theater where *The Strong Man* was previewed, certainly knew what he was getting in the comedian; so did co-writer Vernon Smith, one of the scribes on Langdon's breakthrough Sennett short, *All Night Long*. The end result is a pleasant, entertaining film.

HARRY MOMENT: Harry gets angry during a meeting with his wife and their attorneys. As he gesticulates around the room, his body language is most expressive and reminiscent of his pantomime in the silent films.

WHAT THE CRITICS SAID:
Film Daily, *December 9, 1940*
　Misbehaving Husbands, *Jed Buell's first production for Producer's Releasing Corp., sets an interesting pace for his new association. It's a feature with enough entertainment value to more than satisfy any audience. Harry Langdon, given plenty of leeway, and veteran director Bill Beaudine have concentrated more on sure fire laugh situations than on a startling plot, and a district preview house rewarded them with practically solid laughter. It is completely an audience comedy and will do best when booked for nights when a heavy house is likely. It is excellent counter material for any dramatic feature. Production values, never elaborate, are adequate, and the large number of old-time favorites in the cast offers opportunity for exploitation plants on the drama pages. Vernon Smith and Clarie Parrish have fashioned a swell screenplay, based on an original by Cea Sabin.*
　Direction: Okay, Photography: Good.

Hollywood Reporter, *December 9, 1940*
　This is a strikingly good little picture, a rollicking, high-speed, domestic comedy, so well done and played with such zest that the laughs stumble over each other to provide 65 minutes of unadulterated entertainment. Looking vastly more expensive than it actually is, Misbehaving Husbands *is worthy of a spot on any bill.*

The customers are going to like it plenty and it should be a mop-up for its makers.

It is also extremely probable that this picture will be pegged as the one which brought about Harry Langdon as a top flight screen comedian. Producer Jed Buell wisely took away all the grotesque costume appurtenances which marked Langdon's silent films characterization, kept him away from slapstick and gave him the opportunity to play straight comedy. The result is a brilliant success. It is a new Harry Langdon which emerges, one who demonstrates solid, laugh-provoking ability which will make him a welcome re-entry on the all-too-brief list of present day film comics. After this one, more Langdon pictures will simply be compulsory.

The featherweight story presents the first rift in the lute of domestic felicity between a slightly wacky department store owner, played by Langdon, and his wife, Betty Blythe, who sues him for divorce... But the lightness of the thread does not matter under the expert laugh treatment it has been given.

The entire cast is good, with Betty Blythe, Gayne Whitman, as the lawyer, Esther Muir, Ralph Byrd, Luana Walters, Charlotte Treadway, Nan Blake and Frank Hagney registering solidly in Langdon's support.

William Beaudine did an excellent directorial job, making the most of the unusually good script written by Clarie Parrish and Vernon Smith from Cea Sabin's original. On the production side, Jed Buell has provided a superlative effort in all departments, particularly notable for the exceptional results he achieved on a low budget.

Box Office, *December 14, 1940*

In his first film for Producers Releasing Corp., Jed Buell obviously stretched to the limit every penny of a modest budget. The result is a compact little domestic comedy, well equipped to perform yeoman service in the market for which it was geared. Harry Langdon, a comedy favorite of silent films, is featured and contributes creditably as do other members of an acceptable cast. Story is a bit broad and develops around a standard plot situation to travesty marital misunderstandings and divorce.

Motion Picture Herald, *December 21, 1940; Reviewed by William R. Weaver*

Introducing Harry Langdon in [a] type of portrayal he has not executed in the past, but may be expected to in future if the reaction of an audience attending the preview at midweek in a Los Angeles theatre serving a residential area may be taken as indication, this production by Jed Buell of a comedy predicated on divorce and reconciliation could be starting-point of a career for the comedian in the field of the humor of domesticity not invaded with success by anyone since Sidney Drew.

The character created by Mr. Langdon is a store-keeper indicted by circumstance, not supported by facts, for infidelity on his twentieth wedding anniversary. Upcropping from the episode is a snarl of events surrounding attempts of a lawyer to promote a divorce action, a knot untied by a spot of imbibing and some coincidence. The star turns out to be an expert in this type of delineation.

Direction by William Beaudine, using a script by Vernon Smith and Claire Parrish which distributes laughs throughout the length of the picture, is of a sort to deliver a maximum of entertainment for the ingredients utilized.

Previewed at the Forum Theatre, Los Angeles, where it kept the audience in a burble of amusement throughout its distance.

Variety, *January 15, 1941; Reviewed by Wear*

About the only redeeming features of this absurd comedy drama on the divorce racket are Harry Langdon's sprightly comedy characterization and Betty Blythe's re-entry to the Hollywood scene as a promising actress. The Sea (sic) Sabin-Vernon Smith original story is mostly wretchedly acted, feebly presented and haphazardly directed. It's dual fare of the most ordinary sort.

The crooked divorce formula, with unhappy wives who are consoled and gypped by handsome, thieving attorneys, has been used countless times on the screen, but it's questionable if the theme ever has been projected so insipidly....

Understood that Jed Buell may carry out a series with Harry Langdon and Betty Blythe teamed as man and wife. They'll have to do better by Langdon than they did in this picture — also more plausible plots are needed. Langdon shows possibilities in getting away from his former pantomimic type of clowning, although not capably directed here. Betty Blythe, beauty of silent films, appears a future bet. Esther Muir walks through her characterization as the divorcée who eggs her friend on to seek a divorce. Ralph Byrd does fairly well in a minor role spotted opposite Luana Walters in the sadly neglected romantic phase of the film.

Harrison's Reports, *February 8, 1941*

A fair program marital comedy, suitable for neighborhood theatres. Although the story is not unusual, it has several amusing situations; and it gives Harry Langdon a chance to show his ability as a comedian, without the use of his customary silly makeup. The production values are fair, too. A mild romance is worked into the plot....

Suitability: Class A.

All-American Co-Ed

A Hal Roach Production. 48 minutes. PRODUCED AND DIRECTED BY LeRoy Prinz. ORIGINAL STORY BY LeRoy Prinz and Hal Roach, Jr. SCREENPLAY BY Cortland Fitzsimmons. ADAPTED BY Kenneth Higgins. PHOTOGRAPHY BY Robert Pittack. EDITED BY Bert Jordan. ART DIRECTION BY Charles D. Hall. SONGS BY Walter G. Samuels, Charles Newman, Lloyd R. Norlin. CAST: Frances Langford, Johnny Downs, Marjorie Woodworth, Noah Beery, Jr., Esther Dale, Harry Langdon, Alan Hale, Jr., Kent Rogers, Allan Lane, Joe Brown, Jr., Irving Mitchell, Lillian Randolph, Carlyle Blackwell, Jr. Copyright October 30, 1941, Registration Number LP10814. Released by United Artists, Inc., October 7, 1941.

SYNOPSIS: Bob Sheppard and his college fraternity, Zeta, have just garnered a slew of publicity for their college, Quinceton University, with a revue in which they all sing and dance in drag. Press agent "Hap" Holden (Harry Langdon) wants to do something similar to get publicity for floundering girl's horticultural college Mar Brynn, run by Miss Matilda. They start by giving out twelve scholarships to accomplished gardeners/beauty queens. In order to get attention for themselves and their scholarship program, they release statements to the press calling Zeta "The Men Least Likely to Succeed." Wishing to exact revenge, the men of Zeta have Bob pose as "the Flower Queen" so he can get a scholarship and ruin the school's reputation. Bob attends Mar Brynn as Bobbi de Wolfe, and falls in love with Virginia, a Mar Brynn student and Miss Matilda's niece. Mar Brynn's revue is almost ruined when Bunny, one of the students, comes down with measles and the school is quarantined, but by persuading them to do the show from inside the greenhouse, Bob manages to stage a successful revue and win Virginia, while still one-upping the girls' school on behalf of his brothers.

ANALYSIS: Most 1940s musicals are dated, but *All-American Co-Ed* is especially afflicted. Although the production values are handsome, it's definitely a film of its time. Johnny Downs handles his drag scenes capably, but with little in the way of personal

Alan Hale Jr., Marjorie Woodworth, Noah Beery Jr., Esther Dale and Langdon.

charisma; the same is true when he's in everyday garb and romancing Frances Langford's Virginia. Miss Langford is a fine vocalist, but the songs are unmemorable; as for her acting, she barely has a moment to emote before the film moves on to something else.

As a fast-talking press agent, Langdon is not exactly in his element, yet leaves a favorable impression with the little he has to do. Basically, he's given a few double takes and a much-too-brief scene in which he offers his sandwich to a Venus flytrap, which takes a healthy bite. The rest of the comedy is pure slapstick: Downs's struggles getting in and out of his "Bobbi de Wolfe" garb; two dimwit "spies" knocking each other around while flirting with the co-eds, and a distasteful vignette with a black laundrywoman who comes across men's clothing and is driven to distraction as Downs surreptitiously retrieves it. Kent Rogers, as a Zeta man who likes to impersonate celebrities, does a halfway decent Gary Cooper and James Cagney, but his choicest moment is as Edgar Bergen and Charlie McCarthy, which, like the rest of *All-American Co-Ed*, speaks to a time fast fading from memory.

WHAT THE CRITICS SAID:
Variety, *October 8, 1941; Reviewed by Herb*

Third of Hal Roach's new "streamlined" features is a lively 48-minute entry that should do satisfactorily in its stated niche as dual bill filler. While considerably better than the 60-minute B's often allocated to the supporting role, this is not up to the standard that has led the Criterion, N.Y., to book in Roach's first featurette, Tanks a Million, as a single biller.

As in the two earlier "streamliners," Roach in All-American Co-Ed *harks back to the slapstick that made him as a producer of two-reelers in the silent days. Trouble is he's gone too far on the obvious tricks for getting a laugh (pushing a guy into a lily pool) and not strong enough on genuine gags. Sloppy construction of the story in several spots easily could be overlooked were the laughs thick enough to cover the lapses.*

Definitely on the credit side are the four tunes in the film. Also the speed with which the story moves, the heavy cutting to keep down the length obviating the possibility of slowness although, as a result, there's a weighty call on the audience's imagination to fill in spots in the plot.

Johnny Downs, who was once one of Roach's "Our Gang" kids, fits neatly as the "Quinceton" man selected by his fraternity brothers to even the score with "Mar Brynn" for a slight to his university. He's rigged up as a blonde femme and entered in a beauty scholarship contest at the co-ed school. It's the old boy-in-girls-clothes gag with a few new angles.

Frances Langford warbles a couple pleasant tunes as Downs's singing vis-à-vis. Tanner Sisters (3) also contribute to the vocalizing. Harry Langdon's [okay] as the press agent who dreams up the beauty contest for the college, while Marjorie Woodworth, Noah Beery, Jr., and Esther Dale slide satisfactorily into supporting roles. Kent Rogers is good for giggles in going through the film imitating Hollywoodites (Gary Cooper, Bergen-McCarthy, etc.). It's especially funny while reading his regular lines and it isn't tipped off.

Of the tunes, "I'm a Chap with a Chip on My Shoulder" and "The Farmer's Daughter" are both sure to be heard from. They are by Walter G. Samuels and Charles Newman, who also contributed "Up at the Crack of Dawn." Lloyd B. Norlin provided the one ballad, "Out of the Silence."

LeRoy Prinz, who produced and directed, apparently did little skimping on production costs, with sets and costuming both extensive. Packed in a bit tighter with better gags, the film would rate high for this type product. It adds proof, however, that Roach has something in the "streamlined" featurette idea.

Hollywood Reporter, *October 8, 1941*

This Hal Roach streamlined feature starts off at a neat, entertaining clip. Even the opening titles build into a laugh and for the first fifteen minutes of the brief running time the show holds every promise of being an outstanding attraction in its class. But the female impersonation premise soon breaks down and the story automatically goes to pieces. Unfortunately, the gags come too infrequently thereafter to bolster it. This will just get by as a companion offering on the dual bills of lesser theatres.

On the credit side of the ledger are the principals, mostly young performers who do nobly by the inadequate material. Frances Langford's throaty contralto is heard to advantage and her performance of a slight role is satisfactory. Johnny Downs clicks, as usual, in the very difficult role of the goat of a college jest who is forced to don female attire and enroll in a girls' college where men have never set foot. Marjorie Woodworth is a stunning young lady, if somewhat deficient in the vocal department. Noah Beery, Jr. continues to be sadly wasted in roles unworthy [of] his talent. Esther Dale makes the most of a fool-proof assignment as a stern, old school marm.

Harry Langdon's pantomime is given scant opportunity but in the few moments when the camera pans up close enough to permit a few of his inimitable facial gestures, he's good for a solid laugh. A young chap called Kent Rogers does some excellent impersonations of infrequently mimicked stars but the script never avails itself fully of his talents. The Tanner Sisters are a personable vocal trio.

LeRoy Prinz, as director, did the best possible with the material; as producer, he should never have okayed the script.

Box Office, *October 11, 1941*

Third in Hal Roach's so-called "streamliners" of shorter-than-average running time, this is a surefire winner in its bracket — a brisk and breezy musical, packed with gags, a frail but entertaining story, and a collegiate background which gave Producer-Director Leroy Prinz an opportunity to stage several original dance routines. It features songbird Frances Langford and finds Johnny Downs in his most ingratiating role to date. On all counts the entry should prove capable of doing top business.

Film Daily, *October 13, 1941*

This is the second "capsule" in the Hal Roach series of short features, and, like its predecessor, Tanks a Million, it should bring favorable reaction from film buyers. Like Tanks it has discarded all but the essentials — in this case musical entertainment — and is just bare "college show" numbers with just enough story and sketchy plot to keep it out of the short subject class.

In the cast, Frances Langford, with first-class warbling, stands out. The support, including Johnny Downs, Marjorie Woodworth, Esther Dale, Kent Rogers, and Noah Beery, Jr., all perform admirably. Harry Langdon, who makes one of his rare appearances, in this, is still a top-notch comic.

Direction: Good, Photography: Good.

Harrison's Reports, *October 18, 1941*

A lightweight comedy with music; it should please young folk, first, because of the youthfulness of the players, and, secondly, because of the music. Theatres that cater

Harry welcomes a disguised Johnny Downs aboard, as Dudley Dickerson carries "her" luggage, in All-American Co-Ed.

to adult audiences that are not too discriminating about story values may find it satisfactory as a program filler. The main selling points are Frances Langford's singing, and Johnny Downs's amusing impersonation of a young college girl....

Morally suitable for all.

Motion Picture Herald, *October 18, 1941; Reviewed by William R. Weaver*

Hal Roach's third streamline feature surpasses his second in screen worthiness and crowds his first, Tanks a Million, in point of fitness for today's requirements. It supplies more marquee material than either of the others, offering Frances Langford, Harry Langdon, Johnny Downs, Marjorie Woodworth and Noah Beery, Jr., for ad copy as well as entertainment.

The story utilizes without embarrassment the essentials of the Charley's Aunt *pattern, modernizing the general idea profitably by placing the masquerading college boy in a girls' school as an enrollee pledged to avenge a publicity stunt committed by that institution at expense of his fraternity. The modernization is in the nature of an improvement and, although comparisons are for an audience to make, it was remarked by many present at the preview that the dependable old formula profited by the swift and agile handling of the Roach experts.*

Four songs worked into the proceedings snap it up whenever a lull threatens.

Production and direction by LeRoy Prinz make every inch of film and dialogue click.

Previewed at the Alexander Theatre, Glendale, to a general audience which gave every indication of enjoying the show immensely.

Cleveland Plain Dealer, *December 5, 1938; Reviewed by Glenn C. Pullen*

Jack Benny did Charley's Aunt *in hoopskirts, but Johnny Downs becomes more modern in the Circle's new comedy by impersonating a blonde co-ed who causes a slapstick feud between two colleges.*

Downs, who looks as if he hasn't had his first shave yet, has enough farcical and vocal talent to perpetrate this masquerade fairly amusingly.

The hoax is cooked up by his fraternity brothers at dear old Quinceton U., which may make Princeton's Triangle Club boys burn, to get even with the snooty girls at "Mar Brynn" college. These not-so-subtle digs follow the general tone of the tale's broad travesty, which gets even daffier when Downs enters a beauty scholarship contest at the exclusive co-educational school.

Frances Langford is the object of Johnny's feud but romance, of course, gets the best of him. After a number of typical Hal Roach gags, some of which are droll, the fight ends in a songfest when the two get together in several very tuneful songs.

Three Tanner Sisters swing a couple of them. Harry Langdon, now on the comeback trail, cuts up as an addleheaded press agent. The picture features the sons of several stars — Alan Hale, Jr., Noah Beery, Jr., Joe Brown, Jr. and Carlyle Blackwell, Jr.

Double Trouble

A Monogram Production. 63 minutes. **PRODUCED BY** Dixon R. Harwin. **DIRECTED BY** William West. **ASSOCIATE PRODUCER:** Barney A. Sarecky. **SCREENPLAY BY** Jack Natteford. **PHOTOGRAPHY BY** Arthur Martinelli. **EDITOR:** Carl Pierson. **ART DIRECTOR:** David Milton. **MUSICAL DIRECTOR:** Ross DiMaggio. **SOUND DIRECTOR:** Corson Jowett. **CAST:** Harry Langdon, Charles Rogers, Catherine Lewis, Dave O'Brien, Louise Currie, Benny Rubin, Mira McKinney, Frank Jaquet, Wheeler Oakman, David Cavendish, Edward Kane, Dick Alexander, Ruth Hiatt, Alfred Hall, Guy Kingsford, Fred Santley, Richard Cramer, Art Hamberger. **WORKING TITLES:** "Here We Go Again," "Bundles From Britain." Copyright November 21, 1941, Registration Number LP10915; Renewed March 14, 1965, Number R457685. Released by Monogram Pictures, Inc., November 17, 1941.

SYNOPSIS: Mr. Whitmore, owner of a baked bean cannery, is struggling to continue to do business his way, while his marketing man, Barton, wants him to sell his product with goofy slogans and gimmicks. A competitor threatens to drive him out of business unless he helps them profit by selling beans to the Army at gouged prices. The patriotic Whitmore refuses.

In keeping with his support during wartime, Whitmore has agreed to play host to two British refugees who haven't a home of their own, as a favor to a friend, Lady Prattle. He assumes they are children, but the Prattle Boys, Bert (Harry Langdon) and Alf (Charles Rogers), turn out to be two grown men. They receive Mrs. Whitmore's sympathies with a story about their boat being hit by torpedoes. Mr. Whitmore is decidedly less than sympathetic, and threatens to tell off Lady Prattle for misleading him.

While Whitmore deals with the Prattle situation, his competitor plots to take over his business through the assistance of Kimble, an agent of theirs who is currently working for Whitmore. Barton comes to Whitmore's home to present another marketing idea, which his uncomprehending boss rejects. Whitmore's daughter, Peggy, wants him to get in her father's good graces, so they can ask his permission to wed.

Bert and Alf are anxious to get in touch with Lady Prattle to explain their side of the story before Whitmore can speak with her. Alf has Bert telephone Whitmore from the kitchen, pretending to be Lady Prattle in London, while Alf provides sound effects mimicking an air raid. Unfortunately, the butler catches them at it and alerts his employers. As a sort of revenge, Whitmore makes them sleep in the nursery he'd prepared for the "children." An inflatable toy that looks like a shark blows into the nursery while they're sleeping; it awakens them, gets hooked on Bert's pants and chases them downstairs.

Despite all the shenanigans, Whitmore finds himself in a forgiving mood the next morning, and decides to give the boys jobs at his plant. Alf is put out by the whole "nursery" business and wants to leave, but they let Whitmore's plant manager show them around the cannery and ultimately accept the jobs. Meanwhile, Peggy visits Barton and the two commiserate on having to keep their romance a secret. Peggy wishes she were a working girl instead of the boss's daughter, so they could have a normal relationship. After Peggy leaves, an attractive model points out that *she* is not the boss's daughter, and is perfectly available for Barton to court normally. Instead, Barton gets an inspiration for a new marketing campaign involving the famous Kimberly Diamond, a bracelet that has never been photographed, and which is going on display the next day.

While Bert is working at an assembly line, he starts flirting with an attractive blonde, and does some sleight-of-hand with the empty cans. The blonde buys the boys boxed lunches, with a love note in Bert's. Barton obtains a license to use the Kimberly Diamond in an advertisement, to be worn by the model, but only after Whitmore signs a contract making his company responsible for the gem, which Kimble encourages him to do. After the shoot, the model leaves the bracelet unattended on a desk, and Kimble surreptitiously drops it in the trash.

Bert, having been "promoted" to janitor, collects the trash from the studio. He finds the bracelet and mistakes it for costume jewelry. He decides to give the bracelet to his pretty blonde friend, Tillie, as a thank you for the lunches. He slips the bracelet into an empty can, writes a love note ("Love and Kisses XXX from Bert and Alf") on the base of the can, and sends it down the assembly line. But Tillie is fixing her make-up and the unseen can slips by into the filling station, where it gets lost amid thousands of cans of beans.

Barton discovers the bracelet is missing, and chaos erupts as they search for it. Alf and Bert overhear the commotion and find out what's going on. Realizing that the bracelet they accidentally canned is worth $100,000, they rush back to the cannery and wreak havoc trying to find it. Unsuccessful, they assume that the can is already out for delivery, and explain to Whitmore what happened. Barton gets the "brilliant" idea to get the whole nation to buy beans in an attempt to find the bracelet, for which they will offer $100,000 reward, but Whitmore rejects the idea as "one crack-brained scheme too many" and fires him.

The detective in charge of protecting the diamond tells Whitmore he has 24 hours to find the bracelet, or he owes the owners $100,000. Alf and Bert flee the office in search of the diamond. The incident makes headlines the next day, and orders for beans skyrocket, to the delight of Mr. Whitmore. He sends Peggy to find Barton so he can rehire him. Meanwhile, Mrs. Whitmore calls the police to search for the Prattle boys, who have been out all night searching for the missing can.

A radio broadcast reveals that Alf and Bert are considered responsible for the bracelet's disappearance, and that the public is as eager for them to be apprehended as they are to buy beans. Alf and Bert overhear this and make themselves scarce. At the same time, Peggy catches up to Barton and asks him to come back to work for her father, insinuating that the boost in sales will give him the leverage he needs to get permission to marry her. Barton initially refuses, but Peggy convinces him otherwise, and Whitmore makes him vice president.

Meanwhile, the unscrupulous competitor brings in the Federal Business Bureau to charge Whitmore with false advertising. They claim he made up the story of the diamond being in the can to boost sales. When asked to produce the men responsible for canning the bracelet, Whitmore admits that they disappeared. The Bureau serves Whitmore with a court order to close the plant at midnight. This means the plant will be unable to fill any of their orders, setting them back millions of dollars in sales, *and* holding them liable for the $100,000 diamond.

Alf and Bert find themselves on the docks, evading the police. They sneak into a store bearing a sign that reads "Costumes for Rent," and disguise themselves as women, though Alf has to knock Bert senseless to get him into a dress. They find a café which has the beans in stock, and Alf spies the one with Bert's note scrawled on the bottom. The café is hiring a waitress, so Alf gets the job in order to retrieve the can. He then calls Barton, explains the situation and tells him to hurry over. While Alf is playing at waitress, a sailor takes a shine to Bert. Alf tries to get to the can, but the chef in charge doesn't allow women in his kitchen and rudely tosses "her" out, while the sailor takes Bert to the bar, where he gets a little tipsy.

Louise Currie, Langdon and Charley Rogers in Double Trouble.

Bert stumbles away with another man holding a rucksack, which is filled with cans of beans. Bert believes the one holding the diamond bracelet is inside, and tries to lure him into the kitchen, but gets caught by the chef. Because Bert is apparently a customer, the chef gently lectures "her" about staying out of his kitchen. Taking advantage of the distraction, Alf sneaks into the kitchen and finds the can on a shelf. He sneaks away with it and hides it in Bert's dress so they can leave without causing suspicion.

Barton arrives and looks for the can in Bert's dress. The man with the sack of beans assumes Barton is assaulting "her," and belts him. Bert pulls out the can, and the man assumes "she" stole it from his sack and gives chase. Bert tosses the can to Alf, who accidentally catches a *hot* can of beans that the chef tosses from the kitchen. The hot can gets tossed and dropped by multiple parties, including a mounted moose head. A pie flies out of the kitchen and hits a patron. Finally, Barton finds the correct can of beans on the floor and escapes with Peggy as a bar fight erupts.

With the diamond recovered, the plant is saved and Peggy and Barton's future is assured. As for the Prattle boys, they try to hitchhike their way onto a ship bound for London, but the Whitmores pick them up in a limousine.

ANALYSIS: *Double Trouble* is an unpretentious, low-budget affair with a lot of charm. When we first meet Bert and Alf, at the same time as do Mrs. Whitmore and Peggy, it's a very amusing sequence; both visually and verbally clever. The two women are stunned that the "children" are grown men, whereupon Bert and Alf immediately rise and walk out of the house. This happens more than once, and each time Bert takes some fruit from a bowl for their journey. Eventually, the women adjust to the two "refugee children," especially when they explain how their ship was torpedoed. Twice during this, Bert gets hiccups and Alf frightens them away by simply saying, "Boo!" When Peggy offers to get Bert a glass of water, he replies, "I prefer his boos."

As Bert, Langdon's Elfish persona is brought into the modern era. Although beginning to look old and absent the extreme facial make-up, he's once more the perplexing man-child of many facets: stealing fruit and hiding it in his umbrella; opening and closing a refrigerator door in hopes of seeing if the light actually goes out; juggling cans to impress a young woman on the assembly line. Of course it's his childish crush that sets the plot in motion, when he drops the necklace into an empty can and sends it her way. Two highlights are his impersonation of Lady Prattle and a marvelous portrayal of a woman trying to stave off a persistent waterfront suitor.

Rogers, as Alf, makes a fine foil and is not without his own charm. Others in the cast perform adequately, although Dave O'Brien, best remembered as the perpetrator of several eye-popping stunts in M.G.M.'s Pete Smith Specialties, is wasted as the go-getter marketing executive enamored of the boss's daughter. William West's direction is sharp and Ross DiMaggio's background score complements the goings-on quite nicely. All in all, *Double Trouble* is one of Langdon's few triumphs of the 1940s, and is well worth anyone's time.

HARRY MOMENT: When Bert refuses to dress as a woman, Alf conks him on the head. As he rises, he begins chirping gibberish, while Alf dresses him. Langdon is hilarious in this brief bit, which is the highlight of the picture.

WHAT THE CRITICS SAID:
Hollywood Reporter, *November 10, 1941*

The teaming of Harry Langdon and Charles Rogers appears to be a promising one from comedy contained in Double Trouble. *When this twosome is on the screen, there is a constant supply of chuckling antics which, kept in the proper groove, should delight audiences in the houses where Monogram product is played. Fortunately, Langdon and Rogers are seen in most of the picture's footage, the pace dropping almost to a standstill when they are not involved.*

A farcical sequence that will convulse practically all audiences depicts Langdon and Rogers during a hoax telephone call from London providing sound effects of an air raid with kitchen implements.

Performances throughout are adequate. David O'Brien, in the role of a young advertising executive, delivers a solid characterization that speeds up the story's tempo. Louise Curry and Catherine Lewis are attractive femmes, and Benny Rubin's brief spot is highly effective.

Dixon Harwin was given excellent assistance by associate producer Barney Sarecky, who mounted the production admirably. Direction by William West shows careful attention to the comedy angles. Jack Natteford's screenplay is well stocked with gags. Process shots in the factory could be eliminated without injury to the picture's entertainment.

Daily Variety, *November 10, 1941*

After many years of absence, Harry Langdon is brought back to pictures in Monogram's Double Trouble. *Those who remember the wistful, whimsical little comedian who had no peer but Chaplin in the silent days, and the younger generation which enjoys slapstick as much as the oldsters, will like this film. It is expertly aimed for a certain market and ought to do rollicking business in those spots where it is booked.*

Although Jack Natteford's adequate screenplay has just a little too much slapstick for the slow, pathetic, likable characterization Langdon does best, there is some opportunity afforded by his particular talents. In a role which requires him to be at a loss to understand American customs, and one in which he has to dress in women's clothing while hunting for the diamond in a waterfront dive, Langdon is superb when the script allows him to be. Rogers, a little gent with a Cockney accent and the face of a cadaver, is a good running mate for Langdon.

Dixon R. Hardwin, the producer, is to be congratulated for having the good sense to make use of Langdon's talent as a comedian. William West, the director, milks the script for all possible laughs and makes the comedy a thumping good, old-fashioned killer-diller. Technical assistance is passable.

Motion Picture Herald, *November 15, 1941*

With Double Trouble, *Monogram introduces the first of a series of comedies starring Harry Langdon and Charlie (sic) Rogers, veteran cinematic fun-makes. More or less in the nature of a comeback for both, the picture drew a number of laughs at its preview, held on a Friday night at a neighborhood house before an audience of young and old…*

William West directed the film, which is heavy on the slapstick.

Previewed at the Fox Uptown theatre, Los Angeles, to a mixed audience which showed it had a good time.

Film Daily, *November 17, 1941*

This picture, Harry Langdon's return to films in a story which allows his particular brand of comedy to run free, will find ready reception as supporting fare, with the possibility of a series of this type finding a ready market.

Given a solid story background and above average production values for its bracket…Langdon, under Megger West's skillful direction, turns in a performance that should please "remembering" fans and attract many new ones.

Charles Rogers, too, is deserving of plaudits for his able comedy, as is Frank Jaquet, Catherine Lewis, Dave O'Brien, Benny Rubin and the rest of the supporting cast.

Hedda Hopper's Hollywood, *November 17, 1941*

Double Trouble, *with Harry Langdon, contains a good plot idea, but suffers from a bad script. It shows though that Harry's lost none of his comedy talent. His female impersonation is a riot.*

Box Office, *November 22, 1941*

It is lamentable that story weaknesses and a dearth of gag situations and an insufficient budget should have combined in this, the first in a scheduled series starring Harry Langdon, to drag it down to below-average levels in point of general audience entertainment content. Juveniles probably will find it acceptable.

WHAT THE EXHIBITORS SAID:
Motion Picture Herald, *October 31, 1942*

(Shown with Arizona Bound*) Did fair business with these two. Harry Langdon made them laugh and Rough Riders pleased the Western fans.*
Mrs. Carroll Michael, Freeburn Theater, Freeburn, KY.

Beautiful Clothes (Make Beautiful Girls)

An R.C.M. Production. Three minutes, 40 seconds. **PRODUCED BY** Sam Coslow. **DIRECTED BY** Josef Berne. **CAST:** Harry Langdon, Cliff Nazarro (soundtrack only). Copyright November 24, 1941, Registration Number MP11770. Released by Soundies Distributing Corporation of America, Inc., December 1941.

SYNOPSIS: While dressing mannequins for a department store window display, Harry lip-synchs to Cliff Nazarro's recording of "Beautiful Clothes." Soon, live models join the mannequins in the display, leading to some confusion on Harry's part. Female customers pass through a revolving door, and emerge wearing gorgeous eveningwear. Harry goes through the door and emerges in a prim old woman's outfit. Perplexed, he leaves as the song ends.

ANALYSIS: This 1940s "music video" is a cute diversion, but lip-synching is clearly not Langdon's forte; he looks slightly uncomfortable and doesn't try to inject his performance with any comic exaggeration. Some of his facial reactions to the models are delightful, but as a whole the idea misses the mark and it's not surprising that he never did another. Produced concurrently with Monogram's *Double Trouble,* the film ends with Harry dressed in the same "old lady" outfit he wears in that feature.

House of Errors

A Beaumont Production. 63 minutes. **PRODUCED AND DIRECTED BY** Bernard B. Ray. **ORIGINAL STORY BY** Harry Langdon. **SCREENPLAY BY** Ewart Adamson and Eddie M. Davis. **PHOTOGRAPHY BY** Robert Cline. **EDITED BY** Dan Milner. **ART DIRECTOR:** Fred Prebble. **MUSICAL DIRECTOR:** Lee Zahler. **SOUND ENGINEER:** Corson Jowett. **PRODUCTION MANAGER:** Robert Ray. **CAST:** Harry Langdon, Charles Rogers, Marian Marsh, Ray Walker, Betty Blythe, John Holland, Guy Kingsford, Roy Butler, Gwen Gazo, Monty Collins, Vernon Dent, Bob Baron, Lynn Star, Ed Cassidy, Snub Pollard. Copyright February 20, 1942, Registration Number LP11183; Renewed March 14, 1969, Number R457687. Released by Producers' Releasing Corporation, Inc., March 26, 1942.

SYNOPSIS: Alf (Charles Rogers) and Bert (Harry Langdon) are messenger boys for a paper called *The News.* They're in the loading dock; Alf is napping and Bert is trying to silence a loud, *very* obnoxious truck horn that is disrupting Carr, the editor, who is on the phone. Bert tries "shushing" the offending horn, but that's only a temporary fix, and he finally has to beat it with a hammer. Carr hollers for his star reporter, Jerry Fitzgerald, who turns up in the loading dock. Alf and Bert try to get back some money that they loaned him the week before, but fast-talking Fitzgerald manages to get another ten dollars from them instead.

Alf and Bert approach the editor while he's in a bad mood and are fired. Alf bemoans the fact that they aren't reporters like Fitzgerald. He decides that they'll write a story and sell it to the highest bidder; he hands Bert a little memo pad and tells him to write down everything that happens. Meanwhile, Carr wants Fitzgerald to get an important scoop: an interview with the inventor of a deadly new machine gun. Randall, the inventor, hates newspapers, so the chief wants to send a reporter that Randall doesn't know. Alf and Bert overhear everything and head to Randall's house in order to beat Fitzgerald to the story. One of the office ladies tells Carr to try searching for Fitzgerald at the hospital, where he can often be found trying to win the affections of one of the nurses.

Fitzgerald dodges calls at the hospital to continue to flirt with the nurse, whose name he doesn't even know. The nurse will only tell him her number, 22. Fitzgerald keeps insisting he loves and wants to marry her. When he tries to dodge another call, "Nurse 22" forces him to take it so she can sneak out of the room. Carr gives Fitzgerald the assignment, warning him not to let Randall know that he's with a newspaper.

Alf and Bert beat Fitzgerald to the Randall home and pretend to be temporary servants from an employment agency so they can get into the house. Alf becomes the butler and Bert the houseboy. Bert's servant jacket is so tight his heartbeat is visible. His heart is on the right instead of the left, so Alf knocks it over to the correct side. Mr. and Mrs. Randall discuss their financial situation: they are going to go bankrupt unless Randall can sell his new machine gun. Mrs. Randall has hocked all their furniture to pay for the servants. She wants to make a good impression on potential manufacturers; otherwise, her husband might not receive a fair offer.

Fitzgerald goes to Mr. Randall and pretends to be from the *War Veterans' Bulletin*. Randall, being a veteran himself, agrees to the interview. He brings Fitzgerald into the parlor and explains that his new gun fires 50 percent more rounds and is 100 percent more powerful, while still being lighter than a conventional machine gun.

During all this, Bert cleans the house none too competently, and he and Alf admire Mr. Randall's extensive gun collection. Bert finds some money on the floor and Alf orders him to return it to Mr. Randall. When Alf and Bert see Fitzgerald, he frantically invents a cover story about them serving at his birthday party to explain why he knows them. While Randall is speaking privately with an associate, Paul Gordon, Alf demands the money Fitzgerald owes and threatens to blow his cover if he doesn't pay up. Fitzgerald has no cash, so one by one the boys take his fountain pen, his wristwatch, and, finally, his suit.

Mr. Randall talks to Mr. Drake, the owner of a munitions company that is preparing to purchase the machine gun. Gordon vouches for Randall to Drake, and Randall mentions that Gordon has been courting his daughter. Just then, Florence Randall arrives; in addition to being Randall's daughter, she's also Nurse 22.

Florence goes upstairs to change, and Randall leads Drake and Gordon back into the parlor to introduce them to Fitzgerald, who has to hide behind the sofa since Alf and Bert have taken his suit. As Randall goes out in the hall to look for Fitzgerald,

Drake and Gordon converse about their plan to sabotage the gun so that it fails all its tests, at which point Drake will buy the gun for a fraction of what it's worth. He and Gordon would then split the manufacturing profits, and Gordon will marry Florence so her family won't go bankrupt. Fitzgerald, of course, overhears.

Drake and Gordon go into the workshop, and Randall finds Fitzgerald in his underwear. Fitzgerald fast-talks his way out of it, claiming to have been robbed as a prank by the other members of the *Bulletin*, so Randall loans Fitzgerald a suit. He then shows the men his machine gun. Meanwhile, Bert steals some sugar cubes for his tea out of a safe in the library. In the kitchen, Florence literally runs into

Bert, knocking him over. When he mentions that his nose hurts, she transfers a kiss to it with her finger. Bert falls in love with her, much to Alf's disgust. Bert writes in his little pad, "Bert loves Florence."

Fitzgerald thanks Alf for stealing his clothes, since it has led to a bigger story than he expected. As Alf leaves, Florence enters the room and Fitzgerald learns who she is. He hints about what he knows and proclaims himself the hero who will rescue her from the villain. Gordon walks in on Fitzgerald trying to kiss Florence and knocks him down. Fitzgerald pretends to be unconscious and then kisses Florence once they're alone; as they kiss, *she* faints. Randall finds out Fitzgerald is from *The News* and throws him out, but he promises to return.

That afternoon, during the machine gun test, Florence permits Fitzgerald to drive her to the store. He tells her that he doesn't like Gordon, but can't yet tell her why. Back at Randall's house, Gordon, Drake and Randall discuss the failed test. Drake "regretfully" has to withdraw his offer to buy the gun. After Drake leaves, Gordon offers to loan Randall some money. Randall graciously declines, so Gordon offers $5,000 for the "useless" gun. Shortly afterwards, Bert spies on Gordon as he comforts Florence and proposes marriage, explaining that if they're married, her father might allow him to help the family financially. Bert writes, "Gordon kissed Florence" in his pad, reads what he wrote and reacts. When Gordon leaves the house, Bert drops a flowerpot on his head from an upstairs window, and writes, "Gordon has a headache."

Randall decides to go to Springfield with his wife to see their old friend Daniels, in hopes he can spot the flaw in the gun design. Florence is on night duty at the hospital, so they instruct the servants to guard the house. Fitzgerald visits Florence at the hospital, and she tells him that "things have changed" since last night, implying that she is now engaged to Gordon. He predicts that the gun test was a flop, but can't share anything more until he's through investigating Gordon and Drake. Florence accuses him of being a scandal monger and asks him to stay out of her family's affairs.

Alf and Bert are left guarding Randall's workshop while the Randalls are in Springfield. Drake has hired a burglar to help him break in and steal the gun. His

Vernon Dent has the drop on Harry and Charley in this lobby card.

plan is to replace it with a dummy, so that he won't have to split the take with Gordon. As a thunderstorm rolls in and the power goes out, Drake and his accomplice try to get into the house. Alf and Bert keep getting glimpses of them and assume they're seeing things. The burglars try to get the workshop keys with a fishing hook and line, but that doesn't work.

Both men finally break into the house and steal the gun, leaving the dummy in its place, but Alf and Bert spot them. Bert retrieves Randall's antique blunderbuss, but Alf tells him it's not loaded. Bert fires it anyway, and as smoke and gunpowder fill the room, he and Alf manage to steal the gun back while the crooks are rubbing their eyes and coughing. They run off to find someplace to hide for the night, planning to return before the Randalls get home.

Fitzgerald enters the house, sees the commotion, and rushes to the workshop to check on the gun. He finds the dummy and tosses it out the window to hide it. As it happens, Gordon is right outside; he takes the dummy, believing it to be real. He intends to double-cross Drake, and instructs his driver to put it into his private plane. The Randalls come home, and when Fitzgerald cannot produce the gun, they assume he has stolen it and call the police. Fitzgerald escapes to pursue Gordon.

Gordon is on the phone with Florence, making plans to elope, when Fitzgerald breaks into his house. Fitzgerald threatens Gordon at gunpoint, but he's been tailed by a policeman and gets arrested. At the station, he calls Carr, who agrees to bail him out.

Alf and Bert are spending the night at a flophouse, but must contend with two roughnecks who eject them from their beds, a fellow with a flea circus who keeps losing his "star performers," and other unpleasantries. Alf decides the only safe place to sleep is under Bert's bed, but Bert becomes distracted by a painting that is hanging askew on the wall overhead. He stands upon the bed to straighten the picture, and winds up falling on top of one of the toughs, causing his bed to collapse. The two get chased out of the place. Outside, Bert notices that something has fallen out of the gun, and Alf instructs him to put it in his pocket. They decide to head back to the house.

Once bailed out, Fitzgerald breaks into the Randalls' home to inform them that Florence is

eloping with Gordon. The three rush out of the house, intending to go to the airport, but Gordon and Florence are already overhead in a two-man plane. Outside the house, Alf and Bert run up with the gun. In returning it, Bert accidentally shoots down the plane, which descends into the Randalls' house. Florence emerges unharmed and kisses Fitzgerald, disappointing Bert. Then something makes a loud explosion in the wreckage of the plane, and Florence faints, falling into Bert's arms. Bert steals a few kisses from her lips with his fingers.

ANALYSIS: *House of Errors* is a frustrating film, in that it has good and bad points. Among the good: Langdon and Rogers continue to display a great rapport, even though the bulk of the comedy is thrown to Langdon. The plot is interesting and, as with *Double Trouble*, the two are actually the (accidental) heroes of the day, rather than simply two nitwits who gum things up. Comedy routines are plentiful, and Langdon scores in pretty much all of them, particularly during the scene in the flophouse as he interacts with the flea circus owner, played by Monty Collins. Langdon's expressions and gestures evoke the Elf, although he's dressed more nattily than in *Double Trouble*, with an ordinary suit and hat à la his 1940s Columbia shorts.

The bad points, though, are plentiful. Ray Walker, as Jerry Fitzgerald, is abrasive and unlikable, particularly when coming on to Marian Marsh, the mysterious Nurse 22, who happens to be the inventor's daughter. As Mr. Carr, editor of *The News*, Roy Butler overacts to an annoying degree. Charming Miss Marsh and Betty Blythe are wasted in minor roles, as is Vernon Dent in a bit part as one of the flophouse toughs; meanwhile, John Holland and Guy Kingsford as Gordon and Drake fail to make much of an impression. Bernard Ray's direction is uninspired, and some of the special effects, such as a lightning strike, are too obviously phony. The stock footage of automobiles and airplanes is laughable, coming as it does from old Mascot serials of the early 1930s.

HARRY MOMENTS: The scene in the flophouse is quite funny. As Bert contends with the disheveled flea circus owner, Langdon's pantomime reactions are superb. He also revives a gag from *Tramp, Tramp, Tramp*, when he tries to straighten the crooked picture and ends up falling onto (and destroying) the bed in which Vernon Dent is trying to sleep. The scenes in which he receives a finger-kiss from Florence, and later "steals" them from her at the picture's end, are charming and reflect the Elf's fundamental innocence.

WHAT THE CRITICS SAID:
Film Daily, *March 26, 1942*

House of Errors *should prove one of PRC's most successful releases. It's loaded with laughs and is held together nicely by a strong thread of plot from the pens of Ewart Adamson and Eddie Davis. Bernard B. Ray's direction is excellent; his production, on a limited budget, is amazing. Standout work is also credited to Cameraman Bob Cline and Musical Director Lee Zahler.*

The leading players, Harry Langdon and Charles Rogers, make a great team. They work as smoothly as though they had been together for years. In support they are abetted by good performers Marian Marsh, Ray Walker and Betty Blythe.

The story concerns itself with the adventures of a pair of messenger boys on the Daily News who wish to become reporters. They gain entrance to the house of an inventor of a new type machine gun by posing as servants. The inventor's daughter, Marian Marsh, is being courted by crook John Holland, and the boys, assisted by Ray Walker, set out to foil the crook and win the girl.

Of course, they succeed — except that Langdon doesn't get the girl. Their antics in the House of Errors *and in the flophouse in which they take refuge from the crooks are classic examples of well-timed and studied slapstick routines. These sequences can't fail to draw belly laughs from any audience.*

This one can be recommended for all audiences. It's a great bet as a strong support for a weak top feature.

Hollywood Reporter, *March 30, 1942*

Somehow a Harry Langdon two-reel comedy got itself puffed to an hour's running time. The sketchy material is no more than enough for a short, and House of Errors *offers a paraphrase upon its title that is all too obvious for a reviewer to accept. The picture gets audience laughs only on its physical gags, otherwise is a completely amateurish effort. The dialogue sounds like producer-director Bernard B. Ray gave disorganized permission to his none-too-gifted actors to ad lib as they went along.*

Langdon assumes responsibility for authorship of the original story, Ewart Adamson and Eddie M. Davis for its screenplay…

Langdon is still a very funny clown, although this appearance allows him little opportunity to demonstrate his abilities. With Charles Rogers as his teammate, his routines in silencing an auto horn, the interlude by candlelight, and a tag sequence in a flophouse are the show's highlights. Marian Marsh and Ray Walker are at personal advantage in romantic roles, but the balance of the cast range from passable to incredibly awful. Photography is as flat as its lighting, and production values simply do not exist.

What Makes Lizzy Dizzy?

A Columbia Short Subject Released in Two Reels. PRODUCED AND DIRECTED BY Jules White. SCREENPLAY BY Ewart Adamson. STORY BY Philip L. Leslie. PHOTOGRAPHY BY Benjamin Kline. EDITED BY Jerome Thoms. CAST: Harry Langdon, Elsie Ames, Dorothy Appleby, Monty Collins, Lorin Raker, Bud Jamison, Kathryn Sabichi, Kay Vallon. Copyright March 12, 1942, Registration Number LP11168; Renewed February 20, 1970, Number R479836. Released by Columbia Pictures Corporation, March 26, 1942.

SYNOPSIS: In Kelley's Klassy Laundry and Dry Cleaning shop, Harry and Bill, two detectives, are investigating an attempted robbery. The boss of the shop suspects it was the work of Vittorio, the dynamiter. Liz, Harry's fiancée, and her girlfriend arrive and flirt with their boyfriends. Later, the girls are working in the laundry and Liz is swamped with work. She wrecks her boss's clothes and eventually ends up dumping him in a large washer.

Later that evening, the finals of a bowling tournament are taking place. Kelley's laundry is competing against the Snowite laundry. Liz is added to Kelley's team at the last minute, even though she doesn't know how to bowl. The boss says that if their team wins he'll share the $1,000 prize with Liz. She tells Harry that they can then be married. Liz throws her first ball and completely misses the pins, then gets a strike with her second ball. Harry advises Liz as a rival from the opposing team puts glue in a bowling ball. Harry grabs the ball to demonstrate the right way to throw and gets his fingers stuck. He then bumps Liz, causing her to throw another strike. Meanwhile, Vittiorio, the dynamiter, arrives and hides among the spectators. A cop appears and asks Harry and Bill if they've seen anyone suspicious. They say they haven't, and the cop leaves.

An aging Harry with Elsie Ames in What Makes Lizzy Dizzy?

The rival uses the glue again and Harry gets stuck to a second ball as Liz laughs at his predicament. As Liz throws another strike, her boss picks up Vittorio's bag by mistake. He gives Liz the ball from the bag for her next throw. She grabs a large hammer and intends to hit the ball like a golfer. Meanwhile, the cop returns and scuffles with Vittorio. Harry manages to knock down the cop and Bill with the bowling balls stuck to his hands. Liz sends the new ball, which is really a bomb, down the lane, and it explodes upon contact with the pins. The bowling alley is wrecked, and Harry, Bill and the girls emerge from the wreckage. Liz sees that the pins have become embedded in the wall and spell "you win." She announces to Harry that they now can be married, and then all four discover that bowling balls are stuck to their fingers.

ANALYSIS: Jules White had some strange ideas about women and comedy, and films like *What Makes Lizzy Dizzy?* would often result. Elsie Ames, whose frenetic screen presence made Martha Raye look genteel, was a particular favorite of the director. The previous year she'd paired with Buster Keaton in five of his Columbia two-reelers, and this is her first of a deuce with Langdon. As Liz, Ames dominates the proceedings, most of which are painful. Keaton admired her acrobatic ability (she'd begun in vaudeville as a dancer), but with paper-thin material such as in this short, there's nothing the viewer can do but wince at her overacting and the sheer tastelessness of the violence she engenders and endures. Langdon is basically a supporting player with little to do, none of it memorable, and among his "O-Ouch-O comedies," *What Makes Lizzy Dizzy?* is probably the worst.

WHAT THE CRITICS SAID:
Film Daily, *March 26, 1942*

Question posed by the title can be readily answered: It's this short's corny story. Cut out the sound track, and the situations and un-clever gags have the aroma of an undistinguished slapstick offering of a few decades ago. Cast members are found frolicking in a laundry, and later in a bowling alley. In vastly original scenes, they slip on soap, become incarcerated in washing machines, get blueing on clothes, get trousers bathed in acid, and bean one another with bowling balls. America's sense of humor is so wide and varied that What Makes Lizzy Dizzy? *is almost certain to find a few devotees. As long as there is no shortage of raw film stock, pictures like this are apt to emerge occasionally. Let's be brave in such crises!*

Box Office, *April 4, 1942*

If it's wide-open slapstick the patrons want, this is it. In the hands of a group of capable whacks, this traverses a laundry and bowling alley with all waystops contributing gags that are too goofy to attempt description. Most of them should get laughs with average audiences, but not so with discriminating patrons.

The Exhibitor, *April 8, 1942*

Elsie Ames and her friend, Dorothy Appleby, work in a laundry. Their boyfriends are Harry Langdon and Monty Collins. After generally slopping up the laundry, the girls bowl in a contest on which the boss has bet plenty of money. But a bowling ball gets mixed up with a bomb, and the result is an explosion. Perhaps low class audiences might get some laughs out of this. BAD.

Tireman, Spare My Tires

A Columbia Short Subject Released in Two Reels. **PRODUCED AND DIRECTED BY** Jules White. **SCREENPLAY BY** Clyde Bruckman. **STORY BY** Felix Adler. **PHOTOGRAPHY BY** Benjamin Kline. **EDITED BY** Jerome Thoms. **CAST:** Harry Langdon, Louise Currie, Emmett Lynn, Bud Jamison. Copyright June 4, 1942, Registration Number LP11578; Renewed May 15, 1970, Number R484631. Released by Columbia Pictures Corporation, June 4, 1942.

SYNOPSIS: In a diner, Harry is reading a newspaper that mentions a $5,000 reward being offered for missing heiress Fay Springer. While engrossed in his reading, he pours syrup down his sleeve. Later, Harry is driving and stops to pick up a girl, clad in a bathing suit. It seems that she is the missing heiress. Fay tells Harry that she ran away from home because her father wouldn't let her marry the man she loves. He says he'll take her home, but she tricks him into putting his fingerprints on a locket that contains a photo of her boyfriend. Fay threatens to tell the police that he kidnapped her. An official stops the car and demands Harry's new tires for defense purposes. He's given a coupon for reconditioned tires. Later, a local sheriff stops them and Fay announces that she and Harry are newlyweds. The lawman tells them to go to his auto court. Inside a room at the court, Fay cleans her dress with gasoline. After the sheriff leaves, Fay offers to cook an omelet. She mistakenly mixes in the wrong ingredients. Harry makes the coffee and manages to drop two cigars into the pot. At the table they both pretend that the omelet is good, even though it tastes terrible. They continue to eat and Harry becomes nauseated by the omelet and coffee, plus a small plug of chewing tobacco the sheriff left behind. He eventually keels over in a faint.

Later that evening, Fay tells Harry that it was her brother's picture in the locket. A blanket on a string separates two beds as they prepare to retire. Fay warns Harry not to leave. When he is asleep she puts carpet tacks in front of the door. When Harry sees that she is asleep, he attempts to leave, and steps on the tacks. He screams in pain and falls on them. Fay laughs as Harry pulls tacks out of his rear and tells her to keep quiet. Fay's father and two cops arrive the next morning. Harry tells them that he was holding the daughter and claims the $5,000 reward. Fay's father hands over the money and Harry announces that, with the money, he and Fay *can* get married. They escape from the room as Fay's father and the cops get tangled up in one another's clothes.

ANALYSIS: Langdon teams up with two old hands from his Sennett days, Felix Adler and Clyde Bruckman, and together they pull off the conceit of remaking Frank Capra's Oscar-winning feature *It Happened One Night* in two reels. The physical gags are mostly mild and believable, and Langdon handles them all well. He reuses the balky fountain bit from *Johnny's New Car* in the form of a water faucet that won't allow him to fill his coffee pot. There's also a marvelous eating scene where, once again, chewing tobacco gets mixed up with his food. Louise Currie is the anti-Elsie Ames: attractive, demure, and a good foil. The only downside is that by now Harry looks old enough to be her father; fortunately, they don't fall in love until the final 45 seconds of the film.

HARRY MOMENT: Langdon's facial pantomime at the table as he becomes ill reveals his skills to be intact. Despite encroaching age, he is very funny in this sequence.

WHAT THE CRITICS SAID:
The Exhibitor, *June 3, 1942*

Along the lines of It Happened One Night, *this has Harry Langdon meeting up with an heiress, whose father*

Louise Currie, Bud Jamison, Langdon and Emmett Lynn.

has put up a $5,000 reward for her return. A rustic policeman complicates the adventure. They spend the night at an auto camp, and the wind up finds Langdon not only winning the $5,000 but also the girl, Louise Currie. FAIR.

Carry Harry

A Columbia Short Subject Released in Two Reels. PRODUCED BY Del Lord and Hugh McCollum. DIRECTED BY Harry Edwards. STORY AND SCREENPLAY BY Harry Edwards. PHOTOGRAPHY BY L.W. O'Connell. EDITED BY Paul Borofsky. CAST: Harry Langdon, Elsie Ames, Barbara Pepper, Stanley Blystone, Marjorie Deanne, Dave O'Brien. Copyright September 3, 1942, Registration Number LP12029; Renewed August 24, 1970, Number R490030. Released by Columbia Pictures Corporation, September 3, 1942.

SYNOPSIS: An inebriated Harry exits the Yogi-Palmist's establishment and tells his friend Arthur that he's just had his palm read. He's been told to marry his girlfriend, Edith, right away. Arthur tells him not to marry her because she's domineering and just after his money. Harry then tells his friend that the palmist said that good luck will follow him. He immediately slips on a banana peel. Harry gets into the wrong car by mistake and is warned by Elsie, who is inside, to leave. It seems that her sweetie is very jealous. Harry's car leaves, and Elsie's dress is torn. Her boyfriend arrives and gets angry about the situation. Later, Harry causes them both to be sprayed with water. He attempts to dry the man with a piece of the torn dress and gets punched in the nose. As the cops approach, Arthur tells Harry to go to his apartment and hide. Harry enters Elsie's apartment by mistake and has trouble with a phone. A mousetrap gives him some difficulty, but he gets rid of it. He finally calls Edith, gives the apartment number, and says he's at Arthur's place. Harry is told to never mention Arthur's name again. He wanders around the apartment and discovers Elsie's wet clothes. Realizing that he's in the wrong apartment, he tries to leave and gets pushed in a revolving upright bed. He spots

Harry, Marjorie Deanne and Barbara Pepper try to untangle Elsie Ames from her ironing board in Carry Harry.

Elsie struggling with an ironing board. Vicki, Elsie's girlfriend, returns as Harry hides under a birdcage cover. A cat enters the cage and they struggle, which causes Vicki to faint. Harry goes for some smelling salts and manages to bump Elsie into a tub of water. He applies the salts to Vicki but she doesn't react, and the bottle gets stuck on his nose. Edith arrives and Harry hides Vicki under a sofa bed.

His girlfriend finds some women's clothes lying about, and Harry gets clobbered with a vase. Edith sits on the couch and manages to stick Vicki with a pin. Her screams propel Harry's girl into the air. In the confusion, Harry hides Vicki in the kitchen and pushes Edith into the tub of water. Elsie's boyfriend arrives and shoots a pistol at Harry, who slides down a wire to safety. He ends up in front of the Yogi's place and starts to heave a brick through the window. He then decides to toss the brick aside. It hits the back of a truck and barrels roll down and smash up the shop. Harry quickly runs away.

ANALYSIS: Another in the "animated suit of clothes" series, *Carry Harry* has a few genuine laughs and some interesting stunts, but is a far cry from the character comedy of the Elf, despite the presence of director Harry Edwards. A cartoony gag from *The Chaser* is repeated when the telephone receiver falls into a wastebasket and the scolding that Harry's girlfriend Edith is administering on the other end sends paper flying around the room. Elsie Ames is her usual catastrophic self, getting tangled in an ironing board and otherwise knocked about her own apartment. Thankfully, the two aren't teamed as Harry has his own mishaps with mousetraps, cats and smelling salts. The closing scene is a poorly executed version of the payoff from *Three's a Crowd*, utterly lacking in finesse. Sadly, the gap between that film and *Carry Harry* is far and wide.

HARRY MOMENT: Harry's brief struggle with the mousetrap in the kitchen reveals that his strange rhythms are intact. Walter Kerr, in *The Silent Clowns*, commented on these odd movements that were unique to Langdon.

WHAT THE CRITICS SAID:
Variety, *September 23, 1942*
Langdon looks older, but he's a kid alongside some of the gags foisted on him here. Couple of femme lookers are wasted as Langdon strives to overcome ancient vintage

Marjorie Deane, Langdon and Stanley Blystone in Carry Harry.

material. Premise that if one slapstick fall causes a laugh, three in succession will triple the laughter is proved fallacious in this short.

Box Office, *September 26, 1942*

All the comic antics that make Harry Langdon the laughable comedian he is are included in this farce about a pair of tipplers who dash about the apartment of a couple of girls while an irate fiancée chases Langdon. It has laugh value. Rating: Fair.

The Exhibitor, *October 7, 1942*

Harry Langdon is a bit potted the night before his wedding, and he gets into plenty of jams, in the wrong apt., etc., etc. Barbara Pepper adds some attraction. FAIR.

WHAT THE EXHIBITORS SAID:
Motion Picture Herald, *March 27, 1943*

Right up the alley for small towns such as mine. This comedy sure got the laughs out of my patrons. G. Tewksbury, Harbor Theatre, Deer Isle, ME.

Piano Mooner

A Columbia Short Subject Released in Two Reels. **PRODUCED BY** Hugh McCollum. **DIRECTED BY** Harry Edwards. **STORY AND SCREENPLAY BY** Harry Langdon. **PHOTOGRAPHY BY** Philip Tannura. **EDITED BY** Paul Borofsky. **CAST:** Harry Langdon, Fifi D'Orsay, Gwen Kenyon, Betty Blythe, Chester Conklin, Stanley Blystone. Copyright December 11, 1942, Registration Number LP12047; Renewed November 19, 1970, Number R495125. Released by Columbia Pictures Corporation, December 11, 1942.

SYNOPSIS: Mildred, who is clad in her wedding gown, is told by her brother that Harry the piano tuner will never marry her. She says he will, but that he won't get married until he gets a dress suit. Harry arrives and announces that he's going to swap piano tuning for a full dress suit, and that he has taken out an ad. The brother advises Harry that he had better be married by three o'clock that afternoon — or else. A phone call comes from a lady who read the ad and invites Harry to come over and tune her piano in exchange for a suit. Both Harry and the brother write down the address. He arrives sometime later at the house and notices that the yard is set for a wedding. He begins to play the piano, which is horribly out of tune.

Harry shows the lady's daughter, who is to be married, how to do the wedding march. He bumps into a lever and a sprinkler soaks them both. Later, Harry tunes the piano as dust flies out of it whenever he strikes a key. A maid interrupts him and Harry tells her that he's to be married by three o'clock. She thinks he's proposing and pursues him but winds up being propelled into the house. The lady tosses down Harry's suit and tells him to get on with the tuning. A man from a mission arrives and asks Harry if there are any old clothes that could be obtained. The lady tosses down a huge pile of clothes and the man takes them away. Harry panics when he realizes that the man has removed his suit; he tackles him. He gets his suit back but the maid — determined to woo Harry — takes it inside the house. After a struggle, Harry gets it back, and then receives a call from Mildred's brother asking why he is late. He's soon dressed and attempts to leave for his wedding. Harry tells the lady that the piano is tuned as her daughter grabs him to rehearse the wedding march. As they walk down the aisle, Mildred and her brother arrive. He threatens to murder Harry, who bumps into a motorcycle, causing it to run amok. As the brother shoots at him, Harry gets on the motorcycle, picks up Mildred and drives away, managing also to deposit the annoying maid into a birdbath.

ANALYSIS: Written by Langdon, *Piano Mooner* is less hectic than recent shorts, although it contains a fair amount of slapstick. As the abrasive maid, Fifi D'Orsay, a star of the early talkie era, is reduced to a role better suited for Elsie Ames, as she makes herself generally obnoxious and is continually knocked about in the process. However, Harry Edwards does what he can to give Langdon some time for his particular brand of pantomime. There are two set pieces: first, as Harry sits on his girlfriend's couch, hoping for a tuning job, he plays around with the sofa cushions, which causes a pair of springs to emerge. His struggles to put them back into place are good for laughs, as is his facial pantomime during the second sequence, as he's tuning the piano. Unfortunately, the effects of advancing age show through his still-expressive face. Had *Piano Mooner* been produced five or ten years earlier, it might have been one of Langdon's best talkie two-reelers.

HARRY MOMENT: Harry's reactions to the dust and the sour notes while tuning the piano are quite enjoyable.

WHAT THE CRITICS SAID:
The Exhibitor, *December 16, 1942*

Harry Langdon has plenty of trouble. He needs a dress suit, so he makes a deal to tune the piano for one so he can be married. Then the trouble starts with Fifi D'Orsay, an old clothes collector, his intended brother-in-law, his bride-to-be all involved. He manages to get away with her after plenty of slapstick. FAIR.

A Blitz on the Fritz

A Columbia Short Subject Released in Two Reels. PRODUCED AND DIRECTED BY Jules White. STORY AND SCREENPLAY BY Clyde Bruckman. PHOTOGRAPHY BY Arthur Martinelli. EDITED BY Edwin Bryant. ART DIRECTOR: Carl Anderson. CAST: Harry Langdon, Louise Currie, Douglas Leavitt, Vernon Dent, Bud Jamison, Jack "Tiny" Lipson, Blanche Payson, Charles Betty, Al Hill, Al Thompson, Beatrice Blinn, Joe Palma, Stanley Blystone, Bud Fine, Kit Guard. WORKING TITLE: "Swat That Spy." Copyright January 22, 1943, Registration Number LP12057; Renewed December 16, 1970, Number R496546. Released by Columbia Pictures Corporation, January 22, 1943.

SYNOPSIS: Egbert (Harry Langdon) is eating breakfast as his wife is telling him that everyone should be on the lookout for spies. She also suggests that he help the Red Cross gather rubber and tin. While collecting scrap, Egbert tries to remove a mattress and gets stuck in a tire. He gets out, but the tire rolls away and Egbert pursues it, almost getting hit by a car in the process. It bounces up and goes through an apartment window. Egbert enters the room to retrieve the tire and is met by a group of angry Germans. They let him go with his tire, but soon discover that a paper detailing their plans for sabotage is missing. When Egbert returns home, his mother-in-law, his wife and her friend announce that he's to be their test subject for first aid. With little skill, they apply splints and bandage rolls to his arms, legs and head. He eventually gets loose and his wife finds the Germans' plans to attack shipyards, munitions plants and other industries in the tire. Egbert gets his gun and goes back to the Germans' apartment. He gets punched in the nose and tells a cop that there are spies in the building. The policeman thinks Egbert's a drunk and tells him to beat it. Desperate, Egbert attacks several men, who chase him into the apartment, where they get into a brawl with the spies. With Egbert's help they beat the spies as the cops arrive. Egbert tells the police that he and his guys whipped the Germans. He gives the evidence to the head cop, who tells Egbert and the men that they're all heroes. The men lift Egbert on their shoulders and carry him out of the room, causing him to bump his head on the doorframe.

ANALYSIS: Those who appreciate good wartime entertainment had better steer clear of this lame-brained exercise in tasteless knockabout. Everyone seems to have forgotten that Langdon's comedic strength was keyed to his reactions; here, he does nothing but create havoc, and his individuality gets lost in the shuffle. Distaff viewers will derive no amusement from the women in this short, depicted as stupid and needlessly cruel. As for the conclusion, there's little satisfaction in seeing the nest of fifth columnists get taken down, because they aren't on screen long enough to pose a credible threat. It's all violence for the sake of violence, with nothing original in the gags or execution, and certainly nothing that makes Langdon stand out from the pack. The script may have been better suited for Shemp Howard.

"I had a theory," Jules White told author Leonard Maltin, "make 'em move so fast, if they're not funny, no one will have time to realize it or get bored." *A Blitz on the Fritz* is Exhibit A for White's theory: it moves fast and it's not funny.

WHAT THE CRITICS SAID:
The Exhibitor, *February 24, 1943*

Harry Langdon decides to do something to win the war while collecting scrap. He unearthed a spy ring, and, in order to capture them, he has to start a fight with everyone he meets. This is about par for this slapstick nonsense. FAIR.

WHAT THE EXHIBITORS SAID:
Motion Picture Herald, *April 15, 1944*

Our patrons love these comedies and actually ask for more in preference to some of the so-called features which we are forced to show to them.
Robert E. Floeter, Burton Theatre, Flint, MI.

Blonde and Groom

A Columbia Short Subject Released in Two Reels. **PRODUCED BY** Hugh McCollum. **DIRECTED BY** Harry Edwards. **STORY AND SCREENPLAY BY** Harry Langdon. **PHOTOGRAPHY BY** L.W. O'Connell. **EDITED BY** Paul Borofsky. **ART DIRECTOR:** Arthur Royce. **CAST:** Harry Langdon, Gwen Kenyon, Barbara Pepper, Eddy Chandler, Stanley Blystone. Copyright March 30, 1943, Registration Number LP11944; Renewed February 19, 1971, Number R500614. Released by Columbia Pictures Corporation, April 16, 1943.

SYNOPSIS: Harry, an air raid warden, is moving a bucket of sand to the roof. He ends up with sand running down his back. His wife, to whom he's been married for only a month, is leaving on a business trip and warns him not to meet up with any other women. As she leaves, he goes up to the roof to put down the sand, but ends up causing an alarm to clatter. A soldier arrives with his fiancée and tells her that she can stay at Harry's house until the morning. He will then bring the minister and they can be married.

"Tiny" Lipson and Bud Jamison crowd Harry in this lobby card.

Harry agrees to let the soldier's "friend" stay overnight. When he sees that the friend is a beautiful blonde he says that she can't stay because his wife will get mad. The soldier reminds Harry that he saved his life and therefore owes him this favor.

Harry agrees to let her stay the night. Later that evening, the woman takes both his pillow and blanket. Harry struggles with another pillow that turns out to be a pincushion. He kicks it away and it hits her in the rear. Harry barricades the door of his room to keep her out but she forces her way in. She eventually gets his pistol and fires shots at him. Harry retreats to the roof and falls down the chimney. As the woman is cleaning him off, his wife calls and gets enraged when she hears the guest's voice. The woman's jealous ex-boyfriend also shows up and she masquerades as a nurse getting a blood donation from Harry. She uses a huge needle and draws a lot of blood, causing her ex-boyfriend to faint. Harry's wife arrives, sees the "nurse" taking a blood donation, and remarks that Harry looks weak. After the blonde leaves, he floats around the room. When his wife embraces him, he turns to dust.

ANALYSIS: A pathetically unfunny two reels, *Blonde and Groom,* although penned by Langdon, has nothing to recommend it. Subtlety is completely dispensed with as both Harry and blonde Barbara Pepper get knocked around. Although some footage is spent on Harry's facial expressions, his actions are so brainless there's no possibility of anyone relating to him or the trite and tasteless predicaments into which he puts himself. The Stooges' influence is at its peak, with exaggerated sound effects accompanying such unamusing "gags" as Harry stepping on a pincushion or getting pushed and pulled to and from the floor by his burly "pal." It's hard to believe the same team that created *Piano Mooner,* which at least had a modicum or two of charm, is responsible for this waste of celluloid.

WHAT THE CRITICS SAID:
Film Daily, *April 12, 1943*

It's a little sad to see Harry Langdon wasting his time on this sort of thing. A grown-up will be pained rather than amused at the comedian's efforts to be funny in a rehash of all the slapstick tricks in the book. Langdon is cast as an idiotic air-raid warden who gets into trouble with his wife over a blonde whom he permits to stay in his home overnight as a favor to a pal. The wife is away for the evening when the gal drops in. Langdon goes through the usual folderol in trying to prevent his wife from thinking the worst. Mark this down as strictly for the kids. Hugh McCollum produced and Harry Edwards directed.

The Exhibitor, *April 21, 1943*

This hits a new low. Harry Langdon, an air raid warden with a jealous wife, gets into a jam when his friend, the sergeant, asks him to put up a friend overnight, and it turns out to be Barbara Pepper. Langdon gets mixed-up with his air raid equipment and when an ex-lover of Pepper turns up, he is taken for a blood donor. As his wife returns, Langdon crumbles to dust, his blood gone, when his wife kisses him. BAD.

WHAT THE EXHIBITORS SAID:
Motion Picture Herald, *June 5, 1943*

Very funny. This type of comedy goes over well here.
V. C. Kinchen, Avon Theatre, Poteet, TX.

Motion Picture Herald, *July 17, 1943.*

Old stuff — very poor. Langdon is all washed out.
Wilson T. Cottrell, Carolina Theatre, Oxford, NC.

Here Comes Mr. Zerk

A Columbia Short Subject Released in Two Reels. PRODUCED AND DIRECTED BY Jules White. STORY AND SCREENPLAY BY Jack White. PHOTOGRAPHY BY Benjamin Kline. EDITED BY Charles Hochberg. ART DIRECTOR: Victor Greene. CAST: Harry Langdon, Shirley Patterson, John T. Murray, Fred Kelsey, Bob McKenzie, Dudley Dickerson, Hank Mann, Vernon Dent, Charles "Heine" Conklin, Eva McKenzie, Blanche Payson. WORKING TITLE: "Sue You Later." Copyright July 20, 1943, Registration Number LP12140; Renewed May 27, 1971, Number R506402. Released by Columbia Pictures Corporation, July 23, 1943.

SYNOPSIS: In an editor's office, the boss complains that two photos on the front page were switched by mistake. Egbert (Harry Langdon) is pictured as an insane killer who has escaped and the killer is shown to be a scientist about to be wed. Meanwhile, Egbert is grooming himself in preparation for his forthcoming wedding. He gets a call from his intended bride informing him that he's late for the wedding. Egbert enters an elevator and the operator, glancing at a newspaper, screams at the sight of the "killer." He then bumps into a man who recognizes "him." The man flees in terror as Egbert encounters a woman, who hits him with her umbrella. After another woman and her child run away, he's chased by a hotel detective throughout the building.

Later, Egbert arrives for the wedding and greets his bride-to-be as her father accidentally knocks her

out while trying to crown him. A cop arrives, and he escapes through a window. Egbert ends up in a shooting gallery alongside stand-up targets of Hitler, Mussolini and Hirohito. Two men pick up rifles and begin to fire, but they panic and run away as they see target Egbert move about. The cop encounters the real escaped lunatic, but fails to recognize him. The nut gets into his car and drives away, with Egbert in the back seat. The scientist crawls into the passenger seat and ends up smoking an imaginary cigar offered by the nut. Egbert then sees a newspaper and realizes that he's in the car with a lunatic killer. The crazy man announces that he's Paul Revere and pulls up to a house. He tells Egbert that his horse is waiting for them. It seems that a line of clothes in the back yard is the horse, and the nut attempts to put Egbert on his steed. The clothesline collapses; they are soon back in the car. Egbert winds up in the back seat, and the crazy soon joins him.

The car careens out of control and narrowly misses hitting other cars. His bride and her father pull up alongside in another car. Egbert announces that it's all been a mistake. His bride replies that she's seen the papers. Egbert ends up caught between the two moving cars, which leads to an interesting collision.

ANALYSIS: The clever, if not exactly original, concept of an innocent man mistaken for an escaped lunatic is overly seasoned with the usual Jules White recipe of slapstick and sadism in *Here Comes Mr. Zerk*. One can only imagine what Mack Sennett or Arvid Gillstrom would have done with the idea; it's a cinch the results would have been several degrees better than this tired short. To the role of Zerk, the genuine lunatic, John T. Murray brings a decent crazy chuckle and not much else. Although Egbert's reactions to Zerk's ability to light and smoke a nonexistent cigar are good for a few smiles, things might have worked out better had Vernon Dent played Murray's part, instead of being wasted in a brief bit as the newspaper editor. The end result is another lame, labored "comedy," all too typical of Columbia during this period.

WHAT THE CRITICS SAID:
Film Daily, *July 12, 1943*

Harry Langdon, out of traditional "white face," cavorts through this slapstick offering with spirit and abandon, getting about the most from a pretty good yarn penned by Jack White. Essentially it's for the folks who like their humor clear of any subtlety. Here and there are mirthful situations, but for the most part the footage is just so-so... Stands going in for raucous reels should find it okay.

The Exhibitor, *July 14, 1943*

A mistake is made by a new paper in the captions under two photos, which labels Harry Langdon as an escaped lunatic known as Zerk, and the lunatic is labeled Langdon. In trying to get to the church where he is about to be married, he encounters numerous persons who react in various ways to him. Arriving at the church, the bride's father, who never met Langdon, also thinks he is the escaped lunatic, and has him arrested. However, he gets away from the cop and meets up with the real lunatic, who is eventually captured. FAIR.

Box Office, *July 17, 1943*

Slapstick comedy of bygone days appears in this Harry Langdon two-reeler. The comedy situation hinges on a mixup of photos in the newspapers announcing the forthcoming marriage of Langdon portraying a zany scientist. Langdon's photo is switched with that of an escaped lunatic…that's about the extent of the plot. The comedian now works without the white makeup he formerly used. Rating: Fair.

Spotlight Scandals

A Banner Production. 79 minutes. PRODUCED BY Sam Katzman and Jack Dietz. DIRECTED BY William Beaudine. ASSOCIATE PRODUCER: Barney Sarecky. SCREENPLAY BY William X. Crowley and Beryl Sachs. PHOTOGRAPHY BY Mack Stengler. EDITED BY Carl Pierson. ART DIRECTOR: David Milton. MUSICAL DIRECTOR: Edward Kay. Dance Director: Jack Boyle. CAST: Billy Gilbert, Frank Fay, Bonnie Baker, Harry Langdon, Iris Adrian, James Bush, Betty Blythe, Jim Hope, Claudia Dell, Eddie Parks, Wheeler Oakman, The Radio Rogues, Henry King and Orchestra, Herb Miller and Orchestra. Reissue Title: "Spotlight Revue." Copyright August 13, 1943, Registration Number LP12396. Released by Monogram Pictures, Inc., July 26, 1943.

SYNOPSIS: Mr. Frank Fay is an entertainer and sometime con artist down on his luck. He can't pay his hotel bill, and the manager has confiscated his belongings. One day he runs into a barber named Bill Gilbert, a jovial bumpkin that Frank proceeds to fleece for ten dollars, but Bill is just too sweet for Frank to go through with the con, and he returns the money. Bill invites Frank to dine with his family, and the two talk about Bill's dream to get into show business. The pair travels to New York, where Frank sets up an audition with one of the agents he knows. Bill sings and Frank cracks wise about the lyrics, and their accidental comic act lands them a $300-per-week job on the stage. The act is a variation on their relationship, with Frank acting the fast-talking sharpie and Bill as his stooge. They are a huge hit, and move up to higher- and higher-class theaters. Eventually they get their own show, produced by Oscar Hammond (Harry Langdon), who installs his blonde girlfriend Bernice as a lead dancer.

The show, *Spotlight Revue*, opens to enormous critical and commercial success, and Frank Fay attracts the attentions of both Bernice and a singer, Bonnie Baker,

Iris Adrian forces herself onto an uncomfortable Frank Fay as boyfriend Harry watches in this lobby card.

who offers Frank a job on her radio show. Frank refuses since the offer doesn't include Bill. The night the show closes, the partners' agent pulls Bill aside and asks him to convince Frank to accept the offer. Bill's been living pretty much the same modest lifestyle as always, while money just burns a hole in Frank's pocket. Radio could mean national exposure for Frank, and a better career than he could get if he stayed in vaudeville. Convinced, Bill stages an argument, telling Frank he wants to split up the act and go solo. Hurt and angered, Frank walks out and takes Baker's offer. The two hit it off both professionally and as a couple, becoming known as "The Sweethearts of the Airwaves," while Bill goes back to his family and barbershop.

Meanwhile, Bernice becomes increasingly angry and jealous. She starts stalking and harassing Frank, gets drunk and attacks Baker and finally breaks into Frank's apartment while he's out. He finds her sprawled on his couch and tries to get her to leave. She tussles with him as he attempts to drag her out the door, and she tumbles over the balcony to her death. With no witnesses, Frank is in deep trouble, but as his spending habits have not improved, he can't afford a lawyer.

Bill learns of Frank's dilemma and pours all his savings into getting him the best lawyer available. Frank is acquitted, but the bad press has left him unable to get booking in any big-time theaters, leaving him doing his stand-up to audiences that don't get his sophisticated humor. However, Bill is looking to get back into show business, having mortgaged everything he owns to pay for the lawyer. Frank sees Bill on the stage doing their old act, steps in, and the two have a touching reunion.

ANALYSIS: *Spotlight Scandals*, presented by the same production company responsible for Monogram's East Side Kids, begins as a lighthearted musical comedy that takes a surprising turn toward melodrama when a tertiary character, portrayed by Iris Adrian, is accidentally killed. This gives it a cache that other, similar low-budget musicals can't match. It is also a showcase for a type of humor and music that tickled the fancy of wartime audiences, making it a sort of time capsule of a bygone era, especially for old-time radio and dance band aficionados.

Unfortunately, the film has two strikes against it. First, Frank Fay, ostensibly playing himself, is not exactly likable; his humor is abrasive and occasionally pretentious, especially when he refers to himself in the third person. Billy Gilbert's joviality provides a measure of balance, but their scenes together are usually smothered by Fay's caustic retorts. Consequently, Fay's professions of warmth and friendship toward his partner aren't very convincing.

Second, *Spotlight Scandals* is also a vehicle for radio's "Wee" Bonnie Baker, who has no screen presence at all. Halfway through, the film stops dead as Fay, Gilbert, Langdon and Adrian sit in a nightclub, watching Baker's act. The Radio Rogues, a trio of celebrity impersonators, open with their shtick; luckily most of the figures they mimic are still well known. Then Baker comes on, singing two numbers in a row, including her million-selling smash of 1940, "Oh, Johnny," and she's stiff as a board. When, five minutes later, she's at a radio microphone singing a third tune, her tendency to stand stone still, with only her eyes moving from left to right and back again, distracts from her vocalizing.

On the whole, Langdon isn't given much to do as Oscar, Adrian's boyfriend-financier. He gets one comic vignette: when Adrian, as the spoiled Bernice, argues with the dance director about the routine, Oscar steps in to mediate. He watches the director do the routine in full and decides, "Say, that's marvelous!" Then Bernice goes into her less impressive version, and Oscar stops her after about one second: "That's enough. I like her's best." It's funny, but Langdon brings nothing distinctive to it.

Intended as the first in a series of Fay-Gilbert vehicles, *Spotlight Scandals* understandably failed to set the world on fire. Luckily, one year later Fay won the role of Elwood P. Dowd in the original Broadway production of Mary Chase's Pulitzer Prize-winning play, *Harvey*, which briefly placed his star back into orbit.

WHAT THE CRITICS SAID:
Daily Variety, *July 16, 1943*
First of the Billy Gilbert-Frank Fay series of co-starring comedy dramas, take-off number gives promise of the future and is a melodic potpourri of entertainment which should be reflected favorably at the box office. Here is a homely little film with elements of popular appeal, and both stars register soundly, ably complemented by Bonnie Baker, the radio chantress. Top supporting cast, with Radio Rogues to evoke laughs for their impersonations and music by two orch leaders, Henry King and Herb Miller, all combined to give class to this medium budgeted picture.

Both Gilbert and Fay are perfectly cast, Gilbert the small town barber with theatrical aspirations, Fay the polished ham, quick to seize upon opportunity. By a fluke, they're engaged as a vaude comedy team, instantly score a hit and soon thereafter star in their own musical show on Broadway, angled by Harry Langdon in a brief but memorable portrayal…

Screenplay is tightly knit and pointed toward general consumption, with both stars awarded comedic opportunities for laughs aplenty. Their routines together particularly Fay's as a monologist are excellently presented. Bonnie Baker's singing of "The Restless Age," "Oh, Johnny," "The Lilac Tree" are pleasant interpolations. Atmospherically the backstage spirit is there in full measure, direction by William Beaudine, taking every advantage of the story's theme. Butch and Buddy, growing up, draw clever portrayals, Eddie Parks is immense for his comedy, James Busch, Betty Blythe, Iris Adrian and Jim Hope for personable support.

Production is well contrived by the two producers, Sam Katzman and Jack Dietz, and associate, Barney Sarecky. Photography of Mack Stengler is entirely up to standard. Picture should draw a repeat request for Gilbert and Fay.

Box Office, *July 24, 1943*

This shows for better results than most of Hollywood's attempts to produce musicals on short budgets and largely because Producer Sam Katzman limited its so-called production numbers to one, which, parenthetically, is no asset. Instead, the picture assembles several familiar performers and specialties and uses their diversified talents as a backdrop for the teaming of Billy Gilbert and Frank Fay, whose respective brands of comedy nicely complement one another and provide a dual delivery that is amusing and indicates a market for more co-starring features. The film should be welcome as supporting fare on most any program. It has a human, believable story of the show world which more than suffices to logically connect the entertainment elements.

Harrison's Reports, *July 24, 1943*

Frank Fay and Billy Gilbert emerge as a good comedy team in this diverting comedy with music. Although there is nothing novel either in the story or its treatment, it should serve fairly well as a supporting feature. Added to Fay's smooth delivery of gags, and Gilbert's blustering antics, are a number of specialty acts headed by Bonnie Baker, who sings a few popular tunes. The Radio Rogues' impersonations of famous stars are good. The orchestras of Henry King and Herb Miller provide the music.…

Morally suitable for all.

Motion Picture Herald, *July 24, 1943; Reviewed by William R. Weaver*

The House of Monogram presents now for your consideration, Ladies and Gentlemen of show business, a pair of comedians equipped with all the prerequisites of popularity and commanding attention of everybody in range of their introductory endeavor, inside or outside the trade. They are Frank Fay and Billy Gilbert, each a known equation, both experts in and veterans of the art of comedy, and they are, in the paired aggregate, a total quantity which is several times greater than the sum of its component parts. The pair is, in this first offering, a force of merriment that can be compared with any other pair you are likely to think of off-hand, on the basis of first offerings, and if that pair happens to be present holders of the Number One Box Office Attraction title for 1942 the foregoing statement stands.

The House of Monogram put this introductory Fay-Gilbert film to a severe test on the occasion of its press by screening it at the Hollywood Paramount between performances of Five Graves to Cairo *for a top-scale audience that hasn't been told what was coming.*

In that fast company it proved itself to the satisfaction of the capacity crowd without straining a stitch…

On the framework is hung various other items of entertainment. Bonnie Baker sings several songs, from her repertoire, and the Radio Rogues do their impersonations. Henry King and his orchestra supply their brand of music. So do Butch and Buddy. Eddie Parks entertains virtually en solo for a memorable sequence, and Harry Langdon amuses in a semi-straight performance. Iris Adrian portrays with glitter a jealous showgirl. Lots of others figure in the total.

Production by Sam Katzman and Jack Dietz, with Barney Sarecky in association, is well above par, and direction by William Beaudine reflects the proficiency of long experience.

Reviewer's Rating: Good.

Film Daily, *July 26, 1943*

This is a new type of picture for Banner Productions. Yes, it is a class low-budget with a good cast of performers. Ably made, and so decorative that the only way you could tell its cost is small, would be to get a peek at Banner's ledgers.

Frank Fay and Billy Gilbert make a great comedy team. It's not so much that these gentlemen are masters of the art of milking lines and situations — but their experiences, which if combined would stretch from here to who-knows-where, give the entire proceedings a polish not often found in the work and best efforts of neophytes…

The tale smacks slightly of the Hal Skelly hit "Burlesque" — with the girl part toned down. Frank Fay, the none too successful vaudeville comic, finds himself stranded in a small mid-western city. He is thrown in with the local barber, Billy Gilbert, who one night helps him out with his act as a stooge from the audience. Accidentally the team catches on, and by fluke gets big time booking. Then comes success for the broken down actor and the barber.

They hit the heights and are finally playing their own show on Broadway, under the sponsorship of a very clever producer, namely, Harry Langdon.

This is a good picture. It will make any buyer happy, be it exhibitor, or a guy who buys his look at it from the little ticket booth out front.

Direction: Good, Photography: Good.

New York Post, *September 25, 1943; Reviewed by Irene Thirer*

Spotlight Scandals, *now showing at the Brooklyn Fabian-Fox Theatre with the second-run* Destroyer, *utilizes one of the oldest of the vaudeville situations. Frank Fay is the "wanted" member of an act, and Billy Gilbert is the other. Frank says no, he won't go without Billy. But Billy, learning of his partner's self-sacrifice through their manager, pretends that he wants to break up the act.*

Later, as in all such situations, Frank gets in trouble and has to be rescued by Billy.

So much, which is quite enough, for the plot. The performers are as expected. Frank Fay is suave, Gilbert explosively simple. Wee Bonnie Baker sings her numbers in her little girl style, including "Oh, Johnny." Harry Langdon brings back his expressively vapid face from the old silent days, and Iris Adrian portrays a very forward girl. The Radio Rogues, and two orchestras, Henry King and Herb Miller, fill the interstices with imitations and music.

To Heir Is Human

A Columbia Short Subject Released in Two Reels. **PRODUCED BY** Hugh McCollum. **DIRECTED BY** Harold Godsoe. **STORY AND SCREENPLAY BY** Elwood Ullman and Monty Collins. **PHOTOGRAPHY BY** George Meehan. **EDITED BY** Paul Borofsky. **ART DIRECTOR:** Charles Clague. **CAST:** Harry Langdon, Una Merkel, Christine McIntyre, Lew Kelly, Eddie Gribbon, John Tyrell, Vernon Dent, Snub Pollard. Copyright January 14, 1944, Registration Number LP12478; Renewed December 10, 1971, Number R517052. Released by Columbia Pictures Corporation, January 14, 1944.

SYNOPSIS: Una is giving out new phone books and ends up knocked into the office the Hide and Seek Missing Persons Bureau. She meets A. Raven Sparrow, who mistakes her for an employee of the Bureau. He tells her that the Funevsic estate is being settled, and offers her $1,000 to locate missing heir Harry, a photograph of whom is provided. She soon notices that the window cleaner outside the building is none other

than Harry. She tells him about the fortune but he's not interested. She chases him around another office and eventually leads him away.

Una calls Sparrow and tells him that she's located the missing heir. He hangs up and tells a female accomplice that if cousin Harry is still alive by the next evening he'll get everything. They discuss methods of doing him in with a third accomplice and agree on a rigged bed that will electrocute him. Sparrow ends up on the bed by mistake and is catapulted into the air. The female accomplice suggests using poison.

When Harry and Una arrive, he's pulled into the house while she is looking the other way. Inside, he's greeted by his cousin, who offers a drink. She puts poison in the drink and gives it to her hapless cousin. As Harry raises it, he pokes a hole in the glass by mistake and the poison leaks out, causing the rug to burn. Una eventually gets inside the building as Harry is offered a second drink. He pours it into a planter, and the flower wilts. He then encounters Una and knocks her out by mistake. Harry puts her on the rigged bed and she flies into the air. A short time later, Sparrow and the cousin are knocked unconscious. Harry and Una leave the house as the third accomplice tries to rope them. He's pulled to the ground and dragged behind them as they run away.

ANALYSIS: A clever plot, handsome production values and the use of mood music lift *To Heir is Human* above the usual Columbia level, but the crux of it is still crude knockabout. Una Merkel's mere presence also adds a touch of class to the proceedings, but she's given little opportunity to shine. Right from the start she gets two blows to the backside, one off-camera and one on, and the abuse doesn't let up. As for Langdon, he can still do a few wondrous things with his body — there's a marvelous moment where he runs down a corridor, skids to a stop while leaning to the left, then turns right and proceeds — but age has thoroughly overtaken his baby face and most of his performance. In every close-up, he looks wan; with each line of dialogue, he sounds worn out.

WHAT THE CRITICS SAID:
The Exhibitor, *January 26, 1944*

Una Merkel is mistaken for proprietor of a missing persons bureau, and hired to locate Harry Langdon a missing heir. She finds him, and takes him to her client, who proves to be a screwy relative, who, with other equally maniacal relatives, are bent upon murdering him so that they will in turn become heirs. Their poisoning, hanging and electrocuting fail, and Langdon and Merkel get out of it all. This is slapstick all the way, but has a few laughs. FAIR.

Film Daily, *February 7, 1944*

Although this one is described as a "comedy," it will be tough even for a kid to work himself into a state of hilarity over what goes on in the two-reeler. The short has a lot of

Una Merkel's search for Harry takes no time at all in To Heir is Human.

commotion, to be sure, but not much of it that can be taken for funny...Little can be said in favor of the performances. Hugh McCollum produced and Harold Godsoe directed.

Box Office, *February 19, 1944*
Una Merkel and Harry Langdon are involved in a series of misadventures concerning the acquisition of a fortune to which Harry is the rightful heir. However, a gang of thieves are intent on destroying him, and getting the money for themselves. The humor was intended to evolve from the situations built on the narrow escapes of the principal players, but few laughs can materialize from the weak script and unimaginative business. Rating: Fair.

Hot Rhythm

A Monogram Production. 77 minutes. PRODUCED BY Lindsley Parsons. DIRECTED BY William Beaudine. Original SCREENPLAY BY Tim Ryan, Charles R. Marion. PHOTOGRAPHY BY Ira Morgan. ASSISTANT DIRECTOR: Edward Davis. PRODUCTION MANAGER: William Strohbach. TECHNICAL DIRECTOR: David Milton. ART DIRECTOR: E.R. Hickson. Settings: Al Greenwood. SOUND ENGINEER: Tom Lambert. Music Director: Edward Kay. Songs: Virginia Wicks-Nacio Porter Brown, Lou Herscher, Edward Cherkose-Edward Kay. CAST: Dona Drake, Robert Lowery, Tim Ryan, Irene Ryan, Sidney Miller, Robert Kent, Jerry Cooper, Harry Langdon, Paul Porcast, Jean Curtis, Lloyd Ingraham, Cyril Ring, Robert C. Bruce. Copyright February 26, 1944, Registration Number LP12535; Renewed January 7, 1972, Number R521029. Released by Monogram Pictures, Inc., March 14, 1944.

SYNOPSIS: The Berken Recording Company is teetering on the edge of bankruptcy. Their most successful records are of the Tommy Taylor Band, and their agent, "Honest Herman" Strowback, has demanded double the agreed upon amount to renew the contract. O'Hara, who runs the company, refuses the offer. To increase the band's marketability, Strowback wants Taylor to consider adding a girl vocalist, but Taylor refuses. Meanwhile, O'Hara instructs his assistant, Mr. Whiffle (Harry Langdon), to engage a new secretary. Whiffle pulls out his little

Harry and Irene Ryan tussle for the microphone in this lobby card.

black book and eventually turns up with Polly Kane, who's a bit of an airhead.

As it happens, there's a new singer at Berken: Mary Adams, who is recording jingles to be used over the radio. The jingle writer, Jimmy O'Brien, is smitten, but when she gripes about the silly material she has to sing, he hides his occupation from her. Jimmy offers to record an audition record and personally deliver it to O'Hara. But as they're doing the recording after hours, there is no band to back her up, so Jimmy has Mary sing along with the radio; specifically, the Tommy Taylor Band playing a new song live from the Orchid Room. Afterwards, Mary agrees to go on a date with Jimmy.

The audition is pressed and Jimmy secretly leaves it with O'Hara, who mistakes it for a genuine Tommy Taylor record and has 10,000 copies printed up and distributed. The next day, O'Hara and Whiffle discover the extra record and deduce that the music was taken off the radio, and that the company is now in huge legal trouble. After sending Whiffle out to recall the record, O'Hara and Polly visit all the local record stores, buying up copies and smashing them, an act that ultimately gets them arrested. Jimmy and his partner, Sammy Rubin, head down to the station to bail him out, with Mary tagging along. They hear about the record from O'Hara, but since he's grateful that his "jingle writers" have come to his rescue, they don't reveal that they are the culprits. Angered that Jimmy lied to get her to go out with him, Mary breaks off the relationship.

Despite O'Hara's effort, Strowback and Taylor end up with a copy of the record. Taylor loves Mary's singing and instructs his agent to get her for their band, while Strowback sees an opportunity to destroy O'Hara financially. He arrives to threaten O'Hara with legal action, but after talking with the dizzy Polly, he comes away with the belief that she's the singer on Mary's record. He takes her out clubbing and offers her a contract for $500 a week, which she doesn't yet sign because she's been drinking. Meanwhile, Jimmy follows Mary to her night job (dragging the hapless Sammy along with him) and tries to make amends, ultimately getting them thrown out and Mary fired. Despite that, Mary agrees to give him another chance if he tells O'Hara the truth about the record.

The next day, Polly tells O'Hara about the contract Herman offered her, and O'Hara also believes Polly was the girl on the record. He offers her the same contract with his company, and when Jimmy arrives in the office to come clean, he cuts him off and tells him to take Polly and make a record with her immediately. Polly's singing is predictably awful, and Sammy fears O'Hara has made a mistake. Jimmy has more faith in O'Hara's judgment, and offers Polly a particular song to sing. Polly cuts a record called "The Happiest Girl in Town." Blubbering throughout, even bringing Sammy and Jimmy to tears, Polly turns in a bravura performance.

Jimmy orders a rush order of 10,000 copies, hoping this will help O'Hara out of his financial woes. When O'Hara hears the record, he compares it to the one of Mary and realizes there's been a huge mistake. Not wanting to pay $500 a week to the wrong girl, he convinces Polly that she needs a "real big man" like Herman Strowback, and convinces her to sign with him. However, the rush order of Polly's record has already been shipped, so O'Hara drags Sammy with him to break all the copies of the record, and once again lands in jail. Jimmy and Mary bail them out, and Jimmy finally confesses to being the cause of all the trouble. O'Hara fires him. Mary believes that Jimmy set out to ruin O'Hara on purpose and storms out on him.

Sammy meets up with Mary at her apartment and talks her around, and the two come up with a plan to help Jimmy and O'Hara. They audition for Tommy Taylor, while Strowback is elsewhere, signing Polly. Strowback calls Taylor to say he's found "the Mystery Girl" and wants to arrange for her to sing the next time the band plays the Orchid Room; instead, Taylor arranges for Mary to sing. Upon hearing Mary at the Orchid Room, Strowback realizes he's signed the wrong girl and passes out. O'Hara takes him aside and cheerfully offers to take Polly's contract off his hands if he calls off the lawsuit, to which Strowback gratefully agrees. O'Hara takes the contract, then shows Strowback a clipping that labels Polly Kane's "Happiest Girl in Town" a comedy smash.

ANALYSIS: *Hot Rhythm* is a swiftly paced mélange of music and comedy in which Langdon mainly serves as foil for the scatterbrained Irene Ryan. Things move so quickly that on two separate occasions, Dona Drake's Mary gets angry with her would-be beau, Robert Lowrey's Jimmy, then reneges on her threat not to see him again within a few minutes' screen time. Fortunately, the actors are so appealing that most of the film's contrivances are easily overlooked.

Apart from mock frustration at Ryan's brainlessness, Langdon's big laugh moment comes when he's assisting in the recording of a commercial for "Perkins' Powder," an Alka-Seltzer-like stomach remedy. The announcer's "Just listen to it fizz" is Whiffle's cue to bring a fizzing tumbler of water to the microphone, only the powders aren't cooperating. As the announcer uncomfortably ad-libs, Whiffle empties several packets into the glass, but it's no use and he finally makes an unconvincing fizzing noise with his mouth. The over-loaded tumbler finally does fizz, but by the time Whiffle brings it up to the microphone, it's bubbling over like a churning volcano and he has to put it inside his jacket, much to his discomfort. (The announcer, incidentally, is Robert C. Bruce, better known as the narrator on most of the mock-documentary cartoons produced by Leon Schlesinger for Warner Bros.)

HARRY MOMENT: Langdon is very funny during the scene with the powders. His pantomimed nervousness is exactly right as he struggles to get the concoction to fizz. When it does, he gives a big relieved smile, until the fizzing becomes uncontrollable and he becomes nervous again while trying to quell it. Finally, when the recording is done, he passes out in the announcer's arms.

WHAT THE CRITICS SAID:
Daily Variety, *February 29, 1944*

Comedy antics of Tim and Irene (Ryan) and interesting Dona Drake give a lift to Monogram's Hot Rhythm *for okay returns as supporting material. Talent generally overcomes technical handicaps to give the material a working over for good response. Musically, the picture has five tunes. Miss Drake and Jerry Cooper handle the romantic sides while Irene Ryan makes a riot out of a comedy ditty, "The Happiest Girl in Town."*

Original script by Tim Ryan and Charles R. Marion backgrounds itself in a recording studio, offering ample opportunity for the slapstick comedy which Tim and Irene do so well...

Dona Drake sparks her assignment both vocally and in the playing. Lowery shows well in the other romantic slot. Tim and Irene knock their way around in the funning for excellent laughs. Sidney Miller has several well-done

Langdon and Tim Ryan in Hot Rhythm.

sequences. Cooper's voice registers and his straight playing shows judgment. Harry Langdon takes hold of a funny character and milks the laughs.

Hollywood Reporter, *February 29, 1944*

Hot Rhythm loads a lot of talent into a budget musical that will do very well as an attraction in its market…

Direction by William Beaudine is up to his usual smooth standard, and he makes a very pelasant thing of the romantic teaming of Dona Drake and Robert Lowery, both of whom have a great deal to offer the screen. Accent in this film, however, is heavier on the clowning roles of Tim and Irene Ryan, who repeat their sock appearances for the expected amount of audience laughs. Irene pretty well wraps up the show with her pixie Dumb Dora antics. She is the secretary who is mistaken for the mystery voice, and takes it straight because she has filled in on one of the ad jingles which she thinks is bringing all the praise for her singing.

Sidney Miller plays for a standout his brief part of the ad tunesmith. Jerry Cooper is good as a band leader, and Robert Kent serves effectively as a business agent. Harry Langdon opens promisingly as a flustered office manager, then surprisingly disappears from the latter half of the story…

All of the technical contributions are strictly okay.

Motion Picture Herald, *March 4, 1944; Reviewed by Thalia Bell*

Producer Lindsley Parsons achieved here a refreshing little comedy which is better-than-average merchandise in its bracket. Five song numbers are tuneful…Some effective comedy by Tim and Irene, and dialogue that keeps the chuckles coming brings the story to a logical and satisfactory finish with love triumphing.

William Beaudine directed with a fine sense of timing. The supporting cast of able and experienced players add polish. Harry Langdon's comedy is especially effective, as is Miss Ryan's portrayal of a temperamental executive.

Previewed at the Hawaii Theatre, Hollywood. Reviewer's Rating: Good.

Box Office, *March 11, 1944*

A pleasant little programmer, produced by Lindsley Parsons, this should do all right in its prescribed market. Film boasts four new, nice-to-listen-to tunes, capably delivered by Jerry Cooper and Dona Drake, and a ditty, "The Happiest Girl in Town," which Irene Ryan tearfully sings into a comedy bit. Most of the laughs result from the clowning of Tim and Irene with the script providing them ample opportunity for their zany antics.

Harrison's Reports, *March 11, 1944*

A typical program comedy with popular music, which should get by in theaters that cater to the followers of this type of entertainment. The story is somewhat inane, and most of the comedy is ineffective because it is forced, but the action moves along at a fast pace and it manages to be fairly amusing. Irene Ryan, as a scatterbrain secretary, provokes most of the laughs, making more of the material than what it really offers. The music is tuneful….

Morally suitable for all.

Film Daily, *March 14, 1944*

This is a pleasing modest-budget offering highlighted by the comedy antics of Tim and Irene. Irene is especially effective, scoring heavily with her singing of "The Happiest Girl in Town," by Edward Cherkose and Edward Kay.

Dona Drake, formerly with Paramount, is decorative and puts over her songs nicely, including "You Gotta Talk Me Into It, Baby," by Virginia Wicks and Nacio Herb Brown, which has had several radio plugs; "Where Were You?" by Lou Herscher, "Say It With Your Heart" and "Right Under My Nose," by Edward Cherkose and Edward Kay. Jerry Cooper also does some pleasing warbling.

Robert Lowery, Sidney Miller, Robert Kent, Jerry Cooper and Harry Langdon are among the principals who do good work. Producer Lindsley Parsons has supplied good production values, while Director William Beaudine has stressed comedy and gained a heavy quota of laughs. Charles R. Marion and Tim Ryan wrote the original screenplay…

Direction: Good, Photography: Good.

Defective Detectives

A Columbia Short Subject Released in Two Reels. PRODUCED BY Hugh McCollum. Written and DIRECTED BY Harry Edwards. PHOTOGRAPHY BY Burnett Guffey. EDITED BY Henry Batista. ART DIRECTOR: Charles Clague. CAST: El Brendel, Harry Langdon, Christine McIntyre, Vernon Dent, John Tyrrell, Eddie Laughton, Snub Pollard, Dick Botiller. Copyright March 22, 1944, Registration Number LP12551; Renewed January 3, 1972, Number R519959. Released by Columbia Pictures Corporation, April 3, 1944.

SYNOPSIS: In the Peek and Boos Detective Agency, El is scraping glass on a bureau while Harry is painting a fan. El puts the paintbrush in front of the fan and the boss is covered in paint. They are fired and leave quickly.

Rodney Boodle of the bank arrives and announces that Harry the Hacker has escaped. It seems that Boodle's testimony sent Hacker to jail and he and his gang have threatened revenge. Leena the Leech,

Hacker's girlfriend, arrives at the agency's front office. Boodle suggests to Boos that he put two men on Lena's trail. He's told that she knows all of the agency's men. Harry and El return and Boos hires them as detectives. He tells them to follow Lena to Harry the Hacker's hideout. Mrs. Boodle arrives as Lena storms out of the office. Harry and El think Mrs. Boodle is Lena, and they follow her. She meets with Boodle, and the dicks think he's Hacker and frighten him into running away. El manages to get the Boodles' address, believing it to be Hacker's. He gets stuck under a couch. Harry sits on it and is soon moved down the hall until he's dumped on the floor. Later, at the "Hacker's" apartment, Harry calls Boos for assistance with the captives. The boss wants to know how they captured the crooks. They demonstrate with a rigged club by the door, and El is knocked out by mistake. The cops arrive and a phone call announces that the agency has captured Hacker and Lena. The two "captives" are brought out and are revealed to be Mr. and Mrs. Boodle. The irate banker fires a gun at the detectives as they leap out a window.

ANALYSIS: Whatever potential Columbia expected in teaming Langdon with El Brendel is totally obscured in *Defective Detectives*. In their better days, both Langdon and Brendel were masters of gentle innocence and charm; in this film, charm is utterly absent while the two comedians fail to generate any chemistry or appeal. Perhaps because the short was intended as a showcase that would lead to features, Langdon displays a bit more life and enthusiasm than in recent shorts, but the material just isn't there; *Defective Detectives* emerges as yet another exercise in heavy-handed slapstick.

WHAT THE CRITICS SAID:
The Exhibitor, *May 17, 1944*

El Brendel and Harry Langdon, jacks of all trades, are hired as detectives to keep their eyes on the notorious Hacker and his gang, including Lensa, the leech. They follow, instead, the threatened banker and his wife, capture them after much slapstick, and have the dream of being ace detectives and heroes shattered when they learn of their mistake, and learn that police have rounded up the real bad 'uns. FAIR.

Mopey Dope

A Columbia Short Subject Released in Two Reels.
PRODUCED BY Hugh McCollum. **DIRECTED BY** Del Lord. **STORY BY** Del Lord and Ellwood Ullman. **CAST:** Harry Langdon, Christine McIntyre, Arthur Q. Bryan, Claire Rochelle, Al Thompson, Johnny Kascier. Copyright May 20, 1944, Registration Number LP12677; Renewed January 3, 1972, Number R519973. Released by Columbia Pictures Corporation, June 16, 1944.

SYNOPSIS: This film was unavailable for viewing. The following description is derived from the picture and dialogue continuities:

Louise, wife of Edwin (Harry Langdon), rises in the morning to find a birthday present on the table beside the bed. Pleased that her husband's memory problems may be improving, she wakes him, and sees that not only is his head at the foot of their bed, he's also slept in his daytime clothes. She tells him he needs to see a doctor; he explains that he's seen one but has forgotten the diagnosis.

Louise goes to the kitchen to make breakfast, while Edwin prepares for work. She finds his hat in the freezer, and throws it on the floor, where it shatters. After struggling with his suspenders, which keep getting caught on the bathroom door, he enters the kitchen, while Louise answers the telephone. Holding an egg in one hand and his watch in the other, he drops the watch into a pot of boiling water and puts the egg in his pocket. As he sits at the table, he reaches for his "watch," and crushes the egg in his pocket. Meanwhile, Louise has returned and finds the watch in the boiling water. She removes it with a spoon and places it on Edwin's plate. He finds that it has stopped and is very hot, so he opens the casing in order to wind it, and gets squirted in the face with water. He asks Louise what she did to it, and she reacts angrily.

In the apartment next door, Mr. Ryan is kissing his wife goodbye, but returns inside to answer the telephone. At the same time, Edwin is leaving his front door. Louise and Mrs. Ryan greet each other, and Louise introduces her husband. Confused, Edwin shakes hands with Louise, then kisses Mrs. Ryan goodbye just as Mr. Ryan returns. Apologetic, Edwin explains that he's absent-minded. Mr. Ryan says he's "got a cure for that," and brings back his fist to strike Edwin. Edwin ducks and Ryan strikes a lamp, which hits Edwin on the head.

Edwin decides it's too warm for the overcoat he's wearing, so he removes it; however, it turns out he's not wearing any trousers. Men and women on the street react in various ways until Edwin notices the problem. He ducks behind two mannequins dressed in menswear that are displayed in front of a store. As he does, a store detective approaches and stands

Harry's forgotten something, much to the amusement of Al Thompson and Johnny Kascier in Mopey Dope.

beside one of the mannequins. Believing it to be one of the models, Edwin pulls down the detective's pants. The detective reacts and Edwin runs off; when the detective tries to follow, he trips and falls.

Back at the duplex, Edwin mistakenly enters the Ryans' apartment. He sees a pair of trousers draped over a chair and starts to put them on, just as Mr. Ryan enters the room. Noticing Mr. Ryan, Edwin darts out the door. He picks up a potted plant from the entrance of Ryan's apartment and places it in front of his own as a sort of "marker." Giving up on chasing Edwin, Ryan notices the switch and returns the plant nearer to his own door.

Edwin returns with a bouquet of flowers for his wife, sees the plant in front of the Ryans' door and assumes this is his apartment. Inside, he cuts the flowers off and inhales the stems, then notices his mistake. He takes some flowers from a nearby vase and places them on a table in the bedroom, then enters the bathroom, intending to take a bath. Mrs. Ryan enters the bedroom and calls out her thanks for the flowers. She leaves the room just as Edwin enters it. He returns to the bathroom as Mr. Ryan enters the bedroom. He assumes his wife is in the bathroom and calls out to "her," and Edwin realizes to his horror that he's in the wrong house again. Still in his underwear, he turns on a faucet to muffle his voice, but it's hot water and he's standing in steam.

Ryan, preparing for a hunting trip, is cleaning his shotgun. Trying to leave the bathroom, Edwin sees the rifle and panics. When Ryan isn't looking, he ducks into the bed and pulls up the covers. Ryan speaks to "her" with baby talk, but Edwin is unresponsive. Hurt, Ryan leaves to retrieve clothes from his closet as Edwin sneaks off. Mrs. Ryan enters and thanks him for the flowers. Realizing his wife isn't angry with him, he heads to the kitchen to retrieve his coat from the clothesline outside. However, Edwin is hiding in the coat and tries to keep Ryan from pulling in the line. Eventually, Ryan takes in the coat and sees Edwin, who dashes outside. Ryan chases and shoots at him with his gun.

In the other apartment, Louise is telling someone on the telephone that if Edwin "isn't home in one minute, I'm leaving for good!" As Ryan continues shooting, Edwin enters through the window in his underwear.

"Honey, I'm just in time," he tells her.

"You said it," she replies, and hits him over the head with the telephone.

WHAT THE CRITICS SAID:
The Exhibitor, *June 28, 1944*

Harry Langdon is an absent-minded husband. Among many other things, he can't remember his own house. He tangles with his jealous neighbor when caught in his house without his pants. This is typical Langdon slapstick, plus lots of running around in underwear. FAIR.

Film Daily, *August 28, 1944*

This might well be classed as a modern version of silent day slapstick comedy with the same type of acting and direction. Although Harry Langdon, its star, may be the excuse for the production, certainly he is deserving of a much better break. The situations which are not only incredible, but corny and dull, have Langdon portraying an absent minded husband whose poor memory gets him in trouble with the neighbors.

Box Office, *September 9, 1944*

Harry Langdon demonstrates into what difficulties a man can fall when afflicted with absent-mindedness and a very weak memory. The situations run the gamut from confusion to contusion, the latter being more than plentiful, and poor Harry the unwilling recipient. All of the comic business will doubtless be pleasing to Langdon fans. Rating: Good.

Block Busters

A Banner Production. 60 minutes. PRODUCED BY Sam Katzman and Jack Dietz. DIRECTED BY Wallace Fox. ASSOCIATE PRODUCER: Barney Sarecky. ORIGINAL STORY AND SCREENPLAY BY Houston Branch. PHOTOGRAPHY BY Marcel LePicard. EDITED BY Carl Pierson. Sound Recorder: Harold McNiff. ASSISTANT DIRECTOR: Arthur Hammond. MUSICAL DIRECTOR: Edward Kay. CAST: Leo Gorcey, Huntz Hall, Gabriel Dell, Billy Benedict, Frederick Pressel, Jimmy Strand, Bill Chaney, Roberta Smith, Noah Beery, Sr., Harry Langdon, Minerva Urecal, Kay Marvis, Tom Herbert, Bernard Gorcey, Jack Gilman, Charles Murray, Jr., Jimmie Noone and His Orchestra, The Ashburns. Copyright July 22, 1944, Registration Number LP12749; Renewed June 15, 1972, Number R530953. Released by Monogram Pictures, Inc. August 15, 1944.

SYNOPSIS: The East Side Kids are alarmed when realtor Higgins (Harry Langdon) attempts to spruce up their neighborhood in order to impress Mrs. Rogiet, a wealthy renter. They stage a gang fight with the Five Points in an attempt to dissuade her from moving in, but it backfires, as she is a native and knows what the area is like. When her grandson, a boy named Jean who speaks with a thick French accent, criticizes Muggs on his poor aim, Muggs picks a fight. The two are arrested and brought to court, where the judge rules that, in order to prevent further fighting, he will give them each a suspended six-month sentence and make them responsible for one another's behavior: if Muggs causes trouble, Jean goes to jail, and vice versa. This prompts Jean to spend all his time with the Kids so he can keep an eye on Muggs. In an attempt to get him out of their hair, the Kids start teaching Jean all the roughest American pastimes they can think of, including boxing, wrestling, and football, but Jean excels and enjoys himself. The Kids then try crashing some parties held by Jean's family, but they just become a very popular source of entertainment to the guests. The last straw is when Jean plays shortstop for the Kids in the neighborhood baseball game and becomes a star player overnight. Muggs orders him off the team and forbids him from coming back to the club. But when the team starts losing badly at the next game, Muggs allows Jean to play. Jean hits a walk-off grand slam, and this prompts the team's grateful sponsor to send all the Kids to a mountain retreat for the summer, which benefits a sickly member of the club. The next day, Jean is officially inducted into the gang.

ANALYSIS: Fans of Leo Gorcey, Huntz Hall and the rest of the East Side Kids will probably find *Block Busters* a typically enjoyable film. Fans of Harry Langdon will not be as satisfied. As the fussy Higgins, Langdon has little to do except pontificate to the boys and attempt to convince the wealthy Mrs. Rogiet that the neighborhood is clean and populated with "lovely children." Apart from a double take or two, he isn't even given a chance to react to the disintegration of his grand scheme. Once the gang war is over, he vanishes from the film.

WHAT THE CRITICS SAID:
Daily Variety, *July 27, 1944*
Block Busters *is typical of Monogram's East Side Kids releases, which means ample return from the market in which it will play. Plot fights a losing battle with the East Siders' antics, but that make little difference since such prime muggers as Leo Gorcey, Huntz Hall, et al, need scant assistance from story in these little commercial film epics. Wallace Fox's direction gives the youngsters free rein and Barney Sarecky's associate producer duties takes suitable care of the mounting.*

Plot, whenever it manages to intrude for a losing fight, concerns the Americanizing of a rich, European-raised youth, plus a side plot dealing with the raising of funds to send a sick boy to the country for a month. He wants to play baseball again. On that basis, Gorcey and his cohorts run through their standard shenanigans, seemingly ad-libbing for a fare-you-well and pleasing the paying customers when reviewed.

Such regular members of the East Side screen ventures as Gabriel Dell, Billy Benedict, etc., are present. Minerva Urecal, Roberta Smith, Noah Beery, Sr., Kay Marvis, Fred Pressel, good as the rich boy, Harry Langdon, with a nice bit, Jimmy Strand, Bill Chaney and others turn in okay work.

Marcel LePicard's photography was just fair.

Film Daily, *August 14, 1944*
Leo Gorcey's delivery of "Malapropian" dialogue is the highlight of this latest East Side Kids effort. Some due consideration on stronger, credible story material could do much to build further and keep the combination intact.

Huntz Hall and Gabriel Dell add their "Dead End" talents in easy, humorous style.

Direction: Fair, Photography: Fair.

Box Office, *August 19, 1944*
The East Side Kids lend their exuberant talents to the latest vehicle devoted to their escapades, and in their earthy style, provide exhibitors with a satisfactory film for the supporting spot in double bills. Had the script writers been more generous with their better situations, and discarded some of the old wheezes which unfortunately crop up from time to time, the entire film might have gone better. After hearing Leo Gorcey, the leader of the Kids, mutilate some of the English language, there is no doubt that subtleties and refinements of speech and manner are not the strong points of the boys. Nevertheless, the younger element will find much amusement in the film, and the adults will marvel at the change in the younger generation. Slanted towards the youngsters, the film should do all right at the box office.

Snooper Service

A Columbia Short Subject Released in Two Reels. **PRODUCED BY** Hugh McCollum. **DIRECTED BY** Harry Edwards. **STORY BY** Harry Edwards. **CAST:** El Brendel, Harry Langdon, Rebel Randall, Dick Curtis, Vernon Dent, Fred Kelsey, Buddy Yarus. Copyright February 2, 1945, Registration Number LP13141; Renewed May 19, 1972, Number R529208. Released by Columbia Pictures Corporation, February 4, 1945.

SYNOPSIS: This film was unavailable for viewing. The following description is derived from the picture and dialogue continuities:

El and Harry have opened a detective agency. Harry is painting the sign ("ONE SCENT DETECTIVE AGENCY. I. SNIFF U. SNUFF — WE SMELL TROUBLE") on a piece of cellophane placed over the desk, during which he accidentally paints El's eye shut. After cleaning off, El tries to attach the cellophane to the glass on their office door by using a hammer; he breaks the glass and strikes Harry on the head. While they're placing the sign, Horace and his son, Frank, are walking down the hall toward their office, and are introduced to "Sniff" and "Snuff."

In his office, Horace sees that Frank has purchased a fancy negligee and learns that his son is serious about a young woman. He gives his son some money from a wad of bills, totaling $500. However, when he learns that his son is planning to wed a showgirl named Maisie LaBelle, Horace objects strenuously and demands that Frank break the engagement. Frank agrees, but surreptitiously takes the roll of bills from his father and leaves.

Horace decides to hire Harry and El to "romance" Maisie in order to show his son that she is the wrong kind of woman. When he enters their office, Harry is typing and gets his fingers tangled up in the ribbon. Horace explains what he wants and gives them Maisie's address. He offers to pay them $500 in advance and discovers that his bankroll is missing. El and Harry search his pockets thoroughly, as well as each other's pockets, and then push him onto the

Langdon had been dead for about six weeks when this film was released, hence the absence of his name on this lobby card.

couch and proceed to remove his clothing. El even pulls a medicinal plaster from Horace's back. Horace tells them he'll pay by check in the morning; he then leaves, wearing only undergarments.

At the hotel, Frank has given Maisie a fancy robe and cash, and tells her it's from his father. She wants to call and thank him, but Frank discourages her: "Dad'll drop in tonight. He'll tell you then what

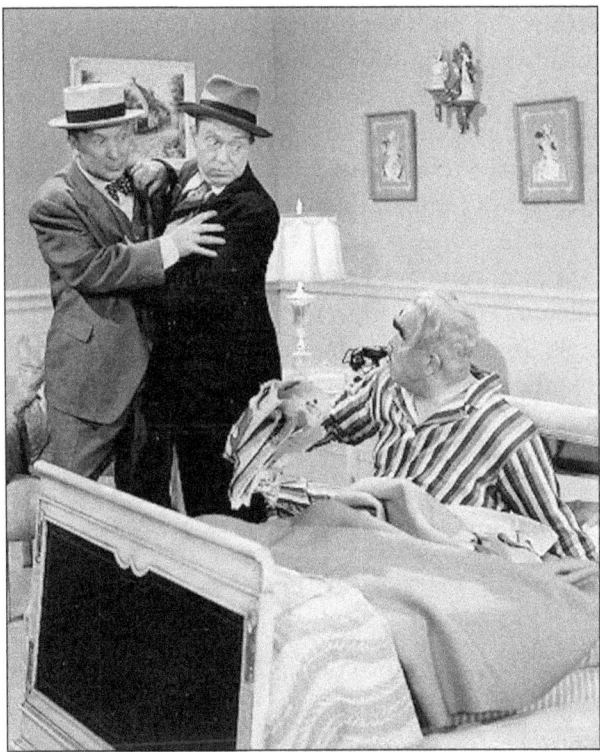

Fred Kelsey, in one of his few non-cop roles, is rudely awakened by Harry and El in Snooper Service.

he thinks of you." She insists, and he lunges for the phone but trips and knocks over Maisie, who screams and drops the phone on Frank's head.

El and Harry arrive at the hotel and argue about which floor and room they're supposed to investigate. They try El's suggestion first, and El produces a skeleton key to open the door. In the bedroom, an old man has fallen asleep in bed while reading a newspaper, which covers his face. Harry and El enter the room and proceed to snuggle up next to the man, professing their love to "her." The old man awakens and sees Harry and El. In their scramble to get out of his room, the bed collapses.

Next, they try Harry's suggested room. El opens the door with his skeleton key. This time there is a woman present, Gertrude, who runs into the bathroom and hides behind the shower curtain. Harry and El chase after her, and Harry helps El try to get through the transom above the door. At that moment, Mickey, her husband, enters and sees the two. Harry runs off, leaving El stuck in the transom, and Mickey grabs El's legs and starts twisting them. El kicks Mickey away, and breaks loose. After some commotion, Mickey finds Harry hiding in a closet. Harry hands him a coat hanger and runs off. Mickey and Gertrude argue about why the two were there.

The third room they try is that of Joe and Flo, another romantic couple. Horace leads Frank to this room, and overhears Joe sweet-talking Flo, while Maisie spies from her real room. They barge in. Horace flings Joe away, where he lands on the bed, under which Harry and El are hiding. Eventually, Joe discovers them under the bed, grabs a baseball bat, and a mad chase ensues. During the chase, Frank and Maisie slip away to elope, suitcases in hand. Finally, Joe corners Harry and Horace, but El grabs the bat and knocks him down, so the three can escape.

WHAT THE CRITICS SAID:
The Exhibitor, *March 21, 1945*

El Brendel and Harry Langdon form a detective agency. When they are engaged by an irate father to frame a showgirl in whom his son is interested, they botch it up by breaking into the wrong apartment and getting chased all over the place by a jealous husband. FAIR.

Box Office, *March 24, 1945*

Harry Langdon and El Brendel go through their usual antics. This time they have formed a detective agency and when they are engaged to get the goods on a show girl proceed to get things in a state of complete confusion. They get the address mixed up and the resultant scraps as they go about breaking into the wrong apartments provides the action for this rather weak film. Rating: Mediocre.

Film Daily, *April 2, 1945*

A labored comedy, this short pairing El Brendel and Harry Langdon is a slapstick item offering no new material. Definitely the film is not entertainment for intelligent persons. Brendel and Langdon are seen as a couple of bungling private detectives hired to gather dope on a show gal. They cause themselves plenty of trouble by forcing their way into places where they shouldn't be.

Pistol Packin' Nitwits

A Columbia Short Subject Released in Two Reels. PRODUCED BY Hugh McCollum. DIRECTED BY Harry Edwards. SCREENPLAY BY Harry Edwards. STORY BY Edward Bernds and Harry Langdon. PHOTOGRAPHY BY L.W. O'Connell. EDITED BY Henry Batista. ART DIRECTOR: Jerome Pycha, Jr. CAST: Harry Langdon, El Brendel, Christine McIntyre, Brad King, Dick Curtis, Tex Cooper, Victor Cox, Charles "Heine" Conklin. WORKING TITLES: "Out Vest," "Tenderfeet." Copyright April 4, 1945, Registration Number LP13538; Renewed June 14, 1972, Number R532250. Released by Columbia Pictures Corporation, April 4, 1945.

SYNOPSIS: In Hangman's Gulch, Nevada, Harry and El approach Queenie's Place, a local saloon. They are soap salesmen and witness gunplay by Rawhide Pete and his gang. Harry thinks a celebration is going on, so he lights a firecracker. The explosion causes their horse to scamper away. Later, Harry puts soap on the axle of a wagon wheel in preparation for their pitch. He plays the banjo as "Professor" Brendel makes his spiel to the crowd. They pick Rawhide Pete as a subject to show the effectiveness of their soap. He says he doesn't have any stains on his clothes, and the professor gets some "axle grease" for a wagon wheel. He doesn't realize that the original wagon has left and he's getting real grease. The salesmen rub the grease on Pete's shirt and fail to remove it with their efforts. Rawhide goes berserk with anger, and Queenie, the saloon's owner, orders the hapless salesmen into the bar. She hires them to help run the joint. Later, Pete arrives and has a triple bourbon. Harry and the professor then do a dance while each alternates playing the piano. Pete tells Queenie that if she doesn't marry him by that evening, he is going to foreclose on the saloon. She refuses, and a handsome cowboy named Jack knocks Pete to the floor. Queenie tells him she needs $2,500; he promises to get the money by 12:00.

Later, Pete and his cronies are drinking in the saloon. Harry tells Queenie to entertain Pete and his gang; it seems he has an idea. She sings a sad ballad, and the patrons are moved by her delivery. Harry then introduces the professor, whom he says can hit harder than a mule can kick. El hits a "Test Your Punch" machine and beats Pete's record. Pete then punches the machine and gets his hand stuck inside. Harry

and El appear to lift the mortgage paper from Pete's coat, but it's an ad for Sunflower cough syrup. A bee flies down Pete's collar, and his cronies remove his coat. Harry and El retrieve the mortgage and Pete begins to shoot up the saloon. Cowboy Jack arrives and shoots the guns out of Pete's hands. Jack bests Pete in a fight and as he kisses Queenie, he fires his pistol, causing Harry and El to run away.

A weary Harry poses with Dick Curtis. Publicity still for Pistol Packin' Nitwits.

ANALYSIS: *Pistol Packin' Nitwits* is an over-the-top western parody. It explodes practically every cliché known to the genre: the tough female saloon owner with a heart of gold, the villain who holds the mortgage on the place, the handsome hero who saves the day, and Harry and El as a couple of tenderfeet who go to work in the saloon. A running gag has the film periodically cutting to Jack, the hero, riding to the rescue to the strains of "The William Tell Overture," which was, of course, the theme to radio's *The Lone Ranger*. However, the cuts appear at ridiculous moments, such as in the middle of Queenie's song, and last for exactly one bar of music! Another absurd touch is that Jack seems to be Superman: bullets bounce off of him (while he stands with chest thrust forward, smiling) and objects are smashed over his head, with no impact.

Langdon and Brendel do some nice work; the film is much more agreeable than their previous two. As a pair of traveling soap salesmen, Harry plays banjo while El goes into his sales pitch. Later, the two perform a soft-shoe routine. For the most part, Langdon is the straight man, formulating plans that are thwarted either by circumstance or his pal's stupidity. As the simpleton of the team, Brendel and his Swedish malapropisms carry the comedy load, while Rawhide Pete endures most of the slapstick indignities.

HARRY MOMENT: Harry and El do a cute soft-shoe routine, each one taking a turn dancing while the other plays the piano. Although not laugh-out-loud funny, it's amusing and showcases the versatility and charm of both men. If, as Mabel Langdon asserted, this was the last scene in which Harry would ever play, it's fitting that he ended his career as he began it: performing comedy, music and dance with a partner.

WHAT THE CRITICS SAID:
The Exhibitor, *April 4, 1945*

El Brendel and Harry Langdon, two phoney soap peddlers, arrive in a wild and wooley western town only to have the tables turned on them when they try to sell their soap, and they are forced to go to work in a saloon owned by a boisterous blonde. When a villain asks the proprietress to marry him, she refuses, and he threatens to foreclose unless she can come through with the necessary cash. While her lover rides off to seek the cash, Brendel and Langdon stall the villain, until the lover returns to throw the would-be-saloon owner off the premises. FAIR.

Box Office, *April 28, 1945*

El Brendel and Harry Langdon go through their paces in a real old-fashioned western complete with villain, mortgage, frightened heroine and handsome hero who arrives in time to save the day. The two comedians are bartenders in a smoke-and-gunshot filled saloon of the early West. Lots of down-to-earth horseplay in this. Rating: Amusing.

Swingin' On A Rainbow

A Republic Production. 72 minutes. **PRODUCED BY** Eddy White. **DIRECTED BY** William Beaudine. **STORY BY** Olive Cooper. **SCREENPLAY BY** Olive Cooper and John Grey. **PHOTOGRAPHY BY** Marcel LePicard. **EDITED BY** Fred Allen. **MUSICAL DIRECTOR:** Morton Scott. Art Directors: Russell Kimball and Gano Chittenden. Sound by Tom Carman. CAST: Jane Frazee, Brad Taylor, Harry Langdon, Minna Gombell, Amelia Ward, Paul Harvey, Tim Ryan, Wendell Niles, Richard Davies, Helen Talbot. WORKING TITLE: "Moonlight and Roses." Copyright July 27, 1945, Registration Number LP13424; Renewed March 29, 1973, Number R548957. Released by Republic Pictures, Inc., August 27, 1945.

SYNOPSIS: Lynn Ford, an aspiring composer who works for a small radio station in Nebraska, has submitted an original song to bandleader Jimmy Rhodes, part of the latter's weekly contest in which winning compositions are played on the air for a $1,000 prize. The "contest" is actually just a publicity stunt, and Lynn has received a rejection letter, but then she hears her tune on the program. She withdraws her savings and heads to New York to confront Rhodes. He refuses to see her, and his manager, Huston Greer, takes him out of town. As he is leaving, however, she gets Rhodes's autograph on a piece of paper by posing as a fan. She then forges a letter above his signature that will introduce her as his niece, enabling her to use his apartment while he's away. There, she gets into a wall-pounding feud with her neighbor, aspiring lyricist Steve Ames.

Meanwhile, an advertising man prepares a radio program for Minnie Regan, the owner of "Lady Minerva's Beauty Aids," for which Jimmy Rhodes is to provide music. The show's star vocalist, Barbara Marsden — who is also the ad man's daughter — has designs on Ames and insists he be hired as lyricist. Her agent, Chester Willoby (Harry Langdon), calls at Rhodes's apartment to pick up the music, and discovers Lynn in the midst of a wall-pounding argument with Ames. Lynn pretends she is Rhodes's collaborator, and gives him her own compositions. Aware that her annoying neighbor is the program's lyricist, Willoby resolves to keep them from meeting. Later on, though, they meet at the radio station to work on the program. Not realizing each is the other's noisy neighbor, romance blooms, much to the annoyance of Barbara Marsden. Eventually, Lynn discovers that Ames is her neighbor; fearful of losing him if he finds this out, she avoids him while at the apartment.

It isn't long before Jimmy Rhodes discovers that "his" songs are being used on the Lady Minerva program, and he rushes back to New York to investigate. He learns about his "niece and collaborator," and heads to his apartment, but Lynn manages an escape. She rushes to the radio station, with Rhodes in hot pursuit. There, both Ames and Minnie Regan want her to sing on the show in place of Barbara. Rhodes arrives just as Lynn goes on the air, and as he hears the songs, he decides they are good. By the time the show ends, Rhodes forgets his anger and sees to it that Lynn gets the $1,000 prize, while Ames sees to it that she gets him.

ANALYSIS: *Swingin' on a Rainbow* is another bargain-basement musical in the same vein as *Spotlight Scandals* and *Hot Rhythm*, although it lacks Monogram's penchant for swiftness. Republic had hoped to build vocalist Jane Frazee as a musical star along the lines of Universal's Gloria Jean, but within a year she'd be fulfilling the balance of her contract as Roy Rogers's leading lady, before moving on to supporting roles in television. (Baby Boomers know her best as the lady farmer who gives an amnesiac Clark Kent a ride to Metropolis after Superman's initial encounter with a deadly asteroid, in the *Adventures of Superman* episode "Panic in the Sky.") Langdon, playing his eccentric milquetoast character, has a few amusing moments thrown his way, particularly when contending with the feud between Frazee and Brad Taylor as unseen neighbors, but once again a mustache detracts from his expressive face.

WHAT THE CRITICS SAID:
Film Daily, *August 17, 1945*

No better than mild entertainment is delivered by this mixture of comedy, music and romance. As directed by William Beaudine, Swingin' on a Rainbow *moves at a feverish pace, and tries awfully hard to be diverting, but its story has been weakly developed, the acting is indifferent in most instances and the production is more or less haphazard. Family audiences in the smaller houses are the ones who will find this film to their taste…*

The music is routine and the picture's attempts to be funny often miss fire, a failing due in a measure of the direction.

Direction: So-so, Photography: Okay.

Variety, *August 29, 1945*

Story line is a complicated but unamusing affair about a girl who tries to collect $1,000 from a bandleader who has plagiarized her song. He leaves town to dodge her; she bluffs her way into living in his apartment during his absence. Here she also carries on a banging-on-the-wall feud with a neighbor with whom, she is then unaware, she's been collaborating on songs. Jane Frazee is satisfactory, but, with script being what it is, few others have a chance. Film looks lightly budgeted.

Box Office, *September 1, 1945*

It took a lot of formula to string together two catchy songs, which latter, incidentally, are the picture's sole claim to praise. All other phases of the vertiginous procedure are hopelessly handicapped from scratch by the story, which abounds in clichés and corny comedy. Against such odds, a willing, hard-working cast is helpless, as is the impressive production mountings with which the effort was endowed. Fortunately, the offering was designed for second picture spotting and in that position it may slide by in most theatres.

Harrison's Reports, *September 1, 1945*

Just a moderately entertaining program comedy with music. Here and there it has situations that will provoke laughs, but for the most part the comedy, some of it slapstick, is so forced that it fails to make much of an impression. In its favor are the tuneful songs and the swift-moving pace, as well as the very pleasant singing of Jane Frazee. The story, which revolves around Miss Frazee's efforts to outwit an unscrupulous bandleader who had plagiarized one of her songs, is rather complicated and contrived, but it will probably amuse audiences that are not too hard to please.…

Unobjectionable morally.

Brooklyn Daily Eagle, *September 20, 1945; Reviewed by Jane Corby*

Swingin' on a Rainbow *shares the new Strand program with* Why Girls Leave Home, *and between them the two films provide the customers with a lot of musical entertainment.* Swingin' on a Rainbow, *having its first metropolitan run here, is a Republic picture, with Jane Frazee, Brad Taylor and the late Harry Langdon.*

Jane Frazee helps Langdon with his tie between scenes for Swingin' on a Rainbow. *Most newspapers received this rare publicity photo a few days after Langdon's passing.*

Miss Frazee has a big stint to do, for besides carrying the main acting role she also sings several songs. She tops the rest of the cast on both counts, and is much better than the story she has to work with. However, with Langdon's comedy and Taylor's romancing to assist her, she succeeds in making a familiar type of plot seem almost new.

New York Post, *September 20, 1945; Reviewed by Irene Thirer*

Swingin' on a Rainbow *is the very minor musical from Republic which now is having its local premiere at the Brooklyn Strand.*

Best thing about it is the score — especially the tunes "Wrap Up Your Troubles in a Rainbow" and "Music in Your Heart," which pretty Jane Frazee renders in pleasant torchy tones. Otherwise, it's a foolish and implausible screen session, hardly worth the footage it takes to unreel its slapstick action. Jane is cast as Lynn Ford, a composer-warbler whose song is stolen by a big-shot radio bandsman. She journeys all the way from Bellflower, Nebraska, to New York to speak up for her rights. But Jimmy Rhodes (Richard Davies) won't see her — in spite of her threatened suit for plagiarism.

When she learns of his departure for a couple of weeks, she inveigles her way into his apartment and remains housed there for the time being, posing as his niece. That's how she meets up with the representative (the late Harry Langdon) of a big advertising agency who comes calling on Jimmy with a program offer and is convinced by the gal that she's the great Rhodes's femme collaborator. When she plays some tunes for the sponsor, she's requested to work with a certain lyricist named Steve Ames (Brad Taylor), current flame of the gal who'll star on the new air show.

Since Lynn and Steve are next-door neighbors — he occupies apartment 803; she's (Jimmy) 801, and they're both, no doubt, good 802'rs — you'd think they'd get together easily. But they don't. This adds further complication to the plot which is at its thickest, of course, when Jimmy Rhodes returns from his little trip.

Langdon was the credited director, but did not appear in, the following:

Wise Guys

A Fox-British Production. 83 minutes. PRODUCED BY Ivor MacLaren. DIRECTED BY Harry Langdon. ORIGINAL STORY BY Alison Booth. SCREENPLAY BY David Evans. CAST: Charlie Naughton, Jimmy Gold, Andrene Brier, Robert Nainby, Walter Roy, Sydney Keith, David Keir. Released August 1937.

SYNOPSIS: This film was unavailable for viewing. Following is the plot description given in the *Monthly Film Bulletin* of the British Film Institute:

Phineas Macnaughton, wishing to retire, decides to trace his relatives and hand over to them the family business. His two nephews, Charlie and Jimmy, living in London and very hard up, see his advertisement and go to the races determined to make enough money to go to Edinburgh. On the course they pick up a sweepstake ticket dropped by an American girl, Flo. She and her tough friend, Eddy, also see the advertisement and Flo decides to become a Macnaughton temporarily and succeeds in convincing old Phineas that she is a genuine claimant. Charlie and Jimmy arrive eventually, but before they can take over the business they find that they must deposit a 500 pound fidelity bond. By many devices they try to raise money, but one of them misfires and Uncle Phineas orders them out. They then clash with Flo and Eddy over the ticket, which proves to be a winning one. That settled, they proceed back to London on foot.

WHAT THE CRITICS SAID:
Monthly Film Bulletin of the British Film Institute, *August 1937*

Knockabout farce. The various episodes of the film strung on the slender theme of securing Uncle Phineas's fortune are amusing, being turns complete in themselves. The direction is good, and some of the backgrounds are excellent — as for example the crowd and bookies at the races. The acting is good, Naughton and Gold giving their usual expressive performances and being well supported by the rest of the cast.

Langdon was a credited writer, but did not appear in, the following:

Block-Heads

A Hal Roach Production. 55 minutes. DIRECTED BY John G. Blystone. SCREENPLAY BY James Parrott, Harry Langdon, Felix Adler, Charles Rogers, Arnold Belgard. PHOTOGRAPHY BY Art Lloyd. CAST: Stan Laurel, Oliver Hardy, Billy Gilbert, Patricia Ellis, James Finlayson, Minna Gombell, Harry Woods, Harry Stubbs, William Royle. Working titles: "Meet the Missus," "Just a Jiffy." Copyright August 17, 1938, Registration Number LP8463; Renewed December 2, 1965, Number R374810. Released by Metro-Goldwyn-Mayer, Inc., August 19, 1938.

SYNOPSIS: Fighting in No-Man's Land in 1918, Stan and Ollie's platoon will soon be going over the top. Stan is requested to remain in the trench and guard his position, which he does — for the next 20 years. When he guns down a private flyer, it is discovered that he was never told the war was over.

The story makes the news and Ollie hears about it. He visits Stan at the Soldiers' Home and invites him to his apartment for a meal. After a mishap involving the car and an automatic garage door, Ollie brings Stan inside, where his wife strenuously objects to Stan's presence. Husband and wife quarrel, and she leaves in a huff. Ollie attempts to cook their dinner himself, but makes a mess of things, and his neighbor, Mrs. Gilbert, offers to help. However, her jealous husband returns home early from a hunting trip, which complicates matters, as does the return of the penitent Mrs. Hardy.

WHAT THE CRITICS SAID:
Film Daily, *August 19, 1938*

Those who like the Laurel and Hardy type of slapstick will find this 55 minutes of enjoyable fun. The boys have made two-reelers like it, but this offering has a greater number of gags. As a pleasant piece of diversion on the program, it should take care of its spot nicely. A capable cast supports the boys. Billy Gilbert, with his German dialect, has a good part as does Minna Gombell as Hardy's argumentative gabby wife. Patricia Ellis and James Finlayson have lesser roles. John Blystone, the director, paced the piece well.

As associate producer, Hal Roach, Jr., handled his first production most capably. The main purpose of the plot is to serve as a medium to work the gags. In 1918, Hardy, Laurel's army buddy, goes over the top. Laurel is left behind to guard the vacated trench and twenty years later he is still there, when he shoots down a passing airplane, whose pilot tells him the war is over. Returning home, Laurel and Hardy renew their friendship, which nearly breaks up Hardy's household. The end has the boys dashing away from a scrape with Billy Gilbert, the husband of the woman in the case, hot after them with a shotgun.

Direction: Well-paced, Photography: Good.

Box Office, *August 20, 1938*

Infinitely better than their last effort, Laurel and Hardy turn in a job which should be a field day for their fans and at the same time deliver value received in abdominal guffaws for all customers. The past masters of slapstick return to the tried and true tricks in which they formerly specialized and, additionally, give out with a fair measure of bright, new gags. The result is a short and snappy feature which more closely resembles their earlier and more widely acclaimed pictures and which should enjoy proportionate patronage. John G. Blystone's unusual understanding direction contributes a large measure to the feature's speed. Buddies during the war, Stan and Oliver are reunited after 20 years to get into more trouble than normally comes in a lifetime.

Ollie assures Stanley, "We'll all be back!" in this Langdon-inspired scene from Block-Heads.

New York Herald-Tribune, *August 1938; Reviewed by R.W.D.*

The fine Italian hand of Harry Langdon is discernable in the latest Laurel and Hardy feature-length film at the Rialto. Langdon, who in his heyday was undoubtedly a greater comedian than either the sad-faced man or the fat fellow ever could be, helps to create a comic tour-de-force which lifts this offering well above the entertainment level of the recent Swiss Miss. Block-Heads is, pardonably enough, a film without a point, unless it is to massage the spectator's stomach muscles, so the other four authors may breathe freely with Mr. Langdon.

New York Post, *August 30, 1938; Reviewed by Irene Thirer*

Block-Heads *is the Laurel and Hardy swansong. Henceforth it will be Langdon and Hardy — or maybe Hardy and Langdon, giving Ollie lead billing over Harry on account of his lengthy association with Producer Hal Roach and the exiting Stanley.*

They were working on Block-Heads *during our recent tour of the Hollywood studios. At that time, all seemed serene between the dead-pan comic and his rotund playmate. Just proves you never can tell what's going on behind the scenes. We're sorry they're washed up as a team but welcome back to frozen-faced Harry Langdon, and here's hoping the initial Langdon-Hardy opus will be worthier than* Block-Heads.

At best, the Rialto's current offering is a stretched-out two-reeler, with insufficient gags to keep it amusing for a full hour, and hardly a smattering of a plot to hang the gags together.... One bit we fell for particularly: Laurel and Hardy are forced to climb thirteen flights of stairs when the apartment-house elevator doesn't work. At each landing Stan pulls down the shadow of a window shade by its string. On one flight it flings itself up again — the shadow, yes! Sorry, but there aren't enough such laugh moments to make Block-Heads *better than passing fairly funny.*

Hollywood Film Archive, *September 1, 1938*

An overlong two-reeler, this has about the same measure, type of fun, slapstick, in the Laurel-Hardy style. It depends on their draw. Story has Hardy find his long lost war-time buddy, Laurel, bring him home to enjoy mean by "loving wife" Minna Gombell, a typical shrew. Gombell blows up, leaves; the pair try to cook their own meals. The kitchen stove blows up; Patricia Ellis, the neighbor, tries to help them clean up; Gombell returns; they try to hide Ellis; then Gilbert, Ellis's husband, who is a big game hunter, arrives as the boys try to lug out a trunk, in which sits Ellis. Gilbert finds her in the trunk, runs for his elephant gun, chases them, the picture ends.

Estimate: Routine Laurel-Hardy.

Harrison's Reports, *September 10, 1938*

A good slapstick comedy. It is filled with gags, both old and new, some of which are extremely comical. From the first scene, which shows Laurel guarding a trench for twenty years without realizing that the war was over, to the last one, the picture offers situations that keep the audience laughing throughout. As a matter of fact, some of the scenes are so comical that one does not have to be a Laurel-Hardy fan to enjoy them....

Suitability: Class A.

Cleveland Plain Dealer, *October 12, 1938; Reviewed by Glenn C. Pullen*

This is not only the last picture made by Laurel and Hardy, who have split, but it also marks the once-famous team's final appearance under Producer Hal Roach, whose comedies gave them too much money and domestic dissension.

Their swan-song movie shown by Loew's Granada is a fairly amusing farce with a two-reel plot that was stretched to the limit by five gagsmiths. When that many writers get together, the results are bound to be rather thin and daffy and slapstick in humor, with more knock-'em-down action than coherence.

Here the pudgy Oliver Hardy and thin Stan Laurel, who has been replaced by Harry Langdon, revive the classic gag about a henpecked husband who brings an unbidden guest home. Hardy this time is married to the grim and husky Minna Gombell, who quickly shows Stan he isn't welcome.

Between these domestic battles the two clown with shotguns, a water hose and smash an auto to pieces. Brightest fun revolves around the episode in which Hardy mistakes Laurel for a mained, one-legged victim of the war. Billy Gilbert as a jealous bombastic big-game hunter and Patricia Ellis as his wife are of service in adding laughs to some of the nuttiest moments.

WHAT THE EXHIBITORS SAID:
Motion Picture Herald, *September 24, 1938*

For slapstick I guess this is about as good as you'll find. Kids loved it and though adults had little comment, they laughed long and heartily.
James I. Denham, Rex Theatre, Port Lavaca, TX. General patronage.

Without a doubt the best in some time from these boys. Sorry to hear it'll be their last. The house was in one big uproar from start to finish and everyone went out laughing. Finish of picture rather abrupt, otherwise fine for us little town boys.
A. E. Eliasen Rialto Theatre, Paynesville, MN.
Small town and rural patronage.

Motion Picture Herald, *October 1, 1938*
The usual Laurel & Hardy comedy that they all seem to like. Personally, I think it is zero in entertainment, but the patrons like them.
Gladys E. McArdle, Owl Theatre, Lebanon, KS.
Small town patronage.

Motion Picture Herald, *October 8, 1938*
Out of the ordinary Saturday night business and audience in an uproar. Why anybody would knock this picture we cannot understand. It has its place and wish we could buy more of them.
C. L. Niles, Niles Theatre, Anamose, IA.
General patronage.

Laurel and Hardy are still popular around here. Too bad they plan to break up.
Floyd Faubion, Long's Theatre, Angleton, TX.
General patronage.

Motion Picture Herald, *October 29, 1938*
Played this comedy riot on Merchant Night and it seemed to give the bargain hunters what they wanted, plenty of laughs. I for one am sorry this team has split up.
C. R. Greeg, Liberty Theatre, Caney, KS.
Small town patronage.

Motion Picture Herald, *November 5, 1938*
It is remarkable the thin stories that Metro builds these comedies on and the business that they do. There just doesn't seem to more than a two-reel comedy material. This one dragged terribly and yet they ate it up.
A. E. Hancock, Columbia Theatre, Columbia City, IN.
General patronage.

Not a big picture but it pleased those who like this type of broad comedy. Average business.
E. M. Freiburger, Paramount Theatre, Dewey, OK.
Small town patronage.

Motion Picture Herald, *November 12, 1938*
Dandy Laurel and Hardy. Will make a live man laugh. The best I have seen them in in a long while. No matter what they say, here's a good one, and McPhee knows.
W. E. McPhee, Strand Theatre, Old Town, ME.
General patronage.

Motion Picture Herald, *November 19, 1938*
The answer to a showman's prayer. Excellent box office, and less slapstick than usual made this the best Laurel and Hardy we have played. Minna Gombell and Billy Gilbert were excellent in their parts. All in all just a good show.
A. J. Inks, Crystal Theatre, Ligonier, IN.
Small town patronage.

Motion Picture Herald, *December 3, 1938*
I disagree with you, Mr. Inks of the Crystal Theatre. This wasn't any showman's prayer, at least to me. I will agree with you, though, and say it was a good Laurel and Hardy picture. But upon second thought, pardon me, Mr. Inks, maybe your prayer was different from mine. Would you be good enough to inform me what your prayer was? We played this one on a double feature and did a nice little business, that because our feature was Metro's *The Crowd Roars* with Robert Taylor, but alone, when I played in Schroon Lake, NY, it flopped. I will end the way you did, too, Mr. Inks. All in all, just a good show.
Pearce Parkhurst, State Theatre, Torrington, CT.
General patronage.

Motion Picture Herald, *December 17, 1938*
Double billed this with *Meet the Girls* and did under average business. A bunch of good shorts with either of these would have made a far better combination. We're glad this pair is through at MGM.
Horn and Morgan, Inc., Star Theatre, Hay Springs, NE.
Small town patronage.

Motion Picture Herald, *January 24, 1939*
Had a full house on this picture. If that is what the people want, make more of them. Some people like spinach.
A. H. Records, Majestic Theatre, Hebron, NE
Rural patronage.

Motion Picture Herald, *April 1, 1939.*

Absolutely the weakest picture I ever saw. There weren't any laughs in the entire picture. The worst Laurel and Hardy ever made.
Leon C. Boldue, Majestic Theatre, Conway, NH. General patronage.

Motion Picture Herald, *April 22, 1939*

This comedy has its moments, and when it got funny there were plenty of good old belly laughs. Sorry to see this team split up because they have made some good comedies. Swell for your weekend double bill and I'd say play it.
Mayme O. Musselman, Princess Theatre, Lincoln, KS. Small town patronage.

Motion Picture Herald, *May 6, 1939*

This okay fun. Pleased generally. Sorry to see them split up.
L. A. Irwin, Palace Theatre, Penacock, NH. General patronage.

The Flying Deuces

A Boris Morros Production. 69 minutes. **PRODUCED BY** Boris Morros. **DIRECTED BY** A. Edward Sutherland. **SCREENPLAY BY** Ralph Spence, Harry Langdon, Charles Rogers and Alfred Schiller. **PHOTOGRAPHY BY** Art Lloyd and Elmer Dyer. **EDITED BY** Jack Dennis. **CAST**: Stan Laurel, Oliver Hardy, Jean Parker, Reginald Gardiner, Charles Middleton, James Finlayson, Jean Del Val, Clem Wilenchick. **WORKING TITLE**: "Deuces Wild." Copyright November 3, 1939, Registration Number LP9209. Released by R.K.O. Radio Pictures, Inc., October 14, 1939.

SYNOPSIS: The boys are in Paris, and Ollie is deeply smitten by Georgette, the daughter of their innkeeper. When he learns she already has a sweetheart, he is crestfallen and decides to end it all. He opts to jump in the Seine with a boulder tied to him, and he fully expects Stan to join him. Stan, however, is not so eager to die. Before they can finish the fatal task, Francois, an officer, arrives and encourages Ollie to forget his heartache by joining the Foreign Legion. Stan and Ollie do so, but find circumstances not to their liking and decide to leave. For this, they are put on laundry duty. Soon Georgette visits the camp, and Ollie tries once more to woo her, much to the chagrin of Francois, who is her sweetheart. He and Stan are placed under arrest and sentenced to execution. To escape their fate, they commandeer an airplane, which they are ill-equipped to fly.

WHAT THE CRITICS SAID:
Film Daily, *October 10, 1939*

Laurel and Hardy's newest picture is full of laughs and should be popular with lovers of comedy everywhere. It has much fresh material and some sequences that should score in any theater. It has been given splendid direction by Edward Sutherland, who has injected several whimsical touches. The picture marks an auspicious debut for Boris Morros as a producer and he, no doubt, had a hand in some of the novel melodic quartet material provided Laurel and Hardy. A quartet of writers — Ralph Spence, Alfred Schiller, Charles Rogers and Harry Langdon — wrote the original story and screenplay. John Leipold and Lee Shuken furnished the musical score and Edward Paul functioned as musical director. One of the funniest and most original gags ever screened has Laurel converting a prison cot bedspread into a harp and playing it à la Harpo Marx. Another sequence has Laurel and Hardy doing a song and dance.

Direction: Splendid, Photography: Very Good.

Box Office, *October 14, 1939*

Laurel and Hardy employ every reliable, time-tested gag in their bag of slapstick tricks in this, the initial Boris Morros production venture, and add a few new ones besides. The moderately entertaining result would be vastly more amusing with the elimination of several draggy sequences. The picture's best market will be with the kids and the confirmed comedy fans, but its slender story — merely a framework for the Laurel-Hardy antics — mark it as only average merchandise for general audience consumption.

Hollywood Film Archive, *October 18, 1939*

While this one contains a couple of new gags, it is more or less a rubber-stamp effort of the comedians' past screen antics…The usual Laurel and Hardy pantomime still seems to have an audience appeal. Especially funny is the final airplane sequence that ends in Hardy's ascension as an angel, and his transmigration back to earth as a mule, the mule displaying a Hardy mustache and derby. Jean Parker, as the girl, Georgette, gives the one legitimate touch to the offering and plays with her usual charm and sincerity. In the final analysis, it is typical Laurel and Hardy hokum injected into a thin story idea. Audience reaction was fair.

Estimate: Lower bracket attraction; will satisfy confirmed Laurel and Hardy fans.

WHAT THE EXHIBITORS SAID:

Motion Picture Herald, *November 25, 1939*

Swell going, gents. Not a slow or dull moment. Well directed and crammed with gags and action. Let's have more of them.
E. C. Arehart, Strand Theatre, Milford, IA.
General patronage.

Motion Picture Herald, *January 20, 1940*

Good slapstick comedy for the crowd that likes to laugh, and who doesn't? Stan Laurel more like his old self in this one than he has been for a long time. Business good.
L. G. Tewksbury, Opera House, Stonington, ME.
Small town patronage.

Doubled this with *Fifth Avenue Girl* and advertised an all-laugh show. It was highly successful. People seemed glad to have Laurel and Hardy back again and there is lots of good humor in this one. Don't expect too much of it and it will do O.K. From the evident enjoyment of the audience, I would call this a successful screwball comedy.
W. V. Nevins III, Co-Op Theatre, Alfred, NY. Small college town and rural patronage.

Very funny comedy that drew well and pleased. Took a chance on Sunday with these boys and was well satisfied.
Gordon P. Held, Strand Theatre, Griswold, IA.
General patronage.

Motion Picture Herald, *February 17, 1940*

Good light comedy that seemed to please.
Joe E. Edwards, Liberty Theatre, Johnston, SC.
Small town patronage.

Box Office, *March 9, 1940*

This picture can be summed up in one word — "lousy." Laurel and Hardy should confine their so-called acting to single reels and not try to make features. RKO certainly has produced a lemon — and I do mean lemon — with this picture!
John E. Moore, Star Theater, Alberta, Canada;
Population: 850, Theater Capacity: 320.
General patronage.

Box Office, *March 23, 1940*

The rest of the exhibitors who have reported this picture are right — it stinks! Audience Reaction: The kids liked it. Boxoffice: No good.
E. A. Stein, Out-Wickenburg-Way Theater, Wickenburg, AZ; Population: 760, Theater Capacity: 263.
Cosmopolitan Patronage.

Motion Picture Herald, *March 23, 1940*

A good comedy and one that will draw the folks in.
G. J. Abein, May Theatre, Watkins, MN.
General patronage.

Laurel and Hardy's usual style but good entertainment. They go over here so everyone was satisfied.
Coombes and Hudson, Empress Theatre, Lloydminister, Sasakatchewan, Canada. Rural and Small town patronage.

Motion Picture Herald, *April 13, 1940*

Same old Laurel and Hardy with their dead-pan comedy and gags. Proved a welcome change to my audiences, perhaps because they had not seen this pair in several years. Picture well produced and got plenty of laughs; in fact, laughter in last reel of aviation escapades almost drowned out dialogue and sound. Played with *Marshall of Mesa City* to better than average business.
F. O. Slenker, Slenker Theatres, Rock Island, IL.
Small town and rural patronage.

Motion Picture Herald, *April 27, 1940*

Best picture these two have made in quite a while. Was enjoyed by everyone. Did above average for this type of picture. Here's hoping RKO makes more with Laurel and Hardy.
Robert Dittrich, Viking Theatre, Cranfills Gap, TX.
Small town and rural patronage.

Box Office, *May 4, 1940*

Good enough comedy which brought many laughs. My people seem to like comedies, as they generally go over better than average.
Arthur E. Phifield, Park Theater, South Berwick, ME;
Population: 2,600, Theater Capacity: 343.
General patronage.

A Chump At Oxford

A Hal Roach Production. 63 minutes. DIRECTED BY Alfred Goulding. ASSOCIATE PRODUCER: Hal Roach, Jr. SCREENPLAY BY Charles Rogers, Harry Langdon and Felix Adler. PHOTOGRAPHY BY Art Lloyd. EDITED BY Bert Jordan. CAST: Stan Laurel, Oliver Hardy, Forrester Harvey, James Finlayson, Wilfred Lucas, Forbes Murray, Frank Baker, Eddie Borden, Gerald Rogers, Peter Cushing, Victor Kendall, Gerald Fielding and Charles Hall. Copyright January 18, 1940, Registration Number LP9377; Renewed February 9, 1967, Number R403910. Released by United Artists, Inc., February 16, 1940.

SYNOPSIS: After a disastrous situation as maid and butler for a wealthy couple, Stan and Ollie try their hands as street-sweepers. They lament the lack of education that has placed them in such menial employment, but luck is with them when they inadvertently foil a bank robbery. The bank president offers to reward them, and they request an education. He promises them the finest money can buy and sends them to Oxford University.

The two innocents are hazed by their fellow students, causing them serious trouble with the dean, until they explain what happened. The students responsible are punished and plot their revenge. Meanwhile, a window accidentally closes on Stan's head, jarring his memory, and it is revealed that he is actually the long-lost Lord Paddington, finest athletic scholar in Oxford's history. A body of students have gathered to beat up Stan and Ollie for snitching on them, but Lord Paddington handily dispatches them all. Paddington settles in at Oxford, with Ollie acting as his manservant. However, the insufferably stuffy Paddington continually belittles his one-time pal, addressing him as "Fatty, old thing," until Ollie can stand it no more. He abruptly resigns and announces his intention to return to America, but the window crashes down upon Paddington's head, and he is once again Stanley, to Ollie's great joy.

WHAT THE CRITICS SAID:

Box Office, *February 17, 1940*

The exhibitor should be guided by recent past performances of Laurel and Hardy pictures and their reception before he undertakes to show this one. The two comedians are cast in a story that suits their talents well enough but which also spaces their high comic moments too far apart. There are two such sequences which will probably leave the audience well satisfied. At first the pair are a couple of tramps seeking work. Later they become street cleaners. While resting from the ardors of this pursuit, they inadvertently catch a bank robber. The banker, out of gratitude, agrees to sponsor their neglected education and sends them to Oxford. In England they have a time with hazing, the dean and the student body.

Film Daily, *February 20, 1940*

Any audience will get plenty of belly laughs from the newest Laurel and Hardy comedy to reach the screen. Picture is one of their best to date, with good material that lends itself to uproariously funny gag situations. Film has all the well-known antics which made the two comics famous, but they have improved on their own style. Producer Hal Roach has done a first rate job on the production end, and Director Alfred Goulding handles Laurel and Hardy and the gag situations deftly to get a maximum amount of laughs throughout the picture. Charles Rogers, Felix Adler and Harry Langdon get credit for a neat job of writing in turning out the original story and screenplay. Forrester Harvey, James Finlayson and Wilfred Lucas also contribute to the laugh fest in supporting roles. The story, such as it is, ably develops each situation for Laurel and Hardy as they appear progressively as hitchhikers, a servant couple with Laurel made up as a woman, a pair of street cleaners and students at Oxford. Outstanding in the picture is the dinner party which they gum up as hired help and a sequence when they get to Oxford and are being ribbed by the students. Gag used in the Oxford sequence with hands of a third person coming through a bush to help the boys smoke and blow their noses will leave any audience limp with laughter. Another hilarious gag has them in the dean's quarters accidentally.

Direction: Good. Photography: Good.

Hollywood Film Archive, *February 21, 1940*

Comedy trivia which packs just enough laughs to enable it to fill out dual programs, A Chump at Oxford doesn't contain enough meat to stand on its own legs... There are a few spots of real humor, but it's just ordinary comedy for the most part.

Estimate: Just dual support.

Harrison's Reports, *February 24, 1940*

A fairly good comedy. The fact that the story is thin does not matter much, for there are plentiful gags. Some are old, others new, but mostly all are comical. Where these two comedians are popular, it should do better than average business. But it is the type of comedy that need not depend *only on the Laurel-Hardy fans; others should enjoy it as well. The only drawback may be that, aside from Laurel and Hardy, the other players are unknown....*

Charles Rogers, Felix Adler and Harry Langdon wrote the screenplay. Alfred Goulding directed it and Hal Roach produced it. In the cast are Forrester Harvey, Wilfred Lucas, Forbes Murray, and others.

Suitability: Class A.

Motion Picture Herald, *March 2, 1940; Reviewed by George Spires*

The campus of England's decorous Oxford is the locale for the latest Laurel and Hardy pursuit of comedy. With Hal Roach producing and Alfred Goulding directing, Hal Roach, Jr., makes his executive debut as associate producer.

Charles Rogers, Felix Adler and Harry Langdon wrote the story and adapted it. That some of the items are implausible has little to do with the case, for there is abundant comedy. No attempt is made to filter romance into it...

The small parts allotted by Forrester Harvey as the gentleman's gentleman and Wilfred Lucas as the dean are capably enacted.

Reviewed at the Rialto theatre in New York where an afternoon audience enjoyed the antics of the comedians.

WHAT THE EXHIBITORS SAID:
Box Office, *March 16, 1940*

Slapstick as the old days and contains plenty of laughs, but personally can't class it good as Laurel and Hardy's go.
Burris and Henly Smith, Imperial Theater, Pocahontas, AR; Population: 1,800. Rural Patronage.

Motion Picture Herald, *April 6, 1940*

Glad to see Laurel and Hardy teamed again. Business far below average in opposition to *Pinocchio*, but don't think it is the picture's fault. This pair has been separated so long the public has grown cold to them and they will have to be sold all over again.
W. C. Lewellen, Uptown Theatre, Pueblo, CO. General patronage.

Motion Picture Herald, *April 27, 1940*

The funniest Laurel and Hardy picture I've ever seen. It kept the crowd in an uproar. The story was weak but that is not unusual for the type of picture. Our patrons would like them better in two-reelers.
J. J. Sanderson, State Theatre, Loris, SC. Rural and Small town patronage.

Motion Picture Herald, *May 18, 1940*

Ideal comedy for Friday–Saturday. One of Laurel and Hardy's best. Gave my customers plenty of laughs.
George J. Biehler, Palace Theatre, Hamburg, NY. Small town patronage.

Motion Picture Herald, *June 8, 1940*

The usual Laurel and Hardy line and the picture was okay for we heard the audience laugh once more and believe me they are going to need a lot more of them in the coming season. I'll cheer some light comedies if I get them and I am sure the public will do the same.
A. E. Hancock, Columbia Theatre, Columbia City, IN. General patronage.

Motion Picture Herald, *June 14, 1940*

This is just what the doctor ordered. A lot of hokum thrown together in a disjointed picture that drew extra business and plenty of laughs.
A. J. Inks, Crystal Theatre, Ligonier, IN. Small town patronage.

Motion Picture Herald, *June 29, 1940*

A very fine Laurel and Hardy comedy slapstick picture and the audience enjoyed it.
C. L. Niles, Niles Theatre, Anamosa, IA. General patronage.

Motion Picture Herald, *July 6, 1940*

Good business; fair picture. Seems like they want comedies here. Why doesn't Hollywood wise up to itself and make pictures the masses of the people will enjoy and lay off the stuff that's supposed to appeal to the intelligentsia who never go to shows.
A. E. Eliasen, Rialto Theatre, Paynesville, MN. Rural and Small town patronage.

Box Office, *July 20, 1940*

Just a fair Laurel and Hardy. There are a few good laughs and some slapstick situations that got good rises out of the audience and I believe most of them went home satisfied they got what they expected and paid for. Boxoffice: Below Saturday average.
E. A. Stein, Out-Wickenburg-Way Theater, Wickenburg, AZ.

Motion Picture Herald, *August 3, 1940*

Doubled this with *Shooting High* and was well received. I believe Hal Roach should continue with this series because the public still enjoys these comedians.

R. Navari, Liberty Theatre, Verona, PA. City and suburban patronage.

Saps at Sea

A Hal Roach Production. 57 minutes. DIRECTED BY Gordon Douglas. SCREENPLAY BY Charles Rogers, Harry Langdon, Gil Pratt and Felix Adler. PHOTOGRAPHY BY Art Lloyd. EDITED BY William Ziegler. CAST: Stan Laurel, Oliver Hardy, James Finlayson, Rychard Cramer, Ben Turpin, Harry Bernard, Eddie Conrad. Copyright April 26, 1940, Registration Number LP9591; Renewed November 1, 1967, Number R420754. Released by United Artists, Inc., May 3, 1940.

SYNOPSIS: Stan and Ollie work in a horn factory, but the constant noise causes Ollie to have a breakdown, which results in his going violently berserk at the sound of a horn. His doctor recommends an ocean voyage to steady his nerves, but he and Stan are dubious about going to sea; instead, they rent a boat and keep it tied to the dock. Unfortunately, Nick Grainger, an escaped convict, is eluding the police, and he finds the boat and unties it while the boys are sleeping. Once they discover this, they try to subdue Grainger by cooking him a thoroughly inedible meal, in hopes of making him sick. However, he overhears their scheme and forces them to eat it. Finally, they figure out how to overpower Grainger: Stan blows a trombone, which sends Ollie into a violent rage.

WHAT THE CRITICS SAID:

Film Daily, *May 3, 1940*

Generous slapstick, this latest Hal Roach concoction can be set down as the vehicle which finds the clowning team of Stan Laurel and Oliver Hardy at its best and funniest. Virtually every ingredient known to the cookers of comedy is employed at one stage or another of the footage. Therein lies much of the secret of this attraction's appeal, namely unflagging action and superlative silly situations devised to whisk the audience along at a slaphappy pace. The Laurel and Hardy duo will add, as a result of *Saps at Sea*, to their already generous following of folks who enjoy laughing over and above all other reactions induced by screen entertainment...Ben Turpin is among the cast members, and another famous film comedian, Harry Langdon, is a co-author of the original story and screenplay. Gordon Douglas directed skillfully, and Art Lloyd's photography is fine.

Box Office, *May 4, 1940*

Straining any number of gags and comic business to their limits, Laurel and Hardy manage at the same time to deliver a rib-tickler that should satisfy their own particular following and liberally entertain others. The laughs, in view of the comedians' particular type of comedy, come off easy. A Broadway audience, about one-third consisting of children, guffawed and howled all over the place.

Harrison's Reports, *May 4, 1940*

Wherever Laurel and Hardy are popular, this comedy should go over well. It is comprised mostly of gags, some of which, though old, are still comical, and some novel and amusing. Most of the action revolves around Laurel and Hardy; only on occasion do other players appear with them. One of the most comical situations is that in which Laurel and Hardy, stranded on a boat without any food, and threatened with death by a gangster, who had sneaked on the boat when it was still at the dock, unless they would cook a meal for him, put together a synthetic meal, which the gangster finally forces them to eat. The production is not lavish, nor can much be said for the story; yet it is a fairly diverting hour's entertainment....

Charles Rogers, Felix Adler, Gil Pratt, and Harry Langdon wrote the original screenplay, Gordon Douglas directed it, and Hal Roach produced it. In the cast are James Finlayson, Ben Turpin, Dick Cramer, Eddie Conrad and others.

Suitability: Class A.

Motion Picture Herald, *May 4, 1940; Reviewed by George Spires*

Reminiscent of the Mack Sennett form of slapstick comedy, the latest Laurel and Hardy endeavor resorts to exploding gas stoves, gas burning electric light sockets, refrigerators that play music, and ice producing radios. Spiced throughout with gags, both old and new.

This type of comedy is still mirth-provoking for the audience who appreciate it, and judging from the reaction of an early afternoon congregation on a Broadway theatre, those who enjoyed it were in the majority.

Directed by Gordon Douglas and with an original story by Charles Rogers, Felix Adler, Gil Pratt and the one-time famous comedian of the silent screen, Harry Langdon, the picture is typical of many of the Laurel and Hardy predecessors…

The comedy team is supported by two additional comedians of the silent era, Ben Turpin and James Finlayson.

Reviewed at the Rialto Theatre in New York in the reaction noted.

Hollywood Film Archive, *May 15, 1940*

For the Laurel and Hardy fans this is a perfect full-length story to satisfy their whacky sense of slapstick humor. Early morning patrons at a metropolitan grind house laughed themselves silly during its unreeling, so exhibitors should have no fear of spotting it on the supporting dualler space. Hardy, suffering from a malady which causes him to go stark [raving] mad whenever he hears a horn, is ordered to rest at sea to get back to normal. Gangster Dick Cramer is found aboard their unshipworthy tub and he is captured by the simple expedient of Laurel tooting a trombone while Hardy slaps the stuffings out of Cramer. Oldtimers Ben Turpin and James Finlayson also come in for their share of fun.

Estimate: Okay for the Laurel-Hardy fans.

WHAT THE EXHIBITORS SAID:
Motion Picture Herald, *July 20, 1940*

90 per cent of my customers thought this was a real treat and we did extra business on gift night. The other 10 per cent walked out in disgust. Too short for single feature, however.
Ritz Amusements, Inc., Park Theatre, North Vernon, IN.
Small town patronage.

Motion Picture Herald, *July 27, 1940*

Not up to the standard of their previous pictures. A few good laughs.
Joe Schindele, Granite Theatre, Granite Falls, MN.
Small town patronage.

Motion Picture Herald, *August 3, 1940*

Was very well enjoyed on a bargain night. This house hasn't heard so much laughing for quite some time, and how they did laugh. Good business and lots of happy and carefree people made this a grand show for us.
A. E. Eliasen, Rialto Theatre, Paynesville, MN.
Small town patronage.

As poor as *Our Town* was, this little comedy was just as good. Our people like something to laugh at and they certainly got it in this comedy. Not the best they have made, but still good enough to bring them in. Extra business on this one.
A. J. Inks, Crystal Theatre, Ligonier, IN.
Small town patronage.

Motion Picture Herald, *August 31, 1940*

These feature comedies are well received and enjoyed by our patrons. They are also well suited for double feature, especially with heavy duds of which we have been getting too many.
Neighborhood patronage.

Motion Picture Herald, *October 5, 1940*

A good little comedy. Audience showed their approval by laughing most of the time. Played on a double feature program with *Anne of Windy Poplars*.
Irvin Baker, Jr., Roaring Spring Theatre, Roaring Spring, PA. Rural and
Small town patronage.

Road Show

A Hal Roach Production. 85 minutes. **PRODUCED AND DIRECTED BY** Hal Roach. Based on the Novel by Eric Hatch. **SCREENPLAY BY** Arnold Belgard, Harry Langdon, and Mickell Novak. **PHOTOGRAPHY BY** Norbert Brodine. **CAST:** Adolphe Menjou, Carole Landis, Joan Hubbard, Charles Butterworth, Patsy Kelly, George E. Stone, Margaret Roach, Polly Ann Young. Menjou and Butterworth roles originally conceived for Oliver Hardy and Harry Langdon. Copyright January 9, 1941, Registration Number LP10169. Released by United Artists, Inc., January 24, 1941.

SYNOPSIS: Millionaire Drogo Gaines gets cold feet at the altar and ducks out of the wedding by pretending to have a mental breakdown. He soon learns that his fiancée is only interested in his money, and when he attempts to call off the wedding, she schemes to have him committed for insanity. At the mental hospital, he encounters another patient, Colonel Carroway, an eccentric inventor. Carroway, dreading that he is soon to be sent to live with his equally eccentric nephew, plots an escape and takes Gaines with him. On the lam, the two hook up with a traveling carnival owned by the lovely "Penguin" Moore.

The carnival is heavily in debt and Carroway doesn't help matters by setting up a crooked shell game to raise money. It gets him and Gaines arrested; Moore helps them escape, but now the police are pursuing the carnival along with Moore's debtors and Gaines's doctor, manservant and fiancée.

Gaines, who has never held a real job, begins working at the carnival in hopes of impressing Moore, with whom he's fallen in love. Gaines secretly purchases a new carnival for her, but Moore is determined to make a success of the one she has. After some complications that find Gaines having to perform a lion-taming act, the colonel decides that the carnival should set up at his nephew's estate. While there, the lion escapes, a riot breaks out (which ultimately rids Gaines of his larcenous fiancée) and Moore's carnival is burned to the ground. Fortunately, the new carnival arrives in town; Gaines brings her to it and she sees he has named it for both of them, which seals their romance.

WHAT THE CRITICS SAID:
Brooklyn Eagle, *February 18, 1941; Reviewed by Herbert Cohn*

Adolphe Menjou has a trick camera in Road Show, *yesterday's arrival at the Rialto. It's laden down with wheels and gadgets, and it develops its own pictures as soon as Adolphe turns a crank. Sometimes. Sometimes when Adolphe turns the crank the picture gets developed and there's nothing on it.*

Road Show itself is very much like Mr. Menjou's camera. It has a lot of comic stuff hung around on its frame. There is George E. Stone, for instance, as a mute Indian tirelessly wooing Patsy Kelly, the phony-Indian medicine girl in the carnival that Carol Landis runs. There's the taffy-pulling machine that so fascinates Charles Butterworth, and there's the scene with Willie Best besting a rampant lion. There is a lot of material in Road Show *that should make it very funny. But like Mr. Menjou's camera, when Director Hal Roach sets it spinning, the expected fun sometimes doesn't develop, and what promised to be very funny turns out to be not funny at all.*

However, Road Show *gets to be moderately amusing, in a screwball way, often enough to survive its little plot about a millionaire playboy who escapes from a swank bughouse and joins Miss Landis's road show. And that — even with the practiced Harry Langdon supplying part of the script and Hoagy Carmichael doing some minor songs — is probably a major achievement.*

Box Office, *February 22, 1941*

The action starts in a nut house and gets nuttier every foot of the way. There have been countless screwball comedies about allegedly sane people but this is probably the first one in which the leading characters are admittedly screwballs. There are no limits to the number of laughs it will furnish the customers who relish their humor in the broadest possible vein with gags and slapstick predominating. Although unstintingly and modernly mounted, the production is reminiscent of the early-day screen funfests which prevailed before art came to the industry. Adolphe Menjou justifies his place in the topline by proving the greatest laugh-garnerer, although he is pressed by Patsy Kelly and Charles Butterworth. Properly merchandised, the feature should pay its way handsomely. Escaping from an asylum, Menjou and a young companion find refuge in a broken-down traveling carnival, owned and operated by Carole Landis. They are put to work and the motivation from that point forward serves only as a frail framework upon which are plastered the fast flow of gag situations.

Theatrical Compilations

The Golden Age of Comedy

Distributed by Distribution Corporation of America. 78 minutes. WRITTEN AND PRODUCED BY Robert Youngson. NARRATED BY Dwight Weist and Ward Wilson. Released January 8, 1958.

A compilation of scenes from Mack Sennett and Hal Roach comedies. Langdon is seen briefly at the opening in footage from *Remember When?* and in an excerpt from reel one of *Luck o' the Foolish*.

When Comedy Was King

Distributed by 20th Century-Fox. 81 minutes. WRITTEN AND PRODUCED BY Robert Youngson. NARRATED BY Dwight Weist. Released February 29, 1960.

A compilation of scenes from Mack Sennett and Hal Roach comedies, plus one Buster Keaton comedy (*Cops*, 1922). Langdon is featured in about 12 minutes of *The First 100 Years*.

The Days of Thrills and Laughter

Distributed by 20th Century-Fox. 93 minutes. WRITTEN AND PRODUCED BY Robert Youngson. NARRATED BY Jay Jackson. MUSIC BY Jack Shaindlin. Released March 21, 1961.

A compilation of scenes from various silent comedies and serial chapters. Battle scenes from Langdon's *All Night Long* are featured.

Laughter Then and Now

Distributed by Union Films. Released in 1962.

Publicity materials would indicate that this is an altered version of Robert Youngson's *The Golden Age of Comedy*, with added footage of Charlie Chaplin and Peter Sellers, the latter presumably representing the "Now." The authors have been unable to ascertain if this film was ever exhibited theatrically in the U.S.

30 Years of Fun

Distributed by 20th Century-Fox. 85 minutes. WRITTEN AND PRODUCED BY Robert Youngson. NARRATED BY Jay Jackson. Released February 12, 1963.

A compilation of scenes from various silent comedies, both domestic and foreign. Langdon appears during the opening credits in a brief street-sweeping scene from *Feet of Mud*, and later on he's seen photographing a baby from *Smile Please*.

The Sound of Laughter

Distributed by Union Films. HOST: Ed Wynn. Released in 1963.

A compilation of scenes from talking shorts released by Educational Films Corporation, also including Bing Crosby, Bob Hope, Buster Keaton, Shirley Temple and Danny Kaye. Langdon is seen in clips from *The Hitch Hiker*.

This Sennett publicity still of Langdon looking over his various guises for His First Flame *was used to promote Robert Youngson's* 30 Years of Fun.

Television Programs

Howdy Doody
NBC-TV, 1947–60

Excerpts from Langdon's Sennett-Pathé comedies were used in an unknown number of episodes during the early years of this daily afternoon children's program. Host "Buffalo Bob" Smith would narrate each film.

Comedy Capers
National Telepix, 1960-62; Syndicated

Langdon appeared in the following six programs in this 92-episode series:

"The Football Hero" *(Feet of Mud)*
"Tall Timber" *(Boobs in the Wood)*
"Tin Pan Alley" *(Fiddlesticks)*
"Watch the Birdie" *(Smile Please)*
"His Wedding Day" *(His Marriage Wow)*
"Lost and Found" *(Remember When?)*

The Funny Manns
California National Productions, 1960; Syndicated

This series, consisting of 130 ten-minute episodes, starred Cliff Norton and utilized footage from various Sennett-Pathé comedies. Excerpted Langdon films include *His New Mamma, Luck o' the Foolish, The Cat's Meow* and *Shanghaied Lovers*.

Silents, Please
Paul Killiam Productions, 1960–61; ABC-TV

This half-hour series, hosted by Ernie Kovacs, presented scenes from various silent films within a documentary setting. Langdon, along with Charlie Chaplin and Buster Keaton, appeared in the episode "The Sad Clowns," which aired on May 25, 1961.

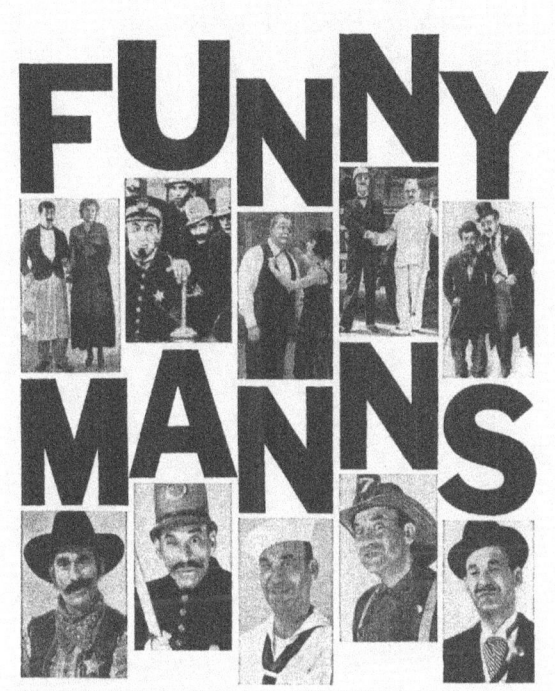

Fractured Flickers
Jay Ward Productions, 1963; Syndicated

This series of 26 half-hour episodes utilized clips, often lasting only a few seconds long, from various silent films, including Sennett's Keystone and Pathé comedies. Hans Conreid hosted each episode; the silent footage utilized voice-over dialogue by Paul Frees, Bill Scott and June Foray, the latter two better known as the voices of Bullwinkle and Rocky in Ward's *The Bullwinkle Show*. Langdon footage appeared in the following episode numbers (the episodes themselves were untitled):

4. *Picking Peaches*
8. *Saturday Afternoon*
14. *Soldier Man*
15. *Boobs in the Wood*
17. *Boobs in the Wood, Feet of Mud*
18. *Feet of Mud*
19. *Boobs in the Wood, Feet of Mud*
20. *Picking Peaches*
21. *Boobs in the Wood*
23. *Boobs in the Wood, Picking Peaches*
24. *Boobs in the Wood*
26. *Feet of Mud*

Hollywood

Thames Television, 1980

This 13-episode mini-series, produced by Kevin Brownlow and David Gill for British television, celebrated the American silent film. Langdon appeared in the episode "Comedy: A Serious Business," which aired on February 26, 1980. The series would appear in the United States on Public Television later in the decade.

Advertisement in the 1923 National Vaudeville Artists' Souvenir Program.

APPENDIX I
A Night on the Bouelvard 1912

By the time this script was submitted to the Library of Congress for copyright protection, The Langdons had been performing *A Night on the Boulevard* for nearly two seasons. Although it contains most of the same situations and visual comedy as its more famous counterpart, *Johnny's New Car*, this version is notable in that Langdon went to the trouble of detailing exactly how the special effects were accomplished. Aspiring performers desiring to recreate one of vaudeville's classic turns may wish to pay close attention.

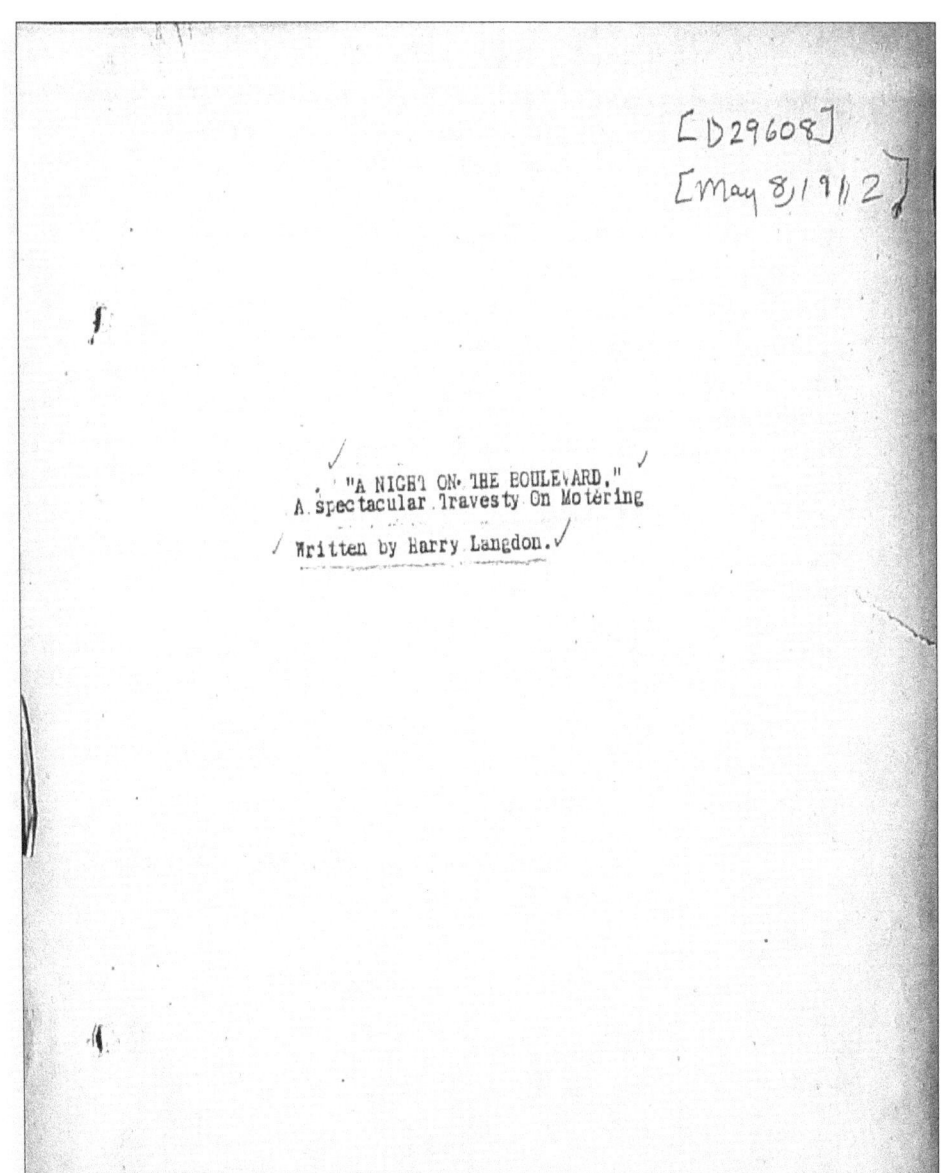

THE LANGDONS PRESENT

A comedy spectacular travesty on ~~horseless~~ Motering,
Intitled
"A Night On The Boulevard,"

Scene_____Boulevard, New York City.
Time_____Midnight

Characters.

Katie Speedington,_____Rose Langdon
Johnie Flat tire,_____Harry Langdon
Policeman
Waiter _____Tulley Langdon
Chauffeur.

Act runs from 15 to 20 minutes, written by Harry Langdon.
Scenery, Automobiles, and trick stuff used in the Act
are painted and built by The Langdons.

Curtain rises slowly with lively music, gong off stage
representing town clock strikes twelve. the scene is a
drop in three, representing a Boulevard with street lamps
illuminated from back with electric lights, a set cafe on
left of stage (looking from Auditorium) with set lamp post
at the corner of Cafe. A set wall is on the right with lamp
post on top , and a horses head sticking out of wall
to represent a fountain. a blue light from Auditorium floods
the stage as curtain rises, then Johnie and Katie enter
from left stage in a white touring car (prop) with ~~~~
search light on front end of Auto, and four difernt kinds of
Auto horns atached to the side of the Auto, one is a bass
horn another a very small horn with a very high tone,
and one french horn that produces four different notes
while pressing bulb. a tool box on the runing board,
two regular head lights iluminated with electric lights.
~~~~ a prop dog is tied behind Automobile, Katie is
seated in the back seat , Johnie as the Chauffeur. as car
enters Johnie blows the serene on front of Auto. as the
Auto stops all lights come up (lights were out as curtain
rises,) Katie looks about her laughing,

Katie,------- (calling) Johnie," Johnie," (third time very
          loud) JOHNIE,"

Johnie,------(a droll eccentric comedian) looks around
          towards audience)------Khatie,"

Katie,------ Johnie were we scorching,?

Johnie,------ No,

Katie,-------Well, what are we stoping here for ? -cant we go any farther,?

Johnie,------ No,-

Katie,-------Well whats the matter,?

Johnie,------The wheels are all tired,(bus" muging and honking horns,)

Katie,-------(looking about her, then discovers Cafe,) Oh Johnie how nice of you to stop right here in front of this Cafe,"

Johnie,------(looks around sees Cafe honks horn says getap as if talking to a horse,)

Katie,-------Now hont try and get out of it, I knew you were going to buy me a supper to night wont you call a waiter,?

Johnie,------ Call a waiter," sure,(bus" calling waiter softly, Waiter,waiter,waiter,

Waiter,------(jumps out quickly and surprises Johnie,)

Johnie,------(Looks around surprised that the waiter heard him,)

Katie,------zWaiter you may bring me a ~~////~~ Cream-De-minth,"

Waiter,------(looking at Johnie,) and what will you have,?

Johnie,------ Tooth-pick,"

Waiter,-------any thing else you would like,?

Katie,--------yes you may bring me some wine for my dog,

Waiter,1------(looking from dog tied on back of Auto and Johnie,) Which one,??

Johnie,------(bus" looks around quickly,)

Waiter,------(speaking to Johnie) Come on and have somthing,"

Johnie,------Got a monkey wrench in your pocket,?

Waiter,why what do you want with a monkey wrench,"

Johnie,------I want to monkey with it,

Waiter,------(looks at Katie,) did you say you wanted a Cream-De-Minth,??

Katie,------Yes a Cream-De-Minth will do.

Waiter,------And what will you have,??

Johnie,------Bring me a nice high cold one (meaning Beer,)

Waiter,------(Exits in Cafe,)

Katie,------Oh Johnie I am so ~~hungry~~ hungry, I be-leave I will Order some kind of game, I just love game dont you,?

Johnie,----- Oh yes,"

Katie,-------What kind of game do you like,??

Johnie,------Base ball and Pool,""

Comedy Sketch.
Entitled, Johnny's New Car.
Written By-Harry Langdon.

Cast

Johnny,----------------------------------Chauffer.
Katie,----------------------------------His sweetheart.
Waitress,----------------------at road side Inn.

Scene,

At the end of Boulevard, Road house at right stage.

Enter Johnny and katie in runabout Automoble from left stage, stop center stage.

Katie.
Johnny, your tail light is out,

Johnny.
How did that get out,?

Katie
And your head lights are out too,"

Johnny
I'll bet they went out with the tail light.

Katie
You had better get out and light up,

Johnny
I don't need any lights on this car,

Katie
Why,?

Johnny
This is a Pathfinder, (pointing to car)

Katie
Now that you have stopped what do you think I am going to do?

Johnny
Light my Tail light,

Katie
no, I am going to take your picture,

Johnny
Yes, wait and I will take one with you.

Katie
no I am going to take a picture of your car.

Johnny
I'll bet the picture will be a tin type. shall I put the awning up,?

Katie
No, never mind the Awning,

Johnny
gets out of Car, slipping on running board) oh,oh, I will have to have that fixed,

Katie
Now stand right down there, put your hat back,

Johnny
shall I put the Awning,?

Katie
Never mind the Awning, now put your feet together,

Johnny
(stands with feet spread apart, one foot pointing one way the other the other way.)

2

Katie
Well make up your mind which way you are going,

Johnny
(pointing to feet) Where they go I go, shall I put up the awning,?

Katie
Never mind the awning,

Johnny
Then be sure and get all the excesories in the picture,

Katie
Why the head lights are not in,?

Johnny
How did they get out,(jars Machine and head-lights light up.) Put the Awning up,?

Katie
All right, put it up,

Johnny
(Puts up the top of car, which is painted like a striped awning)

Katie
Is that a one man top,?

Johnny
No, that is my old shirt,

Katie
(walks over to Johnny and pulls up his coat as if it was a dress, ad lib, talk. johnny keeps pulling down his coat every time that she pulls it up)

Johnny
(backs away from her bashfuly) I don't know you very well.

Katie
Well then stand down here till I take your picture, now smile,

Johnny
What for,

Katie
For the picture,

Johnny
Oh, then I will have to smile inwardly,

Katie
All right .

Johnny
Laughs with out smileing.

Katie
Now lean on the car as if you owned it.

Johnny
Oh I can't lean on it,

Katie
Why not,?

Johnny
It is all damp,

Katie
(feels of car) say it is damp is'nt it, What makes it so damp,?

Johnny
There is so much due on it.

Katie
(takes hispicture) I've got you,(closeing camera)

Johnny
Lets see it,

Katie
no wait until I gat it developed.

3

Johnny
Let me see the synopsis, (gets into car with katie, falls through the bottom of car so that his feet are seen beneath car,) now what do you know about that,

Katie
What's the matter Johnny,?

Johnny
Some one went and opend up my Cut-out, and I fell right thru it,

Katie
And you brought me out with you, and you don't know a thing about running an Automobile, and if I had that wheel I would show you how to run this car,

Johnny
all right here is the wheel,(hands her the steering wheel)

Katie
well get out and crank it,

Johnny
I refuse to crank it, you have the wheel now you will have to crank it.

Katie
(see's the road house at her right) Oh Johnny how nice of you to stop right in front of this cafe,

Johnny
looks around at Cafe) I'll crank it for you this time. (starts to get out of car, Katie pulls hom back into car)

Katie
Now don't try to get out of it, I knew you were going to buy me a dinner, wont you call a waiter,?

Johnny
Sure, (calls waiter very softly) waiter waiter,

Waitress
(jumps out of Cafe very quickly,)

Johnny
You are not very hard of hearing are you,

Katie
Johnny, there is the waiter,

Johnny
yes, what do you know about that, is there any thing else you would like,? (to Katie)

Katie
No,

Johnny
(to waitress) That's all,

Waitress
Is there any thing you wish,?

Johnny
Yes, I wish you a happy New Year.(to waitress) How do you like my little Run-a-bout,?

Waitress
Why, the last time I saw her she was a Brunett. (exits)

Johnny
Yes I had her all over hauld,---(looks at Katie)

Katie
Are you going to sit here and let her insult me like that,?

Johnny
No, I'll get out. (gets out of car)

Katie
The very Idea of her talking to me like that,

Johnn
Yes, what do you know about that,

4

Katie
Why, she insulted me,

Johnny
What do you know about that, I'll get even with her, (walks back and forth in front of Cafe) This place is unfair to organised labor, this place is un fair to organised labor. (to Katie) what did she say to you,?

Katie
She said the last time she saw me I was a brunett,

Johnny
Yes,? well just wait right here and I will settle this, (walks up to door of Cafe and Knocks very loudly)

Waitress
(comes out) Well what do you want,?

Johnny
(very meakly) Can I have a drink of water,?

Waitress
Yes,(exits and returns) with pitcher of wter and a glass)

Katie
(to waitress) can you tell me if there are any nice roads around here,?

Waitress
(pointing with glass of wter in her hand) oh yes there are some very nice roads down that way, (adlib talk about the roads while Johnny has business trying to get the drink of water.) when he finds he can not get the drink he goes to his car and opens up the radister, which dicloses three Whiskey bottles, then he closes it up again quickly, Rose sees him do it, walks around car and opens up the radiater, speaking)

Katie
Johnny, What is this,?

Johnny
Tom Dick and harry,

Katie
to me it looks like WHISKEY,

Johnny
Don't say that,(bis, looking around to see if any one is listing, Don't you ever say what you said there,

Katie
What, WHISKEY,?

Johnny
Don't say that, can't you say SNOPS.(bis, takeing cup off the hub of wheel,) You'll find your cup on the other wheel. Bis, pututting his foot on Bumper useing it for the bar rail)

Katie
Johnny, any kick,?

Johnny
Oh, no one has said any thing so far, have you got enough,?

Katie
Oh plenty,

Johnny
Well after you drink that, just lay the money down any place but don't give it to me directly.(walks to left side of car) Well here's ago, (lifting his cup to her)

Katie
Here's ago,

5

Waitress
(doubles as Policeman) enters and stands behind Johnny)

Katie
(see's Policeman, points to her, Johnny just looks at her as if he don't know what she means,)

Johnny
(talks to her with his fingers, like a deaf and dumb person) then looks aroud and see's Policeman, tries to hide his cup then finds he can not hide it he dips his fingers into it and wipes his hands on his coat, then on his face, puts the cup in his pocket, acts innocent, turns to look at policeman (policeman walks around to the right of him as he looks at the left, he turns and sees her, tips his hat to Katie, Policeman turns to look at Kati, as he does, Johnny steals her star from her coat and pins it to his vest, Policeman turns to Johnny, Johnny pulls back his coat and shows the star, Policeman sulutes him and walks off stage.)

Katie
(to Johnny) Come on now and crank up and get away before the policeman gets back,

Johnny
(cranks his car, after cranking car or rather turning crank to the right, he reverses it and turns crank to the left. gets tired cranking, and walks away in the same stooped position as when cranking.)

Katie
Johnny, you told me this was the best car on the market,

Johnny
On the market but not on the road.(this is the away I start it,(turns fake combination starter on front of radiater, little dog on radiator cap looks down at the combination. Johnny jars the car and the engine starts, he runs and gets in into car, useing the rosome can for effect of meshing gears. engine stops. Johnny gets out of car, slipping on step as he does he pulls the door off the car with him, puts it back on. speaking,) leave the door open now, I want to get in quick. Say when I crank the car will you push that button there,

Katie
This button here,(pointing to button)

Johnny
Yes, NO, not that button,

Katie
Well what is this button for,?

Johnny
That throws the hind wheel off.

Katie
Rings a bell in car.)

Johnny
Picks up exost pipe as if it was a telephone,) Hello, how are you , good bye, gets out again and cranks car, engine runs again, (Johnny, takes out a piece of the engine and throws it away, then takes out another part and throws it away, and the next part he takes out the engine stops, and he puts the part back in again and the starts again. he jumps into car, as he does the hood of the Motor raises and out jumps two tin cans, johnny acts frighten and trys to run away calling to Katie to) Come on thats all, every man for himself.

Katie

6

Katie
(looking into hood of Engine) Why Johnny, there is nothing in there,

Johnny
No it is all out here now,(pointing to the cans Etc.)

Katie
Why where is the Magineto,?

Johnny
Where is the what,?

Katie
Where's the Magy neat toe,?

Johnny
It went out with Dardenelle.

Katie
I suppose you will have a blow out next,

Johnny
Well I've got an extra tire,(takes tire from rear of car, tire is full of blow outs)

Katie
Thats some tire,

Johnny
Yea, some of it, it's got a lot of rubber in it yet, see how it bounces,(bis, discovers a hole in tire) Oh,Oh,

Katie
Why whats the matter,

Johnny
I've got a leak in it,(shows it to Katie,) can you notice it,?

Katie
I can see it,

Johnny
(Puts his ear to hole in tire as if listening where the leak is) Yep, slow leak, do you know what that hole reminds me of,?

Katie
No, what,

Johnny
That one,(points to another hole)

Katie
Never mind the tire whats the matter here,

Johnny
Theres somthing wrong with it, (cranks car again)(engine stats) (Johnny runs to pick up somthing, as he does large flash of flame comes out of side of car and hits Johnny in the seat of his Pants, he runs about faning him self, then goes to door of car and fans himself with door.

Waitress
(enters from Cafe) see here young man this noise will have to stop,

Johnny
It has stopped, I have been trying to start it,

Waitress
Well don't start any thing around here,(hits the hood of his car with lead pencil)

Katie
(jumps up and argues with the Waitress about hitting his car, adlib, -Johnny has bis, trying to say something,)

Waitress
(kicks the spokes out of the front wheel)

7
Johnny
(yells out, as he does he coughs useing auto horn in car for the effect of coughing, honk-honk-honk.
Waitress
(exits)
Katie
What was she kicking about,?
Johnny
She was kicking my runabout, like this,(kicks spoke out of wheel) Oh, any body can do that,(kicks another spoke out, as he does the engine starts , johnny runs and jumps into car, as he sits down the stearing wheel flys out into the air, takeing Johnny's hat with it, Johnny gets out puts his hat on and starts to sneak away, Rose sees him and hollers at him)
Katie
JOHNNY,"
Johnny
Well where do you want to go now,?This ride has got you all tired out,(Johnny picks up all the parts that are laying around and puts them at the bottom of Parking sign, that reads" Auto's Park Here," then he lays grass matt over the parts which resembles a grave, with the sign as the toombe stone, the he places the old tire over the top of sign for the wreath, takes his hat off in prayer, -speaks to Katie-)
I'll bet you are disgusted,
Katie
Yes this think has gone far enough,
Johnny
Yes this is all the farther we will go,
Katie
Do you think I will have to walk home,?
Johnny
Noooo, don't be silly,(picks up the spokes and puts them in his arms as if carrieing in the wood)
Katie
Well I want to go home in the worst way,
Johnny
We'll go in the car, do you realy want to go home,?
Katie
Certainly,
Johnny
Give us a kiss kiddo, give us a kiss,
Katie
kiss you,?
Johnny
Do you want to go home,?
Katie
Yes,
Johnny
Give us a kiss kiddo, give us a kiss.
Katie
Why what girl would kiss that face,?
Johnny
All the Girls kiss me when they go out in my Auto,

8
Katie
They do,?

Johnny
Yep, they kiss me or get out and walk home, I don't burn my gas for nothing,

Katie
Well I would rather walk home,

Johnny
Thats funny they all walk home. I think I will buy a Motor-Boat. what would you do if I would kiss you up there, (pointing to her forhead)

Katie
Why I would call you down,

Johnny
(kisses her, lights go out, Music plays, Auto backs up stage, as if turning around to leave, as curtain falls, curtain up showing red tail light of Automobile in the dark going up the Boulevard, red tail light diminishes to small light as it gets further away, when it is out of sight curtain falls,

Finish

APPENDIX III
After the Ball 1921

As noted in the text, *After the Ball* was not very successful, at least with critics, during most of its first season, and Langdon had to work on it a bit before the 1922–23 season. At least one 1922 reviewer noted that the action in Act III replaced the hospital with the old roadhouse from *Johnny's New Car*. This script, submitted around the same time as its stage debut, demonstrates Langdon's reliance on visual comedy. It's not difficult to imagine the fully formed Little Elf performing these routines.

Scene One.

Rose and Cecil enter with golf bag and sticks,

Rose - Cecil have you seen Johnny any where,?
Cecil- No I have'nt seen him, I suppose he is out in the ruff again.
Rose - (calling out) --Johnny,; oh Johnny,-
Johnny- (back of drop) What do you want,?
Rose - Where are you,?
Johnny, I'm in here,
Rose- In where,?
Johnny- Appears at door in drop) --In here,-
Rose-what are you doing in there,?
Johnny-I'm looking for my Golf ball it went in here,(meaning the house)
Rose - did you find it,?
Johnny- No I have'nt looked yet,
Rose and Cecil start to swing there Golf sticks back and forth in front of the door in drop.
Rose- Come on out and play Johnny,-
Johnny trys to come out but is unable to on account of the clubs swinging in front of him.
Johnny- Lets play in here,
Rose-(still swinging the club) No come on out here and play with us.
Johnny makes another attempt to get out of the door, then he covers his eyes and walks through the swinging clubs.

Goes to pick up Roses golf ball.
Rose-AH ah, did'nt I tell you not to pick up other peoples golf balls
    on this course,?
Johnny- I don't pick them up till they've stopped rolling.
Cecil- Oh look he's for got his Golf bag,
Johnny looks around for the bag, then goes to the door in the house and takes out a large bag,

Cecil- Johnny come here, will you let me take your putter,?
    Your putter,-- you know your putter- putter putter putter,
Johnny-(puts out his hand and says) PUTTER THERE.
Cecil- (takes golf stick out of his bag)
Johnny be careful of that stick,
Cecil- Oh I will johnny, (then she swings with the stick hitting the
    stage and breaking the stick)
Cecil- I'm sorry Johnny,-
Johnny- Oh thats all right,
Cecil- I did not mean to do it,
Johnny- Oh thats all right,
Cecil-I'm very very sorry,
Johnny- Oh thats all right.
Cecil- But I'll buy you a new one,
Johnny- Oh thats--all right.
Cecil (Exits) Rose trys to hit her golf bag but misses it)
 Rose-(swinging at ball) Missed it again,(repeats this three or four
    times) Johnny what is the cause of me missing,?
Johnny- What kind of gas do you use,? you must keep your eye on the ball
Rose-(swings back to hit it,Johnny interupts her saying-missed it again,
Rose-what is the cause of me missing,?
Johnny- Did you ever miss a train,?
Rose- Yes I have missed a train,
Johnny-Well how do you expect to hit that little ball.

2

Rose- what kind of a game did you play this Morning Johnny,?
Johnny- Oh I played a Civil War game, I went out in Sixty one and came back in Sixty four. I should of had the Spirits of seventy six. one good thing about golf, you can play it on Sunday with out sinning, because a golf course is Holy,
Rose- (turns her back to Johnny as if counting up her score)
Johnny(takes a tea pot from his Golf bag, a string or a rope is tied from the tea pot to the golf bag. he places the tea pot the strings length from the bag, puts a golf ball on top of the tea pot, then gets ready to hit the ball, calling <u>fore</u>, in swinging to hit the ball his club strikes the bag, he moves the bag away at the same time draging the tea pot after it, makeing it still the same distant away from the bag. Johnny repeats this bit, moveing the tea pot, then the bag. (speaking) FORE- FORE FORE,- say you women don't pay any attention to that figure do you, FORE- why don't you look around FORE, THREE NINTY EIGHT.
Rose-(looks around) wher did my golf ball go to, you can't turn your head on this golf course or some one will take your golf ball.
Johnny- was it the ball you was just playing with,?
Rose- Yes,
Johnny- Oh you have been missing that all day. (throws his bag over his bag, takes out a long stick with a nail on the end of it and picks up pieces of paper putting the paper in the bag.
Rose- (keeps on talking about looseing her golf balls every time she plays golf with Johnny.
Johnny- Whats seems to be the touble with you,
Rose- every time out play golf with you I loose all my Golf balls,
Johnny- say do you mean to insinuate that I take your golf balls,
Rose- I am not only insinuateing but I am positive.
Johnny- well then you be a little more careful what you say after this.
Rose- well you just stand there till I search you,(feels all about him but does not find any golf balls) Well johnny I am sorry that I accused you of stealing my golf balls and I am going to apologize to you, realy it was my mistake, wont you for give me? (puts out her hand to shake hands)
Johnny-(puts out his hand but discovers that his glove is on backwards, enstead of the black stripes being on the back of his hand they are in the palm of his hand, he hides his hand then tips HIS HAT TO HER. AS HE DOES A BUNCH OF GOLF BALLS ROOL OUT OF HIS HAT,- he gets excited grabs his bag and walks off stage.

2d, Scene,

Scene,Country golf club, door, tee box, running fountain Etc.
Johnny enters with his golf bag, a golf ball flys across stage just missing his head, then another one fly's accross, each one missing him , he takes out his club as if he is going to bat them when on hits him from the rear.
Cecil enters and dumps a lot of rubbish in his golf bag, johnny is just going to hit a ball when Cecil stoops over to pick it up, Johnny just misses hitting her in the back. Cecil gets on tee box and addresses the ball in an an eccentric manner, moveing her body back and forth. Rose enters with her score card and trys to get Johnny's attention , but Johnny is to busy watching Cecil, Rose exits,Johnny goes over in front of Cecil watching her, Cecil Hits the tee knocking dirt all over Johnny, he spits the dirt out of his mouth and dust him self,
Cecil- How do you like our Golf course Johnny, ?
Johnny- It is the best I ever tasted.

3

Cecil strikes another ball, this one goes into club house window, Glass crash is heard, she hands Johnny the Golf club and pushes him on the tee box, insisting that he play Golf, The Manager of club house comes rushing out looking up at the Broken window, seeing Johnny on the tee box with a Golf club in his hand he thinks he broke the window.-Manager calls Johnny and wants to know if he is going to pay him for the Broken glass. Johnny replys that <u>he can't expect him to pay for some thing that is Broke</u>. manager says-Well you broke it,' Johnny says how do you know I broke it,? because you have a club in your hand, replys the manager, yes says johnny-you bet I've got a club in my hand. Manager getting mad says-what are you going to do about it," Johnny, hits the ball and the ball goes into the club house breaking another window, Johnny lays his club down -motions to Cecil to come with him, both start to walk off stage, Manager blocks Johnny's way-Cecil Exits. Manager grabs hold of Johnny's coat walking him back and forth,

Manager- Let me see where can I knock you,;
Johnny- Knock me,? are you looking for a place to knock me,? You know where I come from they knock each other,(laughs) I was only kidding.--I can tell by looking at you -you are sore about something, I can tell by the expression on your voice.(johnnu seeing his coat up to high in front pulls it down, manager pulls it down again, Etc,) ---I don't know you very well,(pulls his coat down like a girl would her skirt) "Well I got to go now(repeats this several times)(then spreads his feet- one pointing one way and the other the opposit direction)
Manager well if your going to go make up your mind which way your going,-
Johnny, Well I guess I'll go this way,(starts to go, manager grabs him by the back of the collar and holds him)
Johnny- No-I don't like that hold as well as I do this one(hands the manager the front of his coat as he was holding before.)
Manager-(Shakes his coat)Johnny make sound with his mouth as if he had a bottle of whisky in his pocket, gurgles.) What have you got in there,?
Johnny- Whist broom,--(shows the audience the print of a bottle through his coat)--See the neck of the whist broom,???
Manager-Take it out," (Johnny takes the bottle out of his pocket) What does this bottle contain,?
Johnny- CONTENTS.-
Manager- Any Kick,?
Johnny- No body has said any thing so far,---After you drink that Just lay the money down any place,but don't give it to me directly. (Manager exits)

(enter Cecil and Rose with capes on, as if leaveing the club House)
Rose- Well Johnny we are going home in our car, do you want to go along with us.
Johnny- sure- but wait till I get a drink of water. (Steps to the fountain to get a drink- just as he stoops to drink the water stops running. Johnny then sneaks up on the fountain and fountain stops running-but Johnny passes right by it as though he did'nt see it. this is kept up to get the laughs.- stoops to drink water stops- water shoots up in the air strikeing Johnny in the face,-- he sits on the fountain. some on throws a golf ball at the club house breaking a window, Johnny hears it and runs off stage.

Scene ~~Four~~ Three.

Exterior of a Hospital.

(Rose Cecil and Johnny enter in an Automobile, Rose and Cecil are seated in the front seat, and Johnny in a little extra seat in the rear of car.-- Car stops in front of the hospital. Rose and Cecil argueing as to who knows more about running the car, they talk very loud, Johnny looks around at the sign on the Hospital and trys to caution Rose and Cecil in regards to the Zone of Quiet sign, but they don't seem to pay any attention to him untill he taps Rose on the sholder speaking.)

Johnny- Would you mind pulling your car up a little further,?
Rose-   Why,?
Johnny- Because I can't stand that smell that comes out of that door.
Cecil - (Jumping up in her seat) Well if you don't like it get out,
Johnny- (starts to climb out) Rose says -Sit down Cecil says- Get out, In getting up and down so much Johnny falls through the bottom of car, the audience can see his feet.
Johnny- (rapping Rose on the shoulder) Say you have left your cut-out open.
Cecil- Ah come on start it up,(motor effect, girls make all kind of noise as if striping the gears.- Johnny sits in the back seat as if he was frightened, trys to get out of seat, opens a little door in side of the car but it is only large enough to put his foot through. intrying to get out he knocks the gas tank of the rear of car,-- engine stops--- Girls don't know what the troub-le is,--- Johnny acts as if he is unconcerned.-- Rose and Cecil start to argue again over the car,--Johnny gets out and trys to tell them about the gas tank lying on the floor,- the girls think he is going to tell them what to do wont listen to him, he trys to tell them again but they ball him out each time, Johnny puts the tank back on and as he does a poliwoman enters and writes down the number of the car- Johnny sees him doing it and trys to get the girls attention by winking at them, girls think he is tring to flirt with them and tell him to mind his own business.-- officer walks around to front of car speaking,-
            What do you Girls mean by driveing so fast,?
Rose- how fast were we driveing,?
Officer- You were driveing Fifty miles anhour,-
Rose- Fifty miles anhour,- (turns to Johnny) did you hear what he said,?
Johnny- What did I say,?
Rose - he said we were driveing Fifty miles an hour,
Johnny are you going to let him get away with it, go on and ball him out, if he says any thing just mention my name.(jumping up in his seat) look here officer, we wadnt going fifty miles anhour because we have'nt been gone an hour.
Officer- I'll give you people just five minutes to move away from this hospital, remember just five minutes.
Johnny- Is that R.R. time or central time.?
Rose- Johnny crank the car for us Johnny, Johnny cranks car-just as He is going to get in the hood opens and a lot of tin cans jump out, Johnny runs about as if excited,speaking--
    Come on thats all,
Rose- Wher is the maggie neato,?

5

Johnny- It went out with Dardinelli-
Rose- will you crank it again,?
Johnny- sure,(cranks it again, then runs around to rear of car and
stoops to pick up a part of the engine , as he does a flame
of fire shoots out the back of car hitting Johnny in the seat
of the pants, Johnny runs about faning him self,- then runs
into the hospital and comes out with a thermomter in his
mouth, then he leans against the door of hospital and the
thermomter on the door rise - as he leave it drops.
Cecil- do you smell something burning Rose,?
Rose - yes I smell something burning, Johnny do you smell something
burning, Johnny replys that he felt something burning.
(Rose takes out the book of imformation and on the cover
is the word Packard,- Rose and Cecil read from the book,-
Johnny drinks from a gasoline can that he found in the rear
seat,-- after drinking from the gasoline can he coughs-at
the xame time he honks an automobile horn,- giveing the
effect that the sound is comming from His mouth. he repeats
the coughing and blowing the horn untill the girls get up and
look at him both wondering what is the mwtter with him,--
rose hits him on the back--Johnny coughs again useing the horn.
Cecil hits him on the head and he coughs and blows the horn.
Johnny blows his nose and gives the same horn effect.
Officer interupts them by comming in and tells them that he will
have to hand them a ticket,-- Johnny steals the officers
badge or star-from his coat,---The officer turns to John
Johnny flashes the badge-- the officer sulutes him and Exits,

Rose Cecil and Johnny exit in the car.

Finis.

APPENDIX IV
Dry Goods 1923

Dry Goods is an oddity. It is an "afterpiece" that Langdon wrote during his troupe's final Orpheum tour, and was introduced in Los Angeles at the same performance where he was seen by Sol Lesser, Harold Lloyd, and possibly Mack Sennett and Hal Roach. It utilized other acts on the bill, and reportedly went over well enough to be used during the remainder of the tour.

"DRY GOODS,"

Scene. Interior of a Saloon, with all the Bar room fixtures,
A Bar, Cuspidores, swinging doors, Etc.
Displayed on the bar are Neck Ties, Collars, hats, shirts,
and other garments used in a Dry goods store.

On the Scenery and Bar are signes reading as follows,-

Johnny Walker Whiskey Shoes.
Manhattan Cocktailes Shirts
Green River Whiskey Bathing suites.
Ginger Ale High balls Collars.
Schlitz Beer Underwear.
Pabts Beer Pajammas.
Old Virginia Dares Wine Petticoats.
    HARD WARE DEPARTMENT
OLD Crow-bars
GORDON Gin-erators.
Kentucky Rye-ding habbits.
Eye Glass for Blind pigs.

Charactors.

A Bartender, (or a clerk)
Mr. Rushthe can.
Mr. Barfly.
Mrs. Bargain Huntter.
Mr. Inagain.
Mrs. Charge Account.
Mr. Just One more.
Mr. Have Anotherone.

OPENING.

Bartender.- (steps from behind bar, takes apron out of his pants,
and speaks,-)

    Twas a balmy summers evening
    and a goodly crowd was there,
    Twas July Ninteen eighteen
    In my Bar room on the square,
    And as that Jolly crowd
    drank to the clinking cup,
    a Sheriff crept slowly in
    and closed the darn place up.

(walks back of Bar, wipeing the bar)
(Two of the male charators enter and stand at bar)

BARTENDER,- Well what are you wearoing to day Gentlemen,?

Char'tor, - I'll have a short neck tie,

(Bartender hands him a neck tie)

Bartender,- And what are you going to have,?

Char,-   I'll have a soft collar, I am off the hard stuff.

Character,- Have something your self Bartender,

Bartender,- No, I don't care for a thing to day boys.

Character,- Oh come on have something on us,

Bartender,- all right I'll take a silk shirt.

   (All three hold there articals up)

Bartender,- Well here's ago,

   (All three sing part of any popular song, the two
   customers leave the bar,)

Bartender,- I say boys you have forgotten to pay for that last round.

Character,- Oh I beg your pardon, how much do I owe you,

Bartender,- Ten dollars.

   (Bartender takes the money and places it in a
   stocking that is on a log form.)

Character,- Oh I say Mr. Bartender, have an Over coat,?

Bartenedr,- Yes Sir, I have a dandy right here,

   (puts the Over coat on, Bis. trying to fit the coat
   on him.)

Character,- (Smelling of coat) say what is that terrible odor,?

Bartender,- Its me, I'm the dirtiest thing.

   (Both Characters Exit)

    ENTER Mrs. Bargain Huntter.

Mrs B.H. - (stands at Bar with foot on rail, speaking to the
   Bartender.)

   I purchased a Suite of underwear here, and it does not
   fit me, may I change it at this counter,?

Bartender,- No you will have to go home to do that.

Mrs, B.H. - Well then I want to buy a Camona to put on around the
   house.

Bartender,- How large is the house,?

Mrs.B.H. - (exits, very angry)

3

(A bar room bum, comes up from cellar and walks out the door)

Enter, Customer.

Customer,- Why hello there Johnny I have not seen you for some time,(looks around at the place) well you woul'nt think that this used to be a Bar room would you,?

Bartender,- No, I have changed it all around since you was in here last,- well what are you going to wear,?

Customer,- I want something strong,

Bartender,- Pair of Army socks,?

Customer,- No I'll take a little Scotch,

Bartender,-(Gives him a a piece of Scotch tweed cloth,)

Enter, Henpecked Husband.

Bartender,-(to Hen pecked) You get out of here, go on get out,

Henpecked,- Just one more,?

Bartender,- Not another one, now get out of here,

Henpecked,- Please give me just one more,

Bartender,- Your wife told je to keep you out of here now go, you can not have another one,

Customer,- What does he want Johnny,?

Bartender,- He wants another Handkerchief.

Customer,- Well why don't you give him one,

Bartender,- I can not take a chance, his wife gave me orders to keep him out of here or she would close my place up.
(to Henpeck)
You big brute, your Wife says you don't bring any Money home, you BLOW every thing in Handkerchiefs.

Customer,- Why I know that fellow, he can't stand very much, one pair of pants under his belt and he's done for.

Bartender,- Well beings that you know him I will give him a hat.

Customer,- Oh, no, don't give him a hat, a hat will go right to his head.

Bartender,-Well here is a Neck tie, no here is a piece of soap that will go right to your neck.

Henpeck,- (exits)

4

(Bar room bum enters, again , and goes into basment)

Customer,- I would like to have a suite of under wear,

Bartender,- We have'nt any Union suites,

Customer,- What you have'nt any Union suites,? (walks back and fortg) this place is unfair to Organised labor.(exits)

(Bum comes up out of celler and exits through door)

          Enters another customer.

Customer,- Let me see what did I come in here for, oh yes I want That, (points to night gown on a womens form)

Bartenedr,- Oh you can't have that,

Customer,- well I am going to take it anyhow,(takes the ladies night gown off the form and holds it up)

Bartender,- Well now that you have it what are you going to do with it,

Customer,- I am going to take it out and get it filled, Oh yes there is something else that I want, here it is,(picks up a cuspidore)

Bartender,- Well say what do you want with that cuspidore,?

Customer, I want it for my dog,

Bartenedr,- what kind of a dog have you,?

Customer,- A spits. (exits)

(Bum enters and goes down into celler again)

          Enters,Mrs, Charge account.

Mrs, C.A.- (walks up to the bar and whispers to the bartender)

Bartender,- You go down that way two isles and turn to the right.

MrsM,C.A. (exits)

          Finish with Comedy Quartett or a band.
And as the band plays, or, the Quartette sings, all the other Vaudeville acts on the same program enter and go through their own individual acts, all simualtaneousley. Then at a given cue all the acts on the program change places with the other acts on the program and do each others act.

          FINISH.

APPENDIX V
Heart Trouble *an Illustrated Synopsis*

Harry Langdon in *Heart Trouble*

The Players
Hans Von Hauser — Harry Langdon
His Sweetheart — Doris Dawson
His Father — Lionel Belmore
His Mother — Madge Hunt
The Colonel — Jack Pratt
The Detective — Joseph Girard
A Boss Carpenter — Bud Jamison

OPENING TITLE: Wise men have said you can be whatever you *will* to be — but many a frog has tried to sing soprano — and only croaked.

Hans is sitting in his room reading a book which states: "Face to Face with onrushing death, the stripling youth stood undaunted — as calm and heroic as David, facing the onslaught of Goliath." Hans puts the book down and starts to think…

He imagines himself firing at some enemy soldiers and planes. A plane comes down and his fellow soldiers cheer. Hans fires at some enemy soldiers on a bridge…

INSERT: Defeat turned to victory — despair to triumph! A humble lad of the people had achieved the immortal diadem of valor!

A general is seen pinning medals on Hans…

TITLE: *"We are proud of you and our one regret is that you will have to wait a day for the rest of your medals."*

As Hans is shaking hands with the general, a nurse runs to him and gives him a big kiss.

Back in his room Hans thinks about the soldiers and continues to read….

A soldier is blowing a bugle and Hans hears its blast. In the room he closes the book and goes to a window. A fish wagon is passing by his house.

TITLE: *For a dreamer Hans got off to a pretty good start.*

Hans is holding a girl on his lap; she is asleep. He yawns, looks at her exposed knees and attempts to put her dress down over them. She slaps him.

TITLE: *Then came 1917 and the call to arms! America was in the war!*

A parade of soldiers is marching down the street. Some men go into an enlistment office and approach a big desk.

TITLE: *And the clarion call of opportunity, a sparrow spreads his wings — determined to be at least an eagle.*

Hans runs into the enlistment office and looks around. He fixes his trousers, and runs up and down the room. An officer behind a desk observes him. After sitting and rising he puts on his coat. Hans approaches the officer and puts his shoes and a certificate on the desk. As the officer reads the document, Hans retrieves his shoes, puts them on and stands up straight. The officer speaks…

TITLE: *"Eyes — heart — feet! Everything about you is wrong! You won't do — the Army demands able bodied men."*

The officer gives the certificate back to Hans, who departs.

INSERT OF A HEADLINE: **Girls Give Sweet-hearts to Army. Fair Sex Aid Recruiting by Turning Cold Call of Uncle Sam.**

Doris is reading a newspaper to her friend who asks…

TITLE: *"Wasn't it awfully hard for you to give Hans up?"*

Doris replies…

TITLES: *"It is hard — but gee! Just think of how much nicer he's going to look in a uniform. I can see him on his horse, bounding over the battlefield — leading the Rough Riders."*

Doris sees Hans in the garden and runs up to him. She sits on his lap and coos…

TITLES: *"Before you tell me when you start for France, I want you to know it was wonderful for you to enlist for me. Gee! Aren't we happy!"*

Doris fixes Han's coat as they rise from the bench. She sits him back down…

TITLE: *"I'll see that your suitcase is packed so that you'll look nice and clean at the front."*

After Doris leaves, Hans reads her newspaper's headline and thinks…

TITLE: *It was very difficult for Hans to tell his sweetheart — he wasn't man enough to get into the Army — so he didn't tell her.*

Hans and Doris are at a trolley station as motorman tells him to hurry and get aboard.

Doris, crying and waving tells him…

TITLES: *"Goodbye, Hans! But remember — don't fall in love with any of those French girls! And don't forget your lemon drops. You may get seasick."*

The motorman rings his gong, calling Hans to get on board. A lot of confusion occurs with another customer, and Hans is eventually put off the trolley. The motorman, while fighting with the customer, puts Hans back on the trolley. He tries to stop the trolley from running over the fighting men. As they get out of the way Hans touches a control on the trolley and it moves forward. It hits a barn and explodes. Hans runs away from the commotion.

TITLE: *When your sweetheart expects you to be a General — and you can't even get in the Army — that is when "War is Hell."*

Hans is near a billboard of Uncle Sam, and imitates a soldier.

In a nearby field a scarecrow stands while Hans falls into a ditch. A man is putting an explosive fuse on fire and runs across the field. Hans looks up at the billboard and throws a rock as if it were a hand grenade. Suddenly, an explosion occurs in the field. As dirt and debris rain down on him, Hans ducks in the ditch.

Potts sees an unconscious Hans in the ditch and stops the truck. Later, he arrives at his destination with Hans lying on boards in the back of the truck.

He covers Hans with a canvas as a fish wagon approaches. Potts drives a stake into the ground as the fish man blows a trumpet. Hans awakens and takes the canvas off.

A truck pulls up near the billboard and gets stuck in the sand. The wheels spin and send dirt flying toward Hans as he puts up a stove pipe. He sees the rocks thrown in front of him and picks one up. He hurls it and the rock comes through the pipe and hits him on the nose. More explosions occur and smoke covers the scene as the truck begins to leave.

A sign on the side of the truck reads: **I Need Men — Will Pay Double Wages.**

TITLE: *Ezra Potts had been forced to quit building his house when Uncle Sam started building his Army.*

He stands up in the wagon and salutes. Potts sees this and attempts to call out to Hans. The bugle blowing is too loud and Potts throws a brick at the man, knocking the bugle out of his hand. The man picks up a brick and throws it at Potts. He misses and the brick strikes Hans, who gets on a ladder and hits Potts. Hans falls over, then gets ups and shakes hands with Potts. He attempts to leave and discovers that he is chained. Potts tells him…

TITLE: *"I've got to finish this house by Christmas and you're going to help me."*

Hans refuses and hits Potts in the face with a stick. Potts hits him back and hands him a shovel. He starts to dig.

As a woman arrives on the scene Potts tells her…

TITLE: *"I had to chain him up — stay here and see that he works."*

After Potts leaves Hans asks the woman to untie the chain for him. She refuses and tells him to get back to work. Potts, while working on the roof, falls down and holds on to a rope attached to a scaffold. The woman leaves Hans, who has a board stuck to him. He tells her again to untie him and she pulls the board off him. She tells him to get Potts down from the roof. Hans throws a rope up to the roof and sneaks off to a shack, where, once inside, he locks the door. The woman puts up a ladder and, while holding it steady, Potts begins to descend. Hans comes out of the shack with a rifle. He fires the gun and the ladder begins to sway as the woman faints. Hans rushes to the ladder and attempts to steady it. The ladder falls across the shack with Potts on one end and Hans on the other. Potts lands very near a saw as a horse enters and begins to lick his face.

Hans is thrown from the scene by the cutting action and mounts the horse. He quickly rides away from the commotion.

The ladder swings up and down as Hans laughs at the sight of the horse's licks. Hans repeatedly touches the saw as the ladder swings and begins to scream. He gets off the ladder and approaches the saw. Hans picks up a piece of wood and puts it against the saw, which cuts it in two.

He rides near the billboard and falls off the horse into the ditch. He looks at the billboard of Uncle Sam and salutes before walking away, shaking his head.

At the enlistment office the officer speaks to Hans, who has returned in another attempt to enlist…

TITLE: *"How many times today, do I have to tell you — the Army won't take physically unfit men."*

Hans smiles at the officer and feels his own heart and ribs. The officer angrily tells him…

TITLE: *"I might overlook your other defects — if you were only tall enough."*

Hans rises and walks out of the office.

TITLE: *Eight feet, six and a half inches later.*

Hans peeks around a corner and comes into view, standing on stilts. He has trouble standing up and sways towards a windowsill. As he attempts to steady himself he grabs a woman's dress. She angrily grabs it back from him. A dog bites Hans's trousers and begins to pull them down. He grabs hold of a rope to keep from falling and holds on to his trousers. A cat arrives, which causes the dog to chase it. They both end up in Hans's trousers and begin fighting. As Hans attempts to get rid of them, he grabs hold of a ladder. The dog and cat run out of each of the trousers' legs. Hans falls into a cellar.

A man and an officer enter the recruiting office. Once inside, the man shows the officer a newspaper.

INSERT OF A HEADLINE: **Frantic Search for Secret U-Boat Base Enemy Getting Their War Supplies from U.S. — Desperate effort still fails to end submarine shipment to Central Powers.**

The man speaks to the officer…

TITLE: *"It is rumored that you know something about this."*

The officer nods and affirms that he does.

TITLE: *"Why didn't you notify the Intelligence Department?"*

The officer replies…

TITLE: *"I deemed it best to wait until I had verified my suspicions."*

A man sitting near the desk inquires…

TITLE: *"Then you know the exact location of the house?"*

The officer picks up paper and pencil and begins writing the information. The other man attacks the officer and pulls him out through a window. The two men express satisfaction with their actions.

Meanwhile, a crowd has gathered in the street outside the recruitment office. A patrol wagon arrives on the scene and officers spill out into the crowd. The officers begin putting men into the wagon and this crowd shouts…

TITLE: *"Slackers! Slackers!"*

Fights break out in the crowd as confusion and violence occur. A soldier comes out of the office and speaks to the men in an angry tone. Hans emerges from the basement and approaches the crowd. The soldier pulls him into the line of slackers. A woman shouts at the men from a window…

TITLE: *"Send 'em to the rock pile, the dirty slackers!"*

Hans hears this and looks at the slackers as another woman shouts from her window…

TITLE: *"You're just low things! Worms! Fat, fuzzy worms!"*

Hans hears the woman, points at the slackers and attempts to run away. A soldier tells him to get back in line with the slackers, and he does.

Hans spots a soldier's coat lying on the ground. He picks them up along with a soldier's hat. As Hans rises with the uniform he begins to put it on. After he is dressed, Hans salutes the soldier, who gets angry when he sees a sign on Hans's coat; it reads: Slightly damaged — $1.35. The soldier calls out to Hans, who picks up a brick. As he is about to throw it, the soldier gets out his gun. Hans puts down the brick and jumps over a fence. The soldier fires and hits Hans. He chases Hans down an alley, but loses him. A car pulls up and the soldier enters it and tells the driver and another man about Hans. He then leaves as Hans is revealed, sitting on top of the car. The car leaves the scene.

The car enters a building and drives into the cellar. The man emerges and looks around but doesn't see Hans, who is still on top of the car. The man and his mate walk away from the car. Hans looks around the cellar and sees dynamite, machine guns rifles and torpedoes. Hans stands up on top of the car in surprise at the arsenal. His head goes through the roof of the cellar. He climbs up into the room and sees the officer bound and gagged on some stairs. The officer sees Hans but falls back unconscious. He slowly comes to as Hans salutes him. Hans removes the gag from the officer's mouth. He then proudly shows the officer the uniform he is wearing and salutes with both hands. The officer shows Hans that he is handcuffed. He then tells Hans…

TITLES: *"This is a secret headquarters from which arms, ammunition and concentrated foods are sent to the enemy by submarine. They discovered I had the place under suspicion and trapped me before I could act. You've got to go for help. This den must be destroyed."*

Hans hears all of this and becomes afraid. The officer angrily tells him…

TITLE: *"All depends on your courage and coolness! Failure means — death."*

Hans begins shaking with fear. He picks up a gun and salutes the officer. Some men see Hans on the stairs as he puts his hand to his lips to tell them to be still. The men grab Hans and take the gun away from him as their leader begins to search him. He finds a small American flag as Hans slaps him. He hits Hans, who falls to the floor. Hans picks up a brick and throws it at the leader, but misses him.

The men hold him as the leader reties the officer's gag. The men put a chain around Hans and leave. He attempts to stand, but he falls over. Soon, he rises again and hobbles behind some boxes, where he finds some dynamite. A horse enters the scene. Hans pours the dynamite on the floor and puts some on the chain binding him. He lights the fuse and gets on the horse with a box. The dynamite explodes and the chain, still holding Hans, winds around a chandelier. The horse and Hans are both hanging on the chandelier. Hans holds onto the horse's tail as they revolve around the chandelier. The horse bites Hans, who screams. He grabs some hay and feeds the horse as they continue to revolve. The chain breaks, the horse drops to the ground and runs away.

A man enters and sees Hans still hanging from the chandelier. Hans kicks the man, who falls on some boxes, causing a pail of water to fall on him. The man pulls a gun and shoots at Hans, causing the chain to break. Hans lands in a hall on top of some guns with bayonets. He jumps up, pulling daggers out of his trousers. The man continues to shoot at him. Hans throws a grenade, which explodes. Hans speaks to the bound officer as other men come into the room after knocking down a wall. Hans throws another grenade at the men and they fall to the floor. Hans continues to throw grenades as the men run around in confusion, attempting to get out of the house. He grabs a box of grenades and hurls many of them around the house as smoke envelops the scene.

Sometime later, the men are being led out of the building by officers. They soon drive away. Back inside, Hans emerges from behind a big box of dynamite and notices that the can of dynamite he is holding is on fire. He puts it down and the can rolls down the stairs. The officer emerges from some debris, sees Hans and runs out of the house with him. The can of dynamite explodes and the whole house goes up.

Hans's parents are in bed and they are shaken by the blast; his father falls out, onto the floor. He looks around and says…

TITLE: *"I knew it! Too much yeast again!"*

Inside the Adolph Von Hauser Bakery, Hans's mother is setting the table. His father enters with a newspaper. The father reads…

INSERT: **Destroyed Here — Bomb Duel Ends Submarine Shipment of Arms to Foes — Modest young patriot eludes interviewers and rescues U. S. Officer, blinded by smoke screen, unfortunately is unable to tell Eagle City just how Von Hauser accomplished this daring capture.**

Father and Mother are happy to hear this good news. The father speaks…

TITLE: *"Mama — the day Hans was born I knew he would be as great as Papa."*

Father hears a knock on the front door. He goes to answer it and sees Hans and Doris in wedding attire. They express their pleasure as the couple enters the house. Once inside, the couple and the parents all embrace each other.

The End.

Promotional items advertised in the Heart Trouble *press kit.*

APPENDIX VI

Articles from Vintage Movie Magazines

Like any major star, Harry Langdon was profiled extensively in movie-related magazines over the years. Following are ten examples that cover the spectrum of this attention. The first two, Jean North's "It's No Joke to Be Funny" (*Photoplay*, June 1925) and Doris Curran's "The Sad-Faced Mr. Langdon" (*Motion Picture Classic*, July 1925) capture the beginning of the Langdon phenomenon during his days with Mack Sennett, just as his films were garnering serious critical attention. The majority of Langdon quotes used in the first came from an August 1924 Sennett press release; there are no quotes at all in the second. At the time, Langdon was singularly focused on his career and too shy to hobnob with journalists.

By the time of the next three pieces, Langdon was at First National, *The Strong Man* was in release and garnering near-unanimous critical acclaim, and the comedian was starting to flex his creative muscles. Margaret G. Monks's "Harry, Harry, Quite Contrary" (*Cinema Art*, October 1926) finds him reading *An American Tragedy* and opining on the importance of pathos in comedy. "Harry Langdon Finds Boyhood Play Ground in Pictures" (*Movie Home Journal*, December 1926) provides a brief recap of his vaudeville years and terms him a "master hand" at blending comedy with tragedy, while Madeline Matzen's "That Funny Little Man" (*Motion Picture*, December 1926) presents a career overview from Langdon's point of view.

From the perspective of the trade press, there is Tom Waller's "Harry Langdon: A Serious Man Who Makes the Whole World Laugh" (*Motion Picture World*, March 19, 1927). At the time of publication, *Long Pants* had just scored in its second Los Angeles preview, while Frank Capra had been dismissed about three weeks earlier. The article fails to mention Capra while extolling Langdon's "originality" in creating the film. It's also the piece that concludes with the assertion, "Langdon directs himself in scenes in which he appears," which would cause no end of grief once Capra decided to strike back. Meanwhile, Dorothy Herzog's "The Wistful Mr. Langdon" (*Motion Picture*, October 1927), published just as *Three's a Crowd* was about to debut, is a full-fledged biography of the comedian, the most in-depth piece to date.

Coverage dried up as Langdon's career spiraled downward, until Leonard Hall celebrated an upcoming return to films in "Hey! Hey! Harry's Coming Back" (*Photoplay*, June 1929). It's noteworthy that Hall does not specify any specific picture deal, mainly because there wasn't one — yet. It wasn't for a few weeks after the issue hit the stands that Langdon officially signed with Hal Roach. Katherine Albert's "What Happened to Harry Langdon?" (*Photoplay*, February 1932) appeared when the comedian's fortunes were at their lowest ebb: legally bankrupt as he struggled to free himself from the avaricious Helen Walton and contended with infrequent (and low-paying) vaudeville engagements. Bringing to light the story of Capra's notorious letter, the piece may well have won for Langdon an opportunity to return to films. Finally, the Langdon-related excerpt from Sonia Lee's "Good Luck or Bad Luck: Bebe [Daniels] and Harry Can Take It" (*Motion Picture*, January 1933) was written while *Hallelujah! I'm a Bum* and the early Educational shorts were in production, and captures Langdon at his most introspective.

Image quality varies depending on the source material available.

Harry Langdon has been entertaining the public for years. He was in an Indian medicine show, minstrels, vaudeville, and was a newspaper cartoonist and tumbler and clown in a circus. And here he is with Natalie Kingston in pictures

Harry Langdon

It's No Joke to Be Funny

Especially when the public will cry at the slightest provocation, says Harry Langdon

By Jean North

I WAS chatting with one of our well known Hollywood portrait photographers in his studio one day when in dashed a funny little chap with a full-moon face and large, serious, wistful brown eyes. He was all out of breath and wanted to see his proofs, it seemed.

After one look, he said:

"Well, you didn't make me as pretty as my wife, but they look pretty good, I guess."

And then what happened just took every breath of wind out of my sails and left me flapping.

You've seen a kid in the good old days, when they put candy up in penny instead of nickel and dime packages, come into the corner grocery with a dime clutched in his grimy little fist like he feared a highwayman. You've seen him point the free hand at the counter full of penny treasures and heard:

"Gimmie one of those and those and those"—until the dime was all gone and he grabbed the ten prized packages to his breast as he scuttled out to meet the gang around the corner.

Well, that's just what I saw again—at least so it seemed to me—only in a far different way.

"Gimmie a hundred of those, three hundred of those, hundred of these—better make it two hundred"—and so on until I lost consciousness from trying to add up so many hundreds.

When I came to, the moon-faced little chap with the wistful eyes was gone.

"Did his keeper come for him and who is he?" I hurled at my friend the photographer.

"If he's crazy, I wish I was too," he answered. "That's Harry Langdon, the new Sennett comedian who left vaudeville to knock 'em dead in the pictures. He was just giving me a little order for $1,950.00 worth of pictures for his fan mail. And he's going to send a truck around to carry 'em to the Sennett studio when they're finished."

WELL, I've been around Hollywood for a few years, but I never heard of a $1,950.00 order for fan pictures before in my whole life—not even around the Wally Reid set in the old days nor at any actor's studio today—so right then and there I made up my mind that some day soon I'd dash over to Mr. Sennett's (which has only spelled bathing beauties to me before) and make a little investigation of this Langdon chap on my own. Then, providing the boss was willing, I'd tell you a bit about him.

He was on location near the studio, and at first glance I was sure a circus had come to town. But no, it was only the set for Langdon's new picture, the story of his own life under the Big Top.

Harry seemed as happy as a kid chumming around there with the elephants and lions, the peanuts and the pink lemonade. He was sure right at home and soon made me feel so, too.

He's a mighty regular little chap and thinks a lot with his head, does Harry Langdon. For a long time he'd been wanting to live over his old days with a circus, when he was trapeze performer, tumbler and clown, and now he had the chance and was getting a fat salary for it. No wonder he was happy.

After watching Langdon work for a while, I made up my mind that he thoroughly enjoys [CONTINUED ON PAGE 126]

It's No Joke to Be Funny

[CONTINUED FROM PAGE 86]

this business of making folks laugh and told him so. He does, but assured me that it's no joke to try to make people laugh. His own private opinion is that "It's easy to make 'em cry, but a darn hard job to make 'em laugh."

And Harry should know, for he's spent most of his life as a public entertainer of some sort. He's been with an Indian medicine show, where he did his turn on the bill and then sold medicine in the crowd, in minstrels, a newspaper cartoonist, a circus tumbler and clown, on the big time vaudeville circuit and now in pictures. And he has certainly had plenty of chance to study the great American joke from all its angles.

"Each is hard in its own way," says Langdon. "Newspaper comics are hard because you have four or five frames in which to tell your comedy. You don't have the elbow room of the circus, the stage or the screen. On the other hand, you can get away with jokes in your strip that would be censored as too violent and brutal on the screen. Somehow the public doesn't think it's brutal when they see a ton of coal fall on a fat policeman in a newspaper comic, but they would send you to jail or have you burned alive if you tried it on the screen.

"Vaudeville is sometimes harder and sometimes easier than the newspaper or screen ways of cracking jokes. If you have a good audience it's easier; if you get a cold house it's harder—harder than anything else on earth. The advantage of vaudeville is you can feel out your audience and change your act to suit your crowd. With a picture it's made and there it is—the same for Medicine Hat and Broadway.

"One valuable little thing I learned in vaudeville, and that is you can pretty well control the laughing of your crowd. If things were going well, I'd play along at a fairly slow tempo and keep my voice well down. If the laughs were too few and quiet, I'd increase my speed and raise my voice. It seemed to be infectious, for almost always it would make 'em laugh louder and longer.

"The oddest thing about this whole funny business is that the public really wants to laugh, but it's the hardest thing in the world to make them do it. They don't want to cry, yet they will cry at the slightest provocation. Maybe that's why so many comedians want to play tragedy—they want a sort of vacation."

Like Harold Lloyd's horn-rimmed glasses, Charlie Chaplin's derby hat, bushy hair protruding, and swishing stick; Buster Keaton's frozen face and flat little hat, Langdon also has his "trade mark." Whenever possible he wears a funny little cloth hat, huge overcoat and a pair of broad, flat shoes. These are relics of his days in vaudeville, when he played "Johnnie's New Car" and "After the Ball," both of which sketches he wrote himself.

Not only does he believe them lucky, but he has worn them so long he feels quite at home in them—so much so that he says they help him in his business of being funny.

Langdon was born in Council Bluffs, Iowa, and for a time was a newsboy, but always there was a yearning for the stage. As a kid he wanted to "clown" for the gang, and it wasn't long until he ran away and joined up with a circus. Since then, with the exception of the time spent as a cartoonist, he has been before the public as a funny man in some form or other constantly.

The Sad-Faced MR. LANGDON

By Doris Curran

Harry Langdon disregarded his parents' advice, ran away from home to go on the stage—and succeeded, thus upsetting all the copy-book platitudes

IF Shakespeare had lived a little later he would have written it this way:
"All the world's a screen, and all the men merely Sennett comedians."

Take Harry Langdon, for instance. His life is just one long comedy with custard pies, cops, and chases, n'everything. He began his comedy career by being born in Iowa, pronounced "I-o-way" by its citizens, where at an early age he learned to sing the Iowa National Anthem, "California, Here I Come."

Council Bluffs, I-o-way, at that time was just like the setting for a rural comedy. It had the clothing store with the dummies out in front, the rural hose and ladder department, a bakery displaying custard pies and a force of Keystone cops. Even the slap-stick was not lacking when Henry would play truant from Sunday School to hold the brush for bill-posters plastering the barns and fences with announcements of Kohn's Klassy Kickers, or The Greatest Show on Earth.

Langdon as a Kid Actor

SPENDING money to Harry Langdon meant make-up outfits with Juvenile Complexions, Irish Whiskers and Jewish Nose Putty instead of gum or marbles. He would decorate his round countenance with an impressive array of whiskers and give all-star performances for his friends.

He got a job presently at the Opery House as prop boy, which meant that he had to go out and rent, beg or borrow whatever they needed for traveling shows. But his heart was not in the prop closet with its dusty plaster skulls, plush thrones and gilt-paper shields. That explains why the centurions of Cæsar in one "Quo Vādis" company marched onto the stage somewhat surprisingly armed with Revolutionary muskets while the manager of the company danced with rage and tried to get at a small props perched serenely out of reach high in the flies to watch the performance. Presently he was running away from home to join stock companies whose managers were evidently not superstitious, for the ghost did not walk, and Harry would return via the bumpers of a freight train.

Still he did not know that he was playing a comedy rôle in life, not even when Destiny made him the subject of a gag. There was the time when the Kickapoo Indian Medicine Show with which he was traveling was stranded in a small Nebraska town and the juggler sent him out to buy twenty-five cents worth of yellow kitchen soap with which the two of them concocted a paste.

(*Continued on page 87*)

OPPORTUNITY MARKET

AGENTS WANTED

Agents—Write for Free Samples. Sell Madison "Better-Made" Shirts for large Manufacturer direct to wearer. No capital or experience required. Many earn $100 weekly and bonus. MADISON CORPORATION, 501 Broadway, New York.

Big money and fast sales. Every owner buys gold initials for his auto. You charge $1.50; make $1.35. Ten orders a day easy. Write for particulars and free samples. American Monogram Co., Dept. 239, East Orange, N. J.

Agents wanted to advertise our goods and distribute free samples to consumers. 90 cents an hour; write for full particulars. American Products Co., 2532 American Bldg., Cincinnati, O.

HELP WANTED

Men, Women, 18 up. Get U. S. Government jobs. $95 to $250 month. Steady work. Vacation. Experience unnecessary. Common education sufficient. List positions free. Write immediately. Franklin Institute, Dept. E93, Rochester, N. Y.

HEMSTITCHING AND PICOTING

Hemstitching and Picoting. High grade patent, 1924. Attachment with instructions by mail $2. Works on any machine. Emb. Needle Free. Testimonials. Rebus & Co., Cohoes, N. Y.

MAIL ORDER METHODS

$50 A WEEK EVENINGS HOME. I made it with small mail order business started with $3. Booklet for stamp tells how. Sample and plan 25 cents. One dozen Articles free. I trust you for $3.00. Alupe Scott, Cohoes, N. Y.

OLD GOLD AND SILVER

Mail us your discarded jewelry. Gold crowns and bridges, watches, diamonds, silver, platinum and old false teeth. Money sent at once. Goods returned if offer is refused. U. S. Smelting Works (Old Reliable), Dept. 7, Chicago.

PATENTS

Inventions commercialized on cash or royalty basis. Patented or unpatented. In business 24 years. Complete facilities. References. Write Adam Fisher Mfg. Co., 512 Enright Ave., St. Louis, Mo.

PHOTOGRAPHY

Films Developed.—Special Trial Offer. Any size Kodak film developed 5c, prints 3c each. Trial 6x10 Enlargement in handsome folder 40c. Overnight Service. Roanoke Photo Finishing Co., 207 Bell Ave., Roanoke, Virginia.

PHOTOPLAYS

Successful Photoplays Bring Big Money. Our new book, "Successful Photoplays," gives full instructions for writers. Send for free copy. Successful Photoplays, Box 43, Des Moines, Iowa.

SHORT STORIES

Stories and Photoplay Ideas Wanted by 48 companies; big pay. Details free to beginners. Producers' League, 441, St. Louis, Mo.

Stories, Poems, Plays, Etc., are wanted for publication. Good ideas bring big money. Submit MSS. or write Literary Bureau, 134 Hannibal, Mo.

STAMPING NAMES

Stamp Names On Key Checks. Make $20 per 100. Some make $10 daily. Either sex. Work can be done at home, spare time. Send 25c for sample and instructions. M. Keytag Co., Cohoes, N. Y.

VAUDEVILLE

GET ON THE STAGE. I tell you how! Personality, confidence, skill developed. Experience unnecessary. Send 6c postage for instructive illustrated Stage Book and particulars. O. LaDelle, Box 557, Los Angeles, Cal.

The Sad-Faced Mr. Langdon

(Continued from page 62)

perfumed it and sold it on the street corner as corn salve.

"Dont suffer any more with that corn, ladeez and gentlemen. The Mystic Electric Corn Salve is posi-tively guaranteed to remove the most pernicious corn overnight. Twenty-five cents a box——"

From their quarter's investment they made eight dollars, enough to buy tickets to the next town. But there they found a good old-fashioned Sennett mob of angry villagers waiting, including the stout lady in the sunbonnet and the sheriff with the tin badge, checked shirt and chin whiskers. The purchasers of the corn salve, finding their affliction still with them, had telephoned ahead—and a chase ensued in which Harry Langdon finally made his escape.

Langdon's Audiences Protest

THERE was that other time when he was playing leading man in a one-night stand in Montana and felt he was surpassing himself when a hoarse voice in the audience exclaimed: "Lemme at him! I've stood as much of that damn ham as I can. A little killing 'll be good for him!"

A huge sheep herder had arisen in the audience and was pulling a revolver from his pocket! The noble sentiments of the hero fell from Harry Langdon's lips and he stood open-mouthed staring at the revolver was leveled at him, then, just as death seemed certain, the cop who always stands at the rear of the theater to yell "Hats off, gentlemen," when the curtain goes up, hurled himself upon the critic of the drama. Thus a lot of good laughs were spared to the world.

The Zealous Country Boy

IN any good comedy the poor country boy who has been the butt of the rest of the cast always comes out on top, finally to their discomfiture. Harry Langdon joined the Gus Sun Minstrel Company, did a song-and-dance number, a chair balancing specialty, assisted in a juggling act, took care of the wardrobe, swung a baton in the parade and burnt the cork for the entire company, for the sum of seven a week and cakes. Then one night their special Pullman car burned down after the show. As the minstrels, wearing their tall silk hats above their night-shirts, stood disconsolately watching their lodgings disappear in the flames, Harry was observed starting away.

"Hey, kid, where do you think you're going?" the End Man demanded.

Stranded in Home Town

HARRY pointed to the station sign, "Council Bluffs." "This is my home town," he said, "I'm gonna go home and go to bed, I am." And he departed in triumph, followed by the envious stares of the entire minstrel company, who must spend the night upon the hard benches in the waiting-room.

Langdon's subsequent successful career as laugh-maker on stage and screen is a lesson for children who refuse to heed their parents' admonitions. If Harry Langdon had listened to his family's advice, he might have become a respectable piano-mover or house-painter earning forty dollars a week. He might even have gone to the Senate instead of to Sennett, the difference being a letter or two, and a mere matter of a thousand dollars or so a week!

Whiten Your Skin Almost Over Night!

No more freckles, no more blackheads, no more sallow skin! A new discovery clears and whitens your skin with amazing quickness! Now you can clear your skin of redness, roughness, blotches, muddiness or any blemish.

Make This 3 Minute Test

There is hidden beauty in your skin. Dust, wind, and clogged pores may have injured it. But underneath—just waiting to be brought out—is a clear, vividly beautiful complexion. Banish freckles, pimples and blackheads this new way; don't let liver splotches, moth patches, tan or sallowness mar your beauty. Make this 3-minute-before-bedtime test. Smooth this cool, fragrant creme on your skin. The very next morning look into your mirror.

An Unsolicited Letter
"Almost overnight Golden Peacock Bleach Creme removed all tan from my face, and when I got up in the morning my husband asked if I felt ill because I looked so pale. I told him of the preparation and he said he could hardly believe his eyes. I did not look the same person." Mrs. M. M., Royal Oak, Mich.

Money-Back Guarantee

So wonderful—so quick—are the results of this new scientific cream that we absolutely guarantee it! Send for a jar now—today. Use it for only five nights. Then if you are not delighted and amazed with the transformation, your money will be instantly refunded. Just enclose a $1 bill with your order and mail direct. Don't be without the natural radiant beauty that lies hidden in your skin.

PARIS TOILET CO., 57 Oak Street, Paris, Tenn.

I Can Teach You To Dance Like This
—*Sergei Marinoff*

My wonderful new method makes Classic Dancing easy and fascinating to learn at home. Simple charts and photographs illustrate each lesson; clear, simple text and phonograph records teach the essentials of technique.

Complete Dancing Outfit FREE
With your lessons, I send everything necessary to equip a complete dancing studio in your own house; phonograph records, practice costume, slippers, and dancing bar.

WRITE Send at once for full information about my unique home instruction method. No obligation. Write today!

SERGEI MARINOFF SCHOOL OF CLASSIC DANCING
1924 Sunnyside Avenue, Studio B-127, Chicago, Ill.

30 Days Free Trial

Select from 44 Styles, colors and sizes, famous Ranger bicycles, delivered free to you on approval, express prepaid, at Factory Prices, from $21.50 up.

$5 a Month if desired. Parents often advance first deposit. Boys can earn easy payments.

Tires, wheels, lamps, horns, equipment at half usual prices. Send No Money. Write for our marvelous prices and terms.

Mead CYCLE COMPANY Dept. M-120, CHICAGO

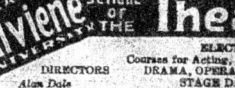

Alviene SCHOOL OF THE Theatre

ELECTIVE Courses for Acting, Teaching, Directing
DRAMA, OPERA, PHOTOPLAY
STAGE DANCING and SINGING. Developing poise and personality essential for any calling in life. Alviene Art Theatre and Stock Co. (appearances while learning). N. Y. debuts and careers stressed. For Prospectus (write study course) to Secretary, 43 West 72nd St., N. Y., EXT. 17.

CINEMA ART

"Harry, Harry, Quite Contrary"

Being the Life History of the Little Man in "Tramp, Tramp, Tramp," and "The Strong Man."

By MARGARET G. MONKS

If his music is as plaintive as he is, we think Harry could quickly collect a fortune with a tin cup and a pack of pencils

"THE greatest comedies of the future will be the saddest stories ever told." With such a contrary remark did Harry Langdon begin our little conversation, a conversation during which I did more digging, hoeing and general coaxing than I ever have needed before to make a celebrity talk. Some of them in fact do nothing better than talk about themselves. But Harry Langdon does nothing so poorly. When he does let a complete sentence drop from those, oh, so wistful lips of his, that sentence carries as great a punch as a paragraph from another man. And this gets us back to his first sentence.

"Humor finds its beginning in pathos," continued Harry. Of course, I am filling in where he merely indicated thoughts by words and gestures. "This is the psychological fact upon which every real comedian builds his laughs. Underlying the necessity for pathos in laughter is the theory of the position of the audience—a theory I have dwelt on for years as a basis of creating chuckles. This theory is simply this. In drama, the audience places itself in the position of the hero or heroine; in comedy, the audience is with the other fellow, the hero is merely another person at whom we can laugh with impunity. Therefore, anything can happen to the other fellow to cause laughter. He can fall from the top of the Woolworth building and still cause nothing but laughter, for he does not concern the onlooker."

SO much for Harry's theory of position. Bit by bit I learned that his whole life has been one of joy for "the other fellow," and that out of a poverty-saddened youth and a grinding existence has come an understanding of the pathetically funny.

Harry Langdon was born in Council Bluffs, Iowa. This is as it should be. An understanding heart such as Harry's could never have matured in a chaotic metropolitan environment. Business would have swallowed up his wistfulness with its practicality. In the dreamy never-moving small-town atmosphere of Council Bluffs there lurked a sweetness which Harry imbibed with his yearly dose of hay-fever, an air of unresisting softness which he inhaled with his country contact.

Let it be understood that Harry's was not a soft or a sweet boyhood. In this as in everything else he is contrary. Harry's was a boyhood such as we would wish to spare our own children. His father's health broke down when the boy was quite young, and in order to keep his little brothers and mother in circumstances a little better than poverty Harry went to work at nine years of age. What work could such a boy do? The work which great men boast of in later years; selling newspapers on the streets. For five years Harry continued to make his thirty and forty-cent wages every day in front of the old Doheny Opera House. It was at this stage of his life, at a time when he should have been enjoying the thrill of the old swimming hole with the other kids, that Harry began to cast around for something better than news-hawking.

THE old theater gave him an idea. His only contact with the theater until now had been received whenever he leaned up against the brick building, hoarse and tired. Watching people enter the doors of this house of magic every day, Harry noticed that they went in careworn, unhappy, frowning, and they came out carefree, happy, grinning. What sort of magic place was this which one entered sad and left glad? In a world of work and care the least bit of joy would have meant much to the little fellow, and the theater offered such a moment. So one day Harry tempted Fate and the doorman, and tried to sneak in. The manager caught him just as he slid past the door. And that was the beginning of Harry's theatrical career.

Even in those days his wistfulness arrested the attention of passersby, and the manager in one glance discovered the ragged boy's remarkable hunger for one glimpse of the performance. So he made a bargain with Harry. He could see all the performances and make a little on the side by working as call-boy. Harry accepted the offer with all the confidence of a star signing a million-dollar contract. Faith such as his couldn't be balked.

ONCE inside the theater Harry learned all the ropes; those behind the curtains as well as in front of them. After being a call-boy he became an usher; and from that he walked into the box-office. Finally he was recognized as a sort of major-domo of the theater, passing out handbills, pulling curtains, selling tickets, and sweeping the floors after the last gallery-god had climbed down from his perch amidst the peanut shells. Harry learned a lot in these years. This was his only school by the way, for the necessity for earning money never allowed him to attend a real school for very long. After his sweeping exercises Harry used to stay in the dark theater until the slam of the outer door told him the manager was gone. Then came his performance, his own; for he was both actors and audience. He would mount the splintery stage and mimic the performers on that week's ten-twenty-thirty bill. From out the deep hollow of the old theater ghostly echoes would applaud his youthful burlesque of "Hamlet," "Pagliacci," or whatever the hashy bill of the house was offering. These one-man performances ruined a perfectly good usher who might some day have become a house manager. Gradually there grew in him a love for acting, which made him useless as anything but an actor.

And one day this longing for acting success made him a failure as an usher. Perched in the wings he lost himself in enjoyment of a performance, and at the same time lost his job. The manager had finally realized that a stage-struck boy was of no more use than a stage-struck girl. So he fired Harry.

To Harry that was the end. He became reckless. Afraid to go home with the bad news, he accompanied a friend across the river to Omaha, which, although in itself an adventure to the boy, was climaxed when the friend led him into the then famous haunt of the Mid-Western great "Mickey Mullin's Music Hall." Nowadays, to the profession, such places are derisively recalled as "honky-tonks." But, to the open-eyed boy from across the river, the table-strewed room with its twenty foot stage was Heaven.

IT was amateur night. A grand prize of twenty-five dollars would go to the amateur who received the most applause for his performance. The music-hall was crowded with carousing farmers, and the commission-girls who ate according to the drinks they injected into the farmers.

Harry's friend, a little under the weather,

Harry, that dressy chap, seems to have discovered something wrong with his hat

OCTOBER, 1926

For once he does not look either tired or hungry. Or perhaps it's only a bluff to impress people while he is doing his stuff in "The Strong Man"

shoved the boy forward, shouting that he was a great little entertainer. Scared, but afraid to retreat before the eyes of the mob, Harry broke into a little jig, a buck and wing, and then an inadequate song. Until he had finished, the house was as still as a muzzled sphinx; but at his conclusion there rose a roar the like of which Mickey Mullin had never before heard in his halls. And as the boy stood there, too frightened to move, the roar swelled until it was obvious that Harry was a hit. He received the first prize.

Once out on the street, he turned to his friend in wonder, asking whether his singing and dancing had been so good that he deserved the prize.

"Your dancing was rotten," admitted the friend candidly. "You got the prize because when you stopped singing you looked scared enough to make a deaf-and-dumb man laugh out loud. It was your funny face that won, not your dancing or singing."

And that was how Harry learned that he had a face which would some day be his fortune. The rest he recited quickly, quietly and without any show of braggadocio. The music hall grew tired of his act, and he finally had to give it up as a means of livelihood. He was becoming known as a "professional amateur." His fame spread to the medicine shows however, and he traveled with one of the best known of these for two years. During this time he gained a world of experience, selling medicines, pantomiming a dozen characters in a night, and at the same time studying the thousands of people with whom he came in contact.

FOLLOWED a couple of years in Mid-Western stock companies. During this time Harry played everything from babies to old men, which accounts for his remarkable adaptability to such a large number of funny characterizations.

Talking of these years reminded Harry of a funny experience. He was playing juveniles with the Metropolitan Stock Company which toured Nebraska, Iowa, Kansas and points thereabouts. In the same company was an old character actor, who knew his lines so well from long repetition that he could ad lib at leisure. He often rattled other actors by his sotto voce lines, and Harry was no exception. It was during a performance of "East Lynne" that the explosion occurred. Harry was to run on the stage, say excitedly, "He jumped in the saddle and galloped off," and then run off again. When he started to speak this time the old character actor whispered, "Come on, hurry up, you're terrible." The boy grew confused and shouted desperately, "He gumped in the jaddle and sallopped off."

This, explains Harry, is one of the reasons why he prefers working in the movies to acting on the stage. "You can say anything, and your audience can't hear you," was his remark.

THIS stock experience was followed by eighteen years in vaudeville in a sketch which he kept always original from the day he first rehearsed it to the last day he played it at the Orpheum Theater, Los Angeles, in 1923. His fame as a vaudevillian was the final step to movie stardom. The rest every movie fan knows. First Mack Sennett featured Harry in two-reelers, then Harry saw a greater field in features, and eventually formed his own corporation to release pictures through First National.

Out of such a past did this comedian come. When one analyzes the vicissitudes through which he struggled before reaching the heights, the sloughs through which he waded before attaining dry-land and peace from poverty's woes, one can hardly understand how he could retain the vitality to make people laugh— with big, healthy guffaws.

Of the necessity for pathos in humor he had more to say. He believes that sadness is the basis of humor, but that there must be a little shy smile to relieve it. First he is pathetic. His big, round, childlike eyes hold your attention and excite your pity. He is hurt. His dignity as a human being has been injured. The audience is very still. Then his mouth twists into an odd little smile, and, reassured, the audience roars.

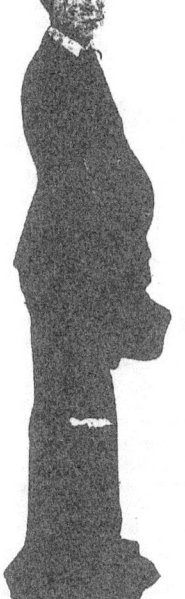

They say that badly assembled haberdashery makes a comedian. Anyway, Harry's trousers would make a Yale sophomore blush with envy

"THE absence of feeling which generally goes with laughter," he said, "is what I find most interesting. In character I am an undying optimist. I always strive to be that. No matter what awful predicament I may find myself in, I must remain that optimist. In "Tramp, Tramp, Tramp," I am chased by a herd of cattle to a high fence which I scale in hope of finding safety on the other side. The fence, however, is built at the very brink of a deep chasm, into the dizzy depths of which I find myself looking. I attempt to make myself safe by pulling out the nails which hold the fence together and nailing my clothes to the sagging boards. Naturally, the fence goes to pieces. Everybody seems agreed that this bit was howlingly funny, but it would not have been if I had been terrified and stumbled as the ordinary person would have. It would have been tragic. It was my apparent indifference to the situation which was funny.

"Laughter is invariably a group matter. You hear a man telling a story to a group, and hear them all laughing, but you are not usually inclined to laugh because you are not one of the company. A man who had attended a very moving church service was asked why he did not weep when everybody else was crying, answered, 'But I'm not a member of this parish.'

"We laugh when we find others in whose intelligence we have confidence, laughing. For instance a very snobbish person might be immensely amused at a street corner scene, but would not join in the laughter unless he saw others of his own social class laughing too. We like to have company in our laughter."

When Harry says the funniest comedies are made from the greatest tragedies, we wonder whether he considers his own life a comedy or a tragedy, for of hard grinding work he has had his share. Certainly his admirers must hope that he will reserve for himself some of that joy which he gives to countless others.

Yet, as I got up to leave him, he picked up a book. I glanced at the cover. It was "An American Tragedy," by Theodore Dreiser. How contrary, Harry.

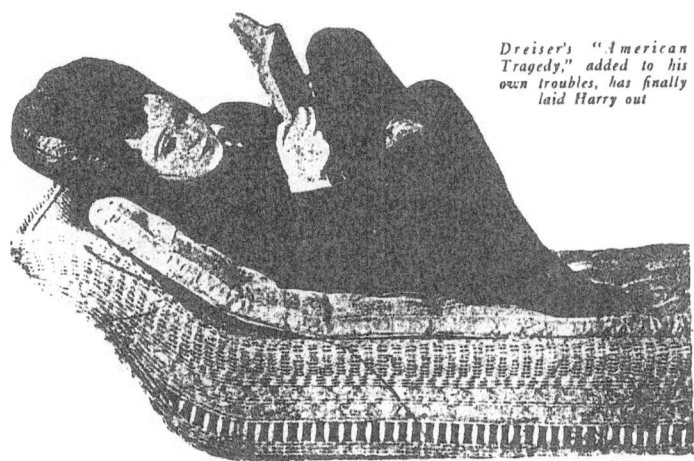

Dreiser's "American Tragedy," added to his own troubles, has finally laid Harry out

Page Nineteen

HARRY LANGDON is the favorite comedian of the movie colony. Ask Harold Lloyd who gives him the biggest celluloid laugh. Ask any star. They will all say Langdon. In a year Langdon has taken up his comedy post right behind Chaplin and Lloyd. Langdon has "gone younger" than any of the other film comics. He plays the comedy infant. In brief, he is the eternal moron. Langdon was once a newspaper cartoonist in Omaha. Now he's the comic idol of Hollywood!

Photoplay, *August 1926*

HARRY LANGDON *Finds Boyhood Play Ground In* PICTURES

Harry LANGDON'S screen cavorting is really the result of repressed desires—boyhood desire to play when it was impossible. Boyhood thirst for laughter and gayety when life held only tears for him. He never had a chance to play when he was young. Now the movies offer a playground where old wishes can come true, and Harry makes a regular romp of his work. But a grown-up boy's play has a certain wistfulness, a wisdom that brews that deep dramatic drink the critics call pathos-humor. That's Langdon. At the age of eight Harry was already helping to support an indigent family by selling newspapers on the cold streets of Council Bluffs, Ia. His stand, strangely enough, was in front of the city's largest legitimate theatre. Many times the boy longed to peep within the portals of the house of drama, but he needed the required thirty cents to help his mother make both ends meet.

Finally, he had his desire by becoming call-boy. Then he rose to the heights of usherdom and later to the post of advertising man, cashier, janitor and the hundreds of other odd jobs a theatre provides. Afraid to disclose his ambition in that theatre, Harry went across the river to Omaha one night and before a jeering audience gave his first performance on any stage. As a singer and dancer he was not a hit, but when he became nervous and a victim of stage fright, Harry was the scream of the evening, taking the first amateur prize. There followed engagements in music halls, with medicine shows and on the legitimate stage; a hard life and a harder struggle out of the rut of the commonplace.

Then Harry conceived an idea, wrote a sketch, and that sketch served him as a vehicle for eighteen years. It was "Johnny's New Car," in which he rose to the heights of vaudeville fame. The rest has often been recited. His attempt at puncturing the movie walls, his failure, his second attempt and success, and the formation of his own company are now merely steps in a triumphal progression.

¶Harry Langdon missed a lot of schooling in his young days, but he's making up for lost time. In fact, the miss is Harry's main concern.

Thus struggle, tragedy and a pathetic boyhood gave Harry Langdon that innate humanness, wistfulness, and appeal which makes him one of today's greatest comedians.

In "The Strong Man," his most recent feature comedy for First National, Harry has shown these human qualities to great advantage. For it is when he drops into an almost autobiographical mood that the greatest laughs are resultant.

Comedy blends with tragedy, laughter with tears to make the pattern of this film so like the pattern of life. It is the mixing of bitter with the sweet, an old recipe for all the great comedies that have always outlived the serious drama from the time of the Greeks, through the glib Moliere, down to our present day. It is a fine art, the proper handling of this mixture, but Langdon's is a master hand.

[11]

  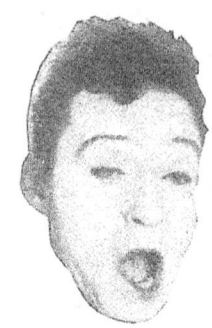

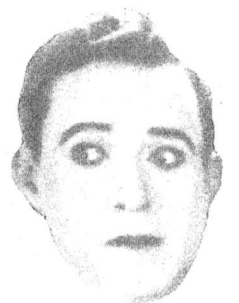

He was a funny little boy, a little boy usually solemn and desperately in earnest, for the wolf of hunger stalked close at his heels. But he had a sudden smile that beguiled the customers who bought his newspapers

That Funny

Or is Harry Langdon sad . . . figure trudging along

By MADELEINE

When he joined a medicine show, he sold unheard-of quantities of medicine, and all by means of laughter. He sang, danced, wisecracked and doubled in the actual selling of the medicine

ONCE upon a time (way back in Council Bluffs, Iowa) there lived a little boy. His parents were very poor and a penny looked to him as big and as exciting as a twenty-dollar gold piece looks to the average boy today.

He went to the public schools until he was ten years old, then the days grew so lean, the struggle so bitter, he was obliged to leave school and sell papers to help out.

He took up his stand opposite the largest theater in town. The selling of papers progressed slowly, for the boy was so thrilled by imagining what went on inside the theater that he would forget to call out his wares and stand there—just dreaming!

He was a funny little boy, a little boy usually solemn and desperately in earnest, for the wolf of hunger stalked close at his heels. Food was scarce and not always forthcoming. But in spite of this he had a sudden smile, a smile that beguiled each customer and made him smile in return.

At home there was a mother, the kind you used to read of but seldom see these days—a mother who made apple pies and cookies when times were plentiful.

To her he brought glamorous tales of stage folk, of kindly actors (who never asked for change); of actresses in gowns that rustled, who carried ermine muffs and smelled of violets even in the dead of winter.

He told his mother of the throngs that crowded past him after each performance, the throngs who left the theater with laughter and tears still lingering in their eyes and blinding them to the small, eager boy who stood there clutching his papers with frost-bitten fingers.

To him the tinsel was gold, the make-believe world of the theater the only real world and a place of growing enchantment.

A chance came to be call-boy in the theater and he grabbed it. Then he became usher, and later filled the positions of cashier, advertising man, and janitor. And, most wonderful of all, several times he filled in for missing actors.

His ambition grew, he entered amateur night contests and came out with honors and prizes which he brought home proudly to his mother.

About this time, a medicine show came to town. There was

Little Man

a Pierrot . . . a gentle, lonely the road of the world?

MATZEN

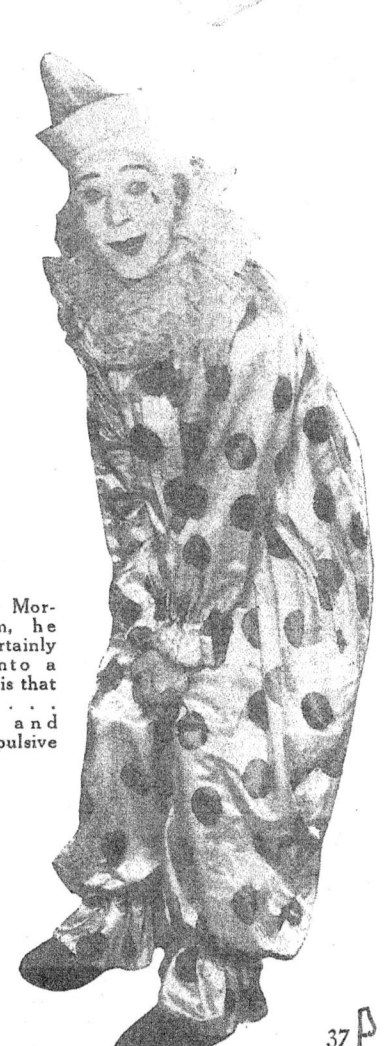

Mack Sennett says that Langdon is the greatest comedian in the world today . . . and that he has only begun . . . and that his future is brighter and more full of promise than that of any star

an opening for someone who could sing, dance, wisecrack and double in selling medicine. Dr. Staley ran the show and he took the boy with him when he left town.

The boy, now almost grown, played for several years with this and other medicine shows.

He sold unheard-of quantities of medicine for them—and all by means of laughter. And the medicine worked wonders, or perhaps it was laughter that made the cures?

From the medicine shows he went into traveling stock company and played every part from *Little Eva* to old character roles. Then came vaudeville on a small-time circuit.

Hard years followed—the struggle for recognition was a heart-rending thing. Laughter and hope almost died for lack of appreciation. Many times the boy walked and bummed his way home—broke. Only to start out again with a new company and the encouragement of his mother to uphold him.

By the time he was twenty-one he had done about everything that was to be done in the way of work connected with the theater.

These years were filled with disappointment, with drudgery without reward. They were years during which ambition faded away to a mere ghost of itself. But, oddly, the tinsel of the stage still shone like a precious thing to him.

Out of the bitterness grew a gentle, unembittered conception of the miseries that beset boys who persist in dreaming. This conception took shape and finally became one of the most lovable and delightful screen characters the world has ever seen. For the boy was Harry Langdon, and the Harry Langdon that you see on the screen today is the boy Harry that smiled his funny crooked smile and refused to give up his dream.

Mack Sennett says that Langdon is the greatest comedian in the world today—and that he has only begun. His future is brighter and more full of promise than that of any star.

And Mr. Sennett should know—if anyone does!

"I couldn't seem to make a dent in the theatrical world," Mr. Langdon told me, "until I wrote a skit of my own, called 'Johnny's New Car.' I toured the Orpheum circuit in that act for nearly ten years. I wasn't a head-liner—but I COULD

(*Continued on page 96*)

If Christopher Morley met him, he would most certainly write him into a story . . . he is that sort of person . . . charmingly and amusingly impulsive

ADVERTISING SECTION

Don't you think?

It is by no means strange that men who want "something better" in cigarettes turn to Fatima. All things considered: tobaccos, aroma, subtle delicacy, it would be extraordinary if they didn't

What a whale of a difference just a few cents make

LIGGETT & MYERS TOBACCO CO.

Beautiful Complexion IN 15 DAYS

Clear your complexion of pimples, blackheads, whiteheads, red spots, enlarged pores, oily skin and other blemishes. I can give you a complexion soft, rosy, clear, velvety beyond your fondest dream. *And I do it in a few days.* My method is different. No cosmetics, lotions, salves, soaps, ointments, plasters, bandages, masks, vapor sprays, massage, rollers or other implements. No diet, no fasting. Nothing to take. Cannot injure the most delicate skin. Send for my Free Booklet. You are not obligated. Send no money. Just get the facts.

Dorothy Ray, 646 N. Michigan Blvd., Suite 499, Chicago

PARKER'S HAIR BALSAM

REMOVES DANDRUFF
STOPS HAIR FALLING

Has been used with success for more than 40 years

RESTORES COLOR AND BEAUTY TO GRAY AND FADED HAIR

60¢ & $1.00 at all druggists

HISCOX CHEMICAL WORKS
PATCHOGUE, N.Y.

Reduce and Shape Your Limbs with Dr. Walter's Medicated Rubber Stockings and Anklets

Light or dark rubber. For over 20 years they have relieved swelling, varicose veins and rheumatism promptly. Worn next to the skin they induce natural heat, stimulate the circulation and give a neat and trim appearance. They give wonderful support and are a protection against cold and dampness. Anklets $7, extra high $9. Stockings $12. Send check or money order—no cash. Write for Booklet.

Dr. Jeanne M.P. Walter, 389 Fifth Ave., N.Y.

ANITA Shapes While You Sleep

Users Praise it as a Priceless Possession

RESHAPE YOUR NOSE!

You can surely and safely mold your nose to beautiful proportions with the

ANITA NOSE ADJUSTER

Shapes while you sleep or work—painlessly, comfortably. Results speedy and *guaranteed*. Physicians praise it highly. No *metal* to harm you.

FREE BOOKLET points way to facial beauty and happiness. *Write for it today.*

The ANITA Co.   Gold Medal Won 1923

That Funny Little Man

(Continued from page 37)

make people laugh, I could eat three meals a day and do some of the things I had always longed to do for my mother.

"Every time I came West I tried to get a hearing in pictures—but no one would listen to me. The less likely my chances became the more enthused I grew over motion pictures.

"Finally Sol Lesser gave me a chance and I made a few comedies for him. Mr. Sennett saw these pictures—and you know the rest!"

If Chaplin is a clown, with trick shoes and a derby—if Lloyd is that nice young man who wears hoot-owl glasses and gets into scrapes—Harry Langdon is a small boy with dreams in his eyes and a shy smile that gets you every time.

We shout with laughter at Chaplin and at Lloyd, we admire them, imitate them —but we love Langdon.

Chaplin is our beloved buffoon, Lloyd our maker of excellent comedies—but Langdon is just himself. His is a sheer triumph of personality.

And with years of training behind it this personality should reach even greater heights.

He is interested in every one whom he meets, he studies them and appreciates them. He is in a sense a humanitarian, as are all truly great people. There is not an ounce of pose about him, he is naive, disconcertingly so—sometimes.

He is well educated tho self-educated. He is humble about his success.

Try as I may, I cannot see him other than a small boy who has suddenly grown up into a *Pierrot*—and is a little bewildered at finding himself as he is.

He adores children, every child he meets delights and enchants him. He has no children of his own and back of this shadow lies an unhappy marriage.

He is taller in real life than he appears to be on the screen; his eyes are, very surprisingly, brown and the saddest eyes I have ever seen.

He is a continual curiosity to his press-agent who worships him and protects him from the sometimes rude public with all the earnestness of a mother.

He is too impulsive at times—but always charmingly and amusing impulsive. He is the sort of person that Christopher Morley would delight in.

The other day a small urchin managed to worm his way into the studio. He spied Langdon's name over the door and rushing over to the screened window pressed his nose against it and stared into the dressing-room.

"You never saw such an excited kid— he watched me as tho I were a wild animal at the Zoo!" Langdon told me.

"I tried to coax him in—but he wouldn't come—I could see he was disappointed. Finally he said hoarse with fear—or something '*smile!*' I grinned and then he gave a relieved giggle. We were friends. He came in and visited, seemed disappointed because I wasn't littler and departed with a sheaf of autographed pictures.

"That little episode convinced me of the folly of personal appearances," he concluded.

A wise man once said that the trait he found most worth while in mankind was gentleness. Harry Langdon has more gentleness in his make-up than most humans.

To me he will always be *Pierrot*—a gentle, lonely figure trudging along the road of the world.

Harry LANGDON

A Serious Man Who Makes the Whole World Laugh

By Tom Waller
West Coast Representative

WHILE interviewing Harry Langdon some one in the room piped up with the boast: "This is my seventeenth day on the wagon." Harry did not even crack a smile. He has been in Hollywood 1,460 nights with not a single party on the record. Harry reads and writes. He operates a typewriter faster than a crack newspaperman. He bubbles over with originality. He jots it down as fast as it bubbles. This, says Harry, prohibits him even time to think about parties.

"Audiences want dumb comedians. They want to be brighter than the comedians. They want comedians to be real. They want comedians to do dumb things the same way that dumb people do in real life."

That's Harry's reason for being dumb on the screen. Not an affected dumbness which would bore and sicken, but a convincing dumbness. A dumbness characteristic of some unfortunate in every day life who blunders in the office, in traffic and in the home but who once in a while meets with the occasional uncanny luck of the dumb.

Harry Langdon as the simp on the screen who simply cannot help himself is as heavy off the set as he is at the box office till. He is the man who gives the thousand and one first impressions. The one that remains indelible, however, is Harry Langdon's sincerity. A sincerity that makes everyone he meets a friend to Harry Langdon whether or not Harry Langdon will accept that friendship.

Analyzed, the thing about Langdon most contagious and that which possibly causes most people to warm up to him even before the conversation is started is Langdon's enthusiasm for his job, always as continuously effervescent as that of the schoolboy who has gotten 100 per cent in all of his exams. Langdon is so in love with his work that after a long day on the set in heat made tropical by electric illumination, he diverts himself in his own home by putting down in black and white his own ideas for his own screen stories.

Langdon's face is contradictory to his mind and his whole being. He isn't absent-minded. He is lonely only when he is not busy. Yet there surely seems to be something pathetic about the man. A trait that automatically arouses sympathy. Harry loves his trait because it is the backbone of his job. It is the trait which enables him to portray the boob; convulsing an intelligent audience, a mediocre audience. The trait which can break off a laugh, almost bring a tear and wind up with a bigger laugh. It is the trait which the many alleged students of psychology believe they can analyze and their analysis, whatever it may be, satisfies Langdon because it satisfies them as patrons of his box office. It is the trait which suggests to other fans someone they have seen before they bought their ticket to the Langdon show; some one of their acquaintances, or, possibly, some one right in their own family.

Although a star and one of the biggest of his kind, Harry Langdon is not even an actor during an interview. To get him to talk the interviewer may often believe it necessary to do the acting. Then Langdon will detect it and close up like the proverbial clam. Loose limbs, plain language and plenty of cigar smoke seem to get the best replies from Langdon. Then his enthusiasm asserts itself and you see before you an entirely different face. It is the Langdon as he really is. Sheer animation because it's the job you're asking him about and not a lot of questions about himself which would cause many others to preen themselves for their best lingo. And Langdon opens up and tells you about that job. And, incidentally, when you are beginning to learn a lot about the man Langdon quite suddenly becomes aware that in talking about the job he is talking about himself. An abrupt apology for being "egotistical" is usually followed by Langdon firmly clamping his lips together. It is more smoke, looser limbs and even plainer language before you can convince him that you are not interested in him; that all you want is to know about the "job."

While smoking a couple of extra cigars we learned that Harry's next picture is going to have a water front tang. That he is now working nightly on the theme which will present him on the screen as a wharf rat—not just a low-minded, low-down, booze-spotted bum—is correct, he told us. He will be the kind of a bum that a newspaperman on a longshoreman strike assignment in New York might have picked out as a drinking partner and cultivated into a "leak" for the "lowdown" on the story. A bum with all the earmarks of a bum but also the kind of a bum who could roll into a gutter, herald the occasion with invectives and at the same time get up and grin over the very thought that wherever there is a gutter there is always a sidewalk.

Harry told us that there will be no leading lady in his next picture. He is planning to have two rather elderly characters tell the romance of the story. He remarked, in fact, that in the future he will try to have as few stories as possible necessitating leading ladies.

Not because Langdon wants to be the side as well as the center of the screen. He is striving to carry on his originality and yet conform with the conventions of the screen. He is doing this because he believes sex is rampant in plays as well as pictures at the present time.

And Harry Langdon is also about to introduce another innovation. He is going to cut his corps of gag men or comedy constructionists, as they have been called of late, down to one man.

Langdon's reasoning in this respect is that the trend of an excellent idea may be lost in its entirety after a half-dozen more or gaggists have made suggestions as to how it could be improved.

And Langdon comes forth again with his originality when he tells how a producer can gauge the success of a picture with a Hollywood preview audience.

"It isn't so much how they applaud out there in Hollywood as it is if the picture has interested them enough to stand out in the street and look for the star," Langdon vouchsafed.

As an instance of how this works Langdon told us about his reaction following two preview showings of his latest picture "Long Pants." The first preview was at the West Lake theatre when "Long Pants," edited for laughs rather than story, was shown in nine reels. The applause was there and probably a lot of people looked around for Langdon after the show but Langdon was not to be seen even though he sat right in the middle of the audience.

"Then 'Long Pants' was taken back to the cutting room and this time edited for story essentials with a maximum length of six short reels. The second preview occurred at the Wilshire. This time the applause thundered and Langdon had a difficult time reaching his car. A few days after he had reached his car it was announced that the picture as seen at the Wilshire would open in the Strand Theatre, Manhattan. And Langdon's business manager personally escorted the Strand print to New York.

We devoted three pages of the Hollywood department recently describing "Long Pants" from the time the story idea was conceived to the time it was brought to the cutting room in 325,000 feet and there made ready for its preview.

At that time, however, we did not know that Langdon one night had conceived the idea for one of the cleverest gags in the picture and that the following morning at eight o'clock, without consulting any of his gag men he put the idea into motion before the camera. He worked until 5:30 the next morning when he had to his credit a record of having shot eighty-five scenes in less than twenty-four hours. And eighty-five scenes which critics now acclaim to constitute one of the best sequences in the picture.

Langdon directs himself in scenes in which he appears. He believes that he can do this best because he knows his story and he knows himself. He ventured the belief that a star, capable in these respects, directing himself would result in the motion picture industry probably turning out better pictures, or at least pictures more truly interpreting emotions as they really are.

The Story Of A Man Who Loves His Work

The Wistful

What He Craves Most of All

By Dorothy

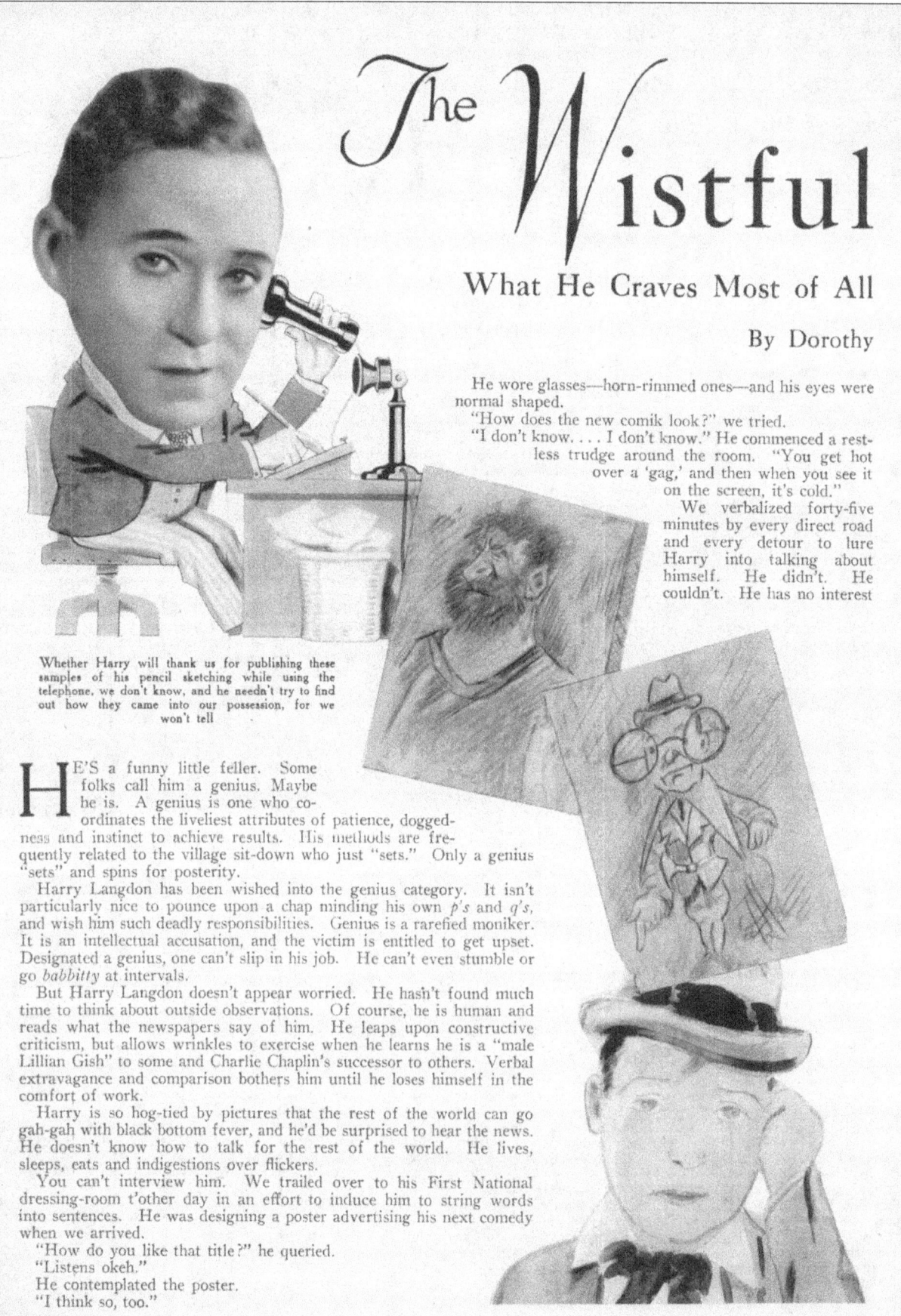

Whether Harry will thank us for publishing these samples of his pencil sketching while using the telephone, we don't know, and he needn't try to find out how they came into our possession, for we won't tell

He wore glasses—horn-rimmed ones—and his eyes were normal shaped.

"How does the new comik look?" we tried.

"I don't know.... I don't know." He commenced a restless trudge around the room. "You get hot over a 'gag,' and then when you see it on the screen, it's cold."

We verbalized forty-five minutes by every direct road and every detour to lure Harry into talking about himself. He didn't. He couldn't. He has no interest

HE'S a funny little feller. Some folks call him a genius. Maybe he is. A genius is one who co-ordinates the liveliest attributes of patience, doggedness and instinct to achieve results. His methods are frequently related to the village sit-down who just "sets." Only a genius "sets" and spins for posterity.

Harry Langdon has been wished into the genius category. It isn't particularly nice to pounce upon a chap minding his own *p's* and *q's*, and wish him such deadly responsibilities. Genius is a rarefied moniker. It is an intellectual accusation, and the victim is entitled to get upset. Designated a genius, one can't slip in his job. He can't even stumble or go *babbitty* at intervals.

But Harry Langdon doesn't appear worried. He hasn't found much time to think about outside observations. Of course, he is human and reads what the newspapers say of him. He leaps upon constructive criticism, but allows wrinkles to exercise when he learns he is a "male Lillian Gish" to some and Charlie Chaplin's successor to others. Verbal extravagance and comparison bothers him until he loses himself in the comfort of work.

Harry is so hog-tied by pictures that the rest of the world can go gah-gah with black bottom fever, and he'd be surprised to hear the news. He doesn't know how to talk for the rest of the world. He lives, sleeps, eats and indigestions over flickers.

You can't interview him. We trailed over to his First National dressing-room t'other day in an effort to induce him to string words into sentences. He was designing a poster advertising his next comedy when we arrived.

"How do you like that title?" he queried.

"Listens okeh."

He contemplated the poster.

"I think so, too."

18

Mr. Langdon

Is to Be Left Alone

Herzog

in his past life, and if others evince any, it makes him fearfully uncomfortable. More, it gets him all hot and bothered and caged as though *Simon Legree* had him cornered at last.

He's a funny little feller, this Harry Langdon chap, inversed within himself, brooding, bubbling, morose, gay. Creating a life of his own, living a life for others, yet curiously isolated, and his isolation respected. He's a whole-hearted emotionalist who soars to the top and thuds to the bottom with unexpected changes of gravitation. He's got himself all bruised with loop-the-loop, nose-dive emotions; but despite this he knows his directions.

People have often soap-boxed about one-track minds, which appear to be a series of brain cells trafficking into a direction unannoyed by stop signals or momentary confusions. Harry has a one-track mind. He started life with it. Ever since he was an inch high to a frog, he craved the grease-paint and the stage.

He was the only one of ten children with such bent. Mrs. Langdon couldn't understand her son. No one in the Langdon family ever craved the make-believe as a livelihood. Harry did. He would mosey around his home town of Council Bluffs, Iowa, scaring up news as to when the next minstrel show was due. When he tacked on a few more years, he trekked

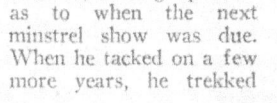

Harry's mother (above) always hid his clothes when a minstrel show came to town, and even at the age of five, as he is pictured below, she often would say, "I don't know what's got into that boy"

across the river to Omaha, Nebraska, to poke around stage doors.

Mrs. Langdon became annoyed with her son. He listened seriously to her lectures on the evils of the stage. He listened until he lost himself in his own thoughts and was spanked for inattentiveness. Harry does precisely the same thing today. Half the time he has no idea what folks talk to him about.

His Mother Hides His Clothes

IN desperation, Mrs. Langdon was compelled to hide her son's clothes when a minstrel aggregation trooped into town. She made Harry change into girl's clothes. He accepted the humiliation as part of the rain that drips into every one's life. No sooner, however, did mother turn her back and go about the business of mending stockings and domesticating a disordered house than Harry was out like a cannon-ball, scurrying around until he found his clothes. He then fast-footed it to the minstrel quarters.

His mother caught him in the act one indigo day and trotted him into the kitchen. Harry was destined to have a tender part of his anatomy soundly walloped. Mrs. Langdon commissioned Jimmy, four years younger than the truant, to go forth and return with a switch. Exit Jimmy, to re-enter with a worn-out weed that cracked after one swipe. Mrs. Langdon locked the boys in a closet, found

(Continued on page 84)

The Wistful Mr. Langdon

(Continued from page 19)

her own switch, and returned to paddle them vigorously.

Harry didn't mind mantelpiece suppers. He had too much to think about.

"I don't know what's got into that boy," Mrs. Langdon often sighed to her husband.

Mothers do get upset and sometimes make the child who is responsible take castor oil for biliousness. Harry had that happen too, but he had a duck's back when it came to punishment.

Came the strawberry season. Harry inveigled Jimmy into the idea of picking berries. Off they trundled, two barefoot boys dressed for muggy business. They always found a farmer to job them for the day and so industriously did they work that they collected forty or fifty cents for their services.

With this Harry organized a stage in the hay-loft. He built miniature wings and a makeshift curtain. He purchased boxes and whatnots from stores that would just as soon sell them as use them for kindling. The children in the neighborhood paid pins or pennies to attend Harry's shows. He offered a pretty good variety bill.

Harry never took dancing lessons or music lessons or even drawing lessons. He just picked these things up. Jimmy was his buddy. He taught Jimmy a dance ending with the split. Also a song or two. If "theatrical funds" were short, Harry piloted his brother to the town restaurant, entering at the most crowded moment.

"Anybody want to hear a song and dance act?" he'd shout in the doorway.

Everybody did. The boys looked so small and determined.

Whereupon Harry pulled out a mouth-harp and commenced to play; Jimmy sang a song and went into his dance, ending with the split. Harry passed the hat around. The pennies and nickels chucked into it swelled the "company's treasury."

Father's Celluloid Collars

Harry dived into hot water over one show. He built a contraption to double for a railroad train. A barrel was wheeled. The front was hollowed to put a coal oil bucket in it. The bucket's funnel poked out. Father's celluloid collars were corralled and placed in the bucket. A match started the fire and clouds of ill-smelling smoke poured forth. Harry hid in the wings and pulled the barrel across the stage with a string. There's a train for you. The act created a sensation in the audience, but when Mr. Langdon discovered to what use his celluloid collars had been put, he took it out on the section of Harry's anatomy that made mantelpiece dining a necessity.

The boy was never a great one at games, but the kids liked him because he was a good scout and gave slick shows. At school, when he was supposed to be cramming his head with reading and writing and arithmetic, he was drawing cartoons. He enjoyed pen pictures as much as stage ones. Harry still draws. Most folks pencil triangles or squares or curlycues when talking over the telephone. Harry draws pictures. You drop into his dressing-room, as we did, and he is usually designing a poster or gagging a scene on paper.

The Spanish-American War. When this broke, Harry was about ten years old. Jimmy ferried across the river to Omaha to sell newspapers. They cost five cents in those days. After earning forty cents Jimmy figured the day okeh and returned home, unsold papers under his arm.

Harry blinked at them and read the searing martial head-line.

"What're you goin' to do with these?"

"Oh, nuthin'. I've sold enough," Jimmy reckoned.

Slapping the papers under his arm, Harry scurried from the house to return a few hours later with a dollar or so profit! He took to selling papers as a regular gadget. It enabled him to spend more time around stage doors.

While waiting for his papers one day, Harry showed a group of newsboys a Theodore Roosevelt cartoon. A reporter chanced by and investigated the interested group:

"Did you do that?" to Harry.

"Um."

The reporter walked him in to see the *Bee's* city editor and the cartoon appeared in the next day's paper. Harry, young as he was, received an offer to cartoon for the *Bee*. He tried it for a while, but the stage yearn made him restless. He resigned.

Seventh heaven was realized when the boy landed an usher job in an Omaha theater. He ate up the amateur contests, flashing his stuff to the amusement of the audience. Harry was small for his age, and when he rounded his eyes—he does the same trick today in pictures—and pantomimed in that wistful, helpless fashion of his, the spectators clapped boisterous approval.

Mrs. Langdon worried over her son and persuaded him to leave the theater. He did, so she didn't object when he started rehearsing Jimmy for a show to be given at the schoolhouse. It was winter—cold, snowy, windy. Harry rigged up posters heralding the gala event and tacked them on fences. The show promised to be worthy of the twenty-five cents admission fee. Came the première. One cash customer dared the iciness of the night. The youngsters went through their rigmarole and had to part with the quarter to pay for coal oil burned in the lamps and messing the room!

Then He Became a Barber

About this time, Mr. Langdon decided to take a hand and pilot his son into the ways of business. Harry was fifteen years old and bound for no decisive profession. Mr. Langdon spoke to the town barber about the boy, and the barber gave him a job. He became pretty good and his chief prognosticated some day Harry would be 'most as good as he.

The Langdon household rested peacefully. Then one day—pandemonium. Harry had disappeared. Days passed. No word from the absentee. At the end of a few months he returned.

"Where have you been?" his mother cried.

"Oh, out with a medicine-show," casually.

That step marked the beginning of his stage career. His mother resigned herself to the inevitable, and when her son asked wistfully if he might have a trunk like the other fellows had in the show, she purchased it for him. His first trunk! Oh, boy, what a thrill! Harry packed his duds, kissed the family good-by and joined the medicine-show again.

His job resembled *Robinson Crusoe's* man—*Friday's*. He rose early and filled bottles with the elixir guaranteed to remove corns, lift long faces, make timid people fight like Jim Jeffries, et cetera, et cetera. When the townspeople gathered to learn what all the shooting was about, Harry stopped bottling to offer a song-and-dance act on the platform, walk through the audience selling the medicine and ballyhoo the show outside. Then back to filling bottles.

For this non-union job he received the magnificent salary of seven dollars a week —when he was paid.

In due time he wearied of philanthropy and crashed into vaudeville in a small town. His act had been planned and rehearsed while with the medicine-show. It consisted of a song and a dance, followed by an acrobatic exhibition. He took four beer bottles and atop these placed a table. Four more beer bottles and another table. Four more upon which rested a chair, with another chair balanced atop this one. He climbed into the second chair and commenced to rock. The act ended with Harry drawing cartoons of a few in the audience and handing the excited ones their likeness.

Life moved smoothly until the day a beer bottle cracked and hurtled Harry to the floor amid the crash and débris. The accident laid him up four weeks with bruises and broken ribs. When he continued vaudeville again, he discarded the rocking stunt.

"Johnny's First Auto"

Came 1902, according to schedule, and with it the first real auto—man's gift to doctors, hospitals, and bigger and better head-lines. On a visit home, Harry busied himself with gathering lumber, nails and hammer in his mother's kitchen. Curious, how boys always dote on sloughing up a kitchen. When they are small, mother prances them into the yard. Grown up, they meet with proper maternal respect.

Harry hammered and sawed and carved, and in due course created a trick auto destined to be the first used on the stage. He called his new act "Johnny's First Auto" and with it rode into a head-liner on the small circuits and later the Orpheum route.

Harry brought this act to Los Angeles in 1912. While there, a celluloid producer with a lean to speculation sketched a proposition to him that promised flicker stardom and wealth—provided Harry invested money in the scheme. He thought it over. No.

On the road again. He joined a company called "The Show Girl," his first and only "legit" play. While with it, he met the girl he later married. He is separated from his wife today and has nothing to say about the matter. Mrs. Langdon lives in Hollywood in a lovely home and draws a handsome income.

Nineteen-fifteen saw Harry vaudevilling in Los Angeles again. Still he refused pictures. His method has always been to think, think again and step gingerly. Not until 1922 did he accept the screen contract that took him to the Mack Sennett lot and paved the way for the popularity that today ranks him with the screen's foremost comedians.

He's a funny fellow, this Harry Langdon chap. He has changed little since his boyhood days. He still runs on a one-track mind. Money, as money, means little to him. He has brought his mother to the cinematropolis and settled her comfortably. As for himself, he lives in a stucco house of semi-Moorish architecture overlooking the bustle of the flicker village.

Yea, verily, he's a funny fellow. A one-track mind mated with whole-hearted emotionalism inversed is unique. Funny, after all, is the word that dulcifies one's reaction to Harry Langdon.

Hey! Hey! Harry's Coming Back

The Great Little Dough-Face, Sane and Peppy, Marches on Hollywood

Yes, it's the same old Harry Langdon, with wide, helpless eyes. After a vaudeville tour, he's moviebound!

By Leonard Hall

FANS, shore up your spare ribs and get your tonsils set for raucous laughter!

Filmland, shine up the Hollywood Athletic Club and dust off the streets for dancing!

Harry Langdon, if God is good, is coming back to pictures!

As far as I am concerned, that's the big news of this or any other month. It has been far too long between howls for the great little doughface who went up like a balloon and came down like a parachute that failed to open.

It's a new Langdon we'll see, too—

A Harry with a well-deflated skull, a head full of smart ideas and a soul that bulges with pepper, hope and the old confy!

Disguised as a Big Reel and Sprocket Man from Culver City, I talked to the beloved Dead-Pan in a suite in the Warwick Hotel, New York. Central Park lay far below us—a relief map high-lighted with spring sunshine.

And Harry's heart was as high as his fancy sitting room!

Though he was nursing a set of clogged pipes, he had just wound up a red-hot week at the Palace Theater—which is to the vaudeville actor what Heaven is to the hell-bent.

A roaring, triumphant week, with the house jammed with Langdon maniacs, a vicious sort of devotee, and yards of blazing praise from press and public in the pews.

Three weeks more of the two a day, and then hey! and a couple of ho's! for the sunburned West and, we hope, the whirr of the old home cameras!

Langdon's vaudeville act, as far as words went, was a weak sister. No, why quibble? It was terrible. But the star, using all the quaint, helpless mannerisms that made him famous in the flickers, was tremendous. In short, it was his superb film pantomime that put him over for ten touchdowns—he didn't have to squeak a note to win his crowd.

Yes, Langdon's simple-sap character is as great as ever—greater, probably, for Harry is an older and wiser boy now.

And Harry, wearing a dressing gown and a set of studious looking cheaters, sat and looked down at sunny Central Park and told me all about it.

I marveled as I listened. Was this the Harry Langdon who everybody said had swell-headed himself out of pictures?

THE story flashed across my mind.

1922—Harry and Rose Langdon, just a good standard vaudeville act kicking around the two a day.

1923—Modestly hooked for the movies by Sol Lesser—a chap who once had a kid named Coogan. "Langdon for Films," said obscure items in the trade press. Who cared?

1924—Success in Sennett two-reelers—one of the greatest series of short films ever produced, and still revived all over the country by managers who know a laugh from a snort.

1925—Bought for long films by First National. One or two ace pictures, then a trey, then a deuce—then a long, steep toboggan for Harry, and the end!

We all remember the yarns that were whispered at the time of his boxoffice collapse—of how he had tried to write, supervise, direct and act—of how he suffered from night sweats, galloping ego, growing pains above the ears, and delusions of grandeur—of how he tried to lead the band, toot the cornet and play the drums and cymbals.

Maybe they were true and maybe they weren't, but they were common, and they hurt plenty.

Even today a tale is told along [PLEASE TURN TO PAGE 102]

Hey! Hey! Harry's Coming Back

[CONTINUED FROM PAGE 59]

Broadway—of how Harry came East with the first print of "Tramp, Tramp, Tramp," his pockets crammed with press clippings from the coast.

"Look!" he said, showing them to a pal, "they say I'm just like Chaplin!"

PERHAPS that was the trouble — that accursed phrase, "Just like Chaplin."

What Harry didn't seem to remember was that Charlie is his own man, and not the slave of a shooting schedule that demands so many pictures a year at so much a picture.

If Chaplin wants to stew two years on a picture, that's his own woe, but Langdon was under the siege guns of his bosses, with eyes on the time-clock and tight fingers on the old family checkbook.

Don't ask me whether or not little doughface suffered from an inflated cranium. Harry himself says it was his tough luck.

His producers, he declares, began clamping down on him as the doubloons started to slip away, until he was under orders to shoot a full length comedy in six weeks—a sheer impossibility where quality product is concerned.

A long comedy sweated out in a month and a half is just 7,000 feet of celluloid that might just as well be made into collars.

All these things raced through my head as Harry talked.

Talked to a purpose, too. For Harry is all broken out with a rash of ideas, and most of them are sound. And he is deadly serious. No fooling now!

"I believe that the day of the long gag comedy, with the whole picture depending on the efforts of a starred comedian, is over," he told me.

"A kick in the pants isn't as funny in pictures as it was in 1910. The gag field has been worked bare.

"The story is the thing of today and tomorrow—the laugh picture with a tale to tell. Look at Lloyd! Has he ever equalled 'Grandma's Boy'?

"Furthermore, no living comic can carry the whole burden of a seven reel comedy and make it one long howl. No man can be that funny and live.

"He must have the help of a good story and two or three all-wool featured actors to help him play it."

IF anyone believes that Harry Langdon's dome is bulged, mark and digest that!

Not only does he want a good story in his pictures—he demands brilliant support from able and well-known actors, and is anxious to share the billing with them!

What price a high hat, now?

Well, I string with Langdon.

I don't believe that even the cleverest comic can make a long gag comedy that has much of anything new to offer.

I agree that the burden of such a film on a star is backbreaking and nonsensical, for we all know that up to the present the support of our leading comedians has consisted of little but animated dummies with nothing to do but hit him on the head.

A great comic can go a couple of fast reels at top speed. Then, like a boxer, he must let down and get his wind. But with the help of good actors, Langdon can let them have their scenes and then come on, building his comedy around the situations instead of framing situations to fit a gag, and simply knock us kicking and screaming into the aisles.

If that isn't sound sense and good business, I wouldn't know them if they came riding up Fifth Avenue on big red motorcycles at high noon!

HARRY LANGDON has his feet on the ground, and his head is hitting on all twelve. He is sane, sensible and determined.

If he makes the business connections he craves, he is as safe for us and for pictures as Congress is for Hoover!

And do we need him?

There's never been a doubt as to Harry's pantomimic genius. He needs pictures and pictures need him.

I believe that he is the greatest living incarnation of harassed, frustrated humanity, and I don't except Chaplin. For very often there is something cocky about Charlie. Occasionally he pulls himself together and takes command of his soul. Not putty-faced Harry.

He is licked before he starts. Forever life's football, kicked around by fate. He is the incarnation of human futility—a grownup Farina with a white skin, chased by bogie men —smacked over by mighty forces he doesn't understand and can't control. His Sennett series of two-reel tragi-comedies stand today as unapproached masterpieces of human frailty.

Who can ever forget the one wherein Harry was left alone in a storm-battered house?

Windows blew in, doors crashed shut on his nose, lights went out, furniture fell—Langdon alone and forlorn, bruised and terrified by all the implacable and irresistible forces of nature gone cuckoo.

At last, scared witless, Harry seeks refuge in the attic. There, seemingly safe, he kneels at the side of a trunk and thanks his Heavenly Protector. At that precise moment, lightning strikes a chimney overhead, and in the midst of his supplications a large, hard brick falls and smacks him fair upon his wide and innocent brow!

IN that one superb moment can be found practically all we can ever know of the dark and devious ways of life and destiny.

And now Harry Langdon is coming back to us—we hope—sane, sound, and full of fight.

Let there be fireworks on the courthouse steps, music by the silver cornet band, and an address by the mayor.

And let yours sincerely be on hand to lead the cheering for the Happy Return of Dead-Pan Harry, whom we have loved long since, and just lost awhile!

What Happened To Harry Langdon

The amazing story of how a two-page letter ruined the career of a grand funny man

By Katherine Albert

HARRY LANGDON'S tragic story has been told in headlines.
"Cash Paid to Hush Love Suit"
"Langdon and Missus Split"
"Actor Denies Paying Balm to Wife's Ex-Mate"
"Langdon Longs for Single Life"
"Funny Man Goes Bankrupt"
And there are dozens more.

But the most amazing story of little Harry Langdon's rise and fall has never been printed. It is as fantastic as Hollywood itself.

Not so many years ago, at least you and I can remember it, Harry Langdon, "the man with the little hat," was one of the big three of comedians. There was Chaplin. There was Lloyd and there was Langdon.

Harry had been knocked around—in films as well as in real life. For every comedy kick received, there were three honest-to-goodness knockout blows. A trouper in a medical show at the age of twelve, an itinerant vaudevillian after that and a Mack Sennett two-reel comic—he learned how to take 'em.

People who couldn't remember him in vaudeville praised him on the screen—and rightly. For here was a real comedian, a man who knew enough about the seamy-side of life to get on the screen that essential comedy quality—a combination of pity and pathos.

REMEMBER his eating the chewing tobacco sandwich in an early Sennett? Remember his being cuffed around by policemen, husky guys and oversized wives? Remember that tragic, futile face?

"Why, the guy's a second Chaplin," everybody said, which was unfair, since Langdon had a style all his own and upon that style he winged his way to the highest comedy heights.

He left Sennett to form his own company and make feature lengths. He produced on the First National lot and released through them. "Tramp, Tramp, Tramp" was a great picture (incidentally a plump almost unknown girl who didn't quite know what to do with her hands played the lead for the great comedian. Her name was Joan Crawford).

The film was fine but Langdon's director had taken too much time on it and run him into the red, so Harry looked about for another director for the next one. And he handed the megaphone to a man who had been a poorly paid gag constructor at Sennett's.

The man, whose name cannot be mentioned here, took over the reins of production and turned out a jim dandy of a piece in "The Strong

Harry Langdon can still give the world the horse laugh. "I know I can act, if I'm not licked," he says

When he married Helen Walton the world looked rosy. But now they're getting a divorce and Harry's bankrupt

Man." It was made in record time, under cost and was a sure fire box-office attraction. It put Langdon right on the top of the heap.

Langdon was delighted with his success. He believed that the troubles he had had—both domestic and professional—were over and that he could take it easy now and things would just sail along on their own momentum. But the poor fellow didn't know that the fates had a little plan up their sleeves that would completely destroy him.

He'd never been able to indulge in rich men's pastimes. He'd never been rich before. So now he took up golf, believing that his picture company was in good hands. The third story of his feature lengths had been doped out. He knew that both his director and writer were able, so he stayed away from the studio for four weeks and followed a little white ball over a green lawn. He could shoot an eighty on a golf course. But he found himself unable to sink the put when he got back to the studio.

THE writer and director had worked for four weeks on the new picture. They had quarreled. The writer thought there was too much footage that retarded the action before Langdon's entrance. The director said he knew his stuff and wouldn't be interfered with. Quite without Langdon who was star as well as producer, they had gone ahead. When he returned, they put their separate cases before him. He strung along with the writer, agreeing with him on almost every point.

The director was furious and the picture was completed in all the maddening discord of a school girl squabble.

And then the fantastic event occurred that was to be the biggest contributing factor in Harry Langdon's downfall.

THE angry director wrote a letter to all the movie columnists. He said that Harry was impossible to work with, that he wanted to have a finger in every pie, that he was conceited, egotistical and considered himself the biggest shot in pictures. That he gave himself airs and wore the high hat instead of the little battered felt of his films. It was a vitriolic letter from a disgruntled man.

But the substance of it got printed. The news was flung all over the world that Langdon was impossible on the set and dabbled in everything. Other writers picked up the story. Almost every newspaper carried it and it gathered power as it went spinning into the world. Movie fans saw it, but more important, it was read by producers.

[PLEASE TURN TO PAGE 106]

What Happened to Harry Langdon

[CONTINUED FROM PAGE 40]

Those who knew nothing about it added incidents to make it all seem more important. It was talked about by everyone, the principal topic in the smart luncheon places and the athletic club locker rooms.

So Langdon thought he was somebody now, did he?

Producing his own pictures had gone to his head.

Wanted to be a big shot, did he?

And the comedian himself was as bewildered by it all as that vague, pitiful little character he played upon the screen might have been when he found himself caught up in a tangled web of circumstance.

Langdon is a highly sensitized fellow. The thing completely got him. It took away his morale, his pep, his enthusiasm. It made him self-conscious. He had a contract to fulfil. He must go on making pictures, but now when he walked on the set he could feel the cold eyes of his co-workers waiting for his interference, already sure that he was going to make himself objectionable.

FEARFUL lest he prove true the statements made in the letter, he took anyone's advice. Trying to overcome and live down his undeserved reputation, he would listen to any prop boy's suggestion for a gag and try to use it. He also heeded the advice of one of the other producers who told him he should shoot his stuff fast, turn out pictures and cash in quick.

Chaplin takes a year and more on one film. Lloyd does the same thing. Langdon was making comedies in six weeks and it was impossible to catch that rare, ephemeral thing that gets laughs—a quality less sustained, more difficult to imprison than tragedy.

He was bewildered. He was miserable. The critics panned these quickly turned out films and everyone added, "Since Langdon has gone high hat his work has suffered."

Well, it got him down—that's all. It simply robbed him of everything he had to give to the screen, which was quite a lot. He couldn't be funny when he knew that they were all whispering about him, that they all believed the stories of his conceit.

It ate into him. He didn't want to see people, he didn't want to be watched on the set. He tried being too friendly and managed to be just a little eccentric instead.

And one letter from an ex-employee of his had done it.

It would be a grand case D for a psychoanalyst if it weren't so pitiful.

AND now here's the ironic part. While the man who wrote that letter has become successful and prosperous and powerful in Hollywood, Langdon is trying desperately in New York to get a job. He is broke. To help himself eke out a living, he draws cartoons for the funny magazines. They're surprisingly good, too.

He plays around in vaudeville. He and his second wife are dickering over a separation.

His life is in a mess. In real life he's playing that beaten, knocked about little fellow he made popular on the screen.

But he says, "Having a jinx follow you is fun. At any rate there's never a dull moment."

But that is not quite true. There have been plenty of dull moments for Harry Langdon, and heartbreaking ones, too.

Not so long ago he signed with Hal Roach to make two-reelers. He'd never met Roach before. The first thing said was, "Now, see here, Langdon, none of that high handed stuff you pulled at First National."

And that was years after the letter had been written.

Nobody has ever forgotten it.

He wants to come back—more than anything else in the world.

And he says, "I can make good comedies, too, if I'm not licked."

HE laughs but he's afraid. He knows he's still a good comedian, but every time anybody looks at him sideways he remembers the letter and its tragic results. At the moment, he's got a swell chance. The talkies need good shorts and they need good comedians to make them. Harry Langdon was, and still is, one of the best—when given the right break, left to work out his gags and not reminded of his supposed egotism.

For, in reality, he is as unassuming and democratic a little person as you'll meet.

And that's the story of how one man was beaten down at the height of a brilliant career, and licked by a letter!

Good Luck or Bad Luck— BEBE and HARRY Can Take It!

By Sonia Lee

STARDOM in Hollywood is built on quicksand. One bad rôle, an ugly bit of gossip, a minor human weakness often is enough to topple the enthroned into oblivion. Few who have reached the heights and who have faltered and fallen have had the courage to tackle again the hazardous road to Fame. They can't start the climb with the shining faith of the struggler. They know the heartaches and disappointments, the fickle illusions that face them.

To struggle back to former glories demands a superlative courage, an ability to withstand the rebuffs of skeptical producers and directors, the intestinal fortitude to take it on the chin! There are now two formerly predominant stars who are seeking a new path toward their once-held unassailable places: Harry Langdon and Bebe Daniels.

Langdon of the baby-face, whose comedy has the divine quality of pathos, is the man who, three brief years ago, was classed with Chaplin and Harold Lloyd. He recently returned to Hollywood to take a supporting rôle in Al Jolson's new picture, "Happy-Go-Lucky," and is making two-reelers for Educational as the first step to re-establishing the name which once magically packed theatres.

Hollywood gossip gave him a reputation for autocracy that was as annihilating as it was undeserved. As a result Langdon's morale was undermined. He lost faith in his own judgment and that sure artistic comedy touch which had spelled success at the box-office. In addition to that, Langdon ran into personal complications concerning his marriage—and it added to his bewilderment. His money was gone, his prestige was shattered. He turned to vaudeville, deserting motion pictures—the field he loved.

He appeared in two talkies—"A Soldier's Plaything" and "See America Thirst"—but began to think he wasn't going to get a real comeback chance unless he started producing some two-reelers, himself, when the "Happy-Go-Lucky" offer came along. Those who have seen the preview say he gives Jolson a merry run for first honors.

Not Bitter About Hard Luck

A NEW, an objectively philosophical Langdon will tell you to-day that nothing matters very much—neither fame, nor wealth, nor luxury. But, strangely enough, he is neither embittered nor prosaically resigned. He knows how to take it.

"The trouble with me," he declares, "was that I was pushed through pictures too fast. I made 'Long Pants' in exactly ten weeks, while Chaplin was taking two years to make one feature and Harold Lloyd an entire year. But I was turning them out without preparation—without giving situations a chance to mature, or to be worked out with the infinite care comedy requires.

"When superlative praise was given to 'Long Pants,' I knew the curtain was slowly coming down for me. The extravagant terms critics used were in reality a death knell for me. I knew, if no one else realized at the moment, the fundamental weakness of the picture—and the difficulties under which it was made.

"I had been talked into producing my own pictures—and they were financially fatal. I trusted directors and writers, and business managers. When I needed every bit of energy for a scene before a camera, I was harassed by business squabbles and by internal strife—as unnecessary as it was selfish. The worries of management destroyed my peace of mind—I couldn't concentrate.

"There's no doubt that fear of criticism licked me. If I had gone ahead, depended on my own judgment, insisted on a schedule of picture-making that would permit me to do good work—I would have continued to be Harry Langdon, the star,

"If once you have succeeded, you can do it again"—that's the slogan of Harry Langdon and Bebe Daniels, and they're out to prove that it's true. A run of hard luck took Harry out of the limelight three years ago, and Bebe has toppled from the heights five times and come back four. And they're happier now than ever before!

Stardom Doesn't Matter Now

"AS it is, I am starting back. Pictures are where I belong. I don't especially care if I'm never a star again. I pity people who grub and grab—the actors who think the world has come to an end if they're not in every close-up.

"I am much happier now—I'm down to earth, to the essential values of living. I enjoy having carpenters shake me by the hand. I get a thrill when the prop boys greet me with the old familiar 'Hello, Harry.' I didn't have that friendliness when I was a star—I haven't had it since those happy and peaceful Sennett days. Somehow, stardom isolated me, removed me from human contacts.

"In reality I don't care how small my rôles are, as long as they give me a chance. And I hope to have time for other things, for art lessons and music and books. I am not afraid of people any more—or even injustice. I've regained my old assurance, my faith in myself. If it's in the cards that some day my name will again be important—that's fine! If not—I'll be content."

Harry Langdon learned in those days when he was medicine-show minstrel, circus clown, balancing artist and vaudevillian, how to take the tricks of life. He laughed at Fate and its obstacles. He kept on going. Fighting. When he finally achieved his desire to go into the movies, his pantomime had that sympathetic eagerness which endeared him to a laugh-hungry world. Fame handed him the short end of the stick when he was at the top.

But he hasn't forgotten how to win.

Or how to take it on the chin—and grin!

Sources

The following sources were extremely helpful in providing historical background, as well as information, articles, quotes and opinions pertaining to Langdon's entire career. Specific articles and reviews are cited elsewhere within the text.

Books:

Bruskin, David N. *Behind the Three Stooges: The White Brothers*; Director's Guild of America, 1993.

Capra, Frank. *The Name Above the Title*; The MacMillan Company, 1971

Csida, Joseph and June Bundy Csida. *American Entertainment: A Unique History of Popular Show Business*; Watson-Guptill Publications, a division of Billboard Publications, Inc., 1978.

Kerr, Walter. *The Silent Clowns*. Alfred A. Knopf, Inc., 1975.

Louvish, Simon. *Stan and Ollie: The Roots of Comedy*; Thomas Dunne Books, 2002.

Louvish, Simon. *Keystone: The Life and Clowns of Mack Sennett*; Faber and Faber, Inc., 2003.

Maltin, Leonard. *The Great Movie Shorts*; Crown Publishers, Inc., 1972.

Maltin, Leonard (Editor). *The Laurel & Hardy Book*, The Curtis Film Series, 1973.

Mast, Gerald. *The Comic Mind: Comedy and the Movies*; The Bobbs-Merrill Company, Inc., 1973.

McBride, Joseph. *Frank Capra: The Catastrophe of Success*; Simon & Schuster, 1992

McCabe, John, with Al Kilgore and Richard W. Bann. *Laurel and Hardy*; E.P. Dutton & Company, Inc., 1975.

McCaffrey, Donald W. *4 Great Comedians*; The Tantivy Press, in association with A. Zwemmer Ltd. and A.S. Barnes & Co. Inc., 1968.

Okuda, Ted and Edward Watz. *The Columbia Comedy Shorts*; McFarland & Company, 1986.

Rheuban, Dr. Joyce. *Harry Langdon: The Comedian as Metteur-en-Scène*; Associated University Presses, Inc., 1983.

Schelly, William. *Harry Langdon: His Life and Films*; Scarecrow Press, Inc., 1982 (First Edition); McFarland & Company, Inc., 2008 (Second Edition).

Sennett, Mack with Cameron Shipp. *King of Comedy*; Doubleday and Company, Inc., 1954.

Stewart, D. Travis (as S.D. Trav). *No Applause — Just Throw Money: The Book That Made Vaudeville Famous*; Faber and Faber, Inc., 2005.

Walker, Brent E. *Mack Sennett's Fun Factory*; McFarland & Company, Inc., 2010.

Ward, Richard Lewis. *A History of the Hal Roach Studios*; Southern Illinois University Press, 2005.

Periodicals:

Billboard, The (1906-1953)
Box Office (1924-1945)
Camera (1923)
Daily Variety (1934-1945)
Exhibitor's Herald (1923-1929)
Exhibitor's Trade Review (1925)
Film Daily (1922-1934)
Film Mercury, The (1924-1928)
Film Spectator, The (1928)
Harrison's Reports (1926-1945)
Hollywood Reporter, The (1933-1944)
Motion Picture (1924-1933)
Motion Picture Classic (1925)
Motion Picture Daily (1931-1933)
Motion Picture Herald (1930-1944)
Motion Picture News (1923-1930)
Motion Picture Times (1928-1930)
Movie Weekly (1924)
Moving Picture World (1923-1927)
Photoplay (1924-1938)
Picture Play (1929)
Variety (1905-1973)
Wild About Harry (1996-2000)

Websites:

Ancestry.com
Feet of Mud *(feetofmud.com)*
Google News Archive *(news.google.com/newspapers)*
Greenbriar Picture Shows *(greenbriarpictureshows.blogspot.com)*
Internet Archive Media History Digital Library *(archive.org/details/mediahistory)*
Library of Congress Historic American Newspapers *(chroniclingamerica.loc.gov)*
NewsLibrary.com *(http://nl.newsbank.com)*
NewspaperArchive *(newspaperarchive.com)*
NitrateVille *(nitrateville.com)*
Old Fulton NY Post Cards *(fultonhistory.com/Fulton.html)*
SilentComedians Forum *(silentcomedians.com/forum/index.php)*
SilentComedyMafia *(silentcomedymafia.com)*

Index

30 Years of Fun 311, 598
Abbott, Bud 302, 470, 519
Adamson, Ewart 276, 527, 552, 556-557
Adler, Felix 118, 274, 285, 367, 370, 372, 558-559, 586, 592-595
After the Ball 75, 79-81, 91, 199, 224, 234, 240, 248, 321, 481, 613, 635
Agee, James 309-310, 314-315, 317, 319, 322, 326-327, 354, 361
All Night Long 114-117, 119, 122-123, 258-259, 311, 324, 356-359, 518, 542, 597
All-American Co-Ed 292, 544-546
American Tragedy, An 155, 164-165, 167, 414, 418, 420, 657
Ames, Elsie 295-296, 557-562
Anything Goes 261-262, 265-268, 299
Arbuckle, Roscoe "Fatty" 5, 84, 92, 114, 138, 297
Armstrong, Billy 335, 338-339
Astaire, Marie 117, 364, 366-367, 467
Astor, Gertrude 122, 145, 147-148, 396, 401-402, 404, 406-409, 523, 539
Atlantic Adventure 260-261, 274, 518-520
Ayres, Lew 247, 499-501
Bailey, Andre 359, 362, 450
Beautiful Clothes (Make Beautiful Girls) 293, 325, 552
Bennett, Alma 156, 162, 183, 411, 415, 417-418, 420
Bennett, Floyd 7, 33, 323
Benny, Jack 324, 547
Bergen, Edgar 545
Berlin, Irving 61, 225
Bernds, Edward 13, 296, 303, 305, 582
Bert, Flo 194
Big Flash, The 239-240, 477-480
Big Kick, The 203-204, 206, 461-462
Blitz on the Fritz, A 297-298, 563-564
Block Busters 303, 578-579
Block-Heads 273-274, 277, 586-588
Blonde and Groom 564-565
Bonner, Priscilla 145, 147-148, 155-156, 158, 168, 200, 307, 326, 396, 401-404, 406, 408, 411, 413, 415, 417-418, 420
Boobs in the Wood 116-117, 122, 364-366, 370, 599-600
Brave Coward, A 80-81
Brendel, El 194, 296, 302-303, 305, 307, 474, 480, 575-576, 580-583
Bride by Mistake 303
Briscoe, Olive 80-81
Brown, Joe E. 70-72, 480

Brownlow, Kevin 18, 161, 322, 600
Bruckman, Clyde 123, 372, 373, 558-559, 563
Capra, Frank R. 11-13, 17-19, 33, 99, 107, 111-114, 116-118, 122-124, 129-131, 137, 141-145, 148, 151, 155-162, 169, 185, 198, 231, 253, 259, 267, 274-276, 307, 310, 312, 314-318-322, 324, 326-327, 366, 368, 370, 376, 378, 380-382, 386, 396, 400, 403, 405, 407, 409, 411, 414, 417, 421, 424-425, 437-438, 450, 528, 559, 657
Carry Harry 295, 297, 298, 560, 561
Cat's Meow, The 99, 101, 102, 107, 343, 344, 345, 346, 599
Chaplin, Charles 11, 13, 17-18, 52, 58, 72, 84, 87, 89-90, 92, 94-95, 103, 106, 116, 119, 128, 131, 139, 143, 150-151, 155, 161, 165, 172, 174, 182, 184-185, 194, 197-198, 241, 271, 278, 287, 293, 307, 309-311, 315, 317-319, 322-323, 325-327, 333-334, 336, 339, 345, 356, 358-359, 367, 372-374, 376, 387-389, 391-392, 394, 401-403, 405-406, 408-410, 414-416, 425-426, 430, 432-433, 435, 443-444, 446, 480, 495, 551, 598-599
Charley's Aunt 292, 547
Chase, Charley 197, 203-204, 207
Chaser, The 178-182, 184, 187, 217, 231, 254, 314, 316-317, 319-320, 323, 326, 368-369, 439-448, 512, 561
Chump at Oxford, A 284-285, 592-593
Circus Hoodoo, A 248-249, 506-508
Clyde, Andy 94, 100, 106, 239-240, 243, 253, 296, 307, 331, 335, 338, 341, 343, 346-348, 354, 357, 376, 378, 450
Colbert, Claudette 12, 111, 265
Cold Turkey 274, 289, 538, 542
Coleman, Caryl 303-304
Coleman, Frank J. 102, 349-350, 352-354
Comedy Capers 312, 325, 599
Comont, Mathilde 88
Conklin, Chester 307, 481, 483-485, 531, 562
Conklin, Hal 114, 118, 137, 145, 356, 382, 396
Coogan, Jackie 87, 91
Cooper, Jack 94-95, 331-332, 335-336, 338, 346-348
Copner, Michael 259, 289, 300, 306-307, 323
Cort, John 70-72
Costello, Lou 302, 470, 519
Counsel on De Fence 254-255, 369, 511-512, 525
Crawford, Joan 138, 140-141, 265, 382, 385, 387, 389-391
Cushman, Claire 122, 359, 370-371
Dawson, Doris 183-184, 448, 450, 647
Day, Alice 99-102, 104, 107, 117, 331, 338-344, 346-351, 362
Day, Marceline 104-107, 138, 331, 352-355

Days of Thrills and Laughter, The 358, 597
Defective Detectives 302, 575-576
Dent, Vernon 11, 51, 94, 107, 114-115, 117, 119-123, 125, 130-133, 237, 239-241, 245, 247-249, 261, 273, 278, 305, 307, 314, 325, 331, 333, 357-359, 361, 364, 367, 370, 372, 374, 376-378, 380, 382, 421, 423, 437, 450, 477-480, 486-495, 502-503, 506-507, 509-511, 518, 521-524, 527, 538, 552, 554, 556, 563, 565-566, 570, 575, 580
Dickason, James F. 223, 225, 228-229
Doggone Mixup, A 271, 524-526, 538, 542
Dooley, Billy 175
Doran, Ann 275-276, 326, 524, 527, 538
Double Trouble 292-293, 309, 547, 549-552, 556
Dover, Nancy 201-204, 455, 457, 460-463, 492
Doyle, Commissioner E.D. 259, 260, 271, 293
Drake, Dona 302, 572-575
Dreiser, Theodore 155, 165, 310, 420
Edwards, Harry J. 18-19, 103-106, 113, 115-116, 120, 123, 130-131, 137, 141-142, 160, 237, 239, 247, 295-296, 302, 305-307, 312, 315, 317-318, 327, 339, 352, 354, 356, 358-359, 361-362, 364, 366-367, 369-370, 372-374, 376-378, 380-382, 386, 391, 421, 423, 425, 437, 450, 492, 538, 560-562, 564-565, 575, 580, 582
Ella Cinders 144, 325, 396
Estaccion de Gasolina 204, 462
Everson, William K. 18, 312
Extra Girl, The 96, 107, 115
Fay, Frank 70-72, 194, 300, 567-570
Feet of Mud 116, 311, 359-361, 363, 598-600
Ferris, Dick 26-30, 33
Fiddlesticks 132-133, 137, 175, 224, 437-438, 451, 599
Fields, W.C. 165, 255, 260
Fighting Parson, The 202-203, 205, 209, 460-461
Finlayson, James 285, 307, 586-587, 590, 592, 594-595
First 100 Years, The 102-103, 311-312, 349-351, 514, 597
Flickering Youth 99-100, 341-342, 346
Flying Deuces, The 285-286, 590
Frazee, Jane 305, 584-586
Funny Manns, The 312, 325, 339, 599
Gable, Clark 265
Garbo, Greta 208, 265, 488
Giebler, Alfred H. 113, 178, 367, 370, 372, 376, 380, 382, 439, 450, 524
Gilbert, Eugenia 97, 107, 272, 331, 333, 341, 346, 359, 362-364
Gill, William 238, 241, 249-250
Gillstrom, Arvid E. 237, 239-242, 244-245, 247-250, 253, 286, 477-480, 486, 488, 491-492, 494, 497, 502-503, 506, 509, 522, 566
Gold Rush, The 143-144, 155, 388-389, 392, 405-406, 415, 433
Golden Age of Comedy, The 104, 311-312, 326, 353, 597-598
Goldwyn, Samuel 92
Goodness! A Ghost 286-287, 537-538
Granger, Dorothy 207-208, 261-262, 466, 509, 521-522
Hallelujah! I'm a Bum 242-244, 314-315, 481-485, 657
Hamilton, Lloyd 84, 91
Hammons, Earle W. 241-242
Hansom Cabman, The 106, 117, 354-356, 495, 515
Hardy, Oliver "Babe" 19, 85, 132, 175, 192, 197, 200, 204, 207, 248-249, 270-275, 277-287, 289, 302, 311, 319, 358, 377, 487-488, 529, 531-537, 586-595

Harry Langdon Announcement 198-199, 325, 452
Harvey, Lilian 247, 499-502
Hayward, Grace 26, 28-29
Hayward, Helen 178, 180, 426, 439, 445-446
He Loved an Actress: see *Mad About Money*
Head Guy, The 202, 204, 322, 457, 459
Heart Trouble 144, 183-187, 191, 231, 316-317, 323, 448-450, 646-656
Hellzapoppin' 291
Hennecke, Clarence 145, 177, 439, 448
Here Comes Mr. Zerk 298, 302, 565-566
Hiatt, Ruth 125, 132, 239, 314, 380, 382, 421, 425, 437, 477-478, 547
His Bridal Sweet 258, 514-516
His First Flame 125-127, 129, 133, 141, 167, 175, 235, 261, 322, 325, 368, 386, 421-426, 522, 598
His Marriage Mix-Up 261-262, 521-522
His Marriage Wow 120-121, 261, 324, 367-369, 442, 492, 522, 599
His New Mamma 101-103, 346-348, 599
Hitch Hiker, The 241, 486-488, 490, 598
Hollywood on Parade 240, 248, 325, 480-481
Hooks and Jabs 245-246, 315, 325, 494-495
Horace Greely Jr. 125, 325, 374
Hot Rhythm 302-303, 305, 309, 572-575, 584
Hotter Than Hot 200-201, 224, 248, 452-453
House of Errors 295, 309, 552-557
Hurlock, Madeline 101-102, 106, 335, 338, 343-344, 346-350, 352, 354
I Don't Remember 261, 263-264, 522-524,
In My Merry Oldsmobile 36, 461
It Happened One Night 12, 274, 529, 559
Jim Jam Jems 70-73, 75, 91, 194, 300
Johnny's New Car 18, 53, 55, 58-63, 65-66, 70, 75, 79-81, 84, 91, 113, 116, 124, 158, 199, 204, 240, 249, 300, 321-322, 326, 462, 480, 559, 603, 613, 635
Jolson, Al 185-186, 234-238, 242-243, 318, 461, 481-486
Jones, F. Richard "Dick" 17, 98, 99, 101-104, 106-107, 113-114, 117-118, 148, 272, 331, 335, 337-338, 341, 343, 346, 349, 352, 354, 356, 359, 362, 364
Kalat, David 325
Kalmar, Bert 280, 285
Karno, Fred 205, 271-272
Keaton, Buster 11, 13, 18, 72, 84, 119, 123, 138-139, 151, 165, 174, 183, 198, 295, 297, 309, 311-313, 315, 317-319, 321-322, 325-327, 337, 350, 356, 359, 373, 376-377, 387-388, 392, 403, 405, 410, 432, 435, 474, 558, 597-599
Kelsey, Fred 260, 539, 541-542, 565, 580-581
Kennedy, Edgar 200-202, 258, 287, 452, 457, 461, 463
Kennedy, Joseph P. 185
Kerr, Walter 18, 319, 320-321, 323, 346, 366, 414, 561
Kickapoo Indian Medicine Show 25, 123-124
Kid, The 87, 430, 432-433
King, The 207-208, 466-467
King of Comedy 17, 98, 310, 312, 314, 316
Kingsford, Guy 295, 547, 552, 556
Kingston, Natalie 114, 116, 121, 123, 125, 128, 130, 169, 346, 357-359, 361, 367-368, 372-374, 376-378, 421, 425, 450-451
Knight Duty 242, 325, 488-490, 538
Koenig, Der 207, 466

Kohler, Fred 208, 467, 471

Lane, Lupino 175

Langdon, Claude 7, 21, 62, 118, 120, 129, 137, 177, 184, 303, 322

Langdon, Edith O'Brien 162, 200, 224, 230

Langdon, Gertrude 21, 62, 71, 145, 303, 309

Langdon, Harry Jr. 258, 260, 262, 265, 268, 289, 291, 293, 299-300, 306-307, 314, 323

Langdon, Helen (Nellie) Laura Walton O'Brien 19, 119-121, 129, 138, 146, 155-158, 161-162, 168, 178, 197, 199-200, 205, 208-216, 223-226, 228-230, 234, 249, 256-257, 259, 264, 271, 274-275, 277, 279, 293, 306, 326-327, 375, 657

Langdon, James Tulley 21, 42-43, 45, 47, 49, 53, 55-56, 59, 61-62, 71, 129, 145, 177, 268

Langdon, John Henry 21, 23, 26, 71, 303, 309

Langdon, Lavina Luchenbill 21-22, 26, 30, 53, 71, 118, 197, 309

Langdon, Mabel Sheldon 11, 13, 238, 242, 249-251, 253, 255, 257-259, 261, 264, 268-269, 271, 274, 278, 289, 291, 303, 305-307, 311, 313-314, 320, 323, 327, 583

Langdon, Rose Frances Musolff 30, 33-37, 39-40, 43, 45-49, 52-53, 55, 58-59, 61-63, 65-66, 70-72, 75-82, 113-114, 120, 129, 138-139, 146, 158, 161-162, 184, 191, 196, 211, 214, 224, 229, 230, 237-238, 249, 253, 255-256, 271, 300, 323-324, 327, 461

Langdon, Virginia O'Brien 120, 121, 146, 158, 162, 178, 200, 210, 224, 230, 234, 306

Langdon, Williamson Worley "W.W." 21-23, 30, 53, 71

Laurel, Stan (Arthur Stanley Jefferson) 11, 19, 85, 89, 132, 175, 192, 197, 200-201, 204, 207, 248-249, 270-275, 277-287, 289, 302, 307, 311, 319, 358, 377, 534-536, 586-595

Leather Necker, The 258-260, 517-518

Lesser, Sol 81-83, 87-88, 90-92, 94, 114, 125, 131, 139, 167, 641

Lessley, Elgin 138, 183, 382, 396, 411, 426, 439, 446

Listen Lester 70-72, 91

Lloyd, Harold 18, 72, 83-84, 89-90, 103, 107, 112, 119, 128, 129, 137, 140, 151, 174, 192, 198, 278, 309, 311, 315, 317-319, 321-322, 325, 327, 337, 341, 345, 356, 359, 364, 367, 369, 376, 386, 388-389, 391-392, 394-395, 400, 405-406, 409, 415, 425, 435, 474, 476-477, 480, 641

Loder, Lotti 208, 210, 467, 470-471

Long Pants 155-167, 169-170, 172, 175, 177, 182-183, 186, 191, 193, 198, 202, 204, 239, 310, 315, 317, 319-320, 323-324, 327, 411-421, 424-426, 433, 443, 446, 490, 512, 526, 657

Love, Honor and Obey (the Law) 256-257, 325, 516

Luck o' the Foolish, The 104-106, 116, 203, 311, 352-354, 363, 492, 597, 599

Lucky Stars 128-129, 315, 376-378

Lyon, Ben 12, 208, 211, 234, 269, 467, 470-471, 519, 526-527

Lytell, Bert 81-82

Mad About Money 269, 526-527

Maltin, Leonard 18, 289, 524, 564

Marriage Humor 247-248, 492-494

Marx Brothers, The 48, 51, 128, 285

Marx, Chico 48, 58

Marx, Groucho 58

Marx, Harpo 311, 499, 590

McConnell, Gladys 168-171, 177-180, 183, 426, 439, 443, 445-447

McCormick, John 131, 144, 167, 396

Merkel, Una 296, 301-302, 570-572

Midnight on the Boulevard 40

Misbehaving Husbands 289-290, 539-543

Monsieur Verdoux 414

Montgomery, Baby Peggy 91-92

Montgomery, Peggy 130-131, 378, 380, 382

Moore, Colleen 131, 144, 151, 396

Mopey Dope 303-304, 576, 577

Morros, Boris 283, 285, 590

Musolff, Cecilia (a.k.a. "Cecil Langdon") 30, 62-66, 70-72, 75-82, 224, 271

My Weakness 247, 314, 494, 497-502

Name Above the Title, The 12, 17, 111, 113, 137, 143, 148, 155, 160, 276, 316

Night on the Boulevard, A 41-42, 45, 48, 49, 51-53, 55, 58, 60, 67, 79, 196, 249, 603

Normand, Mabel 84, 92, 96, 98, 107, 130

O'Day, Nell 242, 244-246, 325-326, 488-491, 494, 503-506

On Ice 248-249, 502-503

O'Brien, Thomas J. 120-121, 146, 157-158, 161-162, 168, 178, 209-216

Parrott, James 207-208, 466, 586

Payson, Blanche 448, 524, 563, 565

Perfect Nuisance, A (see also White Wing's Bride, The) 90-91, 120, 125, 375

Personality Parade 524

Petting Preferred 248-249, 509-511

Piano Mooner 295, 562, 565

Picking Peaches 94-99, 105, 107, 115, 315, 331, 333-334, 336-337, 340, 345, 347, 524, 600

Pistol Packin' Nitwits 305-306, 309, 582-583

Plain Clothes 121-122, 141, 370-372

Pobre Infeliz! 206, 463-464

Quillan, Eddie 175

Rauh, Al 80-81

Reel Virginian, The 107

Remember When? 123-124, 141, 315, 372-373, 474, 597, 599

Ripley, Arthur D. 17-18, 107, 116-118, 121-124, 129-130, 137, 145, 148, 155-159, 162, 168-169, 177, 182, 198, 231, 253-254, 258-259, 300, 307, 315, 327, 364, 366-370, 372-373, 376-378, 380-382, 386-387, 396, 400, 411, 421, 424-426, 437, 439, 448, 450, 511-512, 514-515, 517-518

Roach, Hal 83-84, 89-90, 94, 107, 113, 118, 168, 178, 192, 197-199, 202, 204-205, 207-208, 239, 271-274, 276-277, 279, 281-283, 285-287, 289, 292, 309, 322, 325, 452-455, 457, 460-464, 466, 529-531, 534-536, 544-547, 586, 588, 592-597, 641, 657

Road Show 285-287, 289, 595-596

Roaming Romeo, A 248, 481, 503-506, 524

Rogers, Charles "Charley" 201-203, 206-207, 274, 284-286, 292-293, 295, 307, 314, 454-455, 460, 463, 465-466, 547, 549-552, 556, 586, 590, 592-595

Rohauer, Raymond 13, 305, 312-316, 319-322

Rondeau, Doris 152

Rowland, Richard A. 142, 167, 177, 183, 387

Ruby, Harry 280, 285

Ryan, Irene 302-303, 572-575

Safety Last! 137, 390, 477

Saps at Sea 285, 287, 594

Saturday Afternoon 131-133, 178, 248, 273, 314, 324, 380-382, 442, 451, 600
Scarem Much 337-338
Screen Snapshots 112, 240, 289, 309, 524
Sea Squawk, The 106-107, 122, 125, 362-364
See America Thirst 216-221, 223, 249, 471-477
Seinfeld 325
Semon, Larry 84-85, 92, 119, 175, 309, 337, 377, 442
Sennett, Mack 17-19, 23, 29, 37, 50, 52, 84, 87, 90-92, 94-96, 98-99, 101-104, 106-107, 111, 113-119, 122-124, 128-133, 137, 139, 142, 145, 159, 167, 169, 175, 178, 183, 192, 231, 239, 242, 244, 253, 259, 261, 267, 271-272, 274-275, 283, 297, 307, 309-312, 314-317, 319, 322, 324-327, 331-343, 345-350, 352-354, 356, 358-364, 366-367, 369-373, 375-376, 378, 380, 382, 390, 392, 421, 424-426, 437-438, 442, 450, 457, 464, 522, 536, 538, 542, 559, 566, 594, 597-599, 641, 657
Shanghaied Lovers 96, 98-100, 105, 338-340, 599
Sheekman, Arthur 128
Sheldon, Gene 310-311
Sherwood, Yorke 104-105, 352, 354, 359, 361, 450
Shivers 256, 512-514
Show Girl, The 36-40, 60, 231
Show Goat, The (see also *Stage Hand, The*) 231-232, 234, 245
Shrimp, The 206-207, 463-465, 470, 478, 490
Shubert, Eddie 223-224, 230, 234, 492, 496-497
Silents, Please 312, 599
Sitting Pretty 289, 537
Skirt Shy 201, 203, 455-456, 459
Sky Boy 200-202, 454-455
Skyscraper, The (a.k.a. *The Greenhorn*) 88-92, 331
Smile Please 96-98, 311, 335-336, 339, 345, 598-599
Snooper Service 303-304, 309, 580-581
Soldier Man 130, 132-133, 187, 274, 314-315, 442, 450-451, 600
Soldier's Plaything, A 12, 209-211, 219, 221, 234, 247, 467-471, 474, 519
Sons of the Desert 273
Sparks, Ned 71-72
Spotlight Scandals 299-300, 567-570, 584
Stage Hand, The (see also *Show Goat, The*) 246, 494, 496-497
Strong Man, The 122, 144-148, 150-152, 156, 158-160, 163-165, 170, 174-175, 177, 180, 182, 184, 193, 203, 231, 241, 247, 253, 276, 309-310, 312, 314-316, 318-324, 382, 386, 396, 399-411, 415-416, 418- 420, 424, 426, 432-435, 444, 447, 457, 487, 490, 528, 542, 657
Sue My Lawyer 275-276, 287, 295, 527-528
Summerville, Slim 216-217, 296, 471-472, 474-477
Swanson, Gloria 92
Swingin' on a Rainbow 305, 309, 583-585
Thalasso, Arthur 146-147, 170, 202, 396, 401, 403-404, 408, 426, 455
Thalberg, Irving 116-117

There Goes My Heart 274, 277, 280, 529-530
There He Goes 130-131, 378-379
Thomas, Dan 184-185, 207-209, 253-254
Three Keatons, The 50, 72
Three's a Crowd 168-172, 174-175, 177-178, 180, 184, 187, 198, 203, 310, 314-315, 317-321, 323, 326, 426, 429-436, 442-443, 446, 448, 463, 474, 561, 657
Tied For Life 244-245, 491, 495
Tired Feet 240, 479-480
Tireman, Spare My Tires 558
To Heir is Human 301-302, 570-572
Todd, Thelma 198-201, 205-207, 452-455, 457-461, 463, 466
Tough Tenderfoot, A (See also: *Horace Greely Jr.*) 90-92, 125, 374
Tramp, Tramp, Tramp 122, 124, 138, 140-144, 146-147, 150-151, 155, 158, 171, 185, 193, 200, 242, 247-248, 289, 310, 319-321, 323-324, 376, 382-396, 403, 405-410, 419, 424, 426, 442-444, 474, 484, 556
Turpin, Ben 84, 92, 94, 101, 107, 118, 313, 594-595
Virginian, The 96, 107
Voice of Hollywood 325, 461, 481
Walker, Brent E. 99, 114, 116, 118, 312, 325
Walton, Arthur 120
Walton, Benjamin 120, 214
Walton, Laura Harrison 120, 146, 216
Ward, Alice 131, 380
Ward, Roscoe "Tiny" 102, 331, 333, 335, 338, 341, 343, 346, 348-349, 352, 354, 362, 376, 380, 437
Watz, Edward 145, 156, 169, 177, 238, 242, 245, 249, 258, 268, 289, 291, 305, 307, 319-320, 325, 472, 489
We Faw Down 273
Weber, Harry 43, 45, 50, 61, 63, 84, 397
Weeks, Ada Mae 70-72
West, May (Mae) 50
West, William "Billy" 292-293, 547, 550-551
What Makes Lizzy Dizzy? 295-296, 557-558
Wheeler, Bert 237
When Comedy Was King 311-312, 350, 597
White Wing's Bride, The 90, 119, 125, 375-376
White, Jack 125, 261, 522, 524, 565-566
White, Jules 125, 253, 259, 261, 275, 289, 302, 307, 325-326, 512, 522, 524, 527, 538, 557-558, 563-566
Wise Guys 268-269, 586
Woolsey, Robert 237
Wynn, Ed 51, 598
Youngson, Robert 104, 309, 311-312, 350, 353, 358, 597-598
Zenobia 279-283, 287, 309, 314, 531-537
Zenobia's Infidelity 279-280, 531

About the Authors

CHUCK HARTER (left) is a writer/musician/creative consultant who lives in Los Angeles, California. He is the author of *Superboy & Superpup: The Lost Videos* (Cult Movies Press, 1993), *Superman on Broadway* (Holiday Press, 2003) and *JOHNNIE RAY 1952: The Year of the Atomic Ray* (self published, 2004). He also wrote the critically acclaimed documentary *Hey! Hey! We're the Monkees* (1996) for the Disney Channel.

MICHAEL J. HAYDE (right) is an author/media historian who lives in Manassas, Virginia. He is the author of *My Name's Friday: The Unauthorized but True Story of Dragnet and the Films of Jack Webb* (Cumberland House, 2001) and *Flights of Fantasy: The Unauthorized but True Story of Radio & TV's Adventures of Superman* (BearManor Media, 2009). He has appeared on NBC-TV's *Unsolved Mysteries* and *TV Land's Myths and Legends*.

Bear Manor Media

Classic Cinema.
Timeless TV.
Retro Radio.
www.BEARMANORMEDIA.COM

www.ingramcontent.com/pod-product-compliance
Lightning Source LLC
Chambersburg PA
CBHW081141290426

44108CB00018B/2399